Webster's French-English Dictionary

WEBSTER'S
French-English
English-French
DICTIONARY

for Home, School and Office

Created in Cooperation with the Editors of
MERRIAM-WEBSTER

STRATHEARN

This 2011 edition published by arrangement with Federal Street Press,
a division of Merriam-Webster, Incorporated

Strathearn Books
12 Cranfield Road
Toronto, ON M4B 3G8

ISBN: 978-1-59695-132-7

1st Printing   Craftline, Ft. Wayne, IN   5/2011   NK

Printed in the United States of America

Contents

Preface

This dictionary is a concise reference for the core vocabulary of French and English. Its 40,000 entries and over 50,000 translations provide up-to-date coverage of the basic vocabulary and idioms in both languages. In addition, the book includes vocabulary specific to the Canadian province of Quebec.

IPA (International Phonetic Alphabet) pronunciations are given for all words. Included as well are tables of irregular verbs in both languages and the most common French abbreviations.

This book shares many details of presentation with larger French-English Dictionaries, but for reasons of conciseness it also has a number of features uniquely its own. Users need to be familiar with the following major features of this dictionary.

Main entries follow one another in strict alphabetical order, without regard to intervening spaces or hyphens.

Homographs (words spelled the same but having different meanings or parts of speech) are run on at a single main entry if they are closely related. Run-on homograph entries are replaced in the text by a boldfaced swung dash (as **devoir**. . .*vt*. . . — ~ *nm* . . .). Homographs of distinctly different origin (as **date**[1] and **date**[2]) are given separate entries.

Run-on entries for related words that are not homographs may also follow the main entry. Thus we have the main entry **calculer** *vt* followed by run-on entries for — **calcul** *nm*, — **calculateur, -trice** *adj,* and — **calculatrice** *nf.* However, if a related word falls later in the alphabet than a following unrelated main entry, it will be entered at its own place; **ear** and its run-on — **eardrum** precede the main entry **earl** which is followed by the main entry **earlobe.**

Variant spellings appear at the main entry separated by *or* (as **judgment** *or* **judgement; paralyze** *or Brit* **paralyse;** or **lis** *or* **lys**).

Inflected forms of English verbs, adjectives, adverbs, and nouns are shown when they are irregular (as **wage** . . . **waged; waging; ride** . . . **rode; ridden; good** . . . **better; best;** or **fly** . . . *n, pl* **flies**) or when there might be doubt about their spelling (as **ego** . . . *n, pl* **egos**). Inflected forms of French irregular verbs are shown in the section Conjugation of French Verbs on page 6a; numerical references to this table are included at the main entry (as **tenir** {92} *vt*). Irregular plurals of French nouns or adjectives are shown at the main entry (as **mondial, -diale** *adj, mpl* **-diaux**).

Cross-references are provided to lead the user to the appropriate main entry (as **mice** → **mouse** or **fausse** → **faux**[2]).

Pronunciation information is either given explicitly or implied for all English and French words. A full list of the pronunciation symbols used appears on page 20a.

The grammatical function of entry words is indicated by an italic **functional label** (as *vt, adj,* or *nm*). Italic **usage labels** may be added at the entry or sense as well (as **artilleur** . . . *nm Can* : pitcher (in baseball); **center** *or Brit* **centre** . . . *n* . . .; or **tuyau** . . . *nm* . . . 2 *fam* : tip, advice). These labels are also included in the translations (as **bet** . . . *n* : pari *m,* gageure *f Can*).

Usage notes are occasionally placed before a translation to clarify meaning or use (as **moins** . . . *prep* . . . 2 (*in expressions of time*) : to, of).

Synonyms may appear before the translation word(s) in order to provide context for the meaning of an entry word or sense (as **poursuivre** . . . *vt* . . . 2 CONTINUER : carry on with; or **meet** . . . *vt* . . . 2 SATISFY : satisfaire).

Bold notes are sometimes used before a translation to introduce a plural sense or a common phrase using the main entry word (as **meuble** . . . *nm* . . . 2 ~s *nmpl* : furniture; or **call** . . . *vt* . . . 3 ~ **off** : annuler). Note that when an entry word is repeated in a bold note, it is replaced by a swung dash

Conjugation of French Verbs

Simple Tenses

-ER Verbs (parler)		-IR Verbs (grandir)	
PRESENT INDICATIVE			
je parle	nous parlons	je grandis	nous grandissons
tu parles	vous parlez	tu grandis	vous grandissez
il parle	ils parlent	il grandit	ils grandissent
PRESENT SUBJUNCTIVE			
je parle	nous parlions	je grandisse	nous grandissions
tu parles	vous parliez	tu grandisses	vous grandissiez
il parle	ils parlent	il grandisse	ils grandissent
PRETERIT INDICATIVE			
je parlai	nous parlâmes	je grandis	nous grandîmes
tu parlas	vous parlâtes	tu grandis	vous grandîtes
il parla	ils parlèrent	il grandit	ils grandirent
IMPERFECT INDICATIVE			
je parlais	nous parlions	je grandissais	nous grandissions
tu parlais	vous parliez	tu grandissais	vous grandissiez
il parlait	ils parlaient	il grandissait	ils grandissaient
IMPERFECT SUBJUNCTIVE			
je parlasse	nous parlassions	je grandisse	nous grandissions
tu parlasses	vous parlassiez	tu grandisses	vous grandissiez
il parlât	ils parlassent	il grandît	ils grandissent
FUTURE INDICATIVE			
je parlerai	nous parlerons	je grandirai	nous grandirons
tu parleras	vous parlerez	tu grandiras	vous grandirez
il parlera	ils parleront	il grandira	ils grandiront
CONDITIONAL			
je parlerais	nous parlerions	je grandirais	nous grandirions
tu parlerais	vous parleriez	tu grandirais	vous grandiriez
il parlerait	ils parleraient	il grandirait	ils grandiraient
IMPERATIVE			
	parlons		grandissons
parle, parlez	parlez	grandis, grandissez	grandissez
PRESENT PARTICIPLE (GERUND)			
parlant		grandissant	
PAST PARTICIPLE			
parlé		grandi	

Perfect Tenses

The *perfect* tenses are formed with *avoir* and the past participle:

PRESENT PERFECT
>j'ai parlé, nous avons parlé, etc. (*indicative*)
>j'aie parlé, nous ayons parlé, etc. (*subjunctive*)

PAST PERFECT
>j'avais parlé, nous avions parlé, etc. (*indicative*)
>j'eusse parlé, nous eussions parlé, etc. (*subjunctive*)

PRETERIT PERFECT
>j'eus parlé, nous eûmes parlé, etc.

FUTURE PERFECT
>j'aurai parlé, nous aurons parlé, etc.

CONDITIONAL PERFECT
>j'aurais parlé, nous aurions parlé, etc.
>>*or*
>j'eusse parlé, nous eussions parlé, etc.

PAST IMPERATIVE
>aie parlé, ayons parlé, ayez parlé

The perfect tenses of the following verbs are formed with *être*:
>aller, arriver, décéder, devenir, échoir, éclore, entrer, mourir, naître, partir, repartir, rentrer, rester, retourner, sortir, tomber, venir, revenir, parvenir, survenir

For example, the present perfect of *arriver* would be as follows:
>je suis arrivé, nous sommes arrivés, etc. (*indicative*)

Irregular Verbs

The *imperfect subjunctive*, the *conditional*, and the first and second person plural of the *imperative* are not included in the model conjugations list but can be derived from other verb forms:

The *imperfect subjunctive* is formed by using the second person singular of the preterit indicative, removing the final *s*, and adding the following suffixes: *-sse, -sses, -t* (and adding a circumflex accent on the preceding vowel), *-ssions, -ssiez, -ssent. Servir* is conjugated as follows:

PRETERIT INDICATIVE, SECOND PERSON SINGULAR	servis – *s* = servi
IMPERFECT SUBJUNCTIVE	je servisse, tu servisses, il servît, nous servissions, vous servissiez, ils servissent

The *conditional* is formed by using the stem of the future indicative and adding the following suffixes: *-ais, -ais, -ait, -ions, -iez,- aient. Prendre* is conjugated as follows:

FUTURE INDICATIVE	je prendrai – *ai* = prendr
CONDITIONAL	je prendrais, tu prendrais, il prendrait, nous prendrions, vous prendriez, ils prendraient

The first and second person plural of the *imperative* are the same as the corresponding forms of the present indicative.

Model Conjugations of Irregular Verbs

The model conjugations below include the following simple tenses: the *present indicative* (*IND*), the *present subjunctive* (*SUBJ*), the *preterit indicative* (*PRET*), the *imperfect indicative* (*IMPF*), the *future indicative* (*FUT*), the second person singular form of the *imperative* (*IMPER*), the *present participle* or *gerund* (*PRP*), and the *past participle* (*PP*). Each set of conjugations is preceded by the corresponding infinitive form of the verb, shown in bold type. Only tenses containing irregularities are listed, and the irregular verb forms within each tense are displayed in bold type.

Also note that some conjugated verbs are labeled *defective verb*. This refers to a verb lacking one or more of the usual forms of grammatical inflection (tense, mood, etc.), for example, in French, the verbs *bruire* and *ouïr*.

Each irregular verb entry in the French-English section of this dictionary is cross-referred by number to one of the following model conjugations. These cross-reference numbers are shown in curly braces { } immediately preceding the entry's functional label.

The three main categories of verbs are:

1) Verbs ending in -ER
2) Verbs ending in -IR

Present indicative endings for verbs in these categories are:

-is, -is, -it, -issons, -issez, -issent

For example, *j'arrondis, nous arrondissons*, etc. for infinitive *arrondir*

3) Verbs ending in -IR/-OIR/-RE

Present indicative endings for verbs in these categories are:

-e, -es, -e, -ons, -ez, -ent

For example, *j'accueille, nous accueillons*, etc. for infinitive *accueillir*

or

-s(x), -s(x), -t(d), -ons, -ez, -ent

For example, *je rends, nous rendons*, etc. for infinitive *rendre*

Note that in the third group there are two different sets of endings for both the present indicative and preterit indicative depending on the verb in question, as shown above for the present indicative. For clarity, these forms are included in the model conjugations in an attempt to prevent the reader from inadvertently choosing the wrong endings.

1   **absoudre** : *IND* **j'absous, tu absous, il absout, nous absolvons, vous absolvez, ils absolvent**; *SUBJ* **j'absolve, tu absolves, il absolve, nous absolvions, vous absolviez, ils absolvent**; *PRET* (*not used*); *IMPF* **j'absolvais, tu absolvais, il absolvait, nous absolvions, vous absolviez, ils absolvaient**; *IMPER* **absous**; *PRP* **absolvant**; *PP* **absous**

2   **accroire** (*defective verb*) *Used only in the infinitive*

3   **accueillir** : *IND* **j'accueille, tu accueilles, il accueille**, nous accueillons, vous accueillez, ils accueillent; *PRET* **j'accueillis, tu accueillis, il accueillit, nous accueillîmes, vous accueillîtes, ils accueillirent**; *FUT* **j'accueillerai, tu accueilleras, il accueillera, nous accueillerons, vous accueillerez, ils accueilleront**; *IMPER* **accueille**

4   **advenir** (*defective verb*) *Used only in the infinitive and in the following tenses* : *IND* **il advient**; *SUBJ* **il advienne**; *PRET* **il advint**; *IMPF* **il advenait**; *FUT* **il adviendra**; *PRP* **advenant**; *PP* **advenu**

aller : *IND* **je vais, tu vas, il va, nous allons, vous allez, ils vont**; *SUBJ* **j'aille, tu ailles, il aille, nous allions, vous alliez, ils aillent**; *FUT* **j'irai, tu iras, il ira, nous irons, vous irez, ils iront**; *IMPER* **va**

Conjugation of French Verbs

6 **annoncer** : *IND* j'annonce, tu annonces, il annonce, **nous annonçons,** vous annoncez, ils an-
noncent; *PRET* **j'annonçai, tu annonças, il annonça, nous annonçâmes, vous annonçâtes, ils
annoncèrent;** *IMPF* **j'annonçais, tu annonçais, il annonçait,** nous annoncions, vous annon-
ciez, **ils annonçaient;** *PRP* **annonçant**

7 **apparaître** : *IND* j'apparais, tu apparais, il apparaît, nous apparaissons, vous apparais-
sez, ils apparaissent; *SUBJ* j'apparaisse, tu apparaisses, il apparaisse, nous apparaissions,
vous apparaissiez, ils apparaissent; *PRET* j'apparus, tu apparus, il apparut, nous ap-
parûmes, vous apparûtes, ils apparurent; *IMPF* j'apparaissais, tu apparaissais, il appa-
raissait, nous apparaissions, vous apparaissiez, ils apparaissaient; *IMPER* apparais; *PRP*
apparaissant; *PP* apparu

8 **appeler** : *IND* j'appelle, tu appelles, il appelle, nous appelons, vous appelez, **ils appellent;**
SUBJ **j'appelle, tu appelles, il appelle,** nous appelions, vous appeliez, **ils appellent;** *FUT* **j'ap-
pellerai, tu appelleras, il appellera, nous appellerons, vous appellerez, ils appelleront;**
IMPER **appelle**

9 **asseoir** : *IND* j'assieds *or* j'assois, tu assieds *or* tu assois, il assied *or* il assoit, nous asseyons
or nous assoyons, vous asseyez *or* vous assoyez, ils asseyent *or* ils assoient; *SUBJ* j'asseye *or*
j'assoie, tu asseyes *or* tu assoies, il asseye *or* il assoie, nous asseyions *or* nous assoyions,
vous asseyiez *or* vous assoyiez, ils asseyent *or* ils assoient; *PRET* j'assis, tu assis, il assit,
nous assîmes, vous assîtes, ils assirent; *IMPF* j'asseyais *or* j'assoyais, tu asseyais *or* tu assoyais, il asseyait *or* il assoyait, nous asseyions *or* nous assoyions, vous asseyiez *or* vous assoyiez, ils asseyaient *or* ils assoyaient; *FUT* (*not used*); *IMPER* assieds *or* assois; *PRP* asseyant
or assoyant; *PP* assis

10 **avoir** : *IND* j'ai, tu as, il a, nous avons, vous avez, ils ont; *SUBJ* j'aie, tu aies, il ait, nous
ayons, vous ayez, ils aient; *PRET* j'eus, tu eus, il eut, nous eûmes, vous eûtes, ils eurent;
IMPF j'avais, tu avais, il avait, nous avions, vous aviez, ils avaient; *FUT* j'aurai, tu auras, il
aura, nous aurons, vous aurez, ils auront; *IMPER* aie, ayons, ayez; *PRP* ayant; *PP* eu

11 **balayer** : *IND* je balaie *or* je balaye, **tu balaies** *or* tu balayes, **il balaie** *or* il balaye, nous ba-
layons, vous balayez, **ils balaient** *or* ils balayent; *SUBJ* **je balaie** *or* je balaye, **tu balaies** *or* tu
balayes, **il balaie** *or* il balaye, nous balayions, vous balayiez, **ils balaient** *or* ils balayent; *FUT*
je balaierai *or* je balayerai, **tu balaieras** *or* tu balayeras, **il balaiera** *or* il balayera, **nous ba-
laierons** *or* nous balayerons, **vous balaierez** *or* vous balayerez, **ils balaieront** *or* ils ba-
layeront; *IMPER* **balaie** *or* balaye

12 **battre** : *IND* je bats, tu bats, il bat, nous battons, vous battez, ils battent; *PRET* **je battis, tu battis, il battit, nous battîmes, vous battîtes, ils battirent;** *IMPER* **bats;** *PP* **battu**

13 **boire** : *IND* je bois, tu bois, il boit, **nous buvons, vous buvez, ils boivent;** *SUBJ* **je boive, tu
boives, il boive, nous buvions, vous buviez, ils boivent;** *PRET* **je bus, tu bus, il but, nous
bûmes, vous bûtes, ils burent;** *IMPF* **je buvais, tu buvais, il buvait, nous buvions, vous buviez, ils buvaient;** *PRP* **buvant;** *PP* **bu**

14 **bouillir** : *IND* je bous, tu bous, il bout, nous bouillons, vous bouillez, ils bouillent; *PRET*
bouillis, tu bouillis, il bouillit, nous bouillîmes, vous bouillîtes, ils bouillirent; *IMPER* bou

15 **braire** (*defective verb*) *Used only in the infinitive and in the following tenses* : *IND* **il brait, ils
braient;** *IMPF* **brayait, brayaient;** *FUT* **il braira, ils brairont**

16 **bruire** (*defective verb*) *Used only in the infinitive and in the following tenses* : *IND* **il bruit, il
bruissent;** *SUBJ* (*not used*); *PRET* (*not used*); *IMPF* **il bruissait, ils bruissaient;** *PRP* **bruissant**
PP **bruit**

17 **changer** : *IND* je change, tu changes, il change, **nous changeons,** vous changez, ils changent
PRET **je changeai, tu changeas, il changea, nous changeâmes, vous changeâtes, il
changèrent;** *IMPF* **je changeais, tu changeais, il changeait,** nous changions, vous changiez
ils changeaient; *PRP* **changeant**

18 **choir** (*defective verb*) *Used only in the following tenses* : *IND* **je chois, tu chois, il choit, il**

choient; *SUBJ* (*not used*); *PRET* **il chut**; *IMPF* (*not used*); *FUT* il choira; *IMPER* (*not used*); *PRP* (*not used*); *PP* **chu**

19 **clore** (*defective verb*) *Used only in the following tenses* : *IND* je clos, tu clos, **il clôt, ils closent;** *SUBJ* **je close, tu closes, il close, nous closions, vous closiez, ils closent;** *PRET* (*not used*); *IMPF* (*not used*); *FUT* (*used but regularly formed*); *PRP* **closant;** *PP* **clos**

20 **congeler** : *IND* **je congèle, tu congèles, il congèle,** nous congelons, vous congelez, **ils congèlent;** *SUBJ* **je congèle, tu congèles, il congèle,** nous congelions, vous congeliez, **ils congèlent;** *FUT* **je congèlerai, tu congèleras, il congèlera, nous congèlerons, vous congèlerez, ils congèleront;** *IMPER* **congèle**

21 **conquérir** : *IND* **je conquiers, tu conquiers, il conquiert,** nous conquérons, vous conquérez, **ils conquièrent;** *SUBJ* **je conquière, tu conquières, il conquière,** nous conquérions, vous conquériez, **ils conquièrent;** *PRET* **je conquis, tu conquis, il conquit, nous conquîmes, vous conquîtes, ils conquirent;** *FUT* **je conquerrai, tu conquerras, il conquerra, nous conquerrons, vous conquerrez, ils conquerront;** *IMPER* **conquiers;** *PP* **conquis**

22 **coudre** : *IND* **je couds, tu couds, il coud, nous cousons, vous cousez, ils cousent;** *SUBJ* **je couse, tu couses, il couse, nous cousions, vous cousiez, ils cousent;** *PRET* **je cousis, tu cousis, il cousit, nous cousîmes, vous cousîtes, ils cousirent;** *IMPF* **je cousais, tu cousais, il cousait, nous cousions, vous cousiez, ils cousaient;** *PRP* **cousant;** *PP* **cousu**

23 **courir** : *IND* **je cours, tu cours, il court,** nous courons, vous courez, ils courent; *PRET* **je courus, tu courus, il courut, nous courûmes, vous courûtes, ils coururent;** *FUT* **je courrai, tu courras, il courra, nous courrons, vous courrez, ils courront;** *IMPER* **cours;** *PP* **couru**

24 **croire** : *IND* je crois, tu crois, il croit, **nous croyons, vous croyez,** ils croient; *SUBJ* je croie, tu croies, il croie, **nous croyions, vous croyiez,** ils croient; *PRET* **je crus, tu crus, il crut, nous crûmes, vous crûtes, il crurent;** *IMPF* **je croyais, tu croyais, il croyait, nous croyions, vous croyiez, ils croyaient;** *PRP* **croyant;** *PP* **cru**

25 **croître** : *IND* **je croîs, tu croîs, il croît, nous croissons, vous croissez, ils croissent;** *SUBJ* **je croisse, tu croisses, il croisse, nous croissions, vous croissiez, ils croissent;** *PRET* **je crûs, tu crûs, il crût, nous crûmes, vous crûtes, ils crûrent;** *IMPF* **je croissais, tu croissais, il croissait, nous croissions, vous croissiez, ils croissaient;** *IMPER* **croîs;** *PRP* **croissant;** *PP* **crû**

26 **décevoir** : *IND* **je déçois, tu déçois, il déçoit,** nous décevons, vous décevez, **ils déçoivent;** *SUBJ* **je déçoive, tu déçoives, il déçoive,** nous décevions, vous déceviez, **ils déçoivent;** *PRET* **je déçus, tu déçus, il déçut, nous déçûmes, vous déçûtes, ils déçurent;** *IMPER* **déçois;** *PP* **déçu**

27 **déchoir** (*defective verb*) *Used only in the following tenses* : *IND* je déchois, tu déchois, il déchoit *or* il **déchet, nous déchoyons, vous déchoyez, ils déchoient;** *SUBJ* je déchoie, tu déchoies, il déchoie, **nous déchoyions, vous déchoyiez, ils déchoient;** *PRET* **je déchus, tu déchus, il déchut, nous déchûmes, vous déchûtes, ils déchurent;** *IMPF* (*not used*); *FUT* (*used but regularly formed*); *IMPER* (*not used*); *PRP* (*not used*); *PP* **déchu**

28 **devoir** : *IND* **je dois, tu dois, il doit,** nous devons, vous devez, **ils doivent;** *SUBJ* **je doive, tu doives, il doive,** nous devions, vous deviez, **ils doivent;** *PRET* **je dus, tu dus, il dut, nous dûmes, vous dûtes, ils durent;** *IMPER* **dois;** *PRP* **dû**

29 **dire** : *IND* je dis, tu dis, il dit, **nous disons, vous dites, ils disent;** *SUBJ* **je dise, tu dises, il dise, nous disions, vous disiez, ils disent;** *PRET* **je dis, tu dis, il dit, nous dîmes, vous dîtes, ils dirent;** *IMPF* **je disais, tu disais, il disait, nous disions, vous disiez, ils disent;** *PRP* **disant;** *PP* **dit**

30 **dormir** : *IND* **je dors, tu dors, il dort,** nous dormons, vous dormez, ils dorment; *PRET* **je dormis, tu dormis, il dormit, nous dormîmes, vous dormîtes, ils dormirent;** *IMPER* **dors**

31 **échoir** (*defective verb*) *Used only in the following tenses* : *IND* **il échoit, ils échoient;** *SUBJ* **il échoie;** *PRET* **il échut, ils échurent;** *IMPF* (*not used*); *FUT* il échoira *or* **il écherra;** ils échoiront *or* **ils écherront;** *IMPER* (*not used*); *PRP* **échéant;** *PP* **échu**

32 **éclore** (*defective verb*) *Used only in the following tenses* : *IND* **il éclot;** *PP* **éclos**

33 **écrire** : *IND* j'écris, tu écris, il écrit, **nous écrivons, vous écrivez, ils écrivent**; *SUBJ* **j'écrive, tu écrives, il écrive, nous écrivions, vous écriviez, ils écrivent**; *PRET* **j'écrivis, tu écrivis, il écrivit, nous écrivîmes, vous écrivîtes, ils écrivirent**; *IMPF* **j'écrivais, tu écrivais, il écrivait, nous écrivions, vous écriviez, ils écrivaient**; *PRP* **écrivant**; *PP* **écrit**

34 **enclore** *(defective verb) Used only in the following tenses* : *IND* j'enclos, tu enclos, il enclot, **nous enclosons, vous enclosez, ils enclosent**; *SUBJ* **j'enclose, tu encloses, il enclose, nous enclosions, vous enclosiez, ils enclosent**; *PRET (not used)*; *IMPF (not used)*; *FUT (used but regularly formed)*; *IMPER* enclos; *PRP* **enclosant**; *PP* **enclos**

35 **ensuivre (s')** *(defective verb) Used only in the following tenses* : *IND* il s'ensuit; *SUBJ* **il s'ensuive**; *PRET* il s'ensuivit; *IMPF* il s'ensuivait; *FUT* il s'ensuivra; *PP* s'ensuivi

36 **envoyer** : *IND* j'envoie, tu envoies, il envoie, **nous envoyons, vous envoyez, ils envoient**; *SUBJ* **j'envoie, tu envoies, il envoie, nous envoyions, vous envoyiez, ils envoient**; *FUT* **j'enverrai, tu enverras, il enverra, nous enverrons, vous enverrez, ils enverront**; *IMPER* **envoie**

37 **éteindre** : *IND* j'éteins, tu éteins, il éteint, nous éteignons, vous éteignez, ils éteignent; *SUBJ* **j'éteigne, tu éteignes, il éteigne, nous éteignions, vous éteigniez, ils éteignent**; *PRET* **j'éteignis, tu éteignis, il éteignit, nous éteignîmes, vous éteignîtes, ils éteignirent**; *IMPF* **j'éteignais, tu éteignais, il éteignait, nous éteignions, vous éteigniez, ils éteignaient**; *IMPER* **éteins**; *PRP* **éteignant**; *PP* **éteint**

38 **être** : *IND* je suis, tu es, il est, **nous sommes, vous êtes, ils sont**; *SUBJ* **je sois, tu sois, il soit, nous soyons, vous soyez, ils soient**; *PRET* **je fus, tu fus, il fut, nous fûmes, vous fûtes, ils furent**; *IMPF* **j'étais, tu étais, il était, nous étions, vous étiez, ils étaient**; *FUT* **je serai, tu seras, il sera, nous serons, vous serez, ils seront**; *IMPER* **sois**; *PRP* **étant**; *PP* **été**

39 **exclure** : *IND* j'exclus, tu exclus, il exclut, nous excluons, vous excluez, ils excluent; *PRET* **j'exclus, tu exclus, il exclut, nous exclûmes, vous exclûtes, ils exclurent**; *IMPER* exclus; *PP* **exclu**

40 **extraire** : *IND* j'extrais, tu extrais, il extrait, **nous extrayons, vous extrayez**, ils extraient; *SUBJ* j'extraie, tu extraies, il extraie, **nous extrayions, vous extrayiez**, ils extraient; *PRET (not used)*; *IMPF* **j'extrayais, tu extrayais, il extrayait, nous extrayions, vous extrayiez, ils extrayaient**; *PRP* **extrayant**; *PP* **extrait**

41 **faillir** *(defective verb) Used only in the infinitive and as a PP* **failli**

42 **faire** : *IND* je fais, tu fais, il fait, **nous faisons, vous faites, ils font**; *SUBJ* **je fasse, tu fasses, il fasse, nous fassions, vous fassiez, ils fassent**; *PRET* **je fis, tu fis, il fit, nous fîmes, vous fîtes, ils firent**; *IMPF* **je faisais, tu faisais, il faisait, nous faisions, vous faisiez, ils faisaient**; *FUT* **je ferai, tu feras, il fera, nous ferons, vous ferez, ils feront**; *PRP* **faisant**; *PP* **fait**

43 **falloir** *(defective verb) Used only in the following tenses* : *IND* il faut; *SUBJ* il faille; *PRET* il fallut; *IMPF* il fallait; *FUT* il faudra; *IMPER (not used)*; *PRP (not used)*; *PP* **fallu**

44 **forfaire** *(defective verb) Used only in the infinitive and in the following tenses* : *IND* il forfait; *PP* **forfait**

45 **frire** *(defective verb) Used only in the following tenses* : *IND* **je fris, tu fris, il frit**; *FUT* je frirai, tu friras, il frira, nous frirons, vous frirez, ils friront; *IMPER* **fris**; *PP* **frit**

46 **fuir** : *IND* je fuis, tu fuis, il fuit, **nous fuyons, vous fuyez, ils fuient**; *SUBJ* je fuie, tu fuies, il fuie, **nous fuyions, vous fuyiez, ils fuient**; *PRET* je fuis, tu fuis, il fuit, **nous fuîmes, vous fuîtes, ils fuirent**; *IMPF* **je fuyais, tu fuyais, il fuyait, nous fuyions, vous fuyiez, ils fuyaient**; *PRP* **fuyant**; *PP* **fui**

47 **gésir** *(defective verb) Used only in the following tenses* : *IND* je gis, tu gis, il gît, nous gisons, vous gisez, ils gisent; *IMPF* je gisais, tu gisais, il gisait, nous gisions, vous gisiez, ils gisaient; *PRP* **gisant**

48 **haïr** : *IND* je hais, tu hais, il hait, nous haïssons, vous haïssez, ils haïssent; *SUBJ* je haïsse, tu haïsses, il haïsse, nous haïssions, vous haïssiez, ils haïssent; *PRET* je haïs, tu haïs, il haït,

nous haïmes, vous haïtes, ils haïrent; *IMPF* je haïssais, tu haïssais, il haïssait, nous haïssions, vous haïssiez, ils haïssaient; *IMPER* hais; *PRP* haïssant; *PP* haï

49 **instruire :** *IND* j'instruis, tu instruis, il instruit, **nous instruisons, vous instruisez, ils instruisent;** *SUBJ* j'instruise, tu instruises, il instruise, nous instruisions, vous instruisiez, ils instruisent; *PRET* j'instruisis, tu instruisis, il instruisit, nous instruisîmes, vous instruisîtes, ils instruisirent; *IMPF* j'instruisais, tu instruisais, il instruisait, nous instruisions, vous instruisiez, ils instruisaient; *PRP* instruisant; *PP* instruit

50 **joindre :** *IND* je joins, tu joins, il joint, nous joignons, vous joignez, ils joignent; *SUBJ* je joigne, tu joignes, il joigne, nous joignions, vous joigniez, ils joignent; *PRET* je joignis, tu joignis, il joignit, nous joignîmes, vous joignîtes, ils joignirent; *IMPF* je joignais, tu joignais, il joignait, nous joignions, vous joigniez, ils joignaient; *IMPER* joins; *PRP* joignant; *PP* joint

51 **lire :** *IND* je lis, tu lis, il lit, **nous lisons, vous lisez, ils lisent;** *SUBJ* je lise, tu lises, il lise, nous lisions, vous lisiez, ils lisent; *PRET* je lus, tu lus, il lut, nous lûmes, vous lûtes, ils lurent; *IMPF* je lisais, tu lisais, il lisait, nous lisions, vous lisiez, ils lisaient; *PRP* lisant; *PP* lu

52 **mener :** *IND* je mène, tu mènes, il mène, nous menons, vous menez, ils mènent; *SUBJ* je mène, tu mènes, il mène, nous menions, vous meniez, **ils mènent;** *FUT* je mènerai, tu mèneras, il mènera, nous mènerons, vous mènerez, ils mèneront; *IMPER* mène

53 **mettre :** *IND* je mets, tu mets, il met, nous mettons, vous mettez, ils mettent; *PRET* **je mis, tu mis, il mit, nous mîmes, vous mîtes, ils mirent;** *IMPER* **mets;** *PP* mis

54 **moudre :** *IND* je mouds, tu mouds, il moud, **nous moulons, vous moulez, ils moulent;** *SUBJ* je moule, tu moules, il moule, **nous moulions, vous mouliez, ils moulent;** *PRET* **je moulus, tu moulus, il moulut, nous moulûmes, vous moulûtes, ils moulurent;** *IMPF* je moulais, tu moulais, il moulait, nous moulions, vous mouliez, ils moulaient; *PRP* moulant; *PP* moulu

55 **mourir :** *IND* je meurs, tu meurs, il meurt, nous mourons, vous mourez, **ils meurent;** *SUBJ* je meure, tu meures, il meure, nous mourions, vous mouriez, **ils meurent;** *PRET* je mourus, tu mourus, il mourut, nous mourûmes, vous mourûtes, ils moururent; *FUT* je mourrai, tu mourras, il mourra, nous mourrons, vous mourrez, ils mourront; *IMPER* meurs; *PRP* **mourant;** *PP* mort

56 **mouvoir :** *IND* je meus, tu meus, il meut, nous mouvons, vous mouvez, **ils meuvent;** *SUBJ* je meuve, tu meuves, il meuve, nous mouvions, vous mouviez, **ils meuvent;** *PRET* je mus, tu mus, il mut, nous mûmes, vous mûtes, **ils murent;** *IMPER* meus; *PP* mû

57 **naître :** *IND* je nais, tu nais, il naît, nous naissons, vous naissez, ils naissent; *SUBJ* je naisse, tu naisses, il naisse, nous naissions, vous naissiez, ils naissent; *PRET* je naquis, tu naquis, il naquit, nous naquîmes, vous naquîtes, ils naquirent; *IMPF* je naissais, tu naissais, il naissait, nous naissions, vous naissiez, ils naissaient; *IMPER* nais; *PRP* naissant; *PP* né

58 **nettoyer :** *IND* je nettoie, tu nettoies, il nettoie, nous nettoyons, vous nettoyez, **ils nettoient;** *SUBJ* je nettoie, tu nettoies, il nettoie, nous nettoyions, vous nettoyiez, **ils nettoient;** *FUT* je nettoierai, tu nettoieras, il nettoiera, nous nettoierons, vous nettoierez, ils nettoieront; *IMPER* **nettoie**

59 **oindre** (*defective verb*) *Used only in the infinitive and as a PP* oint

60 **ouïr** (*defective verb*) *Used only in the infinitive and as a pp* ouï

61 **paître** (*defective verb*) *Used only in the following tenses :* *IND* je pais, tu pais, il paît, nous paissons, vous paissez, ils paissent; *SUBJ* je paisse, tu paisses, il paisse, nous paissions, vous paissiez, ils paissent; *PRET* (*not used*); *IMPF* je paissais, tu paissais, il paissait, nous paissions, vous paissiez, ils paissaient; *FUT* (*used but regular*); *IMPER* pais; *PRP* paissant; *PP* (*not used*)

62 **parfaire** (*defective verb*) *Used only in the infinitive and in the following tenses* *IND* il parfait; *PP* parfait

63 **perdre :** *IND* je perds, tu perds, **il perd,** nous perdons, vous perdez, ils perdent; *PRET* **je perdis, tu perdis, il perdit, nous perdîmes, vous perdîtes, ils perdirent;** *PP* perdu

64 **piéger** : *IND* **je piège, tu pièges, il piège, nous piégeons,** vous piégez, **ils piègent;** *SUBJ* **je piège, tu pièges, il piège,** nous piégions, vous piégiez, **ils piègent;** *PRET* **je piégeai, tu piégeas, il piégea, nous piégeâmes, vous piégeâtes, ils piégèrent;** *IMPF* **je piégeais, tu piégeais, il piégeait,** nous piégions, vous piégiez, **ils piégeaient;** *IMPER* **piège;** *PRP* piégeant; *PP* piégé

65 **plaindre** : *IND* je plains, tu plains, il plaint, **nous plaignons, vous plaignez, ils plaignent;** *SUBJ* **je plaigne, tu plaignes, il plaigne, nous plagnions, vous plagniez, ils plaignent;** *PRET* **je plaignis, tu plaignis, il plaignit, nous plaignîmes, vous plaignîtes, ils plaignirent;** *IMPF* **je plaignais, tu plaignais, il plaignait, nous plaignions, vous plaigniez, ils plaignaient;** *PRP* **plaignant;** *PP* **plaint**

66 **plaire** : *IND* je plais, tu plais, **il plaît, nous plaisons, vous plaisez, ils plaisent;** *SUBJ* **je plaise, tu plaises, il plaise, nous plaisions, vous plaisiez, ils plaisent;** *PRET* **je plus, tu plus, il plut, nous plûmes, vous plûtes, ils plurent;** *IMPF* **je plaisais, tu plaisais, il plaisait, nous plaisions, vous plaisiez, ils plaisaient;** *PRP* **plaisant;** *PP* **plu**

67 **pleuvoir** (*defective verb*) *Used in the infinitive and in the following tenses* *IND* **il pleut, ils pleuvent** (*only in the figurative*); *SUBJ* **il pleuve, ils pleuvent** (*only in the figurative*); *PRET* **il plut;** *IMPF* **il pleuvait, ils pleuvaient** (*only in the figurative*); *FUT* **il pleuvra;** *IMPER* (*not used*); *PRP* **pleuvant;** *PP* **plu**

68 **pourvoir** : *IND* **je pourvois, tu pourvois, il pourvoit, nous pourvoyons, vous pourvoyez, ils pourvoient;** *SUBJ* **je pourvoie, tu pourvoies, il pourvoie, nous pourvoyions, vous pourvoyiez, ils pourvoient;** *PRET* **je pourvus, tu pourvus, il pourvut, nous pourvûmes, vous pourvûtes, ils pourvurent;** *IMPF* **je pourvoyais, tu pourvoyais, il pourvoyait, nous pourvoyions, vous pourvoyiez, ils pourvoyaient;** *FUT* **je pourvoirai, tu pourvoiras, il pourvoira, nous pourvoirons, vous pourvoirez, ils pourvoiront;** *IMPER* **pourvois;** *PRP* **pourvoyant;** *PP* **pourvu**

69 **pouvoir** : *IND* **je peux** *or* **je puis, tu peux, il peut,** nous pouvons, vous pouvez, **ils peuvent;** *SUBJ* **je puisse, tu puisses, il puisse, nous puissions, vous puissiez, ils puissent;** *PRET* **je pus, tu pus, il put, nous pûmes, vous pûtes, ils purent;** *FUT* **je pourrai, tu pourras, il pourra, nous pourrons, vous pourrez, ils pourront;** *IMPER* (*not used*); *PP* **pu**

70 **prendre** : *IND* je prends, tu prends, **il prend, nous prenons, vous prenez, ils prennent;** *SUBJ* **je prenne, tu prennes, il prenne, nous prenions, vous preniez, ils prennent;** *PRET* **je pris, tu pris, il prit, nous prîmes, vous prîtes, ils prirent;** *IMPF* **je prenais, tu prenais, il prenait, nous prenions, vous preniez, ils prenaient;** *PRP* **prenant;** *PP* **pris**

71 **prévaloir** : *IND* **je prévaux, tu prévaux, il prévaut,** nous prévalons, vous prévalez, ils prévalent; *PRET* **je prévalus, tu prévalus, il prévalut, nous prévalûmes, vous prévalûtes, ils prévalurent;** *FUT* **je prévaudrai, tu prévaudras, il prévaudra, nous prévaudrons, vous prévaudrez, ils prévaudront;** *IMPER* **prévaux;** *PP* **prévalu**

72 **rassir** (*defective verb*) *Used only in the infinitive and as a* *PP* **rassis**

73 **ravoir** (*defective verb*) *Used only in the infinitive*

74 **résoudre** : *INF* **je résous, tu résous, il résout, nous résolvons, vous résolvez, ils résolvent;** *SUBJ* **je résolve, tu résolves, il résolve, nous résolvions, vous résolviez, ils résolvent;** *PRET* **je résolus, tu résolus, il résolut, nous résolûmes, vous résolûtes, ils résolurent;** *IMPF* **je résolvais, tu résolvais, il résolvait, nous résolvions, vous résolviez, ils résolvaient;** *IMPER* **résous;** *PRP* **résolvant;** *PP* **résolu**

75 **résulter** (*defective verb*) *Used only in the infinitive and in the following tenses* : *IND* **il résulte;** *PRP* **résultant**

76 **rire** : *IND* **je ris, tu ris, il rit, nous rions, vous riez, ils rient;** *SUBJ* je rie, tu ries, il rie, **nous riions, vous riiez,** ils rient; *PRET* **je ris, tu ris, il rit, nous rîmes, vous rîtes, ils rirent;** *IMPER* **ris;** *PP* **ri**

77 **rompre** : *IND* je romps, tu romps, **il rompt,** nous rompons, vous rompez, ils rompent; *PRET* **je rompis, tu rompis, il rompit, nous rompîmes, vous rompîtes, ils rompirent;** *PP* **rompu**

78   saillir : *IND* je saille, tu sailles, il saille, nous saillons, vous saillez, ils saillent; *PRET* je saillis, tu saillis, il saillit, nous saillîmes, vous saillîtes, ils saillirent; *FUT* je saillerai, tu sailleras, il saillera, nous saillerons, vous saillerez, ils sailleront; *IMPER* saille

79   savoir : *IND* je sais, tu sais, il sait, nous savons, vous savez, ils savent; *SUBJ* je sache, tu saches, il sache, nous sachions, vous sachiez, ils sachent; *PRET* je sus, tu sus, il sut, nous sûmes, vous sûtes, ils surent; *FUT* je saurai, tu sauras, il saura, nous saurons, vous saurez, ils sauront; *IMPER* sache, sachons, sachez; *PRP* sachant; *PP* su

80   seoir (*defective verb*) *Used only in the following tenses* : *IND* il sied, ils siéent; *SUBJ* il siée, ils siéent; *PRET* (*not used*); *IMPF* il seyait, ils seyaient; *FUT* il siéra, ils siéront; *IMPER* (*not used*); *PRP* séant *or* seyant; *PP* (*not used*)

81   servir : *IND* je sers, tu sers, il sert, nous servons, vous servez, ils servent; *PRET* je servis, tu servis, il servit, nous servîmes, vous servîtes, ils servirent; *FUT* je servirai, tu serviras, il servira, nous servirons, vous servirez, ils serviront; *IMPER* sers; *PP* servi

82   sortir : *IND* je sors, tu sors, il sort, nous sortons, vous sortez, ils sortent; *PRET* je sortis, tu sortis, il sortit, nous sortîmes, vous sortîtes, ils sortirent; *FUT* je sortirai, tu sortiras, il sortira, nous sortirons, vous sortirez, ils sortiront; *IMPER* sors; *PRP* sortant; *PP* sorti

83   souffrir : *IND* je souffre, tu souffres, il souffre, nous souffrons, vous souffrez, ils souffrent; *PRET* je souffris, tu souffris, il souffrit, nous souffrîmes, vous souffrîtes, ils souffrirent; *FUT* je souffrirai, tu souffriras, il souffrira, nous souffrirons, vous souffrirez, ils souffriront; *IMPER* souffre; *PP* souffert

84   sourdre (*defective verb*) *Used only in the infinitive and in the following tenses* : *IND* il sourd, ils sourdent; *IMPF* il sourdait, ils sourdaient

85   stupéfaire (*defective verb*) *Used only in the following tense* *PP* stupéfié

86   suffire : *IND* je suffis, tu suffis, il suffit, nous suffisons, vous suffisez, ils suffisent; *SUBJ* je suffise, tu suffises, il suffise, nous suffisions, vous suffisiez, ils suffisent; *PRET* je suffis, tu suffis, il suffit, nous suffîmes, vous suffîtes, ils suffirent; *IMPF* je suffisais, tu suffisais, il suffisait, nous suffisions, vous suffisiez, ils suffisaient; *PRP* suffisant; *PP* suffi

87   suggérer : *IND* je suggère, tu suggères, il suggère, nous suggérons, vous suggérez, ils suggèrent; *SUBJ* je suggère, tu suggères, il suggère, nous suggérions, vous suggériez, ils suggèrent; *IMPER* suggère

88   suivre : *IND* je suis, tu suis, il suit, nous suivons, vous suivez, ils suivent; *PRET* je suivis, tu suivis, il suivit, nous suivîmes, vous suivîtes, ils suivirent; *IMPER* suis; *PP* suivi

89   suppléer : *IND* je supplée, tu supplées, il supplée, nous suppléons, vous suppléez, ils suppléent; *SUBJ* je supplée, tu supplées, il supplée, nous suppléions, vous suppléiez, ils suppléent; *PRET* je suppléai, tu suppléas, il suppléa, nous suppléâmes, vous suppléâtes, ils suppléèrent; *FUT* je suppléerai, tu suppléeras, il suppléera, nous suppléerons, vous suppléerez, ils suppléeront; *IMPER* supplée; *PP* suppléé

90   surseoir : *IND* je sursois, tu sursois, il sursoit, nous sursoyons, vous sursoyez, ils sursoient; *SUBJ* je sursoie, tu sursoies, il sursoie, nous sursoyions, vous sursoyiez, ils sursoient; *PRET* je sursis, tu sursis, il sursit, nous sursîmes, vous sursîtes, ils sursirent; *IMPF* je sursoyais, tu sursoyais, il sursoyait, nous sursoyions, vous sursoyiez, ils sursoyaient; *FUT* je surseoirai, tu surseoiras, il surseoira, nous surseoirons, vous surseoirez, ils surseoiront; *IMPER* sursois; *PRP* sursoyant; *PP* sursis

91   taire : *IND* je tais, tu tais, il tait, nous taisons, vous taisez, ils taisent; *SUBJ* je taise, tu taises, il taise, nous taisions, vous taisiez, ils taisent; *PRET* je tus, tu tus, il tut, nous tûmes, vous tûtes, ils turent; *IMPF* je taisais, tu taisais, il taisait, nous taisions, vous taisiez, ils taisaient; *PRP* taisant; *PP* tu

92   tenir : *IND* je tiens, tu tiens, il tient, nous tenons, vous tenez, ils tiennent; *SUBJ* je tienne, tu tiennes, il tienne, nous tenions, vous teniez, ils tiennent; *PRET* je tins, tu tins, il tint, nous

tînmes, vous tîntes, ils tinrent; *FUT* je tiendrai, tu tiendras, il tiendra, nous tiendrons, vous tiendrez, ils tiendront; *IMPER* tiens; *PP* tenu

93 **tressaillir** : *IND* je tressaille, tu tressailles, il tressaille, nous tressaillons, vous tressaillez, ils tressaillent; *PRET* je tressaillis, tu tressaillis, il tressaillit, nous tressaillîmes, vous tressaillites, ils tressaillirent; *FUT* je tressaillirai, tu tressailliras, il tressaillira, nous tressaillirons, vous tressaillirez, ils tressailliront; *IMPF* tressaille; *PP* tressailli

94 **vaincre** : *IND* je vaincs, tu vaincs, il vainc, nous vainquons, vous vainquez, ils vainquent; *SUBJ* je vainque, tu vainques, il vainque, nous vainquions, vous vainquiez, ils vainquent; *PRET* je vainquis, tu vainquis, il vainquit, nous vainquîmes, vous vainquîtes, ils vainquirent; *IMPF* je vainquais, tu vainquais, il vainquait, nous vainquions, vous vainquiez, ils vainquaient; *IMPER* vaincs; *PRP* vainquant; *PP* vaincu

95 **valoir** : *IND* je vaux, tu vaux, il vaut, nous valons, vous valez, ils valent; *SUBJ* je vaille, tu vailles, il vaille, nous valions, vous valiez, ils vaillent; *PRET* je valus, tu valus, il valut, nous valûmes, vous valûtes, ils valurent; *FUT* je vaudrai, tu vaudras, il vaudra, nous vaudrons, vous vaudrez, ils vaudront; *IMPER* vaux; *PP* valu

96 **vérifier** : *SUBJ* je vérifie, tu vérifies, il vérifie, **nous vérifiions, vous vérifiiez**, ils vérifient; *IMPF* je vérifiais, tu vérifiais, il vérifiait, **nous vérifiions, vous vérifiiez**, ils vérifiaient

97 **vêtir** : *IND* je vêts, tu vêts, il vêt, nous vêtons, vous vêtez, ils vêtent; *PRET* je vêtis, tu vêtis, il vêtit, nous vêtîmes, vous vêtîtes, ils vêtirent; *FUT* je vêtirai, tu vêtiras, il vêtira, nous vêtirons, vous vêtirez, ils vêtiront; *IMPER* vêts; *PP* vêtu

98 **vivre** : *IND* je vis, tu vis, il vit, nous vivons, vous vivez, ils vivent; *PRET* je vécus, tu vécus, il vécut, nous vécûmes, vous vécûtes, ils vécurent; *IMPER* vis; *PP* vécu

99 **voir** : *IND* je vois, tu vois, il voit, **nous voyons, vous voyez**, ils voient; *SUBJ* je voie, tu voies, il voie, **nous voyions, vous voyiez**, ils voient; *PRET* je vis, tu vis, il vit, nous vîmes, vous vîtes, ils virent; *IMPF* je voyais, tu voyais, il voyait, nous voyions, vous voyiez, ils voyaient; *FUT* je verrai, tu verras, il verra, nous verrons, vous verrez, ils verront; *PRP* voyant; *PP* vu

100 **vouloir** : *IND* je veux, tu veux, il veut, nous voulons, vous voulez, ils veulent; *SUBJ* je veuille, tu veuilles, il veuille, nous voulions, vous vouliez, ils veuillent; *PRET* je voulus, tu voulus, il voulut, nous voulûmes, vous voulûtes, ils voulurent; *FUT* je voudrai, tu voudras, il voudra, nous voudrons, vous voudrez, ils voudront; *IMPER* veux *or* veuille; *PP* voulu

Irregular English Verbs

INFINITIVE	PAST	PAST PARTICIPLE
arise	arose	arisen
awake	awoke	awoken *or* awaked
be	was, were	been
bear	bore	borne
beat	beat	beaten *or* beat
become	became	become
befall	befell	befallen
begin	began	begun
behold	beheld	beheld
bend	bent	bent
beseech	beseeched *or* besought	beseeched *or* besought
beset	beset	beset
bet	bet	bet
bid	bade *or* bid	bidden *or* bid
bind	bound	bound
bite	bit	bitten
bleed	bled	bled
blow	blew	blown
break	broke	broken
breed	bred	bred
bring	brought	brought
build	built	built
burn	burned *or* burnt	burned *or* burnt
burst	burst	burst
buy	bought	bought
can	could	—
cast	cast	cast
catch	caught	caught
choose	chose	chosen
cling	clung	clung
come	came	come
cost	cost	cost
creep	crept	crept
cut	cut	cut
deal	dealt	dealt
dig	dug	dug
do	did	done
draw	drew	drawn
dream	dreamed *or* dreamt	dreamed *or* dreamt
drink	drank	drunk *or* drank
drive	drove	driven
dwell	dwelled *or* dwelt	dwelled *or* dwelt
eat	ate	eaten
fall	fell	fallen
feed	fed	fed
feel	felt	felt
fight	fought	fought
find	found	found
flee	fled	fled
fling	flung	flung
fly	flew	flown
forbid	forbade	forbidden
forecast	forecast	forecast

INFINITIVE	PAST	PAST PARTICIPLE
forego	forewent	foregone
foresee	foresaw	foreseen
foretell	foretold	foretold
forget	forgot	forgotten *or* forgot
forgive	forgave	forgiven
forsake	forsook	forsaken
freeze	froze	frozen
get	got	got *or* gotten
give	gave	given
go	went	gone
grind	ground	ground
grow	grew	grown
hang	hung	hung
have	had	had
hear	heard	heard
hide	hid	hidden *or* hid
hit	hit	hit
hold	held	held
hurt	hurt	hurt
keep	kept	kept
kneel	knelt *or* kneeled	knelt *or* kneeled
know	knew	known
lay	laid	laid
lead	led	led
leap	leaped *or* leapt	leaped *or* leapt
leave	left	left
lend	lent	lent
let	let	let
lie	lay	lain
light	lit *or* lighted	lit *or* lighted
lose	lost	lost
make	made	made
may	might	—
mean	meant	meant
meet	met	met
mow	mowed	mowed *or* mown
pay	paid	paid
put	put	put
quit	quit	quit
read	read	read
rend	rent	rent
rid	rid	rid
ride	rode	ridden
ring	rang	rung
rise	rose	risen
run	ran	run
saw	sawed	sawed *or* sawn
say	said	said
see	saw	seen
seek	sought	sought
sell	sold	sold
send	sent	sent
set	set	set
shake	shook	shaken
shall	should	—
shear	sheared	sheared *or* shorn
shed	shed	shed
shine	shone *or* shined	shone *or* shined

INFINITIVE	PAST	PAST PARTICIPLE
shoot	shot	shot
show	showed	shown or showed
shrink	shrank or shrunk	shrunk or shrunken
shut	shut	shut
sing	sang or sung	sung
sink	sank or sunk	sunk
sit	sat	sat
slay	slew	slain
sleep	slept	slept
slide	slid	slid
sling	slung	slung
smell	smelled or smelt	smelled or smelt
sow	sowed	sown or sowed
speak	spoke	spoken
speed	sped or speeded	sped or speeded
spell	spelled	spelled
spend	spent	spent
spill	spilled	spilled
spin	spun	spun
spit	spit or spat	spit or spat
split	split	split
spoil	spoiled	spoiled
spread	spread	spread
spring	sprang or sprung	sprung
stand	stood	stood
steal	stole	stolen
stick	stuck	stuck
sting	stung	stung
stink	stank or stunk	stunk
stride	strode	stridden
strike	struck	struck
swear	swore	sworn
sweep	swept	swept
swell	swelled	swelled or swollen
swim	swam	swum
swing	swung	swung
take	took	taken
teach	taught	taught
tear	tore	torn
tell	told	told
think	thought	thought
throw	threw	thrown
thrust	thrust	thrust
tread	trod	trodden or trod
wake	woke	woken or waked
waylay	waylaid	waylaid
wear	wore	worn
weave	wove or weaved	woven or weaved
wed	wedded	wedded
weep	wept	wept
will	would	—
win	won	won
wind	wound	wound
withdraw	withdrew	withdrawn
withhold	withheld	withheld
withstand	withstood	withstood
wring	wrung	wrung
write	wrote	written

French Numbers

Cardinal Numbers

1	un	24	vingt-quatre
2	deux	25	vingt-cinq
3	trois	26	vingt-six
4	quatre	27	vingt-sept
5	cinq	28	vingt-huit
6	six	29	vingt-neuf
7	sept	30	trente
8	huit	31	trente et un
9	neuf	40	quarante
10	dix	50	cinquante
11	onze	60	soixante
12	douze	70	soixante-dix
13	treize	80	quatre-vingts
14	quatorze	90	quatre-vingt-dix
15	quinze	100	cent
16	seize	101	cent un
17	dix-sept	200	deux cents
18	dix-huit	1 000	mille
19	dix-neuf	1 001	mille un
20	vingt	2 000	deux mille
21	vingt et un	100 000	cent mille
22	vingt-deux	1 000 000	un million
23	vingt-trois	1 000 000 000	un milliard

Ordinal Numbers

1st	premier, première	16th	seizième
2nd	deuxième *or* second	17th	dix-septième
3rd	troisième	18th	dix-huitième
4th	quatrième	19th	dix-neuvième
5th	cinquième	20th	vingtième
6th	sixième	21st	vingt et unième
7th	septième	22nd	vingt-deuxième
8th	huitième	30th	trentième
9th	neuvième	40th	quarantième
10th	dixième	50th	cinquantième
11th	onzième	60th	soixantième
12th	douzième	70th	soixante-dixième
13th	treizième	80th	quatre-vingtième
14th	quatorzième	90th	quatre-vingt-dixième
15th	quinzième	100th	centième

Abbreviations in this Work

adj	adjective
adv	adverb
adv phr	adverbial phrase
Bel	Belgium
Brit	Great Britain
Can	Canada
conj	conjunction
conj phr	conjunctive phrase
esp	especially
etc	et cetera
f	feminine
fam	familiar or colloquial
fpl	feminine plural
interj	interjection
m	masculine
mf	masculine or feminine
mpl	masculine plural
n	noun
nf	feminine noun
nfpl	feminine plural noun
nfs & pl	invariable singular or plural feminine noun
nm	masculine noun
nmf	masculine or feminine noun
nmfpl	plural noun invariable for gender

nmfs & pl	noun invariable for both gender and number
nmpl	masculine plural noun
nms & pl	invariable singular or plural masculine noun
npl	plural noun
ns & pl	noun invariable for plural
pl	plural
pp	past participle
prep	preposition
prep phr	prepositional phrase
pron	pronoun
qqch	quelque chose (something)
qqn	quelqu'un (someone)
s	singular
s.o.	someone
sth	something
Switz	Switzerland
usu	usually
v	verb (transitive and intransitive)
v aux	auxiliary verb
vi	intransitive verb
v impers	impersonal verb
vr	reflexive verb
vt	transitive verb

Pronunciation Symbols

VOWELS

æ ask, bat, glad
ɑ cot, bomb
ã *French* chant, ennui
a *New England* aunt, *British* ask, glass
e *French* été, aider, chez
ɛ egg, bet, fed
ɛ̃ *French* lapin, main
ə about, javelin, Alabama
ə when italicized as in əl, əm, ən, indicates a syllabic pronunciation of the consonant as in bottle, prism, button
i very, any, thirty
i: eat, bead, bee
ɪ id, bid, pit
o Ohio, yellower, potato
o: oats, own, zone, blow
ɔ awl, maul, caught, paw
ɔ̃ ombre, mon
ʊ sure, should, could
u *French* ouvert, chou, rouler
u: boot, two, coo
ʌ under, putt, bud
eɪ eight, wade, bay
aɪ ice, bite, tie
aʊ out, gown, plow
ɔɪ oyster, coil, boy
ər further, stir
ø *French* deux, *German* Höhe
œ *French* bœuf, *German* Gött
œ̃ *French* lundi, parfum

CONSONANTS

b baby, labor, cab
d day, ready, kid
dʒ just, badger, fudge
ð then, either, bathe
f foe, tough, buff
g go, bigger, bag
h hot, aha
j yes, vineyard
k cat, keep, lacquer, flock
l law, hollow, boil
m mat, hemp, hammer, rim
n new, tent, tenor, run
ŋ rung, hang, swinger
ɲ *French* digne, agneau
p pay, lapse, top
r rope, burn, tar
s sad, mist, kiss
ʃ shoe, mission, slush
t toe, button, mat
ṭ indicates that some speakers of English pronounce this sound as a voiced alveolar flap, as in later, catty, battle
tʃ choose, batch
θ thin, ether, bath
v vat, never, cave
w wet, software
ɥ *French* cuir, appui
x *German* Bach, *Scottish* loch
z zoo, easy, buzz
ʒ azure, beige
h,k, when italicized indicate sounds which
p,t are present in the pronunciation of some speakers of English but absent in the pronunciation of others, so that *whence* [ˈhwens] can be pronounced as [ˈhwens], [ˈhwɛnts], [ˈwɛnts], or [ˈwɛns].

OTHER SYMBOLS

ˈ high stress **pen**manship
ˌ low stress penman**ship**
ʼ aspiration; when used before French words in *h*-, indicates absence of liaison, as in *le héros* [lə ʼero]
( ) indicate sounds that are present in the pronunciation of some speakers of French but absent in that of others, as in *cenellier* [s(ə)nɛlje], *but* [by(t)]

French-English
Dictionary

A

a [a] *nm* : a, first letter of the alphabet

à [a] *prep* **1** : to **2 ~ deux heures** : at two o'clock **3 ~ la** : in the manner of, like **4 ~ l'heure** : per hour **5 ~ mon avis** : in my opinion **6 ~ pied** : on foot **7 ~ vendre** : for sale **8 la femme aux yeux verts** : the woman with green eyes **9 un ami ~ moi** : a friend of mine **10 voler aux riches** : steal from the rich

abaisser [abese] *vt* **1** : lower, reduce **2** HUMILIER : humble — **s'abaisser** *vr* **1** : lower oneself **2 ~ à** : stoop to

abandonner [abɑ̃dɔne] *vt* : abandon — **s'abandonner** *vr* **1** : neglect oneself **2 ~ à** : give oneself up to — **abandon** [abɑ̃dɔ̃] *nm* **1** : abandonment, neglect **2** DÉSINVOLTURE : abandon

abasourdir [abazurdir] *vt* : stun

abat–jour [abaʒur] *nms & pl* : lampshade

abats [aba] *nmpl* **1** : entrails **2 ~ de volaille** : giblets

abattant [abatɑ̃] *nm* : flap, leaf

abattis [abati] *nmpl* : giblets

abattoir [abatwar] *nm* : slaughterhouse

abattre [abatr] {12} *vt* **1** : knock down, cut down **2** ÉPUISER : wear out **3** DÉMORALISER : dishearten — **s'abattre** *vr* **1** : fall, crash **2 ~ sur** : descend on — **abattement** [abatmɑ̃] *nm* **1** : reduction, allowance **2** : despondency — **abattu, -tue** [abaty] *adj* : downcast

abbaye [abei] *nf* : abbey — **abbé** [abe] *nm* **1** : abbot **2** PRÊTRE : priest

abcès [apsɛ] *nm* : abscess

abdiquer [abdike] *v* : abdicate — **abdication** [abdikasjɔ̃] *nf* : abdication

abdomen [abdɔmɛn] *nm* : abdomen — **abdominal, -nale** [abdɔminal] *adj, mpl* **-naux** [-no] : abdominal

abécédaire [abesedɛr] *nm* : primer, speller

abeille [abɛj] *nf* : bee

aberrant, -rante [abɛrɑ̃, -rɑ̃t] *adj* : absurd — **aberration** [aberasjɔ̃] *nf* : aberration

abêtir [abetir] *vt* : make stupid

abhorrer [abɔre] *vt* : abhor

abîme [abim] *nm* : abyss, depths — **abîmer** [abime] *vt* : spoil, damage — **s'abîmer** *vr* **1** : be spoiled **2** : sink, founder

abject, -jecte [abʒɛkt] *adj* : despicable, abject

abjurer [abʒyre] *vt* : renounce, abjure

abnégation [abnegasjɔ̃] *nf* : self-denial

aboiement [abwamɑ̃] *nm* : barking — **abois** [abwa] *nmpl* **aux ~** : at bay

abolir [abɔlir] *vt* : abolish — **abolition** [abɔlisjɔ̃] *nf* : abolition

abominable [abɔminabl] *adj* : abominable

abonder [abɔ̃de] *vi* : abound — **abondamment** [abɔ̃damɑ̃] *adv* : abundantly — **abondance** [abɔ̃dɑ̃s] *nf* : abundance — **abondant, -dante** [abɔ̃dɑ̃, -dɑ̃t] *adj* : abundant

abonner [abɔne] *vt* : subscribe to — **abonné, -née** [abɔne] *n* : subscriber — **abonnement** [abɔnmɑ̃] *nm* : subscription

aborder [abɔrde] *vt* **1** : approach **2** : tackle, deal with — *vi* : (reach) land — **abord** [abɔr] *nm* **1** : approach **2 d' ~** : at first **3 ~s** *nmpl* : surroundings — **abordable** [abɔrdabl] *adj* **1** : approachable **2** : affordable — **abordage** [abɔrdaʒ] *nm* : boarding

aborigène [abɔriʒɛn] *nmf* : aborigine, native — *adj* : aboriginal

abortif, -tive [abɔrtif, -tiv] *adj* : abortive

aboutir [abutir] *vi* **1** : succeed **2 ~ à** : result in — **aboutissement** [abutismɑ̃] *nm* : result

aboyer [abwaje] {58} *vi* : bark

abraser [abraze] *vt* : abrade — **abrasif, -sive** [abrazif, -ziv] *adj* : abrasive

abréger [abreʒe] {64} *vt* : shorten, abridge — **abrégé** [abreʒe] *nm* : summary — **abrègement** [abrɛʒmɑ̃] *nm* : abridgment

abreuver [abrœve] *vt* **1** : water **2 ~ de** : shower with — **s'abreuver** *vr* : drink — **abreuvoir** [abrœvwar] *nm* : watering place

abréviation [abrevjasjɔ̃] *nf* : abbreviation

abri [abri] *nm* **1** : shelter **2 à l' ~** : under cover — **abriter** [abrite] *vt* **1** : shelter **2** HÉBERGER : house

abricot [abriko] *nm* : apricot

abrier [abrije] {96} *vt Can* : cover

abroger [abrɔʒe] {17} *vt* : repeal

abrupt, -brupte [abrypt] *adj* **1** ESCARPÉ : steep **2** BRUSQUE : abrupt

abrutir [abrytir] *vt* : make stupid — **abruti, -tie** [abryti] *n fam* : fool, idiot

absenter [apsɑ̃te] *v* **s'absenter** *vr* : leave, go away — **absence** [apsɑ̃s] *nf* : absence — **absent, -sente** [apsɑ̃, -sɑ̃t] *adj* : absent — **~** *n* : absentee

absolu, -lue [apsɔly] *adj* : absolute — **absolu** *nm* : absolute — **absolument** [-lymɑ̃] *adv* : absolutely

absolution [apsɔlysjɔ̃] *nf* : absolution

absorber [apsɔrbe] *vt* **1** : absorb **2** : take (medicine) — **absorbant, -bante** [apsɔrbɑ̃, -bɑ̃t] *adj* **1** : absorbent **2** : engrossing — **absorption** [apsɔrpsjɔ̃] *nf* : absorption

absoudre [apsudr] {1} *vt* : absolve

abstenir [apstənir] {92} v **s'abstenir** vr 1 : abstain 2 ～ **de** : refrain from — **abstinence** [apstinãs] nf : abstinence

abstraction [apstraksjõ] nf 1 : abstraction 2 **faire** ～ **de** : set aside — **abstraire** [apstrɛr] {40} vt : abstract — **abstrait, -traite** [apstrɛ, -trɛt] adj : abstract — **abstrait** nm : abstract

absurde [apsyrd] adj : absurd — **absurdité** [apsyrdite] nf : absurdity

abuser [abyze] vt : deceive — vi ～ **de** 1 : misuse 2 : exploit — **s'abuser** vr : be mistaken — **abusif, -sive** [abyzif, -ziv] adj 1 EXAGÉRÉ : excessive 2 IMPROPRE : incorrect

académie [akademi] nf : academy — **académique** [akademik] adj : academic

Acadien, -dienne [akadjɛ̃, -djɛn] n 1 : Acadian 2 : Cajun — **acadien, -dienne** adj 1 : Acadian 2 : Cajun

acajou [akaʒu] nm : mahogany

acariâtre [akarjɑtr] adj : cantankerous

accabler [akable] vt 1 ÉCRASER : overwhelm 2 : condemn — **accablant, -blante** [akablɑ̃, -blɑ̃t] adj : overwhelming — **accablement** [akabləmɑ̃] nm : despondency

accalmie [akalmi] nf : lull

accaparer [akapare] vt : monopolize

accéder [aksede] {87} vi 1 ～ **à** : reach, obtain 2 ～ **à** : accede to

accélérer [akselere] {87} v : accelerate — **accélérateur** nm : accelerator — **accélération** [akselerasjõ] nf : acceleration

accent [aksɑ̃] nm 1 : accent 2 : stress, emphasis — **accentuer** [aksɑ̃tɥe] vt 1 : accent, stress 2 : emphasize — **s'accentuer** vr : become more pronounced

accepter [aksɛpte] vt : accept, agree to — **acceptable** [aksɛptabl] adj : acceptable — **acceptation** [aksɛptasjõ] nf : acceptance

acception [aksɛpsjõ] nf : sense, meaning

accès [aksɛ] nm 1 : access 2 : entry 3 CRISE : fit, attack — **accessible** [aksɛsibl] adj : accessible

accession [aksesjõ] nf ～ **à** : accession to, attainment of

accessoire [aksɛswar] nm 1 : accessory 2 : prop — ～ adj : incidental, secondary

accident [aksidɑ̃] nm : accident — **accidenté, -tée** [aksidɑ̃te] adj 1 : damaged, injured 2 : rough, uneven — ～ n : accident victim — **accidentel, -telle** [aksidɑ̃tɛl] adj : accidental — **accidentellement** [-tɛlmɑ̃] adv : accidentally

acclamer [aklame] vt : acclaim, cheer — **acclamation** [aklamasjõ] nf : cheering

acclimater [aklimate] vt : acclimatize — **s'acclimater** vr : adapt

accolade [akɔlad] nf 1 ÉTREINTE : embrace 2 : brace sign, bracket

accommoder [akɔmɔde] vt : accommodate — **s'accommoder** vr ～ **de** : put up with — **accommodant, -dante** [akɔmɔdɑ̃, -dɑ̃t] adj : obliging — **accommodement** [akɔmɔdmɑ̃] nm : compromise

accompagner [akõpaɲe] vt : accompany — **accompagnement** [akõpaɲmɑ̃] nm : accompaniment

accomplir [akõplir] vt : accomplish — **s'accomplir** vr : take place — **accompli, -plie** [akõpli] adj : finished — **accomplissement** [akõplismɑ̃] nm : accomplishment

accordéon [akɔrdeõ] nm : accordion

accorder [akɔrde] vt 1 : reconcile 2 OCTROYER : grant, bestow — **s'accorder** vr : be in agreement — **accord** [akɔr] nm 1 : agreement 2 : approval, consent 3 : chord (in music)

accoster [akɔste] vt : approach — vi : dock, land

accotement [akɔtmɑ̃] nm : shoulder (of a road)

accoucher [akuʃe] vt : deliver (a baby) — vi 1 : be in labor 2 ～ **de** : give birth to — **accouchement** [akuʃmɑ̃] nm : childbirth

accouder [akude] v **s'accouder** vr ～ **à** or ～ **sur** : lean (one's elbows) on — **accoudoir** [akudwar] nm : armrest

accoupler [akuple] vt : couple, link — **s'accoupler** vr : mate — **accouplement** [akupləmɑ̃] nm 1 : coupling 2 : mating

accourir [akurir] {23} vi : come running

accoutrement [akutrəmɑ̃] nm : outfit

accoutumer [akutyme] vt : accustom — **s'accoutumer** vr ～ **à** : get accustomed to — **accoutumé, -mée** [akutyme] adj : customary

accréditer [akredite] vt 1 : accredit 2 : substantiate (a rumor, etc.)

accroc [akro] nm 1 : rip, tear 2 OBSTACLE : hitch, snag

accrocher [akrɔʃe] vt 1 SUSPENDRE : hang up 2 : hook, hitch 3 HEURTER : bump into 4 ～ **l'œil** : catch the eye — vi : catch, snag — **s'accrocher** vr : hang on, cling — **accrochage** [akrɔʃaʒ] nm 1 : hanging, hooking 2 : collision 3 QUERELLE : dispute — **accrocheur, -cheuse** [akrɔʃœr, -ʃøz] adj 1 OPINIÂTRE : tenacious 2 ATTRAYANT : eye-catching

accroire [akrwar] {2} vt **en faire** ～ **à** : take in, dupe

accroître [akrwatr] {25} vt : increase — **s'accroître** vr : grow — **accroissement** [akrwasmɑ̃] nm : growth, increase

accroupir [akrupir] v **s'accroupir** vr : squat

accueillir [akœjir] {3} vt : greet — **accueil** [akœj] nm : welcome, reception — **accueillant, -lante** [akœjɑ̃, -jɑ̃t] adj : welcoming, hospitable

acculer [akyle] *vt* : corner

accumuler [akymyle] *vt* : accumulate — **s'accumuler** *vr* : pile up — **accumulation** [akymylasjɔ̃] *nf* : accumulation

accuser [akyze] *vt* **1** : accuse **2** ～ **réception de** : acknowledge receipt of — **accusateur, -trice** [akyzatœr, -tris] *adj* : incriminating — **accusation** [akyzasjɔ̃] *nf* : accusation — **accusé, -sée** *n* : defendant, accused

acerbe [asɛrb] *adj* : acerbic

acéré, -rée [asere] *adj* : sharp

acharner [aʃarne] *v* **s'acharner** *vr* **1** s'OBSTINER : persevere **2** ～ **sur** : persecute, hound — **acharné, -née** [aʃarne] *adj* : relentless — **acharnement** [aʃarnəma] *nm* : relentlessness

achat [aʃa] *nm* **1** : purchase **2 faire des** ～**s** : go shopping

acheminer [aʃmine] *vt* **1** : transport **2** : forward (mail) — **s'acheminer** *vr* ～ **vers** : head for — **acheminement** [aʃminma] *nm* : dispatch, routing

acheter [aʃte] {20} *vt* : buy, purchase — **acheteur, -teuse** [aʃtœr, -tøz] *n* : buyer

achever [aʃve] {52} *vt* **1** : complete, finish — **s'achever** *vr* : draw to a close — **achèvement** [aʃɛvma] *nm* : completion

acide [asid] *adj & nm* : acid — **acidité** [asidite] *nf* : sourness, acidity

acier [asje] *nm* : steel — **aciérie** [asjeri] *nf* : steelworks

acné [akne] *nf* : acne

acolyte [akɔlit] *nm* : accomplice

acompte [akɔ̃t] *nm* : deposit, installment

à–côté [akote] *nm, pl* **à–côtés** : extra, perk

à–coup [aku] *nm, pl* **à–coups** : jerk, jolt

acoustique [akustik] *adj* : acoustic — ～ *nf* : acoustics

acquérir [akerir] {21} *vt* **1** : acquire **2** : purchase — **acquéreur, -reuse** [akerœr, -røz] *n* : buyer

acquiescer [akjese] {6} *vi* : agree

acquis, -quise [aki, -kiz] *adj* **1** : acquired **2** : established — **acquis** *nms & pl* : knowledge — **acquisition** [akizisjɔ̃] *nf* : acquisition

acquitter [akite] *vt* **1** : acquit **2** PAYER : pay — **s'acquitter** *vr* ～ **de 1** : carry out **2** : pay off — **acquit** [aki] *nm* : receipt — **acquittement** [akitma] *nm* : payment (of a debt)

acre [akr] *nf* : acre *Can*

âcre [akr] *adj* : acrid — **âcreté** [akrəte] *nf* : bitterness

acrobate [akrɔbat] *nmf* : acrobat — **acrobatie** [akrɔbasi] *nf* : acrobatics — **acrobatique** [akrɔbatik] *adj* : acrobatic

acrylique [akrilik] *adj & nm* : acrylic

acte [akt] *nm* **1** : action, deed **2** : act (in the-

ater) **3** : certificate, document **4** ～**s** *nmpl* : proceedings

acteur, -trice [aktœr, -tris] *n* : actor, actress *f*

actif, -tive [aktif, -tiv] *adj* : active — **actif** *nm* **1** : assets *pl* **2** : active voice

action [aksjɔ̃] *nf* **1** : action, act **2** EFFET : effect **3** : share (in finance) — **actionnaire** [aksjɔnɛr] *nmf* : shareholder — **actionner** [aksjɔne] *vt* **1** : engage, set in motion **2** : sue

activer [aktive] *vt* **1** : activate **2** HÂTER : speed up — **s'activer** *vr* : bustle about

activiste [aktivist] *adj & nmf* : activist — **activisme** [aktivism] *nm* : activism

activité [aktivite] *nf* : activity

actualité [aktɥalite] *nf* **1** : current events *pl* **2** ～**s** *nfpl* : news — **actualiser** [aktɥalize] *vt* : update, modernize

actuel, -tuelle [aktɥɛl] *adj* : current, present — **actuellement** [-tɥɛlma] *adv* : at present

acuité [akɥite] *nf* : acuteness

acupuncture [akypɔ̃ktyr] *nf* : acupuncture

adage [adaʒ] *nm* : adage

adapter [adapte] *vt* : adapt, fit — **s'adapter** *vr* : adapt — **adaptation** [adaptasjɔ̃] *nf* : adaptation — **adaptateur** [adaptatœr] *nm* : adapter

additif [aditif] *nm* : additive

addition [adisjɔ̃] *nf* **1** : addition **2** NOTE : bill, check — **additionnel, -nelle** [adisjɔnɛl] *adj* : additional — **additionner** [adisjɔne] *vt* : add (up)

adepte [adɛpt] *nmf* : follower

adéquat, -quate [adekwa, -kwat] *adj* **1** SUFFISANT : adequate **2** APPROPRIÉ : appropriate

adhérer [adere] {87} *vi* **1** : adhere **2** ～ **à** : join — **adhérence** [aderɑ̃s] *nf* : adhesion, grip — **adhérent, -rente** [aderɑ̃, -rɑ̃t] *adj* : adhering, sticking — ～ *n* : member

adhésif, -sive [adezif, -ziv] *adj* : adhesive — **adhésif** *nm* : adhesive — **adhésion** [adezjɔ̃] *nf* **1** : adhesion **2** : adherence, support **3** AFFILIATION : membership

adieu [adjø] *nm, pl* **adieux** : farewell, goodbye

adjacent, -cente [adʒasɑ̃, -sɑ̃t] *adj* : adjacent

adjectif [adʒɛktif] *nm* : adjective

adjoindre [adʒwɛ̃dr] {50} *vt* **1** : appoint **2** : add, attach — **s'adjoindre** *vr* ～ **qqn** : take s.o. on, hire s.o. — **adjoint, -jointe** [adʒwɛ̃, -ʒwɛ̃t] *adj & n* : assistant

adjonction [adʒɔ̃ksjɔ̃] *nf* : addition

admettre [admɛtr] {53} *vt* : admit

administrer [administre] *vt* : administer — **administrateur, -trice** [administratœr, -tris] *n* : director, administrator — **administratif, -tive** [administratif, -tiv] *adj* : admin-

istrative — **administration** [administrasjɔ̃]
nf : administration

admirer [admire] *vt* : admire — **admirable**
[admirabl] *adj* : admirable — **admirateur,
-trice** [admiratœr, -tris] *n* : admirer — **admiratif, -tive** [admiratif, -tiv] *adj* : admiring
— **admiration** [admirasjɔ̃] *nf* : admiration

admissible [admisibl] *adj* : acceptable, eligible — **admission** [admisjɔ̃] *nf* : admittance

admonester [admɔnɛste] *vt* : admonish

ADN [adeɛn] *nm* (*acide désoxyribonucléique*)
: DNA

adolescence [adɔlesɑ̃s] *nf* : adolescence —
adolescent, -cente [-lesɑ̃, -sɑ̃t] *adj* & *n*
: adolescent

adopter [adɔpte] *vt* : adopt — **adoptif, -tive**
[adɔptif, -tiv] *adj* : adoptive, adopted —
adoption [adɔpsjɔ̃] *nf* : adoption

adorer [adɔre] *vt* : adore, worship —
adorable [adɔrabl] *adj* : adorable

adosser [adose] *vt* : lean — **s'adosser** *vr*
~ **à** *or* ~ **contre** : lean back against

adoucir [adusir] *vt* **1** : soften **2** : alleviate,
ease — **s'adoucir** *vr* : become milder, mellow — **adoucissement** [adusismɑ̃] *nm* **1**
: softening **2** : alleviation

adresser [adrese] *vt* : address — **adresse**
[adrɛs] *nf* **1** : address **2** HABILETÉ : skill —
s'adresser *vr* ~ **à** : speak to

adroit, -droite [adrwa, -drwat] *adj* HABILE
: skillful

adulte [adylt] *adj* & *nmf* : adult

adultère [adyltɛr] *nm* : adultery — ~ *adj*
: adulterous

advenir [advənir] {4} *v impers* **1** : happen,
occur **2** ~ **de** : become of

adverbe [advɛrb] *nm* : adverb

adversaire [advɛrsɛr] *nmf* : opponent — **adverse** [advɛrs] *adj* : opposing — **adversité**
[advɛrsite] *nf* : adversity

aérer [aere] {87} *vt* : air out — **s'aérer** *vr*
: get some fresh air

aérien, -rienne [aerjɛ̃, -rjɛn] *adj* : air, aerial

aérobic [aerɔbik] *nm* : aerobics

aérodynamique [aerɔdinamik] *adj* : aerodynamic

aérogare [aerɔgar] *nf* : air terminal

aéroglisseur [aerɔglisœr] *nm* : hovercraft

aéroport [aerɔpɔr] *nm* : airport

aérosol [aerɔsɔl] *nm* : aerosol

affable [afabl] *adj* : affable

affaiblir [afeblir] *vt* : weaken — **s'affaiblir** *vr*
1 : become weak **2** ATTÉNUER : fade

affaire [afɛr] *nf* **1** : affair **2** CAS : matter **3**
ENTREPRISE : business **4** TRANSACTION
: deal **5** ~**s** *nfpl* : belongings **6** ~**s** *nfpl*
: business **7** **avoir** ~ **à** : deal with — **affairer** [afere] *v* **s'affairer** *vr* : be busy — **af-
fairé, -rée** [afere] *adj* : busy

affaisser [afese] *v* **s'affaisser** *vr* : collapse,

give way — **affaissement** [afɛsmɑ̃] *nm*
: sagging, sinking

affaler [afale] *v* **s'affaler** *vr* : collapse

affamé, -mée [afame] *adj* : famished

affecter [afɛkte] *vt* **1** : affect **2** NOMMER
: appoint **3** ASSIGNER : allocate **4** FEINDRE
: feign — **affectation** [afɛktasjɔ̃] *nf* **1** : appointment **2** ~ **des fonds** : allocation of
funds — **affecté, -tée** [afɛkte] *adj* : mannered, affected

affectif, -tive [afɛktif, -tiv] *adj* : emotional

affection [afɛksjɔ̃] *nf* **1** : affection **2** : ailment — **affectionner** [afɛksjɔne] *vt* : be
fond of — **affectueux, -tueuse** [afɛktɥø,
-tɥøz] *adj* : affectionate — **affectueuse-
ment** [-tɥøzmɑ̃] *adv* : fondly

afférent, -rente [aferɑ̃, -rɑ̃t] *adj* ~ **à** : per-
taining to

affermir [afɛrmir] *vt* : strengthen

affiche [afiʃ] *nf* : poster, notice — **affichage**
[afiʃaʒ] *nm* **1** : posting, publicizing **2** ~
numérique : digital display — **afficher**
[afiʃe] *vt* **1** : post, put up **2** : show, display

affilée [afile] **d'**~ *adv phr* : in a row

affiler [afile] {96} *vt* : sharpen

affilier [afilje] *vt* : affiliate — **s'affilier** *vr* ~
à : join

affiner [afine] *vt* : refine

affinité [afinite] *nf* : affinity

affirmatif, -tive [afirmatif, -tiv] *adj* : affirmative — **affirmative** *nf* : affirmative

affirmer [afirme] *vt* : affirm, assert —
s'affirmer *vr* : assert oneself — **affirmation**
[afirmasjɔ̃] *nf* : assertion

affliger [afliʒe] {17} *vt* : afflict, distress —
affliction [afliksjɔ̃] *nf* : affliction — **af-
fligeant, -geante** [afliʒɑ̃, -ʒɑ̃t] *adj* : distressing

affluer [aflye] *vi* **1** COULER : flow **2** ~ **vers**
: flock to — **affluence** [aflyɑ̃s] *nf* **1** : crowd
2 heure d'~ : rush hour — **affluent** [aflyɑ̃]
nm : tributary

afflux [afly] *nm* : influx, rush

affoler [afɔle] *vt* EFFRAYER : terrify —
s'affoler *vr* : panic — **affolé, -lée** [afɔle] *adj*
: frightened — **affolement** [afɔlmɑ̃] *nm*
: panic

affranchir [afrɑ̃ʃir] *vt* **1** LIBÉRER : liberate,
free **2** : stamp (a letter) — **affranchissement** [afrɑ̃ʃismɑ̃] *nm* **1** : liberation **2**
: stamping, postage

affréter [afrete] {87} *vt* : charter

affreux, -freuse [afrø, -frøz] *adj* : horrible
— **affreusement** [afrøzmɑ̃] *adv* : horribly

affronter [afrɔ̃te] *vt* : confront — **s'affronter**
vr : confront each other — **affront** [afrɔ̃] *nm*
: affront — **affrontement** [afrɔ̃tmɑ̃] *nm*
: confrontation

affûter [afyte] *vt* : sharpen — **affût** [afy] *nm*
être à l'~ **de** : be on the lookout for

afin [afɛ̃] *adv* **1** ~ **de** : in order to **2** ~ **que** : so that

africain, -caine [afrikɛ̃, -kɛn] *adj* : African

agacer [agase] {6} *vt* : irritate — **agaçant, -çante** [agasɑ̃, -sɑ̃t] *adj* : annoying — **agacement** [agasmɑ̃] *nm* : annoyance

âge [aʒ] *nm* **1** : age (of a person) **2** : age, era — **âgé, -gée** [aʒe] *adj* **1** VIEUX : elderly **2** ~ **de 10 ans** : 10 years old

agence [aʒɑ̃s] *nf* : agency, office

agencer [aʒɑ̃se] {6} *vt* : arrange, lay out — **agencement** [aʒɑ̃smɑ̃] *nm* : layout

agenda [aʒɛ̃da] *nm* : appointment book

agenouiller [aʒnuje] *v* **s'agenouiller** *vr* : kneel

agent, -gente [aʒɑ̃, -ʒɑ̃t] *n* **1** : agent **2** ~ **de police** : police officer

agglomération [aglɔmerasjɔ̃] *nf* : urban area

agglutiner [aglytine] *vt* : stick together

aggraver [agrave] *vt* : aggravate, make worse — **s'aggraver** *vr* EMPIRER : worsen — **aggravation** [agravasjɔ̃] *nf* : worsening

agile [aʒil] *adj* : agile — **agilité** [aʒilite] *nf* : agility

agir [aʒir] *vi* **1** : act **2** SE COMPORTER : behave **3** : take effect (of medication) — **s'agir** *vr* **il s'agit de** : it is a question of — **agissements** [aʒismɑ̃] *nmpl* : schemes, dealings

agiter [aʒite] *vt* **1** SECOUER : shake **2** TROUBLER : disturb — **s'agiter** *vr* **1** : bustle about **2** : fidget — **agitation** [aʒitasjɔ̃] *nf* **1** : agitation **2** : (political) unrest — **agité, -tée** [aʒite] *adj* **1** : restless **2** : rough, choppy

agneau [aɲo] *nm, pl* **agneaux** : lamb

agonie [agɔni] *nf* : (death) throes *pl* — **agoniser** [agɔnize] *vi* : be dying

agrafe [agraf] *nf* **1** : hook, fastener **2** : staple — **agrafer** [agrafe] *vt* **1** : fasten **2** : staple — **agrafeuse** [agraføz] *nf* : stapler

agrandir [agrɑ̃dir] *vt* : enlarge — **s'agrandir** *vr* : expand, grow — **agrandissement** [agrɑ̃dismɑ̃] *nm* : enlargement, expansion

agréable [agreabl] *adj* : nice, pleasant — **agréablement** [-abləmɑ̃] *adv* : pleasantly

agréer [agree] *vt* **1** : accept **2 veuillez** ~ **l'expression de mes sentiments distingués** : sincerely yours — **agréé, agréée** [agree] *adj* : authorized

agrégé, -gée [agreʒe] *n France* : certified teacher or professor — **agrégation** [agregasjɔ̃] *nf France* : qualifying exam for teachers or professors

agrément [agremɑ̃] *nm* **1** : charm, appeal **2 voyage d'**~ : pleasure trip — **agrémenter** [agremɑ̃te] *vt* : embellish

agrès [agrɛ] *nmpl* : (gymnastic) apparatus

agresser [agrese] *vt* : attack, assault — **agresseur** [agrɛsœr] *nm* : attacker — **agressif, -sive** [agrɛsif, -siv] *adj* : aggres-

sive — **agression** [agrɛsjɔ̃] *nf* **1** : attack **2** : aggression — **agressivité** [agresivite] *nf* : aggressiveness

agricole [agrikɔl] *adj* : agricultural — **agriculteur, -trice** [agrikyltœr, -tris] *n* : farmer — **agriculture** [agrikyltyr] *nf* : agriculture, farming

agripper [agripe] *vt* : clutch, grab — **s'agripper** *vr* ~ **à** : cling to, clutch

agrumes [agrym] *nmpl* : citrus fruits

aguets [agɛ] **aux** ~ *adv phr* : on the lookout

ah [a] *interj* : oh!, ah!

ahuri, -rie [ayri] *adj* : dumbfounded — **ahurissant, -sante** [ayrisɑ̃, -sɑ̃t] *adj* : astounding

aider [ede] *vt* : help — **aide** *nf* **1** : aid **2 à l'**~ **de** : with the help of — **aide** *nmf* : assistant

aïe [aj] *interj* : ouch!, ow!

aïeux [ajø] *nmpl* : ancestors

aigle [ɛgl] *nm* : eagle

aigre [ɛgr] *adj* : sour, tart — **aigredoux, -douce** [ɛgrədu, -dus] *adj* : bittersweet — **aigreur** [ɛgrœr] *nf* : sourness — **aigri** [egri] *adj* : embittered

aigu, -guë [egy] *adj* **1** : sharp, keen **2** VIF : acute **3** STRIDENT : shrill

aiguille [eguij] *nf* **1** : needle **2** : hand (of a clock)

aiguillon [eguijɔ̃] *nm* **1** : goad **2** : stinger (of an insect)

aiguiser [egize] *vt* **1** : sharpen **2** ~ **l'appétit** : whet the appetite

ail [aj] *nm* : garlic

aile [ɛl] *nf* **1** : wing **2** : fender (of an automobile) — **ailier** [elje] *nm* : wing, end (in sports)

ailleurs [ajœr] *adv* **1** : elsewhere **2 d'**~ : besides, moreover **3 par** ~ : furthermore

aimable [ɛmabl] *adj* : kind — **aimablement** [ɛmabləmɑ̃] *adv* : kindly

aimant¹, -mante [ɛmɑ̃, -mɑ̃t] *adj* : loving, caring

aimant² *nm* : magnet

aimer [eme] *vt* **1** : love, like **2** ~ **mieux** : prefer

aine [ɛn] *nf* : groin

aîné, -née [ene] *adj* **1** : older, oldest **2** : senior — ~ *n* **1** : elder child, eldest child **2** : elder — **aînés** *nmpl* : elders **3 il est mon aîné** : he's older than me

ainsi [ɛ̃si] *adv* **1** : in this way, thus **2** ~ **que** : just as **3** ~ **que** : as well as **4 et** ~ **de suite** : and so on **5 pour** ~ **dire** : so to speak

air [ɛr] *nm* **1** : air **2** MÉLODIE : tune **3** EXPRESSION : air, look **4 avoir l'**~ : look, seem

aire [ɛr] *nf* **1** : area **2 ~ d'atterrissage** : landing strip

aisance [ezɑ̃s] *nf* **1** : ease **2** PROSPÉRITÉ : affluence — **aise** *nf* **1** : ease **2 être à l'~** : be comfortable — **aisé, -sée** [eze] *adj* **1** : easy **2** RICHE : well-off — **aisément** [ezemɑ̃] *adv* : easily

aisselle [ɛsɛl] *nf* : armpit

ajourner [aʒurne] *vt* : adjourn — **ajournement** [aʒurnəmɑ̃] *nm* : adjournment

ajouter [aʒute] *vt* : add — **ajout** [aʒu] *nm* : addition

ajuster [aʒyste] *vt* : adjust — **ajustement** [aʒystəmɑ̃] *nm* : adjustment

alarmer [alarme] *vt* : alarm — **s'alarmer** *vr* : become alarmed — **alarmant, -mante** [alarmɑ̃, -mɑ̃t] *adj* : alarming — **alarme** [alarm] *nf* : alarm

album [albɔm] *nm* : album

alcool [alkɔl] *nm* : alcohol — **alcoolique** [alkɔlik] *adj & nmf* : alcoholic — **alcoolisé, -sée** [alkɔlize] *adj* : alcoholic — **alcoolisme** [-kɔlism] *nm* : alcoholism

alcôve [alkov] *nf* : alcove

aléa [alea] *nm* : risk — **aléatoire** [aleatwar] *adj* **1** : risky, uncertain **2** : random

alentour [alɑ̃tur] *adv* : around, surrounding — **alentours** [alɑ̃tur] *nmpl* **aux ~ de** : around, in the vicinity of

alerter [alɛrte] *vt* : alert, warn — **alerte** [alɛrt] *adj* : alert, lively — **alerte** *nf* : alert, warning

algèbre [alʒɛbr] *nf* : algebra

algérien, -rienne [alʒerjɛ̃, -rjɛn] *adj* : Algerian

algue [alg] *nf* : seaweed

alias [aljas] *adv* : alias

alibi [alibi] *nm* : alibi

aliéner [aljene] {87} *vt* : alienate — **aliénation** [aljenasjɔ̃] *nf* : alienation

aligner [aliɲe] *vt* : align — **s'aligner** *vr* : fall into line — **alignement** [aliɲmɑ̃] *nm* : alignment

alimenter [alimɑ̃te] *vt* **1** : feed **2** APPROVISIONNER : supply — **aliment** [alimɑ̃] *nm* : food — **alimentation** [alimɑ̃tasjɔ̃] *nf* **1** : diet, nourishment **2 magasin d'~** : grocery store

alinéa [alinea] *nm* : paragraph

alité, -tée [alite] *adj* : bedridden

allaiter [alete] *vt* : nurse, breast-feed — **allaitement** [alɛtmɑ̃] *nm* : breast-feeding

allant [alɑ̃] *nm* : drive, spirit

allécher [aleʃe] {87} *vt* : allure, tempt — **alléchant, -chante** [aleʃɑ̃, -ʃɑ̃t] *adj* : tempting

allée [ale] *nf* **1** : path, lane, walk **2** : aisle **3 ~s et venues** : comings and goings

allégation [alegasjɔ̃] *nf* : allegation

allégeance [aleʒɑ̃s] *nf* : allegiance

alléger [aleʒe] {64} *vt* **1** : lighten **2** SOULAGER : alleviate

allègre [alɛgr] *adj* : cheerful, lively — **allégresse** [alegrɛs] *nf* : elation

alléguer [alege] {87} *vt* : allege

allemand, -mande [almɑ̃, -mɑ̃d] *adj* : German — **allemand** *nm* : German (language)

aller [ale] {5} *vi* **1** : go **2** MARCHER : work **3** : proceed, get along **4 ~ à** : fit, suit **5 allons-y** : let's go **6 comment allez-vous?** : how are you? **7 elle va bien** : she is fine — *v aux* : be going to, be about to — **s'en ~** *vr* : go away — *nm* **1** or **~ simple** : one-way (ticket) **2 aller–retour** : round-trip (ticket)

allergie [alɛrʒi] *nf* : allergy — **allergique** [alɛrʒik] *adj* : allergic

alliage [aljaʒ] *nm* : alloy

allier [alje] {96} *vt* : combine — **s'allier** *vr* **~ à** : become allied with — **alliance** [aljɑ̃s] *nf* **1** : alliance **2** : wedding ring **3 par ~** : by marriage — **allié, -liée** *n* : ally

alligator [aligatɔr] *nm* : alligator

allô [alo] *interj* : hello

allocation [alɔkasjɔ̃] *nf* **1** : allocation **2 ~ de chômage** : unemployment benefit

allocution [alɔkysjɔ̃] *nf* : short speech, address

allonger [alɔ̃ʒe] {17} *vt* **1** : lengthen **2** ÉTIRER : stretch (out) — *vi* : get longer — **s'allonger** *vr* SE COUCHER : lie down

allouer [alwe] *vt* : allocate

allumer [alyme] *vt* **1** : light, ignite **2** : turn on, switch on — **s'allumer** *vr* : come on, light (up) — **allumage** *nm* **1** : lighting **2** : (automobile) ignition — **allumette** [alymɛt] *nf* : match

allure [alyr] *nf* **1** APPARENCE : appearance **2** : speed, pace **3 à toute ~** : at full speed

allusion [alyzjɔ̃] *nf* : allusion

almanach [almana] *nm* : almanac

alors [alɔr] *adv* **1** : then **2 ~ que** : while, when **3 ~ que** : even though **4 et ~?** : so?, so what? **5 ou ~** : or else

alouette [alwɛt] *nf* : lark

alourdir [alurdir] *vt* : weigh down — **s'alourdir** *vr* : become heavy

alphabet [alfabɛ] *nm* : alphabet — **alphabétique** [alfabetik] *adj* : alphabetical

alpin, -pine [alpɛ̃, -pin] *adj* : alpine — **alpinisme** [alpinism] *nm* : mountain climbing

altérer [altere] {87} *vt* **1** : distort **2** ABÎMER : spoil — **s'altérer** *vr* : deteriorate

alterner [altɛrne] *vi* : alternate — **alternatif, -tive** [altɛrnatif, -tiv] *adj* : alternative — **alternative** [altɛrnativ] *nf* : alternative

altesse [altɛs] *nf* **son Altesse** : His (Her) Highness

altier, -tière [altje, -tjɛr] *adj* : haughty

altitude [altityd] *nf* : altitude

altruisme [altrɥism] *nm* : altruism

aluminium [alyminjɔm] *nm* : aluminum

amabilité [amabilite] *nf* : kindness

amadouer [amadwe] *vt* : cajole

amaigrir [amegrir] *vt* : make thin — **amaigrissement** [amegrismɑ̃] *nm* : weight loss

amalgame [amalgam] *nm* : mixture

amande [amɑ̃d] *nf* **1** : almond **2** : kernel (of a fruit or nut)

amant, -mante [amɑ̃, -mɑ̃t] *n* : lover

amarrer [amare] *vt* : moor — **amarrage** [amaraʒ] *nm* : mooring

amas [ama] *nm* : pile, heap — **amasser** [amase] *vt* ACCUMULER : amass — **s'amasser** *vr* : pile up

amateur [amatœr] *nm* **1** : enthusiast **2** : amateur

ambages [ɑ̃baʒ] **sans ~** *adv phr* : plainly

ambassade [ɑ̃basad] *nf* : embassy — **ambassadeur, -drice** [ɑ̃basadœr, -dris] *n* : ambassador

ambiance [ɑ̃bjɑ̃s] *nf* : atmosphere — **ambiant, -biante** [ɑ̃bjɑ̃, -bjɑ̃t] *adj* : surrounding

ambigu, -guë [ɑ̃bigy] *adj* : ambiguous — **ambiguïté** [ɑ̃biɡɥite] *nf* : ambiguity

ambitieux, -tieuse [ɑ̃bisjø, -sjøz] *adj* : ambitious — **ambition** [ɑ̃bisjɔ̃] *nf* : ambition

ambivalent, -lente [ɑ̃bivalɑ̃, -lɑ̃t] *adj* : ambivalent

ambre [ɑ̃br] *nm* : amber

ambulant, -lante [ɑ̃bylɑ̃, -lɑ̃t] *adj* : itinerant — **ambulance** [ɑ̃bylɑ̃s] *nf* : ambulance

ambulatoire [ɑ̃bylatwar] *adj* : ambulatory

âme [am] *nf* **1** : soul **2 état d'~** : state of mind

améliorer [ameljɔre] *vt* : improve — **s'améliorer** *vr* : get better — **amélioration** [ameljɔrasjɔ̃] *nf* : improvement

aménager [amenaʒe] {17} *vt* : fit out — **aménagement** [amenaʒmɑ̃] *nm* **1** : fitting out **2** : development (of a region, etc.)

amender [amɑ̃de] *vt* : amend — **amende** [amɑ̃d] *nf* : fine — **amendement** [amɑ̃dmɑ̃] *nm* : amendment

amener [amne] {52} *vt* **1** : bring **2** OCCASIONNER : cause

amenuiser [amənɥize] *v* **s'amenuiser** *vr* : dwindle

amer, -mère [amɛr] *adj* : bitter — **amèrement** [amɛrmɑ̃] *adv* : bitterly

américain, -caine [amerikɛ̃, -kɛn] *adj* : American

amérindien, -dienne [amerɛ̃djɛ̃, -djɛn] *adj* : Native American

amertume [amɛrtym] *nf* : bitterness

ameublement [amœbləmɑ̃] *nm* **1** : furnishing **2** MEUBLES : furniture

ami, -mie [ami] *n* **1** : friend **2** *or* **petit ~** : boyfriend **3** *or* **petite ~e** : girlfriend

amiable [amjabl] *adj* **à l'~** : amicable

amiante [amjɑ̃t] *nm* : asbestos

amibe [amib] *nf* : amoeba

amical, -cale [amikal] *adj, mpl* **-caux** [-ko] : friendly

amidon [amidɔ̃] *nm* : starch — **amidonner** [amidɔne] *vt* : starch

amincir [amɛ̃sir] *vt* : make thinner — **s'amincir** *vr* : get thinner

amiral [amiral] *nm, pl* **-raux** [-ro] : admiral

amitié [amitje] *nf* **1** : friendship **2 ~s** *nfpl* : best regards

ammoniaque [amɔnjak] *nf* : ammonia

amnésie [amnezi] *nf* : amnesia

amnistie [amnisti] *nf* : amnesty

amoindrir [amwɛ̃drir] *vt* : lessen — **s'amoindrir** *vr* : diminish

amollir [amɔlir] *vt* : soften

amonceler [amɔ̃sle] {18} *vt* : accumulate — **s'amonceler** *vr* : pile up — **amoncellement** [amɔ̃sɛlmɑ̃] *nm* : pile, heap

amont [amɔ̃] *nm* **en ~** : upstream

amorce [amɔrs] *nf* **1** DÉBUT : beginning(s) **2** APPÂT **3** : detonator, fuse — **amorcer** [amɔrse] {6} *vt* **1** COMMENCER : begin **2** APPÂTER : bait **3** : boot (a computer) — **s'amorcer** *vr* : begin

amorphe [amɔrf] *adj* : listless

amorti [amɔrti] *nm Can* : bunt (in baseball)

amortir [amɔrtir] *vt* : cushion, deaden — **amortisseur** [amɔrtisœr] *nm* : shock absorber

amour [amur] *nm* : love — **amoureusement** [amurøzmɑ̃] *adv* : lovingly — **amoureux, -reuse** [amurø, -røz] *adj* **1** : loving **2 être ~** : be in love — **~** *n* : lover — **amour–propre** [amurprɔpr] *nm* : self-esteem

amovible [amɔvibl] *adj* : removable

amphibien [ɑ̃fibjɛ̃] *nm* : amphibian

amphithéâtre [ɑ̃fiteatr] *nm* **1** : amphitheater **2** : lecture hall

ample [ɑ̃pl] *adj* : ample — **ampleur** [ɑ̃plœr] *nf* : extent, range

amplifier [ɑ̃plifje] {96} *vt* **1** : amplify **2** : expand — **s'amplifier** *vr* : increase — **amplificateur** [ɑ̃plifikatœr] *nm* : amplifier

ampoule [ɑ̃pul] *nf* **1** : lightbulb **2** CLOQUE : blister **3** : vial (in medicine)

amputer [ɑ̃pyte] *vt* **1** : amputate **2** : cut drastically — **amputation** [ɑ̃pytasjɔ̃] *nf* **1** : amputation **2** : drastic cut

amuse–gueule [amyzɡøl] *nms & pl* : appetizer

amuser [amyze] *vt* : amuse — **s'amuser** *vr* **1** : play **2** : enjoy oneself — **amusant, -sante** [amyzɑ̃, -zɑ̃t] *adj* : amusing — **amusement** [amyzmɑ̃] *nm* : amusement amygdale [amidal] *nf* : tonsil

an [ɑ̃] *nm* **1** : year **2 le Nouvel An** : New Year's Day

analgésique [analʒezik] *adj & nm* : analgesic

analogie [analɔʒi] *nf* : analogy — **analogue** [analɔg] *adj* : similar

analphabète [analfabɛt] *adj* : illiterate — **analphabétisme** [analfabetism] *nm* : illiteracy

analyse [analiz] *nf* **1** : analysis **2** : (blood) test — **analyser** [analize] *vt* : analyze — **analytique** [analitik] *adj* : analytic, analytical

ananas [anana(s)] *nms & pl* : pineapple

anarchie [anarʃi] *nf* : anarchy

anatomie [anatɔmi] *nf* : anatomy — **anatomique** [anatɔmik] *adj* : anatomic(al)

ancêtre [ɑ̃sɛtr] *nmf* : ancestor

anchois [ɑ̃ʃwa] *nms & pl* : anchovy

ancien, -cienne [ɑ̃sjɛ̃, -sjɛn] *adj* **1** : former **2** VIEUX : ancient, old — **anciennement** [ɑ̃sjɛnmɑ̃] *adv* : formerly — **ancienneté** [ɑ̃sjɛnte] *nf* **1** : oldness **2** : seniority

ancre [ɑ̃kr] *nf* : anchor — **ancrer** [ɑ̃kre] *vt* : anchor

andouille [ɑ̃duj] *nf fam* **1** : andouille (sausage) **2** *fam* : fool, sap

âne [an] *nm* : ass, donkey

anéantir [aneɑ̃tir] *vt* **1** DÉTRUIRE : annihilate **2** ACCABLER : overwhelm — **anéantissement** [aneɑ̃tismɑ̃] *nm* : annihilation

anecdote [anɛkdɔt] *nf* : anecdote

anémie [anemi] *nf* : anemia — **anémique** [anemik] *adj* : anemic

ânerie [anri] *nf* : stupid mistake or remark

anesthésie [anɛstezi] *nf* : anesthesia — **anesthésique** [anɛstezik] *adj & nm* : anesthetic

aneth [anɛt] *nm* : dill

ange [ɑ̃ʒ] *nm* : angel — **angélique** [ɑ̃ʒelik] *adj* : angelic

anglais, -glaise [ɑ̃glɛ, -glɛz] *adj* : English — **anglais** *nm* : English (language)

angle [ɑ̃gl] *nm* **1** : angle **2** : corner

anglophone [ɑ̃glɔfɔn] *adj* : English-speaking

anglo–saxon, -saxonne [ɑ̃glɔsaksɔ̃, -saksɔn] *adj* : Anglo-Saxon

angoisser [ɑ̃gwase] *vt* : distress — **angoissant, -sante** [ɑ̃gwasɑ̃, -sɑ̃t] *adj* : agonizing — **angoisse** [ɑ̃gwas] *nf* : anguish

anguille [ɑ̃gij] *nf* : eel

anguleux, -leuse [ɑ̃gylø, -løz] *adj* : angular

animal [animal] *nm, pl* **-maux** [-mo] : animal

animateur, -trice [animatœr, -tris] *n* **1** : moderator **2** : (television show) host

animer [anime] *vt* : enliven — **s'animer** *vr* : come to life — **animation** [animasjɔ̃] *nf* : animation — **animé, -mée** [anime] *adj* : animated, lively

animosité [animɔzite] *nf* : animosity

anis [ani(s)] *nm* : anise

ankyloser [ɑ̃kiloze] *v* **s'ankyloser** *vr* : stiffen (up)

anneau [ano] *nm, pl* **-neaux** : ring

année [ane] *nf* **1** : year **2 ~ bissextile** : leap year

annexe [anɛks] *adj* **1** : adjoining, attached **2** : related — **~** *nf* : annex — **annexer** [anɛkse] *vt* : annex

annihiler [aniile] *vt* : annihilate — **annihilation** [aniilasjɔ̃] *nf* : annihilation

anniversaire [anivɛrsɛr] *nm* **1** : anniversary **2** : birthday

annoncer [anɔ̃se] {6} *vt* **1** : announce **2** DÉNOTER : indicate — **s'annoncer** *vr* : appear (to be) — **annonce** [anɔ̃s] *nf* **1** : announcement **2** : advertisement — **annonceur, -ceuse** [anɔ̃sœr, -søz] *n* **1** : advertiser **2** *Can* : (radio) announcer

annoter [anɔte] *vt* : annotate — **annotation** [anɔtasjɔ̃] *nf* : annotation

annuaire [anɥɛr] *nm* **1** : yearbook **2 ~ téléphonique** : telephone directory

annuel, -nuelle [anɥɛl] *adj* : annual — **annuellement** [anɥɛlmɑ̃] *adv* : annually

annulaire [anɥlɛr] *nm* : ring finger

annuler [anyle] *vt* **1** : cancel **2** RÉVOQUER : annul — **annulation** [anylasjɔ̃] *nf* **1** : cancellation **2** : annulment

anodin, -dine [anɔdɛ̃, -din] *adj* **1** : insignificant **2** : harmless

anomalie [anɔmali] *nf* : anomaly

anonyme [anɔnim] *adj* : anonymous — **anonymat** [anɔnima] *nm* : anonymity

anorexie [anɔrɛksi] *nf* : anorexia

anormal, -male [anɔrmal] *adj, mpl* **-maux** [-mo] : abnormal

anse [ɑ̃s] *nf* **1** : handle **2** : cove

antagoniste [ɑ̃tagɔnist] *adj* : antagonistic

antan [ɑ̃tɑ̃] **d'~** *adj phr* : of yesteryear

antarctique [ɑ̃tarktik] *adj* : antarctic

antécédent, -dente [ɑ̃tesedɑ̃, -dɑ̃t] *adj* : previous — **antécédents** *nmpl* : (medical) history, (criminal) record

antenne [ɑ̃tɛn] *nf* : antenna

antérieur, -rieure [ɑ̃terjœr] *adj* **1** PRÉCÉDENT : previous **2** : front (of a part, etc.) — **antérieurement** [ɑ̃terjœrmɑ̃] *adv* : previously

anthologie [ɑ̃tɔlɔʒi] *nf* : anthology

anthropologie [ɑ̃trɔpɔlɔʒi] *nf* : anthropology

antibiotique [ɑ̃tibiɔtik] *adj & nm* : antibiotic

anticiper [ɑ̃tisipe] *vt* : anticipate — *vi* : think ahead — **anticipation** [ɑ̃tisipasjɔ̃] *nf* : anticipation

anticorps [ɑ̃tikɔr] *nms & pl* : antibody

antidote [ɑ̃tidɔt] *nm* : antidote

antigel [ãtiʒɛl] *nm* : antifreeze

antilope [ãtilɔp] *nf* : antelope

antipathie [ãtipati] *nf* : antipathy

antique [ãtik] *adj* : ancient, antique — **antiquité** [ãtikite] *nf* **1** : antiquity **2** : antique

antisémite [ãtisemit] *adj* : anti-Semitic

antiseptique [ãtisɛptik] *adj & nm* : antiseptic

antonyme [ãtɔnim] *nm* : antonym

antre [ãtr] *nm* : den, lair

anus [anys] *nms & pl* : anus

anxieux, anxieuse [ãksjø, -sjøz] *adj* : anxious — **anxiété** [ãksjete] *nf* : anxiety

août [u(t)] *nm* : August

apaiser [apeze] *vt* : appease — **s'apaiser** *vr* : quiet down — **apaisement** [apɛzmã] *nm* : calming (down)

apanage [apanaʒ] *nm* : prerogative

apathie [apati] *nf* : apathy — **apathique** [apatik] *adj* : apathetic

apercevoir [apɛrsəvwar] {26} *vt* : perceive, see — **s'apercevoir** *vr* **1** ~ **de** : notice **2** ~ **que** : realize that — **aperçu** [apɛrsy] *nm* : general idea, outline

apéritif [aperitif] *nm* : aperitif

à–peu–près [apøprɛ] *nms & pl* : approximation

apeuré, -rée [apœre] *adj* : frightened

apitoyer [apitwaje] {58} *v* **s'apitoyer** *vr* ~ **sur** : feel sorry for — **apitoiement** [apitwamã] *nm* : pity

aplanir [aplanir] *vt* **1** : level **2** : resolve (a problem) — **s'aplanir** *vr* : flatten out

aplatir [aplatir] *vt* : flatten

aplomb [aplɔ̃] *nm* **1** : aplomb, composure **2** d'~ : steady, balanced

apocalypse [apɔkalips] *nf* : apocalypse

apogée [apɔʒe] *nm* : peak

apostrophe [apɔstrɔf] *nf* : apostrophe — **apostropher** [apɔstrɔfe] *vt* : address rudely

apothéose [apɔteoz] *nf* : crowning moment

apôtre [apotr] *nm* : apostle

apparaître [aparɛtr] {73} *vi* : appear — *v impers* **il apparaît que** : it seems that

apparat [apara] *nm* **1** : pomp **2** d'~ : ceremonial

appareiller [apareje] *vi* : set sail — *vt* : match up — **appareil** [aparɛj] *nm* **1** : apparatus, appliance **2** : telephone **3** ~ **auditif** : hearing aid **4** ~ **digestif** : digestive system **5** ~ **photo** : camera

apparence [aparãs] *nf* **1** : appearance **2** en ~ : outwardly — **apparent, -rente** [aparã, -rãt] *adj* : apparent — **apparemment** [aparamã] *adv* : apparently

apparenté, -tée [aparãte] *adj* : related

apparition [aparisjɔ̃] *nf* **1** MANIFESTATION : appearance **2** SPECTRE : apparition

appartement [apartəmã] *nm* : apartment

appartenir [apartənir] {92} *vi* ~ **à** : belong to — *v impers* **il m'appartient de** : it's up to me to — **appartenance** [apartənãs] *nf* : membership, belonging

appâter [apate] *vt* **1** : bait **2** : lure, entice — **appât** [apa] *nm* : bait, lure

appauvrir [apovrir] *vt* : impoverish — **s'appauvrir** *vr* : become impoverished

appeler [aple] {8} *vt* **1** : call **2** NÉCESSITER : call for, require **3** en ~ à : appeal to — *vi* : call — **s'appeler** *vr* : be named, be called — **appel** [apɛl] *nm* **1** : call **2** : appeal

appendice [apãdis] *nm* : appendix — **appendicite** [apãdisit] *nf* : appendicitis

appentis [apãti] *nm* : shed

appesantir [apəzãtir] *vt* : weigh down — **s'appesantir** *vr* **1** : grow heavier **2** ~ **sur** : dwell on

appétit [apeti] *nm* **1** : appetite **2** bon ~! : enjoy your meal! — **appétissant, -sante** [apetisã, -sãt] *adj* : appetizing

applaudir [aplodir] *v* : applaud — **applaudissements** [aplodismã] *nmpl* : applause

appliquer [aplike] *vt* : apply — **s'appliquer** *vr* **1** : apply oneself **2** ~ à CONCERNER : apply to — **applicateur** [aplikatœr] *nm* : applicator — **application** [aplikasjɔ̃] *nf* : application — **appliqué, -quée** [aplike] *adj* : industrious, painstaking

appoint [apwɛ̃] *nm* **1** : contribution, support **2** d'~ : extra **3** faire l'~ : make exact change — **appointements** [apwɛ̃təmã] *nmpl* : salary

apporter [apɔrte] *vt* **1** AMENER : bring **2** FOURNIR : provide — **apport** [apɔr] *nm* : contribution

apposer [apoze] *vt* : put, affix

apprécier [apresje] {96} *vt* **1** : appreciate **2** : appraise — **appréciation** [apresjasjɔ̃] *nf* : assessment, appraisal

appréhender [apreãde] *vt* **1** ARRÊTER : apprehend, arrest **2** : dread — **appréhension** [apreãsjɔ̃] *nf* : apprehension

apprendre [aprãdr] {70} *vt* **1** : learn **2** ENSEIGNER : teach

apprenti, -tie [aprãti] *n* : apprentice — **apprentissage** [aprãtisaʒ] *nm* **1** : apprenticeship **2** : learning

apprêter [aprɛte] *v* **s'apprêter** *vr* : get ready

apprivoiser [aprivwaze] *vt* : tame

approbateur, -trice [aprɔbatœr, -tris] *adj* : approving — **approbation** [aprɔbasjɔ̃] *nf* : approval

approcher [aprɔʃe] *vt* : approach — *vi* : draw near — **s'approcher** *vr* ~ **de** : come up to — **approchant, -chante** [aprɔʃã, -ʃãt] *adj* : similar — **approche** [aprɔʃ] *nf* : approach

approfondir [aprɔfɔ̃dir] *vt* **1** : deepen **2** PÉNÉTRER : delve into — **approfondi, -die** [aprɔfɔ̃di] *adj* : thorough

approprier [aprɔprije] {96} *v* **s'approprier**
vr : appropriate — **approprié, -priée** [aprɔprije] *adj* : appropriate

approuver [apruve] *vt* : approve (of)

approvisionner [aprɔvizjɔne] *vt* : supply — **s'approvisionner** *vr* : stock up — **approvisionnement** [aprɔvizjɔnmɑ̃] *nm* : supply, provision

approximation [aprɔksimasjɔ̃] *nf* : approximation — **approximatif, -tive** [aprɔksimatif, -tiv] *adj* : approximate — **approximativement** [-tivmɑ̃] *adv* : approximately

appuyer [apɥije] {58} *vt* **1** : rest, lean **2** SOUTENIR : support — *vi* ~ **sur** : push, press — **s'appuyer** *vr* **1** ~ **à** *or* ~ **contre** : lean against **2** ~ **sur** : rely on — **appui** [apɥi] *nm* : support

âpre [apr] *adj* : bitter, harsh

après [aprɛ] *adv* : afterwards — ~ *prep* **1** : after **2** : beyond **3** ~ **tout** : after all **4** d'~ : according to — **après-demain** [apredmɛ̃] *adv* : the day after tomorrow — **après-midi** [apremidi] *nmfs & pl* : afternoon

à-propos [aprɔpo] *nm* **1** : aptness **2** : presence of mind

apte [apt] *adj* : capable — **aptitude** [aptityd] *nf* : aptitude

aquarelle [akwarɛl] *nf* : watercolor

aquarium [akwarjɔm] *nm* : aquarium

aquatique [akwatik] *adj* : aquatic

aqueduc [akdyk] *nm* : aqueduct

arabe [arab] *adj* : Arab, Arabic — ~ *nm* : Arabic (language)

arachide [araʃid] *nf* : peanut

araignée [areɲe] *nf* : spider

arbitraire [arbitrɛr] *adj* : arbitrary

arbitre [arbitr] *nm* **1** : arbitrator **2** : referee **3 libre** ~ : free will — **arbitrer** [arbitre] *vt* **1** : arbitrate **2** : referee

arborer [arbɔre] *vt* : bear, display

arbre [arbr] *nm* **1** : tree **2** : shaft

arbrisseau [arbriso] *nm* : shrub

arbuste [arbyst] *nm* : bush

arc [ark] *nm* **1** : arc, curve **2** : bow (in archery)

arcade [arkad] *nf* : arch, archway

arc-boutant [arkbutɑ̃] *nm, pl* **arcs-boutants** : flying buttress

arc-en-ciel [arkɑ̃sjɛl] *nm, pl* **arcs-en-ciel** : rainbow

archaïque [arkaik] *adj* : archaic

arche [arʃ] *nf* **1** : arch **2** : ark

archéologie [arkeɔlɔʒi] *nf* : archaeology

archet [arʃɛ] *nm* : bow (in music)

archevêque [arʃəvɛk] *nm* : archbishop

archipel [arʃipɛl] *nm* : archipelago

architecture [arʃitɛktyr] *nf* : architecture — **architecte** [arʃitɛkt] *nmf* : architect

archives [arʃiv] *nfpl* : archives

arctique [arktik] *adj* : arctic

ardent, -dente [ardɑ̃, -dɑ̃t] *adj* **1** : burning **2** PASSIONNÉ : ardent — **ardemment** [ardamɑ̃] *adv* : ardently — **ardeur** [ardœr] *nf* **1** CHALEUR : heat **2** : ardor

ardoise [ardwaz] *nf* : slate

ardu, -due [ardy] *adj* : arduous

arène [arɛn] *nf* **1** : arena **2** ~**s** : bullring, amphitheater — **aréna** [arena] *nm Can* : arena

arête [arɛt] *nf* **1** : fish bone **2** : ridge, bridge (of the nose)

argent [arʒɑ̃] *nm* **1** : money **2** : silver **3** ~ **comptant** : cash — **argenté, -tée** [arʒɑ̃te] *adj* **1** : silver-plated **2** : silvery — **argenterie** [arʒɑ̃tri] *nf* : silverware

argile [arʒil] *nf* : clay

argot [argo] *nm* : slang

argument [argymɑ̃] *nm* : argument — **argumentation** [argymɑ̃tasjɔ̃] *nf* : rationale — **argumenter** [argymɑ̃te] *vi* : argue

aride [arid] *adj* : arid

aristocrate [aristɔkrat] *nmf* : aristocrat — **aristocratique** [-kratik] *adj* : aristocratic — **aristocratie** [aristɔkrasi] *nf* : aristocracy

arithmétique [aritmetik] *nf* : arithmetic

armature [armatyr] *nf* : framework

armer [arme] *vt* **1** : arm **2** : cock (a gun) — **arme** [arm] *nf* **1** : weapon **2** ~**s** *nfpl* : coat of arms — **armée** [arme] *nf* : army — **armement** [arməmɑ̃] *nm* : armament

armistice [armistis] *nm* : armistice

armoire [armwar] *nf* **1** : cupboard **2** : wardrobe, closet

armoiries [armwari] *nfpl* : coat of arms

armure [armyr] *nf* : armor

arnaquer [arnake] *vt fam* : swindle — **arnaque** [arnak] *nf fam* : swindle

aromate [arɔmat] *nm* : spice, herb

arôme [arom] *nm* **1** : aroma **2** : flavor — **aromatique** [arɔmatik] *adj* : aromatic — **aromatiser** [arɔmatize] *vt* : flavor

arpenter [arpɑ̃te] *vt* **1** : pace up and down **2** MESURER : survey

arqué, -quée [arke] *adj* : curved, arched

arrache-pied [araʃpje] d'~ *adv phr* : relentlessly

arracher [araʃe] *vt* **1** : pull up or out **2** DÉCHIRER : tear off **3** : snatch, grab

arranger [arɑ̃ʒe] {17} *vt* **1** : arrange **2** RÉPARER : fix **3** CONVENIR : suit, please **4** RÉGLER : settle — **s'arranger** *vr* **1** : come to an agreement **2** : get better — **arrangement** [arɑ̃ʒmɑ̃] *nm* : arrangement

arrestation [arɛstasjɔ̃] *nf* : arrest

arrêter [arete] *vt* **1** : stop **2** FIXER : fix **3** APPRÉHENDER : arrest **4** DÉTERMINER : decide on — **s'arrêter** *vr* **1** : stop, cease **2** ~ **de faire** : stop doing — **arrêt** [arɛ] *nm* **1** : stopping, halt **2** : decree **3** ~ **d'autobus** : bus stop

arrhes [ar] *nfpl France* : deposit

arrière [arjɛr] *adj* : back, rear — ~ *nm* **1** : back, rear **2 en** ~ : backwards **3 en** ~ **de** : behind — **arriéré, -rée** [arjere] *adj* **1** : overdue **2** : backward — **arriéré** *nm* **1** : arrears *pl* **2** : backlog — **arrière–goût** [arjɛrgu] *nm, pl* **arrière–goûts** : aftertaste — **arrière–grand–mère** [arjɛrgrɑ̃mɛr] *nf, pl* **arrière–grands–mères** : great-grand-mother — **arrière–grand–père** [arjɛrgrɑ̃pɛr] *nm, pl* **arrière–grands–pères** : great-grandfather — **arrière–pays** [arjɛrpei] *nms & pl* : hinterland — **arrière–pensée** [arjɛrpɑ̃se] *nf, pl* **arrière–pensées** : ulterior motive — **arrière–plan** [arjɛrplɑ̃] *nm, pl* **arrière–plans** : background

arrimer [arime] *vt* **1** : stow **2** FIXER : secure, fix

arriver [arive] *vi* **1** : arrive, come **2** RÉUSSIR : succeed **3** SE PASSER : happen, occur **4** ~ **à** ATTEINDRE : reach — **arrivée** [arive] *nf* **1** : arrival **2** *or* **ligne d'**~ : finish line — **arriviste** [arivist] *adj* : pushy — ~ *nmf* : upstart

arrogant, -gante [arɔgɑ̃, -gɑ̃t] *adj* : arrogant — **arrogance** [arɔgɑ̃s] *nf* : arrogance

arroger [arɔʒe] {17} *v* **s'arroger** *vr* : claim (without right)

arrondir [arɔ̃dir] *vt* **1** : make round **2** : round off (a number)

arrondissement [arɔ̃dismɑ̃] *nm* : district

arroser [aroze] *vt* **1** : water **2** : baste (in cooking) **3** CÉLÉBRER : drink to — **arrosoir** [arozwar] *nm* : watering can

arsenal [arsənal] *nm, pl* **-naux** [-no] **1** : shipyard **2** : arsenal

arsenic [arsənik] *nm* : arsenic

art [ar] *nm* : art

artère [artɛr] *nf* **1** : artery **2** : main road

arthrite [artrit] *nf* : arthritis

artichaut [artiʃo] *nm* : artichoke

article [artikl] *nm* **1** : article **2** ~s **de toilette** : toiletries

articuler [artikyle] *vt* : articulate — **articulation** [artikylasjɔ̃] *nf* **1** : articulation **2** : joint (in anatomy)

artifice [artifis] *nm* : trick, device

artificiel, -cielle [artifisjɛl] *adj* : artificial — **artificiellement** [-sjɛlmɑ̃] *adv* : artificially

artillerie [artijri] *nf* : artillery

artilleur [artijœr] *nm Can* : pitcher (in baseball)

artisan, -sane [artizɑ̃, -zan] *n* : artisan, craftsman — **artisanal, -nale** *adj, pl* **-naux** : made by craftsmen, homemade — **artisanat** [artizana] *nm* **1** : artisans *pl* **2** : arts and crafts *pl*

artiste [artist] *nmf* : artist — **artistique** [artistik] *adj* : artistic

as [ɑs] *nm* : ace

ascendant, -dante [asɑ̃dɑ̃, -dɑ̃t] *adj* : ascending — **ascendant** *nm* **1** : influence **2** ~s *nmpl* : ancestors — **ascendance** [asɑ̃dɑ̃s] *nf* : ancestry

ascenseur [asɑ̃sœr] *nm* : elevator

ascension [asɑ̃sjɔ̃] *nf* : ascent

ascète [asɛt] *nmf* : ascetic — **ascétique** [asetik] *adj* : ascetic

asiatique [azjatik] *adj* : Asian

asile [azil] *nm* **1** : (political) asylum **2** ABRI : refuge

aspect [aspɛ] *nm* **1** : aspect **2** ALLURE : appearance

asperge [aspɛrʒ] *nf* : asparagus

asperger [aspɛrʒe] {17} *vt* : sprinkle, spray

aspérité [asperite] *nf* : bump, protrusion

asphalte [asfalt] *nm* : asphalt

asphyxier [asfiksje] {96} *vt* : asphyxiate, suffocate — **s'asphyxier** *vr* : suffocate — **asphyxie** [asfiksi] *nf* : asphyxiation

aspirer [aspire] *vt* **1** : suck up (a liquid) **2** : inhale — *vi* ~ **à** : aspire to — **aspiration** [aspirasjɔ̃] *nf* **1** AMBITION : aspiration **2** : suction **3** : inhaling — **aspirateur** [aspiratœr] *nm* **1** : vacuum cleaner **2 passer l'**~ : vacuum

aspirine [aspirin] *nf* : aspirin

assagir [asaʒir] *vt* : calm, quiet — **s'assagir** *vr* : quiet down

assaillir [asajir] {93} *vt* : attack — **assaillant, -lante** [asajɑ̃, -jɑ̃t] *n* : attacker

assainir [asenir] *vt* : purify, clean up

assaisonner [asɛzɔne] *vt* : season — **assaisonnement** [asɛzɔnmɑ̃] *nm* : seasoning

assassiner [asasine] *vt* : murder, assassinate — **assassin** *nm* : murderer, assassin

assaut [aso] *nm* **1** : assault **2 prendre d'**~ : storm

assécher [aseʃe] {87} *vt* : drain

assembler [asɑ̃ble] *vt* : assemble — **s'assembler** *vr* : gather — **assemblée** [asɑ̃ble] *nf* **1** RÉUNION : meeting **2** : (political) assembly

asséner [asene] {87} *vt* : strike (a blow)

assentiment [asɑ̃timɑ̃] *nm* : assent, consent

asseoir [aswar] {9} *vt* : seat, sit — **s'asseoir** *vr* : sit down

assermenté, -tée [asɛrmɑ̃te] *adj* : sworn

assertion [asɛrsjɔ̃] *nf* : assertion

asservir [asɛrvir] *vt* : enslave

assez [ase] *adv* **1** SUFFISAMMENT : enough **2** : rather, quite

assidu, -due [asidy] *adj* : diligent — **assiduité** [asidɥite] *nf* : diligence

assiéger [asjeʒe] {64} *vt* : besiege

assiette [asjɛt] *nf* : plate, dish — **assiettée** [asjete] *nf* : plateful

assigner [asiɲe] *vt* : assign, allot — **assi-gnation** [asiɲasjɔ̃] *nf* **1** : allocation **2** : summons, subpoena

assimiler [asimile] *vt* **1** : assimilate **2** ⁓ **à** : equate with, compare to — **assimilation** [asimilasjɔ̃] *nf* : assimilation

assis, -sise [asiz] *adj* : seated, sitting down

assise *nf* **1** : foundation, base **2** ⁓s *nfpl* : court

assister [asiste] *vt* : assist — *vi* ⁓ **à** : attend — **assistance** [asistɑ̃s] *nf* **1** : assistance **2** : audience — **assistant, -tante** [asistɑ̃, -tɑ̃t] *n* : assistant

associer [asɔsje] {96} *vt* **1** : associate **2** ⁓ **qqn à** : include s.o. in — **s'associer** *vr* : join together — **association** [asɔsjasjɔ̃] *nf* : association — **associé, -ciée** [asɔsje] *n* : associate

assoiffé, -fée [aswafe] *adj* : thirsty

assombrir [asɔ̃brir] *vt* : darken — **s'assombrir** *vr* : darken

assommer [asɔme] *vt* **1** : stun, knock out **2** *fam* : bore stiff — **assommant, -mante** [asɔmɑ̃, -mɑ̃t] *adj* : boring

assortir [asɔrtir] *vt* : match — **assorti, -tie** [asɔrti] *adj* **1** : matched **2** : assorted — **assortiment** [asɔrtimɑ̃] *nm* : assortment

assoupir [asupir] *v* **s'assoupir** *vr* : doze off

assouplir [asuplir] *vt* : make supple, soften — **s'assouplir** *vr* : loosen up

assourdir [asurdir] *vt* **1** : deafen **2** ÉTOUF-FER : muffle

assouvir [asuvir] *vt* : appease

assujettir [asyʒetir] *vt* **1** : subjugate **2** ⁓ **à** : subject to

assumer [asyme] *vt* : assume, take on

assurer [asyre] *vt* **1** : assure **2** FOURNIR : provide **3** : insure (one's property, etc.) — **s'assurer** *vr* ⁓ **de** : make sure of — **assurance** [asyrɑ̃s] *nf* **1** : assurance **2** : insurance **3** ⁓-vie : life insurance — **assuré, -rée** [asyre] *adj* : confident, certain — **assurément** [asyremɑ̃] *adv* : certainly

astérisque [asterisk] *nm* : asterisk

asthme [asm] *nm* : asthma

asticot [astiko] *nm* : maggot

astiquer [astike] *vt* : polish

astre [astr] *nm* : star

astreindre [astrɛ̃dr] {37} *vt* : compel — **astreignant, -gnante** [astrɛɲɑ̃, -ɲɑ̃t] *adj* : demanding

astrologie [astrɔlɔʒi] *nf* : astrology

astronaute [astrɔnot] *nmf* : astronaut

astronomie [astrɔnɔmi] *nf* : astronomy

astuce [astys] *nf* **1** : cleverness **2** TRUC : trick **3** PLAISANTERIE : joke — **astucieux, -cieuse** [astysjø, -sjøz] *adj* : astute, clever — **astucieusement** [-sjøzmɑ̃] *adv* : cleverly

atelier [atəlje] *nm* **1** : studio **2** : workshop

athée [ate] *adj* : atheistic — ⁓ *nmf* : atheist

athlète [atlɛt] *nmf* : athlete — **athlétique** [atletik] *adj* : athletic — **athlétisme** [atletism] *nm* : athletics

atlantique [atlɑ̃tik] *adj* : Atlantic

atlas [atlas] *nm* : atlas

atmosphère [atmɔsfɛr] *nf* : atmosphere — **atmosphérique** [atmɔsferik] *adj* : atmospheric

atome [atom] *nm* : atom — **atomique** [atɔmik] *adj* : atomic

atomiseur [atɔmizœr] *nm* : atomizer

atout [atu] *nm* **1** : trump (card) **2** AVANTAGE : asset

âtre [atr] *nm* : hearth

atroce [atrɔs] *adj* : atrocious — **atrocité** [atrɔsite] *nf* : atrocity

atrophier [atrɔfje] {96} *v* **s'atrophier** *vr* : atrophy

attabler [atable] *v* **s'attabler** *vr* : sit down at the table

attacher [ataʃe] *vt* : tie (up), fasten — **s'attacher** *vr* **1** : fasten **2** ⁓ **à** : attach oneself to **3** ⁓ **à** : apply oneself to — **attachant, -chante** [ataʃɑ̃, -ʃɑ̃t] *adj* : appealing, likeable — **attache** [ataʃ] *nf* **1** : fastener **2** LIEN : tie, bond — **attaché, -chée** [ataʃe] *n* : attaché — **attachement** [ataʃmɑ̃] *nm* : attachment

attaquer [atake] *v* : attack — **s'attaquer** *vr* ⁓ **à** : attack — **attaque** [atak] *nf* : attack

attarder [atarde] *v* **s'attarder** *vr* : linger — **attardé** [atarde] *adj* **1** : late **2** : retarded **3** DÉMODÉ : old-fashioned

atteindre [atɛ̃dr] {37} *vt* **1** : reach, attain **2** FRAPPER : strike, hit **3** AFFECTER : affect — **atteinte** [atɛ̃t] *nf* **1** : attack **2** **hors d'**⁓ : out of reach **3** **porter** ⁓ **à** : undermine

atteler [atle] {8} *vt* : harness — **s'atteler** *vr* ⁓ **à** : apply oneself to — **attelage** [atlaʒ] *nm* : team (of animals)

attelle [atɛl] *nf* : splint

attenant, -nante [atnɑ̃, -nɑ̃t] *adj* : adjoining

attendre [atɑ̃dr] {63} *vt* **1** : wait for **2** ESPÉRER : expect — *vi* **1** : wait **2 faire** ⁓ **qqn** : keep s.o. waiting **3 en attendant** : in the meantime — **s'attendre** *vr* ⁓ **à** : expect

attendrir [atɑ̃drir] *vt* **1** ÉMOUVOIR : move **2** : tenderize (meat) — **s'attendrir** *vr* : be moved — **attendrissant, -sante** [atɑ̃drisɑ̃, -sɑ̃t] *adj* : moving, touching

attendu, -due [atɑ̃dy] *adj* **1** : expected **2** : long-awaited — **attendu** *prep* ⁓ **que** : since, considering that

attente [atɑ̃t] *nf* **1** : wait **2** ESPOIR : expectation

attenter [atɑ̃te] *vi* ⁓ **à** : make an attempt on — **attentat** [atɑ̃ta] *nm* : attack

attention [atɑ̃sjɔ̃] *nf* **1** : attention **2** ⁓!

: look out!, beware! **3 faire ∼** : pay attention — **attentionné, -née** [atɑ̃sjɔne] *adj* : considerate — **attentif, -tive** [atɑ̃tif, -tiv] *adj* **1** : attentive **2** : careful **3 être ∼ à** : pay attention to — **attentivement** [-tivmɑ̃] *adv* : attentively

atténuer [atenɥe] *vt* **1** : tone down **2** : ease, allay — **s'atténuer** *vr* : subside

atterrer [atere] *vt* : dismay, appall

atterrir [aterir] *vi* : land — **atterrissage** [aterisaʒ] *nm* : landing

attester [atɛste] *vt* : attest, testify to — **attestation** [atɛstasjɔ̃] *nf* **1** : affidavit **2** : certificate

attirail [atiraj] *nm fam* : gear, paraphernalia

attirer [atire] *vt* : attract, draw — **attirance** [atirɑ̃s] *nf* : attraction — **attirant, -rante** [atirɑ̃, -rɑ̃t] *adj* : attractive

attiser [atize] *vt* : stir up, kindle

attitré, -trée [atitre] *adj* **1** : authorized **2** HABITUEL : regular

attitude [atityd] *nf* : attitude

attouchement [atuʃmɑ̃] *nm* : touching, fondling

attraction [atraksjɔ̃] *nf* : attraction (in science)

attrait [atrɛ] *nm* : appeal, attraction

attraper [atrape] *vt* : catch

attrayant, -trayante [atrɛjɑ̃, -trɛjɑ̃t] *adj* ATTIRANT : attractive

attribuer [atribɥe] *vt* : attribute, assign — **s'attribuer** *vr* : claim for oneself — **attribut** [atriby] *nm* : attribute — **attribution** [atribysjɔ̃] *nf* : allocation, allotment

attrister [atriste] *vt* : sadden

attrouper [atrupe] *v* **s'attrouper** *vr* : gather — **attroupement** [atrupmɑ̃] *nm* : crowd

au [o] → **à, le**

aubaine [obɛn] *nf* : good fortune, godsend

aube [ob] *nf* : dawn, daybreak

aubépine [obepin] *nf* : hawthorn

auberge [obɛrʒ] *nf* **1** : inn **2 ∼ de jeunesse** : youth hostel — **aubergiste** [obɛrʒist] *nmf* : innkeeper

aubergine [obɛrʒin] *nf* : eggplant

auburn [obœrn] *adj* : auburn

aucun, -cune [okœ̃, -kyn] *adj* **1** : no, not any **2 plus qu'aucun autre** : more than any other — **∼ pron 1** : none, not any **2** : any, anyone **3 d'aucuns** : some (people) — **aucunement** [okynmɑ̃] *adv* : not at all

audace [odas] *nf* **1** : audacity **2** COURAGE : boldness — **audacieux, -cieuse** [odasjø, -jøz] *adj* **1** : audacious **2** HARDI : daring

au–dedans [odədɑ̃] *adv* **1** : inside **2 ∼ de** : within

au–dehors [odəɔr] *adv* **1** : outside **2 ∼ de** : outside (of)

au–delà [odəla] *adv* **1** : beyond **2 ∼ de** : beyond

au–dessous [odsu] *adv* **1** : below **2 ∼ de** : below, under

au–dessus [odsy] *adv* **1** : above **2 ∼ de** : above, over

au–devant [odvɑ̃] *adv* **1** : ahead **2 aller ∼ de** : go to meet

audible [odibl] *adj* : audible

audience [odjɑ̃s] *nf* **1** : audience **2 ∼s publiques** : public hearings

audio [odjo] *adj* : audio — **audiovisuel, -suelle** [odjovizɥɛl] *adj* : audiovisual

auditeur, -trice [oditœr, -tris] *n* : listener

audition [odisjɔ̃] *nf* **1** : hearing **2** : audition (in theater) — **auditionner** [odisjɔne] *v* : audition — **auditoire** [oditwar] *nm* : audience — **auditorium** [oditɔrjɔm] *nm* : auditorium

auge [oʒ] *nf* : trough

augmenter [ogmɑ̃te] *v* : increase — **augmentation** [ogmɑ̃tasjɔ̃] *nf* : increase, raise

augurer [ogyre] *vt* : augur — **augure** [ogyr] *nm* : omen

aujourd'hui [oʒurdɥi] *adv & nm* : today

aumône [omon] *nf* : alms *pl*

aumônier [omonje] *nm* : chaplain

auparavant [oparavɑ̃] *adv* : before(hand)

auprès [oprɛ] *adv* **∼ de 1** : beside, near, next to **2** : compared with **3 ambassadeur ∼ des Nations Unies** : ambassador to the United Nations

auquel, -quelle [okɛl] → **lequel**

auréole [oreɔl] *nf* **1** : halo **2** TACHE : ring

auriculaire [orikylɛr] *nm* : little finger

aurore [orɔr] *nf* AUBE : dawn

ausculter [oskylte] *vt* : examine (with a stethoscope)

auspices [ospis] *nmpl* **sous les ∼ de** : under the auspices of

aussi [osi] *adv* **1** : too, also, as well **2** TELLEMENT : so **3 ∼ ... que** : as ... as

aussitôt [osito] *adv* **1** : immediately **2 ∼ que** : as soon as

austère [ostɛr] *adj* : austere — **austérité** [osterite] *nf* : austerity

austral, -trale [ostral] *adj, mpl* **-trals** : southern

australien, -lienne [ostraljɛ̃, -jɛn] *adj* : Australian

autant [otɑ̃] *adv* **1** *or* **∼ de** : as much, as many, so much, so many **2 ∼ que** : as much as, as many as, as far as **3 d'∼ plus** : all the more **4 pour ∼** : for all that

autel [otɛl] *nm* : altar

auteur [otœr] *nm* **1** : author **2** : person responsible, perpetrator

authentique [otɑ̃tik] *adj* : authentic

auto [oto] *nf* : car, automobile

autobiographie [otobjɔgrafi] *nf* : autobiography

autobus [otobys] *nm* : bus

autocar [otɔkar] *nm* : bus, coach

autochtone [otɔktɔn] *adj & nmf* : native

autocollant, -lante [otɔkɔlã, -lãt] *adj* : self-adhesive — **autocollant** *nm* : sticker

autocuiseur [otɔkɥizœr] *nm* : pressure cooker

autodéfense [otɔdefãs] *nf* : self-defense

autodidacte [otɔdidakt] *adj* : self-taught

autodiscipline [otɔdisiplin] *nf* : self-discipline

autographe [otɔgraf] *nm* : autograph

automation [otɔmasjɔ̃] *nf* : automation — **automatique** [otɔmatik] *adj* : automatic — **automatiquement** [-tikmã] *adv* : automatically

automatiser [otɔmatize] *vt* : automate — **automatisation** [otɔmatizasjɔ̃] *nf* : automation

automne [otɔn] *nm* : autumn, fall

automobile [otɔmɔbil] *adj* : automotive — ～ *nf* : automobile, car — **automobiliste** [otɔmɔbilist] *nmf* : motorist, driver

autonome [otɔnɔm] *adj* : autonomous — **autonomie** [otɔnɔmi] *nf* : autonomy

autoportrait [otɔpɔrtrɛ] *nm* : self-portrait

autopsie [otɔpsi] *nf* : autopsy

autoriser [otɔrize] *vt* : authorize — **autorisation** [otɔrizasjɔ̃] *nf* **1** : authorization **2** PERMIS : permit

autorité [otɔrite] *nf* : authority — **autoritaire** [otɔritɛr] *adj* : authoritarian

autoroute [otɔrut] *nf* **1** : highway, freeway **2** ～ **à péage** : turnpike

auto–stop [otɔstɔp] *nm* **faire de l'**～ : hitchhike — **auto–stoppeur, -peuse** [otɔstɔpœr, -pøz] *n* : hitchhiker

autosuffisant, -sante [otɔsyfizã, -zãt] *adj* : self-sufficient

autour [otur] *adv* **1** ～ **de** : around, about **2 tout** ～ : all around

autre [otr] *adj* **1** : other, different **2** ～ **chose** : something else — ～ *pron* : other, another

autrefois [otrəfwa] *adv* : in the past, formerly

autrement [otrəmã] *adv* **1** : differently **2** SINON : otherwise **3** ～ **dit** : in other words

autruche [otryʃ] *nf* : ostrich

autrui [otrɥi] *pron* : others

auvent [ovã] *nm* : awning

auxiliaire [oksiljɛr] *adj & nmf* : auxiliary, assistant — ～ *nm* : auxiliary (verb)

auxquels, -quelles [okɛl] → **lequel**

avachi, -chie [avaʃi] *adj* : shapeless, limp

aval [aval] *nm* **en** ～ : downstream

avalanche [avalãʃ] *nf* : avalanche

avaler [avale] *vt* : swallow

avancer [avãse] {6} *vt* : move forward, put ahead — *vi* **1** : advance, go forward **2** : be fast (of a watch) — **s'avancer** *vr* **1** : move

forward **2** : progress — **avance** [avãs] *nf* **1** : advance **2** : lead **3 à l'**～ *or* **d'**～ : in advance **4 en** ～ : early — **avancé, -cée** [avãse] *adj* : advanced — **avancement** [avãsmã] *nm* : promotion

avant [avã] *adv* **1** : before **2** : first **3** ～ **de** : before **4** ～ **que** : before, until — ～ *adj* : front — ～ *nm* **1** : front **2** : forward (in sports) **3 en** ～ : forward, ahead **4 en** ～ **de** : ahead of — ～ *prep* **1** : before, by **2** ～ **tout** : above all

avantager [avãtaʒe] {17} *vt* **1** FAVORISER : favor **2** : flatter — **avantageux, -geuse** [avãtaʒø, -ʒøz] *adj* : profitable, worthwhile — **avantage** [avãtaʒ] *nm* **1** : advantage **2** ～**s sociaux** : fringe benefits

avant–bras [avãbra] *nms & pl* : forearm

avant–dernier, -nière [avãdɛrnje, -njɛr] *adj* : next to last

avant–garde [avãgard] *nf, pl* **avant–gardes** : avant-garde

avant–goût [avãgu] *nm, pl* **avant–goûts** : foretaste

avant–hier [avãtjɛr] *adv* : the day before yesterday

avant–midi [avãmidi] *nfs & pl Can, nms & pl Bel* : morning

avant–poste [avãpɔst] *nm, pl* **avant–postes** : outpost

avant–première [avãprəmjɛr] *nf, pl* **avant–premières** : preview

avant–propos [avãprɔpo] *nms & pl* : foreword

avant–toit [avãtwa] *nm* : eaves *pl*

avare [avar] *adj* : miserly — ～ *nmf* : miser

avarié [avarje] *adj* : spoiled, rotten

avec [avɛk] *prep* : with — ～ *adv fam* : with it, with them

avenant, -nante [avnã, -nãt] *adj* : pleasant

avènement [avɛnmã] *nm* **1** : accession (to a throne) **2** DÉBUT : advent

avenir [avnir] *nm* **1** : future **2 à l'**～ : in the future

avent [avã] *nm* **l'**～ : Advent

aventure [avãtyr] *nf* **1** : adventure **2** : love affair — **aventurer** [avãtyre] *vt* : risk — **s'aventurer** *vr* : venture — **aventureux, -reuse** [avãtyrø, -røz] *adj* : adventurous

avenu [avny] *adj m* **nul et non** ～ : null and void

avenue [avny] *nf* : avenue

avérer [avere] {87} *v* **s'avérer** *vr* : turn out to be

averse [avɛrs] *nf* : shower, storm

aversion [avɛrsjɔ̃] *nf* : aversion, dislike

avertir [avɛrtir] *vt* **1** : warn **2** INFORMER : inform — **avertissement** [avɛrtismã] *nm* : warning — **avertisseur** [avɛrtisœr] *nm* **1** : (car) horn **2** : alarm

aveu [avø] *nm, pl* **-veux** : confession, admission

aveugle [avœgl] *adj* : blind — ~ *nmf* : blind person — **aveuglant, -glante** [avœglɑ̃, -glɑ̃t] *adj* : blinding — **aveuglement** [avœgləmɑ̃] *nm* : blindness — **aveuglément** [avœglemɑ̃] *adv* : blindly — **aveugler** [avœgle] *vt* : blind

aviateur, -trice [avjatœr, -tris] *n* : pilot — **aviation** [avjasjɔ̃] *nf* : aviation

avide [avid] *adj* **1** CUPIDE : greedy **2** ~ **de** : eager for — **avidité** [avidite] *nf* **1** CUPIDITÉ : greed **2** : eagerness

avilir [avilir] *vt* : debase

avion [avjɔ̃] *nm* : airplane

aviron [avirɔ̃] *nm* RAME : oar

avis [avi] *nm* **1** : opinion **2** ANNONCE : notice **3** CONSEIL : advice — **aviser** [avize] *vt* : inform, notify — **avisé, -sée** [avize] *adj* : sensible

aviver [avive] *vt* : revive

avocat[1], -cate [avɔka, -kat] *n* : lawyer, attorney

avocat[2] *nm* : avocado

avoine [avwan] *nf* : oats *pl*

avoir [avwar] {10} *vt* **1** POSSÉDER : have **2** OBTENIR : get **3** ~ **dix ans** : be ten years old **4** ~ **à** : have to **5** ~ **mal** : be hurt — *v impers* **1** **il y a** : there is, there are **2** **qu'est-ce qu'il y a?** : what's wrong? — *v aux* : have — ~ *nm* : assets *pl*

avoisiner [avwazine] *vt* : be near, border on — **avoisinant, -nante** [avwazinɑ̃] *adj* : neighboring

avorter [avɔrte] *vi* : abort — **avortement** [avɔrtəmɑ̃] *nm* : abortion

avouer [avwe] *vt* : admit, confess to — **s'avouer** *vr* : confess, own up

axe [aks] *nm* **1** : axis **2** ~ **routier** : major road — **axer** [akse] *vt* : center, focus

axiome [aksjom] *nm* : axiom

azote [azɔt] *nm* : nitrogen

azur [azyr] *nm* : sky blue

B

b [be] *nm* : b, second letter of the alphabet

babeurre [babœr] *nm* : buttermilk

babiller [babije] *vi* : babble, chatter — **babillage** [babijaʒ] *nm* : babbling — **babillard** [babijar] *nm* Can : bulletin board

babiole [babjɔl] *nf* : trinket

babouin [babwɛ̃] *nm* : baboon

baby–sitter [bebisitœr] *nmf, pl* **baby–sitters** France : baby-sitter — **baby–sitting** [bebisitiŋ] *nm* **faire du** ~ France : baby-sit

baccalauréat [bakalɔrea] *nm* **1** France : school-leaving certificate **2** Can : bachelor's degree

bâche [baʃ] *nf* : tarpaulin

bâcler [bakle] *vt* : rush through

bacon [bekɔn] *nm* : bacon

bactéries [bakteri] *nfpl* : bacteria

badaud, -daude [bado, -dod] *n* : (curious) onlooker

badge [badʒ] *nm* : badge

badiner [badine] *vi* **1** : joke, jest **2** ~ **avec** : toy with — **badinage** [badinaʒ] *nm* : banter, joking

bafouer [bafwe] *vt* : ridicule, scorn

bafouiller [bafuje] *v* : mumble, stammer — **bafouillage** [bafujaʒ] *nm* : mumbling, gibberish

bagage [bagaʒ] *nm* : baggage, luggage

bagarrer [bagare] *vi* : fight — **se bagarrer** *vr* : fight, brawl — **bagarre** [bagar] *nf* : fight, brawl

bagatelle [bagatɛl] *nf* : trifle, trinket

bagne [baɲ] *nm* : labor camp

bagnole [baɲɔl] *nf fam* : jalopy

bague [bag] *nf* : ring

baguette [bagɛt] *nf* **1** : stick, rod, baton **2** : baguette (loaf of French bread) **3** ~ **de tambour** : drumstick **4** ~**s** *nfpl* : chopsticks

baie [bɛ] *nf* **1** : bay **2** : berry

baigner [beɲe] *vt* : bathe, wash — *vi* : soak, steep — **se baigner** *vr* **1** : take a bath **2** : go swimming — **baignade** [beɲad] *nf* : swimming — **baigneur, -gneuse** [bɛɲœr, -ɲøz] *n* : swimmer, bather — **baignoire** [beɲwar] *nf* : bathtub

bail [baj] *nm, pl* **baux** [bo] : lease

bâiller [baje] *vi* **1** : yawn **2** : be ajar (of a door) — **bâillement** [bajmɑ̃] *nm* : yawn

bâillonner [bajɔne] *vt* : gag, muzzle — **bâillon** [bajɔ̃] *nm* : gag

bain [bɛ̃] *nm* : bath

bain–marie [bɛ̃mari] *nm, pl* **bains–marie** : double boiler

baïonnette [bajɔnɛt] *nf* : bayonet

baiser [beze] *vt* : kiss — ~ *nm* : kiss

baisser [bese] *vt* : lower, reduce (volume, light, etc.) — *vi* : drop, decline — **se**

baisser *vr* : bend down — **baisse** [bɛs] *nf* : fall, drop

bal [bal] *nm* : ball, dance

balader [balade] *v* **se balader** *vr* **1** : go for a walk **2** : go for a drive — **balade** [balad] *nf* **1** : stroll, walk **2** : drive, ride

balafre [balafr] *nf* : gash, slash

balai [balɛ] *nm* : broom, brush

balancer [balɑ̃se] {6} *vt* **1** : sway, swing (one's arms, etc.) **2** : balance (an account) **3** *fam* : chuck, junk — **se balancer** *vr* : rock, sway — **balance** [balɑ̃s] *nf* : scales *pl*, balance

balancier [balɑ̃sje] *nm* : pendulum

balançoire [balɑ̃swar] *nf* **1** : child's swing **2** BASCULE : seesaw

balayer [baleje] {11} *vt* **1** : sweep **2** : scan (in computer science) — **balayage** [balɛjaʒ] *nm* : sweeping — **balayeuse** [balɛjøz] *nf* **1** : street-cleaning truck **2** *Can* : vacuum cleaner

balbutier [balbysje] {96} *v* : stammer, stutter — **balbutiement** [balbysimɑ̃] *nm* **1** : stammering, stuttering **2** ~s *nmpl* : beginnings

balcon [balkɔ̃] *nm* : balcony

baldaquin [baldakɛ̃] *nm* : canopy

baleine [balɛn] *nf* : whale

balise [baliz] *nf* : buoy, beacon — **baliser** [balize] *vt* : mark with beacons

balistique [balistik] *adj* : ballistic

balivernes [balivɛrn] *nfpl* : nonsense

ballade [balad] *nf* : ballad

balle [bal] *nf* **1** : ball (in sports) **2** : bullet **3** *France fam* : franc

balle–molle [balmɔl] *nf Can* : softball

ballet [balɛ] *nm* : ballet — **ballerine** [balrin] *nf* : ballerina

ballon [balɔ̃] *nm* **1** : (foot)ball **2** : balloon — **ballon–panier** [balɔ̃panje] *nm Can* : basketball (game)

ballot [balo] *nm* BALUCHON : pack, bundle

ballotter [balɔte] *vt* SECOUER : shake, toss about — *vi* : toss, roll around

balloune [balun] *nf Can* : balloon

balnéaire [balneɛr] *adj* : seaside

balourd, -lourde [balur, -lurd] *adj* : awkward, clumsy

baluchon [balyʃɔ̃] *nm* : pack, bundle

balustrade [balystrad] *nf* : guardrail

bambin, -bine [bɑ̃bɛ̃, -bin] *n* : child, toddler

bambou [bɑ̃bu] *nm* : bamboo

ban [bɑ̃] *nm* **1** : round of applause **2** ~s *nmpl* : banns **3 mettre au** ~ : ostracize

banal, -nale [banal] *adj, mpl* **-nals** : commonplace, trite — **banalité** [banalite] *nf* : triviality

banane [banan] *nf* : banana

banc [bɑ̃] *nm* **1** : bench **2** : school (of fish) **3** ~ **de sable** : sandbank **4** ~ **de neige** *Can* : snowbank

bancaire [bɑ̃kɛr] *adj* : banking, bank

bancal, -cale [bɑ̃kal] *adj, mpl* **-cals** : wobbly, rickety

bandage [bɑ̃daʒ] *nm* **1** : bandaging **2** PANSEMENT : bandage

bande [bɑ̃d] *nf* **1** : gang, group, pack (of animals) **2** : tape, (reel of) film **3** ~ **dessinée** : comic strip

bandeau [bɑ̃do] *nm, pl* **-deaux 1** : blindfold **2** : headband

bander [bɑ̃de] *vt* **1** : bandage **2** ~ **les yeux à** : blindfold

banderole [bɑ̃drɔl] *nf* : banner, pennant

bandit [bɑ̃di] *nm* VOLEUR : bandit, robber

bandoulière [bɑ̃duljɛr] *nf* : shoulder strap

banlieue [bɑ̃ljø] *nf* : suburbs *pl*

bannière [banjɛr] *nf* : banner

bannir [banir] *vt* : banish, exile

banque [bɑ̃k] *nf* **1** : bank **2 travailler dans la** ~ : work in banking — **banqueroute** [bɑ̃krut] *nf* : bankruptcy

banquet [bɑ̃kɛ] *nm* : banquet, feast

banquette [bɑ̃kɛt] *nf* : bench, seat (in a booth or vehicle)

banquier, -quière [bɑ̃kje, -kjɛr] *n* : banker

baptême [batɛm] *nm* : baptism — **baptiser** [batize] *vt* : baptize, christen

bar [bar] *nm* **1** : sea bass **2** CAFÉ : bar

baragouin [baragwɛ̃] *nm* : gibberish — **baragouiner** [baragwine] *vi* : talk gibberish, jabber

baraque [barak] *nf* **1** : hut, shack **2** : stall, booth (at a fair, etc.)

barbare [barbar] *adj* : barbaric — ~ *nmf* : barbarian

barbe [barb] *nf* : beard

barbecue [barbəkju] *nm* : barbecue

barbelé, -lée [barbəle] *adj* **fil barbelé** : barbed wire

barbiche [barbiʃ] *nf* : goatee

barbier [barbje] *nm Can* : barber

barbouiller [barbuje] *vt* **1** : smear **2** GRIBOUILLER : scribble

bardeau [bardo] *nm, pl* **-deaux** : shingle

barème [barɛm] *nm* : scale, table, list

baril [baril] *nm* TONNELET : barrel, keg

bariolé, -lée [barjɔle] *adj* : multicolored

barman [barman] *nm, pl* **-mans** *or* **-men** : bartender

baromètre [barɔmɛtr] *nm* : barometer

baron, -ronne [barɔ̃, -rɔn] *n* : baron *m*, baroness *f*

barque [bark] *nf* : small boat

barrage [baraʒ] *nm* **1** : dam **2** ~ **routier** : roadblock

barre [bar] *nf* **1** : bar, rod **2** NIVEAU : mark, level **3 prendre la** ~ : take the helm — **barreau** [baro] *nm, pl* **-reaux 1** : bar **2** : rung — **barrer** [bare] *vt* **1** : bar, block **2**

: cross out (a word) **3** : steer (a boat) **4** *Can* : lock

barricader [barikade] *vt* : barricade — **barricade** [barikad] *nf* : barricade

barrière [barjɛr] *nf* : barrier

baryton [baritɔ̃] *nm* : baritone

bas *nms & pl* **1** : bottom, lower part **2** : stocking **3** à ～ : down with **4** en ～ : below **5** en ～ de : at the bottom of — ～ *adv* **1** : low **2** parler tout ～ : whisper, speak softly — **bas, basse** [ba (baz *before a vowel or mute h)*, bas] *adj* **1** : low **2** VIL : base, vile

basané, -née [bazane] *adj* : tanned, sunburned

bascule [baskyl] *nf* **1** BALANCE : balance, scales *pl* **2** BALANÇOIRE : seesaw — **basculer** [baskyle] *vi* : tip, topple

base [baz] *nf* **1** : base **2** FONDEMENT : basis **3** ～ de données : database

baseball *or* **base-ball** [bɛzbol] *nm* : baseball — **baseballeur, -leuse** [bɛzbolœr, -løz] *n Can* : baseball player

baser [baze] *vt* FONDER : base, found

basilic [bazilik] *nm* : basil

basilique [bazilik] *nf* : basilica

basket [baskɛt] *or* **basket-ball** [baskɛtbol] *nm* : basketball — **basketteur, -teuse** [baskɛtœr, -tøz] *n* : basketball player

basque [bask] *adj & nm* : Basque

basse [bas] *nf* : bass (in music)

bassin [basɛ̃] *nm* **1** : basin (in geography) **2** : pond, pool **3** : pelvis — **bassine** [basin] *nf* : bowl

basson [basɔ̃] *nm* : bassoon

bataille [bataj] *nf* : battle, fight — **batailler** [bataje] *vi* : fight, struggle (hard) — **batailleur, -leuse** [batajœr, -jøz] *adj* : quarrelsome — ～ *n* : fighter

bâtard, -tarde [batar, -tard] *adj & n* : bastard

bateau *nm, pl* **-teaux 1** : boat, ship **2** ～ à voiles : sailboat

batifoler [batifole] *vi* : frolic

bâtir [batir] *vt* **1** CONSTRUIRE : build, erect **2** FAUFILER : baste, tack — **bâtiment** [batimɑ̃] *nm* **1** : building, structure **2** NAVIRE : ship — **bâtisseur, -seuse** [batisœr, -søz] *n* : builder

bâton [batɔ̃] *nm* **1** : rod, stick, staff **2** *Can* : bat (in sports) **3** ～ de rouge : lipstick

battre [batr] {12} *vt* **1** FRAPPER : hit, strike **2** VAINCRE : defeat **3** : shuffle (cards) — *vi* : beat (of the heart) — **se battre** *vr* : fight — **battant, -tante** [batɑ̃, -tɑ̃t] *adj* **1** : beating, pounding **2** pluie battante : pouring rain — **batte** [bat] *nf* : bat (in sports) — **battement** [batmɑ̃] *nm* **1** : beating **2** ～ de cœur : heartbeat — **batterie** [batri] *nf* **1** : battery (of a car) **2** ENSEMBLE : set, group **3** : drums, drum set — **batteur** [batœr,

-tøz] *nm* **1** : whisk, eggbeater **2** : drummer **3** : batter (in sports)

baume [bom] *nm* : balm

baux → **bail**

bavard, -varde [bavar, -vard] *adj* : talkative — ～ *n* : chatterbox — **bavarder** [bavarde] *vi* **1** : chatter **2** : gossip — **bavardage** [bavardaʒ] *nm* : idle talk, chatter

bave [bav] *nf* : dribble, spittle — **baver** [bave] *vi* **1** : dribble, drool **2** COULER : leak — **bavoir** [bavwar] *nm* : (baby's) bib

bavure [bavyr] *nf* **1** : smudge **2** GAFFE : blunder

bazar [bazar] *nm* **1** : bazaar **2** *fam* : clutter, mess

beau [bo] (**bel** [bɛl] *before vowel or mute h*), **belle** [bɛl] *adj, mpl* **beaux** [bo] **1** : beautiful, handsome **2** : good (of a performance, etc.) **3** : considerable (in quantity) **4** ～ temps : nice weather — ～ *adv* **1** avoir ～ : do (something) in vain **2** il fait ～ : it's nice outside

beaucoup [boku] *adv* **1** : much, a lot **2** ～ de : much, many, a lot of **3** de ～ : by far

beau-fils [bofis] *nm, pl* **beaux-fils 1** : son-in-law **2** : stepson — **beau-frère** [bofrɛr] *nm, pl* **beaux-frères 1** : brother-in-law **2** : stepbrother — **beau-père** [bopɛr] *nm, pl* **beaux-pères 1** : father-in-law **2** : stepfather

beauté [bote] *nf* : beauty

beaux-arts [bozar] *nmpl* : fine arts

beaux-parents [boparɑ̃] *nmpl* : in-laws

bébé [bebe] *nm* : baby, infant

bec [bɛk] *nm* **1** : beak, bill **2** *fam* : mouth **3** EMBOUCHURE : mouthpiece **4** : point (of a pen) **5** : spout, lip (of a jug, etc.) **6** *Can fam* : kiss

bêche [bɛʃ] *nf* : spade — **bêcher** [beʃe] *vt* : dig (up)

bedaine [bədɛn] *nf fam* : paunch

bée *adj* [be] → **bouche**

beffroi [befrwa] *nm* : belfry

bégayer [begeje] {11} *v* : stutter, stammer

béguin [begɛ̃] *nm fam* : crush, infatuation

beige [bɛʒ] *adj & nm* : beige

beignet [bɛɲɛ] *nm* **1** : doughnut **2** : fritter — **beigne** [bɛɲ] *nm Can* : doughnut

bel [bɛl] → **beau**

bêler [bele] *vi* : bleat — **bêlement** [bɛlmɑ̃] *nm* : bleat

belette [bəlɛt] *nf* : weasel

belge [bɛlʒ] *adj* : Belgian

bélier [belje] *nm* : ram

belle [bɛl] *adj* → **beau**

belle-famille [bɛlfamij] *nf, pl* **belles-familles** : in-laws *pl* — **belle-fille** [bɛlfij] *nf, pl* **belles-filles 1** : daughter-in-law **2** : stepdaughter — **belle-mère** [bɛlmɛr] *nf, pl* **belles-mères 1** : mother-in-law **2** : step-

mother — **belle–sœur** [bɛlsœr] *nf, pl*
belles–sœurs : sister-in-law

belligérant, -rante [beliʒerɑ̃, -rɑ̃t] *adj & n*
: belligerent

belliqueux, -queuse [bɛlikø, -køz] *adj*
GUERRIER : warlike

bémol [bemɔl] *nm* : flat (in music)

bénédiction [benediksjɔ̃] *nf* : blessing,
benediction

bénéfice [benefis] *nm* 1 AVANTAGE : benefit,
advantage 2 GAIN : profit — **bénéficiaire**
[benefisjɛr] *nmf* : beneficiary — **bénéficier**
[benefisje] {96} *vi* ~ **de** : benefit from —
bénéfique [benefik] *adj* : beneficial

bénévole [benevɔl] *adj* : voluntary — ~
nmf : volunteer

bénin, -nigne [benɛ̃, beniɲ] *adj* 1 : slight,
minor 2 : benign (of a tumor)

bénir [benir] *vt* : bless — **bénit, -nite** [beni,
-nit] *adj* : blessed

benjamin, -mine [bɛ̃ʒamɛ̃, -min] *n* CADET
: youngest child

béquille [bekij] *nf* 1 : crutch 2 : kickstand

bercer [bɛrse] {6} *vt* 1 : rock (a baby) 2
APAISER : soothe, lull — **se bercer** *vr*
: rock, swing — **berceau** [bɛrso] *nm, pl*
-ceaux : cradle — **berceuse** [bɛrsøz] *nf* 1
: lullaby 2 : rocking chair

béret [berɛ] *nm* : beret

berge [bɛrʒ] *nf* RIVE : bank (of a river, etc.)

berger, -gère [bɛrʒe, -ʒɛr] *n* : shepherd,
shepherdess *f* — **berger** *nm* : sheepdog

berline [bɛrlin] *nf* : sedan

berlingot [bɛrlɛ̃go] *nm* 1 : carton (for milk,
etc.) 2 : hard candy

berner [bɛrne] *vt* : fool, deceive

besogne [bəzɔɲ] *nf* : task, job

besoin [bəzwɛ̃] *nm* 1 : need 2 **avoir** ~ **de**
: need 3 **dans le** ~ : needy

bestiole [bɛstjɔl] *nf* : bug, tiny creature

bétail [betaj] *nm* : livestock, cattle *pl*

bête [bɛt] *nf* ANIMAL : animal, creature — ~
adj : stupid, silly — **bêtement** [bɛtmɑ̃] *adv*
: foolishly — **bêtise** [betiz] *nf* 1 : stupidity
2 : stupid thing, nonsense

béton [betɔ̃] *nm* : concrete

bette [bɛt] *nf* : Swiss chard

betterave [bɛtrav] *nf* : beet

beugler [bøgle] *vi* 1 : moo, bellow 2 : blare
(of a radio, etc.) — *vt* : bellow out

beurre [bœr] *nm* : butter — **beurrer** [bœre]
vt : butter

bévue [bevy] *nf* : blunder

biais [bjɛ, bjɛz] *nm* 1 : means, way 2 **de** ~
: diagonally — **biaiser** [bjeze] *vi* : hedge,
dodge the issue

bibelot [biblo] *nm* : trinket, curio

biberon [bibrɔ̃] *nm* : baby bottle

Bible [bibl] *nf* **la** ~ : the Bible — **biblique**
[biblik] *adj* : biblical, scriptural

bibliographie [biblijɔgrafi] *nf* : bibliography

bibliothèque [biblijɔtɛk] *nf* 1 : library 2
: bookcase — **bibliothécaire** [biblijɔtekɛr]
nmf : librarian

bicarbonate [bikarbɔnat] *nm* ~ **de soude**
: baking soda

biceps [bisɛps] *nms & pl* : biceps

biche [biʃ] *nf* : doe

bicoque [bikɔk] *nf* : shack, shanty

bicyclette [bisiklɛt] *nf* : bicycle

bidon [bidɔ̃] *nm* : can, flask

bien [bjɛ̃] *adv* 1 : well, satisfactorily 2 TRÈS
: very, quite 3 RÉELLEMENT : definitely, really 4 VOLONTIERS : readily, happily 5 ~
des fois : many times 6 ~ **que** : although
7 ~ **sûr** : of course — ~ *adj* 1 : good,
fine, satisfactory 2 : well, in good health 3
BEAU : good-looking 4 RESPECTABLE : nice
5 : comfortable (of shoes, etc.) — ~ *nm* 1
: good 2 ~**s** *nmpl* : possessions, property
— ~ *interj* : OK, all right, very well —
bien–aimé, -aimée [bjɛ̃neme] *adj & n*
: beloved — **bien–être** [bjɛ̃nɛtr] *nm* 1
: well-being 2 : comfort

bienfaisance [bjɛ̃fəzɑ̃s] *nf* : charity, kindness — **bienfaisant, -sante** [bjɛ̃fəzɑ̃, -zɑ̃t]
adj 1 : charitable 2 BÉNÉFIQUE : beneficial
— **bienfait** [bjɛ̃fɛ] *nm* AVANTAGE : benefit —
bienfaiteur, -trice [bjɛ̃fɛtœr, -tris] *n* : benefactor

bientôt [bjɛ̃to] *adv* : soon, shortly

bienveillance [bjɛ̃vejɑ̃s] *nf* : kindness,
benevolence — **bienveillant, -lante** [bjɛ̃-
vejɑ̃, -jɑ̃t] *adj* : kind, benevolent

bienvenu, -nue [bjɛ̃vny] *adj* : welcome —
~ **n soyez le** ~ : you are welcome (here)
— **bienvenue** *nf* : welcome

bière [bjɛr] *nf* : beer

biffer [bife] *vt* : cross out

bifteck [biftɛk] *nm* : steak

bifurquer [bifyrke] *vi* : to fork — **bifurcation** [bifyrkasjɔ̃] *nf* : fork (in a road)

bigot, -gote [bigo, -ɔt] *adj* : overly devout —
~ *n* : (religious) zealot

bigoudi [bigudi] *nm* : hair curler

bijou [biʒu] *nm, pl* **-joux** 1 : jewel 2 MER-
VEILLE : gem — **bijouterie** [biʒutri] *nf* 1
BIJOUX : jewelry 2 : jewelry store — **bi-
joutier, -tière** [biʒutje, -tjɛr] *n* : jeweler

bilan [bilɑ̃] *nm* 1 : assessment 2 : balance
sheet (in finance)

bilatéral, -rale [bilateral] *adj, mpl* **-raux** [-ro]
: bilateral

bile [bil] *nf* 1 : bile 2 **se faire de la** ~
: worry

bilingue [bilɛ̃g] *adj* : bilingual

billard [bijar] *nm* : billiards *pl*

bille [bij] *nf* 1 : (playing) marble 2 : billiard
ball

billet [bijɛ] *nm* **1** : bill, banknote **2** TICKET : ticket **3** ~ **doux** : love letter — **billetterie** [bijɛtri] *nf* **1** GUICHET : ticket office **2** : automatic teller machine

billion [biljɔ̃] *nm* : trillion (US), billion (Brit)

bimensuel, -suelle [bimɑ̃sɥɛl] *adj* : semimonthly

binette [binɛt] *nf* : hoe

biochimie [bjɔʃimi] *nf* : biochemistry

biographie [bjɔgrafi] *nf* : biography — **biographe** [bjɔgraf] *nmf* : biographer — **biographique** [bjɔgrafik] *adj* : biographical

biologie [bjɔlɔʒi] *nf* : biology — **biologique** [bjɔlɔʒik] *adj* : biological

bis [bis] *adv* **1** : twice (in music) **2** : A (in an address) — ~ *nm & interj* : encore

biscotte [biskɔt] *nf* : cracker

biscuit [biskɥi] *nm* **1** : cookie **2** : sponge cake

bise [biz] *nf* **1** : north wind **2** *fam* : kiss, smack

biseau [bizo] *nm* **1** : bevel **2 en** ~ : beveled

bisexuel, -sexuelle [bisɛksɥɛl] *adj* : bisexual

bison [bizɔ̃] *nm* : bison, buffalo

bissextile [bisɛkstil] *adj* **année** ~ : leap year

bistouri [bisturi] *nm* : lancet

bistro *or* **bistrot** [bistro] *nm* : café

bit [bit] *nm* : bit (unit of information)

bizarre [bizar] *adj* : bizarre, strange — **bizarrement** [-zarmɑ̃] *adv* : oddly, strangely

blafard, -farde [blafar, -fard] *adj* : pale, pallid

blague [blag] *nf* PLAISANTERIE : joke — **blaguer** [blage] *vi* PLAISANTER : joke, kid around — **blagueur, -gueuse** [blagœr, -gøz] *n* : joker

blaireau [blɛro] *nm, pl* **-raux** : badger

blâmer [blame] *vt* : blame, criticize — **blâme** [blam] *nm* DÉSAPPROBATION : blame, censure

blanc, blanche [blɑ̃, blɑ̃ʃ] *adj* **1** : white **2** PÂLE : pale **3** : pure, innocent **4 page blanche** : blank sheet — **blanc** *nm* **1** : white **2** INTERVALLE : gap, blank space — **blanchir** [blɑ̃ʃir] *vt* **1** : whiten, bleach **2** : launder (one's clothes) **3** : blanch (vegetables) — *vi* : turn white — **blanchissage** [blɑ̃ʃisaʒ] *nm* : laundering — **blanchisserie** [blɑ̃ʃisri] *nf* : laundry

blasé, -sée [blaze] *adj* : blasé, jaded

blason [blazɔ̃] *nm* : coat of arms

blasphème [blasfɛm] *nm* : blasphemy

blatte [blat] *nf* : cockroach

blazer [blazɛr] *nm* : blazer

blé [ble] *nm* : wheat

blême [blɛm] *adj* : pale, wan

blesser [blese] *vt* : injure, wound — **blessé,**

-sée [blese] *n* : casualty, injured person — **blessure** [blesyr] *nf* : injury, wound

bleu, bleue [blø] *adj* **1** : blue **2** : very rare (of steak, etc.) — **bleu** *nm* **1** : blue **2** : bruise

bleuet [bløɛ] *nm Can* : blueberry

blindé, -dée [blɛ̃de] *adj* : armored — **blindé** *nm* : armored vehicle

bloc [blɔk] *nm* **1** : block **2 en** ~ : as a whole

blocage [blɔkaʒ] *nm* **1** : obstruction **2** : freezing (of prices, etc.)

blocus [blɔkys] *nm* : blockade

blond, blonde [blɔ̃, blɔ̃d] *adj & n* : blond

blonde *nf Can fam* : girlfriend

bloquer [blɔke] *vt* **1** : block (an entrance) **2** : jam on (the brakes) **3** : freeze (a bank account, etc.), stop (a check) — **se bloquer** *vr* : jam, stick

blottir [blɔtir] *v* **se blottir** *vr* : cuddle, snuggle

blouse [bluz] *nf* **1** CHEMISIER : blouse **2** SARRAU : smock

blouson [bluzɔ̃] *nm* : jacket

blue–jean [bludʒin] *nm, pl* **blue–jeans** : jeans *pl*

bluffer [blœfe] *vi* : bluff — **bluff** [blœf] *nm* : bluff

bobine [bɔbin] *nf* : reel, spool

bocal [bɔkal] *nm, pl* **-caux** [bɔko] : jar

bœuf [bœf] *nm, pl* **bœufs** [bø] : beef

bohème [bɔɛm] *adj* : bohemian — **bohémien, -mienne** [bɔemjɛ̃, -mjɛn] *n* : gypsy

boire [bwar] {13} *vt* **1** : drink **2** ABSORBER : absorb — *vi* : drink

bois [bwa] *nms & pl* **1** : wood **2** FORÊT : woods *pl* **3** ~ **de chauffage** : firewood **4** ~ *nmpl* : antlers — **boisé, -sée** [bwaze] *adj* : wooded — **boisé** *nm Can* : woods *pl*

boisseau [bwaso] *nm* : bushel

boisson [bwasɔ̃] *nf* **1** : drink, beverage **2 en** ~ *Can* : drunk

boîte [bwat] *nf* **1** : (tin) can **2** : box **3** ~ **de nuit** : nightclub

boiter [bwate] *vi* : limp — **boiteux, -teuse** [bwatø, -tøz] *adj* **1** : lame **2** BRANLANT : wobbly, shaky — **boitiller** [bwatije] *vi* : limp slightly, hobble

boîtier [bwatje] *nm* : casing, housing

bol [bɔl] *nm* **1** : bowl **2** : bowlful

bombarder [bɔ̃barde] *vt* : bomb, bombard — **bombardement** [bɔ̃bardəmɑ̃] *nm* : bombing, bombardment — **bombardier** [bɔ̃bardje] *nm* : bomber (plane)

bombe [bɔ̃b] *nf* **1** : bomb **2** ATOMISEUR : aerosol spray

bomber [bɔ̃be] *vt* : puff out, swell

bon, bonne [bɔ̃ (bon *before a vowel or mute h*), bɔn] *adj* **1** : good **2** CORRECT

: correct, proper **3** ~ **marché** : inexpensive **4** ~ **sens** : common sense **5 pour de** ~ : for good, for keeps — **bon** *adv* faire ~ : be nice — ~ *nm* **1** : good thing **2** : voucher, bond

bonbon [bɔ̃bɔ̃] *nm* : candy

bond [bɔ̃] *nm* **1** SAUT : bound, leap **2** : bounce (of a ball)

bondé, -dée [bɔ̃de] *adj* : crammed, packed

bondir [bɔ̃dir] *vi* : jump, leap

bonheur [bɔnœr] *nm* **1** : happiness, pleasure **2 par** ~ : luckily

bonhomme [bɔnɔm] *nm, pl* **bonshommes** **1** *fam* : fellow, guy **2** ~ **de neige** : snowman

bonjour [bɔ̃ʒur] *nm* **1** : hello, good morning, good afternoon **2** *Can* : good-bye

bonne [bɔn] *nf* DOMESTIQUE : maid

bonnement [bɔnmɑ̃] *adv* **tout** ~ : quite simply

bonnet [bɔnɛ] *nm* : cap, hat

bonneterie [bɔnɛtri] *nf* : hosiery

bonsoir [bɔ̃swar] *nm* : good evening, good night

bonté [bɔ̃te] *nf* : goodness, kindness

bord [bɔr] *nm* **1** : edge, rim **2** : bank, shore **3 à** ~ : on board, aboard **4 au** ~ **de** : on the verge of

bordeaux [bɔrdo] *nm* : Bordeaux, claret (wine)

bordée [bɔrde] *nf* **1** : volley **2** ~ **de neige** *Can* : snowstorm

bordel [bɔrdɛl] *nm fam* **1** : brothel **2** PAGAILLE : mess, shambles

border [bɔrde] *vt* **1** : border, line **2** : tuck in

bordereau [bɔrdəro] *nm, pl* **-reaux** [-ro] **1** : note (in finance) **2** ~ **de dépôt** : deposit slip

bordure [bɔrdyr] *nf* : border, edge

borne [bɔrn] *nf* **1** : milestone, landmark **2** ~**s** *nfpl* : limits — **borné, -née** [bɔrne] *adj* : narrow-minded — **borner** [bɔrne] *vt* RESTREINDRE : limit, restrict — **se borner** *vr* : confine oneself

bosquet [bɔske] *nm* : grove, copse

bosse [bɔs] *nf* **1** : hump (of a person or animal) **2 se faire une** ~ : get a bump — **bosseler** [bɔsle] {8} *vt* : dent (a bumper, etc.) — **bosser** [bɔse] *vi France fam* : work, slave away

botanique [bɔtanik] *nf* : botany — ~ *adj* : botanical

botte [bɔt] *nf* **1** : boot **2** : bunch (of radishes), sheaf (of hay) — **botter** [bɔte] *vt* : kick (in sports)

bottin [bɔtɛ̃] *nm* : (telephone) directory

bouche [buʃ] *nf* **1** : mouth **2** ENTRÉE : opening, entrance **3** ~ **bée** : flabbergasted **4** ~ **d'incendie** : fire hydrant — **bouchée** [buʃe] *nf* : mouthful

boucher[1] [buʃe] *vt* : stop up, block — **se boucher** *vr* : become blocked — **bouchon** [buʃɔ̃] *nm* **1** : cork, stopper **2** : float (in fishing) **3** EMBOUTEILLAGE : traffic jam

boucher[2]**, -chère** [buʃe, -ʃɛr] *n* : butcher — **boucherie** [buʃri] *nf* : butcher's shop

boucler [bukle] *vt* **1** : buckle (a belt), fasten (a seat belt) **2** : complete (a task) — *vi* : curl — **boucle** [bukl] *nf* **1** : buckle **2** : curl **3** ~ **d'oreille** : earring — **bouclé, -clée** [bukle] *adj* : curly

bouclier [buklije] *nm* : shield

bouddhiste [budist] *adj & nmf* : Buddhist — **bouddhisme** [budism] *nm* : Buddhism

bouder [bude] *vi* : avoid — *vi* : sulk, pout — **bouderie** [budri] *nf* : sulkiness — **boudeur, -deuse** [budœr, -døz] *adj* : sulky

boudin [budɛ̃] *nm* : blood sausage

boue [bu] *nf* : mud — **boueux, boueuse** [buø, buøz] *adj* : muddy

bouée [bwe] *nf* : buoy

bouffant, -fante [bufɑ̃, -fɑ̃t] *adj* : baggy (of pants) — **bouffi, -fie** [bufi] *adj* : puffy, swollen

bouffe [buf] *nf fam* : grub, chow — **bouffer** [bufe] *vt fam* : eat, gobble up

bouffée [bufe] *nf* **1** : puff, gust **2** : surge, fit (of rage, etc.)

bouffon, -fonne [bufɔ̃, bufɔn] *adj* : comical — **bouffon** *nm* : clown, buffoon

bougeoir [buʒwar] *nm* : candlestick

bouger [buʒe] {17} *vt* : move — *vi* : budge, stir

bougie [buʒi] *nf* **1** : candle **2** : spark plug (of a car)

bougonner [bugɔne] *vi* : grumble — **bougon, -gonne** [bugɔ̃, -gɔn] *adj* : grumpy

bouillabaisse [bujabɛs] *nf* : fish soup

bouillir [bujir] {14} *vi* **1** : boil **2** : seethe (with anger, etc.) — **bouillie** [buji] *nf* : baby cereal, gruel — **bouilloire** [bujwar] *nf* : kettle, teakettle — **bouillon** [bujɔ̃] *nm* : broth, stock — **bouillonner** [bujɔne] *vi* **1** : bubble, foam **2** → **bouillir 2**

boulanger, -gère [bulɑ̃ʒe, -ʒɛr] *n* : baker — **boulangerie** [bulɑ̃ʒri] *nf* : bakery

boule [bul] *nf* **1** : ball **2** ~ **de neige** : snowball

bouleau [bulo] *nm, pl* **-leaux** : birch

bouledogue [buldɔg] *nm* : bulldog

boulet [bulɛ] *nm* **1** : cannonball **2** : ball and chain

boulette [bulɛt] *nf* **1** : pellet **2** : meatball

boulevard [bulvar] *nm* : boulevard

bouleverser [bulverse] *vt* **1** : upset, turn upside down **2** PERTURBER : overwhelm — **bouleversant, -sante** [bulversɑ̃, -sɑ̃t] *adj* : distressing, upsetting — **bouleversement** [bulversəmɑ̃] *nm* : upheaval, upset

boulon [bulõ] *nm* : bolt

boulot [bulo] *nm fam* **1** : work, task **2** EMPLOI : job — **boulot, -lotte** [bulo, -lɔt] *adj* : plump, chubby

boum [bum] *nm* **1** : bang **2** : boom (of business, etc.)

bouquet [bukɛ] *nm* : bouquet, bunch (of flowers)

bouquin [bukɛ̃] *nm fam* : book — **bouquiniste** [bukinist] *nmf* : secondhand bookseller

bourbier [burbje] *nm* : swamp, quagmire

bourde [burd] *nf* : blunder

bourdon [burdõ] *nm* : bumblebee — **bourdonnement** [burdɔnmã] *nm* : buzz, hum, droning — **bourdonner** [burdɔne] *vi* : buzz, hum

bourgeois, -geoise [burʒwa, -ʒwaz] *adj & n* : bourgeois — **bourgeoisie** [burʒwazi] *nf* : bourgeoisie

bourgeon [burʒõ] *nm* : bud — **bourgeonner** [burʒɔne] *vi* : bud

bourgogne [burgɔɲ] *nm* : Burgundy (wine)

bourrage [buraʒ] *nm* : filling, stuffing

bourreau [buro] *nm, pl* **-reaux 1** : executioner **2** ~ **de travail** : workaholic

bourrer [bure] *vt* : fill, stuff, cram — *vi* : be filling — **se bourrer** *vr* : stuff oneself

bourru, -rue [bury] *adj* : gruff, surly

bourse [burs] *nf* **1** PORTE-MONNAIE : purse **2** : scholarship **3 la Bourse** : the stock market — **boursier, -sière** [bursje, -sjɛr] *adj* : stock, stock-market

boursoufler [bursufle] *vt* : puff up, cause to swell — **se boursoufler** *vr* : blister — **boursouflure** [bursuflyr] *nf* : blister (of paint, etc.)

bousculer [buskyle] *vt* **1** : jostle, shove **2** PRESSER : rush — **se bousculer** *vr* : jostle — **bousculade** [buskylad] *nf* : rush, scramble

bousiller [buzije] *vt fam* : bungle, botch

boussole [busɔl] *nf* : compass

bout [bu] *nm* **1** EXTRÉMITÉ : end, tip **2** MORCEAU : bit **3 au** ~ **de** : after **4 à** ~ **portant** : point-blank

bouteille [butɛj] *nf* : bottle

boutique [butik] *nf* : shop, boutique

bouton [butõ] *nm* **1** : button **2** BOURGEON : bud **3** : pimple **4** *or* ~ **de porte** : doorknob — **boutonner** [butɔne] *vt* : button — **boutonnière** *nf* : buttonhole

bovins [bɔvɛ̃] *nmpl* : cattle

bowling [buliɲ] *nm* : bowling

box [bɔks] *nm, pl* **boxes** : stall (for a horse)

boxe [bɔks] *nf* : boxing — **boxer** [bɔkse] *vi* : box — **boxeur** [bɔksœr] *nm* : boxer, fighter

boyau [bwajo] *nm, pl* **boyaux 1** INTESTIN : intestine, gut **2** : inner tube (of a tire)

boycotter [bɔjkɔte] *vt* : boycott — **boycottage** [bɔjkɔtaʒ] *nm* : boycott

bracelet [braslɛ] *nm* : bracelet

braconner [brakɔne] *vi* : poach (of game)

braguette [bragɛt] *nf* : fly (of pants, etc.)

braille [braj] *nm* : braille

brailler [braje] *vi fam* : bawl, howl

braire [brɛr] {15} *vi* : bray

braise [brɛz] *nf* : embers *pl*

brancard [brɑ̃kar] *nm* CIVIÈRE : stretcher

branche [brɑ̃ʃ] *nf* **1** : branch **2** : sidepiece (of eyeglasses) — **branché, -chée** [brɑ̃ʃe] *adj fam* : trendy — **brancher** [brɑ̃ʃe] *vt* **1** : connect (a utility) **2** : plug in (a device)

branchie [brɑ̃ʃi] *nf* : gill (of a fish)

brandir [brɑ̃dir] *vt* : brandish, wave

branler [brɑ̃le] *vi* : wobble, be loose — **branlant, -lante** [brɑ̃lɑ̃, -lɑ̃t] *adj* : unsteady — **branle** [brɑ̃l] *nm* **mettre en** ~ : set in motion

braquer [brake] *vt* **1** DIRIGER : aim **2** : turn (a steering wheel) **3** *fam* : point a gun at **4** ~ **qqn contre qqch** : turn s.o. against sth

bras [bra] *nms & pl* : arm — **brasser** [brase] *vt* **1** : mix **2** : brew (beer) — **brasserie** [brasri] *nf* **1** : brewery **2** : restaurant — **brassière** [brasjɛr] *nf Can* : bra, brassiere

brave [brav] *adj* **1** GENTIL : good, nice **2** COURAGEUX : brave — **bravement** [bravmɑ̃] *adv* : bravely, boldly — **braver** [brave] *vt* : brave

break [brɛk] *nm France* : station wagon — ~ *nm Can* : break, rest

brebis [brəbi] *nf* : ewe

brèche [brɛʃ] *nf* : gap

bredouiller [brəduje] *v* : mumble, mutter

bref, brève [brɛf, brɛv] *adj* : brief, short — **bref** [brɛf] *adv or* **en** ~ : briefly, in short

brésilien, -lienne [breziljɛ̃, -ljɛn] *adj* : Brazilian

bretelle [brətɛl] *nf* **1** : strap **2** : (access) ramp **3** ~**s** *nfpl* : suspenders

breton, -tonne [brətõ, brətɔn] *n* : Breton

breuvage [brœvaʒ] *nm* : beverage

brevet [brəvɛ] *nm* **1** : patent **2** : diploma, certificate — **breveter** [brəvte] {8} *vt* : patent

bribes [brib] *nfpl* : bits, pieces

bric-à-brac [brikabrak] *nms & pl* : odds and ends

bricoler [brikɔle] *vi* : do odd jobs, putter — *vt* : fix up — **bricolage** [brikɔlaʒ] *nm* : do-it-yourself work — **bricoleur, -leuse** [brikɔlœr, -løz] *n* : handyman

bride [brid] *nf* : bridle — **brider** [bride] *vt* **1** : bridle (a horse) **2** CONTENIR : keep in check

bridge [bridʒ] *nm* : bridge (card game)

brièveté [brijɛvte] *nf* : brevity — **brièvement** [brijɛvmã] *adv* : briefly

brigade [brigad] *nf* : brigade, squad
briller [brije] *vi* : shine — **brillant, -lante** [brijɑ̃, -jɑ̃t] *adj* **1** : bright, shiny **2** REMARQUABLE : brilliant, outstanding — **brillant** *nm* : gloss, shine
brimer [brime] *vt* : bully
brin [brɛ̃] *nm* **1** : blade (of grass), sprig **2** : little bit, iota **3** : strand (of thread, etc.)
brindille [brɛ̃dij] *nf* : twig
bringue [brɛ̃g] *nf fam* : binge
brio [brijo] *nm* **1** : brilliance, panache **2** **avec ~** : brilliantly
brioche [brijɔʃ] *nf* **1** : brioche **2** *fam* : paunch
brique [brik] *nf* : brick
briquet [brike] *nm* : (cigarette) lighter
brise [briz] *nf* : breeze
briser [brize] *vt* **1** : break, smash **2** DÉTRUIRE : ruin, wreck — **se briser** *vr* : shatter, break
britannique [britanik] *adj* : British
broche [brɔʃ] *nf* **1** : brooch **2** : spit, skewer (in cooking) — **brochette** [brɔʃɛt] *nf* : skewer
brochure [brɔʃyr] *nf* : brochure, pamphlet
brocoli [brɔkɔli] *nm* : broccoli
broder [brɔde] *vt* : embroider — **broderie** [brɔdri] *nf* : embroidery
bronchite [brɔ̃ʃit] *nf* : bronchitis
bronze [brɔ̃z] *nm* : bronze — **bronzage** [brɔ̃zaʒ] *nm* : suntan — **bronzé, -zée** [brɔ̃ze] *adj* : suntanned — **bronzer** [brɔ̃ze] *vi* : get a suntan
brosse [brɔs] *nf* : brush — **brosser** [brɔse] *vt* **1** : brush **2** : paint (a picture) — **se brosser** *vr* **~ les cheveux** : brush one's hair
brouette [bruɛt] *nf* : wheelbarrow
brouiller [bruje] *vt* **1** : mix up, scramble **2** TROUBLER : blur, cloud — **se brouiller** *vr* **1** : quarrel **2** : cloud over (of the weather) — **brouillard** [brujar] *nm* : fog, mist — **brouillon, -lonne** [brujɔ̃, -jɔn] *adj* : disorganized, untidy — **brouillon** *nm* : rough draft
broussailles [brusaj] *nfpl* : undergrowth
brousse [brus] *nf* **la ~** : bush, wilderness
brouter [brute] *vi* : graze
broyer [brwaje] {58} *vt* : grind, crush
bru [bry] *nf* : daughter-in-law
bruine [bruin] *nf* : drizzle — **bruiner** [bruine] *vi* : drizzle
bruire [bruir] {16} *vi* : rustle, murmur, hum — **bruissement** [bruismɑ̃] *nm* : rustling, murmuring — **bruit** [brui] *nm* **1** : noise **2** VACARME : commotion, fuss **3** RUMEUR : rumor
brûler [bryle] *vt* **1** : burn, scald **2** : run (a red light) — *vi* : burn (up) — **se brûler** *vr* : burn oneself — **brûlant, -lante** [brylɑ̃, -lɑ̃t] *adj* **1** : burning hot **2** : ardent — **brûleur**

[brylœr] *nm* : burner — **brûlure** [brylyr] *nf* **1** : burn **2 ~s d'estomac** : heartburn
brume [brym] *nf* : mist, haze — **brumeux, -meuse** [brymø, -møz] *adj* : misty, foggy
brun, brune [brœ̃, bryn] *adj* : brown — **brun** *n* : brunet — **~** *nm* : brown — **brunette** [brynɛt] *nf* : brunette
brusque [brysk] *adj* : brusque, abrupt — **brusquement** [bryskəmɑ̃] *adv* : abruptly, suddenly — **brusquer** [bryske] *vt* : rush, hurry
brut, brute [bryt] *adj* **1** : raw, crude **2** : dry (of wine) **3 poids ~** : gross weight
brutal, -tale [brytal] *adj, mpl* **-taux** [bryto] : brutal — **brutalement** [-talmɑ̃] *adv* **1** : brutally **2** : suddenly — **brutaliser** [brytalize] *vt* : abuse, mistreat — **brutalité** [brytalite] *nf* : brutality — **brute** [bryt] *nf* : brute
bruyant, bruyante [bruijɑ̃, -jɑ̃t] *adj* : noisy, loud — **bruyamment** [bruijamɑ̃] *adv* : noisily, loudly
bruyère [bruijɛr] *nf* : heather
buanderie [byɑ̃dri] *nf* **1** : laundry room **2** *Can* : self-service laundry
buccal, -cale [bykal] *adj, mpl* **-caux** [byko] : oral
bûche [byʃ] *nf* : log — **bûcher** [byʃe] *vi fam* : work, slave away — **bûcheron, -ronne** [byʃrɔ̃, -rɔn] *n* : logger, lumberjack
budget [bydʒɛ] *nm* : budget — **budgétaire** [bydʒetɛr] *adj* : budgetary — **budgétiser** [bydʒezite] *vt* : budget
buée [bye] *nf* : steam, mist
buffet [byfɛ] *nm* **1** : sideboard **2** : buffet
buffle [byfl] *nm* : buffalo
buisson [buisɔ̃] *nm* : bush, shrub
bulbe [bylb] *nm* : bulb (of a plant)
bulldozer [byldozɛr] *nm* : bulldozer
bulle [byl] *nf* : bubble
bulletin [byltɛ̃] *nm* **1** : report, bulletin **2 ~ de vote** : ballot
bureau [byro] *nm, pl* **-reaux 1** : office, study **2** SECRÉTAIRE : desk **3** : department, bureau — **bureaucrate** [byrokrat] *nmf* : bureaucrat — **bureaucratie** [byrokrasi] *nf* : bureaucracy — **bureaucratique** [-kratik] *adj* : bureaucratic
bus [bys] *nm* AUTOBUS : bus
buste [byst] *nm* **1** : chest, bust **2** : bust (in sculpture)
but [by(t)] *nm* **1** : aim, goal **2** *Can* : base (in baseball)
buter [byte] *vi* **~ contre** *or* **~ sur** : stumble on, trip over — *vt* : antagonize — **se buter** *vr* : become obstinate — **buté, -tée** [byte] *adj* : obstinate
butin [bytɛ̃] *nm* : loot
butte [byt] *nf* **1** : small hill, mound **2 être en ~ à** : come up against
buveur, -veuse [byvœr, -vøz] *n* : drinker

C

c [se] *nm* : c, third letter of the alphabet

ça [sa] *pron* **1** : that, this **2** : it **3** ~ **va?** : how's it going? **4** ~ **y est** : there, that's it

cabane [kaban] *nf* : cabin, hut — **cabanon** [kabanɔ̃] *nm* : shed

cabaret [kabarɛ] *nm* : nightclub

cabine [kabin] *nf* **1** : cabin, cab (of a truck, etc.) **2** ~ **téléphonique** : telephone booth **3** ~ **de pilotage** : cockpit

cabinet [kabinɛ] *nm* **1** : office **2** : cabinet (in government) **3** ~ **de toilette** *France* : toilet

câble [kabl] *nm* **1** : cable **2** : cable television

cabosser [kabɔse] *vt* : dent

cabriole [kabrijɔl] *nf* : somersault

cacahouète [kakaɥɛt] *nf* : peanut

cacao [kakao] *nm* : cocoa

cache–cache [kaʃkaʃ] *nms & pl* : hide-and-seek

cachemire [kaʃmir] *nm* : cashmere

cacher [kaʃe] *vt* : hide, conceal — **se cacher** *vr* : hide

cachet [kaʃɛ] *nm* **1** COMPRIMÉ : tablet, pill **2** *or* ~ **de la poste** : postmark **3** : fee **4** : character, style — **cacheter** [kaʃte] {8} *vt* : seal

cachette [kaʃɛt] *nf* : hiding place

cachot [kaʃo] *nm* : dungeon

cachottier, -tière [kaʃɔtje, -tjɛr] *adj* : secretive — **cachotterie** [kaʃɔtri] *nf* : little secret

cacophonie [kakɔfɔni] *nf* : cacophony

cactus [kaktys] *nms & pl* : cactus

cadavre [kadavr] *nm* : corpse

cadeau [kado] *nm, pl* **-deaux** : gift, present

cadenas [kadna] *nm* : padlock — **cadenasser** [-nase] *vt* : padlock

cadence [kadɑ̃s] *nf* : cadence, rhythm

cadet, -dette [kadɛ, -dɛt] *adj* : younger, youngest — ~ *n* **1** : younger, youngest (son, daughter, child) **2** : junior

cadran [kadrɑ̃] *nm* **1** : dial, face **2** *Can fam* : alarm clock

cadre [kadr] *nm* **1** : frame **2** : setting, surroundings *pl* **3** STRUCTURE : framework **4** : executive

caduc, -duque [kadyk] *adj* **1** : obsolete **2** : deciduous

cafard [kafar] *nm* **1** : cockroach **2 avoir le** ~ : have the blues

café [kafe] *nm* **1** : coffee **2** : café, bar — **caféine** [kafein] *nf* : caffeine — **cafetière** [kaftjɛr] *nf* : coffeepot — **cafétéria** [kafeterja] *nf* : cafeteria

cage [kaʒ] *nf* **1** : cage **2** ~ **d'escalier** : stairwell

cageot [kaʒo] *nm* : crate

cagnotte [kaɲɔt] *nf* : pool, kitty

cagoule [kagul] *nf* : hood

cahier [kaje] *nm* : notebook, exercise book

cahoter [kaɔte] *vi* : bump along — **cahoteux, -teuse** [kaɔtø, -tøz] *adj* : bumpy

cailler [kaje] *vi* **1** : curdle **2** : clot (of blood) — **caillot** [kajo] *nm* : clot

caillou [kaju] *nm, pl* **-loux** : pebble, stone

caisse [kes] *nf* **1** BOÎTE : box, crate **2** *or* ~ **enregistreuse** : cash register **3** ~ **d'épargne** : savings bank **4** ~ **populaire** *Can* : cooperative bank — **caissier, -sière** [kesje, -sjɛr] *n* **1** : cashier **2** : (bank) teller

cajoler [kaʒɔle] *vt* **1** : fuss over, cuddle **2** ENJÔLER : cajole

cajun [kaʒœ̃] *adj* : Cajun

cake [kɛk] *nm* : fruitcake

calamité [kalamite] *nf* : calamity

calcaire [kalkɛr] *nm* : limestone — ~ *adj* : chalky

calciner [kalsine] *vt* : char

calcium [kalsjɔm] *nm* : calcium

calculer [kalkyle] *vt* : calculate — **calcul** [kalkyl] *nm* **1** : calculation, sum **2** : arithmetic **3** ~ **biliaire** : gallstone — **calculateur, -trice** [kalkylatœr, -tris] *adj* : calculating — **calculatrice** *nf* : calculator

cale [kal] *nf* **1** : wedge **2** : hold (of a ship)

calé, -lée [kale] *adj fam* : brainy

calèche [kalɛʃ] *nf* : (horse-drawn) carriage

caleçon [kalsɔ̃] *nm* **1** : boxer shorts *pl* **2** : leggings *pl* **3** *or* ~**s de bain** : swimming trunks

calembour [kalɑ̃bur] *nm* : pun

calendrier [kalɑ̃drije] *nm* : calendar

calepin [kalpɛ̃] *nm* : notebook

caler [kale] *vt* : wedge — *vi* : stall (of an engine)

calibre [kalibr] *nm* **1** : caliber **2** : grade, size — **calibrer** [kalibre] *vt* : calibrate, grade

califourchon [kalifurʃɔ̃] **à** ~**s** *adv phr* : astride

câliner [kaline] *vt* : cuddle — **se câliner** *vr* : cuddle (up)

calmant, -mante [kalmɑ̃, -mɑ̃t] *adj* : soothing — **calmant** *nm* : sedative

calmar [kalmar] *nm* : squid

calme [kalm] *nm* **1** : calm **2 du** ~**!** : quiet down! — ~ *adj* : calm — **calmer** [kalme] *vt* : calm, soothe — **se calmer** *vr* : calm down

calomnie [kalɔmni] *nf* : slander, libel — **calomnier** [kalɔmnje] {96} *vt* : slander, libel

calorie [kalɔri] *nf* : calorie
calorifère [kalɔrifɛr] *nm* : heater, stove
calquer [kalke] *vt* **1** : trace (a drawing) **2** : copy, imitate — **calque** [kalk] *nm* : (exact) copy
calvaire [kalvɛr] *nm* : ordeal, suffering
calvitie [kalvisi] *nf* : baldness
camarade [kamarad] *nmf* **1** : friend **2** ~ **de classe** : classmate — **camaraderie** [kamaradri] *nf* : friendship
cambrer [kãbre] *vt* : curve, arch
cambrioler [kãbrijɔle] *vt* : burglarize — **cambriolage** [kãbrijɔlaʒ] *nm* : burglary — **cambrioleur, -leuse** [kãbrijɔlœr, -løz] *n* : burglar
cambrure [kãbryr] *nf* : arch, curve
camelot [kamlo] *nm Can* : paperboy
camelote [kamlɔt] *nf fam* : trash, junk
caméra [kamera] *nf* : movie or television camera
camion [kamjɔ̃] *nm* : truck — **camionnette** [kamjɔnɛt] *nf* : van — **camionneur, -neuse** [kamjɔnœr, -nøz] *n* : truck driver
camoufler [kamufle] *vt* : camouflage — **camouflage** [kamuflaʒ] *nm* : camouflage
camp [kã] *nm* **1** : camp **2** PARTI : side, team
campagne [kãpaɲ] *nf* **1** : country, countryside **2** : campaign (in politics, etc.) — **campagnard, -gnarde** [kãpaɲar, -ɲard] *adj* : country, rustic
camper [kãpe] *vi* : camp — **campement** [kãpmã] *nm* : encampment — **campeur, -peuse** [kãpœr, -pøz] *n* : camper — **camping** [kãpiŋ] *nm* **1** : camping **2** : campground
campus [kãpys] *nm* : campus
canadien, -dienne [kanadjɛ̃, -djɛn] *adj* : Canadian — **canadien–français, canadienne–française** *adj, pl* **canadiens–français, canadiennes–françaises** : French-Canadian
canal [kanal] *nm, pl* **-naux** [kano] **1** : canal **2** : channel
canapé [kanape] *nm* : sofa, couch
canard [kanar] *nm* : duck
canari [kanari] *nm* : canary
cancer [kãsɛr] *nm* : cancer — **cancéreux, -reuse** [kãserø, -røz] *adj* : cancerous
candeur [kãdœr] *nf* : ingenuousness
candidat, -date [kãdida, -dat] *n* : candidate — **candidature** [kãdidatyr] *nf* : candidacy
candide [kãdid] *adj* : ingenuous, naïve
cane [kan] *nf* : (female) duck — **caneton** [kantɔ̃] *nm* : duckling
canette [kanɛt] *nf* **1** : (small) bottle **2** : can (for a beverage)
caniche [kaniʃ] *nm* : poodle
canicule [kanikyl] *nf* : heat wave
canif [kanif] *nm* : pocketknife
canine [ˈkeɪˌnaɪn] *nf* : canine (tooth)

caniveau [kanivo] *nm, pl* **-veaux** : gutter (in a street)
canne [kan] *nf* **1** : cane **2** ~ **à pêche** : fishing rod **3** ~ **à sucre** : sugar-cane
canneberge [kanbɛrʒ] *nf* : cranberry
cannelle [kanɛl] *nf* : cinnamon
cannibale [kanibal] *nmf* : cannibal
canoë [kanɔe] *nm* : canoe
canon [kanɔ̃] *nm* **1** : cannon **2** : barrel (of a gun) **3** : canon, rule
canot [kano] *nm* **1** *France* : boat **2** *Can* : canoe **3** ~ **de sauvetage** : lifeboat
cantaloup [kãtalu] *nm* : cantaloupe
cantine [kãtin] *nf* : canteen, cafeteria
cantique [kãtik] *nm* : hymn
canton [kãtɔ̃] *nm* **1** *France* : district, canton **2** *Can* : township
canular [kanylar] *nm* : hoax
canyon [kaɲɔ̃] *nm* : canyon
caoutchouc [kautʃu] *nm* **1** : rubber **2** ~**s** *nmpl* : galoshes — **caoutchouteux, -teuse** [kautʃutø, -tøz] *adj* : rubbery
cap [kap] *nm* **1** PROMONTOIRE : cape **2** ÉTAPE : milestone
capable [kapabl] *adj* : capable
capacité [kapasite] *nf* **1** : capacity **2** APTITUDE : ability
cape [kap] *nf* : cape, cloak
capitaine [kapitɛn] *nm* : captain
capital, -tale [kapital] *adj, mpl* **-taux** [-to] **1** : major, crucial **2 peine capitale** : capital punishment — **capital** *nm, pl* **-taux** : capital, assets *pl* — **capitale** *nf* : capital (city)
capitalisme [kapitalism] *nm* : capitalism — **capitaliste** [kapitalist] *adj* : capitalist(ic)
capiteux, -teuse [kapitø, -tøz] *adj* : heady
caporal–chef [kapɔralʃef] *nm, pl* **caporaux–chefs** [-ro] : corporal
capot [kapo] *nm* : hood (of an automobile) — **capoter** [kapɔte] *vt* : overturn, capsize
caprice [kapris] *nm* : whim — **capricieux, -cieuse** [kaprisjø, -sjøz] *adj* : temperamental
capsule [kapsyl] *nf* **1** : capsule **2** : cap (of a bottle)
capter [kapte] *vt* **1** : pick up (radio signals) **2** ~ **l'attention de** : capture the attention of
captif, -tive [kaptif, -tiv] *adj & n* : captive — **captiver** [kaptive] *vt* : captivate — **captivité** [kaptivite] *nf* : captivity
capture [kaptyr] *nf* **1** : capture, seizure **2** ATTRAPE : catch — **capturer** [kaptyre] *vt* : capture, catch
capuche [kapyʃ] *nf* : hood — **capuchon** [kapyʃɔ̃] *nm* **1** : hood **2** : cap, top (of a pen, etc.)
caqueter [kakte] {8} *vi* : cackle
car[1] [kar] *nm* : bus, coach
car[2] *conj* : for, because

carabine [karabin] *nf* : rifle

caractère [karaktɛr] *nm* **1** : letter, character **2** TEMPÉRAMENT : character, nature — **ca-ractériser** [karakterize] *vt* : characterize — **caractéristique** [karakteristik] *adj* & *nf* : characteristic

carafe [karaf] *nf* : carafe, decanter

caramel [karamɛl] *nm* **1** : caramel **2** ∼ **mou** : fudge

carapace [karapas] *nf* : shell

carat [kara] *nm* : carat, karat

caravane [karavan] *nf* **1** : caravan **2** : trailer

carbone [karbɔn] *nm* : carbon — **car-boniser** [karbɔnize] *vt* : burn, char

carburant [karbyrɑ̃] *nm* : fuel — **carbura-teur** [karbyratœr] *nm* : carburetor

carcasse [karkas] *nf* : carcass

cardiaque [kardjak] *adj* : cardiac

cardigan [kardigɑ̃] *nm* : cardigan

cardinal, -nale [kardinal] *adj, mpl* **-naux** [-no] : cardinal, chief — **cardinal** *nm, pl* **-naux 1** : cardinal (in religion) **2** : cardinal number

carence [karɑ̃s] *nf* : lack, deficiency

caresser [karese] *vt* **1** : caress **2** : cherish, dream of — **caresse** [karɛs] *nf* : caress

cargaison [kargɛzɔ̃] *nf* : cargo, freight — **cargo** [kargo] *nm* : freighter

caricature [karikatyr] *nf* : caricature

carie [kari] *nf* : tooth decay, cavity

carillon [karijɔ̃] *nm* : bell, chime — **carillon-ner** [karijɔne] *v* : chime

carnage [karnaʒ] *nm* : carnage, bloodshed

carnaval [karnaval] *nm, pl* **-vals** : carnival

carnet [karnɛ] *nm* **1** : notebook **2** : book (of stamps, tickets, etc.)

carotte [karɔt] *nf* : carrot

carré, -rée [kare] *adj* **1** : square **2** : straight-forward — **carré** *nm* : square

carreau [karo] *nm, pl* **-reaux 1** : tile **2** VITRE : windowpane **3** : diamond (in playing cards) **4 à** ∼**x** : checkered

carrefour [karfur] *nm* : intersection, cross-roads

carreler [karle] {8} *vt* : tile — **carrelage** [karlaʒ] *nm* : tiled floor

carrément [karemɑ̃] *adv* **1** : bluntly, di-rectly **2** : downright

carrière [karjɛr] *nf* **1** : career **2** : stone quarry

carrosse [karɔs] *nm* : (horse-drawn) coach

carrure [karyr] *nf* : build (of the body)

carte [kart] *nf* **1** : card **2** : (road) map **3** : menu (in a restaurant) **4** *or* ∼ **à jouer** : playing card **5** ∼ **de crédit** : credit card **6** ∼ **des vins** : wine list **7** ∼ **postale** : postcard

cartilage [kartilaʒ] *nm* : cartilage, gristle

carton [kartɔ̃] *nm* **1** : cardboard **2** : card-board box

cartouche [kartuʃ] *nf* : cartridge

cas [ka] *nms* & *pl* **1** : case **2 en aucun** ∼ : on no account **3 en** ∼ **de** : in case of

cascade [kaskad] *nf* **1** : cascade, torrent **2** : waterfall

case [kaz] *nf* **1** : box (on a form) **2** ∼ **postale** *Can* : post office box

caserne [kazɛrn] *nf* **1** *France* : barracks *pl* **2** ∼ **de pompiers** *France* : fire station

casier [kazje] *nm* **1** : pigeonhole **2** ∼ **judi-ciaire** : police record

casino [kazino] *nm* : casino

casque [kask] *nm* **1** : helmet **2** : head-phones *pl* — **casquette** [kaskɛt] *nf* : cap

casser [kase] *v* : break — **se casser** *vr* **1** : break (one's leg, etc.) **2 casse-toi!** *fam* : get out of here! — **cassable** [kasabl] *adj* : breakable — **casse—croûte** [kaskrut] *nms* & *pl* **1** : snack **2** *Can* : snack bar — **casse—noix** [kasnwa] *nms* & *pl* : nutcracker

casserole [kasrɔl] *nf* : saucepan

casse—tête [kastɛt] *nms* & *pl* **1** : puzzle **2** PROBLÈME : headache

cassette [kasɛt] *nf* : cassette

cassonade [kasɔnad] *nf* : brown sugar

cassure [kasyr] *nf* : break

castor [kastɔr] *nm* : beaver

catalogue [katalɔg] *nm* : catalog

cataracte [katarakt] *nf* : cataract

catastrophe [katastrɔf] *nf* : catastrophe — **catastrophique** [katastrɔfik] *adj* : cata-strophic

catéchisme [kateʃism] *nm* : catechism

catégorie [kategɔri] *nf* : category — **caté-gorique** [kategɔrik] *adj* : categorical

cathédrale [katedral] *nf* : cathedral

catholique [katɔlik] *adj* : Catholic — **catholicisme** [katɔlisism] *nm* : Catholicism

catimini [katimini] **en** ∼ *adv phr* : on the sly

cauchemar [koʃmar] *nm* : nightmare

cause [koz] *nf* **1** : cause, reason **2** : (legal) case **3 à** ∼ **de** : because of, on account of — **causer** [koze] *vt* PROVOQUER : cause — *vi* : chat — **causerie** [kozri] *nf* : talk, chat

caution [kosjɔ̃] *nf* **1** : surety, guarantee **2 libérer sous** ∼ : release on bail

cavalerie [kavalri] *nf* : cavalry — **cavalier, -lière** [kavalje, -ljɛr] *n* : rider, horseman *m*, horsewoman *f* — **cavalier** *nm* : knight (in chess)

cave [kav] *nf* : cellar

caverne [kavɛrn] *nf* GROTTE : cavern, cave

caviar [kavjar] *nm* : caviar

cavité [kavite] *nf* : cavity, hollow

CD [sede] *nm* (compact *disc*) : CD

ce [sə] (**cet** [sɛt] *before a vowel or mute h*), **cette** [sɛt] *adj, pl* **ces** [se] **1** : this, that, these, those **2 cette fois-ci** : this time **3 cette idée!** : what an idea! — **ce** (**c'** [s] *be-*

fore a vowel) _pron_ **1** : it, that, these, those **2** **~ que**, **~ qui**, **~ dont** : what, which **3** **c'est** : it is **4 ce sont** : they are **5 c'est cela** : that's right

ceci [səsi] _pron_ : this
cécité [sesite] _nf_ : blindness
céder [sede] {87} _vt_ : give up, yield — _vi_ : give in
cédille [sedij] _nf_ : cedilla
cèdre [sɛdr] _nm_ : cedar
cégep [seʒɛp] _nm_ (collège d'enseignement général et professionnel) _Can_ : junior college
ceinture [sɛ̃tyr] _nf_ **1** : belt **2 ~ de sauvetage** : life belt **3 ~ de sécurité** : safety belt
cela [səla] _pron_ : that, it
célébrer [selebre] {87} _vt_ : celebrate — **célébration** [selebrasjɔ̃] _nf_ : celebration — **célèbre** [selɛbr] _adj_ : famous — **célébrité** [selebrite] _nf_ **1** : fame, renown **2** : celebrity (person)
céleri [sɛlri] _nm_ : celery
céleste [selɛst] _adj_ : heavenly
célibataire [selibatɛr] _adj_ : single, unmarried — **~** _nmf_ : single person
celle, celles → **celui**
cellule [selyl] _nf_ : cell
celui [səlɥi], **celle** [sɛl] _pron, pl_ **ceux** [sø], **celles** [sɛl] : the one(s), those — **celui–ci** [səlɥisi], **celle–ci** [sɛlsi] _pron, pl_ **ceux–ci** [søsi], **celles–ci** [sɛlsi] **1** : this (one), these **2** : the latter — **celui–là** [səlɥila], **celle–là** [sɛlla] _pron, pl_ **ceux–là** [søla], **celles–là** [sɛlla] **1** : that (one), those **2** : the former
cendre [sɑ̃dr] _nf_ : ash — **cendrier** [sɑ̃drije] _nm_ : ashtray
censé, -sée [sɑ̃se] _adj_ **être ~ faire** : be supposed to do
censurer [sɑ̃syre] _vt_ : censor, ban — **censure** [sɑ̃syr] _nf_ **1** : censorship **2** : censure
cent [sɑ̃] _adj_ : a hundred, one hundred — **~** _nm_ **1** : hundred **2** : cent **3 pour ~** : percent — **centaine** [sɑ̃tɛn] _nf_ : about a hundred — **centenaire** [sɑ̃tnɛr] _adj_ : hundred-year-old — **~** _nm_ : centennial — **centième** [sɑ̃tjɛm] _adj & nmf & nm_ : hundredth
centigrade [sɑ̃tigrad] _adj_ : centigrade
centime [sɑ̃tim] _nm_ : centime
centimètre [sɑ̃timɛtr] _nm_ **1** : centimeter **2** : tape measure
central, -trale [sɑ̃tral] _adj, mpl_ **-traux** [sɑ̃tro] : central — **central** _nm_ **~ téléphonique** : telephone exchange — **centrale** _nf_ **1** : power plant **2 ~ syndicale** : labor union — **centraliser** [sɑ̃tralize] _vt_ : centralize
centre [sɑ̃tr] _nm_ **1** : center **2 ~ commercial** : shopping center — **centrer** [sɑ̃tre] _vt_ : center — **centre–ville** [sɑ̃trəvil] _nm, pl_ **centres–villes** : downtown
cependant [səpɑ̃dɑ̃] _conj_ : however, yet

céramique [seramik] _nf_ : ceramics
cerceau [sɛrso] _nm, pl_ **-ceaux** : hoop
cercle [sɛrkl] _nm_ **1** : circle **2** : group (of friends, etc.)
cercueil [sɛrkœj] _nm_ : coffin
céréale [sereal] _nf_ : cereal
cérémonie [seremɔni] _nf_ **1** : ceremony **2 sans ~** : informally
cerf [sɛr] _nm_ : stag
cerf–volant [sɛrvɔlɑ̃] _nm, pl_ **cerfs–volants** : kite
cerise [səriz] _nf_ : cherry — **cerisier** [sərizje] _nm_ : cherry tree
cerner [sɛrne] _vt_ **1** : surround **2** DÉFINIR : define, determine — **cerne** [sɛrn] _nm_ **avoir des ~s** : have rings under one's eyes
certain, -taine [sɛrtɛ̃, -tɛn] _adj_ **1** : certain, sure **2** : certain, some — **certainement** [sɛrtɛnmɑ̃] _adv_ : certainly — **certains, certaines** [sɛrtɛ̃, -tɛn] _pron pl_ : some (people), certain (ones)
certes [sɛrt] _adv_ : of course, indeed
certifier [sɛrtifje] {96} _vt_ : certify — **certificat** [sɛrtifika] _nm_ : certificate
certitude [sɛrtityd] _nf_ : certainty
cerveau [sɛrvo] _nm, pl_ **-veaux** : brain
ces → **ce**
cesser [sese] _v_ : cease, stop — **cesse** [sɛs] _nf_ **sans ~** : constantly — **cessez–le–feu** [seselfø] _nms & pl_ : cease-fire
c'est–à–dire [sɛtadir] _conj_ : that is (to say)
cet, cette → **ce** — **ceux** → **celui** — **ceux–ci** → **celui–ci** — **ceux–là** → **celui–là**
chacun, chacune [ʃakœ̃, -kyn] _pron_ **1** : each (one) **2** : everybody, everyone
chagrin [ʃagrɛ̃] _nm_ PEINE : grief, sorrow — **chagriner** [ʃagrine] _vt_ : grieve, distress
chahut [ʃay] _nm_ : uproar, din
chaîne [ʃɛn] _nf_ **1** : chain **2** : (television) channel **3** : (stereo) system — **chaînon** [ʃɛnɔ̃] _nm_ : link
chair [ʃɛr] _nf_ **1** : flesh **2** : meat **3 ~ de poule** : goose bumps
chaire [ʃɛr] _nf_ **1** : (university) chair **2** : pulpit
chaise [ʃɛz] _nf_ **1** : chair, seat **2 ~ roulante** : wheelchair
chaland [ʃalɑ̃] _nm_ : barge
châle [ʃal] _nm_ : shawl
chalet [ʃalɛ] _nm_ **1** : chalet **2** _Can_ : cottage
chaleur [ʃalœr] _nf_ **1** : heat **2** : warmth — **chaleureux, -reuse** [ʃalœrø, -røz] _adj_ : warm, friendly
chaloupe [ʃalup] _nf_ : rowboat
chamailler [ʃamaje] _v_ **se chamailler** _vr_ : bicker
chambarder [ʃɑ̃barde] _vt fam_ : mess up
chambre [ʃɑ̃br] _nf_ **1** : room, bedroom **2** : (legislative) chamber, house
chameau [ʃamo] _nm, pl_ **-meaux** : camel

champ [ʃɑ̃] *nm* **1** : field **2** ~ **de bataille** : battlefield **3** ~ **de courses** : racetrack

champagne [ʃɑ̃paɲ] *nm* : champagne

champêtre [ʃɑ̃pɛtr] *adj* : rural

champignon [ʃɑ̃piɲɔ̃] *nm* : mushroom

champion, -pionne [ʃɑ̃pjɔ̃, -pjɔn] *n* : champion — **championnat** [ʃɑ̃pjɔna] *nm* : championship

chance [ʃɑ̃s] *nf* **1** : luck, fortune **2** POSSIBILITÉ : chance, possibility **3** par ~ : fortunately

chanceler [ʃɑ̃sle] {8} *vi* : stagger — **chancelant, -lante** [ʃɑ̃slɑ̃, -lɑ̃t] *adj* : unsteady

chancelier [ʃɑ̃səlje] *nm* : chancellor

chanceux, -ceuse [ʃɑ̃sø, -søz] *adj* : lucky

chandail [ʃɑ̃daj] *nm* : sweater

chandelle [ʃɑ̃dɛl] *nf* : candle — **chandelier** [ʃɑ̃dəlje] *nm* : candlestick

changer [ʃɑ̃ʒe] {17} *vt* **1** REMPLACER : change **2** MODIFIER : alter — *vi* **1** ~ **de** : change **2** ~ **d'avis** : change one's mind — **se changer** *vr* : change one's clothes — **change** [ʃɑ̃ʒ] *nm* : exchange (in finance) — **changement** [ʃɑ̃ʒmɑ̃] *nm* : change

chanson [ʃɑ̃sɔ̃] *nf* : song — **chant** [ʃɑ̃] *nm* **1** : song, hymn **2** : singing

chantage [ʃɑ̃taʒ] *nm* : blackmail

chanter [ʃɑ̃te] *v* **1** : sing **2** faire ~ : blackmail — **chanteur, -teuse** [ʃɑ̃tœr, -tøz] *n* : singer

chantier [ʃɑ̃tje] *nm* **1** : (construction) site **2** ~ **naval** : shipyard

chantonner [ʃɑ̃tɔne] *v* : hum

chanvre [ʃɑ̃vr] *nm* : hemp

chaos [kao] *nm* : chaos — **chaotique** [kaɔtik] *adj* : chaotic

chapeau [ʃapo] *nm, pl* **-peaux** : hat, cap

chapelet [ʃaplɛ] *nm* : rosary

chapelle [ʃapɛl] *nf* : chapel

chapelure [ʃaplyr] *nf* : bread crumbs *pl*

chaperon [ʃaprɔ̃] *nm* : chaperon

chapiteau [ʃapito] *nm, pl* **-teaux** : circus tent

chapitre [ʃapitr] *nm* **1** : chapter (of a book) **2** : subject matter

chaque [ʃak] *adj* : each, every

char [ʃar] *nm* **1** : chariot **2** : cart, wagon, float (in a parade) **3** ~ **d'assaut** : tank

charabia [ʃarabja] *nm fam* : gibberish

charbon [ʃarbɔ̃] *nm* **1** : coal **2** ~ **de bois** : charcoal

charcuterie [ʃarkytri] *nf* **1** : delicatessen **2** : cooked pork products

charger [ʃarʒe] {17} *vt* **1** : load **2** : charge (a battery) **3** ~ **de** : put in charge of — **se charger** *vr* ~ **de** : take care of — **charge** [ʃarʒ] *nf* **1** : load **2** RESPONSABILITÉ : responsibility **3** : (electrical) charge **4** FONCTION : office **5** ~**s** : costs **6** à la ~ **de** : dependent on — **chargé, -gée** [ʃarʒe] *adj*

: busy — **chargement** [ʃarʒəmɑ̃] *nm* **1** : loading **2** : load, cargo

chariot [ʃarjo] *nm* : cart, wagon

charisme [karism] *nm* : charisma — **charismatique** [-rismatik] *adj* : charismatic

charité [ʃarite] *nf* : charity — **charitable** [ʃaritabl] *adj* : charitable

charlatan [ʃarlatɑ̃] *nm* : charlatan

charmer [ʃarme] *vt* : charm — **charmant, -mante** [ʃarmɑ̃, -mɑ̃t] *adj* : charming, delightful — **charme** [ʃarm] *nm* : charm, attraction — **charmeur, -meuse** [ʃarmœr, -møz] *adj* : charming — ~ *n* : charmer

charnière [ʃarnjɛr] *nf* : hinge

charnu, -nue [ʃarny] *adj* : fleshy

charpente [ʃarpɑ̃t] *nf* **1** : framework **2** : build (of the body) — **charpentier** [ʃarpɑ̃tje] *nm* : carpenter

charrette [ʃarɛt] *nf* : cart

charrue [ʃary] *nf* : plow

charte [ʃart] *nf* : charter — **charter** [ʃarte] *nm* : charter flight

chas [ʃa] *nm* : eye (of a needle)

chasser [ʃase] *vt* **1** : hunt **2** EXPULSER : chase away — **chasse** [ʃas] *nf* **1** : hunting **2** POURSUITE : chase **3** *or* ~ **d'eau** : flush (of a toilet) — **chasse-neige** [ʃasnɛʒ] *nms & pl* : snowplow — **chasseur, -seuse** [ʃasœr, -søz] *n* : hunter

châssis [ʃasi] *nm* : frame (of a window)

chaste [ʃast] *adj* : chaste — **chasteté** [ʃastəte] *nf* : chastity

chat, chatte [ʃa, ʃat] *n* : cat

châtaigne [ʃatɛɲ] *nf* : chestnut

château [ʃato] *nm, pl* **-teaux 1** : castle **2** ~ **fort** : stronghold

châtier [ʃatje] {96} *vt* : chastise — **châtiment** [ʃatimɑ̃] *nm* : punishment

chaton [ʃatɔ̃] *nm* : kitten

chatouiller [ʃatuje] *vt* : tickle — **chatouilleux, -leuse** [ʃatujø, -jøz] *adj* : ticklish

châtrer [ʃatre] *vt* : castrate

chatte → **chat**

chaud, chaude [ʃo, ʃod] *adj* : warm, hot — **chaud** [ʃo] *adv* ~ **1 avoir** ~ : feel warm or hot **2 il fait** ~ : it's warm, it's hot — ~ *nm* : heat, warmth — **chaudière** [ʃodjɛr] *nf* : boiler — **chaudron** [ʃodrɔ̃] *nm* : cauldron

chauffage [ʃofaʒ] *nm* : heating

chauffard [ʃofar] *nm* : reckless driver

chauffer [ʃofe] *vt* : heat, warm — *vi* : warm up — **se chauffer** *vr* : warm (oneself) up

chauffeur [ʃofœr] *nm* : driver, chauffeur

chaussée [ʃose] *nf* : roadway

chausser [ʃose] *vt* **1** : put on (shoes) **2** ~ **du 7** : take size 7 (in shoes) — **chaussette** [ʃosɛt] *nf* : sock — **chausson** [ʃosɔ̃] *nm* **1** : slipper **2** ~ **aux pommes** : apple turnover — **chaussure** [ʃosyr] *nf* : shoe, footwear

chauve [ʃov] *adj* : bald — **chauve–souris** [ʃovsuri] *nf, pl* **chauves–souris** : bat (animal)

chauvin, -vine [ʃovɛ̃, -vin] *adj* : chauvinistic

chaux [ʃo] *nf* **1** : lime **2 lait de ~** : whitewash

chavirer [ʃavire] *v* : capsize

chef [ʃɛf] *nm* **1** : leader, head, chief **2** *or* **~ cuisinier** : chef **3 ~ d'orchestre** : conductor **4 en ~** : (in) chief — **chef–d'œuvre** [ʃɛdœvr] *nm, pl* **chefs–d'œuvre** : masterpiece

chemin [ʃəmɛ̃] *nm* **1** : road, path **2 ~ de fer** : railroad

cheminée [ʃəmine] *nf* **1** : fireplace **2** : chimney

cheminer [ʃəmine] *vi* **1** : walk along **2** PROGRESSER : progress

chemise [ʃəmiz] *nf* **1** : shirt **2** DOSSIER : folder **3 ~ de nuit** : nightgown — **chemisier** [ʃəmizje] *nm* : blouse

chenal [ʃənal] *nm, pl* **-naux** [ʃəno] : channel

chêne [ʃen] *nm* : oak

chenille [ʃənij] *nf* : caterpillar

chèque [ʃɛk] *nm* : check

cher, chère [ʃɛr] *adj* **1** : dear, beloved **2** COÛTEUX : expensive — **~** *n* **mon cher, ma chère** : my dear — **cher** *adv* **coûter ~** : cost a lot

chercher [ʃɛrʃe] *vt* : look for, seek — **chercheur, -cheuse** [ʃɛrʃœr, -ʃøz] *n* : researcher

chérir [ʃerir] *vt* : cherish — **chéri, -rie** [ʃeri] *adj & n* : darling, dear

chétif, -tive [ʃetif, -tiv] *adj* : puny, weak

cheval [ʃəval] *nm, pl* **-vaux** [ʃəvo] **1** : horse **2** *or* **cheval–vapeur** : horsepower

chevalerie [ʃəvalri] *nf* : chivalry

chevalet [ʃəvalɛ] *nm* : easel

chevalier [ʃəvalje] *nm* : knight

chevaucher [ʃəvoʃe] *vt* **1** : straddle **2** : overlap — **se chevaucher** *vr* : overlap

chevelure [ʃəvlyr] *nf* : hair — **chevelu, -lue** [ʃəvly] *adj* : hairy

chevet [ʃəvɛ] *nm* : bedside

cheveu [ʃəvø] *nm, pl* **-veux 1** POIL : hair **2 ~x** *nmpl* : (head of) hair

cheville [ʃəvij] *nf* : ankle

chèvre [ʃɛvr] *nf* : goat — **chevreau** [ʃəvro] *nm, pl* **-vreaux** : kid (goat)

chevreuil [ʃəvrœj] *nm* : roe deer

chevron [ʃəvrɔ̃] *nm* : rafter

chez [ʃe] *prep* **1** : at (the house of) **2** PARMI : among, in **3 ~ soi** : at home

chez–soi [ʃeswa] *nms & pl* : home

chic [ʃik] *adj s & pl* **1** : stylish **2** SYMPATHIQUE : nice

chicane [ʃikan] *nf* : squabble

chicorée [ʃikɔre] *nf* **1** : endive **2** : chicory (for coffee)

chien, chienne [ʃjɛ̃, -ʃjɛn] *n* : dog, bitch *f*

chiffon [ʃifɔ̃] *nm* : rag — **chiffonner** [ʃifɔne] *vt* : crumple

chiffre [ʃifr] *nm* **1** : figure, numeral **2** : amount, sum (in finance) **3** CODE : code **4 ~ d'affaires** : turnover — **chiffrer** [ʃifre] *vt* : calculate, assess — **se chiffrer** *vr* **~ à** : amount to

chignon [ʃiɲɔ̃] *nm* : (hair) bun

chimie [ʃimi] *nf* : chemistry — **chimique** [ʃimik] *adj* : chemical — **chimiste** [ʃimist] *nmf* : chemist

chimpanzé [ʃɛ̃pɑ̃ze] *nm* : chimpanzee

chinois, -noise [ʃinwa, -nwaz] *adj* : Chinese — **chinois** *nm* : Chinese (language)

chiot [ʃjo] *nm* : puppy

chips [ʃips] *nfpl* : potato chips

chirurgie [ʃiryrʒi] *nf* : surgery — **chirurgical, -cale** [ʃiryrʒikal] *adj, mpl* **-caux** [-ko] : surgical — **chirurgien, -gienne** [ʃiryrʒɛ̃, -ʒjɛn] *n* : surgeon

chlore [klɔr] *nm* : chlorine

choc [ʃɔk] *nm* **1** : shock **2** : impact, crash

chocolat [ʃɔkɔla] *nm* : chocolate

chœur [kœr] *nm* **1** : choir **2** : chorus

choir [ʃwar] {18} *vi* : drop, fall

choisir [ʃwazir] *vt* : choose — **choix** [ʃwa] *nm* **1** : choice **2 de ~** : choice, first-rate

cholestérol [kɔlɛsterɔl] *nm* : cholesterol

chômage [ʃomaʒ] *nm* : unemployment — **chômeur, -meuse** [ʃomœr, -møz] *n* : unemployed person

choquer [ʃɔke] *vt* : shock, offend — **choquant, -quante** [ʃɔkɑ̃, -kɑ̃t] *adj* : shocking

choral, -rale [kɔral] *adj, mpl* **-rals** *or* **-raux** [kɔro] : choral — **chorale** *nf* : choir

chose [ʃoz] *nf* **1** : thing **2** AFFAIRE : matter

chou [ʃu] *nm, pl* **choux** : cabbage — **chou-chou, -choute** [ʃuʃu, -ʃut] *n fam* : pet, favorite — **choucroute** [ʃukrut] *nf* : sauerkraut

chouette [ʃwɛt] *nf* : owl — **~** *adj fam* : terrific, neat

chou–fleur [ʃuflœr] *nm, pl* **choux–fleurs** : cauliflower

choyer [ʃwaje] {58} *vt* : pamper

chrétien, -tienne [kretjɛ̃, -tjɛn] *adj & n* : Christian — **christianisme** [kristjanism] *nm* : Christianity

chrome [krom] *nm* **1** : chromium **2 ~s** *nmpl* : chrome

chronique [krɔnik] *adj* : chronic — **~** *nf* : (newspaper) column, (televison) report — **chroniqueur, -queuse** [krɔnikœr, -køz] *n* : columnist

chronologie [krɔnɔlɔʒi] *nf* : chronology — **chronologique** [krɔnɔlɔʒik] *adj* : chronological

chronomètre [krɔnɔmɛtr] *nm* : stopwatch

— **chronométrer** [krɔnɔmetre] {87} *vt* : time

chuchoter [ʃyʃɔte] *v* : whisper **—** **chuchotement** [ʃyʃɔtmã] *nm* : whisper

chum [tʃɔm] *nm Can fam* : boyfriend

chut [ʃyt] *interj* : sh!, hush!

chute [ʃyt] *nf* **1** : fall **2** *or* **~ d'eau** : waterfall **3 ~ de pluie** : rainfall

ci [si] *adv* **1 ce livre-ci** : this book **2 cette fois-ci** : this time **3 ceux-ci** : these ones **4 par-ci par-là** : here and there **— ~ pron 1 ~ et ça** : this and that **2 → comme — ci–après** [siaprɛ] *adv* : hereafter **— ci–bas** [siba] *adv* : below

cible [sibl] *nf* : target

ciboule [sibul] *nf* : scallion **— ciboulette** [sibulɛt] *nf* : chive

cicatrice [sikatris] *nf* : scar **— cicatriser** [sikatrize] *v* **se cicatriser** *vr* : heal (up)

ci–contre [sikɔ̃tr] *adv* : opposite

ci–dessous [sidəsu] *adv* : below

ci–dessus [sidəsy] *adv* : above

cidre [sidr] *nm* : cider

ciel [sjɛl] *nm* **1** *pl* **ciels** : sky **2** *pl* **cieux** [sjø] : heaven

cierge [sjɛrʒ] *nm* : candle (in a church)

cigare [sigar] *nm* : cigar **— cigarette** [sigarɛt] *nf* : cigarette

cigogne [sigɔɲ] *nf* : stork

ci–inclus, -cluse [siɛ̃kly, -klyz] *adj* : enclosed **— ci–inclus** [siɛ̃kly] *adv* : enclosed

ci–joint, -jointe [siʒwɛ̃, -ʒwɛ̃t] *adj* : enclosed **— ci–joint** [siʒwɛ̃] *adv* : enclosed, herewith

cil [sil] *nm* : eyelash

cime [sim] *nf* : summit, peak

ciment [simã] *nm* : cement

cimetière [simtjɛr] *nm* : cemetery

cinéaste [sineast] *nmf* : film director

cinéma [sinema] *nm* **1** : movie theater **2 aller au ~** : go to the movies

cinglant, -glante [sɛ̃glã, -glãt] *adj* : cutting, biting

cinq [sɛ̃k] *adj* **1** : five **2** : fifth (in dates) **— ~ nms & pl** : five

cinquante [sɛ̃kãt] *adj & nms & pl* : fifty **— cinquantaine** [sɛ̃kãten] *nf* **une ~ de** : about fifty **— cinquantième** [sɛ̃kãtjɛm] *adj & nmf & nm* : fiftieth

cinquième [sɛ̃kjɛm] *adj & nmf & nm* : fifth

cintre [sɛ̃tr] *nm* : coat hanger

cirage [siraʒ] *nm* : shoe polish

circoncire [sirkɔ̃sir] {86} *vt* : circumcise **— circoncision** [sirkɔ̃sizjɔ̃] *nf* : circumcision

circonférence [sirkɔ̃ferãs] *nf* : circumference

circonflexe [sirkɔ̃flɛks] *adj* **accent ~** : circumflex (accent)

circonscrire [sirkɔ̃skrir] {33} *vt* : limit, contain **— circonscription** [sirkɔ̃skripsjɔ̃] *nf* : district, ward

circonspect, -specte [sirkɔ̃spɛ, -spɛkt] *adj* : cautious, circumspect

circonstance [sirkɔ̃stãs] *nf* : circumstance, occasion

circuit [sirkɥi] *nm* **1** : circuit **2** *or* **coup de ~** *Can* : home run (in baseball)

circulaire [sirkylɛr] *adj & nf* : circular

circuler [sirkyle] *vi* **1** : circulate **2** SE DÉPLACER : move (along) **3** : run (of buses, etc.) **4 faire ~ des bruits** : spread rumors **— circulation** [sirkylasjɔ̃] *nf* **1** : circulation **2** : traffic

cire [sir] *nf* : wax **— ciré** [sire] *nm* : oilskin **— cirer** [sire] *vt* : wax, polish

cirque [sirk] *nm* **1** : circus **2** *fam* : chaos

cisailles [sizaj] *nfpl* : shears

ciseau [sizo] *nm, pl* **-seaux** **1** : chisel **2 ~x** *nmpl* : scissors **— ciseler** [sizle] {20} *vt* : chisel

citadelle [sitadɛl] *nf* : citadel

citadin, -dine [sitadɛ̃, -din] *n* : city dweller

citation [sitasjɔ̃] *nf* **1** : quotation **2** : summons (in law)

cité [site] *nf* **1** : city **2 ~ universitaire** *France* : college dormitories *pl* **3 ~ universitaire** *Can* : college campus

citer [site] *vt* **1** : quote **2** MENTIONNER : name, cite

citerne [sitɛrn] *nf* : tank, reservoir

citoyen, citoyenne [sitwajɛ̃, -jɛn] *n* : citizen **— citoyenneté** [sitwajɛnte] *nf* : citizenship

citron [sitrɔ̃] *nm* : lemon **— citronnade** [sitrɔnad] *nf* : lemonade

citrouille [sitruj] *nf* : pumpkin

civière [sivjɛr] *nf* : stretcher

civil, -vile [sivil] *adj* **1** : civil **2** : secular **— ~ n** : civilian **— civilisation** [sivilizasjɔ̃] *nf* : civilization **— civiliser** [sivilize] *vt* : civilize **— civilité** [sivilite] *nf* : civility

civique [sivik] *adj* : civic

clair, claire [klɛr] *adj* **1** : clear **2** LUMINEUX : bright **3** PÂLE : light-colored **— clair** *adv* : clearly **— clair** [klɛr] *nm* **1 ~ de lune** : moonlight **2 mettre au ~** : make clear **— clairement** [klɛrmã] *adv* : clearly **— clairière** [klɛrjɛr] *nf* : clearing

clairon [klɛrɔ̃] *nm* : bugle

clairsemé, -mée [klɛrsəme] *adj* : scattered, sparse

clamer [klame] *vt* : proclaim **— clameur** [klamœr] *nf* : clamor

clan [klã] *nm* : clan, clique

clandestin, -tine [klãdɛstɛ̃, -tin] *adj* **1** : clandestine **2 passager ~** : stowaway

clapier [klapje] *nm* : (rabbit) hutch

clapoter [klapɔte] *vi* : lap (of waves)

claque [klak] *nf* **1** : slap, smack **2 ~s** *nfpl* *Can* : rubbers, galoshes **— claquement** [klakmã] *nm* : bang(ing), slam(ming) **— claquer** [klake] *vt* **1** GIFLER : slap **2** : slam (a door) — *vi* **1 faire ~ ses doigts** : snap one's fingers **2 il claque des dents** : his teeth are chattering — **claquettes** [klakɛt] *nfpl* : tap dancing

clarifier [klarifje] {96} *vt* : clarify — **clarification** [-rifikasjɔ̃] *nf* : clarification

clarinette [klarinɛt] *nf* : clarinet

clarté [klarte] *nf* **1** : light, brightness **2** NETTETÉ : clarity

classe [klas] *nf* **1** : class, category **2** : classroom **3 aller en ~** : go to school — **classement** [klasmɑ̃] *nm* **1** : classification **2** RANG : ranking, place — **classer** [klase] *vt* : class, classify — **se classer** *vr* : rank — **classeur** [klasœr] *nm* **1** : binder **2** : filing cabinet

classifier [klasifje] {96} *vt* : classify — **classification** [klasifikasjɔ̃] *nf* : classification

classique [klasik] *adj* : classic(al) — **~** *nm* : classic (of a book, etc.)

clause [kloz] *nf* : clause

claustrophobie [klostrɔfɔbi] *nf* : claustrophobia

clavecin [klavsɛ̃] *nm* : harpsichord

clavicule [klavikyl] *nf* : collarbone

clavier [klavje] *nm* : keyboard

clé *or* **clef** [kle] *nf* **1** : key **2** : clef (in music) **3 ~ anglaise** : monkey wrench — **~** *adj* : key

clément, -mente [klemɑ̃, -mɑ̃t] *adj* **1** : lenient **2** DOUX : mild, clement — **clémence** [klemɑ̃s] *nf* : leniency

clémentine [klemɑ̃tin] *nf* : tangerine

clenche [klɑ̃ʃ] *nf* : latch

clergé [klɛrʒe] *nm* : clergy

clérical, -cale [klerikal] *adj, mpl* **-caux** [-ko] : clerical

cliché [kliʃe] *nm* : cliché

client, cliente [kliɑ̃, kliɑ̃t] *n* **1** : customer, client **2** : patient — **clientèle** [kliɑ̃tɛl] *nf* **1** : customers *pl* **2** : practice (of a doctor)

cligner [kliɲe] *vi* **1 ~ de l'œil** : wink **2 ~ des yeux** : blink — **clignotant** [kliɲɔtɑ̃] *nm* : blinker, directional signal — **clignoter** [kliɲɔte] *vi* **1** : flicker, flash **2 ~ cligner 2**

climat [klima] *nm* : climate — **climatisation** [klimatizasjɔ̃] *nf* : air-conditioning — **climatisé, -sée** [klimatize] *adj* : air-conditioned — **climatiseur** [klimatizœr] *nm* : air conditioner

clin [klɛ̃] *nm* **1 ~ d'œil** : wink **2 en un ~ d'œil** : in a flash

clinique [klinik] *nf* : clinic — **~** *adj* : clinical

cliquer [klike] *vi* : click (on a computer)

cliqueter [klikte] {8} *vi* : clink, jingle, clack — **cliquetis** [klikti] *nm* : jingle, clatter

clochard, -charde [klɔʃar, -ʃard] *n* : tramp

cloche [klɔʃ] *nf* : bell — **clocher** [klɔʃe] *nm* : belfry, steeple

cloison [klwazɔ̃] *nf* : partition — **cloisonner** [klwazɔne] *vt* : partition (off)

cloître [klwatr] *nm* : cloister

cloque [klɔk] *nf* : blister

clore [klɔr] {19} *vt* : close, conclude — **clos, close** [klo, -kloz] *adj* : closed, shut — **clôture** [klotyr] *nf* **1** : fence **2** : end, closure — **clôturer** [klotyre] *vt* **1** : enclose **2** : bring to a close

clou [klu] *nm, pl* **~s 1** : nail **2** : high point **3** FURONCLE : boil **4 ~ de girofle** : clove — **clouer** [klue] *vt* **1** : nail **2** : pin down

clown [klun] *nm* : clown

club [klœb] *nm* : club

coaguler [kɔagyle] *v* : coagulate — **se coaguler** *vr* : coagulate, clot

coalition [kɔalisjɔ̃] *nf* : coalition

coasser [kɔase] *vi* : croak

cobaye [kɔbaj] *nm* : guinea pig

cocaïne [kɔkain] *nf* : cocaine

cocasse [kɔkas] *adj* : comical

coccinelle [kɔksinɛl] *nf* : ladybug

cocher [kɔʃe] *vt* : check (off)

cochon [kɔʃɔ̃] *nm* **1** : pig **2 ~ d'Inde** : guinea pig — **cochonnerie** [kɔʃɔnri] *nf* : junk, trash

cocktail [kɔktɛl] *nm* : cocktail

coco [kɔko] *nm or* **noix de ~** : coconut — **cocotier** [kɔkɔtje] *nm* : coconut palm

cocon [kɔkɔ̃] *nm* : cocoon

cocotte [kɔkɔt] *nf* : casserole dish

code [kɔd] *nm* **1** : code **2 ~ postal** : zip code — **coder** [kɔde] *vt* : code, encode

coéquipier, -pière [kɔekipje, -jɛr] *n* : teammate

cœur [kœr] *nm* **1** : heart **2** : center, core **3** : hearts *pl* (in playing cards) **4** COURAGE : courage **5 à ~ joie** : to one's heart's content **6 avoir mal au ~** : feel sick, feel nauseous **7 de bon ~** : willingly

coffre [kɔfr] *nm* **1** : (toy) chest **2** COFFRE-FORT : safe **3** : trunk (of a car) — **coffre-fort** [kɔfrəfɔr] *nm, pl* **coffres-forts** : safe — **coffret** [kɔfrɛ] *nm* : small box, case

cognac [kɔɲak] *nm* : cognac

cogner [kɔɲe] *vt* : knock, bang — *vi* : knock — **se cogner** *vr* **1** : bump oneself **2 ~ la tête** : hit one's head

cohabiter [kɔabite] *vi* : live together

cohérent, -rente [kɔerɑ̃, -rɑ̃t] *adj* : coherent — **cohérence** [-erɑ̃s] *nf* : coherence

cohue [kɔy] *nf* : crowd

coiffe [kwaf] *nf* : headdress — **coiffer** [kwafe] *v* **se coiffer** *vr* : do one's hair — **coiffeur, -feuse** [kwafœr, -føz] *n* : hairdresser — **coiffure** [kwafyr] *nf* **1** : hairdo **2** : hairdressing

coin [kwɛ̃] *nm* **1** : corner **2** ENDROIT : place, spot

coincer [kwɛ̃se] {6} *vt* **1** : wedge, jam **2** *fam* : corner, nab — *vi* : get stuck

coïncider [kɔɛ̃side] *vi* : coincide — **coïncidence** [kɔɛ̃sidɑ̃s] *nf* : coincidence

col [kɔl] *nm* **1** : collar **2** : neck (of a bottle)

colère [kɔlɛr] *nf* **1** : anger **2 se mettre en ~** : get angry — **coléreux, -reuse** [kɔlerø, -røz] *adj* : bad-tempered, irritable — **colérique** [kɔlerik] *adj* : bad-tempered

colimaçon [kɔlimasɔ̃] *nm* **1** : snail **2 escalier en ~** : spiral staircase

colique [kɔlik] *nf* **1** : diarrhea **2** *or* **~s** *nfpl* : colic

colis [kɔli] *nms & pl* : parcel, package

collaborer [kɔlabɔre] *vi* : collaborate — **collaborateur, -trice** [kɔlabɔratœr, -tris] *n* : colleague — **collaboration** [-bɔrasjɔ̃] *nf* : collaboration

collant, -lante [kɔlɑ̃, -lɑ̃t] *adj* : sticky — **collant** *nm* **1** : panty hose *pl* **2 ~s** *mpl* : tights

collation [kɔlasjɔ̃] *nf* : snack

colle [kɔl] *nf* **1** : paste, glue **2** : trick question

collecte [kɔlɛkt] *nf* : collection — **collecter** [kɔlɛkte] *vt* : collect (funds) — **collectif, -tive** [kɔlɛktif, -tiv] *adj* : collective, joint — **collection** [kɔlɛksjɔ̃] *nf* : collection — **collectionner** [kɔlɛksjɔne] *vt* : collect — **collectionneur, -neuse** [kɔlɛksjɔnœr, -nøz] *n* : collector

collège [kɔlɛʒ] *nm* **1** *France* : junior high school **2** *Can* : vocational college — **collégial, -giale** [kɔleʒjal] *adj, mpl* **-giaux** [-ʒjo] : collegiate — **collégien, -gienne** [kɔleʒjɛ̃, -ʒjɛn] *n* *France* : schoolboy *m*, schoolgirl *f*

collègue [kɔlɛg] *nmf* : colleague

coller [kɔle] *vt* : stick, glue — *vi* **~ à** : stick to, adhere to

collet [kɔlɛ] *nm* **1** : collar (of a shirt) **2 être ~ monté** : be prim and proper

collier [kɔlje] *nm* **1** : necklace **2** : (animal) collar

colline [kɔlin] *nf* : hill

collision [kɔlizjɔ̃] *nf* **1** : collision **2 entrer en ~ avec** : collide with

colloque [kɔlɔk] *nm* : symposium

colombe [kɔlɔ̃b] *nf* : dove

colon [kɔlɔ̃] *nm* : settler

côlon [kolɔ̃] *nm* : colon (in anatomy)

colonel [kɔlɔnɛl] *nm* : colonel

colonie [kɔlɔni] *nf* **1** : colony **2 ~ de vacances** : summer camp — **colonial, -niale** [kɔlɔnjal] *adj, mpl* **-niaux** [-njo] : colonial — **coloniser** [kɔlɔnize] *vt* : colonize, settle

colonne [kɔlɔn] *nf* **1** : column **2 ~ vertébrale** : spine, backbone

colorer [kɔlɔre] *vt* : color, tint — **colorant** [kɔlɔrɑ̃] *nm* : dye, stain — **coloré, -rée** [kɔlɔre] *adj* **1** : colorful **2** : colored — **colorier** [kɔlɔrje] {96} *vt* : color (a drawing) — **coloris** [kɔlɔri] *nm* : shade, color

colporter [kɔlpɔrte] *vt* : hawk, peddle — **colporteur, -teuse** [kɔlpɔrtœr, -tøz] *n* : peddler

coma [kɔma] *nm* : coma

combattre [kɔ̃batr] {12} *v* : fight — **combat** [kɔ̃ba] *nm* **1** : fight(ing) **2 ~ de boxe** : boxing match — **combattant, -tante** [kɔ̃batɑ̃, -tɑ̃t] *n* **1** : combatant, fighter **2 ancien combattant** : veteran — **combatif, -tive** [kɔ̃batif, -tiv] *adj* : combative

combien [kɔ̃bjɛ̃] *adv* **1** : how much, how many **2 ~ de** : how much, how many **3 ~ de fois** : how often **4 ~ de temps** : how long

combiner [kɔ̃bine] *vt* **1** : combine **2** PRÉPARER : work out, devise — **combinaison** [kɔ̃binɛzɔ̃] *nf* **1** : combination **2** : coveralls *pl*, suit — **combiné** [kɔ̃bine] *nm* : (telephone) receiver

combler [kɔ̃ble] *vt* **1** : fill (in) **2** : satisfy, fulfill — **comble** [kɔ̃bl] *adj* : packed — **~** *nm* **le ~ de** : the height of

combustible [kɔ̃bystibl] *adj* : combustible — **~** *nm* : fuel — **combustion** [kɔ̃bystjɔ̃] *nf* : combustion

comédie [kɔmedi] *nf* : comedy — **comédien, -dienne** [kɔmedjɛ̃, -djɛn] *n* : actor *m*, actress *f*

comestible [kɔmɛstibl] *adj* : edible

comète [kɔmɛt] *nf* : comet

comique [kɔmik] *adj* : comic, funny — **~** *nmf* : comedian, comic

comité [kɔmite] *nm* : committee

commander [kɔmɑ̃de] *vt* **1** : command **2** : order (a meal, etc.) — **commandant** [kɔmɑ̃dɑ̃] *nm* **1** : commander **2** : major (in the army) **3 ~ de bord** : captain — **commande** [kɔmɑ̃d] *nf* **1** : order **2 ~ à distance** : remote control — **commandement** [kɔmɑ̃dmɑ̃] *nm* **1** : command, authority **2** : commandment (in religion)

comme [kɔm] *adv* : how — **~** *conj* **1** : as, like **2** : since **3** : when, as **4 ~ ci, ~ ça** : so-so **5 ~ il faut** : properly — **~** *prep* : like, as

commémorer [kɔmemɔre] *vt* : commemorate — **commémoration** [kɔmemɔrasjɔ̃] *nf* : commemoration

commencer [kɔmɑ̃se] {6} *v* : begin, start — **commencement** [kɔmɑ̃smɑ̃] *nm* : beginning, start

comment [kɔmɑ̃] *adv* **1** : how **2** : what **3 ~ ça va?** : how is it going?

commenter [kɔmɑ̃te] *vt* : comment on — **commentaire** [kɔmɑ̃tɛr] *nm* **1** : comment **2** : commentary

commérages [kɔmeraʒ] *nmpl fam* : gossip

commerce [kɔmɛrs] *nm* : business, trade — **commercer** [kɔmɛrse] {6} *vi* : trade, deal — **commerçant, -çante** [kɔmɛrsɑ̃, -sɑ̃t] *n*

: merchant, storekeeper — **commercial** [kɔmɛrsjal] *adj, mpl* **-ciaux** [-sjo] : commercial — **commercialiser** [kɔmɛrsjalize] *vt* : market

commère [kɔmɛr] *nf fam* : gossip (person)

commettre [kɔmɛtr] {53} *vt* : commit

commis [kɔmi] *nm* **1** : clerk **2** ～ **voyageur** : traveling salesman

commissaire [kɔmisɛr] *nm* : superintendent, commissioner — **commissariat** [kɔmisarja] *nm* ～ **de police** : police station

commission [kɔmisjɔ̃] *nf* **1** : committee **2** ～**s** *nfpl* : shopping

commode [kɔmɔd] *adj* **1** : handy **2 pas** ～ : awkward — ～ *nf* : chest of drawers — **commodité** [kɔmɔdite] *nf* : convenience

commotion [kɔmosjɔ̃] *nf* ～ **cérébrale** : concussion

commun, -mune [kɔmœ̃, -myn] *adj* **1** : common, shared **2** : usual, ordinary — **commun** *nm* **1 en** ～ : in common **2 hors du** ～ : out of the ordinary

communauté [kɔmynote] *nf* **1** : community **2** : commune — **communautaire** [kɔmynoter] *adj* : communal

communication [kɔmynikasjɔ̃] *nf* **1** : communication **2** ～ **téléphonique** : telephone call

communion [kɔmynjɔ̃] *nf* : communion

communiquer [kɔmynike] *v* : communicate — **communiqué** [kɔmynike] *nm* : press release

communisme [kɔmynism] *nm* : communism — **communiste** [kɔmynist] *adj & nmf* : communist

commutateur [kɔmytatœr] *nm* : (electric) switch

compact, -pacte [kɔ̃pakt] *adj* : compact, dense — **compact** *nm* : compact disc

compagnie [kɔ̃paɲi] *nf* **1** : company **2 tenir** ～ **à qqn** : keep s.o. company — **compagne** [kɔ̃paɲ] *nf* : (female) companion, partner — **compagnon** [kɔ̃paɲɔ̃] *nm* : companion

comparer [kɔ̃pare] *vt* : compare — **comparaison** [kɔ̃parɛzɔ̃] *nf* : comparison

compartiment [kɔ̃partimɑ̃] *nm* : compartment

compas [kɔ̃pa] *nms & pl* : compass

compassion [kɔ̃pasjɔ̃] *nf* : compassion

compatible [kɔ̃patibl] *adj* : compatible — **compatibilité** [kɔ̃patibilite] *nf* : compatibility

compatir [kɔ̃patir] *vi* : sympathize — **compatissant, -sante** [kɔ̃patisɑ̃, -sɑ̃t] *adj* : compassionate

compatriote [kɔ̃patrijɔt] *nmf* : compatriot

compenser [kɔ̃pɑ̃se] *vt* : compensate for — **compensation** [kɔ̃pɑ̃sasjɔ̃] *nf* : compensation

compétent, -tente [kɔ̃petɑ̃, -tɑ̃t] *adj* : competent — **compétence** [-petɑ̃s] *nf* : competence

compétiteur, -trice [kɔ̃petitœr, -tris] *n* : competitor, rival — **compétitif, -tive** [kɔ̃petitif, -tiv] *adj* : competitive — **compétition** [kɔ̃petisjɔ̃] *nf* : competition

complaisant, -sante [kɔ̃plezɑ̃, -zɑ̃t] *adj* **1** AIMABLE : obliging, kind **2** INDULGENT : indulgent

complément [kɔ̃plemɑ̃] *nm* : complement — **complémentaire** [kɔ̃plemɑ̃tɛr] *adj* : complementary

complet, -plète [kɔ̃plɛ, -plɛt] *adj* **1** : complete **2** PLEIN : full (of a hotel, etc.) — **complet** *nm* : suit — **complètement** [kɔ̃plɛtmɑ̃] *adv* : completely — **compléter** [kɔ̃plete] {87} *vt* : complete

complexe [kɔ̃plɛks] *adj & nm* : complex — **complexité** [kɔ̃plɛksite] *nf* : complexity

complication [kɔ̃plikasjɔ̃] *nf* : complication

complice [kɔ̃plis] *adj* : knowing (of a look, etc.) — ～ *nmf* : accomplice

compliment [kɔ̃plimɑ̃] *nm* : compliment — **complimenter** [kɔ̃plimɑ̃te] *vt* : compliment

compliquer [kɔ̃plike] *vt* : complicate — **compliqué, -quée** [kɔ̃plike] *adj* : complicated

complot [kɔ̃plo] *nm* : plot — **comploter** [kɔ̃plɔte] *v* : plot, scheme

comporter [kɔ̃pɔrte] *vt* **1** CONTENIR : include **2** : entail (risks, etc.) — **se comporter** *vr* : behave — **comportement** [kɔ̃pɔrtəmɑ̃] *nm* : behavior

composer [kɔ̃poze] *vt* **1** : compose (music) **2** : constitute, make up **3** : dial (a number) — **se composer** *vr* ～ **de** : consist of — **composant** [kɔ̃pozɑ̃] *nm* ÉLÉMENT : component — **composé, -sée** [kɔ̃poze] *adj* : compound — **composé** *nm* : compound — **compositeur, -trice** [kɔ̃pozitœr, -tris] *n* : composer — **composition** [kɔ̃pozisjɔ̃] *nf* : composition

compote [kɔ̃pɔt] *nf* ～ **de pommes** : apple sauce

compréhensif, -sive [kɔ̃preɑ̃sif, -siv] *adj* : understanding — **compréhension** [kɔ̃preɑ̃sjɔ̃] *nf* : understanding, comprehension

comprendre [kɔ̃prɑ̃dr] {70} *vt* **1** : consist of, comprise **2** : understand **3 mal** ～ : misunderstand

compression [kɔ̃prɛsjɔ̃] *nf* : compression

comprimer [kɔ̃prime] *vt* : compress — **comprimé** [kɔ̃prime] *nm* : tablet, pill

compris, -prise [kɔ̃pri, -priz] *adj* **1** INCLUS : included **2 y compris** : including

compromettre [kɔ̃prɔmɛtr] {53} *vt* : compromise — **compromis** [kɔ̃prɔmi] *nm* : compromise

comptable [kɔ̃tabl] *nmf* : accountant — **comptabilité** [kɔ̃tabilite] *nf* : accounting

comptant [kɔ̃tɑ̃] *adv* **payer ~** : pay cash

compte [kɔ̃t, -tɛs] *nm* **1** : (bank) account **2 au bout du ~** : in the end **3 ~ à rebours** : countdown **4 se rendre ~ de** : realize — **compter** [kɔ̃te] *vt* **1** : count **2** ESPÉRER : expect **3 ~ faire** : intend to do — *vi* **1** CALCULER : count **2** IMPORTER : matter **3 ~ sur** : count on

compte–rendu [kɔ̃trɑ̃dy] *nm, pl* **comptes–rendus** : report

compteur [kɔ̃tœr] *nm* : meter

comptoir [kɔ̃twar] *nm* : counter, bar

comte, comtesse [kɔ̃t, -tɛs] *n* : count *m*, countess *f*

comté [kɔ̃te] *nm* : county

concave [kɔ̃kav] *adj* : concave

concéder [kɔ̃sede] {87} *vt* : grant, concede

concentrer [kɔ̃sɑ̃tre] *vt* : concentrate — **se concentrer** *vr* **1** : concentrate **2 ~ sur** : center on — **concentration** [kɔ̃sɑ̃trasjɔ̃] *nf* : concentration

concept [kɔ̃sɛpt] *nm* : concept — **conception** [kɔ̃sɛpsjɔ̃] *nf* : conception

concerner [kɔ̃sɛrne] *vt* **1** : concern **2 en ce qui me concerne** : as far as I'm concerned — **concernant** [kɔ̃sɛrnɑ̃] *prep* : concerning, regarding

concert [kɔ̃sɛr] *nm* **1** : concert **2 de ~** : together — **se concerter** [kɔ̃sɛrte] *vr* : consult, confer — **concerté, -tée** [kɔ̃sɛrte] *adj* : concerted

concession [kɔ̃sesjɔ̃] *nf* : concession — **concessionnaire** [kɔ̃sesjɔnɛr] *nmf* : dealer, agent

concevoir [kɔ̃səvwar] {26} *vt* **1** : conceive (a child) **2** IMAGINER : conceive of, design

concierge [kɔ̃sjɛrʒ] *nmf* : janitor

concilier [kɔ̃silje] {96} *vt* : reconcile — **conciliant, -liante** [kɔ̃siljɑ̃, -ljɑ̃t] *adj* : conciliatory

concis, -cise [kɔ̃si, -siz] *adj* : concise — **concision** [kɔ̃sizjɔ̃] *nf* **avec ~** : concisely

conclure [kɔ̃klyr] {39} *vt* : conclude — **concluant, -cluante** [kɔ̃klyɑ̃, -klyɑ̃t] *adj* : conclusive — **conclusion** [kɔ̃klyzjɔ̃] *nf* : conclusion

concombre [kɔ̃kɔ̃br] *nm* : cucumber

concorder [kɔ̃kɔrde] *vi* : agree, match — **concordant, -dante** [kɔ̃kɔrdɑ̃, -dɑ̃t] *adj* : in agreement

concourir [kɔ̃kurir] {23} *vi* **1** : compete **2 ~ à** : work toward — **concours** [kɔ̃kur] *nm* : competition, contest

concret, -crète [kɔ̃krɛ, -krɛt] *adj* : concrete — **concrétiser** [kɔ̃kretize] *vt* : give shape to — **se concrétiser** *vr* : materialize

concurrencer [kɔ̃kyrɑ̃se] {6} *vt* : rival, compete with — **concurrence** [kɔ̃kyrɑ̃s] *nf* : competition, rivalry — **concurrent, -rente** [kɔ̃kyrɑ̃, -rɑ̃t] *adj* : competing, rival — **~** *n* : competitor

condamner [kɔ̃dane] *vt* **1** : condemn **2** : sentence (in law) — **condamnation** [kɔ̃danasjɔ̃] *nf* **1** : condemnation **2** PEINE : sentence

condenser [kɔ̃dɑ̃se] *vt* : condense — **condensation** [kɔ̃dɑ̃sasjɔ̃] *nf* : condensation

condescendant, -dante [kɔ̃desɑ̃dɑ̃, -dɑ̃t] *adj* : condescending

condiment [kɔ̃dimɑ̃] *nm* : condiment

condition [kɔ̃disjɔ̃] *nf* **1** : condition **2 ~s** *nfpl* : conditions, circumstances **3 sous ~ que** : provided that — **conditionnel, -nelle** [kɔ̃disjɔnɛl] *adj* : conditional

condoléances [kɔ̃dɔleɑ̃s] *nfpl* : condolences

conduire [kɔ̃dɥir] {49} *vt* **1** : drive **2 ~ à** : lead to — **se conduire** *vr* : behave — **conducteur, -trice** [kɔ̃dyktœr, -tris] *n* : driver — **conducteur** *nm* : conductor (of electricity) — **conduite** [kɔ̃dɥit] *nf* **1** : behavior, conduct **2** TUYAU : pipe **3 ~ à droite** : right-hand drive

cône [kon] *nm* : cone

confection [kɔ̃fɛksjɔ̃] *nf* **1** : making **2 la ~** : the clothing industry — **confectionner** [kɔ̃fɛksjɔne] *vt* : make (a meal, a garment, etc.)

confédération [kɔ̃federasjɔ̃] *nf* : confederation

conférence [kɔ̃ferɑ̃s] *nf* **1** : conference **2** COURS : lecture — **conférencier, -cière** [kɔ̃ferɑ̃sje, -sjɛr] *n* : lecturer

conférer [kɔ̃fere] {87} *v* : confer

confession [kɔ̃fesjɔ̃] *nf* **1** : confession **2** : denomination — **confesser** [kɔ̃fese] *vt* : confess

confettis [kɔ̃feti] *nmpl* : confetti

confiant, -fiante [kɔ̃fjɑ̃, -fjɑ̃t] *adj* **1** : confident, trusting **2** ASSURÉ : self-confident — **confiance** [kɔ̃fjɑ̃s] *nf* **1** : confidence, trust **2 ~ en soi** : self-confidence

confidence [kɔ̃fidɑ̃s] *nf* **1** : confidence **2 faire des ~s à** : confide in — **confident, -dente** [kɔ̃fidɑ̃, -dɑ̃t] *n* : confidant, confidante *f* — **confidentiel, -tielle** [kɔ̃fidɑ̃sjɛl] *adj* : confidential

confier [kɔ̃fje] {96} *vt* **1 ~ à qqn** : confide to s.o. **2 ~ (qqch) à qqn** : entrust (sth) to s.o. — **se confier** *vr* **~ à qqn** : confide in s.o.

confiner [kɔ̃fine] *vt* : confine — **confins** [kɔ̃fɛ̃] *nmpl* : limits, confines

confirmer [kɔ̃firme] *vt* : confirm — **confirmation** [kɔ̃firmasjɔ̃] *nf* : confirmation

confiserie [kɔ̃fizri] *nf* **1** : candy store **2** : candy

confisquer [kɔ̃fiske] *vt* : confiscate

confiture [kɔ̃fityr] *nf* : jam, preserves *pl*

conflit [kɔ̃fli] *nm* : conflict

confondre [kɔ̃fɔ̃dr] {63} *vt* **1** : confuse, mix up **2** ÉTONNER : baffle

conformer [kɔ̃fɔrme] *v* **se conformer** *vr* ~ **à** : conform to — **conforme** [kɔ̃fɔrm] *adj* **1** ~ **à** : in keeping with **2** ~ **à** : true to — **conformément** [kɔ̃fɔrmemɑ̃] *adv* ~ **à** : in accordance with — **conformité** [kɔ̃fɔrmite] *nf* : conformity

confort [kɔ̃fɔr] *nm* : comfort — **confortable** [kɔ̃fɔrtabl] *adj* : comfortable

confrère [kɔ̃frɛr] *nm* : colleague

confronter [kɔ̃frɔ̃te] *vt* **1** : confront **2** COMPARER : compare

confus [kɔ̃fy] *adj* **1** : confused **2** : embarrassed — **confusion** [kɔ̃fyzjɔ̃] *nf* **1** DÉSORDRE : confusion **2** GÊNE : embarrassment **3** ERREUR : mix-up

congé [kɔ̃ʒe] *nm* **1** VACANCES : vacation **2** : leave, time off — **congédier** [kɔ̃ʒedje] {96} *vt* : dismiss (an employee)

congeler [kɔ̃ʒle] {20} *vt* : freeze — **congélateur** [kɔ̃ʒelatœr] *nm* : freezer

congestion [kɔ̃ʒɛstjɔ̃] *nf* : congestion — **congestionner** [kɔ̃ʒɛstjɔne] *vt* : congest

congrès [kɔ̃grɛ] *nm* : congress, conference

conifère [kɔnifɛr] *nm* : conifer

conjecturer [kɔ̃ʒɛktyre] *v* : conjecture — **conjecture** [kɔ̃ʒɛktyr] *nf* : conjecture

conjoint, -jointe [kɔ̃ʒwɛ̃, -ʒwɛ̃t] *adj* : joint — ~ *n* ÉPOUX : spouse — **conjointement** [-ʒwɛ̃tmɑ̃] *adv* ~ **avec** : in conjunction with

conjonction [kɔ̃ʒɔ̃ksjɔ̃] *nf* : conjunction

conjoncture [kɔ̃ʒɔ̃ktyr] *nf* : circumstances *pl*, juncture

conjugaison [kɔ̃ʒygɛzɔ̃] *nf* : conjugation

conjugal, -gale [kɔ̃ʒygal] *adj, mpl* **-gaux** [-go] : marital

conjuguer [kɔ̃ʒyge] *vt* : conjugate (a verb)

connaître [kɔnɛtr] {7} *vt* **1** : know **2** ÉPROUVER : experience — **se connaître** *vr* **1** : know each other **2** s'y ~ **en** : know about, be an expert in — **connaissance** [kɔnɛsɑ̃s] *nf* **1** : knowledge **2** : acquaintance **3** CONSCIENCE : consciousness **4 à ma** ~ : as far as I know **5 faire** ~ **avec qqn** : meet s.o. **6** ~s *nfpl* : knowledge, learning — **connaisseur, -seuse** [kɔnɛsœr, -søz] *n* : expert

connecter [kɔnɛkte] *vt* : connect

connexe [kɔnɛks] *adj* : related

connu, -nue [kɔny] *adj* : well-known

conquérir [kɔ̃kerir] {21} *vt* **1** : conquer **2** : win over — **conquérant, -rante** [kɔ̃kerɑ̃, -rɑ̃t] *n* : conqueror — **conquête** [kɔ̃kɛt] *nf* : conquest

consacrer [kɔ̃sakre] *vt* **1** : consecrate **2** ~ **à** : devote to — **se consacrer** *vr* ~ **à** : dedicate oneself to

conscience [kɔ̃sjɑ̃s] *nf* **1** : conscience **2** : consciousness — **consciemment** [kɔ̃sjamɑ̃] *adv* : consciously — **consciencieux, -cieuse** [kɔ̃sjɑ̃sjø, -sjøz] *adj* : conscientious — **conscient, -ciente** [kɔ̃sjɑ̃, -sjɑ̃t] *adj* : conscious, aware

consécutif, -tive [kɔ̃sekytif, -tiv] *adj* : consecutive — **consécutivement** [-tivmɑ̃] *adv* : consecutively

conseil [kɔ̃sɛj] *nm* **1** : (piece of) advice **2** : council **3** ~ **d'administration** : board of directors — **conseiller** [kɔ̃seje] *vt* **1** : advise **2** RECOMMANDER : recommend — **conseiller, -ère** [kɔ̃seje, -jɛr] *n* **1** : counselor, advisor **2** : councillor

consentir [kɔ̃sɑ̃tir] {82} *vi* ~ **à** : consent to, agree to — **consentant, -tante** [kɔ̃sɑ̃tɑ̃, -tɑ̃t] *adj* : willing — **consentement** [kɔ̃sɑ̃tmɑ̃] *nm* : consent

conséquence [kɔ̃sekɑ̃s] *nf* **1** : consequence **2 en** ~ : consequently — **conséquent, -quente** [kɔ̃sekɑ̃, -kɑ̃t] *adj* : consistent, logical — **conséquent** *nm* **par** ~ : consequently

conservateur, -trice [kɔ̃sɛrvatœr, -tris] *adj* : conservative — ~ *n* **1** : conservative **2** : curator — **conservation** [kɔ̃sɛrvasjɔ̃] *nf* : conservation

conservatoire [kɔ̃sɛrvatwar] *nm* : academy, conservatory

conserver [kɔ̃sɛrve] *vt* GARDER : keep, retain — **se conserver** *vr* : keep, stay fresh — **conserve** [kɔ̃sɛrv] *nf* **1** : canned food **2 en** ~ : canned

considérable [kɔ̃siderabl] *adj* : considerable

considérer [kɔ̃sidere] {87} *vt* **1** : consider **2** ESTIMER : think highly of — **considération** [kɔ̃siderasjɔ̃] *nf* **1** : consideration **2** ESTIME : respect

consigner [kɔ̃siɲe] *vt* : check (luggage, etc.) — **consigne** [kɔ̃siɲ] *nf* **1** ORDRE : instructions *pl* **2** : checkroom

consister [kɔ̃siste] *vi* **1** ~ **en** : consist of **2** ~ **dans** : lie in **3** ~ **à faire** : consist in doing — **consistance** [kɔ̃sistɑ̃s] *nf* : consistency — **consistant, -tante** [kɔ̃sistɑ̃, -tɑ̃t] *adj* **1** ÉPAIS : thick **2** NOURRISSANT : substantial

consoler [kɔ̃sɔle] *vt* : console, comfort — **consolation** [kɔ̃sɔlasjɔ̃] *nf* : consolation

consolider [kɔ̃sɔlide] *vt* : consolidate

consommer [kɔ̃sɔme] *vt* : consume — *vi* : have a drink — **consommateur, -trice** [kɔ̃sɔmatœr, -tris] *n* : consumer — **consommation** [kɔ̃sɔmasjɔ̃] *nf* **1** : consumption **2** BOISSON : drink — **consommé** [kɔ̃sɔme] *nm* : clear soup

consonne [kɔ̃sɔn] *nf* : consonant

conspirer [kɔ̃spire] *vi* : conspire, plot — **conspiration** [kɔ̃spirasjɔ̃] *nf* : conspiracy

constant, -tante [kɔ̃stɑ̃, -tɑ̃t] *adj* : constant, continual — **constamment** [kɔ̃stamɑ̃] *adv* : constantly

constater [kɔ̃state] *vt* REMARQUER : notice — **constatation** [kɔ̃statasjɔ̃] *nf* : observation

constellation [kɔ̃stelasjɔ̃] *nf* : constellation

consternation [kɔ̃stɛrnasjɔ̃] *nf* : dismay — **consterner** [kɔ̃stɛrne] *vt* : dismay

constipation [kɔ̃stipasjɔ̃] *nf* : constipation — **constiper** [kɔ̃stipe] *vt* : constipate

constituer [kɔ̃titɥe] *vt* **1** COMPOSER : constitute **2** ÉLABORER : set up, form — **constitution** [kɔ̃stitysjɔ̃] *nf* **1** : constitution **2** ÉTABLISSEMENT : setting up — **constitutionnel, -nelle** [kɔ̃stitysjɔnɛl] *adj* : constitutional

constructeur, -trice [kɔ̃stryktœr, -tris] *n* : builder — **constructif, -tive** [kɔ̃stryktif, -tiv] *adj* : constructive — **construction** [kɔ̃stryksjɔ̃] *nf* : building, construction — **construire** [kɔ̃strɥir] {49} *vt* : construct, build

consulat [kɔ̃syla] *nm* : consulate

consultant, -tante [kɔ̃syltɑ̃, -tɑ̃t] *n* : consultant — **consultation** [kɔ̃syltasjɔ̃] *nf* : consultation (with a doctor, etc.) — **consulter** [kɔ̃sylte] *vt* **1** : consult **2** : refer to — **se consulter** *vr* : confer

consumer [kɔ̃syme] *vt* : burn, destroy

contact [kɔ̃takt] *nm* **1** : contact, touch **2** **couper le ~** : switch off the ignition **3** **rester en ~** : keep in touch — **contacter** [kɔ̃takte] *vt* : get in touch with, contact

contagieux, -gieuse [kɔtaʒjœ, -ʒjøz] *adj* : contagious

contaminer [kɔ̃tamine] *vt* **1** : contaminate **2** INFECTER : infect — **contamination** [-minasjɔ̃] *nf* : contamination

conte [kɔ̃t] *nm* **1** : tale, story **2** **~ de fées** : fairy tale

contempler [kɔ̃tɑ̃ple] *vt* : contemplate — **contemplation** [-tɑ̃plasjɔ̃] *nf* : contemplation

contemporain, -raine [kɔ̃tɑ̃pɔrɛ̃, -rɛn] *adj & n* : contemporary

contenir [kɔ̃tnir] {92} *vt* **1** : hold, contain **2** RETENIR : restrain — **se contenir** *vr* : control oneself — **contenance** [kɔ̃tnɑ̃s] *nf* ALLURE : bearing, attitude

content, -tente [kɔ̃tɑ̃, -tɑ̃t] *adj* : content, pleased — **contentement** [kɔ̃tɑ̃tmɑ̃] *nm* : satisfaction — **contenter** [kɔ̃tɑ̃te] *vt* : satisfy, please — **se contenter** *vr* **~ de** : be contented with

contentieux [kɔ̃tɑ̃sjø] *nm* **1** : dispute **2** : legal department

contenu [kɔ̃tny] *nm* : contents *pl*

conter [kɔ̃te] *vt* : tell (a story)

contester [kɔ̃tɛste] *vt* : contest, dispute — *vi* : protest — **contestation** [kɔ̃tɛstasjɔ̃] *nf* **1** DISPUTE : dispute **2** : (political) protest

conteur, -teuse [kɔ̃tœr, -tøz] *n* : storyteller

contexte [kɔ̃tɛkst] *nm* : context

contigu, -guë [kɔ̃tigy] *adj* : adjacent

continent [kɔ̃tinɑ̃] *nm* : continent — **continental, -tale** [-nɑtal] *adj, mpl* **-taux** [-to] : continental

continuer [kɔ̃tinɥe] *vt* **1** : continue **2** PROLONGER : extend — *vi* : continue, go on — **continu, -nue** [kɔ̃tiny] *adj* : continuous — **continuation** [kɔ̃tinɥasjɔ̃] *nf* : continuation — **continuel, -nuelle** [kɔ̃tinɥel] *adj* : continuous, continual — **continuellement** [kɔ̃tinɥelmɑ̃] *adv* : continually — **continuité** [kɔ̃tinɥite] *nf* : continuity

contorsion [kɔ̃tɔrsjɔ̃] *nf* : contortion — **contorsionner** [kɔ̃tɔrsjɔne] *v* **se contorsionner** *vr* : contort oneself

contour [kɔ̃tur] *nm* : outline, contour — **contourner** [kɔ̃turne] *vt* **1** : bypass **2** : get around (a difficulty, etc.)

contraceptif, -tive [kɔ̃trasɛptif, -tiv] *adj* : contraceptive — **contraceptif** *nm* : contraceptive — **contraception** [kɔ̃trasɛpsjɔ̃] *nf* : contraception

contracter [kɔ̃trakte] *vt* **1** : contract (a muscle) **2** : incur (a debt) **3** : catch (a cold, etc.) — **contraction** [kɔ̃traksjɔ̃] *nf* : contraction, tensing

contradiction [kɔ̃tradiksjɔ̃] *nf* : contradiction — **contradictoire** [kɔ̃tradiktwar] *adj* : contradictory

contraindre [kɔ̃trɛ̃dr] {65} *vt* **~ à** : compel to, force to — **contrainte** [kɔ̃trɛ̃, -trɛt] *nf* : constraint, coertion

contraire [kɔ̃trɛr] *adj & nm* : contrary, opposite — **contrairement** [kɔ̃trɛrmɑ̃] *adv* **~ à** : contrary to

contrarier [kɔ̃trarje] {96} *vt* : annoy, vex — **contrariant, -riante** [kɔ̃trarjɑ̃, -rjɑ̃t] *adj* : annoying — **contrariété** [kɔ̃trarjete] *nf* : annoyance

contraste [kɔ̃trast] *nm* : contrast

contrat [kɔ̃tra] *nm* : contract

contravention [kɔ̃travɑ̃sjɔ̃] *nf* : (parking) ticket

contre [kɔ̃tr] *prep* **1** : against **2** : versus (in law) **3** : (in exchange) for **4 trois ~ un** : three to one — **~** *nm* **le pour et le ~** : the pros and cons — **~** *adv* **1 par ~** : on the other hand **2 parler ~** : speak in opposition — **contre–attaque** [kɔ̃tratake] *nf, pl* **contre–attaques** : counterattack — **contrebande** [kɔ̃trəbɑ̃d] *nf* : smuggling — **contrebandier, -dière** [kɔ̃trəbɑ̃dje, -djɛr] *n* : smuggler — **contrebas** [kɔ̃trəba] **en ~** *adv phr* : (down) below — **contrebasse** [kɔ̃trəbas] *nf* : double bass — **contrecarrer** [kɔ̃trəkare] *vt* : thwart — **contrecœur** [kɔ̃-

trəkœr] **à ~** *adv phr* : unwillingly — **contrecoup** [kɔ̃trəku] *nm* : consequence — **contredire** [kɔ̃trədir] {29} *vt* : contradict — **se contredire** *vr* : contradict oneself — **contrefaire** [kɔ̃trəfɛr] {42} *vt* : counterfeit, forge — **contrefaçon** [kɔ̃trəfasɔ̃] *nf* : counterfeiting, forgery — **contrefort** [kɔ̃trəfɔr] *nm* **1** : buttress **2 ~s** *nmpl* : foothills — **contremaître** [kɔ̃trəmɛtr] *n* : foreman — **contrepartie** [kɔ̃trəparti] *nf* **1** : compensation **2 en ~** : in return — **contrepoids** [kɔ̃trəpwa] *nm* : counterbalance — **contrer** [kɔ̃tre] *vt* : counter — **contresens** [kɔ̃trəsɑ̃s] **à ~** *adv phr* : the wrong way — **contretemps** [kɔ̃trətɑ̃] *nm* : hitch, setback — **contrevenir** [kɔ̃trəvnir] {92} *vi* **~ à** : contravene

contribuer [kɔ̃tribɥe] *vi* : contribute — **contribuable** [kɔ̃tribɥabl] *nmf* : taxpayer — **contribution** [kɔ̃tribysjɔ̃] *nf* : contribution

contrit, -trite [kɔ̃tri, -trit] *adj* : contrite

contrôle [kɔ̃trol] *nm* **1** : checking, inspection **2 ~ de soi-même** : self-control — **contrôler** [kɔ̃trole] *vt* **1** : check, inspect **2** MAÎTRISER : supervise, control — **contrôleur, -leuse** [kɔ̃trolœr, -løz] *n* : (ticket) inspector, (bus) conductor

controverse [kɔ̃trɔvɛrs] *nf* : controversy — **controversé, -sée** [kɔ̃trɔvɛrse] *adj* : controversial

contusionner [kɔ̃tyzjɔne] *vt* : bruise — **contusion** [kɔ̃tyzjɔ̃] *nf* : bruise

convaincre [kɔ̃vɛ̃kr] {94} *vt* : convince — **convaincant, -cante** [kɔ̃vɛ̃kɑ̃, -kɑ̃t] *adj* : convincing

convalescence [kɔ̃valesɑ̃s] *nf* : convalescence

convenir [kɔ̃vnir] {92} *vt* : agree, admit — *vi* **~ à** : suit, fit — *v impers* **il convient de** : it is advisable to — **convenable** [kɔ̃vnabl] *adj* **1** ACCEPTABLE : adequate **2** : proper, decent — **convenance** [kɔ̃vnɑ̃s] *nf* **1 à votre ~** : at your convenience **2 ~s** *nfpl* : conventions, proprieties

convention [kɔ̃vɑ̃sjɔ̃] *nf* **1** USAGE : custom **2** ACCORD : agreement **3** ASSEMBLÉE : convention, assembly — **conventionnel, -nelle** [kɔ̃vɑ̃sjɔnɛl] *adj* : conventional

convenu, -nue [kɔ̃vny] *adj* : agreed

converger [kɔ̃vɛrʒe] {17} *vi* : converge, meet

conversation [kɔ̃vɛrsasjɔ̃] *nf* : conversation — **converser** [kɔ̃vɛrse] *vi* : converse

convertir [kɔ̃vɛrtir] *vt* : convert — **conversion** [kɔ̃vɛrsjɔ̃] *nf* : conversion

conviction [kɔ̃viksjɔ̃] *nf* CERTITUDE : conviction

convier [kɔ̃vje] {96} *vt* : invite

convive [kɔ̃viv] *nmf* : guest (at a meal)

convoi [kɔ̃vwa] *nm* **1** : convoy **2** *or* **~ funèbre** : funeral procession

convoiter [kɔ̃vwate] *vt* : covet

convoquer [kɔ̃vɔke] *vt* **1** : convene **2** : summon

convulsion [kɔ̃vylsjɔ̃] *nf* : convulsion

coopérer [kɔɔpere] {87} *vi* : cooperate — **coopératif, -tive** [kɔɔperatif, -tiv] *adj* : cooperative — **coopération** [-perasjɔ̃] *nf* : cooperation — **coopérative** *nf* : cooperative

coordination [kɔɔrdinasjɔ̃] *nf* : coordination — **coordonner** [kɔɔrdɔne] *vt* : coordinate

copain, -pine [kɔpɛ̃, -pin] *n* **1** : friend, buddy **2** *or* **petit copain, petite copine** : boyfriend *m*, girlfriend *f*

copeau [kɔpo] *nm, pl* **-peaux** : chip (of wood, etc.)

copie [kɔpi] *nf* **1** : copy, duplicate **2** DEVOIR : paper, schoolwork — **copier** [kɔpje] {96} *vt* **1** : copy **2 ~ sur** : copy from, crib from

copieux, -pieuse [kɔpjø, -pjøz] *adj* : plentiful, copious

copilote [kɔpilɔt] *nmf* : copilot

copine → **copain**

copropriété [kɔprɔprijete] *nf* **1** : joint ownership **2 immeuble en ~** : condominium

coq [kɔk] *nm* : rooster

coque [kɔk] *nf* **1** : hull (of a boat) **2 œuf à la ~** : soft-boiled egg

coquelicot [kɔkliko] *nm* : poppy

coquet, -quette [kɔke, -kɛt] *adj* **1** ÉLÉGANT : stylish **2** : attractive **3** *fam* : tidy, considerable

coquille [kɔkij] *nf* **1** : shell **2** FAUTE : misprint **3 ~ Saint-Jacques** : scallop — **coquillage** [kɔkijaʒ] *nm* **1** : shellfish **2** COQUILLE : shell

coquin, -quine [kɔkɛ̃, -kin] *adj* : mischievous — **~** *n* : rascal, scamp

cor [kɔr] *nm* **1** : horn (in music) **2** : corn (on one's foot)

corail [kɔraj] *nm, pl* **-raux** [kɔro] : coral

Coran [kɔrɑ̃] *nm* : Koran

corbeau [kɔrbo] *nm, pl* **-beaux** : crow

corbeille [kɔrbɛj] *nf* **1** : basket **2 ~ à papier** : wastepaper basket

corbillard [kɔrbijar] *nm* : hearse

corde [kɔrd] *nf* **1** : rope **2** : string **3 ~s vocales** : vocal cords — **cordage** [kɔrdaʒ] *nm* **1** : rope **2 ~s** *nmpl* : rigging

cordial, -diale [kɔrdjal] *adj, mpl* **-diaux** [-djo] : cordial — **cordialement** [-djalmɑ̃] *adv* : cordially

cordon [kɔrdɔ̃] *nm* **1** : cord (in anatomy) **2 ~ de soulier** : shoelace — **cordonnerie** [kɔrdɔnri] *nf* : shoe repair shop — **cordonnier, -nière** [kɔrdɔnje, -njɛr] *n* : shoemaker, cobbler

coréen, -réenne [kɔreɛ̃, -reɛn] *adj* : Korean — **coréen** *nm* : Korean (language)

coriace [kɔrjas] *adj* : tough

corne [kɔrn] *nf* **1** : antler, horn **2** : horn (instrument) **3** ~ **de brume** : foghorn

cornée [kɔrne] *nf* : cornea

corneille [kɔrnɛj] *nf* : crow

cornemuse [kɔrnəmyz] *nf* : bagpipes *pl*

cornet [kɔrnɛ] *nm* **1** : cone **2** ~ **de crème glacée** : ice-cream cone

corniche [kɔrniʃ] *nf* : cliff road

cornichon [kɔrniʃɔ̃] *nm* : pickle

corporation [kɔrpɔrasjɔ̃] *nf* : corporation

corporel, -relle [kɔrpɔrɛl] *adj* : bodily

corps [kɔr] *nm* **1** : body **2** : corps (in the army, etc.) **3** : professional body **4 prendre** ~ : take shape

corpulent, -lente [kɔrpylɑ̃, -lɑ̃t] *adj* : stout

correct, -recte [kɔrɛkt] *adj* : correct — **correctement** [-rɛktəmɑ̃] *adv* : correctly — **correcteur, -trice** [kɔrɛktœr, -tris] *adj* : corrective — **correction** [kɔrɛksjɔ̃] *nf* **1** : correction **2** : grading, marking **3** PUNITION : beating

corrélation [kɔrelasjɔ̃] *nf* : correlation

correspondre [kɔrɛspɔ̃dr] {63} *vi* **1** : correspond, write **2** : communicate (by telephone, etc.) **3** ~ **à** : correspond to — **correspondance** [kɔrɛspɔ̃dɑ̃s] *nf* **1** : correspondence **2** : connection (of a plane, etc.) — **correspondant, -dante** [kɔrɛspɔ̃dɑ̃, -dɑ̃t] *n* **1** : correspondent **2** : person being called (on the telephone)

corrida [kɔrida] *nf* : bullfight

corridor [kɔridɔr] *nm* : corridor

corriger [kɔriʒe] {17} *vt* **1** : correct **2** : grade, mark

corroborer [kɔrɔbɔre] *vt* : corroborate

corroder [kɔrɔde] *vt* : corrode

corrompre [kɔrɔ̃pr] {77} *vt* **1** : corrupt **2** SOUDOYER : bribe — **corrompu, -pue** [kɔrɔ̃py] *adj* : corrupt

corrosif, -sive [kɔrɔzif, -ziv] *adj* : corrosive — **corrosion** [kɔrɔzjɔ̃] *nf* : corrosion

corruption [kɔrypsjɔ̃] *nf* **1** : corruption **2** : bribery

corsage [kɔrsaʒ] *nm* **1** : blouse **2** : bodice (of a dress)

corsé, -sée [kɔrse] *adj* : full-bodied (of wine), strong (of coffee, etc.)

corser [kɔrse] *v* **se corser** *vr* : get more complicated

cortège [kɔrtɛʒ] *nm* : procession

corvée [kɔrve] *nf* : chore

cosmétique [kɔsmetik] *nm* : cosmetic — ~ *adj* : cosmetic

cosmique [kɔsmik] *adj* : cosmic

cosmopolite [kɔsmɔpɔlit] *adj* : cosmopolitan

cosmos [kɔsmos] *nm* : universe, cosmos

cosse [kɔs] *nf* : pod, husk

costaud, -taude [kɔsto, -tod] *adj fam* : sturdy, burly

costume [kɔstym] *nm* **1** : costume **2** COMPLET : suit — **costumer** [kɔstyme] *v* **se costumer** *vr* ~ **en** : dress up as

cote [kɔt] *nf* **1** : (stock) quotation **2** CLASSEMENT : rating **3** : call number (of a library book) **4** NIVEAU : level

côte [kot] *nf* **1** : coast **2** : rib (in anatomy) **3** : chop, cutlet **4** PENTE : hill **5** ~ **à** ~ : side by side

côté [kote] *nm* **1** : side **2** : way, direction **3** **à** ~ : nearby **4 à** ~ **de** : next to **5 de** ~ : sideways **6 de mon** ~ : for my part **7 mettre de** ~ : put aside

coteau [kɔto] *nm, pl* **-teaux** : hill, hillside

côtelé, -lée [kotle] *adj* **velours côtelé** : corduroy

côtelette [kotlɛt] *nf* : chop

coter [kɔte] *vt* : quote (in finance)

coterie [kɔtri] *nf* : clique

côteux, -teuse [kotø, -tøz] *adj Can* : hilly

côtier, -tière [kotje, -tjɛr] *adj* : coastal

cotiser [kɔtize] *vi* : subscribe, pay one's dues — **cotisation** [kɔtizasjɔ̃] *nf* : dues *pl*, fee

coton [kɔtɔ̃] *nm* : cotton

côtoyer [kotwaje] {58} *vt* **1** : skirt, run alongside of **2** FRÉQUENTER : mix with

cou [ku] *nm* : neck

coucher [kuʃe] *vt* **1** : put to bed **2** : lay down flat — *vi* : sleep, spend the night — **se coucher** *vr* **1** : lie down, go to bed **2** : set (of the sun) — ~ *nm* **1** : bedtime **2** ~ **du soleil** : sunset — **couche** [kuʃ] *nf* **1** : layer, stratum **2** : coat (of paint) **3** : (baby) diaper **4 fausse** ~ : miscarriage — **couchette** [kuʃɛt] *nf* : berth, bunk

coucou [kuku] *nm* : cuckoo

coude [kud] *nm* **1** : elbow **2** COURBE : bend, angle **3** ~ **à** ~ : shoulder to shoulder

cou–de–pied [kudpje] *nm, pl* **cous–de–pied** : instep

coudre [kudr] {22} *v* : sew

couler [kule] *vt* **1** : sink **2** : cast (metal) — *vi* **1** : flow, run **2** : leak (of a faucet) **3** : sink (of a boat)

couleur [kulœr] *nf* **1** : color **2** : suit (of cards)

coulisser [kulise] *vi* : slide (in a groove) — **coulisses** [kulis] *nfpl* : backstage, wings

couloir [kulwar] *nm* **1** : corridor **2** : lane (in transportation)

coup [ku] *nm* **1** : knock, blow **2** CHOC : shock **3** : stroke, shot (in sports) **4** : (political) coup **5** ~ **de feu** : gunshot **6** ~ **de foudre** : love at first sight **7** ~ **de pied** : kick **8** ~ **de poing** : punch **9** ~ **de soleil** : sunburn **10** ~ **de téléphone** : telephone call **11** ~ **d'œil** : glance **12 tout à** ~ : suddenly

coupable [kupabl] *adj* : guilty — ~ *nmf* : culprit

coupant, -pante [kupɑ̃, -pɑ̃t] *adj* 1 : sharp 2 CAUSTIQUE : cutting, curt

couper [kupe] *vt* 1 : cut, cut up 2 : cut off, block 3 CROISER : intersect 4 DILUER : dilute — *vi* : cut — **se couper** *vr* 1 : cut oneself 2 : intersect — **coupe** [kup] *nf* 1 : fruit dish 2 : cup (in sports) 3 *or* ~ **de cheveux** : haircut 4 *or* ~ **transversale** : cross section — **coupe-ongles** [kupɔ̃gl] *nms & pl* : nail clippers — **coupe-papier** [kuppapje] *nms & pl* : letter opener

couple [kupl] *nm* : couple — **coupler** [kuple] *vt* : pair (up)

coupon [kupɔ̃] *nm* : coupon

coupure [kupyr] *nf* 1 : cut 2 BILLET : banknote

cour [kur] *nf* 1 : court (of law) 2 : courtyard 3 : courtship 4 ~ **de récréation** : playground

courage [kuraʒ] *nm* : courage — **courageux, -geuse** [kuraʒø, -ʒøz] *adj* : courageous

courant, -rante [kurɑ̃, -rɑ̃t] *adj* 1 : (electric) current 2 COMMUN : common, usual — **courant** *nm* 1 : (electric) current 2 : course (of the day, etc.) 3 ~ **d'air** : draft 4 **être au** ~ **de** : know all about — **couramment** [kuramɑ̃] *adv* 1 : fluently 2 SOUVENT : commonly

courbature [kurbatyr] *nf* : stiffness, ache — **courbaturé, -rée** [kurbatyre] *adj* : aching

courber [kurbe] *vt* : bend, curve — **se courber** *vr* : bend, curve — **courbe** [kurb] *nf* : curve

coureur, -reuse [kurœr, -røz] *n* : runner

courge [kurʒ] *nf* : gourd — **courgette** [kurʒɛt] *nf* : zucchini

courir [kurir] {23} *vt* 1 : run in, compete in 2 FRÉQUENTER : frequent 3 PARCOURIR : roam through 4 : run (a risk, etc.) — *vi* 1 : run 2 SE PRESSER : rush

couronner [kurɔne] *vt* : crown — **couronne** [kurɔn] *nf* 1 : crown 2 : wreath — **couronnement** [kurɔnmɑ̃] *nm* 1 : coronation 2 : crowning achievement

courrier [kurje] *nm* 1 : mail, correspondence 2 ~ **électronique** : electronic mail, e-mail — **courriel** [kurjɛl] *nm Can* : electronic mail

courroie [kurwa] *nf* : strap, belt

cours [kur] *nm* 1 : course, class 2 : flow, current 3 **au** ~ **de** : in the course of, during 4 ~ **d'eau** : river, stream 5 ~ **du soir** : night school 6 **en** ~ : in progress

course [kurs] *nf* 1 : running 2 COMPÉTITION : race, competition 3 COMMISSION : errand 4 **faire des** ~**s** : go shopping

court, courte [kur, kurt] *adj* : short — **court**

[kur] *adv* 1 **à** ~ **de** : short of 2 **s'arrêter** ~ : stop short 3 **tout** ~ : simply — **court** *nm* : court (in sports) — **court-circuit** [kursirkɥi] *nm, pl* **courts-circuits** : short circuit

courtier, -tière [kurtje, -tjɛr] *n* : broker, agent

courtiser [kurtize] *vt* : court, woo

courtois, -toise [kurtwa, -twaz] *adj* : courteous — **courtoisie** [kurtwazi] *nf* : courtesy

cousin, -sine [kuzɛ̃, -zin] *n* : cousin

coussin [kusɛ̃] *nm* : cushion

coût [ku] *nm* : cost — **coûtant** [kutɑ̃] **à prix** ~ *adv phr* : at cost

couteau [kuto] *nm, pl* **-teaux** 1 : knife 2 ~ **de poche** : pocketknife

coûter [kute] *vt* 1 : cost 2 ~ **cher** : be expensive 3 **ça coûte combien?** : how much is it? — *vi* : cost — **coûteux, -teuse** [kutø, -tøz] *adj* : costly

coutume [kutym] *nf* : custom — **coutumier, -mière** [kutymje, -mjɛr] *adj* : customary

couture [kutyr] *nf* 1 : sewing 2 : dressmaking 3 : seam (of a garment) — **couturier** [kutyrje] *nm* : fashion designer — **couturière** [kutyrjɛr] *nf* : dressmaker

couvée [kuve] *nf* : brood

couvent [kuvɑ̃] *nm* : convent

couver [kuve] *vt* 1 : hatch 2 PROTÉGER : overprotect 3 : be coming down with (an illness) — *vi* 1 : smolder 2 : be brewing

couvercle [kuvɛrkl] *nm* 1 : lid, cover 2 : top (of a spray can, etc.)

couvert, -verte [kuvɛr, -vɛrt] *adj* 1 : covered 2 NUAGEUX : overcast — **couvert** *nm* 1 : place setting (at a table) 2 ~**s** *nmpl* : flatware 3 **à** ~ : under cover — **couverture** [kuvɛrtyr] *nf* 1 : cover (of a book, etc.) 2 : blanket 3 : roofing 4 : news coverage

couveuse [kuvøz] *nf* : incubator

couvrir [kuvrir] {83} *vt* : cover — **se couvrir** *vr* 1 : dress warmly 2 : become overcast 3 ~ **de** : be covered with — **couvre-feu** [kuvrəfø] *nm, pl* **couvre-feux** : curfew — **couvre-lit** [kuvrəli] *nm, pl* **couvre-lits** : bedspread

cow-boy [kɔbɔj] *nm, pl* **cow-boys** : cowboy

coyote [kɔjɔt] *nm* : coyote

crabe [krab] *nm* : crab

cracher [kraʃe] *v* : spit

craie [krɛ] *nf* : chalk

craindre [krɛ̃dr] {65} *vt* 1 REDOUTER : fear, be afraid of 2 ~ **que** : regret that, fear that — **crainte** [krɛ̃t] *nf* 1 : fear, dread 2 **de** ~ **que** : for fear that — **craintif, -tive** [krɛ̃tif, -tiv] *adj* : fearful, timid

crampe [krɑ̃p] *nf* : cramp

crampon [krɑ̃pɔ̃] *nm* : clamp — **cramponner** [krɑ̃pɔne] *v* **se cramponner** *vr* ~ **à** : cling to

cran [krɑ̃] *nm fam* : courage, guts

crâne [kran] *nm* : skull

crapaud [krapo] *nm* : toad

craquer [krake] *vi* **1** : crack, snap, creak **2** SE DÉCHIRER : tear, rip **3** *fam* : break down — **craquement** [krakmã] *nm* : crack, creak

crasse [kras] *nf* : filth — **crasseux, -seuse** [krasø, -søz] *adj* : filthy

cratère [krater] *nm* : crater

cravache [kravaʃ] *nf* : horsewhip

cravate [kravat] *nf* : necktie

crayon [krɛjɔ̃] *nm* **1** : pencil **2** ~ à bille : ballpoint pen

créancier, -cière [kreãsje, -sjɛr] *n* : creditor

créateur, -trice [kreatœr, -tris] *adj* : creative — ~ *n* : creator — **création** [kreasjɔ̃] *nf* : creation — **créativité** [kreativite] *nf* : creativity

créature [kreatyr] *nf* : creature

crèche [krɛʃ] *nf France* : nursery

crédible [kredibl] *adj* : credible — **crédibilité** [-dibilite] *nf* : credibility

crédit [kredi] *nm* **1** : credit **2** ~s *nmpl* : funds — **créditer** [kredite] *vt* : credit — **créditeur, -trice** [kreditœr, -tris] *n* : creditor

crédule [kredyl] *adj* : credulous — **crédulité** [-dylite] *nf* : credulity

créer [kree] {89} *vt* : create

crémaillère [kremajɛr] *nf* **pendre la** ~ : have a housewarming (party)

crème [krɛm] *nf* **1** : cream **2** ~ glacée *Can* : ice cream — **crémerie** [krɛmri] *nf France* : dairy shop — **crémeux, -meuse** [kremø, -møz] *adj* : creamy

créneau [kreno] *nm, pl* -neaux **1** : slot, gap **2 faire un** ~ : back into a parking space

crêpe [krɛp] *nf* : pancake, crepe — ~ *nm* : crepe (fabric)

crépiter [krepite] *vi* : crackle — **crépitement** [krepitmã] *nm* **1** : crackling **2** : patter (of rain)

crépu, -pue [krepy] *adj* : frizzy

crépuscule [krepyskyl] *nm* : twilight, dusk

cresson [krɛsɔ̃] *nm* : watercress

crête [krɛt] *nf* **1** : crest, peak **2** : comb (of a rooster)

crétin, -tine [kretɛ̃, -tin] *n* : idiot

creuser [krøze] *vt* : dig, hollow out — **se creuser** *vr* ~ la tête *fam* : rack one's brains — **creux, creuse** [krø, krøz] *adj* **1** : hollow **2** : sunken (of eyes) — **creux** *nm* **1** CAVITÉ : hollow, cavity **2** : pit (of the stomach)

crevaison [krəvɛzɔ̃] *nf* : flat tire

crevasse [krəvas] *nf* : crevice, crack

crever [krəve] {52} *vt* : burst, puncture **2** *fam* : wear out — *vi* **1** : burst **2** ~ de faim : be starving — **crevé, -vée** [krəve] *adj* **1** : punctured, flat (of a tire) **2** *fam* : dead tired

crevette [krəvɛt] *nf* : shrimp, prawn

cri [kri] *nm* **1** : cry, shout **2 le dernier** ~ : the latest thing — **criant, criante** [krijã, krijãt] *adj* : glaring, obvious — **criard, criarde** [krijar, krijard] *adj* **1** : shrill **2** : gaudy

cribler [krible] *vt* **1** : sift, screen **2** ~ de : riddle with — **crible** [kribl] *nm* : sieve

cric [krik] *nm* : (car) jack

cricket [krikɛt] *nm* : cricket (sport)

crier [krije] {96} *vi* : shout, yell — *vt* : shout (out)

crime [krim] *nm* **1** : crime **2** MEURTRE : murder — **criminel, -nelle** [kriminɛl] *adj* : criminal — ~ *n* **1** : criminal **2** MEURTRIER : murderer

crinière [krinjɛr] *nf* : mane

criquet [krikɛ] *nm* : locust (insect)

crise [kriz] *nf* **1** : crisis **2** ACCÈS : fit, outburst **3** ~ cardiaque : heart attack

crispé, -pée [krispe] *adj* : tense, clenched

crisser [krise] *vi* : screech, squeal (of tires)

cristal [kristal] *nm, pl* -taux [kristo] : crystal

critère [kritɛr] *nm* : criterion

critique [kritik] *adj* : critical — ~ *nf* **1** : criticism **2** : critique, review — ~ *nmf* : critic, reviewer — **critiquer** [kritike] *vt* : criticize

croasser [krɔase] *vi* : caw, croak

croc [kro] *nm* : fang

crochet [krɔʃɛ] *nm* **1** : hook **2** : square bracket **3 faire du** ~ : crochet **4 faire un** ~ : make a detour — **crochu, -chue** [krɔʃy] *adj* : hooked

crocodile [krɔkɔdil] *nm* : crocodile

croire [krwar] {24} *vt* **1** : believe **2** PENSER : think, believe — *vi* ~ à *or* ~ en : believe in

croisade [krwazad] *nf* : crusade

croiser [krwaze] *vt* **1** : cross **2** : intersect **3** RENCONTRER : pass, meet **4** : crossbreed — *vi* : cruise (of a ship) — **se croiser** *vr* **1** : cross, cut across **2** : pass each other — **croisement** [krwazmã] *nm* **1** : junction **2** : crossbreeding — **croiseur** [krwazœr] *nm* : cruiser (ship) — **croisière** [krwazjɛr] *nf* : cruise

croître [krwatr] {25} *vi* : grow, increase — **croissant, -sante** [krwasã, -sãt] *adj* : growing, increasing — **croissant** *nm* : croissant — **croissance** [krwasãs] *nf* : growth, development

croix [krwa] *nf* : cross

croquer [krɔke] *vt* : crunch, munch — *vi* ~ dans : bite into (an apple, etc.) — **croquant, -quante** [krɔkã, -kãt] *adj* : crunchy — **croque–monsieur** [krɔkməsjø] *nms & pl* : grilled ham and cheese sandwich

croquis [krɔki] *nm* : sketch

crosse [krɔs] *nf* : butt (of a gun)

crotte [krɔt] *nf* : droppings *pl*, dung — **crottin** [krɔtɛ̃] *nm* : (horse) manure

crouler [krule] *vi* S'EFFONDRER : crumble, collapse

croupir [krupir] *vi* **1** : stagnate **2** ~ **dans** : wallow in

croustillant, -lante [krustijã, -jãt] *adj* : crisp, crispy

croûte [krut] *nf* **1** : (pie) crust **2** : scab — **croûton** [krutɔ̃] *nm* **1** : crust (of bread) **2** : crouton

croyance [krwajãs] *nf* : belief — **croyant, croyante** [krwajã, -jãt] *n* : believer

cru, crue [kry] *adj* **1** : raw, uncooked **2** OSÉ : crude **3** : harsh (of light, etc.) — **cru** *nm* **1** VIGNOBLE : vineyard **2** : vintage (of wine)

cruauté [kryote] *nf* : cruelty

cruche [kryʃ] *nf* : jug, pitcher

crucial, -ciale [krysjal] *adj, mpl* **-ciaux** [-sjo] : crucial

crucifier [krysifje] {96} *vt* : crucify — **crucifix** [krysifi] *nms & pl* : crucifix — **crucifixion** [krysifiksjɔ̃] *nf* : crucifixion

crudités [krydite] *nfpl* : raw vegetables

crue [kry] *nf* : rise in water level

cruel, cruelle [kryɛl] *adj* : cruel — **cruellement** [-ɛlmã] *adv* : cruelly

crustacés [krystase] *nmpl* : shellfish

crypte [kript] *nf* : crypt

cube [kyb] *adj* : cubic — ~ *nm* : cube — **cubique** [kybik] *adj* : cubic

cueillir [kœjir] {3} *vt* : pick, gather — **cueillette** [kœjɛt] *nf* : picking, gathering

cuillère *or* **cuiller** [kɥijer] *nf* **1** : spoon **2** : spoonful **3** ~ **à thé** *or* ~ **à café** : teaspoon — **cuillerée** [kɥijere] *nf* **1** : spoonful **2** ~ **à café** : teaspoonful

cuir [kɥir] *nm* **1** : leather **2** ~ **chevelu** : scalp

cuire [kɥir] {49} *vt* : cook, bake — *vi* : cook

cuisine [kɥizin] *nf* **1** : kitchen **2** : cooking, cuisine **3 faire la** ~ : cook — **cuisiner** [kɥizine] *v* **1** : cook **2** *fam* : interrogate, grill — **cuisinier, -nière** [kɥizinje, -njɛr] *n* : chef, cook — **cuisinière** [kɥizinjer] *nf* : stove

cuisse [kɥis] *nf* **1** : thigh **2** : leg (in cooking)

cuisson [kɥisɔ̃] *nf* : cooking, baking

cuit, cuite [kɥi, kɥit] *adj* **1** : cooked **2 bien** ~ : well-done

cuivre [kɥivr] *nm* **1** : copper **2** *or* ~ **jaune** : brass **3** ~**s** *nmpl* : brass (musical instruments)

culbute [kylbyt] *nf* **1** : somersault **2** CHUTE : tumble, fall

cul–de–sac [kydsak] *nm, pl* **culs–de–sac** : dead end

culinaire [kyliner] *adj* : culinary

culminer [kylmine] *vi* : culminate, peak — **culminant, -nante** [kylminã, -nãt] *adj* **point culminant** : high point

culot [kylo] *nm fam* **avoir du** ~ : have a lot of nerve

culotte [kylɔt] *nf* **1** PANTALON : pants *pl* **2** : panties *pl*

culpabilité [kylpabilite] *nf* : guilt

culte [kylt] *nm* **1** VÉNÉRATION : worship, cult **2** : religion

cultiver [kyltive] *vt* : cultivate, grow — **cultivateur, -trice** [kyltivatœr, -tris] *n* AGRICULTEUR : farmer — **cultivé, -vée** [kyltive] *adj* **1** : cultivated **2** : cultured, educated

culture [kyltyr] *nf* **1** CONNAISSANCES : culture **2** : cultivation, growing **3** : crop **4** ~ **physique** : physical education — **culturel, -relle** [kyltyrɛl] *adj* : cultural — **culturisme** [kyltyrism] *nm* : bodybuilding

cumuler [kymyle] *vt* **1** : accumulate **2** : hold concurrently — **cumulatif, -tive** [kymylatif, -tiv] *adj* : cumulative

cupide [kypid] *adj* : greedy — **cupidité** [kypidite] *nf* : greed

cure [kyr] *nf* : treatment, cure

curé [kyre] *nm* : pastor, parish priest

curer [kyre] *v* **se curer** *vr* : clean (one's nails, teeth, etc.) — **cure–dent** *or* **cure–dents** [kyrdã] *nm, pl* **cure–dents** : toothpick

curieux, -rieuse [kyrjø, -rjøz] *adj* **1** : curious **2** ÉTRANGE : strange, odd — ~ *n* : onlooker — **curieusement** [kyrjøzmã] *adv* : curiously, strangely — **curiosité** [kyrjɔzite] *nf* : curiosity

curry [kyri] *nm* : curry

curseur [kyrsœr] *nm* : cursor

cuver [kyve] *vi* : ferment — **cuve** [kyv] *nf* : vat, tank — **cuvée** [kyve] *nf* : vintage — **cuvette** [kyvɛt] *nf* : basin

cyanure [sjanyr] *nm* : cyanide

cycle [sikl] *nm* : cycle — **cyclique** [siklik] *adj* : cyclic, cyclical

cycliste [siklist] *nmf* : cyclist, bicyclist — **cyclisme** [siklism] *nm* : cycling, bicycling

cyclomoteur [siklomotœr] *nm* : moped

cyclone [siklon] *nm* : cyclone

cygne [siɲ] *nm* : swan

cylindre [silɛ̃dr] *nm* : cylinder — **cylindrique** [silɛ̃drik] *adj* : cylindrical

cymbale [sɛ̃bal] *nf* : cymbal

cynique [sinik] *adj* : cynical — ~ *nmf* : cynic — **cynisme** [sinism] *nm* : cynicism

cyprès [siprɛ] *nm* : cypress

D

d [de] *nm* : d, fourth letter of the alphabet
dactylographier [daktilɔgrafje] {96} *vt* : type — **dactylo** [daktilo] *or* **dactylographe** [daktilɔgraf] *nmf* : typist
daigner [deɲe] *vt* : deign
daim [dɛ̃] *nm* 1 : deer 2 : suede
dalle [dal] *nf* : slab, paving stone
daltonien, -nienne [daltɔnjɛ̃, -njɛn] *adj* : color-blind
dame [dam] *nf* 1 : lady 2 : queen (in games) 3 ~s *nfpl or* **jeu de** ~s : checkers — **damier** [damje] *nm* : checkerboard
dandiner [dɑ̃dine] *v* **se dandiner** *vr* : waddle
danger [dɑ̃ʒe] *nm* : danger — **dangereux, -reuse** [dɑ̃ʒrø, -røz] *adj* : dangerous
dans [dɑ̃] *prep* 1 : in 2 : into, inside 3 : from, out of 4 ~ **la journée** : during the day 5 ~ **les 20 ans** : in about 20 years 6 **monter** ~ **l'auto** : get into the car
danser [dɑ̃se] *v* : dance — **danse** [dɑ̃s] *nf* : dance, dancing — **danseur, -seuse** [dɑ̃sœr, -søz] *n* : dancer
dard [dar] *nm* 1 : stinger (of an insect) 2 *Can* : dart
date [dat] *nf* : date — **dater** [date] *vi* 1 : be dated, be old-fashioned 2 ~ **de** : date from
datte [dat] *nf* : date (fruit)
dauphin [dofɛ̃] *nm* : dolphin
davantage [davɑ̃taʒ] *adv* 1 PLUS : more 2 : (any) longer
de [də] (**d'** *before vowels and mute h*) *prep* 1 : of 2 (*before infinitive*) : to, of 3 **de l', de la, du, des** : some, any 4 ~ **Molière** : by Molière 5 ~ **Montréal** : from Montreal 6 **moins** ~ **cinq** : less than five
dé [de] *nm* 1 : die, dice *pl* 2 ~ **à coudre** : thimble
déambuler [deɑ̃byle] *vi* : stroll, wander about
débâcle [debakl] *nf* : fiasco
déballer [debale] *vt* : unpack, unwrap
débandade [debɑ̃dad] *nf* : stampede
débarquer [debarke] *vt* : unload (goods) — *vi* : disembark (of passengers) — **débarquement** [debarkəmɑ̃] *nm* 1 : unloading 2 : landing
débarrasser [debarase] *vt* : clear, rid — **se débarrasser** *vr* ~ **de** : get rid of
débarrer [debare] *vt Can* : unlock
débattre [debatr] {12} *vt* : debate, discuss — **se débattre** *vr* : struggle — **débat** [deba] *nm* 1 : debate, discussion 2 ~s *nmpl* : proceedings
débaucher [deboʃe] *vt* 1 CORROMPRE : cor-

rupt 2 LICENCIER : lay off — **débauche** [deboʃ] *nf* : debauchery
débiliter [debilite] *vt* : debilitate — **débile** [debil] *adj fam* : stupid
débiter [debite] *vt* 1 : debit 2 VENDRE : sell, retail 3 FOURNIR : produce 4 : recite, reel off — **débit** [debi] *nm* 1 : debit 2 : turnover (of merchandise, etc.) 3 : (rate of) flow — **débiteur, -trice** [debitœr, -tris] *n* : debtor
déblayer [debleje] {11} *vt* : clear (away)
débloquer [deblɔke] *vt* : free, release
déboires [debwar] *nmpl* ENNUIS : difficulties
déboîter [debwate] *vt* : dislocate (a joint) — *vi* : pull out, change lanes
débonnaire [debɔnɛr] *adj* : easygoing, good-natured
déborder [debɔrde] *vi* : overflow — *vt* 1 : extend beyond 2 SUBMERGER : overwhelm — **débordé, -dée** [debɔrde] *adj* : overwhelmed
déboucher [debuʃe] *vt* : open, unblock — *vi* ~ **sur** : open onto, lead to — **débouché** [debuʃe] *nm* 1 : outlet, market 2 : opportunity, prospect
débourser [deburse] *vt* : pay out
debout [dəbu] *adv* 1 : standing up 2 : upright, on end 3 : up, out of bed
déboutonner [debutɔne] *vt* : unbutton, undo
débraillé, -lée [debraje] *adj* : disheveled
débrancher [debrɑ̃ʃe] *vt* : unplug, disconnect
débrayer [debreje] {11} *vi* 1 : disengage the clutch 2 : go on strike — **débrayage** [debrejaʒ] *nm* 1 : disengaging the clutch 2 : strike, walkout
débris [debri] *nms & pl* 1 : fragment 2 ~ *nmpl* : rubbish, scraps
débrouiller [debruje] *vt* DÉMÊLER : disentangle — **se débrouiller** *vr* : manage, cope — **débrouillard, -larde** [debrujar, -jard] *adj* : resourceful
débuter [debyte] *v* : begin — **début** [deby] *nm* 1 : beginning 2 ~s *nmpl* : debut, early stages — **débutant, -tante** [debytɑ̃, -tɑ̃t] *n* : beginner, novice
décacheter [dekaʃte] {8} *vt* : unseal, open
décadence [dekadɑ̃s] *nf* : decadence — **décadent, -dente** [dekadɑ̃, -dɑ̃t] *adj* : decadent
décaféiné, -née [dekafeine] *adj* : decaffeinated
décalage [dekalaʒ] *nm* 1 : gap, interval 2 ~ **horaire** : time difference
décamper [dekɑ̃pe] *vi* : clear out
décaper [dekape] *vt* 1 : clean, scour 2

: strip (paint, etc.) — **décapant** [dekɑpɑ̃]
nm : paint stripper

décapotable [dekapɔtabl] *adj & nf* : convertible

décapsuleur [dekapsylœr] *nm* : bottle opener

décéder [desede] {87} *vi* : die — **décédé, -dée** [desede] *adj* : deceased

déceler [desle] {20} *vt* **1** DÉCOUVRIR : detect **2** RÉVÉLER : reveal

décembre [desɑ̃br] *nm* : December

décence [desɑ̃s] *nf* : decency

décennie [deseni] *nf* : decade

décent, -cente [desɑ̃, -sɑ̃t] *adj* : decent

déception [desɛpsjɔ̃] *nf* : disappointment

décerner [deserne] *vt* : award

décès [desɛ] *nm* : death

décevoir [desəvwar] {26} *vt* : disappoint — **décevant, -vante** [desəvɑ̃, -vɑ̃t] *adj* : disappointing

déchaîner [defene] *vt* : unleash — **se déchaîner** *vr* : erupt, burst out — **déchaîné, -née** [defene] *adj* : raging, unbridled — **déchaînement** [defɛnmɑ̃] *nm* : outburst

décharger [defarʒe] {17} *vt* **1** : unload **2** : discharge (a firearm, etc.) **3** SOULAGER : relieve, unburden — **décharge** [defarʒ] *nf* **1** : discharge **2** : garbage dump

décharné, -née [defarne] *adj* : gaunt

déchausser [defose] *v* **se déchausser** *vr* : take off one's shoes

déchéance [defeɑ̃s] *nf* : decay, decline

déchet [defɛ] *nm* **1** : scrap **2** ~ s : waste, refuse

déchiffrer [defifre] *vt* : decipher

déchiqueter [defikte] {8} *vt* : tear into pieces

déchirer [defire] *vt* : tear up, tear apart — **déchirant, -rante** [defirɑ̃, -rɑ̃t] *adj* : heartrending — **déchirure** [defiryr] *nf* : tear

déchoir [defwar] {27} *vi* : fall, decline (in prestige)

décider [deside] *vt* **1** : decide **2** CONVAINCRE : persuade **3** ~ **de** : decide on, determine — **se décider** *vr* : make up one's mind — **décidé, -dée** [deside] *adj* **1** : decided, settled **2** DÉTERMINÉ : determined — **décidément** [desidemɑ̃] *adv* : definitely, really

décimal, -male [desimal] *adj, mpl* **-maux** [-mo] : decimal — **décimale** *nf* : decimal

décision [desizjɔ̃] *nf* **1** : decision **2** : decisiveness — **décisif, -sive** [desizif, -ziv] *adj* : decisive

déclarer [deklare] *vt* **1** PROCLAMER : declare **2** : register, report — **se déclarer** *vr* : break out (of fire, etc.) — **déclaration** [deklarasjɔ̃] *nf* : declaration, statement

déclencher [deklɑ̃fe] *vt* **1** : set off, trigger **2** LANCER : launch — **déclenchement** [deklɑ̃fmɑ̃] *nm* : onset, outbreak

déclic [deklik] *nm* : click

décliner [dekline] *v* : decline — **déclin** [deklɛ̃] *nm* : decline

décoller [dekɔle] *vt* : unstick, remove — *vi* : take off (of an airplane, etc.) — **décollage** [dekɔlaʒ] *nm* : takeoff

décolleté, -tée [dekɔlte] *adj* : low-cut

décolorer [dekɔlore] *vt* : bleach — **se décolorer** *vr* : fade

décombres [dekɔ̃br] *nmpl* : rubble, debris

décommander [dekɔmɑ̃de] *vt* : cancel

décomposer [dekɔ̃poze] *vt* : decompose — **décomposition** [dekɔ̃pozisjɔ̃] *nf* : decomposition, rotting

décompter [dekɔ̃te] *vt* **1** : count, calculate **2** DÉDUIRE : deduct — **décompte** [dekɔ̃t] *nm* **1** : count, breakdown **2** DÉDUCTION : deduction

déconcerter [dekɔ̃serte] *vt* : disconcert

décongeler [dekɔ̃ʒle] {20} *v* : thaw, defrost

déconnecter [dekɔnɛkte] *vt* : disconnect

déconseiller [dekɔ̃seje] *vt* : dissuade, advise against — **déconseillé, -lée** [dekɔ̃seje] *adj* : inadvisable

décontracté, -tée [dekɔ̃trakte] *adj* : relaxed, casual

décorer [dekore] *vt* ORNER : decorate — **décor** [dekɔr] *nm* **1** : decor **2** : scenery (in theater, etc.) — **décoration** [dekɔrasjɔ̃] *nf* : decoration — **décorateur, -trice** [dekɔratœr, -tris] *n* : interior decorator — **décoratif, -tive** [dekɔratif, -tiv] *adj* : decorative

décortiquer [dekɔrtike] *vt* : shell, hull

découler [dekule] *vi* : result, follow

découper [dekupe] *vt* **1** : cut up, carve **2** : cut out (a picture)

décourager [dekuraʒe] {17} *vt* : discourage — **se décourager** *vr* : lose heart — **découragement** [dekuraʒmɑ̃] *nm* : discouragement

décousu, -sue [dekuzy] *adj* **1** : unstitched **2** : disjointed, disconnected

découvrir [dekuvrir] {83} *vt* **1** : discover **2** : uncover — **se découvrir** *vr* : clear up (of weather) — **découvert** [dekuvɛr] *nm* : overdraft (in banking) — **découverte** [dekuvɛrt] *nf* : discovery

décrépit, -pite [dekrepi, -pit] *adj* : decrepit

décret [dekrɛ] *nm* : decree, edict — **décréter** [dekrete] {87} *vt* : decree

décrire [dekrir] {33} *vt* : describe

décrocher [dekrɔfe] *vt* **1** : unhook, take down **2** *fam* : get, land (a job, etc.) — *vi fam* : drop out, give up

décroître [dekrwatr] {25} *vi* : decrease, decline

déçu, -çue [desy] *adj* : disappointed

dédaigner [dedeɲe] *vt* : disdain, scorn — **dédaigneux, -neuse** [dedɛɲø, -ɲøz] *adj*

: disdainful, scornful — **dédain** [dedɛ̃] *nm* MÉPRIS : disdain, scorn

dédale [dedal] *nm* : maze, labyrinth

dedans [dədɑ̃] *adv* **1** : inside, in **2 en ~** : on the inside, within — **~** *nm* : inside, interior

dédicace [dedikas] *nf* : dedication — **dédicacer** [dedikase] {6} *vt* : inscribe, dedicate

dédier [dedje] {96} *vt* : dedicate

dédommager [dedɔmaʒe] {17} *vt* : compensate — **dédommagement** [dedɔmaʒmɑ̃] *nm* INDEMNITÉ : compensation

déduire [deduir] {49} *vt* **1** : deduct **2** CONCLURE : deduce, infer — **déduction** [dedyksjɔ̃] *nf* : deduction

déesse [dees] *nf* : goddess

défaillir [defajir] {93} *vi* : weaken, fail — **défaillance** [defajɑ̃s] *nf* : failing, weakness

défaire [defɛr] {42} *vt* **1** : undo **2** : unpack — **se défaire** *vr* **1** : come undone **2 ~ de** : part with — **défait, -faite** [defɛ, -fɛt] *adj* **1** : undone **2** : defeated — **défaite** *nf* : defeat

défaut [defo] *nm* **1** IMPERFECTION : flaw, defect **2** FAIBLESSE : shortcoming **3** MANQUE : lack **4 faire ~** : be lacking

défavoriser [defavɔrize] *vt* : put at a disadvantage — **défavorable** [defavɔrabl] *adj* : unfavorable

défectueux, -tueuse [defɛktɥø, -tɥøz] *adj* : defective, faulty — **défectuosité** [defɛktɥozite] *nf* **1** : defectiveness **2** DÉFAUT : defect, fault

défendre [defɑ̃dr] {63} *vt* **1** : defend **2** PROTÉGER : protect, uphold **3** INTERDIRE : forbid — **se défendre** *vr* : defend oneself — **défendeur, -deresse** [defɑ̃dœr, -drɛs] *n* : defendant

défense [defɑ̃s] *nf* **1** : defense **2** INTERDICTION : prohibition **3** : tusk (of an elephant, etc.) — **défenseur** [defɑ̃sœr] *nm* : defender — **défensif, -sive** [defɑ̃sif, -siv] *adj* : defensive — **défensive** *nf* : defensive

défi [defi] *nm* : challenge, dare

déficit [defisit] *nm* : deficit

défier [defje] {96} *vt* **1** : challenge, dare **2** BRAVER : defy

défigurer [defigyre] *vt* **1** : disfigure **2 ~ les faits** : distort the facts

défiler [defile] *vi* **1** : march, parade **2** : stream past **3** : scroll (on a computer) — **défilé** [defile] *nm* **1** : parade, procession **2** : stream (of visitors, etc.)

définir [definir] *vt* : define — **défini, -nie** [defini] *adj* **1** : defined **2** : definite — **définitif, -tive** [definitif, -tiv] *adj* : definitive, final — **définition** [definisjɔ̃] *nf* : definition — **définitivement** [definitivmɑ̃] *adv* : definitively, for good

défoncer [defɔ̃se] {6} *vt* : smash, break down

déformer [defɔrme] *vt* : deform, distort — **déformation** [defɔrmasjɔ̃] *nf* : distortion

défraîchi, -chie [defreʃi] *adj* : faded, worn

défrayer [defreje] {11} *vt* : pay (s.o.'s expenses)

défunt, -funte [defœ̃, -fœ̃t] *adj & n* : deceased

dégager [degaʒe] {17} *vt* **1** : free **2** DÉBARRASSER : clear (the way, etc.) **3** EXTRAIRE : bring out **4** ÉMETTRE : emit — **se dégager** *vr* **1** : clear (up) **2** : emanate **3 ~ de** : get free of — **dégagé, -gée** [degaʒe] *adj* **1** : clear, open **2** : free and easy

dégâts [dega] *nmpl* : damage

dégeler [deʒle] {20} *v* : thaw — **dégel** [deʒɛl] *nm* : thaw

dégénérer [deʒenere] {87} *vi* : degenerate

dégingandé, -dée [deʒɛ̃gɑ̃de] *adj* : lanky

dégivrer [deʒivre] *vt* : defrost

dégonfler [degɔ̃fle] *vt* : deflate — **se dégonfler** *vr* : deflate, go flat

dégoûter [degute] *vt* : disgust — **se dégoûter** *vr* **~ de** : get sick of — **dégoût** [degu] *nm* : disgust — **dégoûtant, -tante** [degutɑ̃, -tɑ̃t] *adj* : disgusting

dégoutter [degute] *vi* : drip

dégrader [degrade] *vt* : degrade

dégrafer [degrafe] *vt* : unhook

degré [dəgre] *nm* **1** : degree **2** : step (of a staircase) **3 par ~s** : gradually

dégueulasse [degœlas] *adj fam* : disgusting

déguiser [degize] *vt* : disguise — **se déguiser** *vr* **~ en** : dress up as — **déguisement** [degizmɑ̃] *nm* : disguise

déguster [degyste] *vt* **1** : taste **2** SAVOURER : savor, enjoy

dehors [dəɔr] *adv* **1** : outside **2 en ~** : (toward the) outside **3 en ~ de** : outside of, apart from — **~** *nms & pl* : outside, exterior

déjà [deʒa] *adv* : already

déjeuner [deʒœne] *nm* **1** : lunch **2** *Can* : breakfast — **~** *vi* **1** : have lunch **2** *Can* : have breakfast

déjouer [deʒwe] *vt* : thwart

delà [dəla] *adv* → **au–delà, par–delà**

délabrer [delabre] *v* **se délabrer** *vr* : become dilapidated — **délabrement** [delabrəmɑ̃] *nm* : dilapidation, disrepair

délai [delɛ] *nm* **1** : time limit **2** : extension (of time) **3** : waiting period

délaisser [delese] *vt* **1** ABANDONNER : abandon, desert **2** : neglect

délasser [delase] *vt* : relax — **se délasser** *vr* : relax

délayer [deleje] {11} *vt* **1** DILUER : dilute **2** : drag out (a speech, etc.)

déléguer [delege] {87} *vt* : delegate — **délégué, -guée** [delege] *n* : delegate — **délégation** [delegasjɔ̃] *nf* : delegation

délibérer [delibere] {87} *vi* : deliberate — **délibéré, -rée** [delibere] *adj* **1** : deliberate **2** DÉCIDÉ : determined

délicat, -cate [delika, -kat] *adj* **1** : delicate **2** : tactful **3** EXIGEANT : fussy — **délicatement** [delikatmɑ̃] *adv* **1** : delicately **2** : finely, precisely — **délicatesse** [delikatɛs] *nf* **1** : delicacy **2** : tactfulness

délice [delis] *nm* : delight — **délicieux, -cieuse** [delisjø, -sjøz] *adj* : delicious, delightful

délier [delje] {96} *vt* **1** : untie **2** ~ **de** : release from

délimiter [delimite] *vt* : demarcate

délinquant, -quante [delɛ̃kɑ̃, -kɑ̃t] *adj & n* : delinquent

délire [delir] *nm* **1** : delirium **2 en** ~ : delirious, frenzied — **délirant, -rante** [delirɑ̃, -rɑ̃t] *adj* **1** : delirious **2** : frenzied — **délirer** [delire] *vi* **1** : be delirious **2** : rave

délit [deli] *nm* : crime, offense

délivrer [delivre] *vt* **1** : set free **2** : issue, award **3** ~ **de** : relieve of — **délivrance** [delivrɑ̃s] *nf* **1** : freeing, release **2** : delivery, issue **3** SOULAGEMENT : relief

déloger [delɔʒe] {17} *vt* **1** : evict **2** : remove, dislodge

déloyal, -loyale [delwajal] *adj, mpl* **-loyaux** [-jo] **1** : disloyal **2** : unfair — **déloyauté** [delwajote] *nf* : disloyalty

delta [dɛlta] *nm* : delta

déluge [delyʒ] *nm* **1** : deluge, flood **2** AVERSE : downpour

demain [dəmɛ̃] *adv & nm* : tomorrow

demander [dəmɑ̃de] *vt* **1** : ask for, request **2** : ask (about) **3** NÉCESSITER : call for, require — **se demander** *vr* : wonder — **demande** [dəmɑ̃d] *nf* **1** : request **2** : application (form) **3 l'offre et la** ~ : supply and demand

démanger [demɑ̃ʒe] {17} *vi* : itch — **démangeaison** [demɑ̃ʒezɔ̃] *nf* : itch, itching

démarche [demarʃ] *nf* **1** ALLURE : gait, walk **2** REQUÊTE : step, action

démarrer [demare] *v* : start (up) — **démarreur** [demarœr] *nm* : starter

démêler [demele] *vt* : disentangle — **démêlé** [demele] *nm* **1** : quarrel **2** ~**s** *nmpl* : problems, trouble

déménager [demenaʒe] {17} *v* : move, relocate — **déménagement** [demenaʒmɑ̃] *nm* : moving, relocation

démence [demɑ̃s] *nf* : madness, insanity

démener [demne] {52} *v* **se démener** *vr* : struggle, thrash about

dément, -mente [demɑ̃, -mɑ̃t] *adj* : insane, demented

démentir [demɑ̃tir] {82} *vt* : refute, deny — **démenti** [demɑ̃ti] *nm* : denial

démesuré, -rée [deməzyre] *adj* : excessive, immoderate

démettre [demɛtr] {53} *vt* : dismiss, fire — **se démettre** *vr* **1** : resign **2** : dislocate (one's shoulder, etc.)

demeurer [dəmœre] *vi* **1** (*with* **être**) : remain **2** (*with* **avoir**) : reside — **demeure** [dəmœr] *nf* : residence

demi, -mie *adj* **1** : half **2 et** ~ : and a half, half past — ~ *n* : half — **demi** *nm France* : half-pint (of beer) — **à** ~ *adv phr* : half, halfway

démission [demisjɔ̃] *nf* : resignation — **démissionner** [demisjɔne] *vi* : resign

démocratie [demɔkrasi] *nf* : democracy — **démocratique** [demɔkratik] *adj* : democratic

démodé, -dée [demɔde] *adj* : old-fashioned, out-of-date

demoiselle [demwazɛl] *nf* **1** : young lady **2** ~ **d'honneur** : bridesmaid

démolir [demɔlir] *vt* : demolish — **démolition** [demɔlisjɔ̃] *nf* : demolition

démon [demɔ̃] *nm* : demon

démonstration [demɔ̃strasjɔ̃] *nf* : demonstration — **démonstrateur, -trice** [demɔ̃stratœr, -tris] *n* : demonstrator — **démonstratif, -tive** [demɔ̃stratif, -tiv] *adj* : demonstrative

démonter [demɔ̃te] *vt* : dismantle, take down

démontrer [demɔ̃tre] *vt* : demonstrate, show

démoraliser [demɔralize] *vt* : demoralize

démunir [demynir] *vt* : deprive

dénégation [denegasjɔ̃] *nf* : denial

dénicher [deniʃe] *vt* : unearth

dénier [denje] {96} *vt* : deny

dénigrer [denigre] *vt* : disparage

dénombrer [denɔ̃bre] *vt* : count, enumerate

dénommer [denɔme] *vt* : name, call — **dénomination** [denɔminasjɔ] *nf* : name, designation

dénoncer [denɔ̃se] {6} *vt* : denounce, inform on — **dénonciation** [denɔ̃sjasjɔ̃] *nf* : denunciation

dénoter [denɔte] *vt* : denote

dénouement [denumɑ̃] *nm* : outcome

dénouer [denwe] *vt* : untie, undo

denrée [dɑ̃re] *nf* **1** : commodity **2** ~**s alimentaires** : foods

dense [dɑ̃s] *adj* : dense — **densité** [dɑ̃site] *nf* : density, denseness

dent [dɑ̃] *nf* **1** : tooth **2** : cog (of a wheel), prong (of a fork) — **dentaire** [dɑ̃tɛr] *adj* : dental

dentelé, -lée [dɑ̃tle] *adj* : jagged, serrated

dentelle [dɑ̃tɛl] *nf* : lace

dentiste [dɑ̃tist] *nmf* : dentist — **dentier** [dɑ̃tje] *nm* : dentures *pl* — **dentifrice** [dɑ̃tifris] *nm* : toothpaste — **dentition** [dɑ̃tisjɔ̃] *nf* : teeth *pl*

dénuder [denyde] *vt* **1** : make bare **2** : strip (off)

dénué, -nuée [denчe] *adj* ~ **de** : devoid of, lacking in

déodorant [deɔdɔrɑ̃] *adj & nm* : deodorant

dépanner [depane] *vt* **1** : fix, repair **2** : help out (s.o.) — **dépanneur** [depanœr] *nm Can* : convenience store

dépareillé, -lée [depareje] *adj* : odd, not matching

départ [depar] *nm* **1** : departure **2** : start (in sports)

département [departəmɑ̃] *nm* : department

départir [departir] {82} *v* **se départir** *vr* ~ **de** : abandon, depart from

dépassé, -sée [depase] *adj* : outdated, outmoded

dépasser [depase] *vt* **1** : pass, go past **2** EXCÉDER : exceed **3** SURPASSER : surpass **4 cela me dépasse!** : that's beyond me! — *vi* : stick out — **dépassement** [depasmɑ̃] *nm* : passing

dépayser [depeize] *vt* **1** : disorient **2** : provide with a change of scenery

dépecer [depəse] {6} *and* {52} *vt* : cut up, tear apart

dépêcher [depeʃe] *vt* : dispatch — **se dépêcher** *vr* : hurry up — **dépêche** [depɛʃ] *nf* : dispatch

dépeindre [depɛ̃dr] {37} *vt* : depict, describe

dépendre [depɑ̃dr] {63} *vi* ~ **de** : depend on — *vt* : take down — **dépendance** [depɑ̃dɑ̃s] *nf* : dependence — **dépendant, -dante** [depɑ̃dɑ̃, -dɑ̃t] *adj* : dependent

dépenser [depɑ̃se] *vt* **1** : spend (money) **2** : use up, expend (energy) — **se dépenser** *vr* : exert oneself — **dépens** [depɑ̃] *nmpl* **aux** ~ **de** : at the expense of — **dépense** [depɑ̃s] *nf* **1** : spending, expenditure **2** : expense — **dépensier, -sière** [depɑ̃sje, -sjɛr] *adj* : extravagant

dépérir [deperir] *vi* **1** : wither (of a plant) **2** : waste away (of a person)

dépister [depiste] *vt* **1** : detect, discover **2** : track down (a criminal)

dépit [depi] *nm* **1** : spite **2 en** ~ **de** MALGRÉ : in spite of, despite

déplacer [deplase] {6} *vt* : move, shift — **se déplacer** *vr* : move about — **déplacé, -cée** [deplase] *adj* : out of place

déplaire [deplɛr] {66} *vi* **1** : be disliked **2** ~ **à** : displease — **déplaisant, -sante** [deplɛzɑ̃, -zɑ̃t] *adj* : unpleasant

dépliant [deplijɑ̃] *nm* : brochure, pamphlet

déplier [deplije] {96} *vt* : unfold

déplorer [deplɔre] *vt* : deplore — **déplorable** [deplɔrabl] *adj* : deplorable

déployer [deplwaje] {58} *vt* **1** : deploy **2** DÉPLIER : unfold, spread out

déposer [depoze] *vt* **1** : put down **2** : deposit (a sum of money) **3** : drop off, leave **4** : register, file (a complaint) — *vi* : testify — **se déposer** *vr* : settle

dépôt [depo] *nm* **1** : deposit **2** ENTREPÔT : warehouse, store **3** : (train) station **4** ~ **d'ordures** : (garbage) dump — **dépotoir** [depɔtwar] *nm* : dump

dépouiller [depuje] *vt* ~ **qqn de** : deprive s.o. of

dépourvu, -vue [depurvy] *adj* ~ **de** : without, lacking in — **au dépourvu** *adv phr* : by surprise

déprécier [depresje] {96} *vt* **1** : devalue **2** : disparage — **se déprécier** *vr* : depreciate — **dépréciation** [depresjasjɔ̃] *nf* : depreciation

dépression [depresjɔ̃] *nf* : depression

déprimer [deprime] *vt* : depress — **déprimant, -mante** [deprimɑ̃, -mɑ̃t] *adj* : depressing — **déprimé, -mée** [deprime] *adj* : depressed, dejected

depuis [dəpчi] *prep* **1** : since **2** : from **3** ~ **deux ans** : for two years — ~ *adv* : since (then) — **depuis que** *adv phr* : (ever) since

député, -tée [depyte] *n* : representative (in government)

déraciner [derasine] *vt* : uproot

dérailler [deraje] *vi* : derail — **déraillement** [derajmɑ̃] *nm* : derailment

déraisonnable [derezɔnabl] *adj* : unreasonable

déranger [derɑ̃ʒe] {17} *vt* **1** : bother, disturb **2** DÉRÉGLER : disrupt, upset — **se déranger** *vr* : put oneself out — **dérangement** [derɑ̃ʒmɑ̃] *nm* **1** : trouble, bother **2** : (stomach) upset

déraper [derape] *vi* GLISSER : skid, slip **2** : get out of hand (of a situation)

dérégler [deregle] {87} *vt* **1** : put out of order **2** : upset, disturb — **se dérégler** *vr* : go wrong

dérision [derizjɔ̃] *nf* : derision, mockery — **dérisoire** [derizwar] *adj* : ridiculous, pathetic

dériver [derive] *vt* **1** : divert **2** ~ **de** : derive from — *vi* : drift, be adrift — **dérivé** [derive] *nm* **1** : derivation (of a word) **2** : by-product

dernier, -nière [dɛrnje, -njɛr] *adj* **1** : last, previous **2** : latest (of a novel, etc.) **3** : final, last **4** : lowest (of a step, etc.) — ~ *n* **1** : last (one) **2 ce dernier, cette dernière** : the latter — **dernièrement** [dɛrnjɛrmɑ̃] *adv* : recently

dérobé, -bée [derɔbe] *adj* : hidden — **à la dérobée** *adv phr* : on the sly

dérouler [derule] *vt* : unwind, unroll — **se dérouler** *vr* : take place — **déroulement** [derulmɑ̃] *nm* : development, progress

dérouter [derute] *vt* : disconcert, confuse — **déroute** [derut] *nf* : rout

derrière [dɛrjɛr] *adv & prep* : behind — ～ *nm* **1** : back, rear **2** *fam* : buttocks *pl*, bottom

des → **de**

dès [dɛ] *prep* **1** : from **2** ～ **lors** : from then on **3** ～ **que** : as soon as

désaccord [dezakɔr] *nm* : disagreement

désagréable [dezagreabl] *adj* DÉPLAISANT : disagreeable, unpleasant

désagréger [dezagreʒe] {64} *vt* : break up — **se désagréger** *vr* : disintegrate

désagrément [dezagremã] *nm* : annoyance

désapprouver [dezapruve] *vt* : disapprove of — **désapprobation** [dezaprɔbasjɔ̃] *nf* : disapproval

désarmer [dezarme] *vt* : disarm — **désarmement** [dezarməmã] *nm* : disarmament

désarroi [dezarwa] *nm* : confusion, distress

désastre [dezastr] *nm* : disaster — **désastreux, -treuse** [dezastrø, -trøz] *adj* : disastrous

désavantage [dezavãtaʒ] *nm* : disadvantage — **désavantager** [dezavãtaʒe] {17} *vt* : put at a disadvantage — **désavantageux, -geuse** [dezavãtaʒø, -ʒøz] *adj* : disadvantageous

désaveu [dezavø] *nm, pl* **-veux** : repudiation, denial

désavouer [dezavwe] *vt* RENIER : deny, repudiate

descendre [dəsãdr] {63} *vt* **1** : go down (the stairs, etc.) **2** : take (sth) down — *vi* **1** : go down, come down **2** : get off (of a passenger) **3** ～ **de** : be descended from — **descendant, -dante** [desãdã, -dãt] *n* : descendant — **descente** [desãt] *nf* **1** : descent **2** : (police) raid **3** PENTE : slope

description [dɛskripsjɔ̃] *nf* : description — **descriptif, -tive** [dɛskriptif, -tiv] *adj* : descriptive

désemparé, -rée [dezãpare] *adj* **1** : distraught **2** : in distress

déséquilibrer [dezekilibre] *vt* : unbalance — **déséquilibre** [dezekilibr] *nm* : imbalance

désert, -serte [dezɛr, -zɛrt] *adj* : desert, deserted — **désert** *nm* : desert

déserter [dezɛrte] *v* : desert — **déserteur** [dezɛrtœr] *nm* : deserter

désespérer [dezɛspere] {87} *vi* : despair — *vt* : drive to despair — **désespéré, -rée** [dezɛspere] *adj* : desperate — **désespoir** [dezɛspwar] *nm* : desperation, despair

déshabiller [dezabije] *vt* : undress — **se déshabiller** *vr* : get undressed

déshonneur [dezɔnœr] *nm* : dishonor, disgrace — **déshonorant, -rante** [dezɔnɔrã, -rãt] *adj* : dishonorable — **déshonorer** [dezɔnɔre] *vt* : dishonor, disgrace

déshydrater [dezidrate] *vt* : dehydrate

désigner [deziɲe] *vt* **1** : designate, indicate **2** NOMMER : appoint

désillusion [dezilyzjɔ̃] *nf* : disillusionment — **désillusionner** [dezilyzjɔne] *vt* : disillusion

désinfecter [dezɛ̃fɛkte] *vt* : disinfect — **désinfectant** [dezɛ̃fɛkta] *nm* : disinfectant

désintégrer [dezɛ̃tegre] {87} *v* **se désintégrer** *vr* : disintegrate

désintéressé, -sée [dezɛ̃terese] *adj* : impartial, disinterested

désinvolte [dezɛ̃vɔlt] *adj* : casual, offhand — **désinvolture** [dezɛ̃vɔltyr] *nf* : offhand manner

désirer [dezire] *vt* : want, desire — **désir** [dezir] *nm* : desire — **désireux, -reuse** [dezirø, -røz] *adj* : anxious, eager

désobéir [dezɔbeir] *vi* : disobey — **désobéissance** [dezɔbeisãs] *nf* : disobedience — **désobéissant, -sante** [dezɔbeisã, -sãt] *adj* : disobedient

désobligeant, -geante [dezɔbliʒã, -ʒãt] *adj* : disagreeable

désoler [dezɔle] *vt* : distress — **se désoler** *vr* : be upset — **désolé, -lée** [dezɔle] *adj* **1** : desolate **2** **être** ～ : be sorry

désopilant, -lante [dezɔpilã, -lãt] *adj* : hilarious

désordonné, -née [dezɔrdɔne] *adj* **1** : disorganized **2** : untidy — **désordre** [dezɔrdr] *nm* **1** : disorder **2** : untidiness

désorganiser [dezɔrganize] *vt* : disorganize

désorienté, -tée [dezɔrjãte] *adj* : disoriented, confused

désormais [dezɔrmɛ] *adv* : henceforth, from now on

désosser [dezɔse] *vt* : bone (a fish)

desquels, desquelles → **lequel**

dessécher [deseʃe] {87} *vt* : dry up, parch

desserrer [desere] *vt* : loosen

dessert [desɛr] *nm* : dessert

desservir [deservir] {81} *vt* **1** : serve (by providing transportation) **2** : clear (the table) **3** : do a disservice to

dessin [desɛ̃] *nm* **1** : drawing **2** : design, pattern **3** CONTOUR : outline **4** ～ **animé** : (animated) cartoon — **dessinateur, -trice** [desinatœr, -tris] *n* **1** : artist **2** : designer — **dessiner** [desine] *vt* **1** : draw **2** : outline — *vi* : draw, sketch — **se dessiner** *vr* **1** : stand out **2** APPARAÎTRE : appear, take shape

dessous [dəsu] *adv* : underneath — ～ *nms & pl* **1** : underneath, underside **2** ～ *nmpl* : underwear, lingerie **3 en** ～ : underneath, down below **4 en** ～ **de** : below — **dessous–de–verre** [d(ə)esudvɛr] *nms & pl* : coaster

dessus [dəsy] *adv* : on top, on (it) — **~** *nms & pl* **1** : top **2** : upper (of a shoe) **3** : upper floor, upstairs **4 en ~** : on top, above

destiner [dɛstine] *vt* **1** : destine **2 ~ qqch à qqn** : intend sth for s.o. — **destin** [dɛstɛ̃] *nm* : fate, destiny — **destinataire** [dɛstinatɛr] *nmf* : addressee — **destination** [dɛstinasjɔ̃] *nf* : destination — **destinée** [dɛstine] *nf* : fate, destiny

destruction [dɛstryksjɔ̃] *nf* : destruction — **destructeur, -trice** [dɛstryktœr, -tris] *adj* : destructive

désuet, -suète [dezɥɛ, -zɥɛt] *adj* : outdated, obsolete — **désuétude** [dezɥetyd] *nf* **tomber en ~** : fall into disuse

désunir [dezynir] *vt* : separate, divide

détacher [detaʃe] *vt* **1** : detach, tear off **2** : untie, unfasten — **se détacher** *vr* **1** : come undone **2 ~ de** : grow apart from — **détaché, -chée** [detaʃe] *adj* : detached

détailler [detaje] *vt* **1** : sell retail **2** ÉNUMÉRER : detail, itemize — **détail** [detaj] *nm* **1** : detail **2** : retail

détecter [detɛkte] *vt* : detect — **détecteur** [detɛktœr] *nm* : detector, sensor — **détection** [detɛksjɔ̃] *nf* : detection — **détective** [detɛktiv] *nm* : detective

détendre [detɑ̃dr] {63} *vt* **1** : slacken, loosen **2** : relax, ease — **se détendre** *vr* **1** : become slack **2** : relax, unwind — **détendu, -due** [detɑ̃dy] *adj* : relaxed

détenir [detnir] {92} *vt* **1** POSSÉDER : hold, possess **2** : detain (a suspect)

détente [detɑ̃t] *nf* **1** REPOS : relaxation **2** : trigger (of a firearm)

détenteur, -trice [detɑ̃tœr, -tris] *n* : holder

détention [detɑ̃sjɔ̃] *nf* **1** : possession **2** EMPRISONNEMENT : detention

détenu, -nue [detny] *n* : prisoner

détergent [detɛrʒɑ̃] *nm* : detergent

détériorer [deterjore] *vt* : damage — **se détériorer** *vr* : deteriorate — **détérioration** [deterjorasjɔ̃] *nf* : deterioration

déterminer [detɛrmine] *vt* : determine — **se déterminer** *vr* **~ à** : make up one's mind to — **détermination** [detɛrminasjɔ̃] *nf* : determination — **déterminé, -née** [detɛrmine] *adj* **1** : determined, resolute **2** : specified, definite

déterrer [detere] *vt* : dig up, unearth

détester [detɛste] *vt* : detest — **détestable** [detɛstabl] *adj* : hateful

détoner [detɔne] *vi* : explode — **détonation** [detɔnasjɔ̃] *nf* : explosion

détourner [deturne] *vt* **1** : divert, reroute **2** : hijack (an airplane) **3** : embezzle (funds) — **détour** [detur] *nm* : detour — **détourné, -née** [deturne] *adj* : indirect, roundabout — **détournement** [deturnəmɑ̃] *nm* **1** : diversion, rerouting **2** : hijacking **3** : embezzlement

détraquer [detrake] *vt* **1** : put out of order, break **2** *fam* : upset (one's stomach) — **se détraquer** *vr* : break down, go wrong

détresse [detrɛs] *nf* : distress

détriment [detrimɑ̃] *nm* **au ~ de** : at the cost of

détritus [detrity(s)] *nmpl* : waste, rubbish

détroit [detrwa] *nm* : strait

détruire [detrɥir] {49} *vt* : destroy

dette [dɛt] *nf* : debt

deuil [dœj] *nm* : bereavement, mourning

deux [dø] *adj* **1** : two **2** : second (in dates) **3 ~ fois** : twice — **~** *nm* **1** : two **2 tous les ~** : both (of them) — **deuxième** [døzjɛm] *adj & nmf* : second — **deuxièmement** [døzjɛmmɑ̃] *adv* : secondly, second

deux–points [døpwɛ̃] *nms & pl* : colon

dévaliser [devalize] *vt* : rob (a bank, etc.)

dévaloriser [devalɔrize] *vt* **1** : reduce the value of **2** : belittle (s.o.)

devancer [dəvɑ̃se] {6} *vt* **1** : be ahead of **2** ANTICIPER : anticipate

devant [dəvɑ̃] *adv* : in front, ahead, before — **~** *nm* : front — **~** *prep* **1** : in front of **2** : ahead of

devanture [dəvɑ̃tyr] *nf* **1** : storefront **2** : shopwindow

dévaster [devaste] *vt* : devastate

développer [devlɔpe] *vt* : develop — **se développer** *vr* : develop — **développement** [devlɔpmɑ̃] *nm* : development

devenir [dəvnir] {92} *vi* **1** : become **2 qu'est-ce que tu deviens? :** what are you up to?

déverser [devɛrse] *vt* : pour (out) — **se déverser** *vr* **~ dans** : flow into

déviation [devjasjɔ̃] *nf* **1** : deviation **2** DÉTOUR : detour — **dévier** [devje] {96} *vt* : deflect, divert (traffic) — *vi* **1** : veer, swerve **2 ~ de** : deviate from

deviner [dəvine] *vt* **1** : guess **2** APERCEVOIR : perceive **3** PRÉDIRE : foretell

devinette [dəvinɛt] *nf* : riddle

devis [dəvi] *nms & pl* : estimate

devise [dəviz] *nf* **1** : motto **2** : currency (money)

dévisser [devise] *vt* : unscrew

dévoiler [devwale] *vt* : unveil, reveal

devoir [dəvwar] {28} *vt* : owe — *v aux* **1** : have to, should **2** (*expressing obligation*) : must — **~** *nm* **1** : duty **2 ~s** *nmpl* : homework

dévorer [devɔre] *vt* : devour

dévot, -vote [devo, -vɔt] *adj* : devout, pious — **dévotion** [devosjɔ̃] *nf* : devotion, piety

dévouer [devwe] *vt* : devote — **se dévouer** *vr* : devote oneself — **dévoué, -vouée**

dextérité [dɛksterite] *nf* : dexterity, skill
diabète [djabɛt] *nm* : diabetes — **diabétique** [djabetik] *adj & nmf* : diabetic
diable [djabl] *nm* : devil — **diabolique** [djabɔlik] *adj* : diabolical
diagnostic [djagnɔstik] *nm* : diagnosis — **diagnostiquer** [djagnɔstike] *vt* : diagnose
diagonal, -nale [djagɔnal] *adj, mpl* **-naux** [-no] : diagonal — **diagonale** *nf* 1 : diagonal 2 **en ~** : diagonally
diagramme [djagram] *nm* : graph, chart
dialecte [djalɛkt] *nm* : dialect
dialogue [djalɔg] *nm* : dialogue
diamant [djamɑ̃] *nm* : diamond
diamètre [djamɛtr] *nm* : diameter
diaphragme [djafragm] *nm* : diaphragm
diapositive [djapozitiv] *nf* : slide, transparency
diarrhée [djare] *nf* : diarrhea
dictateur [diktatœr] *nm* : dictator
dicter [dikte] *vt* : dictate — **dictée** [dikte] *nf* : dictation
dictionnaire [diksjɔnɛr] *nm* : dictionary
dièse [djɛz] *nm* 1 : sharp (in music) 2 : pound sign
diesel [djezɛl] *adj & nm* : diesel
diète [djɛt] *nf* RÉGIME : diet
dieu [djø] *nm, pl* **dieux** 1 : god 2 **Dieu** : God
diffamer [difame] *vt* : slander, libel — **diffamation** [difamasjɔ̃] *nf* : slander, libel
différence [diferɑ̃s] *nf* 1 : difference 2 **à la ~ de** : unlike — **différencier** [diferɑ̃sje] {96} *vt* : differentiate — **différend** [diferɑ̃] *nm* : disagreement — **différent, -rente** [diferɑ̃, -rɑ̃t] *adj* : different — **différer** [difere] {87} *vt* : defer, postpone — *vi* : differ, vary
difficile [difisil] *adj* : difficult — **difficilement** [difisilmɑ̃] *adv* : with difficulty — **difficulté** [difikylte] *nf* : difficulty
difforme [difɔrm] *adj* : deformed, misshapen — **difformité** [difɔrmite] *nf* : deformity
diffuser [difyze] *vt* 1 : broadcast 2 PROPAGER : spread, distribute — **diffusion** [difyzjɔ̃] *nf* 1 : broadcasting 2 : distribution
digérer [diʒere] {87} *vt* 1 : digest 2 *fam* : put up with — **digestif, -tive** [diʒɛstif, -tiv] *adj* : digestive — **digestion** [diʒɛstjɔ̃] *nf* : digestion
digital, -tale [diʒital] *adj, mpl* **-taux** [-to] : digital
digne [diɲ] *adj* 1 : dignified 2 **~ de** : worthy of — **dignité** [diɲite] *nf* : dignity
digue [dig] *nf* : dike
dilapider [dilapide] *vt* : squander
dilater [dilate] *vt* : dilate — **se dilater** *vr* : dilate
dilemme [dilɛm] *nm* : dilemma

diluer [dilɥe] *vt* : dilute
dimanche [dimɑ̃ʃ] *nm* : Sunday
dimension [dimɑ̃sjɔ̃] *nf* : dimension
diminuer [diminɥe] *vt* RÉDUIRE : lower, reduce — *vi* : diminish, decrease — **diminution** [diminysjɔ̃] *nf* : reduction, decreasing
dinde [dɛ̃d] *nf* : (female) turkey — **dindon** [dɛ̃dɔ̃] *nm* : (male) turkey
dîner [dine] *vi* 1 : dine, have dinner 2 *Can* : have lunch — **~** *nm* 1 : dinner 2 *Can* : lunch — **dîneur, -neuse** [dinœr, -nœz] *n* : diner (person)
dinosaure [dinozɔr] *nm* : dinosaur
diplomate [diplɔmat] *adj* : diplomatic, tactful — **~** *nmf* : diplomat — **diplomatie** [diplɔmasi] *nf* : diplomacy — **diplomatique** [diplɔmatik] *adj* : diplomatic
diplôme [diplom] *nm* : diploma — **diplômé, -mée** [diplome] *adj* : qualified, certified — **~** *n* : graduate
dire [dir] {29} *vt* 1 : say 2 : tell 3 **qu'en dis-tu?** : what do you think? 4 **vouloir ~** : mean — **se dire** *vr* 1 : tell oneself 2 **comment se dit ... en français?** : how do you say ... in French? — **~** *nm* 1 : statement 2 **au ~ de** : according to
direct, -recte [dirɛkt] *adj* : direct — **direct** *nm* 1 : express train 2 **en ~** : live, in person — **directement** [-təmɑ̃] *adv* : directly, straight
directeur, -trice [dirɛktœr, -tris] *adj* : directing, guiding — **~** *n* 1 : manager, director 2 **directeur général** : chief executive officer
direction [dirɛksjɔ̃] *nf* 1 : direction 2 GESTION : management 3 : steering (mechanism)
directive [dirɛktiv] *nf* : order
dirigeant, -geante [diriʒɑ̃, -ʒɑ̃t] *adj* : ruling — **~** *n* : leader, director
diriger [diriʒe] {17} *vt* 1 : direct, manage 2 CONDUIRE : steer 3 MENER : conduct 4 **~ sur** : aim at — **se diriger** *vr* **~ vers** : head toward
discerner [disɛrne] *vt* : discern — **discernement** [disɛrnəmɑ̃] *nm* : discernment
disciple [disipl] *nm* : disciple
discipline [disiplin] *nf* : discipline — **discipliner** [disipline] *vt* : discipline
discorde [diskɔrd] *nf* : discord
discours [diskur] *nms & pl* : speech
discréditer [diskredite] *vt* : discredit
discret, -crète [diskrɛ, -krɛt] *adj* : discreet — **discrétion** [diskresjɔ̃] *nf* 1 : discretion 2 **à ~** : unlimited, as much as one wants
discrimination [diskriminasjɔ̃] *nf* : discrimination
disculper [diskylpe] *vt* : clear, exonerate
discussion [diskysjɔ̃] *nf* : discussion
discuter [diskyte] *vt* 1 : discuss, debate 2

CONTESTER : question — *vi* **1** : talk **2** PROTESTER : argue **3** ∼ **de** : discuss

diseuse [dizøz] *nf* ∼ **de bonne aventure** : fortune-teller

disgrâce [disgras] *nf* : disgrace

disloquer [dislɔke] *vt* LUXER : dislocate

disparaître [disparɛtr] {7} *vi* **1** : disappear **2** MOURIR : die — **disparition** [disparisjɔ̃] *nf* **1** : disappearance **2** MORT : extinction, death

disparité [disparite] *nf* : disparity

disparu, -rue [dispary] *adj* : missing — ∼ *n* **1** : missing person **2** : dead person

dispenser [dispɑ̃se] *vt* **1** : exempt, excuse **2** DISTRIBUER : dispense — **se dispenser** *vr* ∼ **de** : avoid — **dispense** [dispɑ̃s] *nf* : exemption

disperser [dispɛrse] *vt* : disperse, scatter — **se disperser** *vr* : disperse

disponible [disponibl] *adj* : available — **disponibilité** [disponibilite] *nf* : availability

disposer [dispoze] *vt* **1** PLACER : arrange **2** INCITER : incline, dispose — *vi* ∼ **de** : have at one's disposal — **disposé, -sée** [dispoze] *adj* **1** : arranged **2** ∼ **à** : disposed to, willing to — **dispositif** [dispozitif] *nm* **1** : device, mechanism **2** PLAN : plan of action — **disposition** [dispozisjɔ̃] *nf* **1** : arrangement, layout **2** APTITUDE : aptitude **3** TENDANCE : tendency **4 à la** ∼ **de** : at the disposal of **5** ∼**s** *nfpl* : steps, measures

disproportionné, -née [disproporsjone] *adj* : disproportionate

disputer [dispyte] *vt* **1** : compete in, play **2** *fam* : tell off **3** *Can* : scold — **se disputer** *vr* : quarrel, fight — **dispute** [dispyt] *nf* : argument, quarrel

disqualifier [diskalifje] {96} *vt* : disqualify

disque [disk] *nm* **1** : (phonograph) record **2** : disk — **disquette** [diskɛt] *nf* : floppy disk

disséminer [disemine] *vt* : scatter

dissentiment [disɑ̃timɑ̃] *nm* : dissent

dissertation [disɛrtasjɔ̃] *nf* : essay (in school)

dissimuler [disimyle] *vt* : conceal, hide — **se dissimuler** *vr* : hide oneself — **dissimulation** [disimylasjɔ̃] *nf* **1** : deceit **2** : concealment

dissiper [disipe] *vt* **1** : disperse **2** : squander (one's fortune) — **se dissiper** *vr* : clear (up), vanish

dissolu, -lue [disoly] *adj* : dissolute — **dissolution** [disolysjɔ̃] *nf* **1** : dissolution, breakup **2** : dissolving — **dissolvant** [disolvɑ̃] *nm* **1** : solvent **2** : nail polish remover

dissoudre [disudr] {1} *vt* : dissolve — **se dissoudre** *vr* : dissolve

dissuader [disɥade] *vt* : dissuade, deter

distance [distɑ̃s] *nf* : distance — **distant, -tante** [distɑ̃, -tɑ̃t] *adj* : distant

distiller [distile] *vt* : distill

distinct, -tincte [distɛ̃, -tɛ̃kt] *adj* : distinct — **distinctif, -tive** [distɛ̃ktif, -tiv] *adj* : distinctive — **distinction** [distɛ̃ksjɔ̃] *nf* : distinction

distinguer [distɛ̃ge] *v* : distinguish — **distingué, -guée** [distɛ̃ge] *adj* : distinguished

distraction [distraksjɔ̃] *nf* **1** : distraction **2** PASSE-TEMPS : recreation

distraire [distrɛr] {40} *vt* **1** : distract **2** DIVERTIR : amuse, entertain — **se distraire** *vr* : amuse oneself — **distrait, -traite** [distrɛ, -trɛt] *adj* : distracted, absentminded

distribuer [distribɥe] *vt* **1** : distribute **2** : deliver (mail) — **distributeur** [distribytœr] *nm* **1** : distributor **2** *or* ∼ **automatique** : dispenser, vending machine — **distribution** [distribysjɔ̃] *nf* **1** : distribution **2** : casting, cast (of actors)

district [distrikt] *nm* : district

dit, dite [di, dit] *adj* **1** : agreed upon, stated **2** : called, known as

divaguer [divage] *vi* : rave

divan [divɑ̃] *nm* : couch

divergence [-vɛrʒɑ̃s] *nf* : difference — **diverger** [divɛrʒe] {17} *vi* : diverge

divers, -verse [divɛr, -vɛrs] *adj* **1** VARIÉ : diverse **2** PLUSIEURS : various — **diversifier** [divɛrsifje] {96} *vt* : diversify — **diversion** [divɛrsjɔ̃] *nf* : diversion — **diversité** [divɛrsite] *nf* : diversity, variety

divertir [divɛrtir] *vt* : amuse, entertain — **se divertir** *vr* : amuse oneself — **divertissement** [divɛrtismɑ̃] *nm* : entertainment, pastime

dividende [dividɑ̃d] *nm* : dividend

divine, -vine [divɛ̃, -vin] *adj* : divine — **divinité** [divinite] *nf* : divinity

diviser [divize] *vt* : divide — **se diviser** *vr* : divide — **division** [divizjɔ̃] *nf* : division

divorcer [divorse] {6} *vi* : get a divorce — **divorce** [divors] *nm* : divorce

divulguer [divylge] *vt* : divulge, disclose

dix [dis, *before a consonant* di, *before a vowel or mute h* diz] *adj* **1** : ten **2** : tenth (in dates) — ∼ *nms & pl* : ten

dix–huit [dizɥit] *adj* **1** : eighteen **2** : eighteenth (in dates) — ∼ *nms & pl* : eighteen — **dix–huitième** [dizɥitjɛm] *adj & nmf & nm* : eighteenth

dixième [dizjɛm] *adj & nmf & nm* : tenth

dix–neuf [diznœf] *adj* **1** : nineteen **2** : nineteenth (in dates) — ∼ *nms & pl* : nineteen — **dix–neuvième** [diznœvjɛm] *adj & nmf & nm* : nineteenth

dix–sept [disɛt] *adj* **1** : seventeen **2** : seventeenth (in dates) — ∼ *nms & pl* : seventeen

— **dix–septième** [disɛtjɛm] *adj & nmf & nm* : seventeenth

dizaine [dizɛn] *nf* : ten, about ten

docile [dɔsil] *adj* : obedient

dock [dɔk] *nm* : dock

docteur [dɔktœr] *nm* : doctor

doctrine [dɔktrin] *nf* : doctrine

document [dɔkymɑ̃] *nm* : document — **documentation** [dɔkymɑ̃tasjɔ̃] *nf* : literature, leaflets *pl* — **documenter** [dɔkymɑ̃te] *v se* **documenter** *vr* ~ *sur* : research

dodu, -due [dɔdy] *adj* : plump, chubby

dogme [dɔgm] *nm* : dogma

doigt [dwa] *nm* 1 : finger 2 ~ *de pied* : toe — **doigté** [dwate] *nm* TACT : tact

dollar [dɔlar] *nm* : dollar

domaine [dɔmɛn] *nm* 1 : domain 2 PROPRIÉTÉ : estate

dôme [dom] *nm* : dome

domestique [dɔmɛstik] *adj* 1 : domestic 2 : domesticated — *nmf* : servant — **domestiquer** [dɔmɛstike] *vt* APPRIVOISER : domesticate

domicile [dɔmisil] *nm* : residence, home

dominer [dɔmine] *v* : dominate — **dominant, -nante** [dɔminɑ̃, -nɑ̃t] *adj* : dominant

dommage [dɔmaʒ] *nm* 1 PRÉJUDICE : harm, injury 2 DÉGÂTS : damage 3 *c'est* ~ : that's too bad

dompter [dɔ̃te] *vt* : tame

don [dɔ̃] *nm* : gift — **donateur, -trice** [dɔnatœr, -tris] *n* : donor, giver — **donation** [dɔnasjɔ̃] *nf* : donation

donc [dɔ̃k] *conj* 1 : so, therefore, consequently 2 : so, then

donner [dɔne] *vt* 1 : give 2 : produce, yield 3 MONTRER : indicate, show 4 CAUSER : cause 5 : deal (cards) — *vi* 1 : produce a crop 2 ~ *dans* : fall into 3 ~ *sur* : overlook — **se donner** *vr* ~ *à* : devote oneself to — **donne** [dɔn] *nf* : deal (in card games) — **donné, -née** [dɔne] *adj* 1 : given 2 *c'est* ~ : it's a bargain — **donnée** [dɔne] *nf* 1 : fact 2 ~*s* *nfpl* : data — **donneur, -neuse** [dɔnœr, -nøz] *n* 1 : donor 2 : (card) dealer

dont [dɔ̃] *pron* : of which, of whom, whose

doré, -rée [dɔre] *adj* 1 : gilt 2 : golden

dorénavant [dɔrenavɑ̃] *adv* : henceforth

dorer [dɔre] *vt* 1 : gild 2 BRUNIR : tan — *vi* : brown (in cooking)

dorloter [dɔrlɔte] *vt* : pamper

dormir [dɔrmir] {30} *vi* : sleep, be asleep

dortoir [dɔrtwar] *nm* : dormitory

dorure [dɔryr] *nf* : gilding, gilt

dos [do] *nms & pl* : back

dose [doz] *nf* : dose — **doser** [doze] *vt* : measure out (a dose of medicine)

dossier [dɔsje] *nm* 1 : file, record 2 : back (of a chair)

doter [dɔte] *vt* 1 : endow 2 ÉQUIPER : equip

douane [dwan] *nf* 1 : customs 2 : (import) duty — **douanier, -nière** [dwanje, -njɛr] *adj* : customs — **douanier** *nm* : customs officer

double [dubl] *adv & adj* : double — ~ *nm* 1 : double 2 : copy, duplicate — **doublement** [dubləmɑ̃] *adv* : doubly — **doubler** [duble] *vt* 1 : double 2 : line (fabric) 3 : dub (a film, etc.) 4 DÉPASSER : pass, overtake — *vi* : double — **doublure** [dublyr] *nf* 1 : lining 2 : understudy

douce → **doux** — **doucement** [dusmɑ̃] *adv* 1 : gently, softly 2 LENTEMENT : slowly — **douceur** [dusœr] *nf* 1 : softness, smoothness 2 : gentleness, mildness

douche [duʃ] *nf* : shower — **doucher** [duʃe] *se doucher* *vr* : take a shower

doué, douée [dwe] *adj* 1 : gifted, talented 2 ~ *de* : endowed with

douille [duj] *nf* : electric socket

douillet, -lette [dujɛ, -jɛt] *adj* CONFORTABLE : cozy

douleur [dulœr] *nf* 1 : pain 2 CHAGRIN : grief — **douloureux, -reuse** [dulurø, -røz] *adj* : painful

douter [dute] *vt* 1 : doubt 2 ~ *de* : question — **se douter** *vr* ~ *de* : suspect — **doute** [dut] *nm* : doubt — **douteux, -teuse** [dutø, -tøz] *adj* : doubtful

doux, douce [du, dus] *adj* 1 : sweet 2 : soft (of skin) 3 : mild, gentle

douze [duz] *adj* 1 : twelve 2 : twelfth (in dates) — ~ *nms & pl* : twelve — **douzaine** [duzɛn] *nf* : dozen — **douzième** [duzjɛm] *adj & nmf & nm* : twelfth

doyen, doyenne [dwajɛ̃, -jɛn] *n* : dean

dragon [dragɔ̃] *nm* : dragon

draguer [drage] *vt* : dredge

drainer [drene] *vt* : drain — **drainage** [drenaʒ] *nm* : drainage, draining

drame [dram] *nm* 1 : drama 2 : tragedy — **dramatique** [dramatik] *adj* : dramatic — **dramatiser** [dramatize] *vt* : dramatize — **dramaturge** [dramatyrʒ] *nmf* : playwright

drap [dra] *nm* 1 : sheet 2 : woolen fabric

drapeau [drapo] *nm, pl* **-peaux** : flag

draper [drape] *vt* : drape

drastique [drastik] *adj* : drastic

dresser [drese] *vt* 1 LEVER : raise 2 ÉRIGER : put up, erect 3 ÉTABLIR : draft, draw up 4 : train (an animal) 5 ~ *les oreilles* : cock one's ears — **se dresser** *vr* 1 : stand up 2 : rise up, tower

dribbler [drible] *vi* : dribble (in sports)

drogue [drɔg] *nf* : drug — **drogué, -guée** [drɔge] *n* : drug addict — **droguer** [drɔge] *vt* : drug — **se droguer** *vr* : take drugs

droit [drwa] *nm* 1 : right 2 : fee, tax, duty 3 *le* ~ : law 4 ~*s d'auteur* : copyright — ~ *adv* : straight, directly — **droit, droite**

[drwa, drwat] *adj* **1** : right, right-hand **2** : straight, direct **3** VERTICAL : upright, vertical **4** HONNÊTE : honest — **droite** *nf* **1** : right, right-hand side **2** **la ～** : the right (in politics) — **droitier, -tière** [drwatje, -tjɛr] *adj* : right-handed — **droiture** [drwatyr] *nf* : uprightness, integrity

drôle [drol] *adj* : funny — **drôlement** [drolmɑ̃] *adv* **1** : amusingly **2** BIZARREMENT : strangely, oddly **3** *fam* : really, awfully

dru, drue [dry] *adj* : thick (of hair, etc.)

du → de, le

dû, due [dy] *adj* **1** : due, owing **2 ～ à** : due to — **dû** *nm* : due

duc [dyk] *nm* : duke — **duchesse** [dyʃɛs] *nf* : duchess

duel [dɥɛl] *nm* : duel

dûment [dymɑ̃] *adv* : duly

dune [dyn] *nf* : dune

duo [dyo] *nm* **1** : duet **2** : duo, pair

dupe [dyp] *nf* : dupe — **duper** [dype] *vt* : dupe, deceive

duplex [dyplɛks] *nm* : duplex (apartment)

duplicata [dyplikata] *nms & pl* : duplicate

duquel → lequel

dur, dure [dyr] *adj* **1** : hard, stiff **2** DIFFICILE : difficult **3** SÉVÈRE : harsh — **dur** *adv* : hard

durable [dyrabl] *adj* : durable, lasting

durant [dyrɑ̃] *prep* **1** : for (a period of time) **2** : during

durcir [dyrsir] *v* : harden — **se durcir** *vr* : harden — **durcissement** [dyrsismɑ̃] *nm* : hardening

durée [dyre] *nf* : duration, length

durement [dyrmɑ̃] *adv* : harshly, severely

durer [dyre] *vi* : last, go on

dureté [dyrte] *nf* **1** : hardness **2** SÉVÉRITÉ : harshness

duvet [dyvɛ] *nm* **1** : down (fabric) **2** : sleeping bag

dynamique [dinamik] *adj* : dynamic

dynamite [dinamit] *nf* : dynamite — **dynamiter** [dinamite] *vt* : dynamite, blast

dynastie [dinasti] *nf* : dynasty

E

e [ø] *nm* : e, fifth letter of the alphabet

eau [o] *nf, pl* **eaux** **1** : water **2 ～ de Cologne** : cologne **3 ～ douce** : freshwater **4 ～ de Javel** : bleach **5 ～ oxygénée** : hydrogen peroxide — **eau-de-vie** *nf, pl* **eaux-de-vie** : brandy

ébahir [ebair] *vt* : astound, dumbfound

ébaucher [eboʃe] *vt* : sketch out, outline — **s'ébaucher** *vr* : form, take shape — **ébauche** [eboʃ] *nf* : outline, sketch

ébène [ebɛn] *nf* : ebony — **ébéniste** [ebenist] *nmf* : cabinetmaker

éblouir [ebluir] *vt* : dazzle, stun

ébouler [ebule] *v* **s'ébouler** *vr* : cave in, collapse

ébouriffer [eburife] *vt* : tousle, ruffle

ébranler [ebrɑ̃le] *vt* **1** : shake **2** : weaken, undermine

ébrécher [ebreʃe] {87} *vt* : chip, nick — **ébréchure** [ebreʃyr] *nf* : chip, nick

ébriété [ebrijete] *nf* : inebriation, drunkenness

ébullition [ebylisjɔ̃] *nf* : boil, boiling

écailler [ekaje] *vt* **1** : scale (fish) **2** : open (a shell) **3** : chip (paint) — **s'écailler** *vr* : flake off — **écaille** [ekaj] *nf* **1** : scale (of a fish) **2** : tortoiseshell **3** FRAGMENT : flake, chip

écarlate [ekarlat] *adj & nf* : scarlet

écarquiller [ekarkije] *vt* **～ les yeux** : open one's eyes wide

écarter [ekarte] *vt* **1** : spread, open **2** ÉLOIGNER : move apart **3** EXCLURE : rule out **4** DÉTOURNER : divert, distract — **s'écarter** *vr* **1** : move away **2** SE SÉPARER : part, open — **écart** [ekar] *nm* **1** : distance, gap **2** VARIATION : difference **3** : lapse (of conduct) **4** DÉVIATION : swerve **5 à l'～** : apart, away — **écarté, -tée** [ekarte] *adj* **1** ISOLÉ : remote **2** : wide apart — **écartement** [ekartəmɑ̃] *nm* : gap

ecclésiastique [eklezjastik] *nm* : clergyman

écervelé, -lée [esɛrvəle] *adj* : scatterbrained

échafaud [eʃafo] *nm* : scaffold — **échafaudage** [eʃafodaʒ] *nm* : scaffolding

échalote [eʃalɔt] *nf* **1** : shallot **2** *Can* : scallion

échanger [eʃɑ̃ʒe] {17} *vt* : exchange — **échange** [eʃɑ̃ʒ] *nm* **1** : exchange **2** : trade, commerce — **échangeur** [eʃɑ̃ʒœr] *nm* : (highway) interchange

échantillon [eʃɑ̃tijɔ̃] *nm* : sample

échapper [eʃape] *vi* **1 ～ à** : escape (from) **2 laisser ～** : let out **3 l'～ belle** : have a narrow escape — *vt Can* : drop — **s'échapper** *vr* : escape

écharde [eʃard] *nf* : splinter
écharpe [eʃarp] *nf* **1** : scarf **2 en ~** : in a sling
échasse [eʃas] *nf* : stilt
échauffer [eʃofe] *v* **s'échauffer** *vr* : warm up
échéance [eʃeɑ̃s] *nf* **1** : due date **2** OBLIGATION : financial obligation, payment **3 à longue ~** : in the long run — **échéant** [eʃeɑ̃] **le cas ~** *adv phr* : if need be
échec [eʃɛk] *nm* **1** : failure, setback **2 ~s** *nmpl* : chess **3 ~ et mat** : checkmate **4 en ~** : in check
échelle [eʃɛl] *nf* **1** : ladder **2** MESURE : scale — **échelon** [eʃlɔ̃] *nm* **1** : rung **2** NIVEAU : level — **échelonner** [eʃlɔne] *vt* : space out, spread out
échevelé, -lée [eʃəvle] *adj* : disheveled
échiquier [eʃikje] *nm* : chessboard
écho [eko] *nm* : echo — **échographie** [ekografi] *nf* : ultrasound
échoir [eʃwar] {31} *vi* **1** : fall due **2 ~ à qqn** : fall to s.o.
échouer [eʃwe] *vi* : fail (of an exam) — **s'échouer** *vr* : run aground
éclabousser [eklabuse] *vt* : splash, spatter — **éclaboussure** [eklabusyr] *nf* : splash
éclairer [eklere] *vt* **1** : light (up) **2** INFORMER : enlighten **3** EXPLIQUER : clarify — *vi* : give light — **s'éclairer** *vr* **1** : light up **2** : become clearer — **éclair** [ekler] *nm* **1** ÉCLAT : flash **2** : (flash of) lightning — **éclairage** [eklɛraʒ] *nm* : lighting, illumination — **éclaircie** [eklɛrsi] *nf* **1** : sunny spell **2** : clearing, glade — **éclaircir** [eklɛrsir] **1** : lighten **2** CLARIFIER : clarify **3** : thin (in cooking) — **s'éclaircir** *vr* : clear (up) — **éclaircissement** [eklɛrsismɑ̃] *nm* : explanation, clarification
éclaireur, -reuse [eklɛrœr, -røz] *n* : boy scout *m*, girl scout *f* — **éclaireur** *nm* : (military) scout
éclater [eklate] *vi* **1** : burst, explode **2** : break up, splinter — **éclat** [ekla] *nm* **1** : splinter, chip **2** : brilliance, shine **3** : splendor **4 ~ de rire** : burst (of laughter) — **éclatant, -tante** [eklatɑ̃, -tɑ̃t] *adj* **1** BRILLANT : brilliant **2 un succès éclatant** : a resounding success — **éclatement** [eklatmɑ̃] *nm* **1** : explosion, bursting **2** : rupture, split
éclipse [eklips] *nf* : eclipse — **éclipser** [eklipse] *v* **s'éclipser** *vr* : slip away
éclore [eklɔr] {32} *vi* **1** : hatch **2** : open out, blossom — **éclosion** [eklozjɔ̃] *nf* **1** : hatching **2** : blossoming
écluse [eklyz] *nf* : lock (of a canal)
écœurer [ekœre] *vt* : sicken, disgust — **écœurant, -rante** [ekœrɑ̃, -rɑ̃t] *adj* **1** : cloying, sickening **2** DÉGUEULASSE : disgusting

école [ekɔl] *nf* **1** : school **2 ~ secondaire** *Can* : high school **3 ~ maternelle** *Can* : kindergarten — **écolier, -lière** [ekɔlje, -ljɛr] *n* : schoolboy *m*, schoolgirl *f*
écologie [ekɔlɔʒi] *nf* : ecology — **écologique** [ekɔlɔʒik] *adj* : ecological
économie [ekɔnɔmi] *nf* **1** : economy **2** : economics **3 ~s** *nfpl* : savings — **économe** [ekɔnɔm] *adj* : thrifty, economical — *nmf* : bursar — **économique** [ekɔnɔmik] *adj* : economic — **économiser** [ekɔnɔmize] *v* : save — **économiste** [ekɔnɔmist] *nmf* : economist
écorce [ekɔrs] *nf* **1** : bark (of a tree) **2** : peel (of a fruit)
écorcher [ekɔrʃe] *vt* **1** DÉPOUILLER : skin **2** ÉGRATIGNER : scratch, graze — **écorchure** [ekɔrʃyr] *nf* : graze, scratch
écossais, -saise [ekɔsɛ, -sɛz] *adj* **1** : Scottish **2** : tartan, plaid
écosser [ekɔse] *vt* : shell (peas, etc.)
écosystème [ekɔsistɛm] *nm* : ecosystem
écouler [ekule] *vt* : sell, dispose of — **s'écouler** *vr* **1** : flow (out) **2** PASSER : pass, elapse — **écoulement** [ekulmɑ̃] *nm* : flow
écourter [ekurte] *vt* : cut short, curtail
écouter [ekute] *vt* : listen to — *vi* : listen — **écouteur** [ekutœr] *nm* **1** : (telephone) receiver **2 ~s** *nmpl* : headphones
écoutille [ekutij] *nf* : hatch (of a ship)
écran [ekrɑ̃] *nm* : screen
écraser [ekraze] *vt* **1** : crush, squash, mash **2** : run over (an animal, etc.) **3** ACCABLER : overwhelm — **s'écraser** *vr* : crash (of a plane, etc.) — **écrasant, -sante** [ekrazɑ̃, -zɑ̃t] *adj* : crushing, overwhelming
écrémé, -mée [ekreme] *adj* **lait écrémé** : skim milk
écrevisse [ekrəvis] *nf* : crayfish
écrier [ekrije] {96} *v* **s'écrier** *vr* : exclaim
écrin [ekrɛ̃] *nm* : case, box
écrire [ekrir] {33} *v* : write — **s'écrire** *vr* : be spelled — **écrit** [ekri] *nm* **1** : writing(s) **2** : document **3 par ~** : in writing — **écriteau** [ekrito] *nm, pl* **-teaux** : notice, sign — **écriture** [ekrityr] *nf* : writing — **écrivain** [ekrivɛ̃] *nm* : writer — **écrivaillon** [ekrivajɔ̃] *nm fam* : hack writer
écrou [ekru] *nm* : (metal) nut
écrouler [ekrule] *v* **s'écrouler** *vr* : collapse — **écroulement** [ekrulmɑ̃] *nm* : collapse
écueil [ekœj] *nm* RÉCIF : reef
écume [ekym] *nf* **1** : foam, froth **2** : scum (in cooking) — **écumer** [ekyme] *vi* : foam, froth — **écumeux, -meuse** [ekymø, -møz] *adj* : foamy
écureuil [ekyrœj] *nm* : squirrel
écurie [ekyri] *nf* : stable
écusson [ekysɔ̃] *nm* : badge
édenté, -tée [edɑ̃te] *adj* : toothless

édifice [edifis] *nm* : building — **édifier** [edifje] {96} *vt* CONSTRUIRE : build

éditer [edite] *vt* **1** : publish **2** : edit — **éditeur, -trice** [editœr, -tris] *n* **1** : publisher **2** : editor — **édition** [edisjɔ̃] *nf* **1** : publishing **2** : edition (of a book) — **éditorial** [editɔrjal] *nm, pl* **-riaux** [-rjo] : editorial

édredon [edrədɔ̃] *nm* : comforter

éducation [edykasjɔ̃] *nf* **1** ENSEIGNEMENT : education **2** : upbringing (of children) **3** avoir de l'~ : have good manners — **éducatif, -tive** [edykatif, -tiv] *adj* : educational — **éduquer** [edyke] *vt* **1** : educate **2** ÉLEVER : bring up

effacer [efase] {6} *vt* : erase, delete — **s'effacer** *vr* **1** : fade **2** S'ÉCARTER : stand aside

effectif, -tive [efɛktif, -tiv] *adj* : real, actual — **effectivement** [efɛktivmã] *adv* **1** : indeed, in fact **2** RÉELLEMENT : really

effectuer [efɛktɥe] *vt* EXÉCUTER : carry out, make

efféminé, -née [efemine] *adj* : effeminate

effervescent, -cente [efɛrvesɑ, -sɑ̃t] *adj* : effervescent

effet [efɛ] *nm* **1** RÉSULTAT : effect, result **2** en ~ : indeed, actually **3** faire bon ~ : make a good impression

efficace [efikas] *adj* : efficient — **efficacité** [efikasite] *nf* **1** : efficiency **2** : effectiveness

effilocher [efilɔʃe] *vt* : shred, fray — **s'effilocher** *vr* : fray

effleurer [eflœre] *vt* **1** FRÔLER : touch lightly, graze **2** ça m'a effleuré l'esprit : it crossed my mind

effondrer [efɔ̃dre] *v* **s'effondrer** *vr* : collapse — **effondrement** [efɔ̃drəmã] *nm* : collapse

efforcer [efɔrse] {6} *v* **s'efforcer** *vr* : strive, endeavor

effort [efɔr] *nm* : effort

effrayer [efreje] {11} *vt* : frighten — **effrayant, -frayante** [efrɛjã, -jãt] *adj* : frightening

effréné, -née [efrene] *adj* : wild, unrestrained

effriter [efrite] *vt* : crumble — **s'effriter** *vr* : crumble

effroi [efrwa] *nm* : terror, dread

effronté, -tée [efrɔ̃te] *adj* : impudent

effroyable [efrwajabl] *adj* : dreadful

égal, -gale [egal] *adj, mpl* **égaux** [ego] **1** : equal **2** RÉGULIER : regular, even **3** ça m'est ~ : it makes no difference to me — ~ *n* : equal — **également** [egalmã] *adv* **1** : equally **2** AUSSI : also, as well — **égaler** [egale] *vt* : equal — **égaliser** [egalize] *vt* **1** : equalize **2** : level (out) — **égalité** [egalite] *nf* : equality

égard [egar] *nm* **1** : regard, consideration **2** à cet ~ : in this respect **3** à l'~ de : with regard to

égarer [egare] *vt* **1** : lead astray **2** PERDRE : lose, misplace — **s'égarer** *vr* **1** : lose one's way **2** : be misplaced

égayer [egeje] {11} *vt* : cheer up

églefin [egləfɛ̃] *nm* : haddock

église [egliz] *nf* : church

ego [ego] *nm* : ego — **égoïsme** [egɔism] *nm* : selfishness — **égoïste** [egɔist] *adj* : selfish

égorger [egɔrʒe] {17} *vt* : cut the throat of

égotisme [egɔtism] *nm* : egotism — **égotiste** [egɔtist] *adj* : egotistic(al)

égoutter [egute] *vt* : allow to drip, drain — **s'égoutter** *vr* : drain — **égout** [egu] *nm* : sewer — **égouttoir** [egutwar] *nm* : (dish) drainer

égratigner [egratiɲe] *vt* : scratch, graze — **égratignure** [egratiɲyr] *nf* : scratch

eh [e] *interj* **1** : hey! **2** ~ bien : well

éhonté, -tée [eɔ̃te] *adj* : shameless, brazen

éjaculer [eʒakyle] *v* : ejaculate

éjecter [eʒɛkte] *vt* **1** : eject **2** *fam* : kick out

élaborer [elabɔre] *vt* : develop, put together — **élaboration** [elabɔrasjɔ̃] *nf* : elaboration, development

élan¹ [elã] *nm* **1** : momentum **2** : rush, surge (of energy, etc.)

élan² [elã] *nm* : elk

élancé, -cée [elɑ̃se] *adj* : slender

élancer [elɑ̃se] {6} *v* **s'élancer** *vr* SE PRÉCIPITER : dash, rush — **élancement** [elɑ̃smã] *nm* : shooting pain

élargir [elarʒir] *vt* : widen, broaden — **s'élargir** *vr* : expand, become broader — **élargissement** [elarʒismã] *nm* : widening, expanding

élastique [elastik] *adj* : elastic, flexible — ~ *nm* **1** : elastic **2** : rubber band

électeur, -trice [elɛktœr, -tris] *n* : voter — **élection** [elɛksjɔ̃] *nf* : election — **électoral, -rale** [elɛktɔral] *adj, mpl* **-raux** [-ro] : electoral, election — **électorat** [elɛktɔra] *nm* : electorate

électricité [elɛktrisite] *nf* : electricity — **électricien, -cienne** [elɛktrisjɛ̃, -sjɛn] *n* : electrician — **électrique** [elɛktrik] *adj* : electric(al)

électrocuter [elɛktrɔkyte] *vt* : electrocute

électron [elɛktrɔ̃] *nm* : electron — **électronique** [elɛktrɔnik] *adj* : electronic — ~ *nf* : electronics

élégance [elegãs] *nf* : elegance — **élégant, -gante** [elegã, -gãt] *adj* : elegant

élément [elemã] *nm* **1** : element **2** COMPOSANT : component, part — **élémentaire** [elemãter] *adj* : elementary, basic

éléphant [elefã] *nm* : elephant

élevage [ɛlvaʒ] *nm* : breeding

élévation [elevasjɔ̃] *nf* **1** : elevation **2** AUG-
MENTATION : rise, increase

élève [elɛv] *nmf* : pupil, student

élever [elve] {52} *vt* **1** : raise **2** ÉRIGER
: erect **3** ÉDUQUER : bring up (a child) —
s'élever *vr* **1** : rise (up) **2** ~ **à** : amount to
— **élevé, -vée** [elve] *adj* **1** : high, elevated
2 bien ~ : well-mannered — **éleveur,
-veuse** [elvœr, -vøz] *n* : breeder

éligible [eliʒibl] *adj* : eligible

éliminer [elimine] *vt* : eliminate — **élimination** [eliminasjɔ̃] *nf* : elimination

élire [elir] {51} *vt* : elect

élite [elit] *nf* : elite

elle [ɛl] *pron pl* **1** : she, it **2** : her **3 elles** *pron
pl* : they, them — **elle–même** [ɛlmɛm] *pron*
1 : herself, itself **2 elles–mêmes** *pron pl*
: themselves

éloge [elɔʒ] *nm* : eulogy, praise

éloigner [elwaɲe] *vt* **1** ÉCARTER : push
aside, move away **2** DÉTOURNER : divert,
turn away — **s'éloigner** *vr* : move or go
away — **éloigné, -gnée** [elwaɲe] *adj* : distant, remote — **éloignement** [elwaɲmɑ̃] *nm*
: distance, remoteness

éloquence [elɔkɑ̃s] *nf* : eloquence — **éloquent, -quente** [elɔkɑ̃, -kɑ̃t] *adj* : eloquent

élu, -lue [ely] *adj* : elected — ~ *n* : elected
representative

élucider [elyside] *vt* : elucidate

éluder [elyde] *vt* : elude

émacié, -ciée [emasje] *adj* : emaciated

émail [emaj] *nm, pl* **émaux** [emo] : enamel

émanciper [emɑ̃sipe] *vt* : emancipate —
émancipation [emɑ̃sipasjɔ̃] *nf* : emancipa-
tion

émaner [emane] *vi* ~ **de** : emanate from

emballer [ɑ̃bale] *vt* **1** EMPAQUETER : pack,
wrap **2** *fam* : thrill — **s'emballer** *vr* **1**
: race (of an engine), bolt (of a horse) **2** *fam*
: get carried away — **emballage** [ɑ̃balaʒ]
nm : packing, wrapping

embarcadère [ɑ̃barkadɛr] *nm* : wharf, pier

embarcation [ɑ̃barkasjɔ̃] *nf* : small boat

embardée [ɑ̃barde] *nf* : swerve (of a car)

embargo [ɑ̃bargo] *nm* : embargo

embarquer [ɑ̃barke] *vt* **1** : embark **2**
CHARGER : load — *vi* : board — **s'embarquer** *vr* : board — **embarquement**
[ɑ̃barkəmɑ̃] *nm* **1** : boarding **2** : loading
(on board)

embarrasser [ɑ̃barase] *vt* **1** ENCOMBRER
: clutter **2** ENTRAVER : hinder **3** GÊNER
: embarrass — **s'embarrasser** *vr* ~ **de**
: burden oneself with — **embarras** [ɑ̃bara]
nms & pl **1** : difficulty **2** : embarrassment
— **embarrassant, -sante** [ɑ̃barasɑ̃, -sɑ̃t]
adj **1** : embarrassing, awkward **2** ENCOM-
BRANT : cumbersome

embaucher [ɑ̃boʃe] *vt* : hire — **embauche**
[ɑ̃boʃ] *nf* : hiring, employment

embaumer [ɑ̃bome] *vt* **1** : embalm **2**
: scent, make fragment

embellir [ɑ̃belir] *vt* **1** ENJOLIVER : beautify
2 EXAGÉRER : embellish

embêter [ɑ̃bete] *vt* **1** : annoy, bother **2**
LASSER : bore — **s'embêter** *vr* : be bored —
embêtant, -tante [ɑ̃bɛtɑ̃, -tɑ̃t] *adj* : annoying — **embêtement** [ɑ̃bɛtmɑ̃] *nm* : hassle,
bother

emblée [ɑ̃ble] **d'**~ *adv phr* : right away

emblème [ɑ̃blɛm] *nm* : emblem

embobiner [ɑ̃bɔbine] *vt fam* : bamboozle,
trick

emboîter [ɑ̃bwate] *vt* : fit together — **s'emboîter** *vr* ~ **dans** : fit into

embonpoint [ɑ̃bɔ̃pwɛ̃] *nm* : stoutness, cor-
pulence

embouchure [ɑ̃buʃyr] *nf* **1** : mouth (of a
river) **2** : mouthpiece

embourber [ɑ̃burbe] *v* **s'embourber** *vr*
: get bogged down

embouteillage [ɑ̃butejaʒ] *nm* : traffic jam

emboutir [ɑ̃butir] *vt* HEURTER : crash into,
ram

embranchement [ɑ̃brɑ̃ʃmɑ̃] *nm* : junction,
fork

embraser [ɑ̃braze] *vt* : set on fire — **s'embraser** *vr* : catch fire

embrasser [ɑ̃brase] *vt* **1** : kiss **2** ÉTREIN-
DRE : embrace, hug — **s'embrasser** *vr*
: kiss

embrasure [ɑ̃brazyr] *nf* : doorway

embrayage [ɑ̃brejaʒ] *nm* : clutch (of an automobile) — **embrayer** [ɑ̃breje] {11} *vi*
: engage the clutch

embrocher [ɑ̃brɔʃe] *vt* : skewer (meat on a
spit)

embrouiller [ɑ̃bruje] *vt* **1** : tangle up **2**
COMPLIQUER : confuse — **s'embrouiller** *vr*
: get mixed up

embryon [ɑ̃brijɔ̃] *nm* : embryo

embûche [ɑ̃byʃ] *nf* : trap, pitfall

embuer [ɑ̃bɥe] *vt* : mist up

embuscade [ɑ̃byskad] *nf* : ambush

éméché, -chée [emeʃe] *adj fam* : tipsy

émeraude [emrod] *nf* : emerald

émerger [emɛrʒe] {17} *vi* : emerge — **émer-
gence** [emɛrʒɑ̃s] *nf* : emergence

émeri [emri] *nm* : emery

émerveiller [emɛrveje] *vt* : amaze —
s'émerveiller *vr* ~ **de** : marvel at — **émerveillement** [emɛrvejmɑ̃] *nm* : amazement,
wonder

émettre [emɛtr] {53} *vt* **1** : produce, give
out **2** : issue (a check) **3** TRANSMETTRE
: transmit, broadcast **4** EXPRIMER : express
— **émetteur** [emetœr] *nm* **1** : transmitter **2**
: issuer

émeute [emøt] *nf* : riot — **émeutier, -tière** [emøtje] *n* : rioter

émietter [emjete] *vt* : crumble, break up — **s'émietter** *vr* : crumble

émigrer [emigre] *vi* **1** : emigrate **2** : migrate — **émigrant, -grante** [emigrɑ̃, -grɑ̃t] *n* : emigrant — **émigration** [emigrasjɔ̃] *nf* : emigration — **émigré, -grée** [emigre] *n* : emigrant, émigré

éminence [eminɑ̃s] *nf* : eminence — **éminent, -nente** [eminɑ̃, -nɑ̃t] *adj* : eminent

émission [emisjɔ̃] *nf* **1** : emission **2** : transmission (of a message) **3** : program, broadcast **4** : issue (of a stamp, etc.)

emmagasiner [ɑ̃magazine] *vt* : store (up)

emmêler [ɑ̃mele] *vt* **1** : tangle **2** EMBROUILLER : muddle, mix up

emménager [ɑ̃menaʒe] {17} *vi* : move in

emmener [ɑ̃mne] {52} *vt* : take

emmitoufler [ɑ̃mitufle] *vt* : wrap up, bundle up — **s'emmitoufler** *vr* : bundle (up)

émoi [emwa] *nm* : excitement, turmoil

émotif, -tive [emɔtif, -tiv] *adj* : emotional — **émotion** [emosjɔ̃] *nf* : emotion — **émotionnel, -nelle** [emosjɔnɛl] *adj* : emotional

émousser [emuse] *vt* : blunt, dull

émouvoir [emuvwar] {56} *vt* : move, affect — **s'émouvoir** *vr* **1** : be moved **2** ~ **de** : be concerned about — **émouvant, -vante** [emuvɑ̃, -vɑ̃t] *adj* : moving

empailler [ɑ̃paje] *vt* : stuff

empaqueter [ɑ̃pakte] {8} *vt* : package, wrap up

emparer [ɑ̃pare] *v* **s'emparer** *vr* ~ **de** : seize, take hold of

empathie [ɑ̃pati] *nf* : empathy

empêcher [ɑ̃peʃe] *vt* **1** : prevent, stop **2 il n'empêche que** : nevertheless — **s'empêcher** *vr* : refrain, stop oneself — **empêchement** [ɑ̃peʃmɑ̃] *nm* : hitch, difficulty

empereur [ɑ̃prœr] *nm* : emperor

empester [ɑ̃peste] *vt* : stink up — *vi* : stink

empêtrer [ɑ̃petre] *v* **s'empêtrer** *vr* : become entangled

emphase [ɑ̃faz] *nf* : pomposity

empiéter [ɑ̃pjete] {87} *vi* ~ **sur** : infringe on

empiffrer [ɑ̃pifre] *v* **s'empiffrer** *vr fam* : stuff oneself

empiler [ɑ̃pile] *vt* : pile, stack — **s'empiler** *vr* : pile up

empire [ɑ̃pir] *nm* **1** : empire **2 sous l'**~ **de** : under the influence of

empirer [ɑ̃pire] *v* : worsen

emplacement [ɑ̃plasmɑ̃] *nm* : site, location

emplette [ɑ̃plɛt] *nf* **1** ACHAT : purchase **2 faire ses** ~**s** : go shopping

emplir [ɑ̃plir] *vt* : fill — **s'emplir** *vr* : fill up

employer [ɑ̃plwaje] {58} *vt* **1** UTILISER : use **2** : employ, provide a job for — **s'employer**
vr : be used — **emploi** [ɑ̃plwa] *nm* **1** : use **2** TRAVAIL : employment, job **3** ~ **du temps** : schedule, timetable — **employé, -ployée** [ɑ̃plwaje] *n* : employee — **employeur, -ployeuse** [ɑ̃plwajœr, -plwajøz] *n* : employer

empocher [ɑ̃pɔʃe] *vt* : pocket

empoigner [ɑ̃pwaɲe] *vt* : grasp, seize

empoisonner [ɑ̃pwazɔne] *vt* : poison — **empoisonnement** [ɑ̃pwazɔnmɑ̃] *nm* : poisoning

emporter [ɑ̃pɔrte] *vt* **1** : take (away) **2** ENTRAÎNER : carry away **3 l'**~ **sur** : beat, get the better of — **s'emporter** *vr* : lose one's temper

empreinte [ɑ̃prɛ̃t] *nf* **1** : print, imprint **2** ~ **digitale** : fingerprint

empresser [ɑ̃prese] *v* **s'empresser** *vr* **1** ~ **auprès de** : be attentive toward **2** ~ **de** : be in a hurry to — **empressé, -sée** [ɑ̃prese] *adj* : attentive, eager (to please) — **empressement** [ɑ̃prɛsmɑ̃] *nm* **1** : attentiveness **2** : eagerness

emprise [ɑ̃priz] *nf* : influence, hold

emprisonner [ɑ̃prizɔne] *vt* : imprison — **emprisonnement** [ɑ̃prizɔnmɑ̃] *nm* : imprisonment

emprunter [ɑ̃prœ̃te] *vt* **1** : borrow **2** PRENDRE : take, follow — **emprunt** [ɑ̃prœ̃] *nm* : loan

ému, -mue [emy] *adj* : moved, touched

en [ɑ̃] *prep* **1** : in, into **2 aller** ~ **Belgique** : go to Belgium **3** ~ **guerre** : at war **4** ~ **vacances** : on vacation **5** ~ **voiture** : by car **6 fait** ~ **plastique** : made of plastic — ~ *pron* **1** (*expressing quantity*) : some, any **2** (*representing a noun governed by de*) : it, them **3 qu'**~ **ferons-nous?** : what will we do of it? **4 j'**~ **viens** : I've just come from there

encadrer [ɑ̃kadre] *vt* **1** : frame **2** ENTOURER : surround **3** SURVEILLER : supervise — **encadrement** [ɑ̃kadrəmɑ̃] *nm* : frame

encaisser [ɑ̃kese] *vt* **1** : cash (a check), collect (money) **2** *fam* : take, tolerate

encastrer [ɑ̃kastre] *vt* : embed, build in

enceinte [ɑ̃sɛ̃t] *adj* : pregnant — ~ *nf* **1** : wall, enclosure **2** ~ **acoustique** : speaker

encens [ɑ̃sɑ̃] *nm* : incense

encercler [ɑ̃serkle] *vt* : surround, encircle

enchaîner [ɑ̃ʃene] *vt* **1** : chain (up) **2** LIER : link, connect — **s'enchaîner** *vr* : be connected — **enchaînement** [ɑ̃ʃenmɑ̃] *nm* **1** SÉRIE : series, sequence **2** LIEN : chain, link

enchanter [ɑ̃ʃɑ̃te] *vt* **1** ENSORCELER : enchant, bewitch **2** RAVIR : delight — **enchanté, -tée** [ɑ̃ʃɑ̃te] *adj* **1** : enchanted **2** ~ **de vous connaître** : delighted/pleased to meet you — **enchantement** [ɑ̃ʃɑ̃tmɑ̃] *nm* **1**

: enchantment **2** : delight — **enchanteur, -teresse** [ãʃãtœr, -trɛs] *adj* : enchanting

enchère [ãʃɛr] *nf* **1** : bid, bidding **2 vente aux ～s** : auction

enchevêtrer [ãʃəvetre] *vt* : tangle — **s'enchevêtrer** *vr* : become tangled

enclencher [ãklãʃe] *vt* : engage (a mechanism) — **s'enclencher** *vr* : engage, interlock

enclin, -cline [ãklɛ̃, -klin] *adj* ～ **à** : inclined to

enclore [ãklɔr] {34} *vt* : enclose

enclos [ãklo] *nm* : enclosure

enclume [ãklym] *nf* : anvil

encoche [ãkɔʃ] *nf* : notch

encolure [ãkɔlyr] *nf* : neck (of a dress, etc.)

encombrer [ãkɔ̃bre] *vt* **1** : clutter (up) **2** OBSTRUER : block, hamper — **s'encombrer** *vr* **de** : burden oneself with — **encombrant, -brante** [ãkɔ̃brã, -brãt] *adj* : cumbersome — **encombre** [ãkɔ̃br] **sans ～** *adv phr* : without a hitch — **encombrement** [ãkɔ̃brəmã] *nm* **1** : clutter, congestion **2** EMBOUTEILLAGE : traffic jam

encontre [ãkɔ̃tr] **à l'～ de** *prep phr* : against, contrary to

encore [ãkɔr] *adv* **1** TOUJOURS : still **2** : more, again **3 ～ que** : although **4 pas ～** : not yet **5 si ～** : if only

encourager [ãkuraʒe] {17} *vt* : encourage — **encouragement** [ãkuraʒmã] *nm* : encouragement

encourir [ãkurir] {23} *vt* : incur

encrasser [ãkrase] *vt* **1** SALIR : dirty **2** OBSTRUER : clog up

encre [ãkr] *nf* : ink — **encrer** [ãkre] *vt* : ink — **encrier** [ãkrije] *nm* : inkwell

encyclopédie [ãsiklɔpedi] *nf* : encyclopedia

endetter [ãdete] *v* **s'endetter** *vr* : get into debt

endeuillé, -lée [ãdœje] *adj* : in mourning, bereaved

endive [ãdiv] *nf* : endive, chickory

endoctriner [ãdɔktrine] *vt* : indoctrinate — **endoctrinement** [ãdɔktrinmã] *nm* : indoctrination

endommager [ãdɔmaʒe] {17} *vt* : damage

endormir [ãdɔrmir] {30} *vt* : put to sleep — **s'endormir** *vr* : fall asleep — **endormi, -mie** [ãdɔrmi] *adj* **1** : asleep **2** : sleepy

endosser [ãdose] *vt* **1** : take on, assume **2** : endorse (a check)

endroit [ãdrwa] *nm* **1** : place, spot **2 à l'～** : right side up

enduire [ãdɥir] {49} *vt* : coat, cover — **enduit** [ãdɥi] *nm* : coating

endurance [ãdyrãs] *nf* : endurance

endurcir [ãdyrsir] *vt* : toughen, harden — **s'endurcir** *vr* : harden

endurer [ãdyre] *vt* : endure

énergie [enɛrʒi] *nf* : energy — **énergique** [enɛrʒik] *adj* : energetic

énerver [enɛrve] *vt* : irritate, annoy — **s'énerver** *vr* : get worked up

enfance [ãfãs] *nf* : childhood — **enfant** [ãfã] *nmf* : child — **enfanter** [ãfãte] *vt* : give birth to — **enfantillage** [ãfãtijaʒ] *nm* : childishness — **enfantin, -tine** [ãfãtɛ̃, -tin] *adj* **1** : childlike **2** : childish

enfer [ãfɛr] *nm* : hell

enfermer [ãfɛrme] *vt* : shut up, lock up — **s'enfermer** *vr* **1** : shut oneself away **2 ～ dans** : retreat into

enfiler [ãfile] *vt* **1** : slip on, put on (a garment) **2** : string, thread (a needle)

enfin [ãfɛ̃] *adv* **1** : finally, at last **2** : lastly **3 ～, je crois** : at least I think so **4 mais ～, donne-le-moi!** : come on, give it to me!

enflammer [ãflame] *vt* **1** : ignite, set fire to **2** : inflame (in medicine) — **s'enflammer** *vr* : catch fire

enfler [ãfle] *v* : swell — **s'enfler** *vr* : swell up — **enflure** [ãflyr] *nf* : swelling

enfoncer [ãfɔ̃se] {6} *vt* **1** : drive or push in **2** DÉFONCER : break down — *vi* : sink — **s'enfoncer** *vr* **1** : sink in **2** CÉDER : give way

enfouir [ãfwir] *vt* **1** : bury **2** CACHER : hide

enfreindre [ãfrɛ̃dr] {37} *vt* : infringe

enfuir [ãfɥir] {46} *v* **s'enfuir** *vr* : flee

engager [ãgaʒe] {17} *vt* **1** OBLIGER : bind, commit **2** RECRUTER : hire **3** COMMENCER : start **4 ～ qqn à** : urge s.o. to **5 ～ une vitesse** : put a car in gear — **s'engager** *vr* **1** : commit oneself **2** : enlist (in the army) **3 ～ dans** : enter, turn into (a street) — **engagé, -gée** [ãgaʒe] *adj* **1** : committed **2** *Can fam* : busy — **engageant, -geante** [ãgaʒã, -ʒãt] *adj* : engaging — **engagement** [ãgaʒmã] *nm* **1** PROMESSE : commitment **2** PARTICIPATION : involvement

engin [ãʒɛ̃] *nm* : machine, device

engloutir [ãglutir] *vt* **1** : gobble up, devour **2** : engulf, swallow up

engorger [ãgɔrʒe] {17} *vt* : block, jam up

engouement [ãgumã] *nm* : infatuation

engouffrer [ãgufre] *vt* : devour

engourdir [ãgurdir] *vt* : numb — **s'engourdir** *vr* : go numb — **engourdi, -die** [ãgurdi] *adj* : numb

engraisser [ãgrese] *vt* : fatten — *vi* : put on weight — **engrais** [ãgrɛ] *nm* : fertilizer, manure

engrenage [ãgrənaʒ] *nm* : gears *pl*

engueuler [ãgœle] *vt fam* : yell at, bawl out

énième [enjɛm] *adj* : nth, umpteenth

enivrer [ãnivre] *vt* : intoxicate, make drunk — **s'enivrer** *vr* : get drunk

enjamber [ãʒãbe] *vt* **1** : step over **2** : span — **enjambée** [ãʒãbe] *nf* : stride

enjeu [ɑ̃ʒø] *nm, pl* **-jeux** : stake (in games)

enjôler [ɑ̃ʒole] *vt* : cajole, wheedle

enjoliver [ɑ̃ʒɔlive] *vt* : embellish — **enjoliveur** [ɑ̃jɔlivœr] *nm* : hubcap

enjoué, -jouée [ɑ̃ʒwe] *adj* : cheerful

enlacer [ɑ̃lase] {6} *vt* : embrace, hug

enlaidir [ɑ̃ledir] *vt* : make ugly — *vi* : grow ugly

enlever [ɑ̃lve] {52} *vt* **1** : remove, take away **2** KIDNAPPER : abduct — **enlèvement** [ɑ̃lɛvmɑ̃] *nm* **1** : removal **2** : abduction

enliser *v* **s'enliser** *vr* : sink, get stuck

ennemi, -mie [ɛnmi] *n* : enemy

ennui [ɑ̃nɥi] *nm* **1** PROBLÈME : trouble, problem **2** : boredom — **ennuyant, -nuyante** [ɑ̃nɥijɑ̃, ɑ̃nɥijɑ̃t] *adj Can* **1** : annoying **2** : boring — **ennuyer** [ɑ̃nɥije] {58} *vt* **1** AGACER : annoy **2** : bore — **s'ennuyer** *vr* : be bored — **ennuyeux, -nuyeuse** [ɑ̃nɥijø, ɑ̃nɥijøz] *adj* **1** : annoying **2** : boring

énoncer [enɔ̃se] {6} *vt* : express, state — **énoncé** [enɔ̃se] *nm* **1** : statement **2** LIBELLÉ : wording

énorme [enɔrm] *adj* : enormous, huge — **énormément** [enɔrmemɑ̃] *adv* **~ de** : a great number of

enquête [ɑ̃kɛt] *nf* **1** INVESTIGATION : investigation, inquiry **2** SONDAGE : survey — **enquêter** [ɑ̃kete] *vi* : investigate

enraciner [ɑ̃rasine] *vt* : root — **s'enraciner** *vr* : take root

enrager [ɑ̃raʒe] {17} *vi* : be furious — **enragé, -gée** [ɑ̃raʒe] *adj* **1** : rabid (of an animal) **2** : furious (of a person)

enrayer [ɑ̃reje] {11} *vt* **1** : check, curb **2** BLOQUER : jam

enregistrer [ɑ̃rəʒistre] *vt* **1** : record **2** INSCRIRE : register **3** : check in (baggage) — **enregistrement** [ɑ̃rəʒistrəmɑ̃] *nm* **1** : registration **2** : (tape) recording

enrhumer [ɑ̃ryme] *v* **s'enrhumer** *vr* : catch a cold

enrichir [ɑ̃riʃir] *vt* : enrich — **s'enrichir** *vr* : grow rich — **enrichissement** [ɑ̃riʃismɑ̃] *nm* : enrichment

enrober [ɑ̃rɔbe] *vt* : coat

enrôler [ɑ̃role] *vt* : enroll, enlist — **s'enrôler** *vr* : enlist

enroué, -rouée [ɑ̃rwe] *adj* : hoarse

enrouler [ɑ̃rule] *vt* : wind, coil — **s'enrouler** *vr* **~ dans** : wrap oneself in (a blanket)

ensanglanté, -tée [ɑ̃sɑ̃glɑ̃te] *adj* : bloody, bloodstained

enseignant, -gnante [ɑ̃sɛɲɑ̃, -ɲɑ̃t] *adj* : teaching — **~** *n* : teacher

enseigne [ɑ̃sɛɲ] *nf* : sign

enseigner [ɑ̃seɲe] *v* : to teach — **enseignement** [ɑ̃sɛɲmɑ̃] *nm* **1** : teaching **2** : education

ensemble [ɑ̃sɑ̃bl] *adv* : together — **~** *nm* **1** : group, set **2** TOTALITÉ : whole **3** : (musical) ensemble **4** : suit, outfit **5 dans l'~** : on the whole

ensemencer [ɑ̃səmɑ̃se] {6} *vt* : sow

ensoleillé, -lée [ɑ̃sɔleje] *adj* : sunny

ensorceler [ɑ̃sɔrsəle] {8} *vt* : bewitch, charm

ensuite [ɑ̃sɥit] *adv* **1** : then, next **2** : afterwards, later

ensuivre [ɑ̃sɥivr] {35} *v* **s'ensuivre** *vr* : ensue, follow

entailler [ɑ̃taje] *vt* : gash, cut — **entaille** [ɑ̃taj] *nf* **1** : cut, gash **2** ENCOCHE : notch

entamer [ɑ̃tame] *vt* **1** : cut into, eat into **2** : start, enter into (negotiations)

entasser [ɑ̃tase] *vt* **1** : pile (up) **2** SERRER : cram — **s'entasser** *vr* : pile up

entendre [ɑ̃tɑ̃dr] {63} *vt* **1** : hear **2** COMPRENDRE : understand **3** VOULOIR : intend — **s'entendre** *vr* **1** : agree **2 ~ avec** : get along with — **entendement** [ɑ̃tɑ̃dmɑ̃] *nm* : understanding — **entendu, -due** [ɑ̃tɑ̃dy] *adj* **1** : agreed, understood **2 bien ~** : of course — **entente** [ɑ̃tɑ̃t] *nf* **1** : harmony **2** ACCORD : agreement, understanding

entériner [ɑ̃terine] *vt* : ratify

enterrer [ɑ̃tere] *vt* : bury — **enterrement** [ɑ̃tɛrmɑ̃] *nm* **1** : burial **2** FUNÉRAILLES : funeral

en–tête [ɑ̃tɛt] *nm, pl* **en–têtes** : heading

entêter [ɑ̃tete] *v* **s'entêter** *vr* : be obstinate, persist — **entêté, -tée** [ɑ̃tete] *adj* : stubborn, obstinate — **entêtement** [ɑ̃tɛtmɑ̃] *nm* : stubbornness

enthousiasme [ɑ̃tuzjasm] *nm* : enthusiasm — **enthousiasmer** [ɑ̃tuzjasme] *vt* : fill with enthusiasm, excite — **enthousiaste** [ɑ̃tuzjast] *adj* : enthusiastic — **~** *nmf* : enthusiast, fan

entier, -tière [ɑ̃tje, -tjɛr] *adj* : entire, whole — **entier** *nm* **en ~** : totally, in its entirety — **entièrement** [ɑ̃tjɛrmɑ̃] *adv* : entirely, wholly

entité [ɑ̃tite] *nf* : entity

entonnoir [ɑ̃tɔnwar] *nm* : funnel (utensil)

entorse [ɑ̃tɔrs] *nf* : sprain

entortiller [ɑ̃tɔrtije] *vt* : twist, wind

entourer [ɑ̃ture] *vt* : surround — **entourage** [ɑ̃turaʒ] *nm* : circle (of friends or family)

entracte [ɑ̃trakt] *nm* : intermission

entraide [ɑ̃trɛd] *nf* : mutual aid

entrailles [ɑ̃traj] *nfpl* **1** : entrails **2** PROFONDEURS : depths

entrain [ɑ̃trɛ̃] *nm* : liveliness, spirit

entraîner [ɑ̃trene] *vt* **1** EMPORTER : carry away **2** OCCASIONNER : lead to, involve **3** FORMER : train, coach — **s'entraîner** *vr* : train, practice — **entraînant, -nante** [ɑ̃trenɑ̃, -nɑ̃t] *adj* : lively — **entraînement** [ɑ̃trɛnmɑ̃]

[ātrɛnmā] *nm* **1** : training, coaching **2** PRATIQUE : practice — **entraîneur, -neuse** [ātrɛnœr, -nøz] *n* : trainer, coach
entraver [ātrave] *vt* : hinder — **entrave** [ātrav] *nf* : hindrance
entre [ātr] *prep* **1** : between **2** PARMI : among
entrecôte [ātrəkot] *nf* : rib steak
entrecroiser [ātrəkrwaze] *v* **s'entrecroiser** *vr* : intersect
entrée [ātre] *nf* **1** : entrance, entry **2** ACCÈS : admission **3** BILLET : ticket **4** : first course (of a meal) **5** : entry (in a text), input (of information)
entre-jambes [ātrəʒāb] *nms & pl* : crotch (of clothing)
entrelacer [ātrəlase] {6} *vt* : intertwine
entremêler [ātrəmele] *vt* : mix together
entremets [ātrəmɛ] *nms & pl* : dessert
entreposer [ātrəpoze] *vt* : store — **entrepôt** [ātrəpo] *nm* : warehouse
entreprendre [ātrəprādr] {70} *vt* : undertake, start — **entreprenant, -nante** [ātrəprənā, -nāt] *adj* : enterprising — **entrepreneur, -neuse** [ātrəprənœr, -nøz] *n* : contractor — **entreprise** [ātrəpriz] *nf* **1** : enterprise, undertaking **2** : business, firm
entrer [ātre] *vi* **1** : enter, go in, come in **2** ça n'entre pas : it doesn't fit **3** ~ dans : join, go into — *vt* **1** : bring in, take in **2** : enter, input (data, etc.)
entre-temps [ātrətā] *adv* : meanwhile
entretenir [ātrətnir] {92} *vt* **1** MAINTENIR : maintain **2** ~ qqn de : speak to s.o. about — **s'entretenir** *vr* **1** ~ avec : consult with, converse with **2** ~ de : discuss, talk about — **entretenu, -nue** [ātrətny] *adj* : kept, maintained — **entretien** [ātrətjɛ̃] *nm* **1** : maintenance **2** CONVERSATION : talk, interview
entrevoir [ātrəvwar] {99} *vt* **1** : glimpse, make out **2** PRÉSAGER : foresee, anticipate — **entrevue** [ātrəvy] *nf* : meeting, interview
entrouvert, -verte [ātruvɛr, -vɛrt] *adj & adv* : half open, ajar
énumérer [enymere] {87} *vt* : enumerate — **énumération** [-merasjɔ̃] *nf* : enumeration
envahir [āvair] *vt* **1** : invade **2** : overcome (fear, etc.)
envelopper [āvlɔpe] *vt* **1** : envelop **2** RECOUVRIR : wrap up, cover — **enveloppe** [āvlɔp] *nf* : envelope
envergure [āvɛrgyr] *nf* **1** : wingspan **2** IMPORTANCE : breadth, scope
envers [āvɛr] *prep* : toward, to — ~ *nm* **1** REVERS : back, reverse **2** à l'~ : inside out, upside down, backward
envie [āvi] *nf* **1** DÉSIR : desire, wish — **envier** [āvje] {96} *vt* : envy — **envieux, -vieuse** [āvjø, -vjøz] *adj* : envious

environ [āvirɔ̃] *adv* : about, approximately — **environnement** [āvirɔnmā] *nm* : environment, surroundings — **environnant, -nante** [āvirɔnā, -nāt] *adj* : surrounding — **environs** [āvirɔ̃] *nmpl* **1** : surroundings **2** aux ~ de : around, about
envisager [āvizaʒe] {17} *vt* : consider, imagine
envoi [āvwa] *nm* **1** : sending, dispatching **2** COLIS : parcel, package
envoler [āvɔle] *v* **s'envoler** *vr* **1** : take off (of a plane) **2** : fly away (of a bird) — **envol** [āvɔl] *nm* : takeoff — **envolée** [āvɔle] *nf* **1** : flight **2** AUGMENTATION : rise, surge
envoyer [āvwaje] {36} *vt* **1** : send (out) **2** LANCER : throw **3** ~ par la poste : mail — **envoyé, -voyée** [āvwaje] *n* : envoy
enzyme [āzim] *nf* : enzyme
épagneul, -gneule [epaɲœl] *n* : spaniel
épais, -paisse [epɛ, -pɛs] *adj* : thick — **épaisseur** [epɛsœr] *nf* **1** : thickness **2** : layer — **épaissir** [epesir] *v* **s'épaissir** *vr* : thicken
épancher [epāʃe] *vt* : give vent to — **s'épancher** *vr* : pour one's heart out
épanouir [epanwir] *v* **s'épanouir** *vr* **1** : bloom **2** S'ÉCLAIRER : light up **3** SE DÉVELOPPER : develop, flourish — **épanouissement** [epanwismā] *nm* : blossoming
épargner [eparɲe] *vt* **1** ÉCONOMISER : save **2** : spare (s.o.'s life, etc.) — **s'épargner** *vr* : spare oneself — **épargne** [eparɲ] *nf* **1** : saving **2** : savings *pl*
éparpiller [eparpije] *vt* : scatter, disperse — **s'éparpiller** *vr* : dissipate — **épars, -parse** [epar, -pars] *adj* : scattered
épater [epate] *vt fam* : amaze — **épatant, -tante** [epatā, -tāt] *adj fam* : amazing
épaule [epol] *nf* : shoulder — **épaulette** [epolɛt] *nf* : shoulder strap
épave [epav] *nf* : wreck (of a ship)
épée [epe] *nf* : sword
épeler [eple] {8} *vt* : spell
éperdu, -due [epɛrdy] *adj* **1** : intense, passionate **2** ~ de peur : overcome with fear — **éperdument** [epɛrdymā] *adv* : frantically, desperately
éperon [eprɔ̃] *nm* : spur — **éperonner** [eprɔne] *vt* : spur (on)
éphémère [efemɛr] *adj* : ephemeral
épi [epi] *nm* **1** : ear, cob **2** : tuft (of hair)
épice [epis] *nf* : spice — **épicé, -cée** [epise] *adj* : spicy — **épicer** [epise] {6} *vt* : spice — **épicerie** [episri] *nf* **1** : grocery store **2** ~s *nfpl* : groceries *pl* — **épicier, -cière** [episje, -sjɛr] *n* : grocer
épidémie [epidemi] *nf* : epidemic — **épidémique** [-demik] *adj* : epidemic
épiderme [epidɛrm] *nm* : skin

épier [epje] {96} *vt* **1** : spy on **2** ATTENDRE : watch out for

épilepsie [epilɛpsi] *nf* : epilepsy — **épileptique** [epilɛptik] *adj & nmf* : epileptic

épiler [epile] *vt* : remove hair from, pluck

épilogue [epilɔg] *nm* **1** : epilogue **2** : conclusion, outcome

épinards [epinar] *nmpl* : spinach

épine [epin] *nf* **1** : thorn **2** ~ **dorsale** : spine, backbone — **épineux, -neuse** [epinø, -nøz] *adj* : thorny

épingle [epɛ̃gl] *nf* **1** : pin **2** ~ **à cheveux** : hairpin **3** ~ **de sûreté** : safety pin

épique [epik] *adj* : epic

épisode [epizɔd] *nm* : episode

épitaphe [epitaf] *nf* : epitaph

épithète [epitɛt] *nf* : epithet

éplucher [eplyʃe] *vt* **1** PELER : peel **2** EXAMINER : scrutinize

éponge [epɔ̃ʒ] *nf* : sponge — **éponger** [epɔ̃ʒe] {17} *vt* : sponge up, mop up

épopée [epɔpe] *nf* : epic

époque [epɔk] *nf* **1** : age, era **2** : time, period

épouse [epuz] *nf* → **époux** — **épouser** [epuze] *vt* : marry, wed

épousseter [epuste] {8} *vt* : dust

époustouflant, -flante [epustuflɑ̃, -flɑ̃t] *adj fam* : amazing

épouvantable [epuvɑ̃tabl] *adj* : dreadful, horrible

épouvantail [epuvɑ̃taj] *nm* : scarecrow

épouvanter [epuvɑ̃te] *vt* : terrify — **épouvante** [epuvɑ̃t] *nf* : horror

époux, -pouse [epu, -puz] *n* : spouse, husband *m*, wife *f*

éprendre [eprɑ̃dr] {70} *v* **s'éprendre** *vr* ~ **de** : fall in love with

épreuve [eprœv] *nf* **1** ESSAI : test **2** : ordeal, trial **3** : event (in sports) **4** : proof, print (in printing)

éprouver [epruve] *vt* **1** : test, try **2** RESSENTIR : feel, experience **3** AFFECTER : distress

épuiser [epɥize] *vt* : exhaust — **épuisé, -sée** [epɥize] *adj* **1** : exhausted **2** : out of stock — **épuisement** [epɥizmɑ̃] *nm* : exhaustion

épurer [epyre] *vt* **1** : purify, refine **2** : purge (in politics) — **épuration** [epyrasjɔ̃] *nf* **1** : purification **2** : purge

équateur [ekwatœr] *nm* : equator

équation [ekwasjɔ̃] *nf* : equation

équerre [ekɛr] *nf* **1** : square **2** d'~ : square, straight

équestre [ekɛstr] *adj* : equestrian

équilibre [ekilibr] *nm* : equilibrium, balance — **équilibré, -brée** [ekilibre] *adj* : well-balanced — **équilibrer** [ekilibre] *vt* : balance

équinoxe [ekinɔks] *nm* : equinox

équipage [ekipaʒ] *nm* : crew

équiper [ekipe] *vt* : equip, outfit — **équipe**

[ekip] *nf* : team — **équipement** [ekipmɑ̃] *nm* : equipment — **équipier, -pière** [ekipje, -pjɛr] *n* : team member

équitable [ekitabl] *adj* : fair, equitable — **équitablement** [-tabləmɑ̃] *adv* : fairly

équitation [ekitasjɔ̃] *nf* : horseback riding

équité [ekite] *nf* : equity, fairness

équivalence [ekivalɑ̃s] *nf* : equivalence — **équivalent, -lente** [ekivalɑ̃, -lɑ̃t] *adj* : equivalent — **équivalent** *nm* : equivalent — **équivaloir** [ekivalwar] {95} *vi* ~ **à** : be equivalent to

équivoque [ekivɔk] *adj* **1** : equivocal, ambiguous **2** DOUTEUX : questionable

érable [erabl] *nm* : maple

éradiquer [eradike] *vt* : eradicate

érafler [erafle] *vt* : scratch — **éraflure** [eraflyr] *nf* : scratch, scrape

ère [ɛr] *nf* : era

érection [erɛksjɔ̃] *nf* : erection

éreinter [erɛ̃te] *vt* **1** ÉPUISER : exhaust **2** CRITIQUER : criticize — **s'éreinter** *vr* : wear oneself out — **éreintant, -tante** [erɛ̃tɑ̃, -tɑ̃t] *adj* : exhausting

ergoter [ɛrgote] *vi* : quibble

ériger [eriʒe] {17} *vt* : erect — **s'ériger** *vr* ~ **en** : set oneself up as

ermite [ɛrmit] *nm* : hermit

éroder [erɔde] *vt* : erode — **érosion** [erozjɔ̃] *nf* : erosion

érotique [erɔtik] *adj* : erotic — **érotisme** [erɔtism] *nm* : eroticism

errer [ere] *vi* : wander, roam — **erreur** [erœr] *nf* : error, mistake — **erroné, -née** [erɔne] *adj* : erroneous

érudit, -dite [erydi, -dit] *adj* : scholarly — ~ *n* : scholar — **érudition** [erydisjɔ̃] *nf* : learning, scholarship

éruption [erypsjɔ̃] *nf* **1** : eruption **2** : rash (in medicine)

escabeau [ɛskabo] *nm, pl* **-beaux 1** : stool **2** ÉCHELLE : stepladder

escadre [ɛskadr] *nf* : squadron — **escadrille** [ɛskadrij] *nf* : squadron — **escadron** [ɛskadrɔ̃] *nm* : squadron, squad

escalader [ɛskalade] *vt* : climb — **escalade** [ɛskalad] *nf* : (rock) climbing

escale [ɛskal] *nf* : stopover

escalier [ɛskalje] *nm* **1** : stairs *pl*, steps *pl* **2** ~ **de secours** : fire escape **3** ~ **mécanique** : escalator

escalope [ɛskalɔp] *nf* : cutlet

escamoter [ɛskamɔte] *vt* **1** : fold away, retract **2** ÉVITER : evade — **escamotable** [ɛskamɔtabl] *adj* : retractable, foldaway

escargot [ɛskargo] *nm* : snail

escarmouche [ɛskarmuʃ] *nf* : skirmish

escarpé, -pée [ɛskarpe] *adj* : steep

esclaffer [ɛsklafe] *v* **s'esclaffer** *vr* : burst out laughing

esclave [ɛsklav] *adj & nmf* : slave — **es-clavage** [ɛsklavaʒ] *nm* : slavery

escompter [ɛskɔ̃te] *vt* **1** : discount **2** ES-PÉRER : count on, expect — **escompte** [ɛskɔ̃t] *nm* : discount

escorter [ɛskɔrte] *vt* : escort — **escorte** [ɛskɔrt] *nf* : escort

escrime [ɛskrim] *nf* : fencing

escroc [ɛskro] *nm* : swindler, crook — **es-croquer** [ɛskroke] *vt* : swindle, defraud — **escroquerie** [ɛskrokri] *nf* : swindle, fraud

eskimo [ɛskimo] → **esquimau**

ésotérique [ezoterik] *adj* : esoteric

espace [ɛspas] *nm* : space — **espacer** [ɛspase] {6} *vt* : space (out)

espadon [ɛspadɔ̃] *nm* : swordfish

espadrilles [ɛspadrij] *nfpl Can* : sneakers *pl*

espagnol, -gnole [ɛspaɲɔl] *adj* : Spanish — **espagnol** *nm* : Spanish (language)

espèce [ɛspɛs] *nf* **1** : species **2** SORTE : sort, kind **3** ~**s** *nfpl* : cash

espérer [ɛspere] {87} *vt* **1** : hope for **2** ES-COMPTER : expect — **espérance** [ɛsperɑ̃s] *nf* : hope

espiègle [ɛspjɛgl] *adj* : mischievous

espion, -pionne [ɛspjɔ̃, -pjɔn] *n* : spy — **es-pionnage** [ɛspjɔnaʒ] *nm* : espionage — **es-pionner** [ɛspjone] *vt* : spy on

espoir [ɛspwar] *nm* : hope

esprit [ɛspri] *nm* **1** : mind **2** ATTITUDE : spirit **3** HUMOUR : wit **4** FANTÔME : ghost

esquimau, -maude [ɛskimo, -mod] *adj, mpl* **-maux** [-mo] : Eskimo

esquisse [ɛskis] *nf* : sketch — **esquisser** [ɛskise] *vt* : sketch

esquiver [ɛskive] *vt* : avoid, dodge — **es-quive** [ɛskiv] *nf* : dodge

essai [ɛsɛ] *nm* **1** TENTATIVE : attempt, try **2** ÉPREUVE : trial, test **3** : (literary) essay

essaim [ɛsɛ̃] *nm* : swarm

essayer [ɛseje] {11} *vt* : try

essence [ɛsɑ̃s] *nf* : gasoline — **essentiel, -tielle** [ɛsɑ̃sjɛl] *adj* : essential — **essentiel** *nm* : main part, essentials *pl* — **essentielle-ment** [-sjɛlmɑ̃] *adv* : essentially

essieu [ɛsjø] *nm, pl* **-sieux** : axle

essor [ɛsɔr] *nm* **1** : flight (of a bird) **2** : ex-pansion, growth

essouffler [ɛsufle] *vt* : make breathless — **s'essouffler** *vr* : get out of breath

essuyer [ɛsɥije] {58} *vt* **1** : wipe, dry **2** SUBIR : suffer, endure — **essuie–glace** [ɛsɥiglas] *nm, pl* **essuie–glaces** : wind-shield wiper — **essuie–mains** [ɛsɥimɛ̃] *nms & pl* : hand towel — **essuie–tout** [ɛsɥitu] *nms & pl* : paper towel

est [ɛst] *adj* : east, eastern — ~ *nm* **1** : east **2** **l'Est** : the East

estampe [ɛstɑ̃p] *nf* : engraving, print — **es-tampille** [ɛstɑ̃pij] *nf* : stamp

esthétique [ɛstetik] *adj* : aesthetic — **es-théticien, -cienne** [ɛstetisjɛ̃, -sjɛn] *n* : beautician

estimer [ɛstime] *vt* **1** : assess, evaluate **2** CALCULER : estimate **3** RESPECTER : esteem **4** CONSIDÉRER : consider — **estimation** [ɛstimasjɔ̃] *nf* : estimate — **estime** [ɛstim] *nf* : esteem, respect

estival, -vale [ɛstival] *adj, mpl* **-vaux** [-vo] : summer

estomac [ɛstɔma] *nm* : stomach

estrade [ɛstrad] *nf* : platform, stage

estragon [ɛstragɔ̃] *nm* : tarragon

estropié, -piée [ɛstrɔpje] *adj* : crippled, maimed

estuaire [ɛstɥɛr] *nm* : estuary

esturgeon [ɛstyrʒɔ̃] *nm* : sturgeon

et [e] *conj* : and

étable [etabl] *nf* : cowshed

établi [etabli] *nm* : workbench

établir [etablir] *vt* **1** : establish, set up **2** : draw up (a list, etc.) — **s'établir** *vr* : be-come established, get set up — **établisse-ment** [etablismɑ̃] *nm* : establishment

étage [etaʒ] *nm* **1** : story, floor **2** : tier, level — **étagère** [etaʒɛr] *nf* : shelf, bookshelf

étai [etɛ] *nm* : prop, support

étain [etɛ̃] *nm* **1** : tin **2** : pewter

étaler [etale] *vt* **1** : display **2** ÉTENDRE : spread (out) **3** ÉCHELONNER : space out, stagger — **s'étaler** *vr* **1** S'ÉTENDRE : spread out **2** *fam* : fall flat, sprawl — **étalage** [eta-laʒ] *nm* **1** : display **2** DEVANTURE : shop-window **3** **faire** ~ **de** : flaunt

étalon [etalɔ̃] *nm* **1** : stallion **2** MODÈLE : standard

étancher [etɑ̃ʃe] *vt* **1** : stem, staunch **2** : quench (thirst) — **étanche** [etɑ̃ʃ] *adj* : wa-tertight, waterproof

étang [etɑ̃] *nm* : pond

étape [etap] *nf* **1** ARRÊT : stop, halt **2** : stage (of development)

état [eta] *nm* **1** : state, condition **2** : state-ment (of expenses, etc.) **3** : (social) status **4** MÉTIER : profession, trade

étau [eto] *nm, pl* **-taux** : vise

étayer [eteje] {11} *vt* : prop up

été [ete] *nm* : summer

éteindre [etɛ̃dr] {37} *vt* **1** : put out, extin-guish **2** : turn off, switch off — **s'éteindre** *vr* **1** : go out, die out **2** MOURIR : die

étendard [etɑ̃dar] *nm* : standard, flag

étendre [etɑ̃dr] {63} *vt* **1** ÉTALER : spread (out) **2** : hang up (laundry) **3** ALLONGER : stretch (out) **4** ACCROÎTRE : extend — **s'étendre** *vr* **1** : stretch **2** SE COUCHER : lie down **3** CROÎTRE : spread — **étendu, -due** [etɑ̃dy] *adj* : extensive, wide — **étendue** *nf* **1** : area **2** : extent

éternel, -nelle [etɛrnɛl] *adj* : eternal — **éter-**

nellement [-nɛlmɑ̃] *adv* : eternally, forever — **éternité** [etɛrnite] *nf* : eternity

éternuer [etɛrnɥe] *vi* : sneeze — **éternuement** [etɛrnymɑ̃] *nm* : sneeze

éther [etɛr] *nm* : ether

éthique [etik] *adj* : ethical — ~ *nf* : ethics

ethnique [ɛtnik] *adj* : ethnic

étincelle [etɛ̃sɛl] *nf* : spark — **étinceler** [etɛ̃sle] {8} *vi* : sparkle

étiquette [etikɛt] *nf* **1** : label **2** PROTOCOLE : etiquette — **étiqueter** [etikte] {8} *vt* : label

étirer [etire] *vt* : stretch — **s'étirer** *vr* : stretch (out)

étoffe [etɔf] *nf* : material, fabric

étoile [etwal] *nf* : star — **étoilé, -lée** [etwale] *adj* : starry

étonner [etɔne] *vt* : astonish — **s'étonner** *vr* : be surprised — **étonnant, -nante** [etɔnɑ̃, -nɑ̃t] *adj* : astonishing — **étonnement** [etɔnmɑ̃] *nm* : surprise, astonishment

étouffer [etufe] *vt* **1** : stifle **2** ASPHYXIER : smother **3** : deaden (sound, etc.) — **s'étouffer** *vr* **1** : choke **2** : suffocate

étourderie [eturdəri] *nf* : thoughtlessness

étourdir [eturdir] *vt* **1** ASSOMMER : stun **2** : make dizzy — **étourdi, -die** [eturdi] *adj* : absentminded, scatterbrained — **étourdissant, -sante** [eturdisɑ̃, -sɑ̃t] *adj* **1** BRUYANT : deafening **2** : stunning — **étourdissement** [eturdismɑ̃] *nm* VERTIGE : dizziness

étourneau [eturno] *nm, pl* **-neaux** [-no] : starling

étrange [etrɑ̃ʒ] *adj* : strange — **étrangement** [etrɑ̃ʒmɑ̃] *adv* : oddly, strangely — **étrangeté** [etrɑ̃ʒte] *nf* : strangeness, oddity — **étranger, -gère** [etrɑ̃ʒe, -ʒɛr] *adj* **1** : foreign (of a country, etc.) **2** : unfamiliar, strange — ~ *n* **1** : foreigner **2** : stranger **3** **à l'étranger** : abroad

étrangler [etrɑ̃gle] *vt* **1** : strangle **2** SERRER : constrict — **s'étrangler** *vr* : choke

être [ɛtr] {38} *vi* **1** : be, exist **2** ~ **à** : belong to — *v aux* : have — ~ *nm* **1** : being **2** PERSONNE : person

étreindre [etrɛ̃dr] {37} *vt* **1** : embrace, hug **2** SERRER : grip — **étreinte** [etrɛ̃t] *nf* **1** : embrace, hug **2 sous l'~ de** : in the grip of

étrenner [etrene] *vt* : use for the first time

étrier [etrije] *nm* : stirrup

étriqué, -quée [etrike] *adj* **1** : skimpy **2** MESQUIN : petty

étroit, -troite [etrwa, -trwat] *adj* **1** : narrow **2** SERRÉ : tight — **étroitesse** [etrwatɛs] *nf* : narrowness

étude [etyd] *nf* **1** : study, studying **2** BUREAU : office — **étudiant, -diante** [etydjɑ̃, -djɑ̃t] *adj & n* : student — **étudier** [etydje] {96} *v* : study

étui [etɥi] *nm* : case

euphémisme [øfemism] *nm* : euphemism

euphorie [øfɔri] *nf* : euphoria

euro [øro] *nm* : euro (monetary unit)

européen, -péenne [ørɔpeɛ̃, -peɛn] *adj* : European

eux [ø] *pron* : they, them — **eux–mêmes** [ømɛm] *pron pl* : themselves

évacuer [evakɥe] *vt* : evacuate — **évacuation** [evakɥasjɔ̃] *nf* : evacuation

évader [evade] *v* **s'évader** *vr* : escape — **évadé, -dée** [evade] *n* : fugitive

évaluer [evalɥe] *vt* : evaluate, assess — **évaluation** [evalɥasjɔ̃] *nf* : evaluation, assessment

évangile [evɑ̃ʒil] *nm* **1** : gospel **2 l'Évangile** : the Gospel

évanouir [evanwir] *v* **s'évanouir** *vr* : faint — **évanouissement** [evanwismɑ̃] *nm* : fainting, faint

évaporer [evapɔre] *v* **s'évaporer** *vr* : evaporate — **évaporation** [evapɔrasjɔ̃] *nf* : evaporation

évasif, -sive [evazif, -ziv] *adj* : evasive — **évasion** [evazjɔ̃] *nf* : escape

éveiller [eveje] *vt* **1** RÉVEILLER : awaken **2** : arouse (curiosity, etc.) — **s'éveiller** *vr* **1** : wake up **2** : be aroused — **éveil** [evɛj] *nm* **1** : awakening **2 en** ~ : on the alert — **éveillé, -lée** [eveje] *adj* **1** : awake **2** ALERTE : alert

événement [evenmɑ̃] *nm* : event

éventail [evɑ̃taj] *nm* **1** : fan **2** GAMME : range, spread

éventaire [evɑ̃tɛr] *nm* : stall, stand

éventé, -tée [evɑ̃te] *adj* : stale, flat

éventrer [evɑ̃tre] *vt* : tear open

éventualité [evɑ̃tɥalite] *nf* : eventuality, possibility — **éventuel, -tuelle** [evɑ̃tɥɛl] *adj* : possible — **éventuellement** [-tɥɛlmɑ̃] *adv* : possibly

évêque [evɛk] *nm* : bishop

évertuer [evɛrtɥe] *v* **s'évertuer** *vr* : strive, do one's best

éviction [eviksjɔ̃] *nf* : eviction

évidemment [evidamɑ̃] *adv* : obviously, of course

évidence [evidɑ̃s] *nf* : obviousness — **évident, -dente** [evidɑ̃, -dɑ̃t] *adj* : obvious, evident

évider [evide] *vt* : hollow out

évier [evje] *nm* : sink

évincer [evɛ̃se] {6} *vt* : oust

éviter [evite] *vt* **1** : avoid **2** ~ **à qqn de faire qqch** : save s.o. from (doing) sth

évoluer [evolɥe] *vi* **1** : evolve, develop **2** SE DÉPLACER : maneuver, move about — **évolution** [evolɥsjɔ̃] *nf* **1** : evolution **2** CHANGEMENT : development, change

évoquer [evɔke] *vt* : evoke, call to mind

exacerber [ɛgzaserbe] *vt* : exacerbate

exact, exacte [ɛgzakt] *adj* **1** : exact **2** JUSTE

: correct **3** PONCTUEL : punctual — **exactement** [ɛgzaktəmɑ̃] *adv* : exactly — **exactitude** [ɛgzaktityd] *nf* **1** : accuracy **2** PONC-
TUALITÉ : punctuality

ex aequo [ɛgzeko] *adv* : equal

exagérer [ɛgzaʒere] {87} *vt* : exaggerate —
vi : go too far, overdo it — **exagération**
[ɛgzaʒerasjɔ̃] *nf* : exaggeration — **exagéré,
-rée** [ɛgzaʒere] *adj* : exaggerated, excessive

exalter [ɛgzalte] *vt* **1** : excite, stir **2** GLORI-
FIER : exalt — **s'exalter** *vr* : get excited

examiner [ɛgzamine] *vt* : examine — **examen** [ɛgzamɛ̃] *nm* : examination

exaspérer [ɛgzaspere] {87} *vt* : exasperate
— **exaspération** [ɛgzasperasjɔ̃] *nf* : exasperation

exaucer [ɛgzose] {6} *vt* : grant

excaver [ɛkskave] *vt* : excavate — **excavation** [ɛkskavasjɔ̃] *nf* : excavation

excéder [ɛksede] {87} *vt* **1** : exceed **2**
EXASPÉRER : exasperate — **excédent**
[ɛksedɑ̃] *nm* : surplus, excess — **excédentaire** [ɛksedɑ̃tɛr] *adj* : surplus, excess

exceller [ɛksele] *vi* : excel — **excellence**
[ɛkselɑ̃s] *nf* : excellence — **excellent,
-lente** [ɛkselɑ̃, -lɑ̃t] *adj* : excellent

excentrique [ɛksɑ̃trik] *adj & nmf* : eccentric
— **excentricité** [ɛksɑ̃trisite] *nf* : eccentricity

excepter [ɛksɛpte] *vt* : except, exclude —
excepté [ɛksɛpte] *prep* SAUF : except, apart
from — **exception** [ɛksɛpsjɔ̃] *nf* **1** : exception **2** à l'**~** **de** : except for — **exceptionnel, -nelle** [ɛksɛpsjɔnɛl] *adj* : exceptional

excès [ɛksɛ] *nm* **1** : excess **2 ~** **de vitesse**
: speeding — **excessif, -sive** [ɛksɛsif, -siv]
adj : excessive

exciter [ɛksite] *vt* **1** : excite **2** STIMULER
: stimulate — **s'exciter** *vr* : get excited —
excitant, -tante [ɛksitɑ̃, -tɑ̃t] *adj* : exciting
— **excitation** [ɛksitasjɔ̃] *nf* : excitement

exclamer [ɛksklame] *v* **s'exclamer** *vr* : exclaim — **exclamation** [ɛksklamasjɔ̃] *nf*
: exclamation

exclure [ɛksklyr] {39} *vt* **1** : exclude **2** EX-
PULSER : expel — **exclusif, -sive** [ɛksklyzif,
-ziv] *adj* : exclusive — **exclusivement**
[-sivmɑ̃] *adv* : exclusively — **exclusion**
[ɛksklyzjɔ̃] *nf* **1** : exclusion **2** EXPULSION
: expulsion — **exclusivité** [ɛksklyzivite] *nf*
1 : exclusive rights *pl* **2 en ~** : exclusively

excréments [ɛkskremɑ̃] *nmpl* : excrement,
feces

excroissance [ɛkskrwasɑ̃s] *nf* : outgrowth

excursion [ɛkskyrsjɔ̃] *nf* : excursion, trip

excuser [ɛkskyze] *vt* : excuse — **s'excuser**
vr : apologize — **excuse** [ɛkskyz] *nf* **1**
: excuse **2 ~s** *nfpl* : apology

exécrer [ɛgzekre] {87} *vt* : abhor, loathe —

exécrable [ɛgzekrabl] *adj* : atrocious,
awful

exécuter [ɛgzekyte] *vt* **1** : execute **2** EF-
FECTUER : perform — **s'exécuter** *vr* : comply — **exécutant, -tante** [ɛgzekytɑ̃, -tɑ̃t] *n*
: performer — **exécutif, -tive** [ɛgzekytif,
-tiv] *adj* : executive — **exécution**
[ɛgzekysjɔ̃] *nf* : execution

exemple [ɛgzɑ̃pl] *nm* **1** : example **2 par ~**
: for example, for instance — **exemplaire**
[ɛgzɑ̃plɛr] *adj* : exemplary — **~** *nm* **1**
: copy **2** : specimen, example

exempt, exempte [ɛgzɑ̃, ɛgzɑ̃t] *adj* : exempt — **exempter** [ɛgzɑ̃te] *vt* : exempt —
exemption [ɛgzɑ̃psjɔ̃] *nf* : exemption

exercer [ɛgzɛrse] {6} *vt* **1** : exercise, train **2**
: exert (control, influence, etc.) **3** : practice
(a profession) — **s'exercer** *vr* : practice —
exercice [ɛgzɛrsis] *nm* **1** : exercise **2 en
~** : in office

exhaler [ɛgzale] *vt* **1** : exhale **2** ÉMETTRE
: utter, breathe

exhaustif, -tive [ɛgzostif, -tiv] *adj* : exhaustive

exhiber [ɛgzibe] *vt* : exhibit, show off — **exhibition** [ɛgzibisjɔ̃] *nf* : display, exhibition

exhorter [ɛgzɔrte] *vt* : exhort, urge

exiger [ɛgziʒe] {17} *vt* : demand, require —
exigeant, -geante [ɛgziʒɑ̃, -ʒɑ̃t] *adj* : demanding, choosy — **exigence** [ɛgziʒɑ̃s] *nf*
: demand, requirement

exigu, -guë [ɛgzigy] *adj* : cramped, tiny

exil [ɛgzil] *nm* : exile — **exilé, -lée** [ɛgzile] *n*
: exile — **exiler** [ɛgzile] *vt* : exile — **s'exiler**
vr : go into exile, isolate oneself

exister [ɛgziste] *vi* : exist — **existant, -tante**
[ɛgzistɑ̃, -tɑ̃t] *adj* : existing — **existence**
[ɛgzistɑ̃s] *nf* : existence

exode [ɛgzɔd] *nm* : exodus

exonérer [ɛgzɔnere] {87} *vt* : exempt —
exonération [ɛgzɔnerasjɔ̃] *nf* : exemption

exorbitant, -tante [ɛgzɔrbitɑ̃, -tɑ̃t] *adj* : exorbitant

exotique [ɛgzɔtik] *adj* : exotic

expansion [ɛkspɑ̃sjɔ̃] *nf* : expansion — **ex-
pansif, -sive** [ɛkspɑ̃sif, -siv] *adj* : expan-
sive

expatrier [ɛkspatrije] {96} *vt* : expatriate —
s'expatrier *vr* : emigrate — **expatrié, -triée**
[ɛkspatrije] *adj & n* : expatriate

expédient, -diente [ɛkspedjɑ̃, -djɑ̃t] *adj*
: expedient — **expédient** *nm* : expedient

expédier [ɛkspedje] {96} *vt* : send, dispatch
— **expéditeur, -trice** [ɛkspeditœr, -tris] *n*
: sender — **expéditif, -tive** [ɛkspeditif,
-tiv] *adj* : quick — **expédition** [ɛkspedisjɔ̃]
nf **1** : sending, shipment **2** VOYAGE : expedition

expérience [ɛksperjɑ̃s] *nf* **1** : experience **2**
ESSAI : experiment — **expérimental, -tale**

[ɛksperimɑ̃tal] *adj, mpl* **-taux** [-to] : experimental — **expérimentation** [ɛksperimɑ̃tasjɔ̃] *nf* : experimentation — **expérimenté, -tée** [ɛksperimɑ̃te] *adj* : experienced — **expérimenter** [ɛksperimɑ̃te] *vt* : test, experiment with

expert, -perte [ɛkspɛr, -pɛrt] *adj & n* : expert — **expertise** [ɛkspɛrtiz] *nf* **1** : expert appraisal **2** COMPÉTENCE : expertise

expier [ɛkspje] {96} *vt* : atone for

expirer [ɛkspire] *vi* **1** : breathe out **2** : expire (of a contract) — *vt* : exhale — **expiration** [ɛkspirasjɔ̃] *nf* **1** ÉCHÉANCE : expiration **2** : exhalation (of breath)

explication [ɛksplikasjɔ̃] *nf* : explanation — **explicatif, -tive** [ɛksplikatif, -tiv] *adj* : explanatory

explicite [ɛksplisit] *adj* : explicit

expliquer [ɛksplike] *vt* : explain — **s'expliquer** *vr* **1** : explain oneself **2** : be explained

exploiter [ɛksplwate] *vt* **1** : exploit **2** : work (a field, a mine, etc.), run (a business, etc.) — **exploit** [ɛksplwa] *nm* : exploit — **exploitation** [ɛksplwatasjɔ̃] *nf* **1** : exploitation **2** : running, management (of a farm, mine, etc.) **3** ~ **agricole** : (small) farm

explorer [ɛksplɔre] *vt* : explore — **explorateur, -trice** [ɛksplɔratœr, -tris] *n* : explorer — **exploration** [ɛksplɔrasjɔ̃] *nf* : exploration

exploser [ɛksploze] *vi* **1** : explode **2** : burst out, flare up (with anger, etc.) — **explosif, -sive** [ɛksplozif, -ziv] *adj* : explosive — **explosif** *nm* : explosive — **explosion** [ɛksplozjɔ̃] *nf* **1** : explosion **2** : outburst (of anger, joy, etc.)

exporter [ɛkspɔrte] *vt* : export — **exportateur, -trice** [ɛkspɔrtatœr, -tris] *adj* : exporting — ~ *n* : exporter — **exportation** [ɛkspɔrtasjɔ̃] *nf* : export, exportation

exposer [ɛkspoze] *vt* **1** : exhibit **2** EXPLIQUER : explain **3** ORIENTER : orient **4** : expose (to danger), risk (one's life, reputation, etc.) — **s'exposer** *vr* : expose oneself — **exposant, -sante** [ɛkspozɑ̃, -zɑ̃t] *n* : exhibitor — **exposé** [ɛkspoze] *nm* **1** : lecture, talk **2** : account, report — **exposition** [ɛkspozisjɔ̃] *nf* **1** : exhibition **2** PRÉSENTATION : exposition **3** ORIENTATION : orientation, aspect

exprès [ɛksprɛ] *adv* **1** : on purpose, intentionally **2** SPÉCIALEMENT : specially — **exprès, -presse** [ɛksprɛs] *adj* **1** : express, explicit **2** : special delivery — **express** [ɛksprɛs] *adj* : express — ~ *nm* **1** : express (train) **2** *or* **café** ~ : espresso — **expressément** [ɛksprɛsemɑ̃] *adv* : expressly — **expressif, -sive** [ɛksprɛsif, -siv] *adj* : expressive — **expression** [ɛksprɛsjɔ̃] *nf* : expression

exprimer [ɛksprime] *vt* **1** : express **2** EXTRAIRE : squeeze, extract — **s'exprimer** *vr* : express oneself

expulser [ɛkspylse] *vt* : expel, evict — **expulsion** [ɛkspylsjɔ̃] *nf* : expulsion, eviction

exquis, -quise [ɛkski, -kiz] *adj* : exquisite

extase [ɛkstaz] *nf* : ecstasy — **extasier** [ɛkstazje] {96} *v* **s'extasier** *vr* : be in ecstasy — **extatique** [ɛkstatik] *adj* : ecstatic

extension [ɛkstɑ̃sjɔ̃] *nf* **1** : stretching (of a muscle, etc.) **2** ÉLARGISSEMENT : extension, expansion — **extensif, -sive** [ɛkstɑ̃sif, -siv] *adj* : extensive

exténuer [ɛkstenɥe] *vt* : exhaust, tire out — **exténuant, -ante** [ɛkstenɥɑ̃, -ɥɑ̃t] *adj* : exhausting

extérieur, -rieure [ɛksterjœr] *adj* **1** : exterior, outside **2** APPARENT : apparent **3** ÉTRANGER : foreign — **extérieur** *nm* **1** : exterior **2 à l'**~ : abroad — **extérieurement** [ɛksterjœrmɑ̃] *adv* **1** : externally **2** APPAREMMENT : outwardly — **extérioriser** [ɛksterjɔrize] *vt* : show, express

exterminer [ɛkstɛrmine] *vt* : exterminate — **extermination** [ɛkstɛrminasjɔ̃] *nf* : extermination

externe [ɛkstɛrn] *adj* : external

extinction [ɛkstɛ̃ksjɔ̃] *nf* **1** : extinction **2** : extinguishing — **extincteur** [ɛkstɛ̃ktœr] *nm* : fire extinguisher

extirper [ɛkstirpe] *vt* : eradicate

extorquer [ɛkstɔrke] *vt* : extort — **extorsion** [ɛkstɔrsjɔ̃] *nf* : extortion

extra [ɛkstra] *adj* **1** : first-rate **2** *fam* : fantastic — ~ *nms & pl* **1** : extra person **2** : extra thing or amount

extraction [ɛstraksjɔ̃] *nf* : extraction

extrader [ɛkstrade] *vt* : extradite

extraire [ɛkstrɛr] {40} *vt* : extract — **extrait** [ɛkstrɛ] *nm* **1** : extract, essence **2** : excerpt (of a speech, etc.)

extraordinaire [ɛkstraɔrdinɛr] *adj* : extraordinary

extraterrestre [ɛkstratɛrɛstr] *adj & nmf* : extraterrestrial

extravagant, -gante [ɛkstravagɑ̃, -gɑ̃t] *adj* : extravagant — **extravagance** [-vagɑ̃s] *nf* : extravagance

extraverti, -tie [ɛkstravɛrti] *adj* : extroverted — ~ *n* : extrovert

extrême [ɛkstrɛm] *adj* : extreme — ~ *nm* : extreme — **extrêmement** [ɛkstrɛmmɑ̃] *adv* : extremely — **extrémité** [ɛkstremite] *nf* : extremity

exubérant, -rante [ɛgzyberɑ̃, -rɑ̃t] *adj* : exuberant — **exubérance** [-berɑ̃s] *nf* : exuberance

exulter [ɛgzylte] *vi* : exult

exutoire [ɛgzytwar] *nm* : outlet

F

f [ɛf] *nm* : f, sixth letter of the alphabet

fable [fabl] *nf* : fable

fabriquer [fabrike] *vt* 1 : make, manufacture 2 INVENTER : fabricate — **fabricant, -cante** [fabrikɑ̃, -kɑ̃t] *n* : manufacturer — **fabrication** [fabrikasjɔ̃] *nf* : manufacture, making — **fabrique** [fabrik] *nf* : factory

fabuleux, -leuse [fabylø, -løz] *adj* : fabulous

façade [fasad] *nf* : façade, front

face [fas] *nf* 1 VISAGE : face 2 CÔTÉ : side 3 en ~ : opposite 4 ~ à ~ : face-to-face 5 faire ~ à : face — **facette** [fasɛt] *nf* : facet

facétieux, -tieuse [fasesjø, -sjøz] *adj* : facetious

fâcher [faʃe] *vt* : anger — **se fâcher** *vr* : get angry — **fâché, -chée** [faʃe] *adj* : angry — **fâcheux, -cheuse** [faʃø, -ʃøz] *adj* : unfortunate

facile [fasil] *adj* 1 : easy 2 : easygoing — **facilement** [fasilmɑ̃] *adv* : easily — **facilité** [fasilite] *nf* 1 : easiness 2 APTITUDE : aptitude — **faciliter** [fasilite] *vt* : facilitate

façon [fasɔ̃] *nf* 1 : way, manner 2 ~s *nfpl* : behavior, manners 3 de ~ à : so as to 4 de toute ~ : in any case 5 faire des ~s : put on airs — **façonner** [fasɔne] *vt* 1 FORMER : shape 2 FABRIQUER : manufacture

fac–similé [faksimile] *nm, pl* **fac–similés** : facsimile, copy

facteur¹, -trice [faktœr, -tris] *n* : mailman

facteur² *nm* : factor

faction [faksjɔ̃] *nf* 1 GROUPE : faction 2 : guard (duty)

factuel, -tuelle [faktɥɛl] *adj* : factual

facture [faktyr] *nf* : bill, invoice — **facturer** [faktyre] *vt* : bill

facultatif, -tive [fakyltatif, -tiv] *adj* : optional

faculté [fakylte] *nf* 1 : faculty, ability 2 LIBERTÉ : option 3 : faculty (of a university)

fade [fad] *adj* : bland

faible [fɛbl] *adj* 1 : weak, feeble 2 : small (in quantity) 3 PÂLE : faint, light — ~ *nmf* : weakling — ~ *nm* : weakness — **faiblesse** [fɛbles] *nf* : weakness — **faiblir** [feblir] *vi* 1 : weaken 2 DIMINUER : die down

faïence [fajɑ̃s] *nf* : earthenware

faillir [fajir] {41} *vi* ~ à : fail to — *vt* 1 : narrowly miss 2 ~ faire qqch : nearly do sth — **faille** [faj] *nf* 1 : fault (in geology) 2 FAIBLESSE : flaw — **faillible** [fajibl] *adj* : fallible — **faillite** [fajit] *nf* 1 ÉCHEC : failure 2 faire ~ : go bankrupt

faim [fɛ̃] *nf* 1 : hunger 2 avoir ~ : be hungry

fainéant, -néante [feneɑ̃, -neɑ̃t] *adj* : lazy — ~ *n* : loafer, idler

faire [fɛr] {42} *vt* 1 : do 2 : make 3 : equal, amount to 4 DIRE : say 5 cela ne fait rien : it doesn't matter 6 ~ du football : play football 7 ~ mal à : hurt 8 ~ soleil : be sunny 9 ~ un rêve : have a dream — **se faire** *vr* 1 ~ à : get used to 2 s'en faire : worry — **faire–part** [fɛrpar] *nms & pl* : announcement (of marriage, etc.) — **faisable** [fəzabl] *adj* : feasible

faisan, -sane [fəzɑ̃] *n* : pheasant

faisceau [feso] *nm, pl* **-ceaux** : beam (of light)

fait, faite [fɛ, fɛt] *adj* 1 : made, done 2 : ripe (of cheese) 3 tout fait : ready-made — **fait** *nm* 1 : fact 2 ÉVÉNEMENT : event 3 au ~ : by the way 4 sur le ~ : red-handed

faîte [fɛt] *nm* 1 SOMMET : summit, top 2 APOGÉE : pinnacle

falaise [falɛz] *nf* : cliff

falloir [falwar] {43} *v impers* 1 comme il faut : proper(ly) 2 il fallait le faire : it had to be done 3 il fallait me le dire! : you should have said so! 4 il faut partir : we must go 5 il faut que je ... : I need to ... — **s'en falloir** *vr* 1 peu s'en faut : very nearly 2 tant s'en faut : far from it

falsifier [falsifje] {96} *vt* : falsify

famé, -mée [fame] *adj* mal famé : disreputable

famélique [famelik] *adj* : starving

fameux, -meuse [famø, -møz] *adj* 1 CÉLÈBRE : famous 2 *fam* : first-rate

familial, -liale [familjal] *adj, mpl* **-liaux** [-ljo] : family — **familiale** *nf* : station wagon

familiariser [familjarize] *v* **se familiariser** *vr* : familiarize oneself — **familiarité** [familjarite] *nf* : familiarity — **familier, -lière** [familje, -ljer] *adj* 1 : familiar 2 : informal

famille [famij] *nf* : family

famine [famin] *nf* : famine

fanatique [fanatik] *adj* : fanatic(al) — ~ *nmf* : fanatic — **fanatisme** [-natism] *nm* : fanaticism

faner [fane] *v* **se faner** *vr* : fade

fanfare [fɑ̃far] *nf* 1 : fanfare 2 : brass band

fanfaron, -ronne [fɑ̃farɔ̃, -rɔn] *adj* : boastful — ~ *n* : braggart

fantaisie [fɑ̃tezi] *nf* 1 : fantasy 2 CAPRICE : whim — **fantaisiste** [fɑ̃tezist] *adj* : fanciful

fantasme [fɑ̃tasm] *nm* : fantasy — **fantas-**

mer [fɑ̃tasme] *vi* : fantasize — **fantasque** [fɑ̃task] *adj* **1** CAPRICIEUX : whimsical **2** BIZARRE : strange, weird — **fantastique** [fɑ̃tastik] *adj* : fantastic

fantoche [fɑ̃tɔʃ] *adj & nm* : puppet

fantôme [fɑ̃tom] *nm* : ghost

faon [fɑ̃] *nm* : fawn

farce [fars] *nf* **1** : practical joke **2** : farce (in theater) — **farceur, -ceuse** [farsœr, -søz] *n* : prankster

farcir [farsir] *vt* : stuff (in cooking)

fard [far] *nm* : makeup

fardeau [fardo] *nm, pl* **-deaux** : load, burden

farfelu, -lue [farfəly] *adj fam* : wacky

farine [farin] *nf* : flour

farouche [faruʃ] *adj* **1** SAUVAGE : wild **2** TIMIDE : shy **3** ACHARNÉ : fierce

fascicule [fasikyl] *nm* **1** : section (of a book) **2** LIVRET : booklet

fasciner [fasine] *vt* : fascinate — **fascinant, -nante** [fasinɑ̃, -nɑ̃t] *adj* : fascinating — **fascination** [fasinasjɔ̃] *nf* : fascination

fascisme [faʃism] *nm* : fascism — **fasciste** [faʃist] *adj & nmf* : fascist

faste[1] [fast] *adj* : lucky

faste[2] *nm* : pomp, splendor

fastidieux, -dieuse [fastidjø, -djøz] *adj* : tedious

fatal, -tale [fatal] *adj, mpl* **-tals 1** MORTEL : fatal **2** INÉVITABLE : inevitable — **fatalement** [fatalmɑ̃] *adv* : inevitably — **fatalité** [fatalite] *nf* **1** SORT : fate **2** : inevitability

fatidique [fatidik] *adj* : fateful

fatiguer [fatige] *vt* **1** : fatigue, tire **2** ENNUYER : annoy **3** : strain (an engine, etc.) — *vi* : grow tired — **se fatiguer** *vr* : wear oneself out — **fatigant, -gante** [fatigɑ̃, -gɑ̃t] *adj* **1** : tiring **2** ENNUYEUX : tiresome — **fatigue** [fatig] *nf* : fatigue — **fatigué, -guée** [fatige] *adj* : tired

faubourg [fobur] *nm* : suburb

faucher [foʃe] *vt* **1** : mow, cut **2** *fam* : swipe, pinch — **fauché, -chée** [foʃe] *adj fam* : broke, penniless

faucille [fosij] *nf* : sickle

faucon [fokɔ̃] *nm* : falcon, hawk

faufiler [fofile] *vt* : baste (in sewing) — **se faufiler** *vr* : weave one's way

faune [fon] *nf* : fauna, wildlife

faussaire [fosɛr] *nmf* : forger

fausse → **faux**[2]

fausser [fose] *vt* **1** : distort **2** DÉFORMER : bend — **faussement** [fosmɑ̃] *adv* **1** : falsely **2** : wrongfully — **fausseté** [foste] *nf* **1** : falseness **2** DUPLICITÉ : duplicity

faute [fot] *nf* **1** : fault **2** ERREUR : mistake **3** ~ **de** : for lack of

fauteuil [fotœj] *nm* **1** : armchair **2** ~ **roulant** : wheelchair

fautif, -tive [fotif, -tiv] *adj* **1** COUPABLE : at fault **2** ERRONÉ : faulty

fauve [fov] *nm* : big cat

faux[1] [fo] *nfs & pl* : scythe

faux[2], **fausse** [fos] *adj* **1** : false **2** INCORRECT : wrong **3** FALSIFIÉ : counterfeit, fake **4 fausse couche** : miscarriage **5 faire un faux pas** : stumble **6 faux nom** : alias — ~ *nm* : forgery — ~ *adv* : out of tune — **faux–filet** [fofilɛ] *nm, pl* **faux–filets** : sirloin — **faux–monnayeur** [fomɔnɛjœr] *nm, pl* **faux–monnayeurs** : forger

faveur [favœr] *nf* **1** : favor **2 en ~ de** : in favor of — **favorable** [favɔrabl] *adj* : favorable — **favori, -rite** [favɔri, -rit] *adj & n* : favorite — **favoris** [favɔri] *nmpl* : sideburns — **favoriser** [favɔrize] *vt* **1** : favor **2** ENCOURAGER : promote — **favoritisme** [favɔritism] *nm* : favoritism

fax [faks] *nm* : fax — **faxer** [fakse] *vt* : fax

fébrile [febril] *adj* : feverish

fécond, -conde [fekɔ̃, -kɔ̃d] *adj* : fertile — **féconder** [fekɔ̃de] *vt* : fertilize, impregnate — **fécondité** [fekɔ̃dite] *nf* : fertility

fécule [fekyl] *nf* : starch — **féculent, -lente** [fekylɑ̃, -lɑ̃t] *adj* : starchy — **féculent** [fekylɑ̃] *nm* : starchy food

fédéral, -rale [federal] *adj, mpl* **-raux** [-ro] : federal — **fédération** [federasjɔ̃] *nf* : federation

fée [fe] *nf* : fairy — **féerie** [fe(e)ri] *nf* : enchantment — **féerique** [fe(e)rik] *adj* : magical, enchanting

feindre [fɛ̃dr] {37} *vt* : feign — *vi* : pretend — **feinte** [fɛ̃t] *nf* : trick, ruse

fêler [fele] *vt* : crack

féliciter [felisite] *vt* : congratulate — **félicitations** [felisitasjɔ̃] *nfpl* : congratulations

félin, -line [felɛ̃, -lin] *adj & nm* : feline

fêlure [felyr] *nf* : crack

femelle [fəmɛl] *adj & nf* : female

féminin, -nine [feminɛ̃, -nin] *adj* : feminine — **féminisme** [feminism] *nm* : feminism — **féministe** [feminist] *adj & nmf* : feminist — **féminité** [feminite] *nf* : femininity

femme [fam] *nf* **1** : woman **2** ÉPOUSE : wife **3** ~ **au foyer** : homemaker **4** ~ **d'affaires** : businesswoman

fendre [fɑ̃dr] {63} *vt* : split, break — **se fendre** *vr* : crack

fenêtre [fənɛtr] *nf* : window

fenouil [fənuj] *nm* : fennel

fente [fɑ̃t] *nf* **1** : slit, slot **2** FISSURE : crack

féodal, -dale [feɔdal] *adj, mpl* **-daux** [-do] : feudal

fer [fɛr] *nm* **1** : iron **2** ~ **à cheval** : horseshoe **3** ~ **à repasser** : iron (for clothes)

férié, -riée [ferje] *adj* **jour férié** : holiday

ferme [fɛrm] *adj* : firm — ~ *adv* : firmly,

hard — **~** *nf* : farm — **fermement** [fɛrməmɑ̃] *adv* : firmly

fermé, -mée [fɛrme] *adj* **1** : closed, shut (off) **2** EXCLUSIF : exclusive

fermenter [fɛrmɑ̃te] *vi* : ferment — **fermentation** [fɛrmɑ̃tasjɔ̃] *nf* : fermentation

fermer [fɛrme] *vt* **1** : close, shut **2** : close down (a factory, etc.) **3** ÉTEINDRE : turn off **4 ~ à clef** : lock up — **se fermer** *vr* : close (up)

fermeté [fɛrməte] *nf* : firmness

fermeture [fɛrmətyr] *nf* **1** : closing, shutting **2 ~ à glissière** : zipper

fermier, -mière [fɛrmje, -mjɛr] *n* : farmer

fermoir [fɛrmwar] *nm* : clasp

féroce [ferɔs] *adj* : ferocious — **férocité** [ferɔsite] *nf* : ferocity, ferociousness

ferraille [fɛraj] *nf* : scrap iron

ferronnerie [fɛrɔnri] *nf* **1** : ironworks **2** : wrought iron

ferroviaire [fɛrɔvjɛr] *adj* : rail, railroad

ferry–boat [fɛribot] *nm, pl* **ferry–boats** : ferry

fertile [fɛrtil] *adj* : fertile — **fertiliser** [fɛrtilize] *vt* : fertilize — **fertilité** [fɛrtilite] *nf* : fertility

fervent, -vente [fɛrvɑ̃, -vɑ̃t] *adj* : fervent — **~** *n* : enthusiast — **ferveur** [fɛrvœr] *nf* : fervor

fesses [fɛs] *nfpl* : buttocks — **fessée** [fese] *nf* : spanking — **fesser** [fese] *vt* : spank

festin [fɛstɛ̃] *nm* : feast

festival [fɛstival] *nm, pl* **-vals** : festival — **festivités** [fɛstivite] *nfpl* : festivities

fête [fɛt] *nf* **1** : holiday **2** : party **3** FOIRE : fair **4 de ~** : festive **5 faire la ~** : have a good time — **fêter** [fete] *vt* : celebrate

fétiche [fetiʃ] *nm* : fetish

fétide [fetid] *adj* : fetid

feu[1] [fø] *nm, pl* **feux 1** : fire **2** *or* **~ de circulation** : traffic light **3** : burner (of a stove) **4** : light (for a cigarette, etc.) **5** TIR : fire, shooting **6 ~ de joie** : bonfire **7 feux d'artifice** : fireworks **8 mettre le ~ à** : set fire to **9 prendre ~** : catch fire

feu[2]**, feue** [fø] *adj* : late, deceased

feuille [fœj] *nf* **1** : leaf **2** : sheet (of paper, etc.) — **feuillage** [fœjaʒ] *nm* : foliage — **feuillet** [fœjɛ] *nm* : page, leaf — **feuilleter** [fœjte] {8} *vt* : leaf through — **feuilleton** [fœjtɔ̃] *nm* : series, serial

feutre [føtr] *nm* : felt — **feutré, -trée** [føtre] *adj* : muffled, hushed

fève [fɛv] *nf* : broad bean

février [fevrije] *nm* : February

fiable [fjabl] *adj* : reliable — **fiabilité** [fjabilite] *nf* : reliability

fiancer [fijɑ̃se] {6} *v* **se fiancer** *vr* : get engaged — **fiançailles** [fijɑ̃saj] *nfpl* : engage-ment — **fiancé, -cée** [fijɑ̃se] *n* : fiancé *m*, fiancée *f*

fibre [fibr] *nf* **1** : fiber **2 ~ de verre** : fiberglass — **fibreux, -breuse** [fibrø, -brøz] *adj* : fibrous

ficelle [fisɛl] *nf* : string, twine — **ficeler** [fisle] {8} *vt* : tie up

fiche [fiʃ] *nf* **1** : index card **2** FORMULAIRE : form **3** : (electric) plug

ficher [fiʃe] *vt* **1** : drive (in) **2** *fam* : do **3** *fam* : give **4 ~ qqn dehors** *fam* : kick s.o. out — **se ficher** *vr* **1 ~ de** *fam* : make fun of **2 je m'en fiche** *fam* : I don't give a damn

fichier [fiʃje] *nm* : file, index

fichu[1]**, -chue** [fiʃy] *adj fam* **1** : lousy, awful **2** CONDAMNÉ : done for

fichu[2] *nm* : scarf, kerchief

fiction [fiksjɔ̃] *nf* : fiction — **fictif, -tive** [fiktif, -tiv] *adj* : fictional, fictitious

fidèle [fidɛl] *adj* : faithful — **~** *nmf* **1** : follower **2** : regular (customer) **3 les ~s** : the faithful — **fidèlement** [-dɛlmɑ̃] *adv* : faithfully — **fidélité** [fidelite] *nf* : fidelity

fier[1] [fje] *v* **se fier** *vr* **~ à** : trust, rely on

fier[2]**, fière** [fjɛr] *adj* : proud — **fièrement** [fjɛrmɑ̃] *adv* : proudly — **fierté** [fjɛrte] *nf* : pride

fièvre [fjɛvr] *nf* : fever — **fiévreux, -vreuse** [fjɛvrø, -vrøz] *adj* : feverish

figer [fiʒe] {17} *v* **se figer** *vr* : coagulate

figue [fig] *nf* : fig

figure [figyr] *nf* **1** VISAGE : face **2** PERSONNAGE : figure **3** ILLUSTRATION : illustration — **figurant, -rante** [figyrɑ̃, -rɑ̃t] *n* : extra (in theater) — **figurer** [figyre] *vi* : appear — *vt* : represent — **se figurer** *vr* : imagine

fil [fil] *nm* **1** : thread **2** : wire **3 au ~ de** : in the course of **4 coup de ~** *fam* : phone call **5 ~ dentaire** : dental floss — **file** [fil] *nf* **1** : line, file, row **2** : lane (of a highway) **3 en ~** *or* **à la ~** : one after another — **filer** [file] *vt* **1** : spin (yarn) **2** SUIVRE : shadow **3** *fam* : give — *vi* **1** : run (of stockings) **2** *fam* : dash off **3** *fam* : fly by, slip away **4 ~ bien** *Can fam* : be doing fine

filet [filɛ] *nm* **1** : net **2** : fillet (of beef, etc.) **3** : trickle (of water)

filiale [filjal] *nf* : subsidiary (company)

filière [filjɛr] *nf* : (official) channels *pl*

filigrane [filigran] *nm* : watermark

fille [fij] *nf* **1** : girl **2** : daughter — **fillette** [fijɛt] *nf* : little girl

filleul, -leule [fijœl] *n* : godchild, godson *m*, goddaughter *f*

film [film] *nm* : film — **filmer** [filme] *vt* : film

filon [filɔ̃] *nm* : vein, lode

fils [fis] *nm* : son

filtre [filtr] *nm* : filter — **filtrer** [filtre] *vt* **1** : filter **2** : screen (visitors, etc.) — *vi* : filter through

fin¹, fine [fɛ̃, fin] *adj* **1** : fine **2** MINCE : thin **3** : excellent (in quality) **4** : sharp, keen **5** *Can* : nice — **fin** *adv* : finely

fin² *nf* **1** : end **2 à la ～** : in the end **3 prendre ～** : come to an end **4 sans ～** : endless(ly)

final, -nale [final] *adj, mpl* **-nals** *or* **-naux** [fino] : final — **finale** *nf* : finals *pl* (in sports) — **finalement** [finalmɑ̃] *adv* **1** : finally **2** : after all — **finaliste** [finalist] *nmf* : finalist

finance [finɑ̃s] *nf* **1** : finance **2 ～s** *nfpl* : finances — **financer** [finɑ̃se] {6} *vt* : finance — **financier, -cière** [finɑ̃sje, -sjɛr] *adj* : financial

finesse [fines] *nf* **1** : finesse, delicacy **2** PERSPICACITÉ : shrewdness

finir [finir] *vt* : finish — *vi* **1** : finish **2 en ～ avec** : be done with **3 ～ par faire** : end up doing — **fini, -nie** [fini] *adj* **1** : finished **2** : finite — **finition** [finisjɔ̃] *nf* : finish

fiole [fjɔl] *nf* : vial

firme [firm] *nf* : firm

fisc [fisk] *nm* : tax collection agency — **fiscal, -cale** [fiskal] *adj, mpl* **-caux** [fisko] : fiscal — **fiscalité** [fiskalite] *nf* : tax system

fissure [fisyr] *nf* : crack

fiston [fistɔ̃] *nm fam* : son, youngster

fixe [fiks] *adj* **1** IMMOBILE : fixed **2** INVARIABLE : invariable, set — **fixer** [fikse] *vt* **1** ATTACHER : fix, fasten **2** DÉCIDER : determine **3** ÉTABLIR : establish **4 ～ son regard sur** : stare at — **se fixer** *vr* **1** : settle down **2** SE DÉCIDER : decide

flacon [flakɔ̃] *nm* : small bottle

flageller [flaʒele] *vt* : flog, whip

flagrant [flagrɑ̃] *adj* **1** : flagrant **2 en ～ délit** : red-handed

flairer [flɛre] *vt* **1** : sniff, smell **2** DISCERNER : detect, sense — **flair** [flɛr] *nm* **1** : sense of smell **2** INTUITION : intuition

flamand, -mande [flamɑ̃, -mɑ̃d] *adj* : Flemish

flamant [flamɑ̃] *nm* : flamingo

flambant, -bante [flɑ̃bɑ̃, -bɑ̃t] *adj* **flambant neuf** : brand-new

flambeau [flɑ̃bo] *nm, pl* **-beaux** : torch

flamber [flɑ̃be] *vi* : burn, blaze — **flambée** [flɑ̃be] *nf* **1** : blaze, fire **2** : outburst (of anger, etc.)

flamboyer [flɑ̃bwaje] {58} *vi* : blaze, flame — **flamboyant, -boyante** [flɑ̃bwajɑ̃, -bwajɑ̃t] *adj* : blazing

flamme [flam] *nf* **1** : flame **2** FERVEUR : passion, fervor **3 en ～s** : on fire

flan [flɑ̃] *nm* : baked custard

flanc [flɑ̃] *nm* : side, flank

flancher [flɑ̃ʃe] *vi fam* **1** : give in **2** : give out, fail

flanelle [flanɛl] *nf* : flannel

flâner [flane] *vi* **1** SE BALADER : stroll **2** PARESSER : loaf around

flanquer [flɑ̃ke] *vt* **1** : flank **2 ～ par terre** : fling to the ground **3 ～ un coup à** *fam* : punch

flaque [flak] *nf* : puddle, pool

flash [flaʃ] *nm, pl* **flashs** *or* **flashes** [flaʃ] **1** : flash (in photography) **2** : news flash

flasque [flask] *adj* : flabby, limp

flatter [flate] *vt* **1** : flatter **2** CARESSER : stroke — **se flatter** *vr* : pride oneself — **flatterie** [flatri] *nf* : flattery — **flatteur, -teuse** [flatœr, -tøz] *adj* : flattering — **～** *n* : flatterer

fléau [fleo] *nm, pl* **fléaux** : calamity, scourge

flèche [flɛʃ] *nf* **1** : arrow **2** : spire (of a church) — **fléchette** [fleʃet] *nf* : dart

fléchir [fleʃir] *vt* PLIER : bend, flex — *vi* **1** : bend, give way **2** FAIBLIR : weaken

flegme [flɛgm] *nm* : composure — **flegmatique** [flɛgmatik] *adj* : phlegmatic

flemme [flɛm] *nf France fam* : laziness

flétan [fletɑ̃] *nm* : halibut

flétrir [fletrir] *v* **se flétrir** *vr* : wither, fade

fleur [flœr] *nf* **1** : flower **2 en ～** : in blossom — **fleuri, -rie** [flœri] *adj* **1** : flowered **2** : flowery — **fleurir** [flœrir] *vi* **1** : flower, blossom **2** PROSPÉRER : flourish — **fleuriste** [flœrist] *nmf* : florist

fleuve [flœv] *nm* : river

flexible [flɛksibl] *adj* : flexible — **flexibilité** [flɛksibilite] *nf* : flexibility — **flexion** [flɛksjɔ̃] *nf* : bending, flexing

flic [flik] *nm fam* : cop

flirter [flœrte] *vi* : flirt

flocon [flɔkɔ̃] *nm* **1** : flake **2 ～ de neige** : snowflake **3 ～s de maïs** : cornflakes

floraison [flɔrezɔ̃] *nf* : flowering, blossoming — **floral, -rale** [flɔral] *adj, mpl* **-raux** [flɔro] : floral — **flore** [flɔr] *nf* : flora — **florissant, -sante** [flɔrisɑ̃, -sɑ̃t] *adj* : flourishing

flot [flo] *nm* **1** : flood, stream **2 à ～** : afloat

flotter [flɔte] *vi* **1** : float **2** : flutter (of a flag) — **flotte** [flɔt] *nf* : fleet — **flotteur** [flɔtœr] *nm* : float

flou, floue [flu] *adj* **1** : blurred **2** : vague, hazy (of ideas, etc.)

fluctuer [flyktɥe] *vi* : fluctuate — **fluctuation** [flyktɥasjɔ̃] *nf* : fluctuation

fluide [flɥid] *adj* **1** : fluid **2** : flowing freely — **～** *nm* : fluid — **fluidité** [flɥidite] *nf* : fluidity

fluor [flyɔr] *nm* : fluorine

fluorescent, -cente [flyɔresɑ̃, -sɑ̃t] *adj* : fluorescent — **fluorescence** [-sɑ̃s] *nf* : fluorescence

flûte [flyt] *nf* **1** : flute **2** : baguette — **～** *interj* **～ alors!** : nonsense!

fluvial, -viale [flyvjal] *adj, mpl* **-viaux** [-vjo]
: river

flux [fly] *nm* **1** : flow **2** MARÉE : flood tide **3**
le ~ et le reflux : the ebb and flow

fœtus [fetys] *nms & pl* : fetus

foi [fwa] *nf* **1** : faith **2 bonne ~** : honesty,
sincerity **3 digne de ~** : reliable **4 ma
~ !** : well!

foie [fwa] *nm* : liver

foin [fwɛ̃] *nm* : hay

foire [fwar] *nf* : fair, market

fois [fwa] *nf* **1** : time, occasion **2 à la ~** : at
the same time, together **3 des ~** : some-
times **4 il était une ~** : once upon a time

foison [fwazɔ̃] **à ~** *adv phr* : in abundance
— **foisonner** [fwazɔne] *vi* : abound

fol → **fou**

folâtrer [folatre] *vi* : frolic — **folâtre** [folatr]
adj : playful, frisky

folie [foli] *nf* **1** : craziness, madness **2 à la
~** : madly

folklore [folklor] *nm* : folklore — **folklorique** [folklɔrik] *adj* : folk (of music,
dance, etc.)

folle → **fou** — **follement** [fɔlmɑ̃] *adv*
: madly, wildly

foncer [fɔ̃se] {6} *vt* : darken — *vi* **~ sur**
: rush at — **foncé, -cée** [fɔ̃se] *adj* : dark (of
colors)

foncier, -cière [fɔ̃sje, -sjɛr] *adj* **1** : land,
property **2** FONDAMENTAL : fundamental —
foncièrement [fɔ̃sjɛrmɑ̃] *adv* : fundamen-
tally

fonction [fɔ̃ksjɔ̃] *nf* **1** : function **2** EMPLOI
: job, post **3 faire ~ de** : serve as **4 en ~
de** : according to **5 ~ publique** : civil
service — **fonctionnaire** [fɔ̃ksjɔnɛr] *nmf*
: official, civil servant — **fonctionnel,
-nelle** [fɔ̃ksjɔnɛl] *adj* : functional — **fonctionnement** [fɔ̃ksjɔnmɑ̃] *nm* : functioning,
working — **fonctionner** [fɔ̃ksjɔne] *vi*
: function, work

fond [fɔ̃] *nm* **1** : bottom, back **2** CŒUR
: heart, root **3** ARRIÈRE-PLAN : background
4 à ~ : thoroughly **5 au ~** : in fact **6 au
~ de** : at the bottom of, in the depths of

fondamental, -tale [fɔ̃damɑ̃tal] *adj, mpl*
-taux [-to] : fundamental — **fondamentalement** [-talmɑ̃] *adv* : basically

fonder [fɔ̃de] *vt* **1** : found **2** BASER : base —
se fonder *vr* **~ sur** : be based on — **fondateur, -trice** [fɔ̃datœr, -tris] *n* : founder
— **fondation** [fɔ̃dasjɔ̃] *nf* : foundation —
fondé, -dée [fɔ̃de] *adj* : well-founded —
fondement [fɔ̃dmɑ̃] *nm* **1** : foundation **2
sans ~** : groundless

fondre [fɔ̃dr] {63} *vt* **1** : melt, smelt **2** : cast
(a statue, etc.) — *vi* **1** : melt **2 ~ en
larmes** : dissolve into tears

fonds [fɔ̃] *nms & pl* **1** : fund **2 ~** *nmpl*

: funds, capital **3** *or* **~ de commerce**
: business

fontaine [fɔ̃tɛn] *nf* **1** : fountain **2** SOURCE
: spring

fonte [fɔ̃t] *nf* **1** : melting, smelting **2** : thaw-
ing (of snow) **3** : cast iron

football [futbol] *nm* **1** : soccer **2** *Can* : football **3 ~ américain** *France* : football —
footballeur, -leuse [futbolœr, -løz] *n* : soccer player, football player

footing [futiŋ] *France* : jogging

forage [foraʒ] *nm* : drilling

forçat [forsa] *nm* : convict

force [fors] *nf* **1** : force **2** PUISSANCE
: strength **3 à ~ de** : as a result of **4 les
~s armées** : the armed forces — **forcé,
-cée** [forse] *adj* **1** : forced **2** INÉVITABLE
: inevitable — **forcément** [forsemɑ̃] *adv*
: inevitably — **forcer** [forse] {6} *vt* **1**
: force, compel **2** : force open **3** : strain,
overtax (one's voice, etc.) — *vi* : overdo it
— **se forcer** *vr* : force oneself

forer [fore] *vt* : drill, bore

forêt [forɛ] *nf* : forest — **foresterie**
[forɛstəri] *nf* : forestry — **forestier, -tière**
[forɛstje, -tjɛr] *adj* : forest

forfaire [forfɛr] {44} *vi* **~ à** : fail in

forfait [forfɛ] *nm* **1** : fixed price **2 déclarer
~** : withdraw — **forfaitaire** [forfɛtɛr] *adj*
: inclusive

forge [forʒ] *nf* : forge — **forger** [forʒe] {16}
vt : forge — **forgeron** [forʒərɔ̃] *nm* : blacksmith

formaliser [formalize] *v* **se formaliser** *vr*
: take offense

formalité [formalite] *nf* : formality

format [forma] *nm* : format — **formater**
[formate] *vt* : format (a computer disk)

formation [formasjɔ̃] *nf* **1** : formation **2** AP-
PRENTISSAGE : education, training — **forme**
[form] *nf* **1** : form, shape **2 ~s** *nfpl*
: (human) figure **3 ~s** *nfpl* : proprieties **4
en ~** : fit, in shape — **formel, -melle**
[formɛl] *adj* **1** : formal **2** CATÉGORIQUE
: definitive — **formellement** [-mɛlmɑ̃] *adv*
: strictly, absolutely — **former** [forme] *vt* **1**
: form **2** : train, educate, develop

formidable [formidabl] *adj* **1** : tremendous
2 *fam* : great, terrific

formulaire [formylɛr] *nm* : form, questionnaire

formule [formyl] *nf* **1** : formula **2** MÉTHODE
: way, method **3** FORMULAIRE : form **4 ~
de politesse** : polite phrase, closing (of a
letter) — **formuler** [formyle] *vt* : formulate,
express

fort, forte [for, fort] *adj* **1** PUISSANT : strong
2 : loud **3** CONSIDÉRABLE : large **4** DOUÉ
: gifted — **fort** [for] *adv* **1** : strongly, loudly,
hard **2** TRÈS : very — **fort** *nm* **1** : fort,

fortress 2 : strong point — **forteresse** [fɔrtərɛs] *nf* : fortress — **fortifier** [fɔrtifje] {96} *vt* : fortify, strengthen — **fortification** [fɔrtifikasjɔ̃] *nf* : fortification

fortuit, -tuite [fɔrtɥi, -tɥit] *adj* : fortuitous, chance

fortune [fɔrtyn] *nf* : fortune — **fortuné, -née** [fɔrtyne] *adj* : wealthy

forum [fɔrɔm] *nm* : forum

fosse [fos] *nf* 1 : pit 2 TOMBE : grave 3 ~ **septique** : septic tank — **fossé** [fose] *nm* 1 : ditch, trench 2 ~ **de générations** : generation gap — **fossette** [fosɛt] *nf* : dimple

fossile [fosil] *nm* : fossil

fou [fu] (**fol** [fɔl] *before a vowel or mute h*), **folle** [fɔl] *adj* 1 : mad, crazy 2 *fam* : tremendous — ~ *n* : crazy person, lunatic — **fou** *nm* 1 : fool, jester 2 : bishop (in chess)

foudre [fudr] *nf* : lightning — **foudroyant, -droyante** [fudrwajɑ̃, fudrwajɑ̃t] *adj* 1 : overwhelming 2 SOUDAIN : sudden — **foudroyer** [fudrwaje] {58} *vt* : strike down

fouet [fwɛ] *nm* 1 : whip 2 : whisk 3 **de plein** ~ : head-on — **fouetter** [fwete] *vt* : whip

fougère [fuʒɛr] *nf* : fern

fougue [fug] *nf* : ardor, spirit — **fougueux, -geuse** [fugø, -gøz] *adj* : fiery

fouiller [fuje] *vt* 1 : search 2 CREUSER : excavate, dig — *vi* ~ **dans** : rummage through — **fouille** [fuj] *nf* 1 : search 2 ~**s** *nfpl* : excavations — **fouillis** [fuji] *nm* : jumble

fouiner [fwine] *vi fam* : snoop around

foulard [fular] *nm* : scarf

foule [ful] *nf* 1 : crowd 2 **une** ~ **de** : masses of, lots of

fouler [fule] *vt* : press, tread on — **se fouler** *vr* : sprain (one's ankle, etc.) — **foulée** [fule] *nf* **dans la** ~ **de** : in the aftermath of — **foulure** [fulyr] *nf* : sprain

four [fur] *nm* 1 : oven 2 *fam* : flop (in theater, etc.)

fourbu, -bue [furby] *adj* : exhausted

fourche [furʃ] *nf* 1 : pitchfork 2 : fork (of a road) — **fourchette** [furʃɛt] *nf* : fork

fourgon [furgɔ̃] *nm* : van, truck — **fourgonnette** [furgɔnɛt] *nf* : minivan

fourmi [furmi] *nf* : ant — **fourmilière** [furmiljɛr] *nf* : anthill — **fourmiller** [furmije] *vi* 1 : swarm 2 ~ **de** : be teeming with

fourneau [furno] *nm, pl* **-neaux** [furno] 1 : stove 2 CUISINIÈRE : furnace

fournée [furne] *nf* : batch

fournir [furnir] *vt* 1 : supply, provide (with) 2 ~ **un effort** : make an effort — **fourni, -nie** [furni] *adj* : thick, bushy — **fournisseur, -seuse** [furnisœr, -søz] *n* : supplier — **fournitures** [furnityr] *nfpl* : equipment, supplies

fourrage [furaʒ] *nm* : fodder — **fourrager** [furaʒe] {17} *vi* : forage

fourré [fure] *nm* : thicket

fourreau [furo] *nm, pl* **-reaux** : sheath

fourrer [fure] *vt* 1 : stuff, fill 2 *fam* : thrust, stick — **fourre–tout** [furtu] *nms & pl* : tote bag, carryall

fourrière [furjɛr] *nf* : pound (for animals or vehicles)

fourrure [furyr] *nf* : fur

fourvoyer [furvwaje] {58} *v* **se fourvoyer** *vr* 1 : lead astray 2 ~ **dans** : get involved in

foyer [fwaje] *nm* 1 : hearth 2 DOMICILE : home 3 RÉSIDENCE : residence, hall 4 : foyer (of a theater) 5 **lunettes à double** ~ : bifocals

fracas [fraka] *nms & pl* : crash, din — **fracasser** [frakase] *vt* : shatter, smash

fraction [fraksjɔ̃] *nf* : fraction

fracture [fraktyr] *nf* : fracture — **fracturer** [fraktyre] *vt* : fracture

fragile [fraʒil] *adj* 1 : fragile 2 FAIBLE : frail — **fragilité** [fraʒilite] *nf* 1 : fragility 2 FAIBLESSE : frailty

fragment [fragmɑ̃] *nm* : fragment

frais, fraîche [frɛ, frɛʃ] *adj* 1 : fresh 2 : cool (of weather) 3 **peinture fraîche** : wet paint — **frais** *nm* 1 **mettre au** ~ : put in a cool place 2 **prendre le** ~ : take a breath of fresh air 3 **frais** *nmpl* : expenses, fees — ~ [frɛ] *adv* 1 : freshly 2 **il fait** ~ : it's cool outside — **fraîcheur** [frɛʃœr] *nf* 1 : freshness 2 : coolness — **fraîchir** [frɛʃir] *vi* : cool off (of weather)

fraise [frɛz] *nf* : strawberry

framboise [frɑ̃bwaz] *nf* : raspberry

franc, franche [frɑ̃, frɑ̃ʃ] *adj* 1 HONNÊTE : frank 2 VÉRITABLE : utter, downright — **franc** [frɑ̃] *nm* : franc

français, -çaise [frɑ̃sɛ, -sɛz] *adj* : French — **français** *nm* : French (language)

franchement [frɑ̃ʃmɑ̃] *adv* 1 SINCÈREMENT : frankly 2 NETTEMENT : clearly 3 VRAIMENT : downright, really

franchir [frɑ̃ʃir] *vt* 1 : cross (over) 2 : cover (a distance)

franchise [frɑ̃ʃiz] *nf* 1 SINCÉRITÉ : frankness 2 EXONÉRATION : exemption, allowance 3 : franchise

franco–canadien, -dienne [frɑ̃kokanadjɛ̃, -djɛn] *adj* : French-Canadian

francophone [frɑ̃kɔfɔn] *adj* : French-speaking

frange [frɑ̃ʒ] *nf* 1 : fringe 2 : bangs (of hair)

frapper [frape] *vt* 1 : strike, hit 2 IMPRESSIONNER : impress — *vi* : bang, knock — **frappant, -pante** [frapɑ̃, -pɑ̃t] *adj* : striking

fraternel, -nelle [fratɛrnɛl] *adj* : fraternal, brotherly — **fraterniser** [fratɛrnize] *vi*

: fraternize — **fraternité** [fratɛrnite] *nf*
: fraternity, brother-hood

fraude [frod] *nf* : fraud — **frauder** [frode] *v*
: cheat — **fraudeur, -deuse** [frodœr, -døz]
n : cheat, swindler — **frauduleux, -leuse**
[frodylø, -løz] *adj* : fraudulent

frayer [freje] {11} *v* **se frayer** *vr* ~ **un**
chemin : make one's way

frayeur [frejœr] *nf* : fright

fredonner [frədɔne] *vt* : hum

frégate [fregat] *nf* : frigate

frein [frɛ̃] *nm* **1** : brake **2 mettre un ~ à**
: curb, block — **freiner** [frene] *vt* : slow
down, check — *vi* : brake

frêle [frɛl] *adj* : frail

frelon [frəlɔ̃] *nm* : hornet

frémir [fremir] *vi* **1** FRISSONNER : shiver **2**
TREMBLER : quiver, flutter **3** : simmer (in
cooking)

frêne [frɛn] *nm* : ash (tree or wood)

frénésie [frenezi] *nf* : frenzy — **frénétique**
[frenetik] *adj* : frantic, frenzied

fréquenter [frekɑ̃te] *vt* **1** : frequent **2** : attend (school, etc.) **3** CÔTOYER : associate
with, see — **fréquemment** [frekamɑ̃] *adv*
: frequently — **fréquence** [frekɑ̃s] *nf* : frequency — **fréquent, -quente** [frekɑ̃, -kɑ̃t]
adj : frequent — **fréquentation** [frekɑ̃tasjɔ̃]
nf **1** : frequenting **2** PRÉSENCE : attendance
3 RELATION : acquaintance

frère [frɛr] *nm* **1** : brother **2** : friar

fresque [frɛsk] *nf* : fresco

fret [frɛ] *nm* : freight

fretin [frətɛ̃] *nm* **menu ~** : small fry

friable [frijabl] *adj* : crumbly

friand, friande [frijɑ̃, -jɑ̃d] *adj* ~ **de** : fond
of

friandise [frijɑ̃diz] *nf* **1** : delicacy **2** ~**s**
nfpl : sweets

fric [frik] *nm fam* : dough, cash

friction [friksjɔ̃] *nf* **1** : friction **2** MASSAGE
: massage — **frictionner** [friksjɔne] *vt* : rub,
massage

frigide [friʒid] *adj* : frigid

frigo [frigo] *nm fam* : fridge

frileux, -leuse [frilø, -løz] *adj* **1** : sensitive
to cold **2** PRUDENT : cautious

frimer [frime] *vi fam* : show off

fringale [frɛ̃gal] *nf* **avoir la ~** *fam* : be ravenous

fringant, -gante [frɛ̃gɑ̃, -gɑ̃t] *adj* : dashing

fripon, -ponne [fripɔ̃, -pɔn] *adj* : mischievous — ~ *n* : rascal

fripouille [fripuj] *nf fam* : scoundrel

frire [frir] {45} *v* : fry

friser [frize] *vt* **1** BOUCLER : curl **2** : border
on, be close to — *vi* : curl — **frisé, -sée**
[frize] *adj* : curly, curly-haired

frisquet, -quette [friskɛ, -kɛt] *adj* : chilly,
nippy

frisson [frisɔ̃] *nm* : shiver, shudder — **frissonner** [frisɔne] *vi* : shiver, shudder

friture [frityr] *nf* **1** : frying **2** : deep fat, oil
3 : fried food — **frites** [frit] *nfpl* : french
fries

frivole [frivɔl] *adj* : frivolous — **frivolité**
[frivɔlite] *nf* : frivolity

froid, froide [frwa, frwad] *adj* : cold — **froid**
[frwa] *adv* **il fait ~** : it's cold (outside) —
~ *nm* **1** : cold **2 être en ~ avec** : be on
bad terms with **3 prendre ~** : catch cold
— **froidement** [frwadmɑ̃] *adv* : coldly,
coolly — **froideur** [frwadœr] *nf* : coldness,
coolness

froisser [frwase] *vt* **1** : crumple, crease **2**
BLESSER : offend — **se froisser** *vr* **1**
: crease, crumple (up) **2** ~ **un muscle**
: strain a muscle

frôler [frole] *vt* : brush against, touch lightly

fromage [frɔmaʒ] *nm* **1** : cheese **2** ~
blanc : cottage cheese — **fromagerie**
[frɔmaʒri] *nf* : cheese shop

fronce [frɔ̃s] *nf* : gather, crease — **froncement** [frɔ̃smɑ̃] *nm* ~ **de sourcils** : frown

froncer [frɔ̃se] {6} *vt* **1** : gather (fabric) **2**
~ **les sourcils** : frown

fronde [frɔ̃d] *nf* **1** : rebellion, revolt **2**
LANCE-PIERRES : slingshot

front [frɔ̃] *nm* **1** : forehead **2** : front (in
politics, war, etc.) **3** AUDACE : audacity,
cheek **4 de ~** : head-on **5 faire ~ à**
: confront — **frontal, -tale** [frɔ̃tal] *adj, mpl*
-taux [frɔ̃to] : frontal — **frontalier, -lière**
[frɔ̃talje, -ljer] *adj* : frontier — **frontière**
[frɔ̃tjer] *nf* : frontier, border

frotter [frɔte] *vt* **1** : rub **2** NETTOYER : polish, scrub — *vi* : rub — **frottement** [frɔtmɑ̃]
nm **1** : rubbing **2** ~**s** *nmpl* : friction, disagreement

frousse [frus] *nf fam* : scare, fright

fructueux, -tueuse [fryktɥø, -tɥøz] *adj*
: fruitful

frugal, -gale [frygal] *adj, mpl* **-gaux** [frygo]
: frugal — **frugalité** [frygalite] *nf* : frugality

fruit [frɥi] *nm* **1** : fruit **2** ~**s de mer**
: seafood — **fruité, -tée** [frɥite] *adj* : fruity
— **fruitier, -tière** [frɥitje, -tjer] *adj* : fruit

frustrer [frystre] *vt* **1** : frustrate **2** ~ **de**
: deprive of — **frustrant, -trante** [frystrɑ̃,
-trɑ̃t] *adj* : frustrating — **frustration** [frys-
trasjɔ̃] *nf* : frustration

fugace [fygas] *adj* : fleeting

fugitif, -tive [fyʒitif, -tiv] *n* : fugitive, runaway

fugue [fyg] *nf* **1 faire une ~** : run away **2**
~ **amoureuse** : elopement

fuir [fɥir] {46} *vi* **1** : flee **2** SUINTER : leak
— *vt* : avoid, shun — **fuite** [fɥit] *nf* **1**
: flight, escape **2** : leak (of water, information, etc.)

fulgurant, -rante [fylgyrã, -rãt] *adj* : dazzling, vivid

fulminer [fylmine] *vi* : be enraged

fumer [fyme] *vt* : smoke — *vi* **1** : smoke **2** : give off steam — **fumé, -mée** [fyme] *adj* **1** : smoked **2** : tinted (of glass, etc.) — **fumée** *nf* **1** : smoke **2** VAPEUR : steam — **fumeur, -meuse** [fymœr, -møz] *n* : smoker

fumier [fymje] *nm* : dung, manure

fumigation [fymigasjɔ̃] *nf* : fumigation

funambule [fynãbyl] *nmf* : tightrope walker

funèbre [fynɛbr] *adj* **1** : funeral **2** LUGUBRE : gloomy — **funérailles** [fy-neraj] *nfpl* : funeral — **funéraire** [fynerɛr] *adj* : funeral

funeste [fynɛst] *adj* DÉSASTREUX : disastrous

fur [fyr] **au ~ et à mesure** *adv phr* : little by little

furet [fyrɛ] *nm* : ferret

fureter [fyrte] {20} *vi* : pry

fureur [fyrœr] *nf* **1** : rage, fury **2 faire ~** : be all the rage

furibond, -bonde [fyribɔ̃, -bɔ̃d] *adj* : furious

— **furie** [fyri] *nf* : fury, rage — **furieux, -rieuse** [fyrjø, -jøz] *adj* : furious

furoncle [fyrɔ̃kl] *nm* : boil

furtif, -tive [fyrtif, -tiv] *adj* : furtive, sly

fusain [fyzɛ̃] *nm* : charcoal

fuseau [fyzo] *nm, pl* **-seaux 1** : spindle **2 ~ horaire** : time zone

fusée [fyze] *nf* **1** : rocket **2 ~ éclairante** : flare

fuselé, -lée [fyzle] *adj* : slender, tapering

fusible [fyzibl] *nm* : fuse

fusil [fyzi] *nm* : gun, rifle — **fusillade** [fyzijad] *nf* : gunfire — **fusiller** [fyzije] *vt* : shoot

fusion [fyzjɔ̃] *nf* : fusion — **fusionner** [fyzɔnje] *v* : merge

fût [fy] *nm* : barrel, cask

futé, -tée [fyte] *adj* : cunning, crafty

futile [fytil] *adj* : futile — **futilité** [fytilite] *nf* : futility

futur, -ture [fytyr] *adj & nm* : future

fuyant, fuyante [fɥijã, fɥijãt] *adj* : elusive, shifty

G

g [ʒe] *nm* : g, seventh letter of the alphabet

gabarit [gabari] *nm* **1** : size, dimensions *pl* **2** *fam* : caliber, type

gâcher [gɑʃe] *vt* : spoil, ruin

gâchette [gɑʃɛt] *nf* : trigger

gâchis [gɑʃi] *nm* **1** DÉSORDRE : mess **2** GASPILLAGE : waste

gadget [gadʒɛt] *nm* : gadget

gadoue [gadu] *nf* : mud, muck

gaffe [gaf] *nf fam* : blunder — **gaffer** [gafe] *vi fam* : blunder, goof (up)

gage [gaʒ] *nm* **1** : security **2** GARANTIE : pledge, guarantee **3 ~s** *nmpl* : wages, pay **4 en ~ de** : as a token of **5 mettre en ~** : pawn — **gager** [gaʒe] {17} *vt* **1** : bet, wager **2** : guarantee (a loan, etc.) — **gageure** [gaʒœr] *nf* **1** : challenge **2** *Can* : bet, wager

gagner [gaɲe] *vt* **1** : win **2** : earn (one's living, etc.) **3** : gain (speed, etc.) **4** : save (time, space, etc.) **5** ATTEINDRE : reach — *vi* **1** : win **2 ~ en** : increase in **3 y ~** : be better off — **gagnant, -gnante** [gaɲã, -ɲãt] *adj* : winning — **~** *n* : winner — **gagne-pain** [gaɲpɛ̃] *nms & pl* : job, livelihood

gai, gaie [gɛ] *adj* : cheerful, merry — **gaieté** [gete] *nf* : cheerfulness

gaillard, -larde [gajar, -jard] *adj* **1** : sprightly **2** GRIVOIS : ribald — **~** *nmf* : vigorous person

gain [gɛ̃] *nm* **1** : earnings *pl* **2** PROFIT : gain **3** ÉCONOMIE : saving

gaine [gɛn] *nf* **1** : girdle **2** : sheath (of a dagger)

gala [gala] *nm* : gala, reception

galant, -lante [galã, -lãt] *adj* : courteous, gallant

galaxie [galaksi] *nf* : galaxy

galbe [galb] *nm* : curve, shapeliness

galerie [galri] *nf* **1** : gallery **2** : balcony (in a theater) **3** : roof rack (of an automobile)

galet [galɛ] *nm* : pebble

galette [galɛt] *nf* : flat round cake

gallois, -loise [galwa, -lwaz] *adj* : Welsh — **gallois** *nm* : Welsh (language)

gallon [galɔ̃] *nm* : gallon

galoper [galɔpe] *vi* : gallop — **galop** [galo] *nm* : gallop

galopin [galɔpɛ̃] *nm* : rascal

galvaniser [galvanize] *vt* : galvanize

galvauder [galvode] *vt* : sully, tarnish

gambade [gãbad] *nf* : leap, skip — **gambader** [gãbade] *vi* : leap about

gamelle [gamɛl] *nf* : mess kit

gamin, -mine [gamɛ̃, -min] *adj* : mischievous — **~** *n* : kid, youngster

gamme [gam] *nf* **1** : scale (in music) **2** SÉRIE : range, gamut

ganglion [gɑ̃glijɔ̃] *nm* **avoir des ～s** : have swollen glands

gangrène [gɑ̃grɛn] *nf* : gangrene

gangster [gɑ̃gstɛr] *nm* : gangster

gant [gɑ̃] *nm* **1** : glove **2 ～ de toilette** : washcloth

garage [garaʒ] *nm* : garage — **garagiste** [garaʒist] *nmf* **1** : garage owner **2** : (garage) mechanic

garant, -rante [garɑ̃, -rɑ̃t] *n* : guarantor — **garant** *nm* : guarantee (in law) — **garantie** [garɑ̃ti] *nf* : guarantee, warranty — **garantir** [garɑ̃tir] *vt* **1** : guarantee **2 ～ de** : protect from

garçon [garsɔ̃] *nm* **1** : boy, young man **2** SERVEUR : waiter **3 ～ manqué** : tomboy

garder [garde] *vt* **1** : keep **2** SURVEILLER : watch over **3 ～ de** : protect from — **se garder** *vr* **1** : keep **2 ～ de** : be careful not to — **garde** [gard] *nm* **1** : guard **2 ～ du corps** : bodyguard — **～** *nf* **1** : nurse **2** : (military) guard **3** : custody, care **4 de ～** : on duty **5 mettre en ～** : warn **6 prendre ～** : be careful — **garde-fou** [gardəfu] *nm, pl* **garde-fous** : railing — **garde-manger** [gardəmɑ̃ʒe] *nms & pl* : pantry — **garderie** [gardəri] *nf* : day-care center — **garde-robe** [gardərɔb] *nf, pl* **garde-robes** : wardrobe, closet — **gardien, -dienne** [gardjɛ̃, -djɛn] *n* **1** : warden, custodian **2** PROTECTEUR : guardian — **gardien** *nm* **1 ～ de but** : goalkeeper **2 ～ de la paix** *France* : police officer — **gardienne** *nf* **～ d'enfants** : day-care worker

gare[1] [gar] *nf* **1** : station **2 ～ routière** *France or* **～ d'autobus** *Can* : bus station

gare[2] *interj* **1 ～ à toi!** : watch out! **2 sans crier ～** : without warning

garer [gare] *vt* STATIONNER : park — **se garer** *vr* **1** : park **2** S'ÉCARTER : move away

gargariser [gargarize] *v* **se gargariser** *vr* : gargle

gargouiller [garguje] *vi* : gurgle, rumble

garnement [garnəmɑ̃] *nm* : rascal

garnir [garnir] *vt* **1** REMPLIR : fill **2** COUVRIR : cover **3** DÉCORER : decorate, trim — **garni, -nie** [garni] *adj* : served with vegetables

garnison [garnizɔ̃] *nf* : garrison

garniture [garnityr] *nf* **1** : filling (in cooking) **2** DÉCORATION : trimming, garnish

gars [ga] *nm fam* **1** : boy, lad **2** TYPE : guy, fellow

gaspiller [gaspije] *vt* : waste, squander — **gaspillage** [gaspijaʒ] *nm* : waste

gastrique [gastrik] *adj* : gastric

gastronomie [gastrɔnɔmi] *nf* : gastronomy

gâteau [gato] *nm, pl* **-teaux 1** : cake **2 ～ sec** *France* : cookie

gâter [gate] *vt* **1** : pamper **2** ABÎMER : spoil, ruin — **se gâter** *vr* **1** : go bad **2** SE DÉTÉRIORER : deteriorate

gâterie [gatri] *nf* : little treat, delicacy

gâteux, -teuse [gatø, -tøz] *adj* : senile

gauche [goʃ] *adj* **1** : left **2** MALADROIT : clumsy — **～** *nf* **1** : left **2 la ～** : the left (wing) — **gaucher, -chère** [goʃe, -ʃɛr] *adj* : left-handed — **gaucherie** [goʃri] *nf* : awkwardness

gaufre [gofr] *nf* : waffle — **gaufrette** [gofrɛt] *nf* : wafer

gausser [gose] *v* **se gausser** *vr* **～ de** : deride, make fun of

gaver [gave] *v* **se gaver** *vr* : stuff oneself

gay [gɛ] *adj* : gay (homosexual)

gaz [gaz] *nms & pl* : gas

gaze [gaz] *nf* : gauze

gazer [gaze] *vi fam* **ça gaze?** : how are things going?

gazette [gazɛt] *nf* : newspaper

gazeux, -zeuse [gazø, -zøz] *adj* : fizzy, carbonated

gazon [gazɔ̃] *nm* **1** : grass, turf **2** PELOUSE : lawn

gazouiller [gazuje] *vi* **1** : chirp **2** : gurgle, babble (of a baby)

geai [ʒɛ] *nm* : jay

géant, géante [ʒeɑ̃, -ɑ̃t] *adj* : giant, gigantic — **～** *n* : giant

geler [ʒəle] {20} *v* : freeze — *v impers* **on gèle!** : it's freezing! — **gel** [ʒɛl] *nm* **1** : frost **2** : gel **3** : freezing (of prices, etc.) — **gélatine** [ʒelatin] *nf* : gelatin — **gelée** *nf* **1** : (hoar)frost **2** : jelly — **gelure** [ʒəlyr] *nf* : frostbite

gémir [ʒemir] *vi* : groan, moan — **gémissement** [ʒemismɑ̃] *nm* : groan(ing), moan(ing)

gemme [ʒɛm] *nf* : gem

gênant, -nante [ʒenɑ̃, -nɑ̃t] *adj* **1** : embarrassing **2** ENCOMBRANT : cumbersome **3** ENNUYEUX : annoying

gencives [ʒɑ̃siv] *nfpl* : gums

gendarme [ʒɑ̃darm] *nm* : police officer — **gendarmerie** [ʒɑ̃darməri] *nf* **1** *France* : police force **2** *France* : police station **3** *Can* : federal police force

gendre [ʒɑ̃dr] *nm* : son-in-law

gène [ʒɛn] *nm* : gene

généalogie [ʒenealɔʒi] *nf* : genealogy

gêner [ʒene] *vt* **1** : embarrass, make uncomfortable **2** DÉRANGER : bother **3** ENCOMBRER : hamper — **se gêner** *vr* : put oneself out — **gêne** [ʒɛn] *nf* **1** : inconvenience **2** : embarrassment **3** : (physical) discomfort — **gêné, -née** [ʒene] *adj* **1** : embarrassed **2** *Can* : shy

général, -rale [ʒeneral] *adj, mpl* **-raux** [-ro] : general — **général** *nm, pl* **-raux** : general — **généralement** [-ralmɑ̃] *adv* : generally, usually — **généraliser** [ʒeneralize] *v* : generalize — **se généraliser** *vr* : become widespread — **généraliste** [ʒeneralist] *nmf* : general practitioner — **généralité** [ʒeneralite] *nf* : majority

générateur [ʒeneratœr] *nm* : generator

génération [ʒenerasjɔ̃] *nf* : generation

génératrice [ʒeneratris] *nf* : (electric) generator

générer [ʒenere] {87} *vt* : generate

généreux, -reuse [ʒenerø, -røz] *adj* : generous — **généreusement** [-røzmɑ̃] *adv* : generously

générique [ʒenerik] *adj* : generic — ~ *nm* : credits *pl* (in movies)

générosité [ʒenerozite] *nf* : generosity

génétique [ʒenetik] *adj* : genetic — ~ *nf* : genetics

génie [ʒeni] *nm* **1** : genius **2** INGÉNIERIE : engineering — **génial, -niale** [ʒenjal] *adj, mpl* **-niaux** [-njo] **1** : brilliant **2** *fam* : fantastic, great

génisse [ʒenis] *nf* : heifer

génital, -tale [ʒenital] *adj, mpl* **-taux** [-to] : genital

genou [ʒənu] *nm, pl* **-noux 1** : knee **2 se mettre à ~x** : kneel down

genre [ʒɑ̃r] *nm* **1** SORTE : kind, type **2** ATTITUDE : style, manner **3** : gender (in grammar)

gens [ʒɑ̃] *nmfpl* **1** : people **2 ~ d'affaires** : businesspeople **3 jeunes ~** : teenagers

gentil, -tille [ʒɑ̃ti, -tij] *adj* **1** : kind, nice **2** SAGE : well-behaved — **gentillesse** [ʒɑ̃tijes] *nf* : kindness, niceness — **gentiment** [ʒɑ̃timɑ̃] *adv* : nicely, kindly

géographie [ʒeografi] *nf* : geography — **géographique** [ʒeografik] *adj* : geographic(al)

geôlier, -lière [ʒolje, -ljɛr] *n* : jailer

géologie [ʒeolɔʒi] *nf* : geology — **géologique** [ʒeolɔʒik] *adj* : geologic(al)

géométrie [ʒeɔmetri] *nf* : geometry — **géométrique** [ʒeɔmetrik] *adj* : geometric(al)

géranium [ʒeranjɔm] *nm* : geranium

gérant, -rante [ʒerɑ̃, -rɑ̃t] *n* : manager

gerbe [ʒɛrb] *nf* **1** : sheaf (of wheat) **2** : bunch (of flowers, etc.)

gercer [ʒɛrse] {6} *v* **se gercer** *vr* : chap, crack — **gerçure** [ʒɛrsyr] *nf* : crack (in the skin)

gérer [ʒere] {87} *vt* : manage

germain, -maine [ʒɛrmɛ̃, -mɛn] *adj* **cousin germain** : first cousin

germe [ʒɛrm] *nm* **1** : germ **2** POUSSE : sprout

germer [ʒɛrme] *vi* **1** : sprout, germinate **2** : form (of ideas, etc.)

gésier [ʒezje] *nm* : gizzard

gésir [ʒezir] {47} *vi* : lie, be lying

gestation [ʒɛstasjɔ̃] *nf* : gestation

geste [ʒɛst] *nm* : gesture, movement

gestion [ʒɛstjɔ̃] *nf* : management — **gestionnaire** [ʒɛstjɔnɛr] *nmf* : administrator

geyser [ʒezɛr] *nm* : geyser

gibet [ʒibɛ] *nm* : gallows

gibier [ʒibje] *nm* **1** : game (animals) **2** *fam* : prey

giboulée [ʒibule] *nf* : sudden shower

gicler [ʒikle] *vi* : spurt, squirt, spatter — **giclée** [ʒikle] *nf* : spurt, squirt

gifle [ʒifl] *nf* : slap (in the face) — **gifler** [ʒifle] *vt* : slap

gigantesque [ʒigɑ̃tɛsk] *adj* : gigantic, huge

gigot [ʒigo] *nm* : leg (of lamb) — **gigoter** [ʒigɔte] *vi fam* : wriggle, fidget

gilet [ʒilɛ] *nm* **1** : vest **2** : cardigan (sweater) **3 ~ de sauvetage** : life jacket

gin [dʒin] *nm* : gin

gingembre [ʒɛ̃ʒɑ̃br] *nm* : ginger

girafe [ʒiraf] *nf* : giraffe

giratoire [ʒiratwar] *adj* **sens ~** : rotary, traffic circle

girofle [ʒirɔfl] *nm* **clou de ~** : clove

girouette [ʒirwɛt] *nf* : weather vane

gisement [ʒizmɑ̃] *nm* : deposit (in geology)

gitan, -tane [ʒitɑ̃, -tan] *n* : Gypsy

gîte [ʒit] *nm* **1** : shelter, lodging **2 le ~ et le couvert** : room and board

givre [ʒivr] *nm* : frost — **givrer** [ʒivre] *v* **se givrer** *vr* : frost (up)

glabre [glabr] *adj* : hairless

glacer [glase] {6} *vt* **1** : freeze, chill **2** : frost (a cake) — **glaçage** [glasaʒ] *nm* : frosting — **glace** [glas] *nf* **1** : ice **2** *France* : ice cream **3** MIROIR : mirror **4** VITRE : glass — **glacé, -cée** [glase] *adj* **1** : icy, chilly **2** : iced — **glacial, -ciale** [glasjal] *adj, mpl* **-cials** *or* **-ciaux** [-sjo] : icy, frigid — **glacier** [glasje] *nm* : glacier — **glacière** [glasjɛr] *nf* : cooler, icebox — **glaçon** [glasɔ̃] *nm* **1** : block of ice **2** : icicle **3** : ice cube

glaise [glɛz] *nf* : clay

gland [glɑ̃] *nm* **1** : acorn **2** : tassel (ornament)

glande [glɑ̃d] *nf* : gland

glapir [glapir] *vi* : yelp

glas [gla] *nm* **sonner le ~** : toll the bell

glauque [glok] *adj* : gloomy, dreary

glisser [glise] *vi* **1** : slide, slip **2** DÉRAPER : skid — *vt* : slip, slide — **se glisser** *vr* **~ dans** : slip into, creep into — **glissant, -sante** [glisɑ̃, -sɑ̃t] *adj* : slippery — **glissement** [glismɑ̃] *nm* **1** : sliding, gliding **2** ÉVOLUTION : shift — **glissière** [glisjɛr] *nf* **1**

: slide, groove, chute **2 à ~** : sliding —
glissoire [gliswar] *nf* : slide
globe [glɔb] *nm* **1** : globe **2 ~ oculaire**
: eyeball **3 le ~ terrestre** : the earth —
global, -bale [glɔbal] *adj, mpl* **-baux**
[glɔbo] : overall, total — **globalement**
[glɔbalmã] *adv* : as a whole
gloire [glwar] *nf* **1** : glory, fame **2** MÉRITE
: credit — **glorieux, -rieuse** [glɔrjø, -rjøz]
adj : glorious — **glorifier** [glɔrifje] {96} *vt*
: glorify
glossaire [glɔsɛr] *nm* : glossary
glousser [gluse] *vi* **1** : cluck **2** : chuckle —
gloussement [glusmã] *nm* **1** : cluck,
clucking **2** : chuckling
glouton, -tonne [glutɔ̃, -tɔn] *adj* : gluttonous, greedy — **~** *n* : glutton — **gloutonnerie** [glutɔnri] *nf* : gluttony
gluant, gluante [glyã, glyãt] *adj* : sticky
glucose [glykoz] *nm* : glucose
gobelet [gɔblɛ] *nm* : tumbler, beaker
gober [gɔbe] *vt* **1** : swallow whole **2** *fam*
: swallow, fall for
godasse [gɔdas] *nf fam* : shoe
goéland [gɔelã] *nm* : gull
goguenard, -narde [gognar, -nard] *adj*
: mocking
goinfre [gwɛ̃fr] *nm fam* : pig, glutton
golf [gɔlf] *nm* : golf
golfe [gɔlf] *nm* : gulf, bay
gomme [gɔm] *nf* **1** : gum, resin **2** : eraser **3**
~ à mâcher : chewing gum — **gommer**
[gɔme] *vt* : erase
gond [gɔ̃] *nm* : hinge
gondole [gɔ̃dɔl] *nf* : gondola
gondoler [gɔ̃dɔle] *v* **se gondoler** *vr* : warp,
buckle
gonfler [gɔ̃fle] *vt* **1** : swell **2** : blow up, inflate (a balloon, etc.) **3** GROSSIR : exaggerate — *vi* : swell — **se gonfler** *vr* **1** : swell
up **2 ~ de** : swell up with, be filled with —
gonflé, -flée [gɔ̃fle] *adj* : swollen, bloated
— **gonflement** [gɔ̃fləmã] *nm* : swelling
gorge [gɔrʒ] *nf* **1** : throat **2** POITRINE
: bosom, chest **3** : gorge (in geography) —
gorgée [gɔrʒe] *nf* : mouthful, sip — **gorger**
[gɔrʒe] {17} *v* **se gorger** *vr* : gorge oneself
gorille [gɔrij] *nm* : gorilla
gosier [gozje] *nm* : throat
gosse [gɔs] *nmf France fam* : kid, youngster
gothique [gɔtik] *adj* : Gothic
goudron [gudrɔ̃] *nm* : tar — **goudronner**
[gudrɔne] *vt* : tar (a road)
gouffre [gufr] *nm* : gulf, abyss
goujat [guʒa] *nm* : boor
goulot [gulo] *nm* **1** : neck (of a bottle) **2 ~
d'étranglement** : bottleneck
goulu, -lue [guly] *adj* : greedy
gourde [gurd] *nf* **1** : flask **2** : gourd **3** *fam*
: dope, dumbbell

gourdin [gurdɛ̃] *nm* : cudgel, club
gourmand, -mande [gurmã, -mãd] *adj*
GLOUTON : greedy — **~** *n* : glutton —
gourmandise [gurmãdiz] *nf* **1** : greed **2**
~s *nfpl* : sweets, delicacies
gousse [gus] *nf* **~ d'ail** : clove of garlic
goût [gu] *nm* **1** : taste **2** SAVEUR : flavor **3**
GRÉ : fondness, liking **4 de bon ~** : tasteful — **goûter** [gute] *vt* : taste — *vi* **1** : have
an afternoon snack **2 ~ à** *or* **~ de** : try
out, sample — **~** *nm* : afternoon snack
goutte [gut] *nf* : drop (of water, etc.) —
gouttelette [gutlɛt] *nf* : droplet — **goutter**
[gute] *vi* : drip — **gouttière** [gutjɛr] *nf*
: gutter (on a roof)
gouvernail [guvɛrnaj] *nm* **1** : rudder **2**
BARRE : helm
gouverner [guvɛrne] *vt* : govern, rule —
gouvernante [guvɛrnãt] *nf* **1** : governess
2 : housekeeper — **gouvernement** [gu-
vɛrnəmã] *nm* : government — **gouvernemental, -tale** [-mãtal] *adj* : governmental
— **gouverneur** [guvɛrnœr] *nm* : governor
grâce [gras] *nf* **1** : gracefulness **2** FAVEUR
: favor **3** PARDON : mercy, pardon **4 de
bonne ~** : willingly **5 ~ à** : thanks to
— **gracier** [grasje] {96} *vt* : pardon —
gracieux, -cieuse [grasjø, -sjøz] *adj* **1**
: graceful **2** AIMABLE : gracious **3** GRATUIT
: free
grade [grad] *nm* **1** : rank **2 monter en ~**
: be promoted
gradin [gradɛ̃] *nm* **1** : tier **2 ~s** *nmpl*
: bleachers, stands
graduel, -duelle [gradɥɛl] *adj* : gradual —
graduellement [-dɥɛlmã] *adv* : gradually
graduer [gradɥe] *vt* **1** : graduate (a measur-
ing instrument) **2** : increase gradually
graffiti [grafiti] *nmpl* : graffiti
grain [grɛ̃] *nm* **1** : (cereal) grain **2** : speck,
particle (of sand, salt, dust, etc.) **3 ~ de
café** : coffee bean **4 ~ de poivre** : pep-
percorn **5 ~ de beauté** : mole — **graine**
[grɛn] *nf* : seed
graisse [grɛs] *nf* **1** : fat **2** LUBRIFIANT
: grease — **graisser** [grɛse] *vt* : lubricate,
grease — **graisseux, -seuse** [grɛsø, -søz]
adj : greasy
grammaire [gramɛr] *nf* : grammar — **grammatical, -cale** [gramatikal] *adj, mpl* **-caux**
[-ko] : grammatical
gramme [gram] *nm* : gram
grand, grande [grã, grãd] *adj* **1** : tall **2**
GROS : big, large **3** IMPORTANT : great, important **4** : elder, older, grown-up — **grand**
[grã] *adv* **1** : wide **2 ~ ouvert** : wide-
open — **grand–chose** [grãʃoz] *pron* **pas
~** : not much — **grandeur** [grãdœr] *nf* **1**
DIMENSION : size **2** : greatness —
grandiose [grãdjoz] *adj* : grandiose —

grandir [grɑ̃dir] *vt* **1** : make (look) taller **2** EXAGÉRER : exaggerate — *vi* **1** : grow **2** AUGMENTER : increase — **grand–mère** [grɑ̃mɛr] *nf, pl* **grands–mères** : grandmother — **grand–père** [grɑ̃pɛr] *nm, pl* **grands–pères** : grandfather — **grands–parents** [grɑ̃parɑ̃] *nmpl* : grandparents

grange [grɑ̃ʒ] *nf* : barn

granit *or* **granite** [granit] *nm* : granite

granulé [granyle] *nm* : tablet (in medicine) — **granuleux, -leuse** [granylø, -løz] *adj* : granular

graphique [grafik] *adj* : graphic — ~ *nm* : graph, chart

grappe [grap] *nf* : cluster (of grapes, etc.)

grappin [grapɛ̃] *nm* **1** : grapnel **2 mettre le ~ sur** : get one's hooks into

gras, grasse [gra, gras] *adj* **1** : fatty **2** GROS : fat (of persons) **3** HUILEUX : greasy, oily **4** VULGAIRE : crude, coarse **5** : bold (of type) — **gras** *nm* **1** : (animal) fat **2** : grease — **grassouillet, -lette** [grasujɛ, -jɛt] *adj* : pudgy, plump

gratifier [gratifje] {96} *vt* ~ **de** : reward with — **gratification** [gratifikasjɔ̃] *nf* : bonus

gratin [gratɛ̃] *nm* : dish baked with cheese or crumb topping

gratis [gratis] *adv* : free

gratitude [gratityd] *nf* : gratitude

gratte–ciel [gratsjɛl] *nms & pl* : skyscraper

gratter [grate] *vt* : scratch, scrape — **se gratter** *vr* : scratch oneself

gratuit, -tuite [gratɥi, -tɥit] *adj* **1** : free **2** : gratuitous — **gratuitement** [-tɥitmɑ̃] *adv* : free (of charge)

gravats [grava] *nmpl* : rubble

grave [grav] *adj* **1** : serious, grave **2** SOLENNEL : solemn **3 voix** ~ : deep voice — **gravement** [gravmɑ̃] *adv* : seriously

graver [grave] *vt* **1** : engrave **2** : carve **3** ENREGISTRER : cut, record

gravier [gravje] *nm* : gravel

gravillon [gravijɔ̃] *nm* : (fine) gravel, grit

gravir [gravir] *vt* : climb (up)

gravité [gravite] *nf* **1** : gravity (in physics) **2** IMPORTANCE : seriousness — **graviter** [gravite] *vi* : gravitate

gravure [gravyr] *nf* **1** : engraving **2** : print (of a picture), plate (in a book)

gré [gre] *nm* **1** VOLONTÉ : will **2** GOÛT : taste, liking **3 à votre** ~ : as you wish

grec, grecque [grɛk] *adj* : Greek — **grec** *nm* : Greek (language)

greffe [grɛf] *nf* **1** : graft (in botany) **2** : graft, transplant (in medicine) — **greffer** [grɛfe] *vt* **1** : graft **2** : transplant (an organ)

greffier, -fière [grɛfje, -fjɛr] *n* : clerk of court

grêle[1] [grɛl] *adj* **1** : lanky, lean **2** AIGU : shrill

grêle[2] *nf* : hail — **grêler** [grele] *v impers* **il grêle** : it's hailing — **grêlon** [grɛlɔ̃] *nm* : hailstone

grelot [grəlo] *nm* : small bell — **grelotter** [grələte] *vi* : shiver

grenade [grənad] *nf* **1** : pomegranate **2** : grenade (weapon)

grenier [grənje] *nm* : attic, loft

grenouille [grənuj] *nf* : frog

grès [grɛ] *nm* **1** : sandstone **2** POTERIE : stoneware

grésiller [grezije] *vi* : crackle, sizzle

grève [grɛv] *nf* **1** RIVAGE : shore **2** : strike — **gréviste** [grevist] *nmf* : striker

gribouiller [gribuje] *v* : scribble — **gribouillage** [gribujaʒ] *nm* : scribble, scrawl

grief [grijɛf] *nm* : grievance — **grièvement** [grijɛvmɑ̃] *adv* : seriously, severely

griffe [grif] *nf* **1** : claw **2** : signature, label (of a product) — **griffer** [grife] *vt* : scratch — **griffonner** [grifɔne] *vt* : scribble, jot down

grignoter [griɲɔte] *vt* **1** : nibble **2** AMOINDRIR : erode, eat away (at)

gril [gril] *nm* **1** : broiler **2** : grill (for cooking) — **grillade** [grijad] *nf* : grilled meat, grill

grille [grij] *nf* **1** : metal fencing, gate, bars *pl* **2** : grate (of a sewer, etc.) **3** : grid (in games) — **grillage** [grijaʒ] *nm* : wire fencing

griller [grije] *vt* **1** : toast, grill, broil **2** : burn out (a fuse, etc.) — *vi* : broil — **grille–pain** [grijpɛ̃] *nms & pl* : toaster

grillon [grijɔ̃] *nm* : cricket

grimace [grimas] *nf* : grimace — **grimacer** [grimase] {6} *vi* : grimace

grimper [grɛ̃pe] *v* : climb

grincer [grɛ̃se] {6} *vi* **1** : creak, grate **2** ~ **des dents** : grind one's teeth — **grincement** [grɛ̃smɑ̃] *nm* : creak, squeak

grincheux, -cheuse [grɛ̃ʃø, -ʃøz] *adj* : grumpy

grippe [grip] *nf* **1** : flu, influenza **2 prendre qqn en** ~ : take a sudden dislike to s.o. — **grippé, -pée** [gripe] *adj* **être** ~ : have the flu

gris, grise [gri, griz] *adj* **1** : gray **2** MORNE : dull, dreary **3** *fam* : tipsy — **gris** *nm* : gray — **grisaille** [grizaj] *nf* **1** : grayness (of weather) **2** MONOTONIE : dullness

griser [grize] *vt* : intoxicate — **grisant, -sante** [grizɑ̃, -zɑ̃t] *adj* : intoxicating, heady

grisonner [grizɔne] *vi* : turn gray, go gray

grive [griv] *nf* : thrush

grivois, -voise [grivwa, -waz] *adj* : bawdy

grogner [grɔɲe] *vi* **1** : growl **2** : grumble — **grognement** [grɔɲmɑ̃] *nm* **1** : growling **2** : rumbling, roar — **grognon, -gnonne** [grɔɲɔ̃, -ɲɔn] *adj* : grumpy, grouchy

groin [grwɛ̃] *nm* : snout
grommeler [grɔmle] {8} *v* : mutter
gronder [grɔde] *vt* : scold — *vi* **1** : rumble, roar **2** GROGNER : growl — **grondement** [grɔdmɑ̃] *nm* **1** : roar, rumble **2** GROGNEMENT : growling
gros, grosse [gro, gros] *adj* **1** : big, large **2** ÉPAIS : thick **3** CORPULENT : fat **4** GRAVE : serious **5** LOURD : heavy **6** ~ **lot** : jackpot — **gros** [gro] *adv* BEAUCOUP : a lot — ~ *nm* **1** **en** ~ : roughly, in general **2** **le** ~ **de** : the bulk of
groseille [grozɛj] *nf* **1** : currant **2** ~ **à maquereau** : gooseberry
grossir [grosir] *vt* **1** AUGMENTER : increase **2** EXAGÉRER : exaggerate **3** AGRANDIR : magnify — *vi* **1** : put on weight **2** : grow larger — **grossesse** [grosɛs] *nf* : pregnancy — **grosseur** [grosœr] *nf* **1** : fatness **2** VOLUME : size **3** : lump (in medicine) — **grossier, -sière** [grosje, -sjɛr] *adj* **1** APPROXIMATIF : coarse, rough **2** VULGAIRE : crude, vulgar **3** FLAGRANT : gross, glaring — **grossièrement** [grosjɛrmɑ̃] *adv* **1** APPROXIMATIVEMENT : roughly **2** VULGAIREMENT : crudely — **grossièreté** [grosjɛrte] *nf* **1** : coarseness **2** : rudeness — **grossiste** [grosist] *nmf* : wholesaler
grosso modo [grosomodo] *adv* : more or less, roughly
grotesque [grotɛsk] *adj* **1** : grotesque **2** RIDICULE : absurd, ridiculous
grotte [grɔt] *nf* : cave
grouiller [gruje] *vi* ~ **de** : swarm with — **se grouiller** *vr fam* : hurry, get a move on
groupe [grup] *nm* **1** : group **2** ~ **sanguin** : blood type — **groupement** [grupmɑ̃] *nm* : grouping, group — **grouper** [grupe] *vt* : group — **se grouper** *vr* : gather, get together
gruau [gryo] *nm Can* : oatmeal
grue [gry] *nf* : crane
grumeau [grymo] *nm, pl* **-meaux** : lump (in sauce, etc.)
gruyère [gryjɛr] *nm* : Gruyère (cheese)
gué [ge] *nm* : ford, crossing
guenilles [gənij] *nfpl* : rags and tatters
guenon [gənɔ̃] *nf* : female monkey
guépard [gepar] *nm* : cheetah

guêpe [gɛp] *nf* : wasp — **guêpier** [gepje] *nm* **1** : wasps' nest **2** : tight spot, trap
guère [gɛr] *adv* **ne . . . guère** : hardly, scarcely, rarely
guérilla [gerija] *nf* : guerilla warfare — **guérillero** [gerijero] *nm* : guerilla
guérir [gerir] *vt* : cure, heal — *vi* : get better, heal — **guérison** [gerizɔ̃] *nf* **1** : cure, healing **2** RÉTABLISSEMENT : recovery
guérite [gerit] *nf* : sentry box
guerre [gɛr] *nf* : war — **guerrier, -rière** [gɛrje, -jɛr] *adj* : warlike — ~ *n* : warrior
guetter [gete] *vt* **1** : watch (intently) **2** ATTENDRE : watch out for **3** MENACER : threaten — **guet** [gɛ] *nm* **faire le** ~ : be on the lookout — **guet-apens** [gɛtapɑ̃] *nm, pl* **guets-apens** : ambush
gueule [gœl] *nf* **1** : mouth (of an animal, a tunnel, etc.) **2** *fam* : face **3** **ta** ~! *fam* : shut up! **4** ~ **de bois** : hangover — **gueuler** [gœle] *v fam* : bawl, bellow
gui [gi] *nm* : mistletoe
guichet [giʃɛ] *nm* **1** : window, counter **2** : box office **3** ~ **automatique** : automatic teller machine — **guichetier, -tière** [giʃtje, -tjɛr] *n* : counter clerk, teller
guide [gid] *nm* **1** : guide **2** : guidebook — **guider** [gide] *vt* : guide — **guides** *nfpl* : reins
guidon [gidɔ̃] *nm* : handlebars *pl*
guignol [giɲɔl] *nm* **1** : puppet show **2** **faire le** ~ : clown around
guillemets [gijmɛ] *nmpl* : quotation marks
guilleret, -rette [gijrɛ, -rɛt] *adj* : sprightly, perky
guillotine [gijotin] *nf* : guillotine
guimauve [gimov] *nf* : marshmallow
guindé, -dée [gɛ̃de] *adj* : stiff, prim
guirlande [girlɑ̃d] *nf* **1** : garland **2** ~s **de Noël** : tinsel
guise [giz] *nf* **1** **à ta** ~ : as you wish **2** **en** ~ **de** : by way of
guitare [gitar] *nf* : guitar — **guitariste** [gitarist] *nmf* : guitarist
gymnase [ʒimnaz] *nm* : gymnasium — **gymnaste** [ʒimnast] *nmf* : gymnast
gymnastique [ʒimnastik] *nf* : gymnastics
gynécologie [ʒinekɔlɔʒi] *nf* : gynecology — **gynécologue** [ʒinekɔlɔg] *nmf* : gynecologist

H

h [aʃ] *nm* : h, eighth letter of the alphabet

habile [abil] *adj* : skillful, clever — **habilement** [abilmɑ̃] *adv* : skillfully, cleverly — **habileté** [abilte] *nf* : skill, cleverness

habilité, -tée [abilite] *adj* ~ **à** : entitled to

habiller [abije] *vt* : dress, clothe — **s'habiller** *vr* **1** : get dressed **2** ~ **en** : dress up as — **habillé, -lée** [abije] *adj* **1** : dressed **2** ÉLÉGANT : dressy — **habillement** [abijmɑ̃] *nm* : clothes *pl*, clothing

habit [abi] *nm* **1** : outfit, costume **2** : (religious) habit **3** *or* ~ **de soirée** : evening dress, tails *pl* **4** ~**s** *nmpl* : clothes

habiter [abite] *vt* : live in, inhabit — *vi* : live, reside — **habitant, -tante** [abitɑ̃, -tɑ̃t] *n* **1** : inhabitant **2** : occupant — **habitat** [abita] *nm* **1** : habitat **2** : housing — **habitation** [abitasjɔ̃] *nf* **1** : house, home **2 conditions d'**~ : living conditions

habitude [abityd] *nf* **1** : habit **2** COUTUME : custom **3 comme d'**~ : as usual **4 d'**~ : usually — **habitué, -tuée** [abitɥe] *n* : regular (customer) — **habituel, -tuelle** [abitɥɛl] *adj* : usual, regular — **habituellement** [-tɥɛlmɑ̃] *adv* : usually — **habituer** [abitɥe] *vt* : accustom — **s'habituer** *vr* ~ **à** : get used to

hache [ʼaʃ] *nf* : ax — **haché, -chée** [ʼaʃe] *adj* **1** : chopped, minced, ground **2** SACCADÉ : jerky — **hacher** [ʼaʃe] *vt* : chop, mince, grind — **hachette** [aʃɛt] *nf* : hatchet — **hachis** [ʼaʃi] *nms & pl* : ground or minced food — **hachoir** [ʼaʃwar] *nm* **1** : meat grinder **2** : chopper, cleaver **3** : cutting board

hagard, -garde [ʼagar, -gard] *adj* : distraught, wild

haie [ʼɛ] *nf* **1** : hedge **2** : hurdle (in sports) **3** : line, row (of persons)

haillons [ʼajɔ̃] *nmpl* : rags, tatters

haïr [ʼair] {48} *vt* : hate — **haine** [ʼɛn] *nf* : hatred, hate — **haineux, -neuse** [ʼɛnø, -nøz] *adj* : full of hatred

haïtien, -tienne [aisjɛ̃, -sjɛn] *adj* : Haitian

hâle [ʼal] *nm* : suntan — **hâlé, -lée** [ʼale] *adj* : (sun)tanned

haleine [alɛn] *nf* **1** : breath **2 hors d'**~ : out of breath

haleter [ʼalte] {20} *vi* : pant, gasp — **haletant, -tante** [ʼaltɑ̃, -tɑ̃t] *adj* : panting, breathless — **halètement** [ʼalɛtmɑ̃] *nm* : gasp

hall [ʼol] *nm* : hall, lobby

halle [ʼal] *nf France* : covered market

allucination [alysinasjɔ̃] *nf* : hallucination

halte [ʼalt] *nf* **1** ARRÊT : stop, halt **2** : stopping place **3** ~ **routière** *Can* : rest area (on a highway)

haltère [altɛr] *nm* : dumbbell — **haltérophilie** [alterɔfili] *nf* : weightlifting

hamac [ʼamak] *nm* : hammock

hamburger [ʼɑ̃bœrgœr] *nm* : hamburger (cooked)

hameçon [amsɔ̃] *nm* : fishhook

hamster [ʼamstɛr] *nm* : hamster

hanche [ʼɑ̃ʃ] *nf* : hip

handball [ʼɑ̃dbal] *nm* : handball

handicap [ʼɑ̃dikap] *nm* : handicap — **handicapé, -pée** [ʼɑ̃dikape] *adj* : handicapped — ~ *n* : handicapped person — **handicaper** [ʼɑ̃dikape] *vt* : handicap

hangar [ʼɑ̃gar] *nm* **1** : (large) shed **2** *or* ~ **d'aviation** : hangar

hanter [ʼɑ̃te] *vt* : haunt — **hantise** [ʼɑ̃tiz] *nf* : dread

happer [ʼape] *vt* **1** : seize, snatch **2 être happé par** : be hit by (a car, etc.)

harceler [ʼarsəle] {8 *and* 20} *vt* : harass — **harcèlement** [ʼarsɛlmɑ̃] *nm* : harassment

hardi, -die [ʼardi] *adj* : bold, daring — **hardiesse** [ʼardjɛs] *nf* : boldness, audacity — **hardiment** [ʼardimɑ̃] *adv* : boldly

hareng [ʼarɑ̃] *nm* : herring

hargne [ʼarɲ] *nf* : aggressiveness — **hargneux, -neuse** [ʼarɲø, -ɲøz] *adj* : aggressive, bad-tempered

haricot [ʼariko] *nm* **1** : bean **2** ~ **vert** : string bean

harmonica [armɔnika] *nm* : harmonica

harmonie [armɔni] *nf* : harmony — **harmonieux, -nieuse** [armɔnjø, -njøz] *adj* : harmonious — **harmoniser** [armɔnize] *vt* : harmonize — **s'harmoniser** *vr* : go well together

harnais [ʼarnɛ] *nm* : harness — **harnacher** [ʼarnaʃe] *vt* : harness (an animal)

harpe [ʼarp] *nf* : harp

harpon [ʼarpɔ̃] *nm* : harpoon — **harponner** [ʼarpɔne] *vt fam* : nab, collar

hasard [ʼazar] *nm* **1** : chance, luck **2** ~**s** *nmpl* : hazards, danger **3 au** ~ : at random — **hasarder** [ʼazarde] *vt* : risk, venture — **se hasarder** *vr* ~ **à faire** : risk doing — **hasardeux, -deuse** [ʼazardø, -døz] *adj* : risky

hâte [ʼat] *nf* **1** : haste, hurry **2 avoir** ~ **de** : be eager to — **hâter** [ʼate] *vt* : hasten, hurry — **se hâter** *vr* : hurry — **hâtif, -tive** [ʼatif, -tiv] *adj* **1** : hasty, rash **2** PRÉCOCE : early

hausser [ʼose] *vt* **1** : raise **2** ~ **les épaules**

: shrug one's shoulders — **se hausser** *vr*
: stand up, reach up — **hausse** ['os] *nf* **1**
: rise, increase **2 à la ~** *or* **en ~** : rising,
up

haut, haute ['o, 'ot] *adj* **1** : high **2** : high-
ranking — **haut** ['o] *adv* **1** : high **2** FORT
: loud, loudly — **~** *nm* **1** SOMMET : top **2**
des ~s et des bas : ups and downs **3 en
~** : upstairs **4 en ~ de** : on top of **5 un
mètre de ~** : one meter high — **hautain,
-taine** ['otɛ̃, -tɛn] *adj* : haughty — **hautbois**
['obwa] *nms & pl* : oboe — **hautement**
['otmã] *adv* : highly — **hauteur** ['otœr] *nf*
1 : height **2** ARROGANCE : haughtiness —
haut-le-cœur ['olkœr] *nms & pl* **avoir des
~** : retch, gag — **haut-parleur** ['oparlœr]
nm, pl **haut-parleurs** : loudspeaker

hâve ['av] *adj* : gaunt

havre ['avr] *nm* : haven

hayon ['ajɔ̃] *nm* : tailgate

hé ['e] *interj* : hey

hebdomadaire [ɛbdɔmadɛr] *adj & nm*
: weekly

héberger [ebɛrʒe] {17} *vt* : accommodate,
put up — **hébergement** [ebɛrʒəmã] *nm*
: accommodations *pl*

hébété, -tée [ebete] *adj* : dazed — **hébétude**
[ebetyd] *nf* : stupor

hébreu [ebrø] *adj m, pl* **-breux** : Hebrew —
~ *nm* : Hebrew (language) — **hébraïque**
[ebraik] *adj* : Hebrew, Hebraic

hein ['ɛ̃] *interj* : eh?, what?

hélas ['elas] *interj* : alas!

héler ['ele] {87} *vt* : hail, summon

hélice [elis] *nf* : propeller

hélicoptère [elikɔptɛr] *nm* : helicopter

hémisphère [emisfɛr] *nm* : hemisphere

hémorragie [emɔraʒi] *nf* : bleeding, hemorrhage

hémorroïdes [emɔrɔid] *nfpl* : hemorrhoids

hennir ['enir] *vi* : neigh — **hennissement**
['enismã] *nm* : neighing

hépatite [epatit] *nf* : hepatitis

herbe [ɛrb] *nf* **1** : grass **2** : herb (in cooking)
3 en ~ : budding **4 mauvaise ~** : weed
— **herbage** [ɛrbaʒ] *nm* : pasture — **her-
beux, -beuse** [ɛrbø, -bøz] *adj* : grassy —
herbicide [ɛrbisid] *nm* : weed killer

héréditaire [ereditɛr] *adj* : hereditary —
hérédité [eredite] *nf* : heredity

hérésie [erezi] *nf* : heresy

hérisser ['erise] *vt* **1** : ruffle up (fur, feathers, etc.) **2 ~ qqn** *fam* : irritate s.o. — **se
hérisser** *vr* **1** : stand on end **2** *fam* : bristle
(with annoyance) — **hérisson** ['erisɔ̃] *nm*
: hedgehog

hériter [erite] *vi* — **de** : inherit — *vt* : inherit
— **héritage** [eritaʒ] *nm* **1** : inheritance **2**
: (cultural) heritage — **héritier, -tière** [er-
itje, -tjɛr] *n* : heir, heiress *f*

hermétique [ɛrmetik] *adj* **1** ÉTANCHE : airtight, watertight **2** OBSCUR : obscure

hernie ['ɛrni] *nf* : hernia

héroïne [erɔin] *nf* **1** : heroine **2** : heroin —
héroïque [erɔik] *adj* : heroic — **héroïsme**
[erɔism] *nm* : heroism

héron ['erɔ̃] *nm* : heron

héros ['erɔ] *nm* : hero

hésiter [ezite] *vi* : hesitate — **hésitant,
-tante** [ezitã, -tãt] *adj* : hesitant — **hésitation** [ezitasjɔ̃] *nf* : hesitation

hétérogène [eterɔʒɛn] *adj* : heterogeneous

hétérosexuel, -sexuelle [eterɔsɛksyɛl] *adj
& n* : heterosexual

hêtre ['ɛtr] *nm* : beech

heure ['œr] *nf* **1** : time **2** : hour **3 ~ de
pointe** : rush hour **4 ~s supplémen-
taires** : overtime **5 quelle ~ est-il?** : what
time is it? **6 tout à l'~** : later on

heureux, -reuse ['œrø, -røz] *adj* **1** : happy
2 SATISFAIT : glad, pleased **3** CHANCEUX
: fortunate, lucky — **heureusement**
['œrøzmã] *adv* : fortunately, luckily

heurter ['œrte] *vt* **1** : strike, collide with **2**
OFFENSER : offend, go against — *vi* : hit,
collide — **se heurter** *vr* **~ à** : come up
against — **heurt** ['œr] *nm* **1** : collision,
crash **2** CONFLIT : conflict

hexagone [ɛgzagɔn] *nm* : hexagon

hiberner [ibɛrne] *vi* : hibernate

hibou ['ibu] *nm, pl* **-boux** [ibu] : owl

hic ['ik] *nm fam* **1** : snag **2 voilà le ~**
: that's the trouble

hideux, -deuse ['idø, -døz] *adj* : hideous

hier [ijɛr] *adv* : yesterday

hiérarchie ['jerarʃi] *nf* : hierarchy — **hiérarchique** ['jerarʃik] *adj* : hierarchical

hilarité [ilarite] *nf* : hilarity, mirth — **hilarant, -rante** [ilarã, -rãt] *adj* : hilarious —
hilare [ilar] *adj* : mirthful, merry

hindou, -doue [ɛ̃du] *adj* : Hindu

hippie *or* **hippy** ['ipi] *nmf, pl* **-pies** : hippie

hippique [ipik] *adj* : equestrian, horse —
hippodrome [ipɔdrom] *nm* : racecourse

hippopotame [ipɔpɔtam] *nm* : hippopotamus

hirondelle [irɔ̃dɛl] *nf* : swallow

hirsute [irsyt] *adj* : hairy, shaggy

hispanique [ispanik] *adj* : Hispanic

hisser ['ise] *vt* : hoist, haul up — **se hisser**
vr : raise oneself up

histoire [istwar] *nf* **1** : history **2** RÉCIT
: story **3** AFFAIRE : affair, matter **4 ~s** *nfpl*
: trouble, problems — **historien, -rienne**
[istɔrjɛ̃, -rjɛn] *n* : historian — **historique**
[istɔrik] *adj* : historical, historic

hiver [ivɛr] *nm* : winter — **hivernal, -nale**
[ivɛrnal] *adj, mpl* **-naux** [-no] : winter, wintry

hocher ['ɔʃe] *vt* ~ **la tête** : nod, shake one's head

hochet ['ɔʃɛ] *nm* : rattle

hockey ['ɔkɛ] *nm* : hockey

hollandais, -daise ['ɔlɑ̃dɛ, -dɛz] *adj* : Dutch

holocauste [ɔlɔkost] *nm* : holocaust

homard ['ɔmar] *nm* : lobster

homélie [ɔmeli] *nf* : homily

homéopathie [ɔmeɔpati] *nf* : homeopathy

homicide [ɔmisid] *nm* : homicide

hommage [ɔmaʒ] *nm* **1** : homage **2 rendre ~ à** : pay tribute to

homme [ɔm] *nm* **1** : man **2 l'~** : man, mankind **3 ~ d'affaires** : businessman

homme–grenouille [ɔmgrənuj] *nm, pl* **hommes–grenouilles** : frogman

homogène [ɔmɔʒɛn] *adj* : homogeneous

homologue [ɔmɔlɔg] *nmf* : counterpart

homologuer [ɔmɔlɔge] *vt* : ratify, approve

homonyme [ɔmɔnim] *nm* **1** : homonym **2** : namesake

homosexuel, -sexuelle [ɔmɔsɛksyɛl] *adj & n* : homosexual — **homosexualité** [ɔmɔsɛksyalite] *nf* : homosexuality

honnête [ɔnɛt] *adj* **1** : honest **2** JUSTE : reasonable, fair — **honnêtement** [ɔnɛtmɑ̃] *adv* **1** : honestly **2** DÉCEMMENT : fairly, decently — **honnêteté** [ɔnɛtte] *nf* : honesty

honneur [ɔnœr] *nm* **1** : honor **2** MÉRITE : credit

honorer [ɔnɔre] *vt* **1** : honor **2** : be a credit to **3** PAYER : pay (a debt) — **honorable** [ɔnɔrabl] *adj* **1** : honorable **2** CONVENABLE : respectable, decent — **honorablement** [-rabləmɑ̃] *adv* **1** : honorably **2** SUFFISAMMENT : respectably, decently — **honoraire** [ɔnɔrɛr] *adj* : honorary — **honoraires** *nmpl* : fees — **honorifique** [ɔnɔrifik] *adj* : honorary

honte ['ɔ̃t] *nf* **1** : shame **2 avoir ~** : be ashamed — **honteux, -teuse** ['ɔ̃tø, -tøz] *adj* **1** : ashamed **2** DÉSHONORANT : shameful

hôpital [ɔpital] *nm, pl* **-taux** [-to] : hospital

hoquet [ɔkɛ] *nm* **1** : hiccup **2 avoir le ~** : have the hiccups — **hoqueter** ['ɔkte] {8} *vi* : hiccup

horaire [ɔrɛr] *adj* : hourly — ~ *nm* : timetable, schedule

horizon [ɔrizɔ̃] *nm* **1** : horizon **2** : view, vista — **horizontal, -tale** [ɔrizɔ̃tal] *adj, mpl* **-taux** [-to] : horizontal

horloge [ɔrlɔʒ] *nf* : clock — **horloger, -gère** [ɔrlɔʒe, -ʒɛr] *n* : watchmaker

hormone [ɔrmɔn] *nf* : hormone

horoscope [ɔrɔskɔp] *nm* : horoscope

horreur [ɔrœr] *nf* **1** : horror **2 avoir ~ de** : detest — **horrible** [ɔribl] *adj* : horrible — **horrifiant, -fiante** [ɔrifjɑ̃, -fjɑ̃t] *adj* : horrifying — **horrifier** [ɔrifje] {96} *vt* : horrify

hors ['ɔr] *prep* **1** : except for, save **2 ~ de** : out of, outside, beyond **3 être ~ de soi** : be beside oneself — **hors–bord** ['ɔrbɔr] *nms & pl* **1** : outboard motor **2** : speedboat — **hors–d'œuvre** ['ɔrdœvr] *nms & pl* : hors d'oeuvre — **hors–la–loi** ['ɔrlalwa] *nms & pl* : outlaw

horticulture [ɔrtikyltyr] *nf* : horticulture

hospice [ɔspis] *nm France* **1** : home (for the elderly, etc.) **2** : hospice

hospitalier, -lière [ɔspitalje, -jɛr] *adj* **1** : hospital **2** ACCUEILLANT : hospitable — **hospitaliser** [ɔspitalize] *vt* : hospitalize — **hospitalité** [ɔspitalite] *nf* : hospitality

hostie [ɔsti] *nf* : host (in religion)

hostile [ɔstil] *adj* : hostile — **hostilité** [ɔstilite] *nf* **1** : hostility **2 ~s** *nfpl* : hostilities, war

hot–dog ['ɔtdɔg] *nm, pl* **hot–dogs** : hot dog

hôte, hôtesse [ot, otɛs] *n* : host, hostess *f* — **hôte** *nmf* : guest

hôtel [otɛl] *nm* **1** : hotel **2 ~ de ville** : town hall — **hôtelier, -lière** [otəlje, -jɛr] *adj* : hotel — ~ *n* : hotel manager, innkeeper — **hôtellerie** [otɛlri] *nf* : hotel business

hôtesse [otɛs] *nf* **1** → **hôte 2** : receptionist **3 ~ de l'air** : stewardess

hotte ['ɔt] *nf* **1** : basket (carried on the back) **2** : hood (of a chimney or stove)

houblon ['ublɔ̃] *nm* : hops *pl*

houe ['u] *nf* : hoe

houille ['uj] *nf* : coal — **houiller, -lère** ['uje, -jɛr] *adj* : coal, coal-mining — **houillère** *nf* : coal mine

houle ['ul] *nf* : swell, surge

houlette ['ulɛt] *nf* **sous la ~ de** : under the guidance of

houleux, -leuse ['ulø, -løz] *adj* : stormy

houppe ['up] *or* **houppette** ['upɛt] *nf* : powder puff

hourra ['ura] *nm & interj* : hurrah

housse ['us] *nf* : cover, dust cover

houx ['u] *nms & pl* : holly

huard *or* **huart** ['yar] *nm Can* : loon

hublot ['yblo] *nm* : porthole

huche ['yʃ] *nf* **~ à pain** : bread box

huer ['ɥe] *vt* : boo — *vi* : hoot — **huées** ['ɥe] *nfpl* : boos, booing

huile [ɥil] *nf* **1** : oil **2** : oil painting — **huiler** [ɥile] *vt* : oil — **huileux, -leuse** [ɥilø, -løz] *adj* : oily — **huilier** [ɥilje] *nm* : cruet

huis [ɥi] *nm* **à ~ clos** : behind closed doors

huissier [ɥisje] *nm* **1** : usher **2** *or* **~ de justice** : bailiff

huit ['ɥit, *before consonant* 'ɥi] *adj* **1** : eight **2** : eighth (in dates) — ~ *nms & pl* : eight — **huitaine** ['ɥiten] *nf* **une ~ (de jours)** : about a week — **huitième** ['ɥitjɛm] *adj & nmf & nm* : eighth

huître [ɥitr] *nf* : oyster

hululer [′ylyle] *vi* : hoot — **hululement** [′ylylmɑ̃] *nm* : hoot (of an owl)

humain, -maine [ymɛ̃, -mɛn] *adj* 1 : human 2 BIENVEILLANT : humane — **humain** *nm* : human being — **humanitaire** [ymanitɛr] *adj* : humanitarian — **humanité** [ymanite] *nf* : humanity

humble [œ̃bl] *adj* : humble — **humblement** [œ̃bləmɑ̃] *adv* : humbly

humecter [ymɛkte] *vt* : dampen, moisten

humer [′yme] *vt* 1 : breathe in, inhale 2 : smell

humeur [ymœr] *nf* 1 : mood, humor 2 CA-RACTÈRE : temperament

humide [ymid] *adj* 1 : moist, damp 2 : humid — **humidité** [ymidite] *nf* 1 : dampness 2 : humidity

humilier [ymilje] {96} *vt* : humiliate — **s'humilier** *vr* : humble oneself — **humiliant, -liante** [ymiljɑ̃, -jɑ̃t] *adj* : humiliating — **humiliation** [ymiljasjɔ̃] *nf* : humiliation — **humilité** [ymilite] *nf* : humility

humour [ymur] *nm* 1 : humor, wit 2 **avoir de l'~** : have a sense of humor — **humoriste** [ymɔrist] *nmf* : humorist — **humoristique** [ymɔristik] *adj* : humorous

huppé, -pée [′ype] *adj fam* : posh, high-class

hurler [′yrle] *vt* : yell out — *vi* 1 : howl, roar 2 CRIER : yell, shout — **hurlement** [′yrləmɑ̃] *nm* : howl, yell

hutte [′yt] *nf* : hut

hybride [ibrid] *adj & nm* : hybrid

hydratant, -tante [idratɑ̃, -tɑ̃t] *adj* : moisturizing — **hydratant** *nm* : moisturizer

hydrate [idrat] *nm* **~ de carbon** : carbohydrate

hydraulique [idrolik] *adj* : hydraulic

hydroélectrique *or* **hydro–électrique** [idroelɛktrik] *adj* : hydroelectric

hydrogène [idrɔʒɛn] *nm* : hydrogen

hyène [jɛn] *nf* : hyena

hygiène [iʒjɛn] *nf* : hygiene — **hygiénique** [iʒjenik] *adj* : hygienic

hymne [imn] *nm* 1 : hymn 2 **~ nationale** : national anthem

hyperactif, -tive [iperaktif, tiv] *adj* : hyperactive

hypermétrope [ipermetrɔp] *adj* : farsighted

hypertension [ipertɑ̃sjɔ̃] *nf* : high blood pressure

hypnotiser [ipnɔtize] *vt* : hypnotize — **hypnose** [ipnoz] *nf* : hypnosis

hypocrisie [ipɔkrizi] *nf* : hypocrisy — **hypocrite** [ipɔkrit] *adj* : hypocritical — **~** *nmf* : hypocrite

hypothèque [ipɔtɛk] *nf* : mortgage — **hypothéquer** [ipɔteke] {87} *vt* : mortgage

hypothèse [ipɔtɛz] *nf* : hypothesis — **hypothétique** [ipɔtetik] *adj* : hypothetical

hystérie [isteri] *nf* : hysteria — **hystérique** [isterik] *adj* : hysterical

I

i [i] *nm* : i, ninth letter of the alphabet

iceberg [ajsbɛrg] *nm* : iceberg

ici [isi] *adv* 1 : here 2 : now 3 **d'~ là** : by then 4 **par ~** : this way

icône [ikon] *nf* : icon

idéal, idéale [ideal] *adj, mpl* **idéals** *or* **idéaux** [ideo] : ideal — **idéal** *nm* : ideal — **idéaliser** [idealize] *vt* : idealize — **idéaliste** [idealist] *adj* : idealistic — **~** *nmf* : idealist

idée [ide] *nf* : idea

identifier [idɑ̃tifje] {96} *vt* : identify — **s'identifier** *vr* **~ à** : identify with — **identification** [idɑ̃tifikasjɔ̃] *nf* : identification — **identique** [idɑ̃tik] *adj* : identical — **identité** [idɑ̃tite] *nf* : identity

idéologie [ideɔlɔʒi] *nf* : ideology — **idéologique** [ideɔlɔʒik] *adj* : ideological

idiome [idjom] *nm* : idiom (language) — **idiomatique** [idjɔmatik] *adj* : idiomatic

idiot, -diote [idjo, -djɔt] *adj* : idiotic — **~** *n* : idiot, fool — **idiotie** [idjɔsi] *nf* : idiocy

idole [idɔl] *nf* : idol — **idolâtrer** [idɔlatre] *vt* : idolize

idyllique [idilik] *adj* : idyllic

igloo [iglu] *nm* : igloo

ignifuge [iɲifyʒ] *adj* : fireproof

ignoble [iɲɔbl] *adj* : base, vile

ignorance [iɲɔrɑ̃s] *nf* : ignorance — **ignorant, -rante** [iɲɔrɑ̃, -rɑ̃t] *adj* : ignorant — **ignorer** [iɲɔre] *vt* 1 : be unaware of 2 : ignore

il [il] *pron* 1 : he, it 2 (*as subject of an impersonal verb*) : it 3 **ils** *pron pl* : they 4 **il y a** : there is, there are

île [il] *nf* : island, isle

illégal, -gale [ilegal] *adj, mpl* **-gaux** [-go] : illegal — **illégalité** [ilegalite] *nf* : illegality

illégitime [ileʒitim] *adj* : illegitimate — **illégitimité** [ileʒitimite] *nf* : illegitimacy

illettré, -trée [iletre] *adj & n* : illiterate

illicite [ilisit] *adj* : illicit

illimité, -tée [ilimite] *adj* : unlimited

illisible [ilizibl] *adj* : illegible
illogique [ilɔʒik] *adj* : illogical
illuminer [ilymine] *vt* : illuminate, light up —
 illumination [ilyminasjɔ̃] *nf* : illumination
illusion [ilyzjɔ̃] *nf* : illusion — **illusoire**
 [ilyzwar] *adj* : illusory
illustration [ilystrasjɔ̃] *nf* : illustration — **illustre** [ilystr] *adj* : illustrious, renowned —
 illustré, -trée [ilystre] *adj* : illustrated — **illustrer** [ilystre] *vt* : illustrate
îlot [ilo] *nm* **1** : small island **2** : block (of
 houses)
ils [il] → **il**
image [imaʒ] *nf* **1** : image **2** DESSIN : picture
imaginer [imaʒine] *vt* **1** : imagine **2** INVEN-
 TER : devise, think up — **s'imaginer** *vr*
 : picture oneself — **imaginaire** [imaʒinɛr]
 adj : imaginary — **imaginatif, -tive** [imaʒi-
 natif, -tiv] *adj* : imaginative — **imagination**
 [imaʒinasjɔ̃] *nf* : imagination
imbattable [ɛ̃batabl] *adj* : unbeatable
imbécile [ɛ̃besil] *adj* : stupid, idiotic — ∼
 nmf : fool, idiot — **imbécillité** [ɛ̃besilite] *nf*
 : idiocy, stupidity
imbiber [ɛ̃bibe] *vt* : soak — **s'imbiber** *vr*
 : get soaked
imbuvable [ɛ̃byvabl] *adj* : undrinkable
imiter [imite] *vt* **1** COPIER : imitate, mimic **2**
 : look (just) like — **imitateur, -trice** [imi-
 tatœr, -tris] *n* **1** : imitator **2** : impersonator
 — **imitation** [imitasjɔ̃] *nf* **1** : imitation **2**
 : impersonation
immaculé, -lée [imakyle] *adj* : immaculate
immangeable [ɛ̃mɑ̃ʒabl] *adj* : inedible
immanquable [ɛ̃mɑ̃kabl] *adj* **1** : impossible
 to miss **2** INÉVITABLE : inevitable
immatriculer [imatrikyle] *vt* : register —
 immatriculation [imatrikylasjɔ̃] *nf* **1** : registration **2 plaque d'**∼ : license plate
immature [imatyr] *adj* : immature — **immaturité** [imatyrite] *nf* : immaturity
immédiat, -diate [imedja, -djat] *adj* : immediate — **immédiatement** [-djatmɑ̃] *adv*
 : immediately
immense [imɑ̃s] *adj* : immense — **immensité** [imɑ̃site] *nf* : immensity
immerger [imɛrʒe] {17} *vt* : immerse, submerge — **immersion** [imɛrsjɔ̃] *nf* : immersion
immeuble [imœbl] *nm* : building
immigrer [imigre] *vi* : immigrate — **immigrant, -grante** [imigrɑ̃, -grɑ̃t] *adj & n* : immigrant — **immigration** [imigrasjɔ̃] *nf* : immigration — **immigré, -grée** [imigre] *n*
 : immigrant
imminent, -nente [iminɑ̃, -nɑ̃t] *adj* : imminent — **imminence** [iminɑ̃s] *nf* : imminence
immiscer [imise] {6} *v* **s'immiscer** *vr* ∼
 dans : interfere with

immobile [imɔbil] *adj* : motionless
immobilier, -lière [imɔbilje, -ljɛr] *adj* : real
 estate, property
immobiliser [imɔbilize] *vt* **1** : immobilize **2**
 ARRÊTER : bring to a halt — **s'immobiliser**
 vr : stop — **immobilité** [imɔbilite] *nf* : immobility, stillness
immodéré, -rée [imɔdere] *adj* : immoderate,
 excessive
immonde [imɔ̃d] *adj* : foul, filthy
immoral, -rale [imɔral] *adj, mpl* **-raux** [-ro]
 : immoral — **immoralité** [imɔralite] *nf* : immorality
immortalité [imɔrtalite] *nf* : immortality —
 immortel, -telle [imɔrtɛl] *adj* : immortal
immuable [imɥabl] *adj* : unchanging
immuniser [imynize] *vt* : immunize — **immunisation** [-nizasjɔ̃] *nf* : immunization —
 immunité [imynite] *nf* : immunity
impact [ɛ̃pakt] *nm* : impact
impair, -paire [ɛ̃pɛr] *adj* : odd, uneven — **impair** *nm* : blunder
impardonnable [ɛ̃pardɔnabl] *adj* : unforgivable
imparfait, -faite [ɛ̃parfɛ, -fɛt] *adj* : imperfect
 — **imparfait** *nm* : imperfect (tense)
impartial, -tiale [ɛ̃parsjal] *adj, mpl* **-tiaux**
 [-sjo] : unbiased, impartial — **impartialité**
 [ɛ̃parsjalite] *nf* : impartiality
impartir [ɛ̃partir] *vt* : grant, bestow
impasse [ɛ̃pas] *nf* **1** : impasse, deadlock **2**
 CUL-DE-SAC : dead end
impassible [ɛ̃pasibl] *adj* : impassive
impatient, -tiente [ɛ̃pasjɑ̃, -sjɑ̃t] *adj* : impatient — **impatiemment** [ɛ̃pasjamɑ̃] *adv*
 : impatiently — **impatience** [-sjɑ̃s] *nf* : impatience — **impatienter** [ɛ̃pasjɑ̃te] *vt*
 : annoy — **s'impatienter** *vr* : lose patience
impeccable [ɛ̃pekabl] *adj* : impeccable,
 faultless
impénétrable [ɛ̃penetrabl] *adj* **1** : impenetrable **2** : inscrutable
impénitent, -tente [ɛ̃penitɑ̃, -tɑ̃t] *adj* : unrepentant
impensable [ɛ̃pɑ̃sabl] *adj* : unthinkable
impératif, -tive [ɛ̃peratif, -tiv] *adj* : imperative — **impératif** *nm* : imperative (mood)
impératrice [ɛ̃peratris] *nf* : empress
imperceptible [ɛ̃pɛrsɛptibl] *adj* : imperceptible
imperfection [ɛ̃pɛrfɛksjɔ̃] *nf* : imperfection
impérial, -riale [ɛ̃perjal] *adj, mpl* **-riaux**
 [-rjo] : imperial — **impérialisme** [ɛ̃perja-
 lism] *nm* : imperialism
impérieux, -rieuse [ɛ̃perjø, -jøz] *adj* **1** : imperious **2** PRESSANT : urgent
impérissable [ɛ̃perisabl] *adj* : imperishable
imperméable [ɛ̃pɛrmeabl] *adj* : waterproof
 — ∼ *nm* : raincoat

impersonnel, -nelle [ε̃pεrsɔnεl] *adj* : impersonal

impertinent, -nente [ε̃pεrtinɑ̃, -nɑ̃t] *adj* : impertinent — **impertinence** [-tinɑ̃s] *nf* : impertinence

imperturbable [ε̃pεrtyrbabl] *adj* : unflappable

impétueux, -tueuse, [ε̃petɥø, -tɥøz] *adj* : impetuous

impitoyable [ε̃pitwajabl] *adj* : merciless, pitiless

implacable [ε̃plakabl] *adj* : implacable

implanter [ε̃plɑ̃te] *vt* **1** : establish **2** : implant (in medicine) — **s'implanter** *vr* : be set up — **implantation** [ε̃plɑ̃tasjɔ̃] *nf* : establishment

implication [ε̃plikasjɔ̃] *nf* : implication

implicite [ε̃plisit] *adj* : implicit

impliquer [ε̃plike] *vt* **1** : implicate **2** SUPPOSER : imply **3** ENTRAÎNER : entail, involve — **s'impliquer** *vr* : become involved

implorer [ε̃plɔre] *vt* : implore

imploser [ε̃plɔze] *vi* : implode

impoli, -lie [ε̃pɔli] *adj* : impolite, rude — **impolitesse** [ε̃pɔlitεs] *nf* : rudeness

impopulaire [ε̃pɔpylεr] *adj* : unpopular

importer[1] [ε̃pɔrte] *vi* **1** : matter, be important **2** n'**importe qui** : anyone, anybody **3** n'**importe quoi** : anything **4** peu **importe** : no matter — **importance** [ε̃pɔrtɑ̃s] *nf* : importance — **important, -tante** [ε̃pɔrtɑ̃, -tɑ̃t] *adj* **1** : important **2** LARGE : considerable — **important** *nm* l'~ : the important thing, the main thing

importer[2] *vt* : import — **importateur, -trice** [ε̃pɔrtatœr, -tris] *n* : importer — **importation** [ε̃pɔrtasjɔ̃] *nf* **1** : importing **2** : import

importun, -tune [ε̃pɔrtœ̃, -tyn] *adj* : troublesome, unwelcome — ~ *n* : nuisance, pest — **importuner** [ε̃pɔrtyne] *vt* : pester

imposer [ε̃pɔze] *vt* **1** : impose **2** TAXER : tax — **s'imposer** *vr* **1** : be essential **2** : stand out — **imposable** [ε̃pɔzabl] *adj* : taxable — **imposant, -sante** [ε̃pɔzɑ̃, -zɑ̃t] *adj* : imposing

impossible [ε̃pɔsibl] *adj* : impossible — ~ *nm* l'~ : the impossible — **impossibilité** [ε̃pɔsibilite] *nf* : impossibility

imposteur [ε̃pɔstœr] *nm* : impostor

impôt [ε̃po] *nm* : tax, duty

impotent, -tente [ε̃pɔtɑ̃, -tɑ̃t] *adj* : infirm, disabled

impraticable [ε̃pratikabl] *adj* : impassable (of a road, etc.)

imprécis, -cise [ε̃presi, -siz] *adj* : imprecise — **imprécision** [ε̃presizjɔ̃] *nf* : imprecision

imprégner [ε̃preɲe] {87} *vt* IMBIBER : impregnate, soak — **s'imprégner** *vr* ~ de : become filled with

impression [ε̃presjɔ̃] *nf* **1** : impression **2** : printing — **impressionnable** [ε̃presjɔnabl] *adj* : impressionable — **impressionnant, -nante** [ε̃presjɔnɑ̃, -nɑ̃t] *adj* : impressive — **impressionner** [ε̃presjɔne] *vt* : impress

imprévisible [ε̃previzibl] *adj* : unpredictable

imprévoyance [ε̃prevwajɑ̃s] *nf* : lack of foresight — **imprévu, -vue** [ε̃prevy] *adj* : unforeseen, unexpected

imprimer [ε̃prime] *vt* **1** : print **2** : imprint — **imprimante** [ε̃primɑ̃t] *nf* : printer — **imprimé, -mée** [ε̃prime] *adj* : printed (of fabric, etc.) — **imprimerie** [ε̃primri] *nf* **1** : printing **2** : print shop — **imprimeur, -meuse** [ε̃primœr, -møz] *n* : printer

improbable [ε̃prɔbabl] *adj* : improbable, unlikely — **improbabilité** [-babilite] *nf* : unlikelihood

impromptu, -tue [ε̃prɔ̃pty] *adj* : impromptu

impropre [ε̃prɔpr] *adj* **1** INCORRECT : incorrect **2** INADAPTÉ : unsuitable

improviser [ε̃prɔvize] *v* : improvise — **improvisation** [ε̃prɔvizasjɔ̃] *nf* : improvisation

improviste [ε̃prɔvist] à l'~ *adv phr* : unexpectedly

imprudent, -dente [ε̃prydɑ̃, -dɑ̃t] *adj* : rash, careless — **imprudemment** [ε̃prydamɑ̃] *adv* : carelessly — **imprudence** [ε̃prydɑ̃s] *nf* : carelessness

impudent, -dente [ε̃pydɑ̃, -dɑ̃t] *adj* : impudent — **impudence** [ε̃pydɑ̃s] *nf* : impudence

impudique [ε̃pydik] *adj* : immodest, indecent

impuissance [ε̃pɥisɑ̃s] *nf* **1** : helplessness **2** : (physical) impotence — **impuissant, -sante** [ε̃pɥisɑ̃, -sɑ̃t] *adj* **1** : helpless **2** : impotent (in medicine)

impulsion [ε̃pylsjɔ̃] *nf* **1** : impulse **2** POUSSÉE : impetus — **impulsif, -sive** [ε̃pylsif, -siv] *adj* : impulsive — **impulsivité** [ε̃pylsivite] *nf* : impulsiveness

impuni, -nie [ε̃pyni] *adj* : unpunished — **impunément** [ε̃pynemɑ̃] *adv* : with impunity — **impunité** [ε̃pynite] *nf* : impunity

impur, -pure [ε̃pyr] *adj* : impure — **impureté** [ε̃pyrte] *nf* : impurity

imputer [ε̃pyte] *vt* : impute

inabordable [inabɔrdabl] *adj* : inaccessible

inacceptable [inaksεptabl] *adj* : unacceptable

inaccessible [inaksesibl] *adj* : inaccessible

inaccoutumé, -mée [inakutyme] *adj* : unaccustomed

inachevé, -vée [inaʃve] *adj* : unfinished

inaction [inaksjɔ̃] *nf* : inaction, inactivity — **inactif, -tive** [inaktif, -tiv] *adj* : inactive — **inactivité** [inaktivite] *nf* : inactivity

inadapté, -tée [inadapte] *adj* **1** : maladjusted **2** ~ à : unsuited to, unsuitable for

inadéquat, -quate [inadekwa, -kwat] *adj* : inadequate

inadmissible [inadmisibl] *adj* : unacceptable

inadvertance [inadvɛrtãs] *nf* **par ~** : inadvertently

inaltérable [inalterabl] *adj* : stable, unchanging

inamovible [inamɔvibl] *adj* : fixed, permanent

inanimé, -mée [inanime] *adj* **1** : inanimate **2** INCONSCIENT : unconscious

inaperçu, -çue [inapɛrsy] *adj* : unseen, unnoticed

inapplicable [inaplikabl] *adj* : inapplicable

inapte [inapt] *adj* : unfit, unsuited

inarticulé, -lée [inartikyle] *adj* : inarticulate

inassouvi, -vie [inasuvi] *adj* : unsatisfied, unfulfilled

inattaquable [inatakabl] *adj* **1** : irreproachable **2** IRRÉFUTABLE : irrefutable

inattendu, -due [inatãdy] *adj* : unexpected

inattention [inatãsjɔ̃] *nf* **1** : inattention **2** **faute d'~** : careless error — **inattentif, -tive** [inatãtif, -tiv] *adj* : inattentive, distracted

inaudible [inodibl] *adj* : inaudible

inaugurer [inogyre] *vt* : inaugurate — **inaugural, -rale** [inogyral] *adj, mpl* **-raux** [-ro] : inaugural — **inauguration** [inogyrasjɔ̃] *nf* : inauguration

incalculable [ɛ̃kalkylabl] *adj* : incalculable, countless

incapable [ɛ̃kapabl] *adj* : incapable, unable — **incapacité** [ɛ̃kapasite] *nf* : incapacity, inability

incarcérer [ɛ̃karsere] {87} *vt* : incarcerate

incarner [ɛ̃karne] *vt* : play (a role)

incassable [ɛ̃kasabl] *adj* : unbreakable

incendie [ɛ̃sãdi] *nm* : fire — **incendiaire** [ɛ̃sãdjɛr] *adj* : inflammatory

incendier [ɛ̃sãdje] {96} *vt* : set on fire

incertain, -taine [ɛ̃sɛrtɛ̃, -tɛn] *adj* **1** : uncertain **2** VAGUE : indistinct — **incertitude** [ɛ̃sɛrtityd] *nf* : uncertainty

incessant, -sante [ɛ̃sesã, -sãt] *adj* : incessant

inceste [ɛ̃sɛst] *nm* : incest — **incestueux, -tueuse** [ɛ̃sɛstɥø, -tɥøz] *adj* : incestuous

inchangé, -gée [ɛ̃ʃãʒe] *adj* : unchanged

incidence [ɛ̃sidãs] *nf* : effect, impact

incident [ɛ̃sidɑ̃] *nm* : incident

incinérer [ɛ̃sinere] *vt* **1** : incinerate **2** : cremate — **incinérateur** [ɛ̃sineratœr] *nm* : incinerator — **incinération** [ɛ̃sinerasjɔ̃] *nf* **1** : incineration **2** : cremation

incision [ɛ̃sizjɔ̃] *nf* : incision

inciter [ɛ̃site] *vt* : incite

incliner [ɛ̃kline] *vt* **1** PENCHER : tilt, bend **2** INCITER : incline, prompt — *vi* **~ à** : be inclined to — **s'incliner** *vr* **1** : tilt, lean **2 ~ devant** : bow to — **inclinaison** [ɛ̃klinɛzɔ̃] *nf* : incline, slope — **inclination** [ɛ̃klinasjɔ̃] *nf* **1** : nod, bow **2** TENDANCE : inclination, tendency

inclure [ɛ̃klyr] {39} *vt* **1** : include **2** JOINDRE : enclose — **inclus, -cluse** [ɛ̃kly, -klyz] *adj* : inclusive — **inclusion** [ɛ̃klyzjɔ̃] *nf* : inclusion

incognito [ɛ̃kɔɲito] *adv & adj* : incognito

incohérent, -rente [ɛ̃kɔerã, -rãt] *adj* : incoherent — **incohérence** [ɛ̃kɔerãs] *nf* : incoherence

incolore [ɛ̃kɔlɔr] *adj* : colorless

incommensurable [ɛ̃kɔmãsyrabl] *adj* : immeasurable

incommode [ɛ̃kɔmɔd] *adj* **1** : inconvenient **2** INCONFORTABLE : uncomfortable — **incommoder** [ɛ̃kɔmɔde] *vt* : inconvenience

incomparable [ɛ̃kɔ̃parabl] *adj* : incomparable

incompatible [ɛ̃kɔ̃patibl] *adj* : incompatible

incompétent, -tente [ɛ̃kɔ̃petã, -tãt] *adj* : incompetent — **incompétence** [ɛ̃kɔ̃petãs] *nf* : incompetence

incomplet, -plète [ɛ̃kɔ̃plɛ, -plɛt] *adj* : incomplete

incompréhensible [ɛ̃kɔ̃preãsibl] *adj* : incomprehensible — **incompréhension** [ɛ̃kɔ̃preãsjɔ̃] *nf* : lack of understanding — **incompris, -prise** [ɛ̃kɔ̃pri, -priz] *adj* : misunderstood

inconcevable [ɛ̃kɔ̃svabl] *adj* : inconceivable

inconciliable [ɛ̃kɔ̃siljabl] *adj* : irreconcilable

inconditionnel, -nelle [ɛ̃kɔ̃disjɔnɛl] *adj* : unconditional — **~** *n* : enthusiast

inconduite [ɛ̃kɔ̃dɥit] *nf* : misconduct

inconfort [ɛ̃kɔ̃fɔr] *nm* : discomfort — **inconfortable** [ɛ̃kɔ̃fɔrtabl] *adj* : uncomfortable

incongru, -grue [ɛ̃kɔ̃gry] *adj* **1** : incongruous **2** : unseemly, inappropriate

inconnu, -nue [ɛ̃kɔny] *adj* : unknown — **~** *n* **1** : unknown (person) **2** ÉTRANGER : stranger

inconscient, -ciente [ɛ̃kɔ̃sjã, -sjãt] *adj* **1** : unaware **2** : unconscious — **inconsciemment** [ɛ̃kɔ̃sjamã] *adv* **1** : unconsciously **2** : thoughtlessly — **inconscience** [ɛ̃kɔ̃sjãs] *nf* **1** : unconsciousness **2** : thoughtlessness

inconsidéré, -rée [ɛ̃kɔ̃sidere] *adj* : thoughtless

inconsistant, -tante [ɛ̃kɔ̃sistã, -tãt] *adj* : flimsy, weak

inconsolable [ɛ̃kɔ̃sɔlabl] *adj* : inconsolable

inconstant, -stante [ɛ̃kɔ̃stã, -stãt] *adj* : fickle

incontestable [ɛ̃kɔ̃tɛstabl] *adj* : unquestionable, indisputable — **incontesté, -tée** [ɛ̃kɔ̃teste] *adj* : undisputed

incontournable [ɛ̃kɔ̃turnabl] *adj* : essential, that cannot be ignored

inconvenant, -nante [ɛ̃kɔ̃vnɑ̃, -nɑ̃t] *adj* : improper, unseemly — **inconvenance** [ɛ̃kɔ̃vnɑ̃s] *nf* : impropriety

inconvénient [ɛ̃kɔ̃venjɑ̃] *nm* : disadvantage, drawback

incorporer [ɛ̃kɔrpɔre] *vt* : incorporate

incorrect, -recte [ɛ̃kɔrɛkt] *adj* **1** ERRONÉ : incorrect **2** INCONVENANT : improper — **incorrectement** [ɛ̃kɔrɛktəmɑ̃] *adv* : wrongly

incorrigible [ɛ̃kɔriʒibl] *adj* : incorrigible

incrédule [ɛ̃kredyl] *adj* : incredulous

incriminer [ɛ̃krimine] *vt* : incriminate — **incrimination** [ɛ̃kriminasjɔ̃] *nf* : incrimination

incroyable [ɛ̃krwajabl] *adj* : unbelievable, incredible — **incroyant, -croyante** [ɛ̃krwajɑ̃, -jɑ̃t] *n* : unbeliever

inculper [ɛ̃kylpe] *vt* : indict, charge — **inculpation** [ɛ̃kylpasjɔ̃] *nf* : indictment, charge — **inculpé, -pée** [ɛ̃kylpe] *n* : accused, defendant

inculquer [ɛ̃kylke] *vt* : instill

inculte [ɛ̃kylt] *adj* **1** : uncultivated **2** : uneducated

incurable [ɛ̃kyrabl] *adj* : incurable

incursion [ɛ̃kyrsjɔ̃] *nf* : incursion, foray

indécent, -cente [ɛ̃desɑ̃, -sɑ̃t] *adj* : indecent — **indécence** [ɛ̃desɑ̃s] *nf* : indecency

indéchiffrable [ɛ̃deʃifrabl] *adj* : indecipherable

indécis, -cise [ɛ̃desi, -siz] *adj* **1** : indecisive **2** INCERTAIN : undecided — **indécision** [ɛ̃desizjɔ̃] *nf* : indecision

indéfini, -nie [ɛ̃defini] *adj* **1** : indefinite **2** VAGUE : ill-defined — **indéfinissable** [ɛ̃definisabl] *adj* : indefinable

indélébile [ɛ̃delebil] *adj* : indelible

indélicat, -cate [ɛ̃delika, -kat] *adj* **1** : indelicate **2** MALHONNÊTE : dishonest

indemne [ɛ̃dɛmn] *adj* : unharmed

indemnité [ɛ̃dɛmnite] *nf* **1** : indemnity **2** ALLOCATION : allowance — **indemniser** [ɛ̃dɛmnize] *vt* : indemnify, compensate

indéniable [ɛ̃denjabl] *adj* : undeniable

indépendant, -dante [ɛ̃depɑ̃dɑ̃, -dɑ̃t] *adj* : independent — **indépendamment** [ɛ̃depɑ̃damɑ̃] *adv* : independently — **indépendance** [-pɑ̃dɑ̃s] *nf* : independence

indescriptible [ɛ̃dɛskriptibl] *adj* : indescribable

indésirable [ɛ̃dezirabl] *adj* : undesirable

indestructible [ɛ̃dɛstryktibl] *adj* : indestructible

indéterminé, -née [ɛ̃detɛrmine] *adj* : indeterminate, unspecified

index [ɛ̃dɛks] *nm* **1** : index **2** : forefinger, index finger — **indexer** [ɛ̃dɛkse] *vt* : index

indication [ɛ̃dikasjɔ̃] *nf* **1** : indication **2** RENSEIGNEMENT : information **3** ~**s** *nfpl* : instructions, directions — **indicateur, -trice** [ɛ̃dikatœr, -tris] *adj* → **panneau, poteau** — ~ *n* : informer — **indicateur** *nm* **1** GUIDE : guide, directory **2** : gauge, meter — **indicatif, -tive** [ɛ̃dikatif, -tiv] *adj* : indicative — **indicatif** *nm* : indicative (mood)

indice [ɛ̃dis] *nm* **1** SIGNE : sign, indication **2** : clue **3** : index (of prices, etc.) **4** ÉVALUATION : rating

indicible [ɛ̃disibl] *adj* : inexpressible

indien, -dienne [ɛ̃djɛ̃, -djɛn] *adj* : Indian

indifférent, -rente [ɛ̃diferɑ̃, -rɑ̃t] *adj* : indifferent — **indifférence** [ɛ̃diferɑ̃s] *nf* : indifference

indigène [ɛ̃diʒɛn] *adj* : indigenous, native — ~ *nmf* : native

indigent, -gente [ɛ̃diʒɑ̃, -ʒɑ̃t] *adj* : destitute

indigestion [ɛ̃diʒɛstjɔ̃] *nf* : indigestion — **indigeste** [ɛ̃diʒɛst] *adj* : indigestible

indignation [ɛ̃diɲasjɔ̃] *nf* : indignation — **indigne** [ɛ̃diɲ] *adj* **1** : unworthy **2** MÉPRISABLE : shameful — **indigné, -gnée** [ɛ̃diɲe] *adj* : indignant — **indigner** [ɛ̃diɲe] *vt* : outrage — **s'indigner** *vr* : be indignant — **indignité** [ɛ̃diɲite] *nf* **1** : unworthiness **2** : indignity

indigo [ɛ̃digo] *adj & nm* : indigo

indiquer [ɛ̃dike] *vt* **1** : indicate, point out **2** DIRE : give, state — **indiqué, -quée** [ɛ̃dike] *adj* **1** : given, specified **2** RECOMMANDÉ : advisable **3** APPROPRIÉ : appropriate

indirect, -recte [ɛ̃dirɛkt] *adj* : indirect — **indirectement** [-rɛktəmɑ̃] *adv* : indirectly

indiscipliné, -née [ɛ̃disipline] *adj* : undisciplined, unruly

indiscrétion [ɛ̃diskresjɔ̃] *nf* : indiscretion — **indiscret, -crète** [ɛ̃diskrɛ, -krɛt] *adj* : indiscreet

indispensable [ɛ̃dispɑ̃sabl] *adj* : indispensable

indisponible [ɛ̃dispɔnibl] *adj* : unavailable

indisposer [ɛ̃dispoze] *vt* : upset, make ill — **indisposé, -sée** [ɛ̃dispoze] *adj* : unwell — **indisposition** [ɛ̃dispozisjɔ̃] *nf* : ailment, indisposition

indissociable [ɛ̃disɔsjabl] *adj* : inseparable

indistinct, -tincte [ɛ̃distɛ̃(kt), -tɛ̃kt] *adj* : indistinct

individu [ɛ̃dividy] *nm* : individual — **individualité** [ɛ̃dividɥalite] *nf* : individuality — **individuel, -duelle** [ɛ̃dividɥɛl] *adj* **1** : individual **2** PARTICULIER : personal, private — **individuellement** [ɛ̃dividɥɛlmɑ̃] *adv* : individually

indolent, -lente [ɛ̃dɔlɑ̃, -lɑ̃t] *adj* : lazy — **indolence** [ɛ̃dɔlɑ̃s] *nf* : laziness

indolore [ɛ̃dɔlɔr] *adj* : painless

indomptable [ɛ̃dɔ̃tabl] *adj* : indomitable

indu, -due [ɛ̃dy] *adj* : unseemly, ungodly

induire [ɛ̃dɥir] {49} *vt* **1** INCITER : incite, induce **2** CONCLURE : infer, conclude

indulgence [ɛ̃dylʒɑ̃s] *nf* : indulgence — **indulgent, -gente** [ɛ̃dylʒɑ̃, -ʒɑ̃t] *adj* : indulgent

indûment [ɛ̃dymɑ̃] *adv* : unduly

industrie [ɛ̃dystri] *nf* : industry — **industrialiser** [ɛ̃dystrijalize] *vt* : industrialize — **industriel, -trielle** [ɛ̃dystrijɛl] *adj* : industrial — **industrieux, -trieuse** [ɛ̃dystrijø, -trijøz] *adj* : industrious

inébranlable [inebrɑ̃labl] *adj* : unshakeable

inédit, -dite [inedi, -dit] *adj* **1** : unpublished **2** ORIGINAL : novel, original

inefficace [inefikas] *adj* **1** : inefficient **2** : ineffective — **inefficacité** [inefikasite] *nf* **1** : inefficiency **2** : ineffectiveness

inégal, -gale [inegal] *adj, mpl* **-gaux** [-go] **1** : unequal **2** IRRÉGULIER : uneven — **inégalé, -lée** [inegale] *adj* : unequaled — **inégalité** [inegalite] *nf* **1** : inequality **2** IRRÉGULARITÉ : unevenness, irregularity

inéligible [ineliʒibl] *adj* : ineligible

inéluctable [inelyktabl] *adj* : inescapable

inepte [inɛpt] *adj* : inept

inépuisable [inepɥizabl] *adj* : inexhaustible

inerte [inɛrt] *adj* **1** : inert, lifeless **2** APATHIQUE : apathetic — **inertie** [inɛrsi] *nf* **1** : inertia **2** APATHIE : apathy

inespéré, -rée [inɛspere] *adj* : unhoped for, unexpected

inestimable [inɛstimabl] *adj* : inestimable

inévitable [inevitabl] *adj* : inevitable — **inévitablement** [-tabləmɑ̃] *adv* : inevitably

inexact, -exacte [inɛgza(kt), -ɛgzakt] *adj* : inaccurate, incorrect

inexcusable [inɛkskyzabl] *adj* : inexcusable

inexistant, -tante [inɛgzistɑ̃, -tɑ̃t] *adj* : nonexistent

inexpérience [inɛksperjɑ̃s] *nf* : inexperience — **inexpérimenté, -tée** [inɛksperimɑ̃te] *adj* : inexperienced

inexplicable [inɛksplikabl] *adj* : inexplicable — **inexpliqué, -quée** [inɛksplike] *adj* : unexplained

inexprimable [inɛksprimabl] *adj* : inexpressible

infaillible [ɛ̃fajibl] *adj* : infallible

infâme [ɛ̃fam] *adj* : vile — **infamie** [ɛ̃fam] *adj* : infamy

infanterie [ɛ̃fɑ̃tri] *nf* : infantry

infantile [ɛ̃fɑ̃til] *adj* : infantile, childish

infarctus [ɛ̃farktys] *nm or* ~ **myocarde** : heart attack

infatigable [ɛ̃fatigabl] *adj* : tireless

infect, -fecte [ɛ̃fɛkt] *adj* : revolting, foul — **infecter** [ɛ̃fɛkte] *vt* **1** : infect **2** : contami-

nate — **s'infecter** *vr* : become infected

infectieux, -tieuse [ɛ̃fɛksjø, -tjøz] *adj* : infectious — **infection** [ɛ̃fɛksjɔ̃] *nf* **1** : infection **2** PUANTEUR : stench

inférieur, -rieure [ɛ̃ferjœr] *adj & n* : inferior — **infériorité** [ɛ̃ferjɔrite] *nf* : inferiority

infernal, -nale [ɛ̃fɛrnal] *adj, mpl* **-naux** [-no] : infernal

infertile [ɛ̃fɛrtil] *adj* : infertile — **infertilité** [-tilite] *nf* : infertility

infester [ɛ̃fɛste] *vt* : infest

infidèle [ɛ̃fidɛl] *adj* : unfaithful — **infidélité** [ɛ̃fidelite] *nf* : infidelity

infiltrer [ɛ̃filtre] *vt* : infiltrate — **s'infiltrer** *vr* ~ **dans** : seep into, penetrate — **infiltration** [ɛ̃filtrasjɔ̃] *nf* : infiltration

infime [ɛ̃fim] *adj* : minute, tiny

infini, -nie [ɛ̃fini] *adj* : infinite — **infini** *nm* **1** : infinity **2 à l'**~ : endlessly — **infinité** [ɛ̃finite] *nf* **1** : infinity **2** : infinite number

infinitif [ɛ̃finitif] *nm* : infinitive

infirme [ɛ̃firm] *adj* : disabled, infirm — ~ *nmf* : disabled person — **infirmerie** [ɛ̃firməri] *nf* : infirmary — **infirmier, -mière** [ɛ̃firmje, -mjɛr] *n* : nurse — **infirmité** [ɛ̃firmite] *nf* : disability

inflammable [ɛ̃flamabl] *adj* : inflammable, flammable — **inflammation** [ɛ̃flamasjɔ̃] *nf* : inflammation

inflation [ɛ̃flasjɔ̃] *nf* : inflation — **inflationniste** [ɛ̃flasjɔnist] *adj* : inflationary

inflexible [ɛ̃flɛksibl] *adj* : inflexible, unbending — **inflexion** [ɛ̃flɛksjɔ̃] *nf* **1** : inflection (of the voice) **2** : nod (of the head)

infliger [ɛ̃fliʒe] {17} *vt* **1** : inflict **2** : impose (a penalty, etc.)

influence [ɛ̃flyɑ̃s] *nf* : influence — **influencer** [ɛ̃flyɑ̃se] {6} *vt* : influence — **influent, -fluente** [ɛ̃flyɑ̃, -flyɑ̃t] *adj* : influential — **influer** [ɛ̃flye] *vi* ~ **sur** : have an influence on

informateur, -trice [ɛ̃fɔrmatœr, -tris] *n* : informant, informer

informaticien, -cienne [ɛ̃fɔrmatisjɛ̃, -sjɛn] *n* : computer programmer

information [ɛ̃fɔrmasjɔ̃] *nf* **1** : information **2** ~**s** *nfpl* : news — **informatif, -tive** [ɛ̃fɔrmatif, -tiv] *adj* : informative

informatique [ɛ̃fɔrmatik] *adj* : computer — ~ *nf* : computer science — **informatiser** [ɛ̃fɔrmatize] *vt* : computerize

informe [ɛ̃fɔrm] *adj* : shapeless

informer [ɛ̃fɔrme] *vt* : inform — **s'informer** *vr* : inquire

infortune [ɛ̃fɔrtyn] *nf* : misfortune — **infortuné, -née** [ɛ̃fɔrtyne] *adj* : unfortunate

infraction [ɛ̃fraksjɔ̃] *nf* : breach (in law)

infranchissable [ɛ̃frɑ̃ʃisabl] *adj* **1** : insurmountable **2** IMPRACTICABLE : impassable

infrarouge [ɛ̃fraruʒ] *adj* : infrared

infrastructure [ɛ̃frastryktyr] *nf* : infrastructure

infructueux, -tueuse [ɛ̃fryktɥø, -tɥøz] *adj* : fruitless

infuser [ɛ̃fyze] *v* **1** : infuse **2** : brew (tea, etc.) — **infusion** [ɛ̃fyzjɔ̃] *nf* : infusion

ingénieur, -nieure [ɛ̃ʒenjœr] *n* : engineer — **ingénierie** [ɛ̃ʒeniri] *nf* : engineering

ingénieux, -nieuse [ɛ̃ʒenjø, -njøz] *adj* : ingenious — **ingéniosité** [ɛ̃ʒenjozite] *nf* : ingenuity

ingénu, -nue [ɛ̃ʒeny] *adj* : ingenuous, naive

ingérence [ɛ̃ʒerɑ̃s] *nf* : interference

ingratitude [ɛ̃gratityd] *nf* : ingratitude — **ingrat, -grate** [ɛ̃gra, -grat] *adj* **1** : ungrateful **2** : thankless

ingrédient [ɛ̃gredjɑ̃] *nm* : ingredient

inhabitable [inabitabl] *adj* : uninhabitable — **inhabité, -tée** [inabite] *adj* : uninhabited

inhabituel, -tuelle [inabitɥel] *adj* : unusual

inhaler [inale] *vt* : inhale — **inhalation** [-alasjɔ̃] *nf* : inhaling

inhérent, -rente [inerɑ̃, -rɑ̃t] *adj* : inherent

inhiber [inibe] *vt* : inhibit — **inhibition** [inibisjɔ̃] *nf* : inhibition

inhumain, -maine [inymɛ̃, -mɛn] *adj* : inhuman — **inhumanité** [inymanite] *nf* : inhumanity

inhumer [inyme] *vt* : bury — **inhumation** [inymasjɔ̃] *nf* : burial

initial, -tiale [inisjal] *adj, mpl* **-tiaux** [-sjo] : initial — **initiale** [inisjal] *nf* : initial

initiative [inisjativ] *nf* : initiative

initier [inisje] {96} *vt* : initiate — **initiateur, -trice** [inisjatœr, -tris] *n* **1** : initiator **2** NOVATEUR : innovator — **initiation** [inisjasjɔ̃] *nf* : initiation

injecter [ɛ̃ʒɛkte] *vt* : inject — **injection** [ɛ̃ʒɛksjɔ̃] *nf* : injection

injonction [ɛ̃ʒɔ̃ksjɔ̃] *nf* : order, injunction

injure [ɛ̃ʒyr] *nf* : insult, abuse — **injurier** [ɛ̃ʒyrje] {96} *vt* : insult — **injurieux, -rieuse** [ɛ̃ʒyrjø, -rjøz] *adj* : insulting, abusive

injuste [ɛ̃ʒyst] *adj* : unjust, unfair — **injustice** [ɛ̃ʒystis] *nf* : injustice

injustifié, -fiée [ɛ̃ʒystifje] *adj* : unjustified

inlassable [ɛ̃lasabl] *adj* : tireless

inné, -née [ine] *adj* : innate, inborn

innocent, -cente [inɔsɑ̃, -sɑ̃t] *adj & n* : innocent — **innocence** [inɔsɑ̃s] *nf* : innocence — **innocenter** [inɔsɑ̃te] *vt* : clear, exonerate

innombrable [inɔ̃brabl] *adj* : innumerable, countless

innover [inɔve] *v* : innovate — **innovateur, -trice** [inɔvatœr, -tris] *adj* : innovative — ∼ *n* : innovator — **innovation** [inɔvasjɔ̃] *nf* : innovation

inoccupé, -pée [inɔkype] *adj* : unoccupied

inoculer [inɔkyle] *vt* : inoculate — **inoculation** [-kylasjɔ̃] *nf* : inoculation

inodore [inɔdɔr] *adj* : odorless

inoffensif, -sive [inɔfɑ̃sif, -siv] *adj* : inoffensive, harmless

inonder [inɔ̃de] *vt* : flood, inundate — **inondation** [inɔ̃dasjɔ̃] *nf* : flood

inopiné, -née [inɔpine] *adj* : unexpected

inopportun, -tune [inɔpɔrtœ̃, -tyn] *adj* : untimely

inoubliable [inublijabl] *adj* : unforgettable

inouï, inouïe [inwi] *adj* : incredible, unheard of

inquiet, -quiète [ɛ̃kjɛ, -kjɛt] *adj* : anxious, worried — **inquiétant, -tante** [ɛ̃kjetɑ̃, -tɑ̃t] *adj* : worrisome — **inquiéter** [ɛ̃kjete] {87} *vt* **1** : worry **2** DÉRANGER : bother, disturb — **s'inquiéter** *vr* : be worried — **inquiétude** [ɛ̃kjetyd] *nf* : worry, anxiety

inquisition [ɛ̃kizisjɔ̃] *nf* : inquisition

insaisissable [ɛ̃sezisabl] *adj* : elusive

insalubre [ɛ̃salybr] *adj* : unhealthy

insanité [ɛ̃sanite] *nf* : insanity

insatiable [ɛ̃sasjabl] *adj* : insatiable

insatisfait, -faite [ɛ̃satisfɛ, -fɛt] *adj* : dissatisfied — **insatisfaction** [ɛ̃satisfaksjɔ̃] *nf* : dissatisfaction

inscrire [ɛ̃skrir] {33} *vt* **1** ÉCRIRE : write down **2** ENREGISTRER : register, enroll — **s'inscrire** *vr* : register, enroll — **inscription** [ɛ̃skripsjɔ̃] *nf* **1** : inscription **2** : registration, enrollment

insecte [ɛ̃sɛkt] *nm* : insect — **insecticide** [ɛ̃sɛktisid] *nm* : insecticide

insécurité [ɛ̃sekyrite] *nf* : insecurity

insensé, -sée [ɛ̃sɑ̃se] *adj* : crazy, foolish

insensible [ɛ̃sɑ̃sibl] *adj* : insensitive — **insensibilité** [ɛ̃sɑ̃sibilite] *nf* : insensitivity

inséparable [ɛ̃separabl] *adj* : inseparable

insérer [ɛ̃sere] {87} *vt* : insert

insidieux, -dieuse [ɛ̃sidjø, -djøz] *adj* : insidious

insigne [ɛ̃siɲ] *nm* **1** : badge **2** *or* ∼**s** *nmpl* : insignia

insignifiant, -fiante [ɛ̃siɲifjɑ̃, -fjɑ̃t] *adj* : insignificant — **insignifiance** [-ɲifjɑ̃s] *nf* : insignificance

insinuation [ɛ̃sinɥasjɔ̃] *nf* : insinuation — **insinuer** [ɛ̃sinɥe] *vt* : insinuate — **s'insinuer** *vr* ∼ **dans** : insinuate oneself into, penetrate

insipide [ɛ̃sipid] *adj* : insipid

insister [ɛ̃siste] *vi* **1** : insist **2** ∼ **sur** : emphasize, stress — **insistance** [ɛ̃sistɑ̃s] *nf* : insistence — **insistant, -tante** [ɛ̃sistɑ̃, -tɑ̃t] *adj* : insistent

insociable [ɛ̃sɔsjabl] *adj* : unsociable

insolation [ɛ̃sɔlasjɔ̃] *nf* : sunstroke

insolent, -lente [ɛ̃sɔlɑ̃, -lɑ̃t] *adj* : insolent — **insolence** [ɛ̃sɔlɑ̃s] *nf* : insolence

insolite [ɛ̃sɔlit] *adj* : unusual, bizarre

insoluble [ɛ̃sɔlybl] *adj* : insoluble

insolvable [ɛ̃sɔlvabl] *adj* : insolvent

insomnie [ɛ̃sɔmni] *nf* : insomnia

insondable [ɛ̃sɔ̃dabl] *adj* **1** : bottomless **2** IMPÉNÉTRABLE : unfathomable

insonoriser [ɛ̃sɔnɔrize] *vt* : soundproof

insouciant, -ciante [ɛ̃susjɑ̃, -sjɑ̃t] *adj* : carefree — **insouciance** [ɛ̃susjɑ̃s] *nf* : carefree attitude

insoutenable [ɛ̃sutnabl] *adj* **1** : untenable **2** INTOLÉRABLE : unbearable

inspecter [ɛ̃spɛkte] *vt* : inspect — **inspecteur, -trice** [ɛ̃spɛktœr, -tris] *n* : inspector — **inspection** [ɛ̃spɛksjɔ̃] *nf* : inspection

inspirer [ɛ̃spire] *vt* : inspire — *vi* : inhale — **s'inspirer** *vr* ~ **de** : be inspired by — **inspirant, -rante** [ɛ̃spirɑ̃, -rɑ̃t] *adj* : inspirational — **inspiration** [ɛ̃spirasjɔ̃] *nf* **1** : inspiration **2** : breathing in

instable [ɛ̃stabl] *adj* **1** BRANLANT : unsteady **2** : unstable, unsettled — **instabilité** [ɛ̃stabilite] *nf* : instability

installer [ɛ̃stale] *vt* : install, set up — **s'installer** *vr* : settle (in) — **installation** [ɛ̃stalasjɔ̃] *nf* **1** : installation **2** ~**s** *nfpl* : installations, facilities

instance [ɛ̃stɑ̃s] *nf* **1** AUTORITÉ : authority **2** : legal proceedings **3 en** ~ : pending

instant [ɛ̃stɑ̃, -tɑ̃t] *nm* : instant, moment — **instantané, -née** [ɛ̃stɑ̃tane] *adj* : instantaneous, instant — **instantané** *nm* : snapshot

instar [ɛ̃star] **à l'**~ **de** *prep phr* : following the example of, like

instaurer [ɛ̃store] *vt* : institute, establish — **instauration** [ɛ̃storasjɔ̃] *nf* : institution

instigateur, -trice [ɛ̃stigatœr, -tris] *n* : instigator — **instigation** [ɛ̃stigasjɔ̃] *nf* : instigation

instinct [ɛ̃stɛ̃] *nm* : instinct — **instinctif, -tive** [ɛ̃stɛ̃ktif, -tiv] *adj* : instinctive, instinctual

instituer [ɛ̃stitɥe] *vt* **1** : institute, establish **2** NOMMER : appoint — **institut** [ɛ̃stity] *nm* : institute — **instituteur, -trice** [ɛ̃stitytœr, -tris] *n* : schoolteacher — **institution** [ɛ̃stitysjɔ̃] *nf* : institution

instruction [ɛ̃stryksjɔ̃] *nf* **1** : instruction, education **2** ~**s** *nfpl* : instructions — **instruire** [ɛ̃strɥir] {49} *vt* **1** : instruct **2** ~ **de** : inform of — **s'instruire** *vr* **1** : educate oneself **2** ~ **de** : find out about — **instruit, -truite** [ɛ̃strɥi, -trɥit] *adj* : learned, educated

instrument [ɛ̃strymɑ̃] *nm* : instrument — **instrumental, -tale** [ɛ̃strymɑ̃tal] *adj, mpl* **-taux** [-to] : instrumental

insu [ɛ̃sy] **à l'**~ **de** *prep phr* : without the knowledge of, unknown to

insuffisant, -sante [ɛ̃syfizɑ̃, -zɑ̃t] *adj* : insufficient, inadequate — **insuffisance** [ɛ̃syfizɑ̃s] *nf* : inadequacy

insulaire [ɛ̃sylɛr] *adj* : island, insular — ~ *nmf* : islander

insuline [ɛ̃sylin] *nf* : insulin

insulter [ɛ̃sylte] *vt* : insult — **insulte** [ɛ̃sylt] *nf* : insult

insupportable [ɛ̃syportabl] *adj* : unbearable

insurger [ɛ̃syrʒe] {17} *v* **s'insurger** *vr* : rebel, rise up — **insurgé, -gée** [ɛ̃syrʒe] *n* : insurgent, rebel

insurmontable [ɛ̃syrmɔ̃tabl] *adj* : insurmountable

insurrection [ɛ̃syrɛksjɔ̃] *nf* : insurrection

intact, -tacte [ɛ̃takt] *adj* : intact

intangible [ɛ̃tɑ̃ʒibl] *adj* : intangible

intarissable [ɛ̃tarisabl] *adj* : inexhaustible

intégral, -grale [ɛ̃tegral] *adj, mpl* **-graux** [-gro] **1** : complete **2** : unabridged — **intégralité** [ɛ̃tegralite] *nf* : whole — **intégrant, -grante** [ɛ̃tegrɑ̃, -grɑ̃t] *adj* **faire partie intégrante de** : be an integral part of

intègre [ɛ̃tɛgr] *adj* : honest, upright

intégrer [ɛ̃tegre] {87} *vt* : integrate — **s'intégrer** *vr* : integrate

intégrité [ɛ̃tegrite] *nf* : integrity

intellect [ɛ̃telɛkt] *nm* : intellect — **intellectuel, -tuelle** [ɛ̃telɛktɥel] *adj & n* : intellectual

intelligent, -gente [ɛ̃teliʒɑ̃, -ʒɑ̃t] *adj* : intelligent — **intelligence** [ɛ̃teliʒɑ̃s] *nf* **1** : intelligence **2** COMPRÉHENSION : understanding — **intelligible** [ɛ̃teliʒibl] *adj* : intelligible, comprehensible

intempéries [ɛtɑ̃peri] *nfpl* : bad weather

intempestif, -tive [ɛ̃tɑ̃pɛstif, -tiv] *adj* : untimely

intense [ɛ̃tɑ̃s] *adj* : intense — **intensément** [ɛ̃tɑ̃semɑ̃] *adv* : intensely — **intensif, -sive** [ɛ̃tɑ̃sif, -siv] *adj* : intensive — **intensifier** [ɛ̃tɑ̃sifje] {96} *vt* : intensify — **intensité** [ɛ̃tɑ̃site] *nf* : intensity

intenter [ɛ̃tɑ̃te] *vt* : initiate, pursue (legal action)

intention [ɛ̃tɑ̃sjɔ̃] *nf* : intention, intent — **intentionnel, -nelle** [ɛ̃tɑ̃sjɔnɛl] *adj* : intentional

interactif, -tive [ɛ̃teraktif, -tiv] *adj* : interactive — **interaction** [ɛ̃teraksjɔ̃] *nf* : interaction

intercaler [ɛ̃tɛrkale] *vt* : insert

intercéder [ɛ̃tɛrsede] {87} *vi* : intercede

intercepter [ɛ̃tɛrsɛpte] *vt* : intercept

interchangeable [ɛ̃tɛrʃɑ̃ʒabl] *adj* : interchangeable

intercontinental, -tale [ɛ̃tɛrkɔ̃tinɑ̃tal] *adj, mpl* **-taux** [-to] : intercontinental

interdire [ɛ̃tɛrdir] {29} *vt* **1** : ban, prohibit **2** EMPÊCHER : prevent — **interdiction** [ɛ̃tɛrdiksjɔ̃] *nf* : ban, prohibition — **interdit, -dite** [ɛ̃tɛrdi, -dit] *adj* **1** : prohibited **2** STUPÉFAIT : dumbfounded

intéresser [ɛ̃terese] *vt* **1** : interest **2** CON-CERNER : concern — **s'intéresser** *vr* ~ **à** : be interested in — **intéressant, -sante** [ɛ̃teresɑ̃, -sɑ̃t] *adj* **1** : interesting **2** AVAN-TAGEUX : attractive, worthwhile — **intéressé, -sée** *adj* **1** : self-interested **2** CONCERNÉ : concerned — ~ *n* : interested party — **intérêt** [ɛ̃tere] *nm* : interest
interface [ɛ̃terfas] *nf* : interface
interférence [ɛ̃terferɑ̃s] *nf* : interference — **interférer** [ɛ̃terfere] {87} *vi* : interfere
intérieur, -rieure [ɛ̃terjœr] *adj* **1** : inner, inside **2** : internal, domestic (in politics) — **intérieur** *nm* **1** : inside (of a drawer, etc.) **2** : interior, home **3 à l'**~ : indoors **4 d'**~ : indoor — **intérieurement** [ɛ̃terjœrmɑ̃] *adv* : inwardly, internally
intérim [ɛ̃terim] *nm* **1** : interim (period) **2** : temporary activity — **intérimaire** [ɛ̃terimɛr] *adj* : temporary, acting — ~ *nmf* : temporary employee
interjection [ɛ̃terʒɛksjɔ̃] *nf* : interjection
interlocuteur, -trice [ɛ̃terlɔkytœr, -tris] *n* : speaker
intermède [ɛ̃termɛd] *nm* : interlude
intermédiaire [ɛ̃termedjɛr] *adj* : intermediate — ~ *nmf* : intermediary, go-between
interminable [ɛ̃terminabl] *adj* : interminable
intermittent, -tente [ɛ̃termitɑ̃, -tɑ̃t] *adj* : intermittent, sporadic — **intermittence** [ɛ̃termitɑ̃s] *nf* **par** ~ : intermittently
international, -nale [ɛ̃ternasjɔnal] *adj, mpl* **-naux** [-no] : international
interne [ɛ̃tɛrn] *adj* : internal
interner [ɛ̃terne] *vt* **1** : intern (in politics) **2** : confine (in medicine)
interpeller [ɛ̃terpəle] *vt* **1** : shout at, call out to **2** INTERROGER : question
interphone [ɛ̃terfɔn] *nm* : intercom
interposer [ɛ̃terpoze] *v* **s'interposer** *vr* : intervene
interpréter [ɛ̃terprete] {87} *vt* **1** : interpret **2** : perform, play (a role) — **interprétation** [ɛ̃terpretasjɔ̃] *nf* : interpretation — **interprète** [ɛ̃terprɛt] *nmf* **1** : interpreter **2** REPRÉSENTANT : spokesperson **3** : performer (in theater, etc.)
interroger [ɛ̃terɔʒe] {17} *vt* : interrogate, question — **s'interroger** *vr* ~ **sur** : wonder about — **interrogateur, -trice** [ɛ̃terɔgatœr, -tris] *adj* : questioning — **interrogatif, -tive** [ɛ̃terɔgatif, -tiv] *adj* : interrogative — **interrogation** [ɛ̃terɔgasjɔ̃] *nf* **1** : interrogation **2** : test (in school) — **interrogatoire** [ɛ̃terɔgatwar] *nm* : interrogation, questioning
interrompre [ɛ̃terɔ̃pr] {77} *v* : interrupt — **s'interrompre** *vr* : break off — **interrupteur** [ɛ̃teryptœr] *nm* : switch — **interrup-**

tion [ɛ̃terypsjɔ̃] *nf* **1** : interruption **2 sans** ~ : continuously
intersection [ɛ̃tersɛksjɔ̃] *nf* : intersection
interurbain, -baine [ɛ̃teryrbɛ̃, -bɛn] *adj* : long-distance — **interurbain** *nm* **l'**~ : long-distance telephone service
intervalle [ɛ̃terval] *nm* **1** : space, gap **2** : interval (of time) **3 dans l'**~ : in the meantime
intervenir [ɛ̃tervənir] {92} *vi* **1** : intervene **2** SURVENIR : take place **3** : operate (in medicine) — **intervention** [ɛ̃tervɑ̃sjɔ̃] *nf* **1** : intervention **2** OPERATION : (medical) operation
intervertir [ɛ̃tervertir] *vt* : invert, reverse
interview [ɛ̃tervju] *nf* : interview — **interviewer** [ɛ̃tervjuve] *vt* : interview
intestin [ɛ̃testɛ̃] *nm* : intestine — **intestinal, -nale** [ɛ̃testinal] *adj, mpl* **-naux** [-no] : intestinal
intime [ɛ̃tim] *adj* **1** : intimate **2** PERSONNEL : private — ~ *nmf* : close friend
intimider [ɛ̃timide] *vt* : intimidate — **intimidant, -dante** [ɛ̃timidɑ̃, -dɑ̃t] *adj* : intimidating — **intimidation** [-midasjɔ̃] *nf* : intimidation
intimité [ɛ̃timite] *nf* : intimacy
intituler [ɛ̃tityle] *vt* : call, title — **s'intituler** *vr* : be called
intolérable [ɛ̃tɔlerabl] *adj* : intolerable, unbearable — **intolérant, -rante** [ɛ̃tɔlerɑ̃, -rɑ̃t] *adj* : intolerant — **intolérance** [-rɑ̃s] *nf* : intolerance
intonation [ɛ̃tɔnasjɔ̃] *nf* : intonation
intoxiquer [ɛ̃tɔksike] *vt* EMPOISONNER : poison — **intoxication** [ɛ̃tɔksikasjɔ̃] *nf* : poisoning
intransigeant, -geante [ɛ̃trɑ̃ziʒɑ, -ʒɑ̃t] *adj* : uncompromising
intransitif, -tive [ɛ̃trɑ̃zitif, -tiv] *adj* : intransitive
intraveineux, -neuse [ɛ̃travɛnø, -nøz] *adj* : intravenous
intrépide [ɛ̃trepid] *adj* : intrepid, fearless
intriguer [ɛ̃trige] *vt* : intrigue, puzzle — *vi* : plot, scheme — **intrigue** [ɛ̃trig] *nf* **1** : intrigue **2** : plot (of a story)
intrinsèque [ɛ̃trɛ̃sɛk] *adj* : intrinsic
introduire [ɛ̃trɔdɥir] {49} *vt* **1** : introduce **2** : show in, bring in **3** INSÉRER : insert **4** : enter, input (data) — **s'introduire** *vr* : penetrate, get in — **introduction** [ɛ̃trɔdyksjɔ̃] *nf* **1** : introduction **2** : insertion
introuvable [ɛ̃truvabl] *adj* : unobtainable, nowhere to be found
introverti, -tie [ɛ̃trɔverti] *adj* : introverted — ~ *n* : introvert
intrusion [ɛ̃tryzjɔ̃] *nf* : intrusion — **intrus, -truse** [ɛ̃try, -tryz] *n* : intruder

intuition [ɛ̃tɥisjɔ̃] *nf* : intuition — **intuitif, -tive** [ɛ̃tɥitif, -tiv] *adj* : intuitive

inuit [inɥi] *adj* : Inuit

inusable [inyzabl] *adj* : durable

inusité, -tée [inyzite] *adj* : unusual, uncommon

inutile [inytil] *adj* **1** : useless **2** SUPERFLU : pointless — **inutilement** [inytilmɑ̃] *adv* : needlessly — **inutilisable** [inytilizabl] *adj* : unusable — **inutilité** [inytilite] *nf* : uselessness

invalide [ɛ̃valid] *adj* : disabled — ∼ *nmf* : disabled person — **invalidité** [ɛ̃validite] *nf* : disability

invariable [ɛ̃varjabl] *adj* : invariable

invasion [ɛ̃vazjɔ̃] *nf* : invasion

inventaire [ɛ̃vɑ̃tɛr] *nm* **1** : inventory **2 faire l'**∼ : take stock

invention [ɛ̃vɑ̃sjɔ̃] *nf* : invention — **inventer** [ɛ̃vɑ̃te] *vt* : invent — **inventeur, -trice** [ɛ̃vɑ̃tœr, -tris] *n* : inventor — **inventif, -tive** [ɛ̃vɑ̃tif, -tiv] *adj* : inventive

inverse [ɛ̃vɛrs] *adj* : reverse, opposite — ∼ *nm* : reverse, opposite — **inversement** [ɛ̃vɛrsəmɑ̃] *adv* : conversely — **inverser** [ɛ̃vɛrse] *vt* : reverse, invert

invertébré, -brée [ɛ̃vɛrtebre] *adj* : invertebrate — **invertébré** *nm* : invertebrate

investigation [ɛ̃vɛstigasjɔ̃] *nf* : investigation

investir [ɛ̃vɛstir] *v* : invest — **investissement** [ɛ̃vɛstismɑ̃] *nm* : investment — **investisseur, -seuse** [ɛ̃vɛstisœr, -søz] *n* : investor

invétéré, -rée [ɛ̃vetere] *adj* : inveterate

invincible [ɛ̃vɛ̃sibl] *adj* : invincible

invisible [ɛ̃vizibl] *adj* : invisible

inviter [ɛ̃vite] *vt* : invite — **invitation** [ɛ̃vitasjɔ̃] *nf* : invitation — **invité, -tée** [ɛ̃vite] *n* : guest

involontaire [ɛ̃vɔlɔ̃tɛr] *adj* : involuntary

invoquer [ɛ̃vɔke] *vt* : invoke

invraisemblable [ɛ̃vrɛsɑ̃blabl] *adj* : improbable, unlikely

invulnérable [ɛ̃vylnerabl] *adj* : invulnerable

iode [jɔd] *nm* : iodine

ion [jɔ̃] *nm* : ion

iris [iris] *nm* : iris

irlandais, -daise [irlɑ̃dɛ, -dɛz] *adj* : Irish

ironie [irɔni] *nf* : irony — **ironique** [irɔnik] *adj* : ironic(al)

irradier [iradje] {96} *vt* : irradiate — *vi* : radiate

irrationnel, -nelle [irasjɔnɛl] *adj* : irrational

irréalisable [irealizabl] *adj* : unworkable

irréconciliable [irekɔ̃siljabl] *adj* : irreconcilable

irrécupérable [irekyperabl] *adj* : irretrievable, beyond repair

irréel, -réelle [ireɛl] *adj* : unreal

irréfléchi, -chie [irefleʃi] *adj* : thoughtless, rash

irréfutable [irefytabl] *adj* : irrefutable

irrégulier, -lière [iregylje, -ljɛr] *adj* : irregular — **irrégularité** [iregylarite] *nf* : irregularity

irrémédiable [iremedjabl] *adj* : irreparable

irremplaçable [irɑ̃plasabl] *adj* : irreplaceable

irréparable [ireparabl] *adj* : irreparable

irréprochable [ireprɔʃabl] *adj* : irreproachable, blameless

irrésistible [irezistibl] *adj* : irresistible

irrésolu, -lue [irezɔly] *adj* **1** INDÉCIS : irresolute **2** : unresolved (of a problem)

irrespectueux, -tueuse [irɛspɛktɥø, -tɥøz] *adj* : disrespectful

irresponsable [irɛspɔ̃sabl] *adj* : irresponsible — **irresponsabilité** [irɛspɔ̃sabilite] *nf* : irresponsibility

irrigation [irigasjɔ̃] *nf* : irrigation — **irriguer** [irige] *vt* : irrigate

irriter [irite] *vt* : irritate — **s'irriter** *vr* : get irritated — **irritable** [iritabl] *adj* : irritable — **irritation** [iritasjɔ̃] *nf* : irritation

irruption [irypsjɔ̃] *nf* : bursting in

islam [islam] *nm* : Islam — **islamique** [islamik] *adj* : Islamic

isoler [izɔle] *vt* **1** : isolate **2** : insulate — **s'isoler** *vr* : isolate oneself — **isolation** [izɔlasjɔ̃] *nf* : insulation — **isolement** [izɔlmɑ̃] *nm* **1** : isolation **2** ISOLATION : insulation — **isolément** [izɔlemɑ̃] *adv* : separately, individually

israélien, -lienne [israeljɛ̃, -ljɛn] *adj* : Israeli

issu, -sue [isy] *adj* ∼ **de 1** : descended from **2** : resulting from

issue *nf* **1** SORTIE : exit **2** SOLUTION : solution **3** FIN : ending, outcome

isthme [ism] *nm* : isthmus

italien, -lienne [italjɛ̃, -ljɛn] *adj* : Italian — **italien** *nm* : Italian (language)

italique [italik] *nm* : italics *pl*

itinéraire [itinerɛr] *nm* : itinerary

itinérant, -rante [itinerɑ̃, -rɑ̃t] *adj* : itinerant

ivoire [ivwar] *adj & nm* : ivory

ivre [ivr] *adj* : drunk — **ivresse** [ivrɛs] *nf* : drunkenness — **ivrogne, ivrognesse** [ivrɔɲ, -ɲɛs] *n* : drunkard

J

j [ʒi] *nm* : j, 10th letter of the alphabet
jacasser [ʒakase] *vi* : chatter, jabber
jachère [ʒaʃɛr] *nf* : fallow land
jacinthe [ʒasɛ̃t] *nf* : hyacinth
jadis [ʒadis] *adv* : in times past, formerly
jaillir [ʒajir] *vi* **1** : spurt out, gush (out) **2** AP-PARAÎTRE : spring up, emerge
jais [ʒɛ] *nms & pl* **1** : jet (stone) **2 de ~** : jet-black
jalon [ʒalɔ̃] *nm* : marker, milestone — **jalon-ner** [ʒalɔne] *vt* **1** : mark out (a route, etc.) **2** LONGER : line
jaloux, -louse [ʒalu, -luz] *adj* : jealous — **jalouser** [ʒaluze] *vt* : be jealous of — **jalousie** [ʒaluzi] *nf* **1** : jealousy **2** : venetian blind
jamais [ʒamɛ] *adv* **1** : ever **2 ne ... ~** : never **3 à ~** *or* **pour ~** : forever
jambe [ʒɑ̃b] *nf* : leg
jambon [ʒɑ̃bɔ̃] *nm* : ham
jante [ʒɑ̃t] *nf* : rim (of a wheel)
janvier [ʒɑ̃vje] *nm* : January
japonais, -naise [ʒaponɛ, -nɛz] *adj* : Japan-ese — **japonais** *nm* : Japanese (language)
japper [ʒape] *vi* : yap, yelp
jaquette [ʒakɛt] *nf* **1** : dust jacket **2** : jacket (for women)
jardin [ʒardɛ̃] *nm* **1** : garden **2 ~ d'enfants** *France* : kindergarten **3 ~ zoologique** : zoo — **jardinage** [ʒardinaʒ] *nm* : garden-ing — **jardiner** [ʒardine] *vi* : garden — **jar-dinier, -nière** [ʒardinje, -njɛr] *n* : gardener — **jardinière** *nf* : plant stand, window box
jargon [ʒargɔ̃] *nm* **1** : jargon **2** CHARABIA : gibberish
jarre [ʒar] *nf* : (earthenware) jar
jarret [ʒarɛ] *nm* **1** : back of the knee **2** : shank (in cooking) — **jarretelle** [ʒartɛl] *nf* : garter belt — **jarretière** [ʒartjɛr] *nf* : garter
jaser [ʒaze] *vi* **1** : chatter, prattle **2** MÉDIRE : gossip
jatte [ʒat] *nf* : bowl, basin
jauge [ʒoʒ] *nf* **1** : capacity **2** INDICATEUR : gauge — **jauger** [ʒoʒe] {17} *vt* : gauge
jaune [ʒon] *adj* : yellow — **~** *nm* **1** : yellow **2** *or* **~ d'œuf** : egg yolk — **jaunir** [ʒonir] *v* : turn yellow — **jaunisse** [ʒonis] *nf* : jaun-dice
Javel [ʒavɛl] *nf* → **eau**
javelot [ʒavlo] *nm* : javelin
jazz [dʒaz] *nm* : jazz
je [ʒə] (**j'** *before vowel or mute h*) *pron* : I
jean [dʒin] *nm* **1** : denim **2** : (blue) jeans *pl*
jeep [dʒip] *nf* : jeep
jersey [ʒɛrzɛ] *nm* : jersey (fabric)

Jésus [ʒezy] *nm* : Jesus
jeter [ʒəte] {8} *vt* **1** LANCER : throw **2** : throw away **3** ÉMETTRE : give off **4 ~ l'éponge** : throw in the towel **5 ~ un coup d'œil** : take a look at **6 ~ un sort** : cast a spell — **se jeter** *vr* **1 ~ dans** : flow into **2 ~ sur** : pounce on — **jet** [ʒɛ] *nm* **1** : jet, spurt **2** LANCER : throw, throw-ing **3** : jet (airplane) **4 ~ d'eau** : fountain — **jetable** [ʒətabl] *adj* : disposable — **jetée** [ʒəte] *nf* : pier, jetty
jeton [ʒətɔ̃] *nm* : token, counter
jeu [ʒø] *nm, pl* **jeux 1** DIVERTISSEMENT : play **2** : game **3** : set (of chess, etc.), deck (of playing cards) **4 ~ de dames** : checkers **5 ~ de mots** : pun **6 en ~** : at stake **7 le ~** : gambling
jeudi [ʒødi] *nm* : Thursday
jeun [ʒœ̃] **à ~** *adv phr* : on an empty stom-ach
jeune [ʒœn] *adj* **1** : young **2** CADET : younger **3** RÉCENT : new, recent — **~** *nmf* **1** : young person **2 les ~s** : young people
jeûner [ʒøne] *vi* : fast — **jeûne** [ʒøn] *nm* : fast
jeunesse [ʒœnɛs] *nf* **1** : youth **2** : youthful-ness **3** JEUNES : young people
joaillier, -lière [ʒɔaje, -jɛr] *n* : jeweler — **joaillerie** [ʒɔajri] *nf* **1** : jewelry store **2** : jewelry
job [dʒɔb] *nm fam* : job
jockey [ʒɔkɛ] *nm* : jockey
jogging [dʒɔgiŋ] *nm* **1** : jogging **2** : sweat suit
joie [ʒwa] *nf* : joy
joindre [ʒwɛ̃dr] {50} *vt* **1** : join, link, com-bine **2** INCLURE : enclose, attach **3** CON-TACTER : reach, contact — **se joindre** *vr* **1** : join together **2 ~ à** : join in — **joint** [ʒwɛ̃] *nm* **1** : joint **2** : seal, washer
joker [ʒɔkɛr] *nm* : joker (in playing cards)
joli, -lie [ʒɔli] *adj* **1** BEAU : pretty, attractive **2** : nice — **joliment** [ʒɔlimɑ̃] *adv* **1** : nicely **2** *fam* : really, awfully
jonc [ʒɔ̃] *nm* **1** : reed, rush **2** : (wedding) band
joncher [ʒɔ̃ʃe] *vt* **~ de** : strew with, litter with
jonction [ʒɔ̃ksjɔ̃] *nf* : junction
jongler [ʒɔ̃gle] *vi* : juggle — **jongleur, -gleuse** [ʒɔ̃glœr, -gløz] *n* : juggler
jonquille [ʒɔ̃kij] *nf* : daffodil
joue [ʒu] *nf* : cheek
jouer [ʒwe] *vi* **1** : play **2** : act, perform **3** PARIER : gamble **4 faire ~** : flex — *vt* **1** : play **2** PARIER : bet, wager **3** : perform —

jouet [ʒwɛ] *nm* : toy, plaything — **joueur, joueuse** [ʒwœr, ʒwøz] *n* **1** : player **2** : gambler

joufflu, -flue [ʒufly] *adj* : chubby-cheeked

joug [ʒu] *nm* : yoke

jouir [ʒwir] *vi* ~ **de** : enjoy — **jouissance** [ʒwisɑ̃s] *nf* **1** : pleasure **2** : use, (legal) possession

jour [ʒur] *nm* **1** : day **2** : daylight, daytime **3** ASPECT : aspect, light **4** ~ **de l'An** : New Year's Day **5 de nos** ~**s** : nowadays **6 donner le** ~ **à** : give birth to **7 mettre à** ~ : update

journal [ʒurnal] *nm, pl* **-naux 1** : diary, journal **2** : newspaper **3** ~ **télévisé** : television news

journalier, -lière [ʒurnalje, -ljɛr] *adj* : daily — ~ *n* : day worker, laborer

journaliste [ʒurnalist] *nmf* : journalist — **journalisme** [ʒurnalism] *nm* : journalism

journée [ʒurne] *nf* **1** : day **2 toute la** ~ : all day long

jovial, -viale [ʒɔvjal] *adj, mpl* **-vials** or **-viaux** [-vjo] : jovial

joyau [ʒwajo] *nm, pl* **joyaux** : jewel, gem

joyeux, joyeuse [ʒwajø, -jøz] *adj* **1** : joyful, happy **2 Joyeux Noël!** : Merry Christmas!

jubiler [ʒybile] *vi* : rejoice, be jubilant — **jubilé** [ʒybile] *nm* : jubilee — **jubilation** [ʒybilasjɔ̃] *nf* : jubilation

jucher [ʒyʃe] *v* **se jucher** *vr* ~ **sur** : perch on

judaïque [ʒydaik] *adj* : Judaic — **judaïsme** [ʒydaism] *nm* : Judaism

judiciaire [ʒydisjɛr] *adj* : judicial — **judicieux, -cieuse** [ʒydisjø, -sjøz] *adj* : judicious

judo [ʒydo] *nm* : judo

juger [ʒyʒe] {17} *vt* **1** ÉVALUER : judge **2** CONSIDÉRER : think, consider **3** : try (in law) **4** ~ **de** : assess — **se juger** *vr* : consider oneself — **juge** [ʒyʒ] *nm* : judge — **jugement** [ʒyʒmɑ̃] *nm* **1** : judgment, opinion **2** VERDICT : verdict, sentence

juguler [ʒygyle] *vt* : stifle, suppress

juif, juive [ʒɥif, ʒɥiv] *adj* : Jewish

juillet [ʒɥijɛ] *nm* : July

juin [ʒɥɛ̃] *nm* : June

jumeau, -melle [ʒymo, -mɛl] *adj & n, mpl* **-meaux** : twin — **jumeler** [ʒymle] {8} *vt* : twin, couple — **jumelles** [ʒymɛl] *nfpl* : binoculars, field glasses

jument [ʒymɑ̃] *nf* : mare

jungle [ʒœ̃gl] *nf* : jungle

junior [ʒynjɔr] *adj & nmf* : junior

jupe [ʒyp] *nf* : skirt — **jupon** [ʒypɔ̃] *nm* : slip, petticoat

jurer [ʒyre] *vt* : swear, vow — *vi* **1** : swear, curse **2** ~ **avec** : clash with **3** ~ **de** : swear to — **juré, -rée** [ʒyre] *n* : juror

juridiction [ʒyridiksjɔ̃] *nf* : jurisdiction

juridique [ʒyridik] *adj* : legal

juriste [ʒyrist] *nmf* : legal expert, lawyer

juron [ʒyrɔ̃] *nm* : swearword

jury [ʒyri] *nm* : jury

jus [ʒy] *nms & pl* **1** : juice **2** : gravy

jusque [ʒyskə] (**jusqu'** [ʒysk] *before a vowel*) *prep* **1** : even **2** *or* **jusqu'à** : up to, as far as **3 jusqu'à** *or* **jusqu'en** : until **4 jusqu'à présent** : up to now **5 jusqu'où?** : how far?

justaucorps [ʒystokɔr] *nms & pl* : leotard

juste [ʒyst] *adj* **1** ÉQUITABLE : just, fair **2** EXACT : correct, accurate **3** SERRÉ : tight **4 au** ~ : exactly, precisely — ~ *adv* **1** : just, exactly **2** : in tune **3** *or* **tout** ~ : only just, barely — **justement** [ʒystəmɑ̃] *adv* **1** EXACTEMENT : exactly, precisely **2** ÉQUITABLEMENT : justly **3** : just now — **justesse** [ʒystɛs] *nf* **1** PRÉCISION : accuracy **2** : soundness (of reasoning, etc.) **3 de** ~ : just barely

justice [ʒystis] *nf* **1** ÉQUITÉ : fairness **2** : law, justice

justifier [ʒystifje] {96} *vt* : justify — *vi* ~ **de** : give proof of — **se justifier** *vr* : justify oneself — **justification** [ʒystifikasjɔ̃] *nf* : justification

juteux, -teuse [ʒytø, -tøz] *adj* : juicy

juvénile [ʒyvenil] *adj* : youthful, juvenile

juxtaposer [ʒykstapoze] *vt* : juxtapose

K

k [ka] *nm* : k, 11th letter of the alphabet

kaki [kaki] *adj* : khaki

kangourou [kɑ̃guru] *nm* : kangaroo

karaté [karate] *nm* : karate

kascher [kaʃɛr] *adj* : kosher

kayak *or* **kayac** [kajak] *nm* : kayak

kermesse [kɛrmɛs] *nf* : fair, bazaar

kérosène [kerozɛn] *nm* : kerosene

ketchup [kɛtʃœp] *nm* : ketchup

kidnapper [kidnape] *vt* : kidnap — **kidnappeur, -peuse** [kidnapœr, -pøz] *n* : kidnapper

kilo [kilo] *nm* : kilo — **kilogramme** [kilɔgram] *nm* : kilogram — **kilomètre** [kilɔmɛtr] *nm* : kilometer — **kilométrage** [kilɔmetraʒ] *nm* : distance in kilometers, mileage — **kilowatt** [kilɔwat] *nm* : kilowatt
kimono [kimɔno] *nm* : kimono
kinésithérapie [kineziterapi] *nf* : physical therapy

kiosque [kjɔsk] *nm* **1** : kiosk, stall **2** ~ **à musique** : bandstand
kiwi [kiwi] *nm* : kiwi
klaxon [klaksɔn] *nm* : horn — **klaxonner** [klaksɔne] *vi* : honk
kyrielle [kirjɛl] *nf* **une** ~ **de** : a string of
kyste [kist] *nm* : cyst

L

l [ɛl] *nm* : l, 12th letter of the alphabet
l' *pron & art* → **le**
la *pron & art* → **le**
là [la] *adv* **1** (*indicating a place*) : there, here **2** : then **3** (*indicating a situation or a certain point*) : when **4 de** ~ : hence **5** ~ **où** : where **6 par** ~ : over there, that way — **là–bas** [laba] *adv* : over there
label [labɛl] *nm* : label
labeur [labœr] *nm* : toil, labor
laboratoire [labɔratwar] *nm* : laboratory
laborieux, -rieuse [labɔrjø, -rjøz] *adj* **1** : laborious **2** INDUSTRIEUX : hardworking
labourer [labure] *vt* : plow — **labour** [labur] *nm* : plowing
labyrinthe [labirɛ̃t] *nm* : labyrinth, maze
lac [lak] *nm* : lake
lacer [lase] {6} *vt* : lace up
lacérer [lasere] {87} *vt* : tear up, shred
lacet [lasɛ] *nm* **1** : shoelace **2** : sharp bend (in a road)
lâcher [laʃe] *vt* **1** RELÂCHER : loosen **2** LIBÉRER : release **3** : let out (a word, etc.) **4** *fam* : drop (someone) — *vi* : give way — **lâche** [laʃ] *adj* **1** : loose, slack **2** POLTRON : cowardly — ~ *nmf* : coward — **lâcheté** [laʃte] *nf* : cowardice
laconique [lakɔnik] *adj* : laconic
lacrymogène [lakrimɔʒɛn] *adj* **gaz** ~ : tear gas
lacune [lakyn] *nf* : gap
là–dedans [laddɑ̃] *adv* : in here, in there
là–dessous [ladsu] *adv* : under here, under there
là–dessus [ladsy] *adv* **1** : on here, on there **2 il n'y a aucun doute** ~ : there's no doubt about it
ladite → **ledit**
lagune [lagyn] *nf* : lagoon
là–haut [lao] *adv* **1** : up there **2** : upstairs
laïc [laik] *nm* **les** ~**s** : the laity
laid, laide [lɛ, lɛd] *adj* **1** : ugly **2** : despica-

ble (of an action) — **laideur** [lɛdœr] *nf* : ugliness
laine [lɛn] *nf* : wool — **lainage** [lɛnaʒ] *nm* **1** : woolen fabric **2** : woolen garment
laïque [laik] *adj* : lay, secular — ~ *nmf* : layman, laywoman
laisse [lɛs] *nf* : lead, leash
laisser [lese] *vt* : leave — *v aux* **1** : let, allow **2** ~ **faire** : not interfere — **se laisser** *vr* **1** : allow oneself **2** ~ **aller** : let oneself go — **laisser–aller** [lɛseale] *nms & pl* : carelessness — **laissez–passer** [lɛsepase] *nms & pl* : pass, permit
lait [lɛ] *nm* : milk — **laiterie** [lɛtri] *nf* **1** : dairy industry **2** : dairy — **laiteux, -teuse** [lɛtø, -tøz] *adj* : milky — **laitier, -tière** [lɛtje, -tjɛr] *adj* : dairy — ~ *n* **1** : milkman **2** : dairyman
laiton [lɛtɔ̃] *nm* : brass
laitue [lɛty] *nf* : lettuce
lambeau [lɑ̃bo] *nm*, *pl* **-beaux 1** : rag, scrap **2 en** ~**x** : in tatters
lambiner [lɑ̃bine] *vi fam* : dawdle
lambris [lɑ̃bri] *nms & pl* : paneling
lame [lam] *nf* **1** : strip, slat **2** ~ **de razoir** : razor blade — **lamelle** [lamɛl] *nf* : thin strip
lamenter [lamɑ̃te] *v* **se lamenter** *vr* : lament — **lamentable** [lamɑ̃tabl] *adj* **1** : deplorable **2** PITOYABLE : pitiful, pathetic
lampe [lɑ̃p] *nf* **1** : lamp **2** ~ **de poche** : flashlight — **lampadaire** [lɑ̃padɛr] *nm* **1** : floor lamp **2** : streetlight — **lampion** [lɑ̃pjɔ̃] *nm* : Chinese lantern
lance [lɑ̃s] *nf* **1** : spear, lance **2** *or* ~ **à eau** : hose
lancée [lɑ̃se] *nf* **1** : momentum **2 continuer sur sa** ~ : keep going
lancer [lɑ̃se] {6} *vt* **1** : throw, hurl **2** : launch **3** ÉMETTRE : issue, give out **4** : start up (a motor) — **se lancer** *vr* ~ **dans** : launch into — ~ *nm* : throw, throwing — **lancement** [lɑ̃smɑ̃] *nm* **1** : throwing **2** : launch-

ing — **lance–pierres** [lãspjɛr] *nms & pl* : slingshot

lanciner [lãsine] *vi* : throb — *vt* : haunt, obsess — **lancinant, -nante** [lãsinã, -nãt] *adj* : shooting, throbbing

landau [lãdo] *nm France* : baby carriage

lande [lãd] *nf* : moor, heath

langage [lãgaʒ] *nm* : language

lange [lãʒ] *nm* : baby blanket

langouste [lãgust] *nf* : crayfish — **langoustine** [lãgustin] *nf* : prawn

langue [lãg] *nf* **1** : tongue **2** : language — **languette** [lãgɛt] *nf* **1** : tongue (of a shoe) **2** : strip

langueur [lãgœr] *nf* : languor, lethargy — **languir** [lãgir] *vi* **1** : languish, pine **2** : flag (of conversation, etc.) — **languissant, -sante** [lãgisã, -sãt] *adj* : languid, listless

lanière [lanjɛr] *nf* : strap, lash, thong

lanterne [lãtɛrn] *nf* **1** LAMPE : lantern **2** : parking light

laper [lape] *vt* : lap up

lapider [lapide] *vt* : stone

lapin, -pine [lapɛ̃, -pin] *n* **1** : rabbit **2 poser un ~ à qqn** : stand s.o. up

laps [laps] *nms & pl* : lapse (of time) — **lapsus** [lapsys] *nms & pl* : slip, error

laque [lak] *nf* **1** : lacquer **2** : hair spray

laquelle → **lequel**

larcin [larsɛ̃] *nm* : petty theft

lard [lar] *nm* **1** : fat, lard **2** : bacon

large [larʒ] *adj* **1** : wide, broad **2** CONSIDÉRABLE : extensive **3** AMPLE : loose-fitting **4** GÉNÉREUX : generous — **~** *nm* **1 de ~** : wide, in width **2 le ~** : the open sea — **~** *adv* : on a large scale, generously — **largement** [larʒəmã] *adv* **1** : widely **2** DE BEAUCOUP : greatly, by far **3** GÉNÉREUSEMENT : generously **4** AU MOINS : easily — **largesse** [larʒɛs] *nf* : generosity — **largeur** [larʒœr] *nf* **1** : width, breadth **2 ~ d'esprit** : broad-mindedness

larguer [large] *vt* **1** : release, drop **2** *fam* : ditch, get rid of

larme [larm] *nf* **1** : tear **2** *fam* : drop, small quantity — **larmoyant, -moyante** [larmwajã, -mwajãt] *adj* : tearful

larve [larv] *nf* : larva

larynx [larɛ̃ks] *nms & pl* : larynx — **laryngite** [larɛ̃ʒit] *nf* : laryngitis

las, lasse [la, las] *adj* : weary

lasagne [lazaɲ] *nf* : lasagna

laser [lazɛr] *nm* : laser

lasser [lase] *vt* **1** : weary, tire out **2** ENNUYER : bore — **se lasser** *vr* **~ de** : grow weary of — **lassitude** [lasityd] *nf* : weariness

latent, -tente [latã, -tãt] *adj* : latent

latéral, -rale [lateral] *adj, mpl* **-raux** [-ro] : side, lateral

latex [latɛks] *nms & pl* : latex

latin, -tine [latɛ̃, -tin] *adj* : Latin — **latin** *nm* : Latin (language)

latitude [latityd] *nf* : latitude

latte [lat] *nf* : lath, floorboard

lauréat, -réate [lɔrea, -reat] *n* : prizewinner

laurier [lɔrje] *nm* **1** : laurel **2 feuille de ~** : bay leaf

lavable [lavabl] *adj* : washable

lavabo [lavabo] *nm* **1** : (bathroom) sink **2 ~s** *nmpl France* : toilets

lavage [lavaʒ] *nm* **1** : wash, washing **2 ~ de cerveau** : brainwashing

lavande [lavãd] *nf* : lavender

lave [lav] *nf* : lava

laver [lave] *vt* : wash — **se laver** *vr* **1** : wash oneself **2 ~ les mains** : wash one's hands — **lave-linge** [lavlɛ̃ʒ] *nms & pl France* : washing machine — **laverie** [lavri] *nf* : self-service laundry — **lavette** [lavɛt] *nf* : dishcloth — **laveur, -veuse** [lavœr, -vøz] *n* : washer, cleaner — **lave-vaisselle** [lavvɛsɛl] *nms & pl* : dishwasher — **lavoir** [lavwar] *nm Can* : self-service laundry

laxatif [laksatif] *nm* : laxative

le, la [lə, la] (**l'** [l] *before a vowel or mute h*) *pron, pl* **les** [le] : him, her, it, them — **~** *art* **1** : the **2** : a, an, per

lécher [leʃe] {87} *vt* : lick, lap — **se lécher** *vr* : lick (one's fingers, etc.) — **lèche–vitrines** [lɛʃvitrin] *nms & pl* **faire du ~** : window-shop

leçon [ləsɔ̃] *nf* : lesson

lecteur, -trice [lɛktœr, -tris] *n* : reader — **lecteur** *nm* **1 ~ de disquettes** : disk drive **2 ~ laser** : CD player — **lecture** [lɛktyr] *nf* : reading

ledit, ladite [lədi, ladit] *adj, pl* **lesdits, lesdites** [ledi, ledit] : the aforesaid

légal, -gale [legal] *adj, mpl* **-gaux** [lego] : legal, lawful — **légaliser** [legalize] *vt* : legalize — **légalité** [legalite] *nf* : lawfulness

légende [leʒãd] *nf* **1** : legend, tale **2** : caption (of an illustration) — **légendaire** [leʒãdɛr] *adj* : legendary

léger, -gère [leʒe, -ʒɛr] *adj* **1** : light **2** FAIBLE : slight, faint **3** IMPRUDENT : thoughtless **4 à la légère** : rashly — **légèrement** [leʒɛrmã] *adv* **1** : lightly **2** : slightly — **légèreté** [leʒɛrte] *nf* **1** : lightness **2** : thoughtlessness

légiférer [leʒifere] {87} *vi* : legislate

légion [leʒjɔ̃] *nf* : legion

législation [leʒislasjɔ̃] *nf* : legislation — **législateur, -trice** [leʒislatœr, -tris] *n* : legislator, lawmaker — **législatif, -tive** [leʒislatif, -tiv] *adj* : legislative — **législatif** *nm* : legislature — **législature** [leʒislatyr] *nf* : term (of office)

légitime [leʒitim] *adj* **1** LÉGAL : lawful **2**

: rightful, legitimate **3 ~ défense** : self-defense

legs [lɛg] *nms & pl* : legacy — **léguer** [lege] {87} *vt* **1** : bequeath **2** TRANSMETTRE : pass on

légume [legym] *nm* : vegetable

lendemain [lãdmɛ̃] *nm* **1** : next day **2 au ~ de** : just after, following **3 du jour au ~** : in a very short time **4 le ~ matin** : the next morning

lent, lente [lã, lãt] *adj* : slow — **lenteur** [lãtœr] *nf* : slowness

lentille [lãtij] *nf* **1** : lentil **2** : (optical) lens

léopard [leɔpar] *nm* : leopard

lèpre [lɛpr] *nf* : leprosy

lequel, laquelle [ləkɛl, lakɛl] *pron, pl* **lesquels, lesquelles** [lekɛl] (*with* **à** *and* **de** *contracted to* **auquel, auxquels, aux-quelles; duquel, desquels, desquelles**) **1** : which **2** : who, whom **3 lequel préférez-vous?** : which one do you prefer?

les → le

lesbienne [lɛsbjɛn] *nf* : lesbian

lesdits, lesdites → ledit

léser [leze] {87} *vt* **1** : wrong **2** BLESSER : injure

lésiner [lezine] *vi* **~ sur** : skimp on

lésion [lezjɔ̃] *nf* : lesion

lesquels, lesquelles → lequel

lessive [lɛsiv] *nf* **1** LAVAGE : washing, wash **2** : laundry detergent — **lessiver** [lɛsive] *vt* **1** : wash, scrub **2 être lessivé** *fam* : be exhausted

lest [lɛst] *nm* : ballast

leste [lɛst] *adj* : nimble

léthargie [letarʒi] *nf* : lethargy — **léthargique** [letarʒik] *adj* : lethargic

lettre [lɛtr] *nf* **1** : letter (of the alphabet) **2** CORRESPONDANCE : letter **3 ~s** *nfpl* : arts, humanities **4 à la ~** : exactly **5 en toutes ~s** : in full — **lettré, -trée** [lɛtre] *adj* : well-read

leucémie [løsemi] *nf* : leukemia

leur [lœr] *adj, pl* **leurs** : their — **~** *pron* **1** : (to) them **2 le ~, la ~, les ~s** : theirs

leurre [lœr] *nm* **1** : (fishing) lure **2** ILLUSION : illusion, deception — **leurrer** [lœre] *vt* : deceive, delude — **se leurrer** *vr* : delude oneself

levain [ləvɛ̃] *nm* **1** : leaven **2 sans ~** : unleavened

lever [ləve] {52} *vt* **1** : lift **2** : raise **3** : close (a meeting), lift (a ban) — *vi* **1** : come up (of plants) **2** : rise (in cooking) — **se lever** *vr* **1** : get up **2** : stand up **3** : rise (of the sun) **4 le jour se lève** : day is breaking — **~** *nm* **1** : rising, rise **2 ~ du soleil** : sunrise — **levée** [ləve] *nf* **1** SUPPRESSION : lifting **2** : collection (of mail, etc.)

levier [ləvje] *nm* **1** : lever **2 ~ de vitesse** : gearshift

lèvre [lɛvr] *nf* : lip

lévrier [levrije] *nm* : greyhound

levure [ləvyr] *nf* **1** : yeast **2 ~ chimique** : baking powder

lexique [lɛksik] *nm* **1** : glossary, lexicon **2** VOCABULAIRE : vocabulary

lézard [lezar] *nm* : lizard

lézarder [lezarde] *v* **se lézarder** *vr* : crack

liaison [ljɛzɔ̃] *nf* : liaison

liant, liante [ljã, ljãt] *adj* : sociable

liasse [ljas] *nf* : bundle, wad

libanais, -naise [libanɛ, -nɛz] *adj* : Lebanese

libeller [libele] *vt* : draw up (a document), make out (a check)

libellule [libelyl] *nf* : dragonfly

libéral, -rale [liberal] *adj & n, mpl* **-raux** [-ro] : liberal

libérer [libere] {87} *vt* : free, release, liberate — **se libérer** *vr* : free oneself — **libération** [liberasjɔ̃] *nf* : liberation, freeing — **libéré, -rée** [libere] *adj* **~ de** : free from

liberté [libɛrte] *nf* **1** : freedom, liberty **2 en ~ conditionnelle** : on probation **3 mettre en ~** : set free

libido [libido] *nf* : libido

libraire [librɛr] *nmf* : bookseller — **librairie** [libreri] *nf* : bookstore

libre [libr] *adj* **1** : free **2** DISPONIBLE : available, unoccupied **3** DÉGAGÉ : clear, free **4 ~ arbitre** : free will — **libre–échange** [librefɑ̃ʒ] *nm, pl* **libres–échanges** [librəzefɑ̃ʒ] : free trade — **librement** [librəmã] *adv* : freely — **libre–service** [librəsɛrvis] *nm, pl* **libres–services** : self-service

licence [lisãs] *nf* **1** : (bachelor's) degree **2** : license, permit **3 prendre des ~s avec** : take liberties with — **licencié, -ciée** [lisãsje] *n* : (university) graduate

licencier [lisãsje] {96} *vt* : lay off, dismiss — **licenciement** [lisãsimã] *nm* : layoff, dismissal

lichen [likɛn] *nm* : lichen

licite [lisit] *adj* : lawful

lie [li] *nf* : sediment, dregs

liège [ljɛʒ] *nm* : cork

lien [ljɛ̃] *nm* **1** ATTACHE : bond, strap **2** RAPPORT : link **3** RELATION : tie, relationship — **lier** [lje] {96} *vt* **1** : bind, tie up **2** RELIER : link up **3** : strike up (a friendship, etc.) **4** UNIR : unite — **se lier** *vr* **~ avec** : become friends with

lierre [ljɛr] *nm* : ivy

liesse [ljɛs] *nf* : jubilation

lieu [ljø] *nm, pl* **lieux 1** ENDROIT : place **2 au ~ de** : instead of **3 avoir ~** : take place **4 avoir ~ de** : have reason to **5 en premier ~** : in the first place **6 tenir ~ de** : serve as **7 ~x** *nmpl* : premises — **lieu–dit** *or*

lieudit [ljødi] *nm, pl* **lieux–dits** *or* **lieudits** : locality

lieutenant [ljøtnɑ̃] *nm* : lieutenant

lièvre [ljɛvr] *nm* : hare

ligament [ligamɑ̃] *nm* : ligament

ligne [liɲ] *nf* **1** : line **2** PARCOURS : route **3 en ~** : online (in computers) **4 ~ droite** : beeline — **lignée** [liɲe] *nf* **1** : line, lineage **2** DESCENDANTS : descendants *pl*

ligoter [ligɔte] *vt* : tie up, bind

ligue [lig] *nf* : league, alliance — **liguer** [lige] *v* **se liguer** *vr* **1** : join forces **2 ~ contre** : conspire against

lilas [lila] *nms & pl* : lilac

limace [limas] *nf* : slug (mollusk)

lime [lim] *nf* **1** : file **2 ~ à ongles** : nail file — **limer** [lime] *vt* : file — **se limer** *vr* **~ les ongles** : file one's nails

limiter [limite] *vt* : limit — **limitation** [limitasjɔ̃] *nf* : limitation — **limite** [limit] *adj* **1 cas ~** : borderline case **2 date ~** : deadline **3 vitesse ~** : speed limit — **~** *nf* **1** : limit **2** : border, boundary

limitrophe [limitrɔf] *adj* : bordering, adjacent

limoger [limɔʒe] {17} *vt* : dismiss

limon [limɔ̃] *nm* : silt

limonade [limɔnad] *nf* : lemonade

limousine [limuzin] *nf* : limousine

limpide [lɛ̃pid] *adj* : (crystal) clear — **limpidité** [lɛ̃pidite] *nf* : clearness

lin [lɛ̃] *nm* **1** : flax **2** : linen

linceul [lɛ̃sœl] *nm* : shroud

linéaire [lineɛr] *adj* : linear

linge [lɛ̃ʒ] *nm* **1** : (household) linen **2** LESSIVE : wash, washing **3** CHIFFON : cloth **4** *or* **~ de corps** : underwear **5** *Can fam* : clothes *pl*, clothing — **lingerie** [lɛ̃ʒri] *nf* **1** : lingerie **2** *Can* : linen closet

lingot [lɛ̃go] *nm* : ingot

linguistique [lɛ̃gɥistik] *adj* : linguistic — **~** *nf* : linguistics — **linguiste** [lɛ̃gɥist] *nmf* : linguist

linoléum [linɔleɔm] *nm* : linoleum

lion, lionne [ljɔ̃, ljɔn] *n* : lion, lioness *f* — **lionceau** [ljɔ̃so] *nm, pl* **-ceaux** : lion cub

liqueur [likœr] *nf* **1** : liqueur **2** *Can* : soft drink

liquide [likid] *adj* : liquid — **~** *nm* **1** : liquid **2** ARGENT : cash — **liquidation** [likidasjɔ̃] *nf* **1** : liquidation **2** : clearance sale — **liquider** [likide] *vt* **1** : liquidate **2** : eliminate — **liquidités** [likidite] *nfpl* : liquid assets

lire [lir] {51} *vt* : read

lis *or* **lys** [lis] *nms & pl* : lily

lisible [lizibl] *adj* : legible — **lisibilité** [-zibilite] *nf* : legibility

lisière [lizjɛr] *nf* : edge, outskirts *pl*

lisse [lis] *adj* : smooth, sleek

liste [list] *nf* : list

lit [li] *nm* **1** : bed **2 ~ de camp** : cot — **literie** [litri] *nf* : bedding — **litière** [litjɛr] *nf* : litter

litige [litiʒ] *nm* : dispute

litre [litr] *nm* : liter

littérature [literatyr] *nf* : literature — **littéraire** [literer] *adj* : literary — **littéral, -rale** [literal] *adj, mpl* **-raux** [-ro] : literal

littoral [litɔral] *nm* : coast(line) — **~** *adj* : coastal

liturgie [lityrʒi] *nf* : liturgy — **liturgique** [lityrʒik] *adj* : liturgical

livide [livid] *adj* : pallid, pale

livraison [livrɛzɔ̃] *nf* : delivery

livre[1] [livr] *nm* **1** : book **2 ~ de poche** : paperback **3 ~ de recettes** : cookbook

livre[2] *nf* **1** : pound **2** *or* **~ sterling** : pound (monetary unit)

livrer [livre] *vt* **1** : deliver **2** REMETTRE : hand over — **se livrer** *vr* **1 ~ à** : devote oneself to **2 ~ à** : surrender to **3 ~ à** : confide in

livret [livre] *nm* : booklet

livreur, -vreuse [livrœr, -vrøz] *n* : deliveryman *m*, delivery woman *f*

lobe [lɔb] *nm* : lobe

local, -cale [lɔkal] *adj, mpl* **-caux** [lɔko] : local — **local** *nm, pl* **-caux** : place, premises *pl* — **localiser** [lɔkalize] *vt* **1** SITUER : locate **2** LIMITER : localize — **localité** [lɔkalite] *nf* : locality

location [lɔkasjɔ̃] *nf* **1** : renting, leasing **2** : rented property — **locataire** [lɔkater] *nmf* : tenant

locomotive [lɔkɔmɔtiv] *nf* : locomotive, engine

locution [lɔkysjɔ̃] *nf* : phrase, idiom

loge [lɔʒ] *nf* **1** : dressing room **2** : box (at the theater) **3** : lodge

loger [lɔʒe] {17} *vt* **1** : lodge **2** CONTENIR : accommodate — **se loger** *vr* **1** : find accommodations **2 ~ dans** : lodge itself in — **logement** [lɔʒmɑ̃] *nm* **1** : accommodation **2** : apartment **3** HABITAT : housing

logiciel [lɔʒisjɛl] *nm* : software

logique [lɔʒik] *adj* : logical — **~** *nf* : logic

logis [lɔʒi] *nms & pl* : dwelling, abode

logistique [lɔʒistik] *nf* : logistics

loi [lwa] *nf* : law

loin [lwɛ̃] *adv* **1** : far **2** : a long time ago **3 ~ de** : far from **4 plus ~** : further — **~** *nm* **1 au ~** : in the distance **2 de ~** : from a distance **3 de ~** : by far — **lointain, -taine** [lwɛ̃tɛ̃, -tɛn] *adj* : distant — **lointain** *nm* : distance

loisir [lwazir] *nm* **1** : leisure **2 ~s** *nmpl* : leisure activities

long, longue [lɔ̃, lɔ̃g] *adj* : long — **long** [lɔ̃] *adv* : much, a lot — **~** *nm* **1** : length **2 de**

~ : long, in length **3 le ~ de** : along — **à la longue** *adv phr* : in the long run
longer [lɔ̃ʒe] {17} *vt* **1** : walk along, follow **2** LIMITER : border
longévité [lɔ̃ʒevite] *nf* : longevity
longitude [lɔ̃ʒityd] *nf* : longitude
longtemps [lɔ̃tɑ̃] *adv* **1** : a long time **2 avant ~** : before long
longue → long — **longuement** [lɔ̃gmɑ̃] *adv* **1** : for a long time **2** : at length — **longueur** [lɔ̃gœr] *nf* **1** : length **2 à ~ de journée** : all day long **3 ~ d'onde** : wavelength **4 ~s** *nfpl* : tedious parts (of a film, etc.) — **longue–vue** [lɔ̃gvy] *nf, pl* **longues–vues** : telescope
lopin [lɔpɛ̃] *nm* **~ de terre** : plot of land
loquace [lɔkas] *adj* : talkative
loque [lɔk] *nf* **1** : wreck (person) **2 ~s** *nfpl* : rags
loquet [lɔkɛ] *nm* : latch
lorgner [lɔrɲe] *vt* : eye, ogle
lors [lɔr] *adv* **~ de 1** : at the time of **2** : during
lorsque [lɔrskə] (**lorsqu'** [lɔrsk] *before a vowel or mute h*) *conj* : when
losange [lɔzɑ̃ʒ] *nm* **1** : lozenge, diamond shape **2** *Can* : (baseball) diamond
lot [lo] *nm* **1** SORT : fate, lot **2** PRIX : prize **3** PART : share
loterie [lɔtri] *nf* : lottery
lotion [lɔsjɔ̃] *nf* : lotion
lotissement [lɔtismɑ̃] *nm* : (housing) development
louange [lwɑ̃ʒ] *nf* : praise — **louable** [lwabl] *adj* : praiseworthy
louche[1] [luʃ] *nf* : ladle
louche[2] *adj* : shady, suspicious — **loucher** [luʃe] *vi* **1** : be cross-eyed **2** : squint
louer[1] [lwe] *vt* : praise — **se louer** *vr* **~ de** : be satisfied about
louer[2] *vt* : rent, lease — **se louer** *vr* : be for rent
loufoque [lufɔk] *adj fam* : crazy, zany
loup [lu] *nm* : wolf
loupe [lup] *nf* : magnifying glass
louper [lupe] *vt fam* **1** : bungle, mess up **2** : miss (a train, etc.)
lourd, lourde [lur, lurd] *adj* : heavy — **lourd** *adv* **peser ~** : be heavy — **lourdement** [lurdəmɑ̃] *adv* : heavily — **lourdeur** [lurdœr] *nf* : heaviness
loutre [lutr] *nf* : otter
louvoyer [luvwaje] {58} *vi* : hedge, equivocate
loyal, loyale [lwajal] *adj, mpl* **loyaux** [lwajo] **1** : loyal **2** HONNÊTE : fair — **loyauté** [lwajote] *nf* **1** : loyalty **2** : fairness
loyer [lwaje] *nm* : rent
lu [ly] *pp* → **lire**
lubie [lybi] *nf* : whim

lubrifier [lybrifje] {96} *vt* : lubricate — **lubrifiant** [lybrifjɑ̃] *nm* : lubricant
lucarne [lykarn] *nf* : skylight
lucide [lysid] *adj* : lucid — **lucidité** [lysidite] *nf* : lucidity
lucratif, -tive [lykratif, -tiv] *adj* : lucrative, profitable
ludique [lydik] *adj* : play, playing
lueur [lɥœr] *nf* **1** : faint light **2** : glimmer (of hope, etc.)
luge [lyʒ] *nf* : sled
lugubre [lygybr] *adj* : gloomy, dismal
lui [lɥi] *pron* **1** (*used as indirect object*) : (to) him, (to) her, (to) it **2** (*used as object of a preposition*) : him, it **3** (*used as subject or for emphasis*) : he **4** (*used as a reflexive pronoun*) : himself — **lui–même** [lɥimɛm] *pron* : himself, itself
luire [lɥir] {49} *vi* : shine, gleam — **luisant, -sante** [lɥizɑ̃, -zɑ̃t] *adj* : shining, gleaming
lumière [lymjɛr] *nf* : light — **luminaire** [lyminɛr] *nm* : lamp, light — **lumineux, -neuse** [lyminø, -nøz] *adj* **1** : luminous **2** RADIEUX : radiant, bright
lunaire [lynɛr] *adj* : lunar, moon
lunatique [lynatik] *adj* : whimsical
lunch [lœ̃ʃ] *nm, pl* **lunchs** or **lunches 1** BUFFET : buffet **2** *Can* : lunch
lundi [lœ̃di] *nm* : Monday
lune [lyn] *nf* **1** : moon **2 ~ de miel** : honeymoon
lunette [lynɛt] *nf* **1** : telescope **2 ~ arrière** : rear window (of an automobile) **3 ~s** *nfpl* : glasses **4 ~s bifocales** : bifocals
lurette [lyrɛt] *nf* **il y a belle ~** *fam* : ages ago
lustre [lystr] *nm* **1** : luster, sheen **2** : chandelier — **lustré, -trée** [lystre] *adj* : shiny, glossy
luth [lyt] *nm* : lute
lutin [lytɛ̃] *nm* : imp, goblin
lutrin [lytrɛ̃] *nm* : lectern
lutte [lyt] *nf* **1** : fight, struggle **2** : wrestling — **lutter** [lyte] *vi* **1** SE BATTRE : fight, struggle **2** : wrestle — **lutteur, -teuse** [lytœr, -tøz] *n* **1** : fighter **2** : wrestler
luxation [lyksasjɔ̃] *nf* : dislocation (of a joint)
luxe [lyks] *nm* : luxury
luxer [lykse] *v* **se luxer** *vr* : dislocate (one's shoulder, etc.)
luxueux, -xueuse [lyksɥø, -sɥøz] *adj* : luxurious
luxure [lyksyr] *nf* : lust — **luxurieux, -rieuse** [lyksyrjø, -rjøz] *adj* : lustful
luzerne [lyzɛrn] *nf* : alfalfa
lycée [lise] *nm France* : high school — **lycéen, -céenne** [liseɛ̃, -seɛn] *n France* : high school student
lynx [lɛ̃ks] *nm* : lynx
lyrique [lirik] *adj* : lyric(al)
lys → lis

M

m [ɛm] *nm* : m, 13th letter of the alphabet
ma → **mon**
macabre [makabr] *adj* : macabre
macaron [makarɔ̃] *nm* **1** : macaroon **2** IN-SIGNE : badge, sticker
macaronis [makarɔni] *nmpl* : macaroni
macédoine [masedwan] *nf* : mixture (of fruits or vegetables)
macérer [masere] {87} *v* : steep, soak
mâcher [maʃe] *vt* : chew
machin [maʃɛ̃] *nm fam* : thingamajig, thing
machine [maʃin] *nf* **1** : machine **2** : engine (of a ship, a train, etc.) **3** ~ **à écrire** : type-writer **4** ~ **à laver** : washing machine —
machiniste [maʃinist] *nmf* : (bus) driver
mâchoire [maʃwar] *nf* : jaw
mâchonner [maʃɔne] *vt* : chew
maçon [masɔ̃] *nm* : bricklayer, mason —
maçonnerie [masɔnri] *nf* : masonry
maculer [makyle] *vt* : stain
madame [madam] *nf, pl* **mesdames** [medam] **1** : Mrs., Ms., Madam **2** : lady —
mademoiselle [madmwazɛl] *nf, pl* **mesde-moiselles** [medmwazɛl] **1** : Miss, Ms. **2** : young lady
mafia *or* **maffia** [mafja] *nf* : Mafia
magasin [magazɛ̃] *nm* **1** : shop, store **2** ENTREPÔT : warehouse **3** : magazine (of a gun or camera) **4 grand** ~ : department store
magazine [magazin] *nm* REVUE : magazine
magie [maʒi] *nf* : magic — **magicien, -cienne** [maʒisjɛ̃, -sjɛn] *n* : magician — **magique** [maʒik] *adj* : magic(al)
magistral, -trale [maʒistral] *adj, mpl* **-traux** [-tro] **1** : brilliant, masterly **2 cours magistral** : lecture
magistrat [maʒistra] *nm* : magistrate
magnanime [mananim] *adj* : magnanimous
magnat [mana] *nm* : magnate, tycoon
magnétique [manetik] *adj* : magnetic — **magnétiser** [manetize] *vt* : magnetize — **magnétisme** [manetism] *nm* : magnetism
magnétophone [manetɔfɔn] *nm* : tape recorder
magnétoscope [manetɔskɔp] *nm* : video-cassette recorder, VCR
magnifique [manifik] *adj* : magnificent
magnolia [manɔlja] *nm* : magnolia
mai [mɛ] *nm* : May
maigre [mɛgr] *adj* **1** MINCE : thin **2** INSUF-FISANT : meager **3** : low-fat, lean (of meat) — **maigrir** [megrir] *vi* : lose weight, reduce
maille [maj] *nf* **1** : stitch (in knitting) **2** : mesh (of a net)

maillot [majo] *nm* **1** : jersey **2** ~ **de bain** : bathing suit
main [mɛ̃] *nf* **1** : hand **2** SAVOIR-FAIRE : know-how, skill **3 de première** ~ : first-hand **4 donner un coup de** ~ **à** : lend a helping hand to **5** ~ **courante** : handrail — **main–d'œuvre** [mɛ̃dœvr] *nf, pl* **mains–d'œuvre** : manpower, workforce
maint, mainte [mɛ̃, mɛ̃t] *adj* : many a
maintenant [mɛ̃tnɑ̃] *adv* **1** : now **2** : nowa-days
maintenir [mɛ̃tnir] {92} *vt* **1** : maintain **2** SOUTENIR : support — **se maintenir** *vr* : re-main, persist — **maintien** [mɛ̃tjɛ̃] *nm* **1** : maintaining, maintenance **2** PORT : bear-ing, deportment
maire, mairesse [mɛr, mɛrɛs] *n* : mayor — **mairie** [meri] *nf* : town hall, city hall
mais [mɛ] *conj* **1** : but **2** ~ **oui** : certainly, of course
maïs [mais] *nm* : corn, maize
maison [mɛzɔ̃] *nf* **1** : house, home **2** SO-CIÉTÉ : firm — ~ *adj* **1** : homemade **2** : in-house (of an employee) — **maisonnée** [mɛzɔne] *nf* : household
maître, -tresse [mɛtr, -trɛs] *n* **1** : master, mistress **2** ~ **d'école** : schoolteacher — ~ *adj* : main, key — **maître** [mɛtr] *nm* **1** : master (of a pet, etc.) **2** EXPERT : expert — **maîtrise** [metriz] *nf* **1** : skill, mastery **2** : master's degree **3** ~ **de soi** : self-control — **maîtriser** [metrize] *vt* **1** : master **2** CON-TENIR : control, restrain
majesté [maʒeste] *nf* : majesty — **ma-jestueux, -tueuse** [maʒɛstɥø, -tɥøz] *adj* : majestic
majeur, -jeure [maʒœr] *adj* **1** : major, main **2** : of age (in law) — **majeur** *nm* : middle finger — **majorité** [maʒɔrite] *nf* : majority
majuscule [maʒyskyl] *adj* : capital, upper-case — ~ *nf* : capital letter
mal [mal] *adv* **1** : poorly, badly **2** INCOR-RECTEMENT : wrongly **3 aller** ~ : be un-well — ~ *adj* **1** : wrong **2** MAUVAIS : bad — ~ *nm, pl* **maux** [mo] **1** DOULEUR : pain **2** MALADIE : sickness **3** DOMMAGE : harm **4** : evil **5** PEINE : trouble, difficulty
malade [malad] *adj* : sick, ill — ~ *nmf* : sick person, patient — **maladie** [maladi] *nf* : illness, disease — **maladif, -dive** [ma-ladif, -div] *adj* : sickly
maladresse [maladrɛs] *nf* **1** : clumsiness **2** BÉVUE : blunder — **maladroit, -droite** [maladrwa, -drwat] *adj* : clumsy, awkward

malaise [malɛz] *nm* **1** : dizziness **2** GÊNE : uneasiness, malaise

malaxer [malakse] *vt* **1** : knead **2** MÉLANGER : mix

malchance [malʃɑ̃s] *nf* : bad luck, misfortune — **malchanceux, -ceuse** [malʃɑ̃sø, -søz] *adj* : unfortunate

mâle [mal] *adj* **1** : male **2** : manly — ~ *nm* : male

malédiction [malediksjɔ̃] *nf* : curse

maléfique [malefik] *adj* : evil

malencontreux, -treuse [malɑ̃kɔ̃trø, -trøz] *adj* : unfortunate, untoward

malentendu [malɑ̃tɑ̃dy] *nm* : misunderstanding

malfaçon [malfasɔ̃] *nf* : fault, defect

malfaisant, -sante [malfəzɑ̃, -zɑ̃t] *adj* : evil, harmful — **malfaiteur** [malfɛtœr] *nm* : criminal

malgré [malgre] *prep* **1** : in spite of, despite **2** ~ **tout** : nevertheless, even so

malheur [malœr] *nm* : misfortune — **malheureux, -reuse** [malœrø, -røz] *adj* **1** : unhappy **2** MALCHANCEUX : unfortunate — ~ *n* : unfortunate person — **malheureusement** [malœrøzmɑ̃] *adv* : unfortunately

malhonnête [malɔnɛt] *adj* : dishonest — **malhonnêteté** [malɔnɛtte] *nf* : dishonesty

malice [malis] *nf* : mischief, mischievousness — **malicieux, -cieuse** [malisjø, -sjøz] *adj* : mischievous

malin, -ligne [malɛ̃, -liɲ] *adj* **1** : clever **2** *fam* : difficult **3** MÉCHANT : malicious **4** : malignant (in medicine)

malle [mal] *nf* : trunk

malléable [maleabl] *adj* : malleable

mallette [malɛt] *nf* : small suitcase, valise

malnutrition [malnytrisjɔ̃] *nf* : malnutrition

malodorant, -rante [malɔdɔrɑ̃, -rɑ̃t] *adj* : foul-smelling, smelly

malpropre [malprɔpr] *adj* : dirty — **malpropreté** [malprɔprəte] *nf* : dirtiness

malsain, -saine [malsɛ̃, -sɛn] *adj* : unhealthy

malt [malt] *nm* : malt

maltraiter [maltrete] *vt* : mistreat

malveillance [malvɛjɑ̃s] *nf* : spite, malevolence — **malveillant, -lante** [malvɛjɑ̃, -jɑ̃t] *adj* : spiteful

maman [mamɑ̃] *nf* : mom, mommy

mamelle [mamɛl] *nf* **1** : teat **2** PIS : udder — **mamelon** [mamlɔ̃] *nm* : nipple

mammifère [mamifɛr] *nm* : mammal

mammouth [mamut] *nm* : mammoth

manche [mɑ̃ʃ] *nf* **1** : sleeve (of a shirt) **2** : round (in sports), set (in tennis) **3** *Can* : inning (in baseball) **4 la Manche** : the English Channel — ~ *nm* **1** : handle, neck, shaft **2** ~ **à balai** : broomstick — **manchette** [mɑ̃ʃɛt] *nf* **1** : cuff **2** : headline (in the press)

manchot [mɑ̃ʃo] *nm* : penguin

mandarine [mɑ̃darin] *nf* : tangerine, mandarin orange

mandat [mɑ̃da] *nm* **1** : mandate **2** *or* ~ **d'arrêt** : (arrest) warrant **3** *or* ~ **postal** : money order — **mandataire** [mɑ̃datɛr] *nmf* REPRÉSENTANT : representative, agent **2** : proxy (in politics)

manège [manɛʒ] *nm* **1** : riding school **2** : merry-go-round

manette [manɛt] *nf* : lever

manger [mɑ̃ʒe] {17} *vt* **1** : eat **2** DÉPENSER : consume, use up — *vi* : eat — ~ *nm* : food — **mangeable** [mɑ̃ʒabl] *adj* : edible — **mangeoire** [mɑ̃ʒwar] *nf* : feeding trough

mangue [mɑ̃g] *nf* : mango

maniable [manjabl] *adj* : easy to handle, manageable

maniaque [manjak] *adj* : fussy — ~ *nmf* : fussy person **2** : fanatic — **manie** [mani] *nf* **1** HABITUDE : habit **2** : quirk, obsession

manier [manje] {96} *vt* **1** MANIPULER : handle **2** UTILISER : use — **maniement** [manimɑ̃] *nm* : handling, use, operation

manière [manjɛr] *nf* **1** : manner, way **2 de** ~ **à** : so as to **3 de toute** ~ : in any case, anyway **4** ~ **s** *nfpl* : manners — **maniéré, -rée** [manjere] *adj* : affected, mannered

manifester [manifɛste] *vt* **1** : express **2** RÉVÉLER : reveal, show — *vi* : demonstrate — **se manifester** *vr* : appear — **manifestation** [manifɛstasjɔ̃] *nf* **1** : (political) demonstration **2** MARQUE : indication **3** : appearance (of an illness, etc.) — **manifestant, -tante** [manifɛstɑ̃, -tɑ̃t] *n* : demonstrator — **manifeste** [manifɛst] *adj* : obvious — ~ *nm* : manifesto

manigance [manigɑ̃s] *nf* : scheme, trick — **manigancer** [manigɑ̃se] {6} *vt* : plot

manipuler [manipyle] *vt* **1** MANIER : handle **2** : manipulate — **manipulation** [manipylasjɔ̃] *nf* **1** MANIEMENT : handling **2** : manipulation

manivelle [manivɛl] *nf* : crank

mannequin [mankɛ̃] *nm* **1** : dummy, mannequin **2** : (fashion) model

manœuvre [manœvr] *nf* : maneuver — **manœuvrer** [manœvre] *vt* **1** : maneuver **2** : operate (a machine, etc.) **3** MANIPULER : manipulate — *vi* : maneuver

manoir [manwar] *nm* : manor

manquer [mɑ̃ke] *vt* : miss (an opportunity, etc.) — *vi* **1** : lack, be missing **2** ÉCHOUER : fail, be short of — **manque** [mɑ̃k] *nm* **1** : lack **2** LACUNE : gap — **manqué, -quée** [mɑ̃ke] *adj* **1** : failed **2** : missed

mansarde [mɑ̃sard] *nf* : attic

manteau [mɑ̃to] *nm*, *pl* **-teaux** [-to] : coat

manucure [manykyr] *nf* : manicure — ~ *nmf* : manicurist

manuel, -elle [manɥɛl] *adj* : manual — **manuel** *nm* : manual, handbook

manufacture [manyfaktyr] *nf* : factory — **manufacturer** [manyfaktyre] *vt* : manufacture

manuscrit, -scrite [manyskri, -skrit] *adj* : handwritten — **manuscrit** *nm* : manuscript

manutention [manytɑ̃sjɔ̃] *nf* 1 : handling 2 **frais de** ~ : handling charges

maquereau [makro] *nm, pl* **-reaux** [-ro] : mackerel

maquette [makɛt] *nf* : (scale) model

maquiller [makije] *vt* : make up (one's face) — **se maquiller** *vr* : put on makeup — **maquillage** [makijaʒ] *nm* : makeup

maquis [maki] *nm France* : brush, undergrowth

marais [marɛ] *nm* : marsh, swamp

marasme [marasm] *nm* 1 : dejection, depression 2 : (economic) stagnation

marathon [maratɔ̃] *nm* : marathon

marauder [marode] *vi* VOLER : pilfer, thieve

marbre [marbr] *nm* 1 : marble 2 *Can* : home plate (in baseball)

marchand, -chande [marʃɑ̃, -ʃɑ̃d] *n* : storekeeper, merchant — ~ *adj* : market — **marchander** [marʃɑ̃de] *vt* : haggle over — *vi* : haggle, bargain — **marchandises** [marʃɑ̃diz] *nfpl* : goods, merchandise

marche [marʃ] *nf* 1 : step, stair 2 PROMENADE : walk, walking 3 RYTHME : pace 4 : march (in music) 5 ~ **arrière** : reverse 6 **en** ~ : running, operating 7 **mettre en** ~ : start up

marché [marʃe] *nm* 1 : market 2 ACCORD : deal 3 **bon** ~ : cheap 4 ~ **noir** : black market

marchepied [marʃəpje] *nm* : step, steps *pl*

marcher [marʃe] *vi* 1 : walk, march 2 ~ **sur** : step on, tread on 3 FONCTIONNER : work, go, run — **marcheur, -cheuse** [marʃœr, -ʃøz] *n* : walker

mardi [mardi] *nm* 1 : Tuesday 2 ~ **gras** : Mardi Gras

mare [mar] *nf* 1 : pond 2 ~ **de** : pool of

marécage [marekaʒ] *nm* : marsh, swamp — **marécageux, -geuse** [marekaʒø, -ʒøz] *adj* : marshy, swampy

maréchal [mareʃal] *nm, pl* **-chaux** [-ʃo] : marshal

marée [mare] *nf* 1 : tide 2 ~ **noire** : oil slick

marelle [marɛl] *nf* : hopscotch

margarine [margarin] *nf* : margarine

marge [marʒ] *nf* : margin — **marginal, -nale** [marʒinal] *adj, mpl* **-naux** [-no] : marginal

marguerite [margərit] *nf* : daisy

marier [marje] {96} *vt* 1 : marry 2 : blend (colors, etc.) — **se marier** *vr* : get married — **mari** [mari] *nm* : husband — **mariage** [marjaʒ] *nm* 1 : marriage 2 : wedding — **marié, -riée** [marje] *adj* : married — ~ *n* 1 : groom *m*, bride *f* 2 **les mariés** : the newlyweds

marin, -rine [marɛ̃, -rin] *adj* : sea, marine — **marin** *nm* : sailor — **marine** *nf* : navy

mariner [marine] *v* : marinate

marionnette [marjɔnɛt] *nf* 1 : puppet 2 ~ **à fils** : marionette

maritime [maritim] *adj* : maritime, coastal

marmelade [marməlad] *nf* 1 : stewed fruit 2 : marmalade

marmite [marmit] *nf* : cooking pot

marmonner [marmɔne] *v* : mutter, mumble

marmot [marmo] *nm fam* : kid, brat

marmotte [marmɔt] *nf* : woodchuck

marmotter [marmɔte] *v* : mutter, mumble

marocain, -caine [marɔkɛ̃, -kɛn] *adj* : Moroccan

marotte [marɔt] *nf* : craze, fad

marquer [marke] *vt* 1 : mark 2 INDIQUER : show, indicate 3 ÉCRIRE : note (down) 4 : score (in sports) — *vi* 1 : leave a mark 2 : stand out (of an event, etc.) — **marquant, -quante** [markɑ̃, -kɑ̃t] *adj* : memorable, outstanding — **marque** [mark] *nf* 1 : mark, trace 2 : brand, make 3 : score (in sports) 4 ~ **déposée** : registered trademark — **marqué, -quée** [marke] *adj* : marked, distinct

marquisse [markiz] *nf* : canopy, marquee

marraine [marɛn] *nf* : godmother

marrant, -rante [marɑ̃, -rɑ̃t] *adj fam* : amusing, funny

marre [mar] *adv* **en avoir** ~ *fam* : be fed up

marron, -ronne [marɔ̃, -rɔn] *adj* : brown — **marron** *nm* 1 : chestnut 2 : brown — **marronnier** [marɔnje] *nm* : chestnut tree

mars [mars] *nm* : March

Mars *nf* : Mars (planet)

marsouin [marswɛ̃] *nm* : porpoise

marteau [marto] *nm, pl* **-teaux** [marto] 1 : hammer 2 ~ **pneumatique** : pneumatic drill — **marteau–piqueur** [martopikœr] *nm, pl* **marteaux–piqueurs** : jackhammer — **marteler** [martəle] {20} *vt* : hammer

martial, -tiale [marsjal] *adj, mpl* **-tiaux** [-sjo] : martial

martyr, -tyre [martir] *n* : martyr — **martyriser** [martirize] *vt* : martyr

mascarade [maskarad] *nf* : masquerade

mascotte [maskɔt] *nf* : mascot

masculin, -line [maskylɛ̃, -lin] *adj* : male, masculine — **masculin** *nm* : masculine

masque [mask] *nm* : mask — **masquer** [maske] *vt* : mask, conceal

massacrer [masakre] *vt* : massacre — **massacre** [masakr] *nm* : massacre

massage [masaʒ] *nm* : massage

masse [mas] *nf* **1** : mass, body (of water, etc.) **2** : sledgehammer **3 les ~s** : the masses

masser [mase] *vt* **1** : massage **2** ASSEMBLER : gather — **masseur, -seuse** [masœr, -søz] *n* : masseur *m*, masseuse *f*

massif, -sive [masif, -siv] *adj* **1** : massive **2** : solid (of gold, silver, etc.) — **massif** *nm* **1** : clump (of trees)

massue [masy] *nf* : club, bludgeon

mastic [mastik] *nm* : putty — **mastiquer** [mastike] *vt* : chew

masturber [mastyrbe] *v* **se masturber** *vr* : masturbate — **masturbation** [mastyrbasjɔ̃] *nf* : masturbation

mat, mate [mat] *adj* **1** : dull, matte (of a finish, etc.) **2** : checkmated (in chess)

mât [ma] *nm* **1** : mast **2** POTEAU : pole, post

match [matʃ] *nm* : match, game

matelas [matla] *nm* : mattress — **matelasser** [matlase] *vt* REMBOURRER : pad

matelot [matlo] *nm* : sailor, seaman

mater [mate] *vt* DOMPTER : subdue, curb

matériaux [materjo] *nmpl* : materials

matériel, -rielle [materjɛl] *adj* : material — **matériel** *nm* **1** : equipment, material(s) **2** : computer hardware — **matérialiser** [materjalize] *vt* : realize, make happen — **se matérialiser** *vr* : materialize — **matérialiste** [materjalist] *adj* : materialistic

maternel, -nelle [matɛrnɛl] *adj* : maternal, motherly — **maternelle** *nf or* **école ~** : nursery school — **maternité** [matɛrnite] *nf* **1** : maternity **2** GROSSESSE : pregnancy

mathématique [matematik] *adj* : mathematical — **mathématicien, -cienne** [matematisjɛ̃, -sjɛn] *n* : mathematician — **mathématiques** [matematik] *nfpl* : mathematics — **maths** *or* **math** [mat] *nfpl fam* : math

matière [matjɛr] *nf* **1** : matter, substance **2** SUJET : subject **3 ~s premières** : raw materials

matin [matɛ̃] *nm* : morning — **matinal, -nale** [matinal] *adj, mpl* **-naux** [-no] **1** : morning **2 être ~** : be up early — **matinée** [matine] *nf* **1** : morning **2** : matinee

matraque [matrak] *nf* : club — **matraquer** [matrake] *vt* **1** : club, bludgeon **2** : plug (a product)

matrice [matris] *nf* : matrix

matricule [matrikyl] *nf* : register, roll

matrimonial, -niale [matrimɔnjal] *adj, mpl* **-niaux** [-njo] : matrimonial

maturité [matyrite] *nf* : maturity

maudire [modir] *vt* : curse, damn — **maudit, -dite** [modi, -dit] *adj* : damned

maugréer [mogree] {89} *vi* GROGNER : grumble

maussade [mosad] *adj* **1** MOROSE : sullen **2 temps ~** : dismal weather

mauvais, -vaise [movɛ, -vɛz] *adj* **1** : bad (of a grade, etc.) **2** : wrong (of an answer, etc.) **3** DÉPLAISANT : nasty, unpleasant

mauve [mov] *adj & nm* : mauve

mauviette [movjɛt] *nf* : weakling

maux → **mal**

maxillaire [maksilɛr] *nm* : jawbone

maxime [maksim] *nf* ADAGE : maxim, proverb

maximum [maksimɔm] *adj & nm, pl* **-mums** [-mɔm] *or* **-ma** [-ma] : maximum

mayonnaise [majɔnɛz] *nf* : mayonnaise

mazout [mazut] *nm* : heating oil

me [mə] *pron* (**m'** [m] *before a vowel or mute* **h**) **1** : me, to me **2** : myself, to myself

mec [mɛk] *nm fam* : guy

mécanique [mekanik] *nf* **1** : mechanics **2** : mechanism — **~** *adj* : mechanical — **mécanicien, -cienne** [mekanisjɛ̃, -sjɛn] *n* **1** : mechanic **2** : (railway or flight) engineer — **mécanisme** [mekanism] *nm* : mechanism

méchant, -chante [meʃɑ̃, -ʃɑ̃t] *adj* **1** : nasty, malicious **2** : naughty, bad (of a child) **3** : vicious (of a dog) — **~** *n* **1** : villain (in a book or film) **2** : naughty child — **méchamment** [meʃamɑ̃] *adv* : nastily — **méchanceté** [meʃɑ̃ste] *nf* : nastiness

mèche [mɛʃ] *nf* **1** : wick (of a candle) **2** : lock (of hair) **3** : bit (of a drill)

méconnaissable [mekɔnɛsabl] *adj* : unrecognizable

mécontent, -tente [mekɔ̃tɑ̃, -tɑ̃t] *adj* : discontented, dissatisfied — **mécontentement** [mekɔ̃tɑ̃tmɑ̃] *nm* : discontent, dissatisfaction

médaille [medaj] *nf* : medal — **médaillé, -lée** [medaje] *n* : medalist — **médaillon** [medajɔ̃] *nm* **1** : medallion **2** : locket

médecin [medsɛ̃] *nm* : doctor, physician — **médecine** [medsin] *nf* : medicine

média [medja] *nm* **1** : medium **2 les ~s** : the media

médian, -diane [medjɑ̃, -djan] *adj* : median

médiation [medjasjɔ̃] *nf* : mediation, arbitration — **médiateur, -trice** [medjatœr, -tris] *n* : mediator, arbitrator

médical, -cale [medikal] *adj, mpl* **-caux** [-ko] : medical — **médicament** [medikamɑ̃] *nm* : medicine, drug — **médication** [medikasjɔ̃] *nf* : medication — **médicinal, -nale** [medisinal] *adj, mpl* **-naux** [-no] : medicinal

médiéval, -vale [medjeval] *adj, mpl* **-vaux** [-vo] : medieval

médiocre [medjɔkr] *adj* : mediocre — **médiocrité** [medjɔkrite] *nf* : mediocrity

méditer [medite] *vt* : reflect on, think over

— *vi* : meditate — **méditation** [meditasjɔ̃]
nf : meditation
médium [medjɔm] *nm* : medium, psychic
méduse [medyz] *nf* : jellyfish
meeting [mitiŋ] *nm* **1** : meeting **2** : meet (in
sports)
méfait [mefɛ] *nm* **1** : misdeed, misde-
meanour **2 ~s** *nmpl* : ravages
méfier [mefje] {96} *v* **se méfier** *vr* **1** : be
careful, beware **2 ~ de** : distrust — **méfiance** [mefjɑ̃s] *nf* : distrust — **méfiant,
-fiante** [mefjɑ̃, -fjɑ̃t] *adj* : distrustful
mégarde [megard] *nf* **par ~** : inadvertently
mégot [mego] *nm* : cigarette butt
meilleur, -leure [mɛjœr] *adj* **1** : better **2**
: best — **~** *n* : best (one) — **meilleur** *adv*
: better
mélancolie [melɑ̃kɔli] *nf* : melancholy —
mélancolique [melɑ̃kɔlik] *adj* : melancholy
mélanger [melɑ̃ʒe] {17} *vt* **1** : mix, blend **2**
CONFONDRE : mix up, confuse — **se
mélanger** *vr* **1** : blend (with) **2** : get mixed
up — **mélange** [melɑ̃ʒ] *nm* **1** : mixing,
blending **2** : mixture, blend
mélasse [melas] *nf* : molasses
mêlée [mele] *nf* **~ générale** : free-for-all
mêler [mele] *vt* : mix — **se mêler** *vr* **1** : mix,
mingle **2 mêlez-vous de vos affaires**
: mind your own business
mélodie [melɔdi] *nf* : melody
mélomane [melɔman] *nmf* : music lover
melon [məlɔ̃] *nm* : melon
membrane [mɑ̃bran] *nf* : membrane
membre [mɑ̃br] *nm* **1** : limb **2** : member (of
a group)
même [mɛm] *adj* **1** : same, identical **2** (*used
as an intensifier*) : very, actual **3** →
elle–même, lui–même, eux–mêmes —
~ *pron* **le ~, la ~, les ~s** : the same
(one, ones) — **~** *adv* **1** : even **2 de ~**
: likewise, the same
mémère [memɛr] *nf fam* **1** : grandma **2** *Can*
: gossip
mémoire [memwar] *nf* : memory — **~** *nm*
1 : dissertation, thesis **2 ~s** *nmpl* : memoirs
mémorable [memɔrabl] *adj* : memorable
mémorandum [memɔrɑ̃dɔm] *nm* : memorandum
mémoriser [memɔrize] *vt* : memorize
menacer [mənase] {6} *v* : threaten —
menaçant, -çante [mənasɑ̃, -sɑ̃t] *adj*
: threatening — **menace** [mənas] *nf* : threat
ménage [menaʒ] *nm* **1** : household, family
2 faire le ~ : do the housework **3 un
heureux ~** : a happy couple — **ménage-
ment** [menaʒmɑ̃] *nm* : consideration, care
— **ménager** [menaʒe] {17} *vt* **1** ÉPARGNER
: save **2** : handle or treat with care — **se**

ménager *vr* : take it easy — **ménager,
-gère** [menaʒe, -ʒɛr] *adj* : household, domestic — **ménagère** [menaʒɛr] *nf* : housewife
mendier [mɑ̃dje] {96} *v* : beg — **mendiant,
-diante** [mɑ̃djɑ̃, -djɑ̃t] *n* : beggar
menées [məne] *nfpl* : scheming, intrigues
mener [məne] {52} *vt* **1** : lead **2** DIRIGER
: conduct, run **3 ~ qqch à terme** : see sth
through — **meneur, -neuse** [mənœr, -nøz]
n **1** : leader **2 meneuse de claque** *Can*
: cheerleader
méningite [menɛ̃ʒit] *nf* : meningitis
ménopause [menɔpoz] *nf* : menopause
menottes [mənɔt] *nfpl* : handcuffs
mensonge [mɑ̃sɔ̃ʒ] *nm* **1** : lie **2 le ~**
: lying — **mensonger, -gère** [mɑ̃sɔ̃ʒe,
-ʒɛr] *adj* : false, misleading
menstruation [mɑ̃stryasjɔ̃] *nf* RÈGLES
: menstruation — **menstruel, -struelle**
[mɑ̃stryɛl] *adj* : menstrual
mensuel, -suelle [mɑ̃sɥɛl] *adj* : monthly —
mensuel *nm* : monthly (magazine)
mensurations [mɑ̃syrasjɔ̃] *nfpl* : measurements
mental, -tale [mɑ̃tal] *adj, mpl* **-taux** [-to]
: mental — **mentalité** [mɑ̃talite] *nf* : mentality
menteur, -teuse [mɑ̃tœr, -tøz] *adj* : untruth-
ful, false — **~** *n* : liar
menthe [mɑ̃t] *nf* : mint
mention [mɑ̃sjɔ̃] *nf* **1** : mention **2** : (academic) distinction — **mentionner**
[mɑ̃sjɔne] *vt* : mention
mentir [mɑ̃tir] {82} *vi* : lie
menton [mɑ̃tɔ̃] *nm* : chin
menu, -nue [məny] *adj* **1** PETIT : tiny **2**
: minor, trifling — **menu** *adv* : finely — **~**
nm : menu
menuiserie [mənɥizri] *nf* : woodworking,
carpentry — **menuisier** [mənɥizje] *nm*
: woodworker, carpenter
méprendre [meprɑ̃dr] {70} *v* **se méprendre** *vr* **~ sur** : be mistaken about
mépris [mepri] *nm* **1** DÉDAIN : contempt **2
au ~ de** : regardless of — **méprisable**
[meprizabl] *adj* : despicable, contemptible
— **méprisant, -sante** [meprizɑ̃, -zɑ̃t] *adj*
: contemptuous, scornful — **mépriser**
[meprize] *vt* : despise, scorn
mer [mɛr] *nf* **1** : sea **2** MARÉE : tide
mercenaire [mɛrsənɛr] *adj & nmf* : mercenary
mercerie [mɛrsəri] *nf* : notions *pl*
merci [mɛrsi] *interj* : thank you!, thanks! —
~ *nm* : thank-you — **~** *nf* : mercy
mercredi [mɛrkrədi] *nm* : Wednesday
mercure [mɛrkyr] *nm* : mercury
Mercure *nf* : Mercury (planet)
mère [mɛr] *nf* : mother

méridional, -nale [meridjɔnal] *adj*, *mpl*
-naux [-no] : southern

meringue [mərɛ̃g] *nf* : meringue

mérite [merit] *nm* : merit, credit — **mériter**
[merite] *vt* : deserve, merit — **méritoire**
[meritwar] *adj* : commendable

merle [mɛrl] *nm* : blackbird

merveille [mɛrvɛj] *nf* **1** : wonder, marvel **2**
à ~ : wonderfully — **merveilleux, -leuse**
[mɛrvɛjø, -jøz] *adj* : wonderful, marvelous

mes → **mon**

mésaventure [mezavãtyr] *nf* : misfortune,
mishap

mesdames → **madame**

mesdemoiselles → **mademoiselle**

mésentente [mezãtãt] *nf* DÉSACCORD : misunderstanding, disagreement

mesquin, -quine [mɛskɛ̃, -kin] *adj* **1**
: mean, petty **2** : cheap, stingy — **mes-
quinerie** [mɛskinri] *nf* **1** : pettiness **2**
AVARICE : stinginess

message [mɛsaʒ] *nm* : message — **messager, -gère** [mɛsaʒe, -ʒɛr] *n* : messenger
— **messagerie** [mɛsaʒri] *nf* : parcel delivery service

messe [mɛs] *nf* : Mass

mesure [məzyr] *nf* **1** : measure, measurement **2** RETENUE : moderation **3 à la ~ de**
: worthy of **4 à ~ que** : as **5 dans la ~**
où : insofar as — **mesuré, -rée** [məzyre]
adj : measured, restrained — **mesurer**
[məzyre] *vt* **1** : measure **2** ÉVALUER : assess

métabolisme [metabɔlism] *nm* : metabolism

métal [metal] *nm, pl* **-taux** [meto] : metal —
métallique [metalik] *adj* : metallic

métamorphose [metamɔrfoz] *nf* : metamorphosis

métaphore [metafɔr] *nf* : metaphor

météo [meteo] *nf fam* : weather forecast

météore [meteɔr] *nm* : meteor

météorologie [meteɔrɔlɔʒi] *nf* : meteorology — **météorologique** [meteɔrɔlɔʒik] *adj*
: meteorological, weather — **météorologiste** [meteɔrɔlɔʒist] *nmf* : meteorologist

méthode [metɔd] *nf* **1** : method, system **2**
MANUEL : primer — **méthodique** [metɔ-
dik] *adj* : methodical

méticuleux, -leuse [metikylø, -løz] *adj*
: meticulous

métier [metje] *nm* **1** : job, profession **2** : experience, skill **3** *or* **~ à tisser** : loom

métis, -tisse [metis] *adj & n* : half-breed,
half-caste

métrage [metraʒ] *nm* **1** : length (of an object) **2** : footage (of a film)

mètre [mɛtr] *nm* **1** : meter **2 ~ ruban**
: tape measure — **métrique** [metrik] *adj*
: metric

métro [metro] *nm* : subway

métropole [metrɔpɔl] *nf* : city, metropolis —
métropolitain, -taine [metrɔpɔlitɛ̃, -tɛn]
adj : metropolitan

mets [mɛ] *nm* PLAT : dish

metteur [metœr] *nm* **~ en scène** : producer, director

mettre [mɛtr] {53} *vt* **1** PLACER : put, place
2 : put on, wear **3** AJOUTER : add (in), put in
4 DISPOSER : prepare, arrange **5 ~ au**
point : develop, finalize **6 ~ en marche**
: turn on, switch on — **se mettre** *vr* **1** : become, get **2** : put on, wear **3 ~ à faire**
: start doing **4 ~ à table** : sit down at the
table

meuble [mœbl] *nm* **1** : piece of furniture **2**
~s *nmpl* : furniture — **meublé, -blée**
[mœble] *adj* : furnished — **meubler**
[mœble] *vt* : furnish

meugler [møgle] *vi* : moo, low — **meugle-
ment** [møgləmã] *nm* : mooing, lowing

meule [møl] *nf* **1** : millstone **2 ~ de foin**
: haystack

meurtre [mœrtr] *nm* : murder — **meurtrier,
-trière** [mœrtrije, -trijer] *adj* : deadly — **~**
n ASSASSIN : murderer

meurtrir [mœrtrir] *vt* : bruise — **meurtris-
sure** [mœrtrisyr] *nf* : bruise

meute [møt] *nf* : pack (of hounds)

mexicain, -caine [meksikɛ̃, -kɛn] *adj*
: Mexican

miaou [mjau] *nm* : meow — **miauler** [mjole]
vi : meow

mi-bas [miba] *nms & pl* : kneesock

miche [miʃ] *nf* : round loaf of bread

mi-chemin [miʃmɛ̃] **à ~** *adv phr* : halfway,
midway

microbe [mikrɔb] *nm* : germ, microbe

microfilm [mikrɔfilm] *nm* : microfilm

micro-ondes [mikrɔõd] *nms & pl* : microwave oven

microphone [mikrɔfɔn] *nm* : microphone

microscope [mikrɔskɔp] *nm* : microscope
— **microscopique** [mikrɔskɔpik] *adj* : microscopic

microsillon [mikrɔsijõ] *nm* : long-playing
record

midi [midi] *nm* **1** : midday, noon **2**
: lunchtime **3** SUD : south

mie [mi] *nf* : inside, soft part (of a loaf of
bread)

miel [mjɛl] *nm* : honey — **mielleux, -leuse**
[mjɛlø, -løz] *adj* : sickly sweet

mien, mienne [mjɛ̃, mjɛn] *adj* : mine, my
own — **~** *pron* **le mien, la mienne, les
miens, les miennes** : mine

miette [mjɛt] *nf* **1** : crumb **2 en ~s** : in
pieces

mieux [mjø] *adv & adj* **1** (*comparative of*
bien) : better **2** (*superlative of* **bien**) **le ~,**

la ~, les ~ : the best — ~ *nm* **1** : best **2**
il y a du ~ : there's some improvement
mignon, -gnonne [miɲɔ̃, -ɲɔn] *adj* **1**
: sweet, cute **2** GENTIL : nice, kind
migraine [migrɛn] *nf* : headache, migraine
migration [migrasjɔ̃] *nf* : migration — **mi-
grateur, -trice** [migratœr, -tris] *adj* : mi-
gratory
mijoter [miʒɔte] *vt* **1** : simmer **2** MANI-
GANCER : plot, cook up — *vi* : simmer, stew
mil [mil] → **mille**
mile [majl] *nm* : mile
milice [milis] *nf* : militia
milieu [miljø] *nm, pl* -**lieux 1** CENTRE : middle **2** ENTOURAGE : environment **3 au ~
de** : among, in the midst of
militaire [militɛr] *adj* : military — ~ *nm*
SOLDAT : soldier, serviceman
militant, -tante [militɑ̃, -tɑ̃t] *adj & n* : militant
millage [milaʒ] *nm Can* : mileage (of a motor
vehicle)
mille [mil] *adj* : one thousand — ~ *nm or*
~ **marin** : nautical mile
millénaire [milenɛr] *nm* : millennium
mille–pattes [milpat] *nms & pl* **1** : centipede
2 : millipede
millésime [milezim] *nm* **1** : year (of manufacture) **2** : vintage year
millet [mijɛ] *nm* : millet
milliard [miljar] *nm* : billion — **milliardaire**
[miljardɛr] *nmf* : billionaire
millier [milje] *nm* : thousand
milligramme [miligram] *nm* : milligram
millimètre [milimɛtr] *nm* : millimeter
million [miljɔ̃] *nm* : million — **millionnaire**
[miljɔnɛr] *nmf* : millionaire
mime [mim] *nmf* : mime — **mimer** [mime] *vt*
: mimic
mimique [mimik] *nf* GRIMACE : face
minable [minabl] *adj* : shabby
mince [mɛ̃s] *adj* **1** : thin, slender **2** IN-
SIGNIFIANT : meager, scanty — **minceur**
[mɛ̃sœr] *nf* : thinness, slenderness
mine¹ [min] *nf* : appearance, look
mine² *nf* **1** : (coal) mine **2** : (pencil) lead —
miner [mine] *vt* : undermine, weaken —
minerai [minrɛ] *nm* : ore
minéral, -rale [mineral] *adj, mpl* -**raux** [-ro]
: mineral — **minéral** *nm* : mineral
minet, -nette [minɛ, -nɛt] *n fam* : pussycat
mineur¹, -neure [minœr] *adj & nmf* : minor
mineur² *nm* : miner
miniature [minjatyr] *adj & nf* : miniature
minimal, -male [minimal] *adj, mpl* -**maux**
[-mo] : minimal, minimum — **minime**
[minim] *adj* : minimal, negligible — **minimiser** [minimize] *vt* : minimize — **minimum** [minimɔm] *adj & nm, pl* -**mums**
[-mɔm] *or* -**ma** [-ma] : minimum

ministère [ministɛr] *nm* **1** : department,
ministry **2** CABINET : government — **ministériel, -rielle** [ministerjɛl] *adj* : governmental — **ministre** [ministr] *nm* : minister,
secretary
minorité [minɔrite] *nf* : minority — **minori-
taire** [minɔritɛr] *adj* : minority
minou [minu] *nm fam* : pussycat
minuit [minɥi] *nm* : midnight
minuscule [minyskyl] *adj* : minute, tiny —
~ *nf* : small (lowercase) letter
minute [minyt] *nf* : minute — **minuter**
[minyte] *vt* : time — **minuterie** [minytri] *nf*
: timer
minutieux, -tieuse [minysjø, -sjøz] *adj* **1**
MÉTICULEUX : meticulous **2** : detailed (of
work, etc.) — **minutie** [minysi] *nf* : meticu-
lousness
miracle [mirakl] *nm* : miracle — **miraculeux, -leuse** [mirakylø, -løz] *adj* : miraculous
mirage [miraʒ] *nm* : mirage
mire [mir] *nf* **point de** ~ : target
miroir [mirwar] *nm* : mirror
miroiter [mirwate] *vi* BRILLER : sparkle,
shimmer — **miroitement** [mirwatmɑ̃] *nm*
: sparkling, shimmering
mis, mise [mi, miz] *adj* **1** : clad **2 bien** ~
: well-dressed
mise [miz] *nf* **1** : putting, placing **2** : stake
(in games of chance) **3** TENUE : dress, attire
— **miser** [mize] *vt* : bet — *vi* ~ **sur** : bet
on, count on
misérable [mizerabl] *adj* **1** PITOYABLE
: wretched, pitiful **2** INSIGNIFIANT : meager,
paltry — ~ *nmf* **1** : wretch **2** : scoundrel
— **misère** [mizɛr] *nf* **1** : poverty **2** : misery
miséricorde [mizerikɔrd] *nf* : mercy, forgiveness
missile [misil] *nm* : missile
mission [misjɔ̃] *nf* : mission — **missionnaire** [misjɔnɛr] *adj & nmf* : missionary
mitaine [mitɛn] *nf Can, Switz* : mitten
mite [mit] *nf* : clothes moth
mi–temps [mitɑ̃] *nms & pl* : part-time job —
~ *nfs & pl* : halftime (in sports)
miteux, -teuse [mitø, -tøz] *adj* : seedy,
shabby
mitigé, -gée [mitiʒe] *adj* **1** : lukewarm, reserved **2 sentiments mitigés** : mixed feelings
mitoyen, -toyenne [mitwajɛ̃, -jɛn] *adj*
: common, dividing
mitrailleuse [mitrajøz] *nf* : machine gun
mi–voix [mivwa] **à** ~ *adv phr* : in a low
voice
mixeur [miksœr] *or* **mixer** [miksɛr] *nm*
: mixer, blender
mixte [mikst] *adj* **1** : mixed **2 école** ~
: coeducational school

mobile [mɔbil] *adj* **1** : mobile, moving **2**
feuilles ~s : loose-leaf paper — ~ *nm* **1**
: motive (of a crime) **2** : (paper) mobile —
mobilier [mɔbilje] *nm* MEUBLES : furniture
mobiliser [mɔbilize] *vt* : mobilize
mobilité [mɔbilite] *nf* : mobility
mocassin [mɔkasɛ̃] *nm* : moccasin
moche [mɔʃ] *adj fam* **1** : ugly **2** MAUVAIS
: lousy
modalité [mɔdalite] *nf* : form, mode
mode [mɔd] *nm* **1** : mode, method **2** ~
d'emploi : directions for use — ~ *nf*
: fashion
modèle [mɔdɛl] *nm* : model — ~ *adj*
: model, exemplary — **modeler** [mɔdle]
{20} *vt* : mold, shape
modem [mɔdɛm] *nm* : modem
modérer [mɔdere] {87} *vt* : moderate, restrain — **modérateur, -trice** [mɔderatœr,
-tris] *adj* : moderating — **modération**
[mɔderasjɔ̃] *nf* MESURE : moderation, restraint — **modéré, -rée** [mɔdere] *adj* : moderate
moderne [mɔdɛrn] *adj* : modern — **moderniser** [mɔdɛrnize] *vt* : modernize
modeste [mɔdɛst] *adj* : modest — **modestie**
[mɔdɛsti] *nf* : modesty
modifier [mɔdifje] {96} *vt* : modify — **se
modifier** *vr* : change — **modification**
[mɔdifikasjɔ̃] *nf* : modification
modique [mɔdik] *adj* : modest, low
moduler [mɔdyle] *vt* : modulate, adjust
moelle [mwal] *nf* **1** : marrow **2** ~ **épinière**
: spinal cord — **moelleux, -leuse** [mwalø,
-løz] *adj* **1** DOUX : soft **2** : moist (of a cake)
mœurs [mœr(s)] *nfpl* **1** : morals **2** USAGES
: customs, habits
moi [mwa] *pron* **1** : I **2** : me **3 à** ~ : mine
— ~ *nm* **le** ~ : the self, the ego —
moi–même [mwamɛm] *pron* : myself
moindre [mwɛ̃dr] *adj* **1** : lesser, smaller,
lower **2 le** ~, **la** ~ : the least, the slightest
moine [mwan] *nm* : monk
moineau [mwano] *nm, pl* **-neaux** : sparrow
moins [mwɛ̃] *adv* **1** : less **2 le** ~ : least, the
least **3** ~ **de** : less than, fewer **4 à** ~ **que**
: unless **5 en** ~ : missing — ~ *nm* **1**
: minus (sign) **2 au** ~ *or* **du** ~ : at least **3**
pour le ~ : at (the very) least — ~ *prep* **1**
: minus **2** *(in expressions of time)* : to, of **3**
(in expressions of temperature) : below
mois [mwa] *nm* : month
moisi, -sie [mwazi] *adj* : moldy — **moisi** *nm*
: mold, mildew — **moisir** [mwazir] *vi* **1**
: become moldy **2** *fam* : stagnate — **moisissure** [mwazisyr] *nf* : mold, mildew
moisson [mwasɔ̃] *nf* : harvest, crop —
moissonner [mwasɔne] *vt* : harvest, reap
— **moissonneuse** [mwasɔnøz] *nf* : harvester, reaper — **moissonneuse–batteuse**

[mwasɔnøzbatøz] *nf, pl* **moisson-
neuses–batteuses** : combine (harvester)
moite [mwat] *adj* : damp, clammy
moitié [mwatje] *nf* **1** : half **2 à** ~ : half,
halfway — **moitié–moitié** *adv* : fifty-fifty
moka [mɔka] *nm* : mocha
mol → **mou**
molaire [mɔlɛr] *nf* : molar
molécule [mɔlekyl] *nf* : molecule
molle → **mou** — **mollesse** [mɔlɛs] *adj* **1**
: softness **2** INDOLENCE : indolence, apathy
— **mollement** [mɔlmɑ̃] *adv* **1** DOUCEMENT
: softly, gently **2** : weakly, feebly
mollet [mɔlɛ] *nm* : calf (of the leg)
mollir [mɔlir] *vi* **1** : soften, go soft **2** FAIBLIR
: weaken, slacken
mollusque [mɔlysk] *nm* : mollusk
môme [mom] *nmf France fam* : kid, youngster
moment [mɔmɑ̃] *nm* **1** : moment, while **2**
INSTANT : minute, instant **3** OCCASION
: time, occasion **4** : present (time) **5 du** ~
que : since — **momentané, -née** [mɔmɑ̃-
tane] *adj* : momentary, temporary — **momentanément** [-nemɑ̃] *adv* **1** : momentarily **2** : at the moment
momie [mɔmi] *nf* : mummy
mon [mɔ̃], **ma** [ma] *adj, pl* **mes** [mɛ] : my
monarchie [mɔnarʃi] *nf* : monarchy —
monarque [mɔnark] *nm* : monarch
monastère [mɔnaster] *nm* : monastery
monceau [mɔ̃so] *nm, pl* **-ceaux** [mɔ̃so]
: heap, pile
mondain, -daine [mɔ̃dɛ̃, -dɛn] *adj* **1** : society, social **2** RAFFINÉ : fashionable
monde [mɔ̃d] *nm* **1** : world **2** : society, people *pl* **3 tout le** ~ : everyone — **mondial,
-diale** [mɔ̃djal] *adj, mpl* **-diaux** [-djo] **1**
: world **2** : worldwide, global — **mondiale-
ment** [mɔ̃djalmɑ̃] *adv* : throughout the
world
monétaire [mɔnetɛr] *adj* : monetary
moniteur, -trice [mɔnitœr, -tris] *n* : instructor, coach — **moniteur** *nm* : monitor, screen
monnaie [mɔnɛ] *nf* **1** : money, currency **2**
PIÈCE : coin — **monnayer** [mɔneje] {11} *vt*
1 : convert into cash **2** : capitalize on (experience, etc.) — **monnayeur** [mɔnejœr]
nm → **faux–monnayeur**
monocorde [mɔnɔkɔrd] *adj* : droning, monotonous
monogramme [mɔnɔgram] *nm* : monogram
monologue [mɔnɔlɔg] *nm* : monologue, so-
liloquy
monopole [mɔnɔpɔl] *nm* : monopoly — **monopoliser** [mɔnɔpɔlize] *vt* : monopolize
monotone [mɔnɔtɔn] *adj* : monotonous, dull
— **monotonie** [mɔnɔtɔni] *nf* : monotony
monsieur [məsjø] *nm, pl* **messieurs** [mɛsjø]
1 : Mr., sir **2** : man, gentleman

monstre [mɔ̃str] *nm* : monster — ~ *adj* : huge, colossal — **monstrueux, -trueuse** [mɔ̃stryø, -tryøz] *adj* **1** : monstrous, huge **2** TERRIBLE : hideous — **monstruosité** [mɔ̃stryozite] *nf* : monstrosity

mont [mɔ̃] *nm* : mount, mountain

montage [mɔ̃taʒ] *nm* **1** : editing (of a film) **2 chaîne de** ~ : assembly line

montagne [mɔ̃taɲ] *nf* **1** : mountain **2 la** ~ : the mountains **3** ~**s russes** : roller coaster — **montagneux, -gneuse** [mɔ̃taɲø, -ɲøz] *adj* : mountainous

montant, -tante [mɔ̃tɑ̃, -tɑ̃t] *adj* : uphill, rising — **montant** *nm* **1** : upright, post **2** SOMME : total, sum

mont–de–piété [mɔ̃dpjete] *nm, pl* **monts–de–piété** *France* : pawnshop

monte–charge [mɔ̃tʃarʒ] *nms & pl* : freight elevator

monter [mɔ̃te] *vi* **1** : go up, come up, climb (up) **2** : rise (of temperature, etc.) **3** ~ **à** : ride (a bicycle, etc.) **4** ~ **dans** : get into, board **5** ~ **sur** : mount, get on (a horse) — *vt (with auxiliary verb* **avoir***)* **1** : take up, bring up **2** : raise, turn up (volume, etc.) **3** : go up, climb (up) **4** : assemble, put together **5** ~ **à cheval** : ride a horse — **se monter** *vr* ~ **à** : amount to — **montée** [mɔ̃te] *nf* **1** : rise, rising **2** : ascent, climb **3** PENTE : slope

montre [mɔ̃tr] *nf* **1** : watch **2 faire** ~ **de** : show, display

montréalais, -laise [mɔreale, -lɛz] *adj* : of or from Montreal

montre–bracelet [mɔ̃trəbraslɛ] *nf, pl* **montres–bracelets** : wristwatch

montrer [mɔ̃tre] *vt* **1** : show, reveal **2** INDIQUER : point out — **se montrer** *vr* **1** : show oneself **2** : prove to be

monture [mɔ̃tyr] *nf* **1** : mount, horse **2** : setting (for jewelry) **3** : frames *pl* (for eyeglasses)

monument [mɔnymɑ̃] *nm* : monument — **monumental, -tale** [mɔnymɑ̃tal] *adj, mpl* **-taux** [-to] : monumental

moquer [mɔke] *v* **se moquer** *vr* **1** ~ **de** : make fun of, mock **2 je m'en moque** : I couldn't care less — **moquerie** [mɔkri] *nf* : mockery

moquette [mɔkɛt] *nf* : wall-to-wall carpeting

moral, -rale [mɔral] *adj, mpl* **-raux** [mɔro] : moral — **moral** *nm* : morale, spirits *pl* — **morale** *nf* **1** : morals *pl*, morality **2** : moral (of a story) — **moralisateur, -trice** [mɔralizatœr, -tris] *adj* : moralizing — **moralité** [mɔralite] *nf* : morality

morbide [mɔrbid] *adj* : morbid

morceau [mɔrso] *nm, pl* **-ceaux** : piece, bit — **morceler** [mɔrsəle] {8} *vt* : break up, divide

mordant, -dante [mɔrdɑ̃, -dɑ̃t] *adj* : biting, scathing — **mordant** *nm* : bite, punch

mordiller [mɔrdije] *vt* : nibble at

mordre [mɔrdr] {63} *v* : bite — **se mordre** *vr* ~ **la langue** : bite one's tongue — **mordu, -due** *adj* : smitten (with love) — ~ *n fam* : fan, buff

morfondre [mɔrfɔ̃dr] {63} *v* **se morfondre** *vr* **1** : mope **2** *Can* : wear oneself out

morgue [mɔrg] *nf* **1** : morgue, mortuary **2** ARROGANCE : arrogance

morille [mɔrij] *nf* : type of mushroom

morne [mɔrn] *adj* **1** SOMBRE : gloomy, glum **2** MAUSSADE : dismal, dreary

morose [mɔroz] *adj* : morose, sullen

morphine [mɔrfin] *nf* : morphine

mors [mɔr] *nm* : bit (of a bridle)

morse [mɔrs] *nm* **1** : walrus **2** : Morse code

morsure [mɔrsyr] *nf* : bite

mort, morte [mɔr, mɔrt] *adj* : dead — ~ *n* **1** : dead person, corpse **2** VICTIME : fatality — **mort** *nf* : death — **mortalité** [mɔrtalite] *nf* : mortality — **mortel, -telle** [mɔrtɛl] *adj* **1** : mortal **2** FATAL : fatal — ~ *n* : mortal

mortier [mɔrtje] *nm* : mortar

mortifier [mɔrtifje] {96} *vt* : mortify

mortuaire [mɔrtɥɛr] *adj* **1** FUNÈBRE : funeral **2 salon** ~ *Can* : funeral home

morue [mɔry] *nf* : cod

mosaïque [mɔzaik] *adj & nf* : mosaic

mosquée [mɔske] *nf* : mosque

mot [mo] *nm* **1** : word **2** : note, line **3** ~ **de passe** : password **4** ~**s croisés** : crossword puzzle

motel [mɔtɛl] *nm* : motel

moteur [mɔtœr] *nm* : engine, motor — **moteur, -trice** [mɔtœr, -tris] *adj* **1** : motor **2 force motrice** : driving force

motif [mɔtif] *nm* **1** RAISON : motive, grounds *pl* **2** DESSIN : pattern, design

motion [mɔsjɔ̃] *nf* : motion (in politics)

motiver [mɔtive] *vt* **1** : motivate **2** EXPLIQUER : justify, explain — **motivation** [mɔtivasjɔ̃] *nf* : motivation, incentive

moto [mɔto] *nf* : bike, motorbike — **motocyclette** [mɔtɔsiklɛt] *nf* : motorcycle

motoriser [mɔtɔrize] *vt* : motorize

motte [mɔt] *nf* : clod, lump (of earth, etc.)

mou [mu] (**mol** [mɔl] *before vowel or mute h*), **molle** [mɔl] *adj* **1** : soft **2** FLASQUE : flabby, limp **3** LÂCHE : slack **4 avoir les jambes molles** : be weak in the knees

mouchard, -charde [muʃar, -ʃard] *n fam* : informer, stool pigeon

mouche [muʃ] *nf* : fly

moucher [muʃe] *v* **se moucher** *vr* : blow one's nose

moucheron [muʃrɔ̃] *nm* : gnat
moucheté [muʃte] *adj* : speckled, flecked
mouchoir [muʃwar] *nm* : handkerchief
moudre [mudr] {54} *vt* : grind
moue [mu] *nf* **1** : pout **2 faire la ~** : pout
mouette [mwɛt] *nf* : gull, seagull
mouffette *or* **moufette** [mufɛt] *nf* : skunk
moufle [mufl] *nf* : mitten
mouiller [muje] *vt* **1** : wet, moisten **2 ~ l'ancre** : drop anchor — **se mouiller** *vr* **1** : get wet **2** *fam* : become involved — **mouillage** [mujaʒ] *nm* : anchorage, berth — **mouillé, -lée** [muje] *adj* : wet
moulage [mulaʒ] *nm* **1** : molding, casting **2 faire un ~ de** : take a cast of
moulant, -lante [mulɑ̃, -lɑ̃t] *adj* : tight-fitting (of clothes, etc.)
moule[1] [mul] *nf* : mussel
moule[2] *nm* **1** : mold, matrix **2 ~ à gâteaux** : cake pan — **mouler** [mule] *vt* **1** : mold **2** : cast (a statue)
moulin [mulɛ̃] *nm* **1** : mill **2 ~ à café** : coffee grinder **3 ~ à paroles** *fam* : chatterbox — **moulinet** [mulinɛ] *nm* : reel, winch
moulu, -lue [muly] *adj* **1** : ground (of coffee, etc.) **2** *fam* : worn-out
moulure [mulyr] *nf* : molding
mourir [murir] {55} *vi* **1** : die **2** : die out (of a sound, etc.) **3 ~ de faim** : be dying of hunger — **mourant, -rante** [murɑ̃, -rɑ̃t] *n* : dying person
mousquet [muskɛ] *nm* : musket — **mousquetaire** [muskətɛr] *nm* : musketeer
mousse [mus] *nf* **1** : moss (in botany) **2** : foam, lather **3** : mousse (in cooking) — **moussant, -sante** [musɑ̃, -sɑ̃t] *adj* : foaming — **mousser** [muse] *vi* : foam, froth, lather — **mousseux, -seuse** [musø, -søz] *adj* **1** : foaming, frothy **2 vin ~** : sparkling wine
moustache [mustaʃ] *nf* **1** : mustache **2 ~s** *nfpl* : whiskers (of an animal)
moustique [mustik] *nm* : mosquito — **moustiquaire** [mustikɛr] *nf* **1** : mosquito net **2** : screen (for a window, etc.)
moutarde [mutard] *nf* : mustard
mouton [mutɔ̃] *nm* **1** : sheep, sheepskin **2** : mutton (in cooking)
mouvement [muvmɑ̃] *nm* **1** : movement **2** ACTIVITÉ : activity, bustle **3** IMPULSION : impulse, reaction — **mouvementé, -tée** [muvmɑ̃te] *adj* **1** : eventful, hectic **2** ACCIDENTÉ : rough, uneven — **mouvoir** [muvwar] {56} *vt* : move, prompt
moyen, moyenne [mwajɛ̃, -jɛn] *adj* **1** : medium **2** : average **3 Moyen Âge** : Middle Ages *pl* — **moyen** *nm* **1** : way, means (*pl* **2** : possibility **3 ~s** *nmpl* : means, resources — **moyenne** *nf* : average —

moyennement [mwajɛnmɑ̃] *adv* MODÉRÉMENT : fairly, moderately
moyeu [mwajø] *nm, pl* **moyeux** : hub (of a wheel)
muer [mɥe] *vi* **1** : molt, shed **2** : change, break (of the voice) — **mue** [my] *nf* : molting, shedding
muet, muette [mɥɛ, mɥɛt] *adj* **1** : dumb **2** SILENCIEUX : silent — **~** *n* : mute, dumb person
muffin [mɔfœn] *nm Can* : muffin
muguet [mygɛ] *nm* : lily of the valley
mule [myl] *nf* : female mule — **mulet** [mylɛ] *nm* : male mule
multicolore [myltikɔlɔr] *adj* : multicolored
multimédia [myltimedja] *adj* : multimedia
multinational, -nale [myltinasjɔnal] *adj, mpl* **-naux** [-no] : multinational
multiple [myltipl] *adj* **1** : multiple **2** DIVERS : many — **~** *nm* : multiple — **multiplication** [myltiplikasjɔ̃] *nf* : multiplication — **multiplier** [myltiplije] {96} *vt* : multiply — **se multiplier** *vr* : proliferate
multitude [myltityd] *nf* : multitude, mass
municipal, -pale [mynisipal] *adj, mpl* **-paux** [-po] : municipal, town — **municipalité** [mynisipalite] *nf* **1** : municipality, town **2** : town council
munir [mynir] *vt* : equip, provide — **se munir** *vr* **~ de** : equip oneself with
munitions [mynisjɔ̃] *nfpl* : ammunition, munitions
mur [myr] *nm* : wall
mûr, mûre [myr] *adj* **1** : ripe (of a fruit) **2** : mature (of a person)
muraille [myraj] *nf* : (high) wall — **mural, -rale** [myral] *adj, mpl* **-raux** [myro] : wall, mural — **murale** [myral] *nf* : mural
mûre [myr] *nf* : blackberry
mûrir [myrir] *v* **1** : ripen **2** ÉVOLUER : mature, develop
murmure [myrmyr] *nm* : murmur — **murmurer** [myrmyre] *v* : murmur
muscade [myskad] *nf or* **noix ~** : nutmeg
muscle [myskl] *nm* : muscle — **musclé, -clée** [myskle] *adj* : muscular, powerful — **musculaire** [myskyler] *adj* : muscular — **musculature** [myskylatyr] *nf* : muscles *pl*
muse [myz] *nf* : muse
museau [myzo] *nm, pl* **-seaux** : muzzle, snout
musée [myze] *nm* : museum
museler [myzle] {8} *vt* : muzzle — **muselière** [myzəljɛr] *nf* : muzzle
musique [myzik] *nf* : music — **musical, -cale** [myzikal] *adj* **-caux** [-ko] : musical — **musicien, -cienne** [myzisjɛ̃, -sjɛn] *n* : musician
musulman, -mane [myzylmɑ̃, -man] *adj & n* : Muslim

mutant, -tante [mytɑ̃, -tɑ̃t] *adj & n* : mutant — **mutation** [mytasjɔ̃] *nf* **1** : transformation **2** : transfer (of an employee) — **muter** [myte] *vt* : transfer (an employee)

mutiler [mytile] *vt* : mutilate

mutiner [mytine] *v* **se mutiner** *vr* : mutiny, rebel — **mutinerie** [mytinri] *nf* RÉBELLION : mutiny, rebellion

mutuel, -tuelle [mytɥɛl] *adj* : mutual

myope [mjɔp] *adj* : nearsighted — **myopie** [mjɔpi] *nf* : myopia, nearsightedness

myrtille [mirtil] *nf France* : blueberry

mystère [mistɛr] *nm* : mystery — **mystérieux, -rieuse** [misterjø, -rjøz] *adj* : mysterious

mystifier [mistifje] {96} *vt* DUPER : deceive, dupe

mystique [mistik] *adj* : mystic, mystical

mythe [mit] *nm* : myth — **mythique** [mitik] *adj* : mythic(al) — **mythologie** [mitɔlɔʒi] *nf* : mythology

N

n [ɛn] *nm* : n, 14th letter of the alphabet

nacre [nakr] *nf* : mother-of-pearl — **nacré, -crée** [nakre] *adj* : pearly

nager [naʒe] {17} *v* : swim — **nage** [naʒ] *nf* **1** : swimming **2** : stroke (in swimming) **3** **en** ⁓ : dripping with sweat — **nageoire** [naʒwar] *nf* : fin, flipper — **nageur, -geuse** [naʒœr, -ʒøz] *n* : swimmer

naguère [nager] *adv* **1** RÉCEMMENT : recently **2** AUTREFOIS : formerly

naïf, naïve [naif, naiv] *adj* **1** INGÉNU : naive **2** CRÉDULE : gullible

nain, naine [nɛ̃, nɛn] *n* : dwarf, midget

naître [nɛtr] {57} *vi* **1** : be born **2** : rise, originate — **naissance** [nɛsɑ̃s] *nf* **1** : birth **2 donner** ⁓ **à** : give rise to — **naissant, -sante** [nɛsɑ̃, -sɑ̃t] *adj* : incipient

naïveté [naivte] *nf* : naïveté

nantir [nɑ̃tir] *vt* ⁓ **de** : provide with — **nanti, -tie** [nɑ̃ti] *adj* : affluent, well-to-do — **nantissement** [nɑ̃tismɑ̃] *nm* : collateral

nappe [nap] *nf* **1** : tablecloth **2** : layer, sheet (of water, oil, etc.) — **napper** [nape] *vt* : coat, cover — **napperon** [naprɔ̃] *nm* : mat, doily

narcotique [narkɔtik] *nm* : narcotic

narguer [narge] *vt* : mock, taunt

narine [narin] *nf* : nostril

narquois, -quoise [narkwa, -kwaz] *adj* : sneering, derisive

narrer [nare] *vt* : narrate, tell — **narrateur, -trice** [naratœr, -tris] *n* : narrator — **narration** [narasjɔ̃] *nf* : narration, narrative

nasal, -sale [nazal] *adj, mpl* **-saux** [nazo] : nasal — **naseau** [nazo] *nm, pl* **-seaux** : nostril (of an animal) — **nasillard, -larde** [nazijar, -jard] *adj* : nasal (in tone)

natal, -tale [natal] *adj, mpl* **-tals** : native (of a country, etc.) — **natalité** [natalite] *nf* : birthrate

natation [natasjɔ̃] *nf* : swimming

natif¹, -tive [natif, -tiv] *adj* ⁓ **de** : be born in

natif², -tive *n* : native

nation [nasjɔ̃] *nf* : nation — **national, -nale** [nasjɔnal] *adj, mpl* **-naux** [-no] : national — **nationale** *nf France* : highway — **nationaliser** [nasjɔnalize] *vt* : nationalize — **nationalisme** [nasjɔnalism] *nm* : nationalism — **nationalité** [nasjɔnalite] *nf* : nationality

nativité [nativite] *nf* : nativity

natte [nat] *nf* **1** : (straw) mat **2** : braid (of hair) — **natter** [nate] *vt* : braid, plait

naturaliser [natyralize] *vt* : naturalize

nature [natyr] *nf* **1** : nature **2** ⁓ **morte** : still life — ⁓ *adj* : plain (of yogurt, etc.) — **naturel, -relle** [natyrɛl] *adj* : natural — **naturel** *nm* **1** : nature, disposition **2** AISANCE : naturalness — **naturellement** [natyrɛlmɑ̃] *adv* **1** : naturally **2** : of course

naufrage [nofraʒ] *nm* : shipwreck — **naufragé, -gée** [nofraʒe] *adj & n* : castaway

nausée [noze] *nf* : nausea — **nauséabond, -bonde** [nozeabɔ̃, -bɔnd] *adj* : nauseating, revolting

nautique [notik] *adj* : nautical

naval, -vale [naval] *adj, mpl* **-vals** : naval

navet [navɛ] *nm* **1** : turnip **2** *fam* : third-rate film, novel, etc.

navette [navɛt] *nf* **1** : shuttle **2 faire la** ⁓ : shuttle back and forth, commute

naviguer [navige] *vi* : sail, navigate — **navigable** [navigabl] *adj* : navigable — **navigateur, -trice** [navigatœr, -tris] *n* : navigator — **navigation** [navigasjɔ̃] *nf* : navigation

navire [navir] *nm* : ship, vessel

navrant, -vrante [navrɑ̃, -vrɑ̃t] *adj* **1** : upsetting, distressing **2** REGRETTABLE : unfortunate — **navré, -vrée** [navre] *adj* **être** ⁓ **de** : be sorry about

ne [nə] (**n'** *before a vowel or mute h*) *adv* **1**
~ **pas** : not **2** ~ **jamais** : never **3** ~
plus : no longer **4** ~ **que** : only

né, née [ne] *adj* : born

néanmoins [neɑ̃mwɛ̃] *adv* : nevertheless,
yet

néant [neɑ̃] *nm* : emptiness, nothingness

nébuleux, -leuse [nebylø, -løz] *adj* **1**
: cloudy (of the sky) **2** VAGUE : nebulous

nécessaire [neseseʀ] *adj* : necessary — ~
nm **1** : necessity, need **2** TROUSSE : bag, kit
— **nécessairement** [neseseʀmɑ̃] *adv* : necessarily — **nécessité** [nesesite] *nf* : necessity, need — **nécessiter** [nesesite] *vt* EX-
IGER : require, call for

nécrologie [nekʀɔlɔʒi] *nf* : obituary

nectar [nɛktaʀ] *nm* : nectar

nectarine [nɛktaʀin] *nf* : nectarine

nef [nɛf] *nf* : nave

néfaste [nefast] *adj* NUISIBLE : harmful

négatif, -tive [negatif, -tiv] *adj* : negative —
négatif *nm* : negative (in photography) —
négative *nf* **répondre par la** ~ : reply in
the negative — **négation** [negasjɔ̃] *nf* : negative (in grammar)

négliger [negliʒe] {17} *vt* **1** : neglect **2**
IGNORER : disregard — **négligé, -gée**
[negliʒe] *adj* : untidy (of appearance, etc.)
— **négligé** *nm* : negligee — **négligeable**
[negliʒabl] *adj* : negligible — **négligence**
[negliʒɑ̃s] *nf* : negligence, carelessness —
négligent, -gente [negliʒɑ̃, -ʒɑ̃t] *adj* : negligent

négoce [negɔs] *nm* : business, trade — **négociant, -ciante** [negɔsjɑ̃, -sjɑ̃t] *n* : merchant

négocier [negɔsje] {96} *v* : negotiate — **négociable** [negɔsjabl] *adj* : negotiable —
négociateur, -trice [negɔsjatœʀ, -tʀis] *n*
: negotiator — **négociation** [negɔsjasjɔ̃] *nf*
: negotiation

nègre, négresse [nɛgʀ, negʀɛs] *adj & n*
(*sometimes considered offensive*) : Negro

neige [nɛʒ] *nf* **1** : snow **2** ~ **fondue** : slush
— **neiger** [neʒe] {17} *v impers* : snow —
neigeux, -geuse [nɛʒø, -ʒøz] *adj* : snowy

nénuphar [nenyfaʀ] *nm* : water lily

néon [neɔ̃] *nm* : neon

néophyte [neɔfit] *nmf* : novice, beginner

Neptune [nɛptyn] *nf* : Neptune (planet)

nerf [nɛʀ] *nm* **1** : nerve **2** VIGUEUR : vigor,
spirit — **nerveux, -veuse** [nɛʀvø, -vøz] *adj*
: nervous, tense — **nervosité** [nɛʀvozite] *nf*
: nervousness

nervure [nɛʀvyʀ] *nf* : vein (of a leaf)

n'est–ce pas [nɛspa] *adv* : no?, isn't that
right?, isn't it?

net, nette [nɛt] *adj* **1** PROPRE : clean, tidy **2**
CLAIR : clear, distinct — **net** *adv* : plainly,
flatly — **nettement** [nɛtmɑ̃] *adv* **1** : clearly,

distinctly **2** : definitely — **netteté** [nɛtte] *nf*
1 : cleanness **2** : clearness, sharpness

nettoyer [nɛtwaje] {58} *vt* **1** : clean (up) **2**
~ **à sec** : dry-clean — **nettoyage** [nɛtwa-
jaʒ] *nm* : cleaning — **nettoyant** [nɛtwajɑ̃]
nm : cleaning agent

neuf[1] [nœf] *adj* **1** : nine **2** : ninth (in dates)
— ~ *nms & pl* : nine

neuf[2]**, neuve** [nœf, nœv] *adj* : new — **neuf**
nm **quoi de** ~? : what's new?

neurologie [nøʀɔlɔʒi] *nf* : neurology

neutre [nøtʀ] *adj* **1** : neuter (in grammar) **2**
: neutral — **neutraliser** [nøtʀalize] *vt* : neutralize — **neutralité** [nøtʀalite] *nf* : neutrality

neutron [nøtʀɔ̃] *nm* : neutron

neuvième [nœvjɛm] *adj & nmf & nm* : ninth

neveu [nəvø] *nm, pl* **-veux** : nephew

névrosé, -sée [nevʀoze] *adj & n* : neurotic
— **névrotique** [nevʀɔtik] *adj* : neurotic

nez [ne] *nm* : nose

ni [ni] *conj* **1** ~ . . . ~ : neither . . . nor **2**
~ **plus** ~ **moins** : no more, no less

niais, niaise [njɛ, njɛz] *adj* : simple, foolish
— **niaiserie** [njɛzʀi] *nf* : foolishness

niche [niʃ] *nf* **1** : niche, recess **2** : kennel —
nicher [niʃe] *vi* : nest

nickel [nikɛl] *nm* : nickel

nicotine [nikɔtin] *nf* : nicotine

nid [ni] *nm* **1** : nest **2** ~ **de brigands** : den
of thieves

nièce [njɛs] *nf* : niece

nier [nje] {96} *vt* : deny

nigaud, -gaude [nigo, -god] *n* : simpleton,
fool

niveau [nivo] *nm, pl* **-veaux** [nivo] **1** : level
2 ~ **de vie** : standard of living — **niveler**
[nivle] {8} *vt* : level

noble [nɔbl] *adj* : noble — ~ *nmf* : noble,
nobleman *m*, noblewoman *f* — **noblesse**
[nɔblɛs] *nf* : nobility

noce [nɔs] *nf* **1** : wedding, wedding party **2**
~**s** *nfpl* : wedding

nocif, -cive [nɔsif, -siv] *adj* : noxious, harmful

nocturne [nɔktyʀn] *adj* : nocturnal, night

Noël [nɔɛl] *nm* **1** : Christmas **2** **père** ~
: Santa Claus

nœud [nø] *nm* **1** : knot, tie **2** : knot (nautical
speed) **3** ~ **coulant** : noose **4** ~ **papillon** : bow tie

noir, noire [nwaʀ] *adj* **1** : black **2** SALE
: dirty, grimy **3** OBSCUR : dark — **noir** *nm*
1 : black **2** **dans le** ~ : in the dark, in
darkness — **Noir, Noire** *n* : black man,
black woman — **noirceur** [nwaʀsœʀ] *nf* **1**
: blackness **2** *Can* : darkness — **noircir**
[nwaʀsiʀ] *vi* : grow dark, darken — *vt*
: blacken

noisette [nwazɛt] *nf* : hazelnut

noix [nwa] *nfs & pl* **1** : nut, walnut **2** : piece, lump (of butter, etc.) **3** ~ **de cajou** : cashew (nut)

nom [nɔ̃] *nm* **1** : name **2** : (proper) noun

nomade [nɔmad] *nmf* : nomad — ~ *adj* : nomadic

nombre [nɔ̃br] *nm* : number — **nombreux, -breuse** [nɔ̃brø, -brøz] *adj* : numerous

nombril [nɔ̃bril] *nm* : navel

nominal, -nale [nɔminal] *adj, mpl* **-naux** [-no] : nominal

nommer [nɔme] *vt* **1** : name, call **2** : appoint, nominate **3** CITER : mention — **se nommer** *vr* **1** S'APPELER : be named **2** : introduce oneself — **nommément** [nɔmemɑ̃] *adv* : by name, namely

non [nɔ̃] *adv* **1** : no **2 je pense que** ~ : I don't think so **3** ~ **plus** : neither, either — ~ *nm* : no

nonchalance [nɔ̃ʃalɑ̃s] *nf* : nonchalance — **nonchalant, -lante** [nɔ̃ʃalɑ̃, -lɑ̃t] *adj* : nonchalant

non–sens [nɔsɑ̃s] *nms & pl* ABSURDITÉ : nonsense, absurdity

nord [nɔr] *adj* : north, northern — ~ *nm* **1** : north **2 le Nord** : the North

nord–est [nɔrɛst] *adj s & pl* : northeast, northeastern — ~ *nm* : northeast

nord–ouest [nɔrwɛst] *adj s & pl* : northwest, northwestern — ~ *nm* : northwest

normal, -male [nɔrmal] *adj, mpl* **-maux** [nɔrmo] : normal — **normale** *nf* **1** : average **2** NORME : norm — **normalement** [nɔrmalmɑ̃] *adv* : normally, usually — **normaliser** [nɔrmalize] *vt* : normalize, standardize — **normalité** [nɔrmalite] *nf* : normality — **norme** [nɔrm] *nf* : norm, standard

nos → **notre**

nostalgie [nɔstalʒi] *nf* : nostalgia — **nostalgique** [nɔstalʒik] *adj* : nostalgic

notable [nɔtabl] *adj & nm* : notable

notaire [nɔtɛr] *nm* : notary public

notamment [nɔtamɑ̃] *adv* : especially, particularly

notation [nɔtasjɔ̃] *nf* : notation

note [nɔt] *nf* **1** : note **2** ADDITION : bill, check **3** : mark, grade (in school) — **noter** [nɔte] *vt* **1** REMARQUER : note, notice **2** MARQUER : mark, write (down) **3** : mark, grade (an exam)

notice [nɔtis] *nf* : instructions *pl*

notifier [nɔtifje] {96} *vt* : notify

notion [nɔsjɔ̃] *nf* : notion, idea

notoire [nɔtwar] *adj* **1** CONNU : well-known **2** : notorious (of a criminal) — **notoriété** [nɔtɔrjete] *nf* : notoriety

notre [nɔtr] *adj, pl* **nos** [no] : our

nôtre [notr] *pron* **le** ~, **la** ~, **les** ~**s** : ours

nouer [nwe] *vt* : tie, knot — **noueux, noueuse** [nwø, nwøz] *adj* : gnarled

nougat [nuga] *nm* : nougat

nouille [nuj] *nf* **1** *fam* : nitwit, idiot **2** ~**s** *nfpl* : noodles, pasta

nourrir [nurir] *vt* **1** ALIMENTER : feed, nourish **2** : provide for (a family, etc.) **3** : nurse, harbor (a grudge, etc.) — **se nourrir** *vr* : eat — **nourrice** [nuris] *nf* : wet nurse — **nourrissant, -sante** [nurisɑ̃, -sɑ̃t] *adj* : nourishing, nutritious — **nourrisson** [nurisɔ̃] *nm* : infant — **nourriture** [nurityr] *nf* : food

nous [nu] *pron* **1** : we **2** : us **3** ~**-mêmes** : ourselves

nouveau [nuvo] (**-vel** [-vɛl] *before a vowel or mute h*), **-velle** [-vɛl] *adj, mpl* **-veaux** [nuvo] **1** : new **2 de** ~ *or* à ~ : again, once again **3** ~ **venu** : newcomer — **nouveau** *nm* **1 du** ~ : something new **2 le** ~ : the new — **nouveau–né, -née** [nuvone] *adj & n, mpl* **nouveau–nés** : newborn — **nouveauté** [nuvote] *nf* **1** : newness, novelty **2** INNOVATION : innovation

nouvelle [nuvɛl] *nf* **1** : piece of news **2** : short story **3** ~**s** *nfpl* : news — **nouvellement** [nuvɛlmɑ̃] *adv* : newly, recently

novateur, -trice [nɔvatœr, -tris] *adj* : innovative — ~ *n* : innovator

novembre [nɔvɑ̃br] *nm* : November

novice [nɔvis] *adj* : inexperienced — ~ *nmf* : novice, beginner

noyau [nwajo] *nm, pl* **noyaux** [nwajo] **1** : pit, stone (of a fruit) **2** : nucleus, core (in science)

noyauter [nwajote] *vt* : infiltrate

noyer[1] [nwaje] {58} *vt* **1** : drown **2** : flood (an engine) — **se noyer** *vr* : drown — **noyé, noyée** [nwaje] *n* : drowning victim

noyer[2] *nm* : walnut tree

nu, nue [ny] *adj* **1** : naked, nude **2** : plain, bare (of a wall) — **nu** *nm* **1** : nude **2 à** ~ : bare, exposed

nuage [nɥaʒ] *nm* : cloud — **nuageux, -geuse** [nɥaʒø, -ʒøz] *adj* : cloudy

nuance [nɥɑ̃s] *nf* **1** TON : hue, shade **2** SUBTILITÉ : nuance — **nuancer** [nɥɑ̃se] {6} *vt* : qualify (opinions, etc.)

nucléaire [nykleɛr] *adj* : nuclear

nudité [nydite] *nf* : nudity, nakedness

nuée [nɥe] *nf* : horde, swarm

nuire [nɥir] {49} *vi* ~ **à** : harm, injure — **nuisible** [nɥizibl] *adj* : harmful

nuit [nɥi] *nf* **1** : night, nighttime **2 faire** ~ : be dark out

nul, nulle [nyl] *adj* **1** AUCUN : no **2** : null, invalid **3 être nul en maths** : be hopeless in math **5 nulle part** : nowhere — **nul** *pron* : no one, nobody — **nullement** [nylmɑ̃] *adv* : by no means

numéraire [nymerɛr] *nm* : cash

numéral, -rale [nymeral] *adj, mpl* **-raux** [-ro] : numeral — **numéral** *nm, pl* **-raux** : nu-

meral — **numérique** [nymerik] *adj* **1** : numerical **2** : digital — **numéro** [nymero] *nm* **1** : number **2** : issue (of a periodical) — **numéroter** [nymerɔte] *vt* : number
nuptial, -tiale [nypsjal] *adj, mpl* **-tiaux** [-sjo] : nuptial, wedding

nuque [nyk] *nf* : nape of the neck
nutrition [nytrisjɔ̃] *nf* : nutrition — **nutritif, -tive** [nytritif, -tiv] *adj* **1** : nutritious **2** : nutritional
nylon [nilɔ̃] *nm* : nylon
nymphe [nɛ̃f] *nf* : nymph

O

o [o] *nm* : o, 15th letter of the alphabet
oasis [ɔazis] *nf* : oasis
obéir [ɔbeir] *vi* ~ **à 1** : obey **2** : respond to — **obéissance** [ɔbeisɑ̃s] *nf* : obedience — **obéissant, -sante** [ɔbeisɑ̃, -sɑ̃t] *adj* : obedient
obélisque [ɔbelisk] *nm* : obelisk
obèse [ɔbɛz] *adj* : obese — **obésité** [ɔbezite] *nf* : obesity
objecter [ɔbʒɛkte] *vt* **1** : raise as an objection **2** PRÉTEXTER : plead (as an excuse) — **objectif, -tive** [ɔbʒɛktif, -tiv] *adj* : objective — **objectif** *nm* **1** BUT : objective, goal **2** : lens (of an optical instrument) — **objectivité** [ɔbʒɛktivite] *nf* : objectivity — **objection** [ɔbʒɛksjɔ̃] *nf* : objection — **objet** [ɔbʒɛ] *nm* **1** : object, thing **2** : subject, topic **3** BUT : aim, purpose **4 complément d'**~ : object (in grammar)
obligation [ɔbligasjɔ̃] *nf* **1** : obligation **2** : (savings) bond — **obligatoire** [ɔbligatwar] *adj* : compulsory, obligatory — **obligatoirement** [ɔbligatwarmɑ̃] *adv* : necessarily
obliger [ɔbliʒe] {17} *vt* **1** : oblige **2** CONTRAINDRE : force, compel — **obligé, -gée** [ɔbliʒe] *adj* **1 c'est obligé** *fam* : it's bound to happen, it's inevitable **2 être obligé de** : have to — **obligeance** [ɔbliʒɑ̃s] *nf* AMABILITÉ : kindness — **obligeant, -geante** [ɔbliʒɑ̃, -ʒɑ̃t] *adj* : obliging, kind
oblique [ɔblik] *adj* **1** : oblique **2 en** ~ : crosswise, diagonally — **obliquer** [ɔblike] *vi* : bear, turn (off)
oblitérer [ɔblitere] {87} *vt* : cancel (a stamp)
oblong, oblongue [ɔblɔ̃, ɔblɔ̃g] *adj* : oblong
obscène [ɔpsɛn] *adj* : obscene — **obscénité** [ɔpsenite] *nf* : obscenity
obscur, -cure [ɔpskyr] *adj* **1** SOMBRE : dark **2** VAGUE : obscure — **obscurcir** [ɔpskyrsir] *vt* **1** ASSOMBRIR : darken **2** : obscure, blur — **s'obscurcir** *vr* **1** : grow dark **2** : become obscure — **obscurité** [ɔpskyrite] *nf* **1** : darkness **2** : obscurity

obséder [ɔpsede] {87} *vt* : obsess — **obsédant, -dante** [ɔpsedɑ̃, -dɑ̃t] *adj* : haunting, obsessive — **obsédé, -dée** [ɔpsede] *n* : obsessive, fanatic
obsèques [ɔpsɛk] *nfpl* : funeral
observer [ɔpsɛrve] *vt* : observe — **observateur, -trice** [ɔpsɛrvatœr, -tris] *adj* : observant, perceptive — ~ *n* : observer — **observation** [ɔpsɛrvasjɔ̃] *nf* **1** : observance **2** : observation — **observatoire** [ɔpsɛrvatwar] *nm* **1** : observatory **2** : observation post
obsession [ɔpsesjɔ̃] *nf* : obsession — **obsessionnel, -nelle** [ɔpsesjɔnɛl] *adj* : obsessive
obsolète [ɔpsɔlɛt] *adj* : obsolete
obstacle [ɔpstakl] *nm* : obstacle
obstétrique [ɔpstetrik] *nf* : obstetrics
obstiner [ɔpstine] *v* **s'obstiner** *vr* ~ **à** : persist in — **obstiné, -née** [ɔpstine] *adj* ENTÊTÉ : obstinate, stubborn
obstruction [ɔpstryksjɔ̃] *nf* : obstruction — **obstruer** [ɔpstrye] *vt* : obstruct
obtenir [ɔptənir] {92} *vt* : obtain, get — **obtention** [ɔptɑ̃sjɔ̃] *nf* : obtaining
obturer [ɔptyre] *vt* **1** : seal, stop up **2** : fill (a tooth)
obtus, -tuse [ɔpty, -tyz] *adj* : obtuse
obus [ɔby] *nm* **1** : (mortar) shell **2 éclats d'**~ : shrapnel
occasion [ɔkazjɔ̃] *nf* **1** : opportunity **2** CIRCONSTANCE : occasion **3** : bargain **4 d'**~ : secondhand — **occasionnel, -nelle** [ɔkazjɔnɛl] *adj* : occasional — **occasionnel, -nelle** *n Can* : temp, temporary employee — **occasionner** [ɔkazjɔne] *vt* CAUSER : cause
occident [ɔksidɑ̃] *nm* **1** : west **2 l'Occident** : the West — **occidental, -tale** [ɔksidɑtal] *adj, mpl* **-taux** [-to] : western, Western
occulte [ɔkylt] *adj* : occult
occuper [ɔkype] *vt* **1** : occupy **2** REMPLIR : take up, fill **3** ~ **un poste** : hold a job — **s'occuper** *vr* **1** : keep busy **2** ~ **de** : han-

dle, take care of — **occupant, -pante** [ɔkypɑ̃,-pɑ̃t] *n* : occupant — **occupation** [ɔkypasjɔ̃] *nf* **1** : occupation **2** : occupancy — **occupé, -pée** [ɔkype] *adj* **1** : busy **2 zone occupée** : occupied zone

occurrence [ɔkyrɑ̃s] *nf* **1** : instance, occurrence **2 en l'～** : in this case

océan [ɔseɑ̃] *nm* : ocean — **océanique** [ɔseanik] *adj* : oceanic, ocean

ocre [ɔkr] *nmf* : ocher, ochre

octave [ɔktav] *nf* : octave

octet [ɔktɛ] *nm* : byte

octobre [ɔktɔbr] *nm* : October

octogone [ɔktɔgon] *nm* : octagon

octroyer [ɔktrwaje] {58} *vt* : grant, bestow

oculaire [ɔkylɛr] *adj* : ocular, eye — **oculiste** [ɔkylist] *nmf* : oculist

ode [ɔd] *nf* : ode

odeur [ɔdœr] *nf* : odor, smell

odieux, -dieuse [ɔdjø, -djøz] *adj* EXÉCRABLE : odious, hateful

odorant, -rante [ɔdɔrɑ̃, -rɑ̃t] *adj* PARFUMÉ : fragrant

odorat [ɔdɔra] *nm* : sense of smell

œil [œj] *nm, pl* **yeux** [jø] **1** : eye **2 coup d'～** : glance — **œillade** [œjad] *nf* : wink — **œillères** [œjɛr] *nfpl* : blinders — **œillet** [œjɛ] *nm* : carnation

œsophage [ezɔfaʒ] *nm* : esophagus

œstrogène [ɛstrɔʒɛn] *nm* : estrogen

œuf [œf] *nm, pl* **œufs** [ø] : egg

œuvre [œvr] *nm* : (body of) work — **～** *nf* **1** : work, undertaking, task **2 ～ d'art** : work of art — **œuvrer** [œvre] *vi* : work

offense [ɔfɑ̃s] *nf* : insult, offense — **offenser** [ɔfɑ̃se] *vt* : offend — **s'offenser** *vr* **～ de** : take offense at — **offensif, -sive** [ɔfɑ̃sif, -siv] *adj* : offensive, attacking — **offensive** *nf* : offensive

office [ɔfis] *nm* **1** : service (in religion) **2 faire ～ de** : act as

officiel, -cielle [ɔfisjɛl] *adj & n* : official — **officialiser** [ɔfisjalize] *vt* : make official — **officier** [ɔfisje] *nm* : officer (in the armed forces) — **officieux, -cieuse** [ɔfisjø, -sjøz] *adj* : unofficial, informal

offrande [ɔfrɑ̃d] *nf* : offering

offre [ɔfr] *nf* **1** : offer, bid **2 l'～ et la demande** : supply and demand

offrir [ɔfrir] {83} *vt* : offer, give — **s'offrir** *vr* **1** : treat oneself to **2** SE PRÉSENTER : present itself

offusquer [ɔfyske] *vt* : offend — **s'offusquer** *vr* : take offense

ogive [ɔʒiv] *nf* : warhead

ogre, ogresse [ɔgr, ɔgrɛs] *n* : ogre

oh [o] *interj* : oh — **ohé** [ɔe] *interj* : hey

oie [wa] *nf* : goose

oignon [ɔɲɔ̃] *nm* **1** : onion **2** : bulb (of a tulip, etc.) **3** : bunion (in medicine)

oindre [wɛ̃dr] {59} *vt* : anoint

oiseau [wazo] *nm, pl* **oiseaux** : bird

oisif, -sive [wazif, -ziv] *adj* : idle — **oisiveté** [wazivte] *nf* : idleness

oisillon [wazijɔ̃] *nm* : fledgling

oléoduc [ɔleɔdyk] *nm* : (oil) pipeline

olfactif, -tive [ɔlfaktif, -tiv] *adj* : olfactory

olive [ɔliv] *nf* : olive

olympique [ɔlɛ̃pik] *adj* : Olympic

ombilical, -cale [ɔ̃bilikal] *adj, mpl* **-caux** [-ko] : umbilical

ombrage [ɔ̃braʒ] *nm* **1** OMBRE : shade **2 porter ～ à** : offend — **ombragé, -gée** [ɔ̃braʒe] *adj* : shady, shaded — **ombre** [ɔ̃br] *nf* **1** : shadow **2** SOUPÇON : hint, trace **3 à l'～** : in the shade

omelette [ɔmlɛt] *nf* : omelet

omettre [ɔmɛtr] {53} *vt* : omit, leave out — **omission** [ɔmisjɔ̃] *nf* : omission

omnibus [ɔmnibys] *nm* : local train

omnipotent, -tente [ɔmnipɔtɑ̃, -tɑ̃t] *adj* : omnipotent

omoplate [ɔmɔplat] *nf* : shoulder blade

on [ɔ̃] *pron* **1** : one, we, you **2** : they, people **3** QUELQU'UN : someone

once [ɔ̃s] *nf* : ounce

oncle [ɔ̃kl] *nm* : uncle

onctueux, -tueuse [ɔ̃ktɥø, -tɥøz] *adj* : smooth, creamy

onde [ɔ̃d] *nf* : wave

on-dit [ɔ̃di] *nms & pl* : rumor

onduler [ɔ̃dyle] *vi* **1** : undulate, sway **2** : be wavy (of hair) — **ondulation** [ɔ̃dylasjɔ̃] *nf* : undulation, wave — **ondulé, -lée** [ɔ̃dyle] *adj* **1** : wavy **2 carton ondulé** : corrugated cardboard

onéreux, -reuse [ɔnerø, -røz] *adj* COÛTEUX : costly

ongle [ɔ̃gl] *nm* : nail, fingernail

onguent [ɔ̃gɑ̃] *nm* : ointment

onyx [ɔniks] *nm* : onyx

onze [ɔ̃z] *adj* **1** : eleven **2** : eleventh (in dates) — **～** *nms & pl* : eleven — **onzième** [ɔ̃zjɛm] *adj & nmf & nm* : eleventh

opale [ɔpal] *nf* : opal

opaque [ɔpak] *adj* : opaque

opéra [ɔpera] *nm* **1** : opera **2** : opera house

opération [ɔperasjɔ̃] *nf* **1** : operation **2** : transaction (in banking, etc.) — **opérateur, -trice** [ɔperatœr, -tris] *n* : operator — **opérationnel, -nelle** [ɔperasjɔnɛl] *adj* : operational — **opérer** [ɔpere] {87} *vt* : operate on (a patient) — *vi* **1** : take effect, work **2** INTERVENIR : act

opiner [ɔpine] *vi* **～ de la tête** : nod in agreement

opiniâtre [ɔpinjatr] *adj* OBSTINÉ : stubborn, persistent

opinion [ɔpinjɔ̃] *nf* : opinion, belief

opium [ɔpjɔm] *nm* : opium

opportun, -tune [ɔpɔrtœ̃, -tyn] *adj* : opportune, timely — **opportunisme** [ɔpɔrtynism] *nm* : opportunism — **opportuniste** [ɔpɔrtynist] *adj* : opportunist, opportunistic — ~ *nmf* : opportunist

opposer [ɔpoze] *vt* **1** : put up (an objection, etc.) **2** : contrast (ideas, etc.) **3** DIVISER : divide — **s'opposer** *vr* **1** : clash, conflict **2** ~ **à** : be opposed to — **opposant, -sante** [ɔpozɑ̃, -zɑ̃t] *n* ADVERSAIRE : opponent — **opposé, -sée** [ɔpoze] *adj* **1** : opposing **2** : opposite **3** ~ **à** : opposed to — **opposé** *nm* **1** : opposite **2 à l'**~ **de** : contrary to — **opposition** [ɔpozisjɔ̃] *nf* **1** : opposition **2** : objection (in law)

oppresser [ɔprese] *vt* : oppress, burden — **oppressif, -sive** [ɔpresif, -siv] *adj* : oppressive — **oppresseur** [ɔpresœr] *nm* : oppressor — **oppression** [ɔpresjɔ̃] *nf* : oppression

opprimer [ɔprime] *vt* : oppress

opter [ɔpte] *vi* ~ **pour** : opt for, choose

opticien, -cienne [ɔptisjɛ̃, -sjɛn] *n* : optician

optimisme [ɔptimism] *nm* : optimism — **optimiste** [ɔptimist] *adj* : optimistic — ~ *nmf* : optimist

optimum [ɔptimɔm] *adj & adv* : optimum

option [ɔpsjɔ̃] *nf* : option, choice — **optionnel, -nelle** [ɔpsjɔnɛl] *adj* FACULTATIF : optional

optique [ɔptik] *adj* : optic(al) — ~ *nf* **1** : optics **2** PERSPECTIVE : viewpoint

opulent, -lente [ɔpylɑ̃, -lɑ̃t] *adj* : opulent — **opulence** [-lɑ̃s] *nf* : opulence

or[1] [ɔr] *nm* : gold

or[2] *conj* **1** : but, yet **2** : now

oracle [ɔrakl] *nm* : oracle

orage [ɔraʒ] *nm* : storm, thunderstorm — **orageux, -geuse** [ɔraʒø, -ʒøz] *adj* : stormy

oral, -rale [ɔral] *adj, mpl* **oraux** [ɔro] : oral

orange [ɔrɑ̃ʒ] *adj* : orange — ~ *nf* : orange (fruit) — ~ *nm* : orange (color) — **oranger** [ɔrɑ̃ʒe] *nm* : orange tree

orateur, -trice [ɔratœr, -tris] *n* : orator, speaker

orbite [ɔrbit] *nf* **1** : orbit **2** : eye socket

orchestre [ɔrkɛstr] *nm* : orchestra

orchidée [ɔrkide] *nf* : orchid

ordinaire [ɔrdinɛr] *adj* **1** : ordinary, common **2** HABITUEL : usual — ~ *nm* **1 l'**~ : the ordinary **2 d'**~ : usually, as a rule — **ordinairement** [-nɛrmɑ̃] *adv* : usually

ordinateur [ɔrdinatœr] *nm* : computer

ordonnance [ɔrdonɑ̃s] *nf* **1** : order **2** : (medical) prescription

ordonner [ɔrdone] *vt* **1** : put in order, arrange **2** COMMANDER : order **3** : ordain (in religion) — **ordonné, -née** [ɔrdone] *adj* : tidy, orderly

ordre [ɔrdr] *nm* **1** : order **2** PROPRETÉ : tidi-

ness **3** NATURE : nature, sort **4** ~ **du jour** : agenda

ordure [ɔrdyr] *nf* **1** : filth **2** ~**s** *nfpl* : trash, garbage — **ordurier, -rière** [ɔrdyrje] *adj* : filthy

oreille [ɔrej] *nf* **1** : ear **2** OUÏE : hearing

oreiller [ɔreje] *nm* : pillow

oreillons [ɔrejɔ̃] *nmpl* : mumps

orfèvre [ɔrfɛvr] *nm* : goldsmith

organe [ɔrgan] *nm* : organ (of the body) — **organique** [ɔrganik] *adj* : organic

organiser [ɔrganize] *vt* : organize — **s'organiser** *vr* : get organized — **organisateur, -trice** [ɔrganizatœr, -tris] *n* : organizer — **organisation** [ɔrganizasjɔ̃] *nf* : organization

organisme [ɔrganism] *nm* **1** : organism (in biology) **2** : organization, body

organiste [ɔrganist] *nmf* : organist

orgasme [ɔrgasm] *nm* : orgasm

orge [ɔrʒ] *nf* : barley

orgelet [ɔrʒəlɛ] *nm* : sty (in medicine)

orgie [ɔrʒi] *nf* : orgy

orgue [ɔrg] *nm* : organ (musical instrument)

orgueil [ɔrgœj] *nm* : pride — **orgueilleux, -leuse** [ɔrgœjø, -jøz] *adj* : proud

orient [ɔrjɑ̃] *nm* **1** : east **2 l'Orient** : the Orient, the East — **oriental, -tale** [ɔrjɑ̃tal] *adj, mpl* **-taux** [-to] : **1** : eastern **2** : oriental

orienter [ɔrjɑ̃te] *vt* **1** : position, orient **2** GUIDER : guide, direct — **s'orienter** *vr* : find one's bearings — **orientation** [ɔrjɑ̃tasjɔ̃] *nf* **1** : orientation, direction, aspect **2** : guidance, (career) counseling

orifice [ɔrifis] *nm* : orifice

originaire [ɔriʒinɛr] *adj* **être** ~ **de** : be a native of

original, -nale [ɔriʒinal, -nal] *adj, mpl* **-naux** [-no] **1** : original **2** EXCENTRIQUE : eccentric — ~ *n* : character, eccentric — **original** *nm, pl* **-naux** : original — **originalité** [ɔriʒinalite] *nf* **1** : originality **2** : eccentricity — **origine** [ɔriʒin] *nf* **1** : origin **2 à l'**~ : originally — **originel, -nelle** [ɔriʒinɛl] *adj* : original, primary

orignal [ɔriɲal] *nm, pl* **-naux** [-no] : moose

orme [ɔrm] *nm* : elm

orner [ɔrne] *vt* DÉCORER : decorate, adorn — **orné, -née** [ɔrne] *adj* : ornate, flowery — **ornement** [ɔrnəmɑ̃] *nm* : ornament, adornment — **ornemental, -tale** [ɔrnəmɑ̃tal] *adj, mpl* **-taux** [-to] : ornamental

ornière [ɔrnjɛr] *nf* : rut

ornithologie [ɔrnitɔlɔʒi] *nf* : ornithology

orphelin, -line [ɔrfəlɛ̃, -lin] *n* : orphan

orteil [ɔrtɛj] *nm* : toe

orthodoxe [ɔrtɔdɔks] *adj* : orthodox — **orthodoxie** [ɔrtɔdɔksi] *nf* : orthodoxy

orthographe [ɔrtɔgraf] *nf* : spelling, orthography — **orthographier** [ɔrtɔgrafje] {96} *vt* : spell

orthopédie [ɔrtɔpedi] *nf* : orthopedics — **orthopédique** [ɔrtɔpedik] *adj* : orthopedic

ortie [ɔrti] *nf* : nettle

os [ɔs] *nm* : bone

osciller [ɔsile] *vi* **1** : oscillate **2** HESITATE : vacillate, waver — **oscillation** [ɔsilasjɔ̃] *nf* : oscillation

oser [oze] *vt* **1** : dare **2 si j'ose dire** : if I may say so — **osé, -sée** [oze] *adj* : daring, bold

osier [ozje] *nm* **1** : willow (tree) **2** : wicker (furniture)

osmose [ɔsmoz] *nf* : osmosis

ossature [ɔsatyr] *nf* **1** : skeleton, bone structure **2** : frame(work) — **ossements** [ɔsmɑ̃] *nmpl* : remains, bones — **osseux, -seuse** [ɔsø, -søz] *adj* : bony

ostensible [ɔstɑ̃sibl] *adj* : conspicuous, obvious — **ostentation** [ɔstɑ̃tasjɔ̃] *nf* : ostentation

ostéopathe [ɔsteɔpat] *nmf* : osteopath

ostracisme [ɔstrasism] *nm* : ostracism

otage [ɔtaʒ] *nm* : hostage

ôter [ote] *vt* **1** RETIRER : remove, take away **2** SOUSTRAIRE : subtract

otite [ɔtit] *nf* : ear infection

ou [u] *conj* **1** : or **2 ou . . . ou . . .** : either . . . or . . .

où [u] *adv* **1** : where, wherever **2 d'~** : from which, from where — *~ pron* : where, that, in which, on which, to which

ouate [wat] *nf* **1** : absorbent cotton **2** BOURRE : padding, wadding — **ouaté, -tée** [wate] *adj* : padded, quilted

oublier [ublije] {96} *vt* : forget — **s'oublier** *vr* **1** : be forgotten **2** : forget oneself — **oubli** [ubli] *nm* **1** : forgetfulness **2** : oversight — **oublieux, -blieuse** [ublijø, -blijøz] *adj* : forgetful

ouest [wɛst] *adj* : west, western — *~ nm* **1** : west **2 l'Ouest** : the West

oui [wi] *adv & nms & pl* : yes

ouïe [wi] *nf* **1** : (sense of) hearing **2 ~s** *nfpl* : gills — **ouï-dire** [widir] *nms & pl* : hearsay

ouïr [wir] {60} *vt* : hear

ouragan [uragɑ̃] *nm* : hurricane

ourler [urle] *vt* : hem — **ourlet** [urlɛ] *nm* : hem

ours [urs] *nm* **1** : bear **2 ~ blanc** *or* **~ polaire** : polar bear — **ourse** [urs] *nf* : she-bear

outil [uti] *nm* : tool — **outillage** [utijaʒ] *nm* **1** : set of tools **2** : equipment — **outiller** [utije] *vt* ÉQUIPER : equip

outrager [utraʒe] {17} *vt* INSULTER : offend, insult — **outrage** [utraʒ] *nm* : insult

outrance [utrɑ̃s] *nf* : excess — **outrancier, -cière** [utrɑ̃sje, -sjɛr] *adj* : excessive, extreme

outre [utr] *adv* **1 en ~** : in addition, besides **2 ~ mesure** : overly, unduly **3 passer ~ à** : disregard — *~ prep* : besides, in addition to — **outre-mer** [utrəmɛr] *adv* : overseas — **outrepasser** [utrəpase] *vt* : exceed, overstep

outrer [utre] *vt* **1** EXAGÉRER : exaggerate **2** INDIGNER : outrage

ouvert, -verte [uvɛr, -vɛrt] *adj* **1** : open **2** : on, running (of a light, a faucet, etc.) — **ouverture** [uvɛrtyr] *nf* **1** : opening **2** : overture (in music) **3 ~ d'esprit** : open-mindedness

ouvrable [uvrabl] *adj* **1 jour ~** : weekday, working day **2 heures ~s** : business hours

ouvrage [uvraʒ] *nm* : work

ouvre-boîtes [uvrəbwat] *nms & pl* : can opener — **ouvre-bouteilles** [uvrəbutɛj] *nms & pl* : bottle opener

ouvreur, -vreuse [uvrœr, -vrøz] *n* : usher, usherette *f*

ouvrier, -vrière [uvrije, -vrijɛr] *n* : worker — *~ adj* : working-class

ouvrir [uvrir] {83} *vt* **1** : open **2** : turn on (a light, a radio, etc.) — *vi* : open — **s'ouvrir** *vr* : open (up)

ovaire [ɔvɛr] *nm* : ovary

ovale [ɔval] *adj & nm* : oval

ovation [ɔvasjɔ̃] *nf* : ovation

overdose [ɔvœrdoz] *nf* : overdose

oxyde [ɔksid] *nm* **~ de carbone** : carbon monoxide — **oxyder** [ɔkside] *v* **s'oxyder** *vr* : rust

oxygène [ɔksiʒɛn] *nm* : oxygen

ozone [ozɔn] *nm* : ozone

P

p [pe] *nm* : p, 16th letter of the alphabet
pacifier [pasifje] {96} *vt* : pacify, calm —
  pacifique [pasifik] *adj* **1** : peaceful **2**
  l'océan Pacifique : the Pacific Ocean —
  pacifiste [pasifist] *nmf* : pacifist
pacotille [pakɔtij] *nf* **1** : shoddy goods **2 de**
  ~ : cheap
pacte [pakt] *nm* ACCORD : pact, agreement
pagaie [pagɛ] *nf* : paddle
pagaille *or* **pagaïe** [pagaj] *nf fam* **1** : mess,
  chaos **2 en ~** : in great quantities
pagayer [pagaje] {11} *vi* : paddle
page [paʒ] *nf* : page
paie [pɛ] *nf* : pay, wages *pl* — **paiement**
  [pɛmɑ̃] *nm* : payment
païen, païenne [pajɛ̃, pajɛn] *adj & n*
  : pagan, heathen
paillard, -larde [pajar, -jard] *adj* : bawdy
paillasson [pajasɔ̃] *nm* : doormat
paille [paj] *nf* **1** : (piece of) straw **2** : (drinking) straw
paillette [pajɛt] *nf* : sequin
pain [pɛ̃] *nm* **1** : bread **2** : loaf (of bread) **3**
  : cake, bar (of soap, etc.)
pair, paire [pɛr] *adj* : even — **pair** *nm* **1**
  : peer **2 aller de ~** : go hand in hand **3**
  hors ~ : without equal — **paire** [pɛr] *nf*
  : pair
paisible [pezibl] *adj* : peaceful, quiet
paître [pɛtr] {61} *vi* : graze
paix [pɛ] *nf* : peace
palace [palas] *nm* : luxury hotel
palais [palɛ] *nms & pl* **1** : palace **2** : palate
  3 ~ de justice : courts of law
palan [palɑ̃] *nm* : hoist
pale [pal] *nf* : blade (of a propeller, etc.)
pâle [pal] *adj* **1** BLÊME : pale **2** CLAIR
  : light, pale
palet [palɛ] *nm* : puck (in ice hockey)
paletot [palto] *nm* : short coat
palette [palɛt] *nf* **1** : palette **2** : shoulder (of
  pork, etc.)
pâleur [palœr] *nf* : paleness
palier [palje] *nm* **1** : landing, floor **2** NIVEAU
  : level, stage
pâlir [palir] *vi* : turn pale
palissade [palisad] *nf* : fence
pallier [palje] {96} *vt* : alleviate, compensate
  for
palmarès [palmarɛs] *nms & pl* : list of win-
  ners
palme [palm] *nf* **1** : palm leaf **2** NAGEOIRE
  : flipper **3 remporter la ~** : be victorious
palmé, -mée [palme] *adj* : webbed
palmier [palmje] *nm* : palm tree

palourde [palurd] *nf* : clam
palper [palpe] *vt* : feel, finger — **palpable**
  [palpabl] *adj* : tangible
palpiter [palpite] *vi* : palpitate, throb — **pal-
  pitant, -tante** [palpitɑ̃, -tɑ̃t] *adj* : thrilling,
  exciting
paludisme [palydism] *nm* : malaria
pâmer [pame] *v* **se pâmer** *vr* : be ecstatic,
  swoon
pamphlet [pɑ̃flɛ] *nm* : lampoon
pamplemousse [pɑ̃pləmus] *nmf* : grapefruit
pan [pɑ̃] *nm* **1** : section, piece **2** : tail (of a
  garment)
panacée [panase] *nf* : panacea
panais [panɛ] *nm* : parsnip
pancarte [pɑ̃kart] *nf* : sign, placard
pancréas [pɑ̃kreas] *nm* : pancreas
panda [pɑ̃da] *nm* : panda
paner [pane] *vt* : coat with breadcrumbs
panier [panje] *nm* : basket
panique [panik] *nf* : panic — **paniquer**
  [panike] *vi* : panic
panne [pan] *nf* **1** : breakdown **2 ~ d'électricité** : power failure, blackout
panneau [pano] *nm, pl* **-neaux 1** : panel **2**
  : sign, signpost **3 ~ de signalisation**
  : road sign **4 ~ publicitaire** : billboard
panoplie [panɔpli] *nf* **1** GAMME : array,
  range **2** DÉGUISEMENT : outfit, costume
panorama [panɔrama] *nm* : panorama —
  panoramique [panɔramik] *adj* : panoramic
panser [pɑ̃se] *vt* **1** : groom (a horse) **2**
  : dress, bandage (a wound) — **pansement**
  [pɑ̃smɑ̃] *nm* : dressing, bandage
pantalon [pɑ̃talɔ̃] *nm* : pants *pl*, trousers *pl*
panthère [pɑ̃tɛr] *nf* : panther
pantin [pɑ̃tɛ̃] *nm* FANTOCHE : puppet (person)
pantomime [pɑ̃tɔmim] *nf* : pantomime
pantoufle [pɑ̃tufl] *nf* : slipper
panure [panyr] *nf* : bread crumbs *pl*
paon [pɑ̃] *nm* : peacock
papa [papa] *nm fam* : dad, daddy
pape [pap] *nm* : pope
paperasse [papras] *nf* : papers *pl*, paper-
  work
papeterie [papɛtri] *nf* : stationery
papier [papje] *nm* **1** : paper **2** : document,
  paper **3 ~ d'aluminium** : aluminum foil,
  tinfoil **4 ~ hygiénique** : toilet paper **5 ~**
  mouchoir *Can* : tissue **6 ~ peint** : wallpaper **7 ~s** *nmpl* : (identification) papers
papillon [papijɔ̃] *nm* **1** : butterfly **2 ~ de**
  nuit : moth
papoter [papɔte] *vi* : gab, chatter
Pâque [pak] *nf* : Passover

paquebot [pakbo] *nm* : liner, ship
pâquerette [pakrɛt] *nf* : daisy
Pâques [pak] *nm & nfpl* : Easter
paquet [pakɛ] *nm* **1** : package, parcel **2** : pack (of cigarettes, etc.) **3 un ~ de** : a heap of, a pile of
par [par] *prep* **1** : through **2** : by, by means of **3** : as, for **4** : at, during **5 ~ avion** : by airmail **6 ~ exemple** : for example **7 ~ ici** : around here **8 ~ moments** : at times **9 ~ personne** : per person **10 de ~** : throughout
parabole [parabɔl] *nf* : parable
parachever [paraʃve] {52} *vt* : complete, perfect
parachute [paraʃyt] *nm* : parachute — **parachutiste** [paraʃytist] *nmf* : paratrooper
parade [parad] *nf* : parade — **parader** [parade] *vi* : strut, show off
paradis [paradi] *nm* : paradise, heaven
paradoxe [paradɔks] *nm* : paradox — **paradoxal, -xale** [paradɔksal] *adj, mpl* **-xaux** [-kso] : paradoxical
paraffine [parafin] *nf* : paraffin (wax)
parages [paraʒ] *nmpl* **dans les ~** : in the vicinity
paragraphe [paragraf] *nm* : paragraph
paraître [parɛtr] {7} *vi* **1** : appear **2** : show, be visible **3** SEMBLER : seem, look **4 à ~** : forthcoming — *v impers* **il paraît que** : it seems that, apparently
parallèle [paralɛl] *adj* : parallel — **~** *nm* **1** : parallel **2 mettre en ~** : compare — **~** *nf* : parallel (line)
paralyser [paralize] *vt* : paralyze — **paralysie** [paralizi] *nf* : paralysis
paramètre [paramɛtr] *nm* : parameter
paranoïa [paranɔja] *nf* : paranoia
parapet [parapɛ] *nm* : parapet
paraphe [paraf] *nm* **1** : initials *pl* **2** : signature — **parapher** [parafe] *vt* : initial
paraphrase [parafraz] *nf* : paraphrase
parapluie [paraplɥi] *nm* : umbrella
parascolaire [paraskɔlɛr] *adj* : extracurricular
parasite [parazit] *nm* **1** : parasite **2 ~s** *nmpl* : (radio) interference
parasol [parasɔl] *nm* : parasol, sunshade
paravent [paravɑ̃] *nm* : screen, partition
parc [park] *nm* **1** : park **2** : grounds *pl* **3** ENCLOS : pen, playpen **4** : fleet (of automobiles) **5 ~ d'attractions** : amusement park
parcelle [parsɛl] *nf* **1** : fragment **2** : plot (of land)
parce que [parskə] *conj* : because
parchemin [parʃəmɛ̃] *nm* : parchment
parcimonieux, -nieuse [parsimɔnjø, -njøz] *adj* : parsimonious
par–ci, par–là [parsiparla] *adv* : here and there

parcmètre [parkmɛtr] *nm France* : parking meter
parcomètre [parkɔmɛtr] *nm Can* : parking meter
parcourir [parkurir] {23} *vt* **1** : cover (a distance), travel through **2** : leaf through (a text)
parcours [parkur] *nm* **1** : course (of a river), route (of a bus, etc.) **2** : course (in sports)
par–delà *or* **par delà** [pardəla] *prep* : beyond
par–dessous [pardəsu] *adv & prep* : underneath
pardessus [pardəsy] *nms & pl* : overcoat
par–dessus [pardəsy] *adv* : over, above, on top — **~** *prep* **1** : over, above **2 ~ bord** : overboard **3 ~ tout** : above all
par–devant [pardəvɑ̃] *adv* : in front, at the front
pardonner [pardɔne] *vt* **1** : forgive, pardon **2 pardonnez-moi** : excuse me — **pardon** [pardɔ̃] *nm* **1** : forgiveness, pardon **2 ~?** : pardon?, what did you say? **3 ~** : pardon me, sorry
pare–balles [parbal] *adj s & pl* : bulletproof
pare–brise [parbriz] *nms & pl* : windshield
pare–chocs [parʃɔk] *nms & pl* : bumper
pareil, -reille [parɛj] *adj* **1** SEMBLABLE : similar, alike **2** TEL : such — **~** *n* **1** ÉGAL : equal, peer **2 sans pareil** : unequaled — **pareil** [parɛj] *adv fam* : in the same way
parent, -rente [parɑ̃, -rɑ̃t] *adj* : similar, related — **~** *n* **1** : relative, relation **2 parents** *nmpl* : parents — **parenté** [parɑ̃te] *nf* **1** : relationship **2** : family, relations *pl*
parenthèse [parɑ̃tɛz] *nf* : parenthesis, bracket
parer [pare] *vt* **1** : adorn, array **2** : ward off, parry — *vi* **~ à** : deal with
paresser [parɛse] *vi* : laze around — **paresse** [parɛs] *nf* : laziness, idleness — **paresseux, -seuse** [parɛsø, -søz] *adj* : lazy — **paresseux** *nm* : sloth (animal)
parfaire [parfɛr] {62} *vt* : perfect, refine — **parfait, -faite** [parfɛ, -fɛt] *adj* **1** : perfect **2** TOTAL : absolute, complete — **parfaitement** [-fɛtmɑ̃] *adv* **1** : perfectly **2** ABSOLUMENT : definitely
parfois [parfwa] *adv* : sometimes
parfumer [parfyme] *vt* **1** : scent, perfume **2** : flavor (ice cream, etc.) — **se parfumer** *vr* : wear perfume — **parfum** [parfœ̃] *nm* **1** : scent, fragrance **2** : perfume **3** GOÛT : flavor — **parfumé, -mée** [parfyme] *adj* **1** : fragrant, scented **2** : flavored — **parfumerie** [parfymri] *nf* : perfume shop
pari [pari] *nm* : bet, wager — **parier** [parje] {96} *vt* : bet, wager
paria [parja] *nm* : outcast
parisien, -sienne [parizjɛ̃, -zjɛn] *adj* : Parisian

parjurer [parʒyre] *v* **se parjurer** *vr* : perjure oneself

parking [parkiŋ] *nm* : parking lot

parlant, -lante [parlɑ̃, -lɑ̃t] *adj* : vivid, eloquent

parlement [parləmɑ̃] *nm* : parliament — **parlementaire** [parləmɑ̃tɛr] *adj* : parliamentary — **parlementer** [parləmɑ̃te] *vi* : negotiate

parler [parle] *vt* : talk, speak — *vi* **1** : talk, speak **2 ~ à** : talk to **3 ~ de** : mention, refer to — **se parler** *vr* **1** : speak to each other **2** : be spoken (of a language) — **~** *nm* : speech, way of speaking

parloir [parlwar] *nm* : parlor

parmi [parmi] *prep* : among

parodie [parɔdi] *nf* : parody — **parodier** [parɔdje] {96} *vt* : parody, mimic

paroi [parwa] *nf* **1** : partition **2** : wall (in anatomy, etc.) **3 ~ rocheuse** : rock face

paroisse [parwas] *nf* : parish — **paroissien, -sienne** [parwasjɛ̃, -sjɛn] *n* : parishioner

parole [parɔl] *nf* **1** : (spoken) word **2** PROMESSE : word, promise **3** : speech **4 ~s** *nfpl* : lyrics **5 prendre la ~** : speak

paroxysme [parɔksism] *nm* : height, climax

parquer [parke] *vt* **1** : pen (cattle, etc.) **2** GARER : park

parquet [parkɛ] *nm* : parquet (floor)

parrain [parɛ̃] *nm* **1** : godfather **2** : sponsor, patron — **parrainer** [parɛne] *vt* : sponsor

parsemer [parsəme] {52} *vt* **~ de** : scatter with, strew with

part [par] *nf* **1** : portion, piece **2** : part, share **3** : side, position **4 à ~** : apart from **5 de la ~ de** : on behalf of **6 de toutes ~s** : from all sides **7 d'une ~** : on (the) one hand **8 faire sa ~** : do one's share **9 prendre ~ à** : take part in

partager [partaʒe] {17} *vt* **1** : divide up **2** RÉPARTIR : share — **se partager** *vr* : share — **partage** [partaʒ] *nm* : sharing, dividing

partance [partɑ̃s] *nf* **1 en ~** : ready to depart **2 en ~ pour** : bound for — **partant, -tante** [partɑ̃, -tɑ̃t] *adj* : ready, willing

partenaire [partənɛr] *nmf* : partner

parterre [partɛr] *nm* **1** : flower bed **2** : orchestra section (in a theater)

parti [parti] *nm* **1** : group, camp **2** : (political) party **3 ~ pris** : bias **4 prendre ~** : take a stand **5 prendre son ~** : make up one's mind **6 tirer ~ de** : take advantage of — **parti, -tie** [parti] *adj fam* : intoxicated, high

partial, -tiale [parsjal] *adj, mpl* **-tiaux** [-sjo] : biased, partial

participe [partisip] *nm* : participle

participer [partisipe] *vi* **~ à 1** : participate in **2** : contribute to — **participant, -pante** [partisipɑ̃, -pɑ̃t] *n* : participant — **partici-**

pation [partisipasjɔ̃] *nf* **1** : participation **2** : contribution

particule [partikyl] *nf* : particle

particulier, -lière [partikylje, -ljɛr] *adj* **1** : particular, specific **2** SINGULIER : peculiar **3** PRIVÉ : private, personal **4 en ~** : especially, in particular — **particularité** [partikylarite] *nf* : idiosyncrasy — **particulier** [partikylje] *nm* : individual — **particulièrement** [partikyljɛrmɑ̃] *adv* : especially, particularly

partie [parti] *nf* **1** : part **2** : game, match **3** : party, participant **4** SORTIE : outing **5 en ~** : partly, in part **6 faire ~ de** : be a part of — **partiel, -tielle** [parsjɛl] *adj* : partial

partir [partir] {82} *vi* **1** : leave, depart **2** : start up, go off **3** COMMENCER : start **4** S'ENLEVER : come out (of a stain, etc.) **5 à ~ de** : from

partisan, -sane [partizɑ̃, -zan] *adj & n* : partisan

partition [partisjɔ̃] *nf* : score (in music)

partout [partu] *adv* **1** : everywhere **2** : all (in sports)

parure [paryr] *nf* **1** : finery **2** ENSEMBLE : set

parution [parysjɔ̃] *nf* : publication, launch

parvenir [parvənir] {92} *vi* **1 ~ à** : reach, arrive at **2 ~ à faire** : manage to do

parvis [parvi] *nm* : square (in front of a church)

pas¹ [pa] *adv* **1** → **ne 2** : not **3 ~ du tout** : not at all **4 ~ mal de** : quite a lot of

pas² *nms & pl* **1** : step, footstep **2** : footprint **3** : pace, gait **4** : step (in dancing) **5 de ce ~** : right away **6 ~ de la porte** : doorstep

passable [pasabl] *adj* : passable, fair — **passablement** [pasabləmɑ̃] **1** : quite, rather **2** : reasonably well

passage [pasaʒ] *nm* **1** : passing, crossing **2** SÉJOUR : stay, visit **3** CHEMIN : route, way **4** : passage (in a text) **5 ~ pour piétons** : pedestrian crossing **6 ~ interdit** : do not enter — **passager, -gère** [pasaʒe, -ʒɛr] *adj* : passing, temporary — **~** *n* **1** : passenger **2 ~ clandestin** : stowaway — **passant, -sante** [pasɑ̃, -sɑ̃t] *adj* : busy, crowded — **~** *n* : passerby

passe [pas] *nf* **1** : pass (in sports) **2 mauvaise ~** : difficult time

passé, -sée [pase] *adj* **1** : last, past **2** DÉCOLORÉ : faded — **passé** *nm* **1** : past **2** : past tense — **~** *prep* : after, beyond

passe–partout [paspartu] *nms & pl* : master key

passeport [paspɔr] *nm* : passport

passer [pase] *vt* **1** : cross, go over **2** : pass, go past **3** : hand over **4** : put through to (on the telephone) **5** : take (an exam, etc.) **6** : spend (time) **7** : skip, pass over **8** ENFILER

: slip on **9** : show (a film), play (a cassette, etc.) — *vi* **1** : pass, go past, go by **2** : drop by **3** ALLER : go **4 en passant** : incidentally **5 laissez-moi passer** : let me through — **se passer** *vr* **1** : take place **2** SE DÉROULER : turn out **3** : pass, go by (of time) **4 ~ de** : dispense with, do without
passereau [pasro] *nm, pl* **-reaux** : sparrow
passerelle [pasrɛl] *nf* **1** : footbridge **2** : gangplank
passe–temps [pastã] *nms & pl* : hobby, pastime
passeur, -seuse [pascœr, -søz] *n* : smuggler
passible [pasibl] *adj* **~ de** : liable to
passif, -sive [pasif, -siv] *adj* : passive — **passif** *nm* **1** : passive voice **2** : liabilities *pl*
passionner [pasjone] *vt* : fascinate, captivate — **se passionner** *vr* **~ pour** : have a passion for — **passion** [pasjɔ̃] *nf* : passion — **passionnant, -nante** [pasjɔnã, -nãt] *adj* : exciting, fascinating — **passionné, -née** [pasjɔne] *adj* : passionate — **~** *n* : enthusiast
passoire [paswar] *nf* : sieve, colander
pastel [pastɛl] *adj & nm* : pastel
pastèque [pastɛk] *nf* : watermelon
pasteur [pastœr] *nm* : minister, pastor
pasteuriser [pastœrize] *vt* : pasteurize
pastille [pastij] *nf* : lozenge
patate [patat] *nf* **1** *fam* : potato **2** *or* **~ douce** : sweet potato
patauger [patoʒe] {17} *vi* : splash about, paddle
pâte [pat] *nf* **1** : dough, batter **2 ~ à modeler** : modeling clay **3 ~ dentifrice** : toothpaste **4 ~s** *nfpl* : pasta
pâté [pate] *nm* **1** : pâté **2** *or* **~ de maisons** : block (of houses)
patelin [patlɛ̃] *nm fam* : little village
patent, -tente [patã, -tãt] *adj* : obvious, patent
patère [patɛr] *nf* : peg, hook
paternel, -nelle [patɛrnɛl] *adj* : paternal, fatherly — **paternité** [patɛrnite] *nf* : fatherhood
pâteux, -teuse [patø, -tøz] *adj* **1** : pasty, doughy **2 avoir la langue pâteuse** : have a coated tongue
pathologie [patɔlɔʒi] *nf* : pathology
patience [pasjãs] *nf* **1** : patience **2 jeu de ~** : solitaire — **patient, -tiente** [pasjã, -sjãt] *adj & n* : patient — **patiemment** [pasjamã] *adv* : patiently — **patienter** [pasjãte] *vi* : wait
patin [patɛ̃] *nm* **1** : skate **2 ~s à glace** : ice skates **3 ~s à roulettes** : roller skates — **patinage** [patinaʒ] *nm* : skating — **patiner** [patine] *vi* **1** : skate **2** : skid — **patineur, -neuse** [patinœr, -nøz] *n* : skater — **patinoire** [patinwar] *nf* : skating rink

pâtisserie [patisri] *nf* **1** : cake, pastry **2** : pastry shop, bakery
patrie [patri] *nf* : homeland
patrimoine [patrimwan] *nm* **1** : inheritance **2** HÉRITAGE : heritage
patriote [patrijɔt] *adj* : patriotic — **~** *nmf* : patriot — **patriotique** [patrijɔtik] *adj* : patriotic
patron, -tronne [patrɔ̃, -trɔn] *n* : boss, manager — **patron** *nm* : pattern (in sewing) — **patronner** [patrɔne] *vt* : support, sponsor
patrouille [patruj] *nf* : patrol — **patrouiller** [patruje] *vi* : patrol
patte [pat] *nf* **1** : paw, hoof, foot **2** *fam* : leg, foot (of a person) **3** : tab, flap
pâturage [patyraʒ] *nm* : pasture
paume [pom] *nf* : palm (of the hand)
paumer [pome] *v fam* : lose — **se paumer** *vr fam* : get lost
paupière [popjɛr] *nf* : eyelid
pause [poz] *nf* **1** : pause **2** : break (from work)
pauvre [povr] *adj* : poor — **~** *nmf* : poor man, poor woman — **pauvreté** [povrəte] *nf* : poverty
pavaner [pavane] *v* **se pavaner** *vr* : strut about
paver [pave] *vt* : pave — **pavé** [pave] *nm* **1** : pavement **2** : cobblestone
pavillon [pavijɔ̃] *nm* **1** : pavilion **2** *France* : (detached) house **3** : ward, wing (in a hospital) **4** : flag (on a ship)
pavoiser [pavwaze] *vi fam* : rejoice
pavot [pavo] *nm* : poppy
paye [pɛj] → **paie**
payement [pɛmã] → **paiement**
payer [peje] {11} *vt* : pay (for) — *vi* : pay — **se payer** *vr* : treat oneself
pays [pei] *nm* **1** : country **2** : region, area **3 du ~** : local — **paysage** [peizaʒ] *nm* : scenery, landscape — **paysan, -sanne** [peizã, -zan] *adj* **1** : agricultural, farming **2** : rural, rustic — **~** *n* **1** : small farmer **2** : peasant
péage [peaʒ] *nm* **1** : toll **2** : tollbooth
peau [po] *nf, pl* **peaux 1** : (human) skin **2** : hide, pelt **3** : peel, skin (of a fruit) **4 petites peaux** : cuticle
pêche [pɛʃ] *nf* **1** : peach **2** : fishing
péché [peʃe] *nm* : sin — **pécher** [peʃe] {87} *vi* : sin
pêcher[1] [peʃe] *vt* **1** : fish for **2** *fam* : get, dig up — *vi* : fish
pêcher[2] [peʃe] *nm* : peach tree
pécheur[1], **-cheresse** [peʃœr, -ʃrɛs] *n* : sinner
pêcheur[2], **-cheuse** [peʃœr, -ʃøz] *n* **1** : fisherman **2 pêcheur à la ligne** : angler
pécule [pekyl] *nm* : savings *pl*
pécuniaire [pekynjɛr] *adj* : financial

pédagogie [pedagɔʒi] *nf* : education — **pédagogique** [pedagɔʒik] *adj* : educational

pédale [pedal] *nf* : pedal — **pédaler** [pedale] *vi* : pedal — **pédalo** [pedalo] *nm* : pedal boat

pédant, -dante [pedɑ̃, -dɑ̃t] *adj* : pedantic — **~** *n* : pedant

pédestre [pedɛstr] *adj* **randonnée ~** : hike

pédiatre [pedjatr] *nmf* : pediatrician

pédicure [pedikyr] *nmf* : chiropodist

pègre [pɛgr] *nf* : (criminal) underworld

peigne [pɛɲ] *nm* : comb — **peigner** [peɲe] *vt* : comb — **se peigner** *vr* : comb one's hair — **peignoir** [pɛɲwar] *nm* : bathrobe

peindre [pɛ̃dr] {37} *vt* **1** : paint **2** DÉCRIRE : depict, portray

peine [pɛn] *nf* **1** : sorrow, sadness **2** EFFORT : trouble **3** : punishment **4 à ~** : hardly, barely — **peiner** [pene] *vt* ATTRISTER : sadden, distress — *vi* **1** : struggle **2** : labor (of an engine, etc.)

peintre [pɛ̃tr] *nm* : painter — **peinture** [pɛ̃tyr] *nf* **1** : paint **2** : painting

péjoratif, -tive [peʒɔratif, -tiv] *adj* : derogatory

pelage [pəlaʒ] *nm* : coat, fur (of an animal)

pêle-mêle [pɛlmɛl] *adv* : every which way

peler [pəle] {20} *v* : peel

pèlerin, -rine [pɛlrɛ̃] *n* : pilgrim — **pèlerinage** [pɛlrinaʒ] *nm* : pilgrimage — **pèlerine** [pɛlrin] *nf* : cape

pélican [pelikɑ̃] *nm* : pelican

pelle [pɛl] *nf* **1** : shovel **2 ~ à poussière** : dustpan — **pelletée** [pɛlte] *nf* : shovelful — **pelleter** [pɛlte] {8} *vt* : shovel

pellicule [pelikyl] *nf* **1** : (photographic) film **2** : thin layer, film **3 ~s** *nfpl* : dandruff

pelote [pəlɔt] *nf* : ball (of string, etc.) — **peloton** [plɔtɔ̃] *nm* **1** : pack, group **2** : squad, platoon **3 ~ de tête** : front runners — **pelotonner** [pələtɔne] *v* **se pelotonner** *vr* : curl up (into a ball)

pelouse [pəluz] *nf* **1** : lawn, grass **2** : field (in sports)

peluche [pəlyʃ] *nf* **1** : plush **2 ~s** *nfpl* : fluff, lint **3** *or* **animal en ~** : stuffed animal

pelure [pəlyr] *nf* : peel, skin

pénal, -nale [penal] *adj, mpl* **-naux** [peno] : penal — **pénaliser** [penalize] *vt* : penalize — **pénalité** [penalite] *nf* : penalty

penaud, -naude [pəno, -nod] *adj* : sheepish

penchant [pɑ̃ʃɑ̃] *nm* : tendency, inclination — **pencher** [pɑ̃ʃe] *vt* INCLINER : tilt, tip — *vi* **1** : slant, lean **2 ~ pour** : favor — **se pencher** *vr* : hunch over

pendaison [pɑ̃dɛzɔ̃] *nf* **1** : hanging **2 ~ de crémaillère** : housewarming

pendant, -dante [pɑ̃dɑ̃, -dɑ̃t] *adj* : hanging, dangling — **pendant** *nm* **1** *or* **~ d'oreille** : drop earring **2** CONTREPARTIE : counterpart — **~** *prep* **1** : during, for **2 ~ que** : while — **pendentif** [pɑ̃dɑ̃tif] *nm* : pendant

penderie [pɑ̃dri] *nf* : closet, wardrobe

pendre [pɑ̃dr] {63} *v* : hang — **se pendre** *vr* : hang oneself

pendule [pɑ̃dyl] *nm* : pendulum — **~** *nf* : clock

pêne [pɛn] *nm* : bolt (of a lock)

pénétrer [penetre] {87} *vt* : penetrate — *vi* **~ dans** : enter

pénible [penibl] *adj* **1** : painful, distressing **2** ARDU : difficult — **péniblement** [peniblǝmɑ̃] *adv* : with difficulty

péniche [peniʃ] *nf* **1** : barge **2 ~ aménagée** : houseboat

pénicilline [penisilin] *nf* : penicillin

péninsule [penɛ̃syl] *nf* : peninsula

pénis [penis] *nm* : penis

pénitent, -tente [penitɑ̃, -tɑ̃t] *adj* : repentant — **pénitencier** [penitɑ̃sje] *nm* : penitentiary

pénombre [penɔ̃br] *nf* : half-light

pensée [pɑ̃se] *nf* **1** IDÉE : thought **2** ESPRIT : mind **3** : pansy — **penser** [pɑ̃se] *vt* **1** : think **2** CROIRE : believe, suppose **3 ~ faire** : plan on doing — *vi* **~ à** : think about — **pensif, -sive** [pɑ̃sif, -siv] *adj* : pensive

pension [pɑ̃sjɔ̃] *nf* **1** : pension **2** : boardinghouse **3** : room and board **4 ~ alimentaire** : alimony — **pensionnaire** [pɑ̃sjɔnɛr] *nmf* : boarder, roomer — **pensionnat** [pɑ̃sjɔna] *nm* : boarding school

pentagone [pɛ̃tagon] *nm* : pentagon

pente [pɑ̃t] *nf* **1** : slope **2 en ~** : sloping

pénurie [penyri] *nf* : shortage, scarcity

pépé [pepe] *nm France fam* : grandpa

pépier [pepje] {96} *vi* : chirp, tweet — **pépiement** [pepimɑ̃] *nm* : peep (of a bird)

pépin [pepɛ̃] *nm* **1** : seed (of a fruit) **2** *fam* : snag, hitch — **pépinière** [pepinjɛr] *nf* : (tree) nursery

pépite [pepit] *nf* : nugget

perçant, -çante [pɛrsɑ̃, -sɑ̃t] *adj* **1** : piercing **2** : sharp, keen (of vision)

percée [pɛrse] *nf* **1** : opening, gap **2** DÉCOUVERTE : breakthrough

percepteur [pɛrsɛptœr] *nm* : tax collector

perceptible [pɛrsɛptibl] *adj* : perceptible, noticeable

perception [pɛrsɛpsjɔ̃] *nf* **1** : perception **2** RECOUVREMENT : collection (of taxes)

percer [pɛrse] {6} *vt* **1** : pierce, puncture **2** PÉNÉTRER : penetrate **3 ~ ses dents** : be teething — *vi* **1** : break through **2** : come through (of a tooth) — **perceuse** [pɛrsøz] *nf* : drill

percevoir [pɛrsǝvwar] {26} *vt* **1** : perceive **2** : collect (taxes)

perche [pɛrʃ] *nf* **1** : pole, rod **2** : perch, bass (fish)

percher [pɛrʃe] *v* **se percher** *vr* : perch, roost — **perchoir** [pɛrʃwar] *nm* : perch, roost

percussion [pɛrkysjɔ̃] *nf* : percussion

percuter [pɛrkyte] *vt* : strike, crash into — **percutant, -tante** [pɛrkytɑ̃, -tɑ̃t] *adj* : forceful, striking

perdre [pɛrdr] {63} *vt* **1** : lose **2** GASPILLER : waste **3** MANQUER : miss **4** : ruin (one's reputation, etc.) — *vi* : lose — **se perdre** *vr* : get lost — **perdant, -dante** [pɛrdɑ̃, -dɑ̃t] *adj* : losing — ~ *n* : loser

perdrix [pɛrdri] *nfs & pl* : partridge

perdu, -due [pɛrdy] *adj* **1** : lost **2 temps perdu** : wasted time

père [pɛr] *nm* **1** : father **2** ~**s** *nmpl* : ancestors

perfectionner [pɛrfɛksjɔne] *vt* : perfect, improve — **se perfectionner** *vr* : improve — **perfection** [pɛrfɛksjɔ̃] *nf* **1** : perfection **2 à la** ~ : perfectly — **perfectionné, -née** [pɛrfɛksjɔne] *adj* : sophisticated — **perfectionnement** [pɛrfɛksjɔnmɑ̃] *nm* : improvement

perforer [pɛrfɔre] *vt* : perforate, pierce

performance [pɛrfɔrmɑ̃s] *nf* **1** : performance **2** RÉUSSITE : achievement — **performant, -mante** [pɛrfɔrmɑ̃, -mɑ̃t] *adj* : high-performance

péril [peril] *nm* : peril, danger — **périlleux, -leuse** [perijø, -jøz] *adj* : perilous

périmé, -mée [perime] *adj* : out-of-date, expired

périmètre [perimɛtr] *nm* : perimeter

période [perjɔd] *nf* **1** : period, time **2 par** ~**s** : periodically — **périodique** [perjɔdik] *adj* : periodic, periodical — ~ *nm* : periodical

péripétie [peripesi] *nf* : incident, event

périphérie [periferi] *nf* **1** : periphery, circumference **2** : outskirts *pl* (of a city) — **périphérique** [periferik] *adj* **1** : peripheral **2** : outlying (areas)

périple [peripl] *nm* : journey

périr [perir] *vi* : perish

périssable [perisabl] *adj* : perishable

perle [pɛrl] *nf* **1** : pearl **2** : gem, treasure (of a person)

permanent, -nente [pɛrmanɑ̃, -nɑ̃t] *adj* : permanent — **permanente** *nf* : perm, permanent — **permanence** [pɛrmanɑ̃s] *nf* : permanence

permettre [pɛrmɛtr] {53} *vt* **1** : allow, permit **2** : enable, make possible — **se permettre** *vr* **1** : allow oneself **2** ~ **de** : take the liberty of — **permis** [pɛrmi] *nm* : license, permit — **permission** [pɛrmisjɔ̃] *nf* **1** : permission **2** : leave (in the military)

permuter [pɛrmyte] *vt* : switch around — *vi* : switch places

pernicieux, -cieuse [pɛrnisjø, -sjøz] *adj* : pernicious

peroxyde [pɛrɔksid] *nm* : peroxide

perpendiculaire [pɛrpɑ̃dikylɛr] *adj* : perpendicular

perpétrer [pɛrpetre] {87} *vt* : perpetrate, commit

perpétuer [pɛrpetɥe] *vt* : perpetuate — **perpétuel, -tuelle** [pɛrpetɥɛl] *adj* **1** : perpetual **2** : permanent — **perpétuité** [pɛrpetɥite] *nf* **à** ~ : for life

perplexe [pɛrplɛks] *adj* : perplexed, puzzled — **perplexité** [pɛrplɛksite] *nf* : perplexity

perquisition [pɛrkizisjɔ̃] *nf* : (police) search

perron [pɛrɔ̃] *nm* : (front) steps

perroquet [pɛrɔkɛ] *nm* : parrot

perruche [pɛryʃ] *nf* : parakeet

perruque [pɛryk] *nf* : wig

persécuter [pɛrsekyte] *vt* **1** : persecute **2** HARCELER : harass — **persécution** [pɛrsekysjɔ̃] *nf* : persecution

persévérer [pɛrsevere] {87} *vi* : persevere, persist — **persévérance** [pɛrseverɑ̃s] *nf* : perseverance

persienne [pɛrsjɛn] *nf* : shutter

persil [pɛrsi] *nm* : parsley

persister [pɛrsiste] *vi* : persist — **persistant, -tante** [pɛrsistɑ̃, -tɑ̃t] *adj* : persistent — **persistance** [-tɑ̃s] *nf* : persistence

personnage [pɛrsɔnaʒ] *nm* **1** : (fictional) character **2** : character, individual

personnalité [pɛrsɔnalite] *nf* **1** : personality **2** : celebrity

personne [pɛrsɔn] *nf* : person — ~ *pron* **1** : no one, nobody **2** : anyone, anybody — **personnel, -nelle** [pɛrsɔnɛl] *adj* : personal, private — **personnel** *nm* : personnel, staff

perspective [pɛrspɛktiv] *nf* **1** : perspective (in art) **2** : point of view **3** POSSIBILITÉ : outlook, prospect

perspicace [pɛrspikas] *adj* : insightful, shrewd — **perspicacité** [pɛrspikasite] *nf* : shrewdness

persuader [pɛrsɥade] *vt* : persuade, convince — **persuasion** [pɛrsɥazjɔ̃] *nf* : persuasion

perte [pɛrt] *nf* **1** : loss **2** GASPILLAGE : waste **3 à** ~ **de vue** : as far as the eye can see

pertinent, -nente [pɛrtinɑ̃, -nɑ̃t] *adj* : pertinent — **pertinence** [pɛrtinɑ̃s] *nf* : pertinence

perturber [pɛrtyrbe] *vt* **1** INTERROMPRE : disrupt **2** DÉRANGER : disturb, upset — **perturbation** [pɛrtyrbasjɔ̃] *nf* : disruption

pervertir [pɛrvɛrtir] *vt* : pervert, corrupt — **pervers, -verse** [pɛrvɛr, -vɛrs] *adj* : perverse

peser [pəze] {52} *vt* **1** : weigh **2** EXAMINER

: consider — *vi* 1 : weigh 2 INFLUER : carry weight 3 ~ **sur** : press, push — **pesamment** [pəzamɑ̃] *adv* : heavily — **pesant, -sante** [pəzɑ̃, -zɑ̃t] *adj* 1 : heavy 2 : burdensome — **pesanteur** [pəzɑ̃tœr] *nf* 1 : gravity (in physics) 2 LOURDEUR : heaviness, weight — **pesée** [pəze] *nf* : weighing
pèse-personne [pɛzpɛrsɔn] *nm, pl* **pèse-personnes** : (bathroom) scales
pessimiste [pesimist] *adj* : pessimistic — ~ *nmf* : pessimist — **pessimisme** [pesimism] *nm* : pessimism
peste [pɛst] *nf* 1 : plague 2 : pest (person)
pesticide [pɛstisid] *nm* : pesticide
pétale [petal] *nm* : petal
pétarader [petarade] *vi* : backfire — **pétard** [petar] *nm* : firecracker
péter [pete] {87} *vi fam* : go off, explode — *vt fam* : bust, break
pétiller [petije] *vi* 1 : sparkle 2 : bubble, fizz 3 : crackle (of fire) — **pétillant, -lante** [petijɑ̃, -jɑ̃t] *adj* 1 : sparkling 2 : bubbly
petit, -tite [p(ə)ti, -tit] *adj* 1 : small, little 2 COURT : short 3 : young (of an animal) 4 **ma petite sœur** : my little sister 5 **petit ami, petite amie** : boyfriend, girlfriend 6 **petit déjeuner** : breakfast — ~ *n* : little boy *m*, little girl *f* — **petit** *nm* : cub
petit-fils, petite-fille [p(ə)tifis, p(ə)titfij] *n* : grandson *m*, granddaughter *f*
pétition [petisjɔ̃] *nf* : petition
petits-enfants [p(ə)tizɑ̃fɑ̃] *nmpl* : grandchildren
pétrifier [petrifje] {96} *vt* : petrify
pétrin [petrɛ̃] *nm fam* : fix, jam
pétrir [petrir] *vt* : knead
pétrole [petrɔl] *nm* 1 : oil, petroleum 2 *or* ~ **lampant** : kerosene — **pétrolier, -lière** [petrɔlje, -ljɛr] *adj* : oil, petroleum — **pétrolier** *nm* 1 : oil tanker 2 : oilman
pétulant, -lante [petylɑ̃, -lɑ̃t] *adj* : vivacious
peu [pø] *adv* 1 : little, not much 2 : not very 3 ~ **après** : shortly after — ~ *nm* 1 ~ **à** ~ : little by little 2 **le** ~ **de** : the few, the little 3 **un** ~ : a little, a bit — ~ *pron* 1 : few (people) 2 ~ **de** : few
peupler [pœple] *vt* : populate, inhabit — **se peupler** *vr* : become populated — **peuple** [pœpl] *nm* : people *pl*
peuplier [pøplije] *nm* : poplar
peur [pœr] *nf* 1 : fear 2 **avoir** ~ **de** : be afraid of 3 **de** ~ **que** : lest 4 **faire** ~ **à** : frighten — **peureux, -reuse** [pœrø, -røz] *adj* : fearful, afraid
peut-être [pøtɛtr] *adv* : perhaps, maybe
pharaon [faraɔ̃] *nm* : pharaoh
phare [far] *nm* 1 : lighthouse 2 : headlight
pharmacie [farmasi] *nf* : pharmacy, drugstore — **pharmacien, -cienne** [farmasjɛ̃, -sjɛn] *n* : pharmacist

phase [faz] *nf* : phase, stage
phénomène [fenɔmɛn] *nm* : phenomenon
philanthrope [filɑ̃trɔp] *nmf* : philanthropist
philatélie [filateli] *nf* : stamp collecting
philosophe [filɔzɔf] *nmf* : philosopher — **philosophie** [filɔzɔfi] *nf* : philosophy
phobie [fɔbi] *nf* : phobia
phonétique [fɔnetik] *adj* : phonetic — ~ *nf* : phonetics
phoque [fɔk] *nm* : seal
phosphore [fɔsfɔr] *nm* : phosphorous
photo [fɔto] *nf* : photo
photocopie [fɔtɔkɔpi] *nf* : photocopy — **photocopier** [fɔtɔkɔpje] {96} *vt* : photocopy — **photocopieur** [fɔtɔkɔpjœr] *nm or* **photocopieuse** [fɔtɔkɔpjøz] *nf* : photocopier
photographie [fɔtɔgrafi] *nf* 1 : photography 2 : photograph — **photographe** [fɔtɔgraf] *nmf* : photographer — **photographier** [fɔtɔgrafje] {96} *vt* : photograph
phrase [fraz] *nf* : sentence
physicien, -cienne [fizisjɛ̃, -sjɛn] *n* : physicist
physiologie [fizjɔlɔʒi] *nf* : physiology
physionomie [fizjɔnɔmi] *nf* : face
physique [fizik] *adj* : physical — ~ *nm* : physique — ~ *nf* : physics
piailler [pjaje] *vi* : squawk
piano [pjano] *nm* 1 : piano 2 ~ **à queue** : grand piano — **pianiste** [pjanist] *nmf* : pianist
pic [pik] *nm* 1 : woodpecker 2 CIME : peak 3 : pick(ax)
pichet [piʃɛ] *nm* : pitcher, jug
pickpocket [pikpɔkɛt] *nm* : pickpocket
picorer [pikɔre] *v* : peck
picoter [pikɔte] *vi* : prickle, sting — **picotement** [pikɔtmɑ̃] *nm* : prickling, stinging
pie [pi] *nf* 1 : magpie 2 *fam* : chatterbox
pièce [pjɛs] *nf* 1 : piece, bit 2 : part, item 3 : room, bedroom 4 : piece (in music) 5 ~ **de théâtre** : play 6 *or* ~ **de monnaie** : coin 7 ~ **jointe** : enclosure (in correspondence)
pied [pje] *nm* 1 : foot 2 : base, bottom, leg (of a table, etc.) 3 : stalk, head (of lettuce) 4 **aux** ~**s nus** : barefoot 5 **coup de** ~ : kick 6 **mettre sur** ~ : set up, get off the ground — **piédestal** [pjedɛstal] *nm, pl* **-taux** [-to] : pedestal
piège [pjɛʒ] *nm* 1 : trap, snare 2 : pitfall 3 **prendre au** ~ : entrap — **piéger** [pjeʒe] {64} *vt* 1 : trap 2 : booby-trap
pierre [pjɛr] *nf* 1 : stone 2 ~ **de touche** : touchstone 3 ~ **tombale** : tombstone — **pierreries** [pjɛrri] *nfpl* : precious stones, gems — **pierreux, -reuse** [pjɛrø, -røz] *adj* : stony
piété [pjete] *nf* : piety

piétiner [pjetine] *vt* : trample on — *vi* **1** : stamp one's feet **2** STAGNER : make no headway

piéton, -tonne [pjetɔ̃, -tɔn] *n* : pedestrian — **piétonnier, -nière** [pjetɔnje, -njɛr] *adj* : pedestrian

piètre [pjɛtr] *adj* : poor, wretched

pieu [pjø] *nm, pl* **pieux** : post, stake

pieuvre [pjøvr] *nf* : octopus

pieux, pieuse [pjø, pjøz] *adj* : pious

pige [piʒ] *nf* à la ~ : freelance

pigeon [piʒɔ̃] *nm* : pigeon

piger [piʒe] {17} *vt fam* **1** : understand **2** *Can* : to pick (a card, a number, etc.) **3 tu piges?** : get it?

pigment [pigmɑ̃] *nm* : pigment

pignon [piɲɔ̃] *nm* **1** : gable **2** : cogwheel

pile [pil] *nf* **1** : pile, heap **2** (storage) battery **3** ~ **ou face?** : heads or tails? — ~ *adv fam* **1** : abruptly **2** JUSTE : exactly, right **3 à l'heure** ~ : on the dot

piler [pile] *vt* **1** : crush, pound **2** *Can* : mash (potatoes, etc.)

pilier [pilje] *nm* : pillar, column

piller [pije] *vt* : loot, pillage — **pillage** [pijaʒ] *nm* : looting — **pillard, -larde** [pijar, -jard] *n* : looter

pilon [pilɔ̃] *nm* **1** : pestle **2** : (chicken) drumstick — **pilonner** [pilɔne] *vt* **1** : crush, pound **2** : bombard, shell

pilote [pilɔt] *adj* : pilot, test — ~ *nm* **1** : pilot, driver **2** GUIDE : guide — **pilotage** [pilɔtaʒ] *nm* : piloting, flying — **piloter** [pilɔte] *vt* **1** : pilot, fly, drive **2** GUIDER : show around

pilule [pilyl] *nf* : pill

piment [pimɑ̃] *nm* **1** : pepper **2** ~ **rouge** : hot pepper **3** ~ **doux** : sweet pepper

pin [pɛ̃] *nm* : pine

pinard [pinar] *nm fam* : (cheap) wine

pince [pɛ̃s] *nf* **1** : pliers *pl* **2** : tongs *pl* **3** : pincer, claw **4** : dart, fold **5** ~ **à épiler** : tweezers *pl* **6** ~ **à linge** : clothespin

pinceau [pɛ̃so] *nm, pl* **-ceaux** : paintbrush

pincer [pɛ̃se] {6} *vt* **1** : pinch **2** : nip at, sting (of wind, etc.) **3** *fam* : nab — *vi* : be nippy (of weather) — **pincé, -cée** [pɛ̃se] *adj* : forced, stiff — **pincée** [pɛ̃se] *nf* : pinch, small amount — **pincement** [pɛ̃smɑ̃] *nm* **1** : pinch **2** : twinge — **pincettes** [pɛ̃sɛt] *nfpl* **1** : small tweezers **2** : (fire) tongs

pinède [pinɛd] *nf* : pine forest

pingouin [pɛ̃gwɛ̃] *nm* : auk

pingre [pɛ̃gr] *adj* : stingy

pintade [pɛ̃tad] *nf* : guinea fowl

pinte [pɛ̃t] *nf* : pint

pioche [pjɔʃ] *nf* : pickax, pick — **piocher** [pjɔʃe] *vt* : dig (up)

pion, pionne [pjɔ̃, pjɔn] *n France fam* : student monitor — **pion** *nm* **1** : pawn (in chess) **2** : piece (in checkers)

pionnier, -nière [pjɔnje, -njɛr] *n* : pioneer

pipe [pip] *nf* : pipe

pipeline [pajplajn] *nm* : pipeline

piquant, -quante [pikɑ̃, -kɑ̃t] *adj* **1** : prickly, bristly **2** ÉPICÉ : hot, spicy — **piquant** *nm* **1** : prickle, thorn **2** : spine, quill

pique [pik] *nm* : spade (in playing cards) — ~ *nf* : cutting remark

pique–assiette [pikasjɛt] *nmfs & pl* : freeloader

pique–nique [piknik] *nm, pl* **pique–niques** : picnic

piquer [pike] *vt* **1** : prick, puncture **2** : sting, bite **3** : stick (into) **4** ÉVEILLER : arouse (interest, etc.) **5** *fam* : pinch, swipe **6** *fam* : nab, catch — *vi* **1** : sting, burn **2** : dive, swoop down — **se piquer** *vr* ~ **de** : pride oneself on — **piquet** [pikɛ] *nm* **1** : post, stake, peg **2** ~ **de grève** : picket line — **piqûre** [pikyr] *nf* **1** : prick **2** : sting, bite **3** : injection, shot

pirate [pirat] *nm* **1** : pirate **2** ~ **de l'air** : hijacker

pire [pir] *adj* **1** : worse **2 le** ~, **la** ~, **les** ~**s** : the worst — ~ *nm* **1 le** ~ : the worst **2 au** ~ : at the worst

pis [pi] *adv* **1** : worse **2 de mal en** ~ : from bad to worse — ~ *adj* : worse — ~ *nms & pl* **1** : udder **2 le** ~ : the worst

pis–aller [pizale] *nms & pl* : last resort

piscine [pisin] *nf* : swimming pool

pissenlit [pisɑ̃li] *nm* : dandelion

pistache [pistaʃ] *nf* : pistachio

piste [pist] *nf* **1** TRACE : track, trail **2** : path, route **3** : (ski) slope **4** : racetrack **5** INDICE : lead, clue **6** *or* ~ **d'atterrissage** : runway, airstrip

pistolet [pistɔlɛ] *nm* **1** : pistol, handgun **2** : spray gun

piston [pistɔ̃] *nm* : piston

pitié [pitje] *nf* : pity, mercy — **piteux, -teuse** [pitø, -tøz] *adj* : pitiful

piton [pitɔ̃] *nm* **1** : eye, hook **2** *Can fam* : button, switch

pitoyable [pitwajabl] *adj* : pitiful

pitre [pitr] *nm* : clown

pittoresque [pitɔrɛsk] *adj* : picturesque

pivot [pivo] *nm* : pivot — **pivoter** [pivɔte] *vi* : pivot, revolve

pizza [pidza] *nf* : pizza — **pizzeria** [pidzerja] *nf* : pizzeria

placage [plakaʒ] *nm* : veneer

placard [plakar] *nm* **1** : cupboard, closet **2** AFFICHE : poster — **placarder** [plakarde] *vt* : post, put up

placer [plase] {6} *vt* **1** : place, set, put **2** : seat (s.o.) **3** : put in, interject **4** : invest (money, etc.) — **se placer** *vr* **1** : position oneself **2** : get a job **3** ~ **premier** : finish first — **place** [plas] *nf* **1** : place, spot **2** : room, space **3** : seat (at the theater) **4** : rank, position **5** : (public) square **6** EMPLOI : job, position **7 à la ~ de** : instead of **8 mettre en ~** : set up — **placement** [plasmã] *nm* **1** : investment **2 bureau de ~** : placement agency

placide [plasid] *adj* : placid, calm

plafond [plafɔ̃] *nm* : ceiling — **plafonner** [plafɔne] *vi* : reach a maximum, peak

plage [plaʒ] *nf* **1** : beach, shore **2** : seaside resort

plagier [plaʒje] {96} *vt* : plagiarize — **plagiat** [plaʒja] *nm* : plagiarism

plaider [plede] *vi* : plead, litigate — *vt* : plead (a case)

plaie [plɛ] *nf* : wound, cut

plaignant, -gnante [plɛɲã, -ɲãt] *n* : plaintiff

plaindre [plɛ̃dr] {65} *vt* : pity — **se plaindre** *vr* **1** : moan **2 ~ de** : complain about — **plainte** [plɛ̃t] *nf* **1** : moan **2** : complaint

plaire [plɛr] {66} *vi* **1** : be pleasing **2 ~ à** : please, suit — *v impers* **1** : please **2 s'il vous plaît** : please — **se plaire** *vr* **~ à** : like, enjoy — **plaisance** [plɛzãs] *nf or* **navigation de ~** : sailing, boating — **plaisant, -sante** [plɛzã, -zãt] *adj* **1** AGRÉABLE : pleasant **2** AMUSANT : amusing, funny — **plaisanter** [plɛzãte] *vi* : joke, jest — **plaisanterie** [plɛzãtri] *nf* **1** BLAGUE : joke, jest **2** FARCE : prank — **plaisantin** [plɛzãtɛ̃] *nm* : practical joker — **plaisir** [plezir] *nm* **1** : pleasure **2 au ~** : see you soon **3 avec ~!** : of course! **4 faire ~ à** : please

plan, plane [plã, plan] *adj* : flat, level — **plan** *nm* **1** : plane (in geometry) **2** : plan, strategy **3** : map, diagram **4 premier ~** : foreground

planche [plãʃ] *nf* **1** : board, plank **2 ~ à repasser** : ironing board **3 ~ à roulettes** : skateboard — **plancher** [plãʃe] *nm* : floor

planer [plane] *vi* **1** : glide, soar **2 ~ sur** : hover over

planète [planɛt] *nf* : planet — **planétaire** [planetɛr] *adj* : planetary

planeur [planœr] *nm* : glider

planifier [planifje] {96} *vt* : plan — **planification** [planifikasjɔ̃] *nf* : planning

planque [plãk] *nf fam* : hideout — **planquer** [plãke] *vt fam* : hide away, stash

planter [plãte] *vt* **1** : plant **2** ENFONCER : drive in **3** INSTALLER : put up, set up **4** *fam* : ditch, drop — **se planter** *vr* **1** *fam* : stand, plant oneself **2** *fam* : get it wrong, mess up — **plant** [plã] *nm* : seedling, young plant — **plantation** [plãtasjɔ̃] *nf* **1** : planting **2** : plantation — **plante** [plãt] *nf* **1** : sole (of the foot) **2** : plant

plaquer [plake] *vt* **1** : veneer, plate **2** APLATIR : stick (down), flatten **3** : tackle (in football) **4** *fam* : ditch, get rid of — **plaque** [plak] *nf* **1** : plate, sheet **2** : plaque, name-plate **3** : patch (of ice, etc.) **4 ~ chauffante** : hotplate **5 ~ d'immatriculation** : license plate — **plaqué, -quée** [plake] *adj* : plated — **plaquette** [plakɛt] *nf* **1** : slab (of butter, etc.) **2** : pamphlet

plastique [plastik] *adj & nm* : plastic

plat, plate [pla, plat] *adj* **1** : flat, level **2** : dull, bland — **plat** *nm* **1** : plate, dish **2** : course (of a meal) **3 à ~** : flat down **4 à ~** : dead (of a battery) **5 ~ de résistance** : main course

platane [platan] *nm* : plane tree

plateau [plato] *nm, pl* **-teaux 1** : tray, platter **2** : plateau (in geography) **3** : stage, set (in theater)

plate–bande [platbãd] *nf, pl* **plates–bandes** : flower bed

plate–forme [platfɔrm] *nf, pl* **plates–formes** : platform

platine[1] [platin] *nm* : platinum

platine[2] *nf* : turntable

platitude [platityd] *nf* : trite remark

platonique [platɔnik] *adj* : platonic

plâtre [platr] *nm* **1** : plaster **2** : plaster cast — **plâtrer** [platre] *vt* **1** : plaster **2** : put in a (plaster) cast

plausible [plozibl] *adj* : plausible, likely

plein, pleine [plɛ̃, plɛn] *adj* **1** REMPLI : full, filled (up) **2** : rounded, full **3** : pregnant (of an animal) **4 en plein jour** : in broad daylight **5 le plein air** : the outdoors — **plein** *nm* **1 à ~** : fully, totally **2 faire le ~** : fill up — **plénitude** [plenityd] *nf* : fullness

pleurer [plœre] *vt* **1** : weep for, mourn **2** : shed (tears) — *vi* **1** : cry, weep **2** : water (of eyes) **3 ~ sur** : bemoan — **pleurnicher** [plœrniʃe] *vi fam* : whine, snivel — **pleurs** [plœr] *nfpl* **en ~** : in tears

pleuvoir [plœvwar] {67} *v impers* **1** : rain **2 il pleut** : it's raining — *vi* : rain down, pour down

plier [plije] {96} *vt* **1** : fold (up) **2** : bend — *vi* **1** : bend, sag **2** : yield, give in — **se plier** *vr* **1** : fold **2 ~ à** : submit to — **pli** [pli] *nm* **1** : fold, pleat, crease **2** HABITUDE : habit **3 sous ce ~** : enclosed — **pliant, pliante** [plijã, plijãt] *adj* : folding, collapsible

plinthe [plɛ̃t] *nf* : baseboard

plisser [plise] *vt* **1** : pleat, fold, crease **2** FRONCER : wrinkle (one's brow), pucker (one's lips)

plomb [plɔ̃] *nm* **1** : lead **2** : (lead) pellet **3** FUSIBLE : fuse — **plombage** [plɔ̃baʒ] *nm* : filling (of a tooth) — **plomber** [plɔ̃be] *vt* **1** : weight with lead **2** : fill (a tooth) —

plomberie [plɔ̃bri] *nf* : plumbing — **plom-bier** [plɔ̃bje] *nm* : plumber
plonger [plɔ̃ʒe] {17} *vt* : thrust, plunge — *vi* **1** : dive **2** ~ **dans** : plunge into — **se plonger** *vr* ~ **dans** : immerse oneself into — **plongeant, -geante** [plɔ̃ʒɑ̃, -ʒɑ̃t] *adj* **1** : plunging **2 vue plongeante** : bird's-eye view — **plongée** [plɔ̃ʒe] *nf* **1** : diving **2** ~ **sous–marine** : skin diving — **plongeoir** [plɔ̃ʒwar] *nm* : diving board — **plongeon** [plɔ̃ʒɔ̃] *nm* **1** : dive **2** : loon (bird) — **plongeur, -geuse** [plɔ̃ʒœr, -ʒøz] *n* **1** : diver **2** : dishwasher (person)
plouf [pluf] *nm* : splash
ployer [plwaje] {58} *v* : bow, bend
pluie [plɥi] *nf* **1** : rain, rainfall **2 une** ~ **de** : a stream of
plume [plym] *nf* **1** : feather **2** : quill pen — **plumage** [plymaʒ] *nm* : feathers *pl* — **plumeau** [plymo] *nm, pl* **-meaux** [plymo] : feather duster — **plumer** [plyme] *vt* : pluck
plupart [plypar] *nf* **1 la** ~ **des** : most, the majority of **2 pour la** ~ : for the most part, mostly
pluriel, -rielle [plyrjɛl] *adj & nm* : plural — **pluriel** *nm* : plural
plus [ply(s)] *adv* **1** : more **2** (*used with* **ne**) : no more, no longer **3** ~ **de** : more (than) **4 de** ~ : in addition, furthermore **5 de** ~ **en** ~ : increasingly **6 en** ~ : as well **7 le** ~ : the most **8 non** ~ : neither, either — ~ *nm* **1** : plus (sign) **2 fam** : plus, advantage — ~ *conj* : plus (in calculations)
plusieurs [plyzjœr] *adj & pron* : several
plutôt [plyto] *adv* **1** : rather, instead **2** ~ **que** : rather than
pluvieux, -vieuse [plyvjø, -vjøz] *adj* : rainy, wet
pneu [pnø] *nm, pl* **pneus** : tire — **pneumatique** [pnømatik] *adj* : inflatable
pneumonie [pnømɔni] *nf* : pneumonia
poche [pɔʃ] *nf* **1** : pocket (in clothing) **2** ~**s** *nfpl* CERNES : bags (under the eyes) — **pocher** [pɔʃe] *vt* : poach (in cooking) — **pochette** [pɔʃɛt] *nf* **1** : folder, case, sleeve **2** : book (of matches) **3** : pocket handkerchief
poêle [pwal] *nm* : stove — ~ *nf or* ~ **à frire** : frying pan
poème [pɔɛm] *nm* : poem — **poésie** [pɔezi] *nf* **1** : poetry **2** : poem — **poète** [pɔɛt] *nmf* : poet — **poétique** [pɔetik] *adj* : poetic(al)
poids [pwa] *nms & pl* **1** : weight, heaviness **2** FARDEAU : burden **3** IMPORTANCE : meaning, influence **4** ~ **et mesures** : weights and measures **5** ~ **et haltères** : weight lifting
poignant, -gnante [pwaɲɑ̃, -ɲɑ̃t] *adj* : moving, poignant

poignard [pwaɲar] *nm* : dagger — **poignarder** [pwaɲarde] *vt* : stab
poigne [pwaɲ] *nf* **1** : grip, grasp **2 à** ~ : firm, forceful
poignée [pwaɲe] *nf* **1** : handful **2** : handle, knob **3** ~ **de main** : handshake
poignet [pwaɲɛ] *nm* **1** : wrist **2** : cuff
poil [pwal] *nm* **1** : hair **2** : fur, coat **3** : bristle (of a brush) **4 à** ~ *fam* : stark naked — **poilu, -lue** [pwaly] *adj* : hairy
poinçon [pwɛ̃sɔ̃] *nm* **1** : awl, punch **2** MARQUE : hallmark, stamp — **poinçonner** [pwɛ̃sɔne] *vt* : punch, perforate
poing [pwɛ̃] *nm* **1** : fist **2 coup de** ~ : punch
point [pwɛ̃] *nm* **1** : point, position **2** DEGRÉ : degree, extent **3** : period (in punctuation) **4** QUESTION : matter **5** : point (in sports) **6** : stitch (in sewing) **7 à** ~ : just right, just in time **8 mettre au** ~ : adjust, perfect **9** ~ **culminant** : highlight **10** ~ **de vue** : point of view **11** ~ **du jour** : daybreak **12** ~ **mort** : neutral (gear) **13** ~**s cardinaux** : points of the compass — ~ *adv* **1** (*used with* **ne**) : not **2** ~ **du tout** : not at all
pointe [pwɛ̃t] *nf* **1** : point, tip **2** SOUPÇON : touch, hint **3 de** ~ : state-of-the-art **4 heures de** ~ : rush hour **5 sur la** ~ **des pieds** : on tiptoe
pointer [pwɛ̃te] *vt* **1** COCHER : check, mark off **2** : aim (a rifle at), point (a finger at) — *vi* **1** : clock in **2** : break, dawn (of a new day) — **se pointer** *vr fam* : show up
pointillé [pwɛ̃tije] *nm* : dotted line
pointilleux, -leuse [pwɛ̃tijø, -jøz] *adj* : finicky, fussy
pointu, -tue [pwɛ̃ty] *adj* : pointed, sharp
pointure [pwɛ̃tyr] *nf* : size (of clothing)
point–virgule [pwɛ̃virgyl] *nm, pl* **points–virgules** : semicolon
poire [pwar] *nf* : pear
poireau [pwaro] *nm, pl* **-reaux** : leek — **poireauter** [pwarote] *vi fam* : hang around
poirier [pwarje] *nm* : pear tree
pois [pwa] *nms & pl* **1** : pea **2 à** ~ : spotted, polka-dot
poison [pwazɔ̃] *nm* : poison
poisse [pwas] *nf fam* : bad luck
poisseux, -seuse [pwasø, -søz] *adj* : sticky
poisson [pwasɔ̃] *nm* **1** : fish **2** ~ **d'avril!** : April fool! — **poissonnerie** [pwasɔnri] *nf* : fish market — **poissonnier, -nière** [pwasɔnje, -njɛr] *n* : fish merchant
poitrine [pwatrin] *nf* **1** : chest **2** : breasts *pl*, bosom **3** : breast (in cooking)
poivre [pwavr] *nm* : pepper — **poivré, -vrée** [pwavre] *adj* : peppery — **poivrer** [pwavre] *vt* : pepper — **poivrier** [pwavrije] *nm or* **poivrière** [pwavrijɛr] *nf* : pepper shaker — **poivron** [pwavrɔ̃] *nm* : pepper (vegetable)

poker [pɔkɛr] *nm* : poker

pôle [pol] *nm* : pole — **polaire** [pɔlɛr] *adj* : polar

polémique [pɔlemik] *adj* : controversial — ~ *nf* : debate, controversy

poli, -lie [pɔli] *adj* **1** COURTOIS : polite **2** LISSE : polished, smooth

police [pɔlis] *nf* **1** : police, police force **2** ~ d'assurance : insurance policy — **policier, -cière** [pɔlisje, -sjɛr] *adj* **1** : police **2** roman policier : detective novel — **policier** *nm* : police officer

poliomyélite [pɔljɔmjelit] *nf* : poliomyelitis

polir [pɔlir] *vt* : polish, shine

polisson, -sonne [pɔlisɔ̃, -sɔn] *n* : naughty child, rascal

politesse [pɔlitɛs] *nf* **1** : politeness **2** : polite remark

politique [pɔlitik] *adj* : political — ~ *nf* **1** : politics **2** : policy, procedure — **politicien, -cienne** [pɔlitisjɛ̃, -sjɛn] *n* : politician

pollen [pɔlɛn] *nm* : pollen

polluer [pɔlɥe] *vt* : pollute — **polluant** [pɔlɥɑ̃] *nm* : pollutant — **pollution** [pɔlysjɔ̃] *nf*

polo [pɔlo] *nm* **1** : polo **2** : polo shirt

poltron, -tronne [pɔltrɔ̃, -trɔn] *adj* : cowardly — ~ *n* : coward

polyester [pɔljɛstɛr] *nm* : polyester

polyvalent, -lente [pɔlivalɑ̃, -lɑ̃t] *adj* : versatile, multipurpose

pommade [pɔmad] *nf* : ointment

pomme [pɔm] *nf* **1** : apple **2** ~ d'Adam : Adam's apple **3** ~ de pin : pinecone **4** ~ de terre : potato **5** ~s frites : French fries — **pommeau** [pɔmo] *nm* : knob (of a cane) — **pommette** [pɔmɛt] *nf* : cheekbone — **pommier** [pɔmje] *nm* : apple tree

pompe [pɔ̃p] *nf* **1** : pump **2** APPARAT : pomp, ceremony **3** ~s funèbres : funeral home — **pomper** [pɔ̃pe] *vt* : pump

pompette [pɔ̃pɛt] *adj fam* : tipsy

pompeux, -peuse [pɔ̃pø, -pøz] *adj* : pompous

pompier [pɔ̃pje] *nm* : firefighter, fireman

pompiste [pɔ̃pist] *nmf* : service station attendant

pompon [pɔ̃pɔ̃] *nm* : pompom

pomponner [pɔ̃pɔne] *v* se pomponner *vr* : get all dressed up

poncer [pɔ̃se] {6} *vt* : sand (down)

ponctualité [pɔ̃ktɥalite] *nf* : punctuality

ponctuation [pɔ̃ktɥasjɔ̃] *nf* : punctuation

ponctuel, -tuelle [pɔ̃ktɥɛl] *adj* **1** : prompt, punctual **2** : limited, selective

ponctuer [pɔ̃ktɥe] *vt* : punctuate

pondéré, -rée [pɔ̃dere] *adj* : levelheaded, sensible

pondre [pɔ̃dr] {63} *vt* : lay (eggs)

poney [pɔnɛ] *nm* : pony

pont [pɔ̃] *nm* **1** : bridge **2** : deck (of a ship)

ponte [pɔ̃t] *nf* : laying (of eggs)

pont–levis [pɔ̃levi] *nm, pl* **ponts–levis** : drawbridge

ponton [pɔ̃tɔ̃] *nm* : pontoon

pop [pɔp] *adj s & pl* : pop

pop–corn [pɔpkɔrn] *nms & pl* : popcorn

popote [pɔpɔt] *nf* **1** : mess (in the military) **2** *fam* : cooking

populaire [pɔpylɛr] *adj* **1** : popular **2** : working-class — **popularité** [pɔpylarite] *nf* : popularity

population [pɔpylasjɔ̃] *nf* : population — **populeux, -leuse** [pɔpylø, -løz] *adj* : densely populated

porc [pɔr] *nm* **1** : pig, hog **2** : pork (in cooking)

porcelaine [pɔrsəlɛn] *nf* **1** : porcelain **2** : china, chinaware

porc–épic [pɔrkepik] *nm, pl* **porcs–épics** : porcupine

porche [pɔrʃ] *nm* : porch

porcherie [pɔrʃəri] *nf* : pigpen, pigsty

pore [pɔr] *nm* : pore — **poreux, -reuse** [pɔrø, -røz] *adj* : porous

pornographie [pɔrnɔgrafi] *nf* : pornography — **pornographique** [-grafik] *adj* : pornographic

port [pɔr] *nm* **1** : port, harbor **2** : wearing, carrying (of arms, etc.) **3** MAINTIEN : bearing **4** ~ payé : postpaid

portable [pɔrtabl] *adj* : portable

portail [pɔrtaj] *nm* : gate

portant, -tante [pɔrtɑ̃, -tɑ̃t] *adj* bien portant : in good health

portatif, -tive [pɔrtatif, -tiv] *adj* : portable

porte [pɔrt] *nf* **1** : door, doorway **2** : gate (at an airport, etc.) **3** ~ de sortie : exit, way out

porte–avions [pɔrtavjɔ̃] *nms & pl* : aircraft carrier

porte–bagages [pɔrtbagaʒ] *nms & pl* : luggage rack

porte–bonheur [pɔrtbɔnœr] *nms & pl* : lucky charm

porte–clés *or* **porte–clefs** [pɔrtəkle] *nms & pl* : key ring

porte–documents [pɔrtdɔkymɑ̃] *nms & pl* : briefcase

portée [pɔrte] *nf* **1** : range **2** : impact, significance **3** : litter (of kittens, etc.) **4** à ~ de : within reach of

portefeuille [pɔrtəfœj] *nm* **1** : wallet **2** : portfolio (in finance or politics)

portemanteau [pɔrtmɑ̃to] *nm, pl* **-teaux** [-to] : coat rack

porte–monnaie [pɔrtmɔnɛ] *nms & pl* : change purse

porte–parole [pɔrtparɔl] *nms & pl* : spokesperson

porter [pɔrte] *vt* **1** TRANSPORTER : carry **2** : wear, have on **3** APPORTER : bring **4** : bear (responsibility, etc.) **5 être porté à** : be inclined to — *vi* **1** : carry (of a voice) **2 ∼ sur** CONCERNER : be about — **se porter** *vr* **1** : be worn **2 ∼ bien** : be (feel, go) well

porte–savon [pɔrtsavõ] *nms & pl* : soap dish

porte–serviettes [pɔrtsɛrvjɛt] *nms & pl* : towel rack

porteur, -teuse [pɔrtœr, -tøz] *n* **1** : porter **2** : holder, bearer (of news, etc.) **3** : carrier (of disease)

porte–voix [pɔrtəvwa] *nms & pl* : megaphone

portier, -tière [pɔrtje, -tjɛr] *n* : doorman

portière *nf* : door (of an automobile)

portillon [pɔrtijõ] *nm* : gate

portion [pɔrsjõ] *nf* : portion

porto [pɔrto] *nm* : port (wine)

portrait [pɔrtrɛ] *nm* : portrait

portuaire [pɔrtɥɛr] *adj* : harbor, port

portugais, -gaise [pɔrtygɛ, -gɛz] *adj* : Portuguese — **portugais** *nm* : Portuguese (language)

poser [poze] *vt* **1** : put (down), place **2** INSTALLER : put up, install **3** : pose (a problem) **4 ∼ sa candidature** : apply (for a job) — *vi* : pose, sit — **se poser** *vr* **1** : land, alight **2** : arise, come up — **pose** [poz] *nf* **1** : installing **2** : pose, posture — **posé, -sée** [poze] *adj* : composed, calm

positif, -tive [pozitif, -tiv] *adj* : positive

position [pozisjõ] *nf* **1** : position **2 prendre ∼** : take a stand — **positionner** [pozisjɔne] *vt* : position, place

posologie [pozɔlɔʒi] *nf* : dosage

posséder [posede] {87} *vt* **1** AVOIR : possess, have **2** MAÎTRISER : know thoroughly — **possesseur** [posesœr] *nm* : owner, possessor — **possessif, -sive** [posesif, -siv] *adj* : possessive — **possession** [posesjõ] *nf* : ownership, possession

possible [posibl] *adj* : possible — **∼** *nm* **1 dans la mesure du ∼** : as far as possible **2 faire son ∼** : do one's utmost — **possibilité** [posibilite] *nf* **1** : possibility **2 ∼s** *nfpl* : means, resources

poste [pɔst] *nm* **1** : job, position **2** : post, station **3** : (telephone) extension **4 ∼ d'essence** : gas station **5 ∼ de pilotage** : cockpit **6 ∼ de pompiers** *Can* : fire station **7 ∼ de télévision** : television set — **∼** *nf* **1** : mail service **2** : post office — **postal, -tale** [pɔstal] *adj, mpl* **-taux** [pɔsto] : postal, mail — **poster** [pɔste] *vt* **1** : post, station **2** : mail

postérieur, -rieure [pɔsterjœr] *adj* **1** : later (of a date, etc.) **2** : rear, back — **postérieur** *nm fam* : bottom, buttocks *pl*

postérité [pɔsterite] *nf* : posterity

posthume [pɔstym] *adj* : posthumous

postiche [pɔstiʃ] *adj* : false, fake

postier, -tière [pɔstje, -tjɛr] *n* : postal worker

post–scriptum [pɔstskriptɔm] *nms & pl* : postscript

postuler [pɔstyle] *vt* : apply for (a position) — **postulant, -lante** [pɔstylã, -lãt] *n* : candidate, contestant

posture [pɔstyr] *nf* : posture

pot [po] *nm* **1** : pot, jar, container **2** *fam* : drink, glass **3 ∼ d'échappement** : muffler (of an automobile)

potable [pɔtabl] *adj* **1** : drinkable **2** *fam* : fair, passable

potage [pɔtaʒ] *nm* : soup — **potager** [pɔtaʒe] *adj* **jardin ∼** : vegetable garden

pot–au–feu [pɔtofø] *nms & pl* : beef stew

pot–de–vin [podvɛ̃] *nm, pl* **pots–de–vin** : bribe

pote [pɔt] *nm fam* : pal, buddy

poteau [pɔto] *nm, pl* **-teaux 1** : post, pole **2 ∼ indicateur** : signpost

potelé, -lée [pɔtle] *adj* : chubby, plump

potence [pɔtãs] *nf* : gallows

potentiel, -tielle [pɔtãsjɛl] *adj & nm* : potential

poterie [pɔtri] *nf* : pottery

potin [pɔtɛ̃] *nm fam* **1** *France* : noise, racket **2 ∼s** *nmpl* : gossip

potion [posjõ] *nf* : potion

potiron [pɔtirõ] *nm* : large pumpkin

pot–pourri [popuri] *nm, pl* **pots–pourris** : potpourri

pou [pu] *nm, pl* **poux** : louse

poubelle [pubɛl] *nf* : garbage can

pouce [pus] *nm* **1** : thumb **2** : big toe **3** : inch (measurement) **4 faire du ∼** *Can* : hitchhike

poudre [pudr] *nf* : powder — **poudrer** [pudre] *vt* : powder — **poudrerie** [pudrəri] *nf Can* : (snow) flurries *pl* — **poudreux, -dreuse** [pudrø, -drøz] *adj* : powdery — **poudrier** [pudrije] *nm* : (powder) compact

pouffer [pufe] *vi* **∼ de rire** : burst out laughing

pouilleux, -leuse [pujø, -jøz] *adj* **1** : lousy, flea-ridden **2** : seedy (of a neighborhood)

poulailler [pulaje] *nm* : henhouse, chicken coop

poulain [pulɛ̃] *nm* **1** : colt, foal **2** PROTÉGÉ : protégé

poule [pul] *nf* **1** : hen **2** : fowl (in cooking) — **poulet** [pulɛ] *nm* : chicken

pouliche [puliʃ] *nf* : filly

poulie [puli] *nf* : pulley

pouls [pu] *nm* : pulse

poumon [pumõ] *nm* : lung

poupe [pup] *nf* : stern

poupée [pupe] *nf* : doll

poupon [pupɔ̃] *nm* **1** : tiny baby **2** : baby doll — **pouponnière** [pupɔnjɛr] *nf* : nursery (for babies)

pour [pur] *prep* **1** : for **2** : to, in order to **3** ～ **cent** : percent **4** ～ **que** : in order that, so that — ～ *nm* **le** ～ **et le contre** : the pros and cons

pourboire [purbwar] *nm* : tip

pourcentage [pursɑ̃taʒ] *nm* : percentage

pourchasser [purʃase] *vt* : pursue, hunt down

pourparlers [purparle] *nmpl* : talks, negotiations

pourquoi [purkwa] *adv & conj* : why — ～ *nms & pl* : reason, cause

pourrir [purir] *v* : rot, decay — **pourri, -rie** [puri] *adj* : rotten — **pourriture** [purityr] *nf* : rot, decay

poursuivre [pursɥivr] {88} *vt* **1** : pursue, chase **2** CONTINUER : carry on with **3** ～ **en justice** : sue, prosecute **4** HARCELER : hound — *vi* : continue — **poursuite** [pursɥit] *nf* **1** : pursuit **2** ～**s** *nfpl* : legal proceedings, lawsuit — **poursuivant, -vante** [pursɥivɑ̃, -vɑ̃t] *n* **1** : pursuer **2** : plaintiff

pourtant [purtɑ̃] *adv* : however, yet

pourtour [purtur] *nm* : perimeter

pourvoir [purvwar] {68} *vt* ～ **de** : provide with — *vi* ～ **à** : provide for — **pourvu** [purvy] *conj* ～ **que 1** : provided that **2** : let's hope (that)

pousser [puse] *vt* **1** : push, shove **2** INCITER : encourage, urge **3** POURSUIVRE : pursue, continue (with) **4** : let out (a scream) — *vi* **1** : push **2** CROÎTRE : grow — **se pousser** *vr* : move over — **pousse** [pus] *nf* **1** : growth **2** BOURGEON : shoot, sprout — **poussé, -sée** [puse] *adj* : advanced, extensive — **poussée** [puse] *nf* **1** : pressure **2** IMPULSION : push **3** AUGMENTATION : upsurge **4** ACCÈS : attack, outbreak (in medicine) — **poussette** [pusɛt] *nf* : stroller

poussière [pusjɛr] *nf* : dust — **poussiéreux, -reuse** [pusjerø, -røz] *adj* : dusty

poussin [pusɛ̃] *nm* : chick

poutre [putr] *nf* : beam, girder

pouvoir [puvwar] {69} *v aux* **1** : be able to **2** : be permitted to — *v impers* : be possible — *vt* **1** : be able to do **2 je n'en peux plus!** : I can't take anymore! — **se pouvoir** *v impers* : be possible — ～ *nm* : power

pragmatique [pragmatik] *adj* : pragmatic

prairie [preri] *nf* : meadow

pratiquer [pratike] *vt* **1** : practice **2** : play (a sport) **3** : use, apply **4** EFFECTUER : carry out — **praticable** [pratikabl] *adj* **1** : feasible **2** : passable (of a road, etc.) — **praticien, -cienne** [pratisjɛ̃, -sjɛn] *n* : practitioner — **pratiquant, -quante** [pratikɑ̃,

-kɑ̃t] *adj* : practicing — ～ *n* : churchgoer, follower — **pratique** [pratik] *adj* : practical — ～ *nf* : practice

pré [pre] *nm* : meadow

préalable [prealabl] *adj* **1** : preliminary **2 sans avis** ～ : without prior notice — ～ *nm* **1** : prerequisite **2 au** ～ : beforehand

préambule [preɑ̃byl] *nm* **1** : preamble **2 sans** ～ : without warning

préau [preo] *nm, pl* **préaux** [preo] : (covered) playground, courtyard

préavis [preavi] *nm* : (prior) notice

précaire [prekɛr] *adj* : precarious

précaution [prekosjɔ̃] *nf* **1** : precaution **2** PRUDENCE : caution, care

précéder [presede] {87} *vt* : precede — **précédemment** [presedamɑ̃] *adv* : previously — **précédent, -dente** [presedɑ̃, -dɑ̃t] *adj* : previous, prior — **précédent** *nm* : precedent

prêcher [preʃe] *v* : preach

précieux, -cieuse [presjø, -sjøz] *adj* **1** : precious **2** UTILE : valuable

précipice [presipis] *nm* : abyss, chasm

précipiter [presipite] *vt* **1** : hurl, throw **2** HÂTER : hasten, speed up — **se précipiter** *vr* **1** : hasten, rush **2** ～ **sur** : throw oneself on — **précipitation** [presipitasjɔ̃] *nf* **1** : hurry, haste **2** ～**s** *nfpl* : precipitation (in meteorology) — **précipité, -tée** [presipite] *adj* **1** : rapid **2** HÂTIF : hasty, rash

préciser [presize] *vt* : specify, make clear — **se préciser** *vr* : become clearer — **précis, -cise** [presi, -siz] *adj* **1** : precise, accurate **2** : clear, specific — **précis** *nms & pl* **1** : summary **2** MANUEL : handbook — **précisément** [presizemɑ̃] *adv* : precisely, exactly — **précision** [presizjɔ̃] *nf* **1** : precision **2** : clarity

précoce [prekɔs] *adj* **1** : early **2** : precocious (of a child, etc.)

préconçu, -cue [prekɔ̃sy] *adj* : preconceived

préconiser [prekɔnize] *vt* : recommend, advocate

précurseur [prekyrsœr] *nm* : forerunner

prédateur [predatœr] *nm* : predator

prédécesseur [predesesœr] *nm* : predecessor

prédilection [predilɛksjɔ̃] *nf* **1** : partiality **2 de** ～ : favorite

prédire [predir] {29} *vt* : predict — **prédiction** [prediksjɔ̃] *nf* : prediction

prédisposer [predispoze] *vt* : predispose

prédominant, -nante [predɔminɑ̃, -nɑ̃t] *adj* : predominant

préfabriqué, -quée [prefabrike] *adj* : prefabricated

préface [prefas] *nf* : preface

préfecture [prefɛktyr] *nf* ～ **de police** *France* : police headquarters

préférer [prefere] {87} *vt* : prefer —
préférable [preferabl] *adj* : preferable —
préféré, -rée [prefere] *adj & n* : favorite —
préférence [preferãs] *nf* : preference
préfet [prefɛ] *nm* ~ **de police** *France* : police commissioner
préfixe [prefiks] *nm* : prefix
préhistorique [preistɔrik] *adj* : prehistoric
préjudice [preʒydis] *nm* **1** : harm, damage
2 porter ~ **à** : cause harm to — **préjudi-
ciable** [preʒydisjabl] *adj* : harmful, detri-
mental
préjugé [preʒyʒe] *nm* : prejudice
prélasser [prelase] *v* **se prélasser** *vr*
: lounge (around)
prélever [preləve] {52} *vt* **1** : withdraw,
deduct **2** : take (a sample of) — **prélève-
ment** [prelɛvmã] *nm* **1** : withdrawal, deduction **2** : (blood) sample
préliminaire [preliminɛr] *adj* : preliminary
prélude [prelyd] *nm* : prelude
prématuré, -rée [prematyre] *adj* : premature
prémédité [premedite] *adj* : premeditated
premier, -mière [prəmje, -mjɛr] *adj* **1** : first
2 : top, leading **3 premier ministre** : prime
minister — ~ *n* : first (one) — **premier** *nm*
: first (in dates) — **première** *nf* **1** : first
class **2** : premiere (of a show) — **premièrement** [prəmjɛrmã] *adv* : in the first place,
firstly
prémunir [premynir] *v* **se prémunir** *vr* ~
contre : protect oneself against
prendre [prãdr] {70} *vt* **1** : take **2** ACHETER
: get, pick up **3** : take on (responsibility) **4**
ATTRAPER : catch, capture **5** : put on, gain
(weight) **6** : have (a meal) — *vi* **1** : set,
thicken **2** : break out (of fire) **3** ~ **à droite**
: bear right **4** ~ **sur soi** : take upon oneself — **se prendre** *vr* **1** : be taken **2** : get
caught **3** ~ **les doigts dans** : catch one's
fingers in **4** ~ **pour** : consider oneself **5**
s'en ~ **à** : attack — **preneur, -neuse**
[prənœr, -nøz] *n* : buyer, taker
prénom [prenõ] *nm* : given name, first name
préoccuper [preɔkype] *vt* : worry, preoc-
cupy — **préoccupation** [preɔkypasjõ] *nf*
: worry, concern
préparer [prepare] *vt* **1** : prepare, make
ready **2** ~ **qqn à** : prepare s.o. for — **se
préparer** *vr* : prepare oneself, get ready —
préparatifs [preparatif] *nmpl* : preparations
— **préparation** [preparasjõ] *nf* : preparation
prépondérant, -rante [prepõderã, -rãt] *adj*
: predominant
préposer [prepoze] *vt* ~ **à** : put in charge of
— **préposé, -sée** [prepoze] *n* **1** : employee, clerk **2** *France* : mailman
préposition [prepozisjõ] *nf* : preposition

prérogative [prerɔgativ] *nf* : prerogative
près [prɛ] *adv* **1** : close, near(by) **2** : near,
soon **3 à...** ~ : more or less, within about
4 à peu ~ : almost, just about **5 de** ~
: closely **6** ~ **de** : near
présage [prezaʒ] *nm* : omen — **présager**
[prezaʒe] {17} *vt* **1** : foresee **2** : portend,
bode
presbyte [prɛsbit] *adj* : farsighted
presbytère [prɛsbiter] *nm* : rectory
prescrire [prɛskrir] {33} *vt* : prescribe —
prescription [prɛskripsjõ] *nf* : prescription
préséance [preseãs] *nf* : precedence
présent, -sente [prezã, -zãt] *adj* : present —
~ *nm* : present (time) — **présence**
[prezãs] *nf* **1** : presence **2 en** ~ : face to
face **3** ~ **d'esprit** : presence of mind —
présentement [prezãtmã] *adv* : at the moment, now
présenter [prezãte] *vt* **1** MONTRER : present,
show **2** : introduce (to) **3** : pay, offer (one's
condolences) **4** : submit (a proposal, etc.)
— **se présenter** *vr* **1** : go, come, appear **2**
: introduce oneself **3** ~ **à** : run for (an office) — **présentateur, -trice** [prezãtatœr,
-tris] *n* : newscaster, anchor — **présentation** [prezãtasjõ] *nf* **1** : presentation **2** : introduction — **présentoir** [prezãtwar] *nm*
: display shelf
préserver [prezerve] *vt* **1** : protect **2** CON-
SERVER : preserve — **préservatif** [prezer-
vatif] *nm* : condom — **préservation** [pre-
zervasjõ] *nf* : protection, preservation
présider [prezide] *vt* : preside over, chair —
vi ~ **à** : rule over, govern — **président,
-dente** [prezidã, -dãt] *n* **1** : president **2**
: chairperson — **présidence** [prezidãs] *nf* **1**
: presidency **2** : chairmanship — **présidentiel, -tielle** [prezidãsjel] *adj* : presidential
présomption [prezõpsjõ] *nf* : presumption
— **présomptueux, -tueuse** [prezõptɥø,
-tɥøz] *adj* : presumptuous
presque [prɛsk] *adv* : almost, nearly
presqu'île [prɛskil] *nf* : peninsula
pressant, -sante [presã, -sãt] *adj* : urgent,
pressing
presse [prɛs] *nf* : press
pressé, -sée [prese] *adj* **1** : hurried **2** : urgent **3** : freshly squeezed
pressentir [presãtir] {82} *vt* : sense, have a
premonition about — **pressentiment**
[presãtimã] *nm* : premonition
presse–papiers [prɛspapje] *nms & pl* : pa-
perweight
presser [prese] *vt* **1** : press, squeeze **2** IN-
CITER : urge **3** HÂTER : hurry, rush — *vi* : be
pressing, be urgent — **se presser** *vr* **1** SE
HÂTER : hurry up **2** ~ **contre** *or* ~ **sur**
: snuggle up against — **pression** [presjõ] *nf*
: pressure

prestance [prɛstãs] *nf* : (imposing) presence

prestation [prɛstasjɔ̃] *nf* : benefit, allowance — **prestataire** [prɛstatɛr] *nm* : recipient

prestidigitateur, -trice [prɛstidiʒitatœr, -tris] *n* : magician, conjurer

prestige [prɛstiʒ] *nm* : prestige — **prestigieux, -gieuse** [prɛstiʒjø, -ʒjøz] *adj* : prestigious

présumer [prezyme] *vt* : presume, suppose — *vi* ~ **de** : overestimate, overrate

prêt¹, prête [prɛ, prɛt] *adj* **1** : ready, prepared **2** DISPOSÉ : willing

prêt² *nm* : loan

prêt–à–porter [prɛtaporte] *nm, pl* **prêts-à–porter** : ready-to-wear (clothing)

prétendre [pretãdr] {63} *vt* **1** : claim, maintain **2** VOULOIR : intend — **prétendant, -dante** [pretãdã, -dãt] *n* : pretender (to a throne) — **prétendant** *nm* : suitor — **prétendu, -due** [pretãdy] *adj* : so-called, alleged

prétention [pretãsjɔ̃] *nf* : pretentiousness — **prétentieux, -tieuse** [pretãsjø, -sjøz] *adj* : pretentious

prêter [prete] *vt* **1** : lend **2** ~ **à** : attribute to **3** ~ **attention** : pay attention **4** ~ **l'oreille** : listen — *vi* ~ **à** : give rise to, cause — **se prêter** *vr* ~ **à** : lend itself to, suit — **prêteur, -teuse** [pretœr, -tøz] *n* **prêteur sur gages** : pawnbroker

prétexte [pretɛkst] *nm* : pretext, excuse — **prétexter** [pretɛkste] *vt* : use as an excuse

prêtre [prɛtr] *nm* : priest

preuve [prœv] *nf* **1** : proof, evidence **2 faire** ~ **de** : show

prévaloir [prevalwar] {71} *vi* : prevail — **se prévaloir** *vr* **1** ~ **de** : take advantage of **2** ~ **de** : boast of

prévenant, -nante [prevnã, -nãt] *adj* : considerate, thoughtful

prévenir [prevnir] {92} *vt* **1** ÉVITER : prevent **2** AVISER : tell, inform **3** AVERTIR : warn **4** ANTICIPER : anticipate — **prévention** [prevãsjɔ̃] *nf* : prevention — **prévenu, -nue** [prevny] *n* : defendant, accused

prévoir [prevwar] {99} *vt* **1** : predict, anticipate **2** : plan (on), schedule **3** : provide for, allow (for) — **prévisible** [previzibl] *adj* : foreseeable — **prévision** [previzjɔ̃] *nf* **1** : prediction **2** ~**s** *nfpl* : forecast — **prévoyant, -voyante** [prevwajã, -vwajãt] *adj* : provident, farsighted — **prévoyance** [prevwajãs] *nf* : foresight

prier [prije] {96} *vi* : pray — *vt* **1** ~ **de** : ask to, request to **2 je vous en prie** : please **3 je vous en prie** : don't mention it, you're welcome — **prière** [prijɛr] *nf* : prayer

primaire [primɛr] *adj* : primary, elementary

prime¹ [prim] *adj* **1** : early, first **2 de** ~ **abord** : at first

prime² *nf* **1** : premium, allowance **2** RÉCOMPENSE : bonus, gift

primer [prime] *vt* : prevail over — *vi* : be of primary importance

primeurs [primœr] *nfpl* : early produce

primevère [primvɛr] *nf* : primrose

primitif, -tive [primitif, -tiv] *adj* : primitive

primordial, -diale [primɔrdjal] *adj, mpl* **-diaux** [-djo] : essential, vital

prince [prɛ̃s] *nm* : prince — **princesse** [prɛ̃sɛs] *nf* : princess

principal, -pale [prɛ̃sipal] *adj, mpl* **-paux** [-po] : main, principal — **principal** *nm* ESSENTIEL : main thing — **principalement** [prɛ̃sipalmã] *adv* : primarily, mainly

principe [prɛ̃sip] *nm* : principle, rule

printemps [prɛ̃tã] *nm* : spring

priorité [prijɔrite] *nf* **1** : priority **2** : right-of-way **3 en** ~ : first

pris¹ [pri] *pp* → **prendre**

pris², prise [pri, priz] *adj* **1** : taken, sold **2** OCCUPÉ : busy **3** ~ **de** : afflicted with

prise [priz] *nf* **1** : capture, catch **2** : hold, grip **3** *Can* : strike (in baseball) **4** ~ **de courant** : (electrical) outlet **5** ~ **de sang** : blood test

priser [prize] *vt* : prize, value

prison [prizɔ̃] *nf* : prison — **prisonnier, -nière** [prizɔnje, -njɛr] *adj* : captive — ~ *n* : prisoner

priver [prive] *vt* : deprive — **se priver** *vr* ~ **de** : go without — **privé, -vée** [prive] *adj* : private — **privé** *nm* **1** : private sector **2 en** ~ : in private

privilégier [privileʒje] {96} *vt* : privilege, favor — **privilège** [privilɛʒ] *nm* : privilege

prix [pri] *nms & pl* **1** : price, cost **2** : prize **3 à tout** ~ : at all costs

probable [prɔbabl] *adj* : probable, likely — **probabilité** [prɔbabilite] *nf* : probability — **probablement** [prɔbabləmã] *adv* : probably

problème [prɔblɛm] *nm* : problem

procéder [prɔsede] {87} *vi* **1** : proceed **2** ~ **à** : carry out — **procédé** [prɔsede] *nm* : process, procedure — **procédure** [prɔsedyr] *nf* **1** : procedure **2** : proceedings *pl* (in law)

procès [prɔsɛ] *nm* **1** : lawsuit **2** : (criminal) trial

procession [prɔsesjɔ̃] *nf* : procession

processus [prɔsesys] *nms & pl* : process, system

procès–verbal [prɔsɛverbal] *nm, pl* **procès–verbaux** [-verbo] **1** : minutes *pl* (of a meeting) **2** *France* : (parking) ticket

prochain, -chaine [prɔʃɛ̃, -ʃɛn] *adj* **1** SUIVANT : next, following **2** PROCHE : imminent, forthcoming **3 à la prochaine!** *fam*

: see you!, until next time! — **prochain** *nm*
: fellowman — **prochainement** [prɔ-
ʃɛnmɑ̃] *adv* : soon, shortly
proche [prɔʃ] *adj* **1** : near(by) **2** : imminent,
near **3** ~ **de** : close to — **proches** [prɔʃ]
nmpl : close relatives
proclamer [prɔklame] *vt* : proclaim, declare
— **proclamation** [prɔklamasjɔ̃] *nf* : proclamation, declaration
procuration [prɔkyrasjɔ̃] *nf* : proxy (in an
election)
procurer [prɔkyre] *vt* : provide, give — **se
procurer** *vr* : get, obtain — **procureur**
[prɔkyrœr] *nm or* ~ **général** : prosecutor
prodige [prɔdiʒ] *nm* : prodigy — **prodigieux, -gieuse** [prɔdiʒjø, -ʒjøz] *adj* : prodigious, extraordinary
prodigue [prɔdig] *adj* **1** : extravagant **2**
GÉNÉREUX : lavish — **prodiguer** [prɔdige]
vt : lavish
produire [prɔdɥir] {49} *vt* **1** : produce **2**
CAUSER : bring about — **se produire** *vr* **1**
: occur, happen **2** : perform (on stage) —
producteur [prɔdyktœr] *nm* : producer
— **production** [prɔdyksjɔ̃] *nf* : production
— **produit** [prɔdɥi] *nm* : product
profaner [prɔfane] *vt* : defile, desecrate —
profane [prɔfan] *adj* : secular — ~ *nmf*
: layperson
proférer [prɔfere] {87} *vt* : utter
professer [prɔfese] *vt* : profess
professeur [prɔfesœr] *nm* **1** : (school)-
teacher **2** : professor
profession [prɔfesjɔ̃] *nf* : occupation, trade
— **professionnel, -nelle** [prɔfɛsjɔnɛl] *adj
& n* : professional
profil [prɔfil] *nm* : profile
profit [prɔfi] *nm* **1** : profit **2** AVANTAGE
: benefit — **profiter** [prɔfite] *vi* **1** ~ **à** : be
of benefit to **2** ~ **de** : take advantage of
profond, -fonde [prɔfɔ̃, -fɔ̃d] *adj* **1** : deep **2**
: profound — **profondément** [prɔfɔ̃demɑ̃]
adv : profoundly, deeply — **profondeur**
[prɔfɔ̃dœr] *nf* : depth
profusion [prɔfyzjɔ̃] *nf* : profusion
progéniture [prɔʒenityr] *nf* : offspring
programme [prɔgram] *nm* **1** : program **2**
: plan, schedule **3** : curriculum, syllabus (in
academics) — **programmer** [prɔgrame] *vt*
1 : program (a computer) **2** : plan, schedule
— **programmeur, -meuse** [prɔgramœr,
-møz] *n* : (computer) programmer
progrès [prɔgrɛ] *nm* : progress — **progresser** [prɔgrese] *vi* : make progress —
progressif, -sive [prɔgresif, -siv] *adj* : progressive — **progressivement** [-sivmɑ̃] *adv*
: progressively, gradually
prohiber [prɔibe] *vt* : prohibit — **prohibition** [prɔibisjɔ̃] *nf* : prohibition
proie [prwa] *nf* : prey

projecteur [prɔʒɛktœr] *nm* **1** : projector **2**
: spotlight — **projectile** [prɔʒɛktil] *nm*
: missile, projectile — **projection**
[prɔʒɛksjɔ̃] *nf* : projection, showing
projeter [prɔʃte] {8} *vt* **1** LANCER : throw **2**
: project, show (a film, etc.) **3** : cast, project
(light) **4** PRÉVOIR : plan — **projet** [prɔʒɛ]
nm **1** : plan, project **2** ÉBAUCHE : draft, outline
proliférer [prɔlifere] {87} *vi* : proliferate —
prolifération [-ferasjɔ̃] *nf* : proliferation —
prolifique [prɔlifik] *adj* : prolific
prologue [prɔlɔg] *nm* : prologue
prolonger [prɔlɔ̃ʒe] {17} *vt* : prolong, extend — **se prolonger** *vr* : continue — **pro-
longation** [prɔlɔ̃gasjɔ̃] *nf* : extension (of
time) — **prolongement** [prɔlɔ̃ʒmɑ̃] *nm*
: extension (of a road, etc.)
promener [prɔmne] {52} *vt* : take for a walk
— **se promener** *vr* : go for a walk —
promenade [prɔmnad] *nf* **1** : walk, stroll **2**
: trip, ride (in a car, etc.) **3** : walkway,
promenade — **promeneur, -neuse**
[prɔmnœr, -nøz] *n* : walker
promettre [prɔmɛtr] {53} *v* : promise — **se
promettre** *vr* ~ **de** : resolve to —
promesse [prɔmɛs] *nf* : promise —
prometteur, -teuse [prɔmɛtœr, -tøz] *adj*
: promising
promontoire [prɔmɔ̃twar] *nm* : headland
promouvoir [prɔmuvwar] {56} *vt* : promote
— **promotion** [prɔmɔsjɔ̃] *nf* : promotion
prompt, prompte [prɔ̃, prɔ̃t] *adj* : prompt,
quick
prôner [prone] *vt* : advocate
pronom [prɔnɔ̃] *nm* : pronoun
prononcer [prɔnɔ̃se] {6} *vt* : pronounce —
vi : hand down a decision (in law) — **se
prononcer** *vr* : give one's opinion — **prononciation** [prɔnɔ̃sjasjɔ̃] *nf* : pronunciation
pronostic [prɔnɔstik] *nm* **1** : prognosis **2**
PRÉVISION : forecast
propagande [prɔpagɑ̃d] *nf* : propaganda
propager [prɔpaʒe] {17} *vt* : propagate,
spread — **se propager** *vr* : spread — **propagation** [prɔpagasjɔ̃] *nf* : propagation
prophète [prɔfɛt] *nm* : prophet — **prophétie**
[prɔfesi] *nf* : prophecy — **prophétique**
[prɔfetik] *adj* : prophetic — **prophétiser**
[prɔfetize] *vt* : prophesy
propice [prɔpis] *adj* : favorable
proportion [prɔpɔrsjɔ̃] *nf* **1** : proportion,
ratio **2** ~**s** *nfpl* : dimensions, size — **proportionnel, -nelle** [prɔpɔrsjɔnɛl] *adj* : proportional
proposer [prɔpoze] *vt* **1** : suggest, propose
2 OFFRIR : offer **3** : nominate (for election)
— **se proposer** *vr* ~ **de** : intend to — **propos** [prɔpo] *nms & pl* **1** : subject **2** BUT
: intention, point **3** ~ *nmpl* : comments,

talk **4** à ~ : appropriate **5** à ~ **de** : regarding, about — **proposition** [prɔpozisjɔ̃] *nf* **1** : suggestion **2** OFFRE : offer, proposal
propre [prɔpr] *adj* **1** : clean, neat **2** : proper, correct (of a word) **3** ~ à : characteristic of **4** ~ à : suitable for **5** par sa ~ **faute** : through his own fault — **proprement** [prɔprəmã] *adv* à ~ **parler** : strictly speaking — **propreté** [prɔprəte] *nf* : cleanliness, neatness
propriété [prɔprijete] *nf* **1** : property **2** : ownership — **propriétaire** [prɔprijetɛr] *nmf* **1** : owner **2** : landlord, landlady *f*
propulser [prɔpylse] *vt* : propel
prorata [prɔrata] *nms & pl* **au** ~ **de** : in proportion to
proscrire [prɔskrir] {33} *vt* **1** INTERDIRE : ban, prohibit **2** BANNIR : banish — **proscrit, -scrite** [prɔskri, -skrit] *n* : outcast
prose [proz] *nf* : prose
prospectus [prɔspɛktys] *nms & pl* : leaflet
prospérer [prɔspere] {87} *vi* : flourish, thrive — **prospérité** [prɔsperite] *nf* : prosperity
prosterner [prɔstɛrne] *v* **se prosterner** *vr* : bow down
prostituée [prɔstitɥe] *nf* : prostitute — **prostitution** [prɔstitysjɔ̃] *nf* : prostitution
prostré, -trée [prɔstre] *adj* : prostrate
protagoniste [prɔtagɔnist] *nmf* : protagonist
protéger [prɔteʒe] {64} *vt* **1** : protect **2** PATRONNER : support — **se protéger** *vr* ~ **de** : protect oneself from — **protecteur, -trice** [prɔtɛktœr, -tris] *adj* : protective — ~ *n* **1** : protector **2** : patron — **protection** [prɔtɛksjɔ̃] *nf* : protection
protéine [prɔtein] *nf* : protein
protestant, -tante [prɔtɛstã, -tãt] *adj & n* : Protestant
protester [prɔtɛste] *vi* : protest — **protestation** [prɔtɛstasjɔ̃] *nf* : protest
prothèse [prɔtɛz] *nf* **1** : prosthesis **2** ~ **dentaire** : denture
protocole [prɔtɔkɔl] *nm* : protocol
protubérant, -rante [prɔtyberã, -rãt] *adj* : protruding — **protubérance** [prɔtyberãs] *nf* : protuberance
proue [pru] *nf* : prow, bow (of a ship)
prouesse [prɥɛs] *nf* : feat
prouver [pruve] *vt* **1** ÉTABLIR : prove **2** MONTRER : show, demonstrate
provenance [prɔvnãs] *nf* **1** : source, origin **2 en** ~ **de** : from
provenir [prɔvnir] {92} *vi* ~ **de 1** : come from **2** : result from
proverbe [prɔvɛrb] *nm* : proverb
providence [prɔvidãs] *nf* : providence
province [prɔvɛ̃s] *nf* : province — **provincial, -ciale** [-vɛ̃sjal] *adj, mpl* **-ciaux** [-sjo] : provincial

proviseur [prɔvizœr] *nm France* : principal (of a school)
provision [prɔvizjɔ̃] *nf* **1** : stock, supply **2** ~**s** *nfpl* : provisions, food
provisoire [prɔvizwar] *adj* : temporary
provoquer [prɔvɔke] *vt* **1** : give rise to **2** DÉFIER : provoke — **provocant, -cante** [prɔvɔkã, -kãt] *adj* : provocative — **provocation** [prɔvɔkasjɔ̃] *nf* : provocation
proximité [prɔksimite] *nf* : closeness, proximity
prude [pryd] *nf* : prude
prudent, -dente [prydã, -dãt] *adj* : careful, cautious — **prudemment** [prydamã] *adv* : carefully, cautiously — **prudence** [prydãs] *nf* : care, caution
prune [pryn] *nf* : plum — **pruneau** [pryno] *nm, pl* **-neaux** : prune
prunelle [prynɛl] *nf* : pupil (of the eye)
psaume [psom] *nm* : psalm
pseudonyme [psødɔnim] *nm* : pseudonym
psychanalyser [psikanalize] *vt* : psychoanalyze — **psychanalyse** [psikanaliz] *nf* : psychoanalysis — **psychanalyste** [-list] *nmf* : psychoanalyst
psychiatrie [psikjatri] *nf* : psychiatry — **psychiatre** [psikjatr] *nmf* : psychiatrist — **psychiatrique** [psikjatrik] *adj* : psychiatric
psychologie [psikɔlɔʒi] *nf* : psychology — **psychologique** [psikɔlɔʒik] *adj* : psychological — **psychologue** [psikɔlɔg] *nmf* : psychologist
puant, puante [pɥã, -ãt] *adj* : foul, stinking — **puanteur** [pɥãtœr] *nf* : stink, stench
puberté [pybɛrte] *nf* : puberty
public, -blique [pyblik] *adj* : public — **public** *nm* **1** : public **2** : audience, spectators *pl*
publication [pyblikasjɔ̃] *nf* : publication
publicité [pyblisite] *nf* **1** : publicity **2** : (television) commercial — **publicitaire** [pyblisitɛr] *adj* : advertising
publier [pyblije] {96} *vt* : publish
puce [pys] *nf* **1** : flea **2** : computer chip
pudeur [pydœr] *nf* : modesty — **pudique** [pydik] *adj* : modest, decent
puer [pɥe] *vi* : smell, stink — *vt* : reek of
puéril, -rile [pɥeril] *adj* : childish
puis [pɥi] *adv* : then, afterwards
puiser [pɥize] *vt* ~ **dans** : draw from, dip into
puisque [pɥiskə] *conj* : since, as, because
puissant, -sante [pɥisã, -sãt] *adj* : powerful — **puissance** [pɥisãs] *nf* : power
puits [pɥi] *nm* **1** : well **2** : (mine) shaft
pull *or* **pull-over** [pyl, pylɔvɛr] *nm France* : pullover sweater
pulpe [pylp] *nf* : pulp
pulsation [pylsasjɔ̃] *nf* BATTEMENT : beat
pulsion [pylsjɔ̃] *nf* : drive, urge

pulvériser [pylverize] *vt* **1** : pulverize **2** VA-
PORISER : spray
punaise [pynɛz] *nf* **1** : (bed)bug **2** : thumbtack
punch [pɔ̃ʃ] *nm* : punch (drink)
punir [pynir] *vt* : punish — **punition**
[pynisjɔ̃] *nf* : punishment
pupille[1] [pypij] *nmf* : ward (of the court)
pupille[2] *nf* : pupil (of the eye)
pupitre [pypitr] *nm* **1** : music stand **2** BU-
REAU : desk
pur, pure [pyr] *adj* : pure — **pureté** [pyrte]
nf : purity
purée [pyre] *nf* **1** : puree **2** ~ **de pommes**
de terre : mashed potatoes
purgatoire [pyrgatwar] *nm* : purgatory

purger [pyrʒe] {17} *vt* **1** : drain (a radiator,
etc.) **2** : rid of, purge **3** : serve (a sentence)
— **purge** [pyrʒ] *nf* : purge
purifier [pyrifje] {96} *vt* : purify — **purification** [pyrifikasjɔ̃] *nf* : purification
puritain, -taine [pyritɛ̃, -tɛn] *n* : puritan —
~ *adj* : puritanical
pur–sang [pyrsɑ̃] *nms & pl* : Thoroughbred
pus [py] *nm* : pus
putride [pytrid] *adj* : rotten
puzzle [pœzl] *nm* : (jigsaw) puzzle
pyjama [piʒama] *nm* : pajamas *pl*
pylône [pilon] *nm* : pylon
pyramide [piramid] *nf* : pyramid
pyromane [piroman] *nmf* : arsonist
python [pitɔ̃] *nm* : python

Q

q [ky] *nm* : q, 17th letter of the alphabet
quadriller [kadrije] *vt* : surround, take control of — **quadrillage** [kadrijaʒ] *nm* : crisscross pattern, grid — **quadrillé, -lée**
[kadrije] *adj* : squared
quadrupède [k(w)adrypɛd] *nm* : quadruped
quadruple [k(w)adrypl] *adj* : quadruple
quai [kɛ] *nm* **1** : quay, wharf **2** : platform (at
a railway station)
qualifier [kalifje] {96} *vt* **1** : qualify **2**
DÉCRIRE : describe — **qualification** [kali-
fikasjɔ̃] *nf* : qualification
qualité [kalite] *nf* **1** : quality, excellence **2**
: quality, property **3** en ~ de : in one's
role as
quand [kɑ̃] *adv & conj* **1** : when **2** ~
même : all the same, even so
quant [kɑ̃] ~ **à** *prep phr* : as for, as to, regarding
quantité [kɑ̃tite] *nf* : quantity
quarantaine [karɑ̃tɛn] *nf* **1** : quarantine **2**
une ~ **de** : about forty
quarante [karɑ̃t] *adj & nms & pl* : forty —
quarantième [karɑ̃tjɛm] *adj & nmf & nm*
: fortieth
quart [kar] *nm* **1** : quarter, fourth **2** un ~
d'heure : fifteen minutes
quartier [kartje] *nm* **1** : piece, segment,
quarter **2** : area, district **3** ~ **général**
: (military) headquarters
quartz [kwarts] *nm* : quartz
quasi [kazi] *adv* : nearly, almost
quatorze [katorz] *adj* **1** : fourteen **2** : fourteenth (in dates) — ~ *nms & pl* : fourteen

— **quatorzième** [katɔrzjɛm] *adj & nmf &
nm* : fourteenth
quatre [katr] *adj* **1** : four **2** : fourth (in
dates) — ~ *nms & pl* : four
quatre–vingt–dix [katrəvɛ̃dis] *adj & nms &
pl* : ninety
quatre–vingts [katrəvɛ̃] (**quatre-vingt** *with
another numeral adjective*) *adj & nms & pl*
: eighty
quatrième [katrijɛm] *adj & nmf* : fourth
quatuor [kwatɥɔr] *nm* : quartet
que [kə] *conj* **1** : that **2 plus** ~ **nécessaire**
: more than necessary **3 qu'il fasse soleil**
ou non : whether it's sunny or not **4 → ne**
— ~ *pron* **1** : who, whom, that **2** : which
3 ~ **faire?** : what should we do? — ~ *adv*
: how (much), how (many)
québécois, -coise [kebekwa, -kwaz] *adj*
: Quebecer, Quebecois
quel, quelle [kɛl] *adj* **1** : what, which **2**
: whatever, whichever, whoever — ~ *pron*
: who, which one
quelconque [kɛlkɔ̃k] *adj* **1** : some sort of,
any **2 un être** ~ : an ordinary person
quelque [kɛlk(ə)] *adj* **1** : a few, several,
some **2** ~ **chose** : something **3** ~ **part**
: somewhere **4** ~ **peu** : somewhat — ~
adv : about, approximately
quelquefois [kɛlkəfwa] *adv* : sometimes
quelques–uns, quelques–unes [kɛlkəzœ̃,
kɛlkəzyn] *pron* : some, a few
quelqu'un [kɛlkœ̃] *pron* **1** : someone,
somebody **2** : anyone, anybody **3 y a-t-il**
quelqu'un? : is anybody there?
quémander [kemɑ̃de] *vt* : beg for

qu'en–dira–t–on [kɑ̃diratɔ̃] *nms & pl* : gossip

querelle [kərɛl] *nf* : quarrel — **quereller** [kərele] *v* **se quereller** *vr* : quarrel — **querelleur, -leuse** [kərɛlœr, -løz] *adj* : quarrelsome

question [kɛstjɔ̃] *nf* **1** : question **2** : matter, issue — **questionnaire** [kɛstjɔnɛr] *nm* : questionnaire — **questionner** [kɛstjɔne] *vt* : question

quête [kœ̃] *nf* **1** : quest, search **2** : collection (of money) — **quêter** [kete] *vt* : look for, seek — *vi* : take a collection

queue [kø] *nf* **1** : tail **2** : tail end, rear, bottom **3** : handle (of a pot) **4** ~ **de billard** : cue (stick) **5** ~ **de cheval** : ponytail **6 faire la** ~ : stand in line

qui [ki] *pron* **1** : who, whom **2** : which, that **3** ~ **que** : whoever, whomever

quiconque [kikɔ̃k] *pron* **1** : whoever, whomever **2** : anyone, anybody

quiétude [kjetyd] *nf* : quiet, tranquility

quille [kij] *nf* **1** : keel **2** ~**s** *nfpl* : ninepins

quincaillerie [kɛ̃kajri] *nf* **1** : hardware **2** : hardware store

quinte [kɛ̃t] *nf or* ~ **de toux** : coughing fit

quintuple [kɛ̃typl] *adj* : fivefold

quinzaine [kɛ̃zɛn] *nf* **1 une** ~ **de** : about fifteen **2 une** ~ **de jours** : two weeks

quinze [kɛ̃z] *adj* **1** : fifteen **2** : fifteenth (in dates) — ~ *nms & pl* : fifteen — **quinzième** [kɛ̃zjɛm] *adj & nmf & nm* : fifteenth

quiproquo [kiprɔko] *nm* : misunderstanding

quittance [kitɑ̃s] *nf* : receipt

quitte [kit] *adj* **1** : even, quits **2** ~ **à** : even if, at the risk of

quitter [kite] *vt* **1** : leave, depart from **2** : take off (a hat, etc.) **3 ne quittez pas** : hold the (telephone) line — **se quitter** *vr* : part, separate

qui-vive [kiviv] *nms & pl* **être sur le** ~ : be on the alert

quoi [kwa] *pron* **1** : what **2** (*after a pronoun*) : which **3** ~ **que** : whatever

quoique [kwakə] *conj* : although, though

quota [kɔta] *nm* : quota

quotidien, -dienne [kɔtidjɛ̃, -djɛn] *adj* **1** : daily **2** : everyday, routine — **quotidien** *nm* **1** : daily (newspaper) **2 au** ~ : on a daily basis — **quotidiennement** [kɔtidjɛnmɑ̃] *adv* : daily

quotient [kɔsjɑ̃] *nm* : quotient

R

r [ɛr] *nm* : r, 18th letter of the alphabet

rabâcher [rabaʃe] *vt* : repeat over and over

rabaisser [rabese] *vt* **1** : reduce **2** DÉPRÉCIER : belittle, degrade — **rabais** [rabɛ] *nms & pl* RÉDUCTION : reduction, discount

rabat [raba] *nm* : flap

rabat–joie [rabaʒwa] *nms & pl* : killjoy, spoilsport

rabattre [rabatr] {12} *vt* **1** : reduce, diminish **2** : bring down, pull down — **se rabattre** *vr* **1** : fold up, shut **2** ~ **sur** : make do with

rabbin [rabɛ̃] *nm* : rabbi

rabot [rabo] *nm* : plane (tool) — **raboter** [rabɔte] *vt* : plane

raboteux, -teuse [rabɔtø, -tøz] *adj* INÉGAL : rough, uneven

rabougri, -grie [rabugri] *adj* **1** : stunted **2** : shriveled (up)

rabrouer [rabrue] *vt* : snub

raccommoder [rakɔmɔde] *vt* : mend, patch up

raccompagner [rakɔ̃paɲe] *vt* : take (someone) back, see home

raccorder [rakɔrde] *vt* : connect, link up — **raccord** [rakɔr] *nm* : link, connection — **raccordement** [rakɔr-dəmɑ̃] *nm* : linking, connection

raccourcir [rakursir] *vt* : shorten — *vi* : become shorter, shrink — **raccourci** [rakursi] *nm* **1** : shortcut **2 en** ~ : in short, briefly

raccrocher [rakrɔʃe] *vt* ~ **le récepteur** : hang up (a telephone receiver) — *vi* : hang up (on s.o.) — **se raccrocher** *vr* ~ **à** : hang on to

race [ras] *nf* **1** : (human) race **2** : breed (of animals) **3 de** ~ : thoroughbred

racheter [raʃte] {20} *vt* **1** : buy back **2** : buy more of **3** : redeem (in religion) **4** COMPENSER : make up for — **rachat** [raʃa] *nm* : buying back

racial, -ciale [rasjal] *adj, mpl* -**ciaux** [rasjo] : racial

racine [rasin] *nf* : root

racisme [rasism] *nm* : racism — **raciste** [rasist] *adj & nmf* : racist

racler [rakle] *vt* **1** : scrape (off) — **raclée** [rakle] *nf fam* : beating, thrashing

racoler [rakɔle] *vt* : solicit

raconter [rakɔ̃te] *vt* **1** CONTER : tell, relate **2** : say, talk about — **racontars** [rakɔ̃tar] *nmpl* : gossip — **raconteur, -teuse** [rakɔ̃tœr, -tøz] *n* : storyteller

radar [radar] *nm* : radar

rade [rad] *nf* en ~ : stranded

radeau [rado] *nm, pl* **-deaux** : raft

radiateur [radjatœr] *nm* **1** : radiator **2** : heater

radical, -cale [radikal] *adj, mpl* **-caux** [-ko] : radical — ~ *n* : radical

radier [radje] {96} *vt* : cross off

radieux, -dieuse [radjø, -djøz] *adj* : radiant, dazzling

radin, -dine [radɛ̃] *adj fam* : stingy — ~ *n fam* : cheapskate

radio [radjo] *nf* **1** : radio **2** RADIOGRAPHIE : X ray

radioactif, -tive [radjoaktif, -tiv] *adj* : radioactive

radiodiffuser [radjodifyze] *vt* : broadcast — **radiodiffusion** [radjodifyzjɔ̃] *nf* : broadcasting

radiographie [radjografi] *nf* : X ray — **radiographier** [radjografje] {96} *vt* : X-ray

radis [radi] *nm* : radish

radoter [radɔte] *vi* : ramble on

radoucir [radusir] *vt* : soften (up) — **se radoucir** *vr* : grow milder

rafale [rafal] *nf* **1** : gust (of wind, etc.) **2** : burst (of gunfire)

raffermir [rafermir] *vt* : firm up, tone up

raffiner [rafine] *vt* : refine — **raffinage** [rafinaʒ] *nm* : refining — **raffiné, -née** [rafine] *adj* : refined — **raffinement** [rafinmɑ̃] *nm* : refinement — **raffinerie** [rafinri] *nf* : refinery

raffoler [rafɔle] *vi* ~ de : adore, be crazy about

rafistoler [rafistɔle] *vt fam* : patch up, fix up

rafler [rafle] *vt fam* : swipe, steal — **rafle** [rafl] *nf* : (police) raid

rafraîchir [rafreʃir] *vt* : refresh, cool — **se rafraîchir** *vr* **1** : get cooler **2** : freshen up — **rafraîchissant, -sante** [rafreʃisɑ̃, -sɑ̃t] *adj* : refreshing — **rafraîchissement** [rafreʃismɑ̃] *nm* **1** : cooling **2** ~s *nmpl* : cool drinks, refreshments

rage [raʒ] *nf* **1** : rabies **2** FUREUR : rage — **rager** [raʒe] {17} *vi* : rage, fume

ragot [rago] *nm fam* : gossip

ragoût [ragu] *nm* : ragout, stew

raide [red] *adj* **1** : stiff (of muscles) **2** : tight, taut (of a rope) **3** : steep (of a hill) **4** : straight (of hair) — ~ *adv* : steeply — **raideur** [redœr] *nf* **1** : stiffness **2** : steepness — **raidir** [redir] *vt* : stiffen, tighten — **se raidir** *vr* : tighten, tense up

raie [re] *nf* **1** : stripe **2** : part (in hair)

raifort [refɔr] *nm* : horseradish

rail [raj] *nm* : rail, track

railler [raje] *vt* : make fun of — **raillerie** [rajri] *nf* : mockery — **railleur, -leuse** [rajœr, -jøz] *adj* MOQUEUR : mocking

rainure [renyr] *nf* : groove, slot

raisin [rezɛ̃] *nm* **1** : grape **2** ~ de Corinthe : currant **3** ~ sec : raisin

raison [rezɔ̃] *nf* **1** : reason **2** avoir ~ : be right **3** en ~ de : because of **4** perdre la ~ : lose one's mind — **raisonnable** [rezɔnabl] *adj* : sensible, reasonable — **raisonnement** [rezɔnmɑ̃] *nm* **1** : reasoning **2** : argument — **raisonner** [rezɔne] *vi* : reason — *vt* : reason with

rajeunir [raʒœnir] *vt* : make look younger — *vi* : look younger

rajouter [raʒute] *vt* **1** : add **2** en ~ : exaggerate — **rajout** [raʒu] *nm* : addition

rajuster [raʒyste] *vt* : (re)adjust

râle [ral] *nm* : groan

ralentir [ralɑ̃tir] *v* : slow down — **ralenti, -tie** [ralɑ̃ti] *adj* : slow — **ralenti** *nm* **1** : slow motion **2** : idling speed (of a car) — **ralentissement** [ralɑ̃tismɑ̃] *nm* : slowing down

râler [rale] *vi* **1** : groan **2** *fam* : grumble

rallier [ralje] {96} *vt* : rally (troops) — **se rallier** *vr* : rally

rallonger [ralɔ̃ʒe] {17} *vt* : lengthen — *vi* : get longer — **rallonge** [ralɔ̃ʒ] *nf* : extension (cord)

rallumer [ralyme] *vt* **1** : turn back on **2** RANIMER : revive

ramasser [ramase] *vt* **1** : pick up, collect **2** CUEILLIR : pick, gather — **se ramasser** *vr* : crouch — **ramassage** [ramasaʒ] *nm* : picking up, collection

rambarde [rɑ̃bard] *nf* : guardrail

rame [ram] *nf* **1** AVIRON : oar **2** : (subway) train **3** : ream (of paper)

rameau [ramo] *nm, pl* **-meaux** : branch, bough

ramener [ramne] {52} *vt* **1** : bring back, take back **2** RÉDUIRE : reduce

ramer [rame] *vi* : row

ramification [ramifikasjɔ̃] *nf* : offshoot

ramollir [ramɔlir] *vt* : soften — **se ramollir** *vr* : soften

ramoner [ramɔne] *vt* : sweep (a chimney), clean out (pipes) — **ramoneur** [ramɔnœr] *nm* : chimney sweep

rampe [rɑ̃p] *nf* **1** : (access) ramp **2** : banister, handrail **3** : footlights *pl* **4** ~ de lancement : launching pad

ramper [rɑ̃pe] *vi* **1** : crawl, creep **2** S'ABAISSER : grovel

rancart [rɑ̃kar] *nm* mettre au ~ *fam* : discard, scrap

rance [rɑ̃s] *adj* : rancid — **rancir** [rɑ̃sir] *vi* : turn rancid

rancœur [răkœr] *nf* RESSENTIMENT : rancor, resentment

rançon [răsɔ̃] *nf* : ransom — **rançonner** [răsɔne] *vt* : hold to ransom

rancune [răkyn] *nf* 1 : rancor, resentment 2 **garder** ∼ **à** : hold a grudge against

randonnée [rădɔne] *nf* 1 : ride, trip 2 : walk, hike — **randonneur, -neuse** [rădɔnœr, -nøz] *n* : hiker

rang [rɑ̃] *nm* 1 RANGÉE : row 2 : rank (in a hierarchy) — **rangée** [rɑ̃ʒe] *nf* : row, line — **rangement** [rɑ̃ʒmɑ̃] *nm* 1 : tidying up 2 : storage space — **ranger** [rɑ̃ʒe] {17} *vt* 1 : tidy up 2 CLASSER : put in order 3 : put away (objects), park (a vehicle) — **se ranger** *vr* 1 : line up 2 SE GARER : park 3 S'ASSAGIR : settle down 4 ∼ **à** : go along with

ranimer [ranime] *vt* 1 : revive 2 : rekindle (a fire)

rapace [rapas] *adj* : rapacious — ∼ *nm* : bird of prey

rapatrier [rapatrije] {96} *vt* : repatriate, send home

râper [rape] *vt* : grate (cheese, etc.) — **râpe** [rap] *nf* : grater

rapetisser [raptise] *vt* : shorten — *vi* : shrink — **se rapetisser** *vr* : shrink

râpeux, -peuse [rapø, -pøz] *adj* : rough

rapide [rapid] *adj* 1 : quick, rapid 2 : steep — ∼ *nm* 1 : rapids *pl* 2 : express train — **rapidement** [rapidmɑ̃] *adv* : rapidly, swiftly — **rapidité** [rapidite] *nf* : rapidity, speed

rapiécer [rapjese] {6} *vt* : patch (up)

rappeler [raple] {8} *vt* 1 : remind 2 : call back — **se rappeler** *vr* : remember, recall — **rappel** [rapɛl] *nm* 1 : reminder 2 : recall

rapporter [rapɔrte] *vt* 1 : bring back, take back 2 : yield (in finance) 3 RELATER : tell, report — *vi* 1 : yield a profit 2 *fam* : tell tales — **se rapporter** *vr* ∼ **à** : relate to — **rapport** [rapɔr] *nm* 1 : report 2 LIEN : connection 3 RENDEMENT : return, yield 4 PROPORTION : ratio 5 ∼**s** *nmpl* : relations 6 ∼**s** *nmpl* : sexual intercourse — **rapporteur, -teuse** [rapɔrtœr, -tøz] *n* : tattletale

rapprocher [raprɔʃe] *vt* 1 : bring closer 2 COMPARER : compare — **se rapprocher** *vr* 1 ∼ **de** : approach, come closer to 2 ∼ **de** : resemble — **rapproché, -chée** [raprɔʃe] *adj* : close

raquette [rakɛt] *nf* 1 : (tennis) racket 2 : snowshoe

rare [rar] *adj* 1 : rare, uncommon 2 : infrequent 3 CLAIRSEMÉ : sparse — **rarement** [rarmɑ̃] *adv* : seldom, rarely — **rareté** [rarte] *nf* : rarity, scarcity

ras [ra] *adv* : short — **ras, rase** [ra, raz] *adj* : short (of hair)

raser [raze] {87} *vt* 1 : shave 2 DÉTRUIRE : raze 3 FRÔLER : graze, skim — **se raser** *vr* : shave — **rasage** [razaʒ] *nm* : shaving —

rasoir [razwar] *nm* : razor

raseur, -seuse [razœr, -zøz] *n fam* : bore

rassasier [rasazje] {96} *vt* : satisfy — **se rassasier** *vr* : eat one's fill

rassembler [rasɑ̃ble] *vt* : gather, collect — **se rassembler** *vr* : gather, assemble — **rassemblement** [rasɑ̃bləmɑ̃] *nm* : gathering, assembly

rasseoir [raswar] {9} *v* **se rasseoir** *vr* : sit down again

rassir [rasir] {72} *vi* : go stale

rassis, -sise [rasi, -siz] *adj* : stale

rassurer [rasyre] *vt* : reassure — **rassurant, -rante** [rasyrɑ̃, -rɑ̃t] *adj* : reassuring

rat [ra] *nm* : rat

ratatiner [ratatine] *v* **se ratatiner** *vr* : shrivel up

rate [rat] *nf* : spleen

râteau [rato] *nm, pl* **-teaux** : rake

rater [rate] *vt* 1 MANQUER : miss 2 : fail (an exam, etc.) — *vi* ÉCHOUER : fail, go wrong

ratifier [ratifje] {96} *vt* : ratify — **ratification** [-tifikasjɔ̃] *nf* : ratification

ration [rasjɔ̃] *nf* : share, ration

rationaliser [rasjɔnalize] *vt* : rationalize — **rationnel, -nelle** [rasjɔnɛl] *adj* : rational

rationner [rasjɔne] *vt* : ration

ratisser [ratise] *vt* : rake

raton [ratɔ̃] *nm* ∼ **laveur** : raccoon

rattacher [rataʃe] *vt* 1 : tie up again 2 RELIER : link, connect

rattraper [ratrape] *vt* 1 : recapture 2 : catch up with (s.o.) 3 ∼ **le temps perdu** : make up for lost time

raturer [ratyre] *vt* BIFFER : delete — **rature** [ratyr] *nf* : deletion

rauque [rok] *adj* ENROUÉ : hoarse

ravager [ravaʒe] {17} *vt* : ravage, devastate — **ravages** [ravaʒ] *nmpl* **faire des** ∼ : wreak havoc

ravaler [ravale] *vt* 1 : restore (a building) 2 : stifle (one's anger)

ravi, -vie [ravi] *adj* ENCHANTÉ : delighted

ravin [ravɛ̃] *nm* : ravine

ravir [ravir] *vt* : delight

raviser [ravize] *v* **se raviser** *vr* : change one's mind

ravisseur, -seuse [ravisœr, -søz] *n* : kidnapper

ravitailler [ravitaje] *vt* 1 : supply (with food) 2 : refuel

raviver [ravive] *vt* : revive

ravoir [ravwar] {73} *vt* : get back

rayer [reje] {11} *vt* 1 ÉRAFLER : scratch 2 BARRER : cross out, erase — **rayé, rayée** [reje] *adj* : striped

rayon [rejɔ̃] *nm* 1 : ray 2 : radius (of a circle) 3 : range, scope 4 ÉTAGÈRE : shelf 5

: department (in a store) **6 ~ de miel** : honeycomb

rayonnant, -nante [rɛjɔnɑ̃, -nɑ̃t] *adj* : radiant

rayonne [rɛjɔn] *nf* : rayon

rayonner [rɛjɔne] *vi* **1** : radiate **2** BRILLER : shine **3** : tour around **4 ~ sur** : exert influence on — **rayonnement** [rɛjɔnmɑ̃] *nm* : radiation

rayure [rɛjyr] *nf* **1** : stripe **2** ÉRAFLURE : scratch

raz–de–marée [radmare] *nms & pl* : tidal wave

réagir [reaʒir] *vi* : react — **réacteur** [reaktœr] *nm* **1** : jet engine **2** : (nuclear) reactor — **réaction** [reaksjɔ̃] *nf* **1** : reaction **2 à ~** : jet-propelled — **réactionnaire** [reaksjɔnɛr] *adj & nmf* : reactionary

réaliser [realize] *vt* **1** : carry out, execute **2** ACCOMPLIR : achieve **3** : direct (a film) **4** : realize (a profit) — **se réaliser** *vr* : materialize, come true — **réalisateur, -trice** [realizatœr, -tris] *n* : director (in movies, television, etc.) — **réalisation** [realizasjɔ̃] *nf* **1** EXÉCUTION : execution, carrying out **2** : accomplishment **3** : production (of a film)

réaliste [realist] *adj* : realistic

réalité [realite] *nf* **1** : reality **2 en ~** : in fact, actually

réanimer [reanime] *vt* : resuscitate

réapparaître [reaparɛtr] {7} *vi* : reappear

rébarbatif, -tive [rebarbatif, -tiv] *adj* : forbidding, daunting

rebâtir [rəbatir] *vt* : rebuild

rebattu, -tue [rəbaty] *adj* : hackneyed

rebelle [rəbɛl] *nmf* : rebel — **~** *adj* : rebellious — **rebeller** [rəbɛle] *v* **se rebeller** *vr* : rebel — **rébellion** [rebɛljɔ̃] *nf* : rebellion

rebondir [rəbɔ̃dir] *vi* **1** : bounce, rebound **2** : start (up) again — **rebond** [rəbɔ̃] *nm* : bounce, rebound

rebord [rəbɔr] *nm* : edge, sill (of a window)

rebours [rəbur] **à ~** *adv phr* : the wrong way

rebrousse–poil [rəbruspwal] **à ~** *adv phr* : the wrong way

rebrousser [rəbruse] *vt* **1** : brush back **2 ~ chemin** : turn back

rebuffade [rəbyfad] *nf* : rebuff, snub

rebut [rəby] *nm* **1** : trash, scrap **2 mettre au ~** : discard — **rebutant, -tante** [rəbytɑ̃, -tɑ̃t] *adj* : repellent, disagreeable — **rebuter** [rəbyte] *vt* : put off, discourage

récalcitrant, -trante [rekalsitrɑ̃, -trɑ̃t] *adj* : stubborn

récapituler [rekapityle] *vt* RÉSUMER : recapitulate, sum up

recel [rəsɛl] *nm* : possession of stolen goods

récemment [resamɑ̃] *adv* DERNIÈREMENT : recently

recensement [rəsɑ̃smɑ̃] *nm* : census

récent, -cente [resɑ̃, -sɑ̃t] *adj* : recent

récépissé [resepise] *nm* : receipt

récepteur [reseptœr] *nm* : receiver

réception [resɛpsjɔ̃] *nf* : reception — **réceptionniste** [resɛpsjɔnist] *nmf* : receptionist

récession [resesjɔ̃] *nf* : recession

recette [rəsɛt] *nf* **1** : recipe (in cooking) **2** : take, receipts *pl*

recevoir [rəsəvwar] {26} *vt* **1** : receive, get **2** ACCUEILLIR : welcome **3** : see (a client, etc.) **4** : accommodate, hold — **receveur, -veuse** [rəsəvœr, -vøz] *n* **1** *Can* : catcher (in sports) **2 ~ des contributions** : tax collector

rechange [rəʃɑ̃ʒ] *nm* **de ~ 1** : spare, extra **2** : alternative

réchapper [reʃape] *vi* **~ de** : come through, survive

recharger [rəʃarʒe] {17} *vt* **1** : refill **2** : recharge — **recharge** [rəʃarʒ] *nf* **1** : refill **2** : recharging

réchaud [reʃo] *nm* : (portable) stove

réchauffer [reʃofe] *vt* : reheat — **se réchauffer** *vr* : warm up, get warmer

rêche [rɛʃ] *adj* : rough, prickly

rechercher [rəʃɛrʃe] *vt* : search for, seek — **recherche** [rəʃɛrʃ] *nf* **1** : search **2** : (academic) research — **recherché, -chée** [rəʃɛrʃe] *adj* : sought-after, in demand

rechigner [rəʃiɲe] *vi* **1** : grumble **2 ~ à** : balk at

rechute [rəʃyt] *nf* : relapse

récif [resif] *nm* : reef

récipient [resipjɑ̃] *nm* : container

réciproque [resiprɔk] *adj* : reciprocal

réciter [resite] *vt* : recite — **récit** [resi] *nm* : account, story — **récital** [resital] *nm, pl* **-tals** : recital

réclamer [reklame] *vt* **1** : call for, demand **2** REVENDIQUER : claim — **réclamation** [reklamasjɔ̃] *nf* PLAINTE : complaint — **réclame** [reklam] *nf* **1** : advertisement **2** : advertising

reclus, -cluse [rəkly, -klyz] *n* : recluse

recoin [rəkwɛ̃] *nm* : nook, corner

récolte [rekɔlt] *nf* **1** : harvesting **2** : harvest, crop — **récolter** [rekɔlte] *vt* **1** : harvest **2** RAMASSER : gather, collect

recommander [rəkɔmɑ̃de] *vt* **1** : recommend **2** : register (a letter, etc.) — **recommandation** [rəkɔmɑ̃dasjɔ̃] *nf* : recommendation

recommencer [rəkɔmɑ̃se] {6} *v* : begin again

récompenser [rekɔ̃pɑ̃se] *vt* : reward — **récompense** [rekɔ̃pɑ̃s] *nf* : reward

réconcilier [rekɔ̃silje] {96} *vt* : reconcile — **réconciliation** [rekɔ̃siljasjɔ̃] *nf* : reconciliation

reconduire [rəkɔ̃dɥir] {49} *vt* RACCOMPA-
GNER : see home, accompany

réconforter [rekɔ̃fɔrte] *vt* : comfort — **réconfort** [rekɔ̃fɔr] *nm* : comfort — **récon-
fortant, -tante** [rekɔ̃fɔrtɑ̃, -tɑ̃t] *adj* : com-
forting, heartwarming

reconnaître [rəkɔnɛtr] {7} *vt* 1 : recognize
2 ADMETTRE : acknowledge — **reconnaissance** [rekɔnɛsɑ̃s] *nf* 1 : recognition 2
GRATITUDE : gratitude — **reconnaissable**
[rəkɔnɛsabl] *adj* : recognizable — **reconnaissant, -sante** [rəkɔnɛsɑ̃, -sɑ̃t] *adj*
: grateful — **reconnu, -nue** [rəkɔny] *adj*
: well-known

reconsidérer [rəkɔ̃sidere] {87} *vt* : reconsider

reconstituer [rəkɔ̃stitɥe] *vt* : recreate, reconstruct

reconstruire [rəkɔ̃strɥir] {49} *vt* : reconstruct, rebuild

record [rəkɔr] *nm* : record

recouper [rəkupe] *v* **se recouper** *vr* : tally,
match up

recourbé, -bée [rəkurbe] *adj* : curved,
hooked

recourir [rəkurir] {23} *vi* ~ **à** : resort to —
recours [rəkur] *nm* : recourse, resort

recouvrer [rəkuvre] *vt* : recover, regain

recouvrir [rəkuvrir] {83} *vt* : cover (up)

récréation [rekreasjɔ̃] *nf* 1 LOISIRS : recreation 2 : recess, break — **récréatif, -tive**
[rekreatif, -tiv] *adj* : recreational

recréer [rəkree] {89} *vt* : re-create

récrier [rekrije] {96} *v* **se récrier** *vr* : exclaim

récrimination [rekriminasjɔ̃] *nf* : reproach

récrire [rekrir] {33} *vt* : rewrite

recroqueviller [rəkrɔkvije] *v* **se recroqueviller** *vr* 1 : curl up 2 : shrivel up

recruter [rəkryte] *vt* : recruit — **recrue**
[rəkry] *nf* : recruit — **recrutement**
[rəkrytmɑ̃] *nm* : recruitment

rectangle [rɛktɑ̃gl] *nm* : rectangle — **rectangulaire** [-tɑ̃gylɛr] *adj* : rectangular

rectifier [rɛktifje] {96} *vt* : rectify, correct —
rectification [rɛktifikasjɔ̃] *nf* : correction

recto [rɛkto] *nm* : right side (of a page)

rectum [rɛktɔm] *nm* : rectum

reçu, -cue [rəsy] *adj* : accepted, approved —
reçu *nm* : receipt

recueillir [rəkœjir] {3} *vt* 1 : collect, gather
2 : obtain (information) — **se recueillir** *vr*
: meditate — **recueil** [rəkœj] *nm* : collection

reculer [rəkyle] *v* 1 REPOUSSER : move
back, push back 2 DIFFÉRER : postpone —
vi 1 : move back, back up 2 ~ **devant**
: shrink from — **recul** [rəkyl] *nm* 1 : recoil
(of a fire arm) 2 **avec le** ~ : with hindsight
— **reculons** [rəkylɔ̃] **à** ~ *adv phr* : backward

récupérer [rekypere] {87} *vt* 1 : recover,
get back 2 : salvage 3 : make up (hours of
work, etc.) — *vi* SE RÉTABLIR : recover, recuperate

récurer [rekyre] *vt* : scour

recycler [rəsikle] *vt* 1 : retrain (personnel)
2 : recycle — **se recycler** *vr* : retrain

rédacteur, -trice [redaktœr, -tris] *n* : editor
— **rédaction** [redaksjɔ̃] *nf* 1 : writing, editing 2 : editorial staff

reddition [redisjɔ̃] *nf* : surrender

rédemption [redɑ̃psjɔ̃] *nf* : redemption

redevable [rədəvabl] *adj* **être** ~ **à** : be indebted to — **redevance** [rədəvɑ̃s] *nf* : dues
pl, fees *pl*

rédiger [rediʒe] {17} *vt* : draw up, write

redire [rədir] {29} *vt* RÉPÉTER : repeat

redondant, -dante [rədɔ̃dɑ̃, -dɑ̃t] *adj* SUPER-
FLU : redundant

redonner [rədɔne] *vt* 1 RENDRE : give back
2 RÉTABLIR : restore (confidence)

redoubler [rəduble] *vt* 1 DOUBLER : double
2 : repeat (a year in school) 3 ~ **ses efforts** : intensify one's efforts

redouter [rədute] *vt* : fear — **redoutable**
[rədutabl] *adj* : formidable

redresser [rədrɛse] *vt* 1 : straighten (up) 2
: rectify, redress (wrongs, etc.) — **se redresser** *vr* : straighten up

réduction [redyksjɔ̃] *nf* : reduction

réduire [redɥir] {49} *vt* 1 : reduce 2 ~ **en**
: crush to — **réduit, -duite** [redɥi, -dɥit] *adj*
1 : reduced (of speed) 2 : small, limited —
réduit *nm* : recess, nook

rééduquer [reedyke] *vt* : rehabilitate —
rééducation [reedykasjɔ̃] *nf* : rehabilitation

réel, -elle [reɛl] *adj* : real — **réel** *nm* : reality
— **réellement** [reɛlmɑ̃] *adv* : really

refaire [rəfɛr] {42} *vt* : do again, redo — **ré-
fection** [refɛksjɔ̃] *nf* : repair

référence [referɑ̃s] *nf* : reference

référendum [referɛ̃dɔm] *nm* : referendum

référer [refere] {87} *v* **se référer** *vr* ~ **à**
: refer to

réfléchir [refleʃir] *vt* : reflect — *vi* PENSER
: think — **réfléchi, -chie** [refleʃi] *adj* 1
: thoughtful 2 : reflexive (of a verb)

refléter [rəflete] {87} *vt* : reflect, mirror —
reflet [rəflɛ] *nm* : reflection, image

réflexe [reflɛks] *adj & nm* : reflex

réflexion [reflɛksjɔ̃] *nf* 1 : reflection (of
light, etc.) 2 PENSÉE : thought

refluer [rəflye] *vi* 1 : ebb, flow back 2
: surge back (of crowds, etc.) — **reflux**
[rəflys] *nm* : ebb

réformer [rəfɔrme] *vt* : reform — **réformateur, -trice** [refɔrmatœr, -tris] *n* : reformer
— **réforme** [refɔrm] *nf* : reform

refouler [rəfule] *vt* 1 : drive back (a crowd)
2 ~ **ses larmes** : hold back tears

réfractaire [refraktɛr] *adj* ~ **à** : resistant to

refrain [rəfrɛ̃] *nm* : refrain, chorus

refréner [rəfrene] *or* **réfréner** [refrene] {87} *vt* : curb, check

réfrigérer [refriʒere] {87} *vt* : refrigerate — **réfrigérateur** [refriʒeratœr] *nm* : refrigerator

refroidir [rəfrwadir] *v* : cool (down) — **refroidissement** [rəfrwadismɑ̃] *nm* **1** : cooling **2** RHUME : cold, chill

refuge [rəfyʒ] *nm* : refuge — **réfugié, -giée** [refyʒje] *n* : refugee — **réfugier** [refyʒje] {96} *v* **se réfugier** *vr* : take refuge

refuser [rəfyze] *vt* : refuse — **refus** [rəfy] *nm* : refusal

réfuter [refyte] *vt* : refute

regagner [rəgaɲe] *vt* **1** : win back **2** ~ **son domicile** : return home

régal [regal] *nm, pl* **-gals** DÉLICE : delight, treat — **régaler** [regale] *vt* : treat — **se régaler** *vr* **1** : enjoy oneself **2** ~ **de** : feast on

regard [rəgar] *nm* **1** : look **2 au** ~ **de** : in regard to — **regarder** [rəgarde] *vt* **1** : look at, watch **2** CONSIDÉRER : consider **3** CONCERNER : concern — *vi* : look — **se regarder** *vr* **1** : look at oneself **2** : look at each other

régénérer [reʒenere] {87} *vt* : regenerate

régie [reʒi] *nf* **1** *France* : public corporation **2** *Can* : provincial public-service agency

régime [reʒim] *nm* **1** : (political) regime **2** : system **3** : cluster, bunch (of bananas) **4 au** ~ : on a diet

région [reʒjɔ̃] *nf* : region, area — **régional, -nale** [reʒjɔnal] *adj, mpl* **-naux** [-no] : regional

régir [reʒir] *vt* : govern

registre [rəʒistr] *nm* : register

réglable [reglabl] *adj* **1** : adjustable **2** : payable — **réglage** [reglaʒ] *nm* : adjustment

règle [rɛgl] *nf* **1** : ruler (instrument) **2** LOI : rule **3** ~**s** *nfpl* : menstrual period **4 en** ~ : in order, valid — **réglé, -glée** [regle] *adj* ORGANISÉ : orderly, organized — **règlement** [rɛgləmɑ̃] *nm* **1** : regulations *pl* **2** RÉSOLUTION : settlement — **réglementation** [rɛgləmɑ̃tasjɔ̃] *nf* : regulation — **régler** [regle] {87} *vt* **1** : adjust, regulate **2** : settle (a dispute)

réglisse [reglis] *nf* : licorice

régner [reɲe] {87} *vi* : reign — **règne** [rɛɲ] *nm* : reign, rule

regorger [rəgɔrʒe] {17} *vi* ~ **de** : overflow with

regretter [rəgrɛte] *vt* **1** : regret, be sorry about **2** : miss (s.o.) — **regret** [rəgrɛ] *nm* : regret

régularité [regylarite] *nf* : regularity — **régulier, -lière** [regylje, -ljɛr] *adj* **1** : regular **2** CONSTANT : even, steady

réhabiliter [reabilite] *vt* **1** : rehabilitate **2** RÉNOVER : renovate — **réhabilitation** [reabilitasjɔ̃] *nf* : rehabilitation

rein [rɛ̃] *nm* **1** : kidney **2** ~**s** *nmpl* DOS : back

reine [rɛn] *nf* : queen

réinsérer [reẽsere] {87} *vt* : rehabilitate

réitérer [reitere] {87} *vt* : reiterate, repeat

rejeter [rəʒte] {8} *vt* **1** RENVOYER : throw back **2** REFUSER : reject — **rejet** [rəʒɛ] *nm* : rejection

rejoindre [rəʒwɛ̃dr] {50} *vt* **1** RENCONTRER : join, meet **2** RATTRAPER : catch up with **3** REGAGNER : return to — **se rejoindre** *vr* : meet

réjouir [reʒwir] *vt* : delight — **se réjouir** *vr* : rejoice, be delighted — **réjouissance** [reʒwisɑ̃s] *nf* **1** : rejoicing **2** ~**s** *nfpl* : festivities — **réjouissant, -sante** [reʒwisɑ̃, -sɑ̃t] *adj* : cheering, delightful

relâcher [rəlɑʃe] *vt* **1** DESSERRER : loosen (up), slacken **2** LIBÉRER : release — **se relâcher** *vr* **1** : loosen **2** : become lax — **relâche** [rəlɑʃ] *nf* : respite

relais [rəlɛ] *nm* **1** : relay **2** ~ **routier** : truck stop

relancer [rəlɑ̃se] {6} *vt* **1** : throw back **2** : revive, boost (the economy, etc.) — **relance** [rəlɑ̃s] *nf* : boost

relatif, -tive [rəlatif, -tiv] *adj* : relative — **relativité** [rəlativite] *nf* : relativity

relation [rəlasjɔ̃] *nf* **1** : connection, relation **2** : relationship **3** CONNAISSANCE : acquaintance **4** ~**s** *nfpl* : relations

relaxer [rəlakse] *vt* : relax — **relaxation** [rəlaksasjɔ̃] *nf* : relaxation

relayer [rəlɛje] {11} *vt* : relieve — **se relayer** *vr* : take turns

reléguer [rəlege] {87} *vt* : relegate

relent [rəlɑ̃] *nm* : stench

relève [rəlɛv] *nf* **1** : relief **2 prendre la** ~ : take over

relever [rəlve] {52} *vt* **1** : pick up, raise (up) **2** AUGMENTER : increase **3** RELAYER : relieve **4** : bring out, enhance — **se relever** *vr* : get up (again) — **relevé** [rəlɛve] *nm* **1** : (bank) statement **2** : reading (of a meter)

relief [rəljɛf] *nm* **1** : relief **2 mettre en** ~ : highlight

relier [rəlje] {96} *vt* **1** : link, join **2** : bind (a book)

religion [rəliʒjɔ̃] *nf* : religion — **religieux, -gieuse** [rəliʒjø, -ʒjøz] *adj* : religious — ~ *n* : monk *m*, nun *f*

relique [rəlik] *nf* : relic

reliure [rəljyr] *nf* : binding

reluire [rəlɥir] {49} *vi* BRILLER : glisten,

shine — **reluisant, -sante** [rəlɥizɑ̃, -zɑ̃t]
adj : gleaming

remanier [rəmanje] {96} *vt* : revise, modify

remarquer [rəmarke] *vt* **1** : remark, observe
2 CONSTATER : notice — **remarquable**
[rəmarkabl] *adj* : remarkable — **remarque**
[rəmark] *nf* : remark

remblai [rɑ̃blɛ] *nm* : embankment

rembobiner [rɑ̃bɔbine] *vt* : rewind

rembourrer [rɑ̃bure] *vt* : pad

rembourser [rɑ̃burse] *vt* **1** : repay (a debt)
2 : refund, reimburse — **remboursement**
[rɑ̃bursəmɑ̃] *nm* : refund, reimbursement

remède [rəmɛd] *nm* : remedy, cure —
remédier [rəmedje] {96} *vi* **~ à** : remedy,
cure

remercier [rəmɛrsje] {96} *vt* **1** : thank **2**
CONGÉDIER : dismiss, fire — **remer-**
ciement [rəmɛrsimɑ̃] *nm* **1** : thanking **2**
~s *nmpl* : thanks

remettre [rəmɛtr] {53} *vt* **1** REMPLACER
: replace **2** RAJOUTER : add **3** : put back
(on) **4** DONNER : deliver, hand over **5**
: postpone **6** RECONNAÎTRE : recognize,
place — **se remettre** *vr* **1** : go back, get
back **2** : put on again **3** : recover, get better
4 ~ à : begin again **5 ~ de** : get over —
remise [rəmiz] *nf* **1** : postponement **2**
LIVRAISON : delivery **3** : remission (of a
debt, etc.) **4** RABAIS : discount **5** : shed —
rémission [remisjɔ̃] *nf* : remission

remonter [rəmɔ̃te] *vt* **1** : take back up,
bring back up, raise up (again) **2** : go back
up (the stairs, etc.) **3** : cheer up, invigorate
— *vi* **1** : go back up, rise (again) **2 ~ à**
: date back to — **remontée** [rəmɔ̃te] *nf* **1**
: climb, ascent **2 ~ mécanique** : ski lift
— **remonte–pente** [rəmɔ̃tpɑ̃t] *nm, pl* **re-**
monte–pentes : ski lift

remords [rəmɔr] *nm* : remorse

remorquer [rəmɔrke] *vt* : tow — **remorque**
[rəmɔrk] *nf* : trailer — **remorqueuse**
[rəmɔrkøz] *nf Can* : tow truck

remous [rəmu] *nm* : (back)wash

remplacer [rɑ̃plase] {6} *vt* : replace — **rem-**
plaçant, -çante [rɑ̃plasɑ̃, -sɑ̃t] *n* : substitute — **remplacement** [rɑ̃-plasmɑ̃] *nm* : replacement

remplir [rɑ̃plir] *vt* **1** : fill (up) **2** : fill out (a
form, etc.) **3** : carry out, fulfill — **remplis-**
sage [rɑ̃plisaʒ] *nm* : filling, filler

remporter [rɑ̃pɔrte] *vt* **1** REPRENDRE : take
back **2** : win (a prize, etc.)

remue–ménage [rəmymenaʒ] *nms & pl*
: commotion, fuss

remuer [rəmɥe] *vt* **1** MÉLANGER : stir, mix
2 ~ la queue : wag its tail — *vi* : fidget,
squirm

rémunérer [remynere] {87} *vt* : pay (for) —
rémunération [remynerasjɔ̃] *nf* : payment

renâcler [rənakle] *vi* **1** : snort **2 ~ à** : balk
at

renaître [rənɛtr] {57} *vi* : be reborn — **re-**
naissance [rənɛsɑ̃s] *nf* : rebirth, revival

renard [rənar] *nm* : fox

renchérir [rɑ̃ʃerir] *vi* **1** : become more expensive **2 ~ sur** : go (one step) further
than

rencontrer [rɑ̃kɔ̃tre] *vt* **1** : meet **2** TROUVER
: come across, encounter — **se rencontrer**
vr **1** : meet **2** SE TROUVER : be found —
rencontre [rɑ̃kɔ̃tr] *nf* **1** : meeting, encounter **2** : match, game

rendement [rɑ̃dmɑ̃] *nm* **1** : output **2** RAP-
PORT : yield

rendez–vous [rɑ̃devu] *nms & pl* **1** : appointment, meeting **2** : meeting place

rendre [rɑ̃dr] {63} *vt* **1** : give back, return **2**
: pronounce (a verdict) **3** EXPRIMER : con-
vey **4 ~ grâces** : give thanks — *vi* VOMIR
: vomit — **se rendre** *vr* **1** : surrender **2 ~**
à : go to **3 ~ compte de** : realize, be
aware of

rêne [rɛn] *nf* : rein

renfermer [rɑ̃fɛrme] *vt* : contain — **se ren-**
fermer *vr* : withdraw (into oneself) — **ren-**
fermé [rɑ̃fɛrme] *nm* : mustiness

renfler [rɑ̃fle] *v* **se renfler** *vr* : bulge, swell
— **renflement** [rɑ̃fləmɑ̃] *nm* : bulge

renforcer [rɑ̃fɔrse] {6} *vt* : reinforce — **ren-**
fort [rɑ̃fɔr] *nm* : reinforcement

renfrogné, -gnée [rɑ̃frɔɲe] *adj* : sullen,
scowling

rengaine [rɑ̃gɛn] *nf* **la même ~** : the same
old story

renier [rənje] {96} *vt* : deny, disown

renifler [rənifle] *v* : sniff

renne [rɛn] *nm* : reindeer

renom [rənɔ̃] *nm* : renown, fame —
renommé, -mée [rənɔme] *adj* : renowned
— **renommée** *nf* : fame, renown

renoncer [rənɔ̃se] {6} *vi* **~ à** : renounce,
give up — **renonciation** [rənɔ̃sjasjɔ̃] *nf* : renunciation

renouer [rənwe] *vt* REPRENDRE : renew, resume

renouveau [rənuvo] *nm, pl* **-veaux** : revival

renouveler [rənuvle] {8} *vt* : renew — **re-**
nouvellement [rənuvɛlmɑ̃] *nm* : renewal

rénover [renɔve] *vt* : renovate — **rénovation**
[renɔvasjɔ̃] *nf* : renovation

renseigner [rɑ̃seɲe] *vt* : inform — **se ren-**
seigner *vr* : ask, make inquiries — **ren-**
seignement [rɑ̃sɛɲəmɑ̃] *nm* : information

rentable [rɑ̃tabl] *adj* : profitable

rente [rɑ̃t] *nf* **1** : (private) income **2 ~**
viagère : annuity

rentrer [rɑ̃tre] *vi* **1** : go in, get in **2** : go back
in **3** RETOURNER : return — *vt* **1** : bring in,
take in **2** : pull in (one's stomach) — **ren-**

trée [rãtre] *nf* **1** : return (to work, etc.) **2** ~ **scolaire** : start of the new school year
renverser [rãverse] *vt* **1** : knock down, overturn **2** RÉPANDRE : spill **3** : overthrow (a regime) **4** STUPÉFIER : astonish — **se renverser** *vr* : fall over, overturn — **renversement** [rãversəmã] *nm* : reversal
renvoyer [rãvwaje] {36} *vt* **1** : send back, throw back **2** CONGÉDIER : dismiss **3** REMETTRE : postpone **4** ~ **à** : refer to **5** *Can fam* : throw up — **renvoi** [rãvwa] *nm* **1** : return (of a package) **2** LICENCIEMENT : dismissal **3** : cross-reference **4** REMISE : postponement **5** : belch, burp
réorganiser [reorganize] *vt* : reorganize
repaire [rəpɛr] *nm* : den, lair
répandre [repãdr] {63} *vt* **1** : spill **2** : shed (blood, tears, etc.) **3** : spread (the news) **4** : give off, emit — **se répandre** *vr* **1** : spill **2** SE PROPAGER : spread — **répandu, -due** [repãdy] *adj* : widespread
réparer [repare] *vt* **1** : repair **2** : make up for (an error) — **réparation** [reparasjɔ̃] *nf* : repair, repairing
repartir [rəpartir] {82} *vt* : retort — *vi* **1** : leave again **2** : start again
répartir [repartir] *vt* **1** : divide up, distribute **2** : spread (out) — **se répartir** *vr* : divide — **répartition** [repartisjɔ̃] *nf* : distribution
repas [rəpa] *nm* : meal
repasser [rəpase] *vt* **1** : pass again, take again, show again **2** : iron, press **3** : go (back) over — *vi* : pass by again, come again — **repassage** [rəpasaʒ] *nm* : ironing
repentir [rəpãtir] {82} *v* **se repentir** *vr* : repent — ~ *nm* : repentance
répercuter [repɛrkyte] *v* **se répercuter** *vr* **1** : echo **2** ~ **sur** : have repercussions on — **répercussion** [repɛrkysjɔ̃] *nf* : repercussion
repère [rəpɛr] *nm* **1** : line, mark **2 point de** ~ : landmark — **repérer** [rəpere] {87} *vt* **1** : mark **2** SITUER : locate — **se repérer** *vr* : find one's way
répertoire [repɛrtwar] *nm* **1** : list, index **2** : repertoire (in theater) **3** ~ **d'adresses** : address book **4** ~ **téléphonique** : telephone directory
répéter [repete] {87} *vt* **1** : repeat **2** : rehearse (in theater) — **répétitif, -tive** [repetitif, -tiv] *adj* : repetitive, repetitious — **répétition** [repetisjɔ̃] *nf* **1** : repetition **2** : rehearsal
répit [repi] *nm* : respite
replacer [rəplase] {6} *vt* : replace
replier [rəplije] {96} *vt* : fold up, fold over — **se replier** *vr* **1** : fold up **2** ~ **sur soi-même** : withdraw into oneself
répliquer [replike] *vt* RÉPONDRE : reply — *vi* **1** : respond **2** RIPOSTER : retort — **réplique**

[replik] *nf* **1** : reply **2** : line (in a play) **3** : replica (in art)
répondre [repɔ̃dr] {63} *v* : answer, reply — **répondeur** [repɔ̃dœr] *nm* : answering machine — **réponse** [repɔ̃s] *nf* : answer, response
report [rəpɔr] *nm* RENVOI : postponement
reportage [rəpɔrtaʒ] *nm* : report
reporter[1] [rəpɔrte] *vt* **1** : take back **2** REMETTRE : postpone **3** : carry forward (a calculation, etc.)
reporter[2] [rəpɔrtɛr] *nm* : reporter
reposer [rəpoze] *v* : rest — **se reposer** *vr* **1** : rest **2** ~ **sur** : rely on — **repos** [rəpo] *nm* : rest — **reposant, -sante** [rəpozã, -zãt] *nm* : restful
repousser [rəpuse] *vi* : grow back — *vt* **1** : push back **2** DÉGOÛTER : disgust **3** : turn down (an offer) **4** REPORTER : postpone — **repoussant, -sante** [rəpusã, -sãt] *adj* DÉGOÛTANT : repulsive
reprendre [rəprãdr] {70} *vt* **1** : take (up) again **2** : take back, return **3** RETROUVER : regain **4** RECOMMENCER : resume **5** : repair, alter (a garment) — *vi* **1** : pick up, improve **2** : resume
représailles [rəprezaj] *nfpl* : reprisals
représenter [rəprezãte] *vt* **1** : represent **2** JOUER : perform — **représentant, -tante** [rəprezãtã, -tãt] *n* : representative — **représentatif, -tive** [rəprezãtatif, -tiv] *adj* : representative — **représentation** [rəprezãtasjɔ̃] *nf* **1** : representation **2** : performance (in theater)
réprimander [reprimãde] *vt* : reprimand — **réprimande** [reprimãd] *nf* : reprimand
réprimer [reprime] *vt* : repress, suppress
reprise [rəpriz] *nf* **1** : recapture **2** : resumption **3** : repeat, revival **4** : recovery **5** : trade-in (of goods) **6** : round (in sports) **7** : darn, mend — **repriser** [rəprize] *vt* : darn, mend
reprocher [rəprɔʃe] *vt* ~ **à** : reproach — **reproche** [rəprɔʃ] *nm* : reproach
reproduire [rəprɔdɥir] {49} *vt* : reproduce — **se reproduire** *vr* **1** : reproduce **2** SE RÉPÉTER : recur — **reproduction** [rəprɔdyksjɔ̃] *nf* : reproduction
réprouver [repruve] *vt* : condemn
reptile [rɛptil] *nm* : reptile
repu, -pue [rəpy] *adj* : satiated, full
république [repyblik] *nf* : republic — **républicain, -caine** [repyblikɛ̃, -kɛn] *adj & n* : republican
répudier [repydje] {96} *vt* : repudiate
répugner [repyɲe] *vt* : disgust — *vi* ~ **à** : be averse to — **répugnance** [repyɲãs] *nf* **1** : repugnance **2** : reluctance — **répugnant, -gnante** [repyɲã, -ɲãt] *adj* : repugnant
réputation [repytasjɔ̃] *nf* : reputation —

réputé, -tée [repyte] *adj* : renowned, famous

requérir [rəkerir] {21} *vt* : require

requête [rəkɛt] *nf* : request

requin [rəkɛ̃] *nm* : shark

requis, -quise [rəki, -kiz] *adj* : required

rescapé, -pée [rɛskape] *n* : survivor

rescousse [rɛskus] *nf* : rescue, aid

réseau [rezo] *nm, pl* **-seaux** : network

réserver [rezɛrve] *vt* : reserve — **réservation** [rezɛrvasjɔ̃] *nf* : reservation — **réserve** [rezɛrv] *nf* **1** PROVISION : stock **2** RETENUE : reserve **3** : (Indian) reservation **4** : (game) preserve **5 sous ~ de** : subject to — **réservé, -vée** [rezɛrve] *adj* : reserved

réservoir [rezɛrvwar] *nm* **1** : tank **2** : reservoir

résidence [rezidɑ̃s] *nf* : residence — **résident, -dente** [rezidɑ̃, -dɑ̃t] *n* : resident — **résidentiel, -tielle** [rezidɑ̃sjɛl] *adj* : residential — **résider** [rezide] *vi* : reside

résidu [rezidy] *nm* : residue

résigner [reziɲe] *vt* : resign — **se résigner** *vr* **~ à** : resign oneself to — **résignation** [reziɲasjɔ̃] *nf* : resignation

résilier [rezilje] {96} *vt* : terminate

résine [rezin] *nf* : resin

résister [reziste] *vi* **~ à** : resist — **résistance** [rezistɑ̃s] *nf* : resistance — **résistant, -tante** [rezistɑ̃, -tɑ̃t] *adj* : tough, durable

résolu, -lue [rezɔly] *adj* : resolute, resolved — **résolution** [rezɔlysjɔ̃] *nf* **1** : resolution **2** DÉTERMINATION : resolve

résonner [rezɔne] *vi* : resound — **résonance** [rezɔnɑ̃s] *nf* : resonance — **résonnant, -nante** [rezɔnɑ̃, -nɑ̃t] *adj* : resonant

résorber [rezɔrbe] *vt* : absorb, reduce

résoudre [rezudr] {74} *vt* : solve, resolve — **se résoudre** *vr* **~ à** : decide to

respect [rɛspɛ] *nm* : respect — **respectable** [rɛspɛktabl] *adj* : respectable — **respecter** [rɛspɛkte] *vt* : respect

respectif, -tive [rɛspɛktif, -tiv] *adj* : respective

respectueux, -tueuse [rɛspɛktɥø, -tɥøz] *adj* : respectful

respirer [rɛspire] *v* : breathe — **respiration** [rɛspirasjɔ̃] *nf* : breathing

resplendir [rɛsplɑ̃dir] *vi* : shine — **resplendissant, -sante** [rɛsplɑ̃disɑ̃, -sɑ̃t] *adj* : radiant

responsable [rɛspɔ̃sabl] *adj* : responsible — **responsabilité** [rɛspɔ̃sabilite] *nf* **1** : responsibility **2** : liability

resquiller [rɛskije] *vi fam* **1** : sneak in (without paying) **2** : cut in line

ressaisir [rəsezir] *v* **se ressaisir** *vr* : pull oneself together

ressasser [rəsase] *vt* : keep going over

ressembler [rəsɑ̃ble] *vi* **~ à** : resemble — **se ressembler** *vr* : resemble each other, look alike — **ressemblance** [rəsɑ̃blɑ̃s] *nf* **1** : resemblance, likeness **2** SIMILITUDE : similarity

ressentir [rəsɑ̃tir] {82} *vt* : feel — **se ressentir** *vr* : feel the effects of — **ressentiment** [rəsɑ̃timɑ̃] *nm* : resentment

resserrer [rəsere] *vt* : tighten (a knot, etc.) — **se resserrer** *vr* **1** : tighten (up) **2** : narrow

ressortir [rəsɔrtir] {82} *vt* : take out again, bring out again — *vi* **1** : go out again **2** : stand out — *v impers* : emerge, be evident — **ressort** [rəsɔr] *nm* **1** : spring (of a mattress, etc.) **2** : impulse, motivation **3 en dernier ~** : as a last resort — **ressortissant, -sante** [rəsɔrtisɑ̃, -sɑ̃t] *n* : national

ressource [rəsurs] *nf* : resource

ressusciter [resysite] *vt* : resuscitate — *vi* : come back to life, revive

restant, -tante [rɛstɑ̃, -tɑ̃t] *adj* : remaining — **restant** *nm* : remainder

restaurant [rɛstɔrɑ̃] *nm* : restaurant

restaurer [rɛstɔre] *vt* : restore

rester [rɛste] *vi* **1** : stay, remain **2** : be left — *v impers* **il reste** : there remains — **reste** [rɛst] *nm* **1** : remainder, rest **2 au ~** *or* **du ~** : besides, moreover **3 ~s** *nmpl* : leftovers **4 ~s** *nmpl* : remains

restituer [rɛstitɥe] *vt* **1** : restore, return **2** : reproduce (sound, etc.)

restreindre [rɛstrɛ̃dr] {37} *vt* : restrict — **restrictif, -tive** [rɛstriktif, -tiv] *adj* : restrictive — **restriction** [rɛstriksjɔ̃] *nf* : restriction

résultat [rezylta] *nm* : result — **résulter** [rezylte] {75} *vi* **~ de** : result from — *v impers* **il résulte** : it follows

résumer [rezyme] *vt* : summarize, sum up — **résumé** [rezyme] *nm* **1** : summary **2 en ~** : in short

résurrection [rezyrɛksjɔ̃] *nf* : resurrection

rétablir [retablir] *vt* : restore — **se rétablir** *vr* **1** : be restored **2** GUÉRIR : recover — **rétablissement** [reta-blismɑ̃] *nm* **1** : restoration **2** GUÉRISON : recovery

retarder [rətarde] *vt* **1** : delay **2** REPORTER : postpone **3** : set back (a clock, etc.) — *vi* : be slow — **retard** [rətar] *nm* **1** : lateness, delay **2** : backwardness — **retardataire** [rətardatɛr] *nmf* : latecomer

retenir [rətənir] {92} *vt* **1** : hold back, stop **2** RETARDER : keep, detain **3** GARDER : retain **4** RÉSERVER : reserve, book **5** SE RAPPELER : remember **6** : carry (in mathematics) — **se retenir** *vr* **1** : restrain oneself **2 ~ à** : hold on to

retentir [rətɑ̃tir] *vi* : ring, resound — **retentissant, -sante** [rətɑ̃tisɑ̃, -sɑ̃t] *adj* : resounding — **retentissement** [rətɑ̃tismɑ̃] *nm* : effect, impact

retenue [rətəny] *nf* **1** : deduction **2** : detention (in school) **3** RÉSERVE : reserve, restraint

réticent, -cente [retisɑ̃, -sɑ̃t] *adj* : reticent, reluctant — **réticence** [-tisɑ̃s] *nf* : reticence, reluctance

rétine [retin] *nf* : retina

retiré, -rée [rətire] *adj* : remote, secluded

retirer [rətire] *vt* **1** : take off (clothing, etc.) **2** : take away, remove **3** : withdraw (money, support, etc.) **4** : collect (baggage, etc.) **5** *Can* : retire, put out (in baseball) — **se retirer** *vr* : withdraw, retreat

retomber [rətɔ̃be] *vi* : fall again, fall back — **retombées** [rətɔ̃be] *nfpl* : repercussions, consequences

rétorquer [retɔrke] *vt* : retort

rétorsion [retɔrsjɔ̃] *nf* : retaliation

retoucher [rətuʃe] *vt* **1** : touch up **2** : alter (a dress, etc.) — **retouche** [rətuʃ] *nf* **1** : touching up **2** : alteration

retour [rətur] *nm* **1** : return **2 de ~** : back

retourner [rəturne] *vt* **1** : turn over **2** : return (a compliment, etc.) — *vi* REVENIR : return — **se retourner** *vr* **1** : turn around **2** : overturn (of a boat, etc.) **3 ~ contre** : turn against

retrait [rətrɛ] *nm* **1** : withdrawal **2 en ~** : set back **3** *Can* : out (in baseball)

retraite [rətrɛt] *nf* **1** : retirement **2** : retreat (in religion, etc.) **3** PENSION : pension

retransmettre [rətrɑ̃smɛtr] {53} *vt* : broadcast — **retransmission** [rətrɑ̃smisjɔ̃] *nf* : broadcast

rétrécir [retresir] *vi* : shrink

rétribuer [retribɥe] *vt* : pay — **rétribution** [retribysjɔ̃] *nf* RÉMUNÉRATION : payment

rétroactif, -tive [retrɔaktif, -tiv] *adj* : retroactive

rétrograder [retrɔgrade] *vt* : demote — *vi* : downshift (of a gear)

retrousser [rətruse] *vt* : turn up, roll up

retrouvailles [rətruvaj] *nfpl* : reunion

retrouver [rətruve] *vt* **1** : find (again) **2** REVOIR : see again **3** SE RAPPELER : remember — **se retrouver** *vr* **1** : meet again **2** : find one's way

rétroviseur [retrɔvizœr] *nm* : rearview mirror

réunir [reynir] *vt* RASSEMBLER : gather, collect — **se réunir** *vr* : meet — **réunion** [reynjɔ̃] *nf* : meeting

réussir [reysir] *vi* : succeed — *vt* **1** : make a success of **2** : pass (an exam) — **réussi, -sie** [reysi] *adj* : successful — **réussite** [reysit] *nf* : success

revanche [rəvɑ̃ʃ] *nf* **1** : revenge **2 en ~** : on the other hand

rêve [rɛv] *nm* : dream

réveiller [reveje] *vt* **1** : wake up **2** : awaken

— **se réveiller** *vr* : wake up — **réveil** [revɛj] *nm* **1** : waking up, awakening **2** : alarm clock — **réveille-matin** [revɛjmatɛ̃] *nms & pl* : alarm clock

révéler [revele] {87} *vt* **1** : reveal **2** INDIQUER : show — **se révéler** *vr* : prove to be — **révélation** [revelasjɔ̃] *nf* : revelation

revendiquer [rəvɑ̃dike] *vt* **1** : claim **2** EXIGER : demand — **revendication** [rəvɑ̃dikasjɔ̃] *nf* : claim

revendre [rəvɑ̃dr] {63} *vt* : sell

revenir [rəvnir] {92} *vi* **1** : come back, return **2 ~ à** : return to, go back to **3 ~ à** : come down to, amount to **4 ~ de** : get over

revente [rəvɑ̃t] *nf* : resale

revenu [rəvəny] *nm* : revenue, income

rêver [rɛve] *v* : dream

réverbère [reverbɛr] *nm* : streetlight

révérence [reverɑ̃s] *nf* **1** VÉNÉRATION : reverence **2** : bow, curtsy

révérend, -rende [reverɑ̃, -rɑ̃d] *adj* : reverend

rêverie [rɛvri] *nf* : daydreaming

revers [rəvɛr] *nm* **1** ENVERS : back, reverse **2** : lapel (of a jacket), cuff (of trousers) **3** : backhand (in tennis) **4** ÉCHEC : setback

réversible [reversibl] *adj* : reversible

revêtement [rəvɛtmɑ̃] *nm* **1** : facing (in construction) **2** : surface (of a road)

rêveur, -veuse [rɛvœr, -vøz] *adj* : dreamy — **~** *n* : dreamer

revirement [rəvirmɑ̃] *nm* : reversal, turnabout

réviser [revize] *vt* **1** : revise, review **2** : overhaul (a vehicle) — **révision** [revizjɔ̃] *nf* **1** : review, revision **2** : service (of a vehicle)

révocation [revɔkasjɔ̃] *nf* **1** : dismissal **2** : repeal

revoir [rəvwar] {99} *vt* **1** : see again **2** RÉVISER : review — **se revoir** *vr* : meet (each other) again — **~** *nm* **au ~** : goodbye

révolter [revɔlte] *vt* : revolt, outrage — **se révolter** *vr* : rebel — **révolte** [revɔlt] *nf* : revolt

révolu, -lue [revɔly] *adj* : past

révolution [revɔlysjɔ̃] *nf* : revolution — **révolutionnaire** [revɔlysjɔnɛr] *adj & nmf* : revolutionary — **révolutionner** [revɔlysjɔne] *vt* : revolutionize

revolver [revɔlvɛr] *nm* : revolver

révoquer [revɔke] *vt* **1** : dismiss **2** : revoke (a privilege, etc.)

revue [rəvy] *nf* **1** : magazine **2 passer en ~** : go over

rez-de-chaussée [redʃose] *nms & pl* : first floor, ground floor

rhabiller [rabije] *v* **se rhabiller** *vr* : get dressed again

rhétorique [retɔrik] *adj* : rhetorical — ~ *nf* : rhetoric

rhinocéros [rinɔserɔs] *nm* : rhinoceros

rhubarbe [rybarb] *nf* : rhubarb

rhum [rɔm] *nm* : rum

rhumatisme [rymatism] *nm* : rheumatism

rhume [rym] *nm* : cold

ricaner [rikane] *vi* : snicker, giggle

riche [riʃ] *adj* : rich — ~ *nmf* : rich person — **richesse** [riʃɛs] *nf* **1** : wealth **2** : richness

ricocher [rikɔʃe] *vi* : ricochet — **ricochet** [rikɔʃɛ] *nm* : ricochet

ride [rid] *nf* **1** : wrinkle **2** : ripple (on water)

rideau [rido] *nm, pl* **-deaux** : curtain

rider [ride] *vt* **1** : wrinkle **2** : ripple (water)

ridicule [ridikyl] *adj* ABSURDE : ridiculous — ~ *nm* : ridicule — **ridiculiser** [ridikylize] *vt* : ridicule

rien [rjɛ̃] *pron* **1** : nothing **2** : anything **3 de** ~ : don't mention it, you're welcome **4** ~ **que** : only, just — ~ *nm* : trifle

rigide [riʒid] *adj* **1** : rigid **2** RIGOUREUX : strict — **rigidité** [riʒidite] *nf* : rigidity

rigoler [rigɔle] *vi fam* **1** : have fun **2** PLAISANTER : laugh, joke — **rigolo, -lote** [rigɔlo, -lɔt] *adj fam* : funny, comical

rigueur [rigœr] *nf* **1** SÉVÉRITÉ : rigor, harshness **2** : precision **3 à la** ~ : if absolutely necessary **4 de** ~ : obligatory — **rigoureux, -reuse** [rigurø, -røz] *adj* **1** : rigorous **2** : harsh (of climate)

rimer [rime] *vi* : rhyme — **rime** [rim] *nf* : rhyme

rincer [rɛ̃se] {6} *vt* : rinse — **rinçage** [rɛ̃saʒ] *nm* : rinsing, rinse

riposte [ripɔst] *nf* **1** RÉPLIQUE : retort **2** CONTRE-ATTAQUE : counterattack — **riposter** [ripɔste] *vt* : retort — *vi* : counter, retaliate

rire [rir] {76} *vi* **1** : laugh **2** S'AMUSER : joke, have fun **3** ~ **de** : mock, make fun of — ~ *nm* : laugh, laughter

risque [risk] *nm* : risk — **risqué, -quée** [riske] *adj* : risky — **risquer** [riske] *vt* **1** : risk **2 ça risque d'arriver** : it may very well happen — **se risquer** *vr* : venture

rissoler [risɔle] *v* : brown (in cooking)

ristourne [risturn] *nf* REMISE : discount

rite [rit] *nm* : rite, ritual — **rituel, -tuelle** [rituɛl] *adj* : ritual — **rituel** *nm* : rite, ritual

rivage [rivaʒ] *nm* : shore

rival, -vale [rival] *adj & n, mpl* **-vaux** [rivo] : rival — **rivaliser** [rivalize] *vi* ~ **avec** : compete with, rival — **rivalité** [rivalite] *nf* : rivalry

rive [riv] *nf* : bank, shore

river [rive] *vt* : rivet

riverain, -raine [rivrɛ̃, -rɛn] *n* : resident (on a street)

rivet [rivɛ] *nm* : rivet

rivière [rivjɛr] *nf* : river

rixe [riks] *nf* BAGARRE : brawl, fight

riz [ri] *nm* : rice — **rizière** [rizjɛr] *nf* : (rice) paddy

robe [rɔb] *nf* **1** : dress **2** PELAGE : coat **3** ~ **de mariée** : wedding gown **4** ~ **de nuit** *Can* : nightgown

robinet [rɔbinɛ] *nm* : faucet

robot [rɔbo] *nm* : robot

robuste [rɔbyst] *adj* : robust

roc [rɔk] *nm* : rock — **roche** [rɔʃ] *nf* : rock — **rocher** [rɔʃe] *nm* : rock — **rocheux, -cheuse** [rɔʃø, -ʃøz] *adj* : rocky

roder [rɔde] *vt* **1** : break in (a vehicle) **2** *fam* : polish up (a performance, etc.)

rôder [rode] *vi* **1** : prowl **2** ERRER : wander about — **rôdeur, -deuse** [rodœr, -døz] *n* : prowler

rogne [rɔɲ] *nf fam* : anger

rognon [rɔɲɔ̃] *nm* : kidney (in cooking)

roi [rwa] *nm* : king

rôle [rol] *nm* : role, part

roman [rɔmɑ̃] *nm* : novel — **romancier, -cière** [rɔmɑ̃sje, -sjɛr] *n* : novelist

romantique [rɔmɑ̃tik] *adj* : romantic

rompre [rɔ̃pr] {77} *vt* : break (off) — *vi* : break up

ronce [rɔ̃s] *nf* : bramble

rond, ronde [rɔ̃, rɔ̃d] *adj* : round — **rond** *nm* **1** : circle, ring **2** : (round) slice **3** *Can* : burner (of a stove) — **ronde** *nf* : rounds *pl*, patrol

rondelet, -lette [rɔ̃dlɛ, -lɛt] *adj fam* : plump

rondelle [rɔ̃dɛl] *nf* **1** : washer **2** TRANCHE : slice **3** *Can* : (hockey) puck

rondeur [rɔ̃dœr] *nf* : roundness

rondin [rɔ̃dɛ̃] *nm* : log

rond-point [rɔ̃pwɛ̃] *nm, pl* **ronds-points** : traffic circle, rotary

ronfler [rɔ̃fle] *vi* : snore — **ronflement** [rɔ̃fləmɑ̃] *nm* : snore, snoring

ronger [rɔ̃ʒe] {17} *vt* **1** : gnaw, nibble **2** : eat away at — **se ronger** *vr* ~ **les ongles** : bite one's nails — **rongeur** [rɔ̃ʒœr] *nm* : rodent

ronronner [rɔ̃rɔne] *vi* **1** : purr **2** : hum (of an engine, etc.)

rosbif [rɔzbif] *nm* : roast beef

rose [roz] *nf* : rose — ~ *adj & nm* : rose, pink (color) — **rosé, -sée** [roze] *adj* : rosy, pinkish

roseau [rozo] *nm, pl* **-seaux** : reed

rosée [roze] *nf* : dew

rosier [rozje] *nm* : rosebush

rosser [rɔse] *vt* : beat, thrash

rossignol [rɔsiɲɔl] *nm* : nightingale

rotatif, -tive [rɔtatif, -tiv] *adj* : rotary — **rotation** [rɔtasjɔ̃] *nf* : rotation

roter [rote] *vi fam* : burp, belch

rôti [roti] *nm* : roast (meat)

rotin [rɔtɛ̃] *nm* : rattan

rôtir [rotir] *v* : roast — **rôtissoire** [rotiswar] *nf* : rotisserie

rotule [rɔtyl] *nf* : kneecap

rouage [rwaʒ] *nm* **1** : cogwheel **2 ~s** *nmpl* : workings

roucouler [rukule] *vi* : coo

roue [ru] *nf* **1** : wheel **2 grande ~** : Ferris wheel

rouer [rwe] *vt* **~ de coups** : thrash, beat

rouet [rwɛ] *nm* : spinning wheel

rouge [ruʒ] *adj* : red — **~** *n* **1** : red **2 ~ à lèvres** : lipstick — **rougeâtre** [ruʒatr] *adj* : reddish — **rougeaud, -geaude** [ruʒo, -ʒod] *adj* : ruddy

rouge–gorge [ruʒgɔrʒ] *nm, pl* **rouges–gorges** : robin

rougeole [ruʒɔl] *nf* : measles

rougeoyer [ruʒwaje] {58} *vi* : turn red, glow

rougeur [ruʒœr] *nf* **1** : redness **2 ~s** *nfpl* : red blotches (on skin)

rougir [ruʒir] *vt* : make red — *vi* **1** : redden, turn red **2** : blush (with shame, etc.)

rouille [ruj] *nf* : rust — **rouillé, -lée** [ruje] *adj* : rusty — **rouiller** [ruje] *v* : rust

rouler [rule] *vt* : roll (up) — *vi* **1** : roll **2** : go, run (of a car) **3** CONDUIRE : drive — **roulant, -lante** [rulɑ̃, -lɑ̃t] *adj* : on wheels — **rouleau** [rulo] *nm, pl* **-leaux 1** : roller **2** : roll (of paper) — **roulement** [rulmɑ̃] *nm* **1** : roll, rolling **2** : rumble (of thunder) **3** : turnover (in finance) **4 ~ à billes** : ball bearing **5 ~ de tambour** : drum roll

roulette [rulɛt] *nf* : roulette

roulotte [rulɔt] *nf Can* : trailer, camper

rouspéter [ruspete] {87} *vi fam* RONCHONNER : grumble — **rouspéteur, -teuse** [ruspetœr, -tøz] *n* : grouch

roussir [rusir] *vt* : scorch, singe

route [rut] *nf* **1** : road **2** : route, highway **3** CHEMIN : way, path **4 bonne ~ !** : have a good trip! **5 se mettre en ~** : set out, get going

routier, -tière [rutje, -tjɛr] *adj* : road — **routier** *nm* **1** : truck driver **2** : truck stop

routine [rutin] *nf* : routine — **routinier, -nière** [rutinje, -njɛr] *adj* : routine

roux, rousse [ru, rus] *adj* : russet, red — **~** *n* : redhead

royal, royale [rwajal] *adj, mpl* **royaux** [rwajo] : royal, regal — **royaume** [rwajom] *nm* : kingdom, realm — **royauté** [rwajote] *nf* : royalty

ruban [rybɑ̃] *nm* **1** : ribbon **2 ~ adhésif** : adhesive tape

rubéole [rybeɔl] *nf* : German measles

rubis [rybi] *nms & pl* : ruby

rubrique [rybrik] *nf* **1** : column (in a newspaper) **2** : heading

ruche [ryʃ] *nf* : hive, beehive

rude [ryd] *adj* **1** : rough (of a surface, etc.) **2** PÉNIBLE : hard, tough **3** : severe, harsh (of winter) — **rudement** [rydmɑ̃] *adv* **1** : roughly, harshly **2** *fam* DRÔLEMENT : awfully, terribly

rudimentaire [rydimɑ̃tɛr] *adj* : rudimentary — **rudiments** [rydimɑ̃] *nmpl* : rudiments

rue [ry] *nf* : street

ruée [rɥe] *nf* : rush

ruelle [rɥɛl] *nf* : alley(way)

ruer [rɥe] *vi* : buck (of a horse) — **se ruer** *vr* **1 ~ sur** : fling oneself at **2 ~ vers** : rush toward

rugir [ryʒir] *vt* : bellow out — *vi* : roar — **rugissement** [ryʒismɑ̃] *nm* **1** : roar **2** : howling

ruine [rɥin] *nf* **1** : ruin **2 tomber en ~** : fall into ruin — **ruiner** [rɥine] *vt* **1** : ruin **2** DÉTRUIRE : wreck

ruisseau [rɥiso] *nm, pl* **-seaux** : stream, creek

ruisseler [rɥisle] {8} *vi* : stream, flood

rumeur [rymœr] *nf* : rumor

ruminer [rymine] *vt* : ponder — *vi* : brood

rupture [ryptyr] *nf* **1** : break, breaking **2** : breakup (of a relationship) **3** : breach (of contract)

rural, -rale [ryral] *adj, mpl* **-raux** [ryro] : rural

ruse [ryz] *nf* **1** : trick **2** : cunning — **rusé, -sée** [ryze] *adj* MALIN : cunning

russe [rys] *adj* : Russian — **~** *nm* : Russian (language)

rustique [rystik] *adj* : rustic

rythme [ritm] *nm* **1** : rhythm, beat **2** : rate, pace — **rythmique** [ritmik] *adj* : rhythmic, rhythmical

S

s [ɛs] *nm* : s, 19th letter of the alphabet

sa → son

sabbat [saba] *nm* : Sabbath

sable [sabl] *nm* 1 : sand 2 ∼s mouvants : quicksand — **sablé** [sable] *nm* : shortbread (cookie) — **sabler** [sable] *vt* : sand — **sablonneux, -neuse** [sablɔnø, -nøz] *adj* : sandy

saborder [sabɔrde] *vt* : scuttle (a ship)

sabot [sabo] *nm* 1 : clog, wooden shoe 2 : hoof

saboter [sabɔte] *vt* 1 : sabotage 2 : botch up — **sabotage** [sabɔtaʒ] *nm* : sabotage — **saboteur, -teuse** [sabɔtœr, -tøz] *n* : saboteur

sabre [sabr] *nm* : saber

sac [sak] *nm* 1 : sack, bag 2 ∼ à dos : backpack, knapsack 3 ∼ à main : handbag, purse

saccade [sakad] *nf* : jerk, jolt — **saccadé, -dée** [sakade] *adj* : jerky

saccager [sakaʒe] {17} *vt* 1 : sack 2 DÉVASTER : devastate, wreck

sacerdoce [sasɛrdɔs] *nm* 1 : priesthood 2 : vocation

sachet [saʃɛ] *nm* 1 : packet, small bag 2 : sachet

sacoche [sakɔʃ] *nf* : bag, satchel

sacrer [sakre] *vt* 1 : crown 2 : consecrate — **sacre** [sakr] *nm* 1 : coronation 2 : consecration — **sacré, -crée** [sakre] *adj* 1 : sacred, holy 2 *fam* : damned, heck of a — **sacrement** [sakrəmɑ̃] *nm* : sacrament

sacrifier [sakrifje] {96} *vt* : sacrifice — *vi* ∼ à : conform to — **se sacrifier** *vr* : sacrifice oneself — **sacrifice** [sakrifis] *nm* : sacrifice

sacrilège [sakrilɛʒ] *nm* : sacrilege — ∼ *adj* : sacrilegious

sadique [sadik] *adj* : sadistic — **sadisme** [sadism] *nm* : sadism

safari [safari] *nm* : safari

sagace [sagas] *adj* : shrewd

sage [saʒ] *adj* 1 : wise 2 DOCILE : well-behaved — ∼ *n* : wise person, sage — **sage-femme** [saʒfam] *nf*, *pl* **sages-femmes** : midwife — **sagesse** [saʒɛs] *nf* : wisdom

saigner [seɲe] *v* : bleed — **saignant, -gnante** [seɲɑ̃, -ɲɑ̃t] *adj* : rare, undercooked — **saignement** [seɲmɑ̃] *nm* : bleeding

saillir [sajir] {78} *vi* : project — **saillant, -lante** [sajɑ̃, -jɑ̃t] *adj* 1 : projecting 2 : salient — **saillie** [saji] *nf* 1 : projection 2 faire ∼ : project

sain, saine [sɛ̃, sɛn] *adj* 1 : healthy, sound 2 : wholesome

saindoux [sɛ̃du] *nm* : lard

saint, sainte [sɛ̃, sɛ̃t] *adj* : holy — ∼ *n* : saint

saisir [sezir] *vt* 1 : seize, grab 2 COMPRENDRE : grasp 3 IMPRESSIONNER : strike, impress 4 : enter (data) — **se saisir** *vr* ∼ de : seize — **saisie** [sezi] *nf* : seizure (of property) — **saisissant, -sante** [sezisɑ̃, -sɑ̃t] *adj* : striking

saison [sezɔ̃] *nf* : season — **saisonnier, -nière** [sezɔnje, -njɛr] *adj* : seasonal

salade [salad] *nf* : salad — **saladier** [saladje] *nm* : salad bowl

salaire [salɛr] *nm* : salary, wages — **salarié, -riée** [salarje] *n* : salaried employee

salaud [salo] *nm usu vulgar* : bastard

sale [sal] *adj* : dirty — **saleté** [salte] *nf* 1 : dirt 2 : dirtiness 3 *fam* : dirty trick

saler [sale] *vt* : salt — **salé, -lée** [sale] *adj* 1 : salty 2 : salted 3 *fam* : steep — **salière** [saljɛr] *nf* : saltshaker

salir [salir] *vt* : soil — **se salir** *vr* : get dirty

salive [saliv] *nf* : saliva

salle [sal] *nf* 1 : room 2 : auditorium, hall 3 ∼ à manger : dining room 4 ∼ de bains : bathroom

salon [salɔ̃] *nm* 1 : living room 2 : (beauty) salon 3 EXPOSITION : exhibition, show

salopette [salɔpɛt] *nf* : overalls *pl*

salubre [salybr] *adj* : healthy

saluer [salɥe] *vt* 1 : greet 2 : say goodbye to 3 : salute — **salut** [saly] *nm* 1 : greeting 2 : salute 3 : safety 4 : salvation 5 ∼! : hello!, good-bye! — **salutation** [salytasjɔ̃] *nf* : greeting

samedi [samdi] *nm* : Saturday

sanction [sɑ̃ksjɔ̃] *nf* : sanction — **sanctionner** [sɑ̃ksjɔne] *vt* 1 : sanction 2 : punish

sanctuaire [sɑ̃ktɥɛr] *nm* : sanctuary

sandale [sɑ̃dal] *nf* : sandal

sandwich [sɑ̃dwitʃ] *nm*, *pl* **-wiches** *or* **-wichs** [-witʃ] : sandwich

sang [sɑ̃] *nm* : blood — **sang-froid** [sɑ̃frwa] *nms & pl* 1 : composure, calm 2 de ∼ : in cold blood — **sanglant, -glante** [sɑ̃glɑ̃, -glɑ̃t] *adj* 1 : bloody 2 : cruel

sangle [sɑ̃gl] *nf* : strap

sanglot [sɑ̃glo] *nm* : sob — **sangloter** [sɑ̃glɔte] *vi* : sob

sangsue [sɑ̃sy] *nf* : leech

sanguin, -guine [sɑ̃gɛ̃, -gin] *adj* 1 : blood 2 : sanguine

sanitaire [sanitɛr] *adj* **1** : sanitary **2** : health — **~s** *nmpl* : bathroom

sans [sɑ̃] *adv & prep* **1** : without **2 ~ que** : without

santé [sɑ̃te] *nf* **1** : health **2 à votre ~ !** : to your health!, cheers!

saper [sape] *vt* MINER : undermine

sapeur–pompier [sapœrpɔ̃pje] *nm, pl* **sapeurs–pompiers** *France* : firefighter

saphir [safir] *nm* : sapphire

sapin [sapɛ̃] *nm* : fir

sarcastique [sarkastik] *adj* : sarcastic — **sarcasme** [sarkasm] *nm* : sarcasm

sarcler [sarkle] *vt* : weed

sardine [sardin] *nf* : sardine

satellite [satelit] *nm* : satellite

satin [satɛ̃] *nm* : satin

satire [satir] *nf* : satire — **satirique** [satirik] *adj* : satirical

satisfaire [satisfɛr] {42} *vt* : satisfy — *vi* **~ à** : satisfy — **se satisfaire** *vr* **~ de** : be content with — **satisfaction** [satisfaksjɔ̃] *nf* : satisfaction — **satisfaisant, -sante** [satisfəzɑ̃, -zɑ̃t] *adj* **1** : satisfactory **2** : satisfying — **satisfait, -faite** [satisfɛ, -fɛt] *adj* : satisfied

saturer [satyre] *vt* : saturate

Saturne [satyrn] *nf* : Saturn

sauce [sos] *nf* : sauce

saucisse [sosis] *nf* : sausage — **saucisson** [sosisɔ̃] *nm* : sausage, cold cut

sauf, sauve [sof, sov] *adj* : safe — **sauf** *prep* **1** : except (for), apart from **2 ~ si** : unless

sauge [soʒ] *nf* : sage (herb)

saugrenu, -nue [sogrəny] *adj* : preposterous

saule [sol] *nm* : willow

saumon [somɔ̃] *nm* : salmon

sauna [sona] *nm* : sauna

saupoudrer [sopudre] *vt* : sprinkle

saut [so] *nm* **1** : jump, leap **2 faire un ~ chez qqn** : drop in on s.o. — **sauter** [sote] *vt* **1** : jump over **2** OMETTRE : skip — *vi* **1** BONDIR : jump, leap **2** EXPLOSER : blow up — **sauterelle** [sotrɛl] *nf* : grasshopper — **sauteur, -teuse** [sotœr, -tøz] *n* : jumper — **sautiller** [sotije] *vi* : hop

sauvage [sovaʒ] *adj* **1** CRUEL : savage **2** : wild **3** FAROUCHE : shy — **~** *nmf* : savage — **sauvagerie** [sovaʒri] *nf* **1** : savagery **2** : unsociability

sauvegarde [sovgard] *nf* **1** : safeguard **2** : backup (of a computer file) — **sauvegarder** [sovgarde] *vt* **1** : safeguard **2** : save (a computer file)

sauver [sove] *vt* : save, rescue — **se sauver** *vr* **1** : escape **2** *fam* : leave, rush off — **sauve–qui–peut** [sovkipø] *nms & pl* : stampede, panic — **sauvetage** [sovtaʒ] *nm* : rescue — **sauveteur** [sovtœr] *nm* : rescuer, lifesaver — **sauvette** [sovɛt] **à la ~**

adv phr : hastily — **sauveur** [sovœr] *nm* : savior

savant, -vante [savɑ̃, -vɑ̃t] *adj* : learned, scholarly — **~** *n* : scholar — **savant** *nm* : scientist

saveur [savœr] *nf* : flavor, savor

savoir [savwar] {79} *vt* **1** : know **2** : be able to, know how to — **~** *nm* **1** : learning, knowledge **2 à ~** : namely — **savoir–faire** [savwarfɛr] *nms & pl* : know-how, expertise

savon [savɔ̃] *nm* : soap — **savonner** [savone] *vt* : soap (up), lather — **savonnette** [savonɛt] *nf* : bar of soap — **savonneux, -neuse** [savonø, -nøz] *adj* : soapy

savourer [savure] *vt* : savor — **savoureux, -reuse** [savurø, -røz] *adj* : savory, tasty

saxophone [saksofon] *nm* : saxophone

scandale [skɑ̃dal] *nf* **1** : scandal **2** SCÈNE : scene, row — **scandaleux, -leuse** [skɑ̃dalø, -løz] *adj* : scandalous — **scandaliser** [skɑ̃dalize] *vt* : scandalize

scandinave [skɑ̃dinav] *adj* : Scandinavian

scarabée [skarabe] *nm* : beetle

scarlatine [skarlatin] *nf* : scarlet fever

sceau [so] *nm* **1** : seal **2** : hallmark, stamp

scélérat, -rate [selera, -rat] *n* : villain

sceller [sele] *vt* : seal — **scellé** [sele] *nm* : seal

scène [sɛn] *nf* **1** : scene **2** : stage (in theater) — **scénario** [senarjo] *nm* : scenario

sceptique [sɛptik] *adj* : skeptical — **~** *nmf* : skeptic

schéma [ʃema] *nm* : diagram — **schématique** [ʃematik] *adj* : schematic

schisme [ʃism] *nm* : schism

scie [si] *nf* : saw

sciemment [sjamɑ̃] *adv* : knowingly

science [sjɑ̃s] *nf* **1** : science **2** SAVOIR : learning, knowledge — **scientifique** [sjɑ̃tifik] *adj* : scientific — **~** *nmf* : scientist

scier [sje] {96} *vt* : saw — **scierie** [siri] *nf* : sawmill

scinder [sɛ̃de] *vt* : split, divide — **se scinder** *vr* : be divided, split up

scintiller [sɛ̃tije] *vi* : sparkle — **scintillement** [sɛ̃tijmɑ̃] *nm* : sparkling, twinkling

scission [sisjɔ̃] *nf* : split

scolaire [skɔlɛr] *adj* : school — **scolarité** [skɔlarite] *nf* : schooling

score [skɔr] *nm* : score

scotch [skɔtʃ] *nm* : Scotch whiskey

scrupule [skrypyl] *nm* : scruple — **scrupuleux, -leuse** [skrypylø, -løz] *adj* : scrupulous

scruter [skryte] *vt* : scrutinize — **scrutin** [skrytɛ̃] *nm* **1** : ballot **2** : polls *pl*

sculpter [skylte] *vt* : sculpt, sculpture — **sculpteur** [skyltœr] *nm* : sculptor — **sculpture** [skyltyr] *nf* : sculpture

se [sə] (**s'** *before a vowel or mute h*) *pron* **1**

: oneself, himself, herself, themselves, itself 2 : each other, one another

séance [seɑ̃s] *nf* 1 : session, meeting 2 : performance

seau [so] *nm, pl* **seaux** : bucket, pail

sec, sèche [sɛk, sɛʃ] *adj* 1 : dry 2 : dried (of fruit) 3 DUR : harsh, sharp — **sec** [sɛk] *adv* BRUSQUEMENT : abruptly, hard — ~ *nm* 1 : dryness 2 à ~ : dried up 3 à ~ *fam* : broke — **sèche–cheveux** [sɛʃʃəvø] *nms & pl* : hairdryer — **sécher** [seʃe] {87} *vt* 1 : dry 2 *France fam* : skip (a class, etc.) — *vi* : dry (up), dry out — **sécheresse** [seʃrɛs] *nf* 1 : drought 2 : dryness — **séchoir** [seʃwar] *nm* : dryer

second, -conde [səɡɔ̃, -ɡɔ̃d] *adj & nmf* : second — **second** *nm* 1 : assistant, helper 2 : third floor — **secondaire** [səɡɔ̃dɛr] *adj* : secondary — **seconde** [səɡɔ̃d] *nf* : second — **seconder** [səɡɔ̃de] *vt* : assist

secouer [səkwe] *vt* 1 : shake (one's head, etc.) 2 : shake off

secourir [səkurir] {23} *vt* 1 : help, aid 2 : rescue — **secouriste** [səkurist] *nmf* : first aid worker — **secours** [səkur] *nms & pl* 1 : help, aid 2 au ~! : help! 3 de ~ : (for) emergency 4 **premiers** ~ : first aid 5 **secours** *nmpl* : rescuers

secousse [səkus] *nf* 1 SACCADE : jolt, jerk 2 CHOC : shock 3 : tremor

secret, -crète [səkrɛ, -krɛt] *adj* : secret — **secret** *nm* 1 : secret 2 : secrecy

secrétaire [səkretɛr] *nmf* : secretary — **secrétariat** [səkretarjat] *nm* : secretary's office

sécréter [sekrete] {87} *vt* : secrete — **sécrétion** [-resjɔ̃] *nf* : secretion

secte [sɛkt] *nm* : sect

secteur [sɛktœr] *nm* : sector, area

section [sɛksjɔ̃] *nf* : section — **sectionner** [sɛksjone] *vt* 1 DIVISER : divide 2 : sever

séculaire [sekylɛr] *adj* : age-old

sécurité [sekyrite] *nf* 1 : security 2 : safety — **sécuriser** [sekyrize] *vt* : reassure

sédatif, -tive [sedatif, -tiv] *adj* : sedative — **sédatif** *nm* : sedative

sédentaire [sedɑ̃tɛr] *adj* : sedentary

sédiment [sedimɑ̃] *nm* : sediment

séduire [seduir] {49} *vt* 1 : seduce 2 : charm 3 : appeal to — **séducteur, -trice** [sedyktœr, -tris] *adj* : seductive — ~ *n* : seducer — **séduction** [sedyksjɔ̃] *nf* 1 : seduction 2 : charm, appeal — **séduisant, -sante** [seduizɑ̃, -zɑ̃t] *adj* : seductive, attractive

segment [sɛɡmɑ̃] *nm* : segment

ségrégation [segregasjɔ̃] *nf* : segregation

seigle [sɛɡl] *nm* : rye

seigneur [sɛɲœr] *nm* 1 : lord 2 **le Seigneur** : the Lord

sein [sɛ̃] *nm* 1 : breast, bosom 2 au ~ de : within

séisme [seism] *nm* : earthquake

seize [sɛz] *adj* 1 : sixteen 2 : sixteenth (in dates) — ~ *nms & pl* : sixteen — **seizième** [sɛzjɛm] *adj & nmf & nm* : sixteenth

séjour [seʒur] *nm* : stay — **séjourner** [seʒurne] *vi* : stay (at a hotel, etc.)

sel [sɛl] *nm* : salt

sélection [selɛksjɔ̃] *nf* : selection — **sélectionner** [selɛksjone] *vt* : select, choose

selle [sɛl] *nf* : saddle

sellette [sɛlɛt] *nf* **être sur la** ~ : be in the hot seat

selon [səlɔ̃] *prep* 1 : according to 2 ~ **que** : depending on whether

semaine [səmɛn] *nf* : week

sémantique [semɑ̃tik] *adj* : semantic — ~ *nf* : semantics

sembler [sɑ̃ble] *vi* : seem — *v impers* **il semble que** : it seems that — **semblable** [sɑ̃blabl] *adj* 1 : similar, like 2 TEL : such — ~ *nmf* : fellow creature — **semblant** [sɑ̃blɑ̃] *nm* 1 : semblance, appearance 2 **faire** ~ : pretend

semelle [səmɛl] *nf* : sole

semer [səme] {52} *vt* 1 : sow, seed 2 RÉPANDRE : scatter — **semence** [səmɑ̃s] *nf* : seed

semestre [səmɛstr] *nm* : semester — **semestriel, -trielle** [səmɛstrijɛl] *adj* : semiannual

séminaire [seminɛr] *nm* 1 : seminary 2 : seminar

semi–remorque [səmirəmɔrk] *nm, pl* **semi–remorques** : semitrailer

semis [səmi] *nm* 1 : seedling 2 : seedbed

semonce [səmɔ̃s] *nf* RÉPRIMANDE : reprimand

semoule [səmul] *nf* : semolina

sénat [sena] *nm* : senate — **sénateur** [senatœr] *nm* : senator

sénile [senil] *adj* : senile — **sénilité** [senilite] *nf* : senility

sens [sɑ̃s] *nms & pl* 1 : sense 2 SIGNIFICATION : meaning 3 DIRECTION : direction, way 4 à mon ~ : in my opinion 5 ~ **dessus dessous** : upside down

sensation [sɑ̃sasjɔ̃] *nf* : sensation — **sensationnel, -nelle** [sɑ̃sasjonɛl] *adj* : sensational

sensé, -sée [sɑ̃se] *adj* : sensible

sensibiliser [sɑ̃sibilize] *vt* ~ à : make sensitive to — **sensibilité** [sɑ̃sibilite] *nf* : sensitivity — **sensible** [sɑ̃sibl] *adj* 1 : sensitive 2 APPRÉCIABLE : noticeable — **sensiblement** [sɑ̃sibləmɑ̃] *adv* 1 : noticeably 2 : approximately

sensoriel, -rielle [sɑ̃sɔrjɛl] *adj* : sensory

sensuel, -suelle [sɑ̃sɥɛl] *adj* : sensual, sensuous — **sensualité** [sɑ̃sɥalite] *nf* : sensuality

sentence [sãtãs] *nf* JUGEMENT : sentence

senteur [sãtœr] *nf* : scent

sentier [sãtje] *nm* : path

sentiment [sãtimã] *nm* **1** : sentiment, feeling **2** recevez l'expression de mes ~s respectueux : yours truly — **sentimental, -tale** [sãtimãtal] *adj, mpl* **-taux** [-to] : sentimental — **sentimentalité** [-talite] *nf* : sentimentality

sentinelle [sãtinɛl] *nf* : sentinel

sentir [sãtir] {82} *vt* **1** : smell, taste **2** : feel **3** : appreciate **4** PRESSENTIR : sense — *vi* : smell — **se sentir** *vr* : feel (tired, sick, etc.)

seoir [swar] {80} *vi* ~ **à** : suit

séparer [separe] *vt* **1** DÉTACHER : separate **2** : divide — **se séparer** *vr* **1** : separate **2** ~ **de** : part with, be without — **séparation** [separasjɔ̃] *nf* : separation — **séparé, -rée** [separe] *adj* **1** : separate **2** : separated — **séparément** [separemã] *adv* : separately

sept [sɛt] *adj* **1** : seven **2** : seventh (in dates) — ~ *nms & pl* : seven

septante [sɛptãt] *adj* Bel, Switz **1** : seventy **2** : seventieth — ~ *nms & pl* Bel, Switz : seventy

septembre [sɛptãbr] *nm* : September

septième [sɛtjɛm] *adj & nmf & nm* : seventh

sépulture [sepyltyr] *nf* TOMBE : grave

séquelle [sekɛl] *nf* **1** : consequence **2** ~s *nfpl* : aftereffects

séquence [sekãs] *nf* : sequence

séquestrer [sekɛstre] *nm* : confine, sequester

serein, -reine [sərɛ̃, -rɛn] *adj* CALME : serene, calm — **sérénité** [serenite] *nf* : serenity

sergent [sɛrʒã] *nm* : sergeant

série [seri] *nf* **1** : series **2** : set **3** de ~ : mass-produced, standard **4** fabrication en ~ : mass production

sérieux, -rieuse [serjø, -rjøz] *adj* : serious — **sérieux** *nm* **1** : seriousness **2** prendre au ~ : take seriously — **sérieusement** [serjøzmã] *adv* : seriously

serin [sərɛ̃] *nm* : canary

seringue [sərɛ̃g] *nf* : syringe

serment [sɛrmã] *nm* **1** : oath **2** : vow, promise

sermon [sɛrmɔ̃] *nm* : sermon

serpent [sɛrpã] *nm* **1** : snake **2** ~ à sonnettes : rattlesnake — **serpenter** [sɛrpãte] *vi* : meander — **serpentin** [sɛrpãtɛ̃] *nm* : streamer

serre [sɛr] *nf* **1** : greenhouse, hothouse **2** ~s *nfpl* : claws

serré, -rée [sere] *adj* **1** : tight **2** : crowded, cramped, dense

serrer [sere] *vt* **1** : squeeze, grip **2** : clench (one's fists, etc.) **3** : tighten (a knot, etc.) **4** : stay close to **5** : push closer together — **se**

serrer *vr* **1** : huddle up **2** : tighten (up) **3** ~ **la main** : shake hands

serrure [sɛryr] *nf* : lock — **serrurier** [sɛryrje] *nm* : locksmith

sérum [serɔm] *nm* : serum

serveur, -veuse [sɛrvœr, -vøz] *n* : waiter *m*, waitress *f* — **serveur** *nm* : (computer) server

serviable [sɛrvjabl] *adj* : helpful, obliging

service [sɛrvis] *nm* **1** : service **2** FAVEUR : favor **3** : serving, course **4** : department **5** : (coffee) set **6** : serve (in sports) **7** hors ~ : out of order

serviette [sɛrvjɛt] *nf* **1** : napkin **2** : towel **3** : briefcase **4** ~ hygiénique : sanitary napkin

servir [sɛrvir] {81} *vt* **1** : serve **2** : wait on, attend to — *vi* **1** : be useful, serve **2** ~ **de** : serve as — **se servir** *vr* **1** : serve oneself, help oneself **2** ~ **de** : make use of

serviteur [sɛrvitœr] *nm* : servant

ses → **son**

session [sesjɔ̃] *nf* : session

seuil [sœj] *nm* : threshold

seul, seule [sœl] *adj* **1** : alone **2** : lonely **3** UNIQUE : only, sole — ~ *pron* : only one, single one — **seulement** [sœlmã] *adv* **1** : only **2** MÊME : even — ~ *conj* : but, only

sève [sɛv] *nf* : sap

sévère [sever] *adj* : severe — **sévérité** [severite] *nf* : severity

sévir [sevir] *vi* **1** : rage **2** ~ **contre** : punish

sevrer [səvre] *vt* : wean

sexe [sɛks] *nm* **1** : sex **2** : sex organs, genitals — **sexisme** [sɛksism] *nm* : sexism — **sexiste** [sɛksist] *adj & nmf* : sexist — **sexualité** [sɛksɥalite] *nf* : sexuality — **sexuel, sexuelle** [sɛksɥɛl] *adj* : sexual

seyant, seyante [sejã, -jãt] *adj* : becoming, flattering

shampooing [ʃãpwɛ̃] *nm* : shampoo

shérif [ʃerif] *nm* : sheriff

short [ʃort] *nm* : shorts *pl*

si[1] [si] *adv* **1** TELLEMENT : so, such, as **2** : yes **3** ~ **bien que** : with the result that, so

si[2] *conj* : if, whether

sida [sida] *nm* : AIDS

sidérer [sidere] {87} *vt fam* : stagger, amaze

sidérurgie [sideryrʒi] *nf* : steel industry

siècle [sjɛkl] *nm* : century

siège [sjɛʒ] *nm* **1** : seat **2** : siege **3** or ~ **social** : headquarters — **siéger** [sjeʒe] {64} *vi* **1** : sit (in an assembly) **2** : have its headquarters

sien, sienne [sjɛ̃, sjɛn] *adj* : his, hers, its, one's — ~ *pron* le sien, la sienne, les siens, les siennes : his, hers, its, one's, theirs

sieste [sjɛst] *nf* : siesta, nap

siffler [sifle] *vt* **1** : whistle **2** : whistle for, whistle at **3** : boo — *vi* **1** : whistle **2** : hiss **3** : wheeze — **sifflement** [sifləmɑ̃] *nm* : whistling — **sifflet** [sifle] *nm* **1** : whistle **2** ∼s *nmpl* : boos — **siffloter** [siflɔte] *v* : whistle

sigle [sigl] *nm* : acronym

signaler [siɲale] *vt* **1** : signal **2** : point out — **se signaler** *vr* : distinguish oneself — **signal** [siɲal] *nm, pl* **-gnaux** [-ɲo] : signal — **signalement** [siɲalmɑ̃] *nm* : description — **signalisation** [siɲalizasjɔ̃] *nf* : signals *pl*, signs *pl*

signature [siɲatyr] *nf* **1** : signature **2** : signing

signe [siɲ] *nm* **1** : sign **2** : (punctuation) mark — **signer** [siɲe] *vt* : sign — **se signer** *vr* : cross oneself

signifier [siɲifje] {96} *vt* : signify, mean — **significatif, -tive** [siɲifikatif, -tiv] *adj* : significant — **signification** [siɲifikasjɔ̃] *nf* : significance, meaning

silence [silɑ̃s] *nm* **1** : silence **2** : rest (in music) — **silencieux, -cieuse** [silɑ̃sjø, -sjøz] *adj* : silent, quiet — **silencieux** *nm* : muffler

silex [sileks] *nm* : flint

silhouette [silwet] *nf* : silhouette, outline

silicium [silisjɔm] *nm* : silicon

sillage [sijaʒ] *nm* : wake (of a ship)

sillon [sijɔ̃] *nm* **1** : furrow **2** : groove (of a disc, etc.) — **sillonner** [sijɔne] *vt* **1** CREUSER : furrow **2** : crisscross

silo [silo] *nm* : silo

simagrée [simagre] *nf* **faire des** ∼s : put on airs

similaire [similer] *adj* : similar — **similitude** [similityd] *nf* : similarity

simple [sɛ̃pl] *adj* **1** : simple **2** : mere **3 aller** ∼ : one-way ticket — ∼ *nm* : singles (in tennis) — **simplement** [sɛ̃pləmɑ̃] *adv* : simply — **simplicité** [sɛ̃plisite] *nf* : simplicity — **simplifier** [sɛ̃plifje] {96} *vt* : simplify

simulacre [simylakr] *nm* : sham, pretense

simuler [simyle] *vt* : simulate — **simulation** [simylasjɔ̃] *nf* : simulation

simultané, -née [simyltane] *adj* : simultaneous

sincère [sɛ̃ser] *adj* : sincere — **sincèrement** [-sermɑ̃] *adv* : sincerely — **sincérité** [sɛ̃serite] *nf* : sincerity

singe [sɛ̃ʒ] *nm* : monkey — **singer** [sɛ̃ʒe] {17} *vt* **1** IMITER : mimic **2** FEINDRE : feign — **singeries** [sɛ̃ʒri] *nfpl* : antics

singulariser [sɛ̃gylarize] *vt* : draw attention to — **se singulariser** *vr* : call attention to oneself

singularité [sɛ̃gylarite] *nf* : peculiarity

singulier, -lière [sɛ̃gylje, -ljer] *adj* : singular — **singulier** *nm* : singular (in grammar) —

singulièrement [sɛ̃gyljermɑ̃] *nm* **1** : strangely **2** NOTAMMENT : particularly

sinistre [sinistr] *adj* : sinister — ∼ *nm* DÉSASTRE : disaster — **sinistré, -trée** [sinistre] *adj* : damaged, stricken — ∼ *n* : disaster victim

sinon [sinɔ̃] *conj* **1** : or else **2** : if not **3** ∼ **que** : except that

sinueux, -nueuse [sinɥø, -nɥøz] *adj* : winding, meandering

siphon [sifɔ̃] *nm* : siphon

sirène [siren] *nf* **1** : mermaid **2** : siren, alarm

sirop [siro] *nm* : syrup

siroter [sirɔte] *vt fam* : sip

sis, sise [si, siz] *adj* : located (in law)

site [sit] *nm* **1** : site **2** : setting

sitôt [sito] *adv* **1** : as soon as **2** ∼ **après** : immediately after

situer [sitɥe] *vt* : situate, locate — **situation** [sitɥasjɔ̃] *nf* **1** : situation **2** ∼ **de famille** : marital status

six [sis, *before consonant* si, *before vowel* siz] *adj* **1** : six **2** : sixth (in dates) — ∼ *nms & pl* : six — **sixième** [sizjɛm] *adj & nmf & nm* : sixth

ski [ski] *nm* **1** : ski **2** : skiing **3** ∼ **nautique** : waterskiing — **skier** [skje] {96} *vi* : ski — **skieur, skieuse** [skjœr, skjøz] *n* : skier

slip [slip] *nm* **1** : briefs *pl* **2** : panties *pl*

smoking [smɔkiŋ] *nm* : tuxedo

snob [snɔb] *adj* : snobbish — ∼ *nmf* : snob — **snober** [snɔbe] *vt* : snub — **snobisme** [snɔbism] *nm* : snobbery

sobre [sɔbr] *adj* : sober — **sobriété** [sɔbrijete] *nf* : sobriety

soccer [sɔker] *nm Can* : soccer

sociable [sɔsjabl] *adj* : sociable

social, -ciale [sɔsjal] *adj, mpl* **-ciaux** [-sjo] : social — **socialisme** [sɔsjalism] *nm* : socialism — **socialiste** [-sjalist] *adj & nmf* : socialist — **société** [sɔsjete] *nf* **1** : society **2** COMPAGNIE : company, firm

sociologie [sɔsjɔlɔʒi] *nf* : sociology — **sociologique** [sɔsjɔlɔʒik] *adj* : sociological — **sociologue** [sɔsjɔlɔg] *nmf* : sociologist

socle [sɔkl] *nm* : base, pedestal

soda [sɔda] *nm* : soda, soft drink

sodium [sɔdjɔm] *nm* : sodium

sœur [sœr] *nf* **1** : sister **2** : nun

sofa [sɔfa] *nm* : sofa

soi [swa] *pron* : oneself, himself, herself, itself — **soi–disant** [swadizɑ̃] *adv* : supposedly — ∼ *adj* : so-called

soie [swa] *nf* **1** : silk **2** : bristle

soif [swaf] *nf* **1** : thirst **2 avoir** ∼ : be thirsty

soigner [swaɲe] *vt* **1** : treat, nurse, look after **2** : do with care — **se soigner** *vr* : take care of oneself — **soigné, -gnée** [swaɲe] *adj* **1** : carefully done **2** : neat — **soigneux, -gneuse** [swaɲø, -ɲøz] *adj* **1** : careful **2** : neat, tidy

soi—même [swamɛm] *pron* : oneself

soin [swɛ̃] *nm* **1** : care **2** ⁓**s** *nmpl* : care **3 premiers** ⁓**s** : first aid **4 prendre** ⁓ **de** : take care of

soir [swar] *nm* : evening, night — **soirée** [sware] *nf* **1** : evening **2** FÊTE : party

soit [swa] *adv* : so be it, very well — ⁓ *conj* **1** : that is, in other words **2 soit ... soit ...** : either ... or ...

soixante [swasɑ̃t] *adj & nms & pl* : sixty — **soixante—dix** [swasɑ̃tdis] *adj & nms & pl* : seventy — **soixante—dixième** [swasɑ̃t-dizjɛm] *adj & nmf & nm* : seventieth — **soixantième** [swasɑ̃tjɛm] *adj & nmf & nm* : sixtieth

soja [sɔʒa] *nm* : soybean

sol [sɔl] *nm* **1** : ground, floor **2** PLANCHER : flooring **3** TERRE : soil

solaire [sɔlɛr] *adj* **1** : solar **2** : sun

soldat [sɔlda] *nm* : soldier

solde[1] [sɔld] *nf* : pay

solde[2] *nm* **1** : balance (in finance) **2** *or* ⁓**s** *nmpl* : sale — **solder** [sɔlde] *vt* **1** : settle (an account, etc.) **2** : sell off, put on sale — **se solder** *vr* ⁓ **par** : end in

sole [sɔl] *nf* : sole (fish)

soleil [sɔlɛj] *nm* **1** : sun **2** : sunshine, sunlight

solennel, -nelle [sɔlanɛl] *adj* **1** : solemn **2** : formal — **solennité** [sɔlanite] *nf* : solemnity

solidaire [sɔlidɛr] *adj* **1** : united **2** : interdependent — **solidarité** [sɔlidarite] *nf* : solidarity

solide [sɔlid] *adj* : solid — ⁓ *nm* : solid — **solidement** [sɔlidmɑ̃] *adv* : solidly — **solidifier** [sɔlidifje] {96} *v* **se solidifier** *vr* : solidify — **solidité** [sɔlidite] *nf* : solidity

solitaire [sɔlitɛr] *adj* : solitary — ⁓ *nmf* : loner, recluse — ⁓ *nm* : solitaire — **solitude** [sɔlityd] *nf* **1** : solitude **2** : loneliness

solliciter [sɔlisite] *vt* **1** : solicit, seek **2** : appeal to, approach — **sollicitude** [sɔlisityd] *nf* : solicitude, concern

solo [sɔlo] *nm, pl* **solos** *or* **soli** : solo

soluble [sɔlybl] *adj* : soluble — **solution** [sɔlysjɔ̃] *nf* : solution

solvable [sɔlvabl] *adj* : solvent

sombre [sɔ̃br] *adj* **1** OBSCUR : dark **2** TRISTE : gloomy

sombrer [sɔ̃bre] *vi* COULER : sink

sommaire [sɔmɛr] *adj* **1** : brief, concise **2** : summary — ⁓ *nm* : summary

somme[1] [sɔm] *nf* **1** : sum **2 en** ⁓ : in short, all in all

somme[2] *nm* : short nap, catnap

sommeil [sɔmɛj] *nm* : sleep — **sommeiller** [sɔmeje] *vi* **1** : doze **2** : lie dormant

sommer [sɔme] *vt* : summon

sommet [sɔmɛ] *nm* : summit, top

sommier [sɔmje] *nm* : base (of a bed), bedsprings *pl*

somnambule [sɔmnɑ̃byl] *nmf* : sleepwalker

somnifère [sɔmnifɛr] *nm* : sleeping pill

somnolence [sɔmnɔlɑ̃s] *nf* : drowsiness — **somnolent, -lente** [sɔmnɔlɑ̃, -lɑ̃t] *adj* : drowsy — **somnoler** [sɔmnɔle] *vi* : doze

somptueux, -tueuse [sɔ̃ptɥø, -tɥøz] *adj* : sumptuous

son[1]**, sa** [sɔ̃, sa] *adj, pl* **ses** [se] : his, her, its, one's

son[2] *nm* **1** : sound **2** : volume **3** : (wheat) bran

sonde [sɔ̃d] *nf* **1** : probe **2** : sounding line — **sondage** [sɔ̃daʒ] *nm* : poll, survey — **sonder** [sɔ̃de] *vt* **1** : survey, poll **2** : sound, probe

songe [sɔ̃ʒ] *nm* : dream — **songer** [sɔ̃ʒe] {17} *vt* : consider, imagine — *vi* **1** : dream **2** ⁓ **à** : think about — **songeur, -geuse** [sɔ̃ʒœr, -ʒøz] *adj* : pensive

sonner [sɔne] *v* **1** : ring **2** : strike, sound — **sonnant, -nante** [sɔnɑ̃, -nɑ̃t] *adj* **à cinq heures sonnantes** : at five o'clock sharp — **sonné, -née** [sɔne] *adj* **1** *fam* : groggy **2** *fam* : crazy, nuts **3 il est minuit sonné** : it's past midnight — **sonnerie** [sɔnri] *nf* **1** : ringing, ring **2** : alarm (bell)

sonnet [sɔnɛ] *nm* : sonnet

sonnette [sɔnɛt] *nf* : bell, doorbell

sonore [sɔnɔr] *adj* **1** : resonant **2** : sound — **sonorisation** [sɔnɔrizasjɔ̃] *nf* : sound system — **sonorité** [sɔnɔrite] *nf* **1** : tone **2** : resonance, acoustics

sophistiqué, -quée [sɔfistike] *adj* : sophisticated

soporifique [sɔpɔrifik] *adj* : soporific

soprano [sɔprano] *nmf* : soprano

sorbet [sɔrbɛ] *nm* : sorbet

sorcier, -cière [sɔrsje, -sjɛr] *n* : sorcerer, witch — **sorcellerie** [sɔrsɛlri] *nf* : sorcery, witchcraft

sordide [sɔrdid] *adj* **1** : sordid **2** : squalid

sornettes [sɔrnɛt] *nfpl* : nonsense

sort [sɔr] *nm* **1** : fate, lot **2** : spell, hex

sortant, -tante [sɔrtɑ̃, -tɑ̃t] *adj* : outgoing, resigning

sorte [sɔrt] *nf* **1** ESPÈCE : sort, kind **2 de** ⁓ **que** : so that **3 en quelque** ⁓ : in a way

sortie [sɔrti] *nf* **1** : exit **2** DÉPART : departure **3** : launch, release (of a book, etc.) **4** EXCURSION : outing

sortilège [sɔrtilɛʒ] *nm* : spell

sortir [sɔrtir] {82} *vt* **1** : take out, bring out **2** : launch, release — *vi* **1** : go out, come out **2** PARTIR : leave, exit **3** ⁓ **de** : come from,

come out of — se sortir *vr* **1** ~ **de** : get out of **2 s'en sortir** : get by, pull through

sosie [sɔzi] *nm* : double

sot, sotte [so, sɔt] *adj* : foolish, silly — ~ *n* : fool — **sottise** [sɔtiz] *nf* **1** : foolishness **2** : foolish act or remark

sou [su] *nm* **être sans le** ~ : be penniless

soubresaut [subrəso] *nm* : jolt, start

souche [suʃ] *nf* **1** : stump (of a tree) **2** : stock, descent

soucier [susje] {96} *v* **se soucier** *vr* : worry, be concerned — **souci** [susi] *nm* : worry, concern — **soucieux, -cieuse** [susjø, -sjøz] *adj* : anxious, concerned

soucoupe [sukup] *nf* **1** : saucer **2** ~ **volante** : flying saucer

soudain, -daine [sudɛ̃, -dɛn] *adj* : sudden — **soudainement** [-dɛnmɑ̃] *adv* : suddenly

soude [sud] *nf* : soda

souder [sude] *vt* : weld, solder

soudoyer [sudwaje] {58} *vt* : bribe

soudure [sudyr] *nf* **1** : solder **2** : soldering

souffler [sufle] *vt* **1** : wish **2** : blow ÉTEINDRE : blow out **3** CHUCHOTER : whisper — *vi* **1** : blow **2** HALETER : pant, puff — **souffle** [sufl] *nm* **1** : breath, breathing **2** : puff, gust — **soufflé** [sufle] *nm* : soufflé — **soufflet** [suflɛ] *nm* : bellows

souffrir [sufrir] {83} *vt* **1** SUPPORTER : tolerate **2** PERMETTRE : allow — *vi* : suffer — **souffrance** [sufrɑ̃s] *nf* **1** : suffering **2 en** ~ : pending — **souffrant, -frante** [sufrɑ̃, -frɑ̃t] *adj* : unwell

soufre [sufr] *nm* : sulfur

souhait [swɛ] *nm* **1** : wish **2 à vos** ~**s!** : bless you! — **souhaitable** [swɛtabl] *adj* : desirable — **souhaiter** [swete] *vt* : wish, hope for

souiller [suje] *vt* : soil

soûl, soûle [su, sul] *adj* : drunk

soulager [sulaʒe] {17} *vt* : relieve — **soulagement** [sulaʒmɑ̃] *nm* : relief

soûler [sule] *vt* : make drunk, intoxicate — **se soûler** *vr* : get drunk

soulever [sulve] {52} *vt* **1** : lift, raise **2** PROVOQUER : stir up — **se soulever** *vr* **1** : rise up **2** : lift oneself up — **soulèvement** [sulɛvmɑ̃] *nm* : uprising

soulier [sulje] *nm* : shoe

souligner [suliɲe] *vt* **1** : underline **2** : emphasize

soumettre [sumɛtr] {53} *vt* **1** : subjugate **2** PRÉSENTER : submit **3** ~ **à** : subject to — **se soumettre** *vr* : submit — **soumis, -mise** [sumi, -miz] *adj* : submissive — **soumission** [sumisjɔ̃] *nf* : submission

soupape [supap] *nf* : valve

soupçon [supsɔ̃] *nm* **1** : suspicion **2** : hint, touch — **soupçonner** [supsɔne] *vt* : suspect

— soupçonneux, -neuse [supsɔnø, -nøz] *adj* : suspicious

soupe [sup] *nf* : soup

souper [supe] *vi Can* : have supper — ~ *nm Can* : supper

soupeser [supəze] {52} *vt* **1** : feel the weight of **2** PESER : weigh, consider

soupière [supjɛr] *nf* : tureen

soupirer [supire] *vi* : sigh — **soupir** [supir] *nm* : sigh

souple [supl] *adj* : supple, flexible — **souplesse** [suplɛs] *nf* : suppleness, flexibility

source [surs] *nf* **1** : source **2** : spring (of water)

sourcil [sursi] *nm* : eyebrow — **sourciller** [sursije] *vi* **sans** ~ : without batting an eyelid — **sourcilleux, -leuse** [sursijø, -jøz] *adj* **1** : finicky **2** : supercilious

sourd, sourde [sur, surd] *adj* : deaf — ~ *nmf* : deaf person — **sourd–muet, sourde–muette** [surmɥɛ, surdmɥɛt] *n* : deaf-mute

sourdre [surdr] {84} *vi* MONTER : well up

sourire [surir] {76} *vi* : smile — ~ *nm* : smile — **souriant, -riante** [surjɑ̃, -rjɑ̃t] *adj* : smiling, cheerful

souris [suri] *nf* : mouse

sournois, -noise [surnwa, -nwaz] *adj* : sly, underhanded

sous [su] *prep* **1** : under, beneath **2** : during **3** ~ **peu** : shortly

sous–alimenté, -tée [suzalimɑ̃te] *adj* : malnourished

sous–bois [subwa] *nms & pl* : undergrowth

souscrire [suskrir] {33} *vi* ~ **à** : subscribe to — **souscription** [suskripsjɔ̃] *nf* : subscription

sous–développé, -pée [sudevlɔpe] *adj* : underdeveloped

sous–entendre [suzɑ̃tɑ̃dr] {63} *vt* : imply, infer — **sous–entendu** [suzɑ̃tɑ̃dy] *nm* : insinuation

sous–estimer [suzɛstime] *vt* : underestimate

sous–jacent, -cente [suʒasɑ̃, -sɑ̃t] *adj* : underlying

sous–louer [sulwe] *vt* : sublet

sous–marin, -rine [sumarɛ̃, -rin] *adj* : underwater — **sous–marin** *nm* : submarine

sous–officier [suzɔfisje] *nm* : noncommissioned officer

sous–produit [suprɔdɥi] *nm* : by-product

sous–sol [susɔl] *nm* : basement, cellar

sous–titre [sutitr] *nm* : subtitle

soustraire [sustrɛr] {40} *vt* **1** : subtract **2** : remove, take away — **se soustraire** *vr* ~ **à** : escape from — **soustraction** [sustraksjɔ̃] *nf* : subtraction

sous–vêtement [suvɛtmɑ̃] *nm* **1** : undergarment **2** ~**s** *nmpl* : underwear

soutane [sutan] *nf* : cassock

soute [sut] *nf* : hold (of a ship)
soutenir [sutnir] {92} *vt* **1** MAINTENIR : support, hold up **2** RÉSISTER : withstand **3** : sustain — **soutenu, -nue** [sutny] *adj* **1** : formal **2** : sustained
souterrain, -raine [sutɛrɛ̃, -rɛn] *adj* : underground — **souterrain** *nm* : underground passage
soutien [sutjɛ̃] *nm* : support
soutien–gorge [sutjɛ̃gɔrʒ] *nm, pl* **soutiens–gorge** : bra, brassiere
soutirer [sutire] *vt* **~ à** : extract from
souvenir [suvnir] {92} *v* **se souvenir** *vr* **1** **~ de** : remember **2** **~ que** : remember that — **~** *nm* **1** : memory **2** : souvenir **3** **mes meilleurs ~s à** : my best regards to
souvent [suvɑ̃] *adv* : often
souverain, -raine [suvrɛ̃, -rɛn] *adj* **1** : supreme **2** : sovereign — **~** *n* : sovereign — **souveraineté** [suvrɛnte] *nf* : sovereignty
soviétique [sɔvjetik] *adj* : Soviet
soyeux, soyeuse [swajø, swajøz] *adj* : silky
spacieux, -cieuse [spasjø, -sjøz] *adj* : spacious
spaghetti [spageti] *nmpl* : spaghetti
sparadrap [sparadra] *nm* : adhesive tape
spasme [spasm] *nm* : spasm
spatial, -tiale [spasjal] *adj, mpl* **-tiaux 1** : spatial **2 vaisseau spatial** : spaceship
speaker, -kerine [spikœr, -krin] *n France* : announcer (on radio, TV, etc.)
spécial, -ciale [spesjal] *adj, mpl* **-ciaux** [-sjo] **1** : special **2** BIZARRE : odd, peculiar — **spécialement** [spesjalmɑ̃] *adv* **1** EXPRÈS : specially **2** : especially — **spécialiser** [spesjalize] *v* **se spécialiser** *vr* : specialize — **spécialiste** [spesjalist] *nmf* : specialist — **spécialité** [spesjalite] *nf* : specialty
spécifier [spesifje] {96} *vt* : specify — **spécifique** [spesifik] *adj* : specific
spécimen [spesimen] *nm* : specimen
spectacle [spɛktakl] *nm* **1** : spectacle, sight **2** : show — **spectaculaire** [spɛktakylɛr] *adj* : spectacular — **spectateur, -trice** [spɛktatœr, -tris] *n* **1** : spectator **2** : observer, onlooker
spectre [spɛktr] *nm* **1** : specter, ghost **2** : spectrum
spéculer [spekyle] *vi* : speculate — **spéculation** [spekylasjɔ̃] *nf* : speculation
sperme [spɛrm] *nm* : sperm
sphère [sfɛr] *nf* : sphere — **sphérique** [sferik] *adj* : spherical
spirale [spiral] *nf* : spiral
spirituel, -tuelle [spirituɛl] *adj* : spiritual — **spiritualité** [spiritualite] *nf* : spirituality
splendeur [splɑ̃dœr] *nf* : splendor — **splendide** [splɑ̃did] *adj* : splendid
spongieux, -gieuse [spɔ̃ʒjø, -ʒjøz] *adj* : spongy

spontané, -née [spɔ̃tane] *adj* : spontaneous — **spontanéité** [spɔ̃taneite] *nf* : spontaneity — **spontanément** [-nemɑ̃] *adv* : spontaneously
sporadique [spɔradik] *adj* : sporadic
sport [spɔr] *adj* : sport, sports — **~** *nm* **1** : sport **2 ~s d'équipes** : team sports — **sportif, -tive** [spɔrtif, -tiv] *adj* **1** : sport, sports **2** : sportsmanlike **3** : athletic — **~** *n* : sportsman *m*, sportswoman *f*
spot [spɔt] *nm* **1** : spotlight **2** PUBLICITÉ : commercial
sprint [sprint] *nm* : sprint
square [skwar] *nm France* : small public garden
squelette [skəlɛt] *nm* : skeleton
stabiliser [stabilize] *vt* : stabilize — **stabilité** [stabilite] *nf* : stability — **stable** [stabl] *adj* : stable, steady
stade [stad] *nm* **1** : stadium **2** ÉTAPE : stage, phase
stage [staʒ] *nm* **1** : internship **2** : (training) course — **stagiaire** [staʒjɛr] *nmf* : trainee, intern
stagner [stagne] *vi* : stagnate — **stagnant, -gnante** [stagnɑ̃, -gnɑ̃t] *adj* : stagnant
stalle [stal] *nf* : stall
stand [stɑ̃d] *nm* **1** : stand, stall, booth **2 ~ de tir** : shooting range
standard [stɑ̃dar] *adj* : standard — **~** *nm* **1** : standard **2** : (telephone) switchboard — **standardiste** [stɑ̃dardist] *nmf* : switchboard operator
standing [stɑ̃diŋ] *nm* : standing, status
star [star] *nf* VEDETTE : star
station [stasjɔ̃] *nf* **1** : station **2 ~ d'autobus** : bus stop **3 ~ balnéaire** : seaside resort — **stationnaire** [stasjɔnɛr] *adj* : stationary — **stationner** [stasjɔne] *vi* : park — **stationnement** [stasjɔnmɑ̃] *nm* : parking — **station–service** [stasjɔ̃sɛrvis] *nf, pl* **stations–service** : gas station, service station
statistique [statistik] *adj* : statistical — **~** *nf* **1** : statistic **2** : statistics
statue [staty] *nf* : statue
statuer [statɥe] *vi* : decree, ordain
stature [statyr] *nf* : stature
statut [staty] *nm* **1** : statute **2** : status — **statutaire** [statytɛr] *adj* : statutory
steak [stɛk] *nm* : steak
stéréo [stereo] *adj & nf* : stereo
stéréotype [stereotip] *nm* **1** : stereotype **2** : cliché
stérile [steril] *adj* : sterile — **stérilisation** [-lizasjɔ̃] *nf* : sterilization — **stériliser** [sterilize] *vt* : sterilize — **stérilité** [sterilite] *nf* : sterility
stéthoscope [stetɔskɔp] *nm* : stethoscope
stigmate [stigmat] *nm* : mark, stigma — **stigmatiser** [stigmatize] *vt* : stigmatize

stimuler [stimyle] *vt* : stimulate — **stimulation** [-mylasjɔ̃] *nf* : stimulation — **stimulant, -lante** [stimylɑ̃, -lɑ̃t] *adj* : stimulating — **stimulant** *nm* **1** : stimulant **2** : stimulus

stipuler [stipyle] *vt* : stipulate

stock [stɔk] *nm* : stock, goods — **stocker** [stɔke] *vt* : stock

stoïque [stɔik] *adj* : stoic, stoical — ~ *nmf* : stoic

stop [stɔp] *nm* **1** : stop sign **2** : brake light — ~ *interj* : stop — **stopper** [stɔpe] *vt* **1** : stop, halt **2** : mend — *vi* : stop

store [stɔr] *nm* **1** : awning **2** : blind, window shade

strapontin [strapɔ̃tɛ̃] *nm* : folding seat

stratagème [strataʒɛm] *nm* : stratagem — **stratégie** [strateʒi] *nf* : strategy — **stratégique** [strateʒik] *adj* : strategic

stress [strɛs] *nms & pl* : stress — **stressant, -sante** [strɛsɑ̃, -sɑ̃t] *adj* : stressful

strict, stricte [strikt] *adj* **1** : strict **2** : austere, plain

strident, -dente [stridɑ̃, -dɑ̃t] *adj* : strident, shrill

strier [strije] {96} *vt* : streak

strophe [strɔf] *nf* : stanza

structure [stryktyr] *nf* : structure — **structural, -rale** [stryktyral] *adj, mpl* **-raux** [-ro] : structural — **structurer** [stryktyre] *vt* : structure

studieux, -dieuse [stydjø, -djøz] *adj* : studious

studio [stydjo] *nm* **1** : studio **2** : studio apartment

stupéfier [stypefje] {96} *vt* : astonish, stun — **stupéfaction** [stypefaksjɔ̃] *nf* : astonishment — **stupéfait, -faite** [stypefɛ, -fɛt] *adj* : amazed, astounded — **stupéfiant, -fiante** [stypefjɑ̃, -fjɑ̃t] *adj* : amazing, astounding — **stupéfiant** *nm* : drug, narcotic

stupeur [stypœr] *nf* **1** : astonishment **2** : stupor

stupide [stypid] *adj* : stupid — **stupidité** [stypidite] *nf* : stupidity

style [stil] *nm* : style

stylo [stilo] *nm* **1** : pen **2** ~ **à bille** : ballpoint (pen)

suave [sɥav] *adj* **1** : sweet **2** : smooth, suave

subalterne [sybaltɛrn] *adj & nmf* : subordinate

subconscient, -ciente [sybkɔ̃sjɑ̃, -sjɑ̃t] *adj & nm* : subconscious

subdiviser [sybdivize] *vt* : subdivide

subir [sybir] *vt* **1** : undergo **2** : suffer **3** SUPPORTER : put up with **4** : take (an exam)

subit, -bite [sybi, -bit] *adj* : sudden — **subitement** [-bitmɑ̃] *adv* : suddenly

subjectif, -tive [sybʒɛktif, -tiv] *adj* : subjective — **subjectivité** [sybʒɛktivite] *nf* : subjectivity

subjonctif [sybʒɔ̃ktif] *nm* : subjunctive

subjuguer [sybʒuge] *vt* : captivate

sublime [syblim] *adj* : sublime

submerger [sybmɛrʒe] {17} *vt* **1** : submerge, flood **2** : overwhelm

subordonner [sybɔrdɔne] *vt* : subordinate — **subordonné, -née** [sybɔrdɔne] *adj & n* : subordinate

subreptice [sybrɛptis] *adj* : surreptitious

subséquent, -quente [sybsekɑ̃, -kɑ̃t] *adj* : subsequent

subside [sypsid] *nm* : grant, subsidy

subsidiaire [sybzidjɛr] *adj* : subsidiary

subsister [sybziste] *vi* **1** SURVIVRE : subsist, survive (on) **2** DURER : remain

substance [sypstɑ̃s] *nf* : substance — **substantiel, -tielle** [sypstɑ̃sjɛl] *adj* : substantial

substantif [sypstɑ̃tif] *nm* : noun

substituer [sypstitɥe] *vt* : substitute — **se substituer** *vr* ~ **à** : substitute for, replace — **substitut** [sypstity] *nm* : substitute — **substitution** [sypstitysjɔ̃] *nf* : substitution

subterfuge [syptɛrfyʒ] *nm* : ploy, subterfuge

subtil, -tile [syptil] *adj* : subtle — **subtilité** [syptilite] *nf* : subtlety

subvenir [sybvənir] {92} *vi* ~ **à** : provide for, meet — **subvention** [sybvɑ̃sjɔ̃] *nf* : subsidy — **subventionner** [sybvɑ̃sjɔne] *vt* : subsidize

subversif, -sive [sybvɛrsif, -siv] *adj* : subversive — **subversion** [sybvɛrsjɔ̃] *nf* : subversion

suc [syk] *nm* **1** : juice **2** : sap

succédané [syksedane] *nm* : substitute

succéder [syksede] {87} *vi* ~ **à** : succeed, follow — **se succéder** *vr* : follow one another

succès [syksɛ] *nm* : success

successeur [syksesœr] *nm* : successor — **successif, -sive** [syksesif, -siv] *adj* : successive — **succession** [syksesjɔ̃] *nf* : succession

succinct, -cincte [syksɛ̃, -sɛ̃t] *adj* : succinct

succion [syksjɔ̃, sysjɔ̃] *nf* : suction, sucking

succomber [sykɔ̃be] *vi* **1** : die **2** ~ **à** : succumb to

succulent, -lente [sykylɑ̃, -lɑ̃t] *adj* : succulent

succursale [sykyrsal] *nf* : branch (of a bank, etc.)

sucer [syse] {6} *vt* : suck

sucette [sysɛt] *nf* **1** : lollipop **2** : pacifier

sucre [sykr] *nm* : sugar — **sucré, -crée** [sykre] *adj* : sweet, sweetened — **sucrer** [sykre] *vt* : sweeten, add sugar to

sud [syd] *adj* : south, southern, southerly — ~ *nm* **1** : south **2 le Sud** : the South

sud–africain, -caine [sydafrikɛ̃, -kɛn] *adj* : South African

sud–américain, -caine [sydamerikɛ̃, -kɛn] *adj* : South American

sud–est [sydɛst] *adj s & pl* : southeast, southeastern — ⁓ *nm* : southeast

sud–ouest [sydwɛst] *adj s & pl* : southwest, southwestern — ⁓ *nm* : southwest

suédois, -doise [sɥedwa, -dwaz] *adj* : Swedish — **suédois** *nm* : Swedish (language)

suer [sɥe] *vi* : sweat — *vt* : sweat, ooze — **sueur** [sɥœr] *nf* : sweat

suffire [syfir] {86} *vi* : suffice — **se suffire** *vr or* ⁓ **à soi–même** : be self-sufficient — **suffisamment** [syfizamɑ̃] *adv* : sufficiently — **suffisance** [syfizɑ̃s] *nf* : self-importance — **suffisant, -sante** [syfizɑ̃, -zɑ̃t] *adj* 1 : sufficient 2 : conceited

suffixe [syfiks] *nm* : suffix

suffoquer [syfɔke] *v* : suffocate, choke

suffrage [syfraʒ] *nm* : suffrage, vote

suggérer [sygʒere] {86} *vt* : suggest — **suggestion** [sygʒɛstjɔ̃] *nf* : suggestion

suicide [sɥisid] *nm* : suicide — **suicider** [sɥiside] *v* **se suicider** *vr* : commit suicide

suie [sɥi] *nf* : soot

suinter [sɥɛ̃te] *vi* : ooze, seep

suisse [sɥis] *adj* : Swiss

suite [sɥit] *nf* 1 : suite 2 : continuation, sequel 3 SÉRIE : series, sequence 4 CONSÉQUENCE : result 5 **par la** ⁓ : later, afterwards 6 **par** ⁓ **de** : due to, as a result of

suivre [sɥivr] {88} *vt* 1 : follow 2 : take (a course) 3 : keep up with — *vi* 1 : follow 2 : keep up 3 **faire** ⁓ : forward (mail) — **se suivre** *vr* : follow one another — **suivant, -vante** [sɥivɑ̃, -vɑ̃t] *adj* : following, next — ⁓ *n* : next one, following one — **suivant** *prep* : according to — **suivi, -vie** [sɥivi] *adj* 1 : regular, steady 2 : coherent

sujet, -jette [syʒɛ, -ʒɛt] *adj* ⁓ **à** : subject to, prone to — ⁓ *n* : subject (of a state or country) — **sujet** *nm* 1 : subject, topic 2 RAISON : cause

summum [sɔmɔm] *nm* : height, peak

super [sypɛr] *adj s & pl fam* : great, super

superbe [sypɛrb] *adj* : superb

supercherie [sypɛrʃəri] *nf* TROMPERIE : deception

superficie [sypɛrfisi] *nf* : area, surface — **superficiel, -cielle** [sypɛrfisjɛl] *adj* : superficial

superflu, -flue [sypɛrfly] *adj* : superfluous

supérieur, -rieure [syperjœr] *adj* 1 : superior 2 : upper, top 3 ⁓ **à** : higher than — ⁓ *n* : superior — **supériorité** [syperjɔrite] *nf* : superiority

superlative [sypɛrlatif] *nm* : superlative

supermarché [sypɛrmarʃe] *nm* : supermarket

superstitieux, -tieuse [sypɛrstisjø, -sjøz] *adj* : superstitious — **superstition** [sypɛrstisjɔ̃] *nf* : superstition

superviser [sypɛrvize] *vt* : supervise

supplanter [syplɑ̃te] *vt* : supplant

suppléer [syplee] {89} *vt* 1 REMPLA-CER : replace, fill in for 2 : supplement — *vi* ⁓ **à** : make up for — **suppléant, -pléante** [sypleɑ̃, -pleɑ̃t] *adj & n* : substitute, replacement

supplément [syplemɑ̃] *nm* 1 : supplement 2 : extra charge — **supplémentaire** [syplemɑ̃tɛr] *adj* : additional, extra

supplication [syplikasjɔ̃] *nf* : plea

supplice [syplis] *nm* : torture — **supplicier** [syplisje] {96} *vt* TORTURER : torture

supplier [syplije] {96} *vt* : implore, beg

supporter[1] [sypɔrte] *vt* 1 SOUTENIR : support, hold up 2 ENDURER : tolerate, bear — **support** [sypɔr] *nm* : support, prop — **supportable** [sypɔrtabl] *adj* : bearable, tolerable

supporter[2] [sypɔrtɛr] *nm* : supporter, fan

supposer [sypoze] *vt* 1 : suppose, assume 2 IMPLIQUER : imply — **supposition** [sypozisjɔ̃] *nf* : supposition

suppositoire [sypozitwar] *nm* : suppository

supprimer [syprime] *vt* 1 : abolish 2 : take out, delete — **suppression** [sypresjɔ̃] *nf* 1 : removal, elimination 2 : deletion

suppurer [sypyre] *vi* : fester

suprême [syprɛm] *adj* : supreme — **suprématie** [sypremasi] *nf* : supremacy

sur[1] [syr] *prep* 1 : on, upon 2 : over, above 3 : about, on 4 PARMI : out of 5 : by (in measurements)

sur[2], **sure** [syr] *adj* : sour

sûr, sûre [syr] *adj* 1 CERTAIN : sure, certain 2 FIABLE : reliable 3 : safe, secure 4 : sound 5 ⁓ **de soi** : self-confident

surabondance [syrabɔ̃dɑ̃s] *nf* : overabundance

suranné, -née [syrane] *adj* : outdated

surcharger [syrʃarʒe] {17} *vt* 1 : overload 2 : alter — **surcharge** [syrʃarʒ] *nf* : overload

surchauffer [syrʃofe] *vt* : overheat

surclasser [syrklase] *vt* : outclass

surcroît [syrkrwa] *nm* 1 : increase 2 **de** ⁓ : in addition

surdité [syrdite] *nf* : deafness

surélever [syrelve] {52} *vt* : raise, heighten

sûrement [syrmɑ̃] *adv* 1 : surely 2 : safely 3 ⁓ **pas** : certainly not

surenchérir [syrɑ̃ʃerir] *vi* : bid higher

surestimer [syrɛstime] *vt* : overestimate, overrate

sûreté [syrte] *nf* 1 SÉCURITÉ : safety 2 : surety, guarantee (in law)

surexcité, -tée [syrɛksite] *adj* : overexcited

surf [sœrf] *nm* : surfing

surface [syrfas] *nf* : surface
surgelé [syrʒəle] *adj* : frozen (of food)
surgir [syrʒir] *vi* : appear suddenly, arise
surhumain, -maine [syrymɛ̃, -mɛn] *adj* : superhuman
sur–le–champ [syrləʃɑ̃] *adv* : immediately
surlendemain [syrlɑ̃dmɛ̃] *nm* **le ~** : two days later
surmener [syrmǝne] {52} *vt* : overwork — **surmenage** [syrmǝnaʒ] *nm* : overwork
surmonter [syrmɔ̃te] *vt* **1** : overcome **2** : surmount, top
surnager [syrnaʒe] {17} *vi* : float
surnaturel, -relle [syrnatyrɛl] *adj & nm* : supernatural
surnom [syrnɔ̃] *nm* : nickname
surnombre [syrnɔ̃br] *nm* **en ~** : excess, too many
surnommer [syrnɔme] *vt* : nickname
surpasser [syrpase] *vt* : surpass, outdo
surpeuplé, -plée [syrpœple] *adj* : overpopulated
surplomber [syrplɔ̃be] *v* : overhang
surplus [syrply] *nm* : surplus
surprendre [syrprɑ̃dr] {70} *vt* **1** ÉTONNER : surprise **2** : catch, take by surprise **3** : overhear — **surprenant, -nante** [syrprǝnɑ̃, -nɑ̃t] *adj* : surprising — **surprise** [syrpriz] *nf* : surprise
sursaut [syrso] *nm* : start, jump — **sursauter** [syrsote] *vi* : start, jump
surseoir [syrswar] {90} *vi* **~ à** : postpone, defer
sursis [syrsi] *nm* : reprieve
surtaxe [syrtaks] *nf* : surcharge
surtout [syrtu] *adv* **1** : above all **2** : especially, particularly
surveiller [syrveje] *vt* **1** : watch (over) **2** : supervise — **surveillance** [syrvejɑ̃s] *nf* **1** : supervision **2** : watch, surveillance — **surveillant, -lante** [syrvejɑ̃, -jɑ̃t] *n* **1** : supervisor, overseer **2 ~ de prison** : prison guard
survenir [syrvǝnir] {92} *vi* : occur, take place
survivre [syrvivr] {98} *vi* **1** : survive **2 ~ à** : outlive — **survie** [syrvi] *nf* : survival — **survivant, -vante** [syrvivɑ̃, -vɑ̃t] *n* : survivor

survoler [syrvɔle] *vi* **1** : fly over **2** : skim through
sus [sy(s)] *adv* **1 en ~** : extra **2 en ~ de** : in addition to
susceptible [syscptibl] *adj* **1** : sensitive, touchy **2 ~ de** : likely to — **susceptibilité** [syseptibilite] *nf* : susceptibility
susciter [sysite] *vt* : arouse, give rise to
suspect, -pecte [syspε, -pεkt] *adj* : suspicious, suspect — **~ n** : suspect — **suspecter** [syspεkte] *vt* : suspect
suspendre [syspɑ̃dr] {63} *vt* **1** INTERROMPRE : suspend, interrupt **2** PENDRE : hang up — **se suspendre** *vr* **~ à** : hang from — **suspens** [syspɑ̃] *nm* **en ~** : unresolved, uncertain
suspense [syspɑ̃s] *nm* : suspense
suspicion [syspisjɔ̃] *nf* : suspicion
suture [sytyr] *nf* **1** : suture **2 point de ~** : stitch
svelte [zvεlt] *adj* : slender, svelte
syllabe [silab] *nf* : syllable
symbole [sɛ̃bɔl] *nm* : symbol — **symbolique** [sɛ̃bɔlik] *adj* : symbolic — **symboliser** [sɛ̃bɔlize] *vt* : symbolize — **symbolisme** [sɛ̃bɔlism] *nm* : symbolism
symétrie [simetri] *nf* : symmetry — **symétrique** [simetrik] *adj* : symmetrical, symmetric
sympathie [sɛ̃pati] *nf* **1** : liking **2** CONDOLÉANCES : condolences — **sympathique** [sɛ̃patik] *adj* : nice, likeable — **sympathiser** [sɛ̃patize] *vi* **~ avec** : get along with
symphonie [sɛ̃fɔni] *nf* : symphony — **symphonique** [sɛ̃fɔnik] *adj* : symphonic
symptôme [sɛ̃ptom] *nm* : symptom
synagogue [sinagɔg] *nf* : synagogue
syndicat [sɛ̃dika] *nm* : union, labor union — **syndiquer** [sɛ̃dike] *vt* : unionize — **se syndiquer** *vr* : join a union
syndrome [sɛ̃drom] *nm* : syndrome
synonyme [sinɔnim] *nm* : synonym — **~ adj** : synonymous
syntaxe [sɛ̃taks] *nf* : syntax
synthèse [sɛ̃tεz] *nf* : synthesis — **synthétique** [sɛ̃tetik] *adj* : synthetic
système [sistεm] *nm* : system — **systématique** [sistematik] *adj* : systematic

T

t [te] *nm* : t, 20th letter of the alphabet

tabac [taba] *nm* **1** : tobacco **2** ~ **à priser** : snuff **3** *France* : tobacco shop

table [tabl] *nf* **1** : table **2 se mettre à** ~ : sit down to eat **3** ~ **de matières** : table of contents

tableau [tablo] *nm, pl* **-bleaux 1** PEINTURE : painting **2** : picture, scene **3** : table, chart **4** ~ **d'affichage** : bulletin board **5** ~ **de bord** : dashboard **6** ~ **noir** : blackboard

tabler [table] *vt* ~ **sur** : count on

tablette [tablɛt] *nf* **1** : shelf **2** : bar (of candy), stick (of gum)

tablier [tablije] *nm* : apron

tabou, -boue [tabu] *adj* : taboo — **tabou** *nm* : taboo

tabouret [taburɛ] *nm* : stool

tache [taʃ] *nf* **1** : stain, spot **2** ~ **de rousseur** : freckle — **tacher** [taʃe] *vt* SALIR : stain, spot

tâche [taʃ] *nf* : task — **tâcher** [taʃe] *vi* ~ **de** : try to

tacheté [taʃte] *adj* : speckled

tacite [tasit] *adj* : tacit

tact [takt] *nm* : tact

tactique [taktik] *adj* : tactical — ~ *nf* STRATÉGIE : tactics *pl*

taie [tɛ] *nf or* ~ **d'oreiller** : pillowcase

tailler [taje] *vt* **1** : cut, prune, trim **2** : sharpen (a pencil) — **taille** [taj] *nf* **1** : cutting, pruning **2** : size (of clothing, etc.) **3** HAUTEUR : height **4** : waist — **tailleur** [tajœr] *nm* **1** : woman's suit **2** : tailor

taire [tɛr] {91} *vt* : hush up, keep secret — **se taire** *vr* **1** : be quiet **2** : fall silent

talc [talk] *nm* : talcum powder

talent [talɑ̃] *nm* : talent — **talentueux, -tueuse** [talɑ̃tyø, -tyøz] *adj* : talented

talon [talɔ̃] *nm* **1** : heel **2** : stub (of a check) — **talonner** [talɔne] *vt* **1** : follow closely **2** : harass

talus [taly] *nms & pl* : embankment, slope

tambour [tɑ̃bur] *nm* : drum — **tambouriner** [tɑ̃burine] *vt* : drum

tamia [tamja] *nm* : chipmunk

tamis [tami] *nms & pl* : sieve, sifter — **tamiser** [tamize] *vt* **1** : sift **2** : filter

tampon [tɑ̃pɔ̃] *nm* **1** BOUCHON : plug **2** : buffer (of a railway car) **3** : rubber stamp **4** ~ **encreur** : ink pad **5** ~ **hygiénique** : tampon — **tamponner** [tɑ̃pɔne] *vt* **1** : dab **2** HEURTER : crash into **3** : stamp (a document)

tandis [tɑ̃di] ~ **que** *conj phr* **1** : while **2** : whereas

tangente [tɑ̃ʒɑ̃t] *nf* : tangent

tangible [tɑ̃ʒibl] *adj* : tangible

tango [tɑ̃go] *nm* : tango

tanguer [tɑ̃ge] *vi* : pitch (of a ship, etc.)

tanière [tanjɛr] *nf* : lair, den

tanner [tane] *vt* **1** : tan (leather, etc.) **2** *fam* : pester, annoy

tant [tɑ̃] *adv* **1** : so much, so many **2 en** ~ **que** : as, in so far as **3** ~ **mieux!** : so much the better! **4** ~ **pis!** : too bad! **5** ~ **que** : as much as, as long as

tante [tɑ̃t] *nf* : aunt

tantôt [tɑ̃to] *adv* **1** : sometimes **2** *Can* : later **3** *France* : this afternoon

tapage [tapaʒ] *nm* **1** : uproar, din **2** SCANDALE : scandal — **tapageur, -geuse** [tapaʒœr, -ʒøz] *adj* **1** : rowdy **2** TAPE-À-L'ŒIL : flashy

tape [tap] *nf* : slap — **tape-à-l'œil** [tapalœj] *adj* : flashy

taper [tape] *vt* **1** : hit, slap **2** : type — *vi* **1** : hit, bang **2** : beat down (of the sun)

tapir [tapir] *v* **se tapir** *vr* : crouch

tapis [tapi] *nms & pl* **1** : carpet **2** ~ **roulant** : moving walkway, conveyor belt — **tapisser** [tapise] *vt* **1** : wallpaper **2** ~ **de** : cover with — **tapisserie** [tapisri] *nf* **1** : tapestry **2** : wallpaper

tapoter [tapɔte] *vt* : tap, pat

taquiner [takine] *vt* : tease — **taquinerie** [takinri] *nf* : teasing

tarabiscoté, -tée [tarabiskɔte] *adj* : fussy, overelaborate

tard [tar] *adv* : late — **tarder** [tarde] *vi* : take a long time — **tardif, -dive** [tardif, -div] *adj* : late

tare [tar] *nf* DÉFAUT : defect

tarif [tarif] *nm* **1** : rate, fare **2** : price, schedule of prices **3** ~ **douanier** : tariff, customs duty

tarir [tarir] *v* : dry up

tarte [tart] *nf* : tart, pie

tartine [tartin] *nf* : slice of bread (and butter) — **tartiner** [tartine] *vt* : spread (with butter, etc.)

tartre [tartr] *nm* : tartar

tas [ta] *nms & pl* **1** : heap, pile **2 des** ~ **de** : a lot of, piles of

tasse [tas] *nf* : cup

tasser [tase] *vt* **1** : pack down **2** ENTASSER : cram, squeeze **3** *Can* : move over — **se tasser** *vr* **1** : shrink **2** : cram (into a car)

tâter [tate] *vt* **1** : feel **2** ~ **le terrain** : check out the lay of the land — *vi* ~ **de** : try one's hand at

tatillon, -lonne [tatijɔ̃, -jɔn] *adj* : fussy, finicky

tâtonner [tatɔne] *vi* : grope about — **tâtons** [tatɔ̃] **à ~** *adv phr* **avancer à ~** : feel one's way

tatouer [tatwe] *vt* : tattoo — **tatouage** [tatwaʒ] *nm* **1** : tattoo **2** : tattooing

taudis [todi] *nms & pl* : hovel, slum

taule [tol] *nf fam* : prison

taupe [top] *nf* : mole

taureau [tɔro] *nm, pl* **-reaux** : bull

taux [to] *nms & pl* **1** : rate **2** : level **3 ~ de change** : exchange rate **4 ~ de cholestérol** : cholesterol level

taverne [tavɛrn] *nf* : inn, tavern

taxe [taks] *nf* : tax — **taxer** [takse] *vt* : tax

taxi [taksi] *nm* : taxi, taxicab

te [tə] (**t'** *before a vowel or mute h*) *pron* **1** : you, to you **2** (*used as a reflexive pronoun*) : yourself

technique [tɛknik] *nf* : technique — **~** *adj* : technical — **technicien, -cienne** [tɛknisjɛ̃, -sjɛn] *n* : technician

technologie [tɛknɔlɔʒi] *nf* : technology — **technologique** [tɛknɔlɔʒik] *adj* : technological

tee-shirt [tiʃœrt] *nm, pl* **tee-shirts** : T-shirt

teindre [tɛ̃dr] {37} *vt* : dye — **teint** [tɛ̃] *nm* : complexion — **teinte** [tɛ̃t] *nf* **1** : shade, hue **2 une ~ de** : a tinge of — **teinter** [tɛ̃te] *vt* : tint, stain — **teinture** [tɛ̃tyr] *nf* **1** : dye **2** : dyeing — **teinturerie** [tɛ̃tyrri] *nf* **1** : dyeing **2** : dry cleaner's — **teinturier, -rière** [tɛ̃tyrje, -rjɛ] *n* : dry cleaner

tel, telle [tɛl] *adj* **1** : such **2** : such and such, a certain **3 ~ que** : such as, like **4 tel quel** : as (it) is — **~** *pron* **1** : a certain one, someone **2 un tel, une telle** : so-and-so

télé [tele] *nf fam* : TV

télécommande [telekɔmɑ̃d] *nf* : remote control

télécommunication [telekɔmynikas-jɔ̃] *nf* : telecommunication

télécopie [telekɔpi] *nf* : fax — **télécopieur** [telekɔpjœr] *nm* : fax machine

télégramme [telegram] *nm* : telegram

télégraphe [telegraf] *nm* : telegraph

téléphone [telefɔn] *nm* : telephone — **téléphoner** [telefɔne] *vt* : telephone, call — **téléphonique** [telefɔnik] *adj* : telephone

télescope [teleskɔp] *nm* : telescope — **télescoper** [teleskɔpe] *v* **se télescoper** *vr* **1** : collide **2** : overlap — **télescopique** [teleskɔpik] *adj* : telescopic

télésiège [telesjɛʒ] *nm* : chairlift

téléski [teleski] *nm* : ski lift

téléviser [televize] *vt* : televise — **téléviseur** [televizœr] *nm* : television set — **télévision** [televizjɔ̃] *nf* **1** : television **2** TÉLÉVISEUR : television set

tellement [tɛlmɑ̃] *adv* **1** : so, so much **2 ~ de** : so many, so much

téméraire [temerɛr] *adj* : rash, reckless — **témérité** [temerite] *nf* : rashness, recklessness

témoin [temwɛ̃] *nm* **1** : witness **2** : baton (in a relay race) — **témoignage** [temwaɲaʒ] *nm* **1** RÉCIT : account, story **2** : testimony (in court) **3** PREUVE : evidence — **témoigner** [temwaɲe] *vt* **1** : testify, attest **2** MONTRER : show — *vi* : testify

tempe [tɑ̃p] *nf* : temple

tempérament [tɑ̃peramɑ̃] *nm* CARACTÈRE : temperament

température [tɑ̃peratyr] *nf* : temperature

tempéré, -rée [tɑ̃pere] *adj* : temperate

tempête [tɑ̃pɛt] *nf* : storm

temple [tɑ̃pl] *nm* **1** : temple **2** : (protestant) church

temporaire [tɑ̃pɔrɛr] *adj* : temporary

temporel, -relle [tɑ̃pɔrɛl] *adj* : temporal, worldly

temps [tɑ̃] *nms & pl* **1** : time **2** : weather **3** : tense (in grammar) **4 à plein ~** : full-time **5 de ~ à autre** : from time to time **6 quel ~ fait-il?** : what's the weather like?

tenace [tənas] *adj* : tenacious, stubborn — **ténacité** [tenasite] *nf* : tenacity

tenailles [tənaj] *nfpl* : pincers, tongs

tendance [tɑ̃dɑ̃s] *nf* **1** : tendency **2** COURANT : trend

tendon [tɑ̃dɔ̃] *nm* : tendon, sinew

tendre[1] [tɑ̃dr] {63} *vt* **1** : tense, tighten (a rope, etc.) **2 ~ la main** : hold out one's hand **3 ~ un piège à** : set a trap for — *vi* **1 ~ à** : tend to **2 ~ vers** : strive for — **se tendre** *vr* **1** : tighten **2** : become strained — **tendu, -due** [tɑ̃dy] *adj* **1** : tight, taut **2** : tense, strained **3** : outstretched (of a hand)

tendre[2] *adj* **1** : tender, soft **2** : gentle, loving — **tendresse** [tɑ̃drɛs] *nf* : tenderness, affection

ténèbres [tenɛbr] *nfpl* : darkness — **ténébreux, -breuse** [tenebrø, -brøz] *adj* OBSCUR : dark

teneur [tənœr] *nf* : content

tenir [tənir] {92} *vt* **1** : hold, keep **2** : have, catch **3** : run, manage (a hotel, store, etc.) **4** : take up (a space) **5** CONSIDÉRER : hold, regard — *vi* **1** : hold, stay in place **2** DURER : hold up, last **3** : fit (into a space) **4 ~ à** : be fond of **5 ~ à** : be anxious to **6 ~ de** : take after — *v impers* : depend — **se tenir** *vr* **1** : hold, hold up, hold onto **2** RESTER : remain **3** : behave (oneself) **4 ~ debout** : stand still

tennis [tenis] *nm* **1** : tennis **2 ~** *nmpl France* : sneakers

ténor [tenɔr] *nm* : tenor

tension [tɑ̃sjɔ̃] *nf* : tension

tentacule [tɑ̃takyl] *nm* : tentacle
tentation [tɑ̃tasjɔ̃] *nf* : temptation
tentative [tɑ̃tativ] *nf* : attempt
tente [tɑ̃t] *nf* : tent
tenter [tɑ̃te] *vt* **1** : tempt **2** ESSAYER : attempt
tenu, -nue [təny] *adj* **1** : obliged **2 bien ~** : well-kept, tidy
ténu, -nue [teny] *adj* : tenuous
tenue *nf* **1** : conduct, manners *pl* **2** MAINTIEN : posture **3** : clothes *pl*, dress **4 ~ de livres** : bookkeeping
terme [tɛrm] *nm* **1** : term, word **2** ÉCHÉANCE : deadline **3 mettre un ~ à** : put an end to
terminer [tɛrmine] *v* FINIR : finish — **se terminer** *vr* : end — **terminaison** [tɛrminɛzɔ̃] *nf* : ending — **terminal, -nale** [tɛrminal] *adj, mpl* **-naux** [-no] : final, terminal — **terminal** *nm, pl* **-naux** : terminal
terminologie [tɛrminɔlɔʒi] *nf* : terminology
terminus [tɛrminys] *nms & pl* : terminus
terne [tɛrn] *adj* **1** FADE : drab **2** ENNUYEUX : dull
ternir [tɛrnir] *vt* : tarnish
terrain [tɛrɛ̃] *nm* **1** : ground **2** PARCELLE : plot (of land) **3** : land, terrain **4 ~ d'aviation** : airfield **5 ~ de camping** : campsite
terrasse [tɛras] *nf* : terrace — **terrasser** [tɛrase] *vt* : knock down, floor
terre [tɛr] *nf* **1** TERRAIN : land **2** : dirt, soil **3** : earth, world **4 aller à ~** : go ashore **5 la Terre** : the Earth **6 par ~** : on the ground, on the floor **7 sous ~** : underground **8 terre-à-terre** : down-to-earth, matter-of-fact
terrestre [tɛrɛstr] *adj* **1** : earth, terrestrial **2** : earthly, worldly
terreur [tɛrœr] *nf* : terror
terreux, -reuse [tɛrø, -røz] *adj* : earthy
terrible [tɛribl] *adj* **1** : terrible **2** *fam* FORMIDABLE : terrific, great
terrier [tɛrje] *nm* **1** : hole, burrow **2** CHIEN : terrier
terrifier [tɛrifje] {96} *vt* ÉPOUVANTER : terrify
territoire [tɛritwar] *nm* : territory — **territorial, -riale** [tɛritɔrjal] *adj, mpl* **-riaux** [-rjo] : territorial
terroriser [tɛrɔrize] *vt* : terrorize — **terrorisme** [tɛrɔrism] *nm* : terrorism — **terroriste** [-rɔrist] *adj & nmf* : terrorist
tes → ton[1]
tesson [tɛsɔ̃] *nm* : fragment, shard
test [tɛst] *nm* : test
testament [tɛstamɑ̃] *nm* **1** : will, testament **2 Ancien Testament** : Old Testament
tester [tɛste] *vt* : test
testicule [tɛstikyl] *nm* : testicle
tétanos [tetanos] *nms & pl* : tetanus
têtard [tɛtar] *nm* : tadpole

tête [tɛt] *nf* **1** : head **2** VISAGE : face **3** MENEUR : leader **4** : top (of a class, etc.) **5** ESPRIT : mind, brain **6 faire la ~** : sulk **7 tenir ~ à** : stand up to — **tête-à-queue** [tɛtakø] *nms & pl* : spin (of an automobile) — **tête-à-tête** [tɛtatɛt] *nms & pl* : tête-à-tête
téter [tete] {87} *vt* : suck (at) — *vi* : suckle, nurse — **tétine** [tetin] *nf* **1** : teat **2** : nipple (on a baby's bottle), pacifier
têtu, -tue [tety] *adj* : stubborn
texte [tɛkst] *nm* : text
textile [tɛkstil] *nm* : textile
texture [tɛkstyr] *nf* : texture
thé [te] *nm* : tea
théâtre [teatr] *nm* : theater — **théâtral, -trale** [teatral] *adj, mpl* **-traux** [-tro] : theatrical
théière [tejɛr] *nf* : teapot
thème [tɛm] *nm* : theme
théologie [teɔlɔʒi] *nf* : theology
théorie [teɔri] *nf* : theory — **théorique** [teɔrik] *adj* : theoretical
thérapie [terapi] *nf* : therapy — **thérapeute** [terapøt] *nmf* : therapist — **thérapeutique** [terapøtik] *adj* : therapeutic
thermal, -male [tɛrmal] *adj, mpl* **-maux** [tɛrmo] : thermal — **thermique** [tɛrmik] *adj* : thermal
thermomètre [tɛrmɔmɛtr] *nm* : thermometer
thermos [tɛrmos] *nmfs & pl* : thermos
thermostat [tɛrmɔsta] *nm* : thermostat
thèse [tɛz] *nf* : thesis
thon [tɔ̃] *nm* : tuna
thym [tɛ̃] *nm* : thyme
tibia [tibja] *nm* : shin(bone)
tic [tik] *nm* **1** : tic, twitch **2** HABITUDE : mannerism
ticket [tikɛ] *nm* BILLET : ticket
tiède [tjɛd] *adj* : lukewarm — **tiédir** [tjedir] *vi* : warm up, cool down
tien, tienne [tjɛ̃, tjɛn] *adj* : yours, of yours — **~** *pron* **le tien, la tienne, les tiens, les tiennes** : yours
tiers, tierce [tjɛr, tjɛrs] *adj* : third — **tiers** *nm* **1** : third **2** : third party
tige [tiʒ] *nf* **1** : stem, stalk **2** : (metal) rod
tigre [tigr] *nm* : tiger — **tigresse** [tigrɛs] *nf* : tigress
tilleul [tijœl] *nm* : linden (tree)
timbale [tɛ̃bal] *nf* : tumbler, cup
timbre [tɛ̃br] *nm* **1** : (postage) stamp **2** SONNETTE : bell **3** TON : timbre, tone — **timbrer** [tɛ̃bre] *vt* : stamp, postmark
timide [timid] *adj* : timid, shy — **timidité** [timidite] *nf* : shyness
tintamarre [tɛ̃tamar] *nm* : din, racket
tinter [tɛ̃te] *vt* : ring, toll — *vi* **1** : ring, chime **2** : jingle, tinkle — **tintement** [tɛ̃tmɑ̃] *nm* : ringing, chiming

tir [tir] *nm* : shooting, firing

tirage [tiraʒ] *nm* **1** : printing, printout **2** : circulation (of a newspaper, etc.) **3** : drawing (in a lottery)

tirailler [tiraje] *vt* : pull at, tug at

tiré, -rée [tire] *adj* : drawn, haggard

tire–bouchon [tirbuʃɔ̃] *nm, pl* **tire–bouchons** : corkscrew

tirelire [tirlir] *nf* : piggy bank

tirer [tire] *vt* **1** : pull, tug **2** : fire, shoot **3** ~ **de** : pull out of, draw away from **4** ~ **la langue** : stick out one's tongue **5** ~ **une ligne** : draw a line — *vi* **1** : pull **2** : fire, shoot **3** ~ **au sort** : draw lots — **se tirer** *vr* **1** ~ **de** : get through, escape from **2 s'en tirer** *fam* : cope, manage

tiret [tire] *nm* : dash, hyphen

tireur, -reuse [tirœr, -røz] *n* : gunman

tiroir [tirwar] *nm* : drawer

tisane [tizan] *nf* : herbal tea

tisonnier [tizɔnje] *nm* : poker

tisser [tise] *vt* : weave — **tissage** [tisaʒ] *nm* **1** : weaving **2** : weave

tissu [tisy] *nm* **1** : material, fabric **2** : tissue (in biology)

titre [titr] *nm* **1** : title (of a book, etc.) **2** : rank, qualification **3** *or* **gros** ~ : headline **4** : security, bond **5 à** ~ **d'exemple** : as an example

tituber [titybe] *vi* : stagger

titulaire [titylɛr] *adj* : tenured, permanent — ~ *nmf* **1** : holder **2** : tenured professor

toast [tost] *nm* : toast

toboggan [tɔbɔgã] *nm* : toboggan, sleigh

toge [tɔʒ] *nf* : gown, robe (of a judge, etc.)

toi [twa] *pron* **1** : you **2** TOI–MÊME : yourself

toile [twal] *nf* **1** : cloth, fabric **2** TABLEAU : canvas, painting **3** ~ **d'araignée** : spiderweb, cobweb

toilette [twalɛt] *nf* **1** : washing up **2** TENUE : clothing, outfit **3** *Can* : toilet, bathroom **4** ~**s** *nfpl* : toilet, bathroom

toi–même [twamɛm] *pron* : yourself

toison [twazɔ̃] *nf* : fleece

toit [twa] *nm* : roof — **toiture** [twatyr] *nf* : roofing

tôle [tol] *nf* **1** : sheet metal **2** ~ **ondulée** : corrugated iron

tolérer [tɔlere] {87} *vt* : tolerate — **tolérance** [tɔlerãs] *nf* : tolerance — **tolérant, -rante** [tɔlerã, -rãt] *adj* : tolerant

tollé [tɔle] *nm* : outcry

tomate [tɔmat] *nf* : tomato

tombant, -bante [tɔ̃bã, -bãt] *adj* : sloping, drooping

tombe [tɔ̃b] *nf* SÉPULTURE : grave, tomb — **tombeau** [tɔ̃bo] *nm, pl* **-beaux** : tomb, mausoleum

tomber [tɔ̃be] *vi* **1** : fall, drop **2** : die down, subside **3** : droop, sag **4** ~ **amoureux** : fall in love **5** ~ **malade** : fall ill **6** ~ **sur** : run into, come across **7 laisser** ~ : give up — **tombée** [tɔ̃be] *nf* **à la** ~ **du jour** *or* **à la** ~ **de la nuit** : at nightfall, at the close of day

tome [tom] *nm* : volume (of a book)

ton[1] [tɔ̃ (tɔn *before a vowel or mute h*)], **ta** [ta] *adj, pl* **tes** [te] : your

ton[2] [tɔ̃] *nm* **1** : tone, pitch **2** : hue, shade — **tonalité** [tɔnalite] *nf* **1** : tone **2** : tonality, key (in music) **3** : dial tone

tondre [tɔ̃dr] {63} *vt* **1** : mow (the lawn) **2** : shear, clip (hair) — **tondeuse** [tɔ̃døz] *nf* **1** *or* ~ **à gazon** : lawn mower **2** : clippers *pl*, shears *pl*

tonifier [tɔnifje] {96} *vt* REVIGORER : tone up, invigorate — **tonique** [tɔnik] *nm* : tonic

tonne [tɔn] *nf* : ton

tonneau [tɔno] *nm, pl* **-neaux 1** : barrel, cask **2** : rollover (of an automobile) — **tonnelet** [tɔnlɛ] *nm* : keg

tonner [tɔne] *vi* : thunder — **tonnerre** [tɔnɛr] *nm* : thunder

tonton [tɔ̃tɔ̃] *nm fam* : uncle

tonus [tɔnys] *nms & pl* **1** : (muscle) tone **2** : energy, vigor

toqué, -quée [tɔke] *adj fam* : crazy

torche [tɔrʃ] *nf* : torch

torchon [tɔrʃɔ̃] *nm* **1** CHIFFON : rag **2** ~ **à vaisselle** : dishcloth — **torcher** [tɔrʃe] *vt fam* : wipe

tordre [tɔrdr] {63} *vt* : twist, wring — **se tordre** *vr* **1** : twist **2** : double up (with pain, laughter, etc.) — **tordu, -due** [tɔrdy] *adj* : twisted, warped

torero [tɔrero] *nm* : bullfighter

tornade [tɔrnad] *nf* : tornado

torpeur [tɔrpœr] *nf* : lethargy

torpille [tɔrpij] *nf* : torpedo

torrent [tɔrã] *nm* : torrent

torride [tɔrid] *adj* : torrid

torsade [tɔrsad] *nf* : twist, coil

torse [tɔrs] *nm* : torso, chest

tort [tɔr] *nm* **1** : wrong **2 à** ~ : wrongly **3 avoir** ~ : be wrong **4 faire du** ~ **à** : harm

torticolis [tɔrtikɔli] *nms & pl* : stiff neck

tortiller [tɔrtije] *vt* : twist — **se tortiller** *vr* : wriggle, squirm

tortue [tɔrty] *nf* : turtle, tortoise

tortueux, -euse [tɔrtɥø, -øz] *adj* **1** : winding (of a road) **2** : convoluted, tortuous

torture [tɔrtyr] *nf* : torture — **torturer** [tɔrtyre] *vt* : torture

tôt [to] *adv* **1** : soon **2** : early **3** ~ **ou tard** : sooner or later

total, -tale [tɔtal] *adj, mpl* **-taux** [tɔto] : total — **total** *nm, pl* **-taux** : total — **totaliser** [tɔtalize] *vt* : total — **totalitaire** [tɔtalitɛr] *adj* : totalitarian — **totalité** [tɔtalite] *nf* **1 en** ~ : completely **2 la** ~ **de** : all of

toucher [tuʃe] *vt* **1** : touch, handle **2** : hit, strike **3** CONCERNER : affect **4** ÉMOUVOIR : move, touch **5** : receive, earn (a salary) — *vi* ~ **à 1** : touch upon, bring up **2** : relate to — **se toucher** *vr* : touch each other — ~ *nm* **1** : sense of touch **2** SENSATION : feel — **touchant, -chante** [tuʃɑ̃, -ʃɑ̃t] *adj* ÉMOU-VANT : touching — **touche** [tuʃ] *nf* **1** : key (on a keyboard) **2** TRACE : trace, hint

touffe [tuf] *nf* : tuft, clump — **touffu, -fue** [tufy] *adj* : bushy

toujours [tuʒur] *adv* **1** : always, forever **2** ENCORE : still

toupet [tupɛ] *nm fam* : nerve, cheek

toupie [tupi] *nf* : top (toy)

tour[1] [tur] *nm* **1** : tour, circuit **2** : walk, ride **3** ~ **de taille** : girth (of a person) **4 atten-dre son** ~ : wait one's turn **5 jouer un** ~ **à qqn** : play a trick on s.o. **6** : lathe (in car-pentry)

tour[2] *nf* **1** : tower **2** : castle (in chess)

tourbe [turb] *nf* : peat

tourbillon [turbijɔ̃] *nm* **1** : whirlwind, whirl-pool **2** : whirl, bustle — **tourbillonner** [tur-bijɔne] *vi* : whirl, swirl

tourelle [turɛl] *nf* : turret

touriste [turist] *nmf* : tourist — **tourisme** [turism] *nm* : tourism — **touristique** [turis-tik] *adj* : tourist

tourment [turmɑ̃] *nm* : torment — **tour-menter** [turmɑ̃te] *vt* : torment — **se tour-menter** *vr* S'INQUIÉTER : worry

tourner [turne] *vt* **1** : turn, rotate **2** : stir (a sauce), toss (a salad) **3** : shoot, film — *vi* **1** : turn, revolve, spin **2** : run (of an engine, etc.) **3** : make a film **4** : go bad, sour (of milk) **5 bien** ~ : turn out well — **se tourner** *vr* : turn around — **tournant, -nante** [turnɑ̃, -nɑ̃t] *adj* : turning, revolving — **tournant** *nm* **1** : bend **2** : turning point — **tournée** [turne] *nf* **1** : tour **2** *fam* : round (of drinks)

tournesol [turnəsɔl] *nm* : sunflower

tournevis [turnəvis] *nms & pl* : screwdriver

tourniquet [turnikɛ] *nm* : turnstile

tournoi [turnwa] *nm* : tournament

tournoyer [turnwaje] {58} *vi* : whirl, spin

tournure [turnyr] *nf* **1** : turn (of events) **2** : expression

tourterelle [turtərɛl] *nf* : turtledove

tousser [tuse] *vi* : cough

tout [tu] (**toute(s)** [tut] *before feminine adjec-tives beginning with a consonant or an aspi-rate h*) *adv* **1** COMPLÈTEMENT : completely **2** : quite, very, all **3** ~ **à coup** : suddenly **4** ~ **à fait** : completely, entirely **5** ~ **de suite** : immediately — **tout, toute** *adj, pl* **tous, toutes 1** : all **2** : each, every **3 à tout âge** : at any age **4 à toute vitesse** : at full speed **5 tout le monde** : everyone, every-body — **tout** *nm* **1 le** ~ : the whole **2 pas du** ~ : not at all — **tout** *pron, pl* **tous, toutes 1** : all, everything **2** : anyone, every-one

toutefois [tutfwa] *adv* : however

toux [tu] *nfs & pl* : cough

toxicomane [tɔksikɔman] *nmf* : drug addict

toxique [tɔksik] *adj* : toxic, poisonous

trac [trak] *nm* : stage fright, jitters *pl*

tracasser [trakase] *vt* : worry, bother — **se tracasser** *vr* : worry, fret — **tracas** [traka] *nms & pl* **1** : worry **2** ~ *nmpl* ENNUIS : trou-bles, problems

tracer [trase] {6} *vt* **1** : trace **2** DESSINER : draw **3** ~ **le chemin** : pave the way — **trace** [tras] *nf* **1** : track, trail **2** : trace, ves-tige **3** ~**s de pas** : footprints **4 suivre les** ~**s de qqn** : follow in s.o.'s footsteps — **tracé** [trase] *nm* PLAN : plan, layout

trachée [traʃe] *nf* : trachea, windpipe

tract [trakt] *nm* : leaflet

tractations [traktasjɔ̃] *nfpl* : negotiations

tracteur [traktœr] *nm* : tractor

traction [traksjɔ̃] *nf* **1** : traction **2** ~ **avant** : front-wheel drive

tradition [tradisjɔ̃] *nf* : tradition — **tradition-nel, -nelle** [tradisjɔnɛl] *adj* : traditional

traduire [traduir] {49} *vt* : translate — **tra-ducteur, -trice** [tradyktœr, -tris] *n* : trans-lator — **traduction** [tradyksjɔ̃] *nf* : transla-tion

trafic [trafik] *nm* **1** : traffic **2** : (drug) traf-ficking — **trafiquant, -quante** [trafikɑ̃, -kɑ̃t] *n* : dealer, trafficker — **trafiquer** [trafike] *vt* : doctor, tamper with — *vi* : traf-fic, trade

tragédie [traʒedi] *nf* : tragedy — **tragique** [traʒik] *adj* : tragic

trahir [trair] *vt* : betray — **trahison** [traizɔ̃] *nf* **1** : betrayal **2** : treason

train [trɛ̃] *nm* **1** : (passenger) train **2** : pace, rate **3** : set, series **4 en** ~ **de** : in the process of **5** ~ **de vie** : lifestyle

traîner [trene] *vt* **1** : pull, drag **2** ~ **les pieds** : drag one's feet — *vi* **1** : drag **2** : dawdle, lag behind **3** : be lying around (of clothes, etc.) — **se traîner** *vr* : drag oneself, crawl — **traîne** [trɛn] *nf* **1** : train (of a dress) **2** *Can* : toboggan, sled — **traîneau** [treno] *nm, pl* **-neaux** : sled, sleigh — **traînée** [trene] *nf* **1** : streak **2** TRACE : trail **3** : drag (of an airplane, etc.)

train-train [trɛ̃trɛ̃] *nms & pl* ROUTINE : rou-tine

traire [trɛr] {40} *vt* : milk (an animal)

trait [trɛ] *nm* **1** : (character) trait **2** : stroke, line **3 avoir** ~ **à** : relate to **4 d'un** ~ : in one gulp **5** ~ **d'union** : hyphen **6** ~**s** *nmpl* : features

traite [trɛt] *nf* **1** : milking **2** d'une ~ : in one go **3** ~ **bancaire** : bank draft

traité [trete] *nm* **1** : treaty **2** : treatise

traiter [trete] *vt* **1** : treat **2** : process (data) **3** ~ **qqn de menteur** : call s.o. a liar — *vi* — **de** : deal with — **traitement** [trɛtmã] *nm* **1** : treatment **2** ~ **de texte** : word processing

traiteur [trɛtœr] *nm* : caterer

traître, -tresse [trɛtr, -trɛs] *n* : traitor — ~ *adj* : treacherous

trajectoire [traʒɛktwar] *nf* : trajectory

trajet [traʒɛ] *nm* **1** PARCOURS : route **2** VOYAGE : journey

trancher [trãʃe] *vt* **1** COUPER : cut **2** : resolve (an issue) — *vi* **1** : stand out **2** : come to a decision — **tranchant, -chante** [trãʃã, -ʃãt] *adj* : sharp, cutting — **tranchant** *nm* : cutting edge — **tranche** [trãʃ] *nf* **1** : slice (of bread) **2** PARTIE : portion, section **3** : edge (of a book) — **tranchée** *nf* : trench

tranquille [trãkil] *adj* **1** : calm, quiet **2** **tiens-toi** ~! : sit still! — **tranquillisant** [trãkilizã] *nm* : tranquilizer — **tranquilliser** [trãkilize] *vt* RASSURER : reassure — **tranquillité** [trãkilite] *nf* CALME : peacefulness, tranquillity

transaction [trãzaksjõ] *nf* : transaction

transcrire [trãskrir] {33} *vt* : transcribe — **transcription** [trãskripsjõ] *nf* : transcription

transe [trãs] *nf* : trance

transférer [trãsfere] *vt* : transfer — **transfert** [trãsfɛr] *nm* : transfer

transformer [trãsfɔrme] *vt* : transform, change — **se transformer** *vr* ~ **en** : turn into — **transformateur** [trãsfɔrmatœr] *nm* : transformer — **transformation** [trãsfɔrmasjõ] *nf* : transformation

transfusion [trãsfyzjõ] *nf* : transfusion

transgresser [trãsgrese] *vt* ENFREINDRE : infringe, violate

transir [trãzir] *vt* **1** : chill (to the bone) **2** : paralyse (with fear)

transistor [trãzistɔr] *nm* : transistor

transit [trãzit] *nm* : transit

transitif, -tive [trãzitif, -tiv] *adj* : transitive — **transition** [trãzisjõ] *nf* : transition — **transitoire** [trãzitwar] *adj* : transitory, transient

translucide [trãslysid] *adj* : translucent

transmettre [trãsmɛtr] {53} *vt* **1** : transmit (signals, data, etc.) **2** : pass on, convey **3** : broadcast (a show) — **transmission** [trãsmisjõ] *nf* **1** : transmission **2** : broadcasting

transparent, -rente [trãsparã, -rãt] *adj* : transparent — **transparence** [trãsparãs] *nf* : transparency

transpercer [trãspɛrse] {6} *vt* : pierce

transpirer [trãspire] *vi* : perspire — **transpiration** [trãspirasjõ] *nf* : perspiration

transplanter [trãsplãte] *vt* : transplant — **transplantation** [trãsplãtasjõ] *nm* : transplant

transporter [trãspɔrte] *vt* : transport, carry — **transport** [trãspɔr] *nm* : transport — **transporteur** [trãspɔrtœr] *nm* : carrier, transporter

transposer [trãspoze] *vt* : transpose

transversal, -sale [trãsvɛrsal] *adj, mpl* **-saux** [-so] : cross (of a beam)

trapèze [trapɛz] *nm* **1** : trapezoid **2** : trapeze

trappe [trap] *nf* **1** PIÈGE : trap **2** : trapdoor

trapu, -pue [trapy] *adj* : stocky, squat

traquer [trake] *vt* POURSUIVRE : track down

traumatiser [tromatize] *vt* : traumatize — **traumatisant, -sante** [tromatizã, -zãt] *adj* : traumatic — **traumatisme** [tromatism] *nm* : trauma

travailler [travaje] *vt* **1** : work **2** PRATIQUER : work on **3** TRACASSER : worry — *vi* : work — **travail** [travaj] *nm, pl* **-vaux** [travo] **1** : work **2** TÂCHE : task, job **3** EMPLOI : work, employment **4** **travaux** *nmpl* : works, work — **travailleur, -leuse** [travajœr, -jøz] *adj* : hardworking, industrious — ~ *n* : worker

travée [trave] *nf* **1** : row (of seats) **2** : span (of a bridge)

travers [travɛr] *nms & pl* **1** à ~ *or* au ~ : through **2** de ~ : askew, wrongly **3** en ~ : across, sideways — **traverser** [travɛrse] *vt* **1** : cross (the road, etc.) **2** : run through, pass through — **traversée** [travɛrse] *nf* : crossing

trébucher [trebyʃe] *vi* : stumble

trèfle [trɛfl] *nm* **1** : clover, shamrock **2** : clubs *pl* (in playing cards)

treillis [trɛji] *nms & pl* : trellis, lattice

treize [trɛz] *adj* **1** : thirteen **2** : thirteenth (in dates) — ~ *nms & pl* : thirteen — **treizième** [trɛzjɛm] *adj & nmf & nm* : thirteenth

trembler [trãble] *vi* **1** : shake, tremble **2** : quiver (of the voice) — **tremblement** [trãbləmã] *nm* **1** : trembling **2** FRISSON : shiver **3** ~ **de terre** : earthquake — **trembloter** [trãblɔte] *vi* : quaver

trémousser [tremuse] *v* **se trémousser** *vr* : wriggle around

tremper [trãpe] *vt* **1** : soak **2** : dip, dunk — **trempe** [trãp] *nf* : caliber, quality — **trempé, -pée** [trãpe] *adj* : soaked

tremplin [trãplɛ̃] *nm* **1** : springboard **2** *or* ~ **à ski** : ski jump

trente [trãt] *adj* **1** : thirty **2** : thirtieth (in dates) — ~ *nms & pl* : thirty — **trentième** [trãtjɛm] *adj & nmf & nm* : thirtieth

trépied [trepje] *nm* : tripod

trépigner [trepiɲe] *vi* : stamp one's feet

très [trɛ] *adv* : very

trésor [trezɔr] *nm* : treasure

tressaillir [tresajir] {93}*vi* **1** : start (with surprise, etc.), wince (with pain) **2** TREMBLER : quiver, tremble — **tressaillement** [tresajmɑ̃] *nm* : start, wince

tresse [trɛs] *nf* : braid, plait — **tresser** [trese] *vt* **1** : braid, plait **2** : weave (a basket, etc.)

treuil [trœj] *nm* : winch

trêve [trɛv] *nf* **1** : truce **2** : respite

tri [tri] *nm* : sorting (out)

triangle [trijɑ̃gl] *nm* : triangle — **triangulaire** [trijɑ̃gylɛr] *adj* : triangular

tribal, -bale [tribal] *adj, mpl* **-baux** [tribo] : tribal

tribord [tribɔr] *nm* : starboard

tribu [triby] *nf* : tribe

tribulations [tribylasjɔ̃] *nfpl* : tribulations

tribunal [tribynal] *nm, pl* **-naux** [-no] : court

tribune [tribyn] *nf* **1** : gallery, grandstand **2** : rostrum, platform **3** DÉBAT : forum

tribut [triby] *nm* : tribute

tributaire [tribytɛr] *adj* **être ～ de** : be dependent on

tricher [triʃe] *vi* : cheat — **tricherie** [triʃri] *nf* : cheating — **tricheur, -cheuse** [triʃœr, -ʃøz] *n* : cheat

tricoter [trikɔte] *v* : knit — **tricot** [triko] *nm* **1** : knitting **2** : knitted fabric **3** CHANDAIL : sweater

tricycle [trisikl] *nm* : tricycle

trier [trije] {96} *vt* **1** : sort (out) **2** CHOISIR : select

trimbaler *or* **trimballer** [trɛ̃bale] *vt fam* : cart around

trimestre [trimɛstr] *nm* **1** : quarter (in economics, etc.) **2** : term (in school) — **trimestriel, -trielle** [trimɛstrijɛl] *adj* : quarterly

tringle [trɛ̃gl] *nf* : rod

trinité [trinite] *nf* : trinity

trinquer [trɛ̃ke] *vi* : clink glasses, drink (a toast)

trio [trijo] *nm* : trio

triomphe [trijɔ̃f] *nm* : triumph — **triompher** [trijɔ̃fe] *vi* : triumph

tripes [trip] *nfpl* **1** : tripe **2** *fam* : guts

triple [tripl] *adj & nm* : triple, treble — **tripler** [triple] *v* : triple — **triplés, -plées** [triple] *npl* : triplets

tripoter [tripɔte] *vt* : fiddle with

trique [trik] *nf* : cudgel

triste [trist] *adj* **1** : sad **2** : dismal **3** LAMENTABLE : deplorable, sorry — **tristesse** [tristɛs] *nf* : sadness, gloominess

triton [tritɔ̃] *nm* : newt

troc [trɔk] *nm* : swap

trognon [trɔɲɔ̃] *nm* : core (of an apple, etc.)

trois [trwa] *adj* **1** : three **2** : third (in dates)

— **～** *nms & pl* : three — **troisième** [trwazjɛm] *adj & nmf* : third

trombe [trɔ̃b] *nf* **1** : waterspout **2** **～s d'eau** : downpour

trombone [trɔ̃bɔn] *nm* **1** : trombone **2** : paper clip

trompe [trɔ̃p] *nf* **1** : horn **2** : trunk (of an elephant)

tromper [trɔ̃pe] *vt* **1** DUPER : deceive **2** : be unfaithful to (one's spouse) — **se tromper** *vr* : make a mistake — **tromperie** [trɔ̃pri] *nf* : deception, deceit

trompette [trɔ̃pɛt] *nf* : trumpet

trompeur, -peuse [trɔ̃pœr, -pøz] *adj* **1** : deceitful **2** : misleading

tronc [trɔ̃] *nm* **1** : trunk (of a tree) **2** TORSE : torso

tronçon [trɔ̃sɔ̃] *nm* : section — **tronçonneuse** [trɔ̃sɔnøz] *nf* : chain saw

trône [tron] *nm* : throne

tronquer [trɔ̃ke] *vt* : truncate

trop [tro] *adv* **1** : too **2** **～ de** : too many, too much **3** **de ～** *or* **en ～** : too many, extra

trophée [trɔfe] *nm* : trophy

tropique [trɔpik] *nm* **1** : tropic **2** **～s** *nmpl* : tropics — **tropical, -cale** [trɔpikal] *adj, mpl* **-caux** [-ko] : tropical

trop–plein [trɔplɛ̃] *nm, pl* **trop–pleins** **1** : overflow **2** SURPLUS : excess, surplus

troquer [trɔke] *vt* : trade, barter

trotter [trɔte] *vi* : trot

trotteuse [trɔtøz] *nf* : second hand (of a watch)

trottiner [trɔtine] *vi* : scurry along

trottinette [trɔtinɛt] *nf* : scooter

trottoir [trɔtwar] *nm* : sidewalk

trou [tru] *nm* **1** : hole **2** : gap (of time) **3** **～ de mémoire** : memory lapse **4** **～ de (la) serrure** : keyhole

troubler [truble] *vt* **1** : disturb **2** BROUILLER : blur, cloud **3** INQUIÉTER : trouble — **trouble** [trubl] *adj* **1** : cloudy **2** FLOU : blurred, unclear — **～** *nm* **1** : confusion **2** : trouble **3** **～s** *nmpl* : disorder (in medicine) **4** **～s** *nmpl* : unrest

trouer [true] *vt* : make a hole in, pierce — **trouée** [true] *nf* : gap

trouille [truj] *nf fam* : fear, fright

troupe [trup] *nf* **1** : troop **2** **～ de théâtre** : theater company

troupeau [trupo] *nm, pl* **-peaux** : herd, flock

trousse [trus] *nf* **1** : kit, case **2** **aux ～s de** : on the heels of

trousseau [truso] *nm, pl* **-seaux** **1** : trousseau **2** **～ de clefs** : bunch of keys

trouver [truve] *vt* **1** : find **2** ESTIMER : think — **se trouver** *vr* **1** : be (found) **2** : find oneself **3** SE SENTIR : feel — *v impers* **il se**

trouve que : it turns out that — **trouvaille** [truvaj] *nf* DÉCOUVERTE : find
truand [tryɑ̃] *nm* : gangster, crook
truc [tryk] *nm* **1** : trick **2** *fam* MACHIN : thing, thingamajig
truelle [tryɛl] *nf* : trowel
truffe [tryf] *nf* : truffle
truite [truit] *nf* : trout
truquer [tryke] *vt* : fix, rig
trust [trœst] *nm* : trust, cartel
tsar [tsar, dzar] *nm* : czar
t–shirt [tiʃœrt] *nm* → **tee–shirt**
tu [ty] *pron* : you
tuba [tyba] *nm* **1** : tuba **2** : snorkel
tube [tyb] *nm* **1** : tube **2** *fam* : hit (song)
tuberculose [tybɛrkyloz] *nf* : tuberculosis
tuer [tɥe] *vt* **1** : kill **2** ÉPUISER : exhaust — **se tuer** *vr* **1** : be killed, die **2** : kill oneself — **tuerie** [tyri] *nf* CARNAGE : slaughter — **tueur, tueuse** [tɥœr, tɥøz] *n* : killer
tue–tête [tytɛt] **à ~** *adv phr* : at the top of one's lungs
tuile [tɥil] *nf* **1** : tile **2** *fam* : bad luck
tulipe [tylip] *nf* : tulip
tumeur [tymœr] *nf* : tumor
tumulte [tymylt] *nm* : tumult, commotion — **tumultueux, -tueuse** [tymyltɥø, -tɥøz] *adj* : stormy, turbulent

tunique [tynik] *nf* : tunic
tunnel [tynɛl] *nm* : tunnel
tuque [tyk] *nf Can* : stocking cap
turban [tyrbɑ̃] *nm* : turban
turbine [tyrbin] *nf* : turbine
turbulence [tyrbylɑ̃s] *nf* : turbulence — **turbulent, -lente** [tyrbylɑ̃, -lɑ̃t] *adj* **1** : unruly **2** : turbulent
turc, turque [tyrk] *adj* : Turkish — **turc** *nm* : Turkish (language)
turquoise [tyrkwaz] *adj* : turquoise
tutelle [tytɛl] *nf* **1** : guardianship **2** : care, protection
tuteur, -trice [tytœr, -tris] *n* **1** : guardian **2** : tutor — **tuteur** *nm* : stake
tutoyer [tytwaje] {58} *vt* : address someone as *tu*
tuyau [tɥijo] *nm, pl* **tuyaux 1** : pipe, tube **2** *fam* : tip, advice — **tuyauterie** [tɥijotri] *nf* : pipes *pl*, plumbing
tympan [tɛ̃pɑ̃] *nm* : eardrum
type [tip] *nm* **1** : type, kind **2** : example, model **3** : (physical) type **4** *fam* : guy, fellow
typhon [tifɔ̃] *nm* : typhoon
typique [tipik] *adj* : typical
tyran [tirɑ̃] *nm* : tyrant — **tyrannie** [tirani] *nf* : tyranny

U

u [y] *nm* : u, 21st letter of the alphabet
ulcère [ylsɛr] *nm* : ulcer
ultérieur, -rieure [ylterjœr] *adj* : later, subsequent — **ultérieurement** [ylterjœrmɑ̃] *adv* : subsequently
ultimatum [yltimatɔm] *nm* : ultimatum — **ultime** [yltim] *adj* : ultimate, final
ultraviolet, -lette [yltravjolɛ, -lɛt] *adj* : ultraviolet
un, une [œ̃ (œn *before a vowel or mute* h), yn] *adj* : a, an, one — **~** *n & pron* **1** : one **2 une par une** : one by one — **~** *art, pl* **des 1** (*used in the singular*) : a, an **2** (*used in the plural*) : some — **un** *nm* : (number) one
unanime [ynanim] *adj* : unanimous — **unanimité** [ynanimite] *nf* : unanimity
uni, -nie [yni] *adj* **1** : united **2** LISSE : smooth **3** : solid (of a color) **4** : close-knit (of a family)
unifier [ynifje] {96} *vt* : unite, unify — **unification** [ynifikasjɔ̃] *nf* : unification
uniforme [ynifɔrm] *adj* : uniform, even —

~ *nm* : uniform — **uniformiser** *vt* : make uniform, standardize — **uniformité** [yniformite] *nf* : uniformity
unilatéral, -rale [ynilateral] *adj, pl* **-raux** [-ro] : unilateral
union [ynjɔ̃] *nf* : union
unique [ynik] *adj* **1** : unique **2 enfant ~** : only child **3 sens ~** : one-way — **uniquement** [ynikmɑ̃] *adv* : only, solely
unir [ynir] *vt* **1** : unite, connect **2** COMBINER : combine — **s'unir** *vr* : unite
unisson [ynisɔ̃] *nm* : unison
unité [ynite] *nf* **1** : unity **2** : unit
univers [ynivɛr] *nm* : universe — **universel, -selle** [ynivɛrsɛl] *adj* : universal
universitaire [ynivɛrsitɛr] *adj* : university, academic — **université** [yniversite] *nf* : university
uranium [yranjɔm] *nm* : uranium
Uranus [yranys] *nm* : Uranus
urbain, -baine [yrbɛ̃, -bɛn] *adj* : urban, city — **urbanisme** [yrbanism] *nm* : city planning

urgence [yrʒɑ̃s] *nf* **1** : urgency **2** : emergency **3 d'~** : urgently, immediately — **urgent, -gente** [yrʒɑ̃, -ʒɑ̃t] *adj* : urgent

urine [yrin] *nf* : urine — **uriner** [yrine] *vi* : urinate — **urinoir** [yrinwar] *nm* : urinal

urne [yrn] *nf* **1** : urn **2** : ballot box

urticaire [yrtikɛr] *nf* : hives

usage [yzaʒ] *nm* **1** : use **2** : usage (of a word) **3** COUTUME : habit, custom — **usagé, -gée** [yzaʒe] *adj* **1** : worn **2** : used, secondhand — **usager** [yzaʒe] *nm* : user

user [yze] *vt* **1** CONSOMMER : use **2** : wear out, to use up — *vi* **1 ~ de** : exercise (one's rights, etc.) **2 ~ de** : make use of — **usé, -sée** [yze] *adj* **1** : worn-out **2** : hackneyed, trite

usine [yzin] *nf* : factory

usité, -tée [yzite] *adj* : commonly used

ustensile [ystɑ̃sil] *nm* : utensil

usuel, -suelle [yzɥɛl] *adj* : common, usual — **usuellement** [yzɥɛlmɑ̃] *adv* : usually, ordinarily

usure [yzyr] *nm* : wear (and tear)

usurper [yzyrpe] *vt* : usurp

utérus [yterus] *nms & pl* : uterus

utile [ytil] *adj* : useful — **utilisable** [ytilizabl] *adj* : usable — **utiliser** [ytilize] *vt* : use — **utilisateur, -trice** [ytilizatœr, -tris] *n* : user — **utilisation** [ytilizasjɔ̃] *nf* : use — **utilité** [ytilite] *nf* : usefulness

utopie [ytɔpi] *nf* : utopia — **utopique** [ytɔpik] *adj* : utopian

V

v·[ve] *nm* : v, 22d letter of the alphabet

va [va], *etc.* → **aller**

vacances [vakɑ̃s] *nfpl* : vacation — **vacancier, -cière** [vakɑ̃sje, -sjɛr] *n* : vacationer — **vacant, -cante** [vakɑ̃, -kɑ̃t] *adj* : vacant

vacarme [vakarm] *nm* : racket, din

vaccin [vaksɛ̃] *nm* : vaccine — **vacciner** [vaksine] *vt* : vaccinate — **vaccination** [vaksinasjɔ̃] *nf* : vaccination

vache [vaʃ] *nf* : cow — **~** *adj fam* : mean, nasty — **vachement** [vaʃmɑ̃] *adv fam* : really, very — **vacherie** [vaʃri] *nf fam* **1** : nastiness **2** : dirty trick

vaciller [vasije] *vi* **1** : stagger, sway **2** : flicker (of a light) **3** : falter, fail — **vacillant, -lante** [vasijɑ̃, -jɑ̃t] *adj* **1** : unsteady, shaky **2** : wavering, faltering — **vacillement** [vasijmɑ̃] *nm* **1** : flicker **2** : faltering

va–et–vient [vaevjɛ̃] *nms & pl* **1** : comings and goings **2** : to-and-fro motion

vagabond, -bonde [vagabɔ̃, -bɔ̃d] *n* : vagrant, tramp — **vagabonder** [vagabɔ̃de] *vi* : roam, wander

vagin [vaʒɛ̃] *nm* : vagina

vague[1] [vag] *adj* : vague, indistinct — **~** *nm* : vagueness — **vaguement** [vagmɑ̃] *adv* : vaguely, slightly

vague[2] *nf* : wave

vaillant, -lante [vajɑ̃, -jɑ̃t] *adj* **1** : valiant, brave **2** : healthy, robust — **vaillamment** [vajamɑ̃] *adv* : courageously

vain, vaine [vɛ̃, vɛn] *adj* **1** : vain, futile **2 en ~** : in vain

vaincre [vɛ̃kr] {94} *vt* **1** BATTRE : defeat **2**

SURMONTER : overcome — **vaincu, -cue** [vɛ̃ky] *adj* : defeated — **vainqueur** [vɛ̃kœr] *nm* : victor, winner

vaisseau [vɛso] *nm, pl* **-seaux 1** : (blood) vessel **2** : vessel, ship **3 ~ spatial** : spaceship

vaisselle [vɛsɛl] *nf* : crockery, dishes *pl*

valable [valabl] *adj* **1** VALIDE : valid **2** BON : good, worthwhile

valet [valɛ] *nm* **1** : servant **2** : jack (in playing cards)

valeur [valœr] *nf* **1** : value **2** MÉRITE : merit, worth **3 objets de ~** : valuables **4 ~s** *nfpl* : stocks, securities

valide [valid] *adj* : valid — **valider** [valide] *vt* : validate — **validité** [validite] *nf* : validity

valise [valiz] *nf* : suitcase

vallée [vale] *nf* : valley — **vallon** [valɔ̃] *nm* : small valley — **vallonné, -née** [valɔne] *adj* : hilly

valoir [valwar] {95} *vi* **1** : have a (certain) cost **2** : be worth **3** : apply, be valid **4 ça vaut combien?** : how much is it worth? **5 faire ~** : point out, assert — *vt* **1** PROCURER : earn, bring (to) **2 ~ la peine** : be worth the trouble — *v impers* **il vaut mieux** : it's better (to) — **se valoir** *vr* : be equivalent

valoriser [valɔrize] *vt* : increase the value of

valse [vals] *nf* : waltz — **valser** [valse] *vi* : waltz

valve [valv] *nf* : valve

vampire [vɑ̃pir] *nm* : vampire

vandale [vɑ̃dal] *nmf* : vandal — **vandalisme** [vɑ̃dalism] *nm* : vandalism

vanille [vanij] *nf* : vanilla

vanité [vanite] *nf* : vanity — **vaniteux, -teuse** [vanitø, -tøz] *adj* : conceited, vain

vanne [van] *nf* **1** : floodgate **2** *fam* : dig, gibe

vanter [vɑ̃te] *vt* : vaunt, praise — **se vanter** *vr* **1** : boast **2** ~ **de** : pride oneself on — **vantard, -tarde** [vɑ̃tar, -tard] *adj* : boastful — ~ *n* : braggart — **vantardise** [vɑ̃tardiz] *nf* : boast

va-nu-pieds [vanypje] *nmfs & pl* : beggar

vapeur [vapœr] *nf* **1** : steam **2** ~**s** *nfpl* : fumes

vaporiser [vaporize] *vt* : spray — **vaporisateur** [vaporizatœr] *nm* : spray, atomizer

vaquer [vake] *vi* ~ **à** : attend to, see to

varappe [varap] *nf* : rock climbing

variable [varjabl] *adj* : variable, changeable — **variante** [varjɑ̃t] *nf* : variant — **variation** [varjasjɔ̃] *nf* : variation

varice [varis] *nf* : varicose vein

varicelle [varisɛl] *nf* : chicken pox

varier [varje] {96} *v* : vary — **varié, -riée** [varje] *adj* **1** : varied, varying **2** : various, diverse — **variété** [varjete] *nf* : variety

variole [varjɔl] *nf* : smallpox

vase[1] [vaz] *nm* : vase

vase[2] *nf* BOUE : mud, silt — **vaseux, -seuse** [vazø, -zøz] *adj* BOUEUX : muddy

vaste [vast] *adj* : vast, immense

vaurien, -rienne [vorjɛ̃, -rjɛn] *n* : good-for-nothing

vautour [votur] *nm* : vulture

vautrer [votre] *v* **se vautrer** *vr* ~ **dans** : wallow in

veau [vo] *nm, pl* **veaux 1** : calf **2** : veal

vécu [veky] *pp* → **vivre** — **vécu, -cue** [veky] *adj* : real, true

vedette [vədɛt] *nf* **1** : star, celebrity **2 mettre en** ~ : put in the spotlight, feature

végétal, -tale [veʒetal] *adj, mpl* **-taux** : vegetable, plant — **végétal** *nm* : vegetable, plant — **végétarien, -rienne** [veʒetarjɛ̃, -rjɛn] *adj & n* : vegetarian — **végéter** [veʒete] {87} *vi* : vegetate — **végétation** [veʒetasjɔ̃] *nf* : vegetation

véhément, -mente [veemɑ̃, -mɑ̃t] *adj* : vehement — **véhémence** [veemɑ̃s] *nf* : vehemence

véhicule [veikyl] *nm* : vehicle

veiller [veje] *vt* : sit up with, watch over — *vi* **1** : stay awake **2** : keep watch **3** : be vigilant **4** ~ **à** : see to — **veille** [vɛj] *nf* **1** : day before, eve **2** : watch, vigil — **veillée** [veje] *nf* **1** SOIRÉE : evening **2** ~ **funèbre** : wake — **veilleur, -leuse** [vejœr, -jøz] *n* **1** : lookout, sentry **2** ~ **de nuit** : night watchman — **veilleuse** *nf* **1** : night-light **2** : pilot light

veine [vɛn] *nf* **1** : vein **2** *fam* : luck

vélo [velo] *nm* : bike, bicycle

vélomoteur [velomotœr] *nm* : moped

velours [vəlur] *nm* **1** : velvet, velour **2** ~ **côtelé** : corduroy — **velouté, -tée** [vəlute] *adj* : velvety, smooth

velu, -lue [vəly] *adj* : hairy

venaison [vənɛzɔ̃] *nf* : venison

vendange [vɑ̃dɑ̃ʒ] *nf* : grape harvest

vendre [vɑ̃dr] {63} *vt* **1** : sell **2 à** ~ : for sale — **se vendre** : sell — **vendeur, -deuse** [vɑ̃dœr, -døz] *n* : salesperson

vendredi [vɑ̃drədi] *nm* : Friday

vénéneux, -neuse [venenø, -nøz] *adj* : poisonous

vénérer [venere] {87} *vt* : venerate — **vénérable** [venerabl] *adj* : venerable

vénérien, -rienne [venerjɛ̃, -rjɛn] *adj* : venereal

venger [vɑ̃ʒe] {17} *vt* : avenge — **se venger** *vr* : take revenge — **vengeance** [vɑ̃ʒɑ̃s] *nf* : vengeance, revenge — **vengeur, -geresse** [vɑ̃ʒœr, -ʒrɛs] *adj* : vengeful — ~ *n* : avenger

venin [vənɛ̃] *nm* : venom, poison — **venimeux, -meuse** [vənimø, -møz] *adj* : poisonous

venir [vənir] {92} *vi* **1** : come **2** ~ **de** : come from **3 en** ~ **à** : come to (a conclusion, etc.) **4 faire** ~ : send for — *v aux* **1** : come and, come to **2** ~ **de** : have just

vent [vɑ̃] *nm* **1** : wind **2 il y a du** ~ *or* **il fait du** ~ : it's windy — **venteux, -teuse** [vɑ̃tø, -tøz] *adj* : windy

vente [vɑ̃t] *nf* **1** : sale, selling **2 en** ~ : for sale

ventiler [vɑ̃tile] *vt* : ventilate — **ventilateur** [vɑ̃tilatœr] *nm* : (electric) fan, ventilator — **ventilation** [vɑ̃tilasjɔ̃] *nf* : ventilation

ventouse [vɑ̃tuz] *nf* **1** : suction cup **2** : plunger

ventre [vɑ̃tr] *nm* **1** : stomach, belly **2** : womb **3 avoir mal au** ~ : have a stomachache

ventriloque [vɑ̃trilɔk] *nmf* : ventriloquist

venu [vəny] *pp* → **venir** — **venu, -nue** [vəny] *adj* **1 bien venu** : timely **2 mal venu** : ill-advised, unwelcome — **venue** *nf* : coming, arrival

Vénus [venys] *nf* : Venus (planet)

ver [vɛr] *nm* **1** : worm **2** ~ **de terre** : earthworm

véranda [verɑ̃da] *nf* : veranda, porch

verbe [vɛrb] *nm* : verb — **verbal, -bale** [vɛrbal] *adj, mpl* **-baux** [-bo] : verbal

verdeur [vɛrdœr] *nf* : vigor, vitality

verdict [vɛrdikt] *nm* : verdict

verdir [vɛrdir] *v* : turn green — **verdoyant, -doyante** [vɛrdwajɑ̃, -dwajɑ̃t] *adj* : green, verdant — **verdure** [vɛrdyr] *nf* : greenery

verge [vɛrʒ] *nf* : rod, stick

verger [vɛrʒe] *nm* : orchard

verglacé, -cée [vɛrglase] *adj* : icy — **verglas** [vɛrgla] *nm* : black ice

vergogne [vɛrgɔɲ] *nf* **sans ~** : shamelessly

véridique [veridik] *adj* : truthful

vérifier [verifje] {96} *vt* : verify, check — **vérification** [verifikasjɔ̃] *nf* : verification, check

vérité [verite] *nf* **1** : truth **2 en ~** : in fact — **véritable** [veritabl] *adj* **1** RÉEL : true, actual **2** AUTHENTIQUE : genuine **3** (*used as an intensive*) : real — **véritablement** [-tablamɑ̃] *adv* : actually, really

vermine [vɛrmin] *nf* : vermin

vernis [vɛrni] *nms & pl* **1** : varnish **2** : glaze (on pottery) **3** : veneer, facade **4 ~ à ongles** : nail polish — **vernir** [vɛrnir] *vt* : varnish — **vernissage** [vɛrnisaʒ] *nm* **1** : varnishing **2** : opening (of an art exhibition) — **vernisser** [vɛrnise] *vt* : glaze (ceramics)

verre [vɛr] *nm* **1** : glass **2** : (drinking) glass **3 ~s** *nmpl* : eyeglasses, lenses **4 prendre un ~** : have a drink — **verrerie** [vɛrri] *nf* : glassware — **verrière** [vɛrjɛr] *nf* **1** : glass roof **2** : glass wall

verrou [vɛru] *nm* : bolt — **verrouiller** [vɛruje] *vt* : bolt, lock

verrue [vɛry] *nf* : wart

vers[1] [vɛr] *nms & pl* : line, verse (of poetry)

vers[2] *prep* **1** : toward, towards **2** : about, around, near

versant [vɛrsɑ̃] *nm* : slope, side (of a hill, etc.)

versatile [vɛrsatil] *adj* : fickle

verser [vɛrse] *vt* **1** : pour, serve **2** PAYER : pay **3** RÉPANDRE : shed (tears, etc.) — *vi* **1** : overturn **2 ~ dans** : lapse into — **verse** [vɛrs] *nf* **pleuvoir à ~** : pour (rain) — **versé, -sée** [vɛrse] *adj* **~ dans** : (well-) versed in — **versement** [vɛrsamɑ̃] *nm* **1** : payment **2** : installment

verset [vɛrse] *nm* : verse

version [vɛrsjɔ̃] *nf* : version

verso [vɛrso] *nm* : back (of a page)

vert, verte [vɛr, vɛrt] *adj* **1** : green **2** : unripe **3** GAILLARD : sprightly, vigorous — **vert** *nm* : green

vertèbre [vɛrtɛbr] *nf* : vertebra — **vertébral, -brale** [vɛrtebral] *adj, mpl* **-braux** [-bro] : vertebral

vertement [vɛrtamɑ̃] *adv* : sharply, severely

vertical, -cale [vɛrtikal] *adj, mpl* **-caux** [-ko] : vertical — **verticale** *nf* **à la ~** : vertically — **verticalement** [-kalmɑ̃] *adv* : vertically

vertige [vɛrtiʒ] *nm* : dizziness — **vertigineux, -neuse** [vɛrtiʒinø, -nøz] *adj* **1** : dizzy **2** : breathtaking

vertu [vɛrty] *nf* **1** : virtue **2 en ~ de** : by virtue of — **vertueux, -tueuse** [vɛrtɥø, -tɥøz] *adj* : virtuous

verve [vɛrv] *nf* : humor, wit

vésicule [vezikyl] *nf* **~ biliaire** : gallbladder

vessie [vesi] *nf* : bladder

veste [vɛst] *nf* **1** : jacket **2** *Can* : vest

vestiaire [vɛstjɛr] *nm* : locker room

vestibule [vɛstibyl] *nm* : hall

vestige [vɛstiʒ] *nm* **1** : vestige **2** : relic, remains

veston [vɛstɔ̃] *nm* : (man's) jacket

vêtement [vɛtmɑ̃] *nm* **1** : garment, article of clothing **2 ~s** *nmpl* : clothes, clothing

vétéran [veterɑ̃] *nm* : veteran

vétérinaire [veterinɛr] *nmf* : veterinarian

vêtir [vetir] {97} *vt* HABILLER : dress — **se vêtir** *vr* : get dressed — **vêtu, -tue** [vɛty] *adj* : dressed

veto [veto] *nms & pl* : veto

veuf, veuve [vœf, vœv] *adj* : widowed — *n* : widower *m*, widow *f*

vexer [vɛkse] *vt* : vex, upset — **se vexer** *vr* : take offense — **vexant, -ante** [vɛksɑ̃, -sɑ̃t] *adj* : hurtful

via [vja] *prep* : via

viable [vjabl] *adj* : viable

viaduc [vjadyk] *nm* : viaduct

viande [vjɑ̃d] *nf* **1** : meat **2 ~ hachée** : hamburger

vibrer [vibre] *vi* : vibrate — **vibrant, -brante** [vibrɑ̃, -brɑ̃t] *adj* : vibrant — **vibration** [vibrɑsjɔ̃] *nf* : vibration

vicaire [vikɛr] *nm* : vicar, curate

vice [vis] *nm* **1** DÉBAUCHE : vice **2** DÉFAUT : defect

vice–président, -dente [visprezidɑ̃, -dɑ̃t] *n* : vice president

vice versa *or* **vice–versa** [vis(e)vɛrsa] *adv* : vice versa

vicier [visje] {96} *vt* : pollute, taint

vicieux, -cieuse [visjø, -sjøz] *adj* : perverse, depraved

victime [viktim] *nf* : victim

victoire [viktwar] *nf* : victory — **victorieux, -rieuse** [viktɔrjø, -rjøz] *adj* : victorious

vidange [vidɑ̃ʒ] *nf* **1** : emptying, draining **2** : oil change — **vidanger** [vidɑ̃ʒe] {17} *vt* : empty, drain

vide [vid] *adj* : empty — **~** *nm* **1** : emptiness, void **2** LACUNE : gap

vidéo [video] *adj s & pl* : video — **~** *nf* : video

vidéocassette [videokasɛt] *nf* : videocassette, videotape

vider [vide] *vt* **1** : empty **2** : vacate (the premises) **3** : clean (a fowl), gut (a fish) — **videur** [vidœr] *nm* : bouncer

vie [vi] *nf* **1** : life **2** : lifetime **3** : livelihood, living **4 à ~** : for life **5 être en ~** : be alive **6 jamais de la ~!** : never!

vieil → **vieux**

viellard [vjɛjar] *nm* : old man

vieille → **vieux**

vieillir [vjejir] *vt* : make (someone) old, age — *vi* **1** : grow old, age **2** : become outdated — **vieillesse** [vjejɛs] *nf* : old age

vierge [vjɛrʒ] *adj* **1** : virgin **2** : empty, blank (of a tape, etc.) — ~ *nf* : virgin

vieux [vjø] (**vieil** [vjɛj] *before a vowel or mute h*), **vieille** [vjɛj] *adj, mpl* **vieux 1** : old **2 vieille fille** : old maid **3 vieux jeu** : old-fashioned — ~ *n* : old man *m*, old woman *f*

vif, vive [vif, viv] *adj* **1** : lively, animated **2** AIGU : sharp, keen **3** : vivid (of a color) **4** : brisk, bracing (of the wind) — **vif** *nm* **1** à ~ : open, exposed **2 le ~ du sujet** : the heart of the matter **3 sur le** ~ : on the spot, from life

vigilant, -lante [viʒilɑ̃, -lɑ̃t] *adj* : vigilant — **vigilance** [viʒilɑ̃s] *nf* : vigilance

vigne [viɲ] *nf* **1** : grapevine **2** : vineyard — **vigneron, -ronne** [viɲrɔ̃, -rɔn] *n* : wine-grower

vignette [viɲɛt] *nf* : label, sticker

vignoble [viɲɔbl] *nm* : vineyard

vigueur [vigœr] *nf* **1** : vigor **2 en** ~ : in force — **vigoureux, -reuse** [vigurø, -røz] *adj* **1** : vigorous, sturdy **2** : forceful, energetic

VIH [veiaʃ] *nm* (*Virus de l'Immunodéficience Humaine*) : HIV

vil, vile [vil] *adj* : vile, base

vilain, -laine [vilɛ̃, -lɛn] *adj* **1** LAID : ugly **2** MÉCHANT : naughty

villa [vila] *nf* : villa

village [vilaʒ] *nm* : village — **villageois, -geoise** [vilaʒwa, -ʒwaz] *n* : villager

ville [vil] *nf* **1** : city, town **2 en** ~ : downtown

villégiature [vileʒjatyr] *nf* **1** : vacation **2** *or* **lieu de** ~ : resort

vin [vɛ̃] *nm* : wine

vinaigre [vinɛgr] *nm* : vinegar — **vinaigrette** [vinɛgrɛt] *nf* : vinaigrette

vindicatif, -tive [vɛ̃dikatif, -tiv] *adj* : vindictive

vingt [vɛ̃] (**vɛ̃t** *before a vowel, mute h, and the numbers 22-29*)] *adj* **1** : twenty **2** : twentieth (in dates) — ~ *nms & pl* : twenty — **vingtaine** [vɛ̃tɛn] *nf* : about twenty — **vingtième** [vɛ̃tjɛm] *adj & nmf & nm* : twentieth

vinicole [vinikɔl] *adj* : wine, wine-growing

vinyle [vinil] *nm* : vinyl

viol [vjɔl] *nm* : rape — **violation** [vjɔlasjɔ̃] *nf* : violation

violent, -lente [vjɔlɑ̃, -lɑ̃t] *adj* : violent — **violemment** [vjɔlamɑ̃] *adv* : violently — **violence** [vjɔlɑ̃s] *nf* : violence

violer [vjɔle] *vt* **1** : rape **2** : violate, break (a law, etc.)

violet, -lette [vjɔlɛ, -lɛt] *adj* : purple, violet — **violet** *nm* : purple, violet — **violette** *nf* : violet (flower)

violon [vjɔlɔ̃] *nm* : violin — **violoncelle** [vjɔlɔ̃sɛl] *nm* : cello — **violoniste** [vjɔlɔnist] *nmf* : violinist

vipère [vipɛr] *nf* : adder, viper

virer [vire] *vt* **1** : transfer (funds) **2** *fam* : fire, expel — *vi* **1** : veer, turn **2** : change color — **virage** [viraʒ] *nm* **1** COURBE : bend, turn **2** : change, shift (in direction) — **virée** [vire] *nf fam* : outing, trip — **virement** [virmɑ̃] *nm* : (bank) transfer

virevolter [virvɔlte] *vi* : twirl

virginité [virʒinite] *nf* : virginity

virgule [virgyl] *nf* **1** : comma **2** : (decimal) point

viril, -rile [viril] *adj* : virile, manly — **virilité** [virilite] *nf* : virility

virtuel, -tuelle [virtɥɛl] *adj* : virtual

virtuose [virtɥoz] *nmf* : virtuoso

virulent, -lente [virylɑ̃, -lɑ̃t] *adj* : virulent

virus [virys] *nms & pl* : virus

vis [vi] *nfs & pl* : screw

visa [viza] *nm* : visa

visage [vizaʒ] *nm* : face

vis-à-vis [vizavi] *adv* ~ **de 1** : opposite, facing **2** : towards, with respect to — ~ *nms & pl* **en** ~ : facing each other

viscères [visɛr] *nmpl* : innards

viser [vize] *vt* : aim for, aim at — *vi* **1** : aim **2** ~ à : aim at, intend to — **visée** [vize] *nf* : aim, design

visible [vizibl] *adj* **1** : visible **2** : obvious — **visibilité** [vizibilite] *nf* : visibility

visière [vizjɛr] *nf* : visor (of a cap, etc.)

vision [vizjɔ̃] *nf* : vision — **visionnaire** [vizjɔnɛr] *adj & nmf* : visionary — **visionner** [vizjɔne] *vt* : view

visite [vizit] *nf* **1** : visit **2** VISITEUR : visitor **3** : examination, inspection **4 rendre** ~ à **qqn** : visit s.o. — **visiter** [vizite] *vt* **1** : visit **2** EXAMINER : examine, inspect — **visiteur, -teuse** [vizitœr, -tøz] *n* : visitor

vison [vizɔ̃] *nm* : mink

visqueux, -queuse [viskø, -køz] *adj* : viscous

visser [vise] *vt* : screw (on)

visuel, -suelle [vizɥɛl] *adj* : visual — **visualiser** [vizɥalize] *vt* : visualize

vital, -tale [vital] *adj, mpl* **-taux** [vito] : vital — **vitalité** [vitalite] *nf* : vitality

vitamine [vitamin] *nf* : vitamin

vite [vit] *adv* **1** RAPIDEMENT : fast, quickly **2** TÔT : soon — **vitesse** [vitɛs] *nf* **1** : speed **2** : gear (of a car)

viticole [vitikɔl] *adj* : wine, wine-growing — **viticulture** [vitikyltyr] *nf* : wine growing

vitre [vitr] *nf* **1** : pane, windowpane **2** : window (of a car, train, etc.) — **vitrail** [vitraj] *nm, pl* **-traux** [vitro] : stained-glass window — **vitré, -trée** [vitre] *adj* : glass, glazed — **vitrer** [vitre] *vt* : glaze — **vitreux, -treuse** [vitrø, -trøz] *adj* : glassy — **vitrine** [vitrin] *nf* **1** : shop window **2** : display case

vivable [vivabl] *adj* : bearable

vivacité [vivasite] *nf* **1** : vivacity, liveliness **2** AGILITÉ : quickness **3** : sharpness, vividness

vivant, -vante [vivã, -vãt] *adj* **1** : alive, living **2** ANIMÉ : lively — **vivant** *nm* **1 du ~ de** : during the lifetime of **2 les ~s** : the living

vivats [viva] *nmpl* : cheers

vive → vif — **~** [viv] *interj* : long live, three cheers for — **vivement** [vivmã] *adv* **1** : quickly **2** : greatly

vivier [vivje] *nm* : fishpond

vivifier [vivifje] {96} *vt* : invigorate — **vivifiant, -fiante** [vivifjã, -fjãt] *adj* : invigorating

vivre [vivr] {98} *vt* : live through, experience — *vi* **1** : live **2 ~ de** : live on, live by — **vivres** [vivr] *nmpl* : provisions, food

vocabulaire [vɔkabylɛr] *nm* : vocabulary

vocation [vɔkasjɔ̃] *nf* : vocation, calling

vociférer [vɔsifere] {87} *v* : shout, scream

vodka [vɔdka] *nf* : vodka

vœu [vø] *nm, pl* **vœux 1** SOUHAIT : wish **2** SERMENT : vow **3 meilleurs ~x** : best wishes

vogue [vɔg] *nf* : vogue, fashion

voici [vwasi] *prep* **1** : here is, here are **2** : this is, these are **3 me ~** : here I am **4 ~ trois jours** : three days ago

voie [vwa] *nf* **1** : road, route, way **2** : lane (of a highway) **3** : way, course **4** *or* **ferrée** : railroad track, railroad **5 en ~ de** : in the process of **6 la Voie lactée** : the Milky Way

voilà [vwala] *prep* **1** : there is, there are **2** : that is, those are **3** VOICI : here is, here are **4 ~ tout!** : that's all! **5 ~ un an** : a year ago

voile [vwal] *nm* : veil — **~** *nf* **1** : sail **2** : sailing — **voiler** [vwale] *vt* **1** : veil **2** DISSIMULER : conceal — **se voiler** *vr* : warp (of wood) — **voilier** [vwalje] *nm* : sailboat — **voilure** [vwalyr] *nf* : sails *pl*

voir [vwar] {99} *vt* **1** : see **2 faire ~** *or* **laisser ~** : show — *vi* **1** : see **2 ~ à** : see to, make sure that **3 voyons** : let's see — **se voir** *vr* **1** : see oneself **2** : see each other **3 ça se voit** : that's obvious, it shows

voire [vwar] *adv* : indeed, or even

voirie [vwari] *nf* : highway department

voisin, -sine [vwazɛ̃, -zin] *adj* **1** : neighboring, adjoining **2 ~ de** : similar to — **~** *n* : neighbor — **voisinage** [vwazinaʒ] *nm* **1** : neighborhood **2** ENVIRONS : vicinity

voiture [vwatyr] *nf* **1** AUTOMOBILE : car, automobile **2** WAGON : (railroad) car, coach **3 ~ d'enfant** : baby carriage

voix [vwa] *nfs & pl* **1** : voice **2** VOTE : vote **3 à haute ~** : out loud

vol [vɔl] *nm* **1** : (plane) flight **2** : flock (of birds) **3** : theft, robbery

volage [vɔlaʒ] *adj* : fickle, flighty

volaille [vɔlaj] *nf* **1** : poultry **2** : fowl

volant [vɔlã] *nm* **1** : steering wheel **2** : shuttlecock **3** : flounce (of a skirt)

volcan [vɔlkã] *nm* : volcano — **volcanique** [vɔlkanik] *adj* : volcanic

volée [vɔle] *nf* **1** : volley **2** VOL : flock, flight

voler[1] [vɔle] *vt* **1** : steal **2** : rob **3 ~ à l'étalage** : shoplift

voler[2] *vi* : fly — **volet** [vɔlɛ] *nm* **1** : shutter, flap **2** : (detachable) section — **voleter** [vɔlte] {8} *vi* : flutter, flit

voleur, -leuse [vɔlœr, -løz] *adj* : dishonest — **~** *n* : thief, robber

volière [vɔljɛr] *nf* : aviary

volley [vɔlɛ] *or* **volley–ball** [vɔlɛbol] *nm* : volleyball

volontaire [vɔlɔ̃tɛr] *adj* **1** : voluntary **2** : deliberate **3** DÉTERMINÉ : willful — **~** *nmf* : volunteer — **volontairement** [vɔlɔ̃tɛrmã] *adv* **1** : voluntarily **2** : deliberately — **volonté** [vɔlɔ̃te] *nf* **1** : will **2** : willpower **3 à ~** : at will **4 bonne ~** : goodwill — **volontiers** [vɔlɔ̃tje] *adv* : willingly, gladly

volt [vɔlt] *nm* : volt — **voltage** [vɔltaʒ] *nm* : voltage

volte–face [vɔltəfas] *nfs & pl* : about-face

voltiger [vɔltiʒe] {17} *vi* : flutter about — **voltige** [vɔltiʒ] *nf* : acrobatics

volubile [vɔlybil] *adj* : voluble

volume [vɔlym] *nm* : volume — **volumineux, -neuse** [vɔlyminø, -nøz] *adj* : bulky

volupté [vɔlypte] *nf* : sensual pleasure — **voluptueux, -tueuse** [vɔlyptɥø, -tɥøz] *adj* : voluptuous

volute [vɔlyt] *nf* : coil (of smoke, etc.)

vomir [vɔmir] *vt* : vomit — *vi* : vomit

vorace [vɔras] *adj* : voracious

vote [vɔt] *nm* **1** : vote **2** : voting — **voter** [vɔte] *vi* : vote — *vt* : vote for

votre [vɔtr] *adj, pl* **vos** [vo] : your

vôtre [votr] *pron* **le ~, la ~, les ~s** : yours, your own

vouer [vwe] *vt* **1** PROMETTRE : vow, pledge **2** CONSACRER : dedicate, devote **3 voué à** : doomed to

vouloir [vulwar] {100} *vt* **1** : want, wish for **2** CONSENTIR À : agree to, be willing to **3 ~ dire** : mean **4 en ~ à** : bear a grudge against **5 veuillez patienter** : please wait

— **voulu, -lue** [vuly] *adj* **1** DÉLIBÉRÉ : intentional **2** REQUIS : required
vous [vu] *pron* **1** (*as subject or direct object*) : you **2** (*as indirect object*) : you, to you **3** : yourself **4** à ~ : yours — **vous–même** [vumɛm] *pron, pl* **vous–mêmes** : yourself
voûte [vut] *nf* : vault, arch — **voûté, -tée** [vute] *adj* **1** : arched **2** : stooped, bent over
vouvoyer [vuvwaje] {58} *vt* : address as *vous*
voyage [vwajaʒ] *nm* **1** : trip, voyage **2 avoir son** ~ *Can fam* : to be fed up — **voyager** [vwajaʒe] {17} *vi* : travel — **voyageur, -geuse** [vwajaʒœr, -ʒøz] *n* **1** : traveler **2** : passenger
voyance [vwajɑ̃s] *nf* : clairvoyance — **voyant, voyante** [vwajɑ̃, vwajɑ̃t] *adj* : loud, gaudy — ~ *n* : clairvoyant — **voyant** *nm* : warning light
voyelle [vwajɛl] *nf* : vowel
voyou [vwaju] *nm* : thug, hoodlum
vrac [vrak] *adv* **1 en** ~ : loose, in bulk **2 en** ~ : haphazardly

vrai, vraie [vrɛ] *adj* **1** : true **2** : real **3** à **vrai dire** : to tell the truth — **vraiment** [vrɛmɑ̃] *adv* : really
vraisemblable [vrɛzɑ̃blabl] *adj* : likely, probable — **vraisemblance** [vrɛzɑ̃blɑ̃s] *nf* : likelihood, probability
vrombir [vrɔ̃bir] *vi* **1** : hum, buzz **2** : roar (of an engine) — **vrombissement** [vrɔ̃bismɑ̃] *nm* : humming, buzzing, roaring
vu [vy] *pp* → **voir** — ~ *prep* : in view of, considering — **vu, vue** [vy] *adj* **1** : seen, regarded **2 bien vu** : well thought of — **vue** *nf* **1** : sight, eyesight **2** : view, vista **3** IDÉE : opinion, view — **vu que** *conj phr* : seeing that, inasmuch as
vulgaire [vylgɛr] *adj* **1** GROSSIER : vulgar **2** ORDINAIRE : common — **vulgariser** [vylgarize] *vt* : popularize — **vulgarité** [vylgarite] *nf* : vulgarity
vulnérable [vylnerabl] *adj* : vulnerable — **vulnérabilité** [vylnerabilite] *nf* : vulnerability

W

w [dubləve] *nm* : w, 23d letter of the alphabet
wagon [vagɔ̃] *nm* : car (of a train)
wagon–lit [vagɔ̃li] *nm, pl* **wagons–lits** : sleeping car
wagon–restaurant [vagɔ̃rɛstɔrɑ̃] *nm, pl* **wagons–restaurants** : dining car

wallon, -lonne [walɔ̃, -lɔn] *adj* : Walloon
watt [wat] *nm* : watt
w-c [vese] *nmpl* : toilet
week–end [wikɛnd] *nm, pl* **week–ends** : weekend
western [wɛstɛrn] *nm* : western
whisky [wiski] *nm, pl* **-kies** : whiskey

XYZ

x [iks] *nm* : x, 24th letter of the alphabet
xénophobie [gzenɔfɔbi] *nf* : xenophobia
xérès [gzeres, kseres] *nm* : sherry
xylophone [ksilɔfɔn] *nm* : xylophone
y [igrɛk] *nm* : y, 25th letter of the alphabet
y [i] *adv* **1** : there **2 ça** ~ **est !** : finally! **3 il** ~ **a** : there is, there are — ~ *pron* **1** : it, about it, on it, in it **2** : them, about them, on them, in them **3 j'y suis!** : I've got it!
yacht [jot] *nm* : yacht
yaourt [jaurt] *nm* : yogurt
yeux [jø] → **œil**
yoga [jɔga] *nm* : yoga

yogourt *or* **yoghourt** [jɔgurt] → **yaourt**
yo-yo *or* **yoyo** [jojo] *nm* : yo-yo
z [zɛd] *nm* : z, 26th letter of the alphabet
zèbre [zebr] *nm* : zebra — **zébrure** [zebryr] *nf* **1** : stripe **2** : welt
zèle [zɛl] *nm* : zeal — **zélé, -lée** [zele] *adj* : zealous
zénith [zenit] *nm* : zenith
zéro [zero] *adj* **1** : zero **2** : nil, worthless — ~ *nm* : zero, naught
zézayer [zezeje] *vi* : lisp
zigzag [zigzag] *nm* : zigzag — **zigzaguer** [zigzage] *vi* : zigzag

zinc [zɛ̃g] *nm* : zinc
zizanie [zizani] *nf* : discord, conflict
zodiaque [zɔdjak] *nm* : zodiac
zona [zona] *nm* : shingles
zone [zon] *nf* : zone, area — **zonage** [zonaʒ] *nm* : zoning

zoo [zo(o)] *nm* : zoo — **zoologie** [zɔɔlɔʒi] *nf* : zoology
zoom [zum] *nm* **1** : zoom lens **2 faire un ~** : zoom in
zut [zyt] *interj fam* : darn!, damn it!

English-French
Dictionary

A

a¹ [ˈeɪ] *n, pl* **a's** *or* **as** [ˈeɪz] : a *m*, première lettre de l'alphabet

a² [ə, ˈeɪ] *art* (**an** [ən, ˈæn] *before a vowel or silent h*) **1** : un *m*, une *f* **2** PER : par

aback [əˈbæk] *adv* **taken ~** : déconcerté

abandon [əˈbændən] *vt* : abandonner — **~ n** : abandon *m*

abashed [əˈbæʃt] *adj* : décontenancé

abate [əˈbeɪt] *vi* **abated; abating** : s'apaiser, se calmer

abbey [ˈæbi] *n, pl* **-beys** : abbaye *f* — **abbot** [ˈæbət] *n* : abbé *m*

abbreviate [əˈbriːviˌeɪt] *vt* **-ated; -ating** : abréger — **abbreviation** [əˌbriːviˈeɪʃən] *n* : abréviation *f*

abdicate [ˈæbdɪˌkeɪt] *v* **-cated; -cating** : abdiquer

abdomen [ˈæbdəmən, æbˈdoːmən] *n* : abdomen *m* — **abdominal** [æbˈdɑmənəl] *adj* : abdominal

abduct [æbˈdʌkt] *vt* : enlever — **abduction** [æbˈdʌkʃən] *n* : enlèvement *m*

aberration [ˌæbəˈreɪʃən] *n* : aberration *f*

abhor [əbˈhɔr, æb-] *vt* **-horred; -horring** : abhorrer, détester

abide [əˈbaɪd] *v* **abode** [əˈboːd] *or* **abided; abiding** : supporter — *vi* **~ by** : respecter, se conformer à

ability [əˈbɪləti] *n, pl* **-ties** **1** : aptitude *f* **2** SKILL : habileté *f*, talent *m*

ablaze [əˈbleɪz] *adj* : en feu

able [ˈeɪbəl] *adj* **abler; ablest** **1** CAPABLE : capable **2** SKILLED : habile — **ably** [ˈeɪbəli] *adv* : habilement

abnormal [æbˈnɔrmel] *adj* : anormal — **abnormality** [ˌæbnərˈmæləti, -nɔr-] *n, pl* **-ties** : anormalité *f*, anomalie *f*

aboard [əˈbord] *adv* : à bord — **~ prep** : à bord de, dans

abode [əˈboːd] *n* : demeure *f*, domicile *m*

abolish [əˈbɑlɪʃ] *vt* : abolir — **abolition** [ˌæbəˈlɪʃən] *n* : abolition *f*

abominable [əˈbɑmənəbəl] *adj* : abominable

aborigine [ˌæbəˈrɪdʒəni] *n* : aborigène *mf*

abort [əˈbɔrt] *vt* : faire avorter — **abortion** [əˈbɔrʃən] *n* : avortement *m*

abound [əˈbaʊnd] *vi* **~ in** : abonder en

about [əˈbaʊt] *adv* **1** APPROXIMATELY : vers, environ **2** AROUND : autour **3** NEARBY : près **4 be ~ to** : être sur le point de — **~ prep** **1** AROUND : autour de **2** CONCERNING : sur, de

above [əˈbʌv] *adv* **1** OVERHEAD : au-dessus, en haut **2** PREVIOUSLY : ci-dessus — **~**

prep **1** OVER : au-dessus de **2** EXCEEDING : plus de **3 ~ all** : surtout

abrasive [əˈbreɪsɪv] *adj* : abrasif

abreast [əˈbrɛst] *adv* **1** : de front, côte à côte **2 ~ of** : au courant de

abridge [əˈbrɪdʒ] *vt* **abridged; abridging** : abréger

abroad [əˈbrɔd] *adv* **1** : à l'étranger **2** WIDELY : de tous côtés

abrupt [əˈbrʌpt] *adj* **1** SUDDEN : brusque **2** STEEP : abrupt

abscess [ˈæbˌsɛs] *n* : abcès *m*

absence [ˈæbsənts] *n* **1** : absence *f* **2** LACK : manque *m* — **absent** [ˈæbsənt] *adj* : absent — **absentee** [ˌæbsənˈtiː] *n* : absent *m*, -sente *f* — **absentminded** [ˌæbsəntˈmaɪndəd] *adj* : distrait

absolute [ˈæbsəˌluːt, ˌæbsəˈluːt] *adj* : absolu — **absolutely** [ˈæbsəˌluːtli, ˌæbsəˈluːtli] *adv* : absolument

absolve [əbˈzɑlv, æb-, -ˈsɑlv] *vt* **-solved; -solving** : absoudre

absorb [əbˈzɔrb, æb-, -ˈsɔrb] *vt* : absorber — **absorbent** [əbˈzɔrbənt, æb-, -ˈsɔr-] *adj* : absorbant — **absorption** [əbˈzɔrpʃən, æb-, -ˈsɔrp-] *n* : absorption *f*

abstain [əbˈsteɪn, æb-] *vi* **~ from** : s'abstenir de — **abstinence** [ˈæbstənənts] *n* : abstinence *f*

abstract [æbˈstrækt, ˈæbˌ-] *adj* : abstrait — **~ n** SUMMARY : résumé *m*

absurd [əbˈsərd, -ˈzərd] *adj* : absurde — **absurdity** [əbˈsərdəti, -ˈzər-] *n, pl* **-ties** : absurdité *f*

abundant [əˈbʌndənt] *adj* : abondant — **abundance** [əˈbʌndənts] *n* : abondance *f*

abuse [əˈbjuːz] *vt* **abused; abusing** **1** MISUSE : abuser de **2** MISTREAT : maltraiter **3** INSULT : injurier — **~** [əˈbjuːs] *n* **1** MISUSE : abus *m* **2** MISTREATMENT : mauvais traitement *m* **3** INSULTS : insultes *fpl*, injures *fpl* — **abusive** [əˈbjuːsɪv] *adj* : injurieux

abut [əˈbʌt] *vi* **abutted; abutting** **~ on** : être contigu à

abyss [əˈbɪs, ˈæbɪs] *n* : abîme *m*

academy [əˈkædəmi] *n, pl* **-mies** **1** SCHOOL : école *f*, collège *m* **2** SOCIETY : académie *f* — **academic** [ˌækəˈdɛmɪk] *adj* **1** : universitaire **2** THEORETICAL : théorique

accelerate [ɪkˈsɛləˌreɪt, æk-] *v* **-ated; -ating** : accélérer — **acceleration** [ɪkˌsɛləˈreɪʃən, æk-] *n* : accélération *f*

accent [ˈækˌsɛnt, ækˈsɛnt] *vt* : accentuer — **~** [ˈækˌsɛnt, -sənt] *n* : accent *m* — **accen-**

tuate [ɪkˈsɛntʃʊˌeɪt, æk-] vt **-ated; -ating** : accentuer

accept [ɪkˈsɛpt, æk-] vt : accepter — **acceptable** [ɪkˈsɛptəbəl, æk-] adj : acceptable — **acceptance** [ɪkˈsɛptənts, æk-] n **1** : acceptation f **2** APPROVAL : approbation f

access [ˈækˌsɛs] n : accès m — **accessible** [ɪkˈsɛsəbəl, æk-] adj : accessible

accessory [ɪkˈsɛsəri, æk-] n, pl **-ries 1** : accessoire m **2** ACCOMPLICE : complice mf

accident [ˈæksədənt] n **1** : accident m **2 by ~** : par hasard — **accidental** [ˌæksəˈdɛntəl] adj : accidentel — **accidentally** [ˌæksəˈdɛntəli, -ˈdɛntli] adv : accidentellement, par hasard

acclaim [əˈkleɪm] vt : acclamer — **~** n : acclamation f

acclimate [ˈækləˌmeɪt, əˈklaɪmət] vt **-mated; -mating** : acclimater

accommodate [əˈkɑməˌdeɪt] vt **-dated; -dating 1** ADAPT : accommo-der **2** SATISFY : satisfaire **3** LODGE : loger **4** HOLD : contenir — **accommodation** [əˌkɑməˈdeɪʃən] n **1** : accommodation f **2 ~s** npl LODGING : logement m

accompany [əˈkʌmpəni, -ˈkɑm-] vt **-nied; -nying** : accompagner

accomplice [əˈkɑmpləs, -ˈkʌm-] n : complice mf

accomplish [əˈkɑmplɪʃ, -ˈkʌm-] vt **1** : accomplir **2** REALIZE : réaliser — **accomplishment** [əˈkɑmplɪʃmənt, -ˈkʌm-] n : accomplissement m

accord [əˈkɔrd] n **1** AGREEMENT : accord m **2 of one's own ~** : de son plein gré — **accordance** [əˈkɔrdənts] n **in ~ with** : conformément à — **accordingly** [əˈkɔrdɪŋli] adv : en conséquence — **according to** [əˈkɔrdɪŋ] prep : selon, d'après

accordion [əˈkɔrdiən] n : accordéon m

account [əˈkaʊnt] n **1** : compte m **2** REPORT : compte m rendu **3** WORTH : importance f **4 on ~ of** : à cause de **5 on no ~** : en aucun cas **6 take into ~** : tenir compte de — **~** vi **~ for** : expliquer — **accountable** [əˈkaʊntəbəl] adj : responsable — **accountant** [əˈkaʊntənt] n : comptable mf — **accounting** [əˈkaʊntɪŋ] n : comptabilité f

accrue [əˈkru:] vi **-crued; -cruing** : s'accumuler

accumulate [əˈkjuːmjəˌleɪt] v **-lated; -lating** vt : accumuler — vi : s'accumuler — **accumulation** [əˌkjuːmjəˈleɪʃən] n : accumulation f

accurate [ˈækjərət] adj : exact, précis — **accurately** adv : exactement, avec précision — **accuracy** [ˈækjərəsi] n, pl **-cies** : exactitude f, précision f

accuse [əˈkjuːz] vt **-cused; -cusing** : accuser — **accusation** [ˌækyzasjɔ̃] n : accusation f

accustom [əˈkʌstəm] vt : accoutumer — **accustomed** [əˈkʌstəmd] adj **1** CUSTOMARY : habituel **2 become ~ to** : s'habituer à

ace [ˈeɪs] n : as m

ache [eɪk] vi **ached; aching** : faire mal — **~** n : douleur f

achieve [əˈtʃiːv] vt **achieved; achieving** : accomplir, atteindre — **achievement** [əˈtʃiːvmənt] n : accomplissement m, réussite f

acid [ˈæsəd] adj : acide — **~** n : acide m

acknowledge [ɪkˈnɑlɪdʒ, æk-] vt **-edged; -edging 1** ADMIT : admettre **2** RECOGNIZE : reconnaître **3 ~ receipt of** : accuser réception de — **acknowledgment** [ɪkˈnɑlɪdʒmənt, æk-] n **1** : reconnaissance f **2 ~ of receipt** : accusé m de réception

acne [ˈækni] n : acné f

acorn [ˈeɪˌkɔrn, -kərn] n : gland m

acoustic [əˈkuːstɪk] or **acoustical** [əˈkuːstɪkəl] adj : acoustique — **acoustics** [əˈkuːstɪks] ns & pl : acoustique f

acquaint [əˈkweɪnt] vt **1 ~ s.o. with** : mettre qqn au courant de **2 be ~ed with** : connaître (une personne) — **acquaintance** [əˈkweɪntənts] n : connaissance f

acquire [əˈkwaɪr] vt **-quired; -quiring** : acquérir — **acquisition** [ˌækwəˈzɪʃən] n : acquisition f

acquit [əˈkwɪt] vt **-quitted; -quitting** : acquitter

acre [ˈeɪkər] n : acre f — **acreage** [ˈeɪkərɪdʒ] n : superficie f

acrid [ˈækrəd] adj : âcre

acrobat [ˈækrəˌbæt] n : acrobate mf — **acrobatic** [ˌækrəˈbætɪk] adj : acrobatique — **acrobatics** [ˌækrəˈbætɪks] ns & pl : acrobatie f

across [əˈkrɔs] adv **1** : de large, d'un côté à l'autre **2 ~ from** : en face de **3 go ~** : traverser — **~** prep **1 ~ the street** : de l'autre côté de la rue **2 lie ~ sth** : être en travers de qqch

acrylic [əˈkrɪlɪk] n : acrylique m

act [ˈækt] vi **1** : agir **2** PERFORM : jouer, faire du théâtre **3 ~ as** : servir de — vt : jouer (un rôle) — **~** n **1** ACTION : acte m **2** DECREE : loi f **3** : acte m (d'une pièce de théâtre), numéro m (de variétés) **4 put on an ~** : jouer la comédie — **acting** adj : intérimaire

action [ˈækʃən] n **1** : action f **2** DEED : acte m **2** LAWSUIT : procès m, action f

activate [ˈæktəˌveɪt] vt **-vated; -vating** : activer

active [ˈæktɪv] adj : actif — **activity** [ækˈtɪvəti] n, pl **-ties** : activité f

actor [ˈæktər] n : acteur m, -trice f — **actress** [ˈæktrəs] n : actrice f

actual [ˈæktʃʊəl] adj **1** : réel, véritable **2**

VERY : même — **actually** [ˈæktʃʊəli, -ʃəli] *adv* **1** REALLY : vraiment **2** IN FACT : en fait
acupuncture [ˈækjʊˌpʌŋktʃər] *n* : acupuncture *f*
acute [əˈkju:t] *adj* **acuter; acutest 1** : aigu **2** KEEN : fin
ad [ˈæd] *n* → **advertisement**
adamant [ˈædəmənt, -ˌmænt] *adj* : inflexible
adapt [əˈdæpt] *vt* : adapter — *vi* : s'adapter — **adaptable** [əˌdæptəbəl] *adj* : adaptable — **adaptation** [ˌæˌdæpˈteɪʃən, -dəp-] : adaptation *f* — **adapter** [əˈdæptər] *n* : adapteur *m*
add [ˈæd] *vt* **1** : ajouter **2** ∼ **up** : additionner — *vi* : additionner
addict [ˈædɪkt] *n or* **drug** ∼ : toxicomane *mf*; drogué *m*, -guée *f* — **addiction** [əˈdɪkʃən] *n* **1** : dépendance *f* **2** **drug** ∼ : toxicomanie *f*
addition [əˈdɪʃən] *n* **1** : addition *f* **2** **in** ∼ : en plus — **additional** [əˈdɪʃənəl] *adj* : additionnel, supplémentaire — **additive** [ˈædətɪv] *n* : additif *m*
address [əˈdrɛs] *vt* **1** : adresser (une lettre, etc.) **2** : s'adresser à (une personne), aborder (un problème) — ∼ [əˈdrɛs, ˈæˌdrɛs] *n* **1** : adresse *f* **2** SPEECH : discours *m*
adept [əˈdɛpt] *adj* : habile
adequate [ˈædɪkwət] *adj* : adéquat, suffisant — **adequately** [ˈædɪkwətli] *adv* : suffisamment
adhere [ædˈhir, əd-] *vi* **-hered; -hering 1** STICK : adhérer **2** ∼ **to** KEEP : adhé-rer à, observer — **adherence** [ædˈhirənts, əd-] *n* : adhésion *f* — **adhesion** [ædˈhiʒən, əd-] *n* : adhésion *f*, adhérence *f* — **adhesive** [ædˈhi:sɪv, əd-, -zɪv] *adj* : adhésif — ∼ *n* : adhésif *m*
adjacent [əˈʤeɪsənt] *adj* : adjacent, contigu
adjective [ˈæʤɪktɪv] *n* : adjectif *m*
adjoining [əˈʤɔɪnɪŋ] *adj* : contigu
adjourn [əˈʤərn] *vt* : ajourner — *vi* : suspendre la séance
adjust [əˈʤʌst] *vt* : ajuster — *vi* ADAPT : s'adapter — **adjustable** [əˈʤʌstəbəl] *adj* : réglable, ajustable — **adjustment** [əˈʤʌstmənt] *n* **1** : ajustement *m* **2** ADAPTATION : adaptation *f*
ad–lib [ˈædˈlɪb] *vt* **ad–libbed; ad–libbing** : improviser
administer [ædˈmɪnəstər, əd-] *vt* : administrer — **administration** [ædˌmɪnəˈstreɪʃən, əd-] *n* : administration *f* — **administrative** [ædˈmɪnəˌstreɪtɪv, əd-] *adj* : administratif — **administrator** [ædˈmɪnəˌstreɪtər, əd-] *n* : admi-nistrateur *m*, -trice *f*
admirable [ˈædmərəbəl] *adj* : admirable
admiral [ˈædmərəl] *n* : amiral *m*
admire [ædˈmaɪr] *vt* **-mired; -miring** : ad-

mirer — **admiration** [ˌædməˈreɪʃən] *n* : ad-miration *f* — **admirer** [ædˈmaɪrər] *n* : admi-rateur *m*, -trice *f* — **admiring** [ædˈmaɪrɪŋ] *adj* : admiratif
admit [ædˈmɪt, əd-] *vt* **-mitted; -mitting 1** : admettre **2** ACKNOWLEDGE : reconnaître **3** CONFESS : avouer — **admission** [ædˈmɪʃən] *n* **1** ADMITTANCE : admission *f* **2** FEE : entrée *f* **3** CONFESSION : aveu *m* — **admittance** [ædˈmɪtənts, əd-] *n* : entrée *f*
admonish [ædˈmɑnɪʃ, əd-] *vt* : réprimander
ado [əˈdu:] *n* **1** : agitation *f* **2** **without further** ∼ : sans plus de cérémonie
adolescent [ˌædəlˈɛsənt] *n* : adolescent *m*, -cente *f* — **adolescence** [ˌædəlˈɛsənts] *n* : adolescence *f*
adopt [əˈdɑpt] *vt* : adopter — **adoption** [əˈdɑpʃən] *n* : adoption *f*
adore [əˈdor] *vt* **adored; adoring** : adorer — **adorable** [əˈdorəbəl] *adj* : adorable — **adoration** [ˌædəˈreɪʃən] *n* : adoration *f*
adorn [əˈdɔrn] *vt* : orner
adrift [əˈdrɪft] *adv & adj* : à la dérive
adroit [əˈdrɔɪt] *adj* : adroit, habile
adult [əˈdʌlt, ˈæˌdʌlt] *adj* : adulte — ∼ *n* : adulte *mf*
adultery [əˈdʌltəri] *n, pl* **-teries** : adultère *m*
advance [ædˈvænts, əd-] *v* **-vanced; -vancing** *vt* : avancer — *vi* **1** : avancer **2** IMPROVE : progresser — ∼ *n* **1** : avance *f* **2** **in** ∼ : à l'avance, d'avance — **advancement** [ædˈvæntsmənt, əd-] *n* : avancement *m*
advantage [ədˈvæntɪʤ, æd-] *n* **1** : avantage *m* **2** **take** ∼ **of** : profiter de — **advantageous** [ˌædˌvænˈteɪʤəs, -vən-] *adj* : avantageux
advent [ˈædˌvɛnt] *n* **1** : avènement *m* **2** **Advent** : Avent *m*
adventure [ædˈvɛntʃər, əd-] *n* : aventure *f* — **adventurous** [ædˈvɛntʃərəs, əd-] *adj* : aventureux
adverb [ˈædˌvərb] *n* : adverbe *m*
adversary [ˈædvərˌseri] *n, pl* **-saries** : adversaire *mf*
adverse [ædˈvərs, ˈædˌ-] *adj* : défavorable — **adversity** [ædˈvərsəti, əd-] *n, pl* **-ties** : adversité *f*
advertise [ˈædvərˌtaɪz] *v* **-tised; -tising** *vt* : faire de la publicité pour — *vi* : passer une annonce (dans un journal) — **advertisement** [ˈædvərˌtaɪzmənt, ædˈvərtəzmənt] *n* : publicité *f*, annonce *f* — **advertiser** [ˈædvərˌtaɪzər] *n* : annonceur *m* — **advertising** [ˈædvərˌtaɪzɪŋ] *n* : publicité *f*
advice [ædˈvaɪs] *n* : conseils *mpl*
advise [ædˈvaɪz, əd-] *vt* **-vised; -vising 1** : conseiller **2** RECOMMEND : recommander **3** INFORM : aviser — **advisable** [ædˈvaɪzəbəl, əd-] *adj* : recommandé, prudent — **adviser** [ædˈvaɪzər, əd-] *n* : conseiller *m*,

-lère f — **advisory** [æd'vaɪzəri, əd-] adj : consultatif

advocate ['ædvə‚keɪt] vt -cated; -cating : préconiser — ['ædvəkət] n 1 SUPPORTER : défenseur m 2 LAWYER : avocat m, -cate f

aerial ['æriəl] adj : aérien — ～ n : antenne f

aerobics [‚ær'o:bɪks] ns & pl : aérobic m

aerodynamic [‚æro:daɪ'næmɪk] adj : aérodynamique

aerosol ['ærə‚sɔl] n : aérosol m

aesthetic [ɛs'θɛtɪk] adj : esthétique

afar [ə'fɑr] adv from ～ : de loin

affable ['æfəbəl] adj : affable

affair [ə'fær] n 1 : affaire f 2 or love ～ : liaison f, affaire f de cœur

affect [ə'fɛkt, æ-] vt : affecter — **affection** [ə'fɛkʃən] n : affection f — **affectionate** [ə-'fɛkʃənət] adj : affectueux

affirm [ə'fərm] vt : affirmer — **affirmative** [ə'fɔrmətɪv] adj : affirmatif

affix [ə'fɪks] vt : apposer (une signature), coller (un timbre)

afflict [ə'flɪkt] vt : affliger — **affliction** [ə-'flɪkʃən] n : affliction f

affluent ['æ‚flu:ənt; æ'flu:-, ə-] adj : riche

afford [ə'ford] vt 1 : avoir les moyens d'acheter 2 ～ to do : se permettre de faire

affront [ə'frʌnt] n : affront m

afloat [ə'flo:t] adj & adv : à flot

afoot [ə'fʊt] adv & adj : en train, en cours

afraid [ə'freɪd] adj 1 be ～ of : avoir peur de, craindre 2 be ～ that : regretter que 3 I'm ～ not : hélas, non

African ['æfrɪkən] adj : africain

after ['æftər] adv 1 AFTERWARD : après 2 BEHIND : en arrière — ～ conj : après que — ～ prep 1 : après 2 ～ all : après tout 3 it's ten ～ five : il est cinq heures dix

aftereffect ['æftəri‚fɛkt] n : répercussion f

aftermath ['æftər‚mæθ] n : suites fpl

afternoon [‚æftər'nu:n] n : après-midi mf

afterward ['æftərwərd] or **afterwards** [-wərdz] adv : après, ensuite

again [ə'gɛn, -gɪn] adv 1 : encore (une fois), de nouveau 2 ～ and ～ : maintes et maintes fois 3 then ～ : d'autre part

against [ə'gɛntst, -'gɪntst] prep 1 : contre 2 go ～ : aller à l'encontre

age ['eɪʤ] n 1 : âge m 2 ERA : ère f, époque f 3 come of ～ : atteindre la majorité 4 for ～s : depuis longtemps 5 old ～ : vieillesse f — ～ v age; aging : vieillir — **aged** ['eɪʤəd, 'eɪʤd] adj 1 : âgé de 2 ['eɪʤd] OLD : vieux, âgé

agency ['eɪʤəntsi] n, pl -cies : agence f

agenda [ə'ʤɛndə] n : ordre m du jour, programme m

agent ['eɪʤənt] n : agent m

aggravate ['ægrə‚veɪt] vt -vated; -vating 1 WORSEN : aggraver 2 ANNOY : agacer, énerver

aggregate ['ægrɪgət] adj : total, global — ～ n : ensemble m, total m

aggression [ə'grɛʃən] n : agression f — **aggressive** [ə'grɛsɪv] adj : agressif — **aggressor** [ə'grɛsər] n : agresseur m

aghast [ə'gæst] adj : horrifié

agile ['æʤəl] adj : agile — **agility** [ə'ʤɪləti] n, pl -ties : agilité f

agitate ['æʤə‚teɪt] vt -tated; -tating 1 SHAKE : agiter 2 TROUBLE : inquiéter — **agitation** [‚æʤə'teɪʃən] n : agitation f

ago [ə'go:] adv 1 : il y a 2 long ～ : il y a longtemps

agony ['ægəni] n, pl -nies : angoisse f, souffrance f — **agonize** ['ægə‚naɪz] vi -nized; -nizing : se tourmenter — **agonizing** ['ægə‚naɪzɪŋ] adj : déchirant

agree [ə'gri:] v agreed; agreeing vt 1 ADMIT : convenir 2 ～ that : reconnaître que — vi 1 : être d'accord 2 CORRESPOND : concorder 3 ～ to : consentir à — **agreeable** [ə'gri:əbəl] adj 1 PLEASING : agréable 2 WILLING : consentant — **agreement** [ə-'gri:mənt] n : accord m

agriculture ['ægrɪ‚kʌltʃər] n : agriculture f — **agricultural** [‚ægrɪ'kʌltʃərəl] adj : agricole

aground [ə'graʊnd] adv run ～ : s'échouer

ahead [ə'hɛd] adv 1 IN FRONT : en avant, devant 2 BEFOREHAND : à l'avance 3 LEADING : en avance 4 go ～! : allez-y! — **ahead of** prep 1 IN FRONT OF : devant 2 ～ time : avant l'heure

aid ['eɪd] vt : aider — ～ n : aide f, secours m

AIDS ['eɪdz] n (acquired immunodeficiency syndrome) : sida m

ail ['eɪl] vi : être souffrant — **ailment** ['eɪlmənt] n : maladie f

aim ['eɪm] vt : braquer (une arme à feu), diriger (une remarque, etc.) — vi 1 ～ to : avoir l'intention de 2 ～ at or ～ for : viser — ～ n : but m — **aimless** ['eɪmləs] adj : sans but

air ['ær] vt 1 : aérer 2 EXPRESS : exprimer 3 BROADCAST : diffuser — ～ n 1 : air m 2 on the ～ : à l'antenne — **air-conditioned** [‚ærkən'dɪʃənd] adj : climatisé — **air-conditioning** [‚ærkən'dɪʃənɪŋ] n : climatisation f — **aircraft** ['ær‚kræft] ns & pl : avion m — **air force** n : armée f de l'air — **airline** ['ær‚laɪn] n : compagnie f aérienne — **airmail** ['ær‚meɪl] n 1 : poste f aérienne 2 by ～ : par avion — **airplane** ['ær‚pleɪn] n : avion m — **airport** ['ær‚port] n : aéroport m — **airstrip** ['ær‚strɪp] n : piste f d'atterrissage — **airtight** ['ær‚taɪt] adj : hermétique — **airy** ['æri] adj airier; -est : aéré

aisle ['aɪl] *n* : allée *f* (d'un théâtre, etc.), couloir *m* (d'un avion)

ajar [ə'dʒar] *adj & adv* : entrouvert

akin [ə'kɪn] *adj* ~ **to** : semblable à

alarm [ə'lɑrm] *n* **1** : alarme *f* **2** ANXIETY : inquiétude *f* — ~ *vt* : alarmer — **alarm clock** *n* : réveille-matin *m*

alas [ə'læs] *interj* : hélas!

album ['ælbəm] *n* : album *m*

alcohol ['ælkə,hɔl] *n* : alcool *m* — **alcoholic** [,ælkə'hɔlɪk] *adj* : alcoolisé, alcoolique — ~ *n* : alcoolique *mf* — **alcoholism** ['ælkəhɔ,lɪzəm] *n* : alcoolisme *m*

alcove ['æl,ko:v] *n* : alcôve *f*

ale ['eɪl] *n* : bière *f*

alert [ə'lərt] *adj* **1** WATCHFUL : vigilant **2** LIVELY : alerte, éveillé — ~ *n* : alerte *f* — ~ *vt* : alerter — **alertness** [ə'lərtnəs] *n* **1** : vigilance *f* **2** : vivacité *f*

alfalfa [æl'fælfə] *n* : luzerne *f*

alga ['ælgə] *n, pl* **-gae** ['æl,dʒi:] : algue *f*

algebra ['ældʒəbrə] *n* : algèbre *f*

Algerian [æl'dʒɪriən] *adj* : algérien

alias ['eɪliəs] *adv* : alias — ~ *n* : nom *m* d'emprunt, faux nom *m*

alibi ['ælə,baɪ] *n* : alibi *m*

alien ['eɪliən] *adj* : étranger — ~ *n* **1** FOREIGNER : étranger *m*, -gère *f* **2** EXTRATERRESTRIAL : extraterrestre *mf* — **alienate** ['eɪliə,neɪt] *vt* **-ated; -ating** : aliéner — **alienation** [,eɪliə'neɪʃən] *n* : aliénation *f*

alight [ə'laɪt] *vi* : descendre, se poser

align [ə'laɪn] *vt* : aligner — **alignment** [ə'laɪnmənt] *n* : alignement *m*

alike [ə'laɪk] *adv* : de la même façon — ~ *adj* **1** : semblable **2 be** ~ : se ressembler

alimony ['ælə,mo:ni] *n, pl* **-nies** : pension *f* alimentaire

alive [ə'laɪv] *adj* **1** LIVING : vivant, en vie **2** LIVELY : vif, animé

all ['ɔl] *adv* **1** COMPLETELY : tout, complètement **2** ~ **at once** : tout d'un coup **3** ~ **the better** : tant mieux — ~ *adj* : tout — ~ *pron* **1** EVERYTHING : tout **2** EVERYONE : tous, toutes **3** ~ **in** : tout compte fait — **all-around** [,ɔlə'raʊnd] *adj* VERSATILE : complet

allay [ə'leɪ] *vt* : calmer, apaiser

allege [ə'lɛdʒ] *vt* **-leged; -leging** : alléguer, prétendre — **allegation** [,ælɪ'geɪʃən] *n* : allégation *f* — **alleged** [ə'lɛdʒd, ə'lɛdʒəd] *adj* : présumé, prétendu — **allegedly** [ə'lɛdʒədli] *adv* : prétendument

allegiance [ə'li:dʒənts] *n* : allégeance *f*

allergy ['ælərdʒi] *n, pl* **-gies** : allergie *f* — **allergic** [ə'lərdʒɪk] *adj* : allergique

alleviate [ə'li:vi,eɪt] *vt* **-ated; -ating** : soulager, alléger

alley ['æli] *n, pl* **-leys** : ruelle *f*, allée *f*

alliance [ə'laɪənts] *n* : alliance *f*

alligator ['ælə,geɪtər] *n* : alligator *m*

allocate ['ælə,keɪt] *vt* **-cated; -cating** : allouer, assigner

allot [ə'lɑt] *vt* **allotted; allotting 1** ASSIGN : attribuer **2** DISTRIBUTE : répartir — **allotment** [ə'lɑtmənt] *n* : allocation *f*

allow [ə'laʊ] *vt* **1** PERMIT : permettre **2** CONCEDE : admettre **3** GRANT : accorder — *vi* ~ **for** : tenir compte de — **allowance** [ə'laʊənts] *n* **1** : allocation *f* **2** : argent *m* de poche (pour les enfants) **3 make** ~**s for** : tenir compte de

alloy ['æ,lɔɪ] *n* : alliage *m*

all right *adv* **1** YES : d'accord **2** WELL : bien **3** CERTAINLY : bien, sans doute — ~ *adj* : pas mal, bien

allude [ə'lu:d] *vi* **-luded; -luding** ~ **to** : faire allusion à

allure [ə'lʊr] *vt* **-lured; -luring** : attirer

allusion [ə'lu:ʒən] *n* : allusion *f*

ally [ə'laɪ, 'æ,laɪ] *vt* **-lied; -lying 1** : allier **2** ~ **oneself with** : s'allier avec — ~ ['æ,laɪ, ə'laɪ] *n, pl* **allies** : allié *m*, -liée *f*

almanac ['ɔlmə,næk, 'æl-] *n* : almanach *m*

almighty [ɔl'maɪti] *adj* : tout puissant, formidable

almond ['ɑmənd, 'ɑl-, 'æ-, 'æl-] *n* : amande *f*

almost ['ɔl,mo:st, ɔl'mo:st] *adv* : presque

alms ['ɑmz, 'ɑlmz, 'ælmz] *ns & pl* : aumône *f*

alone [ə'lo:n] *adv* **1** : seul **2 leave** ~ : laisser tranquille — ~ *adj* : seul

along [ə'lɔŋ] *adv* **1 all** ~ : tout le temps **2** ~ **with** : avec, accompagné de — ~ *prep* **1** : le long de **2** ON : sur — **alongside** [ə,lɔŋ'saɪd] *adv* : à côté — ~ *or* ~ **of** *prep* : à côté de

aloof [ə'lu:f] *adj* : distant

aloud [ə'laʊd] *adv* : à haute voix

alphabet ['ælfə,bɛt] *n* : alphabet *m* — **alphabetic** [,ælfə'bɛtɪk] *or* **alphabetical** [-tɪkəl] *adj* : alphabétique

already [ɔl'rɛdi] *adv* : déjà

also ['ɔl,so:] *adv* : aussi

altar ['ɔltər] *n* : autel *m*

alter ['ɔltər] *vt* **1** : changer, modifier **2** : retoucher (un vêtement) — **alteration** [,ɔltə'reɪʃən] *n* **1** : changement *m*, modification *f* **2** ~**s** *npl* : retouches *fpl*

alternate ['ɔltərnət] *adj* : alternatif — ~ ['ɔltər,neɪt] *v* **-nated; -nating** *vt* : faire alterner — *vi* : alterner — **alternating current** ['ɔltər,neɪtɪŋ] *n* : courant *m* alternatif — **alternative** [ɔl'tərnətɪv] *adj* : alternatif — ~ *n* : alternative *f*

although [ɔl'ðo:] *conj* : bien que, quoique

altitude ['æltə,tu:d, -,tju:d] *n* : altitude *f*

altogether [,ɔltə'gɛðər] *adv* **1** COMPLETELY : entièrement, tout à fait **2** ON THE WHOLE

: dans l'ensemble **3 how much ~? :** combien en tout?

aluminum [ə'lu:mənəm] *n* : aluminium *m*

always ['ɔlwiz, -ˌweɪz] *adv* **1** : toujours **2** FOREVER : pour toujours

am → **be**

amass [ə'mæs] *vt* : amasser

amateur ['æmətʃər, -tər, -ˌtʊr, -ˌtjʊr] *adj* : amateur — **~** *n* : amateur *m*

amaze [ə'meɪz] *vt* **amazed; amazing** : étonner, stupéfier — **amazement** [ə'meɪzmənt] *n* : stupéfaction *f* — **amazing** [ə'meɪzɪŋ] *adj* : étonnant

ambassador [æm'bæsəˌdər] *n* : ambassadeur *m*, -drice *f*

amber ['æmbər] *n* : ambre *m*

ambiguous [æm'bɪgjuəs] *adj* : ambigu — **ambiguity** [ˌæmbə'gju:əti] *n, pl* **-ties** : ambiguïté *f*

ambition [æm'bɪʃən] *n* : ambition *f* — **ambitious** [æm'bɪʃəs] *adj* : ambitieux

ambivalence [æm'bɪvələnts] *n* : ambivalence *f* — **ambivalent** [æm'bɪvələnt] *adj* : ambivalent

amble ['æmbəl] *vi* **-bled; -bling** : déambuler

ambulance ['æmbjələnts] *n* : ambulance *f*

ambush ['æmbʊʃ] *vt* : tendre une embuscade à — **~** *n* : embuscade *f*

amenable [ə'mi:nəbəl, -'mɛ-] *adj* **1** : accommodant **2 ~ to** : disposé à

amend [ə'mɛnd] *vt* : amender, modifier — **amendment** [ə'mɛndmənt] *n* : amendement *m* — **amends** [ə'mɛndz] *ns & pl* **make ~** : réparer ses torts

amenities [ə'mɛnətis, -'mi:-] *npl* : équipements *mpl*, aménagements *mpl*

American [ə'mɛrɪkən] *adj* : américain

amiable ['eɪmiˌəbəl] *adj* : aimable

amicable ['æmɪkəbəl] *adj* : amical

amid [ə'mɪd] *or* **amidst** [ə'mɪdst] *prep* : au milieu de, parmi

amiss [ə'mɪs] *adv* **1** : mal **2 take sth ~** : prendre qqch de travers — **~** *adj* **something is ~** : quelque chose ne va pas

ammonia [ə'mo:njə] *n* : ammoniaque *f*

ammunition [ˌæmjə'nɪʃən] *n* : munitions *fpl*

amnesia [æm'ni:ʒə] *n* : amnésie *f*

amnesty ['æmnəsti] *n, pl* **-ties** : amnistie *f*

amoeba [ə'mi:bə] *n, pl* **-bas** *or* **-bae** [-bi:] : amibe *f*

among [ə'mʌŋ] *prep* : parmi, entre

amount [ə'maʊnt] *vi* **1 ~ to** TOTAL : s'élever à **2 that ~s to the same thing** : cela revient au même — **~** *n* **1** : quantité *f* **2** SUM : somme *f*, montant *m*

amphibian [æm'fɪbiən] *n* : amphibien *m* — **amphibious** [æm'fɪbiəs] *adj* : amphibie

amphitheater ['æmfəˌθi:ətər] *n* : amphithéâtre *m*

ample ['æmpəl] *adj* **-pler; -plest 1** SPACIOUS : ample **2** PLENTIFUL : abondant

amplify ['æmpləˌfaɪ] *vt* **-fied; -fying** : amplifier — **amplifier** ['æmpləˌfaɪər] *n* : amplificateur *m*

amputate ['æmpjəˌteɪt] *v* **-tated; -tating** : amputer — **amputation** [ˌæmpjə'teɪʃən] *n* : amputation *f*

amuse [ə'mju:z] *vt* **amused; amusing** : amuser — **amusement** [ə'mju:zmənt] *n* **1** ENJOYMENT : amusement *m* **2** DIVERSION : divertissement *m*

an → **a²**

analgesic [ˌænəl'dʒi:zɪk, -sɪk] *n* : analgésique *m*

analogy [ə'nælədʒi] *n, pl* **-gies** : analogie *f* — **analogous** [ə'næləgəs] *adj* : analogue

analysis [ə'næləsəs] *n, pl* **-yses** [-ˌsi:z] : analyse *f* — **analytic** [ˌænə'lɪtɪk] *or* **analytical** [-tɪkəl] *adj* : analytique — **analyze** *or Brit* **analyse** ['ænəˌlaɪz] *vt* **-lyzed** *or Brit* **-lysed; -lyzing** *or Brit* **-lysing** : analyser

anarchy ['ænərki, -ˌnɑr-] *n* : anarchie *f*

anatomy [ə'nætəmi] *n, pl* **-mies** : anatomie *f* — **anatomic** [ˌænə'tɑmɪk] *or* **anatomical** [-mɪkəl] *adj* : anatomique

ancestor ['ænˌsɛstər] *n* : ancêtre *mf* — **ancestral** [æn'sɛstrəl] *adj* : ancestral — **ancestry** ['ænˌsɛstri] *n* **1** LINEAGE : ascendance *f* **2** ANCESTORS : ancêtres *mpl*

anchor ['æŋkər] *n* **1** : ancre *f* **2** : présentateur *m*, -trice *f* (à la télévision) — **~** *vt* : ancrer — *vi* : jeter l'ancre

anchovy ['ænˌtʃo:vi, æn'tʃo:-] *n, pl* **-vies** *or* **-vy** : anchois *m*

ancient ['eɪntʃənt] *adj* : ancien

and ['ænd] *conj* **1** : et **2 come ~ see** : venez voir **3 more ~ more** : de plus en plus **4 try ~ finish it soon** : tâchez de l'achever bientôt

anecdote ['ænɪkˌdo:t] *n* : anecdote *f*

anemia [ə'ni:miə] *n* : anémie *f* — **anemic** [ə'ni:mɪk] *adj* : anémique

anesthesia [ˌænəs'θi:ʒə] *n* : anesthésie *f* — **anesthetic** ['ænəs'θɛtɪk] *adj* : anesthésique — **~** *n* : anesthésique *m*

anew [ə'nu:, -'nju:] *adv* : encore, de nouveau

angel ['eɪndʒəl] *n* : ange *m* — **angelic** [æn'dʒɛlɪk] *or* **angelical** [-lɪkəl] *adj* : angélique

anger ['æŋgər] *vt* : fâcher, mettre en colère — **~** *n* : colère *f*

angle ['æŋgəl] *n* **1** : angle *m* **2 at an ~ :** de biais — **angler** ['æŋglər] *n* : pêcheur *m*, -cheuse *f* à la ligne

Anglo–Saxon [ˌæŋglo'sæksən] *adj* : anglo-saxon

angry ['æŋgri] *adj* **-grier; -est** : fâché, en colère — **angrily** ['æŋgrəli] *adv* : avec colère

anguish ['æŋgwɪʃ] *n* : angoisse *f*

angular [ˈæŋgjələr] *adj* : anguleux
animal [ˈænəməl] *n* : animal *m*
animate [ˈænəˌmeɪt] *vt* **-mated; -mating** : animer, stimuler — ~ [ˈænəmət] *adj* ALIVE : vivant — **animated** [ˈænəˌmeɪtəd] *adj* **1** : animé **2** ~ **cartoon** : dessin *m* animé — **animation** [ˌænəˈmeɪʃən] *n* : animation *f*
animosity [ˌænəˈmɑsəti] *n, pl* **-ties** : animosité *f*
anise [ˈænəs] *n* : anis *m*
ankle [ˈæŋkəl] *n* : cheville *f*
annex [əˈnɛks, ˈæˌnɛks] *vt* : annexer — ~ [ˈæˌnɛks, -nɪks] *n* : annexe *f*
annihilate [əˈnaɪəˌleɪt] *vt* **-lated; -lating** : anéantir, annihiler — **annihilation** [əˌnaɪəˈleɪʃən] *n* : anéantissement *m*
anniversary [ˌænəˈvərsəri] *n, pl* **-ries** : anniversaire *m*
annotate [ˈænəˌteɪt] *vt* **-tated; -tating** : annoter
announce [əˈnaʊnts] *vt* **-nounced; -nouncing** : annoncer — **announcement** [əˈnaʊntsmənt] *n* **1** : annonce *f* **2** NOTIFICATION : avis *m* **3** : faire-part *m* (de mariage, etc.) — **announcer** [əˈnaʊntsər] *n* : présentateur, -trice *f;* speaker *m*, -kerine *f* France
annoy [əˈnɔɪ] *vt* : agacer, ennuyer — **annoyance** [əˈnɔɪənts] *n* : contrariété *f* — **annoying** [əˈnɔɪɪŋ] *adj* : agaçant
annual [ˈænjuəl] *adj* : annuel
annuity [əˈnuːəti] *n, pl* **-ties** : rente *f* (viagère)
annul [əˈnʌl] *vt* **anulled; anulling** : annuler — **annulment** [əˈnʌlmənt] *n* : annulation *f*
anoint [əˈnɔɪnt] *vt* : oindre
anomaly [əˈnɑməli] *n, pl* **-lies** : anomalie *f*
anonymous [əˈnɑnəməs] *adj* : anonyme — **anonymity** [ˌænəˈnɪməti] *n* : anonymat *m*
another [əˈnʌðər] *adj* **1** : un(e) autre **2** ~ **beer** : encore une bière **3 in** ~ **year** : dans un an — ~ *pron* **1** : un autre *m*, une autre *f* **2 one after** ~ : l'un après l'autre
answer [ˈæntsər] *n* **1** REPLY : réponse *f* **2** SOLUTION : solution *f* — ~ *vt* **1** : répondre à **2** ~ **the door** : aller ouvrir la porte — *vi* : répondre
ant [ˈænt] *n* : fourmi *f*
antagonize [ænˈtægəˌnaɪz] *vt* **-nized; -nizing** : éveiller l'hostilité de, contrarier — **antagonistic** [ænˌtægəˈnɪstɪk] *adj* : antagoniste
antarctic [æntˈɑrktɪk, -ˈɑrtɪk] *adj* : antarctique
antelope [ˈæntəlˌoːp] *n, pl* **-lope** *or* **-lopes** : antilope *f*
antenna [ænˈtɛnə] *n, pl* **-nae** *or* **-nas** : antenne *f*
anthem [ˈænθəm] *n* : hymne *m*

anthology [ænˈθɑlədʒi] *n, pl* **-gies** : anthologie *f*
anthropology [ˌænθrəˈpɑlədʒi] *n* : anthropologie *f*
antibiotic [ˌæntibaɪˈɑtɪk, ˌænˌtaɪ-, -bi-] *adj* : antibiotique — ~ *n* : antibiotique *m*
antibody [ˈæntiˌbɑdi] *n, pl* **-bodies** : anticorps *m*
anticipate [ænˈtɪsəˌpeɪt] *vt* **-pated; -pating 1** FORESEE : anticiper **2** EXPECT : s'attendre à — **anticipation** [ænˌtɪsəˈpeɪʃən] *n* : anticipation *f*
antics [ˈæntɪks] *npl* : singeries *fpl*
antidote [ˈæntiˌdoːt] *n* : antidote *m*
antifreeze [ˈæntiˌfriːz] *n* : antigel *m*
antipathy [ænˈtɪpəθi] *n, pl* **-thies** : antipathie *f*
antiquated [ˈæntəˌkweɪtəd] *adj* : dépassé
antique [ænˈtiːk] *adj* : ancien, antique — ~ *n* : antiquité *f* — **antiquity** [ænˈtɪkwəti] *n, pl* **-ties** : antiquité *f*
anti-Semitic [ˌæntisəˈmɪtɪk, ˌænˌtaɪ-] *adj* : antisémite
antiseptic [ˌæntəˈsɛptɪk] *adj* : antiseptique — ~ *n* : antiseptique *m*
antisocial [ˌæntiˈsoːʃəl, ˌænˌtaɪ-] *adj* UNSOCIABLE : peu sociable
antlers [ˈæntlərz] *npl* : bois *mpl*, ramure *f*
antonym [ˈæntəˌnɪm] *n* : antonyme *m*
anus [ˈeɪnəs] *n* : anus *m*
anvil [ˈænvəl, -vɪl] *n* : enclume *f*
anxiety [æŋkˈzaɪəti] *n, pl* **-ties 1** APPREHENSION : anxiété *f* **2** EAGERNESS : impatience *f* — **anxious** [ˈæŋkʃəs] *adj* **1** WORRIED : inquiet, anxieux **2** EAGER : impatient — **anxiously** [ˈæŋkʃəsli] *adv* **1** : anxieusement **2** : avec impatience
any [ˈɛni] *adv* **1** SOMEWHAT : un peu **2** AT ALL : du tout **3 do you want** ~ **more tea?** : voulez-vous encore du thé? **4 she does-n't smoke** ~ **longer** : elle ne fume plus — ~ *adj* **1** : de, de la, du, des **2** WHICHEVER : quelconque, n'importe quel **3 at** ~ **moment** : à tout moment **4 we don't have** ~ **money** : nous n'avons pas d'argent — ~ *pron* **1** WHICHEVER : n'importe lequel **2 do you have** ~ : est-ce que vous en avez?
anybody [ˈɛniˌbʌdi, -ˌbɑ-] → **anyone**
anyhow [ˈɛniˌhaʊ] *adv* **1** : de toute façon, en tout cas **2** HAPHAZARDLY : n'importe comment
anymore [ˌɛniˈmor] *adv* **not** ~ : ne plus
anyone [ˈɛniˌwʌn] *pron* **1** SOMEONE : quelqu'un **2** (*in negative constructions*) : personne **3** ~ **can play** : tout le monde peut jouer, n'importe qui peut jouer
anyplace [ˈɛniˌpleɪs] → **anywhere**
anything [ˈɛniˌθɪŋ] *pron* **1** WHATEVER : n'importe quoi **2** SOMETHING : quelque chose **3** (*in negative constructions*) : rien **4**

~ **but** : tout sauf **5 hardly** ~ : presque rien

anytime ['ɛni,taɪm] *adv* : n'importe quand

anyway ['ɛni,weɪ] → **anyhow**

anywhere ['ɛni,ʰwɛr] *adv* **1** : n'importe où **2** SOMEWHERE : quelque part **3** (*in negative constructions*) : nulle part **4** ~ **else** : partout ailleurs

apart [ə'pɑrt] *adv* **1** ASIDE : à part, à l'écart **2** SEPARATED : éloigné **3** ~ **from** : en dehors de **4 five minutes** ~ : à cinq minutes d'intervalle **5 take** ~ : démonter **6 tell** ~ : distinguer

apartment [ə'pɑrtmənt] *n* : appartement *m*

apathy ['æpəθi] *n* : apathie *f* — **apathetic** [,æpə'θɛtɪk] *adj* : apathique

ape ['eɪp] *n* : grand singe *m*

aperture ['æpərtʃər, -,tʃur] *n* : ouverture *f*

apex ['eɪ,pɛks] *n, pl* **apexes** *or* **apices** ['eɪpə,si:z, 'æ-] : sommet *m*

apiece [ə'pi:s] *adv* **1** : chacun **2 two dollars** ~ : deux dollars la pièce

aplomb [ə'plɑm, -'plʌm] *n* : aplomb *m*

apology [ə'pɑlədʒi] *n, pl* **-gies** : excuses *fpl* — **apologetic** [ə'pɑlə'dʒɛtɪk] *adj* **1** : d'excuse **2 be** ~ : s'excuser — **apologize** [ə-'pɑlə,dʒaɪz] *vi* **-gized; -gizing** : s'excuser, faire des excuses

apostle [ə'pɑsəl] *n* : apôtre *m*

apostrophe [ə'pɑstrə,fi:] *n* : apostrophe *f*

appall *or Brit* **appal** [ə'pɔl] *vt* **-palled; -palling** : épouvanter — **appalling** [ə'pɔlɪŋ] *adj* : épouvantable

apparatus [,æpə'rætəs, -'reɪ-] *n, pl* **-tuses** *or* **-tus** : appareil *m*

apparel [ə'pærəl] *n* : habillement *m*

apparent [ə'pærənt] *adj* **1** OBVIOUS : évident **2** SEEMING : apparent — **apparently** [ə'pærəntli] *adv* : apparemment

apparition [,æpə'rɪʃən] *n* : apparition *f*

appeal [ə'pi:l] *vt* : faire appel contre (un jugement) — *vi* **1** ~ **for** : lancer un appel à **2** ~ **to** ATTRACT : plaire à **3** ~ **to** INVOKE : faire appel à — ~ *n* **1** REQUEST : appel *m* **2** ATTRACTION : attrait *m* — **appealing** [ə-'pi:lɪŋ] *adj* : attrayant, séduisant

appear [ə'pɪr] *vi* **1** : paraître **2** SEEM : paraître, sembler **3** COME OUT : paraître, sortir — **appearance** [ə'pɪrənts] *n* **1** LOOK : apparence *f* **2** ARRIVAL : apparition *f* **3** ~**s** *npl* : apparences *fpl*

appease [ə'pi:z] *vt* **-peased; -peasing** : apaiser

appendix [ə'pɛndɪks] *n, pl* **-dixes** *or* **-dices** [-də,si:z] : appendice *m* — **appendicitis** [ə-,pɛndə'saɪtəs] *n* : appendicite *f*

appetite ['æpə,taɪt] *n* : appétit *m* — **appetizer** ['æpə,taɪzər] *n* : amuse-gueule *m* — **appetizing** ['æpə,taɪzɪŋ] *adj* : appétissant

applaud [ə'plɔd] *v* : applaudir — **applause** [ə'plɔz] *n* : applaudissements *mpl*

apple ['æpəl] *n* : pomme *f*

appliance [ə'plaɪənts] *n* : appareil *m*

apply [ə'plaɪ] *v* **-plied; -plying** *vt* **1** : appliquer **2** EXERT : exercer **3** ~ **oneself** : s'appliquer — *vi* **1** : s'appliquer **2** ~ **for** : poser sa candidature pour — **applicant** ['æplɪkənt] *n* : candidat *m*, -date *f* — **application** [,æplə'keɪʃən] *n* **1** USE : application *f* **2** : demande *f* (d'emploi)

appoint [ə'pɔɪnt] *vt* **1** SET : fixer **2** NAME : nommer — **appointment** [ə'pɔɪntmənt] *n* **1** : nomination *f* **2** MEETING : rendez-vous *m*

apportion [ə'porʃən] *vt* : répartir

appraise [ə'preɪz] *vt* **-praised; -praising** : évaluer — **appraisal** [ə'preɪzəl] *n* : évaluation *f*

appreciate [ə'pri:ʃi,eɪt, -'prɪ-] *vt* **-ated; -ating** **1** VALUE : apprécier **2** REALIZE : comprendre, se rendre compte de **3 I** ~ **your help** : je vous suis reconnaissant de m'avoir aidé — **appreciation** [ə,pri:ʃi-'eɪʃən, -,prɪ-] *n* **1** EVALUATION : appréciation *f* **2** GRATITUDE : reconnaissance *f* — **appreciative** [ə'pri:ʃəṭɪv, -'prɪ-; ə'pri:ʃi,eɪ-] *adj* : reconnaissant

apprehend [,æprɪ'hɛnd] *vt* **1** ARREST : appréhender **2** UNDERSTAND : comprendre **3** DREAD : appréhender — **apprehension** [,æprɪ'hɛntʃən] *n* : appréhension *f* — **apprehensive** [,æprɪ'hɛntsɪv] *adj* : inquiet

apprentice [ə'prɛntɪs] *n* : apprenti *m*, -tie *f* — **apprenticeship** [ə'prɛntɪs,ʃɪp] *n* : apprentissage *m*

approach [ə'pro:tʃ] *vt* **1** NEAR : s'approcher de **2** : s'adresser à (quelqu'un), aborder (un problème, etc.) — *vi* : s'approcher — ~ *n* : approche *f* — **approachable** [ə'pro:tʃəbəl] *adj* : abordable, accessible

appropriate [ə'pro:pri,eɪt] *vt* **-ated; -ating** **1** SEIZE : s'approprier **2** ALLOCATE : affecter — ~ [ə'pro:priət] *adj* : approprié

approve [ə'pru:v] *v* **-proved; -proving** *or* ~ **of** : approuver — **approval** [ə'pru:vəl] *n* : approbation *f*

approximate [ə'prɑksəmət] *adj* : approximatif — ~ [ə'prɑksə,meɪt] *vt* **-mated; -mating** : se rapprocher de — **approximately** [ə'prɑksəmətli] *adv* : à peu près, environ

apricot ['æprə,kɑt, 'eɪ-] *n* : abricot *m*

April ['eɪprəl] *n* : avril *m*

apron ['eɪprən] *n* : tablier *m*

apt ['æpt] *adj* **1** : approprié **2 be** ~ **to** : avoir tendance à — **aptitude** ['æptə,tu:d, -,tju:d] *n* : aptitude *f*

aquarium [ə'kwæriəm] *n, pl* **-iums** *or* **-ia** [-iə] : aquarium *m*

aquatic [ə'kwɑṭɪk, -'kwæ-] *adj* **1** : aquatique **2** : nautique (se dit des sports)
aqueduct ['ækwə,dʌkt] *n* : aqueduc *m*
Arab ['ærəb] *or* **Arabic** ['ærəbɪk] *adj* : arabe — **Arabic** *n* : arabe *m* (langue)
arbitrary ['ɑrbə,treri] *adj* : arbitraire
arbitrate ['ɑrbə,treɪt] *v* **-trated; -trating** : arbitrer — **arbitration** [,ɑrbə'treɪʃən] *n* : arbitrage *m*
arc ['ɑrk] *n* : arc *m*
arcade [ɑr'keɪd] *n* **1** : arcade *f* **2 shopping ~** : galerie *f* marchande
arch ['ɑrtʃ] *n* : voûte *f*, arc *m* — **~** *vt* : arquer, courber
archaeology *or* **archeology** [,ɑrki'ɑlədʒi] *n* : archéologie *f* — **archaeological** [,ɑrkiə'lɑdʒɪkəl] *adj* : archéologique — **archaeologist** [,ɑrki'ɑlədʒɪst] *n* : archéologue *mf*
archaic [ɑr'keɪɪk] *adj* : archaïque
archbishop [ɑrtʃ'bɪʃəp] *n* : archevêque *m*
archery ['ɑrtʃəri] *n* : tir *m* à l'arc
archipelago [,ɑrkə'pelə,go:, ,ɑrtʃə-] *n, pl* **-goes** *or* **-gos** [-go:z] : archipel *m*
architecture ['ɑrkə,tɛktʃər] *n* : architecture *f* — **architect** ['ɑrkə,tɛkt] *n* : architecte *mf* — **architectural** [,ɑrkə'tɛktʃərəl] *adj* : architectural
archives ['ɑr,kaɪvz] *npl* : archives *fpl*
archway ['ɑrtʃ,weɪ] *n* : voûte *f*, arcade *f*
arctic ['ɑrktɪk, 'ɑrt-] *adj* : arctique
ardent ['ɑrdənt] *adj* : ardent — **ardently** ['ɑrdəntli] *adv* : ardemment — **ardor** ['ɑrdər] *n* : ardeur *f*
arduous ['ɑrdʒuəs] *adj* : ardu
are → **be**
area ['æriə] *n* **1** REGION : région *f* **2** SURFACE : aire *f* **3** FIELD : domaine *m* **4 ~ code** : indicatif *m* de zone, indicatif *m* régional *Can*
arena [ə'ri:nə] *n* : arène *f*, aréna *m Can*
aren't ['ɑrnt, 'ɑrənt] (*contraction of* **are not**) → **be**
argue ['ɑr,gju:] *v* **-gued; -guing** *vi* **1** QUARREL : se disputer **2** DEBATE : argumenter — *vt* DEBATE : discuter — **argument** ['ɑrgjəmənt] *n* **1** QUARREL : dispute *f* **2** DEBATE : discussion *f* **3** REASONING : argument *m*
arid ['ærəd] *adj* : aride
arise [ə'raɪz] *vi* **arose** [ə'ro:z]; **arisen** [ə'rɪzən]; **arising 1** : se présenter **2 ~ from** : résulter de
aristocracy [,ærə'stɑkrəsi] *n, pl* **-cies** : aristocratie *f* — **aristocrat** [ə'rɪstə,kræt] *n* : aristocrate *mf* — **aristocratic** [ə,rɪstə'krætɪk] *adj* : aristocratique
arithmetic [ə'rɪθmə,tɪk] *n* : arithmétique *f*
ark ['ɑrk] *n* : arche *f*
arm ['ɑrm] *n* **1** : bras *m* **2** WEAPON : arme *f* — **~** *vt* : armer — **armament** ['ɑrməmənt]

n : armement *m* — **armchair** ['ɑrm,tʃɛr] *n* : fauteuil *m* — **armed** ['ɑrmd] *adj* **1** : armé **2 ~ forces** : forces *fpl* armées **3 ~ robbery** : vol *m* à main armée
armistice ['ɑrməstɪs] *n* : armistice *m*
armor *or Brit* **armour** ['ɑrmər] *n* **1** : armure *f* **2** *or* **~ plating** : blindage *m* — **armored** *or Brit* **armoured** ['ɑrmərd] *adj* : blindé — **armory** *or Brit* **armoury** ['ɑrməri] *n, pl* **-mories** : arsenal *m*
armpit ['ɑrm,pɪt] *n* : aisselle *f*
army ['ɑrmi] *n, pl* **-mies** : armée *f*
aroma [ə'ro:mə] *n* : arôme *m* — **aromatic** [,ærə'mætɪk] *adj* : aromatique
around [ə'raʊnd] *adv* **1** : de circonférence **2** NEARBY : là, dans les parages **3** APPROXIMATELY : environ, à peu près **4 all ~** : tout autour — **~** *prep* **1** SURROUNDING : autour de **2** THROUGHOUT : partout dans **3 ~ here** : par ici **4 ~ noon** : vers midi
arouse [ə'raʊz] *vt* **aroused; arousing 1** AWAKE : réveiller **2** STIMULATE : éveiller
arrange [ə'reɪndʒ] *v* **-ranged; -ranging** *vt* : arranger — *vi* **~ for** : prendre des dispositions pour — **arrangement** [ə'reɪndʒmənt] *n* **1** ORDER : arrangement *m* **2 ~s** *npl* : dispositions *fpl*
array [ə'reɪ] *n* : sélection *f*
arrears [ə'rɪrz] *npl* **1** : arriéré *m* **2 be in ~** : avoir du retard
arrest [ə'rest] *vt* : arrêter — **~** *n* : arrestation *f*
arrive [ə'raɪv] *vi* **-rived; -riving 1** : arriver **2 ~ at** : parvenir à, atteindre — **arrival** [ə'raɪvəl] *n* : arrivée *f*
arrogance ['ærəgənts] *n* : arrogance *f* — **arrogant** ['ærəgənt] *adj* : arrogant
arrow ['æro] *n* : flèche *f*
arsenal ['ɑrsənəl] *n* : arsenal *m*
arsenic ['ɑrsənɪk] *n* : arsenic *m*
arson ['ɑrsən] *n* : incendie *m* criminel
art ['ɑrt] *n* : art *m*
artefact *Brit* → **artifact**
artery ['ɑrtəri] *n, pl* **-teries** : artère *f*
artful ['ɑrtfəl] *adj* : rusé, astucieux
arthritis [ɑr'θraɪṭəs] *n, pl* **-thritides** [-'θrɪṭə,di:z] : arthrite *f* — **arthritic** [ɑr'θrɪṭɪk] *adj* : arthritique
artichoke ['ɑrṭə,tʃo:k] *n* : artichaut *m*
article ['ɑrtɪkəl] *n* : article *m*
articulate [ɑr'tɪkjə,leɪt] *vt* **-lated; -lating** : articuler — [ɑr'tɪkjələt] *adj* **be ~** : s'exprimer bien
artifact *or Brit* **artefact** ['ɑrṭə,fækt] *n* : objet *m* fabriqué
artificial [,ɑrṭə'fɪʃəl] *adj* : artificiel
artillery [ɑr'tɪləri] *n, pl* **-leries** : artillerie *f*
artist ['ɑrtɪst] *n* : artiste *mf* — **artistic** [ɑr'tɪstɪk] *adj* : artistique
as ['æz] *adv* **1 ~ much** : autant **2 ~ tall**

~ : aussi grand que **3 ~ well** : aussi —
~ *conj* **1** LIKE : comme **2** WHILE : tandis
que, alors que **3** SINCE : puisque, comme **4**
~ **is** : tel quel — ~ *prep* : en tant que,
comme — ~ *pron* **1** : que **2 ~ you know**
: comme vous savez

asbestos [æz'bɛstəs, æs-] *n* : amiante *m*

ascend [ə'sɛnd] *vt* : monter (à), gravir — *vi*
: monter — **ascent** [ə'sɛnt] *n* : ascension *f*

ascertain [ˌæsər'teɪn] *vt* : établir

ascribe [ə'skraɪb] *vt* **-cribed; -cribing** ~
to: attribuer à

as for *prep* : quant à

ash[1] ['æʃ] *n* : cendre *f*

ash[2] *n* : frêne *m* (arbre)

ashamed [ə'ʃeɪmd] *adj* **1** : honteux **2 be ~**
: avoir honte

ashore [ə'ʃor] *adv* : à terre

ashtray ['æʃˌtreɪ] *n* : cendrier *m*

Asian ['eɪʒən, -ʃən] *adj* : asiatique

aside [ə'saɪd] *adv* : de côté, à part — **aside
from** *prep* **1** BESIDES : à part **2** EXCEPT
: sauf

as if *conj* : comme si

ask ['æsk] *vt* **1** : demander **2** INVITE : inviter **3 ~ a question** : poser une question
4 ~ s.o. : demandez à qqn — *vi* : demander

askance [ə'skænts] *adv* **look ~** : regarder
du coin de l'œil

askew [ə'skju:] *adv & adj* : de travers

asleep [ə'sli:p] *adj* **1** : endormi **2 fall ~**
: s'endormir

as of *prep* : dès, à partir de

asparagus [ə'spærəgəs] *ns & pl* : asperges
fpl

aspect ['æˌspɛkt] *n* : aspect *m*

asphalt ['æsˌfɔlt] *n* : asphalte *m*

asphyxiate [æ'sfɪksiˌeɪt] *vt* **-ated; -ating**
: asphyxier — **asphyxiation** [æˌsfɪksi-
'eɪʃən] *n* : asphyxie *f*

aspire [ə'spaɪr] *vi* **-pired; -piring ~ to** : aspirer à — **aspiration** [ˌæspə'reɪʃən] *n* : aspiration *f*

aspirin ['æsprən, 'æspə-] *n*, *pl* **aspirin** *or* **as-
pirins** : aspirine *f*

ass ['æs] *n* **1** : âne *m* **2** FOOL : idiot *m*,
-diote *f*

assail [ə'seɪl] *vt* : assaillir — **assailant** [ə-
'seɪlənt] *n* : assaillant *m*, -lante *f*

assassin [ə'sæsən] *n* : assassin *m* — **assassinate** [ə'sæsənˌeɪt] *vt* **-nated; -nating** : assassiner — **assassination** [əˌsæsən'eɪʃən]
n : assassinat *m*

assault [ə'sɔlt] *vt* : agresser — ~ *n* : agression *f*, assaut *m* (militaire)

assemble [ə'sɛmbəl] *v* **-bled; -bling** *vt* **1**
CONSTRUCT : assembler **2** GATHER : rassembler — *vi* CONVENE : se rassembler — **assembly** [ə'sɛmbli] *n*, *pl* **-blies 1** MEETING

: assemblée *f*, réunion *f* **2 ~ line** : chaîne *f*
de montage

assent [ə'sɛnt] *vi* : consentir — ~ *n* : assentiment *m*

assert [ə'sərt] *vt* **1** : affirmer **2 ~ oneself**
: s'imposer — **assertion** [ə'sərʃən] *n* : assertion *f* — **assertive** [ə'sərtɪv] *adj* : assuré

assess [ə'sɛs] *vt* : évaluer — **assessment**
[ə'sɛsmənt] *n* : évaluation *f*

asset ['æˌsɛt] *n* **1** : avantage *m*, atout *m* **2**
~**s** *npl* : biens *mpl*, actif *m*

assiduous [ə'sɪdʒuəs] *adj* : assidu

assign [ə'saɪn] *vt* **1** ALLOT : assigner **2** AP-
POINT : nommer — **assignment** [ə-
'saɪnmənt] *n* **1** TASK : mission *f* **2** HOME-
WORK : devoir *m*

assimilate [ə'sɪməˌleɪt] *vt* **-lated; -lating**
: assimiler

assist [ə'sɪst] *vt* : aider, assister — **assistance** [ə'sɪstənts] *n* : aide *f*, assistance *f* —
assistant [ə'sɪstənt] *n* : assistant *m*, -tante *f*;
adjoint *m*, -jointe *f*

associate [ə'soˌʃiˌeɪt, -si-] *v* **-ated; -ating** *vt*
: associer — *vi* ~ **with** : fréquenter —
[ə'soˌʃiət, -siət] *n* : associé *m*, -ciée *f* — **association** [əˌsoˌʃi'eɪʃən, -si-] *n* : association *f*

as soon as *conj* : aussitôt que

assorted [ə'sɔrtəd] *adj* : assorti — **assortment** [ə'sɔrtmənt] *n* : assortiment *m*

assume [ə'su:m] *vt* **-sumed; -suming 1**
: assumer **2** SUPPOSE : supposer, présumer
— **assumption** [ə'sʌmpʃən] *n* : supposition *f*

assure [ə'ʃur] *vt* **-sured; -suring** : assurer
— **assurance** [ə'ʃurənts] *n* : assurance *f*

asterisk ['æstəˌrɪsk] *n* : astérisque *m*

asthma ['æzmə] *n* : asthme *m*

as though → as if

as to *prep* : sur, concernant

astonish [ə'stanɪʃ] *vt* : étonner — **astonishing** [ə'stanɪʃɪŋ] *adj* : étonnant — **astonishment** [ə'stanɪʃmənt] *n* : étonnement *m*

astound [ə'staund] *vt* : stupéfier — **astounding** [ə'staundɪŋ] *adj* : stupéfiant

astray [ə'streɪ] *adv* **1 go ~** : s'égarer **2
lead ~** : égarer

astrology [ə'straləd͡ʒi] *n* : astrologie *f*

astronaut ['æstrəˌnɔt] *n* : astronaute *mf*

astronomy [ə'stranəmi] *n*, *pl* **-mies** : astronomie *f* — **astronomer** [ə'stranəmər] *n*
: astronome *mf* — **astronomical** [ˌæstrə-
'namɪkəl] *adj* : astronomique

astute [ə'stu:t, -'stju:t] *adj* : astucieux — **as-
tuteness** [ə'stu:tnəs, -'stju:t-] *n* : astuce *f*

as well as *conj* : en plus de — ~ *prep*
: ainsi que, à part

asylum [ə'saɪləm] *n* : asile *m*

at ['æt] *prep* **1** : à **2 ~ the dentist's** : chez
le dentiste **3 ~ three o'clock** : à trois

heures **4** ~ **war** : en guerre **5 be angry** ~ : être fâché contre **6 laugh** ~ : rire de **7 shoot** ~ : tirer sur — **at all** *adv* : du tout

ate ['eɪt] → **eat**

atheist ['eɪθiɪst] *n* : athée *mf* — **atheism** ['eɪθiˌɪzəm] *n* : athéisme *m*

athlete ['æθˌliːt] *n* : athlète *mf* — **athletic** [æθ'lɛtɪk] *adj* : athlétique — **athletics** [æθ-'lɛtɪks] *ns & pl* : athlétisme *m*

atlas ['ætləs] *n* : atlas *m*

atmosphere ['ætməˌsfɪr] *n* : atmosphère *f* — **atmospheric** [ˌætmə'sfɪrɪk, -'sfɛr-] *adj* : atmosphérique

atom ['ætəm] *n* : atome *m* — **atomic** [ə-'tɑmɪk] *adj* : atomique

atomizer ['ætəˌmaɪzər] *n* : atomiseur *m*

atone [ə'toːn] *vi* **atoned; atoning** ~ **for** : expier — **atonement** [ə'toːnmənt] *n* : expiation *f*

atrocious [ə'troːʃəs] *adj* : atroce — **atrocity** [ə'trɑsəti] *n, pl* **-ties** : atrocité *f*

atrophy ['ætrəfi] *vi* **-phied; phying** : s'atrophier

attach [ə'tætʃ] *vt* **1** : attacher **2 become** ~**ed to** : s'attacher à — *vi* ADHERE : s'attacher —**attachment** [ə'tætʃmənt] *n* **1** AFFECTION : attachement *m* **2** ACCESSORY : accessoire *m*

attack [ə'tæk] *v* : attaquer — ~ *n* **1** : attaque *f* **2 heart** ~ : crise *f* cardiaque — **attacker** [ə'tækər] *n* : agresseur *m*

attain [ə'teɪn] *vt* : atteindre — **attainment** [ə-'teɪnmənt] *n* : réalisation *f*

attempt [ə'tɛmpt] *vt* : tenter — ~ *n* : tentative *f*

attend [ə'tɛnd] *vt* **1** : assister à **2** ~ **church** : aller à l'église — *vi* **1** ~ **to** : s'occuper de **2** ~ **to** HEED : prêter attention à — **attendance** [ə'tɛndənts] *n* **1** : présence *f* **2** TURNOUT : assistance *f* — **attendant** [ə-'tɛndənt] *n* **1** : gardien *m*, -dienne *f* **2 service station** ~ : pompiste *mf*

attention [ə'tɛnʧən] *n* **1** : attention *f* **2 pay** ~ **to** : prêter attention à — **attentive** [ə-'tɛntɪv] *adj* : attentif

attest [ə'tɛst] *vt* : attester — *vi* ~ **to** : témoigner de

attic ['ætɪk] *n* : grenier *m*

attitude ['ætəˌtuːd, -ˌtjuːd] *n* : attitude *f*

attorney [ə'tərni] *n, pl* **-neys** : avocat *m*, -cate *f*

attract [ə'trækt] *vt* : attirer — **attraction** [ə-'trækʃən] *n* **1** : attrait *f* **2** : attraction *f* (en science) — **attractive** [ə'træktɪv] *adj* : attirant, attrayant

attribute ['ætrəˌbjuːt] *n* : attribut *m* — ~ [ə-'trɪˌbjuːt] *vt* **-uted; -uting** : attribuer

auburn ['ɔbərn] *adj* : auburn

auction ['ɔkʃən] *vt* : vendre aux enchères — ~ *n* : vente *f* aux enchères

audacious [ɔ'deɪʃəs] *adj* : audacieux — **audacity** [ɔ'dæsəti] *n, pl* **-ties** : audace *f*

audible ['ɔdəbəl] *adj* : audible

audience ['ɔdiənts] *n* : assistance *f*, public *m*

audio ['ɔdiˌoː] *adj* : audio — **audiovisual** [ˌɔdio'vɪʒuəl] *adj* : audiovisuel

audition [ɔ'dɪʃən] *n* : audition *f* — ~ *v* : auditionner

auditor ['ɔdətər] *n* : auditeur *m*, -trice *f*

auditorium [ˌɔdə'tɔriəm] *n, pl* **-riums** *or* **-ria** [-riə] : salle *f*

augment [ɔg'mɛnt] *vt* : augmenter

augur ['ɔgər] *vi* ~ **well** : être de bon augure

August ['ɔgəst] *n* : août *m*

aunt ['ænt, 'ɑnt] *n* : tante *f*

aura ['ɔrə] *n* : aura *f*, atmosphère *f*

auspices ['ɔspəsəz, -ˌsiːz] *npl* : auspices *mpl*

auspicious [ɔ'spɪʃəs] *adj* : favorable

austere [ɔ'stɪr] *adj* : austère — **austerity** [ɔ-'stɛrəti] *n, pl* **-ties** : austérité *f*

Australian [ɔ'streɪljən] *adj* : australien

authentic [ə'θɛntɪk, ɔ-] *adj* : authentique

author ['ɔθər] *n* : auteur *m*

authority [ə'θɔrəti, ɔ-] *n, pl* **-ties** : autorité *f* — **authoritarian** [ɔˌθɔrə'tɛriən, ə-] *adj* : autoritaire — **authoritative** [ə'θɔrəˌteɪtɪv, ɔ-] *adj* **1** DICTATORIAL : autoritaire **2** DEFINITIVE : qui fait autorité — **authorization** [ˌɔθərə'zeɪʃən] *n* : autorisation *f* — **authorize** ['ɔθəˌraɪz] *vt* **-rized; -rizing** : autoriser

autobiography [ˌɔtoˌbaɪ'ɑgrəfi] *n, pl* **-phies** : autobiographie *f* — **autobiographical** [ˌɔtobaɪə'græfɪkəl] *adj* : autobiographique

autograph ['ɔtəˌgræf] *n* : autographe *m*

automate ['ɔtəˌmeɪt] *v* **-mated; -mating** : automatiser — **automatic** [ˌɔtə'mætɪk] *adj* : automatique — **automation** [ˌɔtə-'meɪʃən] *n* : automatisation *f*

automobile [ˌɔtəmo'biːl, -'moːˌbiːl] *n* : automobile *f*, voiture *f*

autonomy [ɔ'tɑnəmi] *n, pl* **-mies** : autonomie *f* — **autonomous** [ɔ'tɑnəməs] *adj* : autonome

autopsy ['ɔˌtɑpsi, -təp-] *n, pl* **-sies** : autopsie *f*

autumn ['ɔtəm] *n* : automne *m*

auxiliary [ɔg'zɪljəri, -'zɪləri] *adj* : auxiliaire — ~ *n, pl* **-ries** : auxiliaire *mf*

avail [ə'veɪl] *vt* ~ **oneself of** : profiter de — ~ *n* **to no** ~ : en vain, sans résultat

available [ə'veɪləbəl] *adj* : disponible — **availability** [əˌveɪlə'bɪləti] *n, pl* **-ties** : disponibilité *f*

avalanche ['ævəˌlænʧ] *n* : avalanche *f*

avarice ['ævərəs] *n* : avarice *f*

avenge [ə'vɛnʤ] *vt* **avenged; avenging** : venger

avenue ['ævəˌnuː, -ˌnjuː] *n* : avenue *f*

average ['ævrɪʤ, 'ævə-] *vt* **-aged; -aging**

: faire en moyenne — ~ *adj* : moyen — ~ *n* : moyenne *f*

averse [ə'vərs] *adj* be ~ to : répugner à — **aversion** [ə'vərʒən] *n* : aversion *f*

avert [ə'vərt] *vt* **1** AVOID : éviter **2** ~ one's eyes : détourner les yeux

aviation [ˌeɪviˈeɪʃən] *n* : aviation *f*

avid [ˈævɪd] *adj* **1** be ~ for : être avide de **2** ENTHUSIASTIC : passionné — **avidly** [ˈævɪdli] *adv* : avidement

avocado [ˌævəˈkɑdo, ˌɑvə-] *n, pl* -dos : avocat *m*

avoid [əˈvɔɪd] *vt* : éviter

await [əˈweɪt] *vt* : attendre

awake [əˈweɪk] *v* **awoke** [əˈwoːk]; **awoken** [əˈwoːkən] *or* **awaked** [əˈweɪkt]; **awaking** *vt* : réveiller, éveiller — *vi* WAKE UP : se réveiller — ~ *adj* : éveillé, réveillé — **awaken** [əˈweɪkən] → **awake**

award [əˈwɔrd] *vt* **1** GRANT : accorder **2** CONFER : décerner — ~ *n* : prix *m*

aware [əˈwær] *adj* **1** : au courant **2** be ~ of : être conscient de — **awareness** [əˈwærnəs] *n* : conscience *f*

awash [əˈwɔʃ] *adj* ~ with : inondé de

away [əˈweɪ] *adv* **1** chatter ~ : bavarder sans arrêt **2** give ~ : donner **3** go ~! : allez-vous en! **4** take ~ : enlever **5** ten kilometers ~ : à dix kilomètres d'ici **6** turn ~ : se détourner — ~ *adj* **1** ABSENT : absent **2** ~ game : match *m* à l'extérieur

awe [ˈɔ] *n* : crainte *f* mêlée de respect — **awesome** [ˈɔsəm] *adj* : impressionnant

awful [ˈɔfəl] *adj* **1** : affreux **2** an ~ lot of : énormément de — **awfully** [ˈɔfəli] *adv* : extrémement

awhile [əˈhwaɪl] *adv* : un moment

awkward [ˈɔkwərd] *adj* **1** : gauche, maladroit **2** EMBARRASSING : gênant **3** DIFFICULT : difficile — **awkwardly** [ˈɔkwərdli] *adv* : maladroitement

awning [ˈɔnɪŋ] *n* : auvent *m*

awoke, awoken → **awake**

awry [əˈraɪ] *adv* go ~ : mal tourner

ax *or* **axe** [ˈæks] *n* : hache *f*

axiom [ˈæksiəm] *n* : axiome *m*

axis [ˈæksɪs] *n, pl* **axes** [-siːz] : axe *m*

axle [ˈæksəl] *n* : essieu *m*

B

b [ˈbiː] *n, pl* **b's** *or* **bs** [ˈbiːz] : b *m*, deu-xième lettre de l'alphabet

babble [ˈbæbəl] *vi* -bled; -bling **1** : babiller, gazouiller **2** MURMUR : murmurer — ~ *n* : babillage *m*

baboon [bæˈbuːn] *n* : babouin *m*

baby [ˈbeɪbi] *n, pl* -bies : bébé *m* — ~ *vt* -bied; -bying : dorloter — **baby carriage** *n* : voiture *f* d'enfant, landau *m France* — **babyish** [ˈbeɪbiɪʃ] *adj* : enfantin — **baby-sit** [ˈbeɪbiˌsɪt] *vi* -sat [-ˌsæt]; -sitting : garder des enfants, faire du baby-sitting *France* — **baby-sitter** [ˈbeɪbiˌsɪtər] *n* : gardienne *f* d'enfants, baby-sitter *mf France*

bachelor [ˈbætʃələr] *n* **1** : célibataire *m* **2** GRADUATE : licencié *m*, -ciée *f*

back [ˈbæk] *n* **1** : dos *m* **2** REVERSE : revers *m*, dos *m* **3** REAR : derrière *m*, arrière *m*, fond *m* **4** : arrière *m* (aux sports) — ~ *adv* **1** : en arrière, vers l'arrière **2** be ~ : être de retour **3** go ~ : retourner **4** two years ~ : il y a deux ans — ~ *adj* **1** REAR : arrière, de derrière **2** OVERDUE : arriéré — ~ *vt* **1** SUPPORT : soutenir, appuyer **2** *or* ~ up : mettre en marche arrière (un véhicule) — *vi* **1** ~ down : céder **2** ~ up : reculer — **backache** [ˈbækˌeɪk] *n* : mal *m* de dos —

backbone [ˈbækˌboːn] *n* : colonne *f* vertébrale — **backfire** [ˈbækˌfaɪr] *vi* -fired; -firing : pétarader — **background** [ˈbækˌɡraʊnd] *n* **1** : arrière-plan *m*, fond *m* (d'un tableau) **2** EXPERIENCE : formation *f* — **backhand** [ˈbækˌhænd] *adj* : de revers — **backhanded** [ˈbækˌhændəd] *adj* : équivoque — **backing** [ˈbækɪŋ] *n* : soutien *m*, appui *m* — **backlash** [ˈbækˌlæʃ] *n* : contrecoup *m*, répercussion *f* — **backlog** [ˈbækˌlɔɡ] *n* : accumulation *f* (de travail, etc.) — **backpack** [ˈbækˌpæk] *n* : sac *m* à dos — **backstage** [ˌbækˈsteɪdʒ, ˈbækˌ-] *adv* : dans les coulisses — **backtrack** [ˈbækˌtræk] *vi* : revenir sur ses pas — **backup** [ˈbækˌʌp] *n* **1** SUPPORT : soutien *m*, appui *m* **2** : sauvegarde *f* (en informatique) — **backward** [ˈbækwərd] *or* **backwards** [-wərdz] *adv* **1** : en arrière **2** bend over ~s : faire tout son possible **3** do it ~ : fais-le à l'envers **4** fall ~ : tomber à la renverse — **backward** *adj* : en arrière

bacon [ˈbeɪkən] *n* : lard *m*, bacon *m*

bacteria [bækˈtɪriə] *npl* : bactéries *fpl*

bad [ˈbæd] *adj* **worse** [ˈwərs]; **worst** [ˈwərst] **1** : mauvais **2** ROTTEN : pourri **3** SEVERE : grave, aigu **4** from ~ to worse : de mal en pis **5 too** ~! : quel dommage! — ~ *adv* → **badly**

badge [ˈbædʒ] *n* : insigne *m*, plaque *f*

badger [ˈbædʒər] *n* : blaireau *m* — ~ *vt* : harceler

badly [ˈbædli] *adv* **1** : mal **2** SEVERELY : gravement **3 need** ~ : avoir grand besoin de

baffle [ˈbæfəl] *vt* **-fled; -fling** : déconcerter

bag [ˈbæg] *n* **1** : sac *m* **2** HANDBAG : sac *m* à main **3** SUITCASE : valise *f* — ~ *vt* **bagged; bagging** : mettre en sac

baggage [ˈbægɪdʒ] *n* : bagages *mpl*

baggy [ˈbægi] *adj* **-gier; -est** : ample, trop grand

bagpipes [ˈbægˌpaɪps] *npl* : cornemuse *f*

bail [ˌbeɪl] *n* : caution *f* — ~ *vt* **1** *or* ~ **out** : vider, écoper (un bateau) **2** *or* ~ **out** RELEASE : mettre en liberté sous caution **3** ~ **out** EXTRICATE : tirer d'affaire

bailiff [ˈbeɪlɪf] *n* : huissier *m*

bait [ˈbeɪt] *vt* **1** : appâter **2** HARASS : tourmenter — ~ *n* : appât *m*

bake [ˈbeɪk] *v* **baked; baking** *vt* : faire cuire au four — *vi* : cuire (au four) — **baker** [ˈbeɪkər] *n* : boulanger *m*, -gère *f* — **bakery** [ˈbeɪkəri] *n, pl* **-ries** : boulangerie *f* — **baking soda** *n* : bicarbonate *m* de soude

balance [ˈbæləns] *n* **1** SCALES : balance *f* **2** COUNTERBALANCE : contrepoids *m* **3** EQUILIBRIUM : équilibre *m* **4** REMAINDER : reste *m* **5** *or* **bank** ~ : solde *m* — ~ *v* **-anced; -ancing** *vt* **1** : faire ses comptes **2** EQUALIZE : équilibrer **3** WEIGH : peser — *vi* : être en équilibre

balcony [ˈbælkəni] *n, pl* **-nies** : balcon *m*

bald [ˈbɔld] *adj* **1** : chauve **2** WORN : usé

balk [ˈbɔk] *vi* ~ **at** : reculer devant

ball [ˈbɔl] *n* **1** : balle *f*, ballon *m*, boule *f* **2** DANCE : bal *m* **3** ~ **of string** : pelote *f* de ficelle

ballad [ˈbæləd] *n* : ballade *f*

ballast [ˈbæləst] *n* : lest *m*, ballast *m*

ballerina [ˌbæləˈriːnə] *n* : ballerine *f*

ballet [bæˈleɪ, ˈbæˌleɪ] *n* : ballet *m*

ballistic [bəˈlɪstɪk] *adj* : balistique

balloon [bəˈluːn] *n* : ballon *m*, balloune *f Can*

ballot [ˈbælət] *n* **1** : bulletin *m* de vote **2** VOTING : scrutin *m*

ballpoint pen [ˈbɔlˌpɔɪnt] *n* : stylo *m* à bille

ballroom [ˈbɔlˌruːm, -ˌrʊm] *n* : salle *f* de danse, salle *f* de bal

balm [ˈbam, ˈbalm] *n* : baume *m* — **balmy** [ˈbami, ˈbal-] *adj* **balmier; -est** : doux, agréable

baloney [bəˈloːni] *n* NONSENSE : balivernes *fpl*

bamboo [bæmˈbuː] *n* : bambou *m*

bamboozle [bæmˈbuːzəl] *vt* **-zled; -zling** : embobiner *fam*

ban [ˈbæn] *vt* **banned; banning** : interdire — ~ *n* : interdiction *f*

banana [bəˈnænə] *n* : banane *f*

band [ˈbænd] *n* **1** STRIP : bande *f* **2** GROUP : groupe *m*, orchestre *m* — ~ *vi* ~ **together** : se réunir, se grouper

bandage [ˈbændɪdʒ] *n* : pansement *m*, bandage *m* — ~ *vt* : bander, panser

bandy [ˈbændi] *vt* **-died; -dying** ~ **about** : faire circuler

bang [ˈbæŋ] *vt* **1** STRIKE : frapper **2** SLAM : claquer — *vi* ~ **on** : cogner sur — ~ *n* **1** BLOW : coup *m* **2** EXPLOSION : détonation *f* **3** SLAM : claquement *m*

bangs [ˈbæŋz] *npl* : frange *f*

banish [ˈbænɪʃ] *vt* : bannir

banister [ˈbænəstər] *n* : rampe *f*

bank [ˈbæŋk] *n* **1** : banque *f* **2** : talus *m*, rive *f* (d'un fleuve) **3** EMBANKMENT : terre-plein *m* — ~ *vt* : déposer — *vi* **1** : avoir un compte en banque **2** ~ **on** : compter sur — **banker** [ˈbæŋkər] *n* : banquier *m* — **banking** [ˈbæŋkɪŋ] *n* : opérations *fpl* bancaires

bankrupt [ˈbæŋˌkrʌpt] *adj* : en faillite — **bankruptcy** [ˈbæŋˌkrʌptsi] *n, pl* **-cies** : faillite *f*

banner [ˈbænər] *n* : bannière *f*

banquet [ˈbæŋkwət] *n* : banquet *m*

banter [ˈbæntər] *n* : plaisanteries *fpl* — ~ *vi* : plaisanter

baptize [bæpˈtaɪz, ˈbæpˌtaɪz] *vt* **-tized; -tizing** : baptiser — **baptism** [ˈbæpˌtɪzəm] *n* : baptême *m*

bar [ˈbar] *n* **1** : barre *f* (de métal), barreau *m* (d'une fenêtre) **2** BARRIER : obstacle *m*, barrière *f* **3** TAVERN : bar *m* **4** **behind** ~**s** : sous les verrous **5** ~ **of soap** : pain *m* de savon — ~ *vt* **barred; barring 1** OBSTRUCT : barrer, bloquer **2** EXCLUDE : exclure **3** PROHIBIT : interdire — ~ *prep* **1** : sauf **2** ~ **none** : sans exception

barbarian [barˈbæriən] *n* : barbare *mf* — **barbaric** [barˈbærɪk] *adj* : barbare

barbecue [ˈbarbɪˌkjuː] *vt* **-cued; -cuing** : griller au charbon de bois — ~ *n* : barbecue *m*

barbed wire [ˈbarbdˈwaɪr] *n* : fil *m* de fer barbelé

barber [ˈbarbər] *n* : coiffeur *m*, -feuse *f*; barbier *m Can*

bare [ˈbær] *adj* **barer; barest 1** : dénudé **2** EMPTY : vide **3** MINIMUM : essentiel — **barefaced** [ˈbærˌfeɪst] *adj* : éhonté — **barefoot** [ˈbærˌfʊt] *or* **barefooted** [-ˌfʊtəd] *adv* : pieds nus — ~ *adj* **be** ~ : être nupieds — **barely** [ˈbærli] *adv* : à peine, tout juste

bargain [ˈbargən] *n* **1** AGREEMENT : marché *m* **2** BUY : aubaine *f* — ~ *vi* **1** : négocier, marchander **2** ~ **for** : s'attendre à

barge ['bɑrdʒ] *n* : chaland *m* — ~ *vi* **barged; barging** ~ **in** : interrompre

baritone ['bærə,to:n] *n* : baryton *m*

bark[1] ['bɑrk] *vi* : aboyer — ~ *n* : aboiement *m* (d'un chien)

bark[2] *n* : écorce *f* (d'un arbre)

barley ['bɑrli] *n* : orge *f*

barn ['bɑrn] *n* : grange *f*

barometer [bə'rɑmətər] *n* : baromètre *m*

baron ['bærən] *n* : baron *m* — **baroness** ['bærənɪs, -nəs, -'nɛs] *n* : baronne *f*

barracks ['bærəks] *npl* : caserne *f*

barrage [bə'rɑʒ, -'rɑdʒ] *n* **1** : tir *m* de barrage **2** : déluge *m* (de questions, etc.)

barrel ['bærəl] *n* **1** : tonneau *m*, fût *m*, baril *m* **2** : canon *m* (d'une arme à feu)

barren ['bærən] *adj* : stérile

barricade *vt* ['bærə,keɪd, ,bærə'-] **-caded; -cading** : barricader — ~ *n* : barricade *f*

barrier ['bæriər] *n* : barrière *f*

barring ['bɑrɪŋ] *prep* : excepté, sauf

bartender ['bɑr,tɛndər] *n* : barman *m*

barter ['bɑrtər] *vt* : échanger, troquer — ~ *n* : échange *m*, troc *m*

base ['beɪs] *n, pl* **bases** : base *f* — ~ *vt* **based; basing** : baser, fonder — ~ *adj* **baser; basest** : bas, vil

baseball ['beɪs,bɔl] *n* : baseball *m*, base-ball *m*

basement ['beɪsmənt] *n* : sous-sol *m*

bash ['bæʃ] *vt* : cogner, frapper — ~ *n* **1** BLOW : coup *m* **2** PARTY : fête *f*

bashful ['bæʃfəl] *adj* : timide, gêné *Can*

basic ['beɪsɪk] *adj* : fondamental, de base — **basically** ['beɪsɪkli] *adv* : au fond, fondamentalement

basil ['beɪzəl, 'bæzəl] *n* : basilic *m*

basin ['beɪsən] *n* : bassin *m* (d'un fleuve)

basis ['beɪsəs] *n, pl* **bases** [-,si:z] : base *f*

bask ['bæsk] *vi* ~ **in the sun** : se chauffer au soleil

basket ['bæskət] *n* : corbeille *f*, panier *m* — **basketball** ['bæskət,bɔl] *n* : basket *m*, basket-ball *m*, ballon-panier *m Can*

bass[1] ['bæs] *n, pl* **bass** *or* **basses** : perche *f*, bar *m* (poisson)

bass[2] ['beɪs] *n* : basse *f* (voix, instrument)

bassoon [bə'su:n, bæ-] *n* : basson *m*

bastard ['bæstərd] *n* : bâtard *m*, -tarde *f*

baste ['beɪst] *vt* **basted; basting 1** STITCH : faufiler, bâtir **2** : arroser (un rôti, etc.)

bat[1] ['bæt] *n* : chauve-souris *f* (animal)

bat[2] *n* : batte *f*, bâton *m Can* — ~ *vt* **batted; batting** : frapper

batch ['bætʃ] *n* : liasse *f* (de papiers, etc.), lot *m* (de marchandises), fournée *f* (de pain, etc.)

bath ['bæθ] *n, pl* **baths** ['bæðz, 'bæθs] **1** : bain *m* **2** BATHROOM : salle *f* de bains **3** **take a** ~ : prendre un bain — **bathe** ['beɪð]

v **bathed; bathing** *vt* : baigner — *vi* : se baigner, prendre un bain — **bathrobe** ['bæθ,ro:b] *n* : peignoir *m* (de bain), robe *f* de chambre — **bathroom** ['bæθ,ru:m, -,rʊm] *n* : salle *f* de bains — **bathtub** ['bæθ,tʌb] *n* : baignoire *f*

baton [bə'tɑn] *n* : bâton *m*

battalion [bə'tæljən] *n* : bataillon *m*

batter ['bætər] *vt* **1** BEAT : battre **2** MISTREAT : maltraiter — ~ *n* **1** : pâte *f* (à cuire) **2** HITTER : batteur *m* (au baseball)

battery ['bætəri] *n, pl* **-teries** : batterie *f*, pile *f* (d'une radio, etc.)

battle ['bætəl] *n* **1** : bataille *f* **2** STRUGGLE : lutte *f* — ~ *vi* **-tled; -tling** : lutter — **battlefield** ['bætəl,fi:ld] *n* : champ *m* de bataille — **battleship** ['bætəl,ʃɪp] *n* : cuirassé *m*

bawdy ['bɔdi] *adj* **bawdier; -est** : paillard, grivois

bawl ['bɔl] *vi* : brailler *fam*

bay[1] ['beɪ] *n* INLET : baie *f*

bay[2] *n or* ~ **leaf** : laurier *m*

bay[3] *vi* : aboyer — ~ *n* : aboiement *m*

bayonet [,beɪə'nɛt, 'beɪə,nɛt] *n* : baïonnette *f*

bay window *n* : fenêtre *f* en saillie

bazaar [bə'zɑr] *n* **1** : bazar *m* **2** SALE : vente *f* (de charité)

be ['bi:] *v* **was** ['wəz, 'wɑz]; **were** ['wər]; **been** ['bɪn]; **being; am** ['æm]; **is** ['ɪz]; **are** ['ɑr] *vi* **1** : être **2** (*expressing a state*) : être, avoir **3** (*expressing age*) : avoir **4** (*expressing equality*) : faire, égaler **5** (*expressing health or well-being*) : aller, se porter — *v aux* **1** : être en train de **2** (*indicating obligation*) : devoir **3** (*used in passive constructions*) : être — *v impers* **1** (*indicating weather*) : faire **2** (*indicating time*) : être

beach ['bi:tʃ] *n* : plage *f*

beacon ['bi:kən] *n* : phare *m*, signal *m* lumineux

bead ['bi:d] *n* **1** : perle *f* **2** DROP : goutte *f* **3** ~**s** *npl* NECKLACE : collier *m*

beak ['bi:k] *n* : bec *m*

beaker ['bi:kər] *n* : gobelet *m*

beam ['bi:m] *n* **1** : poutre *f* (de bois) **2** RAY : rayon *m* — ~ *vi* SHINE : rayonner — ~ *vt* BROADCAST : diffuser, transmettre

bean ['bi:n] *n* **1** : haricot *m* **2** *or* **coffee** ~ : grain *m* (de café)

bear[1] ['bær] *n, pl* **bears** *or* **bear** : ours *m*, ourse *f*

bear[2] *v* **bore** ['bor]; **borne** ['bɔrn]; **bearing** *vt* **1** CARRY : porter **2** ENDURE : supporter — *vi* **1** ~ **in mind** : tenir compte de **2** **left/right** : prendre à gauche, à droite — **bearable** ['bærəbəl] *adj* : supportable

beard ['bɪrd] *n* : barbe *f*

bearer ['bærər] *n* : porteur *m*, -teuse *f*

bearing ['bærɪŋ] *n* **1** MANNER : maintien *m*

2 SIGNIFICANCE : rapport *m* **3 get one's ~s** : s'orienter

beast ['bi:st] *n* : bête *f*

beat ['bi:t] *v* **beat; beaten** ['bi:tən] *or* **beat; beating** : battre — **~** *n* **1** : battement *m* **2** RHYTHM : rythme *m*, temps *m* — **beating** ['bitɪŋ] *n* **1** : raclée *f fam* **2** DEFEAT : défaite *f*

beauty ['bju:ti] *n, pl* **-ties** : beauté *f* — **beautician** [bju:'tɪʃən] *n* : esthéticien *m*, -cienne *f* — **beautiful** ['bju:tɪfəl] *adj* **1** : beau *f* WONDERFUL : merveilleux — **beautifully** ['bju:tɪfəli] *adv* WONDERFULLY : merveilleusement — **beautify** ['bju:tɪ,faɪ] *vt* **-fied; -fying** : embellir

beaver ['bi:vər] *n* : castor *m*

because [bɪ'kʌz, -'kɔz] *conj* : parce que — **because of** *prep* : à cause de

beckon ['bɛkən] *vt* : faire signe à, attirer — *vi* : faire signe

become [bɪ'kʌm] *v* **-came** [-'keɪm]; **-come; -coming** — *vt* SUIT : aller à, convenir à — **becoming** [bɪ'kʌmɪŋ] *adj* **1** SUITABLE : convenable **2** FLATTERING : seyant

bed ['bɛd] *n* **1** : lit *m* **2** BOTTOM : fond *m* (de la mer) **3 go to ~** : se coucher — **bedclothes** ['bɛd,kloːz, -,kloːðz] *npl* : draps *mpl* et couvertures *fpl*

bedridden ['bɛd,rɪdən] *adj* : alité

bedroom ['bɛd,ruːm, -,rʊm] *n* : chambre *f* (à coucher)

bedspread ['bɛd,sprɛd] *n* : couvre-lit *m*

bedtime ['bɛd,taɪm] *n* : heure *f* du coucher

bee ['bi:] *n* : abeille *f*

beech ['bi:ʧ] *n, pl* **beeches** *or* **beech** : hêtre *m*

beef ['bi:f] *n* : bœuf *m* — **beefsteak** ['bif,steɪk] *n* : bifteck *m*

beehive ['bi:,haɪv] *n* : ruche *f*

beeline ['bi:,laɪn] *n* **make a ~ for** : se diriger droit vers

been → **be**

beep ['bi:p] *n* : coup *m* de klaxon, bip *m* — *vi* : klaxonner, faire bip — **beeper** ['bi:pər] *n* : récepteur *m* de radiomessagerie

beer ['bɪr] *n* : bière *f*

beet ['bi:t] *n* : betterave *f*

beetle ['bi:təl] *n* : scarabée *m*

before [bɪ'for] *adv* **1** : avant, auparavant **2 the month ~** : le mois dernier — **~** *prep* **1** (*in space*) : devant **2** (*in time*) : avant **3 ~ my eyes** : sous mes yeux — **~** *conj* : avant de, avant que — **beforehand** [bɪ'for,hænd] *adv* : à l'avance

befriend [bɪ'frɛnd] *vt* : offrir son amitié à

beg ['bɛg] *v* **begged; begging** *vt* **1** : mendier **2** ENTREAT : supplier, prier — *vi* : mendier — **beggar** ['bɛgər] *n* : mendiant *m*, -diante *f*

begin [bɪ'gɪn] *v* **-gan** [-'gæn]; **-gun** [-'gʌn]; **-ginning** : commencer — **beginner** [bɪ'gɪnər] *n* : débutant *m*, -tante *f* — **beginning** [bɪ'gɪnɪŋ] *n* : début *m*, commencement *m*

begrudge [bɪ'grʌʤ] *vt* **-grudged; -grudging 1** : accorder à regret **2** ENVY : envier

behalf [bɪ'hæf, -'haf] *n* **on ~ of** : de la part de, au nom de

behave [bɪ'heɪv] *vi* **-haved; -having** : se conduire, se comporter — **behavior** *or Brit* **behaviour** [bɪ'heɪvjər] *n* : conduite *f*, comportement *m*

behind [bɪ'haɪnd] *adv* **1** : derrière, en arrière **2 fall ~** : prendre du retard — **~** *prep* **1** : derrière, en arrière de **2** : en retard sur (l'horaire, etc.) **3 her friends are ~ her** : elle a l'appui de ses amis

behold [bɪ'hoːld] *vt* **-held; -holding** : contempler

beige ['beɪʒ] *adj & nm* : beige

being ['bi:ɪŋ] *n* **1** : être *m*, créature *f* **2 come into ~** : prendre naissance

belated [bɪ'leɪtəd] *adj* : tardif

belch ['bɛlʧ] *vi* : roter *fam* — **~** *n* : renvoi *m*

belfry ['bɛlfri] *n, pl* **-fries** : beffroi *m*, clocher *m*

Belgian ['bɛlʤən] *adj* : belge

belie [bɪ'laɪ] *vt* **-lied; -lying** : démentir, contredire

belief [bə'li:f] *n* **1** TRUST : confiance *f* **2** CONVICTION : croyance *f* **3** FAITH : foi *f* — **believable** [bə'li:vəbəl] *adj* : croyable — **believe** [bə'li:v] *v* **-lieved; -lieving** : croire — **believer** [bə'li:vər] *n* : croyant *m*, croyante *f*

belittle [bɪ'lɪtəl] *vt* **-tled; -tling** : rabaisser

bell ['bɛl] *n* **1** : cloche *f*, clochette *f* **2** : sonnette *f* (d'une porte, etc.)

belligerent [bə'lɪʤərənt] *adj* : belligérant

bellow ['bɛ,loː] *vi* **1** : beugler **2** HOWL : brailler *fam*, hurler

belly ['bɛli] *n, pl* **-lies** : ventre *m*

belong [bɪ'lɔŋ] *vi* **1 ~ to** : appartenir à, être à **2 ~ to** : être membre de (un club, etc.) **3 where does it ~ ?** : où va-t-il? — **belongings** [bɪ'lɔŋɪŋz] *npl* : affaires *fpl*, effets *mpl* personnels

beloved [bɪ'lʌvəd, -'lʌvd] *adj* : bien-aimé — **~** *n* : bien-aimé *m*, -mée *f*

below [bɪ'loː] *adv* : en dessous, en bas — **~** *prep* : sous, au-dessous de, en dessous de

belt ['bɛlt] *n* **1** : ceinture *f* **2** STRAP : courroie *f* (d'une machine) **3** AREA : zone *f*, région *f* — **~** *vt* THRASH : donner un coup à

bench ['bɛnʧ] *n* **1** : banc *m* **2** WORKBENCH : établi *m* **3** COURT : cour *f*, tribunal *m*

bend ['bɛnd] *v* **bent** ['bɛnt]; **bending** *vt* : plier, courber — *vi* **1** : se plier, se courber **2** *or* **~ over** : se pencher — **~** *n* : virage *m*, coude *m*

beneath [bɪ'ni:θ] *adv* : au-dessous, en bas — ~ *prep* : sous, en dessous de

benediction [,bɛnə'dɪkʃən] *n* : bénédiction *f*

benefactor ['bɛnə,fæktər] *n* : bienfaiteur *m*, -trice *f*

benefit ['bɛnəfɪt] *n* **1** : avantage *m*, bénéfice *m* **2** AID : allocation *f*, prestation *f* — ~ *vt* : profiter à, bénéficier à — *vi* : profiter, tirer avantage — **beneficial** [,bɛnə'fɪʃəl] *adj* : avantageux — **beneficiary** [,bɛnə'fɪʃi,ɛri, -'fɪʃəri] *n*, *pl* **-ries** : bénéficiaire *mf*

benevolent [bə'nɛvələnt] *adj* : bienveillant

benign [bɪ'naɪn] *adj* **1** KIND : bienveillant, aimable **2** : bénin (en médecine)

bent ['bɛnt] *adj* **1** : tordu, courbé **2 be on doing** : être décidé à faire — ~ *n* : aptitude *f*, penchant *m*

bequeath [bɪ'kwi:θ, -kwi:ð] *vt* : léguer — **bequest** [bɪ'kwɛst] *n* : legs *m*

berate [bɪ'reɪt] *vt* **-rated; -rating** : réprimander

bereaved [bɪ'ri:vd] *adj* : endeuillé, attristé — **bereavement** [bɪ'ri:vmənt] *n* : deuil *m*

beret [bə'reɪ] *n* : béret *m*

berry ['bɛri] *n*, *pl* **-ries** : baie *f*

berserk [bər'sərk, -'zərk] *adj* **1** : fou, enragé **2 go** ~ : devenir fou furieux

berth ['bɛrθ] *n* **1** MOORING : mouillage *m* **2** BUNK : couchette *f*

beset [bɪ'sɛt] *vt* **-set; -setting 1** HARASS : assaillir **2** SURROUND : encercler

beside [bɪ'saɪd] *prep* **1** : à côté de, près de **2 be** ~ **oneself** : être hors de soi — **besides** [bɪ'saɪdz] *adv* : en plus — ~ *prep* **1** : en plus de **2** EXCEPT : sauf

besiege [bɪ'si:dʒ] *vt* **-sieged; -sieging** : assiéger

best ['bɛst] *adj* (*superlative of* **good**) **1** : meilleur **2** : plus beau — ~ *adv* (*superlative of* **well**) : le mieux, le plus — ~ *n* **1 at** ~ : au mieux **2 do one's** ~ : faire de son mieux **3 the** ~ : le meilleur — **best man** *n* : garçon *m* d'honneur, témoin *m*

bestow [bɪ'sto:] *vt* : accorder, concéder

bet ['bɛt] *n* : pari *m*, gageure *f Can* — ~ *v* **bet; betting** *vt* : parier, gager *Can* — *vi* ~ **on sth** : parier sur qqch

betray [bɪ'treɪ] *vt* : trahir — **betrayal** [bɪ'treɪəl] *n* : trahison *f*

better ['bɛtər] *adj* (*comparative of* **good**) **1** : meilleur **2 get** ~ : s'améliorer — ~ *adv* (*comparative of* **well**) **1** : mieux **2 all the** ~ : tant mieux — ~ *n* **1 the** ~ : le meilleur, la meilleure **2 get the** ~ **of** : l'emporter sur — ~ *vt* **1** IMPROVE : améliorer **2** SURPASS : surpasser, faire mieux que

between [bɪ'twi:n] *prep* : entre — ~ *adv or* **in** ~ : au milieu

beverage ['bɛvrɪdʒ, 'bɛvə-] *n* : boisson *f*

beware [bɪ'wær] *vi* ~ **of** : prendre garde à, se méfier de

bewilder [bɪ'wɪldər] *vt* : rendre perplexe, déconcerter — **bewilderment** [bɪ'wɪldərmənt] *n* : perplexité *f*, confusion *f*

bewitch [bɪ'wɪtʃ] *vt* : enchanter

beyond [bi'jand] *adv* : au-delà, plus loin — ~ *prep* : au-delà de

bias ['baɪəs] *n* **1** PREJUDICE : préjugé *m* **2** TENDENCY : penchant *m* — **biased** ['baɪəst] *adj* : partial

bib ['bɪb] *n* : bavoir *m* (d'un bébé)

Bible ['baɪbəl] *n* : Bible *f* — **biblical** ['bɪblɪkəl] *adj* : biblique

bibliography [,bɪbli'agrəfi] *n*, *pl* **-phies** : bibliographie *f*

biceps ['baɪ,sɛps] *ns & pl* : biceps *m*

bicker ['bɪkər] *vi* : se chamailler

bicycle ['baɪsɪkəl, -,sɪ-] *n* : bicyclette *f*, vélo *m* — ~ *vi* **-cled; -cling** : faire de la bicyclette, faire du vélo

bid ['bɪd] *vt* **bade** ['bæd, 'beɪd] *or* **bid; bidden** ['bɪdən] *or* **bid; bidding 1** OFFER : offrir **2** ~ **farewell** : dire adieu — ~ *n* **1** OFFER : offre *f*, enchère *f* **2** ATTEMPT : tentative *f*

bide ['baɪd] *vt* **bode** ['bo:d] *or* **bided; biding** ~ **one's time** : attendre le bon moment

bifocals [baɪ'fo:kəlz] *npl* : lunettes *fpl* bifocales

big ['bɪg] *adj* **bigger; biggest** : grand, gros

bigot ['bɪgət] *n* : fanatique *mf* — **bigotry** ['bɪgətri] *n*, *pl* **-tries** : fanatisme *m*

bike ['baɪk] *n* **1** BICYCLE : vélo *m* **2** MOTORCYCLE : moto *f*

bikini [bə'ki:ni] *n* : bikini *m*

bile ['baɪl] *n* : bile *f*

bilingual [baɪ'lɪŋgwəl] *adj* : bilingue

bill ['bɪl] *n* **1** BEAK : bec *m* (d'un oiseau) **2** INVOICE : facture *f*, compte *m*, addition *f* (au restaurant) **3** LAW : projet *m* de loi **4** BANKNOTE : billet *m* (de banque) — ~ *vt* : facturer, envoyer la facture à

billiards ['bɪljərdz] *n* : billard *m*

billion ['bɪljən] *n*, *pl* **billions** *or* **billion** : milliard *m*

billow ['bɪlo] *vi* : onduler (se dit d'un drapeau)

bin ['bɪn] *n* : coffre *m*, boîte *f*

binary ['baɪnəri, -,nɛri] *adj* : binaire

bind ['baɪnd] *vt* **bound** ['baʊnd]; **binding 1** TIE : lier **2** OBLIGE : obliger **3** UNITE : unir **4** : relier (un livre) — **binder** ['baɪndər] *n* FOLDER : classeur *m* — **binding** ['baɪndɪŋ] *n* : reliure *f* (d'un livre)

binge ['bɪndʒ] *n* : bringue *f fam*

bingo ['bɪŋ,go:] *n*, *pl* **-gos** : bingo *m*

binoculars [bə'nakjələrz, baɪ-] *npl* : jumelles *fpl*

biochemistry [ˌbaɪoˈkɛməstri] *n* : biochimie *f*

biography [baɪˈɑgrəfi, bi:-] *n, pl* **-phies** : biographie *f* — **biographer** [baɪˈɑgrəfər] *n* : biographe *mf* — **biographical** [ˌbaɪəˈgræfɪkəl] *adj* : biographique

biology [baɪˈɑləʤi] *n* : biologie *f* — **biological** [-ʤɪkəl] *adj* : biologique — **biologist** [baɪˈɑləʤɪst] *n* : biologiste *mf*

birch [ˈbərʧ] *n* : bouleau *m*

bird [ˈbərd] *n* : oiseau *m*

birth [ˈbərθ] *n* **1** : naissance *f* **2 give ~ to** : accoucher de — **birthday** [ˈbərˌdeɪ] *n* : anniversaire *m* — **birthmark** [ˈbərθˌmɑrk] *n* : tache *f* de vin — **birthplace** [ˈbərθˌpleɪs] *n* : lieu *m* de naissance — **birthrate** [ˈbərθˌreɪt] *n* : natalité *f*

biscuit [ˈbɪskət] *n* : petit pain *m* au lait

bisexual [ˌbaɪˈsɛkʃəwəl, -ˈsɛkʃəl] *adj* : bisexuel

bishop [ˈbɪʃəp] *n* **1** : évêque *m* **2** : fou *m* (aux échecs)

bison [baɪzən, -sən] *ns & pl* : bison *m*

bit[1] [ˈbɪt] *n* : mors *m* (d'une bride)

bit[2] *n* **1** : morceau *m*, bout *m* **2** : bit *m* (en informatique) **3 a ~** : un peu

bitch [ˈbɪʧ] *n* : chienne *f* — **~** *vi* COMPLAIN : râler *fam*

bite [ˈbaɪt] *v* **bit** [ˈbɪt]; **bitten** [ˈbɪtən]; **biting** *vt* **1** : mordre **2** STING : piquer — *vi* : mordre — **~** *n* **1** : piqûre *f* (d'insecte), morsure *f* (de chien, etc.) **2** MOUTHFUL : bouchée *f* — **biting** *adj* **1** PENETRATING : pénétrant **2** SCATHING : mordant

bitter [ˈbɪtər] *adj* **1** : amer **2 it's ~ cold** : il fait un froid glacial — **bitterness** [ˈbɪtərnəs] *n* : amertume *f*

bizarre [bəˈzɑr] *adj* : bizarre

black [ˈblæk] *adj* : noir — **~** *n* **1** : noir *m* (couleur) **2** : Noir *m*, Noire *f* (personne) — **black–and–blue** [ˌblækənˈblu:] *adj* : couvert de bleus — **blackberry** [ˈblækˌbɛri] *n, pl* **-ries** : mûre *f* — **blackboard** [ˈblækˌbord] *n* : tableau *m* (noir) — **blacken** [ˈblækən] *vt* : noircir — **blackmail** [ˈblækˌmeɪl] *n* : chantage *m* — **~** *vi* : faire chanter — **black market** *n* : marché *m* noir — **blackout** [ˈblækˌaʊt] *n* **1** : panne *f* d'électricité **2** FAINT : évanouissement *m* — **blacksmith** [ˈblækˌsmɪθ] *n* : forgeron *m* — **blacktop** [ˈblækˌtɑp] *n* : asphalte *m*

bladder [ˈblædər] *n* : vessie *f*

blade [ˈbleɪd] *n* **1** : lame *f* (de couteau) **2** : pale *f* (d'hélice, de rame, etc.) **3 ~ of grass** : brin *m* d'herbe

blame [ˈbleɪm] *vt* **blamed; blaming** : blâmer, reprocher — **~** *n* : faute *f*, responsabilité *f* — **blameless** [ˈbleɪmləs] *adj* : irréprochable

bland [ˈblænd] *adj* : fade, insipide

blank [ˈblæŋk] *adj* **1** : blanc (se dit d'une page, etc.) **2** EMPTY : vide — **~** *n* : blanc *m*, vide *m*

blanket [ˈblæŋkət] *n* **1** : couverture *f* (d'un lit) **2 ~ of snow** : couche *f* de neige — **~** *vt* : recouvrir

blare [ˈblær] *vi* **blared; blaring** : beugler

blasé [blɑˈzeɪ] *adj* : blasé

blasphemy [ˈblæsfəmi] *n, pl* **-mies** : blasphème *m*

blast [ˈblæst] *n* **1** GUST : rafale *f*, souffle *m* **2** EXPLOSION : explosion *f* **3 at full ~** : à plein volume — **~** *vt* BLOW UP : faire sauter — **blast–off** [ˈblæstˌɔf] *n* : lancement *m*

blatant [ˈbleɪtənt] *adj* : flagrant

blaze [ˈbleɪz] *n* **1** FIRE : incendie *f* **2** BRIGHTNESS : éclat *m* — **~** *v* **blazed; blazing** : flamber

blazer [ˈbleɪzər] *n* : blazer *m*

bleach [ˈbli:ʧ] *vt* : blanchir, décolorer — **~** *n* : décolorant *m*, eau *f* de Javel

bleachers [ˈbli:ʧərz] *npl* : gradins *mpl*

bleak [ˈbli:k] *adj* **1** DESOLATE : désolé **2** GLOOMY : triste, sombre

bleat [ˈbli:t] *vi* : bêler — **~** *n* : bêlement *m*

bleed [ˈbli:d] *v* **bled** [ˈblɛd]; **bleeding** : saigner

blemish [ˈblɛmɪʃ] *vt* : tacher, ternir — **~** *n* : tache *f*, défaut *m*

blend [ˈblɛnd] *vt* : mélanger — **~** *n* : mélange *m*, combinaison *f* — **blender** [ˈblɛndər] *n* : mixer *m*

bless [ˈblɛs] *vt* **blessed** [ˈblɛst]; **blessing** : bénir — **blessed** [ˈblɛsəd] *or* **blest** [ˈblɛst] *adj* : bénit, saint — **blessing** [ˈblɛsɪŋ] *n* : bénédiction *f*

blew → blow

blind [ˈblaɪnd] *adj* : aveugle — **~** *vt* **1** : aveugler **2** DAZZLE : éblouir — **~** *n* **1** : store *m* (d'une fenêtre) **2 the ~** : les non-voyants *mpl* — **blindfold** [ˈblaɪndˌfo:ld] *vt* : bander les yeux à — **~** *n* : bandeau *m* — **blindly** [ˈblaɪndli] *adv* : aveuglément — **blindness** [ˈblaɪndnəs] *n* : cécité *f*

blink [ˈblɪŋk] *vi* **1** : cligner des yeux **2** FLICKER : clignoter — **~** *n* : battement *m* des paupières — **blinker** [ˈblɪŋkər] *n* : clignotant *m*

bliss [ˈblɪs] *n* : félicité *f* — **blissful** [ˈblɪsfəl] *adj* : bienheureux

blister [ˈblɪstər] *n* **1** : ampoule *f*, cloque *f* (sur la peau) **2** : boursouflure *f* (sur une surface peinte) — **~** *vi* **1** : se couvrir d'ampoules *fpl* (se dit de la peau) **2** : se boursoufler (se dit de la peinture, etc.)

blitz [ˈblɪts] *n* : bombardement *m*

blizzard [ˈblɪzərd] *n* : tempête *f* de neige

bloated [ˈblo:təd] *adj* : boursouflé, gonflé

blob [ˈblɑb] *n* **1** DROP : goutte *f* **2** SPOT : tache *f*

block ['blɑk] *n* **1** : bloc *m* **2** OBSTRUCTION : obstruction *f* **3** : pâté *m* de maisons, bloc *m Can* **4** *or* **building** ~ : cube *m* — ~ *vt* : bloquer, boucher — **blockade** [blɑ'keɪd] *n* : blocus *m* — **blockage** ['blɑkɪdʒ] *n* : obstruction *f*

blond *or* **blonde** ['blɑnd] *adj* : blond — ~ *n* : blond *m*, blonde *f*

blood ['blʌd] *n* : sang *m* — **blood pressure** *n* : tension *f* artérielle — **bloodshed** ['blʌd-ˌʃɛd] *n* : carnage *m* — **bloodshot** ['blʌd-ˌʃɑt] *adj* : injecté de sang — **bloodstained** ['blʌd-ˌsteɪnd] *adj* : taché de sang — **bloodstream** ['blʌd-ˌstriːm] *n* : sang *m*, système *m* sanguin — **bloodthirsty** ['blʌd-ˌθərsti] *adj* : sanguinaire — **bloody** ['blʌdi] *adj* **blood-ier; -est** : ensanglanté

bloom ['bluːm] *n* **1** : fleur *f* **2 in full** ~ : en pleine floraison — ~ *vi* : fleurir, éclore

blossom ['blɑsəm] *n* : fleur *f* — ~ *vi* **1** : fleurir **2** MATURE : s'épanouir

blot ['blɑt] *n* : tache *f* (d'encre, etc.) — ~ *vt* **blotted; blotting 1** : tacher **2** DRY : sécher

blotch ['blɑtʃ] *n* : tache *f* — **blotchy** ['blɑ'tʃi] *adj* **blotchier; -est** : tacheté

blouse ['blaʊs, 'blaʊz] *n* : chemisier *m*

blow ['bloː] *v* **blew** ['bluː]; **blown** ['bloːn]; **blowing** *vi* **1** : souffler **2** SOUND : sonner **3** *or* ~ **out** : éclater (se dit d'un pneu), s'éteindre (se dit d'une bougie) — *vt* **1** : souffler **2** SOUND : jouer de (la trompette, etc.) **3** BUNGLE : rater **4** ~ **one's nose** : se moucher — ~ *n* : coup *m* — **blowout** ['bloːˌaʊt] *n* : éclatement *m* — **blow up** *vi* : exploser, sauter — *vt* **1** EXPLODE : faire sauter **2** INFLATE : gonfler

blubber ['blʌbər] *n* : graisse *f* de baleine

bludgeon ['blʌdʒən] *n* : matraque *f* — ~ *vt* : matraquer

blue ['bluː] *adj* **bluer; bluest 1** : bleu **2** MELANCHOLY : triste — ~ *n* : bleu *m* — **blueberry** ['bluːˌbɛri] *n, pl* **-ries** : myrtille *f France*, bleuet *m Can* — **bluebird** ['bluː-ˌbərd] *n* : oiseau *m* bleu — **blue cheese** *n* : (fromage *m*) bleu *m* — **blueprint** ['bluː-ˌprɪnt] *n* : plan *m* (de travail) — **blues** ['bluːz] *ns & pl* **1** : cafard *m* **2** : blues *m* (musique)

bluff ['blʌf] *v* : bluffer — ~ *n* **1** : falaise *f*, escarpement *m* **2** DECEPTION : bluff *m* —

blunder ['blʌndər] *vi* : faire une gaffe — ~ *n* : gaffe *f fam*

blunt ['blʌnt] *adj* **1** DULL : émoussé **2** DIRECT : brusque, franc — ~ *vt* : émousser

blur ['blər] *n* : image *f* floue — ~ *vt* **blurred; blurring** : brouiller, rendre flou

blurb ['blərb] *n* : notice *f* publicitaire

blurt ['blərt] *vt or* ~ **out** : laisser échapper

blush ['blʌʃ] *n* : rougeur *f* — ~ *vi* : rougir

blustery ['blʌstəri] *adj* : venteux, orageux

boar ['bor] *n* : sanglier *m*

board ['bord] *n* **1** PLANK : planche *f* **2** COMMITTEE : conseil *m* **3** : tableau *m* (d'un jeu) **4 room and** ~ : pension *f* complète — ~ *vt* **1** : monter à bord de (un avion, un navire), monter dans (un train) **2** LODGE : prendre en pension **3** ~ **up** : couvrir de planches — **boarder** ['bordər] *n* : pensionnaire *mf*

boast ['boːst] *n* : vantardise *f* — ~ *vi* : se vanter — **boastful** ['boːstfəl] *adj* : vantard

boat ['boːt] *n* : bateau *m*, barque *f*

bob ['bɑb] *vi* **bobbed; bobbing** *or* ~ **up and down** : monter et descendre

bobbin ['bɑbən] *n* : bobine *f*

body ['bɑdi] *n, pl* **bodies 1** : corps *m* **2** CORPSE : cadavre *m* **3** : carrosserie *f* (d'une voiture) **4** ~ **of water** : masse *f* d'eau — **bodily** ['bɑdəli] *adj* : physique, corporel — **bodyguard** ['bɑdiˌgɑrd] *n* : garde *m* du corps

bog ['bɑg, 'bɔg] *n* : marais *m*, marécage *m* — ~ *vi* **bogged; bogging** *or* ~ **down** : s'embourber

bogus ['boːgəs] *adj* : faux

bohemian [boː'hiːmiən] *adj* : bohème

boil ['bɔɪl] *vt* : faire bouillir — *vi* : bouillir — ~ *n* **1** : ébullition *f* **2** : furoncle *m* (en médecine) — **boiler** ['bɔɪlər] *n* : chaudière *f*

boisterous ['bɔɪstərəs] *adj* : bruyant, tapageur

bold ['boːld] *adj* **1** DARING : hardi, audacieux **2** IMPUDENT : effronté — **boldness** ['boːldnəs] *n* : hardiesse *f*, audace *f*

bologna [bə'loːni] *n* : gros *m* saucisson

bolster ['boːlstər] *n* : traversin *m* — ~ *vt* **-stered; -stering** *or* ~ **up** : soutenir

bolt ['boːlt] *n* **1** LOCK : verrou *m* **2** SCREW : boulon *m* **3** ~ **of lightning** : éclair *m*, coup *m* de foudre — ~ *vt* LOCK : verrouiller — *vi* FLEE : se sauver

bomb ['bɑm] *n* : bombe *f* — ~ *vt* : bombarder — **bombard** [bɑm'bɑrd, bəm-] *vt* : bombarder — **bombardment** [bɑm-'bɑrdmənt] *n* : bombardement *m* — **bomber** ['bɑmər] *n* : bombardier *m*

bond ['bɑnd] *n* **1** TIE : lien *m* **2** SECURITY : bon *m* — ~ *vi* ~ **with** : s'attacher à

bondage ['bɑndɪdʒ] *n* : esclavage *m*

bone ['boːn] *n* : os *m*, arête *f* — ~ *vt* **boned; boning** : désosser

bonfire ['bɑnˌfaɪr] *n* : feu *m* de joie

bonus ['boːnəs] *n* : gratification *f*, prime *f*

bony ['boːni] *adj* **bonier; -est** : plein d'os, plein d'arêtes

boo ['buː] *n, pl* **boos** : huée *f* — ~ *vt* : huer, siffler

book ['bʊk] *n* **1** : livre *m* **2** NOTEBOOK : cahier *m* — ~ *vt* : réserver — **bookcase** ['bʊkˌkeɪs] *n* : bibliothèque *f* — **bookkeep-**

ing ['bʊk,kiːpɪŋ] *n* : comptabilité *f* — **booklet** ['bʊklət] *n* : brochure *f* — **bookmark** ['bʊk,mɑrk] *n* : signet *m* — **bookseller** ['bʊk,sɛlər] *n* : libraire *mf* — **bookshelf** ['bʊk,ʃɛlf] *n, pl* **-shelves** : rayon *m*, étagère *f* (à livres) — **bookstore** ['bʊk,stor] *n* : librairie *f*

boom ['buːm] *vi* **1** : gronder, retentir **2** PROSPER : prospérer — ~ *n* **1** : grondement *m* **2** : boom *m* (économique)

boon ['buːn] *n* : bienfait *m*

boost ['buːst] *vt* **1** LIFT : soulever **2** INCREASE : augmenter — ~ *n* **1** INCREASE : augmentation *f* **2** ENCOURAGEMENT : encouragement *m*

boot ['buːt] *n* : botte *f* — ~ *vt* **1** : donner un coup de pied à **2** *or* ~ **up** : amorcer (en informatique)

booth ['buːθ] *n, pl* **booths** ['buːðz, 'buːθs] : baraque *f* (d'un marché), cabine *f* (téléphonique)

booze ['buːz] *n* : alcool *m*, boissons *fpl* alcoolisées

border ['bɔr,dər] *n* **1** EDGE : bord *m* **2** BOUNDARY : frontière *f* **3** : bordure *f* (d'un vêtement, etc.)

bore¹ ['bor] *vt* **bored; boring** DRILL : percer, forer

bore² *vt* TIRE : ennuyer — ~ *n* : raseur *m*, -seuse *f fam* — **boredom** ['bordəm] *n* : ennui *m* — **boring** ['borɪŋ] *adj* : ennuyeux, ennuyant *Can*

born ['bɔrn] *adj* **1** : né **2 be** ~ : naître

borough ['bəro] *n* : arrondissement *m* urbain

borrow ['bɑro] *vt* : emprunter

bosom ['bʊzəm, 'buː-] *n* BREAST : poitrine *f* — ~ *adj* ~ **friend** : ami intime

boss ['bɔs] *n* : patron *m*, -tronne *f*; chef *m* — ~ *vt* SUPERVISE : diriger — **bossy** ['bɔsi] *adj* **bossier; -est** : autoritaire

botany ['bɑtəni] *n* : botanique *f* — **botanical** [bə'tænɪkəl] *adj* : botanique

botch ['bɑtʃ] *vt or* ~ **up** : bousiller *fam*, saboter

both ['boːθ] *adj* : les deux — ~ *conj* : à la fois — ~ *pron* : tous les deux, l'un et l'autre

bother ['bɑðər] *vt* **1** TROUBLE : préoccuper **2** PESTER : harceler — *vi* ~ **to** : se donner la peine de — ~ *n* : ennui *m*

bottle ['bɑtəl] *n* **1** : bouteille *f* **2** *or* **baby** ~ : biberon *m* — ~ *vt* **-tled; -tling** : mettre en bouteille — **bottleneck** ['bɑtəl,nɛk] *n* : embouteillage *m*

bottom ['bɑtəm] *n* **1** : bas *m* (d'une page, etc.), fond *m* (d'une bouteille, d'un lac, etc.), pied *m* (d'un escalier) **2** BUTTOCKS : derrière *m fam* — ~ *adj* : du bas, inférieur — **bottomless** ['bɑtəmləs] *adj* : insondable

bough ['baʊ] *n* : rameau *m*

bought → **buy**

boulder ['boːldər] *n* : rocher *m*

boulevard ['bʊlə,vɑrd, 'buː-] *n* : boulevard *m*

bounce ['baʊnts] *v* **bounced; bouncing** *vt* : faire rebondir — *vi* : rebondir — ~ *n* : bond *m*, rebond *m*

bound¹ ['baʊnd] *adj* ~ **for** : à destination de

bound² *adj* OBLIGED : obligé **2 be** ~ **to** : être certain de

bound³ *n* **out of** ~**s** : interdit — **boundary** ['baʊndri, -dəri] *n, pl* **-aries** : limite *f*, frontière *f* — **boundless** ['baʊndləs] *adj* : sans bornes

bouquet [boː'keɪ, buː-] *n* : bouquet *m*

bourbon ['bərbən, 'bʊr-] *n* : bourbon *m*

bourgeois ['bʊrʒ,wɑ, bʊrʒ'wɑ] *adj* : bourgeois

bout ['baʊt] *n* **1** : combat *m* (aux sports) **2** : accès *m* (de fièvre)

bow¹ ['baʊ] *vi* : s'incliner — *vt* **1** : incliner **2** ~ **one's head** : baisser la tête — ~ ['baʊ] *n* : révérence *f*, salut *m*

bow² ['boː] *n* **1** : arc *m* **2 tie a** ~ : faire un nœud

bow³ ['baʊ] *n* : proue *f* (d'un bateau)

bowels ['baʊəlz] *npl* **1** : intestins *mpl* **2** DEPTHS : entrailles *fpl*

bowl¹ ['boːl] *n* : bol *m*, cuvette *f*

bowl² *vi* : jouer au bowling — **bowling** ['boːlɪŋ] *n* : bowling *m*

box¹ ['bɑks] *vi* FIGHT : boxer, faire de la boxe — **boxer** ['bɑksər] *n* : boxeur *m* — **boxing** ['bɑksɪŋ] *n* : boxe *f*

box² *n* **1** : boîte *f*, caisse *f*, coffre *m* **2** : loge *f* (au théâtre) — ~ *vt* : mettre en boîte — **box office** *n* : guichet *m*, billetterie *f*

boy ['bɔɪ] *n* : garçon *m*

boycott ['bɔɪ,kɑt] *vt* : boycotter — ~ *n* : boycott *m*, boycottage *m*

boyfriend ['bɔɪ,frɛnd] *n* : petit ami *m*

bra ['brɑ] → **brassiere**

brace ['breɪs] *n* **1** SUPPORT : support *m* **2** ~**s** *npl* : appareil *m* orthodontique — ~ *vi* ~ **oneself for** : se préparer pour

bracelet ['breɪslət] *n* : bracelet *m*

bracket ['brækət] *n* **1** SUPPORT : support *m* **2** : parenthèse *f*, crochet *m* (signe de ponctuation) **3** CATEGORY : catégorie *f* — ~ *vt* : mettre entre parenthèses, mettre entre crochets

brag ['bræg] *vi* **bragged; bragging** : se vanter

braid ['breɪd] *vt* : tresser — ~ *n* : tresse *f* (de cheveux)

braille ['breɪl] *n* : braille *m*

brain ['breɪn] *n* **1** : cerveau *m* **2** *or* ~**s** *npl* : intelligence *f* — **brainstorm** ['breɪn,stɔrm] *n* : idée *f* géniale — **brainwash** ['breɪn,wɑʃ, -,wɔʃ] *vt* : faire un lavage de

cerveau à — **brainy** [ˈbreɪni] *adj* **brainier;
-est** : intelligent, calé *fam*
brake [ˈbreɪk] *n* 1 : frein *m* — ∼ *vi* **braked;
braking** : freiner
bramble [ˈbræmbəl] *n* : ronce *f*
bran [ˈbræn] *n* : son *m*
branch [ˈbræntʃ] *n* 1 : branche *f* (d'un arbre)
2 DIVISION : succursale *f* — ∼ *vi or* ∼ **off**
: bifurquer
brand [ˈbrænd] *n* 1 : marque *f* (sur un animal) 2 *or* ∼ **name** : marque *f* déposée —
∼ *vt* 1 : marquer (au fer rouge) 2 LABEL
: étiqueter
brandish [ˈbrændɪʃ] *vt* : brandir
brand–new [ˈbrændˈnu:, -ˈnju:] *adj* : tout
neuf
brandy [ˈbrændi] *n, pl* **-dies** : cognac *m*,
eau-de-vie *f*
brash [ˈbræʃ] *adj* : impertinent
brass [ˈbræs] *n* 1 : cuivre *m* (jaune), laiton
m 2 : cuivres *mpl* (d'un orchestre)
brassiere [brəˈzɪr, brɑ-] *n* : soutien-gorge
m, brassière *f Can*
brat [ˈbræt] *n* : môme *mf France fam;* gosse
mf France fam
bravado [brəˈvɑˈdo] *n, pl* **-does** *or* **-dos**
: bravade *f*
brave [ˈbreɪv] *adj* **braver; bravest**
: courageux, brave — ∼ *vt* **braved; brav-
ing** : braver, défier — **bravery** [ˈbreɪvəri] *n,
pl* **-eries** : courage *m*
brawl [ˈbrɔl] *n* : bagarre *f*
brawn [ˈbrɔn] *n* : muscles *mpl* — **brawny**
[ˈbrɔni] *adj* **brawnier; -est** : musclé
bray [ˈbreɪ] *vi* : braire
brazen [ˈbreɪzən] *adj* : effronté
Brazilian [brəˈzɪljən] *adj* : brésilien
breach [ˈbriːtʃ] *n* 1 VIOLATION : infraction *f*
2 GAP : brèche *f*
bread [ˈbrɛd] *n* 1 : pain *m* 2 ∼ **crumbs**
: chapelure *f*
breadth [ˈbrɛtθ] *n* : largeur *f*
break [ˈbreɪk] *v* **broke** [ˈbroːk]; **broken**
[ˈbroːkən] **breaking** *vt* 1 : casser, briser 2
VIOLATE : violer (la loi) 3 INTERRUPT : interrompre 4 SURPASS : battre (un record,
etc.) 5 ∼ **a habit** : se défaire d'une habitude 6 ∼ **the news** : annoncer la nouvelle
— *vi* 1 : se casser, se briser 2 ∼ **away**
: s'évader 3 ∼ **down** : tomber en panne (se
dit d'une voiture) 4 ∼ **into** : entrer par ef-
fraction 5 ∼ **up** SEPARATE : rompre, se
quitter — ∼ *n* 1 : cassure *f*, rupture *f* 2
GAP : trouée *f*, brèche *f* 3 REST : pause *f*,
break *m Can* 4 **a lucky** ∼ : un coup de
veine — **breakable** [ˈbreɪkəbˈl] *adj* : cassable — **breakdown** [ˈbreɪkˌdaʊn] *n* 1
: panne *f* (d'une machine), rupture *f* (des négociations) 2 *or* **nervous** ∼ : dépression *f*
nerveuse

breakfast [ˈbrɛkfəst] *n* : petit déjeuner *m
France*, déjeuner *Can*
breast [ˈbrɛst] *n* 1 : sein *m* (d'une femme) 2
CHEST : poitrine *f* — **breast–feed** [ˈbrɛst-
ˌfiːd] *vt* **-fed** [-ˌfɛd]; **-feeding** : allaiter
breath [ˈbrɛθ] *n* : souffle *m*, haleine *f*, respiration *f* — **breathe** [ˈbriːð] *v* **breathed;
breathing** : respirer — **breathless** [ˈbrɛθ-
ləs] *adj* : à bout de souffle, hors d'haleine —
breathtaking [ˈbrɛθˌteɪkɪŋ] *adj* : à couper
le souffle
breed [ˈbriːd] *v* **bred** [ˈbrɛd]; **breeding** *vt* 1
: élever (du bétail) 2 CAUSE : engendrer —
vi : se reproduire — ∼ *n* 1 : race *f* 2 CLASS
: espèce *f*, sorte *f*
breeze [ˈbriːz] *n* : brise *f* — **breezy** [ˈbriːzi]
adj **breezier; -est** 1 WINDY : venteux 2
NONCHALANT : désinvolte
brevity [ˈbrɛvəti] *n, pl* **-ties** : brièveté *f*
brew [ˈbruː] *vt* : brasser (de la bière), faire infuser (du thé) — *vi* : fermenter (se dit de la
bière), infuser (se dit du thé, etc.) — **brewery** [ˈbruːəri, ˈbruri] *n, pl* **-eries** : brasserie *f*
bribe [ˈbraɪb] *n* : pot-de-vin *m* — ∼ *vt*
bribed; bribing : soudoyer — **bribery**
[ˈbraɪbəri] *n, pl* **-eries** : corruption *f*
brick [ˈbrɪk] *n* : brique *f* — **bricklayer** [ˈbrɪk-
ˌleɪər] *n* : maçon *m*
bride [ˈbraɪd] *n* : mariée *f* — **bridal** [ˈbraɪdəl]
adj : nuptial — **bridegroom** [ˈbraɪdˌgruːm]
n : marié *m* — **bridesmaid** [ˈbraɪdzˌmeɪd] *n*
: demoiselle *f* d'honneur
bridge [ˈbrɪdʒ] *n* 1 : pont *m* 2 : arête *f* (du
nez) 3 : bridge *m* (jeu de cartes) — ∼ *vt*
bridged; bridging 1 : construire un pont
sur 2 ∼ **the gap** : combler une lacune
bridle [ˈbraɪdəl] *n* : bride *f* — ∼ *vt* **-dled;
-dling** : brider
brief [ˈbriːf] *adj* : bref — ∼ *n* 1 : résumé *m*
2 ∼**s** *npl* UNDERPANTS : slip *m* — ∼ *vt*
: donner des instructions à — **briefcase**
[ˈbriːfˌkeɪs] *n* : serviette *f*, porte-documents
m — **briefly** [ˈbriːfli] *adv* : brièvement
brigade [brɪˈgeɪd] *n* : brigade *f*
bright [ˈbraɪt] *adj* 1 : brillant, éclatant 2
CHEERFUL : joyeux 3 INTELLIGENT : intelligent — **brighten** [ˈbraɪtən] *vi* 1 : s'éclaircir
(se dit du temps) 2 *or* ∼ **up** : s'animer —
vt ENLIVEN : égayer
brilliant [ˈbrɪljənt] *adj* : brillant — **brilliance**
[ˈbrɪljənts] *n* 1 BRIGHTNESS : éclat *m* 2 IN-
TELLIGENCE : intelligence *f*
brim [ˈbrɪm] *n* : bord *m* (d'un chapeau, etc.)
— ∼ *vi* **brimmed; brimming** *or* ∼ **over**
: être plein jusqu'à déborder
brine [ˈbraɪn] *n* : saumure *f*
bring [ˈbrɪŋ] *vt* **brought** [ˈbrɔt]; **bringing** 1
: amener (une personne ou un animal), ap-
porter (une chose) 2 ∼ **about** : occasionner 3 ∼ **around** PERSUADE : convaincre 4

~ **back** : rapporter **5** ~ **down** : faire tomber **6** ~ **on** CAUSE : provoquer **7** ~ **out** : sortir **8** ~ **to an end** : mettre fin à **9** ~ **up** REAR : élever **10** ~ **up** MENTION : mentionner

brink ['brɪŋk] n **1** EDGE : bord m **2 on the** ~ **of** : au bord de

brisk ['brɪsk] adj **1** FAST : rapide **2** LIVELY : vif

bristle ['brɪsəl] n **1** : soie f (d'un animal) **2** : poil m (d'une brosse) — ~ vi -**tled; -tling** : se hérisser

British ['brɪtɪʃ] adj : britannique

brittle ['brɪtəl] adj -**tler; -tlest** : fragile

broach ['broːʧ] vt : entamer

broad ['brɔd] adj **1** WIDE : large **2** GENERAL : grand **3 in** ~ **daylight** : en plein jour

broadcast ['brɔd,kæst] v -**cast; -casting** vt : diffuser, téléviser — vi : émettre — ~ n : émission f

broaden ['brɔdən] vt : élargir — vi : s'élargir — **broadly** ['brɔdli] adv : en général — **broad–minded** ['brɔd'maɪndəd] adj : large d'esprit, tolérant

broccoli ['brɑkəli] n : brocoli m

brochure [broˈʃʊr] n : brochure f, dépliant m

broil ['brɔɪl] v : griller

broke ['broːk] → **break** — ~ adj : fauché fam, cassé Can fam — **broken** ['broːkən] adj : cassé, brisé — **brokenhearted** [ˌbroː-kənˈhɑrtəd] adj : au cœur brisé

broker ['broːkər] n : courtier m, -tière f

bronchitis [brɑnˈkaɪtəs, brɑŋ-] n : bronchite f

bronze ['brɑnz] n : bronze m

brooch ['broːʧ, 'bruːʧ] n : broche f

brood ['bruːd] n : couvée f (d'oiseaux) — ~ vi **1** INCUBATE : couver **2** ~ **about** : ressasser, ruminer

brook ['brʊk] n : ruisseau m

broom ['bruːm, 'brʊm] n : balai m — **broomstick** ['bruːmˌstɪk, 'brʊm-] n : manche m à balai

broth ['brɔθ] n, pl **broths** ['brɔθs, 'brɔðz] : bouillon m

brothel ['brɑθəl, 'brɔ-] n : bordel m fam

brother ['brʌðər] n : frère m — **brother-hood** ['brʌðərˌhʊd] n : fraternité f — **brother–in–law** ['brʌðərɪnˌlɔ] n, pl **broth-ers–in–law** : beau-frère m — **brotherly** ['brʌðərli] adj : fraternel

brought → **bring**

brow ['braʊ] n **1** EYEBROW : sourcil m **2** FOREHEAD : front m **3** : sommet m (d'une colline)

brown ['braʊn] adj : brun, marron — ~ n : brun m, marron m — ~ vt : faire dorer (en cuisine)

browse ['braʊz] vi **browsed; browsing** : re-garder, jeter un coup d'œil

browser ['braʊzər] n : navigateur m (en in-formatique)

bruise ['bruːz] vt **bruised; bruising 1** : faire un bleu à, contusionner **2** : taler (un fruit) — ~ n : bleu m, contusion f, prune f Can

brunch ['brʌnʧ] n : brunch m

brunet or **brunette** [bruːˈnɛt] n : brun m, brune f

brunt ['brʌnt] n **bear the** ~ **of** : subir le plus gros de

brush ['brʌʃ] n **1** : brosse f (à cheveux), pinceau m (de peintre) **2** UNDERGROWTH : brousses fpl — ~ vt **1** : brosser **2** GRAZE : effleurer **3** ~ **off** DISREGARD : écarter — vi ~ **up on** : réviser — **brush–off** ['brʌʃˌɔf] n **give s.o. the** ~ : envoyer promener qqn

brusque ['brʌsk] adj : brusque

brutal ['bruːtəl] adj : brutal — **brutality** [bruːˈtæləti] n, pl -**ties** : brutalité f

brute ['bruːt] adj : brutal — ~ n : brute f

bubble ['bʌbəl] n : bulle f — ~ vi -**bled; -bling** : bouillonner

buck ['bʌk] n, pl **bucks 1** or pl **buck** : mâle m (animal) **2** DOLLAR : dollar m — ~ vi **1** : ruer (se dit d'un cheval) **2** ~ **up** : ne pas se laisser abattre — vt OPPOSE : résister

bucket ['bʌkət] n : seau m

buckle ['bʌkəl] n : boucle f — ~ v -**led; -ling** vt **1** FASTEN : boucler **2** WARP : gauchir — vi BEND : se courber, se voiler

bud ['bʌd] n : bourgeon m (d'une feuille), bouton m (d'une fleur) — ~ vi **budded; budding** : bourgeonner

Buddhism ['buːˌdɪzəm, 'bʊ-] n : boudd-hisme m — **Buddhist** ['buːˌdɪst, 'bʊ-] adj : bouddhiste — ~ n : bouddhiste mf

buddy ['bʌdi] n, pl -**dies** : copain m, -pine f

budge ['bʌʤ] vi **budged; budging 1** MOVE : bouger **2** YIELD : céder

budget ['bʌʤət] n : budget m — ~ vt : budgétiser — vi : dresser un budget — **budgetary** ['bʌʤəˌtɛri] adj : budgétaire

buff ['bʌf] n **1** : chamois m (couleur) **2** EN-THUSIAST : mordu m, -due f fam; fanatique mf — ~ adj : chamois, beige — ~ vt POL-ISH : polir

buffalo ['bʌfəˌloː] n, pl -**lo** or -**loes** : buffle m, bison m (d'Amérique)

buffer ['bʌfər] n : tampon m

buffet [ˌbʌˈfeɪ, ˌbuː-] n : buffet m (repas ou meuble)

buffoon [ˌbʌˈfuːn] n : bouffon m

bug ['bʌg] n **1** INSECT : insecte m, bestiole f **2** FLAW : défaut m **3** GERM : microbe m **4** : bogue m (en informatique) — ~ vt **bugged; bugging 1** : installer un micro-phone dans (une maison, etc.) **2** PESTER : embêter

buggy ['bʌgi] n, pl -**gies 1** CARRIAGE

: calèche *f* **2** *or* **baby ~** : voiture *f* d'enfant, landau *m France*

bugle [ˈbjuːˌgəl] *n* : clairon *m*

build [ˈbɪld] *v* **built** [ˈbɪlt]; **building** *vt* : construire, bâtir **2** DEVELOP : établir — *vi* **1** *or* **~ up** INTENSIFY : augmenter, intensifier **2** *or* **~ up** ACCUMULATE : s'accumuler — **~** *n* PHYSIQUE : carrure *f*, charpente *f* — **builder** [ˈbɪldər] *n* : entrepreneur *m* — **building** [ˈbɪldɪŋ] *n* **1** : bâtiment *m*, immeuble *m* **2** CONSTRUCTION : construction *f* — **built-in** [ˈbɪltˌɪn] *adj* : encastré

bulb [ˈbʌlb] *n* **1** : bulbe *m* **2** LIGHTBULB : ampoule *f*

bulge [ˈbʌldʒ] *vi* **bulged**; **bulging** : être gonflé, se renfler — **~** *n* : renflement *m*

bulk [ˈbʌlk] *n* **1** : masse *f*, volume *m* **2 in ~** : en gros — **bulky** [ˈbʌlki] *adj* **bulkier**; **-est** : volumineux

bull [ˈbʊl] *n* **1** : taureau *m* **2** MALE : mâle *m*

bulldog [ˈbʊlˌdɔg] *n* : bouledogue *m*

bulldozer [ˈbʊlˌdoːzər] *n* : bulldozer *m*

bullet [ˈbʊlət] *n* : balle *f* (d'un fusil)

bulletin [ˈbʊlətən, -lətən] *n* : bulletin *m* — **bulletin board** *n* : tableau *m* d'affichage, babillard *m Can*

bulletproof [ˈbʊlətˌpruːf] *adj* : pare-balles

bullfight [ˈbʊlˌfaɪt] *n* : corrida *f* — **bullfighter** [ˈbʊlˌfaɪtər] *n* : torero *m*

bull's-eye [ˈbʊlzˌaɪ] *n*, *pl* **bull's-eyes** : centre *m* (de la cible)

bully [ˈbʊli] *n*, *pl* **-lies** : tyran *m* — **~** *vt* **-lied**; **-lying** : malmener, maltraiter

bum [ˈbʌm] *n* : clochard *m*, -charde *f*

bumblebee [ˈbʌmbəlˌbiː] *n* : bourdon *m*

bump [ˈbʌmp] *n* **1** BULGE : bosse *f*, protubérance *f* **2** IMPACT : coup *m*, choc *m* **3** JOLT : secousse *f* — **~** *vt* : heurter, cogner — *vi* **~ into** MEET : tomber sur — **bumper** [ˈbʌmpər] *n* : pare-chocs *m* — **~** *adj* : exceptionnel — **bumpy** [ˈbʌmpi] *adj* **bumpier**; **-est** : cahoteux (se dit d'un chemin) **2 a ~ flight** : un vol agité

bun [ˈbʌn] *n* : petit pain *m* (au lait)

bunch [ˈbʌntʃ] *n* **1** : bouquet *m* (de fleurs), grappe *f* (de raisins), botte *f* (de légumes, etc.) **2** GROUP : groupe *m* — **~** *vt* **~ together** : mettre ensemble — *vi* **~ up** : s'entasser

bundle [ˈbʌndəl] *n* **1** : liasse *f* (de papiers, etc.) **2** PARCEL : paquet *m* — **~** *vi* **-dled**; **-dling ~ up** : s'emmitoufler

bungalow [ˈbʌŋgəˌloː] *n* : maison *f* sans étage

bungle [ˈbʌŋgəl] *vt* **-gled**; **-gling** : gâcher

bunion [ˈbʌnjən] *n* : oignon *m*

bunk [ˈbʌŋk] *n* **1** : couchette *f* **2 ~ bed** : lits *mpl* superposés

bunny [ˈbʌni] *n*, *pl* **-nies** : lapin *m*

buoy [ˈbuːi, ˈbɔɪ] *n* : bouée *f* — **~** *vt* *or* **~**

up : revigorer — **buoyant** [ˈbɔɪənt, ˈbuːjənt] *adj* **1** : qui flotte **2** LIGHTHEARTED : allègre, optimiste

burden [ˈbərdən] *n* : fardeau *m* — **~** *vt* **~ sth with** : accabler qqn de — **burdensome** [ˈbərdənsəm] *adj* : lourd

bureau [ˈbjʊro] *n* **1** : commode *f* (meuble) **2** : service *m* (gouvernemental) **3** AGENCY : agence *f* — **bureaucracy** [bjʊˈrakrəsi] *n*, *pl* **-cies** : bureaucratie *f* — **bureaucrat** [ˈbjʊrəˌkræt] *n* : bureaucrate *mf* — **bureaucratic** [ˌbjʊrəˈkrætɪk] *adj* : bureaucratique

burglar [ˈbərglər] *n* : cambrioleur *m*, -leuse *f* — **burglarize** [ˈbərgləˌraɪz] *vt* **-ized**; **-izing** : cambrioler — **burglary** [ˈbərgləri] *n*, *pl* **-glaries** : cambriolage *m*

Burgundy [ˈbərgəndi] *n*, *pl* **-dies** : bourgogne *m* (vin)

burial [ˈbɛriəl] *n* : enterrement *m*

burly [ˈbərli] *adj* **-lier**; **-est** : costaud *fam*

burn [ˈbərn] *v* **burned** [ˈbərnd, ˈbərnt] *or* **burnt** [ˈbərnt]; **burning** : brûler — **~** *n* : brûlure *f* — **burner** [ˈbərnər] *n* : brûleur *m* (d'une cuisinière), rond *m Can*

burnish [ˈbərnɪʃ] *vt* : polir

burp [ˈbərp] *vi* : avoir des renvois, roter *fam* — **~** *n* : renvoi *m*

burrow [ˈbəro] *n* : terrier *m* — **~** *vt* : creuser — *vi* **~ into** : fouiller dans

burst [ˈbərst] *v* **burst** *or* **bursted**; **bursting** *vi* **1** : crever, éclater **2 ~ into tears** : fondre en larmes **3 ~ out laughing** : éclater de rire — **~** *vt* : crever, faire éclater — **~** *n* **1** EXPLOSION : explosion *f* **2** OUTBURST : élan *m* (d'enthousiasme), éclat *m* (de rire)

bury [ˈbɛri] *vt* **buried**; **burying** **1** : enterrer **2** HIDE : enfouir, cacher

bus [ˈbʌs] *n*, *pl* **buses** *or* **busses** : bus *m*, autobus *m* — **~** *v* **bused** *or* **bussed** [ˈbʌst]; **busing** *or* **bussing** [ˈbʌsɪŋ] *vt* : transporter en autobus — *vi* : voyager en autobus

bush [ˈbʊʃ] *n* SHRUB : buisson *m*

bushel [ˈbʊʃəl] *n* : boisseau *m*

bushy [ˈbʊʃi] *adj* **bushier**; **-est** : touffu

busily [ˈbɪzəli] *adv* : activement

business [ˈbɪznəs, -nəz] *n* **1** COMMERCE : affaires *fpl* **2** COMPANY : ent-reprise *f* **3 it's none of your ~** : ce n'est pas de vos affaires — **businessman** [ˈbɪznəsˌmæn, -nəz-] *n*, *pl* **-men** : homme *m* d'affaires — **businesswoman** [ˈbɪznəsˌwʊmən, -nəz-] *n*, *pl* **-women** : femme *f* d'affaires

bust¹ [ˈbʌst] *vt* BREAK : briser

bust² *n* **1** : buste *m* (en sculpture) **2** BREASTS : seins *fpl*, poitrine *f*

bustle [ˈbʌsəl] *vi* **-tled**; **-tling** *or* **~ about** : s'affairer — **~** *n* *or* **hustle and ~** : agitation *f*, activité *f*

busy [ˈbɪzi] *adj* **busier**; **-est** **1** : occupé **2** BUSTLING : animé

but ['bʌt] *conj* : mais — ～ *prep* : sauf, excepté

butcher ['bʊtʃər] *n* : boucher *m*, -chère *f* — ～ *vt* **1** : abattre **2** BOTCH : bousiller *fam*

butler ['bʌtlər] *n* : maître *m* d'hôtel

butt ['bʌt] *vi* ～ **in** : interrompre — ～ *n* **1** : crosse *f* (d'un fusil) **2** : mégot *m* *fam* (de cigarette)

butter ['bʌtər] *n* : beurre *m* — ～ *vt* : beurrer

butterfly ['bʌtər‚flaɪ] *n, pl* **-flies** : papillon *m*

buttermilk ['bʌtər‚mɪlk] *n* : babeurre *m*

buttocks ['bʌtəks, -‚tɑks] *npl* : fesses *fpl*

button ['bʌtən] *n* : bouton *m* — ～ *vi or* ～ **up** : se boutonner — **buttonhole** ['bʌtən‚hoːl] *n* : boutonnière *f*

buttress ['bʌtrəs] *n* : contrefort *m*

buy ['baɪ] *vt* **bought** ['bɔt]; **buying** : acheter — ～ *n* : achat *m* — **buyer** ['baɪər] *n* : acheteur *m*, -teuse *f*

buzz ['bʌz] *vi* : bourdonner — ～ *n* : bourdonnement *m*

buzzer ['bʌzər] *n* : sonnette *f*

by ['baɪ] *prep* **1** NEAR : près de, à côté de **2** VIA : par, en **3** PAST : devant, à côté de **4** DURING : pendant **5** (*in expressions of time*) : avant **6** (*indicating cause or agent*) : par — ～ *adv* **1** ～ **and** ～ : bientôt **2** ～ **and large** : en général **3 go** ～ : passer **4 stop** ～ : arrêter

bygone ['baɪ‚ɡɔn] *adj* **1** : passé, d'autrefois **2 let** ～**s be** ～**s** : enterrer le passé

bypass ['baɪ‚pæs] *n* : route *f* de contournement — ～ *vt* : contourner

by–product ['baɪ‚prɑdəkt] *n* : sous-produit *m*, dérivé *m*

bystander ['baɪ‚stændər] *n* : spectateur *m*, -trice *f*

byte ['baɪt] *n* : octet *m*

C

c ['siː] *n, pl* **c's** *or* **cs** : c *m*, troisième lettre de l'alphabet

cab ['kæb] *n* **1** : taxi *m* **2** : cabine *f* (d'un camion, etc.)

cabbage ['kæbɪʤ] *n* : chou *m*

cabin ['kæbən] *n* **1** : cabane *f* **2** : cabine *f* (d'un navire, d'un avion, etc.)

cabinet ['kæbnət] *n* **1** CUPBOARD : armoire *f* **2** : cabinet *m* (en politique) **3** *or* **medicine** ～ : pharmacie *f*

cable ['keɪbəl] *n* : câble *m* — **cable television** *n* : câble *m*

cackle ['kækəl] *vi* **-led; -ling** : caqueter, glousser

cactus ['kæktəs] *n, pl* **cacti** [-‚taɪ] *or* **-tuses** : cactus *m*

cadence ['keɪdənʦ] *n* : cadence *f*, rythme *m*

cadet [kə'dɛt] *n* : élève *mf* officier

café [kæ'feɪ, kə-] *n* : café *m*, bistrot *m* — **cafeteria** [‚kæfə'tɪriə] *n* : cafétéria *f*

caffeine [kæ'fiːn] *n* : caféine *f*

cage ['keɪʤ] *n* : cage *f*

cajole [kə'ʤoːl] *vt* **-joled; -joling** : cajoler, enjôler

Cajun ['keɪʤən] *adj* : acadien, cajun

cake ['keɪk] *n* **1** : gâteau *m* **2** BAR : pain *m* (de savon) — **caked** ['keɪkt] *adj* ～ **with** : couvert de

calamity [kə'læməti] *n, pl* **-ties** : calamité *f*

calcium ['kælsiəm] *n* : calcium *m*

calculate ['kælkjə‚leɪt] *v* **-lated; -lating** : calculer — **calculating** ['kælkjə‚leɪtɪŋ]

adj : calculateur — **calculation** [‚kælkjə-'leɪʃən] *n* : calcul *m* — **calculator** ['kælkjə-‚leɪtər] *n* : calculatrice *f*

calendar ['kæləndər] *n* : calendrier *m*

calf¹ ['kæf] *n, pl* **calves** ['kævz] : veau *m* (de bovin)

calf² *n, pl* **calves** : mollet *m* (de la jambe)

caliber *or* **calibre** ['kæləbər] *n* : calibre *m*

call ['kɔl] *vi* **1** : appeler **2** VISIT : passer, faire une visite **3** ～ **for** : demander — *vt* **1** : appeler **2** ～ **back** : rappeler **3** ～ **off** : annuler — ～ *n* **1** : appel *m* **2** SHOUT : cri *m* **3** VISIT : visite *f* **4** NEED : demande *f* — **calling** ['kɔlɪŋ] *n* : vocation *f*

callous ['kæləs] *adj* : dur, sans cœur

calm ['kɑm, 'kɑlm] *n* : calme *m*, tranquillité *f* — ～ *vt* : calmer, apaiser — *vi or* ～ **down** : se calmer — ～ *adj* : calme, tranquille

calorie ['kæləri] *n* : calorie *f*

came → **come**

camel ['kæməl] *n* : chameau *m*

camera ['kæmrə, 'kæmərə] *n* : appareil *m* photo, caméra *f*

camouflage ['kæmə‚flɑʒ, -‚flɑʤ] *n* : camouflage *m* — ～ *vt* **-flaged; -flaging** : camoufler

camp ['kæmp] *n* **1** : camp *m* **2** FACTION : parti *m* — ～ *vi* : camper, faire du camping

campaign [kæm'peɪn] *n* : campagne *f* — ～ *vi* : faire campagne

camping ['kæmpɪŋ] *n* : camping *m*
campus ['kæmpəs] *n* : campus *m*, cité *f* universitaire *Can*
can[1] ['kæn] *v aux, past* **could** ['kʊd]; *present s & pl* **can 1** (*expressing possibility or permission*) : pouvoir **2** (*expressing knowledge or ability*) : savoir **3 that cannot be** : cela n'est pas possible
can[2] *n* : boîte *f* (d'aliments), canette *f* (de boisson gazeuse), bidon *m* (d'essence, etc.) — ~ *vt* **canned; canning** : mettre en boîte
Canadian [kə'neɪdiən] *adj* : canadien
canal [kə'næl] *n* : canal *m*
canary [kə'nɛri] *n, pl* **-naries** : canari *m*, serin *m*
cancel ['kæntsəl] *vt* **-celed** *or* **-celled; -celing** *or* **-celling** : annuler — **cancellation** [ˌkæntsə'leɪʃən] *n* : annulation *f*
cancer ['kæntsər] *n* : cancer *m* — **cancerous** ['kæntsərəs] *adj* : cancéreux
candid ['kændɪd] *adj* : franc, sincère
candidate ['kændə,deɪt, -dət] *n* : candidat *m*, -date *f* — **candidacy** ['kændədəsi] *n, pl* **-cies** : candidature *f*
candle ['kændəl] *n* : bougie *f*, chandelle *f* — **candlestick** ['kændəl,stɪk] *n* : chandelier *m*, bougeoir *m*
candor *or Brit* **candour** ['kændər] *n* : franchise *f*
candy ['kændi] *n, pl* **-dies 1** : bonbon *m* **2** ~ **store** : confiserie *f*
cane ['keɪn] *n* : canne *f* — ~ *vt* **caned; caning** FLOG : fouetter
canine ['keɪ,naɪn] *n or* ~ **tooth** : canine *f* — ~ *adj* : canin
canister ['kænəstər] *n* : boîte *f*
cannibal ['kænəbəl] *n* : cannibale *mf*
cannon ['kænən] *n, pl* **-nons** *or* **-non** : canon *m*
cannot (**can not**) ['kæn,ɑt, kə'nɑt] → **can**[1]
canoe [kə'nu:] *n* : canoë *m*, canot *m Can*
canon ['kænən] *n* : canon *m*, règle *f*
can opener *n* : ouvre-boîtes *m*
canopy ['kænəpi] *n, pl* **-pies** : auvent *m*, baldaquin *m*
can't ['kænt, 'kant] (*contraction of* **can not**) → **can**[1]
cantaloupe ['kæntəl,o:p] *n* : cantaloup *m*
cantankerous [kæn'tæŋkərəs] *adj* : acariâtre
canteen [kæn'ti:n] *n* CAFETERIA : cantine *f*
canter ['kæntər] *vi* : aller au petit galop — ~ *n* : petit galop *m*
canvas ['kænvəs] *n* : toile *f*
canvass ['kænvəs] *vt* : solliciter les voix de (les) électeurs) — ~ *n* : démarchage *m* électoral
canyon ['kænjən] *n* : canyon *m*
cap ['kæp] *n* **1** : casquette *f* **2** : capsule *f* (d'une bouteille), capuchon *m* (d'un stylo, etc.) — ~ *vt* **capped; capping** COVER : couvrir
capable ['keɪpəbəl] *adj* : capable — **capability** [ˌkeɪpə'bɪləti] *n, pl* **-ties** : aptitude *f*, capacité *f*
capacity [kə'pæsəti] *n, pl* **-ties 1** : capacité *f* **2** ROLE : qualité *f*
cape[1] ['keɪp] *n* : cap *m* (en géographie)
cape[2] *n* CLOAK : cape *f*, pèlerine *f*
caper ['keɪpər] *n* : câpre *f*
capital ['kæpətəl] *adj* **1** : capital, principal **2** : majuscule (se dit d'une lettre) — ~ *n* **1** *or* ~ **city** : capitale *f* **2** WEALTH : capital *m*, fonds *mpl* **3** *or* ~ **letter** : majuscule *f* — **capitalism** ['kæpətəl,ızəm] *n* : capitalisme *m* — **capitalist** ['kæpətəlıst] *or* **capitalistic** ['kæpətəl'ıstık] *adj* : capitaliste — **capitalize** ['kæpətəl,aız] *v* **-ized; -izing** *vt* : écrire avec une majuscule — *vi* ~ **on** : tirer profit de
capitol ['kæpətəl] *n* : capitole *m*
capsize ['kæp,saız, kæp'saız] *v* **-sized; -sizing** *vt* : faire chavirer — *vi* : chavirer
capsule ['kæpsəl, -,su:l] *n* : capsule *f*
captain ['kæptən] *n* : capitaine *m*
caption ['kæpʃən] *n* **1** : légende *f* (d'une illustration) **2** SUBTITLE : sous-titre *m*
captivate ['kæptə,veɪt] *vt* **-vated; -vating** : captiver, fasciner
captive ['kæptɪv] *adj* : captif — ~ *n* : captif *m*, -tive *f* — **captivity** [kæp'tɪvəti] *n* : captivité *f*
capture ['kæpʃər] *n* : capture *f*, prise *f* — ~ *vt* **-tured; -turing 1** SEIZE : capturer **2** : captiver (l'imagination), capter (l'attention)
car ['kɑr] *n* **1** : voiture *f*, automobile *f* **2** *or* **railroad** ~ : wagon *m*
carafe [kə'ræf, -'rɑf] *n* : carafe *f*
caramel ['kɑrməl; 'kærəməl, -,mɛl] *n* : caramel *m*
carat ['kærət] *n* : carat *m*
caravan ['kærə,væn] *n* : caravane *f*
carbohydrate [ˌkɑrbo'haɪ,dreɪt, -drət] *n* : hydrate *m* de carbone
carbon ['kɑrbən] *n* : carbone *m*
carburetor ['kɑrbə,reɪtər, -bjə-] *n* : carburateur *m*
carcass ['kɑrkəs] *n* : carcasse *f*
card ['kɑrd] *n* : carte *f* — **cardboard** ['kɑrd,bord] *n* : carton *m*
cardiac ['kɑrdi,æk] *adj* : cardiaque
cardigan ['kɑrdɪgən] *n* : cardigan *m*
cardinal ['kɑrdənəl] *n* : cardinal *m* — ~ *adj* : cardinal, essentiel
care ['kær] *n* **1** : soin *m* **2** WORRY : préoccupation *f* — ~ *vi* **cared; caring 1** : se préoccuper, se soucier **2** ~ **for** TEND : prendre soin de **3** ~ **for** LIKE : aimer **4 I don't** ~ : ça m'est égal

career [kə'rır] *n* : carrière *f*, profession *f*

carefree ['kær,fri:, ,kær'-] *adj* : insouciant

careful ['kærfəl] *adj* 1 : prudent 2 **be ~**! : fais attention! — **carefully** ['kærfəli] *adv* : prudemment, avec soin — **careless** ['kærləs] *adj* : négligent — **carelessness** ['kærləsnəs] *n* : négligence *f*

caress [kə'rɛs] *n* : caresse *f* — **~** *vt* : caresser

cargo ['kar,go:] *n, pl* **-goes** *or* **-gos** : chargement *m*, cargaison *f*

Caribbean [,kærə'bi:ən, kə'rıbiən] *adj* : des Caraïbes

caricature ['kærıkə,tʃur] *n* : caricature *f*

caring ['kærıŋ] *adj* : aimant, affectueux

carnage ['karnıdʒ] *n* : carnage *m*

carnation [kar'neıʃən] *n* : œillet *m*

carnival ['karnəvəl] *n* : carnaval *m*

carol ['kærəl] *n* : chant *m* de Noël

carpenter ['karpəntər] *n* : charpentier *m*, menuisier *m* — **carpentry** ['karpəntri] *n* : charpenterie *f*, menuiserie *f*

carpet ['karpət] *n* : tapis *m*

carriage ['kærıdʒ] *n* 1 : transport *m* (de marchandises) 2 BEARING : maintien *m* 3 → baby carriage 4 *or* horse-drawn **~** : calèche *f*, carrosse *m*

carrier ['kæriər] *n* 1 : transporteur *m* 2 : porteur *m*, -teuse *f* (d'une maladie)

carrot ['kærət] *n* : carotte *f*

carry ['kæri] *v* **-ried; -rying** *vt* 1 : porter 2 TRANSPORT : transporter 3 STOCK : vendre 4 ENTAIL : comporter 5 **~ oneself** : se présenter — *vi* : porter (se dit de la voix) — **carry away** *vt* **get carried away** : s'emballer — **carry on** *vt* CONDUCT : réaliser — *vi* 1 : mal se comporter 2 CONTINUE : continuer — **carry out** *vt* 1 : réaliser, effectuer 2 FULFILL : accomplir

cart ['kart] *n* : charrette *f* — **~** *vt or* **~ around** : trimbaler *fam*

carton ['kartən] *n* : boîte *f* de carton

cartoon [kar'tu:n] *n* 1 : dessin *m* humoristique 2 COMIC STRIP : bande *f* dessinée 3 *or* **animated ~** : dessin *m* animé

cartridge ['kartrıdʒ] *n* : cartouche *f*

carve ['karv] *vt* **carved; carving** 1 : tailler (le bois, etc.) 2 : découper (de la viande)

case ['keıs] *n* 1 : boîte *f*, caisse *f* 2 **in any ~** : en tout cas 3 **in ~ of** : au cas de 4 **just in ~** : au cas où

cash ['kæʃ] *n* : espèces *fpl*, argent *m* liquide — **~** *vt* : encaisser

cashew ['kæ,ʃu:, kə'ʃu:] *n* : noix *f* de cajou

cashier [kæ'ʃır] *n* : caissier *m*, -sière *f*

cashmere ['kæʒ,mır, 'kæʃ-] *n* : cachemire *m*

cash register *n* : caisse *f* enregistreuse

casino [kə'si:,no:] *n, pl* **-nos** : casino *m*

cask ['kæsk] *n* : fût *m*, tonneau *f*

casket ['kæskət] *n* : cercueil *m*

casserole ['kæsə,ro:l] *n* : ragoût *m*

cassette [kə'sɛt, kæ-] *n* : cassette *f*

cast ['kæst] *vt* **cast; casting** 1 THROW : jeter, lancer 2 : donner un rôle à (au cinéma, etc.) 3 MOLD : couler (du métal) 4 **~ one's vote** : voter — **~** *n* 1 : distribution *f* (d'acteurs) 2 *or* **plaster ~** : plâtre *m*

cast iron *n* : fonte *f*

castle ['kæsəl] *n* : château *m*

castrate ['kæs,treıt] *vt* **-trated; -trating** : châtrer

casual ['kæʒuəl] *adj* 1 : nonchalant 2 INFORMAL : décontracté — **casually** ['kæʒuəli, 'kæʒəli] *adv* 1 : nonchalamment 2 **~ dressed** : habillé simplement

casualty ['kæʒuəlti, 'kæʒəl-] *n, pl* **-ties** 1 : accident *m* grave, désastre *m* 2 VICTIM : blessé *m*, -sée *f*; accidenté *m*, -tée *f*; mort *m*, morte *f*

cat ['kæt] *n* : chat *m*, chatte *f*

catalog *or* **catalogue** ['kætə,lɔg] *n* : catalogue *m*

cataract ['kætə,rækt] *n* : cataracte *f*

catastrophe [kə'tæstrə,fi:] *n* : catastrophe *f*

catch ['kætʃ, 'kɛtʃ] *v* **caught** ['kɔt]; **catching** *vt* 1 CAPTURE, TRAP : attraper 2 SURPRISE : surprendre 3 GRASP : saisir 4 SNAG : accrocher 5 : prendre (le train, etc.) 6 **~ one's breath** : reprendre son souffle — *vi* 1 SNAG : s'accrocher 2 **~ fire** : prendre feu — **~** *n* 1 : prise *f*, capture *f* 2 PITFALL : piège *f* — **catching** ['kætʃıŋ, 'kɛ-] *adj* : contagieux — **catchy** ['kætʃi, 'kɛ-] *adj* : catchier; -est : entraînant

category ['kætə,gori] *n, pl* **-ries** : catégorie *f*, classe *f* — **categorical** [,kætə'gorıkəl] *adj* : catégorique

cater ['keıtər] *vi* 1 : fournir des repas 2 **~ to** : pourvoir à — **caterer** ['keıtərər] *n* : traiteur *m*

caterpillar ['kætər,pılər] *n* : chenille *f*

cathedral [kə'θi:drəl] *n* : cathédrale *f*

catholic ['kæθəlık] *adj* 1 : universel 2 **Catholic** : catholique — **catholicism** [kə'θalə,sızəm] *n* : catholicisme *m*

cattle ['kætəl] *npl* : bétail *m*, bovins *mpl*

caught → **catch**

cauldron ['kɔldrən] *n* : chaudron *m*

cauliflower ['kalı,flauər, 'kɔ-] *n* : chou-fleur *m*

cause ['kɔz] *n* 1 : cause *f* 2 REASON : raison *f*, motif *m* — **~** *vt* **caused; causing** : causer, occasionner

caution ['kɔʃən] *n* 1 WARNING : avertissement *m* 2 CARE : prudence *f* — **~** *vt* : avertir, mettre en garde — **cautious** ['kɔʃəs] *adj* : prudent, avisé — **cautiously** ['kɔʃəsli] *adv* : prudemment

cavalier [,kævə'lır] *adj* : cavalier, désinvolte

cavalry ['kævəlri] n, pl **-ries** : cavalerie f
cave ['keɪv] n : grotte f, caverne f — ~ vi **caved; caving** or ~ **in** : s'affaisser, s'effondrer
cavern ['kævərn] n : caverne f
caviar or **caviare** ['kævi,ɑr, 'kɑ-] n : caviar m
cavity ['kævəṭi] n, pl **-ties** 1 : cavité f 2 : carie f (dentaire)
CD [,si:'di:] n : CD m, disque m compact
cease ['si:s] v **ceased; ceasing** : cesser — **cease-fire** ['si:s'faɪr] n : cessez-le-feu m — **ceaseless** ['si:sləs] adj : incessant, continuel
cedar ['si:dər] n : cèdre m
cedilla [sɪ'dɪlə] n : cédille nf
ceiling ['si:lɪŋ] n : plafond m
celebrate ['sɛlə,breɪt] v **-brated; -brating** vt : fêter, célébrer — vi : faire le fête — **celebrated** ['sɛlə,breɪṭəd] adj : célèbre — **celebration** [,sɛlə'breɪʃən] n 1 : célébration f 2 FESTIVITY : fête f — **celebrity** [sə'lɛbrəṭi] n, pl **-ties** : célébrité f
celery ['sɛləri] n, pl **-eries** : céleri m
cell ['sɛl] n : cellule f
cellar ['sɛlər] n : cave f
cello ['tʃɛ,lo:] n, pl **-los** : violoncelle m
cellular ['sɛljələr] adj : cellulaire
cement [sɪ'mɛnt] n : ciment m
cemetery ['sɛmə,tɛri] n, pl **-teries** : cimetière m
censor ['sɛntsər] vt : censurer — **censorship** ['sɛntsər,ʃɪp] n : censure f — **censure** ['sɛntʃər] n : censure f, blâme m — ~ vt **-sured; -suring** : critiquer, blâmer
census ['sɛntsəs] n : recensement m
cent ['sɛnt] n : cent m
centennial [sɛn'tɛniəl] n : centenaire m
center or Brit **centre** ['sɛntər] n : centre m — ~ v **centered** or Brit **centred; centering** or Brit **centring** vt : centrer — vi ~ **on** : se concentrer sur
centigrade ['sɛntə,greɪd, 'sɑn-] adj : centigrade
centimeter ['sɛntə,mi:ṭər, 'sɑn-] n : centimètre m
centipede ['sɛntə,pi:d] n : mille-pattes m
central ['sɛntrəl] adj : central — **centralize** ['sɛntrə,laɪz] vt **-ized; -izing** : centraliser
centre → **center**
century ['sɛntʃəri] n, pl **-ries** : siècle m
ceramics [sə'ræmɪks] n : céramique f
cereal ['sɪriəl] n : céréale f
ceremony ['sɛrə,mo:ni] n, pl **-nies** : cérémonie f
certain ['sərṭən] adj 1 : certain 2 be ~ of : être assuré de 3 for ~ : au juste — **certainly** ['sərṭənli] adv : certainement, bien sûr — **certainty** ['sərṭənti] n, pl **-ties** : certitude f

certify ['sərṭə,faɪ] vt **-fied; -fying** : certifier — **certificate** [sər'tɪfɪkət] n : certificat m
chafe ['tʃeɪf] vi **chafed; chafing** 1 RUB : frotter 2 ~ **at** : s'irriter de
chain ['tʃeɪn] n 1 : chaîne f 2 ~ **of events** : série f d'événements — ~ vt : enchaîner
chair ['tʃer] n 1 : chaise f 2 : chaire f (d'une université) — ~ vt : présider — **chairman** ['tʃermən] n, pl **-men** [-mən, -,mɛn] : président m — **chairperson** ['tʃer,pərsən] n : presidente m, -dente f
chalk ['tʃɔk] n : craie f
challenge ['tʃælɪndʒ] vt **-lenged; -lenging** 1 DISPUTE : contester 2 DARE : défier — ~ n : défi m — **challenging** ['tʃælɪndʒɪŋ] adj : stimulant
chamber ['tʃeɪmbər] n : chambre f (de commerce, etc.)
champagne [ʃæm'peɪn] n : champagne m
champion ['tʃæmpiən] n : champion m, -pionne — **championship** ['tʃæmpiən,ʃɪp] n : championnat m
chance ['tʃænts] n 1 LUCK : hasard m 2 OPPORTUNITY : occasion f 3 LIKELIHOOD : chances fpl 4 **by ~** : par hasard 5 **take a ~** : prendre un risque — ~ vt **chanced; chancing** : hasarder, risquer — ~ adj : fortuit
chandelier [,ʃændə'lɪr] n : lustre m
change ['tʃeɪndʒ] v **changed; changing** vt 1 : changer 2 SWITCH : changer de — vi 1 : changer 2 or ~ **clothes** : se changer — ~ n 1 : changement m 2 COINS : monnaie f — **changeable** ['tʃeɪndʒəbəl] adj : changeant
channel ['tʃænəl] n 1 : canal m 2 : chenal m (dans un fleuve, etc.) 3 : chaîne f (de télévision)
chant ['tʃænt] n : chant m
chaos ['keɪ,ɑs] n : chaos m — **chaotic** [keɪ'ɑṭɪk] adj : chaotique
chap[1] ['tʃæp] vi **chapped; chapping** : gercer
chap[2] n : type m fam, bonhomme m fam
chapel ['tʃæpəl] n : chapelle f
chaperon or **chaperone** ['ʃæpə,ro:n] n : chaperon m
chaplain ['tʃæplɪn] n : aumônier m
chapter ['tʃæptər] n : chapitre m
char ['tʃɑr] vt **charred; charring** : carboniser
character ['kærɪktər] n 1 : caractère m 2 : personnage m (d'un roman, etc.) — **characteristic** [,kærɪktə'rɪstɪk] adj : caractéristique — ~ n : caractéristique f — **characterize** ['kærɪktə,raɪz] vt **-ized; -izing** : caractériser
charcoal ['tʃɑr,ko:l] n : charbon m de bois
charge ['tʃɑrdʒ] n 1 : charge f (électrique) 2 COST : prix m, frais mpl 3 ACCUSATION : inculpation f 4 **be in ~** : être responsable —

~ *v* **charged; charging** *vt* **1** : charger (une batterie) **2** ENTRUST : charger, confier **3** ACCUSE : inculper **4** : payer par carte de crédit — *vi* **1** : se précipiter, foncer **2** ~ **too much** : demander trop (d'argent)

charisma [kə'rɪzmə] *n* : charisme *m* — **charismatic** [ˌkærəz'mæţɪk] *adj* : charismatique

charity ['ʧærəţi] *n, pl* **-ties 1** : organisation *f* caritative **2** GOODWILL : charité *f*

charlatan ['ʃɑrləţən] *n* : charlatan *m*

charm ['ʧɑrm] *n* : charme *m* — ~ *vt* : charmer, captiver — **charming** ['ʧɑrmɪŋ] *adj* : charmant

chart ['ʧɑrt] *n* : graphique *m*, tableau *m*

charter ['ʧɑrtər] *n* : charte *f* — ~ *vt* : affréter (un vol, etc.)

chase ['ʧeɪs] *n* : poursuite *f* — ~ *vt* **chased; chasing 1** : poursuivre, courir après **2** *or* ~ **away** : chasser

chasm ['kæzəm] *n* : gouffre *m*, abîme *m*

chaste ['ʧeɪst] *adj* **chaster; chastest** : chaste — **chastity** ['ʧæstəţi] *n* : chasteté *f*

chat ['ʧæt] *vi* **chatted; chatting** : bavarder, causer — ~ *n* : causerie *f* — **chatter** ['ʧæţər] *vi* **1** : bavarder **2** : claquer (se dit des dents) — ~ *n* : bavardage *m* — **chatterbox** ['ʧæţərˌbɑks] *n* : moulin *m* à paroles *fam* — **chatty** ['ʧæţi] *adj* **chattier; -est** : bavard

chauffeur ['ʃo:fər, ʃo'fər] *n* : chauffeur *m*

chauvinist ['ʃo:vənɪst] *or* **chauvinistic** [ˌʃo:və'nɪstɪk] *adj* : chauvin

cheap ['ʧi:p] *adj* **1** INEXPENSIVE : bon marché **2** SHODDY : de mauvaise qualité — ~ *adv* : à bon marché

cheat ['ʧi:t] *vt* : frauder, tromper — *vi* **1** : tricher **2** ~ **on s.o.** : tromper qqn — ~ *or* **cheater** ['ʧi:tər] *n* : tricheur *m*, -cheuse *f*

check ['ʧɛk] *n* **1** HALT : arrêt *m* **2** RESTRAINT : limite *f*, frein *m* **3** INSPECTION : contrôle *m* **4** *or Brit* **cheque** DRAFT : chèque *m* **5** BILL : addition *f* — ~ *vt* **1** HALT : freiner, arrêter **2** RESTRAIN : retenir, contenir **3** VERIFY : vérifier **4** ~ **in** : se présenter à la réception (à l'hôtel) **5** *or* ~ **off** MARK : cocher **6** ~ **out** : quitter (l'hôtel) **7** ~ **out** VERIFY : vérifier — **checkbook** ['ʧɛkˌbʊk] *n* : carnet *m* de chèques

checkers ['ʧɛkərz] *n* : jeu *m* de dames

checkmate ['ʧɛkˌmeɪt] *n* : échec *m* et mat

checkpoint ['ʧɛkˌpɔɪnt] *n* : poste *m* de contrôle

checkup ['ʧɛkˌʌp] *n* : examen *m* médical

cheek ['ʧik] *n* : joue *f*

cheer ['ʧɪr] *n* **1** : gaieté *f* **2** APPLAUSE : acclamation *f* **3** ~**s!** : à votre santé! — ~ *vt* **1** COMFORT : encourager **2** APPLAUD : acclamer — **cheerful** ['ʧɪrfəl] *adj* : de bonne humeur

cheese ['ʧi:z] *n* : fromage *m*

cheetah ['ʧi:ţə] *n* : guépard *m*

chef ['ʃɛf] *n* : cuisinier *m*, -nière *f*; chef *m* (cuisinier)

chemical ['kɛmɪkəl] *adj* : chimique — ~ *n* : produit *m* chimique — **chemist** ['kɛmɪst] *n* : chimiste *mf* — **chemistry** ['kɛmɪstri] *n, pl* **-tries** : chimie *f*

cheque *Brit* → **check**

cherish ['ʧɛrɪʃ] *vt* **1** : chérir, aimer **2** HARBOR : caresser, nourrir (un espoir, etc.)

cherry ['ʧɛri] *n, pl* **-ries** : cerise *f*

chess ['ʧɛs] *n* : échecs *mpl*

chest ['ʧɛst] *n* **1** BOX : coffre *m* **2** : poitrine *f* (du corps) **3** *or* ~ **of drawers** : commode *f*

chestnut ['ʧɛstˌnʌt] *n* : marron *m*, châtaigne *f*

chew ['ʧu:] *vt* : mastiquer, mâcher — **chewing gum** *n* : chewing-gum *m France*, gomme *f* à mâcher

chick ['ʧɪk] *n* : poussin *m* — **chicken** ['ʧɪkən] *n* : poulet *m* — **chicken pox** *n* : varicelle *f*

chicory ['ʧɪkəri] *n, pl* **-ries 1** : endive *f* **2** : chicorée *f*

chief ['ʧi:f] *adj* : principal, en chef — ~ *n* : chef *m* — **chiefly** ['ʧi:fli] *adv* : principalement, surtout

child ['ʧaɪld] *n, pl* **children** ['ʧɪldrən] **1** : enfant *mf* **2** OFFSPRING : fils *m*, fille *f* — **childbirth** ['ʧaɪldˌbərθ] *n* : accouchement *m* — **childhood** ['ʧaɪldˌhʊd] *n* : enfance *f* — **childish** ['ʧaɪldɪʃ] *adj* : puéril, enfantin — **childlike** ['ʧaɪldˌlaɪk] *adj* : innocent, d'enfant — **childproof** ['tlaɪldˌpru:f] *adj* : de sécurité pour enfants

chili *or* **chile** *or* **chilli** ['ʧɪli] *n, pl* **chilies** *or* **chiles** *or* **chillies 1** *or* ~ **pepper** : piment *m* fort **2** : chili *m* con carne

chill ['ʧɪl] *n* **1** : froid *m* **2 catch a** ~ : attraper un coup de froid **3 there's a** ~ **in the air** : il fait un peu froid — ~ *vt* : refroidir, réfrigérer — **chilly** ['ʧɪli] *adj* **chillier; -est** : frais, froid

chime ['ʧaɪm] *v* **chimed; chiming** : carillonner — ~ *n* : carillon *m*

chimney ['ʧɪmni] *n, pl* **-neys** : cheminée *f*

chimpanzee ['ʧɪmˌpæn'zi:, ˌʃɪm-; ʧɪm'pænzi, ʃɪm-] *n* : chimpanzé *m*

chin ['ʧɪn] *n* : menton *m*

china ['ʧaɪnə] *n* : porcelaine *f*

Chinese ['ʧaɪ'ni:z, -'ni:s] *adj* : chinois — ~ *n* : chinois *m* (langue)

chip ['ʧɪp] *n* **1** : éclat *m* (de verre), copeau *m* (de bois) **2** : jeton *m* (de poker, etc.) **3** NICK : ébréchure *f* **4** *or* **computer** ~ : puce *f* — ~ *v* **chipped; chipping** *vt* : ébrécher (de la vaisselle, etc.), écailler (de la peinture) — *vi* ~ **in** : contribuer

chipmunk ['ʧɪpˌmʌŋk] *n* : tamia *m*

chiropodist [kə'rɑpədɪst, ʃə-] *n* : pédicure *mf*

chiropractor ['kaɪrə₁præktər] *n* : chiropracteur *m*

chirp ['tʃərp] *vi* : pépier

chisel ['tʃɪzəl] *n* : ciseau *m* — ～ *vt* **-eled** *or* **-elled; -eling** *or* **-elling** : ciseler

chitchat ['tʃɪt₁tʃæt] *n* : bavardage *m*

chivalry ['ʃɪvəlri] *n, pl* **-ries** : chevalerie *f*

chive ['tʃaɪv] *n* : ciboulette *f*

chlorine ['klɔr₁iːn] *n* : chlore *m*

chock–full ['tʃɑk'fʊl, 'tʃʌk-] *adj* : bondé, plein à craquer

chocolate ['tʃɑkələt, 'tʃɔk-] *n* : chocolat *m*

choice ['tʃɔɪs] *n* : choix *m* — ～ *adj* **choicer; choicest** : de choix, de première qualité

choir ['kwaɪr] *n* : chœur *m*

choke ['tʃoːk] *v* **choked; choking** *vt* **1** : étrangler, étouffer **2** BLOCK : boucher — *vi* : s'étouffer (en mangeant) — ～ *n* : starter *m* (d'une voiture)

cholesterol [kə'lestə₁rɔl] *n* : cholestérol *m*

choose ['tʃuːz] *v* **chose** ['tʃoːz]; **chosen** ['tʃoːzən]; **choosing** *vt* **1** SELECT : choisir **2** DECIDE : décider — *vi* : choisir — **choosy** *or* **choosey** ['tʃuːzi] *adj* **choosier; -est** : exigeant

chop ['tʃɑp] *vt* **chopped; chopping 1** : couper (du bois), hacher (des légumes, etc.) **2** ～ **down** : abattre — ～ *n* : côtelette *f* (de porc, etc.) — **choppy** ['tʃɑpi] *adj* **-pier; -est** : agité (se dit de la mer)

chopsticks ['tʃɑp₁stɪks] *npl* : baguettes *fpl*

chord ['kɔrd] *n* : accord *m* (en musique)

chore ['tʃor] *n* **1** : corvée *f* **2 household** ～**s** : travaux *mpl* ménagers

choreography [₁kori'ɑɡrəfi] *n, pl* **-phies** : chorégraphie *f*

chorus ['korəs] *n* **1** : chœur *m* (de chanteurs) **2** REFRAIN : refrain *m*

chose, chosen → **choose**

christen ['krɪsən] *vt* : baptiser — **christening** ['krɪsənɪŋ] *n* : baptême *m*

Christian ['krɪstʃən] *adj* : chrétien — ～ *n* : chrétien *m*, -tienne *f* — **Christianity** [₁krɪstʃi'ænəti, ₁krɪs'tʃæ-] *n* : christianisme *m*

Christmas ['krɪsməs] *n* : Noël *m*

chrome ['kroːm] *n* : chrome *m* — **chromium** ['kroːmiəm] *n* : chrome *m*

chronic ['krɑnɪk] *adj* : chronique

chronicle ['krɑnɪkəl] *n* : chronique *f*

chronology [krə'nɑlədʒi] *n, pl* **-gies** : chronologie *f* — **chronological** [₁krɑnəl-'ɑdʒɪkəl] *adj* : chronologique

chrysanthemum [krɪ'sæntθəməm] *n* : chrysanthème *m*

chubby ['tʃʌbi] *adj* **-bier; -est** : potelé, dodu

chuck ['tʃʌk] *vt* : tirer, lancer

chuckle ['tʃʌkəl] *vi* **-led; -ling** : glousser, rire tout bas — ～ *n* : petit rire *m*

chum ['tʃʌm] *n* : copain *m*, -pine *f;* camarade *mf*

chunk ['tʃʌŋk] *n* : (gros) morceau *m*

church ['tʃərtʃ] *n* : église *f*

churn ['tʃərn] *vt* **1** : battre (du beurre) **2** STIR : agiter, remuer **3** ～ **out** : produire en série

cider ['saɪdər] *n* : cidre *m*

cigar [sɪ'ɡɑr] *n* : cigare *m* — **cigarette** [₁sɪɡə'rɛt, 'sɪɡə₁rɛt] *n* : cigarette *f*

cinch ['sɪntʃ] *n* **it's a** ～ : c'est du gâteau

cinema ['sɪnəmə] *n* : cinéma *m*

cinnamon ['sɪnəmən] *n* : cannelle *f*

cipher ['saɪfər] *n* **1** ZERO : zéro *m* **2** CODE : chiffre *m*

circa ['sərkə] *prep* : environ, vers

circle ['sərkəl] *n* : cercle *m* — ～ *vt* **-cled; -cling 1** : faire le tour de **2** SURROUND : entourer, encercler

circuit ['sərkət] *n* : circuit *m* — **circuitous** [₁sər'kjuːətəs] *adj* : détourné, indirect

circular ['sərkjələr] *adj* : circulaire — ～ *n* LEAFLET : circulaire *f*

circulate ['sərkjə₁leɪt] *v* **-lated; -lating** : circuler — **circulation** [₁sərkjə'leɪʃən] *n* **1** FLOW : circulation *f* **2** : tirage *m* (d'un journal)

circumcise ['sərkəm₁saɪz] *vt* **-cised; -cising** : circoncire — **circumcision** [₁sərkəm-'sɪʒən, 'sərkəm₁-] *n* : circoncision *f*

circumference [sər'kʌmpfrənts] *n* : circonférence *f*

circumflex ['sərkəm₁flɛks] *n* : accent *m* circonflexe

circumspect ['sərkəm₁spɛkt] *adj* : circonspect, prudent

circumstance ['sərkəm₁stænts] *n* **1** : circonstance *f* **2 under no** ～**s** : en aucun cas

circus ['sərkəs] *n* : cirque *m*

cistern ['sɪstərn] *n* TANK : citerne *f*

cite ['saɪt] *vt* **cited; citing** : citer — **citation** [saɪ'teɪʃən] *n* : citation *f*

citizen ['sɪtəzən] *n* : citoyen *m*, -toyenne *f* — **citizenship** ['sɪtəzən₁ʃɪp] *n* : citoyenneté *f*

citrus ['sɪtrəs] *n, pl* **-rus** *or* **-ruses** *or* ～ **fruit** : agrumes *mpl*

city ['sɪti] *n, pl* **-ties** : ville *f* — **city hall** *n* : hôtel *m* de ville

civic ['sɪvɪk] *adj* : civique — **civics** ['sɪvɪks] *ns & pl* : instruction *f* civique

civil ['sɪvəl] *adj* **1** : civil **2** ～ **rights** : droits *mpl* civiques **3** ～ **service** : fonction *f* publique — **civilian** [sə'vɪljən] *n* : civil *m*, -vile *f* — **civility** [sə'vɪləti] *n, pl* **-ties** : civilité *f*, courtoisie *f* — **civilization** [₁sɪvələ-'zeɪʃən] *n* : civilisation *f* — **civilize** ['sɪvə₁laɪz] *vt* **-lized; -lizing** : civiliser

clad ['klæd] *adj* ～ **in** : vêtu de, habillé de

claim ['kleɪm] *vt* **1** DEMAND : revendiquer,

réclamer **2** MAINTAIN : prétendre — ～ *n*
1 : revendication *f* **2** ASSERTION : affirmation *f*

clam [ˈklæm] *n* : palourde *f*

clamber [ˈklæmbər] *vi* : grimper (avec difficulté)

clammy [ˈklæmi] *adj* **-mier; -est** : moite

clamor *or Brit* **clamour** [ˈklæmər] *n*
: clameur *f*, cris *mpl* — ～ *vi* : vociférer

clamp [ˈklæmp] *n* : crampon *m* — ～ *vt* : attacher, fixer

clan [ˈklæn] *n* : clan *m*

clandestine [klænˈdɛstɪn] *adj* : clandestin, secret

clang [ˈklæŋ] *n* : bruit *m* métallique

clap [ˈklæp] *v* **clapped; clapping** : applaudir — ～ *n* : applaudissement *m*

clarify [ˈklærəˌfaɪ] *vt* **-fied; -fying** : clarifier, éclaircir — **clarification** [ˌklærəfəˈkeɪʃən] *n* : clarification *f*

clarinet [ˌklærəˈnɛt] *n* : clarinette *f*

clarity [ˈklærəti] *n* : clarté *f*

clash [ˈklæʃ] *vi* : s'opposer, se heurter — ～ *n* : conflit *m*

clasp [ˈklæsp] *n* : fermoir *m*, boucle *f* — ～ *vt* **1** FASTEN : attacher **2** HOLD : serrer

class [ˈklæs] *n* **1** : classe *f* **2** COURSE : cours *m* — ～ *vt* : classer, classifier

classic [ˈklæsɪk] *or* **classical** [ˈklæsɪkəl] *adj* : classique — **classic** : classique *m*

classify [ˈklæsəˌfaɪ] *vt* **-fied; -fying** : classer, classifier — **classification** [ˌklæsəfəˈkeɪʃən] *n* : classification *f* — **classified** [ˈklæsəˌfaɪd] *adj* **1** : confidentiel **2** ～ **ads** : petites annonces *fpl*

classmate [ˈklæsˌmeɪt] *n* : compagnon *m*, compagne *f* de classe

classroom [ˈklæsˌruːm] *n* : salle *f* de classe

clatter [ˈklæṭər] *vi* : cliqueter — ～ *n* : bruit *m*, cliquetis *m*

clause [ˈklɔz] *n* : clause *f*

claustrophobia [ˌklɔstrəˈfoːbiə] *n* : claustrophobie *f*

claw [ˈklɔ] *n* : griffe *f* (d'un chat, etc.), pince *f* (d'un crustacé)

clay [ˈkleɪ] *n* : argile *f*

clean [ˈkliːn] *adj* **1** : propre **2** UNADULTERATED : pur — ～ *vt* : nettoyer, laver — **cleanliness** [ˈklɛnlinəs] *n* : propreté *f* — **cleanse** [ˈklɛnz] *vt* **cleansed; cleansing** : nettoyer, purifier

clear [ˈkliːr] *adj* **1** : clair **2** TRANSPARENT : transparent **3** OPEN : libre, dégagé — ～ *vt* **1** : débarrasser (un espace, etc.), dégager (une voie) **2** ～ **a check** : encaisser un chèque **3** ～ **up** RESOLVE : résoudre — *vi* **1** ～ **up** BRIGHTEN : s'éclaircir (se dit du temps, etc.) **2** ～ **up** VANISH : disparaître (se dit d'un symptôme, etc.) — ～ *adv* **1** **hear loud and ～** : entendre très clairement

2 make oneself ～ : s'expliquer — **clearance** [ˈkliːrənts] *n* **1** SPACE : espace *m* libre **2** AUTHORIZATION : autorisation *f* **3** ～ **sale** : liquidation *f* — **clearing** [ˈkliːrɪŋ] *n* : clairière *f* — **clearly** [ˈkliːrli] *adv* **1** DISTINCTLY : clairement **2** OBVIOUSLY : évidemment

cleaver [ˈkliːvər] *n* : couperet *m*

clef [ˈklɛf] *n* : clé *f* (en musique)

clement [ˈklɛmənt] *adj* : doux, clément — **clemency** [ˈklɛməntsi] *n, pl* **-cies** : clémence *f*

clench [ˈklɛntʃ] *vt* : serrer

clergy [ˈklərdʒi] *n, pl* **-gies** : clergé *m* — **clergyman** [ˈklərdʒimən] *n, pl* **-men** [-mən, -ˌmɛn] : ecclésiastique *m* — **clerical** [ˈklɛrɪkəl] *adj* **1** : clérical, du clergé **2** ～ **work** : travail *m* de bureau

clerk [ˈklərk, *Brit* ˈklɑːrk] *n* **1** : employé *m*, -ployée *f* de bureau **2** SALESPERSON : vendeur *m*, -deuse *f*

clever [ˈklɛvər] *adj* **1** SKILLFUL : habile, adroit **2** SMART : astucieux — **cleverly** [ˈklɛvərli] *adv* **1** : habilement **2** : astucieusement — **cleverness** [ˈklɛvərnəs] *n* **1** SKILL : habileté *f* **2** INTELLIGENCE : intelligence *f*

cliché [kliˈʃeɪ] *n* : cliché *m*

click [ˈklɪk] *vt* : faire claquer — *vi* **1** : faire un déclic **2** : cliquer (en informatique) — ～ *n* : déclic *m*

client [ˈklaɪənt] *n* : client *m*, cliente *f* — **clientele** [ˌklaɪənˈtɛl, ˌkli-] *n* : clientèle *f*

cliff [ˈklɪf] *n* : falaise *f*

climate [ˈklaɪmət] *n* : climat *m*

climax [ˈklaɪˌmæks] *n* : point *m* culminant, apogée *m*

climb [ˈklaɪm] *vt* : monter, gravir — *vi* RISE : monter, augmenter — ～ *n* : montée *f*, ascension *f*

cling [ˈklɪŋ] *vi* **clung** [ˈklʌŋ]; **clinging** ～ **to** : s'accrocher à

clinic [ˈklɪnɪk] *n* : clinique *f* — **clinical** [ˈklɪnɪkəl] *adj* : clinique

clink [ˈklɪŋk] *vi* : cliqueter

clip [ˈklɪp] *vt* **clipped; clipping 1** : couper, tailler **2** FASTEN : attacher (avec un trombone) — ～ *n* FASTENER : attache *f*, pince *f* — **clippers** [ˈklɪpərz] *npl* **1** *or* **nail ～** : coupe-ongles *m* **2** SHEARS : tondeuse *f*

cloak [ˈkloːk] *vt* : cape *f*

clock [ˈklɑk] *n* **1** : horloge *f*, pendule *f* **2 around the ～** : d'affilée — **clockwise** [ˈklɑkˌwaɪz] *adv & adj* : dans le sens des aiguilles d'une montre

clog [ˈklɑg] *n* : sabot *m* — ～ *v* **clogged; clogging** *vt* : boucher, bloquer — *vi or* ～ **up** : se boucher

cloister [ˈklɔɪstər] *n* : cloître *m*

close[1] [ˈkloːz] *v* **closed; closing** *vt* : fermer — *vi* **1** : fermer, se fermer **2** TERMINATE

: prendre fin, se terminer **3 ~ in** : se rapprocher — **~** n : fin f, conclusion f
close² [ˈkloːs] adj **closer; closest 1** NEAR : proche **2** INTIMATE : intime **3** STRICT : rigoureux, étroit **4 a ~ game** : une partie serrée — **~** adv : près — **closely** [ˈkloːsli] adv : de près — **closeness** [ˈkloːsnəs] n **1** : proximité f **2** INTIMACY : intimité f
closet [ˈklɑzət] n : placard m, garde-robe f
closure [ˈkloːʒər] n : fermeture f, clôture f
clot [ˈklɑt] n : caillot m — **~** vi **clotted; clotting** : cailler, (sé) coaguler
cloth [ˈklɔθ] n, pl **cloths** [ˈklɔðz, ˈklɔθs] : tissu m
clothe [ˈkloːð] vt **clothed** or **clad** [ˈklæd]; **clothing** : habiller, vêtir — **clothes** [ˈkloːz, ˈkloːðz] npl **1** : vêtements mpl **2 put on one's ~** : s'habiller — **clothespin** [ˈkloːzˌpɪn] n : pince f (à linge) — **clothing** [ˈkloːðɪŋ] n : vêtements mpl
cloud [ˈklaʊd] n : nuage m — **~** vi or **~ over** : se couvrir de nuages — **cloudy** [ˈklaʊdi] adj **cloudier; -est** : nuageux, couvert
clout [ˈklaʊt] n : influence m, poids m
clove [ˈkloːv] n **1** : clou m de girofle **2** or **garlic ~** : gousse f d'ail
clover [ˈkloːvər] n : trèfle m
clown [ˈklaʊn] n : clown m — **~** vi or **~ around** : faire le clown
cloying [ˈklɔɪɪŋ] adj : mièvre
club [ˈklʌb] n **1** : massue f, matraque f **2** ASSOCIATION : club m, groupe m **3 ~s** npl : trèfle m (aux cartes) — **~** vt **clubbed; clubbing** : matraquer
cluck [ˈklʌk] vi : glousser
clue [ˈkluː] n **1** : indice m **2 I haven't got a ~** : je n'ai aucune idée
clump [ˈklʌmp] n : massif m (d'arbres), touffe f (d'herbe)
clumsy [ˈklʌmzi] adj **-sier; -est** : maladroit, gauche
cluster [ˈklʌstər] n : groupe m (de personnes), grappe f (de raisins, etc.) — vi : se rassembler, se grouper
clutch [ˈklʌtʃ] vt : saisir, étreindre — vi **~ at** : s'agripper à — **~** n : embrayage m (d'une voiture)
clutter [ˈklʌtər] vt : encombrer — **~** n : désordre m, fouillis m
coach [ˈkoːtʃ] n **1** CARRIAGE : carrosse m **2** : voiture f, wagon m (d'un train) **3** BUS : autocar m **4** : billet m d'avion de deuxième classe **5** TRAINER : entraîneur m, -neuse f — **~** vt **1** : entraîner (une équipe sportive) **2** TUTOR : donner des leçons à
coagulate [koˈægjəˌleɪt] v **-lated; -lating** vt : coaguler — vi : se coaguler
coal [ˈkoːl] n : charbon m

coalition [ˌkoːəˈlɪʃən] n : coalition f
coarse [ˈkors] adj **coarser; coarsest 1** : gros (se dit du sable, du sel, etc.) **2** CRUDE : grossier, vulgaire — **coarseness** [ˈkorsnəs] n **1** ROUGHNESS : rudesse f **2** CRUDENESS : grossièreté f
coast [ˈkoːst] n : côte f — **coastal** [ˈkoːstəl] adj : côtier, littoral
coaster [ˈkoːstər] n : dessous-de-verre m
coast guard n : gendarmerie f maritime France, garde f côtière Can
coastline [ˈkoːstˌlaɪn] n : littoral m
coat [ˈkoːt] n **1** : manteau m **2** : pelage m (d'un animal) **3** : couche f (de peinture) — **~** vt **with** : couvrir de, recouvrir de — **coat hanger** n : cintre m — **coating** [ˈkoːtɪŋ] n : couche f, revêtement m — **coat of arms** n : blason m, armoiries fpl
coax [ˈkoːks] vt : amadouer, cajoler
cob [ˈkɑb] → corncob
cobblestone [ˈkɑbəlˌstoːn] n : pavé m
cobweb [ˈkɑbˌwɛb] n : toile f d'araignée
cocaine [koːˈkeɪn, ˈkoːˌkeɪn] n : cocaïne f
cock [ˈkɑk] n ROOSTER : coq m — **~** vt **1** : armer (un fusil) **2** TILT : pencher (la tête, etc.) — **cockeyed** [ˈkɑkˌaɪd] adj **1** ASKEW : de travers **2** ABSURD : insensé
cockpit [ˈkɑkˌpɪt] n : poste m de pilotage
cockroach [ˈkɑkˌroːtʃ] n : cafard m
cocktail [ˈkɑkˌteɪl] n : cocktail m
cocoa [ˈkoːˌkoː] n : cacao m
coconut [ˈkoːkəˌnʌt] n : noix f de coco
cocoon [kəˈkuːn] n : cocon m
cod [ˈkɑd] ns & pl : morue f
coddle [ˈkɑdəl] vt **-dled; -dling** : dorloter
code [ˈkoːd] n : code m — **~** vt : coder
coeducational [ˌkoːˌɛdʒəˈkeɪʃənəl] adj : mixte
coerce [koˈ ors] vt **-erced; -ercing** : contraindre — **coercion** [koˈorʒən, -ʃən] n : contrainte f
coffee [ˈkɔfi] n : café m — **coffeepot** [ˈkɔfiˌpɑt] n : cafetière f
coffer [ˈkɔfər] n : coffre m, caisse f
coffin [ˈkɔfən] n : cercueil m, bière f
cog [ˈkɑg] n : dent f (d'une roue)
cogent [ˈkoːdʒənt] adj : convaincant, persuasif
cognac [ˈkoːnˌjæk] n : cognac m
cogwheel [ˈkɑgˌhwiːl] n : pignon m
coherent [koˈhirənt] adj : cohérent
coil [ˈkɔɪl] vt : enrouler — vi : s'enrouler — **~** n **1** : rouleau m **2** : volute f (de fumée)
coin [ˈkɔɪn] n : pièce f de monnaie
coincide [ˌkoːɪnˈsaɪd, ˈkoːɪnˌsaɪd] vi **-cided; -ciding** : coïncider — **coincidence** [koˈɪntsədənts] n : coïncidence f
colander [ˈkɑləndər, ˈkʌ-] n : passoire f
cold [ˈkoːld] adj **1** : froid **2 be ~** : avoir froid **3 it's ~ today** : il fait froid aujour-

d'hui — **~** n **1** : froid m **2** : rhume m (en médecine) **3 catch a ~** : s'enrhumer

coleslaw ['ko:l,slɔ] n : salade f de chou cru

colic ['kɑlik] n : coliques fpl

collaborate [kə'læbə,reɪt] vi **-rated; -rating** : collaborer, coopérer — **collaboration** [kə-,læbə'reɪʃən] n : collaboration f

collapse [kə'læps] vi **-lapsed; -lapsing** : s'effondrer, s'écrouler — **~** n : effondrement m, écroulement m — **collapsible** [kə'læpsəbəl] adj : pliant

collar ['kɑlər] n : col m — **collarbone** ['kɑlər,bo:n] n : clavicule f

collateral [kə'lætərəl] n : nantissement m

colleague ['kɑ,li:g] n : collègue mf

collect [kə'lɛkt] vt **1** GATHER : ramasser, recueillir **2** : percevoir (des impôts), encaisser (une somme d'argent) **3** : collectionner (des objets) — vi **1** ASSEMBLE : se rassembler, se réunir **2** ACCUMULATE : s'accumuler — **~** adv **call ~** : téléphoner en PCV France, téléphoner à frais virés Can — **collection** [kə'lɛkʃən] n **1** : collection f (de livres, etc.) **2** : quête f (à l'église) — **collective** [kə'lɛktɪv] adj : collectif

college ['kɑlɪʤ] n : établissement m d'enseignement supérieur

collide [kə'laɪd] vi **-lided; -liding** : se heurter, entrer en collision — **collision** [kə-'lɪʒən] n : collision f

colloquial [kə'lo:kwiəl] adj : familier

cologne [kə'lo:n] n : eau f de Cologne

colon[1] ['ko:lən] n, pl **colons** or **cola** [-lə] : côlon m (en anatomie)

colon[2] n, pl **colons** : deux-points m

colonel ['kɑrnəl] n : colonel m

colony ['kɑləni] n, pl **-nies** : colonie f — **colonial** [kə'lo:niəl] adj : colonial — **colonize** ['kɑlə,naɪz] vt **-nized; -nizing** : coloniser

color or Brit **colour** ['kʌlər] n : couleur f — **~** vt : colorer — **color–blind** or Brit **colour–blind** ['kʌlər,blaɪnd] adj : daltonien — **colored** or Brit **coloured** ['kʌlərd] adj : coloré — **colorful** or Brit **colourful** ['kʌlərfəl] adj : coloré — **colorless** or Brit **colourless** ['kʌlərləs] adj : incolore

colossal [kə'lɑsəl] adj : colossal

colt ['ko:lt] n : poulain m

column ['kɑləm] n **1** : colonne f **2** : rubrique f (dans la presse) — **columnist** ['kɑləmnɪst, -ləmɪst] n : chroniqueur m, -queuse f

coma ['ko:mə] n : coma m

comb ['ko:m] n **1** : peigne m **2** : crête f (d'un coq) — **~** vt : (se) peigner

combat ['kɑm,bæt] n : combat m — **~** [kəm'bæt, 'kɑm,bæt] vt **-bated** or **-batted; -bating** or **-batting** : combattre — **combatant** [kəm'bætənt] n : combattant m, -tante f

combine [kəm'baɪn] vt **-bined; -bining** : combiner — **~** ['kɑm,baɪn] n HARVESTER : moissonneuse-batteuse f — **combination** [,kɑmbə'neɪʃən] n : combinaison f

combustion [kəm'bʌsʧən] n : combustion f

come ['kʌm] vi **came** ['keɪm]; **come; coming 1** : venir **2** ARRIVE : arriver **3 ~ about** : se produire **4 ~ back** : revenir **5 ~ from** : provenir de **6 ~ in** : entrer **7 ~ out** : sortir **8 ~ to** REVIVE : revenir à soi **9 ~ on!** : allez! **10 ~ up** OCCUR : se présenter **11 how ~?** : comment ça se fait? — **comeback** ['kʌm,bæk] n **1** RETURN : rentrée f **2** RETORT : réplique f

comedy ['kɑmədi] n, pl **-dies** : comédie f — **comedian** [kə'mi:diən] n : comique mf

comet ['kɑmət] n : comète f

comfort ['kʌmpfərt] vt : consoler, réconforter — **~** n **1** : confort m **2** SOLACE : consolation f, réconfort m — **comfortable** ['kʌmpfərtəbəl, 'kʌmpftə-] adj : confortable

comic ['kɑmɪk] or **comical** ['kɑmɪkəl] adj : comique — **~** n : comique mf — **comic strip** n : bande f dessinée

coming ['kʌmɪŋ] adj : à venir

comma ['kɑmə] n : virgule f

command [kə'mænd] vt **1** ORDER : ordonner, commander **2 ~ respect** : inspirer le respect — vi : donner des ordres — **~** n **1** ORDER : ordre m **2** MASTERY : maîtrise f — **commander** [kə'mændər] n : commandant m — **commandment** [kə'mændmənt] n : commandement m (en religion)

commemorate [kə'mɛmə,reɪt] vt **-rated; -rating** : commémorer — **commemoration** [kə,mɛmə'reɪʃən] n : commémoration f

commence [kə'mɛnts] vi **-menced; -mencing** : commencer — **commencement** [kə'mɛntsmənt] n : remise f des diplômes

commend [kə'mɛnd] vt : louer — **commendable** [kə'mɛndəbəl] adj : louable

comment ['kɑ,mɛnt] n : commentaire m, remarque f — **~** vi : faire des commentaires — **commentary** ['kɑmən,tɛri] n, pl **-taries** : commentaire m — **commentator** ['kɑmən,teɪtər] n : commentateur m, -trice f

commerce ['kɑmərs] n : commerce m — **commercial** [kə'mərʃəl] adj : commercial — **~** n : annonce f publicitaire — **commercialize** [kə'mərʃə,laɪz] vt **-ized; -izing** : commercialiser

commiserate [kə'mɪzə,reɪt] vi **-ated; -ating** : compatir

commission [kə'mɪʃən] n : commission f, comité m — **~** vt : commander (une œuvre d'art) — **commissioner** [kə'mɪʃənər] n : commissaire m

commit [kə'mɪt] vt **-mitted; -mitting 1** ENGAGE : confier **2** : commettre (un crime, etc.) **3** ~ **oneself** : s'engager — **commit-ment** [kə'mɪtmənt] *n* **1** PROMISE : engagement *m* **2** OBLIGATION : obligation *f*

committee [kə'mɪti] *n* : comité *m*

commodity [kə'madəti] *n*, *pl* **-ties** : marchandise *f*, denrée *f*

common ['kamən] *adj* **1** : commun **2** WIDESPREAD : universel — ~ *n* **in** ~ : en commun — **commonly** ['kamənli] *adv* : communément — **commonplace** ['kamən,pleɪs] *adj* : commun, banal — **common sense** *n* : bon sens *m*

commotion [kə'moːʃən] *n* : vacarme *m*, brouhaha *m*

commune ['ka,mjuːn, kə'mjuːn] *n* : communauté *f* — **communal** [kə'mjuːnəl] *adj* : communautaire

communicate [kə'mjuːnə,keɪt] *v* **-cated**; **-cating** : communiquer — **communication** [kə,mjuːnə'keɪʃən] *n* : communication *f*

communion [kə'mjuːnjən] *n* : communion *f*

Communism ['kamjə,nɪzəm] *n* : communisme *m* — **Communist** ['kamjə,nɪst] *adj* : communiste

community [kə'mjuːnəti] *n*, *pl* **-ties** : communauté *f*

commute [kə'mjuːt] *vi* **-muted**; **-muting** : faire la navette, faire un trajet journalier

compact [kəm'pækt, 'kam,pækt] *adj* : compact — ~ ['kam,pækt] *n* **1** *or* ~ **car** : voiture *f* compacte **2** *or* **powder** ~ : poudrier *m* — **compact disc** ['kam,pækt-'dɪsk] *n* : disque *m* compact, compact *m*

companion [kəm'pænjən] *n* : compagnon *m*, compagne *f* — **companionship** [kəm-'pænjən,ʃɪp] *n* : compagnie *f*

company ['kʌmpəni] *n*, *pl* **-nies** **1** : compagnie *f*, société *f* **2** : troupe *f* (de théâtre) **3** GUESTS : invités *mpl*

compare [kəm'pær] *v* **-pared**; **-paring** *vt* : comparer — *vi* ~ **with** : être comparable à — **comparative** [kəm'pærətɪv] *adj* : comparatif, relatif — **comparison** [kəm-'pærəsən] *n* : comparaison *f*

compartment [kəm'partmənt] *n* : compartiment *m*

compass ['kʌmpəs, 'kam-] *n* **1** : boussole *f* **2 points of the** ~ : points *mpl* cardinaux

compassion [kəm'pæʃən] *n* : compassion *f* — **compassionate** [kəm'pæʃənət] *adj* : compatissant

compatible [kəm'pætəbəl] *adj* : compatible — **compatibility** [kəm,pætə'bɪləti] *n* : compatibilité *f*

compel [kəm'pɛl] *vt* **-pelled**; **-pelling** : contraindre, obliger — **compelling** [kəm-'pɛlɪŋ] *adj* : irrésistible

compensate ['kampən,seɪt] *v* **-sated**; **-sating** *vi* ~ **for** : compenser — *vt* : indemniser

compensation [,kampən'seɪʃən] *n* : compensation *f*

compete [kəm'piːt] *vi* **-peted**; **-peting** : faire concurrence, rivaliser — **competent** ['kampətənt] *adj* : compétent — **competition** [,kampə'tɪʃən] *n* **1** : concurrence *f* **2** CONTEST : compétition *f* — **competitor** [kəm'pɛtətər] *n* : concurrent *m*, -rente *f*

compile [kəm'paɪl] *vt* **-piled**; **-piling** : dresser (une liste, etc.)

complacency [kəm'pleɪsəntsi] *n* : satisfaction *f* de soi, suffisance *f* — **complacent** [kəm'pleɪsənt] *adj* : content de soi

complain [kəm'pleɪn] *vi* : se plaindre — **complaint** [kəm'pleɪnt] *n* : plainte *f*

complement ['kampləmənt] *n* : complément *m* — ~ ['kamplə,mɛnt] *vt* : aller bien avec — **complementary** [,kamplə-'mɛntəri] *adj* : complémentaire

complete [kəm'pliːt] *adj* **-pleter**; **-est** **1** WHOLE : complet, intégral **2** FINISHED : achevé **3** TOTAL : complet, absolu — ~ *vt* **-pleted**; **-pleting** **1** : compléter (un puzzle, etc.), remplir (un questionnaire) **2** FINISH : achever — **completely** [kəm'pliːtli] *adv* : complètement — **completion** [kəm-'pliːʃən] *n* : achèvement *m*

complex [kam'plɛks, kəm-; 'kam,plɛks] *adj* : complexe — ~ ['kam,plɛks] *n* : complexe *m*

complexion [kəm'plɛkʃən] *n* : teint *m*

complexity [kəm'plɛksəti, kam-] *n*, *pl* **-ties** : complexité *f*

compliance [kəm'plaɪənts] *n* **1** : conformité *f* **2 in** ~ **with** : conformément à — **compliant** [kəm'plaɪənt] *adj* : soumis

complicate ['kamplə,keɪt] *vt* **-cated**; **-cating** : compliquer — **complicated** ['kamplə-,keɪtəd] *adj* : compliqué — **complication** [,kamplə'keɪʃən] *n* : complication *f*

compliment ['kampləmənt] *n* : compliment *m* — ~ ['kamplə,mɛnt] *vt* : complimenter — **complimentary** [,kamplə'mɛntəri] *adj* **1** FLATTERING : flatteur **2** FREE : gratuit

comply [kəm'plaɪ] *vi* **-plied**; **-plying** ~ **with** : se conformer à, respecter

component [kəm'poːnənt, 'kam,poː-] *n* : composant *m*, élément *m*

compose [kəm'poːz] *vt* **-posed**; **-posing** **1** : composer **2** ~ **oneself** : retrouver son calme — **composer** [kəm'poːzər] *n* : compositeur *m*, -trice *f* — **composition** [,kampə'zɪʃən] *n* : composition *f* — **composure** [kəm'poːʒər] *n* : calme *m*, sang-froid *m*

compound[1] [kam'paʊnd, kəm-; 'kam-,paʊnd] *adj* : composé — ~ ['kam,paʊnd] *n* : composé *m* (en chimie)

compound[2] ['kam,paʊnd] *n* ENCLOSURE : enceinte *f*, enclos *m*

comprehend [ˌkɑmprɪ'hɛnd] *vt* : comprendre — **comprehension** [ˌkɑmprɪ'hɛntʃən] *n* : compréhension *f* — **comprehensive** [ˌkɑmprɪ'hɛntsɪv] *adj* : complet, détaillé

compress [kəm'prɛs] *vt* : comprimer — **compression** [kəm'prɛʃən] *n* : compression *f*

comprise [kəm'praɪz] *vt* **-prised; -prising** : comprendre

compromise ['kɑmprəˌmaɪz] *n* : compromis *m* — ~ *v* **-mised; -mising** *vi* : faire un compromis — *vt* : compromettre

compulsion [kəm'pʌlʃən] *n* URGE : envie *f* — **compulsory** [kəm'pʌlsəri] *adj* : obligatoire

compute [kəm'pju:t] *vt* **-puted; -puting** : calculer — **computer** [kəm'pju:t̬ər] *n* **1** : ordinateur *m* **2** ~ **science** : informatique *f* — **computerize** [kəm'pju:t̬əˌraɪz] *vt* **-ized; -izing** : informatiser

con ['kɑn] *vt* **conned; conning** : duper, escroquer — ~ *n* **the pros and** ~**s** : le pour et le contre

concave [kɑn'keɪv, 'kɑnˌkeɪv] *adj* : concave

conceal [kən'si:l] *vt* : dissimuler, cacher

concede [kən'si:d] *vt* **-ceded; -ceding** : accorder, concéder

conceit [kən'si:t] *n* : suffisance *f*, vanité *f* — **conceited** [kən'si:t̬əd] *adj* : suffisant, vaniteux

conceive [kən'si:v] *v* **-ceived; -ceiving** *vt* : concevoir — *vi* ~ **of** : concevoir

concentrate ['kɑntsənˌtreɪt] *v* **-trated; -trating** *vt* : concentrer — *vi* : se concentrer — **concentration** [ˌkɑntsən'treɪʃən] *n* : concentration *f*

concept ['kɑnˌsɛpt] *n* : concept *m* — **conception** [kən'sɛpʃən] *n* : conception *f*

concern [kən'sərn] *vt* **1** : concerner **2** ~ **oneself about** : s'inquiéter de — ~ *n* **1** BUSINESS : affaire *f* **2** WORRY : inquiétude *f* — **concerned** [kən'sərnd] *adj* **1** ANXIOUS : inquiet **2 as far as I'm** ~ : en ce qui me concerne — **concerning** [kən'sərnɪŋ] *prep* : concernant

concert ['kɑnˌsərt] *n* : concert *m* — **concerted** [kən'sərt̬əd] *adj* : concerté

concession [kən'sɛʃən] *n* : concession *f*

concise [kən'saɪs] *adj* : concis

conclude [kən'klu:d] *v* **-cluded; -cluding** *vt* : conclure — *vi* : s'achever, se terminer — **conclusion** [kən'klu:ʒən] *n* : conclusion *f* — **conclusive** [kən'klu:sɪv] *adj* : concluant

concoct [kən'kɑkt, kɑn-] *vt* **1** PREPARE : confectionner **2** DEVISE : fabriquer — **concoction** [kən'kɑkʃən] *n* : mélange *m*

concrete [kɑn'kri:t, 'kɑnˌkri:t] *adj* **1** : de béton **2** REAL : concret, réel — ~ ['kɑnˌkri:t, kɑn'kri:t] *n* : béton *m*

concur [kən'kər] *vi* **-curred; -curring** : être d'accord

concussion [kən'kʌʃən] *n* : commotion *f* cérébrale

condemn [kən'dɛm] *vt* : condamner — **condemnation** [ˌkɑnˌdɛm'neɪʃən] *n* : condamnation *f*

condense [kən'dɛnts] *vt* **-densed; -densing** : condenser — **condensation** [ˌkɑnˌdɛn'seɪʃən, -dən-] *n* : condensation *f*

condescending [ˌkɑk'ndɪ'sɛndɪŋ] *adj* : condescendant

condiment ['kɑndəmənt] *n* : condiment *m*

condition [kən'dɪʃən] *n* **1** : condition *f* **2 in good** ~ : en bon état— **conditional** [kən'dɪʃənəl] *adj* : conditionnel

condolences [kən'do:lənt̬səz] *npl* : condoléances *fpl*

condom ['kɑndəm] *n* : préservatif *m*

condominium [ˌkɑndə'mɪniəm] *n*, *pl* **-ums** : immeuble *m* en copropriété

condone [kən'do:n] *vt* **-doned; -doning** : excuser

conducive [kən'du:sɪv, -'dju:-] *adj* : propice, favorable

conduct ['kɑnˌdʌkt] *n* : comportement *m*, conduite *f* — ~ [kən'dʌkt] *vt* **1** : conduire, diriger **2** ~ **oneself** : se comporter — **conductor** [kən'dʌkt̬ər] *n* **1** : conducteur *m* (d'électricité) **2** : chef *m* d'orchestre **3** : contrôleur *m* (de train, etc.)

cone ['ko:n] *n* **1** : cône *m* **2** *or* **ice-cream** ~ : cornet *m* (de crème glacée)

confection [kən'fɛkʃən] *n* : confiserie *f*, bonbon *m*

confederation [kənˌfɛdə'reɪʃən] *n* : confédération *f*

confer [kən'fər] *v* **-ferred; -ferring** *vt* : conférer — *vi* ~ **with** : conférer avec, s'entretenir avec — **conference** ['kɑnfrənts, -fərənts] *n* : conférence *f*

confess [kən'fɛs] *vt* : confesser, avouer — *vi* ~ **to** : admettre — **confession** [kən'fɛʃən] *n* : confession *f*

confetti [kən'fɛt̬i] *n* : confettis *mpl*

confide [kən'faɪd] *v* **-fided; -fiding** *vt* : confier — *vi* ~ **in** : se confier à — **confidence** ['kɑnfədənts] *n* **1** TRUST : confiance *f* **2** SELF-ASSURANCE : confiance *f* en soi, assurance *f* **3** SECRET : confidence *f* — **confident** ['kɑnfədənt] *adj* **1** SURE : confiant, sûr **2** SELF-ASSURED : sûr de soi — **confidential** [ˌkɑnfə'dɛntʃəl] *adj* : confidentiel

confine [kən'faɪn] *vt* **-fined; -fining 1** LIMIT : confiner, limiter **2** IMPRISON : enfermer — **confines** ['kɑnˌfaɪnz] *npl* : confins *mpl*, limites *fpl*

confirm [kən'fərm] *vt* : confirmer — **confirmation** [ˌkɑnfər'meɪʃən] *n* : confirmation *f*

confiscate ['kɑnfə‚skeɪt] *vt* **-cated; -cating** : confisquer

conflict ['kɑn‚flɪkt] *n* : conflit *m* — **~** [kən-'flɪkt] *vi* : être en conflit, s'opposer

conform [kən'fɔrm] *vi* **~ with** : se conformer à, être conforme à — **conformity** [kən'fɔrməti] *n, pl* **-ties** : conformité *f*

confound [kən'faʊnd, kɑn-] *vt* : confondre, déconcerter

confront [kən'frʌnt] *vt* : affronter, faire face à — **confrontation** [‚kɑnfrən'teɪʃən] *n* : confrontation *f*

confuse [kən'fju:z] *vt* **-fused; -fusing** : troubler, déconcerter — **confusing** [kən-'fju:zɪŋ] *adj* : déroutant — **confusion** [kən-'fju:ʒən] *n* : confusion *f*

congenial [kən'ʤi:niəl] *adj* : sympathique

congested [kən'ʤestəd] *adj* **1** : congestionné (en médecine) **2** OBSTRUCTED : encombré — **congestion** [kən'ʤestʃən] *n* : congestion *f*

Congolese [‚kɑŋgə'li:z,-'li:s] *adj* : congolais

congratulate [kən'græʤə‚leɪt, -'græʧə-] *vt* **-lated; -lating** : féliciter — **congratulations** [kən‚græʤə'leɪʃənz, -‚græʧə-] *npl* : félicitations *fpl*

congregate ['kɑŋgrɪ‚geɪt] *vi* **-gated; -gating** : se rassembler, se réunir — **congregation** [‚kɑŋgrɪ'geɪʃən] *n* : assemblée *f* (de fidèles)

congress ['kɑŋgrəs] *n* : congrès *m* — **congressman** ['kɑŋgrəsmən] *n, pl* **-men** [-mən, -‚mɛn] : membre *m* d'un congrès

conjecture [kən'ʤɛktʃər] *n* : conjecture *f*, supposition *f* — **~** *vt* **-tured; -turing** : conjecturer, présumer

conjugate ['kɑnʤə‚geɪt] *vt* **-gated; -gating** : conjuguer — **conjugation** [‚kɑnʤə-'geɪʃən] *n* : conjugaison *f*

conjunction [kən'ʤʌŋkʃən] *n* : conjonction *f* (en grammaire)

conjure ['kɑnʤər, 'kʌn-] *vt* **-jured; -juring ~ up** : invoquer, évoquer

connect [kə'nɛkt] *vi* : assurer la correspondance (avec un train, etc.) — *vt* **1** JOIN : relier **2** ASSOCIATE : associer **3** : brancher (en électricité) — **connection** [kə'nɛkʃən] *n* **1** : lien *m*, rapport *m* **2** : correspondance *f* (de train, etc.) **3 ~s** *npl* : relations *fpl* (sociales)

connote [kə'no:t] *vt* **-noted; -noting** : évoquer, indiquer

conquer ['kɑŋkər] *vt* : conquérir, vaincre — **conqueror** ['kɑŋkərər] *n* : conquérant *m*, -rante *f* — **conquest** ['kɑn‚kwɛst, 'kɑŋ-] *n* : conquête *f*

conscience ['kɑnʧənts] *n* : conscience *f* — **conscientious** [‚kɑnʧi'ɛntʃəs] *adj* : consciencieux

conscious ['kɑnʧəs] *adj* **1** AWARE : con-

scient **2** INTENTIONAL : délibéré — **consciously** ['kɑnʧəsli] *adv* : consciemment — **consciousness** ['kɑnʧəsnəs] *n* **1** AWARENESS : conscience *f* **2 lose ~** : perdre connaissance

consecrate ['kɑntsə‚kreɪt] *vt* **-crated; -crating** : consacrer

consecutive [kən'sɛkjətɪv] *adj* : consécutif

consensus [kən'sɛntsəs] *n* : consensus *m*

consent [kən'sɛnt] *vi* : consentir — **~** *n* : consentement *m*, accord *m*

consequence ['kɑntsə‚kwɛnts, -kwənts] *n* **1** : conséquence *f* **2 of no ~** : sans importance — **consequently** ['kɑntsəkwəntli, -‚kwɛnt-] *adv* : par conséquent

conserve [kən'sərv] *vt* **-served; -serving** : conserver, préserver — **conservation** [‚kɑntsər'veɪʃən] *n* : conservation *f* — **conservative** [kən'sərvətɪv] *adj* **1** : conservateur **2** CAUTIOUS : modéré, prudent — **~** *n* : conservateur *m*, -trice *f* — **conservatory** [kən'sərvə‚tori] *n, pl* **-ries** : conservatoire *m*

consider [kən'sɪdər] *vt* : considérer — **considerable** [kən'sɪdərəbəl] *adj* : considérable — **considerate** [kən'sɪdərət] *adj* : attentionné, prévenant — **consideration** [kən‚sɪdə'reɪʃən] *n* : considération *f* — **considering** [kən'sɪdərɪŋ] *prep* : étant donné, vu

consign [kən'saɪn] *vt* SEND : expédier, envoyer — **consignment** [kən'saɪnmənt] *n* : envoi *m*

consist [kən'sɪst] *vi* **1 ~ in** : consister à **2 ~ of** : se composer de, consister en — **consistency** [kən'sɪstəntsi] *n, pl* **-cies 1** TEXTURE : consistance *f* **2** COHERENCE : cohérence *f* — **consistent** [kən'sɪstənt] *adj* **1** : constant, régulier **2 ~ with** : en accord avec

console [kən'so:l] *vt* **-soled; -soling** : consoler, réconforter — **consolation** [‚kɑntsə-'leɪʃən] *n* : consolation *f*

consolidate [kən'sɑlə‚deɪt] *vt* **-dated; -dating** : consolider — **consolidation** [kən-‚sɑlə'deɪʃən] *n* : consolidation *f*

consonant ['kɑntsənənt] *n* : consonne *f*

conspicuous [kən'spɪkjuəs] *adj* **1** OBVIOUS : évident, visible **2** STRIKING : voyant

conspire [kən'spaɪr] *vi* **-spired; -spiring** : conspirer, comploter — **conspiracy** [kən-'spɪrəsi] *n, pl* **-cies** : conspiration *f*

constant ['kɑnstənt] *adj* : constant — **constantly** ['kɑnstəntli] *adv* : constamment

constellation [‚kɑnstə'leɪʃən] *n* : constellation *f*

constipated ['kɑnstə‚peɪtəd] *adj* : constipé — **constipation** [‚kɑnstə'peɪʃən] *n* : constipation *f*

constituent [kən'stɪtʃuənt] *n* **1** COMPONENT : composant *m* **2** VOTER : électeur *m*, -trice *f* — **constitute** ['kɑnstə‚tu:t, -tju:t] *vt* **-tuted;**

-tuting : constituer — **constitution** [ˌkɑnt-stə'tuːʃən, -'tjuː-] n : constitution f — **constitutional** [ˌkɑntstə'tuːʃənəl, -'tjuː-] adj : constitutionnel

constraint [kən'streɪnt] n : contrainte f

construct [kən'strʌkt] vt : construire, bâtir — **construction** [kən'strʌkʃən] n : construction f — **constructive** [kən'strʌktɪv] adj : constructif

construe [kən'struː] vt **-strued; -struing** : interpréter

consulate ['kɑntsələt] n : consulat m

consult [kən'sʌlt] vt : consulter — **consultant** [kən'sʌltənt] n : consultant m, -tante f — **consultation** [ˌkɑntsəl'teɪʃən] n : consultation f

consume [kən'suːm] vt **-sumed; -suming** : consommer — **consumer** [kən'suːmər] n : consommateur m, -trice f — **consumption** [kən'sʌmpʃən] n : consommation f

contact ['kɑnˌtækt] n 1 TOUCHING : contact m 2 **be in ~ with** : être en rapport avec 3 **business ~** : relation f de travail — ~ ['kɑnˌtækt, kən'-] vt : contacter — **contact lens** ['kˈnˌtæktˈlenz] n : lentille f (de contact), verre m de contact

contagious [kən'teɪdʒəs] adj : contagieux

contain [kən'teɪn] vt 1 : contenir 2 ~ **oneself** : se contenir, se maîtriser — **container** [kən'teɪnər] n : récipient m

contaminate [kən'tæməˌneɪt] vt **-nated; -nating** : contaminer — **contamination** [kənˌtæmə'neɪʃən] n : contamination f

contemplate ['kɑntəmˌpleɪt] v **-plated; -plating** vt 1 : contempler 2 CONSIDER : envisager, considérer — vi : réfléchir — **contemplation** [ˌkɑntəm'pleɪʃən] n : contemplation f, réflexion f

contemporary [kən'tempəˌreri] adj : contemporain — ~ n, pl **-raries** : contemporain m, -raine f

contempt [kən'tempt] n : mépris m, dédain m — **contemptible** [kən'temptəbəl] adj : méprisable — **contemptuous** [kən'tempʧʊəs] adj : méprisant

contend [kən'tend] vi 1 COMPETE : rivaliser 2 ~ **with** : faire face à — vt : soutenir, maintenir — **contender** [kən'tendər] n : concurrent m, -rente f

content[1] ['kɑnˌtent] n 1 : contenu m 2 **table of ~s** : table f des matières

content[2] [kən'tent] adj : content — ~ vt ~ **oneself with** : se contenter de, être satisfait de — **contented** [kən'tentəd] adj : content, satisfait

contention [kən'tenʧən] n 1 ARGUMENT : dispute f, discussion f 2 OPINION : affirmation f, assertion f

contentment [kən'tentmənt] n : contentement m

contest [kən'test] vt : contester, disputer — ~ ['kɑnˌtest] n 1 STRUGGLE : lutte f 2 COMPETITION : concours m, compétition f — **contestant** [kən'testənt] n : concurrent m, -rente f

context ['kɑnˌtekst] n : contexte m

continent ['kɑntənənt] n : continent m — **continental** [ˌkɑntən'entəl] adj : continental

contingency [kən'tɪndʒəntsi] n, pl **-cies** : éventualité f

continue [kən'tɪnjuː] v **-ued; -uing** vt 1 KEEP UP : continuer (à) 2 RESUME : reprendre — vi : continuer — **continual** [kə'tɪnjuəl] adj : continuel — **continuation** [kənˌtɪnju'eɪʃən] n : continuation f — **continuity** [ˌkɑntən'uːəti, -'juː-] n, pl **-ties** : continuité f — **continuous** [kən'tɪnjuəs] adj : continu

contort [kən'tɔrt] vt : tordre — **contortion** [kən'tɔrʃən] n : contorsion f

contour ['kɑnˌtʊr] n : contour m

contraband ['kɑntrəˌbænd] n : contrebande f

contraception [ˌkɑntrə'sepʃən] n : contraception f — **contraceptive** [ˌkɑntrə'septɪv] adj : contraceptif — ~ n : contraceptif m

contract ['kɑnˌtrækt] n : contrat m — ~ [kən'trækt] vt : contracter — vi : se contracter — **contraction** [kən'trækʃən] n : contraction f — **contractor** ['kɑnˌtræktər, kən'træk-] n : entrepreneur m, -neuse f

contradiction [ˌkɑntrə'dɪkʃən] n : contradiction f — **contradict** [ˌkɑntrə'dɪkt] vt : contredire — **contradictory** [ˌkɑntrə'dɪktəri] adj : contradictoire

contraption [kən'træpʃən] n : truc m fam, machin m fam

contrary ['kɑnˌtreri] n, pl **-traries** 1 : contraire m 2 **on the ~** : au contraire — ~ adj 1 : contraire, opposé 2 ~ **to** : contrairement à

contrast [kən'træst] vi : contraster — ~ ['kɑnˌtræst] n : contraste m

contribute [kən'trɪbjət] v **-uted; -uting** vi : contribuer — vt : apporter, donner — **contribution** [ˌkɑntrə'bjuːʃən] n : contribution f — **contributor** [kən'trɪbjətər] n : collaborateur m, -trice f

contrite ['kɑnˌtraɪt, kən'traɪt] adj : contrit

contrive [kən'traɪv] vt **-trived; -triving** 1 DEVISE : inventer, imaginer 2 ~ **to** : parvenir à, réussir à

control [kən'troːl] vt **-trolled; -trolling** 1 RULE, RUN : diriger 2 REGULATE : contrôler, régler 3 RESTRAIN : maîtriser — ~ n 1 : contrôle m, régulation f 2 RESTRAINT : maîtrise f 3 **remote ~** : commande f à distance

controversy ['kɑntrəˌvərsi] n, pl **-sies**

: controverse *f* — **controversial** [ˌkɑntrə-ˈvərʃəl, -siəl] *adj* : controversé

convalescence [ˌkɑnvəˈlɛsənts] *n* : convalescence *f*

convene [kənˈviːn] *v* **-vened; -vening** *vt* : convoquer — *vi* : se réunir

convenience [kənˈviːnjənts] *n* **1** : commodité *f*, confort *m* **2 at your ~** : quand cela vous conviendra — **convenient** [kənˈviːnjənt] *adj* : commode

convent [ˈkɑnvənt, -ˌvɛnt] *n* : couvent *m*

convention [kənˈvɛnʃən] *n* **1** : convention *f* **2** CUSTOM : usage *m* — **conventional** [kənˈvɛnʃənəl] *adj* : conventionnel

converge [kənˈvərdʒ] *vi* **-verged; -verging** : converger

converse[1] [kənˈvərs] *vi* **-versed; -versing** **~ with** : s'entretenir avec — **conversation** [ˌkɑnvərˈseɪʃən] *n* : conversation *f*

converse[2] [kənˈvərs, ˈkɑnˌvərs] *n* : contraire *m*, inverse *m* — **conversely** [kənˈvərsli, ˈkɑnˌvərs-] *adv* : inversement

conversion [kənˈvərʒən] *n* : conversion *f* — **convert** [kənˈvərt] *vt* : convertir — **convertible** [kənˈvərtəbəl] *adj* : décapotable *f*

convex [kɑnˈvɛks, ˈkɑnˌ-, kənˈ-] *adj* : convexe

convey [kənˈveɪ] *vt* **-veyed; -veying** : transmettre, exprimer

convict [kənˈvɪkt] *vt* : déclarer coupable — **~** [ˈkɑnˌvɪkt] *n* : détenu *m*, -nue *f* — **conviction** [kənˈvɪkʃən] *n* **1** : condamnation *f* **2** BELIEF : conviction *f*

convince [kənˈvɪnts] *vt* **-vinced; -vincing** : convaincre, persuader — **convincing** [kənˈvɪntsɪŋ] *adj* : convaincant

convoluted [ˈkɑnvəˌluːtəd] *adj* : compliqué

convulsion [kənˈvʌlʃən] *n* : convulsion *f*

cook [ˈkʊk] *n* : cuisinier *m*, -nière *f* — **~** *vi* : cuisiner, faire la cuisine — *vt* : préparer (de la nourriture) — **cookbook** [ˈkʊkˌbʊk] *n* : livre *m* de recettes

cookie *or* **cooky** [ˈkʊki] *n*, *pl* **-ies** : biscuit *m*, gâteau *m* sec

cooking [ˈkʊkɪŋ] *n* : cuisine *f*

cool [ˈkuːl] *adj* **1** : frais **2** CALM : calme **3** UNFRIENDLY : indifférent, froid — **~** *vt* : refroidir — *vi or* **~ down** : se refroidir — **~** *n* **1** : fraîcheur *m* **2 lose one's ~** : perdre son sang-froid — **cooler** [ˈkuːlər] *n* : glacière *f* — **coolness** [ˈkuːlnəs] *n* : fraîcheur *f*

coop [ˈkuːp, ˈkʊp] *n or* **chicken ~** : poulailler *m* — **~** *vt or* **~ up** : enfermer

cooperate [koˈɑpəˌreɪt] *vi* **-ated; -ating** : coopérer — **cooperation** [koˌɑpəˈreɪʃən] *n* : coopération *f* — **cooperative** [koˈɑpərəˌtɪv, -ˈɑpəˌreɪtɪv] *adj* : coopératif

coordinate [koˈɔrdənˌeɪt] *vt* **-nated; -nating** : coordonner — **coordination** [koˌɔrdənˈeɪʃən] *n* : coordination *f*

cop [ˈkɑp] *n* **1** : flic *m fam* **2 the ~s** : la police *fam*

cope [ˈkoːp] *vi* **coped; coping 1** : se débrouiller **2 ~ with** : faire face à

copious [ˈkoːpiəs] *adj* : copieux

copper [ˈkɑpər] *n* : cuivre *m*

copy [ˈkɑpi] *n*, *pl* **copies 1** : copie *f*, reproduction *f* **2** : exemplaire *m* (d'un livre, etc.) — **~** *vt* **copied; copying 1** : faire une copie de **2** IMITATE : copier — **copyright** [ˈkɑpiˌraɪt] *n* : droits *mpl* d'auteur

coral [ˈkɔrəl] *n* : corail *m*

cord [ˈkɔrd] *n* : corde *f*, cordon *m*

cordial [ˈkɔrdʒəl] *adj* : cordial, amical

corduroy [ˈkɔrdəˌrɔɪ] *n* : velours *m* côtelé

core [ˈkor] *n* **1** : trognon *m* (d'un fruit) **2** CENTER : cœur *m*, centre *m*

cork [ˈkɔrk] *n* **1** : liège *m* **2** : bouchon *m* (d'une bouteille) — **corkscrew** [ˈkɔrkˌskruː] *n* : tire-bouchon *m*

corn [ˈkɔrn] *n* **1** : grain *m* (de blé, etc.) **2** *or* **Indian ~** : maïs *m* **3** : cor *m* (sur le pied) — **corncob** [ˈkɔrnˌkɑb] *n* : épi *m* de maïs

corner [ˈkɔrnər] *n* **1** : coin *m*, angle *m* **2 around the ~** : à deux pas d'ici — **cornerstone** [ˈkɔrnərˌstoːn] *n* : pierre *f* angulaire

cornmeal [ˈkɔrnˌmiːl] *n* : farine *f* de maïs — **cornstarch** [ˈkɔrnˌstɑrtʃ] *n* : fécule *f* de maïs

corny [ˈkɔrni] *adj* **cornier; -est** : banal, à l'eau de rose

coronary [ˈkɔrəˌnɛri] *n*, *pl* **-naries** : infarctus *m*

coronation [ˌkɔrəˈneɪʃən] *n* : couronnement *m*

corporal [ˈkɔrpərəl] *n* : caporal-chef *m*

corporation [ˌkɔrpəˈreɪʃən] *n* : compagnie *f* commerciale, société *f* — **corporate** [ˈkɔrpərət] *adj* : d'entreprise

corps [ˈkor], *pl* **corps** [ˈkorz] : corps *m*

corpse [ˈkɔrps] *n* : cadavre *m*

corpulent [ˈkɔrpjələnt] *adj* : corpulent, gras

corral [kəˈræl] *n* : corral *m*

correct [kəˈrɛkt] *vt* : corriger — **~** *adj* **1** : juste, correct **2 that's ~** : c'est exact — **correction** [kəˈrɛkʃən] *n* : correction *f*

correlation [ˌkɔrəˈleɪʃən] *n* : corrélation *f*

correspond [ˌkɔrəˈspɑnd] *vi* : correspondre — **correspondence** [ˌkɔrəˈspɑndənts] *n* : correspondance *f* — **correspondent** [ˌkɔrəˈspɑndənt] *n* **1** : correspondant *m*, -dante *f* **2** REPORTER : journaliste *mf*

corridor [ˈkɔrədər, -ˌdor] *n* : corridor *m*

corroborate [kəˈrɑbəˌreɪt] *vt* **-rated; -rating** : corroborer

corrode [kəˈroːd] *vt* **-roded; -roding** : corroder — **corrosion** [kəˈroːʃ'n] *n* : corrosion *f*

corrugated [ˈkɔrəˌgeɪtəd] *adj* : ondulé
corrupt [kəˈrʌpt] *vt* : corrompre — ~ *adj* : corrompu — **corruption** [kəˈrʌpʃən] *n* : corruption *f*
cosmetic [kazˈmɛtɪk] *n* : cosmétique *f* — ~ *adj* : cosmétique
cosmic [ˈkazmɪk] *adj* : cosmique
cosmopolitan [ˌkazməˈpalətən] *adj* : cosmopolite
cosmos [ˈkazməs, -ˌmoːs, -ˌmas] *n* : cosmos *m*, univers *m*
cost [ˈkɔst] *n* : coût *m*, prix *m* — ~ *vi* **cost; costing 1** : coûter **2 how much does it** ~**?** : combien ça coûte? — **costly** [ˈkɔstli] *adj* **-lier; -est** : coûteux, cher
costume [ˈkasˌtuːm, -ˌtjuːm] *n* : costume *m*
cot [ˈkat] *n* : lit *m* de camp
cottage [ˈkatɪdʒ] *n* : petite maison *f* — **cottage cheese** *n* : fromage *m* blanc
cotton [ˈkatən] *n* : coton *m*
couch [ˈkaʊtʃ] *n* : canapé *m*, sofa *m*
cough [ˈkɔf] *vi* : tousser — ~ *n* : toux *f*
could [ˈkʊd] → **can**[1]
council [ˈkaʊnsəl] *n* : conseil *m*, assemblée *f* — **councillor** *or* **councilor** [ˈkaʊnsələr] *n* : conseiller *m*, -lère *f*
counsel [ˈkaʊnsəl] *n* **1** ADVICE : conseil *m* **2** LAWYER : avocat *m*, -cate *f* — ~ *vt* **-seled** *or* **-selled; -seling** *or* **-selling** : conseiller, guider — **counselor** *or* **counsellor** [ˈkaʊnsələr] *n* **1** : conseiller *m*, -lère *f* **2** *or* **camp** ~ : moniteur *m*, -trice *f*
count[1] [ˈkaʊnt] *vt* : compter, énumérer — *vi* **1** : compter **2** ~ **on** : compter sur — ~ *n* : compte *m*, décompte *m*
count[2] *n* : comte *m* (noble)
counter[1] [ˈkaʊntər] *n* **1** : comptoir *m* **2** TOKEN : jeton *m*
counter[2] *vt* : s'opposer à, contrecarrer — *vi* : riposter — ~ *adv* ~ **to** : à l'encontre de — **counteract** [ˌkaʊntərˈækt] *vt* : neutraliser — **counterattack** [ˈkaʊntərəˌtæk] *n* : contre-attaque *f* — **counterbalance** [ˌkaʊntərˈbælənts] *n* : contrepoids *m* — **counterclockwise** [ˌkaʊntərˈklakˌwaɪz] *adv & adj* : dans le sens contraire des aiguilles d'une montre — **counterfeit** [ˈkaʊntərˌfɪt] *vt* : contrefaire — ~ *adj* : faux — **counterpart** [ˈkaʊntərˌpart] *n* : homologue *mf* (d'une personne), équivalent *m* (d'une chose)
countess [ˈkaʊntɪs] *n* : comtesse *f*
countless [ˈkaʊntləs] *adj* : innombrable, incalculable
country [ˈkʌntri] *n*, *pl* **-tries 1** NATION : pays *m*, patrie *f* **2** COUNTRYSIDE : campagne *f* — ~ *adj* : champêtre, rural — **countryside** [ˈkʌntriˌsaɪd] *n* : campagne *f*
county [ˈkaʊnti] *n*, *pl* **-ties** : comté *m*

coup [ˈkuː] *n*, *pl* **coups** [ˈkuːz] *or* ~ **d'état** : coup *m* d'état
couple [ˈkʌpəl] *n* **1** : couple *m* **2 a** ~ **of** : deux ou trois — ~ *v* **-pled; -pling** *vt* : accoupler — *vi* : s'accoupler
coupon [ˈkuːˌpan, ˈkjuː-] *n* : coupon *m*
courage [ˈkərɪdʒ] *n* : courage *m* — **courageous** [kəˈreɪdʒəs] *adj* : courageux
courier [ˈkʊriər, ˈkəriər] *n* : messager *m*, -gère *f*
course [ˈkors] *n* **1** : cours *m* **2** : service *m*, plat *m* (au restaurant) **3** ~ **of action** : ligne *f* de conduite **4 golf** ~ : terrain *m* de golf **5 in the** ~ **of** : au cours de **6 of** ~ : bien sûr
court [ˈkort] *n* **1** : cour *f* (d'un souverain, etc.) **2** : court *m*, terrain *m* (de sports) **3** TRIBUNAL : cour *f*, tribunal *m* — ~ *vt* : courtiser, faire la cour à
courteous [ˈkərtiəs] *adj* : courtois, poli — **courtesy** [ˈkərtəsi] *n*, *pl* **-sies** : courtoisie *f*
courthouse [ˈkortˌhaʊs] *n* : palais *m* de justice — **courtroom** [ˈkortˌruːm] *n* : salle *f* du tribunal
courtship [ˈkortˌʃɪp] *n* : cour *f*
courtyard [ˈkortˌjard] *n* : cour *f*, patio *m*
cousin [ˈkʌzən] *n* : cousin *m*, -sine *f*
cove [ˈkoːv] *n* : anse *f*
covenant [ˈkʌvənənt] *n* : contrat *m*, convention *f*
cover [ˈkʌvər] *vt* **1** : couvrir, recouvrir **2** *or* ~ **up** : cacher **3** DEAL WITH : traiter **4** : parcourir (une distance) **5** INSURE : assurer — ~ *n* **1** LID : couvercle *m* **2** SHELTER : abri *m*, refuge *m* **3** : couverture *f* (d'un livre) **4** ~**s** *npl* BEDCLOTHES : couvertures *fpl* — **coverage** [ˈkʌvərɪdʒ] *n* : reportage *m*, couverture *f* — **covert** [ˈkoːˌvərt, ˈkʌvərt] *adj* : voilé, secret — **cover-up** [ˈkʌvərˌʌp] *n* : opération *f* de camouflage
covet [ˈkʌvət] *vt* : convoiter — **covetous** [ˈkʌvətəs] *adj* : avide, cupide
cow [ˈkaʊ] *n* : vache *f*
coward [ˈkaʊərd] *n* : lâche *mf*; poltron *m*, -tronne *f* — **cowardice** [ˈkaʊərdɪs] *n* : lâcheté *f* — **cowardly** [ˈkaʊərdli] *adj* : lâche
cowboy [ˈkaʊˌbɔɪ] *n* : cow-boy *m*
cower [ˈkaʊər] *vi* : se recroqueviller
coy [ˈkɔɪ] *adj* : faussement timide
coyote [kaɪˈoːti, ˈkaɪˌoːt] *n*, *pl* **coyotes** *or* **coyote** : coyote *m*
cozy [ˈkoːzi] *adj* **-zier; -est** : douillet, confortable
crab [ˈkræb] *n* : crabe *m*
crack [ˈkræk] *vt* **1** SPLIT : fêler, fendre **2** : casser (un œuf, etc.) **3** : faire claquer (un fouet) **4** ~ **down on** : sévir contre — *vi* **1** SPLIT : se fêler, se fendre **2** BREAK : se casser, muer (se dit de la voix) — ~ *n* **1**

: craquement *m*, bruit *m* sec **2** CREVICE
: crevasse *f*, fissure *f*
cracker [ˈkrækər] *n* : biscuit *m* salé
crackle [ˈkrækəl] *vi* **-led; -ling** : crépiter,
pétiller — **~** *n* : crépitement *m*
cradle [ˈkreɪdəl] *n* : berceau *m* — **~** *vt*
-dled; -dling : bercer (un enfant)
craft [ˈkræft] *n* **1** TRADE : métier *m*, art *m* **2**
CUNNING : ruse *f* **3** *pl usu* **craft** BOAT : embarcation *f* — **craftsman** [ˈkræftsmən] *n*, *pl*
-men [-mən, -ˌmɛn] : artisan *m*, -sane *f* —
craftsmanship [ˈkræftsmənˌʃɪp] *n* : artisanat *m* — **crafty** [ˈkræfti] *adj* **craftier; -est**
: astucieux, rusé
cram [ˈkræm] *v* **crammed; cramming** *vt*
: fourrer, entasser — *vi* : étudier à la
dernière minute
cramp [ˈkræmp] *n* : crampe *f*
cranberry [ˈkrænˌbɛri] *n*, *pl* **-ries** : canneberge *f*
crane [ˈkreɪn] *n* : grue *f* — **~** *vt* **craned;**
craning : tendre (le cou, etc.)
crank [ˈkræŋk] *n* **1** : manivelle *f* **2** ECCEN-
TRIC : excentrique *mf* — **cranky** [ˈkræŋki]
adj **crankier; -est** : irritable
crash [ˈkræʃ] *vi* **1** : se fracasser, s'écraser **2**
: faire faillite (se dit d'une banque), s'effondrer (se dit du marché) — *vt* **~ one's car**
: avoir un accident de voiture — **~** *n* **1**
: fracas *m*, bruit *m* sourd **2** COLLISION : accident *m*
crass [ˈkræs] *adj* : grossier
crate [ˈkreɪt] *n* : cageot *m*, caisse *f*
crater [ˈkreɪtər] *n* : cratère *m*
crave [ˈkreɪv] *vt* **craved; craving** : désirer,
avoir très envie de — **craving** [ˈkreɪvɪŋ] *n*
: envie *f* (incontrôlable), soif *f*
crawl [ˈkrɔl] *vi* : ramper, marcher à quatre
pattes — **~** *n* **at a ~** : à un pas de tortue
crayon [ˈkreɪˌɑn, -ən] *n* : crayon *m* de cire
craze [ˈkreɪz] *n* : mode *f* passagère
crazy [ˈkreɪzi] *adj* **-zier; -est 1** : fou **2 go**
~ : devenir fou — **craziness** [ˈkreɪzinəs] *n*
: folie *f*
creak [ˈkriːk] *vi* : grincer, craquer — **~** *n*
: grincement *m*
cream [ˈkriːm] *n* : crème *f* — **creamy**
[ˈkriːmi] *adj* **creamier; -est** : crémeux
crease [ˈkriːs] *n* : (faux) pli *m* — **~** *v*
creased; creasing *vt* : froisser — *vi* : se
froisser
create [kriˈeɪt] *vt* **-ated; -ating** : créer —
creation [kriˈeɪʃən] *n* : création *f* — **cre-**
ative [kriˈeɪtɪv] *adj* : créateur — **creator**
[kriˈeɪtər] *n* : créateur *m*, -trice *f*
creature [ˈkriːtʃər] *n* : créature *f*
credence [ˈkriːdənts] *n* **give ~ to** : accorder du crédit à
credentials [krɪˈdɛntʃəlz] *npl* : références
fpl

credible [ˈkrɛdəbəl] *adj* : crédible — **credi-**
bility [ˌkrɛdəˈbɪləti] *n* : crédibilité *f*
credit [ˈkrɛdɪt] *n* **1** : crédit *m* **2** RECOGNI-
TION : mérite *m* **3 to his ~** : à son honneur
— **~** *vt* **1** : créditer (un compte de banque)
2 ~ with : attribuer à — **credit card** *n*
: carte *f* de crédit — **creditor** [ˈkrɛdɪtər] *n*
: créancier *m*, -cière *f*
credulous [ˈkrɛdʒələs] *adj* : crédule
creed [ˈkriːd] *n* : credo *m*
creek [ˈkriːk, ˈkrɪk] *n* : ruisseau *m*
creep [ˈkriːp] *vi* **crept** [ˈkrɛpt]; **creeping 1**
CRAWL : ramper **2** : avancer sans un bruit —
~ *n* **1 ~s** *npl* : frissons *mpl*, chair *f* de
poule **2 move at a ~** : avancer au ralenti
cremate [ˈkriːˌmeɪt] *vt* **-mated; -mating** : incinérer
crescent [ˈkrɛsənt] *n* : croissant *m*
cress [ˈkrɛs] *n* : cresson *m*
crest [ˈkrɛst] *n* : crête *f*
crevice [ˈkrɛvɪs] *n* : fissure *f*, fente *f*
crew [ˈkruː] *n* **1** : équipage *m* (d'un navire)
2 TEAM : équipe *f*
crib [ˈkrɪb] *n* : lit *m* d'enfant
cricket [ˈkrɪkət] *n* **1** : grillon *m* (insecte) **2**
: cricket *m* (jeu)
crime [ˈkraɪm] *n* : crime *m*, délit *m* — **crimi-**
nal [ˈkrɪmənəl] *adj* : criminel — **~** *n*
: criminel *m*, -nelle *f*
cringe [ˈkrɪndʒ] *vi* **cringed; cringing**
: reculer (devant)
crinkle [ˈkrɪŋkəl] *vt* **-kled; -kling** : froisser,
chiffonner
cripple [ˈkrɪpəl] *vt* **-pled; -pling 1** DISABLE
: estropier **2** INCAPACITATE : paralyser
crisis [ˈkraɪsɪs] *n*, *pl* **-ses** [-ˌsiːz] : crise *f*
crisp [ˈkrɪsp] *adj* : croustillant, croquant —
crispy [ˈkrɪspi] *adj* **crispier; -est** : croustillant, croquant
crisscross [ˈkrɪsˌkrɔs] *vt* : entrecroiser
criterion [kraɪˈtɪriən] *n*, *pl* **-ria** [-riə] : critère
m
critic [ˈkrɪtɪk] *n* : critique *mf* — **critical**
[ˈkrɪtɪkəl] *adj* : critique — **criticism** [ˈkrɪtə-
ˌsɪzəm] *n* : critique *f* — **criticize** [ˈkrɪtə-
ˌsaɪz] *vt* **-cized; -cizing** : critiquer
croak [ˈkroːk] *vi* : coasser
crockery [ˈkrɑkəri] *n* : faïence *f*
crocodile [ˈkrɑkəˌdaɪl] *n* : crocodile *m*
crony [ˈkroːni] *n*, *pl* **-nies** : copain *m*, -pine *f*
crook [ˈkrʊk] *n* **1** STAFF : houlette *f* (d'un
berger) **2** THIEF : escroc *m* **3** BEND
: courbe *f* — **crooked** [ˈkrʊkəd] *adj* **1**
BENT : crochu, courbé **2** DISHONEST : malhonnête
crop [ˈkrɑp] *n* **1** HARVEST : récolte *f*, moisson *f* **2** PRODUCE : culture *f* — **~** *v*
cropped; cropping *vt* TRIM : tailler — *vi*
~ up : surgir, se présenter
cross [ˈkrɔs] *n* : croix *f* — **~** *vt* **1** : traverser

(la rue, etc.) **2** CROSSBREED : croiser **3** OP-POSE : contrarier **4** : croiser (les bras, etc.) **5** ~ **out** : rayer — ~ *adj* **1** ANGRY : fâché, contrarié **2** ~ **street** : rue *f* transversale — **crossbreed** [ˈkrɔsˌbriːd] *vt* **-bred** [-bred]; **-breeding** : croiser (deux espèces) — **cross-eyed** [ˈkrɔsˌaɪd] *adj* : qui louche — **cross fire** *n* : feux *mpl* croisés — **crossing** [ˈkrɔsɪŋ] *n* **1** : croisement *m* **2** → **cross-walk** — **cross-reference** [ˌkrɔsˈrefrənts, -ˈrefərənts] *n* : renvoi *m* — **crossroads** [ˈkrɔsˌroːdz] *n* : carrefour *m* — **cross section** *n* **1** : coupe *f* transversale **2** SAMPLE : échantillon *m* — **crosswalk** [ˈkrɔsˌwɔk] *n* : passage *m* pour piétons — **crossword puzzle** [ˈkrɔsˌwərd] *n* : mots *mpl* croisés

crotch [ˈkrɑtʃ] *n* : entre-jambes *m*

crouch [ˈkraʊtʃ] *vi* : s'accroupir

crow [ˈkroː] *n* : corbeau *m* — ~ *vi* **crowed** *or Brit* **crew**; **crowing** : chanter (se dit du coq)

crowbar [ˈkroːˌbɑr] *n* : (pince à) levier *m*

crowd [ˈkraʊd] *vi* : se presser, s'entasser — *vt* : serrer, entasser — ~ *n* : foule *f*

crown [ˈkraʊn] *n* : couronne *f* — ~ *vt* : couronner

crucial [ˈkruːʃəl] *adj* : crucial

crucify [ˈkruːsəˌfaɪ] *vt* **-fied**; **-fying** : crucifier — **crucifix** [ˈkruːsəˌfɪks] *n* : crucifix *m* — **crucifixion** [ˌkruːsəˈfɪkʃən] *n* : crucifixion *f*

crude [ˈkruːd] *adj* **cruder**; **crudest 1** RAW : brut **2** VULGAR : grossier **3** ROUGH : rudimentaire

cruel [ˈkruːəl] *adj* **-eler** *or* **-eller**; **-elest** *or* **-ellest** : cruel — **cruelty** [ˈkruːəlti] *n, pl* **-ties** : cruauté *f*

cruet [ˈkruːɪt] *n* : huilier *m*, vinaigrier *m*

cruise [ˈkruːz] *vi* **cruised**; **cruising** : rouler à sa vitesse de croisière — ~ *n* : croisière *f* — **cruiser** [ˈkruːzər] *n* **1** WARSHIP : croiseur *m* **2** *or* **police** ~ : véhicule *m* de police

crumb [ˈkrʌm] *n* : miette *f*

crumble [ˈkrʌmbəl] *v* **-bled**; **-bling** *vt* : émietter — *vi* : s'émietter, s'effriter

crumple [ˈkrʌmpəl] *vt* **-pled**; **-pling** : froisser, chiffonner

crunch [ˈkrʌntʃ] *vt* : croquer — **crunchy** [ˈkrʌntʃi] *adj* **crunchier**; **-est** : croquant

crusade [kruːˈseɪd] *n* : croisade *f*, campagne *f*

crush [ˈkrʌʃ] *vt* : écraser, aplatir — ~ *n* **have a** ~ **on s.o.** : avoir le béguin pour qqn

crust [ˈkrʌst] *n* : croûte *f*

crutch [ˈkrʌtʃ] *n* : béquille *f*

crux [ˈkrʌks, ˈkrʊks] *n* : point *m* crucial, cœur *m*

cry [ˈkraɪ] *vi* **cried**; **crying 1** SHOUT : crier,

pousser un cri **2** WEEP : pleurer — ~ *n, pl* **cries** : cri *m*

crypt [ˈkrɪpt] *n* : crypte *f*

crystal [ˈkrɪstəl] *n* : cristal *m*

cub [ˈkʌb] *n* : petit *m* (d'un animal)

cube [ˈkjuːb] *n* : cube *m* — **cubic** [ˈkjuːbɪk] *adj* : cube, cubique

cubicle [ˈkjuːbɪkəl] *n* : box *m*

cuckoo [ˈkuːˌkuː, ˈkʊ-] *n, pl* **-oos** : coucou *m* (oiseau)

cucumber [ˈkjuːˌkʌmbər] *n* : concombre *m*

cuddle [ˈkʌdəl] *v* **-dled**; **-dling** *vt* : caresser, câliner — *vi* : se câliner

cudgel [ˈkʌdʒəl] *n* : gourdin *m*, trique *f*

cue¹ [ˈkjuː] *n* SIGNAL : signal *m*

cue² *n or* ~ **stick** : queue *f* de billard

cuff [ˈkʌf] *n* : poignet *m* (de chemise), revers *m* (de pantalon)

cuisine [kwɪˈziːn] *n* : cuisine *f*

culinary [ˈkʌləˌneri, ˈkjuːlə-] *adj* : culinaire

cull [ˈkʌl] *vt* : choisir, sélectionner

culminate [ˈkʌlməˌneɪt] *vi* **-nated**; **-nating** : culminer — **culmination** [ˌkʌlməˈneɪʃən] *n* : point *m* culminant

culprit [ˈkʌlprɪt] *n* : coupable *mf*

cult [ˈkʌlt] *n* : culte *m*

cultivate [ˈkʌltəˌveɪt] *vt* **-vated**; **-vating** : cultiver — **cultivation** [ˌkʌltəˈveɪʃən] *n* : culture *f* (de la terre)

culture [ˈkʌltʃər] *n* : culture *f* — **cultural** [ˈkʌltʃərəl] *adj* : culturel — **cultured** [ˈkʌltʃərd] *adj* : cultivé

cumbersome [ˈkʌmbərsəm] *adj* : encombrant

cumulative [ˈkjuːmjələtɪv, -ˌleɪtɪv] *adj* : cumulatif

cunning [ˈkʌnɪŋ] *adj* : astucieux — ~ *n* : ruse *f*, astuce *f*

cup [ˈkʌp] *n* **1** : tasse *f* **2** TROPHY : coupe *f*

cupboard [ˈkʌbərd] *n* : placard *m*, armoire *f*

curator [ˈkjʊrˌeɪtər, kjʊˈreɪtər] *n* : conservateur *m*, -trice *f*

curb [ˈkərb] *n* **1** RESTRAINT : contrainte *f*, frein *m* **2** : bord *m* du trottoir — ~ *vt* : mettre un frein à

curdle [ˈkərdəl] *vi* **-dled**; **-dling** : (se) cailler

cure [ˈkjʊr] *n* : remède *m* — ~ *vt* **cured**; **curing** : guérir

curfew [ˈkərˌfjuː] *n* : couvre-feu *m*

curious [ˈkjʊriəs] *adj* : curieux — **curiosity** [ˌkjʊriˈɑsəti] *n, pl* **-ties** : curiosité *f*

curl [ˈkərl] *vt* **1** : friser, boucler **2** COIL : enrouler — *vi* **1** : boucler (se dit des cheveux) **2** ~ **up** : se pelotonner — ~ *n* : boucle *f* (de cheveux) — **curler** [ˈkərlər] *n* : bigoudi *m* — **curly** [ˈkərli] *adj* **curlier**; **-est** : bouclé, frisé

currant [ˈkərənt] *n* **1** BERRY : groseille *f* **2** RAISIN : raisin *m* de Corinthe

currency ['kərəntsi] *n, pl* **-cies 1** : monnaie *f*, devise *f* **2 gain ~** : se répandre

current ['kərənt] *adj* **1** PRESENT : en cours **2** PREVALENT : courant, commun — **~** *n* : courant *m*

curriculum [kə'rıkjələm] *n, pl* **-la** [-lə] : programme *m* (scolaire)

curry ['kəri] *n, pl* **-ries** : curry *m*

curse ['kərs] *n* : malédiction *f* — **~** *v* **cursed; cursing** *vt* : maudire — *vi* SWEAR : sacrer, jurer

cursor ['kərsər] *n* : curseur *m*

cursory ['kərsəri] *adj* : superficiel, hâtif

curt ['kərt] *adj* : brusque

curtail [kər'teıl] *vt* : écourter

curtain ['kərtən] *n* : rideau *m*

curtsy ['kərtsi] *vi* **-sied;** *or* **-seyed;** *or* **-sying** *or* **-seying** : faire une révérence — **~** *n* : révérence *f*

curve ['kərv] *v* **curved; curving** *vt* : courber — *vi* : se courber, faire une courbe — **~** *n* : courbe *f*

cushion ['kuʃən] *n* : coussin *m* — **~** *vt* : amortir

custard ['kʌstərd] *n* : flan *m*

custody ['kʌstədi] *n, pl* **-dies 1** CARE : garde *f* **2 be in ~** : être en détention

custom ['kʌstəm] *n* : coutume *f*, tradition *f* — **~** *adj* : fait sur commande — **custom-**

ary ['kʌstə,mɛri] *adj* : habituel, coutumier — **customer** ['kʌstəmər] *n* : client *m*, cliente *f* — **customs** ['kʌst'mz] *npl* : douane *f*

cut ['kʌt] *v* **cut; cutting** *vt* **1** : couper **2** REDUCE : réduire **3 ~ oneself** : se couper (le doigt, etc.) **4** *or* **~ up** : découper — *vi* **1** : couper **2 ~ in** : interrompre — **~** *n* **1** : coupure *f* **2** REDUCTION : réduction *f*

cute ['kju:t] *adj* **cuter; cutest** : mignon, joli

cutlery ['kʌtləri] *n* : couverts *mpl*

cutlet ['kʌtlət] *n* : escalope *f*

cutting ['kʌtıŋ] *adj* **1** : cinglant (se dit du vent) **2** CURT : mordant, tranchant

cyanide ['saıə,naıd, -nıd] *n* : cyanure *m*

cycle ['saıkəl] *n* : cycle *m* — **~** *vi* **-cled; -cling** : faire de la bicyclette — **cyclic** ['saıklık, 'sı-] *or* **cyclical** [-klıkəl] *adj* : cyclique — **cyclist** ['saıklıst] *n* : cycliste *mf*

cyclone ['saı,klo:n] *n* : cyclone *m*

cylinder ['sıləndər] *n* : cylindre *m* — **cylindrical** [sə'lındrıkəl] *adj* : cylindrique

cymbal ['sımbəl] *n* : cymbale *f*

cynic ['sınık] *n* : cynique *mf* — **cynical** ['sınıkəl] *adj* : cynique — **cynicism** ['sınə,sızəm] *n* : cynisme *m*

cypress ['saıprəs] *n* : cyprès *m*

cyst ['sıst] *n* : kyste *m*

czar ['zɑr, 'sɑr] *n* : tsar *m*

D

d ['di:] *n, pl* **d's** *or* **ds** ['di:z] : d *m*, quatrième lettre de l'alphabet

dab ['dæb] *n* : touche *f*, petite quantité *f* — **~** *vt* **dabbed; dabbing** : appliquer délicatement

dabble ['dæbəl] *vi* **-bled; -bling ~ in** : s'intéresser superficiellement à

dad ['dæd] *n* : papa *m fam* — **daddy** ['dædi] *n, pl* **-dies** : papa *m fam*

daffodil ['dæfə,dıl] *n* : jonquille *f*

dagger ['dægər] *n* : poignard *m*

daily ['deıli] *adj* : quotidien — **~** *adv* : quotidiennement

dainty ['deınti] *adj* **-tier; -est** : délicat

dairy ['dæri] *n, pl* **dairies** : laiterie *f*, crémerie *f France*

daisy ['deızi] *n, pl* **-sies** : marguerite *f*

dam ['dæm] *n* : barrage *m*

damage ['dæmıdʒ] *n* **1** : dégâts *mpl* **2 ~s** *npl* : dommages *mpl* et intérêts *mpl* — **~** *vt* **-aged; -aging** : endommager (des objets), abîmer (sa santé)

damn ['dæm] *vt* **1** CONDEMN : condamner **2** CURSE : maudire — **~** *n* **not give a ~** : s'en ficher *fam* — **~** *or* **damned** ['dæmd] *adj* : fichu *fam*, sacré *fam*

damp ['dæmp] *adj* : humide, moite — **dampen** ['dæmpən] *vt* **1** MOISTEN : humecter **2** DISCOURAGE : décourager — **dampness** ['dæmpnəs] *n* : humidité *f*

dance ['dænts] *v* **danced; dancing** : danser — **~** *n* : danse *f* — **dancer** ['dæntsər] *n* : danseur *m*, -seuse *f*

dandelion ['dænd,laıən] *n* : pissenlit *m*

dandruff ['dændrəf] *n* : pellicules *fpl*

danger ['deındʒər] *n* : danger *m* — **dangerous** ['deındʒərəs] *adj* : dangereux

dangle ['dæŋgəl] *v* **-gled; -gling** *vi* HANG : pendre — *vt* : balancer, laisser pendre

dank ['dæŋk] *adj* : froid et humide

dare ['dær] *v* **dared; daring** *vt* : défier — *vi* : oser — **~** *n* : défi *m* — **daring** ['deırıŋ] *adj* : audacieux, hardi

dark ['dɑrk] *adj* **1** : noir **2** : foncé (se dit des

cheveux, etc.) **3** GLOOMY : sombre **4 get
~** : faire nuit — **darken** ['dɑrkən] *vt* : obscurcir — *vi* : s'obscurcir — **darkness**
['dɑrknəs] *n* : obscurité *f*, noirceur *f Can*
darling ['dɑrlɪŋ] *n* BELOVED : chéri *m*, -rie *f*
— **~s** *adj* : chéri
darn ['dɑrn] *vt* : repriser (en couture) — **~**
adj : sacré
dart ['dɑrt] *n* **1** : fléchette *f*, dard *m Can* **2**
~s *npl* : fléchettes *fpl* (jeu) — **~** *vi* : se
précipiter, s'élancer
dash ['dæʃ] *vt* **~ off** : terminer à la hâte —
vi : se précipiter — **~** *n* **1** : tiret *m* (signe
de ponctuation) **2** PINCH : pincée *f*, soupçon
m **3** RUSH : course *f* folle — **dashboard**
['dæʃ,bord] *n* : tableau *m* de bord — **dashing** ['dæʃɪŋ] *adj* : fringant, élégant
data ['deɪtə, 'dæ-, 'dɑ-] *ns & pl* : données *fpl*
— **database** ['deɪtə,beɪs, 'dæ-, 'dɑ-] *n*
: base *f* de données
date[1] ['deɪt] *n* : datte *f* (fruit)
date[2] *n* **1** : date *f* **2** APPOINTMENT : rendez-
vous *m* — **~** *v* **dated; dating** *vt* **1** : dater
(un chèque, etc.) **2** : sortir avec (qqn) — *vi*
~ from : dater de, remonter à — **dated**
['deɪtəd] *adj* : démodé
daughter ['dɔtər] *n* : fille *f* — **daughter–in–
law** ['dɔtərɪn,lɔ] *n*, *pl* **daughters–in–law**
: belle-fille *f*, bru *f*
daunt ['dɔnt] *vt* : décourager
dawdle ['dɔdəl] *vi* **-dled; -dling** : lambiner
fam, traîner
dawn ['dɔn] *vi* **1** : se lever (se dit du jour) **2**
it ~ed on him that : il s'est rendu compte
que — **~** *n* : aube *f*
day ['deɪ] *n* **1** : jour *m* **2** *or* **working ~**
: journée *f* (de travail) **3 the ~ before** : la
veille **4 the ~ before yesterday** : avant-
hier **5 the ~ after** : le lendemain **6 the ~
after tomorrow** : après-demain — **daybreak** ['deɪ,breɪk] *n* : aube *f* — **daydream**
['deɪ,dri:m] *n* : rêve *m*, rêverie *f* — **~** *vi*
: rêver — **daylight** ['deɪ,laɪt] *n* : lumière *f* du
jour — **daytime** ['deɪ,taɪm] *n* : jour *m*,
journée *f*
daze ['deɪz] *vt* **dazed; dazing** : abasourdir
— **~** *n* **in a ~** : hébété
dazzle ['dæzəl] *vt* **-zled; -zling** : éblouir
dead ['dɛd] *adj* : mort — **~** *n* **the ~** : les
morts — **~** *adv* COMPLETELY : complètement — **deaden** ['dɛdən] *vt* **1** : calmer (une
douleur) **2** MUFFLE : assourdir — **dead end**
['dɛd,ɛnd] *n* : cul-de-sac *m*, impasse *f* —
deadline ['dɛd,laɪn] *n* : date *f* limite —
deadly ['dɛdli] *adj* **-lier; -est** : mortel —
dealings ['di:lɪŋz] *npl* : transactions *fpl*, affaires *fpl*
deaf ['dɛf] *adj* : sourd — **deafen** ['dɛfən] *vt*
: assourdir — **deafness** ['dɛfnəs] *n* : surdité *f*

deal ['di:l] *n* **1** TRANSACTION : affaire *f*,
marché *m* **2** : donne *f* (aux cartes) — **~** *v*
dealt; dealing *vt* **1** : donner **2** : distribuer
(des cartes) **3 ~ a blow** : assener un coup
— *vi* **~ with** CONCERN : traiter de —
dealer ['di:lər] *n* : marchand *m*, -chande *f*;
négociant *m*, -ciante *f*
dean ['di:n] *n* : doyen *m*, doyenne *f*
dear ['dɪr] *adj* : cher — **~** *n* : chéri *m*, -rie *f*
— **dearly** ['dɪrli] *adv* : beaucoup
death ['dɛθ] *n* : mort *f*
debate [dɪ'beɪt] *n* : débat *m*, discussion *f* —
~ *v* **-bated; -bating** : discuter
debit ['dɛbɪt] *vt* : débiter — **~** *n* : débit *m*
debris [də'bri:, deɪ-; 'deɪ,bri:] *n*, *pl* **-bris**
[-'bri:z, -,bri:z] : décombres *mpl*
debt ['dɛt] *n* : dette *f*
debug [,di:'bʌg] *vt* : déboguer
debut [deɪ'bju:, 'deɪ,bju:] *n* : débuts *mpl* —
~ *vi* : débuter
decade ['dɛ,keɪd, dɛ'keɪd] *n* : décennie *f*
decadence ['dɛkədənts] *n* : décadence *f* —
decadent ['dɛkədənt] *adj* : décadent
decanter [dɪ'kæntər] *n* : carafe *f*
decay [dɪ'keɪ] *vi* **1** DECOMPOSE : se décomposer, pourrir **2** : se carier (se dit d'une
dent) — **~** *n* **1** : pourriture *f* **2** *or* **tooth ~**
: carie *f* (dentaire)
deceased [dɪ'si:st] *adj* : décédé, défunt —
~ *n* **the ~** : le défunt, la défunte
deceive [dɪ'si:v] *vt* **-ceived; -ceiving**
: tromper — **deceit** [dɪ'si:t] *n* : tromperie *f*
— **deceitful** [dɪ'si:tfəl] *adj* : trompeur
December [dɪ'sɛmbər] *n* : décembre *m*
decent ['di:sənt] *adj* **1** : décent, convenable
2 KIND : bien, aimable — **decency** ['di:-
səntsi] *n*, *pl* **-cies** : décence *f*
deception [dɪ'sɛpʃən] *n* : tromperie *f* — **de-
ceptive** [dɪ'sɛptɪv] *adj* : trompeur
decide [dɪ'saɪd] *v* **-cided; -ciding** *vt* : décider — *vi* : se décider — **decided** [dɪ-
'saɪdəd] *adj* RESOLUTE : décidé
decimal ['dɛsəməl] *adj* : décimal — **~** *n*
: décimale *f* — **decimal point** *n* : virgule *f*
decipher [dɪ'saɪfər] *vt* : déchiffrer
decision [dɪ'sɪʒən] *n* : décision *f* — **decisive**
[dɪ'saɪsɪv] *adj* **1** RESOLUTE : décidé **2** CON-
CLUSIVE : décisif
deck ['dɛk] *n* **1** : pont *m* (d'un navire) **2** *or*
~ of cards : jeu *m* de cartes
declare [dɪ'klær] *vt* **-clared; -claring** : déclarer — **declaration** [,dɛklə'reɪʃən] *n*
: déclaration *f*
decline [dɪ'klaɪn] *v* **-clined; -clining** : décliner — **~** *n* **1** DETERIORATION : déclin *m*
2 DECREASE : baisse *f*
decompose [,di:kəm'po:z] *vt* **-posed; -pos-
ing** : décomposer — *vi* : se décomposer
decongestant [,di:kən'dʒɛstənt] *n* : décon-
gestif *m*

decorate ['dɛkə,reɪt] *vt* **-rated; -rating** : dé-corer — **decor** *or* **décor** [deɪ'kɔr, 'deɪ,kɔr] *n* : décor *m* — **decoration** [,dɛkə'reɪʃən] *n* : décoration *f* — **decorative** ['dɛkərətɪv, -,reɪ-] *adj* : décoratif — **decorator** ['dɛkə,reɪtər] *n* : décorateur *m*, -trice *f*

decoy ['di,kɔɪ, di'-] *n* : appeau *m*

decrease [di'kri:s] *v* **-creased; -creasing** : diminuer — ~ ['di:,kri:s] *n* : diminution *f*

decree [di'kri:] *n* : décret *m* — ~ *vt* **-creed; -creeing** : décréter

decrepit [di'krɛpɪt] *adj* **1** FEEBLE : décrépit **2** DILAPIDATED : délabré

dedicate ['dɛdɪ,keɪt] *vt* **-cated; -cating 1** : dédier **2** ~ **oneself to** : se consacrer à — **dedication** [dɛdɪ'keɪʃən] *n* **1** DEVOTION : dévouement *m* **2** INSCRIPTION : dédicace *f*

deduce [di'du:s, -'dju:s] *vt* **-duced; -ducing** : déduire — **deduct** [di'dʌkt] *vt* : déduire — **deduction** [di'dʌkʃən] *n* : déduction *f*

deed ['di:d] *n* : action *f*, acte *m*

deem ['di:m] *vt* : juger, considérer

deep ['di:p] *adj* : profond — ~ *adv* **1** DEEPLY : profondément **2** ~ **down** : au fond — **deepen** ['di:pən] *vt* : approfondir — *vi* : devenir plus profond — **deeply** ['di:pli] *adv* : profondément

deer ['dɪr] *ns & pl* : cerf *m*

default [di'fɔlt, 'di:,fɔlt] *n* **by** ~ : par défaut — ~ *vi* **1** : ne pas s'acquitter (d'une dette) **2** : déclarer forfait (aux sports)

defeat [di'fi:t] *vt* : battre, vaincre — ~ *n* : défaite *f*

defect ['di:,fɛkt, di'fɛkt] *n* : défaut *m* — **defective** [di'fɛktɪv] *adj* : défectueux

defence *Brit* → **defense**

defend [di'fɛnd] *vt* : défendre — **defendant** [di'fɛndənt] *n* : défendeur *m*, -deresse *f*; accusé *m*, -sée *f* — **defense** *or Brit* **defence** [di'fɛnts, 'di:,fɛnts] *n* : défense *f* — **defensive** [di'fɛntsɪv] *adj* : défensif — ~ *n* **on the** ~ : sur la défensive

defer [di'fər] *v* **-ferred; -ferring** *vt* : différer — *vi* ~ **to** : s'en remettre à

defiance [di'faɪənts] *n* **1** : défi *m* **2 in** ~ **of** : au mépris de — **defiant** [di'faɪənt] *adj* : de défi

deficient [di'fɪʃənt] *adj* **1** INADEQUATE : insuffisant **2** FAULTY : défectueux — **deficiency** [di'fɪʃəntsi] *n, pl* **-cies 1** LACK : carence *f* **2** FLAW : défaut *m*

deficit ['dɛfəsɪt] *n* : déficit *m*

defile [di'faɪl] *vt* **-filed; -filing** DESECRATE : profaner

define [di'faɪn] *vt* **-fined; -fining** : définir — **definite** ['dɛfənɪt] *adj* **1** : défini, précis **2** CERTAIN : certain, sûr — **definitely** ['dɛfənɪtli] *adv* : certainement — **definition** [,dɛfə'nɪʃən] *n* : définition *f* — **definitive** [də'fɪnətɪv] *adj* : définitif

deflate [di'fleɪt] *v* **-flated; -flating** *vt* : dégonfler (un pneu, etc.) — *vi* : se dégonfler

deflect [di'flɛkt] *vt* : faire dévier — *vi* : dévier

deform [di'fɔrm] *vt* : déformer — **deformity** [di'fɔrməti] *n, pl* **-ties** : difformité *f*

defraud [di'frɔd] *vt* : frauder, escroquer

defrost [di'frɔst] *vt* THAW : décongeler

defy [di'faɪ] *vt* **-fied; -fying 1** CHALLENGE : défier **2** RESIST : résister à

degenerate [di'dʒɛnə,reɪt] *vi* **-ated; -ating** : dégénérer

degrade [di'greɪd] *vt* **-graded; -grading** : dégrader — **degrading** *adj* : dégradant

degree [di'gri:] *n* **1** : degré *m* **2** *or* **academic** ~ : diplôme *m*

dehydrate [di'haɪ,dreɪt] *vt* **-drated; -drating** : déshydrater

deign ['deɪn] *vi* ~ **to** : daigner

deity ['di:əti, 'deɪ-] *n, pl* **-ties** : dieu *m*, déesse *f*

dejected [di'dʒɛktəd] *adj* : abattu — **dejection** [di'dʒɛkʃən] *n* : abattement *m*

delay [di'leɪ] *n* : retard *m*, délai *m* — ~ *vt* **1** POSTPONE : différer **2** HOLD UP : retarder

delectable [di'lɛktəbəl] *adj* : délicieux

delegate ['dɛlɪgət, -,geɪt] *n* : délégué *m*, -guée *f* — ~ ['dɛlɪ,geɪt] *v* **-gated; -gating** : déléguer — **delegation** [,dɛlɪ'geɪʃən] *n* : délégation *f*

delete [di'li:t] *vt* **-leted; -leting** : supprimer, effacer

deliberate [di'lɪbə,reɪt] *v* **-ated; -ating** *vt* : délibérer sur — *vi* : délibérer — ~ [di'lɪbərət] *adj* : délibéré — **deliberately** [di'lɪbərətli] *adv* : exprès

delicacy ['dɛlɪkəsi] *n, pl* **-cies 1** : délicatesse *f* **2** FOOD : mets *m* fin — **delicate** ['dɛlɪkət] *adj* : délicat

delicatessen [,dɛlɪkə'tɛsən] *n* : charcuterie *f*

delicious [di'lɪʃəs] *adj* : délicieux

delight [di'laɪt] *n* : plaisir *m*, joie *f* — ~ *vt* : réjouir — *vi* ~ **in** : prendre plaisir à — **delightful** [di'laɪtfəl] *adj* : charmant, ravissant

delinquent [di'lɪŋkwənt] *adj* : délinquant — ~ *n* : délinquant *m*, -quante *f*

delirious [di'lɪriəs] *adj* : délirant, en délire — **delirium** [di'lɪriəm] *n* : délire *m*

deliver [di'lɪvər] *vt* **1** DISTRIBUTE : livrer **2** FREE : libérer **3** : mettre au monde (un enfant) **4** : prononcer (un discours, etc.) **5** DEAL : asséner (un coup, etc.) — **delivery** [di'lɪvəri] *n, pl* **-eries 1** DISTRIBUTION : livraison *f*, distribution *f* **2** LIBERATION : délivrance *f* **3** CHILDBIRTH : accouchement *m*

delude [di'lu:d] *vt* **-luded; -luding 1** : tromper **2** ~ **oneself** : se faire des illusions

deluge ['dɛl,ju:dʒ, -,ju:ʒ] *n* : déluge *m*

delusion [di'lu:ʒən] n : illusion f

deluxe [di'lʌks, -'cluks] adj : de luxe

delve ['dɛlv] vi **delved; delving** 1 : creuser 2 **~ into** PROBE : fouiller dans

demand [di'mænd] n 1 REQUEST : demande f 2 CLAIM : réclamation f 3 → **supply** — **~** vt : exiger — **demanding** ['di'mændɪŋ] adj : exigeant

demean [di'mi:n] vt **~ oneself** : s'abaisser

demeanor or Brit **demeanour** [di'mi:nər] n : comportement m

demented [di'mɛntəd] adj : dément, fou

democracy [di'mɑkrəsi] n, pl **-cies** : démocratie f — **democrat** ['dɛmə,kræt] n : démocrate mf — **democratic** [,dɛmə'krætɪk] adj : démocratique

demolish [di'mɑlɪʃ] vt : démolir — **demolition** [,dɛmə'lɪʃən, ,di:-] n : démolition f

demon ['di:mən] n : démon m

demonstrate ['dɛmən,streɪt] v **-strated; -strating** vt : démontrer — vi RALLY : manifester — **demonstration** [dɛmən'streɪʃən] n 1 : démonstration f 2 RALLY : manifestation f — **demonstrative** [di'mɑntstrətɪv] adj : démonstratif — **demonstrator** ['dɛmən,streɪtər] n PROTESTOR : manifestant m, -tante f

demoralize [di'mɔrə,laɪz] vt **-ized; -izing** : démoraliser

demote [di'mo:t] vt **-moted; -moting** : rétrograder

demure [di'mjʊr] adj : modeste, réservé

den ['dɛn] n LAIR : antre m, tanière f

denial [di'naɪəl] n 1 : démenti m, dénégation f 2 REFUSAL : refus m

denim ['dɛnəm] n : jean m

denomination [dɪ,nɑmə'neɪʃən] n 1 : confession f (religieuse) 2 : valeur f (monétaire)

denote [di'no:t] vt **-noted; -noting** : dénoter

denounce [di'naʊnts] vt **-nounced; -nouncing** : dénoncer

dense ['dɛnts] adj **denser; -est** 1 THICK : dense 2 STUPID : bête, obtus — **density** ['dɛntsəti] n, pl **-ties** : densité f

dent ['dɛnt] vt : cabosser — **~** n : bosse f

dental ['dɛntəl] adj : dentaire — **dental floss** n : fil m dentaire — **dentist** ['dɛntɪst] n : dentiste mf — **dentures** ['dɛntʃərz] npl : dentier m

denunciation [dɪ,nʌntsi'eɪʃən] n : dénonciation f

deny [di'naɪ] vt **-nied; -nying** 1 : nier 2 REFUSE : refuser

deodorant [di'o:dərənt] n : déodorant m

depart [di'pɑrt] vi 1 : partir 2 **~ from** : s'écarter de

department [di'pɑrtmənt] n : ministère m (gouvernemental), service m (d'un hôpital, etc.), rayon m (d'un magasin) — **department store** n : grand magasin m

departure [di'pɑrtʃər] n 1 : départ m 2 DEVIATION : écart m

depend [di'pɛnd] vi 1 **~ on** : dépendre de, compter sur 2 **~ on s.o.** : compter sur qqn 3 **that ~s** : tout dépend — **dependable** [di'pɛndəbəl] adj : digne de confiance — **dependence** [di'pɛndənts] n : dépendance f — **dependent** [di'pɛndənt] adj : dépendant

depict [di'pɪkt] vt 1 PORTRAY : représenter 2 DESCRIBE : dépeindre

deplete [di'pli:t] vt **-pleted; -pleting** : épuiser, réduire

deplore [di'plor] vt **-plored; -ploring** : déplorer — **deplorable** [di'plorəbəl] adj : déplorable

deploy [di'plɔɪ] vt : déployer

deport [di'port] vt : expulser (d'un pays) — **deportation** [,di,por'teɪʃən] n : expulsion f

deposit [di'pɑzət] vt **-ited; -iting** : déposer — **~** n 1 : dépôt m 2 DOWN PAYMENT : acompte m, arrhes fpl France

depreciate [di'pri:ʃi,eɪt] vi **-ated; -ating** : se déprécier — **depreciation** [di,pri:ʃi'eɪʃən] n : dépréciation f

depress [di'prɛs] vt 1 PRESS : appuyer sur 2 SADDEN : déprimer — **depressed** [di'prɛst] adj : déprimé — **depressing** [di'prɛsɪŋ] adj : déprimant — **depression** [di'prɛʃən] n : dépression f

deprive [di'praɪv] vt **-prived; -priving** : priver

depth ['dɛpθ] n, pl **depths** : profondeur f

deputy ['dɛpjuti] n, pl **-ties** : adjoint m, -jointe f

derail [di'reɪl] vi : dérailler — **derailment** [di'reɪlmənt] n : déraillement m

deride [di'raɪd] vt **-rided; -riding** : railler — **derision** [di'rɪʒən] n : dérision f

derive [di'raɪv] vi **-rived; -riving ~ from** : provenir de

derogatory [di'rɑgə,tori] adj : désobligeant

descend [di'sɛnd] v : descendre — **descendant** [di'sɛndənt] n : descendant m, -dante f — **descent** [di'sɛnt] n 1 : descente f 2 LINEAGE : descendance f

describe [di'skraɪb] vt **-scribed; -scribing** : décrire — **description** [di'skrɪpʃən] n : description f — **descriptive** [di'skrɪptɪv] adj : descriptif

desecrate ['dɛsɪ,kreɪt] vt **-crated; -crating** : profaner

desert ['dɛzərt] n : désert m — **~** adj **~ island** : île f déserte — **~** [di'zərt] vt : abandonner — vi : déserter — **deserter** [di'zərtər] n : déserteur m

deserve [di'zərv] vt **-served; -serving** : mériter

design [di'zaɪn] vt 1 DEVISE : concevoir 2 DRAW : dessiner — **~** n 1 : conception f 2

PLAN : plan *m* **3** SKETCH : dessin *m* **4** PATTERN : motif *m*

designate ['dɛzɪg,neɪt] *vt* **-nated; -nating** : désigner

designer [di'zaɪnər] *n* : dessinateur *m*, -trice *f*

desire [di'zaɪr] *vt* **-sired; -siring** : désirer — ~ *n* : désir *m*

desk ['dɛsk] *n* : bureau *m*, pupitre *m* (d'un élève)

desolate ['dɛsələt, -zə-] *adj* : désolé

despair [di'spær] *vi* : désespérer — ~ *n* : désespoir *m*

desperate ['dɛspərət] *adj* : désespéré — **desperation** [,dɛspə'reɪʃən] *n* : désespoir *m*

despise [di'spaɪz] *vt* **-spised; -spising** : mépriser — **despicable** [di'spɪkəbəl, 'dɛspɪ-] *adj* : méprisable

despite [də'spaɪt] *prep* : malgré

dessert [di'zərt] *n* : dessert *m*

destination [,dɛstɪ'neɪʃən] *n* : destination *f* — **destined** ['dɛstənd] *adj* **1** : destiné **2** ~ **for** : à destination de — **destiny** ['dɛstəni] *n, pl* **-nies** : destin *m*, destinée *f*

destitute ['dɛstə,tu:t, -,tju:t] *adj* : indigent

destroy [di'strɔɪ] *vt* : détruire — **destruction** [di'strʌkʃən] *n* : destruction *f* — **destructive** [di'strʌktɪv] *adj* : destructeur

detach [di'tætʃ] *vt* : détacher — **detached** [di'tætʃt] *adj* : détaché

detail [di'teɪl, 'di:,teɪl] *n* : détail *m* — ~ *vt* : détailler — **detailed** [di'teɪld, 'di:,teɪld] *adj* : détaillé

detain [di'teɪn] *vt* **1** : détenir (un prisonnier) **2** DELAY : retenir

detect [di'tɛkt] *vt* : détecter, déceler — **detection** [di'tɛkʃən] *n* : détection *f* — **detective** [di'tɛktɪv] *n* : détective *m*

detention [di'tɛnʃən] *n* : détention *f*

deter [di'tər] *vt* **-terred; -terring** : dissuader

detergent [di'tərdʒənt] *n* : détergent *m*

deteriorate [di'tɪriə,reɪt] *vi* **-rated; -rating** : se détériorer — **deterioration** [di,tɪriə'reɪʃən] *n* : détérioration *f*

determine [di'tərmən] *vt* **-mined; -mining** **1** : déterminer **2** RESOLVE : décider — **determined** [di'tərmənd] *adj* RESOLUTE : déterminé — **determination** [di,tərmə'neɪʃən] *n* : détermination *f*

detest [di'tɛst] *vt* : détester

detour ['di:,tʊr, di'tʊr] *n* : détour *m* — ~ *vi* : faire un détour

devastate ['dɛvə,steɪt] *vt* **-tated; -tating** : dévaster — **devastating** ['dɛvə,steɪtɪŋ] *adj* : accablant — **devastation** [,dɛvə'steɪʃən] *n* : dévastation *f*

develop [di'vɛləp] *vt* **1** : développer **2** ~ **an illness** : contracter une maladie — *vi* **1** GROW : se développer **2** HAPPEN : se manifester — **developing** [di'vɛləpɪŋ] *adj* **1** : en expansion **2** ~ **country** : pays en voie de développement — **development** [di'vɛləpmənt] *n* : développement *m*

deviate ['di:vi,eɪt] *vi* **-ated; -ating** : dévier, s'écarter

device [di'vaɪs] *n* : appareil *m*, mécanisme *m*

devil ['dɛvəl] *n* : diable *m* — **devilish** ['dɛvəlɪʃ] *adj* : diabolique

devious ['di:viəs] *adj* CRAFTY : sournois

devise [di'vaɪz] *vt* **-vised; -vising** : inventer, concevoir

devoid [di'vɔɪd] *adj* ~ **of** : dépourvu de

devote [di'vo:t] *vt* **-voted; -voting** : consacrer, dédier — **devoted** [di'vo:təd] *adj* : dévoué — **devotion** [di'vo:ʃən] *n* **1** DEDICATION : dévouement *m* **2** PIETY : dévotion *f*

devour [di'vaʊər] *vt* : dévorer

devout [di'vaʊt] *adj* **1** PIOUS : dévot **2** EARNEST : fervent

dew ['du:, 'dju:] *n* : rosée *f*

dexterity [dɛk'stɛrəṭi] *n, pl* **-ties** : dextérité *f*

diabetes [,daɪə'bi:ṭiz] *n* : diabète *m* — **diabetic** [,daɪə'bɛṭɪk] *adj* : diabétique — ~ *n* : diabétique *mf*

diabolic [,daɪə'bɑlɪk] *or* **diabolical** [-lɪkəl] *adj* : diabolique

diagnosis [,daɪɪg'no:sɪs] *n, pl* **-ses** [-'no:,si:z] : diagnostic *m* — **diagnose** ['daɪɪg,no:s, ,daɪɪg'no:s] *vt* **-nosed; -nosing** : diagnostiquer

diagonal [daɪ'ægənəl] *adj* : diagonal — **diagonally** [daɪ'ægənəli] *adv* : en diagonale

diagram ['daɪə,græm] *n* : diagramme *m*

dial ['daɪl] *n* : cadran *m* (d'une horloge), bouton *m* (d'une radio) — ~ *vt* **-aled** *or* **-alled; -aling** *or* **-alling** : faire, composer (un numéro de téléphone)

dialect ['daɪə,lɛkt] *n* : dialecte *m*

dialogue ['daɪə,lɔg] *n* : dialogue *m*

diameter [daɪ'æmətər] *n* : diamètre *m*

diamond ['daɪmənd, 'daɪə-] *n* **1** : diamant *m* **2** : losange *m* (forme géométrique) **3** : carreau *m* (aux cartes) **4** *or* **baseball** ~ : terrain *m* de baseball, losange *m* Can

diaper ['daɪpər, 'daɪə-] *n* : couche *f* (de bébé)

diaphragm ['daɪə,fræm] *n* : diaphragme *m*

diarrhea *or Brit* **diarrhoea** [,daɪə'ri:ə] *n* : diarrhée *f*

diary ['daɪəri:] *n, pl* **-ries** : journal *m* intime

dice ['daɪs] *ns & pl* : dé *m* (à jouer)

dictate ['dɪk,teɪt, dɪk'teɪt] *vt* **-tated; -tating** : dicter — **dictation** [dɪk'teɪʃən] *n* : dictée *f* — **dictator** ['dɪk,teɪtər] *n* : dictateur *m*

dictionary ['dɪkʃə,nɛri] *n, pl* **-naries** : dictionnaire *m*

did → do

die[1] ['daɪ] *vi* **died** ['daɪd]; **dying** ['daɪɪŋ] **1** : mourir, décéder **2** *or* ~ **down** SUBSIDE

: diminuer **3 be dying to** : mourir d'envie de

die² ['daɪ] *n, pl* **dice** ['daɪs] : dé *m* (à jouer)

diesel ['di:zəl, -səl] *n* : diesel *m*

diet ['daɪət] *n* **1** FOOD : alimentation *f* **2 go on a** ~ : être au régime — ~ *vi* : suivre un régime

differ ['dɪfər] *vi* **-ferred; -ferring** : différer — **difference** ['dɪfrənts, 'dɪfərənts] *n* : différence *f* — **different** ['dɪfrənt, 'dɪfərənt] *adj* : différent — **differentiate** [ˌdɪfə'rentʃi,eɪt] *v* **-ated; -ating** *vt* : différencier — *vi* ~ **between** : faire la différence entre — **differently** ['dɪfrəntli, 'dɪfərəntli] *adv* : différemment

difficult ['dɪfɪ,kʌlt] *adj* : difficile — **difficulty** ['dɪfɪ,kʌlti] *n, pl* **-ties** : difficulté *f*

dig ['dɪg] *vt* **dug** ['dʌg]; **digging 1** : creuser **2** ~ **up** : déterrer

digest ['daɪ,dʒest] *n* : résumé *m* — ~ ['daɪ-,dʒest] *vt* **1** : digérer **2** SUMMARIZE : résumer — **digestion** [daɪ'dʒestʃən, dɪ-] *n* : digestion *f* — **digestive** [daɪ'dʒestɪv, dɪ-] *adj* : digestif

digit ['dɪdʒət] *n* NUMERAL : chiffre *m* — **digital** ['dɪdʒətəl] *adj* : digital

dignity ['dɪgnəti] *n, pl* **-ties** : dignité *f* — **dignified** ['dɪgnə,faɪd] *adj* : digne

digress [daɪ'grɛs, də-] *vi* : s'écarter (du sujet)

dike ['daɪk] *n* : digue *f*

dilapidated [də'læpə,deɪtəd] *adj* : délabré

dilate [daɪ'leɪt, 'daɪ,leɪt] *v* **-lated; -lating** *vt* : dilater — *vi* : se dilater

dilemma [dɪ'lɛmə] *n* : dilemme *m*

diligence ['dɪlədʒənts] *n* : assiduité *f* — **diligent** ['dɪlədʒənt] *adj* : assidu, appliqué

dilute [daɪ'lu:t, də-] *vt* **-luted; -luting** : diluer

dim ['dɪm] *v* **dimmed; dimming** *vt* : baisser — *vi* : baisser, s'affaiblir — ~ *adj* **dimmer; dimmest 1** DARK : sombre **2** FAINT : faible, vague

dime ['daɪm] *n* : pièce *f* de dix cents

dimension [də'mentʃən, daɪ-] *n* : dimension *f*

diminish [də'mɪnɪʃ] *v* : diminuer

diminutive [də'mɪnjʊtɪv] *adj* : minuscule

dimple ['dɪmpəl] *n* : fossette *f*

din ['dɪn] *n* : vacarme *m*, tapage *m*

dine ['daɪn] *vi* **dined; dining** : dîner — **diner** ['daɪnər] *n* **1** : dîneur *m*, -neuse *f* **2** : petit restaurant *m* — **dining room** *n* : salle *f* à manger — **dinner** ['dɪnər] *n* : dîner *m*

dinosaur ['daɪnə,sɔr] *n* : dinosaure *m*

dip ['dɪp] *v* **dipped; dipping** *vt* : plonger, tremper — *vi* : baisser, descendre — ~ *n* **1** DROP : déclivité *f* **2** SWIM : petite baignade *f* **3** SAUCE : sauce *f*

diploma [də'plo:mə] *n* : diplôme *m*

diplomacy [də'plo:məsi] *n* : diplomatie *f* — **diplomat** ['dɪplə,mæt] *n* : diplomate *mf* — **diplomatic** [ˌdɪplə'mætɪk] *adj* **1** : diplomatique **2** TACTFUL : diplomate

dire ['daɪr] *adj* **direr; direst 1** : grave, terrible **2** EXTREME : extrême

direct [də'rɛkt, daɪ-] *vt* **1** : diriger **2** ORDER : ordonner — ~ *adj* **1** STRAIGHT : direct **2** FRANK : franc — ~ *adv* : directement — **direct current** *n* : courant *m* continu — **direction** [də'rɛkʃən, daɪ-] *n* **1** : direction *f* **2 ask for** ~**s** : demander des indications — **directly** [də'rɛktli, daɪ-] *adv* **1** STRAIGHT : directement **2** IMMEDIATELY : tout de suite — **director** [də'rɛktər, daɪ-] *n* **1** : directeur *m*, -trice *f* **2 board of** ~**s** : conseil *m* d'administration — **directory** [də'rɛktəri, daɪ-] *n, pl* **-ries** : annuaire *m* (téléphonique)

dirt ['dərt] *n* **1** : saleté *f* **2** SOIL : terre *f* — **dirty** ['dərti] *adj* **dirtier; -est 1** INDECENT : obscène, cochon *fam* — ~ *vt* **dirtied; dirtying** : salir

disability [ˌdɪsə'bɪləti] *n, pl* **-ties** : infirmité *f* — **disable** [dɪs'eɪbəl] *vt* **-abled; -abling** : rendre infirme — **disabled** [dɪs'eɪbəld] *adj* : handicapé, infirme

disadvantage [ˌdɪsəd'væntɪdʒ] *n* : désavantage *m*

disagree [ˌdɪsə'gri:] *vi* **1** : ne pas être d'accord (avec qqn) **2** CONFLICT : ne pas convenir — **disagreeable** [ˌdɪsə'gri:əbəl] *adj* : désagréable — **disagreement** [ˌdɪsə-'gri:mənt] *n* **1** : désaccord *m* **2** ARGUMENT : différend *m*

disappear [ˌdɪsə'pɪr] *vi* : disparaître — **disappearance** [ˌdɪsə'pi:rənts] *n* : disparition *f*

disappoint [ˌdɪsə'pɔɪnt] *vt* : décevoir — **disappointment** [ˌdɪsə'pɔɪntmənt] *n* : déception *f*

disapprove [ˌdɪsə'pru:v] *vi* **-proved; -proving** ~ **of** : désapprouver — **disapproval** [ˌdɪsə'pru:vəl] *n* : désapprobation *f*

disarm [dɪs'ɑrm] *v* : désarmer — **disarmament** [dɪs'ɑrməmənt] *n* : désarmement *m*

disarray [ˌdɪsə'reɪ] *n* : désordre *m*

disaster [dɪ'zæstər] *n* : désastre *m* — **disastrous** [dɪ'zæstrəs] *adj* : désastreux

disbelief [ˌdɪsbɪ'li:f] *n* : incrédulité *f*

disc → **disk**

discard [dɪs'kɑrd, 'dɪs,kɑrd] *vt* : se débarrasser de

discern [dɪ'sərn, -'zərn] *vt* : discerner — **discernible** [dɪ'sərnəbəl, -'zər-] *adj* : perceptible

discharge [dɪs'tʃɑrdʒ, 'dɪs,-] *vt* **-charged; -charging 1** UNLOAD : décharger **2** DISMISS : renvoyer **3** RELEASE : libérer — ~ ['dɪs-,tʃɑrdʒ, dɪs'-] *n* **1** : décharge *f* (électrique) **2** FLOW : écoulement *m* **3** DISMISSAL : renvoi *m* **4** RELEASE : libération *f*

disciple [dɪ'saɪpəl] *n* : disciple *mf*

discipline ['dɪsəplən] *n* : discipline *f* — ~ *vt* **-plined; -plining 1** PUNISH : punir **2** CONTROL : discipliner

disclose [dɪs'klo:z] *vt* **-closed; -closing** : révéler

discomfort [dɪs'kʌmfərt] *n* **1** : malaise *m* **2** UNEASINESS : gêne *f*

disconcert [ˌdɪskən'sərt] *vt* : déconcerter

disconnect [ˌdɪskə'nɛkt] *vt* : débrancher (un appareil électrique), couper (l'électricité, etc.)

discontinue [ˌdɪskən'tɪnˌju:] *vt* **-ued; -uing** : cesser, interrompre

discord ['dɪsˌkɔrd] *n* STRIFE : discorde *m*

discount ['dɪsˌkaʊnt, dɪs'-] *n* : rabais *m*, remise *f* — ~ *vt* : faire une remise de

discourage [dɪs'kərɪdʒ] *vt* **-aged; -aging** : décourager — **discouragement** [dɪs'kərɪdʒmənt] *n* : découragement *m*

discover [dɪs'kʌvər] *vt* : découvrir — **discovery** [dɪs'kʌvəri] *n, pl* **-eries** : découverte *f*

discredit [dɪs'krɛdət] *vt* : discréditer

discreet [dɪ'skri:t] *adj* : discret

discrepancy [dɪs'krɛpəntsi] *n, pl* **-cies** : divergence *f*

discretion [dɪs'krɛʃən] *n* : discrétion *f*

discriminate [dɪs'krɪməˌneɪt] *vi* **-nated; -nating 1** ~ **against** : être l'objet de discriminations **2** ~ **between** : distinguer entre — **discrimination** [dɪsˌkrɪmə'neɪʃən] *n* discrimination *f*, préjugés *mpl*

discuss [dɪs'kʌs] *vt* : discuter de, parler de — **discussion** [dɪs'kʌʃən] *n* : discussion *f*

disdain [dɪs'deɪn] *n* : dédain *m* — ~ *vt* : dédaigner

disease [dɪ'zi:z] *n* : maladie *f*

disembark [ˌdɪsɪm'bark] *vi* : débarquer

disengage [ˌdɪsɪn'geɪdʒ] *vt* **-gaged; -gaging 1** RELEASE : dégager **2** ~ **the clutch** : débrayer

disentangle [ˌdɪsɪn'tæŋgəl] *vt* **-gled; -gling** : démêler

disfigure [dɪs'fɪgjər] *vt* **-ured; -uring** : défigurer

disgrace [dɪs'skreɪs] *vt* **-graced; -gracing** : déshonorer — ~ *n* **1** DISHONOR : disgrâce *f* **2** SHAME : honte *f* — **disgraceful** [dɪ'skreɪsfəl] *adj* : honteux

disgruntled [dɪs'grʌntəld] *adj* : mécontent

disguise [dɪs'skaɪz] *vt* **-guised; -guising** : déguiser — ~ *n* : déguisement *m*

disgust [dɪs'skʌst] *n* : dégoût *m* — ~ *vt* : dégoûter — **disgusting** [dɪs'skʌstɪŋ] *adj* : écœurant, dégoûtant

dish ['dɪʃ] *n* **1** : assiette *f* **2** *or* **serving** ~ : plat *m* de service **3** ~**es** *npl* : vaisselle *f* — ~ *vt or* ~ **out** : servir — **dishcloth** ['dɪʃˌklɔθ] *n* : torchon *m* (à vaisselle), lavette *f*

dishearten [dɪs'hartən] *vt* : décourager

disheveled *or* **dishevelled** [dɪ'ʃɛvəld] *adj* : en désordre (se dit des vêtements, etc.)

dishonest [dɪ'sanəst] *adj* : malhonnête — **dishonesty** [dɪ'sanəsti] *n, pl* **-ties** : malhonnêteté *f*

dishonor [dɪ'sanər] *n* : déshonneur *m* — ~ *vt* : déshonorer — **dishonorable** [dɪ'sanərəbəl] *adj* : déshonorant

dishwasher ['dɪʃˌwɔʃər] *n* : lave-vaisselle *m*

disillusion [ˌdɪsə'lu:ʒən] *vt* : désillusionner — **disillusionment** [ˌdɪsə'lu:ʒənmənt] *n* : désillusion *f*

disinfect [ˌdɪsɪn'fɛkt] *vt* : désinfecter — **disinfectant** [ˌdɪsɪn'fɛktənt] *n* : désinfectant *m*

disintegrate [dɪs'ɪntəˌgreɪt] *vi* **-grated; -grating** : se désagréger, se désintégrer

disinterested [dɪs'ɪntərəstəd, -ˌrɛs-] *adj* : désintéressé

disjointed [dɪs'dʒɔɪntəd] *adj* : décousu, incohérent

disk *or* **disc** ['dɪsk] *n* : disque *m*

dislike [dɪs'laɪk] *n* : aversion *f*, antipathie *f* — ~ *vt* **-liked; -liking** : ne pas aimer

dislocate ['dɪsloˌkeɪt, dɪs'lo:-] *vt* **-cated; -cating** : se démettre, se luxer

dislodge [dɪs'ladʒ] *vt* **-lodged; -lodging** : déplacer, déloger

disloyal [dɪs'lɔɪəl] *adj* : déloyal — **disloyalty** [dɪs'lɔɪəlti] *n, pl* **-ties** : déloyauté *f*

dismal ['dɪzməl] *adj* : sombre, triste

dismantle [dɪs'mæntəl] *vt* **-tled; -tling** : démonter

dismay [dɪs'meɪ] *vt* : consterner — ~ *n* : consternation *f*

dismiss [dɪs'mɪs] *vt* **1** DISCHARGE : renvoyer, congédier **2** REJECT : ne pas tenir compte de — **dismissal** [dɪs'mɪsəl] *n* : renvoi *m*, licenciement *m*

disobey [ˌdɪsə'beɪ] *vt* : désobéir à — *vi* : désobéir — **disobedience** [ˌdɪsə'bi:diənts] *n* : désobéissance *f* — **disobedient** [-ənt] *adj* : désobéissant

disorder [dɪs'ɔrdər] *n* **1** : désordre *m* **2** AILMENT : troubles *mpl*, maladie *f* — **disorderly** [dɪs'ɔrdərli] *adj* : désordonné

disorganize [dɪs'ɔrgəˌnaɪz] *vt* **-nized; -nizing** : désorganiser

disown [dɪs'o:n] *vt* : renier

disparage [dɪs'pærɪdʒ] *vt* **-aged; -aging** : dénigrer

disparity [dɪs'pærəti] *n, pl* **-ties** : disparité *f*

dispatch [dɪs'pætʃ] *vt* : envoyer, expédier

dispel [dɪs'pɛl] *vt* **-pelled; -pelling** : dissiper

dispense [dɪs'pɛnts] *v* **-pensed; -pensing** *vt* : distribuer — *vi* ~ **with** : se passer de

disperse [dɪs'pərs] *v* **-persed; -persing** *vt* : disperser — *vi* : se disperser

display [dɪs'pleɪ] *vt* PRESENT : exposer — ~ *n* : exposition *f*, étalage *m*

dispose [dɪs'po:z] v **-posed; -posing** vt : disposer — vi ~ **of** : se débarrasser de — **disposable** [dɪs'po:zəbəl] adj : jetable — **disposal** [dɪs'po:zəl] n 1 : élimination f (de déchets) 2 **have at one's** ~ : avoir à sa disposition — **disposition** [ˌdɪspə'zɪʃən] n : TEMPERAMENT : caractère m

dispute [dɪs'pju:t] vt **-puted; -puting** : contester — ~ n : dispute f, conflit m

disqualify [dɪs'kwɑlə,faɪ] vt **-fied; -fying** : disqualifier

disregard [ˌdɪsrɪ'gɑrd] vt : ne pas tenir compte de — ~ n : indifférence f

disreputable [dɪs'rɛpjʊtəbəl] adj : mal famé

disrespect [ˌdɪsrɪ'spɛkt] n : manque m de respect — **disrespectful** [ˌdɪsrɪ'spɛktfəl] adj : irrespectueux

disrupt [dɪs'rʌpt] vt : perturber, déranger — **disruption** [dɪs'rʌpʃən] n : perturbation f

dissatisfied [dɪs'sæt̬əs,faɪd] adj : mécontent

disseminate [dɪ'sɛmə,neɪt] vt **-nated; -nating** : disséminer

dissent [dɪ'sɛnt] vi : différer, être en désaccord — ~ n : dissentiment m

dissertation [ˌdɪsər'teɪʃən] n THESIS : thèse f

dissipate ['dɪsə,peɪt] v **-pated; -pating** vt DISPERSE : dissiper — vi : se dissiper

dissolve [dɪ'zɑlv] v **-solved; -solving** vt : dissoudre — vi : se dissoudre

dissuade [dɪ'sweɪd] vt **-suaded; -suading** : dissuader

distance ['dɪstən̩s] n 1 : distance f 2 **in the** ~ : au loin — **distant** ['dɪstənt] adj : distant

distaste [dɪs'teɪst] n : dégoût m — **distasteful** [dɪs'teɪstfəl] adj : déplaisant, répugnant

distill or Brit **distil** [dɪ'stɪl] vt **-tilled; -tilling** : distiller

distinct [dɪ'stɪŋkt] adj 1 CLEAR : distinct 2 DEFINITE : net — **distinction** [dɪ'stɪŋkʃən] n : distinction f — **distinctive** [dɪ'stɪŋktɪv] adj : distinctif

distinguish [dɪ'stɪŋgwɪʃ] vt : distinguer — **distinguished** [dɪ'stɪŋgwɪʃt] adj : distingué

distort [dɪ'stɔrt] vt : déformer — **distortion** [dɪ'stɔrʃən] n : déformation f

distract [dɪ'strækt] vt : distraire — **distraction** [dɪ'strækʃən] n : distraction f

distraught [dɪ'strɔt] adj : éperdu

distress [dɪ'strɛs] n 1 : angoisse f, affliction f 2 **in** ~ : en détresse f — ~ vt : affliger — **distressing** [dɪ'strɛsɪŋ] adj : pénible

distribute [dɪ'strɪ,bju:t, -bjʊt] vt **-uted; -uting** : distribuer, répartir — **distribution** [ˌdɪstrə'bju:ʃən] n : distribution f — **distributor** [dɪ'strɪbjʊt̬ər] n : distributeur m

district ['dɪs,trɪkt] n 1 AREA : région f 2 : quartier m (d'une ville) 3 : district m (administratif)

distrust [dɪs'trʌst] n : méfiance f — ~ vt : se méfier de

disturb [dɪ'stərb] vt 1 BOTHER : déranger 2 WORRY : troubler, inquiéter — **disturbance** [dɪ'stərbən̩s] n **to cause a** ~ : faire du tapage

disuse [dɪs'ju:s] n **fall into** ~ : tomber en désuétude

ditch ['dɪtʃ] n : fossé m

dive ['daɪv] vi **dived** or **dove** ['do:v]; **dived; diving** : plonger — ~ n 1 : plongeon m 2 DESCENT : piqué m — **diver** ['daɪvər] n : plongeur m, -geuse f

diverge [də'vərdʒ, daɪ-] vi **-verged; -verging** : diverger

diverse [daɪ'vərs, də-, 'daɪ,vərs] adj : divers — **diversify** [daɪ'vərsə,faɪ, də-] vt **-fied; -fying** : diversifier

diversion [daɪ'vərʒən, də-] n 1 DEVIATION : déviation f 2 AMUSEMENT : divertissement m

diversity [daɪ'vərsət̬i, də-] n, pl **-ties** : diversité f

divert [də'vərt, daɪ-] vt 1 DEFLECT : détourner 2 AMUSE : divertir

divide [də'vaɪd] v **-vided; -viding** vt : diviser — vi : se diviser

dividend ['dɪvɪ,dɛnd, -dənd] n : dividende m

divine [də'vaɪn] adj **diviner; -est** : divin — **divinity** [də'vɪnət̬i] n, pl **-ties** : divinité f

division [dɪ'vɪʒən] n : division f

divorce [də'vors] n : divorce m — ~ vi **-vorced; -vorcing** : divorcer

divulge [də'vʌldʒ, daɪ-] vt **-vulged; -vulging** : divulguer

dizzy ['dɪzi] adj **dizzier; -est** : vertigineux — **dizziness** ['dɪzinəs] n : vertige m, étourdissement m

DNA [ˌdi:ˌɛn'eɪ] n (deoxyribonucleic acid) : ADN m

do ['du:] v **did** ['dɪd]; **done** ['dʌn]; **doing; does** ['dʌz] vt 1 : faire 2 PREPARE : préparer 3 ~ **one's hair** : se coiffer — vi 1 BEHAVE : faire 2 MANAGE : s'en sortir 3 SUFFICE : suffire 4 ~ **away with** : éliminer 5 **how are you doing?** : comment-vas-tu? — v aux 1 **does he work?** : travaille-t-il? 2 **I don't know** : je ne sais pas 3 ~ **be careful** : fais attention, je t'en prie 4 **he reads more than I** ~ : il lit plus que moi 5 **you know him, don't you?** : vous le connaissez, n'est-ce pas?

dock ['dɑk] n : dock m — ~ vi : se mettre à quai

doctor ['dɑktər] n 1 : docteur m (de droit, etc.) 2 PHYSICIAN : médecin m, docteur m

doctrine ['dɑktrɪn] n : doctrine f

document ['dɑkjʊmənt] n : document m — **documentary** [ˌdɑkjʊ'mɛntəri] n, pl **-ries** : documentaire m

dodge ['dɑdʒ] n : ruse f, truc m — ~ vt **dodged; dodging** : esquiver

doe ['do:] *n, pl* **does** *or* **doe** : biche *f*

does → **do**

doesn't ['dʌzɪnt] (*contraction of* **do not**) → **do**

dog ['dɔg, 'dɑg] *n* : chien *m* — ~ *vt* **dogged; dogging** : poursuivre — **dogged** ['dɔgəd] *adj* : tenace

dogma ['dɔgmə] *n* : dogme *m*

doldrums ['do:ldrəmz, 'dɑl-] *npl* **be in the** ~ : être dans le marasme

doll ['dɑl, 'dɔl] *n* : poupée *f*

dollar ['dɑlər] *n* : dollar *m*

dolphin ['dɑlfən, 'dɔl-] *n* : dauphin *m*

domain [do'meɪn, də-] *n* : domaine *m*

dome ['do:m] *n* : dôme *m*

domestic [də'mɛstɪk] *adj* **1** FAMILY : familial **2** HOUSEHOLD : ménager, domestique **3** INTERNAL : intérieur, du pays — ~ *n* SERVANT : domestique *mf* — **domesticate** [də'mɛstɪˌkeɪt] *vt* **-cated; -cating** : domestiquer

dominant ['dɑmənənt] *adj* : dominant — **dominate** ['dɑməˌneɪt] *v* **-nated; -nating** : dominer — **domineer** [ˌdɑmə'nɪr] *vi* : se montrer autoritaire

donate ['do:ˌneɪt, do:'-] *vt* **-nated; -nating** : faire (un) don de — **donation** [do:'neɪʃən] *n* : don *m*, donation *f*

done ['dʌn] → **do** — ~ *adj* **1** FINISHED : fini, terminé **2** COOKED : cuit

donkey ['dɑŋki, 'dʌŋ] *n, pl* **-keys** : âne *m*

donor ['do:nər] *n* **1** : donateur *m*, -trice *f* **2** **blood** ~ : donneur *m*, -neuse *f* de sang

don't ['do:nt] (*contraction of* **do not**) → **do**

doodle ['du:dəl] *v* **-dled; -dling** : gribouiller

doom ['du:m] *n* : perte *f*, ruine *f* — ~ *vt* : vouer, condamner

door ['dor] *n* **1** : porte *f* **2** : portière *f* (d'une voiture) **3** ENTRANCE : entrée *f* — **doorbell** ['dor,bɛl] *n* : sonnette *f* — **doorknob** ['dor,nɑb] *n* : bouton *m* de porte — **doormat** ['dor,mæt] *n* : paillasson *m* — **doorstep** ['dor,stɛp] *n* : pas *m* de la porte — **doorway** ['dor,weɪ] *n* : porte *f*, embrasure *f* (de la porte)

dope ['do:p] *n* **1** DRUG : drogue *f* **2** IDIOT : imbécile *mf*

dormitory ['dɔrməˌtori] *n, pl* **-ries** : dortoir *m*

dose ['do:s] *n* : dose *f* — **dosage** ['do:sɪdʒ] *n* : posologie *f*

dot ['dɑt] *n* **1** POINT : point *m* **2** **on the** ~ : pile *fam*

dote ['do:t] *vi* **doted; doting** ~ **on** : adorer

double ['dʌbəl] *adj* : double — ~ *v* **-bled; -bling** *vt* **1** : doubler **2** FOLD : plier (en deux) — *vi* : doubler — ~ *adv* **1** : deux fois **2 see** ~ : voir double — ~ *n* : double *m* — **double bass** *n* : contrebasse *f* — **doubly** ['dʌbli] *adv* : doublement, deux fois plus

doubt ['daʊt] *vt* **1** : douter **2** DISTRUST : douter de — ~ *n* : doute *m* — **doubtful** ['daʊtfəl] *adj* : douteux

dough ['do:] *n* : pâte *f* (en cuisine) — **doughnut** ['do:ˌnʌt] *n* : beignet *m*, beigne *m* *Can*

douse ['daʊs, 'daʊz] *vt* **doused; dousing 1** DRENCH : tremper **2** EXTINGUISH : éteindre

dove¹ ['do:v] → **dive**

dove² ['dʌv] *n* : colombe *f*

down ['daʊn] *adv* **1** DOWNWARD : en bas, vers le bas **2 fall** ~ : tomber **3 go** ~ : descendre — ~ *prep* **1** : en bas de **2** ALONG : le long de — ~ *adj* **1** : qui descend **2** DOWNCAST : déprimé, abattu — ~ *n* : duvet *m* — **downcast** ['daʊnˌkæst] *adj* : abattu — **downfall** ['daʊnˌfɔl] *n* : chute *f* — **downhearted** [ˌdaʊn'hɑrtəd] *adj* : découragé — **downhill** ['daʊn'hɪl] *adv* **go** ~ : descendre — **download** ['daʊnˌlo:d] *vt* : télécharger (en informatique) — **down payment** *n* : acompte *m* — **downpour** ['daʊnˌpor] *n* : averse *f* — **downright** ['daʊnˌraɪt] *adv* : carrément — ~ *adj* : véritable, catégorique — **downstairs** [*adv* 'daʊn'stærz, *adj* 'daʊnˌstærz] *adv & adj* : en bas — **downstream** ['daʊn'stri:m] *adv* : en aval — **down-to-earth** [ˌdaʊntu'ərθ] *adj* : terre à terre — **downtown** [ˌdaʊn'taʊn, 'daʊnˌtaʊn] *n* : centre-ville *m* — ~ [ˌdaʊn'taʊn] *adv* : en ville — **downward** ['daʊnwərd] *or* **downwards** [-wərdz] *adv* : en bas, vers le bas — **downward** *adj* : vers le bas

doze ['do:z] *vi* **dozed; dozing** : sommeiller, somnoler

dozen ['dʌzən] *n, pl* **-ens** *or* **-en** : douzaine *f*

drab ['dræb] *adj* **drabber; drabbest** : terne

draft ['dræft, 'drɑft] *n* **1** : courant *m* d'air **2** *or* **rough** ~ : brouillon *m* **3** : conscription *f* (militaire) **4** *or* **bank** ~ : traite *f* bancaire **5** *or* ~ **beer** : bière *f* pression — ~ *vt* **1** OUTLINE : faire le brouillon de **2** : appeler (des soldats) sous les drapeaux — **drafty** ['dræfti] *adj* **draftier; -est** : plein de courants d'air

drag ['dræg] *v* **dragged; dragging** *vt* **1** HAUL : tirer **2** : traîner (les pieds, etc.) **3** : glisser (en informatique) — *vi* TRAIL : traîner — ~ *n* **1** RESISTANCE : résistance *f* (aérodynamique) **2 what a** ~! : quelle barbe!

dragon ['drægən] *n* : dragon *m* — **dragonfly** ['drægənˌflaɪ] *n, pl* **-flies** : libellule *f*

drain ['dreɪn] *vt* **1** EMPTY : vider, drainer **2** EXHAUST : épuiser — *vi* : s'écouler, s'égoutter (se dit de la vaisselle) — ~ *n* **1** : tuyau *m* d'écoulement **2** SEWER : égout *m* **3** DEPLETION : épuisement *m* — **drainage** ['dreɪnɪdʒ] *n* : drainage *m* — **drainpipe** ['dreɪnˌpaɪp] *n* : tuyau *m* d'écoulement

drama ['drɑmə, 'dræ-] *n* : drame *m* — **dra-**

matic [drə'mætɪk] *adj* : dramatique —
dramatize ['dræmə,taɪz, 'drɑ-] *vt* **-tized;
-tizing** : dramatiser

drank → drink

drape ['dreɪp] *vt* **draped; draping** : draper
— **drapes** *npl* CURTAINS : rideaux *mpl*

drastic ['dræstɪk] *adj* : sévère, énergique

draught ['dræft, 'drɑft] → **draft**

draw ['drɔ] *v* **drew** ['dru:]; **drawn** ['drɑʊn];
drawing ['drɔɪŋ] *vt* **1** PULL : tirer **2** AT-
TRACT : attirer **3** SKETCH : dessiner **4**
MAKE : faire (une distinction, etc.) **5** *or ~
up* FORMULATE : rédiger — *vi* **1** SKETCH
: dessiner **2** *~ near* : approcher — *~ n* **1**
DRAWING : tirage *m* (au sort) **2** TIE : match
m nul **3** ATTRACTION : attraction *f* — **drawback** ['drɔ,bæk] *n* : inconvénient *m* —
drawer ['drɔr, 'drɔər] *n* : tiroir *m* — **drawing** ['drɔɪŋ] *n* **1** SKETCH : dessin *m* **2** LOT-
TERY : tirage *m* (au sort)

drawl ['drɔl] *n* : voix *f* traînante

dread ['drɛd] *vt* : redouter, craindre — *~ n*
: crainte *f*, terreur *f* — **dreadful** ['drɛdfəl]
adj : affreux, épouvantable

dream ['dri:m] *n* : rêve *m* — *~ v* **dreamed**
['dri:md] *or* **dreamt** ['drɛmpt]; **dreaming**
: rêver — **dreamer** ['dri:mər] *n* : rêveur *m*,
-veuse *f* — **dreamy** ['dri:mi] *adj* **dreamier;
-est** : rêveur

dreary ['drɪri] *adj* **drearier; -est** : morne,
sombre

dredge ['drɛdʒ] *vt* **dredged; dredging** : draguer

dregs ['drɛgz] *npl* : lie *f*

drench ['drɛntʃ] *vt* : tremper

dress ['drɛs] *vt* **1** CLOTHE : habiller, vêtir **2**
: assaisonner (une salade) **3** BANDAGE
: panser (une blessure) — *vi* **1** : s'habiller **2**
or ~ up : se mettre en grande toilette **3** *~
up as* : se déguiser en — *~ n* **1** CLOTHING
: tenue *f* **2** : robe *f* (de femme) — **dresser**
['drɛsər] *n* : commode *f* à miroir — **dressing** ['drɛsɪŋ] *n* **1** SAUCE : sauce *f*, vinaigrette
f **2** BANDAGE : pansement *m* — **dressmaker**
['drɛs,meɪkər] *n* : couturière *f* — **dressy**
['drɛsi] *adj* **dressier; -est** : habillé, élégant

drew → draw

dribble ['drɪbəl] *vi* **-bled; -bling 1** TRICKLE
: tomber goutte à goutte **2** DROOL : baver **3**
: dribbler (aux sports) — *~ n* **1** TRICKLE
: filet *m* **2** DROOL : bave *f*

drier, driest → dry

drift ['drɪft] *n* **1** MOVEMENT : mouvement *m*
2 HEAP : banc *m* (de neige) *Can* — *~ vi* **1**
: dériver (sur l'eau), être emporté (par le
vent) **2** ACCUMULATE : s'amonceler

drill ['drɪl] *n* **1** : perceuse *f* (outil) **2** EXER-
CISE : exercice *m* — *~ vt* **1** : percer, forer
2 TRAIN : entraîner

drink ['drɪŋk] *v* **drank** ['dræŋk]; **drunk**

['drʌŋk] *or* **drank; drinking** : boire — *~ n*
: boisson *f*

drip ['drɪp] *vi* **dripped; dripping** : tomber
goutte à goutte, dégoutter — *~ n* DROP
: goutte *f*

drive ['draɪv] *v* **drove** ['dro:v]; **driven**
['drɪvən]; **driving** *vt* **1** : conduire **2** COM-
PEL : inciter — *vi* : conduire, rouler — *~ n*
1 : promenade *f* (en voiture) **2** CAMPAIGN
: campagne *f* **3** VIGOR : énergie *f* **4** NEED
: besoin *m* fondamental

driver ['draɪvər] *n* **1** : conducteur *m*, -trice *f*
2 CHAUFFEUR : chauffeur *m*

driveway ['draɪv,weɪ] *n* : allée *f*, entrée *f* (de
garage)

drizzle ['drɪzəl] *n* : bruine *f* — *~ vi* **-zled;
-zling** : bruiner

drone ['dro:n] *n* **1** BEE : abeille *f* mâle **2**
HUM : bourdonnement *m* — *~ vi* **droned;
droning 1** BUZZ : bourdonner **2** *or ~ on*
: parler d'un ton monotone

drool ['dru:l] *vi* : baver — *~ n* : bave *f*

droop ['dru:p] *vi* : pencher, tomber

drop ['drɑp] *n* **1** : goutte *f* (de liquide) **2** DE-
CLINE, FALL : baisse *f* **3** DESCENT : chute *f* —
~ v **dropped; dropping** *vt* **1** : laisser
tomber **2** LOWER : baisser **3** ABANDON
: abandonner **4** *~ off* LEAVE : déposer — *vi*
1 FALL : tomber **2** DECREASE : baisser **3** *~
by* : passer

drought ['draʊt] *n* : sécheresse *f*

drove ['dro:v] → **drive**

droves ['dro:vz] *npl in ~* : en masse

drown ['draʊn] *vt* : noyer — *vi* : se noyer

drowsy ['draʊzi] *adj* **drowsier; -est** : somnolent — **drowsiness** ['draʊzinəs] *n* : somnolence *f*

drudgery ['drʌdʒəri] *n, pl* **-eries** : corvée *f*

drug ['drʌg] *n* **1** MEDICATION : médicament
m **2** NARCOTIC : drogue *f*, stupéfiant *m* —
~ vt **drugged; drugging** : droguer —
drugstore ['drʌg,stor] *n* : pharmacie *f*

drum ['drʌm] *n* **1** : tambour *m* **2** *or oil ~*
: bidon *m* — *~ v* **drummed; drumming** *vi*
: jouer du tambour — *vt* : tambouriner —
drumstick ['drʌm,stɪk] *n* **1** : baguette *f* de
tambour **2** : pilon *m* (de poulet)

drunk ['drʌŋk] → **drink** — *~ adj* : ivre —
~ or **drunkard** ['drʌŋkərd] *n* : ivrogne *m*,
ivrognesse *f* — **drunken** ['drʌŋkən] *adj*
: ivre

dry ['draɪ] *adj* **drier; driest** : sec — *~ v*
dried; drying *vt* **1** : sécher **2** WIPE : essuyer — *vi* : sécher — **dry-clean** ['draɪ-
,kli:n] *vt* : nettoyer à sec — **dry cleaner** *n*
: teinturerie *f* — **dryer** ['draɪər] *n* : séchoir
m — **dryness** ['draɪnəs] *n* : sécheresse *f*

dual ['du:əl, 'dju:-] *adj* : double

dub ['dʌb] *vt* **dubbed; dubbing** : doubler
(un film, etc.)

dubious ['du:biəs, 'dju:-] *adj* **1** DOUBTFUL : douteux **2** QUESTIONABLE : suspect

duck ['dʌk] *n, pl* **ducks** *or* **duck** : canard *m* — ~ *vt* **1** PLUNGE : plonger **2** LOWER : baisser **3** AVOID, DODGE : éviter, esquiver — **duckling** ['dʌklɪŋ] *n* : caneton *m*

duct ['dʌkt] *n* : conduit *m*

due ['du:, 'dju:] *adj* **1** PAYABLE : dû, payable **2** APPROPRIATE : qui convient **3** EXPECTED : attendu **4** ~ **to** : en raison de — ~ *n* **1** : dû *m* **2** ~**s** *npl* FEE : cotisation *f* — ~ *adv* : plein, droit vers

duel ['du:əl, 'dju:-] *n* : duel *m*

duet [du:'ɛt, dju:-] *n* : duo *m*

dug → **dig**

duke ['du:k, 'dju:k] *n* : duc *m*

dull ['dʌl] *adj* **1** STUPID : stupide **2** BLUNT : émoussé **3** BORING : ennuyeux **4** LACKLUSTER : terne — ~ *vt* **1** BLUNT : émousser **2** DIM, TARNISH : ternir

duly ['du:li] *adv* **1** PROPERLY : dûment **2** EXPECTEDLY : comme prévu

dumb ['dʌm] *adj* **1** MUTE : muet **2** STUPID : bête

dumbfound *or* **dumfound** [ˌdʌm'faʊnd] *vt* : abasourdir

dummy ['dʌmi] *n, pl* **-mies** **1** FOOL : imbécile *mf* **2** MANNEQUIN : mannequin *m* — ~ *adj* : faux

dump ['dʌmp] *vt* : déposer, jeter — ~ *n* **1** : décharge *f* (publique) **2 down in the** ~**s** : déprimé

dune ['du:n, 'dju:n] *n* : dune *f*

dung ['dʌŋ] *n* : fumier *m*

dungeon ['dʌndʒən] *n* : cachot *m*

dunk ['dʌŋk] *vt* : tremper

duo ['du:o:, 'dju:-] *n, pl* **duos** : duo *m*

dupe ['du:p, 'dju:p] *n* : dupe *f* — ~ *vt* **duped; duping** : duper

duplex ['du:ˌplɛks, 'dju:-] *n* : duplex *m*, maison *f* jumelée

duplicate ['du:plɪkət, 'dju:-] *adj* : en double — ~ ['du:plɪˌkeɪt, 'dju:-] *vt* **-cated; -cating** : faire un double de, copier — ~ ['du:plɪkət, 'dju:-] *n* : double *m*

durable ['dʊrəbəl, 'djʊr-] *adj* : durable, résistant

duration [dʊ'reɪʃən, djʊ-] *n* : durée *f*

during ['dʊrɪŋ, 'djʊr-] *prep* : pendant

dusk ['dʌsk] *n* : crépuscule *m*

dust ['dʌst] *n* : poussière *f* — ~ *vt* **1** : épousseter **2** SPRINKLE : saupoudrer — **dustpan** ['dʌstˌpæn] *n* : pelle *f* à poussière — **dusty** ['dʌsti] *adj* **dustier; -est** : poussiéreux

duty ['du:ti, 'dju:-] *n, pl* **-ties** **1** TASK : fonction *f* **2** OBLIGATION : devoir *m* **3** TAX : taxe *f*, droit *m* — **dutiful** ['du:tɪfəl, 'dju:-] *adj* : obéissant

dwarf ['dwɔrf] *n* : nain *m*, naine *f*

dwell ['dwɛl] *vi* **dwelled** *or* **dwelt** ['dwɛlt]; **dwelling** **1** RESIDE : demeurer **2** ~ **on** : penser sans cesse à — **dweller** ['dwɛlər] *n* : habitant *m*, -tante *f* — **dwelling** ['dwɛlɪŋ] *n* : habitation *f*

dwindle ['dwɪndəl] *vi* **-dled; -dling** : diminuer

dye ['daɪ] *n* : teinture *f* — ~ *vt* **dyed; dyeing** : teindre

dying → **die**[1]

dynamic [daɪ'næmɪk] *adj* : dynamique

dynamite ['daɪnəˌmaɪt] *n* : dynamite *f* — ~ *vt* **-mited; -miting** : dynamiter

dynasty ['daɪnəsti, -næs-] *n, pl* **-ties** : dynastie *f*

E

e ['i:] *n, pl* **e's** *or* **es** ['i:z] : e *m*, cinquième lettre de l'alphabet

each ['i:tʃ] *adj* : chaque — ~ *pron* **1** : chacun *m*, -cune *f* **2** ~ **other** : l'un l'autre **3 they love** ~ **other** : ils s'aiment — ~ *adv* : chacun, par personne

eager ['i:gər] *adj* **1** ENTHUSIASTIC : avide **2** IMPATIENT : impatient — **eagerness** ['i:gərnəs] *n* : enthousiasme *m*, empressement *m*

eagle ['i:gəl] *n* : aigle *m*

ear ['ɪr] *n* **1** : oreille *f* **2** ~ **of corn** : épi *m* de maïs — **eardrum** ['ɪrˌdrʌm] *n* : tympan *m*

earl ['ərl] *n* : comte *m*

earlobe ['ɪrˌlo:b] *n* : lobe *m* de l'oreille

early ['ərli] *adv* **-lier; -est** **1** : tôt, de bonne heure **2 as** ~ **as possible** : le plus tôt possible **3 ten minutes** ~ : en avance de dix minutes — ~ *adj* **-lier; -est** **1** FIRST : premier **2** ANCIENT : ancien **3 in the** ~ **afternoon** : au début de l'après-midi

earmark ['ɪrˌmɑrk] *vt* : réserver, désigner

earn ['ərn] *vt* **1** : gagner **2** DESERVE : mériter

earnest ['ərnəst] *adj* : sérieux — ~ *n* **in** ~ : sérieusement

earnings ['ərnɪŋz] *npl* **1** WAGES : salaire *m* **2** PROFITS : gains *mpl*

earphone ['ɪr,foːn] *n* : écouteur *m*

earring ['ɪr,rɪŋ] *n* : boucle *f* d'oreille

earshot ['ɪr,ʃat] *n* within ~ : à portée de voix

earth ['ərθ] *n* 1 GROUND : terre *f*, sol *m* 2 **the Earth** : la terre — **earthly** ['ərθli] *adj* : terrestre — **earthquake** ['ərθ,kweɪk] *n* : tremblement *m* de terre — **earthworm** ['ərθ,wərm] *n* : ver *m* de terre — **earthy** ['ərθi] *adj* **earthier; earthiest** : terreux

ease ['iːz] *n* 1 FACILITY : facilité *f* 2 COMFORT : bien-être *m* 3 **feel at** ~ : être à l'aise — ~ *v* **eased; easing** *vt* 1 FACILITATE : faciliter 2 ALLEVIATE : soulager, réduire — *vi* ~ **up** : s'atténuer

easel ['iːzəl] *n* : chevalet *m*

easily ['iːzəli] *adv* 1 : facilement 2 UNQUESTIONABLY : de loin

east ['iːst] *adv* : vers l'est, à l'est — ~ *adj* : est — ~ *n* 1 : est *m* 2 **the East** : l'Est *m*, l'Orient *m*

Easter ['iːstər] *n* : Pâques *m*, Pâques *fpl*

easterly ['iːstərli] *adv* : vers l'est — ~ *adj* : d'est, de l'est

eastern ['iːstərn] *adj* : est, de l'est 2 **Eastern** : de l'Est, oriental

easy ['iːzi] *adj* **easier; easiest** 1 : facile, aisé 2 RELAXED : décontracté — **easygoing** [,iːzi'goːɪŋ] *adj* : accommodant

eat ['iːt] *v* **ate** ['eɪt]; **eaten** ['iːtən]; **eating** : manger

eaves ['iːvz] *npl* : avant-toit *m* — **eavesdrop** ['iːvz,drap] *vi* **-dropped; -dropping** : écouter aux portes

ebb ['ɛb] *n* : reflux *m* — ~ *vi* 1 : refluer 2 DECLINE : décliner

ebony ['ɛbəni] *n, pl* **-nies** : ébène *f*

eccentric [ɪk'sɛntrɪk] *adj* : excentrique — ~ *n* : excentrique *mf* — **eccentricity** [,ɛk,sɛn'trɪsəti] *n, pl* **-ties** : excentricité *f*

echo ['ɛ,koː] *n, pl* **echoes** : écho *m* — ~ *v* **echoed; echoing** *vt* : répéter — *vi* : se répercuter, résonner

eclipse [ɪ'klɪps] *n* : éclipse *f*

ecology [i'kalədʒi, ɛ-] *n, pl* **-gies** : écologie *f* — **ecological** [,iːkə'ladʒɪkəl, ,ɛkə-] *adj* : écologique

economy [i'kanəmi] *n, pl* **-mies** : économie *f* — **economic** [,iːkə'namɪk, ,ɛkə-] *adj* : économique — **economical** [,iːkə'namɪkəl, ,ɛkə-] *adj* THRIFTY : économe — **economics** [,iːkə'namɪks, ,ɛkə-] *ns & pl* : sciences *fpl* économiques, économie *f* — **economist** [i'kanəmɪst] *n* : économiste *mf* — **economize** [i'kanə,maɪz] *v* **-mized; -mizing** : économiser

ecstasy ['ɛkstəsi] *n, pl* **-sies** : extase *f* — **ecstatic** [ɛk'stætɪk, ɪk-] *adj* : extatique

edge ['ɛdʒ] *n* 1 BORDER : bord *m* 2 : tranchant *m* (d'un couteau, etc.) 3 ADVANTAGE : avantage *m* — ~ *vi* : avancer lentement — **edgewise** ['ɛdʒ,waɪz] *adv* : de côté — **edgy** ['ɛdʒi] *adj* **edgier; edgiest** : énervé

edible ['ɛdəbəl] *adj* : comestible

edit ['ɛdɪt] *vt* 1 : réviser, corriger 2 ~ **out** : couper — **edition** [ɪ'dɪʃən] *n* : édition *f* — **editor** ['ɛdɪtər] *n* : rédacteur *m*, -trice *f* (d'un journal); éditeur *m*, -trice *f* (d'un livre) — **editorial** [,ɛdɪ'toriəl] *n* : éditorial *m*

educate ['ɛdʒə,keɪt] *vt* **-cated; -cating** : instruire, éduquer — **education** [,ɛdʒə'keɪʃən] *n* 1 : éducation *f*, études *fpl* 2 TEACHING : enseignement *m*, instruction *f* — **educational** [,ɛdʒə'keɪʃənəl] *adj* 1 : éducatif 2 TEACHING : pédagogique — **educator** ['ɛdʒə,keɪtər] *n* : éducateur *m*, -trice *f*

eel ['iːl] *n* : anguille *f*

eerie ['ɪri] *adj* **eerier; -est** : étrange

effect [ɪ'fɛkt] *n* 1 : effet *m* 2 **go into** ~ : entrer en vigueur — ~ *vt* : effectuer, réaliser — **effective** [ɪ'fɛktɪv] *adj* 1 : efficace 2 **become** ~ : entrer en vigueur — **effectiveness** [ɪ'fɛktɪvnəs] *n* : efficacité *f*

effeminate [ə'fɛmənət] *adj* : efféminé

efficient [ɪ'fɪʃənt] *adj* : efficace — **efficiency** [ɪ'fɪʃəntsi] *n pl* **-cies** : efficacité *f*

effort ['ɛfərt] *n* 1 : effort *m* 2 **it's not worth the** ~ : ça ne vaut pas la peine — **effortless** ['ɛfərtləs] *adj* : facile

egg ['ɛg] *n* : œuf *m* — **eggplant** ['ɛg,plænt] *n* : aubergine *f* — **eggshell** ['ɛg,ʃɛl] *n* : coquille *f* d'œuf

ego ['iː,goː] *n, pl* **egos** 1 SELF : moi *m* 2 SELF-ESTEEM : amour-propre *m* — **egotism** ['iːgə,tɪzəm] *n* : égotisme *m* — **egotistic** [,iːgə'tɪstɪk] *or* **egotistical** [-'tɪstɪkəl] *adj* : égocentrique

Egyptian [i'dʒɪpʃən] *adj* : égyptien

eight ['eɪt] *n* : huit *m* — ~ *adj* : huit — **eighteen** [eɪt'tiːn] *n* : dix-huit *m* — ~ *adj* : dix-huit — **eighteenth** [eɪt'tiːnθ] *n* 1 : dix-huitième *mf* 2 October ~ : le dix-huit octobre — ~ *adj* : dix-huitième — **eighth** ['eɪtθ] *n* 1 : huitième *mf* 2 February ~ : le huit février — ~ *adj* : huitième — **eight hundred** *adj* : huit cents — **eightieth** [eɪtiəθ] *n* : quatre-vingtième *mf* — ~ *adj* : quatre-vingtième — **eighty** [eɪti] *n, pl* **eighties** : quatre-vingts *m* — ~ *adj* : quatre-vingts

either ['iːðər, 'aɪ-] *adj* 1 : l'un ou l'autre 2 EACH : chaque — ~ *pron* : l'un ou l'autre, n'importe lequel — ~ *conj* 1 : ou, soit 2 *(in negative constructions)* : ni

eject [i'dʒɛkt] *vt* : éjecter, expulser

elaborate [i'læbərət] *adj* 1 DETAILED : détaillé 2 COMPLEX : compliqué — ~ [i'læbə,reɪt] *v* **-rated; -rating** *vt* : élaborer — *vi* ~ **on** : donner des détails sur

elapse [i'læps] *vi* **elapsed; elapsing** : s'écouler

elastic [i'læstik] *adj* : élastique — ~ *n* : élastique *m* — **elasticity** [i,læs'tisəti, ,i:,læs-] *n, pl* **-ties** : élasticité *f*

elated [i'leitəd] *adj* : fou de joie — **elation** [i'leiʃən] *n* : allégresse *f*, joie *f*

elbow ['ɛl,boː] *n* : coude *m*

elder ['ɛldər] *adj* : aîné, plus âgé — ~ *n* : aîné *m*, aînée *f* — **elderly** ['ɛldərli] *adj* : âgé

elect [i'lɛkt] *vt* : élire — ~ *adj* : élu, futur — **election** [i'lɛkʃən] *n* : élection *f* — **electoral** [i'lɛktərəl] *adj* : électoral — **electorate** [i'lɛktərət] *n* : électorat *m*

electricity [i,lɛk'trisəti] *n, pl* **-ties** : électricité *f* — **electric** [i'lɛktrik] *or* **electrical** [-trikəl] *adj* : électrique — **electrician** [i,lɛk'triʃən] *n* : électricien *m*, -cienne *f* — **electrocute** [i'lɛktrə,kjuːt] *vt* **-cuted; -cuting** : électrocuter

electron [i'lɛk,tran] *n* : électron *m* — **electronic** [i,lɛk'tranik] *adj* : électronique — **electronic mail** *n* : courrier *m* électronique — **electronics** [i,lɛk'traniks] *n* : électronique *f*

elegant ['ɛligənt] *adj* : élégant — **elegance** ['ɛligənts] *n* : élégance *f*

element ['ɛlə,mənt] *n* **1** : élément *m* **2** ~**s** *npl* BASICS : rudiments *mpl* — **elementary** [,ɛlə'mɛntri] *adj* : élémentaire — **elementary school** *n* : école *f* primaire

elephant ['ɛləfənt] *n* : éléphant *m*

elevate ['ɛlə,veit] *vt* **-vated; -vating** : élever — **elevator** ['ɛlə,veitər] *n* : ascenseur *m*

eleven [i'lɛvən] *n* : onze *m* — ~ *adj* : onze — **eleventh** [i'lɛvəntθ] *n* **1** : onzième *mf* **2 March** ~ : le onze mars — ~ *adj* : onzième

elf ['ɛlf] *n, pl* **elves** ['ɛlvz] : lutin *m*

elicit [i'lisət] *vt* : provoquer

eligible ['ɛlədʒəbəl] *adj* : éligible, admissible

eliminate [i'limə,neit] *vt* **-nated; -nating** : éliminer — **elimination** [i,limə'neiʃən] *n* : élimination *f*

elite [ei'liːt, i-] *n* : élite *f*

elk ['ɛlk] *n* : élan *m* (d'Europe), wapiti *m* (d'Amérique)

elm ['ɛlm] *n* : orme *m*

elongate [i'lɔŋ,geit] *vt* **-gated; -gating** : allonger

elope [i'loːp] *vi* **eloped; eloping** : s'enfuir (pour se marier) — **elopement** [i'loːpmənt] *n* : fugue *f* amoureuse

eloquence ['ɛlə,kwənts] *n* : éloquence *f* — **eloquent** ['ɛlə,kwənt] *adj* : éloquent

else ['ɛls] *adv* **or** ~ : sinon, autrement — ~ *adj* **1 everyone** ~ : tous les autres **2 what** ~ : quoi d'autre — **elsewhere** ['ɛls,hwɛr] *adv* : ailleurs

elude [i'luːd] *vt* **eluded; eluding** : échapper à, éluder — **elusive** [i'luːsiv] *adj* : insaisissable

elves → **elf**

e-mail ['iː,meil] *n* : courriel *m*, e-mail *m France*

emanate ['ɛmə,neit] *vi* **-nated; -nating** : émaner

emancipate [i'mæntsə,peit] *vt* **-pated; -pating** : émanciper

embalm [im'bam, ɛm-, -'balm] *vt* : embaumer

embankment [im'bæŋkmənt, ɛm-] *n* : digue *f* (d'une rivière), remblai *m* (d'une route)

embargo [im'bargo, ɛm-] *n, pl* **-goes** : embargo *m*

embark [im'bark, ɛm-] *vt* : embarquer — *vi* ~ **on** : entreprendre

embarrass [im'bærəs, ɛm-] *vt* : gêner, embarrasser — **embarrassing** [im'bærəsiŋ, ɛm-] *adj* : embarrassant — **embarrassment** [im'bærəsmənt, ɛm-] *n* : gêne *f*, embarras *m*

embassy ['ɛmbəsi] *n, pl* **-sies** : ambassade *f*

embed [im'bɛd, ɛm-] *vt* **-bedded; -bedding** : enfoncer

embellish [im'bɛliʃ, ɛm-] *vt* : embellir — **embellishment** [im'bɛliʃmənt, ɛm-] *n* : ornement *m*

embers ['ɛmbərz] *npl* : braise *f*

embezzle [im'bɛzəl, ɛm-] *vt* **-zled; -zling** : détourner — **embezzlement** [im'bɛzəlmənt, ɛm-] *n* : détournement *m* de fonds

emblem ['ɛmbləm] *n* : emblème *m*

embody [im'badi, ɛm-] *vt* **-bodied; -bodying** : incarner

embrace [im'breis, ɛm-] *v* **-braced; -bracing** *vt* : embrasser — *vi* : s'embrasser — ~ *n* : étreinte *f*

embroider [im'brɔidər, ɛm-] *vt* : broder — **embroidery** [im'brɔidəri, ɛm-] *n, pl* **-deries** : broderie *f*

embryo ['ɛmbri,oː] *n* : embryon *m*

emerald ['ɛmrəld, 'ɛmə-] *n* : émeraude *f*

emerge [i'mərdʒ] *vi* **emerged; emerging 1** APPEAR : apparaître **2** ~ **from** : émerger de — **emergence** [i'mərdʒənts] *n* : apparition *f*

emergency [i'mərdʒəntsi] *n, pl* **-cies 1** : urgence *f* **2** ~ **exit** : sortie *f* de secours **3** ~ **room** : salle *f* des urgences

emery ['ɛməri] *n, pl* **-eries 1** : émeri *m* **2** ~ **board** : lime *f* à ongles

emigrant ['ɛmigrənt] *n* : émigrant *m*, -grante *f* — **emigrate** ['ɛmə,greit] *vi* **-grated; -grating** : émigrer

eminence ['ɛmənənts] *n* : éminence *f* — **eminent** ['ɛmənənt] *adj* : éminent

emission [i'miʃən] *n* : émission *f* — **emit** [i'mit] *vt* **emitted; emitting** : émettre

emotion [i'moːʃən] *n* : émotion *f* — **emotional** [i'moːʃənəl] *adj* **1** : émotif **2** MOVING : émouvant

emperor ['empərər] *n* : empereur *m*

emphasis ['emfəsɪs] *n, pl* **-ses** [-ˌsiːz] : accent *m* — **emphasize** ['emfəˌsaɪz] *vt* **-sized; -sizing** : insister sur — **emphatic** [ɪm'fætɪk, em-] *adj* : énergique, catégorique

empire ['emˌpaɪr] *n* : empire *m*

employ [ɪm'plɔɪ, em-] *vt* : employer — **employee** [ɪm'plɔɪ'iː, em-, ɪm,plɔɪ'iː, -ˌplɔɪ,iː] *n* : employé *m*, -ployée *f* — **employer** [ɪm'plɔɪər, em-] *n* : employeur *m*, -ployeuse *f* — **employment** [ɪm'plɔɪmənt, em-] *n* : emploi *m*, travail *m*

empower [ɪm'pauər, em-] *vt* : autoriser

empress ['emprəs] *n* : impératrice *f*

empty ['empti] *adj* **-tier; -est 1** : vide **2** MEANINGLESS : vain — ~ *v* **-tied; -tying** *vt* : vider — *vi* : se vider — **emptiness** ['emptinəs] *n* : vide *m*

emulate ['emjəˌleɪt] *vt* **-lated; -lating** : imiter

enable [ɪ'neɪbəl, e-] *vt* **-abled; -abling** : permettre

enact [ɪ'nækt, e-] *vt* : promulguer (une loi, etc.)

enamel [ɪ'næməl] *n* : émail *m*

enchant [ɪn'tʃænt, en-] *vt* : enchanter — **enchanting** [ɪn'tʃæntɪŋ, en-] *adj* : enchanteur

encircle [ɪn'sərkəl, en-] *vt* **-cled; -cling** : entourer, encercler

enclose [ɪn'kloːz, en-] *vt* **-closed; -closing 1** SURROUND : entourer **2** INCLUDE : joindre (à une lettre) — **enclosure** [ɪn'kloːʒər, en-] *n* **1** : enceinte *f* **2** : pièce *f* jointe (à une lettre)

encompass [ɪn'kʌmpəs, en-, -'kʌm-] *vt* **1** ENCIRCLE : entourer **2** INCLUDE : inclure

encore ['ɑn,kor] *n* : bis *m*

encounter [ɪn'kauntər, en-] *vt* : rencontrer — ~ *n* : rencontre *f*

encourage [ɪn'kərɪdʒ, en-] *vt* **-aged; -aging** : encourager — **encouragement** [ɪn'kərɪdʒmənt, en-] *n* : encouragement *m*

encroach [ɪn'kroːtʃ, en-] *vi* ~ **on** : empiéter sur

encyclopedia [ɪn,saɪklə'piːdiə, en-] *n* : encyclopédie *f*

end ['end] *n* **1** : fin *f* **2** EXTREMITY : bout *m* **3 come to an** ~ : prendre fin **4 in the** ~ : finalement— ~ *vt* : terminer, mettre fin à — *vi* : se terminer

endanger [ɪn'deɪndʒər, en-] *vt* : mettre en danger

endearing [ɪn'dɪrɪŋ, en-] *adj* : attachant

endeavor *or Brit* **endeavour** [ɪn'devər, en-] *vt* ~ **to** : s'efforcer de — ~ *n* : effort *m*

ending ['endɪŋ] *n* : fin *f*, dénouement *m*

endive ['en,daɪv, ,ɑn'diːv] *n* : endive *f*

endless ['endləs] *adj* **1** INTERMINABLE : in-

terminable **2** INNUMERABLE : innombrable **3** ~ **possibilities** : possibilités *fpl* infinies

endorse [ɪn'dors, en-] *vt* **-dorsed; -dorsing 1** SIGN : endosser **2** APPROVE : approuver — **endorsement** [ɪn'dorsmənt, en-] *n* APPROVAL : approbation *f*

endow [ɪn'dau, en-] *vt* : doter

endure [ɪn'dur, en-, -'djur] *v* **-dured; -during** *vt* : supporter, endurer — *vi* LAST : durer — **endurance** [ɪn'durənts, en-, -'djur-] *n* : endurance *f*

enemy ['enəmi] *n, pl* **-mies** : ennemi *m*, -mie *f*

energy ['enərdʒi] *n, pl* **-gies** : énergie *f* — **energetic** [,enər'dʒetɪk] *adj* : énergique

enforce [ɪn'fors, en-] *vt* **-forced; -forcing 1** : faire respecter (une loi) **2** IMPOSE : imposer — **enforcement** [ɪn'forsmənt, en-] *n* : exécution *f*, application *f*

engage [ɪn'geɪdʒ, en-] *v* **-gaged; -gaging** *vt* **1** : engager (une conversation) **2** ~ **the clutch** : embrayer — *vi* ~ **in** : prendre part à, s'occuper de — **engaged** [ɪn'geɪdʒd, en-] *adj* **get** ~ **to** : se fiancer à — **engagement** [ɪn'geɪdʒmənt, en-] *n* **1** : fiançailles *fpl* **2** APPOINTMENT : rendez-vous *m* — **engaging** [ɪn'geɪdʒɪŋ, en-] *adj* : engageant, attirant

engine ['endʒən] *n* **1** : moteur *m* **2** LOCOMOTIVE : locomotive *f* — **engineer** [,endʒə'nɪr] *n* : ingénieur *m*, -nieure *f* — **engineering** [,endʒə'nɪrɪŋ] *n* : ingénierie *f*

English ['ɪŋglɪʃ, 'ɪŋlɪʃ] *adj* : anglais — ~ *n* : anglais *m* (langue) — **Englishman** ['ɪŋglɪʃmən, 'ɪŋlɪʃ-] *n* : Anglais *m* — **Englishwoman** ['ɪŋglɪʃ,wumən, 'ɪŋlɪʃ-] *n* : Anglaise *f*

engrave [ɪn'greɪv, en-] *vt* **-graved; -graving** : graver — **engraving** [ɪn'greɪvɪŋ, en-] *n* : gravure *f*

engross [ɪn'groːs, en-] *vt* : absorber, occuper

engulf [ɪn'gʌlf, en-] *vt* : engloutir

enhance [ɪn'hænts, en-] *vt* **-hanced; -hancing** : améliorer, rehausser

enjoy [ɪn'dʒɔɪ, en-] *vt* **1** LIKE : aimer **2** POSSESS : jouir de **3** ~ **oneself** : s'amuser — **enjoyable** [ɪn'dʒɔɪəbəl, en-] *adj* : agréable — **enjoyment** [ɪn'dʒɔɪmənt, en-] *n* : plaisir *m*

enlarge [ɪn'lɑrdʒ, en-] *vt* **-larged; -larging** : agrandir — **enlargement** [ɪn'lɑrdʒmənt, en-] *n* : agrandissement *m*

enlighten [ɪn'laɪtən, en-] *vt* : éclairer

enlist [ɪn'lɪst, en-] *vt* **1** ENROLL : enrôler **2** OBTAIN : obtenir — *vi* : s'engager, s'enrôler

enliven [ɪn'laɪvən, en-] *vt* : animer

enormous [ɪ'norməs] *adj* : énorme

enough [i'nʌf] *adj* : assez de — ~ *adv*

: assez — ~ *pron* **have** ~ **of** : en avoir assez de

enquire [ɪnˈkwaɪr, ɛn-], **enquiry** [ˈɪn-ˌkwaɪri, ˈɛn-, -kwəri; ɪnˈkwaɪri, ɛnˈ-] → **inquire, inquiry**

enrage [ɪnˈreɪdʒ, ɛn-] *vt* **-raged; -raging** : rendre furieux

enrich [ɪnˈrɪtʃ, ɛn-] *vt* : enrichir

enroll *or* **enrol** [ɪnˈroːl, ɛn-] *v* **-rolled; -rolling** *vt* **1** : inscrire (à l'école, etc.) **2** ENLIST : enrôler — *vi* : s'inscrire

ensue [ɪnˈsuː, ɛn-] *vi* **-sued; -suing** : s'ensuivre

ensure [ɪnˈʃʊr, ɛn-] *vt* **-sured; -suring** : assurer

entail [ɪnˈteɪl, ɛn-] *vt* : entraîner, comporter

entangle [ɪnˈtæŋɡəl, ɛn-] *vt* **-gled; -gling** : emmêler

enter [ˈɛntər] *vt* **1** : entrer dans **2** RECORD : inscrire — *vi* **1** : entrer **2** ~ **into** : entamer

enterprise [ˈɛntərˌpraɪz] *n* **1** : entreprise *f* **2** INITIATIVE : initiative *f* — **enterprising** [ˈɛntərˌpraɪzɪŋ] *adj* : entreprenant

entertain [ˌɛntərˈteɪn] *vt* **1** AMUSE : amuser, divertir **2** CONSIDER : considérer **3** : recevoir (des invités) — **entertainment** [ˌɛntərˈteɪnmənt] *n* : divertissement *m*

enthrall *or* **enthral** [ɪnˈθrɔl, ɛn-] *vt* **-thralled; -thralling** : captiver

enthusiasm [ɪnˈθuːziˌæzəm, ɛn-, -ˈθjuː-] *n* : enthousiasme *m* — **enthusiast** [ɪnˈθuːziˌæst, ɛn-, -ˈθjuː-, -əst] *n* : enthousiaste *mf*; passionné *m*, -née *f* — **enthusiastic** [ɪnˌθuːziˈæstɪk, ɛn-, -ˈθjuː-] *adj* : enthousiaste

entice [ɪnˈtaɪs, ɛn-] *vt* **-ticed; -ticing** : attirer, entraîner

entire [ɪnˈtaɪr, ɛn-] *adj* : entier, complet — **entirely** [ɪnˈtaɪrli, ɛn-] *adv* : entièrement — **entirety** [ɪnˈtaɪrti, ɛn-, -taɪrəti] *n, pl* **-ties 1** : totalité *f* **2 in its** ~ : dans son ensemble

entitle [ɪnˈtaɪtəl, ɛn-] *vt* **-tled; -tling 1** NAME : intituler **2** AUTHORIZE : autoriser, donner droit à — **entitlement** [ɪnˈtaɪtəlmənt, ɛn-] *n* : droit *m*

entity [ˈɛntəti] *n, pl* **-ties** : entité *f*

entrails [ˈɛnˌtreɪlz, -trəlz] *npl* : entrailles *fpl*

entrance[1] [ɪnˈtrænts, ɛn-] *vt* **-tranced; -trancing** : transporter, ravir

entrance[2] [ˈɛntrənts] *n* : entrée *f*

entreat [ɪnˈtriːt, ɛn-] *vt* : supplier

entrée *or* **entree** [ˈɑnˌtreɪ, ˌɑnˈ-] *n* : entrée *f*, plat *m* principal

entrust [ɪnˈtrʌst, ɛn-] *vt* : confier

entry [ˈɛntri] *n, pl* **-tries** ENTRANCE : entrée *f*

enumerate [ɪˈnuːməˌreɪt, ɛ-, -ˈnjuː-] *vt* **-ated; -ating** : énumérer

enunciate [iˈnʌntsiˌeɪt, ɛ-] *vt* **-ated; -ating 1** STATE : énoncer **2** PRONOUNCE : articuler

envelop [ɪnˈvɛləp, ɛn-] *vt* : envelopper — **envelope** [ˈɛnvəˌloːp, ˈɑnˈ-] *n* : enveloppe *f*

envious [ˈɛnviəs] *adj* : envieux, jaloux — **enviously** [ˈɛnviəsli] *adv* : avec envie

environment [ɪnˈvaɪrənmənt, ɛn-, -ˈvaɪərn-] *n* : environnement *m*, milieu *m* — **environmental** [ɪnˌvaɪrənˈmɛntəl, ɛn-, -ˌvaɪərn-] *adj* : de l'environnement — **environmentalist** [ɪnˌvaɪrənˈmɛntəlɪst, ɛn-, -ˌvaɪərn-] *n* : écologiste *mf*

envision [ɪnˈvɪʒən, ɛn-] *vt* : envisager

envoy [ˈɛnˌvɔɪ, ˈɑn-] *n* : envoyé *m*, -voyée *f*

envy [ˈɛnvi] *n* : envie *f*, jalousie *f* — ~ *vt* **-vied; -vying** : envier

enzyme [ˈɛnˌzaɪm] *n* : enzyme *f*

epic [ˈɛpɪk] *adj* : épique — ~ *n* : épopée *f*

epidemic [ˌɛpəˈdɛmɪk] : épidémie *f* — ~ *adj* : épidémique

epilepsy [ˈɛpəˌlɛpsi] *n, pl* **-sies** : épilepsie *f* — **epileptic** [ˌɛpəˈlɛptɪk] *adj* : épileptique — ~ *n* : épileptique *mf*

episode [ˈɛpəˌsoːd] *n* : épisode *m*

epitaph [ˈɛpəˌtæf] *n* : épitaphe *f*

epitome [ɪˈpɪtəmi] *n* : exemple *m* même, modèle *m* — **epitomize** [ɪˈpɪtəˌmaɪz] *vt* **-mized; -mizing** : incarner

equal [ˈiːkwəl] *adj* **1** SAME : égal **2 be ~ to** : être à la hauteur de — ~ *n* : égal *m*, -gale *f* — ~ *vt* **equaled** *or* **equalled; equaling** *or* **equalling** : égaler — **equality** [ɪˈkwɑləti] *n, pl* **-ties** : égalité *f* — **equalize** [ˈiːkwəˌlaɪz] *vt* **-ized; -izing** : égaliser — **equally** [ˈiːkwəli] *adv* **1** : également **2** ~ **important** : tout aussi important

equate [ɪˈkweɪt] *vt* **equated; equating** ~ **with** : assimiler à — **equation** [ɪˈkweɪʒən] : équation *f*

equator [ɪˈkweɪtər] *n* : équateur *m*

equilibrium [ˌiːkwəˈlɪbriəm, ˌɛ-] *n, pl* **-riums** *or* **-ria** : équilibre *m*

equinox [ˈiːkwəˌnɑks, ˈɛ-] *n* : équinoxe *m*

equip [ɪˈkwɪp] *vt* **equipped; equipping** : équiper — **equipment** [ɪˈkwɪpmənt] *n* : équipement *m*, matériel *m*

equity [ˈɛkwəti] *n, pl* **-ties 1** FAIRNESS : équité *f* **2 equities** *npl* STOCKS : actions *fpl* ordinaires

equivalent [ɪˈkwɪvələnt] *adj* : équivalent — ~ *n* : équivalent *m*

era [ˈɪrə, ˈɛrə, ˈiːrə] *n* : ère *f*, époque *f*

eradicate [ɪˈrædəˌkeɪt] *vt* **-cated; -cating** : éradiquer

erase [ɪˈreɪs] *vt* **erased; erasing** : effacer — **eraser** [ɪˈreɪsər] *n* : gomme *f*, efface *f* Can

erect [ɪˈrɛkt] *adj* : droit — ~ *vt* **1** BUILD : construire **2** RAISE : ériger — **erection** [ɪˈrɛkʃən] *n* **1** BUILDING : construction *f* **2** : érection *f* (en physiologie)

erode [ɪˈroːd] *vt* **eroded; eroding** : éroder, ronger — **erosion** [ɪˈroːʒən] *n* : érosion *f*

erotic [ɪˈrɑtɪk] *adj* : érotique

err [ˈɛr, ˈər] *vi* : se tromper

errand ['ɛrənd] *n* : course *f*, commission *f*
erratic [ɪ'rætɪk] *adj* : irrégulier
error ['ɛrər] *n* : erreur *f* — **erroneous** [ɪ-'roːniəs, ɛ-] *adj* : erroné
erupt [ɪ'rʌpt] *vi* **1** : entrer en éruption (se dit d'un volcan) **2** : éclater (se dit de la guerre, etc.) — **eruption** [ɪ'rʌpʃən] *n* : éruption *f*
escalate ['ɛskə,leɪt] *vi* -**lated; -lating 1** : s'intensifier **2** : monter en flèche (se dit des prix, etc.)
escalator ['ɛskə,leɪtər] *n* : escalier *m* mécanique
escape [ɪ'skeɪp, ɛ-] *v* -**caped; -caping** *vt* : échapper à, éviter — *vi* : s'échapper, s'évader — **~** *n* : fuite *f*, évasion *f*
escort ['ɛs,kɔrt] *n* GUARD : escorte *f* — **~** [ɪ'skɔrt, ɛ-] *vt* : escorter
Eskimo ['ɛskə,moː] *adj* : esquimau
especially [ɪ'spɛʃəli] *adv* : particulièrement
espionage ['ɛspiə,nɑʒ, -,nɑdʒ] *n* : espionnage *m*
espresso [ɛ'sprɛ,soː] *n, pl* -**sos** : express *m*, café *m* express
essay ['ɛ,seɪ] *n* : essai *m* (littéraire), dissertation *f* (académique)
essence ['ɛsənts] *n* : essence *f* — **essential** [ɪ'sɛntʃəl] *adj* : essentiel — **~** *n* **1** : objet *m* essentiel **2 the ~s** : l'essentiel *m*
establish [ɪ'stæblɪʃ, ɛ-] *vt* : établir — **establishment** [ɪ'stæblɪʃmənt, ɛ-] *n* : établissement *m*
estate [ɪ'steɪt, ɛ-] *n* **1** POSSESSIONS : biens *mpl* **2** LAND, PROPERTY : propriété *f*, domaine *m*
esteem [ɪ'stiːm, ɛ-] *n* : estime *f* — **~** *vt* : estimer
esthetic [ɛs'θɛtɪk] → **aesthetic**
estimate ['ɛstə,meɪt] *vt* -**mated; -mating** : estimer — **~** ['ɛstəmət] *n* : estimation *f* — **estimation** [,ɛstə'meɪʃən] *n* **1** JUDGMENT : jugement *m* **2** ESTEEM : estime *f*
estuary ['ɛstʃu,wɛri] *n, pl* -**aries** : estuaire *m*
eternal [ɪ'tərnəl, iː-] *adj* : éternel — **eternity** [ɪ'tərnəti, iː-] *n, pl* -**ties** : éternité *f*
ether ['iː,θər] *n* : éther *m*
ethical ['ɛθɪkəl] *adj* : éthique, moral — **ethics** ['ɛθɪks] *ns & pl* : éthique *f*, morale *f*
ethnic ['ɛθnɪk] *adj* : ethnique
etiquette ['ɛtɪkət, -,kɛt] *n* : étiquette *f*, convenances *fpl*
Eucharist ['juːkərɪst] *n* : Eucharistie *f*
eulogy ['juːlədʒi] *n, pl* -**gies** : éloge *m*
euphemism ['juːfə,mɪzəm] *n* : euphémisme *m*
euphoria [jʊ'foriə] *n* : euphorie *f*
European [,jʊrə'piːən, -,piːn] *adj* : européen
evacuate [ɪ'vækju,eɪt] *vt* -**ated; -ating** : évacuer — **evacuation** [ɪ,vækju'eɪʃən] *n* : évacuation *f*

evade [ɪ'veɪd] *vt* **evaded; evading** : éviter, esquiver
evaluate [ɪ'vælju,eɪt] *vt* -**ated; -ating** : évaluer
evaporate [ɪ'væpə,reɪt] *vi* -**rated; -rating** : s'évaporer
evasion [ɪ'veɪʒən] *n* : évasion *f* — **evasive** [ɪ'veɪsɪv] *adj* : évasif
eve ['iːv] *n* : veille *f*
even ['iːvən] *adj* **1** REGULAR, STEADY : régulier **2** LEVEL : uni, plat **3** EQUAL : égal **4 ~ number** : nombre *m* pair **5 get ~ with** : se venger de — **~** *adv* **1** : même **2 ~ better** : encore mieux **3 ~ so** : quand même — **~** *vt* : égaliser — *vi or* **~ out** : s'égaliser
evening ['iːvnɪŋ] *n* : soir *m*, soirée *f*
event [ɪ'vɛnt] *n* **1** : événement *m* **2** : épreuve *f* (aux sports) **3 in the ~ of** : en cas de — **eventful** [ɪ'vɛntfəl] *adj* : mouvementé
eventual [ɪ'vɛntʃuəl] *adj* : final — **eventuality** [ɪ,vɛntʃu'æləti] *n, pl* -**ties** : éventualité *f* — **eventually** [ɪ'vɛntʃuəli] *adv* : finalement, en fin de compte
ever ['ɛvər] *adv* **1** ALWAYS : toujours **2 ~ since** : depuis **3 hardly ~** : presque jamais
evergreen ['ɛvər,griːn] *n* : plante *f* à feuilles persistantes
everlasting [,ɛvər'læstɪŋ] *adj* : éternel
every ['ɛvri] *adj* **1** EACH : chaque **2 ~ month** : tous les mois — **everybody** ['ɛvri,bʌdi, -'bɑ-] *pron* : tout le monde — **everyday** [,ɛvri'deɪ, 'ɛvri-] *adj* : quotidien, de tous les jours — **everyone** ['ɛvri,wʌn] → **everybody** — **everything** ['ɛvri,θɪŋ] *pron* : tout — **everywhere** ['ɛvri,hwɛr] *adv* : partout
evict [ɪ'vɪkt] *vt* : expulser — **eviction** [ɪ'vɪkʃən] *n* : expulsion *f*
evidence ['ɛvədənts] *n* **1** PROOF : preuve *f* **2** TESTIMONY : témoignage *m* — **evident** ['ɛvɪdənt] *adj* : évident — **evidently** ['ɛvɪdəntli, ,ɛvɪ'dɛntli] *adv* **1** OBVIOUSLY : évidemment, manifestement **2** APPARENTLY : apparemment
evil ['iːvəl, -vɪl] *adj* **eviler** *or* **eviller; evilest** *or* **evillest** : mauvais, méchant — **~** *n* : mal *m*
evoke [i'voːk] *vt* **evoked; evoking** : évoquer
evolution [,ɛvə'luːʃən, ,iː-] *n* : évolution *f* — **evolve** [i'vɑlv] *vi* **evolved; evolving** : évoluer, se développer
exact [ɪg'zækt, ɛg-] *adj* : exact, précis — **~** *vt* : exiger — **exacting** [ɪg'zæktɪŋ, ɛg-] *adj* : exigeant — **exactly** [ɪg'zæktli, ɛg-] *adv* : exactement
exaggerate [ɪg'zædʒə,reɪt, ɛg-] *v* -**ated; -ating** : exagérer — **exaggeration** [ɪg-'zædʒə'reɪʃən, ɛg-] *n* : exagération *f*

examine [ɪg'zæmən, ɛg-] vt **-ined; -ining 1** : examiner **2** QUESTION : interroger — **exam** [ɪg'zæm, ɛg-] n : examen m — **examination** [ɪgˌzæmə'neɪʃən, ɛg-] n : examen m

example [ɪg'zæmpəl, ɛg-] n : exemple m

exasperate [ɪg'zæspəˌreɪt, ɛg-] vt **-ated; -ating** : exaspérer — **exasperation** [ɪgˌzæspə'reɪʃən, ɛg-] n : exaspération f

excavate ['ɛkskəˌveɪt] vt **-vated; -vating** : creuser, excaver

exceed [ɪk'si:d, ɛk-] vt : dépasser — **exceedingly** [ɪk'si:dɪŋli, ɛk-] adv : extrêmement

excel [ɪk'sɛl, ɛk-] vi **-celled; -celling** : exceller — **excellence** ['ɛksələnts] n : excellence f — **excellent** ['ɛksələnt] adj : excellent

except [ɪk'sɛpt] prep **1** : sauf, excepté **2** ∼ **for** : à part — ∼ vt : excepter — **exception** [ɪk'sɛpʃən] n : exception f — **exceptional** [ɪk'sɛpʃənəl] adj : exceptionnel

excerpt [ɛk'sərpt, 'ɛgˌzərpt] n : extrait m

excess [ɪk'sɛs, 'ɛkˌsɛs] n : excès m — ∼ ['ɛkˌsɛs, ɪk'sɛs] adj : excédentaire, en trop — **excessive** [ɪk'sɛsɪv, ɛk-] adj : excessif

exchange [ɪks'tʃeɪndʒ, ɛks-; 'ɛksˌtʃeɪndʒ] n **1** : échange m **2** : change m (en finances) — ∼ vt **-changed; -changing** : échanger

excise ['ɪkˌsaɪz, ɛk-] n or ∼ **tax** : contribution f indirecte

excite [ɪk'saɪt, ɛk-] vt **-cited; -citing** : exciter — **excited** [ɪk'saɪt̬əd, ɛk-] adj : excité, enthousiaste — **excitement** [ɪk'saɪtmənt, ɛk-] n : enthousiasme m — **exciting** [ɪk'saɪt̬ɪŋ, ɛk-] adj : passionnant

exclaim [ɪks'kleɪm, ɛk-] vi : s'exclamer — **exclamation** [ˌɛksklə'meɪʃən] n : exclamation f — **exclamation point** n : point m d'exclamation

exclude [ɪks'klu:d, ɛks-] vt **-cluded; -cluding** : exclure — **excluding** [ɪks'klu:dɪŋ, ɛks-] prep : à part, à l'exclusion de — **exclusion** [ɪks'kluːʃ'n, ɛks-] n : exclusion f — **exclusive** [ɪks'klu:sɪv, ɛks-] adj : exclusif

excrement ['ɛkskrəmənt] n : excréments mpl

excruciating [ɪk'skru:ʃiˌeɪt̬ɪŋ, ɛk-] adj : atroce, insupportable

excursion [ɪk'skərʒən, ɛk-] n : excursion f

excuse [ɪk'skju:z, ɛk-] vt **-cused; -cusing 1** : excuser **2** ∼ **me** : excusez-moi, pardon — ∼ [ɪk'skju:s, ɛk-] n : excuse f

execute ['ɛksɪˌkju:t] vt **-cuted; -cuting** : exécuter — **execution** [ˌɛksɪ'kju:ʃən] n : exécution f — **executioner** [ˌɛksɪ'kju:ʃənər] n : bourreau m

executive [ɪg'zɛkjət̬ɪv, ɛg-] adj : exécutif — ∼ n **1** MANAGER : cadre m **2** or ∼ **branch** : exécutif m, pouvoir m exécutif

exemplify [ɪg'zɛmpləˌfaɪ, ɛg-] vt **-fied; -fying** : illustrer — **exemplary** [ɪg'zɛmpləri, ɛg-] adj : exemplaire

exempt [ɪg'zɛmpt, ɛg-] adj : exempt — ∼ vt : exempter — **exemption** [ɪg'zɛmpʃən, ɛg-] n : exemption f

exercise ['ɛksərˌsaɪz] n : exercice m — ∼ **-cised; -cising** vt : exercer — vi : faire de l'exercice

exert [ɪg'zərt, ɛg-] vt **1** : exercer **2** ∼ **oneself** : se donner de la peine — **exertion** [ɪg'zərʃən, ɛg-] n : effort m

exhale [ɛks'heɪl] v **-haled; -haling** : expirer

exhaust [ɪg'zɔst, ɛg-] vt : épuiser — ∼ n **1** or ∼ **fumes** : gaz m d'échappement **2** or ∼ **pipe** : tuyau m d'échappement — **exhaustion** [ɪg'zɔstʃən, ɛg-] n : épuisement m — **exhaustive** [ɪg'zɔstɪv, ɛg-] adj : exhaustif

exhibit [ɪg'zɪbət, ɛg-] vt **1** DISPLAY : exposer **2** SHOW : montrer — ∼ n **1** : objet m exposé **2** EXHIBITION : exposition f — **exhibition** [ˌɛksə'bɪʃən] n : exposition f

exhilarate [ɪg'zɪləˌreɪt, ɛg-] vt **-rated; -rating** : animer — **exhilaration** [ɪgˌzɪlə'reɪʃən, ɛg-] n : joie f

exile ['ɛgˌzaɪl, 'ɛkˌsaɪl] n **1** : exil m **2** OUTCAST : exilé m, -lée f — ∼ vt **exiled; exiling** : exiler

exist [ɪg'zɪst, ɛg-] vi : exister — **existence** [ɪg'zɪstənts, ɛg-] n : existence f

exit ['ɛgzət, 'ɛksət] n : sortie f — ∼ vi : sortir

exodus ['ɛksədəs] n : exode m

exonerate [ɪg'zɑnəˌreɪt, ɛg-] vt **-ated; -ating** : disculper

exorbitant [ɪg'zɔrbət̬ənt, ɛg-] adj : exorbitant, excessif

exotic [ɪg'zɑtɪk, ɛg-] adj : exotique

expand [ɪk'spænd, ɛk-] vt : étendre, élargir — vi : s'étendre, s'agrandir — **expanse** [ɪk'spænts, ɛk-] n : étendue f — **expansion** [ɪk'spænʃən, ɛk-] n : expansion f

expatriate [ɛks'peɪtriət, -ˌeɪt] n : expatrié m, -triée f — ∼ adj : expatrié

expect [ɪk'spɛkt, ɛk-] vt **1** ANTICIPATE : s'attendre à **2** AWAIT : attendre **3** REQUIRE : exiger, demander — vi **be expecting** : attendre un bébé, être enceinte — **expectancy** [ɪk'spɛktəntsi, ɛk-] n, pl **-cies** : attente f, espérance f — **expectant** [ɪk'spɛktənt, ɛk-] adj **1** : qui attend **2** ∼ **mother** : future mère f — **expectation** [ˌɛkˌspɛk'teɪʃən] n : attente f

expedient [ɪk'spi:diənt, ɛk-] adj : opportun — ∼ n : expédient m

expedition [ˌɛkspə'dɪʃən] n : expédition f

expel [ɪk'spɛl, ɛk-] vt **-pelled; -pelling** : expulser, renvoyer (un élève)

expend [ɪk'spɛnd, ɛk-] vt : dépenser — **expendable** [ɪk'spɛndəbəl, ɛk-] adj : remplacable — **expenditure** [ɪk'spɛndɪtʃər, ɛk-, -tʃʊr] n : dépense f — **expense** [ɪk'spɛnts, ɛk-] n **1** : dépense f **2** **~s** npl : frais mpl **3** **at the ~ of** : aux dépens de — **expensive** [ɪk'spɛnsɪv, ɛk-] adj : cher, coûteux

experience [ɪk'spɪriənts, ɛk-] n : expérience f — **~** vt **-enced; -encing** : éprouver, connaître — **experienced** [ɪk'spɪriəntst, ɛk-] adj : expérimenté — **experiment** [ɪk-'spɛrəmənt, ɛk-, -'spɪr-] n : expérience f — **~** vi : expérimenter — **experimental** [ɪk-,spɛrə'mɛntəl, ɛk-, -,spɪr-] adj : expérimental

expert ['ɛk,spərt, ɪk'spərt] adj : expert — **~** ['ɛk,spərt] n : expert m, -perte f — **expertise** [,ɛkspər'tiːz] n : compétence f

expire [ɪk'spaɪr, ɛk-] vi **-pired; -piring** : expirer — **expiration** [,ɛkspə'reɪʃən] n : expiration f

explain [ɪk'spleɪn, ɛk-] vt **1** : expliquer **2** **~ oneself** : s'expliquer — **explanation** [,ɛksplə'neɪʃən] n : explication f — **explanatory** [ɪk'splænə,tori, ɛk-] adj : explicatif

explicit [ɪk'splɪsət, ɛk-] adj : explicite

explode [ɪk'sploːd, ɛk-] v **-ploded; -ploding** vt : faire exploser — vi : exploser

exploit ['ɛk,splɔɪt] n : exploit m — **~** [ɪk-'splɔɪt, ɛk-] vt : exploiter — **exploitation** [,ɛk,splɔɪ'teɪʃən] n : exploitation f

exploration [,ɛksplə'reɪʃən] n : exploration f — **explore** [ɪk'splor, ɛk-] v **-plored; -ploring** : explorer — **explorer** [ɪk'splorər, ɛk-] n : explorateur m, -trice f

explosion [ɪk'splo:ʒən, ɛk-] n : explosion f — **explosive** [ɪk'splo:sɪv, ɛk-] adj : explosif — **~** n : explosif m

export [ɛk'sport, 'ɛk,sport] vt : exporter — **~** ['ɛk,sport] n : exportation f

expose [ɪk'spoːz, ɛk-] vt **-posed; -posing 1** : exposer **2** REVEAL : révéler — **exposure** [ɪk'spoːʒər, ɛk-] n : exposition f

express [ɪk'sprɛs, ɛk-] adj **1** SPECIFIC : exprès, formel **2** FAST : express — **~** adv **send ~** : envoyer en exprès — **~** n or **~ train** : rapide m, express m — **~** vt : exprimer — **expression** [ɪk'sprɛʃən, ɛk-] n : expression f — **expressive** [ɪk'sprɛsɪv, ɛk-] adj : expressif — **expressly** [ɪk'sprɛsli, ɛk-] adv : expressément — **expressway** [ɪk-'sprɛs,weɪ, ɛk-] n : autoroute f

expulsion [ɪk'spʌlʃən, ɛk-] n : expulsion f, renvoi m (d'un élève)

exquisite [ɛk'skwɪzət, 'ɛk,skwɪ-] adj : exquis

extend [ɪk'stɛnd, ɛk-] vt **1** STRETCH : étendre **2** LENGTHEN : prolonger **3** ENLARGE : agrandir **4 ~ one's hand** : tendre la main — vi : s'étendre — **extension** [ɪk'stɛnʃən, ɛk-] n **1** : extension f **2** LENGTHENING : pro-

longation f **3** ANNEX : annexe f **4** : poste m (de téléphone) **5 ~ cord** : rallonge f — **extensive** [ɪk'stɛntsɪv, ɛk-] adj : étendu, vaste — **extent** [ɪk'stɛnt, ɛk-] n **1** : étendue f, ampleur f **2** DEGREE : mesure f, degré m

exterior [ɛk'stɪriər] adj : extérieur — **~** n : extérieur m

exterminate [ɪk'stərmə,neɪt, ɛk-] vt **-nated; -nating** : exterminer — **extermination** [ɪk-,stərmə'neɪʃən, ɛk-] n : extermination f

external [ɪk'stərnəl, ɛk-] adj : externe — **externally** [ɪk'stərnəli, ɛk-] adv : extérieurement

extinct [ɪk'stɪŋkt, ɛk-] adj : disparu — **extinction** [ɪk'stɪŋkʃən, ɛk-] n : extinction f

extinguish [ɪk'stɪŋgwɪʃ, ɛk-] vt : éteindre — **extinguisher** [ɪk'stɪŋgwɪʃər, ɛk-] n : extincteur m

extol [ɪk'sto:l, ɛk-] vt **-tolled; -tolling** : louer

extort [ɪk'stɔrt, ɛk-] vt : extorquer — **extortion** [ɪk'stɔrʃən, ɛk-] n : extorsion f

extra ['ɛkstrə] adj : supplémentaire, de plus — **~** n : supplément m — **~** adv **1** : plus (que d'habitude) **2 cost ~** : coûter plus cher

extract [ɪk'strækt, ɛk-] vt : extraire, arracher — **~** ['ɛk,strækt] n : extrait m — **extraction** [ɪk'strækʃən, ɛk-] n : extraction f

extracurricular [,ɛkstrəkə'rɪkjələr] adj : parascolaire

extraordinary [ɪk'strɔrdən,ɛri, ,ɛkstrə-'ɔrd-] adj : extraordinaire

extraterrestrial [,ɛkstrətə'rɛstriəl] adj : extraterrestre — **~** n : extraterrestre mf

extravagant [ɪk'strævɪgənt, ɛk-] adj **1** : extravagant **2** WASTEFUL : prodigue — **extravagance** [ɪk'strævɪgənts, ɛk-] n **1** : extravagance f **2** WASTEFULNESS : prodigalité f

extreme [ɪk'striːm, ɛk-] adj : extrême — **~** n : extrême m — **extremity** [ɪk'strɛməti, ɛk-] n, pl **-ties** : extrémité f

extricate ['ɛkstrə,keɪt] vt **-cated; -cating 1** : dégager **2 ~ oneself from** : s'extirper de

extrovert ['ɛkstrə,vərt] n : extraverti m, -tie f — **extroverted** ['ɛkstrə,vərtəd] adj : extraverti

exuberant [ɪg'zuːbərənt, ɛg-] adj : exubérant — **exuberance** [ɪg'zuːbərənts, ɛg-] n : exubérance f

exult [ɪg'zʌlt, ɛg-] vi : exulter

eye ['aɪ] n **1** : œil m **2** VISION : vision f **3** GLANCE : regard m **4 ~ of a needle** : chas m — **~** vt **eyed; eyeing** or **eying** : regarder — **eyeball** ['aɪ,bɔl] n : globe m oculaire — **eyebrow** ['aɪ,braʊ] n : sourcil m — **eyeglasses** ['aɪ,glæsəz] npl : lunettes fpl — **eyelash** ['aɪ,læʃ] n : cil m — **eyelid** [aɪ,lɪd] n : paupière f — **eyesight** ['aɪ,saɪt] n : vue f, vision f — **eyewitness** ['aɪ,wɪtnəs] n : témoin m oculaire

F

f ['ɛf] *n, pl* **f's** *or* **fs** ['ɛfs] : f *m*, sixième lettre de l'alphabet

fable ['feɪbəl] *n* : fable *f*

fabric ['fæbrɪk] *n* : tissu *m*, étoffe *f*

fabulous ['fæbjələs] *adj* : fabuleux

facade [fə'sɑd] *n* : façade *f*

face ['feɪs] *n* **1** : visage *m*, figure *f* **2** EX-PRESSION : mine *f* **3** SURFACE : face *f* (d'une monnaie), façade *f* (d'un bâtiment) **4** ~ **value** : valeur *f* nominale **5 in the** ~ **of** DESPITE : en dépit de **6 lose** ~ : perdre la face **7 make a** ~ : faire la grimace — *vt* **faced; facing 1** CONFRONT : faire face à **2** OVERLOOK : être en face de, donner sur — **faceless** ['feɪsləs] *adj* : anonyme

facet ['fæsət] *n* : facette *f*

face–to–face *adv* : face à face

facial ['feɪʃəl] *adj* : du visage

facetious [fə'si:ʃəs] *adj* : facétieux

facility [fə'sɪləti] *n, pl* **-ties 1** : facilité *f* **2 fa-cilities** *npl* : installations *fpl* — **facilitate** [fə'sɪlə,teɪt] *vt* **-tated; -tating** : faciliter

facsimile [fæk'sɪməli] *n* : fac-similé *m*

fact ['fækt] *n* **1** : fait *m* **2 in** ~ : en fait

faction ['fækʃən] *n* : faction *f*

factor ['fæktər] *n* : facteur *m*

factory ['fæktəri] *n, pl* **-ries** : usine *f*, fa-brique *f*

factual ['fæktʃʊəl] *adj* : factuel, basé sur les faits

faculty ['fækəlti] *n, pl* **-ties** : faculté *f*

fad ['fæd] *n* : mode *f* passagère, manie *f*

fade ['feɪd] *v* **faded; fading** *vi* **1** WITHER : se flétrir, se faner **2** DISCOLOR : se décolorer **3** DIM : s'affaiblir, diminuer **4** VANISH : dis-paraître — *vt* : décolorer

fail ['feɪl] *vi* **1** : échouer **2** WEAKEN : faiblir, baisser **3** BREAK DOWN : tomber en panne **4** ~ **in** : manquer à — *vt* **1** DISAPPOINT : décevoir **2** NEGLECT : manquer, négliger **3** : échouer à (un examen) — ~ *n* **without** ~ : à coup sûr — **failing** ['feɪlɪŋ] *n* : défaut *m* — **failure** ['feɪljər] *n* **1** : échec *m* **2** BREAK-DOWN : panne *f*

faint ['feɪnt] *adj* **1** WEAK : faible **2** INDIS-TINCT : vague **3 feel** ~ : se sentir mal — ~ *vi* : s'évanouir — **fainthearted** ['feɪnt-'hɑrtəd] *adj* : timide — **faintly** ['feɪntli] *adv* **1** WEAKLY : faiblement **2** SLIGHTLY : légère-ment

fair[1] ['fær] *n* : foire *f*

fair[2] *adj* **1** BEAUTIFUL : beau **2** : blond (se dit des cheveux), clair (se dit de la peau) **3** JUST : juste, équitable **4** ADEQUATE : pas-sable **5** LARGE : grand — **fairly** ['færli] *adv*

1 HONESTLY : équitablement **2** QUITE : assez — **fairness** ['færnəs] *n* : équité *f*

fairy ['færi] *n, pl* **fairies 1** : fée *f* **2** ~ **tale** *n* : conte *m* de fées

faith ['feɪθ] *n, pl* **faiths** ['feɪθs, 'feɪðz] : foi *f* — **faithful** ['feɪθfəl] *adj* : fidèle — **faith-fully** *adv* : fidèlement — **faithfulness** ['feɪθfəlnəs] *n* : fidélité *f* —

fake ['feɪk] *v* **faked; faking** *vt* **1** FALSIFY : falsifier **2** FEIGN : simuler — *vi* PRETEND : faire semblant — ~ *adj* : faux — ~ *n* **1** IMITATION : faux *m* **2** IMPOSTER : impos-teur *m*

falcon ['fælkən, 'fɔl-] *n* : faucon *m*

fall ['fɔl] *vi* **fell** ['fɛl]; **fallen** ['fɔlən]; **falling 1** : tomber **2** ~ **asleep** : s'endormir **3** ~ **back** : se retirer **4** ~ **back on** : avoir re-cours à **5** ~ **behind** : prendre du retard **6** ~ **in love** : tomber amoureux **7** ~ **out** QUARREL : se disputer — ~ *n* **1** : chute *f* **2** AUTUMN : automne *m* **3** ~**s** *npl* WATER-FALL : chute *f* (d'eau), cascade *f*

fallacy ['fæləsi] *n, pl* **-cies** : erreur *f*

fallible ['fæləbəl] *adj* : faillible

fallow ['fælo] *adj* : en jachère

false ['fɔls] *adj* **falser; falsest 1** : faux **2** ~ **alarm** : fausse alerte *f* **3** ~ **teeth** : dentier *m* — **falsehood** ['fɔls,hʊd] *n* : mensonge *m* — **falsely** ['fɔlsli] *adv* : faussement — **false-ness** ['fɔlsnəs] *n* : fausseté *f* — **falsify** ['fɔlsə,faɪ] *vt* **-fied; -fying** : falsifier

falter ['fɔltər] *vi* **1** STUMBLE : chanceler **2** WAVER : hésiter

fame ['feɪm] *n* : renommée *f*

familiar [fə'mɪljər] *adj* **1** : familier **2 be** ~ **with** : bien connaître — **familiarity** [fə,mɪli-'ærəti, -,mɪl'jær-] *n, pl* **-ties** : familiarité *f* — **familiarize** [fə'mɪljə,raɪz] *vt* **-ized; -izing** ~ **oneself** : se familiariser

family ['fæmli, 'fæmə-] *n, pl* **-lies** : famille *f*

famine ['fæmən] *n* : famine *f*

famished ['fæmɪʃt] *adj* : affamé

famous ['feɪməs] *adj* : célèbre

fan ['fæn] *n* **1** : éventail *m*, ventilateur *m* (électrique) **2** ENTHUSIAST : enthousiaste *mf* — *vt* **fanned; fanning 1** : attiser (un feu) **2** ~ **oneself** : s'éventer (le visage)

fanatic [fə'nætɪk] *n* : fanatique *mf* — ~ *or* **fanatical** [-tɪkəl] *adj* : fanatique — **fanati-cism** [fə'nætə,sɪzəm] *n* : fanatisme *m*

fancy ['fænsi] *vt* **-cied; -cying 1** LIKE : aimer **2** WANT : avoir envie de **3** IMAGINE : s'imaginer — ~ *adj* **fancier; -est 1** ELAB-ORATE : recherché **2** LUXURIOUS : fin, de luxe — ~ *n, pl* **-cies 1** LIKING : goût *m* **2**

WHIM : fantaisie *f* **3 take a ~ to** : se prendre d'affection pour — **fanciful** [ˈfænɪsɪfəl] *adj* : fantaisiste

fanfare [ˈfænˌfær] *n* : fanfare *f*

fang [ˈfæŋ] *n* : croc *m*, crochet *m* (d'un serpent)

fantasy [ˈfæntəsi] *n, pl* **-sies 1** DREAM : fantasme *m* **2** IMAGINATION : fantaisie *f* — **fantasize** [ˈfæntəˌsaɪz] *vi* **-sized; -sizing** : fantasmer — **fantastic** [fænˈtæstɪk] *adj* : fantastique

far [ˈfɑr] *adv* **farther** [ˈfɑrðər] *or* **further** [ˈfər-]; **farthest** *or* **furthest** [-ðəst] **1** : loin **2 as ~ as** : jusqu'à **3 as ~ as possible** : autant que possible **4 by ~** : de loin **5 ~ away** : au loin **6 ~ from it!** : pas du tout! **7 ~ worse** : bien pire **8 so ~** : jusqu'ici — **~** *adj* **farther** *or* **further; farthest** *or* **furthest 1** : lointain **2 the ~ right** : l'extrême droite **3 the ~ side** : l'autre côté —

faraway [ˈfɑrəˌweɪ] *adj* : éloigné, lointain

farce [ˈfɑrs] *n* : farce *f*

fare [ˈfær] *vi* **fared; faring** : aller — **~** *n* **1** : tarif *m*, prix *m* **2** FOOD : nourriture *f*

farewell [færˈwɛl] *n* : adieu *m* — **~** *adj* : d'adieu

far–fetched [ˈfɑrˈfɛtʃt] *adj* : improbable, bizarre

farm [ˈfɑrm] *n* : ferme *f* — **~** *vt* : cultiver — *vi* : être fermier — **farmer** [ˈfɑrmər] *n* : fermier *m*, -mière *f* — **farmhand** [ˈfɑrmˌhænd] *n* : ouvrier *m*, -vrière *f* agricole — **farmhouse** [ˈfɑrmˌhaʊs] *n* : ferme *f* — **farming** [ˈfɑrmɪŋ] *n* : agriculture *f*, élevage (des animaux) — **farmyard** [ˈfɑrmˌjɑrd] *n* : cour *f* de ferme

far–off [ˈfɑrˌɔf, -ˈɔf] *adj* : lointain

far–reaching [ˈfɑrˈriːtʃɪŋ] *adj* : d'une grande portée

farsighted [ˈfɑrˌsaɪtəd] *adj* **1** : presbyte **2** SHREWD : prévoyant

farther [ˈfɑrðər] *adv* **1** : plus loin **2** MORE : de plus — **~** *adj* : plus éloigné, plus lointain — **farthest** [ˈfɑrðəst] *adv* : le plus loin — **~** *adj* : le plus éloigné

fascinate [ˈfæsənˌeɪt] *vt* **-nated; -nating** : fasciner — **fascination** [ˌfæsənˈeɪʃən] *n* : fascination *f*

fascism [ˈfæʃˌɪzəm] *n* : fascisme *m* — **fascist** [ˈfæʃɪst] *adj* : fasciste — **~** *n* : fasciste *mf*

fashion [ˈfæʃən] *n* **1** MANNER : façon *f* **2** STYLE : mode *f* **3 out of ~** : démodé — **fashionable** [ˈfæʃənəbəl] *adj* : à la mode

fast¹ [ˈfæst] *vi* : jeûner — **~** *n* : jeûne *m*

fast² *adj* **1** SWIFT : rapide **2** SECURE : ferme **3 my watch is ~** : ma montre avance — **~** *adv* **1** SECURELY : solidement, ferme **2** SWIFTLY : rapidement, vite **3 ~ asleep** : profondément endormi

fasten [ˈfæsən] *vt* : attacher, fermer — *vi* : s'attacher, se fermer — **fastener** [ˈfæsənər] *n* : attache *f*, fermeture *f*

fastidious [fæsˈtɪdiəs] *adj* : méticuleux

fat [ˈfæt] *adj* **fatter; fattest 1** : gros, gras **2** THICK : épais — **~** *n* : gras *m* (de la viande), graisse *f* (du corps)

fatal [ˈfeɪtəl] *adj* **1** DEADLY : mortel **2** FATEFUL : fatal — **fatality** [feɪˈtæləti, fə-] *n, pl* **-ties** : mort *m*

fate [ˈfeɪt] *n* **1** DESTINY : destin *m* **2** LOT : sort *m* — **fateful** [ˈfeɪtfəl] *adj* : fatidique

father [ˈfɑðər] *n* : père *m* — **fatherhood** [ˈfɑðərˌhʊd] *n* : paternité *f* — **father–in–law** [ˈfɑðərɪnˌlɔ] *n, pl* **fathers–in–law** : beau-père *m* — **fatherly** [ˈfɑðərli] *adj* : paternel

fathom [ˈfæðəm] *vt* : comprendre

fatigue [fəˈtiːg] *vt* **-tigued; -tiguing** : fatiguer — **~** *n* : fatigue *f*

fatten [ˈfætən] *vt* : engraisser — **fattening** [ˈfætənɪŋ] *n* : qui fait grossir

fatty [ˈfæti] *adj* **fattier; -est** : gras

faucet [ˈfɔsət] *n* : robinet *m*

fault [ˈfɔlt] *n* **1** FLAW : défaut *m* **2** RESPONSIBILITY : faute *f* **3** : faille *f* (géologique) — **~** *vt* : trouver des défauts à, critiquer — **faultless** [ˈfɔltləs] *adj* : irréprochable — **faulty** [ˈfɔlti] *adj* **faultier; -est** : fautif, défectueux

fauna [ˈfɔnə] *n* : faune *f*

favor *or Brit* **favour** [ˈfeɪvər] *n* **1** APPROVAL : faveur *f* **2 do s.o. a ~** : rendre un service à qqn **3 in ~ of** : en faveur de, pour — **~** *vt* **1** : favoriser **2** PREFER : préférer — **favorable** *or Brit* **favourable** [ˈfeɪvərəbəl] *adj* : favorable — **favorite** *or Brit* **favourite** [ˈfeɪvərət] *adj* : favori, préféré — **~** *n* : favori *m*, -rite *f*; préféré *m*, -rée *f* — **favoritism** *or Brit* **favouritism** [ˈfeɪvərəˌtɪzəm] *n* : favoritisme *m*

fawn¹ [ˈfɔn] *vi* **~ upon** : flatter servilement

fawn² *n* : faon *m*

fax [ˈfæks] *n* : fax *m*, télécopie *f* — **~** *vt* : faxer, envoyer par télécopie

fear [ˈfɪr] *vt* : craindre, avoir peur de — *vi* **~ for** : craindre pour — **~** *n* : crainte *f*, peur *f* — **fearful** [ˈfɪrfəl] *adj* **1** FRIGHTENING : effrayant **2** AFRAID : craintif, peureux

feasible [ˈfiːzəbəl] *adj* : faisable

feast [ˈfiːst] *n* : banquet *m*, festin *m* — *vi* **~ on** : se régaler de

feat [ˈfiːt] *n* : exploit *m*, prouesse *f*

feather [ˈfɛðər] *n* : plume *f*

feature [ˈfiːtʃər] *n* **1** : trait *m* (du visage) **2** CHARACTERISTIC : caractéristique *f* — **~** *vt* : mettre en vedette — *vi* : figurer

February [ˈfɛbjuˌɛri, ˈfɛbʊ-, ˈfɛbrʊ-] *n* : février *m*

feces [ˈfiːˌsiːz] *npl* : fèces *fpl*

federal [ˈfɛdrəl, -dərəl] *adj* : fédéral —

federation [ˌfɛdəˈreɪʃən] n : fédération f
fed up [ˈfɛd] adj be ~ : en avoir assez, en avoir marre fam
fee [ˈfiː] n 1 : frais mpl (de scolarité), honoraires mpl (médicaux) 2 or **entrance** ~ : droit m d'entrée
feeble [ˈfiːbəl] adj **-bler; -blest** 1 : faible 2 a ~ **excuse** : une piètre excuse
feed [ˈfiːd] v **fed** [ˈfɛd]; **feeding** vt 1 : nourrir, donner à manger à 2 SUPPLY : alimenter — vi EAT : manger, se nourrir — ~ n : fourrage m
feel [ˈfiːl] v **felt** [ˈfɛlt]; **feeling** vt 1 : sentir 2 TOUCH : toucher 3 EXPERIENCE : ressentir (un sentiment) 4 BELIEVE : croire — vi 1 : se sentir 2 SEEM : sembler 3 ~ **cold/thirsty** : avoir froid, soif 4 ~ **like** WANT : avoir envie de — ~ n : toucher m, sensation f — **feeling** [ˈfiːlɪŋ] n 1 SENSATION : sensation f 2 EMOTION : sentiment m 3 OPINION : avis m 4 ~**s** npl : sentiments mpl
feet → **foot**
feign [ˈfeɪn] vt : feindre
feline [ˈfiːˌlaɪn] adj : félin — ~ n : félin m
fell[1] → **fall**
fell[2] [ˈfɛl] vt : abattre (un arbre)
fellow [ˈfɛˌloː] n 1 COMPANION : compagnon m 2 MAN : gars m fam, type m fam — **fellowship** [ˈfɛloˌʃɪp] n 1 COMPANIONSHIP : camaraderie f 2 GRANT : bourse f universitaire
felon [ˈfɛlən] n : criminel m, -nelle f — **felony** [ˈfɛləni] n, pl **-nies** : crime m
felt[1] → **feel**
felt[2] [ˈfɛlt] n : feutre m
female [ˈfiːˌmeɪl] adj : femelle (se dit des animaux), féminin (se dit des personnes) — ~ n 1 : femelle f (animal) 2 WOMAN : femme f
feminine [ˈfɛmənən] adj : féminin — **femininity** [ˌfɛməˈnɪnəti] n : féminité f — **feminism** [ˈfɛməˌnɪzəm] n : féminisme m — **feminist** [ˈfɛmənɪst] adj : féministe — ~ n : féministe mf
fence [ˈfɛnts] n : clôture f, barrière f — ~ v **fenced; fencing** vt : clôturer — vi : faire de l'escrime — **fencing** [ˈfɛntsɪŋ] n : escrime f
fend [ˈfɛnd] vt or ~ **off** : parer (un coup) — vi ~ **for oneself** : se débrouiller tout seul
fender [ˈfɛndər] n : aile f (d'une voiture)
fennel [ˈfɛnəl] n : fenouil m
ferment [fərˈmɛnt] vi : fermenter — **fermentation** [ˌfərmənˈteɪʃən, -ˌmɛn-] n : fermentation f
fern [ˈfərn] n : fougère f
ferocious [fəˈroːʃəs] adj : féroce — **ferocity** [fəˈrasəti] n : férocité f

ferret [ˈfɛrət] n : furet m — ~ vt ~ **out** : dénicher
Ferris wheel [ˈfɛrɪs] n : grande roue f
ferry [ˈfɛri] vt **-ried; -rying** : transporter — ~ n, pl **-ries** : ferry-boat m
fertile [ˈfərtəl] adj : fertile — **fertility** [fərˈtɪləti] n : fertilité f, fécondité f — **fertilize** [ˈfərtəlˌaɪz] vt **-ized; -izing** : fertiliser (une terre), féconder (un œuf, etc.) — **fertilizer** [ˈfərtəlˌaɪzər] n : engrais m
fervent [ˈfərvənt] adj : fervent — **fervor** or Brit **fervour** [ˈfərvər] n : ferveur f
fester [ˈfɛstər] vi : suppurer
festival [ˈfɛstəvəl] n : festival m — **festive** [ˈfɛstɪv] adj : joyeux, de fête — **festivities** [fɛsˈtɪvətiz] npl : réjouissances fpl
fetch [ˈfɛtʃ] vt 1 BRING : aller chercher 2 REALIZE : rapporter (de l'argent)
fetid [ˈfɛtəd] adj : fétide
fetish [ˈfɛtɪʃ] n : fétiche m
fetter [ˈfɛtər] vt : enchaîner — **fetters** [ˈfɛtərz] npl : fers mpl, chaînes fpl
fetus [ˈfiːtəs] n : fœtus m
feud [ˈfjuːd] n : querelle f — ~ vi : se quereller
feudal [ˈfjuːdəl] adj : féodal
fever [ˈfiːvər] n : fièvre f — **feverish** [ˈfiːvərɪʃ] adj : fiévreux
few [ˈfjuː] adj 1 : peu de 2 a ~ : quelques — ~ pron 1 : peu, quelques-uns, quelques-unes 2 quite a ~ : un assez grand nombre de — **fewer** [ˈfjuːər] adj : moins de — ~ pron : moins
fiancé, fiancée [ˌfiːˌɑnˈseɪ, ˌfiːˈɑnˌseɪ] n : fiancé m, -cée f
fiasco [fiˈæsˌkoː] n, pl **-coes** : fiasco m
fib [ˈfɪb] n : petit mensonge m — ~ vi **fibbed; fibbing** : raconter des histoires
fiber or **fibre** [ˈfaɪbər] n : fibre f — **fiberglass** [ˈfaɪbərˌglæs] n : fibre f de verre — **fibrous** [ˈfaɪbrəs] adj : fibreux
fickle [ˈfɪkəl] adj : volage, inconstant
fiction [ˈfɪkʃən] n : fiction f — **fictional** [ˈfɪkʃənəl] or **fictitious** [fɪkˈtɪʃəs] adj : fictif
fiddle [ˈfɪdəl] n : violon m — ~ vi **-dled; -dling** ~ **with** : tripoter
fidelity [fəˈdɛləti, faɪ-] n, pl **-ties** : fidélité f
fidget [ˈfɪdʒət] vi : remuer — **fidgety** [ˈfɪdʒəti] adj : agité
field [ˈfiːld] n 1 : champ m 2 : terrain m (de sport) 3 SPECIALTY : domaine m — **field glasses** npl : jumelles fpl — **field trip** n : sortie f éducative
fiend [ˈfiːnd] n 1 : diable m 2 FANATIC : mordu m — **fiendish** [ˈfiːndɪʃ] adj : diabolique
fierce [ˈfɪrs] adj **fiercer; -est** 1 FEROCIOUS : féroce 2 INTENSE : violent — **fierceness** [ˈfɪrsnəs] n : férocité f

fiery [ˈfaɪəri] *adj* **fierier; -est 1** BURNING : brûlant **2** SPIRITED : ardent

fifteen [fɪfˈtiːn] *n* : quinze *m* — ~ *adj* : quinze — **fifteenth** [fɪfˈtiːnθ] *n* **1** : quinzième *mf* **2 November** ~ : le 15 novembre — ~ *adj* : quinzième

fifth [ˈfɪfθ] *n* **1** : cinquième *mf* **2 June** ~ : le cinq juin — ~ *adj* : cinquième

fiftieth [ˈfɪftiəθ] *n* : cinquantième *mf* — ~ *adj* : cinquantième

fifty [ˈfɪfti] *n, pl* **-ties** : cinquante *m* — ~ *adj* : cinquante — **fifty–fifty** [ˌfɪftiˈfɪfti] *adv* : moitié-moitié — ~ *adj* **a** ~ **chance** : une chance sur deux

fig [ˈfɪg] *n* : figue *f*

fight [ˈfaɪt] *v* **fought** [ˈfɔt]; **fighting** *vi* **1** BATTLE : se battre **2** QUARREL : se disputer **3** STRUGGLE : lutter — *vt* : se battre contre, combattre — ~ *n* **1** BATTLE : combat *m* **2** BRAWL : bagarre *f* **3** QUARREL : dispute *f* **4** STRUGGLE : lutte *f* — **fighter** [ˈfaɪtər] *n* **1** : combattant *m*, -tante *f* **2** *or* ~ **plane** : avion *m* de chasse

figment [ˈfɪgmənt] *n* ~ **of the imagination** : produit *m* de l'imagination

figurative [ˈfɪgjərətɪv, -gə-] *adj* : figuré

figure [ˈfɪgjər, -gər] *n* **1** : figure *f* **2** NUMBER : chiffre *m* **3** SHAPE : forme *f* **4** ~ **of speech** : façon *f* de parler **5 watch one's** ~ : surveiller sa ligne — *v* **-ured; -uring** *vt* : penser, supposer — *vi* **1** APPEAR : figurer **2 that** ~**s!** : ça se comprend! — **figurehead** [ˈfɪgjərˌhɛd, -gər-] *n* **1** : figure *f* de proue (d'un navire) **2** : homme *m* de paille — **figure out** *vt* : comprendre

file[1] [ˈfaɪl] *n* : lime *f* (outil) — ~ *vt* **filed; filing** : limer

file[2] *v* **filed; filing** *vt* **1** CLASSIFY : classer **2** ~ **charges** : déposer une plainte — ~ *n* **1** : dossier *m* **2** *or* **computer** ~ : fichier *m*

file[3] ROW : file *f* — ~ *vi* ~ **past** : défiler devant

fill [ˈfɪl] *vt* **1** : remplir **2** PLUG : boucher (un trou) **3** : plomber (une dent) **4** ~ **in** IN-FORM : mettre au courant — *vi* **1** *or* ~ **up** : se remplir **2** ~ **in for** : remplacer — ~ *n* **1 eat one's** ~ : se rassasier **2 have had one's** ~ **of** : en avoir assez de

fillet [fɪˈleɪ, ˈfɪˌleɪ, ˈfɪlət] *n* : filet *m*

filling [ˈfɪlɪŋ] *n* **1** : garniture *f* (d'une tarte, etc.) **2** : plombage *m* (d'une dent) **3** ~ **station** → **service station**

filly [ˈfɪli] *n, pl* **-lies** : pouliche *f*

film [ˈfɪlm] *n* **1** : pellicule *f* **2** MOVIE : film *m* — ~ *vt* : filmer

filter [ˈfɪltər] *n* : filtre *m* — ~ *v* : filtrer

filth [ˈfɪlθ] *n* : saleté *f* — **filthiness** [ˈfɪlθɪnəs] *n* : saleté *f* — **filthy** [ˈfɪlθi] *adj* **filthier; -est** : sale, dégoûtant

fin [ˈfɪn] *n* : nageoire *f*

final [ˈfaɪnəl] *adj* **1** LAST : dernier **2** CON-CLUSIVE : définitif **3** ULTIMATE : final — ~ *n* **1** *or* ~ **s** : finale *f* (d'une compétition) **2** ~ **s** *npl* : examens *mpl* de fin de semestre — **finalist** [ˈfaɪnəlɪst] *n* : finaliste *mf* — **finalize** [ˈfaɪnəlˌaɪz] *vt* **-ized; -izing** : mettre au point — **finally** [ˈfaɪnəli] *adv* : enfin, finalement

finance [fəˈnænts, ˈfaɪˌnænts] *n* **1** : finance *f* **2** ~ **s** *npl* RESOURCES : finances *fpl* — ~ *vt* **-nanced; -nancing** : financer — **financial** [fəˈnænʧəl, faɪ-] *adj* : financier

find [ˈfaɪnd] *vt* **found** [ˈfaʊnd]; **finding 1** LO-CATE : trouver **2** REALIZE : s'apercevoir **3** ~ **out** : découvrir **4** ~ **guilty** : prononcer coupable — ~ *n* : trouvaille *f* — **finding** [ˈfaɪndɪŋ] *n* **1** FIND : découverte *f* **2** ~ **s** *npl* : conclusions *fpl*

fine[1] [ˈfaɪn] *n* : amende *f* — ~ *vt* **fined; fin-ing** : condamner à une amende

fine[2] *adj* **finer; -est 1** DELICATE : fin **2** SUB-TLE : subtil **3** EXCELLENT : excellent **4** : beau (se dit du temps) **5 be** ~ : aller bien **6 that's** ~ **with me** : ça me va — ~ *adv* OK : très bien — **fine arts** *npl* : beaux-arts *mpl* — **finely** [ˈfaɪnli] *adv* **1** EXCELLENTLY : exceptionnellement **2** PRECISELY : délicate-ment **3** MINUTELY : finement

finesse [fəˈnɛs] *n* : finesse *f*

finger [ˈfɪŋgər] *n* : doigt *m* — ~ *vt* : toucher, palper — **fingernail** [ˈfɪŋgərˌneɪl] *n* : ongle *m* — **fingerprint** [ˈfɪŋgərˌprɪnt] *n* : em-preinte *f* digitale — **fingertip** [ˈfɪŋgərˌtɪp] *n* : bout *m* du doigt

finicky [ˈfɪnɪki] *adj* : pointilleux

finish [ˈfɪnɪʃ] *vt* : finir, terminer — *vi* : finir, se terminer — ~ *n* **1** END : fin *f* **2** *or* ~ **line** : arrivée *f* **3** SURFACE : finition *f*, fini *m* *Can*

finite [ˈfaɪˌnaɪt] *adj* : fini

fir [ˈfər] *n* : sapin *m*

fire [ˈfaɪr] *n* **1** : feu *m* **2** BLAZE : incendie *m* **3 catch** ~ : prendre feu **4 on** ~ : en feu **5 open** ~ **on** : ouvrir le feu sur — ~ *vt* **fired; firing 1** IGNITE : incendier **2** DISMISS : renvoyer, virer **3** SHOOT : tirer — **fire alarm** *n* : avertisseur *m* d'incendie — **firearm** [ˈfaɪrˌɑrm] *n* : arme *f* à feu — **fire-cracker** [ˈfaɪrˌkrækər] *n* : pétard *m* — **fire engine** *n* : pompe *f* à incendie — **fire escape** *n* : escalier *m* de secours — **fire extin-guisher** *n* : extincteur *m* — **firefighter** [ˈfaɪrˌfaɪtər] *n* : pompier *m*, sapeur-pompier *m France* — **fireman** [ˈfaɪrmən] *n, pl* **-men** [-mən, -ˌmɛn] → **firefighter** — **fireplace** [ˈfaɪrˌpleɪs] *n* : cheminée *f*, foyer *m* — **fire-proof** [ˈfaɪrˌpruːf] *adj* : ignifuge — **fireside** [ˈfaɪrˌsaɪd] *n* : coin *m* du feu — **fire station** *n* : caserne *f* de pompiers *France*, poste *m* de pompiers *Can* — **firewood** [ˈfaɪrˌwʊd] *n* : bois *m* de chauffage — **fireworks** [ˈfaɪrˌwərks] *npl* : feux *mpl* d'artifice

firm[1] ['fərm] *n* : entreprise *f*, firme *f*
firm[2] *adj* **1** : ferme **2** STEADY : solide **3 stand ~** : tenir bon — **firmly** ['fərmli] *adv* : fermement — **firmness** ['fərmnəs] *n* : fermeté *f*
first ['fərst] *adj* **1** : premier **2 at ~ sight** : à première vue — **~** *adv* **1** : d'abord **2 for the ~ time** : pour la première fois **3 ~ of all** : tout d'abord — **~** *n* **1** : premier *m*, -mière *f* **2 or ~ gear** : première *f* **3 at ~** : au début — **first aid** *n* : premiers secours *mpl* — **first-class** ['fərst'klæs] *adv* : en première — **~** *adj* : de première qualité, de première classe — **firstly** ['fərstli] *adv* : premièrement
fiscal ['fɪskəl] *adj* : fiscal
fish ['fɪʃ] *n, pl* **fish** *or* **fishes** : poisson *m* — **~** *vi* **1** : pêcher **2 ~ for** SEEK : chercher **3 go ~ing** : aller à la pêche — **fisherman** ['fɪʃərmən] *n, pl* **-men** [-mən, -mɛn] : pêcheur *m*, -cheuse *f* — **fishhook** ['fɪʃ-,hʊk] *n* : hameçon *m* — **fishing** ['fɪʃɪŋ] *n* : pêche *f* — **fishing pole** *n* : canne *f* à la pêche — **fishy** ['fɪʃi] *adj* **fishier; -est 1** : de poisson **2** SUSPICIOUS : louche
fist ['fɪst] *n* : poing *m*
fit[1] ['fɪt] *n* : crise *f* (épileptique), accès *m* (de colère, etc.)
fit[2] *adj* **fitter; fittest 1** APPROPRIATE : convenable **2** HEALTHY : en forme **3 see ~ to** : trouver bon de — **~** *v* **fitted; fitting** *vt* **1** (*relating to clothing*) : aller à **2** MATCH : correspondre à **3** INSTALL : poser, insérer **4** EQUIP : équiper — *vi* **1** : être de la bonne taille **2 *or* ~ in** BELONG : s'intégrer — **~** *n* : coupe *f* (d'un vêtement) — **fitful** ['fɪtfəl] *adj* : intermittent *or* : agité (se dit du sommeil) — **fitness** ['fɪtnəs] *n* **1** HEALTH : forme *f* physique **2** SUITABILITY : aptitude *f* — **fitting** ['fɪtɪŋ] *adj* : approprié, convenable
five ['faɪv] *n* : cinq *m* — **~** *adj* : cinq — **five hundred** *adj* : cinq cents
fix ['fɪks] *vt* **1** ATTACH : fixer **2** REPAIR : réparer **3** PREPARE : préparer **4** RIG : truquer — **~** *n* **be in a ~** : être dans le pétrin *m* — **fixed** ['fɪkst] *adj* : fixe — **fixture** ['fɪkstʃər] *n* : installation *f*
fizz ['fɪz] *vi* : pétiller — **~** *n* : pétillement *m*
fizzle ['fɪzəl] *vi* **~ out** : s'éteindre
flabbergasted ['flæbər,gæstəd] *adj* : sidéré
flabby ['flæbi] *adj* **flabbier; -est** : mou
flaccid ['flæksəd, 'flæsəd] *adj* : flasque
flag[1] ['flæg] *vi* WEAKEN : faiblir
flag[2] *n* : drapeau *m* — **~** *vt* **flagged; flagging** : faire signe à (un taxi, etc.) — **flagpole** [,flæg,po:l] *n* : mât *m*
flagrant ['fleɪgrənt] *adj* : flagrant
flair ['flær] *n* **1** TALENT : don *m* **2** STYLE : style *m*

flake ['fleɪk] *n* : flocon *m* (de neige), écaille *f* (de peinture) — **~** *vi* **flaked; flaking** *or* **~ off** : s'écailler
flamboyant [flæm'bɔɪənt] *adj* : extravagant
flame ['fleɪm] *n* **1** : flamme *f* **2 burst into ~s** : s'embraser, s'enflammer
flamingo [flə'mɪŋgo] *n, pl* **-gos** : flamant *m*
flammable ['flæməbəl] *adj* : inflammable
flank ['flæŋk] *n* : flanc *m* — **~** *vt* : flanquer
flannel ['flænəl] *n* : flanelle *f*
flap ['flæp] *n* : rabat *m* — **~** *v* **flapped; flapping** *vt* : battre (des ailes) — *vi* **~ in the wind** : claquer au vent
flare ['flær] *vi* **flared; flaring ~ up 1** BLAZE : s'embraser **2** ERUPT : s'emporter (se dit d'une personne), éclater (se dit d'une dispute, etc.) — **~** *n* : fusée *f* éclairante
flash ['flæʃ] *vi* **1** SPARKLE : briller **2** BLINK : clignoter **3 ~ past** : passer comme un éclair — *vt* **1** PROJECT : projeter **2** SHOW : montrer **3 ~ a smile** : lancer un sourire — **~** *n* **1** éclat *m* **2** : flash *m* (d'un appareil photographique) **3 ~ of lightning** : éclair *m* **4 in a ~** : dans un instant — **flashlight** ['flæʃ,laɪt] *n* : lampe *f* de poche — **flashy** ['flæʃi] *adj* **flashier; -est** : tape-à-l'œil, tapageur
flask ['flæsk] *n* : flacon *m*
flat ['flæt] *adj* **flatter; flattest 1** LEVEL : plat **2** DOWNRIGHT : catégorique **3** FIXED : fixe **4** MONOTONOUS : monotone **5** : éventé (se dit d'une boisson) **6** : bémol (en musique) **7 ~ tire** : crevé, à plat — **~** *n* **1** : bémol *m* (en musique) **2** *Brit* APARTMENT : appartement *m* **3** *or* **~ tire** : crevaison *f* — **~** *adv* **1** : à plat **2 ~ broke** : complètement fauché **3 in one hour ~** : dans une heure pile *fam* — **flatly** ['flætli] *adv* : catégoriquement — **flatten** ['flætən] *vt* : aplatir — *vi* *or* **~ out** : s'aplanir
flatter ['flætər] *vt* : flatter — **flatterer** ['flætərər] *n* : flatteur *m*, -teuse *f* — **flattering** ['flætərɪŋ] *adj* : flatteur — **flattery** ['flætəri] *n, pl* **-ries** : flatterie *f*
flaunt ['flɔnt] *vt* : faire étalage de
flavor *or Brit* **flavour** ['fleɪvər] *n* **1** : goût *m* **2** FLAVORING : parfum *m* — **~** *vt* : parfumer — **flavorful** *or Brit* **flavourful** ['fleɪvərfəl] *adj* : savoureux — **flavoring** *or Brit* **flavouring** ['fleɪvərɪŋ] *n* : parfum *m*
flaw ['flɔ] *n* : défaut *m* — **flawless** ['flɔləs] *adj* : sans défaut, parfait
flax ['flæks] *n* : lin *m*
flea ['fli:] *n* : puce *f*
fleck ['flɛk] *n* : petite tache *f*, moucheture *f*
flee ['fli:] *v* **fled** ['flɛd]; **fleeing** : fuir
fleece ['fli:s] *n* : toison *f* — **~** *vt* **fleeced; fleecing** : escroquer
fleet ['fli:t] *n* : flotte *f*
fleeting ['fli:tɪŋ] *adj* : bref

Flemish ['flɛmɪʃ] *adj* : flamand
flesh ['flɛʃ] *n* : chair *f* — **fleshy** ['flɛʃi] *adj*
fleshier; -est : charnu
flew → **fly**[1]
flex ['flɛks] *vt* : fléchir — **flexible** ['flɛksəbəl]
adj : flexible — **flexibility** ['flɛksə'bɪləti] *n*
: flexibilité *f*
flick ['flɪk] *n* : petit coup *m* — ~ *vt* ~ **a**
switch : appuyer sur un bouton — *vi* ~
through : feuilleter
flicker ['flɪkər] *vi* : vaciller — ~ *n* **1** : vacillement *m* **2 a** ~ **of hope** : une lueur d'e-
spoir
flier ['flaɪər] *n* **1** PILOT : aviateur *m*, -trice *f* **2**
or **flyer** LEAFLET : prospectus *m*
flight[1] ['flaɪt] *n* **1** FLYING : vol *m* **2** ~ **of**
stairs : escalier *m*
flight[2] *n* ESCAPE : fuite *f*
flimsy ['flɪmzi] *adj* **flimsier; -est 1** LIGHT
: léger **2** SHAKY : peu solide **3 a** ~ **ex-**
cuse : une pauvre excuse
flinch ['flɪntʃ] *vi* **1** WINCE : tressaillir **2** ~
from : reculer devant
fling ['flɪŋ] *vt* **flung** ['flʌŋ]; **flinging 1**
THROW : lancer **2** ~ **open** : ouvrir
brusquement — ~ *n* **1** AFFAIR : affaire *f*,
aventure *f* **2 have a** ~ **at** : essayer de faire
flint ['flɪnt] *n* : silex *m*
flip ['flɪp] *v* **flipped; flipping** *vt* **1** *or* ~
over : faire sauter **2** ~ **a coin** : jouer à
pile ou face — *vi* **1** *or* ~ **over** : se retourner **2** ~ **through** : feuilleter — ~ *n*
: saut *m* périlleux
flippant ['flɪpənt] *adj* : désinvolte
flipper ['flɪpər] *n* : nageoire *f*
flirt ['flərt] *vi* : flirter — ~ *n* : flirteur *m*,
-teuse *f* — **flirtatious** [,flər'teɪʃəs] *adj*
: charmeur
flit ['flɪt] *vi* **flitted; flitting** : voleter
float ['floːt] *n* **1** RAFT : radeau *m* **2** CORK
: flotteur *m* **3** : char *m* (de carnaval) — ~
vi : flotter — *vt* : faire flotter
flock ['flɑk] *n* **1** : volée *f* (d'oiseaux), troupeau *m* (de moutons) **2** CROWD : foule *f* —
~ *vi* : affluer, venir en foule
flog ['flɑg] *vt* **flogged; flogging** : flageller
flood ['flʌd] *n* **1** : inondation *f* **2** : déluge *m*
(de paroles, de larmes, etc.) — ~ *vt* : inon-
der — *vi* : déborder (se dit d'une rivière) —
floodlight ['flʌd,laɪt] *n* : projecteur *m*
floor ['flor] *n* **1** : plancher *m* **2** GROUND : sol
m **3** STORY : étage *m* **4 dance** ~ : piste *f*
de danse **5 ground** ~ : rez-de-chaussée *m*
— ~ *vt* **1** KNOCK DOWN : terrasser **2** AS-
TOUND : stupéfier — **floorboard** ['flor-
,bord] *n* : planche *f*
flop ['flɑp] *vi* **flopped; flopping 1** : s'agiter
mollement **2** *or* ~ **down** COLLAPSE : s'affaler **3** FAIL : échouer — ~ *n* : fiasco *m* —

floppy ['flɑpi] *adj* **floppier; -est** : mou —
floppy disk *n* : disquette *f*
flora ['florə] *n* : flore *f* — **floral** ['florəl] *adj*
: floral — **florid** ['florɪd] *adj* **1** FLOWERY
: fleuri **2** RUDDY : rougeaud — **florist**
['florɪst] *n* : fleuriste *mf*
floss ['flɔs] → **dental floss**
flounder[1] ['flaʊndər] *n, pl* **flounder** *or*
flounders : flet *m*
flounder[2] *vi* **1** *or* ~ **about** : patauger **2**
FALTER : bredouiller
flour ['flaʊər] *n* : farine *f*
flourish ['flərɪʃ] *vi* **1** PROSPER : prospérer **2**
THRIVE : s'épanouir — *vt* BRANDISH
: brandir — ~ *n* : grand geste *m* — **flour-**
ishing ['flərɪʃɪŋ] *adj* : florissant
flout ['flaʊt] *vt* : bafouer
flow ['floː] *vi* **1** : couler **2** MOVE : s'écouler
3 CIRCULATE : circuler **4** BILLOW : flotter —
~ *n* **1** : écoulement *m* (d'un liquide) **2**
MOVEMENT : circulation *f* **3** : flux *m* (de la
marée)
flower ['flaʊər] *n* : fleur *f* — ~ *vi* : fleurir —
flowering ['flaʊərɪŋ] *n* : floraison *f* — **flow-**
erpot ['flaʊər,pɑt] *n* : pot *m* de fleurs —
flowery ['flaʊəri] *adj* : fleuri
flown → **fly**[1]
flu ['fluː] *n* : grippe *f*
fluctuate ['flʌktʃʊ,eɪt] *vi* **-ated; -ating**
: fluctuer — **fluctuation** [,flʌktʃʊ'eɪʃən] *n*
: fluctuation *f*
fluency ['fluːəntsi] *n* : aisance *f* — **fluent**
['fluːənt] *adj* **1** : coulant, aisé **2 be** ~ **in**
: parler couramment — **fluently** ['fluːəntli]
adv : couramment
fluff ['flʌf] *n* **1** DOWN : duvet *m* **2** FUZZ
: peluches *fpl* — **fluffy** ['flʌfi] *adj* **fluffier;**
-est : duveteux
fluid ['fluːɪd] *adj* : fluide — ~ *n* : fluide *m*
flunk ['flʌŋk] *vt* FAIL : rater
fluorescent [,flʊr'ɛsənt, ,flɔr-] *adj* : fluorescent
flurry ['fləri] *n, pl* **-ries 1** GUST : rafale *f* **2** *or*
snow ~ : poudrerie *f Can* **3** : tourbillon *m*
(d'activité)
flush ['flʌʃ] *vi* BLUSH : rougir — *vt* ~ **the**
toilet : tirer la chasse d'eau — ~ *n* **1**
: chasse *f* (d'eau) **2** BLUSH : rougeur *f* — ~
adj : au même niveau — ~ *adv* : de niveau
fluster ['flʌstər] *vt* : troubler
flute ['fluːt] *n* : flûte *f*
flutter ['flʌtər] *vi* **1** FLAP : battre (se dit des
ailes) **2** FLIT : voleter **3** ~ **about** : s'agiter
— ~ *n* **1** : battement *m* (d'ailes) **2** STIR
: agitation *f*, émoi *m*
flux ['flʌks] *n* **in a state of** ~ : dans un état
de perpétuel changement
fly[1] ['flaɪ] *v* **flew** ['fluː]; **flown** ['floːn]; **flying**
vi **1** : voler **2** TRAVEL : prendre l'avion **3**
: flotter (se dit d'un drapeau) **4** RUSH : filer

5 FLEE : s'enfuir — *vt* : faire voler — ~ *n*, *pl* **flies** : braguette *f* (d'un pantalon)
fly[2] *n*, *pl* **flies** : mouche *f* (insecte)
flyer → **flier**
flying saucer *n* : soucoupe *f* volante
foal ['fo:l] *n* : poulain *m*
foam ['fo:m] *n* : mousse *f*, écume *f* — ~ *vi* : mousser, écumer — **foamy** ['fo:mi] *adj* **foamier; -est** : mousseux, écumeux (se dit de la mer)
focus ['fo:kəs] *n*, *pl* **foci** ['fo:,saɪ, -,kaɪ] **1** : foyer *m* **2 be in** ~ : être au point **3** ~ **of attention** : centre *m* d'attention — ~ *v* **-cused** *or* **-cussed; -cusing** *or* **-cussing** *vt* **1** : mettre au point (un instrument) **2** : fixer (les yeux) — *vi* ~ **on** : se concentrer sur
fodder ['fɑdər] *n* : fourrage *m*
foe ['fo:] *n* : ennemi *m*, -mie *f*
fog ['fɔg, 'fɑg] *n* : brouillard *m* — ~ *vi* **fogged; fogging** *or* ~ **up** : s'embuer — **foggy** ['fɔgi, 'fɑ-] *adj* **foggier; -est** : brumeux — **foghorn** ['fɔg,hɔrn, 'fɑg-] *n* : corne *f* de brume
foil[1] ['fɔɪl] *vt* : déjouer
foil[2] *n* : feuille *f* (d'aluminium, etc.)
fold[1] ['fo:ld] *n* **1** : parc *m* à moutons **2 return to the** ~ : rentrer au bercail
fold[2] *vt* **1** : plier **2** ~ **one's arms** : croiser les bras — *vi* **1** *or* ~ **up** : se plier **2** FAIL : échouer — ~ *n* CREASE : pli *m* — **folder** ['fo:ldər] *n* **1** FILE : chemise *f* **2** PAMPHLET : dépliant *m*
foliage ['fo:liːʤ, -liʤ] *n* : feuillage *m*
folk ['fo:k] *n*, *pl* **folk** *or* **folks 1** PEOPLE : gens *mfpl* **2** ~**s** *npl* PARENTS : famille *f*, parents *mpl* — ~ *adj* : populaire, folklorique — **folklore** ['fo:k,lor] *n* : folklore *m*
follow ['fɑlo] *vt* **1** : suivre **2** PURSUE : poursuivre **3** ~ **up** : donner suite à — *vi* **1** : suivre **2** ENSUE : s'ensuivre — **follower** ['fɑloər] *n* : partisan *m*, -sane *f* — **following** ['fɑloɪŋ] *adj* : suivant — ~ *n* : partisans *mpl* — ~ *prep* : après
folly ['fɑli] *n*, *pl* **-lies** : folie *f*
fond ['fɑnd] *adj* **1** : affectueux **2 be** ~ **of** : aimer beaucoup
fondle ['fɑndəl] *vt* **-dled; -dling** : caresser
fondness ['fɑndnəs] *n* **1** : affection *f* **2 have a** ~ **for** : avoir une prédilection pour
food ['fu:d] *n* : nourriture *f* — **foodstuffs** ['fu:d,stʌfs] *npl* : denrées *fpl* alimentaires
fool ['fu:l] *n* **1** : idiot *m*, -diote *f* **2** JESTER : fou *m* — ~ *vt* DECEIVE : duper — *vi* **1** JOKE : plaisanter **2** ~ **around** : perdre son temps — **foolhardy** ['fu:l,hɑrdi] *adj* : téméraire — **foolish** ['fu:lɪʃ] *adj* : bête, idiot — **foolishness** ['fu:lɪʃnəs] *n* : bêtise *f*, sottise *f* — **foolproof** ['fu:l,pru:f] *adj* : infaillible
foot ['fʊt] *n*, *pl* **feet** ['fiːt] : pied *m* — **footage**

['fʊtɪʤ] *n* : métrage *m* — **football** ['fʊt,bɔl] *n* : football *m* américain, football *m* Can — **footbridge** ['fʊt,brɪʤ] *n* : passerelle *f* — **foothills** ['fʊt,hɪlz] *npl* : contreforts *mpl* — **foothold** ['fʊt,ho:ld] *n* : prise *f* de pied — **footing** ['fʊtɪŋ] *n* **1** → **foothold 2** STATUS : position *f* **3 on equal** ~ : sur pied d'égalité — **footlights** ['fʊt,laɪts] *npl* : rampe *f* — **footnote** ['fʊt,no:t] *n* : note *f* (en bas de la page) — **footpath** ['fʊt,pæθ] *n* : sentier *m* — **footprint** ['fʊt,prɪnt] *n* : empreinte *f* (de pied) — **footstep** ['fʊt,stɛp] *n* : pas *m* — **footwear** ['fʊt,wær] *n* : chaussures *fpl*
for ['fɔr] *prep* **1** : pour **2** BECAUSE OF : de, à cause de **3** (*indicating duration*) : pour, pendant **4** (*indicating destination*) : pour, à destination de **5 a cure** ~ **cancer** : un remède contre le cancer **6** ~ **sale** : à vendre — ~ *conj* BECAUSE : car
forage ['fɔrɪʤ] *vi* **-aged; -aging** : fourrager
foray ['fɔr,eɪ] *n* : incursion *f*
forbid [fər'bɪd] *vt* **-bade** [-'bæd, -'beɪd] *or* **-bad** [-'bæd]; **-bidden** [-'bɪdən]; **-bidding** : interdire, défendre — **forbidding** [fər'bɪdɪŋ] *adj* : menaçant
force ['fors] *n* **1** : force *f* **2** *or* ~**s** *npl* : forces *fpl* **3 by** ~ : de force **4 in** ~ : en vigueur — ~ *vt* **forced; forcing 1** : forcer **2** IMPOSE : imposer — **forceful** ['forsfəl] *adj* : vigoureux
forceps ['forsəps, -,sɛps] *ns & pl* : forceps *m*
forcibly ['forsəbli] *adv* : de force
ford ['ford] *n* : gué *m* — ~ *vt* : passer à gué
fore ['for] *n* **1** : avant *m* (d'un navire) **2 come to the** ~ : se mettre en évidence
forearm ['for,arm] *n* : avant-bras *m*
foreboding [for'bo:dɪŋ] *n* : pressentiment *m*
forecast ['for,kæst] *vt* **-cast; -casting** : prévoir — ~ *n* *or* **weather** ~ : prévisions *fpl* météorologiques, météo *f fam*
forefathers ['for,faðərz] *npl* : ancêtres *mfpl*, aïeux *mpl*
forefinger ['for,fɪŋgər] *n* : index *m*
forefront ['for,frʌnt] *n* : premier rang *m*
forego [for'go:] → **forgo**
foregone [for'gɔn] *adj* **it's a** ~ **conclusion** : c'est gagné d'avance
foreground ['for,graund] *n* : premier plan *m*
forehead ['fored, 'for,hed] *n* : front *m*
foreign ['forən] *adj* **1** : étranger (se dit d'une langue, etc.) **2** ~ **trade** : commerce *m* extérieur — **foreigner** ['forənər] *n* : étranger *m*, -gère *f*
foreman ['formən] *n*, *pl* **-men** [-mən, -,mɛn] : contremaître *m*
foremost ['for,mo:st] *adj* : principal — ~ *adv* **first and** ~ : tout d'abord
forensic [fə'rɛnʦɪk] *adj* : médico-légal
forerunner ['for,rʌnər] *n* : précurseur *m*
foresee [for'si:] *vt* **-saw; -seen; -seeing**

: prévoir — **foreseeable** [for'si:əbəl] *adj* : prévisible

foreshadow [for'ʃædo:] *vt* : présager

foresight ['for,saɪt] *n* : prévoyance *f*

forest ['fɔrəst] *n* : forêt *f* — **forestry** ['fɔrəstri] *n* : sylviculture *f*

foretaste ['for,teɪst] *n* : avant-goût *m*

foretell [for'tɛl] *vt* -**told**; -**telling** : prédire

forethought ['for,θɔt] *n* : prévoyance *f*

forever [fər'ɛvər] *adv* **1** ETERNALLY : toujours **2** CONTINUALLY : sans cesse

forewarn [for'wɔrn] *vt* : avertir, prévenir

foreword ['forwərd] *n* : avant-propos *m*

forfeit ['fɔrfət] *n* **1** PENALTY : peine *f* **2 pay a ~** : avoir un gage — **~** *vt* : perdre

forge ['fɔrdʒ] *n* : forge *f* — **~** *v* **forged**; **forging** *vt* **1** : forger (un métal, etc.) **2** COUNTERFEIT : contrefaire, falsifier — *vi* **~ ahead** : prendre de l'avance — **forger** ['fɔrdʒər] *n* : faussaire *mf*, faux-monnayeur *m* — **forgery** ['fɔrdʒəri] *n*, *pl* -**eries** : faux *m*, contrefaçon *f*

forget [fər'gɛt] *v* -**got** [-'gɑt]; -**gotten** [-'gɑtən] *or* -**got**; -**getting** : oublier — **forgetful** [fər'gɛtfəl] *adj* : distrait

forgive [fər'gɪv] *vt* -**gave** [-'geɪv]; -**given** [-'gɪvən]; -**giving** : pardonner — **forgiveness** [fər'gɪvnəs] *n* : pardon *m*

forgo *or* **forego** [for'go:] *vt* -**went**; -**gone**; -**going** : renoncer à, se priver de

fork ['fɔrk] *n* **1** : fourchette *f* **2** PITCHFORK : fourche *f* **3** JUNCTION : bifurcation *f* (d'une route) — **~** *vt or* **~ over** : allonger *fam* — *vi* : bifurquer

forlorn [fər'lɔrn] *adj* : triste

form ['fɔrm] *n* **1** : forme *f* **2** DOCUMENT : formulaire *m* — **~** *vt* : former — *vi* : se former, prendre forme

formal ['fɔrməl] *adj* **1** : officiel, solennel **2** : soigné, soutenu (se dit du langage) — **~** *n* **1** *or* **~ dance** : bal *m* **2** *or* **~ dress** : tenue *f* de soirée — **formality** [fɔr'mæləti] *n*, *pl* -**ties** : formalité *f*

format ['fɔr,mæt] *n* : format *m* — **~** *vt* -**matted**; -**matting** : formater (une diskette, etc.)

formation [fɔr'meɪʃən] *n* : formation *f*

former ['fɔrmər] *adj* **1** PREVIOUS : ancien **2** FIRST : premier — **formerly** ['fɔrmərli] *adv* : autrefois

formidable ['fɔrmədəbəl, fɔr'mɪdə-] *adj* : redoutable

formula ['fɔrmjələ] *n*, *pl* -**las** *or* -**lae** [-,li:, -,laɪ] **1** : formule *f* **2** *or* **baby ~** : lait *m* reconstitué — **formulate** ['fɔrmjə,leɪt] *vt* -**lated**; -**lating** : formuler

forsake [fər'seɪk] *vt* -**sook** [-'sʊk]; -**saken** [-'seɪkən]; -**saking** : abandonner

fort ['fɔrt] *n* : fort *m*

forth ['forθ] *adv* **1 and so ~** : et ainsi de suite **2 from this day ~** : dorénavant **3 go back and ~** : aller et venir — **forthcoming** [forθ'kʌmɪŋ, 'forθ-] *adj* **1** COMING : prochain, à venir **2** OPEN : communicatif — **forthright** ['forθ,raɪt] *adj* : franc, direct

fortieth ['fɔrtiəθ] *n* : quarantième *mf* — **~** *adj* : quarantième

fortify ['fɔrtə,faɪ] *vt* -**fied**; -**fying** : fortifier — **fortification** [,fɔrtəfə'keɪʃən] *n* : fortification *f*

fortitude ['fɔrtə,tu:d, -,tju:d] *n* : force *f* d'âme

fortnight ['fort,naɪt] *n* : quinzaine *f*, quinze jours *mpl*

fortress ['fɔrtrəs] *n* : forteresse *f*

fortunate ['fɔrtʃənət] *adj* : heureux — **fortunately** ['fɔrtʃənətli] *adv* : heureusement — **fortune** ['fɔrtʃən] *n* **1** : fortune *f* **2** LUCK : chance *f* — **fortune–teller** ['fɔrtʃən,tɛlər] *n* : diseuse *f* de bonne aventure

forty ['fɔrti] *n*, *pl* **forties** : quarante *m* — **~** *adj* : quarante

forum ['forəm] *n*, *pl* -**rums** : forum *m*

forward ['forwərd] *adj* **1** : avant, en avant **2** BRASH : effronté — **~** *adv* : en avant, vers l'avant — **~** *n* : avant *m* (aux sports) — **~** *vt* : expédier (des marchandises), faire suivre (du courrier) — **forwards** ['forwərdz] *adv* → **forward**

fossil ['fɑsəl] *n* : fossile *m*

foster ['fɔstər] *adj* : adoptif, d'accueil — **~** *vt* **1** NURTURE : nourrir **2** ENCOURAGE : encourager

fought → **fight**

foul ['faʊl] *adj* **1** : infect (se dit d'une odeur, etc.) **2 ~ language** : langage *m* ordurier **3 ~ play** : jeu *m* irrégulier **4 ~ weather** : sale temps *m* — **~** *n* : faute *f* (aux sports) — **~** *vt* : salir, souiller

found[1] ['faʊnd] → **find**

found[2] *vt* : fonder, établir — **foundation** [faʊn'deɪʃən] *n* **1** : fondation *f* **2** BASIS : base *f*, fondement *m*

founder[1] ['faʊndər] *n* : fondateur *m*, -trice *f*

founder[2] *vi* **1** SINK : sombrer **2** COLLAPSE : s'effondrer

fountain ['faʊntən] *n* : fontaine *f*

four ['for] *n* : quatre *m* — **~** *adj* : quatre — **fourfold** ['for,fo:ld, -'fo:ld] *adj* : quadruple — **four hundred** *adj* : quatre cents

fourteen [for'ti:n] *n* : quatorze *m* — **~** *adj* : quatorze — **fourteenth** [for'ti:nθ] *n* **1** : quatorzième *mf* **2 June ~** : le quatorze juin — **~** *adj* : quatorzième

fourth ['forθ] *n* **1** : quatrième *mf* (dans une série) **2** : quart *m* (en mathématiques) **3 August ~** : le quatre août — **~** *adj* : quatrième

fowl ['faʊl] *n*, *pl* **fowl** *or* **fowls** : volaille *f*

fox ['fɑks] *n*, *pl* **foxes** : renard *m* — **~** *vt*

TRICK : tromper, berner — **foxy** ['fɑksi] *adj*
foxier; -est SHREWD : rusé
foyer ['fɔɪər, 'fɔɪˌjeɪ] *n* : vestibule *m*, foyer *m*
(d'un théâtre)
fraction ['frækʃən] *n* : fraction *f*
fracture ['fræktʃər] *n* : fracture *f* — ～ *vt*
-tured; -turing : fracturer
fragile ['fræʤəl, -ˌʤaɪl] *adj* : fragile —
fragility [frə'ʤɪləti] *n* : fragilité *f*
fragment ['frægmənt] *n* : fragment *m*
fragrance ['freɪɡrənts] *n* : parfum *m* — **fragrant** ['freɪɡrənt] *adj* : parfumé
frail ['freɪl] *adj* : frêle, fragile
frame ['freɪm] *vt* **framed; framing 1** EN-
CLOSE : encadrer **2** DEVISE : élaborer **3**
FORMULATE : formuler **4** INCRIMINATE
: monter un coup contre — ～ *n* **1** : cadre *m*
(d'un tableau, etc.) **2** : charpente *f* (d'un édifice, etc.) **3** ～**s** *npl* : monture *f* (de
lunettes) **4** ～ **of mind** : état *m* d'esprit —
framework ['freɪmˌwərk] *n* : structure *f*,
cadre *m*
franchise ['frænˌtʃaɪz] *n* **1** : franchise *f* (en
commerce) **2** SUFFRAGE : droit *m* de vote
frank ['fræŋk] *adj* : franc — **frankly**
['fræŋkli] *adv* : franchement — **frankness**
['fræŋknəs] *n* : franchise *f*
frantic ['fræntɪk] *adj* : frénétique
fraternal [frə'tərnəl] *adj* : fraternel — **fraternity** [frə'tərnəti] *n, pl* **-ties** : fraternité *f* —
fraternize ['frætərˌnaɪz] *vi* **-nized; -nizing**
: fraterniser
fraud ['frɔd] *n* **1** DECEIT : fraude *f* **2** IMPOS-
TOR : imposteur *m* — **fraudulent**
['frɔʤələnt] *adj* : frauduleux
fraught ['frɔt] *adj* ～ **with** : chargé de
fray[1] ['freɪ] *n* : bagarre *f*
fray[2] *vt* : mettre (les nerfs) à vif — *vi* : s'effilocher
freak ['fri:k] *n* **1** ODDITY : phénomène *m* **2**
ENTHUSIAST : fana *mf fam* — ～ *adj* : anormal — **freakish** ['fri:kɪʃ] *adj* : anormal,
bizarre
freckle ['frɛkəl] *n* : tache *f* de rousseur
free ['fri:] *adj* **freer; freest 1** : libre **2** *or* ～
of charge : gratuit **3** ～ **from** : dépourvu
de — ～ *vt* **freed; freeing 1** RELEASE
: libérer **2** DISENGAGE : dégager — ～ *adv*
1 : librement **2 for** ～ : gratuitement —
freedom ['fri:dəm] *n* : liberté *f* — **freelance** ['fri:ˌlænts] *adv* : à la pige — **freely**
['fri:li] *adv* **1** : librement **2** LAVISHLY
: largement — **freeway** ['fri:ˌweɪ] *n* : autoroute *f* — **free will** ['fri:ˌwɪl] *n* **1** : libre arbitre *m* **2 of one's own** ～ : de sa propre
volonté
freeze ['fri:z] *v* **froze** ['fro:z]; **frozen**
['fro:zən]; **freezing** *vt* **1** : geler (de l'eau),
congeler (des aliments, etc.) **2** FIX : bloquer
— *vi* : geler — ～ *n* **1** : gel *m* **2** : blocage *m*

(des prix, etc.) — **freeze–dry** ['fri:z'draɪ] *vt*
-dried; -drying : lyophiliser — **freezer**
['fri:zər] *n* : congélateur *m* — **freezing**
['fri:zɪŋ] *adj* **1** : glacial **2 it's** ～ : on gèle
freight ['freɪt] *n* **1** SHIPPING : transport *m* **2**
GOODS : fret *m*, marchandises *fpl*
French ['frɛntʃ] *adj* : français — ～ *n* **1**
: français *m* (langue) **2 the** ～ : les Français
French Canadian *adj* : canadien français —
～ *n* : Canadien *m* français, Canadienne *f*
française
french fries ['frɛntʃˌfraɪz] *npl* : frites *fpl*
Frenchman ['frɛntʃmən] *n, pl* **-men** [-mən,
-ˌmɛn] : Français *m* — **Frenchwoman**
['frɛntʃˌwʊmən] *n, pl* **-women** [-ˌwɪmən]
: Française *f*
frenzy ['frɛnzi] *n, pl* **-zies** : frénésie *f* —
frenzied ['frɛnzid] *adj* : frénétique
frequency ['fri:kwəntsi] *n, pl* **-cies**
: fréquence *f* — **frequent** [fri:kwɛnt,
'fri:kwənt] *vt* : fréquenter — ～ ['fri:kwənt]
adj : fréquent — **frequently** ['fri:kwəntli]
adv : fréquemment
fresco ['frɛsˌko:] *n, pl* **-coes** : fresque *f*
fresh ['frɛʃ] *adj* **1** : frais **2** NEW : nouveau **3**
IMPUDENT : insolent **4** ～ **water** : eau *f*
douce — **freshen** ['frɛʃən] *vt* : rafraîchir —
vi ～ **up** : se rafraîchir — **freshly** ['frɛʃli]
adv : récemment — **freshman** ['frɛʃmən] *n,
pl* **-men** [-mən, -ˌmɛn] : étudiant *m*, -diante
f de première année — **freshness** ['frɛʃnəs]
n : fraîcheur *f*
fret ['frɛt] *vi* **fretted; fretting** : s'inquiéter —
fretful ['frɛtfəl] *adj* : irritable
friar ['fraɪər] *n* : frère *m*
friction ['frɪkʃən] *n* : friction *f*
Friday ['fraɪˌdeɪ, -di] *n* : vendredi *m*
friend ['frɛnd] *n* : ami *m*, amie *f* — **friendli-
ness** ['frɛndlinəs] *n* : gentillesse *f* —
friendly ['frɛndli] *adj* **friendlier; -est** : gentil, amical — **friendship** ['frɛndˌʃɪp] *n*
: amitié *f*
frigate ['frɪɡət] *n* : frégate *f*
fright ['fraɪt] *n* : peur *f*, frayeur *f* — **frighten**
['fraɪtən] *vt* : faire peur à, effrayer — **frightened** ['fraɪt'nd] *adj* : apeuré, effrayé —
frightening ['fraɪt'nɪŋ] *adj* : effrayant —
frightful ['fraɪtfəl] *adj* : terrible, affreux
frigid ['frɪʤɪd] *adj* : glacial
frill ['frɪl] *n* **1** RUFFLE : volant *m* (d'une jupe),
jabot *m* (d'une chemise) **2** LUXURY : luxe *m*
fringe ['frɪnʤ] *n* **1** : frange *f* **2** EDGE : bordure *f* **3** ～ **benefits** : avantages *mpl* sociaux
frisk ['frɪsk] *vt* SEARCH : fouiller — **frisky**
['frɪski] *adj* **friskier; -est** : vif, folâtre
fritter ['frɪtər] *n* : beignet *m* — ～ *vt or* ～
away : gaspiller
frivolous ['frɪvələs] *adj* : frivole — **frivolity**
[frɪ'vɑləti] *n, pl* **-ties** : frivolité *f*

frizzy ['frɪzi] *adj* **frizzier; -est** : crépu
fro ['froː] *adv* → **to**
frock ['frɑk] *n* : robe *f*
frog ['frɔg, 'frɑg] *n* **1** : grenouille *f* **2 have a ~ in one's throat** : avoir un chat dans la gorge — **frogman** ['frɔg,mæn, 'frɑg-, -mən] *n, pl* **-men** [-mən, -,mɛn] : homme-grenouille *m*
frolic ['frɑlɪk] *vi* **-icked; -icking** : folâtrer
from ['frʌm, 'frɑm] *prep* **1** (*indicating a starting point*) : de, à partir de **2** (*indicating a source or cause*) : de, par, à **3 ~ now on** : à partir de maintenant **4 protection ~ the sun** : protection contre le soleil **5 drink ~ a glass** : boire dans un verre
front ['frʌnt] *n* **1** : avant *m*, devant *m* **2** APPEARANCE : air *m*, contenance *f* **3** : front *m* (militaire) **4** : façade *f* (d'un bâtiment) **5 in ~** : à l'avant **6 in ~ of** : devant — **~** *vi* **~ on** : donner sur — **~** *adj* **1** : de devant, (en) avant **2 ~ row** : premier rang *m*
frontier [,frʌn'tɪr] *n* : frontière *f*
frost ['frɔst] *n* **1** : givre *m* **2** FREEZING : gel *m*, gelée *f* — **~** *vt* : glacer (un gâteau) — **frostbite** ['frɔst,baɪt] *n* : gelure *f* — **frosting** ['frɔstɪŋ] *n* ICING : glaçage *m* — **frosty** ['frɔsti] *adj* **frostier; -est 1** : couvert de givre **2** FRIGID : glacial
froth ['frɔθ] *n, pl* **froths** ['frɔθs, 'frɔðz] : écume *f*, mousse *f* — **frothy** ['frɔθi, -ði] *adj* **frothier; -est** : écumeux, mousseux
frown ['fraʊn] *vi* : froncer les sourcils — **~** *n* : froncement *m* de sourcils
froze, frozen → **freeze**
frugal ['fruːgəl] *adj* : économe
fruit ['fruːt] *n* : fruit *m* — **fruitcake** ['fruːt-,keɪk] *n* : cake *m* — **fruitful** ['fruːtfəl] *adj* : fructueux — **fruition** [fruː'ɪʃən] *n* **come to ~** : se réaliser — **fruity** ['fruːti] *adj* **fruitier; -est** : fruité
frustrate ['frʌs,treɪt] *vt* **-trated; -trating** : frustrer — **frustrating** ['frʌs,treɪtɪŋ] *adj* : frustrant — **frustration** [,frʌs'treɪʃən] *n* : frustration *f*
fry ['fraɪ] *v* **fried; frying** : frire — **~** *n, pl* **fries 1** *or* **small ~** : menu fretin *m* **2 fries** → **french fries** — **frying pan** *n* : poêle *f*
fudge ['fʌʤ] *n* : caramel *m* mou — **~** *vt* FALSIFY : truquer
fuel ['fjuːəl] *n* : combustible *m*, carburant *m* — **~** *vt* **-eled** *or* **-elled; -eling** *or* **-elling 1** : alimenter en combustible **2** STIMULATE : aviver
fugitive ['fjuːʤətɪv] *n* : fugitif *m*, -tive *f*
fulfill *or* **fulfil** [fʊl'fɪl] *vt* **-filled; -filling 1** EXECUTE : accomplir, réaliser **2** FILL, MEET : remplir — **fulfillment** [fʊl'fɪlmənt] *n* **1** ACCOMPLISHMENT : réalisation *f* **2** SATISFACTION : contentement *m*
full ['fʊl, 'fʌl] *adj* **1** FILLED : plein **2** COM-

PLETE : entier, total **3** : ample (se dit d'une jupe), rond (se dit d'un visage) **4** : complet (se dit d'un hotel, etc.) — **~** *adv* **1** DIRECTLY : carrément **2 know ~ well** : savoir très bien — **~** *n* **in ~** : entièrement — **full-fledged** ['fʊl'flɛʤd] *adj* : à part entière — **fully** ['fʊli] *adv* : complètement
fumble ['fʌmbəl] *vi* **-bled; -bling** : tâtonner, fouiller
fume ['fjuːm] *vi* **fumed; fuming** RAGE : rager, fulminer — **fumes** ['fjuːmz] *npl* : vapeurs *fpl*
fumigate ['fjuːmə,geɪt] *vt* **-gated; -gating** : désinfecter par fumigation
fun ['fʌn] *n* **1** : amusement *m* **2 have ~** : s'amuser **3 for ~** : pour rire **4 make ~ of** : se moquer de
function ['fʌŋkʃən] *n* **1** : fonction *f* **2** GATHERING : réception *f*, cérémonie *f* — **~** *vi* **1** : fonctionner **2 ~ as** : servir de — **functional** ['fʌŋkʃənəl] *adj* : fonctionnel
fund ['fʌnd] *n* **1** : fonds *m* **2 ~s** *npl* RESOURCES : fonds *mpl* — **~** *vt* : financer
fundamental [,fʌndə'mɛntəl] *adj* : fondamental — **fundamentals** *npl* : principes *mpl* de base
funeral ['fjuːnərəl] *n* : enterrement *m*, funérailles *fpl* — **~** *adj* : funèbre — **funeral home** *or* **funeral parlor** *n* : entreprise *f* de pompes funèbres
fungus ['fʌŋgəs] *n, pl* **fungi** [fʌn,ʤaɪ, 'fʌn-,gaɪ] **1** MUSHROOM : champignon *m* **2** MOLD : moisissure *f*
funnel ['fʌnəl] *n* **1** : entonnoir *m* **2** SMOKESTACK : cheminée *f*
funny ['fʌni] *adj* **funnier; -est 1** : drôle, amusant **2** PECULIAR : bizarre — **funnies** ['fʌniz] *npl* : bandes *fpl* dessinées
fur ['fər] *n* : fourrure *f* — **~** *adj* : de fourrure
furious ['fjʊriəs] *adj* : furieux
furnace ['fərnəs] *n* : fourneau *m*
furnish ['fərnɪʃ] *vt* **1** SUPPLY : fournir **2** : meubler (un appartement, etc.) — **furnishings** ['fərnɪʃɪŋz] *npl* : ameublement *m*, meubles *mpl* — **furniture** ['fərnɪʧər] *n* : meubles *mpl*
furrow ['fəroː] *n* : sillon *m*
furry ['fəri] *adj* **furrier; -est** : au poil touffu (se dit d'un animal), en peluche (se dit d'un jouet, etc.)
further ['fərðər] *adv* **1** FARTHER : plus loin **2** MORE : davantage, plus **3** MOREOVER : de plus — **~** *adj* **1** FARTHER : plus éloigné **2** ADDITIONAL : supplémentaire **3 until ~ notice** : jusqu'à nouvel ordre — **furthermore** ['fərðər,mor] *adv* : en outre, de plus — **furthest** ['fərðəst] *adv & adj* → **farthest**
furtive ['fərtɪv] *adj* : furtif
fury ['fjʊri] *n, pl* **-ries** : fureur *f*

fuse¹ or **fuze** ['fju:z] n : amorce f, détonateur m (d'une bombe, etc.)

fuse² v **fused; fusing** vt **1** MELT : fondre **2** UNITE : fusionner — ~ n **1** : fusible m, plomb m (en électricité) **2 blow a** ~ : faire sauter un plomb — **fusion** ['fju:ʒən] n : fusion f

fuss ['fʌs] n **1** : agitation f, remueménage m **2 make a** ~ : faire des histoires — ~ vi **1** : s'agiter **2** WORRY : s'inquiéter — **fussy**

['fʌsi] adj **fussier; -est 1** FINICKY : tatillon, pointilleux **2** ELABORATE : tarabiscoté

futile ['fju:ṭəl, 'fju:ˌtaɪl] adj : futile, vain — **futility** [fju:'tɪləti] n : futilité f

future ['fju:tʃər] adj : futur — ~ n : avenir m, futur m

fuze n → **fuse**¹

fuzz ['fʌz] n FLUFF : peluches fpl — **fuzzy** ['fʌzi] adj **fuzzier; -est 1** FURRY : duveteux **2** INDISTINCT : flou **3** VAGUE : confus

G

g ['ʤi:] n, pl **g's** or **gs** ['ʤi:z] : g m, septième lettre de l'alphabet

gab ['gæb] vi **gabbed; gabbing** : bavarder — ~ n CHATTER : bavardage m

gable ['geɪbəl] n : pignon m

gadget ['gæʤət] n : gadget m

gag ['gæg] v **gagged; gagging** vt : bâillonner — vi CHOKE : avoir des haut-le-cœur — ~ n **1** : bâillon m **2** JOKE : blague f

gage → **gauge**

gaiety ['geɪəṭi] n, pl **-eties** : gaieté f

gain ['geɪn] n **1** PROFIT : profit m **2** INCREASE : augmentation f — ~ vt **1** OBTAIN : gagner **2** ~ **weight** : prendre du poids — vi **1** PROFIT : gagner **2** : avancer (se dit d'une horloge) — **gainful** ['geɪnfəl] adj : rémunéré

gait ['geɪt] n : démarche f

gala ['geɪlə, 'gæ-, 'gɑ-] n : gala m

galaxy ['gæləksi] n, pl **-axies** : galaxie f

gale ['geɪl] n : coup m de vent

gall ['gɔl] n **have the** ~ **to** : avoir le culot de

gallant ['gælənt] adj : galant

gallbladder ['gɔlˌblædər] n : vesicule f biliaire

gallery ['gæləri] n, pl **-leries** : galerie f

gallon ['gælən] n : gallon m

gallop ['gæləp] vi : galoper — ~ n : galop m

gallows ['gæˌloːz] n, pl **-lows** or **-lowses** [-ˌloːzəz] : gibet m, potence f

gallstone ['gɔlˌstoːn] n : calcul m biliaire

galore [gə'lor] adv : en abondance

galoshes [gə'lɑʃəz] npl : caoutchoucs mpl, claques fpl Can

galvanize ['gælvənˌaɪz] vt **-nized; -nizing** : galvaniser

gamble ['gæmbəl] v **-bled; -bling** vi : jouer — vt WAGER : parier — ~ n **1** BET : pari m **2** RISK : entreprise f risquée — **gambler** ['gæmbələr] n : joueur m, joueuse f

game ['geɪm] n **1** : jeu m **2** MATCH : match m, partie f **3** or ~ **animals** : gibier m — ~ adj READY : partant, prêt

gamut ['gæmət] n : gamme f

gang ['gæŋ] n : bande f — ~ vi ~ **up on** : se liguer contre

gangplank ['gæŋˌplæŋk] n : passerelle f

gangrene ['gæŋˌgriːn, 'gæn-; gæŋ'-, gæn'-] n : gangrène f

gangster ['gæŋstər] n : gangster m

gangway ['gæŋˌweɪ] → **gangplank**

gap ['gæp] n **1** OPENING : trou m **2** INTERVAL : intervalle m **3** DIFFERENCE : écart m **4** DEFICIENCY : lacune f

gape ['geɪp] vi **gaped; gaping 1** OPEN : bâiller **2** STARE : rester bouche bée

garage [gə'rɑʒ, -'rɑʤ] n : garage m

garb ['gɑrb] n : costume m, mise f

garbage ['gɑrbɪʤ] n : ordures fpl — **garbage can** n : poubelle f

garble ['gɑrbəl] vt **-bled; -bling** : embrouiller — **garbled** ['gɑrbəld] adj : confus

garden ['gɑrdən] n : jardin m — ~ vi : jardiner — **gardener** ['gɑrdənər] n : jardinier m, -nière f

gargle ['gɑrgəl] vi **-gled; -gling** : se gargariser

garish ['gærɪʃ] adj : criard, voyant

garland ['gɑrlənd] n : guirlande f

garlic ['gɑrlɪk] n : ail m

garment ['gɑrmənt] n : vêtement m

garnish ['gɑrnɪʃ] vt : garnir — ~ n : garniture f

garret ['gærət] n : mansarde f

garrison ['gærəsən] n : garnison f

garter ['gɑrtər] n : jarretière f

gas ['gæs] n, pl **gases 1** : gaz m **2** GASOLINE : essence f — ~ v **gassed; gassing** vt : asphyxier au gaz — vi ~ **up** : faire le plein d'essence — **gas station** n : station-service f

gash ['gæʃ] n : entaille f — ~ vt : entailler
gasket ['gæskət] n : joint m (d'étanchéité)
gasoline ['gæsə‚li:n, ‚gæsə'-] n : essence f
gasp ['gæsp] vi 1 : avoir le souffle coupé 2
PANT : haleter — ~ n : halètement m
gastric ['gæstrɪk] adj : gastrique
gastronomy [gæs'trɑnəmi] n : gastronomie
f
gate ['geɪt] n 1 DOOR : porte f 2 BARRIER
: barrière f, grille f — **gateway** ['geɪt‚weɪ] n
: porte f, entrée f
gather ['gæðər] vt 1 ASSEMBLE : rassembler
2 COLLECT : ramasser 3 CONCLUDE : déduire — vi ASSEMBLE : se rassembler —
gathering ['gæðərɪŋ] n : rassemblement m
gaudy ['gɔdi] adj -**dier; -est** : criard, tape-à-
l'œil
gauge ['geɪdʒ] n 1 INDICATOR : jauge f, indicateur m 2 CALIBER : calibre m — ~ vt
gauged; gauging 1 MEASURE : jauger 2
ESTIMATE : évaluer
gaunt ['gɔnt] adj : décharné, émacié
gauze ['gɔz] n : gaze f
gave → **give**
gawky ['gɔki] adj **gawkier; gawkiest**
: gauche, maladroit
gay ['geɪ] adj 1 : gai 2 HOMOSEXUAL : gay
gaze ['geɪz] vi **gazed; gazing** : regarder (fixement) — ~ n : regard m
gazette [gə'zɛt] n : journal m officiel
gear ['gɪr] n 1 EQUIPMENT : équipement m
2 POSSESSIONS : effets mpl personnels 3
SPEED : vitesse f 4 or ~ **wheel** : roue f
dentée — ~ vt : adapter — vi ~ **up** : se
préparer — **gearshift** ['gɪr‚ʃɪft] n : levier m
de vitesse
geese → **goose**
gelatin ['dʒɛlətən] n : gélatine f
gem ['dʒɛm] n : pierre f précieuse, gemme f
— **gemstone** ['dʒɛm‚sto:n] n : pierre f précieuse
gender ['dʒɛndər] n 1 SEX : sexe m 2
: genre m (en grammaire)
gene ['dʒi:n] n : gène m
genealogy [‚dʒi:ni'ɑlədʒi, ‚dʒɛ-, -'æ-] n, pl
-**gies** : généalogie f
general ['dʒɛnrəl, 'dʒɛnə-] adj : général —
~ n 1 : général m (militaire) 2 **in** ~ : en
général — **generalize** ['dʒɛnrə‚laɪz,
'dʒɛnərə-] v -**ized; -izing** : généraliser —
generally ['dʒɛnrəli, 'dʒɛnərə-] adv
: généralement, en général — **general prac-**
titioner n : généraliste mf
generate ['dʒɛnə‚reɪt] vt -**ated; -ating**
: générer — **generation** [‚dʒɛnə'reɪʃ ən] n
: génération f — **generator** ['dʒɛnə‚reɪtər] n
1 : générateur m 2 : génératrice f (d'énergie
électrique)
generous ['dʒɛnərəs] adj 1 : généreux 2

AMPLE : copieux — **generosity** [‚dʒɛnə-
'rɑsəti] n, pl -**ties** : générosité f
genetic [dʒə'nɛtɪk] adj : génétique — **genet-**
ics [dʒə'nɛtɪks] n : génétique f
genial ['dʒi:niəl] adj : affable
genital ['dʒɛnətəl] adj : génital — **genitals**
['dʒɛnətəlz] npl : organes mpl génitaux
genius ['dʒi:njəs] n : génie m
genocide ['dʒɛnə‚saɪd] n : génocide m
genteel [dʒɛn'ti:l] adj : distingué
gentle ['dʒɛntəl] adj -**tler; -tlest** 1 MILD
: doux 2 LIGHT : léger — **gentleman**
['dʒɛntəlmən] n, pl -**men** [-mən, -‚mɛn] 1
MAN : monsieur m 2 **act like a** ~ : agir en
gentleman — **gentleness** ['dʒɛntəlnəs] n
: douceur f
genuine [‚dʒɛnjuwən] adj 1 AUTHENTIC
: authentique, véritable 2 SINCERE : sincère
geography [dʒi'ɑgrəfi] n, pl -**phies** : géographie f — **geographic** [‚dʒi:ə'græfɪk] or **ge-**
ographical [-fɪkəl] adj : géographique
geology [dʒi'ɑlədʒi] n : géologie f — **geo-**
logic [‚dʒi:ə'lɑdʒɪk] or **geological** [-dʒɪkəl]
adj : géologique
geometry [dʒi'ɑmətri] n, pl -**tries**
: géométrie f — **geometric** [‚dʒi:ə'mɛtrɪk]
or **geometrical** [-trɪkəl] adj : géométrique
geranium [dʒə'reɪniəm] n : géranium m
geriatric [‚dʒɛri'ætrɪk] adj : gériatrique —
geriatrics [‚dʒɛri'ætrɪks] n : gériatrie f
germ ['dʒərm] n 1 : germe m 2 MICROBE
: microbe m
German ['dʒərmən] adj : allemand — ~ n
: allemand m (langue)
germinate ['dʒərmə‚neɪt] v -**nated; -nating**
vi : germer — vt : faire germer
gestation [dʒɛ'steɪʃ ən] n : gestation f
gesture ['dʒɛstʃ ər] n : geste m — ~ vi
-**tured; -turing** 1 : faire des gestes 2 ~ **to**
: faire signe à
get ['gɛt] v **got** ['gɑt]; **got** or **gotten**
['gɑtən]; **getting** vt 1 OBTAIN : obtenir,
trouver 2 RECEIVE : recevoir, avoir 3 EARN
: gagner 4 FETCH : aller chercher 5 CATCH
: attraper (une maladie) 6 UNDERSTAND
: comprendre 7 PREPARE : préparer 8 ~
one's hair cut : se faire couper les cheveux
9 **have got to** : devoir — vi 1 BECOME : devenir 2 GO, MOVE : aller, arriver 3
PROGRESS : avancer 4 ~ **ahead** : progresser 5 ~ **at** MEAN : vouloir dire 6 ~
away : s'échapper 7 ~ **back at** : se venger
de 8 ~ **by** : s'en sortir 9 ~ **out** : sortir
10 ~ **over** : se remettre de 11 ~ **together**
MEET : se réunir 12 ~ **up** : se lever — **get**
along vi 1 MANAGE : aller 2 **get along**
with : bien s'entendre avec — **getaway**
['gɛtə‚weɪ] n : fuite f — **get–together**
['gɛttə‚gɛðər] n : réunion f
geyser ['gaɪzər] n : geyser m

ghastly ['gæstli] *adj* **-lier; -est** : épouvantable

ghetto ['gɛto:] *n, pl* **-tos** *or* **-toes** : ghetto *m*

ghost ['go:st] *n* : fantôme *m*, spectre *m* — **ghostly** ['go:stli] *adj* **-lier; -est** : spectral

giant ['dʒaɪənt] *n* : géant *m*, géante *f* — **~** *adj* : géant, gigantesque

gibberish ['dʒɪbərɪʃ] *n* : baragouin *m*, charabia *m fam*

gibe ['dʒaɪb] *vi* **gibed; gibing ~ at** : se moquer de — **~** *n* : moquerie *f*

giblets ['dʒɪbləts] *npl* : abats *mpl* (de volaille)

giddy ['gɪdi] *adj* **-dier; -est** : vertigineux — **giddiness** ['gɪdinəs] *n* : vertige *m*

gift ['gɪft] *n* **1** PRESENT : cadeau *m* **2** TALENT : don *m* — **gifted** ['gɪftəd] *adj* : doué

gigantic [dʒaɪ'gæntɪk] *adj* : gigantesque

giggle ['gɪgəl] *vi* **-gled; -gling** : rire bêtement — **~** *n* : petit rire *m*

gild ['gɪld] *vt* **gilded** ['gɪldəd] *or* **gilt** ['gɪlt]; **gilding** : dorer

gill ['gɪl] *n* : branchie *f*, ouïe *f*

gilt ['gɪlt] *adj* : doré

gimmick ['gɪmɪk] *n* : truc *m*, gadget *m*

gin ['dʒɪn] *n* : gin *m*

ginger ['dʒɪndʒər] *n* : gingembre *m* — **ginger ale** *n* : boisson *f* gazeuse au gingembre — **gingerbread** ['dʒɪndʒər,brɛd] *n* : pain *m* d'épice — **gingerly** ['dʒɪndʒərli] *adv* : avec précaution

giraffe [dʒə'ræf] *n* : girafe *f*

girdle ['gərdəl] *n* : gaine *f*

girl ['gərl] *n* : fille *f*, jeune fille *f* — **girlfriend** ['gərl,frɛnd] *n* : copine *f*, petite amie *f*

girth ['gərθ] *n* : circonférence *f*

gist ['dʒɪst] *n* **the ~** : l'essentiel *m*

give ['gɪv] *v* **gave** ['geɪv]; **given** ['gɪvən]; **giving** *vt* **1** : donner **2 ~ out** DISTRIBUTE : distribuer **3 ~ up smoking** : arrêter de fumer — *vi* **1** YIELD : céder **2 ~ in** *or* **~ up** : se rendre — **~** *n* : élasticité *f*, souplesse *f* — **given** ['gɪvən] *adj* **1** SPECIFIED : donné **2** INCLINED : enclin — **given name** *n* : prénom *m*

glacier ['gleɪʃər] *n* : glacier *m*

glad ['glæd] *adj* **gladder; gladdest 1** : content **2 be ~ to** : être heureux de **3 ~ to meet you** : enchanté — **gladden** ['glædən] *vt* : réjouir — **gladly** ['glædli] *adv* : avec plaisir, volontiers

glade ['gleɪd] *n* : clairière *f*

glamour *or* **glamor** ['glæmər] *n* : charme *m* — **glamorous** ['glæmərəs] *adj* : séduisant

glance ['glænts] *vi* **glanced; glancing ~ at** : jeter un coup d'œil à — **~** *n* : coup *m* d'œil

gland ['glænd] *n* : glande *f*

glare ['glær] *vi* **glared; glaring 1** : briller d'un éclat éblouissant **2 ~ at** : lancer un regard furieux à — **~** *n* **1** : lumière *f* éblouissante **2** STARE : regard *m* furieux — **glaring** ['glærɪŋ] *adj* **1** BRIGHT : éblouissant **2** FLAGRANT : flagrant

glass ['glæs] *n* **1** : verre *m* **2 ~es** *npl* SPECTACLES : lunettes *fpl* — **~** *adj* : en verre — **glassware** ['glæs,wær] *n* : verrerie *f* — **glassy** ['glæsi] *adj* **glassier; glassiest** : vitreux

glaze ['gleɪz] *vt* **glazed; glazing** : vernisser (des céramiques) — **~** *n* **1** : vernis *m* **2** FROSTING : glaçage *m*

gleam ['gli:m] *n* : lueur *f* — **~** *vi* : luire, reluire

glee ['gli:] *n* : joie *f* — **gleeful** ['gli:fəl] *adj* : joyeux

glib ['glɪb] *adj* **glibber; glibbest** : désinvolte

glide ['glaɪd] *vi* **glided; gliding** : glisser (sur une surface), planer (en l'air) — **glider** ['glaɪdər] *n* : planeur *m*

glimmer ['glɪmər] *vi* : jeter une faible lueur — **~** *n* : lueur *f*

glimpse ['glɪmps] *vt* **glimpsed; glimpsing** : entrevoir — **~** *n* **1** : aperçu *m* **2 catch a ~ of** : entrevoir

glint ['glɪnt] *vi* : étinceler — **~** *n* : reflet *m*

glisten ['glɪsən] *vi* : briller

glitter ['glɪtər] *vi* : scintiller, étinceler — **~** *n* : scintillement *m*

gloat ['glo:t] *vi* : jubiler

globe ['glo:b] *n* : globe *m* — **global** ['glo:bəl] *adj* : mondial

gloom ['glu:m] *n* **1** DARKNESS : obscurité *f* **2** SADNESS : tristesse *f* — **gloomy** ['glu:mi] *adj* **gloomier; gloomiest 1** DARK : sombre **2** DISMAL : lugubre

glory ['glori] *n, pl* **-ries** : gloire *f* — **glorify** ['glorə,faɪ] *vt* **-fied; -fying** : glorifier — **glorious** ['gloriəs] *adj* : glorieux

gloss ['glɔs, 'glɑs] *n* : brillant *m*, lustre *m*

glossary ['glɔsəri, 'glɑ-] *n, pl* **-ries** : glossaire *m*

glossy ['glɔsi, 'glɑ-] *adj* **glossier; glossiest** : brillant

glove ['glʌv] *n* : gant *m*

glow ['glo:] *vi* **1** : luire **2 ~ with health** : rayonner de santé — **~** *n* : lueur *f*

glue ['glu:] *n* : colle *f* — **~** *vt* **glued; gluing** *or* **glueing** : coller

glum ['glʌm] *adj* **glummer; glummest** : morne, triste

glut ['glʌt] *n* : surabondance *f*

glutton ['glʌtən] *n* : glouton *m*, -tonne *f* — **gluttonous** ['glʌtənəs] *adj* : glouton — **gluttony** ['glʌtəni] *n, pl* **-tonies** : gloutonnerie *f*

gnarled ['nɑrld] *adj* : noueux

gnash ['næʃ] *vt* **~ one's teeth** : grincer des dents

gnat ['næt] *n* : moucheron *m*

gnaw ['nɔ] *vt* : ronger

go ['goː] *v* **went** ['wɛnt]; **gone** ['gɔn, 'gʌn]; **going**; **goes** ['goːz] *vi* **1** : aller **2** LEAVE : partir, s'en aller **3** EXTEND : s'étendre **4** SELL : se vendre **5** FUNCTION : marcher **6** DISAPPEAR : disparaître **7** ~ **back on** : revenir sur **8** ~ **for** FAVOR : aimer **9** ~ **off** EXPLODE : exploser **10** ~ **out** : sortir **11** ~ **with** MATCH : aller avec **12** ~ **without** : se passer de — *v aux* **be going to do** : aller faire — ~ *n, pl* **goes 1** ATTEMPT : essai *m*, tentative *f* **2 be on the** ~ : ne jamais s'arrêter

goad ['goːd] *vt* : aiguillonner (un animal), provoquer (une personne)

goal ['goːl] *n* **1** : but *m* — **goalie** ['goːli] → **goalkeeper** — **goalkeeper** ['goːl,kiːpər] *n* : gardien *m* de but

goat ['goːt] *n* : chèvre *f*

goatee [goː'tiː] *n* : barbiche *f*

gobble ['gabəl] *vt* **-bled; -bling** *or* ~ **up** : engloutir

goblet ['gablət] *n* : verre *m* à pied

goblin ['gablən] *n* : lutin *m*

god ['gad, 'gɔd] *n* **1** : dieu *m* **2 God** : Dieu *m* — **goddess** ['gadəs, 'gɔ-] *n* : déesse *f* — **godchild** ['gad,tʃaɪld, 'gɔd-] *n, pl* **-children** : filleul *m*, -leule *f* — **godfather** ['gad,faðər, 'gɔd-] *n* : parrain *m* — **godmother** ['gad,mʌðər, 'gɔd-] *n* : marraine *f*

goes → **go**

goggles ['gagəlz] *npl* : lunettes *fpl* (protectrices)

gold ['goːld] *n* : or *m* — **golden** ['goːldən] *adj* **1** : en or, d'or **2** : doré, couleur *f* d'or — **goldfish** ['goːld,fɪʃ] *n* : poisson *m* rouge — **goldsmith** ['goːld,smɪθ] *n* : orfèvre *m*

golf ['galf, 'gɔlf] *n* : golf *m* — ~ *vi* : jouer au golf — **golf ball** *n* : balle *f* de golfe — **golf course** *n* : terrain *m* de golf — **golfer** ['galfər, 'gɔl-] *n* : joueur *m*, joueuse *f* de golf

gone ['gɔn] *adj* **1** PAST : passé **2** DEPARTED : parti

good ['gʊd] *adj* **better** ['bɛtər]; **best** ['bɛst] **1** : bon **2** OBEDIENT : sage **3 be** ~ **at** : être bon en **4 feel** ~ : se sentir bien **5** ~ **evening** : bonsoir **6** ~ **morning** : bonjour **7** ~ **night** : bonsoir, bonne nuit **8 have a** ~ **time** : s'amuser — ~ *n* **1** : bien *m* **2** GOODNESS : bonté *f* **3** ~**s** *npl* PROPERTY : biens *mpl* **4** ~**s** *npl* WARES : marchandises *fpl* **5 for** ~ : pour de bon — ~ *adv* : bien — **good–bye** *or* **good–by** ['gʊd'baɪ] *n* : au revoir — **good–looking** ['gʊd'lʊkɪŋ] *adj* : beau — **goodness** ['gʊdnəs] *n* **1** : bonté *f* **2 thank** ~ ! : Dieu merci! — **goodwill** [,gʊd'wɪl] *n* : bienveillance *f* — **goody** ['gʊdi] *n, pl* **goodies 1** ~! : chouette! *fam* **2 goodies** *npl* : friandises *fpl*

goof ['guːf] *n* : gaffe *f fam* — ~ *vi* **1** *or* ~ **up** : gaffer *fam* **2** ~ **around** : faire l'imbécile

goose ['guːs] *n, pl* **geese** ['giːs] : oie *f* — **goose bumps** *npl* : chair *f* de poule

gopher ['goːfər] *n* : gaufre *f*

gore ['gor] *n* BLOOD : sang *m*

gorge ['gɔrdʒ] *n* RAVINE : gorge *f*, défilé *m* — ~ *vt* **gorged; gorging** ~ **oneself** : se gorger

gorgeous ['gɔrdʒəs] *adj* : magnifique, splendide

gorilla [gə'rɪlə] *n* : gorille *m*

gory ['gori] *adj* **gorier; goriest** : sanglant

gospel ['gaspəl] *n* **1** : évangile *m* **2 the Gospel** : l'Évangile

gossip ['gasɪp] *n* : commérages *mpl fam*, ragots *mpl fam* — ~ *vi* : bavarder — **gossipy** ['gasɪpi] *adj* : bavard

got → **get**

Gothic ['gaθɪk] *adj* : gothique

gotten → **get**

gourmet ['gʊr,meɪ, gʊr'meɪ] *n* : gourmet *m*

govern ['gʌvərn] *v* : gouverner — **governess** ['gʌvərnəs] *n* : gouvernante *f* — **government** ['gʌvərmənt] *n* : gouvernement *m* — **governor** ['gʌvənər, 'gʌvərnər] *n* : gouverneur *m*

gown ['gaʊn] *n* **1** : robe *f* **2** : toge *f* (de juge, etc.)

grab ['græb] *vt* **grabbed; grabbing** : saisir

grace ['greɪs] *n* : grâce *f* — ~ *vt* **graced; gracing 1** HONOR : honorer **2** ADORN : orner — **graceful** ['greɪsfəl] *adj* : gracieux — **gracious** ['greɪʃəs] *adj* : courtois, gracieux

grade ['greɪd] *n* **1** QUALITY : catégorie *f*, qualité *f* **2** RANK : grade *m*, rang *m* (militaire) **3** YEAR : classe *f* (à l'école) **4** MARK : note *f* **5** SLOPE : pente *f* — ~ *vt* **graded; grading 1** CLASSIFY : classer **2** MARK : noter (un examen, etc.) — **grade school** → **elementary school**

gradual ['grædʒuəl] *adj* : graduel, progressif — **gradually** ['grædʒuəli, 'grædʃəli] *adv* : petit à petit

graduate ['grædʒuət] *n* : diplômé *m*, -mée *f* — ~ ['grædʒu,eɪt] *vi* **-ated; -ating** : recevoir son diplôme — **graduation** [,grædʒu'eɪʃən] *n* : remise *f* des diplômes

graffiti [grə'fiːti, græ-] *npl* : graffiti *mpl*

graft ['græft] *n* : greffe *f* — ~ *vt* : greffer

grain ['greɪn] *n* **1** : grain *m* **2** CEREAL : céréales *fpl*

gram ['græm] *n* : gramme *m*

grammar ['græmər] *n* : grammaire *f* — **grammar school** → **elementary school**

grand ['grænd] *adj* **1** : grand, magnifique **2** FABULOUS : formidable *fam* — **grandchild** ['grænd,tʃaɪld] *n, pl* **-children** [-,tʃɪldrən]

: petit-fils *m*, petite-fille *f* — **granddaughter** ['grænd,dɔtər] *n* : petite-fille *f* — **grandeur** ['grændʒər] *n* : grandeur *f* — **grandfather** ['grænd,faðər] *n* : grand-père *m* — **grandiose** ['grændi,o:s, ,grændi'-] *adj* : grandiose — **grandmother** ['grænd,mʌðər] *n* : grand-mère *f* — **grandparents** ['grænd,pærənts] *npl* : grands-parents *mpl* — **grandson** ['grænd,sʌn] *n* : petit-fils *m* — **grandstand** ['grænd,stænd] *n* : tribune *f*

granite ['grænɪt] *n* : granit *m*, granite *m*

grant ['grænt] *vt* **1** : accorder **2** ADMIT : admettre **3 take for granted** : prendre pour acquis — **~** *n* **1** SUBSIDY : subvention *f* **2** SCHOLARSHIP : bourse *f*

grape ['greɪp] *n* : raisin *m*

grapefruit ['greɪp,fru:t] *n* : pamplemousse *mf*

grapevine ['greɪp,vaɪn] *n* : vigne *f*

graph ['græf] *n* : graphique *m* — **graphic** ['græfɪk] *adj* : graphique

grapnel ['græpnəl] *n* : grappin *m*

grapple ['græpəl] *vi* **-pled; -pling ~ with** : lutter avec

grasp ['græsp] *vt* **1** : saisir **2** UNDERSTAND : comprendre — **~** *n* **1** : prise *f* **2** UNDERSTANDING : compréhension *f* **3 within s.o.'s ~** : à la portée de qqn

grass ['græs] *n* **1** : herbe *f* **2** LAWN : gazon *m*, pelouse *f* — **grasshopper** ['græs,hɑpər] *n* : sauterelle *f*

grate[1] ['greɪt] *v* **grated; grating** *vt* : râper (du fromage, etc.) — *vi* : grincer

grate[2] *n* : grille *f*

grateful ['greɪtfəl] *adj* : reconnaissant — **gratefully** ['greɪtfəli] *adv* : avec reconnaissance — **gratefulness** ['greɪtfəlnəs] *n* : gratitude *f*, reconnaissance *f*

grater ['greɪtər] *n* : râpe *f*

gratify ['grætə,faɪ] *vt* **-fied; -fying 1** PLEASE : faire plaisir à **2** SATISFY : satisfaire

grating ['greɪtɪŋ] *n* : grille *f*

gratitude ['grætə,tu:d, -,tju:d] *n* : gratitude *f*

gratuitous [grə'tu:ətəs] *adj* : gratuit

gratuity [grə'tu:əti] *n*, *pl* **-ities** TIP : pourboire *m*

grave[1] ['greɪv] *n* : tombe *f*

grave[2] *adj* **graver; gravest** : grave, sérieux

gravel ['grævəl] *n* : gravier *m*

gravestone ['greɪv,sto:n] *n* : pierre *f* tombale — **graveyard** ['greɪv,jɑrd] *n* : cimetière *m*

gravity ['grævəti] *n*, *pl* **-ties 1** SERIOUSNESS : gravité *f* **2** : pesanteur *f* (en physique)

gravy ['greɪvi] *n*, *pl* **-vies** : sauce *f* (au jus de viande)

gray ['greɪ] *adj* **1** : gris **2** GLOOMY : morne — **~** *n* : gris *m* — **~** *vi or* **turn ~** : grisonner

graze[1] ['greɪz] *vi* **grazed; grazing** : paître

graze[2] *vt* **1** TOUCH : frôler **2** SCRATCH : écorcher

grease ['gri:s] *n* : graisse *f* — **~** ['gri:s, 'gri:z] *vt* **greased; greasing** : graisser — **greasy** ['gri:si, -zi] *adj* **greasier; greasiest 1** : graisseux **2** OILY : huileux

great ['greɪt] *adj* **1** : grand **2** FANTASTIC : génial *fam*, formidable *fam* — **great-grandchild** [,greɪt'grænd,tʃaɪld] *n*, *pl* **-children** [-,tʃɪldrən] : arrière-petit-enfant *m*, arrière-petite-enfant *f* — **great-grandfather** [,greɪt'grænd,faðər] *n* : arrière-grand-père *m* — **great-grandmother** [,greɪt'grænd,mʌðər] *n* : arrière-grand-mère *f* — **greatly** ['greɪtli] *adv* **1** MUCH : beaucoup **2** VERY : énormément — **greatness** ['greɪtnəs] *n* : grandeur *f*

greed ['gri:d] *n* **1** : avarice *f*, avidité *f* **2** GLUTTONY : gloutonnerie *f* — **greedily** ['gri:dəli] *adv* : avidement — **greedy** ['gri:di] *adj* **greedier; greediest 1** : avare, avide **2** GLUTTONOUS : glouton

Greek ['gri:k] *adj* : grec — **~** *n* : grec *m* (langue)

green ['gri:n] *adj* **1** : vert **2** INEXPERIENCED : inexpérimenté — **~** *n* **1** : vert *m* (couleur) **2 ~s** *npl* : légumes *mpl* verts — **greenery** ['gri:nəri] *n*, *pl* **-eries** : verdure *f* — **greenhouse** ['gri:n,haʊs] *n* : serre *f*

greet ['gri:t] *vt* **1** : saluer **2** WELCOME : accueillir — **greeting** ['gri:tɪŋ] *n* **1** : salutation *f* **2 ~s** *npl* REGARDS : salutations *fpl* **3 birthday ~s** : vœux *mpl* d'anniversaire

grenade [grə'neɪd] *n* : grenade *f*

grew → grow

grey → gray

greyhound ['greɪ,haʊnd] *n* : lévrier *m*

grid ['grɪd] *n* **1** GRATING : grille *f* **2** : quadrillage *m* (d'une carte, etc.)

griddle ['grɪdəl] *n* : plaque *f* chauffante

grief ['gri:f] *n* : chagrin *m*, douleur *f* — **grievance** ['gri:vənts] *n* : grief *m* — **grieve** ['gri:v] *v* **grieved; grieving** *vt* DISTRESS : peiner, chagriner — *vi* **~ for** : pleurer — **grievous** ['gri:vəs] *adj* : grave, sérieux

grill ['grɪl] *vt* **1** : griller (en cuisine) **2** INTERROGATE : cuisiner *fam* — **~** *n* : gril *m* (de cuisine) — **grille** *or* **grill** ['grɪl] *n* GRATING : grille *f*

grim ['grɪm] *adj* **grimmer; grimmest 1** STERN : sévère **2** GLOOMY : sinistre

grimace ['grɪməs, grɪ'meɪs] *n* : grimace *f* — **~** *vi* **-maced; -macing** : grimacer

grime ['graɪm] *n* : saleté *f*, crasse *f* — **grimy** ['graɪmi] *adj* **grimier; grimiest** : sale, crasseux

grin ['grɪn] *vi* **grinned; grinning** : sourire — **~** *n* : (grand) sourire *m*

grind ['graɪnd] *v* **ground** ['graʊnd]; **grind-**

ing *vt* **1** : moudre (du café, etc.) **2** SHARPEN : aiguiser **3** ~ **one's teeth** : grincer des dents — *vi* : grincer — ~ *n* **the daily** ~ : le train-train quotidien — **grinder** ['graɪndər] *n* : moulin *m*

grip ['grɪp] *vt* **gripped; gripping 1** : serrer, empoigner **2** CAPTIVATE : captiver — ~ *n* **1** : prise *f*, étreinte *f* **2** TRACTION : adhérence *f* **3 come to** ~**s with** : en venir aux prises avec

gripe ['graɪp] *vi* **griped; griping** : rouspéter *fam*, ronchonner *fam* — ~ *n* : plainte *f*

grisly ['grɪzli] *adj* **-lier; -est** : horrible, macabre

gristle ['grɪsəl] *n* : cartilage *m*

grit ['grɪt] *n* **1** : sable *m*, gravillon *m* **2** ~**s** *npl* : gruau *m* de maïs — ~ *vt* **gritted; gritting** ~ **one's teeth** : serrer les dents

groan ['groːn] *vi* : gémir — ~ *n* : gémissement *m*

grocery ['groːsəri, -ʃəri] *n, pl* **-ceries 1** *or* ~ **store** : épicerie *f* **2 groceries** *npl* : épiceries *fpl*, provisions *fpl* — **grocer** ['groːsər] *n* : épicier *m*, -cière *f*

groggy ['grɑgi] *adj* **-gier; -est** : chancelant, sonné *fam*

groin ['grɔɪn] *n* : aine *f*

groom ['gruːm, 'grʊm] *n* BRIDEGROOM : marié *m* — ~ *vt* : panser (un animal)

groove ['gruːv] *n* : rainure *f*, sillon *m*

grope ['groːp] *vi* **groped; groping 1** : tâtonner **2** ~ **for** : chercher à tâtons

gross ['groːs] *adj* **1** SERIOUS : flagrant **2** TOTAL : brut **3** VULGAR : grossier — ~ *n* ~ **income** : recettes *fpl* brutes — **grossly** ['groːsli] *adv* : extrêmement

grotesque [groːˈtɛsk] *adj* : grotesque

grouch ['graʊtʃ] *n* : rouspéteur *m*, -teuse *f fam* — **grouchy** ['graʊtʃi] *adj* **grouchier; grouchiest** : grognon

ground[1] ['graʊnd] → **grind**

ground[2] *n* **1** : sol *m*, terre *f* **2** *or* ~**s** LAND : terrain *m* **3** ~**s** *npl* REASON : raison *f* — ~ *vt* BASE : baser, fonder — **groundhog** ['graʊnd,hɔg] *n* : marmotte *f* d'Amérique — **groundwork** ['graʊnd,wərk] *n* : travail *m* préparatoire

group ['gruːp] *n* : groupe *m* — ~ *vt* : grouper, réunir — *vi or* ~ **together** : se grouper

grove ['groːv] *n* : bosquet *m*

grovel ['grɑvəl, 'grʌ-] *vi* **-eled** *or* **-elled; -eling** *or* **-elling** : ramper

grow ['groː] *v* **grew** ['gruː]; **grown** ['groːn]; **growing** *vi* **1** : pousser (se dit des plantes), grandir (se dit des personnes) **2** INCREASE : croître **3** BECOME : devenir — *vt* **1** CULTIVATE : cultiver **2** : laisser pousser (la barbe, etc.) — **grower** ['groːər] *n* : cultivateur *m*, -trice *f*

growl ['graʊl] *vi* : grogner, gronder — ~ *n* : grognement *m*, grondement *m*

grown-up ['groːn,əp] *adj* : adulte — ~ *n* : adulte *mf*

growth ['groːθ] *n* **1** : croissance *f* **2** INCREASE : augmentation *f* **3** TUMOR : tumeur *f*

grub ['grʌb] *n* FOOD : bouffe *f fam*

grubby ['grʌbi] *adj* **-bier; -est** : sale

grudge ['grʌdʒ] *n* **1** : rancune *f* **2 hold a** ~ : en vouloir à

grueling *or* **gruelling** ['gruːlɪŋ, gruːə-] *adj* : exténuant, épuisant

gruesome ['gruːsəm] *adj* : horrible

gruff ['grʌf] *adj* : bourru, brusque

grumble ['grʌmbəl] *vi* **-bled; -bling** : ronchonner *fam*

grumpy ['grʌmpi] *adj* **grumpier; grumpiest** : grincheux, grognon

grunt ['grʌnt] *vi* : grogner — ~ *n* : grognement *m*

guarantee [ˌgærənˈtiː] *n* : garantie *f* — ~ *vt* **-teed; -teeing** : garantir

guarantor [ˌgærənˈtɔr] *n* : garant *m*, -rante *f*

guard ['gɑrd] *n* **1** : garde *m* (personne) **2 be on one's** ~ : être sur ses gardes — ~ *vt* : garder, surveiller — *vi* ~ **against** : se garder de — **guardian** ['gɑrdiən] *n* **1** : tuteur *m*, -trice *f* (d'un mineur) **2** PROTECTOR : gardien *m*, -dienne *f*

guerrilla *or* **guerilla** [gəˈrɪlə] *n* **1** : guérillero *m* **2** ~ **warfare** : guérilla *f*

guess ['gɛs] *vt* **1** : deviner **2** SUPPOSE : penser — *vi* : deviner — ~ *n* : conjecture *f*

guest ['gɛst] *n* **1** VISITOR : invité *m*, -tée *f* **2** : client *m*, cliente *f* (d'un hôtel)

guide ['gaɪd] *n* **1** : guide *mf* (personne) **2** : guide *m* (livre, etc.) — ~ *vt* **guided; guiding** : guider — **guidance** ['gaɪdənts] *n* : conseils *mpl*, direction *f* — **guidebook** ['gaɪd,bʊk] *n* : guide *m* — **guideline** ['gaɪd,laɪn] *n* : ligne *f* directrice

guild ['gɪld] *n* : association *f*

guile ['gaɪl] *n* : ruse *f*

guilt ['gɪlt] *n* : culpabilité *f* — **guilty** ['gɪlti] *adj* **guiltier; guiltiest** : coupable

guinea pig ['gɪni-] *n* : cobaye *m*

guise ['gaɪz] *n* : apparence *f*

guitar [gəˈtɑr, gɪ-] *n* : guitare *f*

gulf ['gʌlf] *n* : golfe *m*

gull ['gʌl] *n* : mouette *f*

gullible ['gʌlɪbəl] *adj* : crédule

gully ['gʌli] *n, pl* **-lies** : ravin *m*

gulp ['gʌlp] *vt or* ~ **down** : avaler — ~ *n* : gorgée *f*, bouchée *f*

gum[1] ['gʌm] *n* : gencive *f*

gum[2] *n* CHEWING GUM : chewing-gum *m France*, gomme *f* à mâcher

gun ['gʌn] *n* **1** FIREARM : arme *f* à feu, fusil

m **2** or **spray** ~ : pistolet m — ~ vt
gunned; gunning or ~ **down** : abattre —
gunfire ['gʌn,faɪr] n : fusillade f, coups mpl
de feu — **gunman** ['gʌnmən] n, pl **-men**
[-mən, -,mɛn] : personne f armée — **gun-
powder** ['gʌn,paʊdər] n : poudre f (à
canon) — **gunshot** ['gʌn,ʃɑt] n : coup m de
feu
gurgle ['gərgəl] vi **-gled; -gling 1** : gargouiller **2** : gazouiller (se dit d'un bébé)
gush ['gʌʃ] vi **1** SPOUT : jaillir **2** ~ **over**
: s'extasier devant
gust ['gʌst] n : rafale f
gusto ['gʌs,to:] n, pl **-toes** : enthousiasme m
gut ['gʌt] n **1** : intestin m **2** ~**s** npl IN-
NARDS : entrailles fpl **3** ~**s** npl COURAGE

: cran m fam — ~ vt **gutted; gutting**
: détruire l'intérieur de (un édifice)
gutter ['gʌtər] n **1** : gouttière f (d'un toit) **2**
: caniveau m (d'une rue)
guy ['gaɪ] n : type m fam
guzzle ['gʌzəl] vt **-zled; -zling** : bâfrer fam,
engloutir
gym ['dʒɪm] or **gymnasium** [dʒɪm'neɪziəm,
-ʒəm] n, pl **-siums** or **-sia** [-zi:ə, -ʒə] : gymnase m — **gymnast** ['dʒɪmnəst, -,næst] n
: gymnaste mf — **gymnastics** [dʒɪm-
'næstɪks] n : gymnastique f
gynecology [,gaɪnə'kɑlədʒi] n : gynécologie f — **gynecologist** [,gaɪnə'kɑlədʒɪst] n
: gynécologue mf
Gypsy ['dʒɪpsi] n, pl **-sies** : gitan m, -tane f

H

h ['eɪtʃ] n, pl **h's** or **hs** ['eɪtʃəz] : h m, huitième
lettre de l'alphabet
habit ['hæbɪt] n **1** CUSTOM : habitude f, coutume f **2** : habit m (religieux)
habitat ['hæbɪ,tæt] n : habitat m
habitual [hə'bɪtʃuəl] adj **1** CUSTOMARY
: habituel **2** INVETERATE : invétéré
hack[1] ['hæk] n **1** : cheval m de louage **2** or
~ **writer** : écrivaillon m
hack[2] vt CUT : tailler — vi ~ **into** : entrer
dans (en informatique)
hackneyed ['hæknid] adj : rebattu
hacksaw ['hæk,sɔ] n : scie f à métaux
had → **have**
haddock ['hædək] ns & pl : églefin m
hadn't ['hædənt] (contraction of **had not**) →
have
hag ['hæg] n : vieille sorcière f
haggard ['hægərd] adj : hâve, exténué
haggle ['hægəl] vi **-gled; -gling** : marchander
hail[1] ['heɪl] vt **1** ACCLAIM : acclamer **2**
: héler (un taxi)
hail[2] ['heɪl] n : grêle f (en météorologie) —
~ vi : grêler — **hailstone** ['heɪl,sto:n] n
: grêlon m
hair ['hær] n **1** : cheveux mpl (sur la tête) **2**
: poil m (de chien, sur les jambes, etc.) —
hairbrush ['hær,brʌʃ] n : brosse f à cheveux
— **haircut** ['hær,kʌt] n : coupe f de cheveux
— **hairdo** ['hær,du:] n, pl **-dos** : coiffure f —
hairdresser ['hær,drɛsər] n : coiffeur m,
-feuse f — **hairless** ['hærləs] adj : sans
cheveux, glabre — **hairpin** ['hær,pɪn] n
: épingle f à cheveux — **hair–raising** ['hær-

,reɪzɪŋ] adj : à vous faire dresser les cheveux
sur la tête — **hair spray** n : laque f — **hairy**
['hæri] adj **hairier; -est** : poilu, velu
Haitian ['heɪʃən, 'heɪtiən] adj : haïtien
half ['hæf] n, pl **halves** ['hævz] **1** : moitié f,
demi m, -mie f **2** in ~ : en deux **3** or **halftime** : mi-temps f (aux sports) — ~ adj **1**
: demi **2** ~ **an hour** : une demi-heure **3** in
~ : en deux — ~ adv : à demi, à moitié —
halfhearted ['hæf'hɑrtəd] adj : sans enthousiasme — **halfway** ['hæf'weɪ] adv & adj
: à mi-chemin
halibut ['hælɪbət] ns & pl : flétan m
hall ['hɔl] n **1** HALLWAY : couloir m **2** AUDI-
TORIUM : salle f **3** LOBBY : entrée f,
vestibule m **4** DORMITORY : résidence f universitaire
hallmark ['hɔl,mɑrk] n : marque f, sceau m
Halloween [,hælə'wi:n, ,hɑ-] n : Halloween f
hallucination [hə,lu:sən'eɪʃən] n : hallucination f
hallway ['hɔl,weɪ] n **1** ENTRANCE : entrée f,
vestibule m **2** CORRIDOR : couloir m
halo ['heɪ,lo:] n, pl **-los** or **-loes** : auréole f
halt ['hɔlt] n **1** : halte f **2 come to a** ~
: s'arrêter — ~ vi : s'arrêter — vt : arrêter
halve ['hæv] vt **halved; halving 1** DIVIDE
: couper en deux **2** REDUCE : réduire de
moitié — **halves** → **half**
ham ['hæm] n : jambon m
hamburger ['hæm,bərgər] or **hamburg**
[-,bərg] n **1** : viande f hachée (crue) **2**
: hamburger m (cuit)
hammer ['hæmər] n : marteau m — ~ vt
: marteler, enfoncer (à coups de marteau)

hammock ['hæmək] n : hamac m

hamper[1] ['hæmpər] vt : gêner

hamper[2] n : panier m (à linge)

hamster ['hæmpstər] n : hamster m

hand ['hænd] n 1 : main f 2 : aiguille f (d'une montre, etc.) 3 HANDWRITING : écriture f 4 : main f, jeu m (aux cartes) 5 WORKER : ouvrier m, -vrière f 6 by ~ : à la main 7 give s.o. a ~ : donner un coup de main à qqn 8 on ~ : disponible 9 on the other ~ : d'autre part — vt 1 : donner, passer 2 ~ out : distribuer — handbag ['hænd,bæg] n : sac m à main — handbook ['hænd,bʊk] n : manuel m, guide m — handcuffs ['hænd,kʌfs] npl : menottes fpl — handful ['hænd,fʊl] n : poignée f — handgun ['hænd,gʌn] n : pistolet m, revolver m

handicap ['hændi,kæp] n : handicap m — ~ vt -capped; -capping : handicaper — handicapped ['hændi,kæpt] adj : handicapé

handicrafts ['hændi,kræfts] npl : objets mpl artisanaux

handiwork ['hændi,wərk] n : ouvrage m

handkerchief ['hæŋkərtʃəf, -,tʃi:f] n, pl -chiefs : mouchoir m

handle ['hændəl] n : manche m (d'un ustensile), poignée f (de porte), anse f (d'un panier, etc.) — ~ vt -dled; -dling 1 TOUCH : toucher à, manipuler 2 MANAGE : s'occuper de — handlebars ['hændəl,barz] npl : guidon m

handmade ['hænd,meɪd] adj : fait à la main

handout ['hænd,aʊt] n 1 ALMS : aumône f 2 LEAFLET : prospectus m

handrail ['hænd,reɪl] n : rampe f

handshake ['hænd,ʃeɪk] n : poignée f de main

handsome ['hænt̬səm] adj handsomer; -est 1 ATTRACTIVE : beau 2 GENEROUS : généreux 3 LARGE : considérable

handwriting ['hænd,raɪt̬ɪŋ] n : écriture f — handwritten ['hænd,rɪt̬ən] adj : écrit à la main

handy ['hændi] adj handier; -est 1 NEARBY : à portée de la main, proche 2 USEFUL : commode, pratique 3 CLEVER : adroit — handyman ['hændimən] n, pl -men [-mən, -,mɛn] : bricoleur m

hang ['hæŋ] v hung ['hʌŋ]; hanging vt 1 : suspendre, accrocher 2 (past tense often hanged) EXECUTE : pendre 3 ~ one's head : baisser la tête — vi 1 : être accroché, pendre 2 ~ up : raccrocher — ~ n get the ~ of : piger fam

hangar ['hæŋər, 'hæŋgər] n : hangar m

hanger ['hæŋər] n or coat ~ : cintre m

hangover ['hæŋ,o:vər] n : gueule f de bois

hanker ['hæŋkər] vi ~ for : désirer, avoir

envie de — hankering ['hæŋkərɪŋ] n : désir m, envie f

haphazard [hæp'hæzərd] adj : fait au hasard

happen ['hæpən] vi 1 OCCUR : arriver, se passer 2 CHANCE : arriver par hasard 3 it so happens that … : il se trouve que … — happening ['hæpənɪŋ] n : événement m

happy ['hæpi] adj happier; -est 1 : heureux 2 be ~ with : être satisfait de — happily ['hæpəli] adv : heureusement — happiness ['hæpinəs] n : bonheur m — happy–go–lucky ['hæpigo:'lʌki] adj : insouciant

harass [hə'ræs, 'hærəs] vt : harceler — harassment [hə'ræsmənt, 'hærəsmənt] n : harcèlement m

harbor or Brit harbour ['harbər] n : port m — ~ vt 1 SHELTER : héberger 2 ~ a grudge against : garder rancune à

hard ['hard] adj 1 : dur 2 DIFFICULT : difficile 3 ~ water : eau f calcaire — ~ adv 1 : dur 2 FORCEFULLY : fort 3 take sth … : mal prendre qqch — harden ['hardən] vt : durcir, endurcir — vi : s'endurcir — hardheaded ['hard'hɛdəd] adj : têtu, entêté — hard–hearted ['hard'hartəd] adj : dur, insensible — hardly ['hardli] adv 1 BARELY : à peine, ne … guère 2 it's ~ surprising : ce n'est pas surprenant — hardness ['hardnəs] n : dureté f — hardship ['hard-ʃɪp] n : épreuves fpl — hardware ['hard-,wær] n 1 : quincaillerie f 2 : matériel m (en informatique) — hardworking ['hard-'wərkɪŋ] adj : travailleur, travaillant Can

hardy ['hardi] adj hardier; -est 1 BOLD : hardi, intrépide 2 ROBUST : résistant

hare ['hær] n, pl hare or hares : lièvre m

harm ['harm] n 1 INJURY : mal m 2 DAMAGE : dommage m 3 WRONG : tort m — ~ vt : faire du mal à, nuire à — harmful ['harmfəl] adj : nuisible — harmless ['harmləs] adj : inoffensif

harmonica [har'manɪkə] n : harmonica m

harmony ['harməni] n, pl -nies : harmonie f — harmonious [har'mo:niəs] adj : harmonieux — harmonize ['harmə,naɪz] v -nized; -nizing vt : harmoniser — vi : s'harmoniser

harness ['harnəs] n : harnais m — ~ vt 1 : harnacher 2 UTILIZE : exploiter

harp ['harp] n : harpe f — ~ vi ~ on : rabâcher

harpoon [har'pu:n] n : harpon m

harpsichord ['harpsɪ,kɔrd] n : clavecin m

harsh ['harʃ] adj 1 ROUGH : rude 2 SEVERE : dur, sévère 3 : cru (se dit des couleurs), rude (se dit des sons) — harshness ['harʃnəs] n : sévérité f

harvest ['harvəst] n : moisson f, récolte f — ~ vt : moissonner, récolter

has → **have**

hash ['hæʃ] *vt* **1** CHOP : hacher **2** ~ **over** DISCUSS : parler de, discuter — ~ *n* **1** : hachis *m* **2** JUMBLE : gâchis *m*

hasn't ['hæzənt] (*contraction of* **has not**) → **have**

hassle ['hæsəl] *n* : embêtements *mpl*, ennuis *mpl* — ~ *vt* : tracasser

haste ['heɪst] *n* : hâte *f*, précipitation *f* — **hasten** ['heɪsən] *vt* : hâter, précipiter — *vi* : se hâter, se dépêcher — **hastily** ['heɪstəli] *adv* : à la hâte — **hasty** ['heɪsti] *adj* **hastier; -est** : précipité

hat ['hæt] *n* : chapeau *m*

hatch ['hætʃ] *n* : écoutille *f* (d'un navire) — ~ *vt* **1** : couver, faire éclore **2** CONCOCT : tramer (un complot) — *vi* : éclore

hatchet ['hætʃət] *n* : hachette *f*

hate ['heɪt] *n* : haine *f* — ~ *vt* **hated; hating** : haïr — **hateful** ['heɪtfəl] *adj* : odieux — **hatred** ['heɪtrəd] *n* : haine *f*

haughty ['hɔti] *adj* **haughtier; -est** : hautain

haul ['hɔl] *vt* : tirer, traîner — ~ *n* **1** CATCH : prise *f* **2** LOOT : butin *m* **3 it's a long ~** : la route est longue

haunch ['hɔntʃ] *n* : hanche *f* (d'une personne), derrière *m* (d'un animal)

haunt ['hɔnt] *vt* : hanter

have ['hæv, *in sense 2 as an auxiliary verb usu* 'hæf] *v* **had** ['hæd]; **having; has** ['hæz] *vt* **1** : avoir **2** WANT : vouloir, prendre **3** RECEIVE : recevoir **4** ALLOW : permettre, tolérer **5** HOLD : tenir **6** ~ **a sandwich** : manger un sandwich — *v aux* **1** : avoir, être **2** ~ **to** : devoir **3 you've finished, haven't you?** : tu as fini, n'est-ce pas?

haven ['heɪvən] *n* : refuge *m*, havre *m*

havoc ['hævək] *n* : ravages *mpl*, dégâts *mpl*

hawk[1] ['hɔk] *n* : faucon *m* (oiseau)

hawk[2] *vt* : colporter

hay ['heɪ] *n* : foin *m* — **hay fever** *n* : rhume *m* des foins — **haystack** ['heɪˌstæk] *n* : meule *f* de foin — **haywire** ['heɪˌwaɪr] *adj* **go** ~ : se détraquer

hazard ['hæzərd] *n* **1** PERIL : risque *m* **2** CHANCE : hasard *m* — ~ *vt* : hasarder, risquer — **hazardous** ['hæzərdəs] *adj* : dangereux

haze ['heɪz] *n* : brume *f*

hazel ['heɪzəl] *n* : noisette *f* (couleur) — **hazelnut** ['heɪzəlˌnʌt] *n* : noisette *f*

hazy ['heɪzi] *adj* **hazier; -est** **1** : brumeux **2** VAGUE : vague, flou

he ['hi] *pron* **1** : il **2** (*used for emphasis or contrast*) : lui

head ['hɛd] *n* **1** : tête *f* **2** END, TOP : bout *m* (d'une table), chevet *m* (d'un lit) **3** LEADER : chef *m* **4** ~**s or tails** : pile ou face **5 per** ~ : par personne — ~ *adj* MAIN : principal — ~ *vt* **1** LEAD : être en tête de **2** DIRECT : diriger — *vi* : se diriger, aller — **headache** ['hɛdˌeɪk] *n* : mal *m* de tête — **headband** ['hɛdˌbænd] *n* : bandeau *m* — **headdress** ['hɛdˌdrɛs] *n* : coiffe *f* — **headfirst** ['hɛdˈfərst] *adv* : la tête la première — **heading** ['hɛdɪŋ] *n* : titre *m*, rubrique *f* — **headland** ['hɛdlənd, -ˌlænd] *n* : promontoire *m*, cap *m* — **headlight** ['hɛdˌlaɪt] *n* : phare *m* — **headline** ['hɛdˌlaɪn] *n* : (gros) titre *m* — **headlong** ['hɛdˈlɔŋ] *adv* : à toute allure — **headmaster** ['hɛdˌmæstər] *n* : directeur *m* (d'école) — **headmistress** ['hɛdˌmɪstrəs, -'mɪs-] *n* : directrice *f* (d'école) — **head-on** ['hɛdˈɑn, -ˈɔn] *adv & adj* : de plein fouet — **headphones** ['hɛdˌfoːnz] *npl* : casque *m* — **headquarters** ['hɛdˌkwɔrtərz] *ns & pl* : siège *m* (d'une compagnie), quartier *m* général (militaire) — **headstrong** ['hɛdˌstrɔŋ] *adj* : têtu, obstiné — **headwaiter** ['hɛdˈweɪtər] *n* : maître *m* d'hôtel — **headway** ['hɛdˌweɪ] *n* **1** : progrès *m* **2 make** ~ : avancer, progresser — **heady** ['hɛdi] *adj* **headier; -est** **1** : capiteux (se dit du vin) **2** EXCITING : grisant

heal ['hiːl] *v* : guérir

health ['hɛlθ] *n* : santé *f* — **healthy** ['hɛlθi] *adj* **healthier; -est** : sain, en bonne santé

heap ['hiːp] *n* : tas *m* — ~ *vt* : entasser

hear ['hɪr] *v* **heard** ['hərd]; **hearing** *vt* **1** : entendre **2** *or* ~ **about** : apprendre — *vi* **1** : entendre **2** ~ **from** : avoir des nouvelles de — **hearing** ['hɪrɪŋ] *n* **1** : ouïe *f*, audition *f* **2** : audience *f* (d'un tribunal) — **hearing aid** *n* : appareil *m* auditif — **hearsay** ['hɪrˌseɪ] *n* : ouï-dire *m*

hearse ['hərs] *n* : corbillard *m*

heart ['hɑrt] *n* **1** : cœur *m* **2 at** ~ : au fond **3 by** ~ : par cœur **4 lose** ~ : perdre courage — **heartache** ['hɑrtˌeɪk] *n* : chagrin *m*, peine *f* — **heart attack** *n* : crise *f* cardiaque — **heartbeat** ['hɑrtˌbiːt] *n* : battement *m* de cœur — **heartbroken** ['hɑrtˌbroːkən] *adj* **be** ~ : avoir le cœur brisé — **heartburn** ['hɑrtˌbərn] *n* : brûlures *fpl* d'estomac

hearth ['hɑrθ] *n* : foyer *m*

heartily ['hɑrtəli] *adv* **1 eat** ~ : manger avec appétit **2 laugh** ~ : rire de bon cœur — **heartless** ['hɑrtləs] *adj* : sans cœur, cruel — **hearty** ['hɑrti] *adj* **heartier; -est** **1** : cordial, chaleureux **2** : copieux (se dit d'un repas)

heat ['hiːt] *v* : chauffer — ~ *n* **1** : chaleur *f* **2** HEATING : chauffage *m* **3** PASSION : feu *m*, ardeur *f* — **heated** ['hiːtəd] *adj* : animé, passionné — **heater** ['hiːtər] *n* : radiateur *m*, appareil *m* de chauffage

heath ['hiːθ] *n* : lande *f*

heathen ['hiːðən] *adj* : païen — ~ *n, pl* **-thens** *or* **-then** : païen *m*, païenne *f*

heather ['hɛðər] *n* : bruyère *f*

heave ['hi:v] *v* **heaved** *or* **hove** ['ho:v]; **heaving** *vt* **1** LIFT : lever, soulever (avec effort) **2** HURL : lancer **3** ~ **a sigh** : pousser un soupir — *vi* : se soulever — *n* : effort *m*

heaven ['hɛvən] *n* : ciel *m* — **heavenly** ['hɛvənli] *adj* : céleste, divin

heavy ['hɛvi] *adj* **heavier; -est 1** : lourd, pesant **2** : gros (se dit du corps, du cœur, etc.) **3** ~ **sleep** : sommeil *m* profond **4** ~ **smoker** : grand fumeur *m* **5** ~ **traffic** : circulation *f* dense — **heavily** ['hɛvəli] *adv* : lourdement, pesamment — **heaviness** ['hɛvinəs] *n* : lourdeur *f*, pesanteur *f* — **heavyweight** ['hɛvi,weɪt] *n* : poids *m* lourd

Hebrew ['hi:,bru:] *adj* : hébreu — ~ *n* : hébreu *m* (langue)

heckle ['hɛkəl] *vt* **-led; -ling** : interrompre bruyamment

hectic ['hɛktɪk] *adj* : mouvementé, agité

he'd ['hi:d] (*contraction of* **he had** *or* **he would**) → **have, would**

hedge ['hɛdʒ] *n* : haie *f* — ~ *v* **hedged; hedging** *vt* ~ **one's bets** : se couvrir — *vi* : éviter de s'engager — **hedgehog** ['hɛdʒ,hɔg, -,hɑg] *n* : hérisson *m*

heed ['hi:d] *vt* : faire attention à, écouter — ~ *n* **take** ~ **of** : tenir compte de — **heedless** ['hi:dləs] *adj* : insouciant

heel ['hi:l] *n* : talon *m*

hefty ['hɛfti] *adj* **heftier; -est** : gros, lourd

heifer ['hɛfər] *n* : génisse *f*

height ['haɪt] *n* **1** TALLNESS : taille *f* (d'une personne), hauteur *f* (d'un objet) **2** ALTITUDE : élévation *f* **3 the** ~ **of folly** : le comble de la folie **4 what is your** ~? : combien mesures-tu? — **heighten** ['haɪtən] *vt* : augmenter, intensifier

heir ['ær] *n* : héritier *m*, -tière *f* — **heiress** ['ærəs] *n* : héritière *f* — **heirloom** ['ær,lu:m] *n* : objet *m* de famille

held → **hold**

helicopter ['hɛlə,kɑptər] *n* : hélicoptère *m*

hell ['hɛl] *n* : enfer *m* — **hellish** ['hɛlɪʃ] *adj* : infernal

he'll ['hi:l] (*contraction of* **he shall** *or* **he will**) → **shall, will**

hello [hə'lo:, hɛ-] *or Brit* **hullo** [hʌ'leʊ] *interj* : bonjour!, allô! (au téléphone)

helm ['hɛlm] *n* : barre *f*

helmet ['hɛlmət] *n* : casque *m*

help ['hɛlp] *vt* **1** : aider, venir à l'aide de **2** PREVENT : empêcher **3** ~ **yourself** : servez-vous — ~ *n* **1** : aide *f*, secours *m* **2** STAFF : employés *mpl*, -ployées *fpl* **3** ~! : au secours! — **helper** ['hɛlpər] *n* : aide *mf*; assistant *m*, -tante *f* — **helpful** ['hɛlpfəl] *adj* : utile, serviable — **helping** ['hɛlpɪŋ] *n* SERVING : portion *f* — **helpless** ['hɛlpləs] *adj* : impuissant

hem ['hɛm] *n* : ourlet *m* — ~ *vt* **hemmed; hemming** : ourler

hemisphere ['hɛmə,sfɪr] *n* : hémisphère *m*

hemorrhage ['hɛmərɪdʒ] *n* : hémorragie *f*

hemorrhoids ['hɛmə,rɔɪdz, 'hɛm,rɔɪdz] *npl* : hémorroïdes *fpl*

hemp ['hɛmp] *n* : chanvre *m*

hen ['hɛn] *n* : poule *f*

hence ['hɛnts] *adv* **1** : d'où, donc **2 ten years** ~ : d'ici dix ans — **henceforth** ['hɛnts,forθ, ,hɛnts'-] *adv* : dorénavant, désormais

henpeck ['hɛn,pɛk] *vt* : mener par le bout du nez

hepatitis [,hɛpə'taɪtəs] *n, pl* **-titides** [-'tɪtə-,di:z] : hépatite *f*

her ['hər] *adj* : son, sa, ses — ~ ['hər, ər] *pron* **1** (*used as a direct object*) : la, l' **2** (*used as an indirect object*) : lui **3** (*used as object of a preposition*) : elle

herald ['hɛrəld] *vt* : annoncer

herb ['ərb, 'hərb] *n* : herbe *f*

herd ['hərd] *n* : troupeau *m* — ~ *vt* : mener, conduire — *vi or* ~ **together** : s'assembler

here ['hɪr] *adv* **1** : ici, là **2** NOW : alors **3** ~ **is,** ~ **are** : voici, voilà — **hereabouts** ['hɪrə,baʊts] *or* **hereabout** [-,baʊt] *adv* : par ici — **hereafter** [hɪr'æftər] *adv* : ci-après — **hereby** [hɪr'baɪ] *adv* : par la présente

hereditary [hə'rɛdə,tɛri] *adj* : héréditaire — **heredity** [hə'rɛdəti] *n* : hérédité *f*

heresy ['hɛrəsi] *n, pl* **-sies** : hérésie *f*

herewith [hɪr'wɪθ] *adv* : ci-joint

heritage ['hɛrətɪdʒ] *n* : héritage *m*, patrimoine *m*

hermit ['hərmət] *n* : ermite *m*

hernia ['hərniə] *n, pl* **-nias** *or* **-niae** [-ni,i:, -ni,aɪ] : hernie *f*

hero ['hi:,ro:, 'hɪr,o:] *n, pl* **-roes** : héros *m* — **heroic** [hɪ'ro:ɪk] *adj* : héroïque — **heroine** ['hɛroən] *n* : héroïne *f* — **heroism** ['hɛro-,ɪzəm] *n* : héroïsme *m*

heron ['hɛrən] *n* : héron *m*

herring ['hɛrɪŋ] *n, pl* **-ring** *or* **-rings** : hareng *m*

hers ['hərz] *pron* **1** : le sien, la sienne, les siens, les siennes **2 some friends of** ~ : des amis à elle — **herself** [hər'sɛlf] *pron* **1** (*used reflexively*) : se, s' **2** (*used for emphasis*) : elle-même **3** (*used after a preposition*) : elle, elle-même

he's ['hi:z] (*contraction of* **he is** *or* **he has**) → **be, have**

hesitant ['hɛzətənt] *adj* : hésitant, indécis — **hesitate** ['hɛzə,teɪt] *vi* **-tated; -tating** : hésiter — **hesitation** [,hɛzə'teɪʃən] *n* : hésitation *f*

heterogeneous [,hɛtərə'dʒi:niəs, -njəs] *adj* : hétérogène

heterosexual [ˌhɛt̬əroˈsɛkʃʊəl] *adj* : hétérosexuel — ~ *n* : hétérosexuel *m*, -sexuelle *f*
hexagon [ˈhɛksəˌgɑn] *n* : hexagone *m*
hey [ˈheɪ] *interj* : hé!, ohé!
heyday [ˈheɪˌdeɪ] *n* : beaux jours *mpl*,
apogée *f*
hi [ˈhaɪ] *interj* : salut!
hibernate [ˈhaɪbərˌneɪt] *vi* -**nated; -nating**
: hiberner
hiccup [ˈhɪkəp] *vi* -**cuped; -cuping** : hoqueter — ~ *n* **have the ~s** : avoir le hoquet
hide[1] [ˈhaɪd] *n* : peau *f* (d'animal)
hide[2] *v* **hid** [ˈhɪd]; **hidden** [ˈhɪdən] *or* **hid;**
hiding *vt* : cacher — *vi* : se cacher —
hide-and-seek [ˈhaɪdənd̩ˌsiːk] *n* : cache-
cache *m*
hideous [ˈhɪdiəs] *adj* : hideux, affreux
hideout [ˈhaɪdˌaʊt] *n* : cachette *f*
hierarchy [ˈhaɪəˌrɑrki] *n, pl* -**chies** : hiérarchie *f* — **hierarchical** [ˌhaɪəˈrɑrkɪkəl] *adj*
: hiérarchique
high [ˈhaɪ] *adj* **1** : haut **2** : élevé (se dit des
prix, etc.) **3** INTOXICATED : parti *fam*,
drogué **4** ~ **speed** : grande vitesse *f* **5 a**
~ **voice** : une voix aiguë — ~ *adv* : haut
— ~ *n* : record *m*, niveau *m* élevé —
higher [ˈhaɪər] *adj* **1** : plus haut **2** ~ **edu-**
cation : études *fpl* supérieures — **highlight**
[ˈhaɪˌlaɪt] *n* : point *m* culminant — ~ *vt*
EMPHASIZE : souligner — **highly** [ˈhaɪli] *adv*
1 VERY : très, extrêmement **2 think** ~ **of**
: penser du bien de — **highness** [ˈhaɪnəs] *n*
His/Her Highness : son Altesse — **high**
school *n* : lycée *m France*, école *f* secondaire *Can* — **high-strung** [ˈhaɪˈstrʌŋ]
adj : nerveux, très tendu — **highway** [ˈhaɪ-
ˌweɪ] *n* **1** : autoroute *f* **2** → **interstate**
hijack [ˈhaɪˌdʒæk] *vt* : détourner (un avion)
— **hijacker** [ˈhaɪˌdʒækər] *n* : pirate *m* de
l'air — **hijacking** [ˈhaɪˌdʒækɪŋ] *n* : détournement *m*
hike [ˈhaɪk] *v* **hiked; hiking** *vi* : faire une
randonnée — *vt or* ~ **up** RAISE : augmenter — ~ *n* : randonnée *f* — **hiker**
[ˈhaɪkər] *n* : randonneur *m*, -neuse *f*
hilarious [hɪˈlæriəs, haɪ-] *adj* : désopilant,
hilarant — **hilarity** [hɪˈlærət̬i, haɪ-] *n* : hilarité *f*
hill [ˈhɪl] *n* : colline *f* — **hillside** [ˈhɪlˌsaɪd] *n*
: coteau *m* — **hilly** [ˈhɪli] *adj* **hillier; -est**
: vallonné, côteux *Can*
hilt [ˈhɪlt] *n* : poignée *f* (d'une épée)
him [ˈhɪm, əm] *pron* **1** (*used as a direct object*) : le, l' **2** (*used as an indirect object or
as object of a preposition*) : lui — **himself**
[hɪmˈsɛlf] *pron* **1** (*used reflexively*) : se, s'
2 (*used for emphasis*) : lui-même **3** (*used
after a preposition*) : lui, lui-même
hind [ˈhaɪnd] *adj* : de derrière

hinder [ˈhɪndər] *vt* : empêcher, entraver —
hindrance [ˈhɪndrənts] *n* : entrave *f*
hindsight [ˈhaɪndˌsaɪt] *n* **in** ~ : avec du
recul
Hindu [ˈhɪnˌduː] *adj* : hindou
hinge [ˈhɪndʒ] *n* : charnière *f*, gond *m* — ~
vi **hinged; hinging** ~ **on** : dépendre de
hint [ˈhɪnt] *n* **1** INSINUATION : allusion *f* **2**
TRACE : soupçon *m* **3** TIP : conseil *m* — ~
vt : insinuer — *vi* ~ **at** : faire une allusion à
hip [ˈhɪp] *n* : hanche *f*
hippie *or* **hippy** [ˈhɪpi] *n, pl* **hippies** : hippie
mf, hippy *mf*
hippopotamus [ˌhɪpəˈpɑt̬əməs] *n, pl*
-**muses** *or* -**mi** [-ˌmaɪ] : hippopotame *m*
hire [ˈhaɪr] *vt* **hired; hiring 1** : engager, embaucher **2** RENT : louer — ~ *n* **1** WAGES
: gages *mpl* **2 for** ~ : à louer
his [ˈhɪz, ɪz] *adj* **1** : son, sa, ses **2 it's** ~
: c'est à lui — ~ *pron* **1** : le sien, la sienne,
les siens, les siennes **2 a friend of** ~ : un
ami à lui
Hispanic [hɪˈspænɪk] *adj* : hispanique
hiss [ˈhɪs] *vi* : siffler — ~ *n* : sifflement *m*
history [ˈhɪstəri] *n, pl* -**ries 1** : histoire *f* **2**
: antécédents *mpl* (médicaux, etc.) — **histo-**
rian [hɪˈstoriən] *n* : historien *m*, -rienne *f* —
historic [hɪˈstorɪk] *or* **historical** [-ɪkəl] *adj*
: historique
hit [ˈhɪt] *v* **hit; hitting** *vt* **1** : frapper (une
balle, etc.) **2** STRIKE : heurter **3** AFFECT
: toucher **4** REACH : atteindre — *vi* **1** : frapper **2** OCCUR : arriver — ~ *n* **1** : coup *m*
(aux sports, etc.) **2** SUCCESS : succès *m*
hitch [ˈhɪtʃ] *vt* **1** : accrocher **2** *or* ~ **up**
RAISE : remonter **3** ~ **a ride** : faire de
l'auto-stop — ~ *n* PROBLEM : problème *m*
— **hitchhike** [ˈhɪtʃˌhaɪk] *vi* -**hiked; -hiking**
: faire de l'auto-stop — **hitchhiker** [ˈhɪtʃ-
ˌhaɪkər] *n* : auto-stoppeur *m*, -peuse *f*
hitherto [ˈhɪðərˌtuː, ˌhɪðər'-] *adv* : jusqu'à
présent
HIV [ˌeɪtʃˌaɪˈviː] *n* (*human immunodeficiency
virus*) : VIH *m*
hive [ˈhaɪv] *n* : ruche *f*
hives [ˈhaɪvz] *ns & pl* : urticaire *f*
hoard [ˈhord] *n* : réserve *f*, provisions *fpl* —
~ *vt* : accumuler, amasser
hoarse [ˈhors] *adj* **hoarser; -est** : rauque,
enroué
hoax [ˈhoːks] *n* : canular *m*
hobble [ˈhɑbəl] *vi* -**bled; -bling** : boitiller
hobby [ˈhɑbi] *n, pl* -**bies** : passe-temps *m*
hobo [ˈhoːˌboː] *n, pl* -**boes** : vagabond *m*,
-bonde *f*
hockey [ˈhɑki] *n* : hockey *m*
hoe [ˈhoː] *n* : houe *f*, binette *f* — ~ *vi* **hoed;**
hoeing : biner
hog [ˈhɔg, ˈhɑg] *n* : porc *m*, cochon *m* — ~
vt **hogged; hogging** : monopoliser

hoist ['hɔɪst] *vt* : hisser — ～ *n* : palan *m*
hold¹ ['ho:ld] *v* **held** ['hɛld]; **holding** *vt* **1**
: tenir **2** POSSESS : posséder **3** CONTAIN
: contenir **4** *or* ～ **up** SUPPORT : soutenir
5 : détenir (un prisonnier, etc.) **6** ～ **the
line** : ne quittez pas **7** ～ **s.o's attention**
: retenir l'attention de qqn — *vi* **1** LAST
: durer, continuer **2** APPLY : tenir — ～ *n* **1**
GRIP : prise *f*, étreinte *f* **2 get** ～ **of** : trouver
— **holder** ['ho:ldər] *n* : détenteur *m*, -trice *f*;
titulaire *mf* — **holdup** ['ho:ld,ʌp] *n* **1** : vol *m*
à main armée **2** DELAY : retard *m* — **hold up**
vt DELAY : retarder
hold² *n* : cale *f* (d'un navire ou d'un avion)
hole ['ho:l] *n* : trou *m*
holiday ['halə,deɪ] *n* **1** : jour *m* férié **2** *Brit*
VACATION : vacances *fpl*
holiness ['ho:linəs] *n* : sainteté *f*
holler ['halər] *vi* : gueuler *fam*, hurler — ～
n : hurlement *m*
hollow ['hɑ,lo:] *n* : creux *m* — ～ *adj* **hol-
lower; -est 1** : creux **2** FALSE : faux — ～
vt or ～ **out** : creuser
holly ['hali] *n*, *pl* **-lies** : houx *m*
holocaust ['halə,kɔst, 'ho:-, 'hɑ-] *n* : holocauste *m*
holster ['ho:lstər] *n* : étui *m* de revolver
holy ['ho:li] *adj* **holier; -est 1** : saint **2** ～
water : eau *f* bénite
homage ['amɪʤ, 'hɑ-] *n* : hommage *m*
home ['ho:m] *n* **1** RESIDENCE : maison *f* **2**
FAMILY : foyer *m*, chez-soi *m* **3** → **funeral
home, nursing home** — ～ *adv* **go** ～
: rentrer à la maison, rentrer chez soi —
homeland ['ho:m,lænd] *n* : patrie *f* —
homeless ['ho:mləs] *n* **the** ～ : les sans-
abri — **homely** ['ho:mli] *adj* **homelier; -est
1** SIMPLE : simple, ordinaire **2** UGLY : laid
— **homemade** ['ho:m'meɪd] *adj* : fait à la
maison — **homemaker** ['ho:m,meɪkər] *n*
: femme *f* au foyer — **home page** *n* : page *f*
d'accueil — **home run** *n* : coup *m* de circuit
Can — **homesick** ['ho:m,sɪk] *adj* **be** ～
: avoir le mal du pays — **homeward**
['ho:mwərd] *or* **homewards** [-wərdz] *adv*
: vers la maison — **homeward** *adj* : de retour — **homework** ['ho:m,wərk] *n* : devoirs
mpl — **homey** ['ho:mi] *adj* **homier; -est**
COZY, INVITING : accueillant
homicide ['hamə,saɪd, 'ho:-] *n* : homicide *m*
homogeneous [,ho:mə'ʤi:niəs, -njəs] *adj*
: homogène
homosexual [,ho:mə'sɛkʃuəl] *adj* : homosexuel — ～ *n* : homosexuel *m*, -sexuelle *f*
— **homosexuality** [,ho:mə,sɛkʃʊ'æləti] *n*
: homosexualité *f*
honest ['anəst] *adj* : honnête — **honestly**
['anəstli] *adv* : honnêtement — **honesty**
['anəsti] *n* : honnêteté *f*
honey ['hʌni] *n*, *pl* **-eys** : miel *m* — **honey-**

comb ['hʌni,ko:m] *n* : rayon *m* de miel —
honeymoon ['hʌni,mu:n] *n* : lune *f* de miel
honk ['haŋk, 'hɔŋk] *vi* : klaxonner — ～ *n*
: coup *m* de klaxon
honor *or Brit* **honour** ['anər] *n* : honneur *m*
— ～ *vt* : honorer — **honorable** *or Brit* **ho-
nourable** ['anərəbəl] *adj* : honorable —
honorary ['anə,rɛri] *adj* : honoraire, honorifique
hood ['hʊd] *n* **1** : capuchon *m* (d'un vêtement) **2** : capot *m* (d'une voiture)
hoodlum ['hʊdləm, 'hu:d-] *n* : voyou *m*
hoodwink ['hʊd,wɪŋk] *vt* : tromper
hoof ['hʊf, 'hu:f] *n*, *pl* **hooves** ['hʊvz,
'hu:vz] *or* **hoofs** : sabot *m* (d'un animal)
hook ['hʊk] *n* **1** : crochet *m* **2** FASTENER
: agrafe *f* **3** → **fishhook** — ～ *vt* : accrocher
— *vi* : s'accrocher
hoop ['hu:p] *n* : cerceau *m*
hoorah [hʊ'ra], **hooray** [hʊ'reɪ] → **hurrah**
hoot ['hu:t] *vi* **1** : hululer (se dit d'un hibou)
2 ～ **with laughter** : pouffer de rire — ～ *n*
1 : hululement *m* **2 I don't give a** ～ : je
m'en fiche
hop [hap] *v* **hopped; hopping** *vi* : sauter,
sautiller — *vt or* ～ **over** : sauter — ～ *n*
: saut *m*
hope ['ho:p] *v* **hoped; hoping** : espérer —
～ *n* : espoir *m* — **hopeful** ['ho:pfəl] *adj*
OPTIMISTIC : plein d'espoir **2** PROMISING
: encourageant — **hopefully** ['ho:pfəli] *adv*
1 : avec espoir **2** ～ **it will work** : on espère
que cela marche — **hopeless** ['ho:pləs] *adj*
: désespéré — **hopelessly** ['ho:pləsli] *adv*
1 : complètement **2** ～ **in love** : éperdument amoureux
hops ['haps] *nmpl* : houblon *m*
horde ['hord] *n* : horde *f*, foule *f*
horizon [hə'raɪzən] *n* : horizon *m* — **horizontal** [,hɔrə'zantəl] *adj* : horizontal
hormone ['hɔr,mo:n] *n* : hormone *f*
horn ['hɔrn] *n* **1** : corne *f* (d'un animal) **2**
: cor *m* (instrument de musique) **3** : klaxon
m (d'un véhicule)
hornet ['hɔrnət] *n* : frelon *m*
horoscope ['hɔrə,sko:p] *n* : horoscope *m*
horrendous [hə'rɛndəs] *adj* : épouvantable
— **horrible** ['hɔrəbəl] *adj* : horrible, affreux
— **horrid** ['hɔrɪd] *adj* : horrible, hideux —
horrify ['hɔrə,faɪ] *vt* **-fied; -fying** : horrifier
— **horror** ['hɔrər] *n* : horreur *f*
hors d'oeuvre [ɔr'dərv] *n*, *pl* **hors d'oeuvres** [-'dərvz] : hors-d'œuvre *m*
horse ['hɔrs] *n* **1** : cheval *m* — **horseback**
['hɔrs,bæk] **n on** ～ : à cheval — **horsefly**
['hɔrs,flaɪ] *n*, *pl* **-flies** : taon *m* — **horseman**
['hɔrsmən] *n*, *pl* **-men** [-mən, -,mɛn] : cavalier *m* — **horsepower** ['hɔrs,paʊər] *n*
: cheval-vapeur *m* — **horseradish** ['hɔrs-
,rædɪʃ] *n* : raifort *m* — **horseshoe** ['hɔrs-

ˌʃuː] *n* : fer *m* à cheval — **horsewoman** [ˈhɔrsˌwʊmən] *n, pl* **-women** [-ˌwɪmən] : cavalière *f*

horticulture [ˈhɔrtəˌkʌltʃər] *n* : horticulture *f*

hose [ˈhoːz] *n* **1** *pl* **hoses** : tuyau *m* (d'arrosage, etc.) **2** *pl* **hose** STOCKINGS : bas *mpl* — ~ *vt* **hosed; hosing** : arroser — **hosiery** [ˈhoːʒəri, ˈhoːʒə-] *n* : bonneterie *f*

hospice [ˈhɑspəs] *n* : hospice *m*

hospital [ˈhɑsˌpɪtəl] *n* : hôpital *m* — **hospitable** [hɑsˈpɪtəbəl, ˈhɑˌspɪ-] *adj* : hospitalier — **hospitality** [ˌhɑspəˈtæləti] *n, pl* **-ties** : hospitalité *f* — **hospitalize** [ˈhɑsˌpɪtəˌlaɪz] *vt* **-ized; -izing** : hospitaliser

host[1] [ˈhoːst] *n* a ~ **of** : une foule de

host[2] *n* **1** : hôte *mf* **2** : animateur *m*, -trice *f* (de radio, etc.) — ~ *vt* : animer (une émission de télévision, etc.)

host[3] *n* EUCHARIST : hostie *f*

hostage [ˈhɑstɪdʒ] *n* : otage *m*

hostel [ˈhɑstəl] *n* : auberge *f*

hostess [ˈhoːstəs] *n* : hôtesse *f*

hostile [ˈhɑstəl, -ˌtaɪl] *adj* : hostile — **hostility** [hɑsˈtɪləti] *n, pl* **-ties** : hostilité *f*

hot [ˈhɑt] *adj* **hotter; hottest 1** : chaud **2** SPICY : épicé **3** ~ **news** : les dernières nouvelles **4 have a** ~ **temper** : s'emporter facilement **5 it's** ~ **today** : il fait chaud aujourd'hui

hot dog *n* : hot-dog *m*

hotel [hoːˈtɛl] *n* : hôtel *m*

hotheaded [ˈhɑtˈhɛdəd] *adj* : impétueux

hound [ˈhaʊnd] *n* : chien *m* courant — ~ *vt* : traquer, poursuivre

hour [ˈaʊər] *n* : heure *f* — **hourglass** [ˈaʊərˌglæs] *n* : sablier *m* — **hourly** [ˈaʊərli] *adv* & *adj* : toutes les heures

house [ˈhaʊs] *n, pl* **houses** [ˈhaʊzəz, -səz] **1** HOME : maison *f* **2** : chambre *f* (en politique) **3 publishing** ~ : maison *f* d'édition — ~ [ˈhaʊz] *vt* **housed; housing** : loger, héberger — **houseboat** [ˈhaʊsˌboːt] *n* : péniche *f* aménagée — **housefly** [ˈhaʊsˌflaɪ] *n, pl* **-flies** : mouche *f* — **household** [ˈhaʊsˌhoːld] *adj* **1** : ménager **2** ~ **name** : nom *m* connu de tous — ~ *n* : ménage *m*, maison *f* — **housekeeper** [ˈhaʊsˌkiːpər] *n* : gouvernante *f* — **housekeeping** [ˈhaʊsˌkiːpɪŋ] *n* HOUSEWORK : ménage *m* — **housewarming** [ˈhaʊsˌwɔrmɪŋ] *n* : pendaison *f* de crémaillère — **housewife** [ˈhaʊsˌwaɪf] *n, pl* **-wives** : femme *f* au foyer, ménagère *f* — **housework** [ˈhaʊsˌwərk] *n* : travaux *mpl* ménagers, ménage *m* — **housing** [ˈhaʊzɪŋ] *n* : logement *m*

hovel [ˈhʌvəl, ˈhɑ-] *n* : taudis *m*

hover [ˈhʌvər] *vi* **1** : planer **2** *or* ~ **about** : rôder — **hovercraft** [ˈhʌvərˌkræft] *n* : aéroglisseur *m*

how [ˈhaʊ] *adv* **1** : comment **2** (*used in ex-*

clamations) : comme, que **3** ~ **about ... ?** : que dirais-tu de ... ? **4** ~ **come** WHY : comment, pourquoi **5** ~ **much** : combien **6** ~ **do you do?** : comment allez-vous? **7** ~ **old are you?** : quel âge as-tu? — ~ *conj* : comment

however [haʊˈɛvər] *conj* **1** : de quelque manière que **2** ~ **you like** : comme vous voulez — ~ *adv* **1** NEVERTHELESS : cependant, toutefois **2** ~ **important it is** : si important que ce soit **3** ~ **you want** : comme tu veux

howl [ˈhaʊl] *vi* : hurler — ~ *n* : hurlement *m*

hub [ˈhʌb] *n* **1** CENTER : centre *m* **2** : moyeu *m* (d'une roue)

hubbub [ˈhʌˌbʌb] *n* : vacarme *m*, brouhaha *m*

hubcap [ˈhʌbˌkæp] *n* : enjoliveur *m*

huddle [ˈhʌdəl] *vi* **-dled; -dling** *or* ~ **together** : se blottir

hue [ˈhjuː] *n* : couleur *f*, teinte *f*

huff [ˈhʌf] *n* **be in a** ~ : être fâché, être vexé

hug [ˈhʌg] *vt* **hugged; hugging 1** : serrer dans ses bras, étreindre **2** : serrer, longer (un mur, etc.) — ~ *n* : étreinte *f*

huge [ˈhjuːdʒ] *adj* **huger; hugest** : énorme, immense

hull [ˈhʌl] *n* : coque *f* (d'un navire)

hullo *Brit* → **hello**

hum [ˈhʌm] *v* **hummed; humming** *vi* : bourdonner — *vt* : fredonner, chantonner — ~ *n* : bourdonnement *m*

human [ˈhjuːmən, ˈjuː-] *adj* **1** : humain **2** ~ **rights** : droits *mpl* de l'homme, droits *mpl* de la personne *Can* — ~ *n* : humain *m*, être *m* humain — **humane** [hjuːˈmeɪn, juː-] *adj* : humain — **humanitarian** [hjuːˌmænəˈteriən, juː-] *adj* : humanitaire — **humanity** [hjuːˈmænəti, juː-] *n, pl* **-ties** : humanité *f*

humble [ˈhʌmbəl] *adj* **humbler; -blest** : humble, modeste — ~ *vt* **-bled; -bling 1** : humilier **2** ~ **oneself** : s'humilier

humdrum [ˈhʌmˌdrʌm] *adj* : monotone, banal

humid [ˈhjuːməd, ˈjuː-] *adj* : humide — **humidity** [hjuːˈmɪdəˌti, juː-] *n, pl* **-ties** : humidité *f*

humiliate [hjuːˈmɪliˌeɪt, juː-] *vt* **-ated; -ating** : humilier — **humiliating** [hjuːˈmɪliˌeɪtɪŋ, juː-] *adj* : humiliant — **humiliation** [hjuːˌmɪliˈeɪʃən, juː-] *n* : humiliation *f* — **humility** [hjuːˈmɪləti, juː-] *n* : humilité *f*

humor *or Brit* **humour** [ˈhjuːmər, ˈjuː-] *n* **1** WIT : humour *m* **2** MOOD : humeur *f* — ~ *vt* : faire plaisir à, ménager — **humorist** [ˈhjuːmərɪst, ˈjuː-] *n* : humoriste *mf* — **humorous** [ˈhjuːmərəs, ˈjuː-] *adj* : plein d'humour, drôle

hump [ˈhʌmp] *n* : bosse *f*

hunch [ˈhʌntʃ] *vi or* ~ **over** : se pencher — ~ *n* : intuition *f*, petite idée *f*

hundred ['hʌndrəd] *n, pl* **-dreds** *or* **-dred** : cent *m* — ~ *adj* : cent — **hundredth** ['hʌndrədθ] *n* **1** : centième *mf* (dans une série) **2** : centième *m* (en mathématiques) — ~ *adj* : centième

hung → **hang**

hunger ['hʌŋgər] *n* : faim *f* — ~ *vi* ~ **for** : avoir envie de — **hungry** ['hʌŋgri] *adj* **hungrier; -est be** ~ : avoir faim

hunk ['hʌŋk] *n* : gros morceau *m*

hunt ['hʌnt] *vt* **1** : chasser **2** *or* ~ **for** : chercher — ~ *vi* **1** : chasse *f* (sport) **2** SEARCH : recherche *f* — **hunter** ['hʌntər] *n* : chasseur *m*, -seuse *f* — **hunting** ['hʌntɪŋ] *n* : chasse *f*

hurdle ['hərdəl] *n* **1** : haie *f* (aux sports) **2** OBSTACLE : obstacle *m*

hurl ['hərl] *vt* : lancer, jeter

hurrah [hʊ'ra, -'rɔ] *interj* : hourra!

hurricane ['hərə,keɪn] *n* : ouragan *m*

hurry ['həri] *n* : hâte *f*, empressement *m* — ~ *v* **-ried; -rying** *vt* : presser, bousculer — *vi* **1** : se presser, se hâter **2** ~ **up!** : dépêche-toi! — **hurried** ['hərəd] *adj* : précipité — **hurriedly** ['hərədli] *adv* : à la hâte

hurt ['hərt] *v* **hurt; hurting** *vt* **1** INJURE : faire mal à, blesser **2** OFFEND : blesser — *vi* **1** : faire mal **2 my throat** ~**s** : j'ai mal à la gorge — ~ *adj* : blessé — ~ *n* **1** INJURY : blessure *f* **2** PAIN : douleur *f* — **hurtful** ['hərtfəl] *adj* : blessant

hurtle ['hərtəl] *vi* **-tled; -tling** : aller à toute vitesse

husband ['hʌzbənd] *n* : mari *m*

hush ['hʌʃ] *vt or* ~ **up** : faire taire — *vi* **1** : se taire **2** ~**!** : chut! — ~ *n* : silence *m*

husk ['hʌsk] *n* : enveloppe *f*

husky[1] ['hʌski] *adj* **huskier; -est** HOARSE : rauque

husky[2] *n, pl* **-kies** : chien *m* esquimau

husky[3] *n* BURLY : costaud

hustle ['həsəl] *v* **-tled; -tling** *vt* : presser, pousser — *vi* : se dépêcher — ~ *n* ~ **and bustle** : agitation *f*, grande activité *f*

hut ['hʌt] *n* : hutte *f*, cabane *f*

hutch ['hʌtʃ] *n* : clapier *m*

hyacinth ['haɪə,sɪnθ] *n* : jacinthe *f*

hybrid ['haɪbrɪd] *n* : hybride *m* — ~ *adj* : hybride

hydrant ['haɪdrənt] *n or* **fire** ~ : bouche *f* d'incendie

hydraulic [haɪ'drɔlɪk] *adj* : hydraulique

hydroelectric [,haɪdroɪ'lɛktrɪk] *adj* : hydroélectrique

hydrogen ['haɪdrədʒən] *n* : hydrogène *m*

hyena [haɪ'i:nə] *n* : hyène *f*

hygiene ['haɪ,dʒi:n] *n* : hygiène *f* — **hygienic** [haɪ'dʒɛnɪk, -'dʒi:-; ,haɪdʒi:'ɛnɪk] *adj* : hygiénique

hymn ['hɪm] *n* : hymne *m*

hyperactive [,haɪpər'æktɪv] *adj* : hyperactif

hyphen ['haɪfən] *n* : trait *m* d'union

hypnosis [hɪp'no:sɪs] *n, pl* **-noses** [-,si:z] : hypnose *f* — **hypnotic** [hɪp'nɑtɪk] *adj* : hypnotique — **hypnotism** ['hɪpnə,tɪzəm] *n* : hypnotisme *m* — **hypnotize** ['hɪpnə,taɪz] *vt* **-tized; -tizing** : hypnotiser

hypochondriac [,haɪpə'kɑndri,æk] *n* : hypocondriaque *mf*

hypocrisy [hɪ'pɑkrəsi] *n, pl* **-sies** : hypocrisie *f* — **hypocrite** ['hɪpə,krɪt] *n* : hypocrite *mf* — **hypocritical** [,hɪpə'krɪtɪkəl] *adj* : hypocrite

hypothesis [haɪ'pɑθəsɪs] *n, pl* **-eses** [-,si:z] : hypothèse *f* — **hypothetical** [,haɪpə-'θɛtɪkəl] *adj* : hypothétique

hysteria [hɪs'tɛriə, -'tɪr-] *n* : hystérie *f* — **hysterical** [hɪs'tɛrɪkəl] *adj* : hystérique

I

i ['aɪ] *n, pl* **i's** *or* **is** ['aɪz] : i *m*, neuvième lettre de l'alphabet

I ['aɪ] *pron* : je

ice ['aɪs] *n* **1** : glace *f* **2** ~ **cube** : glaçon *m* — ~ *v* **iced; icing** *vt* : glacer — *vi or* ~ **up** : se givrer — **iceberg** ['aɪs,bərg] *n* : iceberg *m* — **icebox** ['aɪs,bɑks] → **refrigerator** — **ice-cold** ['aɪs'ko:ld] *adj* : glacé — **ice cream** *n* : glace *f France*, crème *f* glacée *Can* — **ice–skate** *vi* **-skated; -skating** : patiner — **ice skate** ['aɪs,skeɪt] *n* : patin *m* (à glace) — **icicle** ['aɪ,sɪkəl] *n* : glaçon *m* — **icing** ['aɪsɪŋ] *n* : glaçage *m*

icon ['aɪ,kɑn, -kən] *n* : icône *f* (en informatique)

icy ['aɪsi] *adj* **icier; -est 1** : verglacé (se dit d'une route) **2** FREEZING : glacial, glacé

I'd ['aɪd] (*contraction of* **I should** *or* **I would**) → **should, would**

idea [aɪ'di:ə] *n* : idée *f*

ideal [aɪ'di:əl] *adj* : idéal — ~ *n* : idéal *m* — **idealist** [aɪ'di:ə,lɪst] *n* : idéaliste *mf* — **idealistic** [aɪ,di:ə'lɪstɪk] *adj* : idéaliste —

idealize [aɪˈdiːəˌlaɪz] vt **-ized; -izing** : idéaliser

identity [aɪˈdɛntəṭi] n, pl **-ties** : identité f — **identical** [aɪˈdɛntɪkəl] adj : identique — **identify** [aɪˈdɛntəˌfaɪ] v **-fied; -fying** vt : identifier — vi **~ with** : s'identifier à — **identification** [aɪˌdɛntəfəˈkeɪʃən] n **1** : identification f **2** or **~ card** : carte f d'identité

ideology [ˌaɪdiˈɑləʤi, ˌɪ-] n, pl **-gies** : idéologie f — **ideological** [ˌaɪdiəˈlɑʤɪkəl, ˌɪ-] adj : idéologique

idiocy [ˈɪdiəsi] n, pl **-cies** : idiotie f

idiom [ˈɪdiəm] n **1** : expression f idiomatique **2** LANGUAGE : idiome m — **idiomatic** [ˌɪdiəˈmæṭɪk] adj : idiomatique

idiosyncrasy [ˌɪdioˈsɪŋkrəsi] n, pl **-sies** : particularité f

idiot [ˈɪdiət] n : idiot m, -diote f — **idiotic** [ˌɪdiˈɑṭɪk] adj : idiot

idle [ˈaɪdəl] adj **idler; idlest 1** UNOCCUPIED : désœuvré, oisif **2** LAZY : paresseux **3** VAIN : vain **4 out of ~ curiosity** : par pure curiosité **5 stand ~** : être à l'arrêt — **~** v **idled; idling** vi : tourner au ralenti (se dit d'un moteur) — vt or **~ away** : gaspiller (son temps) — **idleness** [ˈaɪdəlnəs] n : oisiveté f

idol [ˈaɪdəl] n : idole f — **idolize** [ˈaɪdəˌlaɪz] vt **-ized; izing** : idolâtrer

idyllic [aɪˈdɪlɪk] adj : idyllique

if [ˈɪf] conj **1** : si **2** THOUGH : bien que **3 ~ so** : dans ce cas-là **4 ~ not** : sinon

igloo [ˈɪˌgluː] n, pl **-loos** : igloo m

ignite [ɪgˈnaɪt] v **-nited; -niting** vt : enflammer — vi : prendre feu, s'enflammer — **ignition** [ɪgˈnɪʃən] n **1** : allumage m **2** or **~ switch** : contact m

ignorance [ˈɪgnərənts] n : ignorance f — **ignorant** [ˈɪgnərənt] adj : ignorant — **ignore** [ɪgˈnor] vt **-nored; -noring** : ignorer

ilk [ˈɪlk] n : espèce f

ill [ˈɪl] adj **worse; worst 1** SICK : malade **2** BAD : mauvais — **~** adv **worse** [ˈwərs]; **worst** [ˈwərst] : mal — **~** n : mal m — **ill-advised** [ˌɪlædˈvaɪzd, -əd-] adj : peu judicieux — **ill at ease** adj : mal à l'aise

I'll [ˈaɪl] (contraction of **I shall** or **I will**) → **shall, will**

illegal [ɪlˈliːgəl] adj : illégal

illegible [ɪlˈlɛʤəbəl] adj : illisible

illegitimate [ˌɪlɪˈʤɪtəmət] adj : illégitime — **illegitimacy** [ˌɪlɪˈʤɪtəməsi] n : illégitimité f

illicit [ɪlˈlɪsət] adj : illicite

illiterate [ɪlˈlɪṭərət] adj : analphabète, illettré — **illiteracy** [ɪlˈlɪṭərəsi] n, pl **-cies** : analphabétisme m

ill-mannered [ˌɪlˈmænərd] adj : impoli

ill-natured [ˌɪlˈneɪtʃərd] adj : désagréable

illness [ˈɪlnəs] n : maladie f

illogical [ɪlˈlɑʤɪkəl] adj : illogique

ill-treat [ˌɪlˈtriːt] vt : maltraiter

illuminate [ɪˈluːməˌneɪt] vt **-nated; -nating** : éclairer — **illumination** [ɪˌluːməˈneɪʃən] n : éclairage m

illusion [ɪˈluːʒən] n : illusion f — **illusory** [ɪˈluːsəri, -zəri] adj : illusoire

illustrate [ˈɪləsˌtreɪt] v **-trated; -trating** : illustrer — **illustration** [ˌɪləsˈtreɪʃən] n : illustration f — **illustrative** [ɪˈlʌstrəṭɪv, ˈɪləˌstreɪṭɪv] adj : explicatif

illustrious [ɪˈlʌstriəs] adj : illustre

ill will n : malveillance f

I'm [ˈaɪm] (contraction of **I am**) → **be**

image [ˈɪmɪʤ] n : image f — **imagination** [ɪˌmæʤəˈneɪʃən] n : imagination f — **imaginary** [ɪˈmæʤəˌneri] adj : imaginaire — **imaginative** [ɪˈmæʤɪnəṭɪv] adj : imaginatif — **imagine** [ɪˈmæʤən] vt **-ined; -ining** : imaginer, s'imaginer

imbalance [ɪmˈbælənts] n : déséquilibre m

imbecile [ˈɪmbəsəl, -ˌsɪl] n : imbécile mf

imbue [ɪmˈbjuː] vt **-bued; -buing** : imprégner

imitation [ˌɪməˈteɪʃən] n : imitation f — **~** adj : artificiel, faux — **imitate** [ˈɪməˌteɪt] vt **-tated; -tating** : imiter — **imitator** [ˈɪməˌteɪṭər] n : imitateur m, -trice f

immaculate [ɪˈmækjələt] adj : impeccable

immaterial [ˌɪməˈtɪriəl] adj : sans importance

immature [ˌɪməˈtʃʊr, -ˈtjʊr, -ˈtʊr] adj : immature — **immaturity** [ˌɪməˈtʃʊrəṭi, -ˈtjʊr-, -ˈtʊr-] n, pl **-ties** : immaturité f

immediate [ɪˈmiːdiət] adj : immédiat — **immediately** [ɪˈmiːdiətli] adv **1** : immédiatement **2 ~ before** : juste avant

immense [ɪˈmɛnts] adj : immense — **immensity** [ɪˈmɛntsəṭi] n, pl **-ties** : immensité f

immerse [ɪˈmərs] vt **-mersed; -mersing** : plonger, immerger — **immersion** [ɪˈmərʒən] n : immersion f

immigrate [ˈɪməˌgreɪt] vi **-grated; -grating** : immigrer — **immigrant** [ˈɪmɪgrənt] n : immigrant m, -grante f; immigré m, -grée f — **immigration** [ˌɪməˈgreɪʃən] n : immigration f

imminent [ˈɪmənənt] adj : imminent — **imminence** [ˈɪmənənts] n : imminence f

immobile [ɪˈmoːbəl] adj **1** FIXED : fixe **2** MOTIONLESS : immobile — **immobilize** [ɪˈmoːbəˌlaɪz] vt **-ized; -izing** : immobiliser

immoral [ɪˈmorəl] adj : immoral — **immorality** [ˌɪmoˈræləṭi, ˌɪmə-] n : immoralité f

immortal [ɪˈmorṭəl] adj : immortel — **immortality** [ˌɪ.morˈtæləṭi] n : immortalité f

immune [ɪˈmjuːn] adj : immunisé — **immunity** [ɪˈmjuːnəṭi] n, pl **-ties** : immunité f —

immunization [ˌɪmjʊnəˈzeɪʃən] *n* : immunisation *f* — **immunize** [ˈɪmjʊˌnaɪz] *vt* -nized; -nizing : immuniser

imp [ˈɪmp] *n* 1 : lutin *m* 2 RASCAL : polisson *m*, -sonne *f*

impact [ˈɪmˌpækt] *n* : impact *m*

impair [ɪmˈpær] *vt* 1 WEAKEN : affaiblir 2 DAMAGE : détériorer

impart [ɪmˈpɑrt] *vt* : communiquer

impartial [ɪmˈpɑrʃəl] *adj* : impartial — **impartiality** [ɪmˌpɑrʃiˈæləti] *n* : impartialité *f*

impassable [ɪmˈpæsəbəl] *adj* : impraticable

impasse [ˈɪmˌpæs] *n* : impasse *f*

impassive [ɪmˈpæsɪv] *adj* : impassible

impatience [ɪmˈpeɪʃənts] *n* : impatience *f* — **impatient** [ɪmˈpeɪʃənt] *adj* : impatient — **impatiently** [ɪmˈpeɪʃəntli] *adv* : impatiemment

impeccable [ɪmˈpɛkəbəl] *adj* : impeccable

impede [ɪmˈpiːd] *vt* -peded; -peding : entraver, gêner — **impediment** [ɪmˈpɛdəmənt] *n* : entrave *f*, obstacle *m*

impel [ɪmˈpɛl] *vt* -pelled; -pelling 1 : inciter 2 PROPEL : pousser

impending [ɪmˈpɛndɪŋ] *adj* : imminent

impenetrable [ɪmˈpɛnətrəbəl] *adj* : impénétrable

imperative [ɪmˈpɛrətɪv] *adj* 1 COMMANDING : impérieux 2 NECESSARY : impératif — ~ *n* : impératif *m* (en grammaire)

imperceptible [ˌɪmpərˈsɛptəbəl] *adj* : imperceptible

imperfection [ɪmˌpərˈfɛkʃən] *n* : imperfection *f* — **imperfect** [ɪmˈpərfɪkt] *adj* : imparfait — ~ *n or* ~ **tense** : imparfait *m*

imperial [ɪmˈpɪriəl] *adj* : impérial — **imperialism** [ɪmˈpɪriəˌlɪzəm] *n* : impérialisme *m* — **imperious** [ɪmˈpɪriəs] *adj* : impérieux

impersonal [ɪmˈpərsənəl] *adj* : impersonnel

impersonate [ɪmˈpərsənˌeɪt] *vt* -ated; -ating : se faire passer pour — **impersonation** [ɪmˌpərsənˈeɪʃən] *n* : imitation *f* — **impersonator** [ɪmˈpərsənˌeɪtər] *n* : imitateur *m*, -trice *f*

impertinent [ɪmˈpərtənənt] *adj* : impertinent — **impertinence** [ɪmˈpərtənənts] *n* : impertinence *f*

impervious [ɪmˈpərviəs] *adj* ~ **to** : imperméable à

impetuous [ɪmˈpɛtʃuəs] *adj* : impétueux

impetus [ˈɪmpətəs] *n* : impulsion *f*

impinge [ɪmˈpɪndʒ] *vi* -pinged; -pinging 1 ~ **on** : effecter 2 ~ **on s.o.'s rights** : empiéter sur les droits de qqn

impish [ˈɪmpɪʃ] *adj* : espiègle

implant [ɪmˈplænt] *vt* : implanter — ~ [ˈɪmˌplænt] *n* : implant *m*

implausible [ɪmˈplɔzəbəl] *adj* : invraisemblable

implement [ˈɪmpləmənt] *n* : outil *m*, instru-

ment *m* — ~ [ˈɪmpləˌmɛnt] *vt* : mettre en œuvre, appliquer

implicate [ˈɪmpləˌkeɪt] *vt* -cated; -cating : impliquer — **implication** [ˌɪmpləˈkeɪʃən] *n* : implication *f*

implicit [ɪmˈplɪsət] *adj* 1 : implicite 2 UNQUESTIONING : absolu, total

implode [ɪmˈploːd] *vi* -ploded; -ploding : imploser

implore [ɪmˈplor] *vt* -plored; -ploring : implorer

imply [ɪmˈplaɪ] *vt* -plied; -plying : impliquer

impolite [ˌɪmpəˈlaɪt] *adj* : impoli

import [ɪmˈport] *vt* : importer (des marchandises) — ~ [ˈɪmˌport] *n* 1 IMPORTANCE : signification *f* 2 IMPORTATION : importation *f* — **importance** [ɪmˈportənts] *n* : importance *f* — **important** [ɪmˈportənt] *adj* : important — **importation** [ˌɪmˌporˈteɪʃən] *n* : importation *f* — **importer** [ɪmˈportər] *n* : importateur *m*, -trice *f*

impose [ɪmˈpoːz] *v* -posed; -posing *vt* : imposer — *vi* 1 : s'imposer 2 ~ **on** : déranger — **imposing** [ɪmˈpoːzɪŋ] *adj* : imposant — **imposition** [ˌɪmpəˈzɪʃən] *n* : imposition *f*

impossible [ɪmˈpasəbəl] *adj* : impossible — **impossibility** [ɪmˌpasəˈbɪləti] *n, pl* -ties : impossibilité *f*

impostor *or* **imposter** [ɪmˈpastər] *n* : imposteur *m*

impotent [ˈɪmpətənt] *adj* : impuissant — **impotence** [ˈɪmpətənts] *n* : impuissance *f*

impound [ɪmˈpaʊnd] *vt* : saisir, confisquer

impoverished [ɪmˈpavərɪʃt] *adj* : appauvri

impracticable [ɪmˈpræktɪkəbəl] *adj* : impraticable

impractical [ɪmˈpræktɪkəl] *adj* : peu pratique

imprecise [ˌɪmprɪˈsaɪs] *adj* : imprécis

impregnable [ɪmˈprɛgnəbəl] *adj* : imprenable

impregnate [ɪmˈprɛgˌneɪt] *vt* -nated; -nating 1 FERTILIZE : féconder 2 SATURATE : imprégner

impress [ɪmˈprɛs] *vt* 1 IMPRINT : imprimer 2 AFFECT : impressionner 3 ~ **upon s.o.** : faire bien comprendre à qqn — **impression** [ɪmˈprɛʃən] *n* : impression *f* — **impressionable** [ɪmˈprɛʃənəbəl] *adj* : impressionnable — **impressive** [ɪmˈprɛsɪv] *adj* : impressionnant

imprint [ɪmˈprɪnt, ˈɪmˌ-] *vt* : imprimer — ~ [ˈɪmˌprɪnt] *n* MARK : empreinte *f*, marque *f*

imprison [ɪmˈprɪzən] *vt* : emprisonner — **imprisonment** [ɪmˈprɪzənmənt] *n* : emprisonnement *m*

improbable [ɪmˈprabəbəl] *adj* : improbable — **improbability** [ɪmˌprabəˈbɪləti] *n, pl* -ties : improbabilité *f*

impromptu [ɪm'prɑmp,tu:, -,tju:] *adj* : impromptu

improper [ɪm'prɑpər] *adj* **1** UNSEEMLY : peu convenable **2** INCORRECT : incorrect **3** INDECENT : indécent — **impropriety** [,ɪmprə'praɪəṭi] *n, pl* **-ties** : inconvenance *f*

improve [ɪm'pru:v] *v* **-proved; -proving** *vt* : améliorer — *vi* : s'améliorer, faire des progrès — **improvement** [ɪm'pru:vmənt] *n* : amélioration *f*

improvise ['ɪmprə,vaɪz] *v* **-vised; -vising** : improviser — **improvisation** [ɪm,prɑvə'zeɪʃən, ,ɪmprəvə-] *n* : improvisation *f*

impudent ['ɪmpjədənt] *adj* : impudent — **impudence** ['ɪmpjədənts] *n* : impudence *f*

impulse ['ɪm,pʌls] *n* : impulsion *f* — **impulsive** [ɪm'pʌlsɪv] *adj* : impulsif — **impulsiveness** [ɪm'pʌlsɪvnəs] *n* : impulsivité *f*

impunity [ɪm'pju:nəṭi] *n* : impunité *f*

impure [ɪm'pjʊr] *adj* : impur — **impurity** [ɪm'pjʊrəṭi] *n, pl* **-ties** : impureté *f*

impute [ɪm'pju:t] *vt* **-puted; -puting** : imputer

in ['ɪn] *prep* **1** : dans, en, à **2** ～ **1938** : en 1938 **3** ～ **an hour** : dans une heure **4** ～ **Canada** : au Canada **5** ～ **leather** : en cuir **6** ～ **my house** : chez moi **7** ～ **the hospital** : à l'hôpital **8** ～ **the sun** : au soleil **9** ～ **this way** : de cette manière **10** be ～ **a hurry** : être pressé **11** be ～ **luck** : avoir de la chance — ～ *adv* **1** INSIDE : dedans, à l'intérieur **2** be ～ : être là, être chez soi **3** come ～ : entrer **4** she's ～ **for a surprise** : elle va être surprise **5** ～ **power** : au pouvoir — ～ *adj* : à la mode

inability [,ɪnə'bɪləṭi] *n, pl* **-ties** : incapacité *f*

inaccessible [,ɪnɪk'sɛsəbəl] *adj* : inaccessible

inaccurate [ɪn'ækjərət] *adj* : inexact

inactive [ɪn'æktɪv] *adj* : inactif — **inactivity** [,ɪn,æk'tɪvəṭi] *n, pl* **-ties** : inactivité *f*

inadequate [ɪ'nædɪkwət] *adj* : insuffisant

inadvertently [,ɪnəd'vərtəntli] *adv* : par inadvertance

inadvisable [,ɪnæd'vaɪzəbəl] *adj* : déconseillé

inane [ɪ'neɪn] *adj* **inaner; -est** : inepte, stupide

inanimate [ɪ'nænəmət] *adj* : inanimé

inapplicable [ɪ'næplɪkəbəl, ,ɪnə'plɪkəbəl] *adj* : inapplicable

inappropriate [,ɪnə'pro:priət] *adj* : inopportun, peu approprié

inarticulate [,ɪnɑr'tɪkjələt] *adj* **1** : indistinct (se dit des mots, des sons, etc.) **2** be ～ : ne pas savoir s'exprimer

inasmuch as [,ɪnæz'mʌtʃæz] *conj* : vu que

inaudible [ɪn'ɔdəbəl] *adj* : inaudible

inauguration [ɪ,nɔgjə'reɪʃən, -gə-] *n* : inauguration *f* — **inaugural** [ɪ'nɔgjərəl, -gərəl]

adj : inaugural — **inaugurate** [ɪ'nɔgjə,reɪt, -gə-] *vt* **-rated; -rating** : inaugurer

inborn ['ɪn,bɔrn] *adj* : inné

inbred ['ɪn,brɛd] *adj* INNATE : inné

incalculable [ɪn'kælkjələbəl] *adj* : incalculable

incapable [ɪn'keɪpəbəl] *adj* : incapable — **incapacitate** [,ɪnkə'pæsə,teɪt] *vt* **-tated; -tating** : rendre incapable — **incapacity** [,ɪnkə'pæsəṭi] *n, pl* **-ties** : incapacité *f*

incarcerate [ɪn'kɑrsə,reɪt] *vt* **-ated; -ating** : incarcérer

incarnation [,ɪn,kɑr'neɪʃən] *n* : incarnation *f*

incense¹ ['ɪnsɛnts] *n* : encens *m*

incense² [ɪn'sɛnts] *vt* **-censed; -censing** : mettre en fureur

incentive [ɪn'sɛntɪv] *n* : motivation *f*

inception [ɪn'sɛpʃən] *n* : commencement *m*

incessant [ɪn'sɛsənt] *adj* : incessant — **incessantly** [ɪn'sɛsəntli] *adv* : sans cesse

incest ['ɪn,sɛst] *n* : inceste *m* — **incestuous** [ɪn'sɛstʃuəs] *adj* : incestueux

inch ['ɪntʃ] *n* : pouce *m* — ～ *v* : avancer petit à petit

incident ['ɪntsədənt] *n* : incident *m* — **incidental** [,ɪntsə'dɛntəl] *adj* : accessoire — **incidentally** [,ɪntsə'dɛntəli, -'dɛntli] *adv* : à propos

incinerate [ɪn'sɪnə,reɪt] *vt* **-ated; -ating** : incinérer — **incinerator** [ɪn'sɪnə,reɪṭər] *n* : incinérateur *m*

incision [ɪn'sɪʒən] *n* : incision *f*

incite [ɪn'saɪt] *vt* **-cited; -citing** : inciter

incline [ɪn'klaɪn] *v* **-clined; -clining** *vt* **1** BEND : incliner **2** be ～ **d to** : avoir tendance à — *vi* **1** LEAN : s'incliner **2** ～ **towards** : tendre vers — ～ ['ɪn,klaɪn] *n* : inclinaison *f* — **inclination** [,ɪnklə'neɪʃən] *n* : penchant *m*, inclination *f*

include [ɪn'klu:d] *vt* **-cluded; -cluding** : inclure, comprendre — **inclusion** [ɪn'klu:ʒən] *n* : inclusion *f* — **inclusive** [ɪn'klu:sɪv] *adj* : inclus, compris

incognito [,ɪn,kɑg'ni:ṭo, ɪn'kɑgnə,to:] *adv & adj* : incognito

incoherence [,ɪnko'hɪrənts, -'hɛr-] *n* : incohérence *f* — **incoherent** [,ɪnko'hɪrənt, -'hɛr-] *adj* : incohérent

income ['ɪn,kʌm] *n* : revenu *m* — **income tax** *n* : impôt *m* sur le revenu

incomparable [ɪn'kɑmpərəbəl] *adj* : incomparable

incompatible [,ɪnkəm'pæṭəbəl] *adj* : incompatible — **incompatibility** [,ɪnkəm,pæṭə'bɪləṭi] *n* : incompatibilité *f*

incompetent [ɪn'kɑmpəṭənt] *adj* : incompétent — **incompetence** [ɪn'kɑmpəṭənts] *n* : incompétence *f*

incomplete [,ɪnkəm'pli:t] *adj* : incomplet, inachevé

incomprehensible [ˌɪnˌkɑmpriˈhɛntsəbəl] *adj* : incompréhensible

inconceivable [ˌɪnkənˈsiːvəbəl] *adj* : inconcevable

inconclusive [ˌɪnkənˈkluːsɪv] *adj* : peu concluant

incongruous [ɪnˈkɑŋgruəs] *adj* : incongru

inconsiderate [ˌɪnkənˈsɪdərət] *adj* **1** THOUGHTLESS : inconsidéré **2** be ~ toward : manquer d'égards envers

inconsistent [ˌɪnkənˈsɪstənt] *adj* **1** ERRATIC : changeant **2** CONTRADICTORY : contradictoire — **inconsistency** [ˌɪnkənˈsɪstəntsi] *n*, *pl* -cies : incohérence *f*, contradiction *f*

inconspicuous [ˌɪnkənˈspɪkjuəs] *adj* : qui passe inaperçu

inconvenience [ˌɪnkənˈviːnjənts] *n* **1** BOTHER : dérangement *m* **2** DISADVANTAGE : inconvénient *m* — ~ *vt* -nienced; -niencing : déranger — **inconvenient** [ˌɪnkənˈviːnjənt] *adj* : incommode

incorporate [ɪnˈkɔrpəˌreɪt] *vt* -rated; -rating : incorporer

incorrect [ˌɪnkəˈrɛkt] *adj* : incorrect

increase [ˈɪnˌkriːs, ɪnˈkriːs] *n* : augmentation *f* — ~ [ɪnˈkriːs, ˈɪnˌkriːs] *v* -creased; -creasing : augmenter — **increasingly** [ɪnˈkriːsɪŋli] *adv* : de plus en plus

incredible [ɪnˈkrɛdəbəl] *adj* : incroyable

incredulous [ɪnˈkrɛdʒələs] *adj* : incrédule

incriminate [ɪnˈkrɪməˌneɪt] *vt* -nated; -nating : incriminer

incubator [ˈɪŋkjuˌbeɪtər, -ˈɪn-] *n* : incubateur *m*, couveuse *f*

incumbent [ɪnˈkʌmbənt] *n* : titulaire *mf*

incur [ɪnˈkər] *vt* -curred; -curring : encourir (une pénalité, etc.), contracter (une dette)

incurable [ɪnˈkjurəbəl] *adj* : incurable

indebted [ɪnˈdɛtəd] *adj* ~ to : redevable à

indecent [ɪnˈdiːsənt] *adj* : indécent — **indecency** [ɪnˈdiːsəntsi] *n*, *pl* -cies : indécence *f*

indecisive [ˌɪndɪˈsaɪsɪv] *adj* : indécis

indeed [ɪnˈdiːd] *adv* : vraiment, en effet

indefinite [ɪnˈdɛfənət] *adj* **1** : indéfini **2** VAGUE : imprécis — **indefinitely** [ɪnˈdɛfənətli] *adv* : indéfiniment

indelible [ɪnˈdɛləbəl] *adj* : indélébile

indent [ɪnˈdɛnt] *vt* : mettre en alinéa — **indentation** [ˌɪnˌdɛnˈteɪʃən] *n* DENT, NOTCH : creux *m*, bosse *f*

independent [ˌɪndəˈpɛndənt] *adj* : indépendant — **independence** [ˌɪndəˈpɛndənts] *n* : indépendance *f* — **independently** [ˌɪndəˈpɛndəntli] *adv* : de façon indépendante

indescribable [ˌɪndɪˈskraɪbəbəl] *adj* : indescriptible

indestructible [ˌɪndɪˈstrʌktəbəl] *adj* : indestructible

index [ˈɪnˌdɛks] *n*, *pl* -dexes *or* -dices [ˈɪndəˌsiːz] **1** : index *m* (d'un livre, etc.) **2** INDICATOR : indice *m* **3** *or* ~ finger : index *m* — ~ *vt* : classer

Indian [ˈɪndiən] *adj* : indien

indication [ˌɪndəˈkeɪʃən] *n* : indication *f* — **indicate** [ˈɪndəˌkeɪt] *vt* -cated; -cating : indiquer — **indicative** [ɪnˈdɪkətɪv] *adj* : indicatif *m* — **indicator** [ˈɪndəˌkeɪtər] *n* : indicateur *m*

indict [ɪnˈdaɪt] *vt* : inculper — **indictment** [ɪnˈdaɪtmənt] *n* : inculpation *f*

indifferent [ɪnˈdɪfrənt, -ˈdɪfə-] *adj* **1** UNCONCERNED : indifférent **2** MEDIOCRE : médiocre — **indifference** [ɪnˈdɪfrənts, -ˈdɪfə-] *n* : indifférence *f*

indigenous [ɪnˈdɪdʒənəs] *adj* : indigène

indigestion [ˌɪndaɪˈdʒɛstʃən, -dɪ-] *n* : indigestion *f* — **indigestible** [ˌɪndaɪˈdʒɛstəbəl, -dɪ-] *adj* : indigeste

indignation [ˌɪndɪgˈneɪʃən] *n* : indignation *f* — **indignant** [ɪnˈdɪgnənt] *adj* : indigné — **indignity** [ɪnˈdɪgnəti] *n*, *pl* -ties : indignité *f*

indigo [ˈɪndɪˌgoː] *n*, *pl* -gos *or* -goes : indigo *m*

indirect [ˌɪndəˈrɛkt, -daɪ-] *adj* : indirect

indiscreet [ˌɪndɪˈskriːt] *adj* : indiscret — **indiscretion** [ˌɪndɪˈskrɛʃən] *n* : indiscrétion *f*

indiscriminate [ˌɪndɪˈskrɪmənət] *adj* **1** : sans discernement **2** RANDOM : fait au hasard

indispensable [ˌɪndɪˈspɛntsəbəl] *adj* : indispensable

indisputable [ˌɪndɪˈspjuːtəbəl] *adj* : incontestable

indistinct [ˌɪndɪˈstɪŋkt] *adj* : indistinct

individual [ˌɪndəˈvɪdʒuəl] *adj* **1** : individuel **2** SPECIFIC : particulier — ~ *n* : individu *m* — **individuality** [ˌɪndəˌvɪdʒuˈæləti] *n*, *pl* -ties : individualité *f* — **individually** [ˌɪndəˈvɪdʒuəli, -dʒəli] *adv* : individuellement

indoctrinate [ɪnˈdɑktrəˌneɪt] *vt* -nated; -nating : endoctriner — **indoctrination** [ɪnˌdɑktrəˈneɪʃən] *n* : endoctrinement *m*

Indonesian [ˌɪndoˈniːʒən, -ʃən] *adj* : indonésien — ~ *n* : indonésien *m* (langue)

indoor [ˈɪnˈdor] *adj* **1** : d'intérieur **2** ~ pool : piscine *f* couverte **3** ~ sports : sports *mpl* pratiqués en salle — **indoors** [ˈɪnˈdorz] *adv* : à l'intérieur

induce [ɪnˈduːs, -ˈdjuːs] *vt* -duced; -ducing **1** PERSUADE : induire **2** CAUSE : provoquer — **inducement** [ɪnˈduːsmənt, -ˈdjuːs-] *n* : encouragement *m*

indulge [ɪnˈdʌldʒ] *v* -dulged; -dulging *vt* **1** GRATIFY : céder à **2** PAMPER : gâter — *vi* ~ in : se permettre — **indulgence** [ɪnˈdʌldʒənts] *n* : indulgence *f* — **indulgent** [ɪnˈdʌldʒənt] *adj* : indulgent

industrial [ɪnˈdʌstriəl] *adj* : industriel — **industrialize** [ɪnˈdʌstriəˌlaɪz] *vt* -ized; -izing : industrialiser — **industrious** [ɪnˈdʌstriəs]

adj : industrieux, travailleur — **industry**
['ɪndəstri] *n, pl* **-tries** : industrie *f*
inebriated [ɪ'ni:bri,eɪtəd] *adj* : ivre
inedible [ɪ'nɛdəbəl] *adj* : immangeable
ineffective [,ɪnɪ'fɛktɪv] *adj* : inefficace — **in-
effectual** [,ɪnɪ'fɛktʃʊəl] *adj* : inefficace
inefficient [,ɪnɪ'fɪʃənt] *adj* **1** : inefficace **2**
INCOMPETENT : incompétent — **ineffi-
ciency** [,ɪnɪ'fɪʃənsi] *n, pl* **-cies** : inefficacité *f*
ineligible [ɪn'ɛlədʒəbəl] *adj* : inéligible
inept [ɪ'nɛpt] *adj* : inepte
inequality [,ɪnɪ'kwɑləti] *n, pl* **-ties** : inégalité *f*
inert [ɪ'nərt] *adj* : inerte — **inertia** [ɪ'nərʃə] *n*
: inertie *f*
inescapable [,ɪnɪ'skeɪpəbəl] *adj* : inéluctable
inevitable [ɪn'ɛvətəbəl] *adj* : inévitable —
inevitably [-bli] *adv* : inévitablement
inexcusable [,ɪnɪk'skju:zəbəl] *adj* : inexcusable
inexpensive [,ɪnɪk'spɛntsɪv] *adj* : pas cher,
bon marché
inexperienced [,ɪnɪk'spɪriəntst] *adj* : inexpérimenté
inexplicable [,ɪnɪk'splɪkəbəl] *adj* : inexplicable
infallible [ɪn'fæləbəl] *adj* : infaillible
infamous ['ɪnfəməs] *adj* : infâme, notoire
infancy ['ɪnfəntsi] *n, pl* **-cies** : petite enfance
f — **infant** ['ɪnfənt] *n* : petit enfant *m*, petite
enfant *f*; nourrisson *m* — **infantile** ['ɪnfən-
,taɪl, -təl, -,ti:l] *adj* : infantile
infantry ['ɪnfəntri] *n, pl* **-tries** : infanterie *f*
infatuated [ɪn'fætʃʊ,eɪtəd] *adj* **be ~ with**
: être épris de — **infatuation** [ɪn,fætʃʊ-
'eɪʃən] *n* : engouement *m*
infect [ɪn'fɛkt] *vt* : infecter — **infection** [ɪn-
'fɛkʃən] *n* : infection *f* — **infectious** [ɪn-
'fɛkʃəs] *adj* : infectieux, contagieux
infer [ɪn'fər] *vt* **-ferred; -ferring** : déduire —
inference ['ɪnfərənts] *n* : déduction *f*
inferior [ɪn'firiər] *adj* : inférieur — **~** *n* : inférieur *m*, -rieure *f* — **inferiority** [ɪn,firi-
'ɔrəti] *n, pl* **-ties** : infériorité *f*
infernal [ɪn'fərnəl] *adj* : infernal — **inferno**
[ɪn'fər,no:] *n, pl* **-nos** : brasier *m*
infertile [ɪn'fərtəl, -,taɪl] *adj* **1** : infertile **2**
STERILE : stérile — **infertility** [,ɪnfər'tɪləti]
n : infertilité *f*
infest [ɪn'fɛst] *vt* : infester
infidelity [,ɪnfə'dɛləti, -faɪ-] *n, pl* **-ties** : infidélité *f*
infiltrate [ɪn'fɪl,treɪt, 'ɪnfɪl-] *v* **-trated; -trat-
ing** *vt* : infiltrer — *vi* : s'infiltrer
infinite ['ɪnfənət] *adj* : infini — **infinitive**
[ɪn'fɪnətɪv] *n* : infinitif *m* — **infinity** [ɪn-
'fɪnəti] *n, pl* **-ties** : infinité *f*
infirm [ɪn'fərm] *adj* : infirme — **infirmary**

[ɪn'fərməri] *n, pl* **-ries** : infirmerie *f* — **infir-
mity** [ɪn'fərməti] *n, pl* **-ties** : infirmité *f*
inflame [ɪn'fleɪm] *v* **-flamed; -flaming** *vt*
: enflammer — *vi* : s'enflammer — **inflammable** [ɪn'flæməbəl] *adj* : (in)flammable —
inflammation [,ɪnflə'meɪʃən] *n* : inflammation *f* — **inflammatory** [ɪn'flæmə,tori] *adj*
: incendiaire
inflate [ɪn'fleɪt] *v* **-flated; -flating** *vt* : gonfler
— *vi* : se gonfler — **inflatable** [ɪn'fleɪtəbəl]
adj : gonflable — **inflation** [ɪn'fleɪʃən] *n*
: inflation *f* — **inflationary** [ɪn'fleɪʃə,nɛri]
adj : inflationniste
inflexible [ɪn'flɛksɪbəl] *adj* : inflexible
inflict [ɪn'flɪkt] *vt* : infliger
influence ['ɪn,flu:ənts, ɪn'flu:ənts] *n* **1** : influence *f* **2 under the ~ of** : sous l'effet de
— **~** *vt* **-enced; -encing** : influencer, influer sur — **influential** [,ɪnflu'ɛntʃəl] *adj*
: influent
influenza [,ɪnflu'ɛnzə] *n* : grippe *f*
influx ['ɪn,flʌks] *n* : afflux *m*
inform [ɪn'fɔrm] *vt* : informer, renseigner —
vi **~ on** : dénoncer
informal [ɪn'fɔrməl] *adj* **1** : simple **2** CA-
SUAL : familier, décontracté **3** UNOFFICIAL
: officieux — **informally** [ɪn'fɔrməli] *adv*
: sans cérémonie, simplement
information [,ɪnfər'meɪʃən] *n* : renseigne-
ments *mpl*, information *f* — **informative**
[ɪn'fɔrmətɪv] *adj* : informatif — **informer**
[ɪn'fɔrmər] *n* : indicateur *m*, -trice *f*
infrared [,ɪnfrə'rɛd] *adj* : infrarouge
infrastructure ['ɪnfrə,strʌktʃər] *n* : infrastructure *f*
infrequent [ɪn'fri:kwənt] *adj* : rare, peu
fréquent — **infrequently** [ɪn'fri:kwəntli]
adv : rarement
infringe [ɪn'frɪndʒ] *v* **-fringed; -fringing** *vt*
: enfreindre — *vi* **~ on** : empiéter sur — **in-
fringement** [ɪn'frɪndʒmənt] *n* : infraction *f*
(à la loi)
infuriate [ɪn'fjʊri,eɪt] *vt* **-ated; -ating** : rendre furieux — **infuriating** [ɪn'fjʊri,eɪtɪŋ] *adj*
: exaspérant
infuse [ɪn'fju:z] *vt* **-fused; -fusing** : infuser
— **infusion** [ɪn'fju:ʒən] *n* : infusion *f*
ingenious [ɪn'dʒi:njəs] *adj* : ingénieux — **ingenuity** [,ɪndʒə'nu:əti, -'nju:-] *n, pl* **-ties**
: ingéniosité *f*
ingenuous [ɪn'dʒɛnjʊəs] *adj* : ingénu, naïf
ingot ['ɪŋgət] *n* : lingot *m*
ingrained [ɪn'greɪnd] *adj* : enraciné
ingratiate [ɪn'greɪʃi,eɪt] *vt* **-ated; -ating ~
oneself with** : gagner les bonnes grâces de
ingratitude [ɪn'grætə'tu:d, -'tju:d] *n* : ingratitude *f*
ingredient [ɪn'gri:diənt] *n* : ingrédient *m*
inhabit [ɪn'hæbət] *vt* : habiter — **inhabitant**
[ɪn'hæbətənt] *n* : habitant *m*, -tante *f*

inhale [ɪn'heɪl] *v* **-haled; -haling** *vt* : inhaler, respirer — *vi* : inspirer

inherent [ɪn'hɪrənt, -'her-] *adj* : inhérent — **inherently** [ɪn'hɪrəntli, -'her-] *adv* : fondamentalement

inherit [ɪn'herət] *vt* : hériter de — **inheritance** [ɪn'herətənts] *n* : héritage *m*

inhibit [ɪn'hɪbət] *vt* IMPEDE : entraver, gêner — **inhibition** [ˌɪnhə'bɪʃən, ˌɪnə-] *n* : inhibition *f*

inhuman [ɪn'hju:mən, -'ju:-] *adj* : inhumain — **inhumane** [ˌɪnhju'meɪn, -ju-] *adj* : cruel — **inhumanity** [ˌɪnhju'mænəti, -ju-] *n, pl* **-ties** : inhumanité *f*

initial [ɪ'nɪʃəl] *adj* : initial, premier — ~ *n* : initiale *f* — ~ *vt* **-tialed** *or* **-tialled; -tialing** *or* **-tialling** : parapher — **initially** [ɪ'nɪʃəli] *adv* : au départ

initiate [ɪ'nɪʃiˌeɪt] *vt* **-ated; -ating** 1 BEGIN : amorcer, entreprendre 2 ~ **into** : initier à — **initiation** [ɪˌnɪʃi'eɪʃən] *n* : initiation *f* — **initiative** [ɪ'nɪʃətɪv] *n* : initiative *f*

inject [ɪn'dʒekt] *vt* : injecter — **injection** [ɪn'dʒekʃən] *n* : injection *f*

injure ['ɪndʒər] *vt* **-jured; -juring** 1 WOUND : blesser 2 HARM : nuire à 3 ~ **oneself** : se blesser — **injury** ['ɪndʒəri] *n, pl* **-ries** 1 WOUND : blessure *f* 2 WRONG : tort *m*

injustice [ɪn'dʒʌstəs] *n* : injustice *f*

ink ['ɪŋk] *n* : encre *f* — **inkwell** ['ɪŋkˌwel] *n* : encrier *m*

inland ['ɪnˌlænd, -lənd] *adj* : intérieur — ~ *adv* : à l'intérieur, vers l'intérieur

in–laws ['ɪnˌlɔz] *npl* : beaux-parents *mpl*

inlet ['ɪnˌlet, -lət] *n* : bras *m* de mer

inmate ['ɪnˌmeɪt] *n* 1 PRISONER : détenu *m*, -nue *f* 2 PATIENT : interné *m*, -née *f*

inn ['ɪn] *n* : auberge *f*

innards ['ɪnərdz] *npl* : entrailles *fpl*

innate [ɪ'neɪt] *adj* : inné

inner ['ɪnər] *adj* : intérieur, interne — **innermost** ['ɪnərˌmo:st] *adj* : le plus profond

inning ['ɪnɪŋ] *n* : tour *m* de batte, manche *f* Can (au baseball)

innocence ['ɪnəsənts] *n* : innocence *f* — **innocent** ['ɪnəsənt] *adj* : innocent — ~ *n* : innocent *m*, -cente *f*

innocuous [ɪ'nɑkjəwəs] *adj* : inoffensif

innovate ['ɪnəˌveɪt] *v* **-vated; -vating** : innover — **innovation** [ˌɪnə'veɪʃən] *n* : innovation *f* — **innovative** ['ɪnəˌveɪtɪv] *adj* : innovateur — **innovator** ['ɪnəˌveɪtər] *n* : innovateur *m*, -trice *f*

innumerable [ɪ'nu:mərəbəl, -'nju:-] *adj* : innombrable

inoculate [ɪ'nɑkjəˌleɪt] *vt* **-lated; -lating** : inoculer — **inoculation** [ɪˌnɑkjə'leɪʃən] *n* : inoculation *f*

inoffensive [ˌɪnə'fentsɪv] *adj* : inoffensif

inpatient ['ɪnˌpeɪʃənt] *n* : malade *m* hospitalisé, malade *f* hospitalisée

input ['ɪnˌpʊt] *n* 1 : contribution *f* 2 : entrée *f* (de données) — ~ *vt* **-putted** *or* **-put; -putting** : entrer (des données)

inquire [ɪn'kwaɪr] *v* **-quired; -quiring** *vt* : demander — *vi* 1 ~ **about** : se renseigner sur 2 ~ **into** : enquêter sur — **inquiry** [ɪn'kwaɪri, 'ɪnˌkwaɪri; 'ɪnkwəri, 'ɪŋ-] *n, pl* **-ries** 1 QUESTION : demande *f* 2 INVESTIGATION : enquête *f* — **inquisition** [ˌɪnkwə'zɪʃən, ˌɪŋ-] *n* : inquisition *f* — **inquisitive** [ɪn'kwɪzətɪv] *adj* : curieux

insane [ɪn'seɪn] *adj* : fou — **insanity** [ɪn'sænəti] *n, pl* **-ties** : folie *f*

insatiable [ɪn'seɪʃəbəl] *adj* : insatiable

inscribe [ɪn'skraɪb] *vt* **-scribed; -scribing** 1 : inscrire 2 DEDICATE : dédicacer — **inscription** [ɪn'skrɪpʃən] *n* : inscription *f*

inscrutable [ɪn'skru:təbəl] *adj* : impénétrable

insect ['ɪnˌsekt] *n* : insecte *m* — **insecticide** [ɪn'sektəˌsaɪd] *n* : insecticide *m*

insecure [ˌɪnsɪ'kjʊr] *adj* 1 UNSAFE : peu sûr 2 FEARFUL : anxieux — **insecurity** [ˌɪnsɪ'kjʊrəti] *n, pl* **-ties** : insécurité *f*

insensitive [ɪn'sentsətɪv] *adj* : insensible — **insensitivity** [ɪnˌsentsə'tɪvəti] *n* : insensibilité *f*

inseparable [ɪn'sepərəbəl] *adj* : inséparable

insert [ɪn'sert] *vt* : insérer, introduire

inside [ɪn'saɪd, 'ɪnˌsaɪd] *n* 1 : intérieur *m* 2 ~**s** *npl* GUTS : entrailles *fpl* — ~ *adv* 1 : à l'intérieur 2 ~ **out** : à l'envers — ~ *adj* : intérieur — ~ *prep* : à l'intérieur de

insidious [ɪn'sɪdiəs] *adj* : insidieux

insight ['ɪnˌsaɪt] *n* : perspicacité *f* — **insightful** [ɪn'saɪtfəl] *adj* : perspicace

insignia [ɪn'sɪgniə] *or* **insigne** [-ˌni:] *n, pl* **-nia** *or* **-nias** : insigne(s) *m(pl)*

insignificant [ˌɪnsɪg'nɪfɪkənt] *adj* : insignifiant

insincere [ˌɪnsɪn'sɪr] *adj* : pas sincère

insinuate [ɪn'sɪnjuˌeɪt] *vt* **-ated; -ating** : insinuer — **insinuation** [ɪnˌsɪnju'eɪʃən] *n* : insinuation *f*

insipid [ɪn'sɪpəd] *adj* : insipide

insist [ɪn'sɪst] *v* : insister — **insistent** [ɪn'sɪstənt] *adj* : insistant

insofar as [ˌɪnso'fɑrˌæz] *conj* : dans la mesure où

insole ['ɪnˌso:l] *n* : semelle *f* (intérieure)

insolence ['ɪntsələnts] *n* : insolence *f* — **insolent** ['ɪntsələnt] *adj* : insolent

insolvent [ɪn'salvənt] *adj* : insolvable

insomnia [ɪn'samniə] *n* : insomnie *f*

inspect [ɪn'spekt] *vt* : examiner, inspecter — **inspection** [ɪn'spekʃən] *n* : inspection *f* — **inspector** [ɪn'spektər] *n* : inspecteur *m*, -trice *f*

inspire [ɪnˈspaɪr] *vt* **-spired; -spiring** : inspirer — **inspiration** [ˌɪnfspəˈreɪʃən] *n* : inspiration *f* — **inspirational** [ˌɪnfspə-ˈreɪʃənəl] *adj* : inspirant

instability [ˌɪnfstəˈbɪləti] *n* : instabilité *f*

install [ɪnˈstɔl] *vt* **-stalled; -stalling** : installer — **installation** [ˌɪnfstəˈleɪʃən] *n* : installation *f* — **installment** [ɪnˈstɔlmənt] *n* 1 PAYMENT : versement *m*, acompte *m* 2 : épisode *m* (d'un feuilleton)

instance [ˈɪnfstənfs] *n* 1 : cas *m*, exemple *m* 2 **for ~** : par exemple

instant [ˈɪnfstənt] *n* : instant *m*, moment *m* — **~** *adj* 1 IMMEDIATE : immédiat, instantané 2 **~ coffee** : café *m* instantané — **instantaneous** [ˌɪnfstənˈteɪniəs] *adj* : instantané — **instantly** [ˈɪnfstəntli] *adv* : immédiatement, sur-le-champ

instead [ɪnˈsted] *adv* 1 : plutôt **2 I went ~** : j'y suis allé à sa place — **instead of** *prep* : au lieu de, à la place de

instep [ˈɪnˌstep] *n* : cou-de-pied *m*

instigate [ˈɪnfstəˌgeɪt] *vt* **-gated; -gating** : engager, provoquer — **instigation** [ˌɪnfstə-ˈgeɪʃən] *n* : instigation *f* — **instigator** [ˈɪnfstəˌgeɪtər] *n* : instigateur *m*, -trice *f*

instill *or Brit* **instil** [ɪnˈstɪl] *vt* **-stilled; -stilling** : inculquer

instinct [ˈɪnˌstɪŋkt] *n* : instinct *m* — **instinctive** [ɪnˈstɪŋktɪv] *or* **instinctual** [ɪn-ˈstɪŋktʃuəl] *adj* : instinctif

institute [ˈɪnstəˌtuːt, -ˌtjuːt] *vt* **-tuted; -tuting** : instituer — **~** *n* : institut *m* — **institution** [ˌɪnstəˈtuːʃən, -ˈtjuː-] *n* : institution *f*

instruct [ɪnˈstrʌkt] *vt* 1 TEACH : instruire 2 DIRECT : charger — **instruction** [ɪn-ˈstrʌkʃən] *n* : instruction *f* — **instructor** [ɪnˈstrʌktər] *n* : moniteur *m*, -trice *f*

instrument [ˈɪnfstrəmənt] *n* : instrument *m* — **instrumental** [ˌɪnfstrəˈmentəl] *adj* 1 : instrumental **2 be ~ in** : contribuer à

insufferable [ɪnˈsʌfərəbəl] *adj* : insupportable

insufficient [ˌɪnsəˈfɪʃənt] *adj* : insuffisant

insular [ˈɪnfsʊlər, -sjʊ-] *adj* 1 : insulaire 2 NARROW-MINDED : borné

insulate [ˈɪnfsəˌleɪt] *vt* **-lated; -lating** : isoler — **insulation** [ˌɪnfsəˈleɪʃən] *n* : isolation *f*

insulin [ˈɪnfsələn] *n* : insuline *f*

insult [ɪnˈsʌlt] *vt* : insulter — **~** [ˈɪnˌsʌlt] *n* : insulte *f*, injure *f*

insure [ɪnˈʃʊr] *vt* **-sured; -suring** : assurer — **insurance** [ɪnˈʃʊrənfs] *n* : assurance *f*

insurmountable [ˌɪnsərˈmaʊntəbəl] *adj* : insurmontable

intact [ɪnˈtækt] *adj* : intact

intake [ˈɪnˌteɪk] *n* 1 : consommation *f* (de nourriture) 2 ADMISSION : admission *f*

intangible [ɪnˈtændʒəbəl] *adj* : intangible

integral [ˈɪntɪgrəl] *adj* 1 : intégral **2 be an ~ part of** : faire partie intégrante de

integrate [ˈɪntəˌgreɪt] *v* **-grated; -grating** *vt* : intégrer — *vi* : s'intégrer

integrity [ɪnˈtegrəti] *n* : intégrité *f*

intellect [ˈɪntəˌlekt] *n* : intelligence *f* — **intellectual** [ˌɪntəˈlektʃuəl] *adj* : intellectuel — **~** *n* : intellectuel *m*, -tuelle *f* — **intelligence** [ɪnˈtelədʒənfs] *n* : intelligence *f* — **intelligent** [ɪnˈtelədʒənt] *adj* : intelligent — **intelligible** [ɪnˈtelədʒəbəl] *adj* : intelligible

intend [ɪnˈtend] *vt* **1 be ~ed for** : être destiné à **2 ~ to** : avoir l'intention de — **intended** [ɪnˈtendəd] *adj* 1 PLANNED : voulu 2 INTENTIONAL : intentionnel

intense [ɪnˈtenfs] *adj* : intense — **intensely** [ɪnˈtenfsli] *adv* 1 : intensément 2 EXTREMELY : extrêmement — **intensify** [ɪn-ˈtenfsəˌfaɪ] *v* **-fied; -fying** *vt* : intensifier — *vi* : s'intensifier — **intensity** [ɪnˈtenfsəti] *n*, *pl* **-ties** : intensité *f* — **intensive** [ɪnˈtenfsɪv] *adj* : intensif

intent [ɪnˈtent] *n* : intention *f* — **~** *adj* 1 : absorbé, attentif **2 ~ on doing** : résolu à faire — **intention** [ɪnˈtenfʃən] *n* : intention *f* — **intentional** [ɪnˈtenfʃənəl] *adj* : intentionnel — **intently** [ɪnˈtentli] *adv* : attentivement

interact [ˌɪntərˈækt] *vi* 1 : agir l'un sur l'autre **2 ~ with** : communiquer avec — **interaction** [ˌɪntərˈækʃən] *n* : interaction *f*

intercede [ˌɪntərˈsiːd] *vi* **-ceded; -ceding** : intercéder

intercept [ˌɪntərˈsept] *vt* : intercepter

interchange [ˌɪntərˈtʃeɪndʒ] *vt* **-changed; -changing** EXCHANGE : échanger — **~** *n* [ˈɪntərˌtʃeɪndʒ] 1 EXCHANGE : échange *m* 2 JUNCTION : échangeur *m* — **interchangeable** [ˌɪntərˈtʃeɪndʒəbəl] *adj* : interchangeable

intercourse [ˈɪntərˌkors] *n* : rapports *mpl* (sexuels)

interest [ˈɪntrəst, -təˌrest] *n* : intérêt *m* — **~** *vt* : intéresser — **interesting** [ˈɪntrəstɪŋ, -təˌrestɪŋ] *adj* : intéressant

interface [ˈɪntərˌfeɪs] *n* : interface *f*

interfere [ˌɪntərˈfɪr] *vi* **-fered; -fering** 1 INTERVENE : intervenir **2 ~ in** : s'immiscer dans — **interference** [ˌɪntərˈfɪrənfs] *n* 1 : ingérence *f* 2 : interférence *f*, parasites *mpl* (à la radio, etc.)

interim [ˌɪntərəm] *n* 1 : intérim *m* **2 in the ~** : entre-temps — **~** *adj* : provisoire

interior [ɪnˈtɪriər] *adj* : intérieur — **~** *n* : intérieur *m*

interjection [ˌɪntərˈdʒekʃən] *n* : interjection *f*

interlock [ˌɪntərˈlɑk] *vi* : s'enclencher

intermediate [ˌɪntərˈmiːdiət] *adj* : intermédiaire — **intermediary** [ˌɪntərˈmiːdiˌeri] *n*, *pl* **-aries** : intermédiaire *mf*

interminable [ɪn'tərmənəbəl] *adj* : interminable

intermission [ˌɪntər'mɪʃən] *n* **1** : pause *f* **2** : entracte *m* (au théâtre)

intermittent [ˌɪntər'mɪtənt] *adj* : intermittent

intern[1] ['ɪn,tərn, ɪn'tərn] *vt* CONFINE : interner

intern[2] ['ɪn,tərn] *n* : stagiaire *mf*

internal [ɪn'tərnəl] *adj* : interne — **internally** [ɪn'tərnəli] *adv* : intérieurement

international [ˌɪntər'næʃənəl] *adj* : international

Internet ['ɪntər,nɛt] *n* : Internet *m*

interpret [ɪn'tərprət] *vt* : interpréter — **interpretation** [ɪn,tərprə'teɪʃən] *n* : interprétation *f* — **interpreter** [ɪn'tərprətər] *n* : interprète *mf*

interrogate [ɪn'tɛrə,geɪt] *vt* **-gated; -gating** : interroger — **interrogation** [ɪn,tɛrə-'geɪʃən] *n* QUESTIONING : interrogatoire *m* — **interrogative** [ˌɪntə'rɑgətɪv] *adj* : interrogatif

interrupt [ˌɪntə'rʌpt] *v* : interrompre — **interruption** [ˌɪntə'rʌpʃən] *n* : interruption *f*

intersect [ˌɪntər'sɛkt] *vt* : croiser, couper — *vi* : se croiser, se couper — **intersection** [ˌɪntər'sɛkʃən] *n* JUNCTION : croisement *m*, carrefour *m*

intersperse [ˌɪntər'spɛrs] *vt* **-spersed; -spersing** ~ **with** : parsemer de

interstate ['ɪntər,steɪt] *n or* ~ **highway** : autoroute *f*

intertwine [ˌɪntər'twaɪn] *vi* **-twined; -twining** : s'entrelacer

interval ['ɪntərvəl] *n* : intervalle *m*

intervene [ˌɪntər'vi:n] *vi* **-vened; -vening** **1** : intervenir **2** HAPPEN : survenir — **intervention** [ˌɪntər'vɛntʃən] *n* : intervention *f*

interview ['ɪntər,vju:] *n* **1** : entretien *m*, entrevue *f* **2** : interview *f* (à la télévision, etc.) — ~ *vt* **1** : faire passer une entrevue (pour un emploi) **2** : interviewer (à la télévision, etc.)

intestine [ɪn'tɛstən] *n* : intestin *m* — **intestinal** [ɪn'tɛstənəl] *adj* : intestinal

intimate[1] ['ɪntə,meɪt] *vt* **-mated; -mating** : laisser entendre

intimate[2] ['ɪntəmət] *adj* : intime — **intimacy** ['ɪntəməsi] *n, pl* **-cies** : intimité *f*

intimidate [ɪn'tɪmə,deɪt] *vt* **-dated; -dating** : intimider — **intimidation** [ɪn,tɪmə'deɪʃən] *n* : intimidation *f*

into ['ɪn,tu:] *prep* **1** : en, dans **2 bump** ~ : se cogner contre **3** (*used in mathematics*) **4** ~ **12 is 3** : 12 divisé par 4 fait 3

intolerable [ɪn'tɑlərəbəl] *adj* : intolérable — **intolerance** [ɪn'tɑlərənts] *n* : intolérance *f* — **intolerant** [ɪn'tɑlərənt] *adj* : intolérant

intoxicate [ɪn'tɑksə,keɪt] *vt* **-cated; -cating**

: enivrer — **intoxicated** [ɪn'tɑksə,keɪtəd] *adj* : ivre

intransitive [ɪn'træntsətɪv, -'trænzə-] *adj* : intransitif

intravenous [ˌɪntrə'vi:nəs] *adj* : intraveineux

intrepid [ɪn'trɛpəd] *adj* : intrépide

intricate ['ɪntrɪkət] *adj* : compliqué — **intricacy** ['ɪntrɪkəsi] *n, pl* **-cies** : complexité *f*

intrigue ['ɪn,tri:g, ɪn'tri:g] *n* : intrigue *f* — ~ [ɪn'tri:g] *v* **-trigued; -triguing** : intriguer — **intriguing** [ɪn'tri:gɪŋ] *adj* : fascinant

intrinsic [ɪn'trɪnzɪk, -'trɪntsɪk] *adj* : intrinsèque

introduce [ˌɪntrə'du:s, -'dju:s] *vt* **-duced; -ducing** **1** : introduire **2** PRESENT : présenter — **introduction** [ˌɪntrə'dʌkʃən] *n* **1** : introduction *f* **2** PRESENTATION : présentation *f* — **introductory** [ˌɪntrə'dʌktəri] *adj* : d'introduction, préliminaire

introvert ['ɪntrə,vərt] *n* : introverti *m*, -tie *f* — **introverted** ['ɪntrə,vərtəd] *adj* : introverti

intrude [ɪn'tru:d] *vi* **-truded; -truding** : déranger, s'imposer — **intruder** [ɪn'tru:-dər] *n* : intrus *m*, -truse *f* — **intrusion** [ɪn-'tru:ʒən] *n* : intrusion *f* — **intrusive** [ɪn-'tru:sɪv] *adj* : importun, gênant

intuition [ˌɪntu'ɪʃən, -tju-] *n* : intuition *f* — **intuitive** [ɪn'tu:ətɪv, -'tju:-] *adj* : intuitif

inundate ['ɪnən,deɪt] *vt* **-dated; -dating** : inonder

invade [ɪn'veɪd] *vt* **-vaded; -vading** : envahir

invalid[1] [ɪn'væləd] *adj* : non valide, non valable

invalid[2] ['ɪnvələd] *n* : infirme *mf*, invalide *mf*

invaluable [ɪn'væljəbəl, -'væljuə-] *adj* : inestimable, précieux

invariable [ɪn'væriəbəl] *adj* : invariable

invasion [ɪn'veɪʒən] *n* : invasion *f*

invent [ɪn'vɛnt] *vt* : inventer — **invention** [ɪn'vɛntʃən] *n* : invention *f* — **inventive** [ɪn-'vɛntɪv] *adj* : inventif — **inventor** [ɪn-'vɛntər] *n* : inventeur *m*, -trice *f*

inventory ['ɪnvən,tori] *n, pl* **-ries** : inventaire *m*

invert [ɪn'vərt] *vt* : inverser, renverser

invertebrate [ɪn'vərtəbrət, -,breɪt] *adj* : invertébré — ~ *n* : invertébré *m*

invest [ɪn'vɛst] *v* : investir

investigate [ɪn'vɛstə,geɪt] *vt* **-gated; -gating** : enquêter sur, faire une enquête sur — **investigation** [ɪn,vɛstə'geɪʃən] *n* : investigation *f*, enquête *f*

investment [ɪn'vɛstmənt] *n* : investissement *m* — **investor** [ɪn'vɛstər] *n* : investisseur *m*, -seuse *f*

inveterate [ɪn'vɛtərət] *adj* : invétéré

invigorating [ɪn'vɪgə,reɪtɪŋ] *adj* : vivifiant, revigorant

invincible [ɪn'vɪntsəbəl] *adj* : invincible

invisible [ɪnˈvɪzəbəl] *adj* : invisible
invitation [ˌɪnvəˈteɪʃən] *n* : invitation *f* — **invite** [ɪnˈvaɪt] *vt* **-vited; -viting** : inviter — **inviting** [ɪnˈvaɪt̬ɪŋ] *adj* : attrayant, engageant
invoice [ˈɪnˌvɔɪs] *n* : facture *f*
invoke [ɪnˈvoːk] *vt* **-voked; -voking** : invoquer
involuntary [ɪnˈvɑlənˌteri] *adj* : involontaire
involve [ɪnˈvɑlv] *vt* **-volved; -volving 1** ENTAIL : entraîner **2** CONCERN : concerner, toucher — **involved** [ɪnˈvɑlvd] *adj* INTRICATE : complexe — **involvement** [ɪnˈvɑlvmənt] *n* : participation *f*
invulnerable [ɪnˈvʌlnərəbəl] *adj* : invulnérable
inward [ˈɪnwərd] *adj* : intérieur — ∼ *or* **inwards** [ˈɪnwərdz] *adv* : vers l'intérieur
iodine [ˈaɪəˌdaɪn] *n* : iode *m*, teinture *f* d'iode
ion [ˈaɪən, ˈaɪˌɑn] *n* : ion *m*
iota [aɪˈoːt̬ə] *n* : brin *m*
IOU [ˌaɪˌoːˈjuː] *n* : reconnaissance *f* de dette
Iranian [ɪˈreɪniən, -ˈræ-, -ˈrɑ-; aɪˈ-] *adj* : iranien
Iraqi [ɪˈraki, -ˈræ-] *adj* : irakien
irate [aɪˈreɪt] *adj* : furieux
iris [ˈaɪrəs] *n, pl* **irises** *or* **irides** [ˈaɪrəˌdiːz, ˈɪr-] : iris *m*
Irish [ˈaɪrɪʃ] *adj* : irlandais
irksome [ˈərksəm] *adj* : irritant, agaçant
iron [ˈaɪərn] *n* **1** : fer *m* (métal) **2** : fer *m* à repasser — ∼ *vt* PRESS : repasser — **ironing** [ˈaɪərnɪŋ] *n* : repassage *m*
irony [ˈaɪrəni] *n, pl* **-nies** : ironie *f* — **ironic** [aɪˈrɑnɪk] *or* **ironical** [-nɪkəl] *adj* : ironique
irrational [ɪˈræʃənəl] *adj* : irrationnel
irreconcilable [ɪˌrekənˈsaɪləbəl] *adj* : irréconciliable, inconciliable
irrefutable [ˌɪrɪˈfjuːt̬əbəl, ɪrˈrefjə-] *adj* : irréfutable
irregular [ɪˈreɡjələr] *adj* : irrégulier — **irregularity** [ɪˌreɡjəˈlærət̬i] *n, pl* **-ties** : irrégularité *f*
irrelevant [ɪˈreləvənt] *adj* : sans rapport, non pertinent
irreparable [ɪˈrepərəbəl] *adj* : irréparable
irreplaceable [ˌɪrɪˈpleɪsəbəl] *adj* : irremplaçable
irreproachable [ˌɪrɪˈproːtʃəbəl] *adj* : irréprochable
irresistible [ˌɪrɪˈzɪstəbəl] *adj* : irrésistible
irresolute [ɪˈrezəˌluːt] *adj* : irrésolu, indécis
irrespective of [ˌɪrɪˈspektɪvəv] *prep* : sans tenir compte de
irresponsible [ˌɪrɪˈspɑntsəbəl] *adj* : irresponsable — **irresponsibility** [ˌɪrɪˌspɑntsəˈbɪləti] *n* : irresponsabilité *f*
irreverent [ɪˈrevərənt] *adj* : irrévérencieux

irrigate [ˈɪrəˌɡeɪt] *vt* **-gated; -gating** : irriguer — **irrigation** [ˌɪrəˈɡeɪʃən] *n* : irrigation *f*
irritate [ˈɪrəˌteɪt] *vt* **-tated; -tating** : irriter — **irritable** [ˈɪrət̬əbəl] *adj* : irritable — **irritating** [ˈɪrəˌteɪt̬ɪŋ] *adj* : irritant, agaçant — **irritation** [ˌɪrəˈteɪʃən] *n* : irritation *f*
is → **be**
Islam [ɪsˈlɑm, ɪz-, -ˈlæm; ˈɪsˌlɑm, ˈɪz-] *n* : islam *m* — **Islamic** [-mɪk] *adj* : islamique
island [ˈaɪlənd] *n* : île *f* — **isle** [ˈaɪl] *n* : île *f*, îlot *m*
isolate [ˈaɪsəˌleɪt] *vt* **-lated; -lating** : isoler — **isolation** [ˌaɪsəˈleɪʃən] *n* : isolement *m*
Israeli [ɪzˈreɪli] *adj* : israélien
issue [ˈɪˌʃuː] *n* **1** MATTER : question *f*, problème *m* **2** : publication *f* (d'un livre), émission *f* (de timbres, etc.) **3** : numéro *m* (d'une revue, etc.) **4 make an** ∼ **of** : faire des histoires de — ∼ *v* **-sued; -suing** *vt* **1** : émettre (un chèque, etc.), distribuer (des provisions, etc.), donner (un ordre) **2** PUBLISH : publier, sortir — *vi* ∼ **from** : provenir de
isthmus [ˈɪsməs] *n* : isthme *m*
it [ˈɪt] *pron* **1** (*as subject*) : il, elle **2** (*as direct object*) : le, la, l' **3** (*as indirect object*) : lui **4** (*as a nonspecific subject*) : ce, cela, ça **5 it's snowing** : il neige **6 that's** ∼ : c'est ça **7 who is** ∼ ? : qui c'est?
Italian [ɪˈtæliən, aɪ-] *adj* : italien — ∼ *n* : italien *m* (langue)
italics [ɪˈtælɪks] *npl* : italique *m*
itch [ˈɪtʃ] *n* : démangeaison *f* — ∼ *vi* : avoir des démangeaisons — **itchy** [ˈɪtʃi] *adj* **itchier; -est** : qui démange
it'd [ˈɪt̬əd] (*contraction of* **it had** *or* **it would**) → **have, would**
item [ˈaɪt̬əm] *n* **1** : article *m*, chose *f* **2** : point *m* (d'un ordre du jour) **3 news** ∼ : nouvelle *f* — **itemize** [ˈaɪt̬əˌmaɪz] *vt* **-ized; -izing** : détailler
itinerant [aɪˈtɪnərənt] *adj* : itinérant, ambulant
itinerary [aɪˈtɪnəˌreri] *n, pl* **-aries** : itinéraire *m*
it'll [ˈɪt̬l] (*contraction of* **it shall** *or* **it will**) → **shall, will**
its [ˈɪts] *adj* : son, sa, ses
it's [ˈɪts] *contraction of* **it is** *or* **it has** → **be, have**
itself [ɪtˈself] *pron* **1** (*used reflexively*) : se **2** (*for emphasis*) : lui-même, elle-même, soi-même
I've [ˈaɪv] (*contraction of* **I have**) → **have**
Ivorian [aɪˈvoriən] *adj* : ivoirien
ivory [ˈaɪvəri] *n, pl* **-ries** : ivoire *m*
ivy [ˈaɪvi] *n, pl* **ivies** : lierre *m*

J

j [ˈʤeɪ] *n, pl* **j's** *or* **js** [ˈʤeɪz] : j *m*, dixième lettre de l'alphabet

jab [ˈʤæb] *vt* **jabbed; jabbing 1** PIERCE : piquer **2** POKE : enfoncer — **∼** *n* POKE : (petit) coup *m*

jabber [ˈʤæbər] *vi* : jacasser, bavarder

jack [ˈʤæk] *n* **1** : cric *m* (mécanisme) **2** : valet *m* (aux cartes) — **∼** *vt or* **∼ up** : soulever avec un cric

jackass [ˈʤæk,æs] *n* : âne *m*

jacket [ˈʤækət] *n* **1** : veste *f* **2** : jaquette *f* (d'un livre)

jackhammer [ˈʤæk,hæmər] *n* : marteau-piqueur *m*

jackknife [ˈʤæk,naɪf] *n, pl* **-knives** : couteau *m* de poche

jackpot [ˈʤæk,pɑt] *n* : gros lot *m*

jaded [ˈʤeɪdəd] *adj* : blasé

jagged [ˈʤægəd] *adj* : dentelé

jail [ˈʤeɪl] *n* : prison *f* — **∼** *vt* : emprisonner, mettre en prison — **jailer** *or* **jailor** [ˈʤeɪlər] *n* : geôlier *m*, -lière *f*

jam¹ [ˈʤæm] *v* **jammed; jamming** *vt* **1** CRAM : entasser **2** OBSTRUCT : bloquer — *vi* : se bloquer, se coincer — **∼** *n* **1** *or* **traffic ∼** : embouteillage *m* **2** FIX : pétrin *m fam*

jam² *n* PRESERVES : confiture *f*

janitor [ˈʤænətər] *n* : concierge *mf*

January [ˈʤænju,ɛri] *n* : janvier *m*

Japanese [ˌʤæpəˈniːz, -ˈniːs] *adj* : japonais — **∼** *n* : japonais *m* (langue)

jar¹ [ˈʤɑr] *v* **jarred; jarring** *vi* **1** : rendre un son discordant **2 ∼ on** : agacer (qqn) — *vt* JOLT : secouer — **∼** *n* : secousse *f*

jar² *n* : bocal *m*, pot *m*

jargon [ˈʤɑrgən] *n* : jargon *m*

jaundice [ˈʤɔndɪs] *n* : jaunisse *f*

jaunt [ˈʤɔnt] *n* : balade *f*

jaunty [ˈʤɔnti] *adj* **-tier; -est** : allègre, insouciant

jaw [ˈʤɔ] *n* : mâchoire *f* — **jawbone** [ˈʤɔ,boːn] *n* : maxillaire *m*

jay [ˈʤeɪ] *n* : geai *m*

jazz [ˈʤæz] *n* : jazz *m* — **∼** *vt or* **∼ up** : animer — **jazzy** [ˈʤæzi] *adj* **jazzier; jazziest** FLASHY : voyant, tapageur

jealous [ˈʤɛləs] *adj* : jaloux — **jealousy** [ˈʤɛləsi] *n, pl* **-sies** : jalousie *f*

jeans [ˈʤiːnz] *npl* : jean *m*, blue-jean *m*

jeer [ˈʤɪr] *vt* BOO : huer — *vi* **∼ at** : se moquer de — **∼** *n* : raillerie *f*

jelly [ˈʤɛli] *n, pl* **-lies** : gelée *f* — **jellyfish** [ˈʤɛli,fɪʃ] *n* : méduse *f*

jeopardy [ˈʤɛpərdi] *n* : danger *m*, péril *m* —

jeopardize [ˈʤɛpərˌdaɪz] *vt* **-dized; -dizing** : mettre en danger, compromettre

jerk [ˈʤərk] *n* **1** JOLT : saccade *f*, secousse *f* **2** FOOL : idiot *m*, -diote *f* — **∼** *vt* **1** YANK : tirer brusquement **2** JOLT : secouer

jersey [ˈʤərzi] *n, pl* **-seys** : jersey *m* (tissu)

jest [ˈʤɛst] *n* : plaisanterie *f* — **∼** *vi* : plaisanter — **jester** [ˈʤɛstər] *n* : bouffon *m*

Jesus [ˈʤiːzəs, -zəz] *n* : Jésus *m*

jet [ˈʤɛt] *n* **1** STREAM : jet *m* **2** *or* **∼ airplane** : jet *m*, avion *m* à réaction — **jet–propelled** *adj* : à réaction

jettison [ˈʤɛtəsən] *vt* **1** : jeter par-dessus bord **2** DISCARD : se débarrasser de

jetty [ˈʤɛti] *n, pl* **-ties** : jetée *f*

jewel [ˈʤuːəl] *n* : bijou *m* — **jeweler** *or* **jeweller** [ˈʤuːələr] *n* : bijoutier *m*, -tière *f*; joaillier *m*, -lière *f* — **jewelry** *or* **Brit jewellery** [ˈʤuːəlri] *n* : bijoux *mpl*

Jewish [ˈʤuːɪʃ] *adj* : juif

jibe [ˈʤaɪb] *vi* **jibed; jibing** AGREE : concorder

jiffy [ˈʤɪfi] *n, pl* **-fies** : instant *m*

jig [ˈʤɪg] *n* : gigue *f* (danse)

jiggle [ˈʤɪgəl] *vt* **-gled; -gling** : secouer, agiter — **∼** *n* : secousse *f*

jigsaw [ˈʤɪg,sɔ] *n or* **∼ puzzle** : puzzle *m*

jilt [ˈʤɪlt] *vt* : laisser tomber

jingle [ˈʤɪŋgəl] *v* **-gled; -gling** *vi* : tinter — **∼** *vt* : faire tinter — **∼** *n* : tintement *m*

jinx [ˈʤɪŋks] *n* : mauvais sort *m*

jitters [ˈʤɪtərz] *npl* **have the ∼** : être nerveux — **jittery** [ˈʤɪtəri] *adj* : nerveux

job [ˈʤɑb] *n* **1** EMPLOYMENT : emploi *m* **2** TASK : travail *m*, tâche *f*

jockey [ˈʤɑki] *n, pl* **-eys** : jockey *m*

jog [ˈʤɑg] *vi* **jogged; jogging** : faire du jogging — **jogging** [ˈʤɑgɪŋ] *n* : jogging *m*

join [ˈʤɔɪn] *vt* **1** UNITE : joindre, unir **2** MEET : rejoindre **3** : devenir membre de (un club, etc.) — *vi or* **∼ together** : s'unir, se joindre

joint [ˈʤɔɪnt] *n* **1** : articulation *f* (en anatomie) **2** : joint *m* (en menuiserie) — **∼** *adj* : commun

joke [ˈʤoːk] *n* : plaisanterie *f*, blague *f* — **∼** *vi* **joked; joking** : plaisanter — **joker** [ˈʤoːkər] *n* **1** : blagueur *m*, -gueuse *f* **2** : joker *m* (aux cartes)

jolly [ˈʤɑli] *adj* **-lier; -est** : jovial, gai

jolt [ˈʤoːlt] *vt* : secouer — **∼** *n* **1** : secousse *f*, coup *m* **2** SHOCK : choc *m*

jostle [ˈʤɑsəl] *v* **-tled; -tling** *vt* : bousculer — *vi* : se bousculer

jot [ˈdʒɑt] *vt* **jotted; jotting** *or* ~ **down** : prendre note de

journal [ˈdʒərnəl] *n* **1** DIARY : journal *m* (intime) **2** PERIODICAL : revue *f* — **journalism** [ˈdʒərnəlˌızəm] *n* : journalisme *m* — **journalist** [ˈdʒərnəlıst] *n* : journaliste *mf*

journey [ˈdʒərni] *n, pl* **-neys** : voyage *m*

jovial [ˈdʒoːviəl] *adj* : jovial

joy [ˈdʒɔɪ] *n* : joie *f* — **joyful** [ˈdʒɔɪfəl] *adj* : joyeux — **joyous** [ˈdʒɔɪəs] *adj* : joyeux

jubilant [ˈdʒuːbələnt] *adj* : débordant de joie — **jubilee** [ˈdʒuːbəˌliː] *n* : jubilé *m*

Judaism [ˈdʒuːdəˌızəm, ˈdʒuːdiˌ-, ˈdʒuːˌdeɪ-] *n* : judaïsme *m*

judge [ˈdʒʌdʒ] *vt* **judged; judging** : juger — ~ *n* : juge *m* — **judgment** *or* **judgement** [ˈdʒʌdʒmənt] *n* : jugement *m*

judicial [dʒuˈdɪʃəl] *adj* : judiciaire — **judicious** [dʒuˈdɪʃəs] *adj* : judicieux

jug [ˈdʒʌg] *n* : cruche *f*, pichet *m*

juggle [ˈdʒʌgəl] *vi* **-gled; -gling** : jongler — **juggler** [ˈdʒʌgələr] *n* : jongleur *m*, -gleuse *f*

juice [ˈdʒuːs] *n* : jus *m* — **juicy** [ˈdʒuːsi] *adj* **juicier; juiciest** : juteux

July [dʒuˈlaɪ] *n* : juillet *m*

jumble [ˈdʒʌmbəl] *vt* **-bled; -bling** : mélanger — ~ *n* : fouillis *m*, désordre *m*

jumbo [ˈdʒʌmˌboː] *adj* : géant

jump [ˈdʒʌmp] *vi* **1** LEAP : sauter **2** START : sursauter **3** RISE : faire un bond **4** ~ **at** : saisir (une occasion, etc.) — *vt or* ~ **over** : sauter — ~ *n* **1** LEAP : saut *m* **2** INCREASE : hausse *f* — **jumper** [ˈdʒʌmpər] *n* **1** : sauteur *m*, -teuse *f* (aux sports) **2** : robe-

chasuble *f* (vêtement) — **jumpy** [ˈdʒʌmpi] *adj* **jumpier; jumpiest** : nerveux

junction [ˈdʒʌŋkʃən] *n* **1** : jonction *f* **2** : carrefour *m*, embranchement *m* (de deux routes) — **juncture** [ˈdʒʌŋktʃər] *n* : conjoncture *f*

June [ˈdʒuːn] *n* : juin *m*

jungle [ˈdʒʌŋgəl] *n* : jungle *f*

junior [ˈdʒuːnjər] *adj* **1** YOUNGER : cadet, plus jeune **2** SUBORDINATE : subalterne — ~ *n* **1** : cadet *m*, -dette *f* **2** : étudiant *m*, -diante *f* de troisième année

junk [ˈdʒʌŋk] *n* : camelote *f fam*

Jupiter [ˈdʒuːpətər] *n* : Jupiter *f*

jurisdiction [ˌdʒurəsˈdɪkʃən] *n* : juridiction *f*

jury [ˈdʒʊri] *n, pl* **-ries** : jury *m* — **juror** [ˈdʒʊrər] *n* : juré *m*, -rée *f*

just [ˈdʒʌst] *adj* : juste — ~ *adv* **1** BARELY : à peine **2** EXACTLY : exactement **3** ONLY : seulement **4** he has ~ arrived : il vient d'arriver **5** it's ~ perfect : c'est parfait

justice [ˈdʒʌstɪs] *n* **1** : justice *f* **2** JUDGE : juge *m*

justify [ˈdʒʌstəˌfaɪ] *vt* **-fied; -fying** : justifier — **justification** [ˌdʒʌstəfəˈkeɪʃən] *n* : justification *f*

jut [ˈdʒʌt] *vi* **jutted; jutting** *or* ~ **out** : dépasser, faire saillie

juvenile [ˈdʒuːvəˌnaɪl, -vənəl] *adj* **1** YOUNG : jeune **2** CHILDISH : puéril — ~ *n* : jeune *mf*

juxtapose [ˈdʒʌkstəˌpoːz] *vt* **-posed; -posing** : juxtaposer

K

k [ˈkeɪ] *n, pl* **k's** *or* **ks** [ˈkeɪz] : k *m*, onzième lettre de l'alphabet

kangaroo [ˌkæŋgəˈruː] *n, pl* **-roos** : kangourou *m*

karat [ˈkærət] *n* : carat *m*

karate [kəˈrɑti] *n* : karaté *m*

keel [ˈkiːl] *n* : quille *f* — ~ *vi or* ~ **over** : chavirer (se dit d'un bateau), s'écrouler (se dit d'une personne)

keen [ˈkiːn] *adj* **1** PENETRATING : vif, pénétrant **2** ENTHUSIASTIC : enthousiaste

keep [ˈkiːp] *v* **kept** [ˈkɛpt]; **keeping** *vt* **1** : garder **2** : tenir (une promesse, etc.) **3** DETAIN : retenir **4** PREVENT : empêcher **5** ~ **up** : maintenir — *vi* **1** STAY : se tenir, rester **2** LAST : se conserver, se garder **3** *or* ~ **on** CONTINUE : continuer — ~ *n* **for**

~**s** : pour de bon — **keeper** [ˈkiːpər] *n* : gardien *m*, -dienne *f* — **keeping** [ˈkiːpɪŋ] *n* **1** CARE : garde *f* **2 in** ~ **with** : en accord avec — **keepsake** [ˈkiːpˌseɪk] *n* : souvenir *m*

keg [ˈkɛg] *n* : baril *m*, tonnelet *m*

kennel [ˈkɛnəl] *n* : niche *f*

kept → **keep**

kerchief [ˈkərtʃəf, -ˌtʃiːf] *n* : fichu *m*

kernel [ˈkərnəl] *n* **1** : amande *f* **2** CORE : noyau *m*, cœur *m*

kerosene *or* **kerosine** [ˈkɛrəˌsiːn, ˌkɛrəˈ-] *n* : kérosène *m*, pétrole *m* lampant

ketchup [ˈkɛtʃəp, ˈkæ-] *n* : ketchup *m*

kettle [ˈkɛtəl] *n* : bouilloire *f*

key [ˈkiː] *n* **1** : clé *f* **2** : touche *f* (d'un clavier) — ~ *adj* : clé — **keyboard** [ˈkiː-

ˌbord] *n* : clavier *m* — **keyhole** [ˈki:ˌho:l] *n* : trou *m* de serrure

khaki [ˈkæki, ˈkɑ-] *adj* : kaki

kick [ˈkɪk] *vt* : donner un coup de pied à — *vi* : donner un coup de pied — ~ *n* **1** : coup *m* de pied **2** PLEASURE, THRILL : plaisir *m*

kid [ˈkɪd] *n* **1** GOAT : chevreau *m* **2** CHILD : gosse *mf France fam;* flot *m Can* — ~ *v* **kidded; kidding** *vi or* ~ **around** — blaguer, plaisanter — *vt* TEASE : taquiner — **kidnap** [ˈkɪdˌnæp] *vt* **-napped** *or* **-naped** [-ˌnæpt]; **-napping** *or* **-naping** [-ˌnæpɪŋ] : kidnapper, enlever

kidney [ˈkɪdˌni] *n, pl* **-neys** : rein *m*

kill [ˈkɪl] *v* : tuer — ~ *n* **1** KILLING : mise *f* à mort **2** PREY : proie *f* — **killer** [ˈkɪlər] *n* : meurtrier *m,* -trière *f;* tueur *m,* tueuse *f* — **killing** [ˈkɪlɪŋ] *n* : meurtre *m*

kiln [ˈkɪl, ˈkɪln] *n* : four *m*

kilo [ˈki:ˌlo:] *n, pl* **-los** : kilo *m* — **kilogram** [ˈkɪləˌgræm, ˈki:-] *n* : kilogramme *m* — **kilometer** [kɪˈlɑmətər, ˈkɪləˌmi:-] *n* : kilomètre *m* — **kilowatt** [ˈkɪləˌwɑt] *n* : kilowatt *m*

kin [ˈkɪn] *n* : parents *mpl,* famille *f*

kind [ˈkaɪnd] *n* : espèce *f,* genre *m,* sorte *f* — ~ *adj* : gentil, bienveillant

kindergarten [ˈkɪndərˌgɑrtən, -dən] *n* : jardin *m* d'enfants *France,* école *f* maternelle *Can*

kindhearted [ˈkaɪndˈhɑrtəd] *adj* : bon, qui a bon cœur

kindle [ˈkɪndəl] *v* **-dled; -dling** *vt* : allumer — *vi* : s'enflammer

kindly [ˈkaɪndli] *adj* **-lier; -est** : bienveillant — ~ *adv* **1** : avec gentillesse **2** OBLIGINGLY : gentiment — **kindness** [ˈkaɪndnəs] *n* : gentillesse *f,* bonté *f* — **kind of** *adv* SOMEWHAT : quelque peu

kindred [ˈkɪndrəd] *adj* **1** : apparenté **2** ~ **spirit** : âme *f* sœur

king [ˈkɪŋ] *n* : roi *m* — **kingdom** [ˈkɪŋdəm] *n* : royaume *m*

kink [ˈkɪŋk] *n* **1** TWIST : nœud *m* **2** FLAW : défaut *m,* problème *m*

kinship [ˈkɪnˌʃɪp] *n* : parenté *f*

kiss [ˈkɪs] *vt* : embrasser, donner un baiser à — *vi* : s'embrasser — ~ *n* : baiser *m*

kit [ˈkɪt] *n* : trousse *f*

kitchen [ˈkɪtʃən] *n* : cuisine *f*

kite [ˈkaɪt] *n* : cerf-volant *m*

kitten [ˈkɪtən] *n* : chaton *m* — **kitty** [ˈkɪti] *n, pl* **-ties** FUND : cagnotte *f*

knack [ˈnæk] *n* TALENT : don *m*

knapsack [ˈnæpˌsæk] *n* : sac *m* à dos

knead [ˈni:d] *vt* : pétrir

knee [ˈni:] *n* : genou *m* — **kneecap** [ˈni:ˌkæp] *n* : rotule *f*

kneel [ˈni:l] *vi* **knelt** [ˈnɛlt] *or* **kneeled** [ˈni:ld]; **kneeling** : s'agenouiller

knew → **know**

knife [naɪf] *n, pl* **knives** [ˈnaɪvz] : couteau *m* — ~ *vt* **knifed** [naɪft]; **knifing** : donner un coup de couteau à

knight [ˈnaɪt] *n* **1** : chevalier *m* **2** : cavalier *m* (aux échecs) — **knighthood** [ˈnaɪtˌhu:d] *n* : titre *m* de chevalier

knit [ˈnɪt] *v* **knit** *or* **knitted** [ˈnɪtəd]; **knitting** : tricoter — **knitting** [ˈnɪtɪŋ] *n* : tricot *m*

knob [ˈnɑb] *n* : poignée *f,* bouton *m*

knock [ˈnɑk] *vt* **1** HIT : cogner, frapper **2** CRITICIZE : critiquer **3** ~ **down** *or* ~ **over** : renverser **4** ~ **out** : assommer — *vi* **1** : frapper (à la porte) **2** : cogner (se dit d'un moteur) **3** ~ **into** : heurter

knot [ˈnɑt] *n* : nœud *m* — ~ *vt* **knotted; knotting** : nouer, faire un nœud à — **knotty** [ˈnɑti] *adj* **-tier; -est** : épineux (se dit d'un problème)

know [ˈno:] *v* **knew** [ˈnu:, ˈnju:]; **known** [ˈno:n]; **knowing** *vt* **1** : savoir **2** : connaître (une personne, un lieu) **3** UNDERSTAND : comprendre — *vi* **1** : savoir **2** ~ **about** : être au courant de, s'y connaître en (un sujet) — **knowing** [ˈno:ɪŋ] *adj* : entendu — **knowingly** [ˈno:ɪŋli] *adv* INTENTIONALLY : sciemment — **knowledge** [ˈnɑlɪdʒ] *n* **1** : connaissance *f* **2** LEARNING : connaissances *fpl,* savoir *m* — **knowledgeable** [ˈnɑlɪdʒəbəl] *adj* : bien informé

knuckle [ˈnʌkəl] *n* : jointure *f* du doigt, articulation *f* du doigt

Koran [kəˈrɑn, -ˈræn] *n* **the** ~ : le Coran

Korean [kəˈri:ən] *adj* : coréen — ~ *n* : coréen *m* (langue)

kosher [ˈko:ʃər] *adj* : kascher, casher

L

l [ˈɛl] *n, pl* **l's** *or* **ls** [ˈɛlz] : l *m*, douzième lettre de l'alphabet

lab [ˈlæb] → **laboratory**

label [ˈleɪbəl] *n* **1** TAG : étiquette *f* **2** BRAND : marque *f* — ~ *vt* **-beled** *or* **-belled; -beling** *or* **-belling** : étiqueter

labor *or Brit* **labour** [ˈleɪbər] *n* **1** : travail *m* **2** WORKERS : main-d'œuvre *f* **3 in** ~ : en train d'accoucher — ~ *vi* **1** : travailler **2** STRUGGLE : avancer péniblement — *vt* : insister sur (un point)

laboratory [ˈlæbrə,tori, ləˈbɔrə-] *n, pl* **-ries** : laboratoire *m*

laborer *or Brit* **labourer** [ˈleɪbərər] *n* : ouvrier *m*, -vrière *f*

laborious [ləˈbɔriəs] *adj* : laborieux

lace [ˈleɪs] *n* **1** : dentelle *f* **2** SHOELACE : lacet *m* — ~ *vt* **laced; lacing 1** TIE : lacer **2 be laced with** : être mêlé de (se dit d'une boisson)

lacerate [ˈlæsə,reɪt] *vt* **-ated; -ating** : lacérer

lack [ˈlæk] *vt* : manquer de, ne pas avoir — *vi or* **be lacking** : manquer — ~ *n* : manque *m*, carence *f*

lackadaisical [ˌlækəˈdeɪzɪkəl] *adj* : apathique, indolent

lackluster [ˈlæk,lʌstər] *adj* : terne, fade

lacquer [ˈlækər] *n* : laque *m*

lacrosse [ləˈkrɔs] *n* : crosse *f*

lacy [ˈleɪsi] *adj* **lacier; -est** : de dentelle

lad [ˈlæd] *n* : gars *m*, garçon *m*

ladder [ˈlædər] *n* : échelle *f*

laden [ˈleɪdən] *adj* : chargé

ladle [ˈleɪdəl] *n* : louche *f* — ~ *vt* **-dled; -dling** : servir à la louche

lady [ˈleɪdi] *n, pl* **-dies** : dame *f*, madame *f* — **ladybug** [ˈleɪdi,bʌg] *n* : coccinelle *f* — **ladylike** [ˈleɪdi,laɪk] *adj* : élégant, de dame

lag [ˈlæg] *n* **1** DELAY : retard *m* **2** INTERVAL : décalage *m* — ~ *vi* **lagged; lagging** : traîner, être en retard

lager [ˈlɑgər] *n* : bière *f* blonde

lagoon [ləˈguːn] *n* : lagune *f*

laid *pp* → **lay¹**

lain *pp* → **lie¹**

lair [ˈlær] *n* : tanière *f*

lake [ˈleɪk] *n* : lac *m*

lamb [ˈlæm] *n* : agneau *m*

lame [ˈleɪm] *adj* **lamer; lamest 1** : boiteux **2 a** ~ **excuse** : une excuse peu convaincante

lament [ləˈmɛnt] *vt* **1** MOURN : pleurer **2** DEPLORE : déplorer — ~ *n* : lamentation *f* — **lamentable** [ˈlæməntəbəl, ləˈmɛntə-] *adj* : lamentable

laminate [ˈlæmə,neɪt] *vt* **-nated; -nating** : laminer

lamp [ˈlæmp] *n* : lampe *f* — **lamppost** [ˈlæmp,post] *n* : réverbère *m* — **lampshade** [ˈlæmp,ʃeɪd] *n* : abat-jour *m*

lance [ˈlænts] *n* : lance *f* — ~ *vt* **lanced; lancing** : percer (en médecine)

land [ˈlænd] *n* **1** : terre *f* **2** COUNTRY : pays *m* **3** *or* **plot of** ~ : terrain *m* — ~ *vt* **1** : faire un atterrissage, débarquer (des passagers) **2** CATCH : attraper (un poisson) **3** SECURE : décrocher (un emploi, etc.) — *vi* **1** : atterrir (se dit d'un avion) **2** FALL : tomber — **landing** [ˈlændɪŋ] *n* **1** : atterrissage *m* (d'un avion) **2** : débarquement *m* (d'un navire) **3** : palier *m* (d'un escalier) — **landlady** [ˈlænd,leɪdi] *n, pl* **-dies** : propriétaire *f* — **landlord** [ˈlænd,lɔrd] *n* : propriétaire *m* — **landmark** [ˈlænd,mark] *n* **1** : point *m* de repère **2** MONUMENT : monument *m* historique — **landowner** [ˈlænd,oːnər] *n* : propriétaire *m* foncier, propriétaire *f* foncière — **landscape** [ˈlænd,skeɪp] *n* : paysage *m* — ~ *vt* **-scaped; -scaping** : aménager — **landslide** [ˈlænd,slaɪd] *n* **1** : glissement *m* de terrain **2** *or* ~ **victory** : victoire *f* écrasante

lane [ˈleɪn] *n* **1** : voie *f* (d'une autoroute) **2** PATH, ROAD : chemin *m*

language [ˈlæŋgwɪdʒ] *n* **1** : langue *f* **2** SPEECH : langage *m*

languid [ˈlæŋgwɪd] *adj* : languissant — **languish** [ˈlæŋgwɪʃ] *vi* : languir

lanky [ˈlæŋki] *adj* **lankier; -est** : grand et maigre, dégingandé

lantern [ˈlæntərn] *n* : lanterne *f*

lap [ˈlæp] *n* **1** : genoux *mpl* **2** : tour *m* de piste (aux sports) — ~ *v* **lapped; lapping** *vt or* ~ **up** : boire à petites gorgées — *vi* ~ **against** : clapoter

lapel [ləˈpɛl] *n* : revers *m*

lapse [ˈlæps] *n* **1** : trou *m* (de mémoire, etc.) **2** INTERVAL : laps *m*, intervalle *m* — ~ *vi* **lapsed; lapsing 1** EXPIRE : expirer **2** ELAPSE : passer **3** ~ **into** : tomber dans

laptop [ˈlæp,tɑp] *adj* : portable

larceny [ˈlɑrsəni] *n, pl* **-nies** : vol *m*

lard [ˈlɑrd] *n* : saindoux *m*

large [ˈlɑrdʒ] *adj* **larger; largest 1** : grand **2 at** ~ : en liberté **3 by and** ~ : en général — **largely** [ˈlɑrdʒli] *adv* : en grande partie

lark [ˈlɑrk] *n* **1** : alouette *f* (oiseau) **2 for a** ~ : comme divertissement

larva [ˈlɑrvə] *n, pl* **-vae** [-ˌviː, -ˌvaɪ] : larve *f*

larynx [ˈlærɪŋks] *n, pl* **-rynges** [ləˈrɪn,dʒiːz]

or **-ynxes** [ˈlærɪŋksəz] : larynx *m* — **laryn-gitis** [ˌlærənˈdʒaɪtəs] *n* : laryngite *f*

lasagna [ləˈzɑnjə] *n* : lasagnes *fpl*

laser [ˈleɪzər] *n* : laser *m*

lash [ˈlæʃ] *vt* **1** WHIP : fouetter **2** BIND : attacher — *vi* ~ **out at** : invectiver contre — ~ *n* **1** BLOW : coup *m* de fouet **2** EYELASH : cil *m*

lass [ˈlæs] *or* **lassie** [ˈlæsi] *n* : fille *f*

lasso [ˈlæˌsoː, læˈsuː] *n, pl* **-sos** *or* **-soes** : lasso *m*

last [ˈlæst] *vi* : durer — ~ *n* : dernier *m*, -nière *f* **2 at** ~ : enfin, finalement — *adv* **1** : pour la dernière fois, en dernière place **2 arrive** ~ : arriver dernier — ~ *adj* **1** : dernier **2** ~ **year** : l'an passé — **lastly** [ˈlæstli] *adv* : enfin, finalement

latch [ˈlætʃ] *n* : loquet *m*, serrure *f*

late [ˈleɪt] *adj* **later; latest 1** : en retard **2** : avancé (se dit de l'heure) **3** DECEASED : défunt **4** RECENT : récent — ~ *adv* **later; latest** : en retard — **lately** [ˈleɪtli] *adv* : récemment, dernièrement — **lateness** [ˈleɪtnəs] *n* **1** : retard *m* **2** : heure *f* avancée

latent [ˈleɪtənt] *adj* : latent

lateral [ˈlætərəl] *adj* : latéral

latest [ˈleɪtəst] *n* **at the** ~ : au plus tard

lathe [ˈleɪð] *n* : tour *m*

lather [ˈlæðər] *n* : mousse *f* — ~ *vt* : savonner — *vi* : faire mousser

Latin [ˈlætən] *adj* : latin — ~ *n* : latin *m* (langue)

latitude [ˈlætəˌtuːd, -ˌtjuːd] *n* : latitude *f*

latter [ˈlætər] *adj* **1** : dernier **2** SECOND : second — ~ *pron* **the** ~ : ce dernier, cette dernière, ces derniers

lattice [ˈlætəs] *n* : treillis *m*, treillage *m*

laugh [ˈlæf] *vi* : rire — ~ *n* : rire *m* — **laughable** [ˈlæfəbəl] *adj* : risible, ridicule — **laughter** [ˈlæftər] *n* : rire *m*, rires *mpl*

launch [ˈlɔntʃ] *vt* : lancer — ~ *n* : lancement *m*

launder [ˈlɔndər] *vt* **1** : laver et repasser (du linge) **2** : blanchir (de l'argent) — **laundry** [ˈlɔndri] *n, pl* **-dries 1** : linge *m* sale **2** : blanchisserie *f* (service) **3 do the** ~ : faire la lessive

lava [ˈlɑvə, ˈlæ-] *n* : lave *f*

lavatory [ˈlævəˌtori] *n, pl* **-ries** BATHROOM : toilettes *fpl*

lavender [ˈlævəndər] *n* : lavande *f*

lavish [ˈlævɪʃ] *adj* **1** EXTRAVAGANT : prodigue **2** ABUNDANT : abondant **3** LUXURIOUS : luxueux — ~ *vt* : prodiguer

law [ˈlɔ] *n* **1** : loi *f* **2** : droit *m* (profession, etc.) **3 practice** ~ : exercer le droit — **lawful** [ˈlɔfəl] *adj* : légal, légitime

lawn [ˈlɔn] *n* : pelouse *f* — **lawn mower** *n* : tondeuse *f*

lawsuit [ˈlɔˌsuːt] *n* : procès *m*

lawyer [ˈlɔɪər, ˈlɔjər] *n* : avocat *m*, -cate *f*

lax [ˈlæks] *adj* : peu strict, relâché

laxative [ˈlæksətɪv] *n* : laxatif *m*

lay[1] [ˈleɪ] *vt* **laid** [ˈleɪd]; **laying 1** PLACE, PUT : mettre, placer **2** ~ **eggs** : pondre des œufs **3** ~ **off** : licencier (un employé) **4** ~ **out** PRESENT : présenter, exposer **5** ~ **out** DESIGN : concevoir (un plan)

lay[2] → **lie**[1]

lay[3] *adj* **1** SECULAR : laïc **2** NONPROFESSIONAL : profane

layer [ˈleɪər] *n* : couche *f*

layman [ˈleɪmən] *n, pl* **-men** [-mən, -ˌmɛn] : profane *mf*, laïque *mf* (en religion)

layoff [ˈleɪˌɔf] *n* : licenciement *m*, renvoi *m*

layout [ˈleɪˌaʊt] *n* ARRANGEMENT : disposition *f*

lazy [ˈleɪzi] *adj* **-zier; -est** : paresseux — **laziness** [ˈleɪzinəs] *n* : paresse *f*

lead[1] [ˈliːd] *v* **led** [ˈlɛd]; **leading** *vt* **1** GUIDE : conduire **2** DIRECT : diriger **3** HEAD : être à la tête de, aller au devant de — *vi* : mener, conduire (à) — ~ *n* **1** : devant *m* **2 follow s.o.'s** ~ : suivre l'exemple de qqn

lead[2] [ˈlɛd] *n* **1** : plomb *m* (métal) **2** : mine *f* (d'un crayon) — **leaden** [ˈlɛdən] *adj* **1** : de plomb **2** HEAVY : lourd

leader [ˈliːdər] *n* : chef *m*; dirigeant *m*, -geante *f* — **leadership** [ˈliːdərˌʃɪp] *n* : direction *f*, dirigeants *mpl*

leaf [ˈliːf] *n, pl* **leaves** [ˈliːvz] **1** : feuille *f* **2 turn over a new** ~ : tourner la page — ~ *vi* ~ **through** : feuilleter (se dit d'un livre, etc.) — **leaflet** [ˈliːflət] *n* : dépliant *m*, prospectus *m*

league [ˈliːg] *n* **1** : lieue *f* **2 be in** ~ **with** : être de mèche avec

leak [ˈliːk] *vt* **1** : faire couler (un liquide ou un gaz) **2** : divulguer (un secret) — *vi* **1** : fuir, s'échapper (se dit d'un liquide ou d'un gaz) **2** : être divulgué (se dit de l'information) — ~ *n* : fuite *f* — **leaky** [ˈliːki] *adj* **leakier; -est** : qui prend l'eau

lean[1] [ˈliːn] *v* **leaned** *or Brit* **leant** [ˈlɛnt]; **leaning** [ˈliːnɪŋ] *vi* **1** BEND : se pencher **2** ~ **against** : s'appuyer contre — *vt* : appuyer

lean[2] *adj* : mince (se dit d'une personne), maigre (se dit de la viande)

leaning [ˈliːnɪŋ] *n* : tendance *f*

leanness [ˈliːnnəs] *n* : minceur *f* (d'une personne), maigreur *f* (de la viande)

leap [ˈliːp] *vi* **leaped** *or* **leapt** [ˈliːpt, ˈlɛpt]; **leaping** : sauter, bondir — ~ *n* : saut *m*, bond *m* — **leap year** *n* : année *f* bissextile

learn [ˈlərn] *v* **learned** [ˈlərnd, ˈlərnt] *or Brit* **learnt** [ˈlərnt]; **learning** : apprendre — **learned** [ˈlərnəd] *adj* : savant, érudit — **learner** [ˈlərnər] *n* : débutant *m*, -tante *f*;

étudiant *m*, -diante *f* — **learning** ['lərnɪŋ] *n* : savoir *m*, érudition *f*

lease ['li:s] *n* : bail *m* — ~ *vt* **leased; leasing** : louer à bail

leash ['li:ʃ] *n* : laisse *f*

least ['li:st] *adj* **1** : moins **2** SLIGHTEST : moindre — ~ *n* **1 at** ~ : au moins **2 the** ~ : le moins — ~ *adv* : moins

leather ['lɛðər] *n* : cuir *m*

leave ['li:v] *v* **left** ['lɛft]; **leaving** *vt* **1** : quitter **2** : sortir de (un endroit) **3** ~ **out** : omettre — *vi* DEPART : partir — ~ *n or* ~ **of absence** : congé *m*

leaves → **leaf**

lecture ['lɛktʃər] *n* **1** TALK : conférence *f* **2** REPRIMAND : sermon *m*, réprimande *f* — ~ *v* **-tured; -turing** *vt* : sermonner — *vi* : donner un cours, donner une conférence

led → **lead**¹

ledge ['lɛdʒ] *n* : rebord *m* (d'une fenêtre, etc.), saillie *f* (d'une montagne)

leech ['li:tʃ] *n* : sangsue *f*

leek ['li:k] *n* : poireau *m*

leer ['lɪr] *vi* : jeter un regard lascif — ~ *n* : regard *m* lascif

leery ['lɪri] *adj* : méfiant

leeway ['li:,weɪ] *n* : liberté *f* d'action, marge *f* de manœuvre

left¹ → **leave**

left² ['lɛft] *adj* : gauche — ~ *adv* : à gauche — ~ *n* : gauche *f* — **left–handed** ['lɛft-'hændəd] *adj* : gaucher

leftovers ['lɛft,o:vərz] *npl* : restes *mpl*

leg ['lɛg] *n* **1** : patte *f* (d'un animal), jambe *f* (d'une personne ou d'un pantalon), pied *m* (d'une table, etc.) **2** : étape *f* (d'un voyage)

legacy ['lɛgəsi] *n, pl* **-cies** : legs *m*

legal ['li:gəl] *adj* **1** LAWFUL : légitime, légal **2** JUDICIAL : juridique — **legality** [li'gæləti] *n, pl* **-ties** : légalité *f* — **legalize** ['li:gə,laɪz] *vt* **-ized; -izing** : légaliser

legend ['lɛdʒənd] *n* : légende *f* — **legendary** ['lɛdʒən,dɛri] *adj* : légendaire

legible ['lɛdʒəbəl] *adj* : lisible

legion ['li:dʒən] *n* : légion *f*

legislate ['lɛdʒəs,leɪt] *vi* **-lated; -lating** : légiférer — **legislation** [,lɛdʒəs'leɪʃən] *n* : législation *f* — **legislative** ['lɛdʒəs,leɪtɪv] *adj* : législatif — **legislature** ['lɛdʒəs,leɪtʃər] *n* : corps *m* législatif

legitimate [lɪ'dʒɪtəmət] *adj* : légitime — **legitimacy** [lɪ'dʒɪtəməsi] *n* : légitimité *f*

leisure ['li:ʒər, 'lɛ-] *n* **1** : loisir *m*, temps *m* libre **2 at your** ~ : à votre convenance — **leisurely** ['li:ʒərli, 'lɛ-] *adv* : lentement, sans se presser — ~ *adj* : lent

lemon ['lɛmən] *n* : citron *m* — **lemonade** [,lɛmə'neɪd] *n* : limonade *f*

lend ['lɛnd] *vt* **lent** ['lɛnt]; **lending** : prêter

length ['lɛŋkθ] *n* **1** : longueur *f* **2** DURATION : durée *f* **3 at** ~ FINALLY : finalement **4 at** ~ EXTENSIVELY : longuement **5 go to any** ~**s** : faire tout son possible — **lengthen** ['lɛŋkθən] *vt* **1** : rallonger **2** PROLONG : prolonger — *vi* : s'allonger — **lengthways** ['lɛŋkθ,weɪz] *or* **lengthwise** ['lɛŋkθ-,waɪz] *adv* : dans le sens de la longueur — **lengthy** ['lɛŋkθi] *adj* **lengthier; -est** : long

lenient ['li:niənt] *adj* : indulgent — **leniency** ['li:niəntsi] *n* : indulgence *f*

lens ['lɛnz] *n* **1** : lentille *f* (d'un instrument) **2** → **contact lens**

Lent ['lɛnt] *n* : carême *m*

lentil ['lɛntəl] *n* : lentille *f*

leopard ['lɛpərd] *n* : léopard *m*

leotard ['li:ə,tɑrd] *n* : justaucorps *m*

lesbian ['lɛzbiən] *n* : lesbienne *f*

less ['lɛs] *adv & adj* (*comparative of* **little**) : moins — ~ *pron* : moins — ~ *prep* MINUS : moins — **lessen** ['lɛsən] *v* : diminuer — **lesser** ['lɛsər] *adj* : moindre

lesson ['lɛsən] *n* **1** CLASS : classe *f*, cours *m* **2 learn one's** ~ : servir de leçon

lest ['lɛst] *conj* ~ **we forget** : de peur que nous n'oublions

let ['lɛt] *vt* **let; letting 1** ALLOW : laisser, permettre **2** RENT : louer **3** ~**'s go!** : allons-y! **4** ~ **down** DISAPPOINT : décevoir **5** ~ **in** : laisser entrer **6** ~ **off** FORGIVE : pardonner **7** ~ **up** ABATE : diminuer, arrêter

letdown ['lɛt,daʊn] *n* : déception *f*

lethal ['li:θəl] *adj* : mortel

lethargic [lɪ'θɑrdʒɪk] *adj* : léthargique

let's ['lɛts] (*contraction of* **let us**) → **let**

letter ['lɛtər] *n* : lettre *f*

lettuce ['lɛtəs] *n* : laitue *f*

letup ['lɛt,əp] *n* : pause *f*, répit *m*

leukemia [lu:'ki:miə] *n* : leucémie *f*

level ['lɛvəl] *n* **1** : niveau *m* **2 be on the** ~ : être franc — ~ *vt* **-eled** *or* **-elled; -eling** *or* **-elling 1** : niveler **2** AIM : diriger **3** RAZE : raser — ~ *adj* **1** FLAT : plat, plan **2** ~ **with** : au même niveau que — **levelheaded** ['lɛvəl'hɛdəd] *adj* : sensé, équilibré

lever ['lɛvər, 'li:-] *n* : levier *m* — **leverage** ['lɛvərɪdʒ, 'li:-] *n* **1** : force *f* de levier (en physique) **2** INFLUENCE : influence *f*

levity ['lɛvəti] *n* : légèreté *f*

levy ['lɛvi] *n, pl* **levies** : impôt *m* — ~ *vt* **levied; levying** : imposer, prélever (une taxe)

lewd ['lu:d] *adj* : lascif

lexicon ['lɛksɪ,kɑn] *n, pl* **-ica** [-kə] *or* **-icons** : lexique *m*

liable ['laɪəbəl] *adj* **1** : responsable **2** LIKELY : probable **3** SUSCEPTIBLE : sujet — **liability** [,laɪə'bɪləti] *n, pl* **-ties 1** RESPONSIBILITY : responsabilité *f* **2** DRAWBACK : désavantage *m* **3 liabilities** *npl* DEBTS : dettes *fpl*, passif *m*

liaison ['liːəˌzɑn, liˈeɪ-] n : liaison f
liar ['laɪər] n : menteur m, -teuse f
libel ['laɪbəl] n : diffamation f — ~ vt
-beled or -belled; -beling or -belling : diffamer
liberal ['lɪbrəl, 'lɪbərəl] adj : libéral — ~ n
: libéral m, -rale f
liberate ['lɪbəˌreɪt] vt -ated; -ating : libérer
— liberation [ˌlɪbəˈreɪʃən] n : libération f
liberty ['lɪbərti] n, pl -ties : liberté f
library ['laɪˌbreri] n, pl -braries : bibliothèque f — librarian [laɪˈbreriən] n : bibliothécaire mf
lice → louse
license or licence n 1 PERMIT : permis m 2
FREEDOM : licence f 3 AUTHORIZATION
: permission f — ~ ['laɪsənts] vt -censed;
-censing : autoriser
lick ['lɪk] vt 1 : lécher 2 DEFEAT : battre (à
plate couture) — ~ n : coup m de langue
licorice or Brit liquorice ['lɪkərɪʃ, -rəs] n
: réglisse f
lid ['lɪd] n 1 : couvercle m 2 EYELID
: paupière f
lie¹ ['laɪ] vi lay ['leɪ]; lain ['leɪn]; lying
['laɪɪŋ] 1 or ~ down : se coucher, s'allonger 2 BE : être, se trouver
lie² vi lied; lying ['laɪɪŋ] : mentir — ~ n
: mensonge m
lieutenant [luːˈtɛnənt] n : lieutenant m
life ['laɪf] n, pl lives ['laɪvz] : vie f — lifeboat
['laɪfˌboːt] n : canot m de sauvetage — lifeguard ['laɪfˌɡɑrd] n : sauveteur m — lifeless ['laɪfləs] adj : sans vie — lifelike ['laɪfˌlaɪk] adj : naturel, réaliste — lifelong ['laɪfˈlɔŋ] adj : de toute une vie — life preserver n : gilet m de sauvetage — lifestyle ['laɪfˌstaɪl] n : mode m de vie — lifetime ['laɪfˌtaɪm] n : vie f
lift ['lɪft] vt 1 RAISE : lever 2 STEAL : voler
— vi 1 CLEAR UP : se dissiper 2 or ~ off
: décoller (se dit d'un avion, etc.) — ~ n 1
LIFTING : soulèvement m 2 give s.o. a ~
: emmener qqn en voiture — liftoff ['lɪftˌɔf]
n : lancement m
light¹ ['laɪt] n 1 : lumière f 2 LAMP : lampe f
3 HEADLIGHT : phare m 4 do you have a
~? : avez-vous du feu? — ~ adj 1
BRIGHT : bien illuminé 2 : clair (se dit des
couleurs), blond (se dit des cheveux) — ~
v lit ['lɪt] or lighted; lighting vt 1 : allumer
(un feu) 2 ILLUMINATE : éclairer — vi or ~
up : s'illuminer — lightbulb ['laɪtˌbʌlb] n
: ampoule f — lighten ['laɪtən] vt BRIGHTEN
: éclairer — lighter ['laɪtər] n : briquet m —
lighthouse ['laɪtˌhaʊs] n : phare m — lighting ['laɪtɪŋ] n : éclairage m — lightning ['laɪtnɪŋ] n : éclairs mpl, foudre f —
light–year ['laɪtˌjɪr] n : année-lumière f
light² adj : léger — lighten ['laɪtən] vt : al-

léger — lightly ['laɪtli] adv 1 : légèrement
2 let off ~ : traiter avec indulgence —
lightness ['laɪtnəs] n : légèreté f — lightweight ['laɪtˌweɪt] adj : léger
like¹ ['laɪk] v liked; liking vt 1 : aimer (qqn)
2 WANT : vouloir — vi if you ~ : si vous
voulez — likes npl : préférences fpl, goûts
mpl — likable or likeable ['laɪkəbəl] adj
: sympathique
like² adj SIMILAR : pareil — ~ prep : comme
— ~ conj 1 AS : comme 2 AS IF : comme
si — likelihood ['laɪkliˌhʊd] n : probabilité f
— likely ['laɪkli] adj -lier; -est : probable —
liken ['laɪkən] vt : comparer — likeness
['laɪknəs] n : ressemblance f — likewise
['laɪkˌwaɪz] adv 1 : de même 2 ALSO : aussi
liking ['laɪkɪŋ] n : goût m (pour une chose),
affection f (pour une personne)
lilac ['laɪlək, -læk, -lɑk] n : lilas m
lily ['lɪli] n, pl lilies : lis m — lily of the valley n : muguet m
lima bean ['laɪmə] n : haricot m de Lima
limb ['lɪm] n 1 : membre m (en anatomie) 2
: branche f (d'un arbre)
limber ['lɪmbər] vi ~ up : s'échauffer, faire
des exercices d'assouplissement
limbo ['lɪmˌboː] n, pl -bos : limbes mpl
lime ['laɪm] n : lime f, citron m vert
limelight ['laɪmˌlaɪt] n be in the ~ : être en
vedette
limerick ['lɪmərɪk] n : poème m humoristique en cinq vers
limestone ['laɪmˌstoːn] n : pierre f à chaux,
calcaire m
limit ['lɪmət] n : limite f — ~ vt : limiter, restreindre — limitation [ˌlɪməˈteɪʃən] n : limitation f, restriction f — limited ['lɪmətəd]
adj : limité
limousine ['lɪməˌziːn, ˌlɪməˈ-] n : limousine f
limp¹ ['lɪmp] vi : boiter — ~ n have a ~
: boiter
limp² adj : mou, flasque
line ['laɪn] n 1 : ligne f 2 ROPE : corde f 3
ROW : rangée f 4 QUEUE : file f 5 WRINKLE
: ride f 6 drop s.o. a ~ : écrire un mot à
qqn — v lined; lining vt 1 : doubler (un
vêtement, etc.), tapisser (un mur, etc.) 2
MARK : rayer, ligner 3 BORDER : border —
vi ~ up : se mettre en ligne, faire la queue
lineage ['lɪniɪdʒ] n : lignée f
linear ['lɪniər] adj : linéaire
linen ['lɪnən] n : lin m
liner ['laɪnər] n 1 LINING : doublure f 2 SHIP
: paquebot m
lineup ['laɪnˌəp] n 1 or police ~ : rangée f
de suspects 2 : équipe f (aux sports)
linger ['lɪŋɡər] vi 1 : s'attarder, flâner 2
PERSIST : persister
lingerie [ˌlɑndʒəˈreɪ] n : vêtement m intime
féminin, lingerie f

lingo [ˈlɪŋgo] *n, pl* **-goes** JARGON : jargon *m*
linguistics [lɪŋˈgwɪstɪks] *n* : linguistique *f* —
  linguist [ˈlɪŋgwɪst] *n* : linguiste *mf* — **linguistic** [lɪŋˈgwɪstɪk] *adj* : linguistique
lining [ˈlaɪnɪŋ] *n* : doublure *f*
link [ˈlɪŋk] *n* **1** : maillon *m* (d'une chaîne) **2**
  BOND : lien *m* **3** CONNECTION : liaison *f* —
  ~ *vt* : relier, lier — *vi or* ~ **up** : se rejoindre, se relier
linoleum [ləˈnoːliəm] *n* : linoléum *m*, prélart
  m Can
lint [ˈlɪnt] *n* : peluches *fpl*
lion [ˈlaɪən] *n* : lion *m* — **lioness** [ˈlaɪənɪs] *n*
  : lionne *f*
lip [ˈlɪp] *n* **1** : lèvre *f* **2** EDGE : rebord *m* —
  lipstick [ˈlɪpˌstɪk] *n* : rouge *m* à lèvres
liqueur [lɪˈkər, -ˈkʊr, -ˈkjʊr] *n* : liqueur *f*
liquid [ˈlɪkwəd] *adj* : liquide — ~ *n* : liquide
  m — **liquidate** [ˈlɪkwəˌdeɪt] *vt* **-dated; -dat-
  ing** : liquider — **liquidation** [ˌlɪkwəˈdeɪʃən]
  n : liquidation *f*
liquor [ˈlɪkər] *n* : boissons *fpl* alcoolisées
lisp [ˈlɪsp] *vi* : zézayer — ~ *n* : zézaiement
  m
list[1] [ˈlɪst] *n* : liste *f* — ~ *vt* **1** ENUMERATE
  : faire une liste de, énumérer **2** INCLUDE
  : mettre (sur une liste)
list[2] *vi* : gîter (se dit d'un bateau)
listen [ˈlɪsən] *vi* **1** : écouter **2** ~ **to reason**
  : entendre raison — **listener** [ˈlɪsənər] *n*
  : auditeur *m*, -trice *f*
listless [ˈlɪstləs] *adj* : apathique
lit [ˈlɪt] *pp →* **light**[1]
litany [ˈlɪtəni] *n, pl* **-nies** : litanie *f*
liter [ˈliːtər] *n* : litre *m*
literacy [ˈlɪtərəsi] *n* : alphabétisation *f*
literal [ˈlɪtərəl] *adj* : littéral — **literally**
  [ˈlɪtərəli] *adv* : littéralement, au pied de la
  lettre
literate [ˈlɪtərət] *adj* : qui sait lire et écrire
literature [ˈlɪtərəˌtʃur, -tʃər] *n* : littérature *f*
  — **literary** [ˈlɪtəˌreri] *adj* : littéraire
lithe [ˈlaɪð, ˈlaɪθ] *adj* : agile et gracieux
litigation [ˌlɪtəˈgeɪʃən] *n* : litige *m*
litre → **liter**
litter [ˈlɪtər] *n* **1** RUBBISH : ordures *fpl* **2**
  : portée *f* (se dit d'un animal) **3** *or* **kitty** ~
  : litière *f* (de chat) — ~ *vt* : mettre du désordre dans — *vi* : jeter des déchets
little [ˈlɪtəl] *adj* **littler** *or* **less** [ˈles] *or* **lesser**
  [ˈlesər]; **littlest** *or* **least** [ˈliːst] **1** SMALL
  : petit **2** **a** ~ SOME : un peu de **3** **he
  speaks** ~ **English** : il ne parle presque pas
  l'anglais — ~ *adv* **less** [ˈles]; **least** [ˈliːst]
  : peu — ~ *pron* **1** : peu *m* **2** ~ **by** ~
  : peu à peu
liturgy [ˈlɪtərdʒi] *n, pl* **-gies** : liturgie *f* —
  liturgical [ləˈtərdʒɪkəl] *adj* : liturgique
live [ˈlɪv] *v* **lived; living** *vi* **1** : vivre **2** RE-
  SIDE : habiter **3** ~ **on** : vivre de — *vt*

: vivre, mener — ~ [ˈlaɪv] *adj* **1** : vivant **2**
: sous tension (se dit d'un câble électrique)
3 : en direct (se dit d'un programme de
télévision, etc.) — **livelihood** [ˈlaɪvliˌhʊd] *n*
: subsistance *f*, gagne-pain *m* — **lively**
[ˈlaɪvli] *adj* **-lier; -est** : animé, vivant —
liven [ˈlaɪvən] *vt or* ~ **up** : animer, égayer
— *vi* : s'animer
liver [ˈlɪvər] *n* : foie *m*
livestock [ˈlaɪvˌstak] *n* : bétail *m*
livid [ˈlɪvəd] *adj* **1** : livide **2** ENRAGED : furieux
living [ˈlɪvɪŋ] *adj* : vivant — ~ *n* **make a** ~
: gagner sa vie — **living room** *n* : salle *f* de
séjour, salon *m*
lizard [ˈlɪzərd] *n* : lézard *m*
llama [ˈlamə, ˈjɑ-] *n* : lama *m*
load [ˈloːd] *n* **1** CARGO : chargement *m* **2**
BURDEN : charge *f*, poids *m* **3** ~**s of**
: beaucoup de — ~ *vt* : charger
loaf[1] [ˈloːf] *n, pl* **loaves** [ˈloːvz] : pain *m*
loaf[2] *vi* : fainéanter, paresser — **loafer**
[ˈloːfər] *n* **1** : fainéant *m*, fainéante *f* **2** : mocassin *m* (soulier)
loan [ˈloːn] *n* : emprunt *m*, prêt *m* — ~ *vt*
: prêter
loathe [ˈloːð] *vt* **loathed; loathing** : détester
— **loathsome** [ˈloːθsəm, ˈloːð-] *adj* : odieux
lobby [ˈlabi] *n, pl* **-bies** **1** : vestibule *m* **2** *or*
political ~ : groupe *m* de pression, lobby
m — ~ *vt* **-bied; -bying** : faire pression sur
lobe [ˈloːb] *n* : lobe *m*
lobster [ˈlabstər] *n* : homard *m*
local [ˈloːkəl] *adj* : local — ~ *n* **the** ~**s** *npl*
: les gens du coin — **locale** [loˈkæl] *n* : lieu
m — **locality** [loˈkæləti] *n, pl* **-ties** : localité
f
locate [ˈloːˌkeɪt] *vt* **-cated; -cating** **1** SITU-
ATE : situer, établir **2** FIND : trouver — **location** [loˈkeɪʃən] *n* : emplacement *m*, endroit *m*
lock[1] [ˈlak] *n* : mèche *f* (de cheveux)
lock[2] *n* **1** : serrure *f* (d'une porte, etc.) **2**
: écluse *f* (d'un canal) — ~ *vt* **1** : fermer (à
clé) **2** *or* ~ **up** CONFINE : enfermer — *vi* **1**
: se fermer à clé **2** : se bloquer (se dit d'une
roue, etc.) — **locker** [ˈlakər] *n* : vestiaire *m*
— **locket** [ˈlakət] *n* : médaillon *m* — **locksmith** [ˈlakˌsmɪθ] *n* : serrurier *m*
locomotive [ˌloːkəˈmoːtɪv] *n* : locomotive *f*
locust [ˈloːkəst] *n* : criquet *m*, sauterelle *f*
lodge [ˈladʒ] *v* **lodged; lodging** *vt* **1** HOUSE
: loger, héberger **2** FILE : déposer — *vi* : se
loger — ~ *n* : pavillon *m* — **lodger**
[ˈladʒər] *n* : locataire *mf*, pensionnaire *mf* —
lodging [ˈladʒɪŋ] *n* **1** : hébergement *m* **2**
~**s** *npl* : logement *m*
loft [ˈlɔft] *n* : grenier *m* (d'une maison, à foin,
etc.) — **lofty** [ˈlɔfti] *adj* **loftier; -est** **1**
: noble, élevé **2** HAUGHTY : hautain

log ['lɔg, 'lɑg] n 1 : bûche f, rondin m 2 RECORD : registre m de bord — ~ vi **logged; logging** 1 : tronçonner (des arbres) 2 RECORD : enregistrer, noter 3 ~ **on** : entrer (dans le système) 4 ~ **off** : sortir (du système) — **logger** ['lɔgər, 'lɑ-] n : bûcheron m, -ronne f

logic ['lɑʤɪk] n : logique f — **logical** ['lɑʤɪkəl] adj : logique — **logistics** [lə-'ʤɪstɪks, lo-] ns & pl : logistique f

logo ['lo:ˌgo:] n, pl **logos** [-ˌgo:z] : logo m

loin ['lɔɪn] n : filet m

loiter ['lɔɪtər] vi : traîner, flâner

lollipop or **lollypop** ['lɑliˌpɑp] n : sucette f France, suçon m Can

lone ['lo:n] adj : solitaire — **loneliness** ['lo:nlinəs] n : solitude f — **lonely** ['lo:nli] adj **-lier; -est** : solitaire, seul — **loner** ['lo:nər] n : solitaire mf — **lonesome** ['lo:nsəm] adj : seul, solitaire

long[1] ['lɔŋ] adj **longer** ['lɔŋɡər]; **longest** ['lɔŋɡəst] : long — ~ adv 1 : longtemps 2 **all day** ~ : toute la journée 3 **as** ~ **as** : tant que 4 **no** ~**er** : ne…plus 5 **so** ~! : à bientôt! — ~ n 1 **before** ~ : dans peu de temps 2 **the** ~ **and short of it** : l'essentiel m

long[2] vi ~ **for** : avoir envie de, désirer

longevity [lɑn'ʤevəti] n : longévité f

longing ['lɔŋɪŋ] n : envie f

longitude ['lɑnʤəˌtu:d, -ˌtju:d] n : longitude f

look ['lʊk] vi 1 : regarder 2 SEEM : sembler 3 ~ **after** : prendre soin (de) 4 ~ **for** EXPECT : attendre 5 ~ **for** SEEK : chercher 6 ~ **into** : enquêter 7 ~ **out** : faire attention 8 ~ **over** EXAMINE : examiner 9 ~ **up to** : respecter — vt : regarder — ~ n 1 : coup m d'œil, regard m 2 APPEARANCE : aspect m, air m — **lookout** ['lʊkˌaʊt] n 1 : poste m d'observation 2 WATCHMAN : guetteur m 3 **be on the** ~ : faire le guet

loom[1] ['lu:m] n : métier m à tisser

loom[2] vi 1 APPEAR : surgir 2 APPROACH : être imminent

loop ['lu:p] n : boucle f — ~ vt : faire une boucle avec — **loophole** ['lu:pˌho:l] n : échappatoire m

loose ['lu:s] adj **looser; -est** 1 MOVABLE : desserré 2 SLACK : lâche 3 ROOMY : ample 4 APPROXIMATE : approximatif 5 FREE : libre 6 IMMORAL : dissolu — **loosely** ['lu:sli] adv 1 : sans serrer 2 ROUGHLY : approximativement — **loosen** ['lu:sən] vt : desserrer

loot ['lu:t] n : butin m — ~ vt : piller, saccager — **looter** ['lu:tər] n : pillard m, -larde f — **looting** ['lu:tɪŋ] n : pillage m

lop ['lɑp] vt **lopped; lopping** : couper, élaguer

lopsided ['lɑpˌsaɪdəd] adj : de travers, croche Can

lord ['lɔrd] n 1 : seigneur m, noble m 2 **the Lord** : le Seigneur

lore ['lor] n : savoir m populaire, tradition f

lose ['lu:z] v **lost** ['lɔst]; **losing** ['lu:zɪŋ] vt 1 : perdre 2 ~ **one's way** : se perdre 3 ~ **time** : retarder (se dit d'une horloge) — vi : perdre — **loser** ['lu:zər] n : perdant m, -dante f — **loss** ['lɔs] n 1 : perte f 2 DEFEAT : défaite f 3 **be at a** ~ **for words** : ne pas savoir quoi dire — **lost** ['lɔst] adj 1 : perdu 2 **get** ~ : se perdre

lot ['lɑt] n 1 FATE : sort m 2 PLOT : parcelle f 3 **a** ~ **of** or ~**s of** : beaucoup, une montagne de

lotion ['lo:ʃən] n : lotion f

lottery ['lɑtəri] n, pl **-teries** : loterie f

loud ['laʊd] adj 1 : grand, fort 2 NOISY : bruyant 3 FLASHY : criard — ~ adv 1 : fort 2 **out** ~ : à voix haute — **loudly** ['laʊdli] adv : à voix haute — **loudspeaker** ['laʊdˌspi:kər] n : haut-parleur m

lounge ['laʊnʤ] vi **lounged; lounging** 1 : se vautrer 2 ~ **about** : flâner — ~ n : salon m

louse ['laʊs] n, pl **lice** ['laɪs] : pou m — **lousy** ['laʊzi] adj **lousier; -est** 1 : pouilleux 2 BAD : piètre, très mauvais

love ['lʌv] n 1 : amour m 2 **fall in** ~ : tomber amoureux — ~ v **loved; loving** : aimer — **lovable** ['lʌvəbəl] adj : adorable — **lovely** ['lʌvli] adj **-lier; -est** : beau, joli — **lover** ['lʌvər] n : amant m, -mante f — **loving** ['lʌvɪŋ] adj : affectueux

low ['lo:] adj **lower** ['lo:ər]; **lowest** 1 : bas 2 SCARCE : limité 3 DEPRESSED : déprimé — ~ adv 1 : bas 2 **turn the lights** ~ : baisser les lumières — ~ n 1 : point m bas 2 or ~ **gear** : première f — **lower** ['lo:ər] adj : inférieur, plus bas — vt : baisser — **lowly** ['lo:li] adj **-lier; -est** : humble

loyal ['lɔɪəl] adj : loyal, fidèle — **loyalty** ['lɔɪəlti] n, pl **-ties** : loyauté f

lozenge ['lɑzənʤ] n : pastille f

lubricate ['lu:brəˌkeɪt] vt **-cated; -cating** : lubrifier — **lubricant** ['lu:brɪkənt] n : lubrifiant m — **lubrication** [ˌlu:brə'keɪʃən] n : lubrification f

lucid ['lu:səd] adj : lucide — **lucidity** [lu:'sɪdəti] n : lucidité f

luck ['lʌk] n 1 : chance f 2 **good** ~! : bonne chance! — **luckily** ['lʌkəli] adv : heureusement — **lucky** ['lʌki] adj **luckier; -est** 1 : chanceux 2 ~ **charm** : porte-bonheur m

lucrative ['lu:krətɪv] adj : lucratif

ludicrous ['lu:dəkrəs] adj : ridicule, absurde

lug ['lʌg] *vt* **lugged; lugging** : traîner
luggage ['lʌgɪʤ] *n* : bagages *mpl*
lukewarm ['lu:k'wɔrm] *adj* : tiède
lull ['lʌl] *vt* **1** CALM : calmer **2** ~ **to sleep** : endormir — ~ *n* : période *f* de calme, pause *f*
lullaby ['lʌlə,baɪ] *n, pl* **-bies** : berceuse *f*
lumber ['lʌmbər] *n* : bois *m* — **lumberjack** ['lʌmbər,ʤæk] *n* : bûcheron *m*, -ronne *f*
luminous ['lu:mənəs] *adj* : lumineux
lump ['lʌmp] *n* **1** CHUNK, PIECE : morceau *m*, motte *f* **2** SWELLING : bosse *f* **3** : grumeau *m* (dans une sauce) — ~ *vt or* ~ **together** : réunir, regrouper — **lumpy** ['lʌmpi] *adj* **lumpier; -est** : grumeleux (se dit d'une sauce), bosselé (se dit d'un matelas)
lunacy ['lu:nəsi] *n, pl* **-cies** : folie *f*
lunar ['lu:nər] *adj* : lunaire
lunatic ['lu:nə,tɪk] *n* : fou *m*
lunch ['lʌntʃ] *n* : déjeuner *m*, dîner *m Can*, lunch *m Can* — ~ *vi* : déjeuner, dîner *Can* — **luncheon** ['lʌntʃən] *n* : déjeuner *m*
lung ['lʌŋ] *n* : poumon *m*
lunge ['lʌnʤ] *vi* **lunged; lunging 1** : se précipiter **2** ~ **at** : foncer sur

lurch[1] ['lərtʃ] *vi* **1** STAGGER : tituber **2** : faire une embardée (se dit d'une voiture)
lurch[2] *n* **leave in a** ~ : laisser en plan
lure ['lʊr] *n* **1** BAIT : leurre *m* **2** ATTRACTION : attrait *m* — ~ *vt* **lured; luring** : attirer
lurid ['lʊrəd] *adj* **1** GRUESOME : épouvantable **2** SENSATIONAL : à sensation **3** GAUDY : criard
lurk ['lərk] *vi* : être tapi
luscious ['lʌʃəs] *adj* : délicieux, exquis
lush ['lʌʃ] *adj* : luxuriant, somptueux
lust ['lʌst] *n* **1** : luxure *f* **2** CRAVING : envie *f*, désir *m* — ~ *vi* ~ **after** : désirer (une personne), convoiter (des richesses, etc.)
luster *or* **lustre** ['lʌstər] *n* : lustre *m*
lusty ['lʌsti] *adj* **lustier; -est** : robuste, vigoureux
luxurious [,lʌg'ʒʊriəs, ,lʌk'ʃʊr-] *adj* : luxueux — **luxury** ['lʌkʃəri, 'lʌgʒə-] *n, pl* **-ries** : luxe *m*
lye ['laɪ] *n* : lessive *f*
lying → **lie**
lynch ['lɪntʃ] *vt* : lyncher
lynx ['lɪŋks] *n* : lynx *m*
lyric ['lɪrɪk] *or* **lyrical** ['lɪrɪkəl] *adj* : lyrique — **lyrics** *npl* : paroles *fpl* (d'une chanson)

M

m ['ɛm] *n, pl* **m's** *or* **ms** ['ɛmz] : m *m*, treizième lettre de l'alphabet
ma'am ['mæm] → **madam**
macabre [mə'kab, -'kabər, -'kabrə] *adj* : macabre
macaroni [,mækə'ro:ni] *n* : macaronis *mpl*
mace ['meɪs] *n* **1** : masse *f* (arme ou symbole) **2** : macis *m* (épice)
machete [mə'ʃɛti] *n* : machette *f*
machine [mə'ʃi:n] *n* : machine *f* — **machine gun** *n* : mitrailleuse *f* — **machinery** [mə'ʃi:nəri] *n, pl* **-eries 1** : machinerie *f* **2** WORKS : mécanisme *m*
mad ['mæd] *adj* **madder; maddest 1** INSANE : fou **2** FOOLISH : insensé **3** ANGRY : furieux
madam ['mædəm] *n, pl* **mesdames** [meɪ'dam] : madame *f*
madden ['mædən] *vt* : exaspérer
made → **make**
madly ['mædli] *adv* : comme un fou, follement — **madman** ['mæd,mæn, -mən] *n, pl* **-men** [-mən, -,mɛn] : fou *m* — **madness** ['mædnəs] *n* : folie *f*
Mafia ['mafiə] *n* : mafia *f*

magazine ['mægə,zi:n] *n* **1** PERIODICAL : revue *f* **2** : magasin *m* (d'une arme à feu)
maggot ['mægət] *n* : asticot *m*
magic ['mæʤɪk] *n* : magie *f* — ~ *or* **magical** ['mæʤɪkəl] *adj* : magique — **magician** [mə'ʤɪʃən] *n* : magicien *m*, -cienne *f*
magistrate ['mæʤə,streɪt] *n* : magistrat *m*
magnanimous [mæg'nænəməs] *adj* : magnanime
magnate ['mæg,neɪt, -nət] *n* : magnat *m*
magnet ['mægnət] *n* : aimant *m* — **magnetic** [mæg'nɛtɪk] *adj* : magnétique — **magnetism** ['mægnə,tɪzəm] *n* : magnétisme *m* — **magnetize** ['mægnə,taɪz] *vt* **-tized; -tizing** : magnétiser
magnificent [mæg'nɪfəsənt] *adj* : magnifique — **magnificence** [mæg'nɪfəsənts] *n* : splendeur *f*
magnify ['mægnə,faɪ] *vt* **-fied; -fying 1** ENLARGE : amplifier **2** EXAGGERATE : exagérer — **magnifying glass** *n* : loupe *f*
magnitude ['mægnə,tu:d, -,tju:d] *n* : ampleur *f*
magnolia [mæg'no:ljə] *n* : magnolia *m*

mahogany [mə'hɑgəni] *n, pl* **-nies** : acajou *m*

maid ['meɪd] *n* : servante *f,* bonne *f,* domestique *f* — **maiden name** *n* : nom *m* de jeune fille

mail ['meɪl] *n* **1** : poste *f* **2** LETTERS : correspondence *f* — ~ *vt* : envoyer par la poste — **mailbox** ['meɪl,bɑks] *n* : boîte *f* aux lettres — **mailman** ['meɪl,mæn, -mən] *n, pl* **-men** [-mən, -,mɛn] : facteur *m*

maim ['meɪm] *vt* : mutiler

main ['meɪn] *n* : canalisation *f* principale (d'eau ou de gaz) — ~ *adj* : principal — **mainframe** ['meɪn,freɪm] *n* : ordinateur *m* central — **mainland** ['meɪn,lænd, -lənd] *n* : continent *m* — **mainly** ['meɪnli] *adv* : principalement — **mainstay** ['meɪn,steɪ] *n* : soutien *m* prinicpal — **mainstream** ['meɪn,stri:m] *n* : courant *m* dominant — ~ *adj* : dominant, conventionnel

maintain [meɪn'teɪn] *vt* : entretenir, maintenir — **maintenance** ['meɪntənənts] *n* : entretien *m,* maintien *m*

maize ['meɪz] *n* : maïs *m*

majestic [mə'ʤɛstɪk] *adj* : majestueux — **majesty** ['mæʤəsti] *n, pl* **-ties** : majesté *f*

major ['meɪʤər] *adj* **1** : très important, principal **2** : majeur (en musique) — ~ *n* **1** : commandant *m* (des forces armées) **2** : spécialité *f* (à l'université) — ~ *vi* **-jored**; **-joring** : se spécialiser — **majority** [mə'ʤɔrəti] *n, pl* **-ties** : majorité *f*

make ['meɪk] *v* **made** ['meɪd]; **making** *vt* **1** : faire **2** MANUFACTURE : fabriquer **3** CONSTITUTE : constituer **4** PREPARE : préparer **5** RENDER : rendre **6** COMPEL : obliger **7** ~ **a decision** : prendre une décision **8** ~ **a living** : gagner sa vie — *vi* **1** ~ **do** : se débrouiller **2** ~ **for** : se diriger vers **3** ~ **good** SUCCEED : réussir — ~ *n* BRAND : marque *f* — **make–believe** [,meɪkbə'li:v] *n* : fantaisie *f* — ~ *adj* : imaginaire — **make out** *vt* **1** : faire (un chèque, etc.) **2** DISCERN : distinguer **3** UNDERSTAND : comprendre — *vi* **how did you** ~**?** : comment ça s'est passé? — **maker** ['meɪkər] *n* MANUFACTURER : fabricant *m,* -cante *f* — **makeshift** ['meɪk,ʃɪft] *adj* : improvisé — **makeup** ['meɪk,ʌp] *n* **1** COMPOSITION : composition *f* **2** COSMETICS : maquillage *m* — **make up** *vt* **1** PREPARE : préparer **2** INVENT : inventer **3** CONSTITUTE : former — *vi* RECONCILE : faire la paix

maladjusted [,mælə'ʤʌstəd] *adj* : inadapté

malaria [mə'lɛriə] *n* : paludisme *m*

male ['meɪl] *n* : mâle *m,* homme *m* — ~ *adj* **1** : mâle **2** MASCULINE : masculin

malevolent [mə'lɛvələnt] *adj* : malveillant

malfunction [mæl'fʌŋkʃən] *vi* : mal fonctionner — ~ *n* : mauvais fonctionnement *m*

malice ['mælɪs] *n* : mauvaise intention *f,* rancœur *f* — **malicious** [mə'lɪʃəs] *adj* : malveillant

malign [mə'laɪn] *adj* : pernicieux — ~ *vt* : calomnier

malignant [mə'lɪgnənt] *adj* : malveillant

mall ['mɔl] *n or* **shopping** ~ : centre *m* commercial

malleable ['mæliəbəl] *adj* : malléable

mallet ['mælət] *n* : maillet *m*

malnutrition [,mælnʊ'trɪʃən, -njʊ-] *n* : malnutrition *f*

malt ['mɔlt] *n* : malt *m*

mama *or* **mamma** ['mɑmə] *n* : maman *f*

mammal ['mæməl] *n* : mammifère *m*

mammogram ['mæmə,græm] *n* : mammographie *f*

mammoth ['mæməθ] *adj* : gigantesque

man ['mæn] *n, pl* **men** ['mɛn] : homme *m* — ~ *vt* **manned**; **manning** : équiper en personnel

manage ['mænɪʤ] *v* **-aged**; **-aging** *vt* **1** HANDLE : manier **2** DIRECT : gérer, diriger — *vi* COPE : se débrouiller — **manageable** ['mænɪʤəbəl] *adj* : maniable — **management** ['mænɪʤmənt] *n* : gestion *f,* direction *f* — **manager** ['mænɪʤər] *n* : directeur *m,* -trice *f;* gérant *m,* -rante *f;* manager *m* (aux sports) — **managerial** [,mænə'ʤɪriəl] *adj* : de gestion

mandarin ['mændərən] *n or* ~ **orange** : mandarine *f*

mandate ['mæn,deɪt] *n* : mandat *m*

mandatory ['mændə,tori] *adj* : obligatoire

mane ['meɪn] *n* : crinière *f*

maneuver *or Brit* **manoeuvre** [mə'nu:vər, -'nju:-] *n* : manœuvre *f* — ~ *v* **-vered** *or Brit* **-vred**; **-vering** *or Brit* **-vring** : manœuvrer

mangle ['mæŋgəl] *vt* **-gled**; **-gling** : mutiler

mango ['mæŋ,go:] *n, pl* **-goes** : mangue *f*

mangy ['meɪnʤi] *adj* **mangier**; **-est** : galeux

manhandle ['mæn,hændəl] *vt* **-dled**; **-dling** : malmener

manhole ['mæn,ho:l] *n* : bouche *f* d'égout

manhood ['mæn,hʊd] *n* **1** : âge *m* d'homme **2** : virilité *f*

mania ['meɪniə, -njə] *n* : manie *f* — **maniac** ['meɪni,æk] *n* : maniaque *mf*

manicure ['mænə,kjʊr] *n* : manucure *f* — ~ *vt* **-cured**; **-curing** : faire les ongles de

manifest ['mænə,fɛst] *adj* : manifeste, patent — ~ *vt* : manifester — **manifesto** [,mænə'fɛs,to:] *n, pl* **-tos** *or* **-toes** : manifeste *m*

manipulate [mə'nɪpjə,leɪt] *vt* **-lated**; **-lating** : manipuler — **manipulation** [mə,nɪpjə-'leɪʃən] *n* : manipulation *f*

mankind ['mæn'kaɪnd, -ˌkaɪnd] *n* : le genre humain, humanité *f*

manly ['mænli] *adj* **-lier; -est** : viril — **manliness** ['mænlinəs] *n* : virilité *f*

mannequin ['mænɪkən] *n* : mannequin *m*

manner ['mænər] *n* **1** : manière *f* **2** KIND : sorte *f* **3** ∼**s** *npl* ÉTIQUETTE : manières *fpl*, éducation *f* — **mannerism** ['mænəˌrɪzəm] *n* : particularité *f*

manoeuvre *Brit* → **maneuver**

manor ['mænər] *n* : manoir *m*

manpower ['mænˌpaʊər] *n* : main-d'œuvre *f*

mansion ['mæntʃən] *n* : château *m*

manslaughter ['mænˌslɔtər] *n* : homicide *m* involontaire

mantel ['mæntəl] *or* **mantelpiece** ['mæntəlˌpiːs] *n* : cheminée *f*

manual ['mænjʊəl] *adj* : manuel — ∼ *n* : manuel *m*

manufacture [ˌmænjəˈfæktʃər] *n* : fabrication *f* — ∼ *vt* **-tured; -turing** : fabriquer — **manufacturer** [ˌmænjəˈfæktʃərər] *n* : fabricant *m*, -cante *f*

manure [məˈnʊr, -ˈnjʊr] *n* : fumier *m*

manuscript ['mænjəˌskrɪpt] *n* : manuscrit *m*

many ['meni] *adj* **more** ['mor]; **most** ['moːst] **1** : beaucoup de **2 as** ∼ : autant de **3 how** ∼ : combien **4 too** ∼ : trop de — ∼ *pron* : beaucoup

map ['mæp] *n* : carte *f*, plan *m* — ∼ *vt* **mapped; mapping 1** : faire la carte de **2** *or* ∼ **out** : élaborer

maple ['meɪpəl] *n* **1** : érable *m* **2** ∼ **syrup** : sirop *m* d'érable

mar ['mar] *vt* **marred; marring** : estropier

marathon ['mærəˌθɑn] *n* : marathon *m*

marble ['marbəl] *n* **1** : marbre *m* **2** : billes *fpl* (à jouer)

march ['martʃ] *n* : marche *f* — ∼ *vi* : marcher, défiler

March ['martʃ] *n* : mars *m*

mare ['mær] *n* : jument *f*

margarine ['mardʒərən] *n* : margarine *f*

margin ['mardʒən] *n* : marge *f* — **marginal** ['mardʒənəl] *adj* : marginal

marigold ['mærəˌgoːld] *n* : souci *m*

marijuana [ˌmærəˈhwɑnə] *n* : marijuana *f*

marinate ['mærəˌneɪt] *v* **-nated; -nating** : mariner

marine [məˈriːn] *adj* : marin — ∼ *n* : fusilier *m* marin

marital ['mærətəl] *adj* **1** : conjugal **2** ∼ **status** : état *m* civil

maritime ['mærəˌtaɪm] *adj* : maritime

mark ['mark] *n* **1** : marque *f* **2** STAIN : tache *f* **3** IMPRINT : trace *f* **4** TARGET : cible *f* **5** GRADE : note *f* — ∼ *vt* **1** : marquer **2** STAIN : tacher **3** POINT OUT : signaler **4** : corriger (un examen, etc.) **5** COMMEMORATE : com-

mémorer **6** CHARACTERIZE : caractériser **7** ∼ **off** : délimiter — **marked** ['markt] *adj* : marqué, notable — **markedly** ['markədli] *adv* : sensiblement — **marker** ['markər] *n* **1** : repère *m* **2** PEN : marqueur *m*

market ['markət] *n* : marché *m* — ∼ *vt* : vendre, commercialiser — **marketable** ['markətəbəl] *adj* : vendable — **marketplace** ['markətˌpleɪs] *n* : marché *m*

marksman ['marksmən] *n, pl* **-men** [-mən, -ˌmɛn] : tireur *m*, -reuse *f* d'élite — **marksmanship** ['marksmənˌʃɪp] *n* : adresse *f* au tir

marmalade ['marməˌleɪd] *n* : marmelade *f*

maroon[1] [məˈruːn] *vt* : abandonner

maroon[2] *n* : rouge *m* foncé

marquee [marˈkiː] *n* CANOPY : marquise *f*

marriage ['mærɪdʒ] *n* **1** : mariage *m* **2** WEDDING : noces *fpl* — **married** ['mærid] *adj* **1** : marié **2 get** ∼ : se marier

marrow ['mæroː] *n* : moelle *f*

marry ['mæri] *v* **-ried; -rying** *vt* **1** : marier **2** WED : se marier avec, épouser — *vi* : se marier

Mars ['marz] *n* : Mars *f*

marsh ['marʃ] *n* **1** : marécage *m* **2** *or* **salt** ∼ : marais *m* salant

marshal ['marʃəl] *n* : maréchal *m* (militaire), commissaire *m* (de police) — ∼ *vt* **-shaled** *or* **-shalled; -shaling** *or* **-shalling** : rassembler

marshmallow ['marʃˌmɛloː, -ˌmæloː] *n* : guimauve *f*

marshy ['marʃi] *adj* **marshier; -est** : marécageux

mart ['mart] *n* : marché *m*

martial ['marʃəl] *adj* : martial

martyr ['martər] *n* : martyr *m*, -tyre *f* — ∼ *vt* : martyriser

marvel ['marvəl] *n* : merveille *f* — ∼ *vi* **-veled** *or* **-velled; -veling** *or* **-velling** : s'émerveiller — **marvelous** ['marvələs] *or* **marvellous** *adj* : merveilleux

mascara [mæsˈkærə] *n* : mascara *m*

mascot ['mæsˌkat, -kət] *n* : mascotte *f*

masculine ['mæskjələn] *adj* : masculin — **masculinity** [ˌmæskjəˈlɪnəti] *n* : masculinité *f*

mash ['mæʃ] *vt* **1** CRUSH : écraser, aplatir **2** PUREE : faire une purée de, piler *Can* — **mashed potatoes** *npl* : purée *f* de pommes de terre, patates *fpl Can*

mask ['mæsk] *n* : masque *m* — ∼ *vt* : masquer

masochism ['mæsəˌkɪzəm, 'mæzə-] *n* : masochisme *m* — **masochist** ['mæsəˌkɪst, 'mæzə-] *n* : masochiste *mf* — **masochistic** [ˌmæsəˈkɪstɪk] *adj* : masochiste

mason ['meɪsən] *n* : maçon *m* — **masonry** ['meɪsənri] *n, pl* **-ries** : maçonnerie *f*

meanwhile

masquerade [ˌmæskəˈreɪd] n : mascarade f — ~ vi **-aded; -ading** ~ **as** : se déguiser en, se faire passer pour

mass [ˈmæs] n **1** : masse f **2** MULTITUDE : quantité f **3 the** ~**es** : les masses

Mass n : messe f

massacre [ˈmæsɪkər] n : massacre m — ~ vt **-cred; -cring** : massacrer

massage [məˈsɑʃ, -ˈsɑdʒ] n : massage m — ~ vt **-saged; -saging** : donner un massage à, masser — **masseur** [mæˈsər] n : masseur m — **masseuse** [mæˈsøz, -ˈsuːz] n : masseuse f

massive [ˈmæsɪv] adj **1** BULKY : massif **2** HUGE : énorme

mast [ˈmæst] n : mât m

master [ˈmæstər] n **1** : maître m **2** ~**'s degree** : maîtrise f — ~ vt : maîtriser — **masterful** [ˈmæstərfəl] adj : magistral — **masterpiece** [ˈmæstərˌpiːs] n : chef m d'œuvre — **mastery** [ˈmæstəri] n : maîtrise f

masturbate [ˈmæstərˌbeɪt] vi **-bated; -bating** : se masturber — **masturbation** [ˌmæstərˈbeɪʃən] n : masturbation f

mat [ˈmæt] n **1** DOORMAT : paillasson m **2** RUG : tapis m

match [ˈmætʃ] n **1** : allumette f **2** EQUAL : égal m, égale f **3** GAME : match m, combat m (de boxe) **4 be a good** ~ : être un bon parti — ~ vt **1** or ~ **up** : appareiller **2** EQUAL : égaler **3** : s'accorder avec, aller ensemble (vêtements, couleurs, etc.) — vi : correspondre

mate [ˈmeɪt] n **1** COMPANION : compagnon m, -pagne f **2** : mâle m, femelle f (d'un animal) — ~ vi **mated; mating** : s'accoupler

material [məˈtɪriəl] adj **1** : matériel **2** IMPORTANT : important — ~ n **1** : matière f **2** FABRIC : tissu m, étoffe f — **materialistic** [məˌtɪriəˈlɪstɪk] adj : matérialiste — **materialize** [məˈtɪriəˌlaɪz] vi **-ized; -izing** : se matérialiser

maternal [məˈtərnəl] adj : maternel — **maternity** [məˈtərnəti] n, pl **-ties** : maternité f — ~ adj : de maternité

math [ˈmæθ] → **mathematics**

mathematics [ˌmæθəˈmætɪks] ns & pl : mathématiques fpl — **mathematical** [ˌmæθəˈmætɪkəl] adj : mathématique — **mathematician** [ˌmæθəməˈtɪʃən] n : mathématicien m, -cienne f

matinee or **matinée** [ˌmætənˈeɪ] n : matinée f (au cinéma)

matrimony [ˈmætrəˌmoːni] n : mariage m — **matrimonial** [ˌmætrəˈmoːniəl] adj : matrimonial

matrix [ˈmeɪtrɪks] n, pl **-trices** [ˈmeɪtrəˌsiːz, ˈmæ-] or **-trixes** [ˈmeɪtrɪksəz] : matrice f

matte [ˈmæt] adj : mat

matter [ˈmætər] n **1** SUBSTANCE : matière f

2 QUESTION : affaire f, question f **3 as a** ~ **of fact** : en fait, en réalité **4 for that** ~ : d'ailleurs **5 to make** ~**s worse** : pour ne rien arranger **6 what's the** ~? : qu'est-ce qu'il y a? — ~ vi : importer

mattress [ˈmætrəs] n : matelas m

mature [məˈtʊr, -ˈtjʊr, -ˈtʃʊr] adj **-turer; -est** : mûr — ~ vi **-tured; -turing** : mûrir — **maturity** [məˈtʊrəti, -ˈtjʊr-, -ˈtʃʊr-] n : maturité f

maul [ˈmɔl] vt : mutiler

mauve [ˈmoːv, ˈmɔv] n : mauve m

maxim [ˈmæksəm] n : maxime f

maximum [ˈmæksəməm] n, pl **-ma** [ˈmæksəmə] or **-mums** : maximum m — ~ adj : maximum — **maximize** [ˈmæksəˌmaɪz] vt **-mized; -mizing** : porter au maximum

may [ˈmeɪ] v aux, past **might** [ˈmaɪt]; present s & pl **may 1** : pouvoir **2 come what** ~ : quoiqu'il arrive **3 it** ~ **rain** : il se peut qu'il pleuve, il va peut-être pleuvoir **4** ~ **the best man win** : que le meilleur gagne

May [ˈmeɪ] n : mai m

maybe [ˈmeɪbi] adv : peut-être

mayhem [ˈmeɪˌhɛm, ˈmeɪəm] n : pagaille f

mayonnaise [ˈmeɪəˌneɪz] n : mayonnaise f

mayor [ˈmeɪər, ˈmɛr] n : maire m, mairesse f

maze [ˈmeɪz] n : labyrinthe m

me [ˈmiː] pron **1** : moi **2** : me, m' **3 give it to** ~ : donne-le moi **4 will she come with** ~? : m'accompagnera-t-elle?

meadow [ˈmɛdoː] n : pré m, prairie f

meager or **meagre** [ˈmiːgər] adj : maigre

meal [ˈmiːl] n **1** : repas m **2** : farine f (de maïs, etc.) — **mealtime** [ˈmiːlˌtaɪm] n : l'heure f du repas

mean[1] [ˈmiːn] vt **meant** [ˈmɛnt]; **meaning 1** SIGNIFY : vouloir dire **2** INTEND : avoir l'intention de **3 be meant for** : être destiné à **4 he didn't** ~ **it** : il ne l'a pas fait exprès

mean[2] adj **1** UNKIND : méchant **2** STINGY : mesquin

mean[3] adj AVERAGE : moyen — ~ n : moyenne f

meander [miˈændər] vi **1** WIND : serpenter **2** WANDER : errer

meaning [ˈmiːnɪŋ] n : sens m, signification f — **meaningful** [ˈmiːnɪŋfəl] adj : significatif — **meaningless** [ˈmiːnɪŋləs] adj : sans signification

meanness [ˈmiːnnəs] n : méchanceté f

means [ˈmiːnz] n **1** : moyens mpl **2 by all** ~ : certainement **3 by** ~ **of** : au moyen de **4 by no** ~ : d'aucune façon

meantime [ˈmiːnˌtaɪm] n **1** : intervalle m **2 in the** ~ : en attendant — ~ adv → **meanwhile**

meanwhile [ˈmiːnˌʍaɪl] adv : entre-temps — ~ n → **meantime**

measles ['miːzəlz] *npl* : rougeole *f*

measly ['miːzli] *adj* **-slier; -est** : misérable, minable *fam*

measure ['mɛʒər, 'meɪ-] *n* : mesure *f* — ~ *v* **-sured; -suring** : mesurer — **measurable** ['mɛʒərəbəl, 'meɪ-] *adj* : mesurable — **measurement** ['mɛʒərmənt, 'meɪ-] *n* : mesure *f* — **measure up** *vi* ~ **to** : être à la hauteur de

meat ['miːt] *n* : viande *f* — **meatball** ['miːt,bɔl] *n* : boulette *f* de viande — **meaty** ['miːti] *adj* **meatier; -est 1** : de viande **2** SUBSTANTIAL : substantiel

mechanic [mɪ'kænɪk] *n* : mécanicien *m*, -cienne *f* — **mechanical** [mɪ'kænɪkəl] *adj* : mécanique — **mechanics** [mɪ'kænɪks] *ns & pl* **1** : mécanique *f* **2** WORKINGS : mécanisme *m* — **mechanism** ['mɛkə,nɪzəm] *n* : mécanisme *m* — **mechanize** ['mɛkə,naɪz] *vt* **-nized; -nizing** : mécaniser

medal ['mɛdəl] *n* : médaille *f* — **medallion** [mə'dæljən] *n* : médaillon *m*

meddle ['mɛdəl] *vi* **-dled; -dling** : se mêler

media ['miːdiə] *or* **mass ~** *npl* : les médias

median ['miːdiən] *adj* : médian

mediate ['miːdi,eɪt] *vi* **-ated; -ating** : servir de médiateur — **mediation** [,miːdi'eɪʃən] *n* : médiation *f* — **mediator** ['miːdi,eɪtər] *n* : médiateur *m*, -trice *f*

medical ['mɛdɪkəl] *adj* : médical — **medicated** ['mɛdə,keɪtəd] *adj* : médical, traitant — **medication** [,mɛdə'keɪʃən] *n* : médicaments *mpl* — **medicinal** [mə'dɪsənəl] *adj* : médicinal — **medicine** ['mɛdəsən] *n* **1** : médecine *f* **2** MEDICATION : médicament *m*

medieval *or* **mediaeval** [mɪ'diːvəl, ,miː-, ,mɛ-, -di'iːvəl] *adj* : médiéval

mediocre [,miːdi'oːkər] *adj* : médiocre — **mediocrity** [,miːdi'ɑkrəti] *n, pl* **-ties** : médiocrité *f*

meditate ['mɛdə,teɪt] *vi* **-tated; -tating** : méditer — **meditation** [,mɛdə'teɪʃən] *n* : méditation *f*

Mediterranean [,mɛdətə'reɪniən] *adj* : méditerranéen

medium ['miːdiəm] *n, pl* **-diums** *or* **-dia** ['miːdiə] **1** MEANS : moyen *m* **2** MEAN : milieu *m* **3** → **media** — ~ *adj* : moyen

medley ['mɛdli] *n, pl* **-leys 1** : mélange *m* **2** : pot-pourri *m* (de chansons)

meek ['miːk] *adj* : docile

meet ['miːt] *v* **met** ['mɛt]; **meeting** *vt* **1** ENCOUNTER : rencontrer **2** SATISFY : satisfaire **3 pleased to ~ you** : enchanté de faire votre connaissance — *vi* **1** : se rencontrer **2** ASSEMBLE : se réunir **3** : faire connaissance — ~ *n* : rencontre *f* (aux sports) — **meeting** ['miːtɪŋ] *n* : réunion *f*

megabyte ['mɛgə,baɪt] *n* : mégaoctet *m*

megaphone ['mɛgə,foːn] *n* : porte-voix *m*, mégaphone *m*

melancholy ['mɛlən,kɑli] *n, pl* **-cholies** : mélancolie *f* — ~ *adj* : mélancolique, triste

mellow ['mɛloː] *adj* **1** : doux, moelleux **2** CALM : paisible — ~ *vt* : adoucir — *vi* : s'adoucir

melody ['mɛlədi] *n, pl* **-dies** : mélodie *f*

melon ['mɛlən] *n* : melon *m*

melt ['mɛlt] *v* — *vt* : faire fondre

member ['mɛmbər] *n* : membre *m* — **membership** ['mɛmbər,ʃɪp] *n* **1** : adhésion *f* **2** MEMBERS : membres *mpl*

membrane ['mɛm,breɪn] *n* : membrane *f*

memory ['mɛmri, 'mɛmə-] *n, pl* **-ries 1** : mémoire *f* **2** RECOLLECTION : souvenir *m* — **memento** [mɪ'mɛn,toː] *n, pl* **-tos** *or* **-toes** : souvenir *m* — **memo** ['mɛmoː] *n, pl* **memos** *or* **memorandum** [,mɛmə'rændəm] *n, pl* **-dums** *or* **-da** [-də] : mémorandum *m* — **memoirs** ['mɛm,wɑrz] *npl* : mémoires *mpl* — **memorable** ['mɛmərəbəl] *adj* : mémorable — **memorial** [mə'moriəl] *adj* : commémoratif — ~ *n* : monument *m* (commémoratif) — **memorize** ['mɛmə,raɪz] *vt* **-rized; -rizing** : apprendre par cœur

men → **man**

menace ['mɛnəs] *n* : menace *f* — ~ *vt* **-aced; -acing** : menacer — **menacing** ['mɛnəsɪŋ] *adj* : menaçant

mend ['mɛnd] *vt* **1** : réparer, arranger **2** DARN : raccommoder — *vi* HEAL : guérir

menial ['miːniəl] *adj* : servile, bas

meningitis [,mɛnən'dʒaɪtəs] *n, pl* **-gitides** [-'dʒɪtə,diːz] : méningite *f*

menopause ['mɛnə,pɔz] *n* : ménopause *f*

menstruate ['mɛnstrʊ,eɪt] *vi* **-ated; -ating** : avoir ses règles — **menstruation** [,mɛnstrʊ'eɪʃən] *n* : menstruation *f*, règles *fpl*

mental ['mɛntəl] *adj* : mental — **mentality** [mɛn'tæləti] *n, pl* **-ties** : mentalité *f*

mention ['mɛntʃən] *n* : mention *f* — ~ *vt* **1** : mentionner **2 don't ~ it** : il n'y a pas de quoi

menu ['mɛn,juː] *n* : menu *m*

meow [mi'aʊ] *n* : miaulement *m*, miaou *m* — ~ *vi* : miauler

mercenary ['mərsən,ɛri] *n, pl* **-naries** : mercenaire *mf*

merchant ['mərtʃənt] *n* : marchand *m*, -chande *f*; commerçant *m*, -çante *f* — **merchandise** ['mərtʃən,daɪz, -,daɪs] *n* : marchandises *fpl*

merciful ['mərsɪfəl] *adj* : miséricordieux, compatissant — **merciless** ['mərsɪləs] *adj* : impitoyable

mercury ['mərkjəri] *n* : mercure *m*

Mercury ['mərkjəri] *n* : Mercure *f*

mercy ['mɛrsi] *n*, *pl* **-cies 1** : miséricorde *f*, compassion *f* **2 at the ~ of** : à la merci de

mere ['mɪr] *adj*, *superlative* **merest** : simple — **merely** ['mɪrli] *adv* : simplement

merge ['mərʤ] *v* **merged; merging** *vi* : fusionner (se dit d'une compagnie), confluer (se dit d'une rivière, etc.) — *vt* : unir, fusionner — **merger** ['mərʤər] *n* : union *f*, fusion *f*

merit ['mɛrət] *n* : mérite *m* — ~ *vt* : mériter

mermaid ['mər,meɪd] *n* : sirène *f*

merry ['mɛri] *adj* **-rier; -est** : allègre — **merry–go–round** ['mɛrigo,raʊnd] *n* : manège *m*

mesh ['mɛʃ] *n* : maille *f*

mesmerize ['mɛzmə,raɪz] *vt* **-ized; -izing** : hypnotiser

mess ['mɛs] *n* **1** : désordre *m* **2** MUDDLE : gâchis *m* **3** : cantine *f* (ambulante) — *vt* **1 ~ up** : mettre en désordre **2** *or* ~ **up** SOIL : salir **3 ~ up** BUNGLE : gâcher — *vi* **1 ~ around** PUTTER : bricoler **2 ~ with** PROVOKE : embêter

message ['mɛsɪʤ] *n* : message *m* — **messenger** ['mɛsənʤər] *n* : messager *m*, -gère *f*

messy ['mɛsi] *adj* **messier; -est** : désordonné

met → **meet**

metabolism [mə'tæbə,lɪzəm] *n* : métabolisme *m*

metal ['mɛţəl] *n* : métal *m* — **metallic** [mə-'tælɪk] *adj* : métallique

metamorphosis [,mɛţə'mɔrfəsɪs] *n*, *pl* **-phoses** [-'si:z] : métamorphose *f*

metaphor ['mɛţə,fɔr, -fər] *n* : métaphore *f*

meteor ['mi:ţiər, -ţi,ɔr] *n* : météore *m* — **meteorological** [,mi:ţi,ɔrə'lɑʤɪkəl] *adj* : météorologique — **meteorologist** [,mi:ţiə'rɑləʤɪst] *n* : météorologue *mf* — **meteorology** [,mi:ţiə'rɑləʤi] *n* : météorologie *f*

meter *or Brit* **metre** ['mi:ţər] *n* **1** : mètre *m* **2** : compteur *m* (d'électricité, etc.)

method ['mɛθəd] *n* : méthode *f* — **methodical** [mə'θɑdɪkəl] *adj* : méthodique

meticulous [mə'tɪkjələs] *adj* : méticuleux

metric ['mɛtrɪk] *or* **metrical** [-trɪkəl] *adj* : métrique

metropolis [mə'trɑpələs] *n* : métropole *f* — **metropolitan** [,mɛtrə'pɑlətən] *adj* : métropolitain

Mexican ['mɛksɪkən] *adj* : mexicain

mice → **mouse**

microbe ['maɪ,kro:b] *n* : microbe *m*

microfilm ['maɪkro,fɪlm] *n* : microfilm *m*

microphone ['maɪkrə,fo:n] *n* : microphone *m*

microscope ['maɪkrə,sko:p] *n* : microscope

m — **microscopic** [,maɪkrə'skɑpɪk] *adj* : microscopique

microwave ['maɪkrə,weɪv] *n* *or* ~ **oven** : (four *m* à) micro-ondes *m*

mid ['mɪd] *adj* **1 ~-morning** : au milieu de la matinée **2 in ~-June** : à la mi-juin **3 she is in her ~ thirties** : elle est dans la trentaine — **midair** ['mɪd'ær] *n* **in ~** : en plein ciel — **midday** ['mɪd'deɪ] *n* : midi *m*

middle ['mɪdəl] *adj* : du milieu, au milieu — ~ *n* **1** : milieu *m*, centre *m* **2 in the ~ of** : au milieu de (un espace), en train de (faire une activité) — **middle–aged** *adj* : d'un certain age — **Middle Ages** *npl* : Moyen Âge *m* — **middle class** *n* : classe *f* moyenne — **Middle Eastern** *adj* : moyen-oriental — **middleman** ['mɪdəl,mæn] *n*, *pl* **-men** [-mən, -,mɛn] : intermédiaire *mf*

midget ['mɪʤət] *n* : nain *m*, naine *f*

midnight ['mɪd,naɪt] *n* : minuit *m*

midriff ['mɪd,rɪf] *n* : diaphragme *m*

midst ['mɪdst] *n* **1 in the ~ of** : au milieu de **2 in our ~** : parmi nous

midsummer ['mɪd'sʌmər, -,sʌ-] *n* : milieu *m* de l'été

midway ['mɪd,weɪ] *adv* : à mi-chemin

midwife ['mɪd,waɪf] *n*, *pl* **-wives** [-,waɪvz] : sage-femme *f*

midwinter ['mɪd'wɪntər, -,wɪn-] *n* : milieu *m* de l'hiver

miff ['mɪf] *vt* : vexer

might[1] ['maɪt] (*used to express permission or possibility or as a polite alternative to* **may**) → **may**

might[2] *n* : force *f*, pouvoir *m* — **mighty** ['maɪti] *adj* **mightier; -est 1** : fort, puissant **2** GREAT : énorme — ~ *adv* : très, rudement *fam*

migraine ['maɪ,greɪn] *n* : migraine *f*

migrate ['maɪ,greɪt] *vi* **-grated; -grating** : émigrer — **migrant** ['maɪgrənt] *n* : travailleur *m* saisonnier

mild ['maɪld] *adj* **1** GENTLE : doux **2** LIGHT : léger

mildew ['mɪl,du:, -,dju:] *n* : moisissure *f*

mildly ['maɪldli] *adv* : doucement, légèrement — **mildness** ['maɪldnəs] *n* : douceur *f*

mile ['maɪl] *n* : mille *m* — **mileage** ['maɪlɪʤ] *n* : distance *f* parcourue (en milles), kilométrage *m* — **milestone** ['maɪl,sto:n] *n* : jalon *m*

military ['mɪlə,tɛri] *adj* : militaire — ~ *n* **the ~** : les forces armées — **militant** ['mɪlətənt] *adj* : militant — ~ *n* : militant *m*, -tante *f* — **militia** [mə'lɪʃə] *n* : milice *f*

milk ['mɪlk] *n* : lait *m* — ~ *vt* : traire (une vache, etc.) — **milky** ['mɪlki] *adj* **milkier; -est** : laiteux — **Milky Way** *n* **the ~** : la Voie lactée

mill ['mɪl] *n* **1** : moulin *m* **2** FACTORY : usine *f* — ~ *vt* : moudre — *vi or* ~ **about** : grouiller

millennium [mə'lɛniəm] *n, pl* **-nia** [-niə] *or* **-niums** : millénaire *m*

miller ['mɪlər] *n* : meunier *m*, -nière *f*

milligram ['mɪlə,græm] *n* : milligramme *m* — **millimeter** *or Brit* **millimetre** ['mɪlə,miːtər] *n* : millimètre *m*

million ['mɪljən] *n, pl* **millions** *or* **million** : million *m* — ~ *adj* **a** ~ : un million de — **millionaire** [,mɪljə'nær, 'mɪljə,nær] *n* : millionnaire *mf* — **millionth** ['mɪljənθ] *adj* : millionième

mime ['maɪm] *n* **1** : mime *mf* **2** PANTOMIME : pantomime *f* — ~ *v* **mimed; miming** *vt* : imiter — *vi* : faire des mimiques — **mimic** *vt* **-icked; -icking** : imiter, singer

mince ['mɪnts] *vt* **minced; mincing 1** : hacher **2 not to** ~ **one's words** : ne pas mâcher ses mots

mind ['maɪnd] *n* **1** : esprit *m* **2** INTELLECT : capacité *f* intellectuelle **3** OPINION : opinion *f* **4** REASON : raison *f* **5 have a** ~ **to** : avoir l'intention de — ~ *vt* **1** TEND : s'occuper de **2** OBEY : obéir à **3** WATCH : faire attention à **4 I don't** ~ **the heat** : la chaleur ne m'incommode pas — *vi* **1** OBEY : obéir **2 I don't** ~ : ça m'est égal — **mindful** ['maɪndfəl] *adj* : attentif — **mindless** ['maɪndləs] *adj* **1** SENSELESS : stupide **2** DULL : ennuyeux

mine[1] ['maɪn] *pron* **1** : le mien, la mienne, les miens, les miennes **2 a friend of** ~ : un ami à moi

mine[2] *n* : mine *f* — ~ *vt* **mined; mining 1** : extraire (de l'or, etc.) **2** : miner (avec des explosifs) — **minefield** ['maɪn,fiːld] *n* : champ *m* de mines — **miner** ['maɪnər] *n* : mineur *m*

mineral ['mɪnərəl] *n* : minéral *m*

mingle ['mɪŋgəl] *v* **-gled; -gling** *vt* : mêler, mélanger — *vi* : se mêler (à, avec)

miniature ['mɪniə,tʃʊr, 'mɪni,tʃʊr, -tʃər] *n* : miniature *f* — ~ *adj* : en miniature

minimal ['mɪnəməl] *adj* : minimal — **minimize** ['mɪnə,maɪz] *vt* **-mized; -mizing** : minimiser — **minimum** ['mɪnəməm] *adj* : minimum — ~ *n, pl* **-ma** ['mɪnəmə] *or* **-mums** : minimum *m*

minister ['mɪnəstər] *n* **1** : pasteur *m* (d'une église) **2** : ministre *m* (en politique) — ~ *vi* ~ **to** : pourvoir à, donner des soins à — **ministerial** [,mɪnə'stɪriəl] *adj* : ministériel — **ministry** ['mɪnəstri] *n, pl* **-tries** : ministère *m* (gouvernemental), sacerdoce *m* (religieux)

mink ['mɪŋk] *n, pl* **mink** *or* **minks** : vison *m*

minor ['maɪnər] *adj* **1** : mineur **2** INSIGNIFICANT : sans importance — ~ *n* **1** : mineur *m*, -neure *f* **2** : matière *f* secondaire (à l'université) — **minority** [mə'nɔrəti, maɪ-] *n, pl* **-ties** : minorité *f*

mint[1] ['mɪnt] *n* **1** : menthe *f* (plante) **2** : bonbon *m* à la menthe

mint[2] *n* **1 the Mint** : l'Hôtel *m* de la Monnaie **2 worth a** ~ : valoir une fortune — ~ *vt* : frapper (la monnaie) — ~ *adj* **in** ~ **condition** : comme neuf

minus ['maɪnəs] *prep* **1** : moins **2** WITHOUT : sans — ~ *n or* ~ **sign** : moins *m*

minuscule *or* **miniscule** ['mɪnəs,kjuːl] *adj* : minuscule

minute[1] ['mɪnət] *n* **1** : minute *f* **2** MOMENT : moment *m* **3** ~**s** *npl* : procès-verbal *m*

minute[2] [maɪ'nuːt, mɪ-, -'njuːt] *adj* **-nuter; -est 1** TINY : minuscule **2** DETAILED : minutieux

miracle ['mɪrɪkəl] *n* : miracle *m* — **miraculous** [mə'rækjələs] *adj* : miraculeux

mirage [mɪ'rɑʒ, *chiefly Brit* 'mɪr,ɑʒ] *n* : mirage *m*

mire ['maɪr] *n* : boue *f*, fange *f*

mirror ['mɪrər] *n* : miroir *m*, glace *f* — ~ *vt* : refléter, réfléchir

mirth ['mərθ] *n* : allégresse *f*, gaieté *f*

misapprehension [,mɪs,æprə'hɛntʃən] *n* : malentendu *m*

misbehave [,mɪsbi'heɪv] *vi* **-haved; -having** : se conduire mal — **misbehavior** [,mɪsbi'heɪvjər] *n* : mauvaise conduite *f*

miscalculate [mɪs'kælkjə,leɪt] *v* **-lated; -lating** : mal calculer

miscarriage [,mɪs'kærɪdʒ, 'mɪs,kærɪdʒ] *n* **1** : fausse couche *f* **2** ~ **of justice** : erreur *f* judiciaire

miscellaneous [,mɪsə'leɪniəs] *adj* : divers, varié

mischief ['mɪstʃəf] *n* : espièglerie *f* — **mischievous** ['mɪstʃəvəs] *adj* : espiègle

misconception [,mɪskən'sɛpʃən] *n* : concept *m* erroné

misconduct [mɪs'kɑndəkt] *n* : mauvaise conduite *f*

misdeed [mɪs'diːd] *n* : méfait *m*

misdemeanor [,mɪsdɪ'miːnər] *n* : délit *m* judiciaire

miser ['maɪzər] *n* : avare *m*

miserable ['mɪzərəbəl] *adj* **1** UNHAPPY : malheureux **2** WRETCHED : misérable **3** ~ **weather** : temps *m* maussade — **miserly** ['maɪzərli] *adj* : avare

misery ['mɪzəri] *n, pl* **-eries 1** : souffrance *f* **2** WRETCHEDNESS : misère *f*

misfire [mɪs'faɪr] *vi* **-fired; -firing** : échouer

misfit ['mɪs,fɪt] *n* : inadapté *m*, -tée *f*

misfortune [mɪs'fɔrtʃən] *n* : malheur *f*, infortune *f*

misgiving [mɪs'gɪvɪŋ] *n* : doute *m*

misguided [mɪs'gaɪdəd] *adj* : malencontreux, peu judicieux

mishap ['mɪs,hæp] *n* : contretemps *m*

misinform [,mɪsɪn'fɔrm] *vt* : mal renseigner

misinterpret [,mɪsɪn'tərprət] *vt* : mal interpréter

misjudge [mɪs'dʒʌdʒ] *vt* **-judged; -judging** : mal juger

mislay [mɪs'leɪ] *vt* **-laid** [-'leɪd]; **-laying** : égarer

mislead [mɪs'li:d] *vt* **-led** [-'lɛd]; **-leading** : tromper — **misleading** [mɪs'li:dɪŋ] *adj* : trompeur

misnomer [mɪs'no:mər] *n* : terme *m* impropre

misplace [mɪs'pleɪs] *vt* **-placed; -placing** : égarer, perdre

misprint ['mɪs,prɪnt, mɪs'-] *n* : faute *f* typographique, coquille *f*

miss ['mɪs] *vt* **1** : rater, manquer (une occasion, un vol, etc.) **2** OVERLOOK : laisser passer **3** AVOID : éviter **4** OMIT : sauter **5 I ~ you** : tu me manques — ~ *n* **1** : coup *m* manqué **2** FAILURE : échec *m*

Miss ['mɪs] *n* : mademoiselle *f*

missile ['mɪsəl] *n* **1** : missile *m* **2** PROJECTILE : projectile *m*

missing ['mɪsɪŋ] *adj* : perdu, disparu

mission ['mɪʃən] *n* : mission *f* — **missionary** ['mɪʃə,nɛri] *n, pl* **-aries** : missionnaire *mf*

misspell [mɪs'spɛl] *vt* : mal orthographier, mal écrire

mist ['mɪst] *n* : brume *f*

mistake [mɪ'steɪk] *vt* **-took** [-'stʊk]; **-taken** [-'steɪkən]; **-taking 1** MISINTERPRET : mal comprendre **2** CONFUSE : confondre — ~ *n* **1** : faute *f*, erreur *f* **2 make a ~** : se tromper — **mistaken** [mɪ'steɪkən] *adj* : erroné

mister ['mɪstər] *n* : monsieur *m*

mistletoe ['mɪsəl,to:] *n* : gui *m*

mistreat [mɪs'tri:t] *vt* : maltraiter

mistress ['mɪstrəs] *n* **1** : maîtresse *f* (de classe) **2** LOVER : amante *f*

mistrust [mɪs'trʌst] *n* : méfiance *f* — ~ *vt* : se méfier de

misty ['mɪsti] *adj* **mistier; -est** : brumeux

misunderstand [,mɪs,ʌndər'stænd] *vt* **-stood** [-'stʊd]; **-standing** : mal comprendre — **misunderstanding** [,mɪs,ʌndər'stændɪŋ] *n* : malentendu *m*

misuse [mɪs'ju:z] *vt* **-used; -using 1** : mal employer **2** MISTREAT : maltraiter — ~ [mɪs'ju:s] *n* : mauvais emploi *m*, abus *m*

mitigate ['mɪtə,geɪt] *vt* **-gated; -gating** : atténuer

mitt ['mɪt] *n* : gant *m* (de baseball) — **mitten** ['mɪtən] *n* : moufle *f*, mitaine *f* Can

mix ['mɪks] *vt* **1** : mélanger **2 ~ up** : confondre — *vi* : se mélanger — ~ *n* : mélange *m* — **mixture** ['mɪkstʃər] *n* : mélange *m* — **mix–up** ['mɪks,ʌp] *n* : confusion *f*

moan ['mo:n] *n* : gémissement *m* — ~ *vi* : gémir

mob ['mɑb] *n* : foule *f* — ~ *vt* **mobbed; mobbing** : assaillir

mobile ['mo:bəl, -,bi:l, -,baɪl] *adj* : mobile — ~ ['mo:,bi:l] *n* : mobile *m* — **mobile home** *n* : auto-caravane *f* — **mobility** [mo:'bɪləti] *n* : mobilité *f* — **mobilize** ['mo:bə,laɪz] *vt* **-lized; -lizing** : mobiliser

moccasin ['mɑkəsən] *n* : mocassin *m*

mock ['mɑk, 'mɔk] *vt* : se moquer de — ~ *adj* : faux — **mockery** ['mɑkəri, 'mɔ-] *n, pl* **-eries** : moquerie *f*

mode ['mo:d] *n* : mode *m*

model ['mɑdəl] *n* **1** : modèle *m* **2** MOCK-UP : maquette *f* **3** : mannequin *m* (personne) — ~ *v* **-eled** *or* **-elled; -eling** *or* **-elling** *vt* **1** SHAPE : modeler **2** WEAR : porter — *vi* : travailler comme mannequin — ~ *adj* : modèle

modem ['mo:dəm, -,dɛm] *n* : modem *m*

moderate ['mɑdərət] *adj* : modéré — ~ *n* : modéré *m*, -rée *f* — ['mɑdə,reɪt] *v* **-ated; -ating** *vt* : modérer — *vi* : se modérer — **moderation** [,mɑ'də'reɪʃən] *n* : modération *f* — **moderator** ['mɑdə,reɪtər] *n* : animateur *m*, -trice *f*

modern ['mɑdərn] *adj* : moderne — **modernize** ['mɑdər,naɪz] *vt* **-nized; -nizing** : moderniser

modest ['mɑdəst] *adj* : modeste — **modesty** ['mɑdəsti] *n* : modestie *f*

modify ['mɑdə,faɪ] *vt* **-fied; -fying** : modifier

moist ['mɔɪst] *adj* : humide — **moisten** ['mɔɪsən] *vt* : humecter — **moisture** ['mɔɪstʃər] *n* : humidité *f* — **moisturizer** ['mɔɪstʃə,raɪzər] *n* : crème *f* hydratante

molar ['mo:lər] *n* : molaire *f*

molasses [mə'læsəz] *n* : mélasse *f*

mold[1] ['mo:ld] *n* FORM : moule *m* — ~ *vt* : mouler, former

mold[2] *n* : moisissure *f* — **moldy** ['mo:ldi] *adj* **moldier; -est** : moisi

mole[1] ['mo:l] *n* : grain *m* de beauté (sur la peau)

mole[2] *n* : taupe *f* (animal)

molecule ['mɑlɪ,kju:l] *n* : molécule *f*

molest [mə'lɛst] *vt* **1** HARASS : importuner **2** : abuser (sexuellement)

molt ['mo:lt] *vi* : muer

molten ['mo:ltən] *adj* : en fusion

mom ['mɑm] *n* : maman *f*

moment ['mo:mənt] *n* : instant *m*, moment *m* — **momentarily** [,mo:mən'tɛrəli] *adv* **1** : momentanément **2** SOON : dans un instant, immédiatement — **momentary** ['mo:mən,tɛri] *adj* : momentané

momentous [mo'mɛntəs] *adj* : très important, tant

momentum [mo'mɛntəm] *n, pl* **-ta** [-tə] *or*
-tums **1** : moment *m* (en physique) **2** IM-
PETUS : élan *m*

monarch ['mɑ,nɑrk, -nərk] *n* : monarque *m*
— **monarchy** ['mɑ,nɑrki, -nər-] *n, pl*
-chies : monarchie *f*

monastery ['mɑnə,stɛri] *n, pl* **-teries**
: monastère *m*

Monday ['mʌn,deɪ, -di] *n* : lundi *m*

money ['mʌni] *n, pl* **-eys** *or* **-ies** [-iz] : argent
m — **monetary** ['mɑnə,tɛri, 'mʌnə-] *adj*
: monétaire — **money order** *n* : mandat-
poste *m*

mongrel ['mɑŋgrəl, 'mʌn-] *n* : chien *m*
métisse

monitor ['mɑnətər] *n* : moniteur *m* (d'un ordinateur, etc.) — ~ *vt* : surveiller

monk ['mʌŋk] *n* : moine *m*

monkey ['mʌŋki] *n, pl* **-keys** : singe *m* —
monkey wrench : clé *f* à molette

monogram ['mɑnə,græm] *n* : monogramme
m

monologue ['mɑnə,lɔg] *n* : monologue *m*

monopoly [mə'nɑpəli] *n, pl* **-lies** : monopole
pole *m* — **monopolize** [mə'nɑpə,laɪz] *vt*
-lized; -lizing : monopoliser

monotonous [mə'nɑtənəs] *adj* : monotone
— **monotony** [mə'nɑtəni] *n* : monotonie *f*

monster ['mɑntstər] *n* : monstre *m* — **monstrosity** [mɑn'strɑsəti] *n, pl* **-ties** : monstruosité *f* — **monstrous** ['mɑntstrəs] *adj* **1**
: monstrueux **2** HUGE : gigantesque

month ['mʌnθ] *n* : mois *m* — **monthly**
['mʌnθli] *adv* : mensuellement — ~ *adj*
: mensuel

monument ['mɑnjəmənt] *n* : monument *m*
— **monumental** [,mɑnjə'mɛntəl] *adj*
: monumental

moo ['mu:] *vi* : meugler — ~ *n* : meugle-
ment *m*

mood ['mu:d] *n* : humeur *f* — **moody**
['mu:di] *adj* **moodier; -est** **1** GLOOMY
: mélancolique, déprimé **2** IRRITABLE : de
mauvaise humeur **3** TEMPERAMENTAL
: d'humeur changeante

moon ['mu:n] *n* : lune *f* — **moonlight**
['mu:n,laɪt] *n* : clair *m* de lune

moor¹ ['mur] *n* : lande *f*

moor² *vt* : amarrer — **mooring** ['murɪŋ] *n*
: mouillage *m*

moose ['mu:s] *ns & pl* : orignal *m*

moot ['mu:t] *adj* : discutable

mop ['mɑp] *n* **1** : balai *m* à franges **2** *or* ~
of hair : tignasse *f* — ~ *vt* **mopped; mop-
ping** : laver (le plancher, etc.)

mope ['mo:p] *vi* **moped; moping** : être
déprimé

moped ['mo:,pɛd] *n* : cyclomoteur *m*, vélomoteur *m*

moral ['mɔrəl] *adj* : moral — ~ *n* **1**

: morale *f* (d'une histoire, etc.) **2** ~**s** *npl*
: mœurs *fpl* — **morale** [mə'ræl] *n* : moral *m*
— **morality** [mə'ræləti] *n, pl* **-ties** : moralité *f*

morbid ['mɔrbɪd] *adj* : morbide

more ['mor] *adj* : plus de — ~ *adv* **1** : plus,
davantage **2** ~ **and** ~ : de plus en plus **3**
~ **or less** : plus ou moins **4 once** ~ : encore une fois — ~ *n* **the** ~ : le plus — ~
pron : plus — **moreover** [mor'o:vər] *adv*
: de plus

morgue ['mɔrg] *n* : morgue *f*

morning ['mɔrnɪŋ] *n* **1** : matin *m*, avant-
midi *f* Can **2 good** ~ : bonjour **3 in the**
~ : pendant la matinée

Moroccan [mə'rɑkən] *adj* : marocain

moron ['mor,ɑn] *n* : imbécile *mf*

morose [mə'ro:s] *adj* : morose

morphine ['mɔr,fi:n] *n* : morphine *f*

morsel ['mɔrsəl] *n* **1** BITE : bouchée *f* **2**
FRAGMENT : morceau *m*

mortal ['mɔrtəl] *adj* : mortel — ~ *n* : mortel *m*, -telle *f* — **mortality** [mɔr'tæləti] *n*
: mortalité *f*

mortar ['mɔrtər] *n* : mortier *m*

mortgage ['mɔrgɪʤ] *n* : hypothèque *f* — ~
vt **-gaged; -gaging** : hypothéquer

mortify ['mɔrtə,faɪ] *vt* **-fied; -fying** : mortifier

mosaic [mo'zeɪɪk] *n* : mosaïque *f*

Moslem ['mɑzləm] → **Muslim**

mosque ['mɑsk] *n* : mosquée *f*

mosquito [mə'ski:to] *n, pl* **-toes** : moustique
m, maringouin *m* Can

moss ['mɔs] *n* : mousse *f*

most ['mo:st] *adj* **1** : la plupart de **2 (the)** ~
: le plus — ~ *adv* : plus — ~ *n* : plus *m* —
~ *pron* : la plupart — **mostly** ['mo:stli] *adv*
1 MAINLY : principalement, surtout **2** USU-
ALLY : normalement

motel [mo'tɛl] *n* : motel *m*

moth ['mɔθ] *n* : papillon *m* de nuit, mite *f*

mother ['mʌðər] *n* : mère *f* — ~ *vt* **1** : s'occuper de **2** SPOIL : dorloter — **motherhood**
['mʌðər,hud] *n* : maternité *f* — **mother-in-
law** ['mʌðərɪn,lɔ] *n, pl* **mothers-in-law**
: belle-mère *f* — **motherly** ['mʌðərli] *adj*
: maternel — **mother-of-pearl** [,mʌðərəv-
'pərl] *n* : nacre *f*

motif [mo'ti:f] *n* : motif *m*

motion ['mo:ʃən] *n* **1** : mouvement *m* **2**
PROPOSAL : motion *f* **3 set in** ~ : mettre en
marche — ~ *vi* ~ **to** : faire signe à — **motionless** ['mo:ʃənləs] *adj* : immobile —
motion picture *n* : film *m*

motive ['mo:tɪv] *n* : motif *m* — **motivate**
['mo:tə,veɪt] *vt* **-vated; -vating** : motiver —
motivation [,mo:tə'veɪʃən] *n* : motivation *f*

motor ['mo:tər] *n* : moteur *m* — **motorbike**
['mo:tər,baɪk] *n* : moto *f* — **motorboat**

['mo:ʈər,bo:t] *n* : canot *m* à moteur — **motorcycle** ['mo:ʈər,saɪkəl] *n* : motocyclette *f*, moto *f* — **motorcyclist** ['mo:ʈər,saɪkəlɪst] *n* : motocycliste *mf* — **motorist** ['mo:ʈərɪst] *n* : automobiliste *mf*

motto ['mɑʈo:] *n, pl* **-toes** : devise *f*

mould ['mo:ld] → **mold**

mound ['maʊnd] *n* **1** PILE : tas *m* **2** HILL : monticule *m*

mount[1] ['maʊnt] *n* **1** HORSE : monture *f* **2** SUPPORT : support *m* — ～ *vt* : monter sur (un cheval, etc.)

mount[2] *n* HILL : mont *m* — **mountain** ['maʊntən] *n* : montagne *f* — **mountainous** ['maʊntnəs] *adj* : montagneux

mourn ['morn] *vt* ～ **for s.o.** : pleurer qqn — *vi* : porter le deuil — **mournful** ['mornfəl] *adj* : triste — **mourning** ['mornɪŋ] *n* : deuil *m*

mouse ['maʊs] *n, pl* **mice** ['maɪs] : souris *f* — **mousetrap** ['maʊs,træp] *n* : souricière *f*

moustache ['mʌ,stæʃ, mə'stæʃ] → **mustache**

mouth ['maʊθ] *n* : bouche *f* (d'une personne, etc.), gueule *f* (d'un animal) — **mouthful** ['maʊθ,fʊl] *n* : bouchée *f* — **mouthpiece** ['maʊθ,pi:s] *n* : bec *m*, embouchure *f* (d'un instrument de musique)

move ['mu:v] *v* **moved; moving** *vi* **1** GO : aller **2** RELOCATE : déménager **3** STIR : bouger **4** ACT : agir — *vt* **1** : déplacer **2** AFFECT : émouvoir **3** TRANSPORT : transporter **4** PROPOSE : proposer — ～ *n* **1** MOVEMENT : mouvement *m* **2** RELOCATION : déménagement *m* **3** STEP : pas *m*, étape *m* — **movable** *or* **moveable** ['mu:vəbəl] *adj* : mobile — **movement** ['mu:vmənt] *n* : mouvement *m*

movie ['mu:vi] *n* **1** : film *m* **2** ～**s** *npl* : cinéma *m*

mow ['mo:] *vt* **mowed; mowed** *or* **mown** ['mo:n]; **mowing** : tondre — **mower** ['mo:ər] *n* → **lawn mower**

Mr. ['mɪstər] *n, pl* **Messrs.** ['mɛsərz] : Monsieur *m*

Mrs. ['mɪsəz, -səs, *esp South* 'mɪzəz, -zəs] *n, pl* **Mesdames** [meɪ'dɑm, -'dæm] : Madame *f*

Ms. ['mɪz] *n* : Madame *f*, Mademoiselle *f*

much ['mʌtʃ] *adj* **more; most** : beaucoup de — ～ *adv* **more** ['mor]; **most** ['mo:st] **1** : beaucoup **2 as** ～ : autant **3 how** ～? : combien? **4 too** ～ : trop — ～ *pron* : beaucoup

muck ['mʌk] *n* : saleté *f*

mucus ['mju:kəs] *n* : mucus *m*

mud ['mʌd] *n* : boue *f*, bouette *f Can fam*

muddle ['mʌdəl] *v* **-dled; -dling** *vt* **1** CONFUSE : confondre **2** JUMBLE : embrouiller

— *vi* ～ **through** : se tirer d'affaire — ～ *n* : désordre *m*, fouillis *m*

muddy ['mʌdi] *adj* **-dier; -est** : boueux

muffin ['mʌfən] *n* : muffin *m Can*

muffle ['mʌfəl] *vt* **muffled; muffling** : étouffer (des sons) — **muffler** ['mʌflər] *n* : silencieux *m* (d'un véhicule)

mug ['mʌg] *n* CUP : tasse *f* — ～ *vt* **mugged; mugging** : agresser, attaquer — **mugger** ['mʌgər] *n* : agresseur *m*

muggy ['mʌgi] *adj* **-gier; -est** : lourd et humide

mule ['mju:l] *n* : mule *f*, mulet *m*

mull ['mʌl] *vt or* ～ **over** : réfléchir sur

multicolored ['mʌlti,kʌlərd, 'mʌl,taɪ-] *adj* : multicolore

multimedia [,mʌlti'mi:diə, ,mʌl,taɪ-] *adj* : multimédia

multinational [,mʌlti'næʃənəl, ,mʌl,taɪ-] *adj* : multinational

multiple ['mʌltəpəl] *adj* : multiple — ～ *n* : multiple *m* — **multiplication** [,mʌltəplə'keɪʃən] *n* : multiplication *f* — **multiply** ['mʌltə,plaɪ] *v* **-plied; -plying** *vt* : multiplier — *vi* : se multiplier

multitude ['mʌltə,tu:d, -,tju:d] *n* : multitude *f*

mum ['mʌm] *adj* **keep** ～ : garder le silence

mumble ['mʌmbəl] *vi* **-bled; -bling** : marmonner

mummy ['mʌmi] *n, pl* **-mies** : momie *f*

mumps ['mʌmps] *ns & pl* : oreillons *mpl*

munch ['mʌntʃ] *v* : mâcher, mastiquer

mundane [,mʌn'deɪn, 'mʌn,-] *adj* : routinier, ordinaire

municipal [mju'nɪsəpəl] *adj* : municipal — **municipality** [mju,nɪsə'pæləti] *n, pl* **-ties** : municipalité *f*

munitions [mju'nɪʃənz] *npl* : munitions *fpl*

mural ['mjʊrəl] *n* : peinture *f* murale

murder ['mərdər] *n* : meurtre *m* — ～ *vt* : assassiner — **murderer** ['mərdərər] *n* : meurtrier *m*, -trière *f*; assassin *m* — **murderous** ['mərdərəs] *adj* : meurtrier

murky ['mərki] *adj* **murkier; -est** : obscur, sombre

murmur ['mərmər] *n* : murmure *m* — ～ *v* : murmurer

muscle ['mʌsəl] *n* : muscle *m* — ～ *vi* **-cled; -cling** *or* ～ **in** : s'ingérer avec force dans — **muscular** ['mʌskjələr] *adj* **1** : musculaire **2** STRONG : musclé

muse[1] ['mju:z] *n* : muse *f*

muse[2] *vi* **mused; musing** : méditer

museum [mju'zi:əm] *n* : musée *m*

mushroom ['mʌʃ,ru:m, -,rʊm] *n* : champignon *m* — ～ *vi* : proliférer, se multiplier

mushy ['mʌʃi] *adj* **mushier; -est 1** SOFT : mou **2** SENTIMENTAL : mièvre

music ['mjuːzɪk] *n* : musique *f* — **musical** ['mjuːzɪkəl] *adj* : musical — **~** *n* : comédie *f* musicale — **musician** [mjʊ'zɪʃən] *n* : musicien *m*, -cienne *f*

musket ['mʌskət] *n* : mousquet *m*

Muslim ['mʌzləm, 'mʊs-, 'mʊz-] *adj* : musulman — **~** *n* : musulman *m*, -mane *f*

muslin ['mʌzlən] *n* : mousseline *f*

mussel ['mʌsəl] *n* : moule *f*

must ['mʌst] *v aux* **1** : devoir **2 she ~ try** : elle doit essayer **3 you ~ decide** : il faut que tu te décides — **~** *n* : nécessité *f*

mustache ['mʌˌstæʃ, mʌ'stæʃ] *n* : moustache *f*

mustard ['mʌstərd] *n* : moutarde *f*

muster ['mʌstər] *vt* : rassembler, réunir

musty ['mʌsti] *adj* **mustier; -est** : qui sent le renfermé

mute ['mjuːt] *adj* **muter; mutest** : muet — **~** *n* : muet *m*, muette *f*

mutilate ['mjuːtəˌleɪt] *vt* **-lated; -lating** : mutiler

mutiny ['mjuːtəni] *n, pl* **-nies** : mutinerie *f* — **~** *vi* **-nied; -nying** : se mutiner

mutter ['mʌtər] *vi* : marmonner

mutton ['mʌtən] *n* : viande *f* de mouton

mutual ['mjuːtʃʊəl] *adj* **1** : mutuel **2** COMMON : commun — **mutually** ['mjuːtʃʊəli, -tʃəli] *adv* : mutuellement

muzzle ['mʌzəl] *n* **1** SNOUT : museau *m* **2** : muselière *f* (pour un chien, etc.) **3** : gueule *f* (d'une arme à feu) — **~** *vt* **-zled; -zling** : museler

my ['maɪ] *adj* : mon, ma, mes

myopia [maɪ'oːpiə] *n* : myopie *f* — **myopic** [maɪ'oːpɪk, -'ɑ-] *adj* : myope

myself [maɪ'sɛlf] *pron* **1** (*reflexive*) : me **2** (*emphatic*) : moi aussi **3 by ~** : tout seul

mystery ['mɪstəri] *n, pl* **-teries** : mystère *m* — **mysterious** [mɪ'stɪriəs] *adj* : mystérieux

mystic ['mɪstɪk] *adj or* **mystical** ['mɪstɪkəl] : mystique

mystify ['mɪstəˌfaɪ] *vt* **-fied; -fying** : rendre perplexe

myth ['mɪθ] *n* : mythe *m* — **mythical** ['mɪθɪkəl] *adj* : mythique

N

n ['ɛn] *n, pl* **n's** *or* **ns** ['ɛnz] : n *m*, quatorzième lettre de l'alphabet

nab ['næb] *vt* **nabbed; nabbing** : pincer *fam*

nag ['næg] *v* **nagged; nagging** *vi* COMPLAIN : se plaindre — *vt* : harceler — **nagging** ['næɡɪŋ] *adj* : persistant

nail ['neɪl] *n* **1** : clou *m* **2** FINGERNAIL : ongle *m* — **~** *vt or* **~ down** : clouer — **nail file** *n* : lime *f* à ongles — **nail polish** *n* : vernis *m* à ongles

naive *or* **naïve** [nɑ'iːv] *adj* **-iver; -est** : naïf — **naked** ['neɪkəd] *adj* : nu — **nakedness** ['neɪkədnəs] *n* : nudité *f*

name ['neɪm] *n* **1** : nom *m* **2** REPUTATION : réputation *f* **3 what is your ~ ?** : comment vous appelez-vous? — **~** *vt* **named; naming 1** : nommer **2** : fixer (une date, un prix, etc.) — **nameless** ['neɪmləs] *adj* : sans nom, anonyme — **namely** ['neɪmli] *adv* : c'est-à-dire, savoir — **namesake** ['neɪmˌseɪk] *n* : homonyme *m*

nap ['næp] *vi* **napped; napping** : faire un somme — **~** *n* : somme *m*, sieste *f*

nape ['neɪp, 'næp] *n* : nuque *f*

napkin ['næpkən] *n* **1** : serviette *f* **2** → **sanitary napkin**

narcotic [nɑr'kɑtɪk] *n* **1** : narcotique *m* (en pharmacie) **2** DRUG : stupéfiant *m*

narrate ['nærˌeɪt] *vt* **narrated; narrating** : raconter, narrer — **narration** [næ'reɪʃən] *n* : narration *f* — **narrative** ['nærətɪv] *n* : récit *m* — **narrator** ['nærˌeɪtər] *n* : narrateur *m*, -trice *f*

narrow ['nærˌoː] *adj* **1** : étroit **2 by a ~ margin** : de justesse — **~** *vt* : limiter, réduire — *vi* : se rétrécir — **narrowly** ['næroli] *adv* : de justesse, de peu — **narrow–minded** [ˌnæroˈmaɪndəd] *adj* : étroit d'esprit

nasal ['neɪzəl] *adj* : nasal

nasty ['næsti] *adj* **-tier; -est 1** MEAN : mauvais, méchant **2** UNPLEASANT : désagréable, sale **3** SERIOUS : grave — **nastiness** ['næstinəs] *n* : méchanceté *f*

nation ['neɪʃən] *n* : pays *m*, nation *f* — **national** ['næʃənəl] *adj* : national — **nationalism** ['næʃənəˌlɪzəm] *n* : nationalisme *m* — **nationality** [ˌnæʃə'næləti] *n, pl* **-ties** : nationalité *f* — **nationalize** ['næʃənəˌlaɪz] *vt* **-ized; -izing** : nationaliser — **nationwide** ['neɪʃənˌwaɪd] *adj* : dans tout le pays

native ['neɪtɪv] *adj* **1** : natal (se dit d'un pays, etc.) **2** INNATE : inné **3 ~ language**

: langue *f* maternelle — **~** *n* **1** : natif *m*, -tive *f* **2 be a ~ of** : être originaire de — **Native American** *adj* : amérindien *m* — **nativity** [nə'tɪvəti, neɪ-] *n*, *pl* **-ties** : nativité *f*

natural ['nætʃərəl] *adj* **1** : naturel **2** INBORN : né, inné — **naturalize** ['nætʃərə,laɪz] *vt* **-ized; -izing** : naturaliser — **naturally** ['nætʃərəli] *adv* **1** : naturellement **2** OF COURSE : bien sûr — **nature** ['neɪtʃər] *n* : nature *f*

naught ['nɔt] *n* **1** NOTHING : rien *m* **2** ZERO : zéro *m*

naughty ['nɔti] *adj* **-tier; -est** : méchant, vilain

nausea ['nɔziə, 'nɔʃə] *n* : nausée *f* — **nauseating** ['nɔzi,eɪtɪŋ] *adj* : écœurant, nauséabond — **nauseous** ['nɔʃəs, -ziəs] *adj* : écœuré

nautical ['nɔtɪkəl] *adj* : nautique

naval ['neɪvəl] *adj* : naval

nave ['neɪv] *n* : nef *f* (d'une église)

navel ['neɪvəl] *n* : nombril *m*

navigate ['nævə,geɪt] *v* **-gated; -gating** *vi* : naviguer — *vt* : naviguer sur (la mer, etc.), piloter (un avion), gouverner (un bateau) — **navigable** ['nævɪgəbəl] *adj* : navigable — **navigation** [,nævə'geɪʃən] *n* : navigation *f* — **navigator** ['nævə,geɪtər] *n* : navigateur *m*, -trice *f*

navy ['neɪvi] *n*, *pl* **-vies** : marine *f* — **navy blue** *adj* : bleu marine

near ['nɪr] *adv* **1** : près **2 nowhere ~ enough** : loin d'être suffisant — *prep* : près de — **~** *adj* : proche — **~** *vt* : approcher de — **nearby** [nɪr'baɪ, 'nɪr,baɪ] *adv* : tout près — **~** *adj* : voisin, proche — **nearly** ['nɪrli] *adv* : presque — **nearsighted** ['nɪr,saɪtəd] *adj* : myope

neat ['ni:t] *adj* **1** TIDY : soigné, net **2** ORDERLY : bien rangé (se dit d'une chambre, etc.) **3** SKILLFUL : habile — **neatly** ['ni:tli] *adv* **1** : soigneusement **2** SKILLFULLY : habilement — **neatness** ['ni:tnəs] *n* : ordre *m*, propreté *f*

nebulous ['nɛbjʊləs] *adj* : nébuleux

necessary ['nɛsə,sɛri] *adj* : nécessaire — **necessarily** [,nɛsə'sɛrəli] *adv* : nécessairement, forcément — **necessitate** [nɪ'sɛsə,teɪt] *vt* **-tated; -tating** : nécessiter, exiger — **necessity** [nɪ'sɛsəti] *n*, *pl* **-ties 1** : nécessité *f* **2 necessities** *npl* : choses *fpl* essentielles

neck ['nɛk] *n* **1** : cou *m* **2** COLLAR : col *m*, encolure *f* **3** : col *m*, goulot *m* (d'une bouteille) — **necklace** ['nɛkləs] *n* : collier *m* — **necktie** ['nɛk,taɪ] *n* : cravate *f*

nectar ['nɛktər] *n* : nectar *m*

nectarine [,nɛktə'ri:n] *n* : nectarine *f*

need ['ni:d] *n* **1** : besoin *m* **2 if ~ be** : si nécessaire, s'il le faut — **~** *vt* **1** : avoir besoin de **2 ~ to** : devoir — *v aux* **not ~ to** : ne pas être obligé de

needle ['ni:dəl] *n* : aiguille *f* — **~** *vt* **-dled; -dling** : agacer

needless ['ni:dləs] *adj* **1** : inutile **2 ~ to say** : il va sans dire

needlework ['ni:dəl,wərk] *n* : travaux *mpl* d'aiguille

needy ['ni:di] *adj* **needier; -est** : dans le besoin

negative ['nɛgətɪv] *adj* : négatif — **~** *n* **1** : négatif *m* (en photographie) **2** : négation *f* (en grammaire)

neglect [nɪ'glɛkt] *vt* : négliger — **~** *n* : négligence *f*

negligee [,nɛglə'ʒeɪ] *n* : négligé *m*

negligence ['nɛglɪdʒənts] *n* : négligence *f*

negligent ['nɛglɪdʒənt] *adj* : négligent

negligible ['nɛglɪdʒəbəl] *adj* : négligeable

negotiate [nɪ'go:ʃi,eɪt] *v* **-ated; -ating** : négocier — **negotiable** [nɪ'go:ʃəbəl, -ʃiə-] *adj* : négociable — **negotiation** [nɪ,goʃi'eɪʃən, -si'eɪ-] *n* : négociation *f* — **negotiator** [nɪ'go:ʃi,eɪtər, -si,eɪ-] *n* : négociateur *m*, -trice *f*

Negro ['ni:,gro:] *n*, *pl* **-groes** *sometimes considered offensive* : nègre *m*, négresse *f*

neigh ['neɪ] *vi* : hennir — **~** *n* : hennissement *m*

neighbor *or Brit* **neighbour** ['neɪbər] *n* : voisin *m*, -sine *f* — **~** *vt* : avoisiner — *vi* **~ on** : être voisin de — **neighborhood** *or Brit* **neighbourhood** ['neɪbər,hʊd] *n* **1** : quartier *m*, voisinage *m* **2 in the ~ of** : environ — **neighborly** *or Brit* **neighbourly** ['neɪbərli] *adj* : amical

neither ['ni:ðər, 'naɪ-] *conj* **1 ~ . . . nor** : ni . . . ni **2 ~ do I** : moi non plus — **~** *pron* : aucun — **~** *adj* : aucun (des deux)

neon ['ni:,ɑn] *n* : néon *m*

nephew ['nɛ,fju:, *chiefly Brit* 'nɛ,vju:] *n* : neveu *m*

Neptune ['nɛp,tu:n, -,tju:n] *n* : Neptune *f*

nerve ['nərv] *n* **1** : nerf *m* **2** COURAGE : courage *m* **3** GALL : culot *m fam*, toupet *m fam* **4 ~s** *npl* JITTERS : nerfs *mpl* — **nervous** ['nərvəs] *adj* : nerveux — **nervousness** ['nərvəsnəs] *n* : nervosité *f* — **nervy** ['nərvi] *adj* **nervier; -est** : effronté

nest ['nɛst] *n* : nid *m* — **~** *vi* : nicher

nestle ['nɛsəl] *vi* **-tled; -tling** : se blottir

net[1] ['nɛt] *n* : filet *m* — **~** *vt* **netted; netting** : prendre au filet (des poissons)

net[2] *adj* : net — **~** *vt* **netted; netting** YIELD : rapporter

nettle ['nɛtəl] *n* : ortie *f*

network ['nɛt,wərk] *n* : réseau *m*

neurology [nʊ'rɑlədʒi, nju-] *n* : neurologie *f*

neurosis [nʊ'ro:sɪs, nju-] *n*, *pl* **-roses** [-,si:z]

: névrose *f* — **neurotic** [nʊ'rɑṭɪk, njʊ-] *adj* : névrosé

neuter ['nuːṭər, 'njuː-] *adj* : neutre — ~ *vt* : châtrer

neutral ['nuːtrəl, 'njuː-] *adj* : neutre — ~ *n* : point *m* mort, neutre *m Can* — **neutralize** ['nuːtrə,laɪz, 'njuː-] *vt* -ized; -izing : neutraliser — **neutrality** [nuː'træləṭi, njuː-] *n* : neutralité *f*

neutron ['nuː,trɑn, 'njuː-] *n* : neutron *m*

never ['nɛvər] *adv* 1 : jamais 2 I ~ **said a word** : je n'ai rien dit — **nevermore** [,nɛvər'mor] *adv* : plus jamais, jamais plus — **nevertheless** [,nɛvərðə'lɛs] *adv* : néanmoins

new ['nuː, 'njuː] *adj* : neuf, nouveau — **newborn** ['nuː,bɔrn, 'njuː-] *adj* : nouveau-né — **newcomer** ['nuː,kʌmər, 'njuː-] *n* : nouveau venu *m*, nouvelle venue *f* — **newly** ['nuːli, 'njuː-] *adv* : récemment — **newlywed** ['nuːli,wɛd, 'njuː-] *n* : nouveau marié *m*, nouvelle mariée *f* — **news** ['nuːz, 'njuːz] *n* : nouvelles *fpl* — **newscast** ['nuːz,kæst, 'njuːz-] *n* : journal *m* télévisé — **newscaster** ['nuːz,kæstər, 'njuːz-] *n* : présentateur *m*, -trice *f* — **newsgroup** ['nuːz,gruːp, 'njuːz-] *n* : forum *m* (en informatique) — **newsletter** ['nuːz,lɛṭər, 'njuːz-] *n* : bulletin *m* — **newspaper** ['nuːz,peɪpər, 'njuːz-] *n* : journal *m* — **newsstand** ['nuːz,stænd, 'njuːz-] *n* : kiosque *m* à journaux

newt ['nuːt, 'njuːt] *n* : triton *m*

New Year's Day *n* : jour *m* de l'An

next ['nɛkst] *adj* 1 : prochain 2 FOLLOWING : suivant — ~ *adv* 1 : la prochaine fois 2 AFTERWARD : ensuite 3 NOW : maintenant — **next door** ['nɛkst'dor] *adv* : à côté — **next-door** *adj* : voisin, d'à côté — **next to** *prep* 1 BESIDE : à côté de 2 ~ **nothing** : presque rien

nib ['nɪb] *n* : bec *m* (d'un stylo)

nibble ['nɪbəl] *vt* -bled; -bling : grignoter

nice ['naɪs] *adj* **nicer; nicest** 1 PLEASANT : bon, agréable 2 KIND : gentil, aimable — **nicely** ['naɪsli] *adv* 1 WELL : bien 2 KINDLY : gentiment — **niceness** ['naɪsnəs] *n* : gentillesse *f* — **niceties** ['naɪsəṭiz] *npl* : subtilités *fpl*

niche ['nɪtʃ] *n* 1 : niche *f* 2 **find one's** ~ : trouver sa voie

nick ['nɪk] *n* 1 NOTCH : entaille *f*, encoche *f* 2 **in the** ~ **of time** : juste à temps — ~ *vt* : faire une entaille dans

nickel ['nɪkəl] *n* 1 : nickel *m* (métal) 2 : pièce *f* de cinq cents

nickname ['nɪk,neɪm] *n* : surnom *m* — ~ *vt* : surnommer

nicotine ['nɪkə,tiːn] *n* : nicotine *f*

niece ['niːs] *n* : nièce *f*

niggling ['nɪgəlɪŋ] *adj* 1 PETTY : insignifiant 2 NAGGING : persistant

night ['naɪt] *n* 1 : nuit *f*, soir *m* 2 **at** ~ : le soir 3 **tomorrow** ~ : demain soir — ~ *adj* : de nuit — **nightclub** ['naɪt,klʌb] *n* : boîte *f* de nuit — **nightfall** ['naɪt,fɔl] *n* : tombée *f* de la nuit — **nightgown** ['naɪt,gaʊn] *n* : chemise *f* de nuit, robe *f* de nuit *Can* — **nightingale** ['naɪtən,geɪl, 'naɪtɪŋ-] *n* : rossignol *m* — **nightly** ['naɪtli] *adv & adj* : (de) tous les soirs — **nightmare** ['naɪt,mær] *n* : cauchemar *m* — **nighttime** ['naɪt,taɪm] *n* : nuit *f*

nil ['nɪl] *n* NOTHING : zéro *m* — ~ *adj* : nul

nimble ['nɪmbəl] *adj* **-bler; -blest** : agile

nine ['naɪn] *n* : neuf *m* — ~ *adj* : neuf — **nine hundred** *adj* : neuf cents — **nineteen** [naɪn'tiːn] *n* : dix-neuf *m* — ~ *adj* : dix-neuf — **nineteenth** [naɪn'tiːnθ] *n* 1 : dix-neuvième *mf* 2 **January** ~ : le dix-neuf janvier — ~ *adj* : dix-neuvième — **ninetieth** ['naɪntiəθ] *n* : quatre-vingt-dixième *mf* — ~ *adj* : quatre-vingt-dixième — **ninety** ['naɪnti] *n, pl* **-ties** : quatre-vingt-dix *m* — **ninth** ['naɪnθ] *n* 1 : neuvième *mf* 2 **March** ~ : le neuf mars — ~ *adj* : neuvième

nip ['nɪp] *vt* **nipped; nipping** 1 BITE : mordre 2 PINCH : pincer — ~ *n* 1 BITE : morsure *f* 2 PINCH : pincement *m* 3 **there's a** ~ **in the air** : il fait frisquet — **nippy** ['nɪpi] *adj* **-pier; -est** : frisquet

nipple ['nɪpəl] *n* 1 : mamelon *m* (d'une femme) 2 : tétine *f* (d'un biberon)

nitrogen ['naɪtrədʒən] *n* : azote *m*

nitwit ['nɪt,wɪt] *n* : imbécile *mf*

no ['noː] *adv* 1 : non 2 ~ **better** : pas mieux 3 ~ **bigger** : pas plus grand 4 ~ **longer** : ne … plus — ~ *adj* 1 : pas de, aucun 2 ~ **parking** : stationnement interdit 3 ~ **smoking** : défense de fumer — ~ *n, pl* **noes** *or* **nos** ['noːz] : non *m*

noble ['noːbəl] *adj* **-bler; -blest** : noble — ~ *n* : noble *mf* — **nobility** [no'bɪləṭi] *n* : noblesse *f*

nobody ['noː,bɑdi, -,bɑdi] *pron* : personne

nocturnal [nɑk'tərnəl] *adj* : nocturne

nod ['nɑd] *v* **nodded; nodding** *vi* 1 : faire un signe de la tête 2 *or* ~ **off** : s'endormir — *vt* ~ **one's head** : faire un signe de la tête — ~ *n* : signe *m* de la tête

noise ['nɔɪz] *n* : bruit *m* — **noisily** ['nɔɪzəli] *adv* : bruyamment — **noisy** ['nɔɪzi] *adj* **noisier; -est** : bruyant

nomad ['noː,mæd] *n* : nomade *mf* — **nomadic** [no'mædɪk] *adj* : nomade

nominal ['nɑmənəl] *adj* : nominal

nominate ['nɑmə,neɪt] *vt* **-nated; -nating** 1 PROPOSE : proposer 2 APPOINT : nommer — **nomination** [,nɑmə'neɪʃən] *n* : nomination *f*

nonalcoholic [ˌnɑn͵ælkəˈhɔlɪk] *adj* : non al-coolisé

nonchalant [ˌnɑnʃəˈlɑnt] *adj* : nonchalant — **nonchalance** [ˌnɑnʃəˈlɑnts] *n* : nonchalance *f*

noncommissioned officer [ˌnɑnkə-ˈmɪʃənd] *n* : sous-officier *m*

noncommittal [ˌnɑnkəˈmɪtəl] *adj* : évasif

nondescript [ˌnɑndɪˈskrɪpt] *adj* : quel-conque

none [ˈnʌn] *pron* : aucun, aucune — ~ *adv* **1** ~ **too** : pas tellement **2** ~ **the worse** : pas plus mal

nonentity [ˌnɑnˈɛntəti] *n, pl* **-ties** : être *m* in-signifiant

nonetheless [ˌnʌnðəˈlɛs] *adv* : néanmoins

nonexistent [ˌnɑnɪgˈzɪstənt] *adj* : inexistant

nonfat [ˌnɑnˈfæt] *adj* : sans matière grasse

nonfiction [ˌnɑnˈfɪkʃən] *n* : œuvres *fpl* non romanesques

nonprofit [ˌnɑnˈprɑfət] *adj* : à but non lu-cratif

nonsense [ˈnɑn͵sɛnts, -sənts] *n* : absurdités *fpl*, sottises *fpl* — **nonsensical** [nɑn-ˈsɛntsɪkəl] *adj* : absurde

nonstop [ˌnɑnˈstɑp] *adj* **1** : sans arrêt **2** ~ **flight** : vol *m* direct

noodle [ˈnuːdəl] *n* : nouille *f*

nook [ˈnʊk] *n* : coin *m*, recoin *m*

noon [ˈnuːn] *n* : midi *m* — ~ *adj* : de midi

no one *pron* : personne *f*

noose [ˈnuːs] *n* : nœud *m* coulant

nor [ˈnɔr] *conj* **1** : ni **2** ~ **can I** : moi non plus

norm [ˈnɔrm] *n* : norme *f* — **normal** [ˈnɔrməl] *adj* : normal — **normality** [nɔr-ˈmæləti] *n* : normalité *f* — **normally** [ˈnɔrməli] *adv* : normalement

north [ˈnɔrθ] *adv* : au nord, vers le nord — ~ *adj* : nord, du nord — ~ *n* **1** : nord *m* **2 the North** : le Nord — **North American** *adj* : nord-américain — ~ *n* : Nord-Américain *m*, -caine *f* — **northeast** [nɔrθˈiːst] *adv* : au nord-est, vers le nord-est — ~ *adj* : nord-est, du nord-est — ~ *n* : nord-est *m* — **northeastern** [nɔrθˈiːstərn] *adj* : nord-est, du nord-est — **northerly** [ˈnɔrðərli] *adj* : du nord — **northern** [ˈnɔrðərn] *adj* : nord, du nord — **northwest** [nɔrθˈwɛst] *adv* : au nord-ouest, vers le nord-ouest — ~ *adj* : nord-ouest, du nord-ouest — ~ *n* : nord-ouest *m* — **northwestern** [nɔrθˈwɛstərn] *adj* : nord-ouest, du nord-ouest

Norwegian [nɔrˈwiːʤən] *adj* : norvégien

nose [ˈnoːz] *n* **1** : nez *m* **2 blow one's** ~ : se moucher — ~ *vi* **nosed; nosing** *or* ~ **around** : fouiner *fam* — **nosebleed** [ˈnoːz͵bliːd] *n* : saignement *m* de nez — **nosedive** [ˈnoːz͵daɪv] *n* : piqué *m*

nostalgia [nɑˈstælʤə, nə-] *n* : nostalgie *f* — **nostalgic** [-ʤɪk] *adj* : nostalgique

nostril [ˈnɑstrəl] *n* : narine *f* (d'une per-sonne), naseau *m* (d'un animal)

nosy *or* **nosey** [ˈnoːzi] *adj* **nosier; -est** : curieux, fureteur

not [ˈnɑt] *adv* **1** (*used to form a negative*) : ne...pas **2** (*used to replace a negative clause*) : non, pas **3** ~ **at all** : pas du tout **4 I hope** ~ : j'espère que non

notable [ˈnoːtəbəl] *adj* : notable — ~ *n* : notable *m* — **notably** [ˈnoːtəbli] *adv* : no-tamment

notary public [ˈnoːtəri] *n, pl* **notaries pub-lic** *or* **notary publics** : notaire *m*

notation [noˈteɪʃən] *n* : notation *f*

notch [ˈnɑtʃ] *n* : entaille *f*, encoche *f*

note [ˈnoːt] *vt* **noted; noting 1** NOTICE : re-marquer **2** *or* ~ **down** : noter — ~ *n* **1** : note *f* **2** LETTER : mot *m* **3 an artist of** ~ : un artiste de renom — **notebook** [ˈnoːt-͵bʊk] *n* : carnet *m* — **noted** [ˈnoːtəd] *adj* : éminent, célèbre — **noteworthy** [ˈnoːt-͵wərði] *adj* : notable, remarquable

nothing [ˈnʌθɪŋ] *pron* : rien — ~ *adv* ~ **like** : pas du tout comme — ~ *n* **1** TRIFLE : rien *m* **2** ZERO : zéro *m*

notice [ˈnoːtɪs] *n* **1** : avis *m*, annonce *f* **2 be given one's** ~ : recevoir son congé **3 take** ~ **of** : faire attention à — ~ *vt* **-ticed; -ticing** : s'apercevoir de, remarquer — **no-ticeable** [ˈnoːtɪsəbəl] *adj* : visible

notify [ˈnoːtə͵faɪ] *vt* **-fied; -fying** : aviser, no-tifier — **notification** [ˌnoːtəfəˈkeɪʃən] *n* : avis *m*

notion [ˈnoːʃən] *n* **1** : notion *f*, idée *f* **2** ~**s** *npl* : mercerie *f*

notorious [noˈtoːriəs] *adj* : notoire — **noto-riety** [ˌnoːtəˈraɪəti] *n, pl* **-ties** : notoriété *f*

notwithstanding [ˌnɑtwɪθˈstændɪŋ, -wɪð-] *adv* : néanmoins — ~ *prep* : malgré

nougat [ˈnuːgət] *n* : nougat *m*

nought [ˈnɔt, ˈnɑt] → **naught**

noun [ˈnaʊn] *n* : nom *m*, substantif *m*

nourish [ˈnərɪʃ] *vt* : nourrir — **nourishing** [ˈnərɪʃɪŋ] *adj* : nourrissant — **nourishment** [ˈnərɪʃmənt] *n* : nourriture *f*, alimentation *f*

novel [ˈnɑvəl] *adj* : nouveau, original — ~ *n* : roman *m* — **novelist** [ˈnɑvəlɪst] *n* : ro-mancier *m*, -cière *f* — **novelty** [ˈnɑvəlti] *n, pl* **-ties** : nouveauté *f*

November [noˈvɛmbər] *n* : novembre *m*

novice [ˈnɑvɪs] *n* : novice *mf*; débutant *m*, -tante *f*

now [ˈnaʊ] *adv* **1** : maintenant **2** ~ **and then** : de temps à autre — ~ *conj* ~ **that** : maintenant que — ~ *n* **1 by** ~ : déjà **2 for** ~ : pour le moment **3 up until** ~ : jusqu'à maintenant — **nowadays** [ˈnaʊə-͵deɪz] *adv* : de nos jours

nowhere [ˈnoːˌhwɛr] *adv* **1** : nulle part **2** ∼ **near** : loin de

noxious [ˈnɑkʃəs] *adj* : nocif

nozzle [ˈnɑzəl] *n* : ajutage *m*

nuance [ˈnuːˌɑnts, ˈnjuː-] *n* : nuance *f*

nucleus [ˈnuːkliəs, ˈnjuː-] *n, pl* **-clei** [-kliˌaɪ] : noyau *m* — **nuclear** [ˈnuːkliər, ˈnjuː-] *adj* : nucléaire

nude [ˈnuːd, ˈnjuːd] *adj* **nuder; nudest** : nu — ∼ *n* : nu *m*

nudge [ˈnʌʤ] *vt* **nudged; nudging** : donner un coup de coude à — ∼ *n* : coup *m* de coude

nudity [ˈnuːdəti, ˈnjuː-] *n* : nudité *f*

nugget [ˈnʌɡət] *n* : pépite *f*

nuisance [ˈnuːsənts, ˈnjuː-] *n* **1** ANNOYANCE : ennui *m* **2** PEST : peste *f*

null [ˈnʌl] *adj* ∼ **and void** : nul et non avenu

numb [ˈnʌm] *adj* **1** : engourdi **2** ∼ **with fear** : paralysé par la peur — ∼ *vt* : engourdir

number [ˈnʌmbər] *n* **1** : nombre *m*, numéro *m* **2** NUMERAL : chiffre *m* **3** **a** ∼ **of** : un certain nombre de — ∼ *vt* **1** : numéroter **2** INCLUDE : compter — **numeral** [ˈnuːmərəl, ˈnjuː-] *n* : chiffre *m* — **numerical** [nuˈmɛrɪkəl, nyu-] *adj* : numérique — **numerous** [ˈnuːmərəs, ˈnjuː-] *adj* : nombreux

nun [ˈnʌn] *n* : religieuse *f*

nuptial [ˈnʌpʃəl] *adj* : nuptial

nurse [ˈnərs] *n* : infirmier *m*, -mière *f* — ∼ *v* **nursed; nursing** *vt* **1** : soigner (un malade) **2** BREAST-FEED : allaiter — *vi* SUCKLE : téter — **nursery** [ˈnərsəri] *n, pl* **-eries 1** : crèche *f France*, garderie *f Can* **2** : pépinière *f* (pour les plantes) — **nursing home** *n* : maison *f* de retraite, centre *m* d'accueil *Can*

nurture [ˈnərtʃər] *vt* **-tured; -turing 1** : élever **2** : nourrir (des espoirs, etc.)

nut [ˈnʌt] *n* **1** : noix *f* **2** LUNATIC : fou *m*, folie *f* **3** ENTHUSIAST : mordu *m*, -due *f fam* **4** ∼**s and bolts** : des écrous et des boulons — **nutcracker** [ˈnʌtˌkrækər] *n* : casse-noix *m* — **nutmeg** [ˈnʌtˌmɛɡ] *n* : muscade *f*

nutrient [ˈnuːtriənt, ˈnjuː-] *n* : substance *f* nutritive — **nutrition** [nuˈtrɪʃən, njuː-] *n* : nutrition *f*, alimentation *f* — **nutritional** [nuˈtrɪʃənəl, njuː-] *adj* : nutritif — **nutritious** [nuˈtrɪʃəs, njuː-] *adj* : nourrissant, nutritif

nuts [ˈnʌts] *adj* : fou, cinglé *fam*

nutshell [ˈnʌtˌʃɛl] *n* **1** : coquille *f* de noix **2** **in a** ∼ : en un mot

nuzzle [ˈnʌzəl] *v* **-zled; -zling** *vt* : frotter son nez contre — *vi* : se blottir

nylon [ˈnaɪˌlɑn] *n* **1** : nylon *m* **2** ∼**s** *npl* : bas *mpl* de nylon

nymph [ˈnɪmpf] *n* : nymphe *f*

O

o [ˈoː] *n, pl* **o's** *or* **os** [ˈoːz] **1** : o *m*, quinzième lettre de l'alphabet **2** ZERO : zéro *m*

O [ˈoː] → **oh**

oak [ˈoːk] *n, pl* **oaks** *or* **oak** : chêne *m*

oar [ˈor] *n* : rame *f*, aviron *m*

oasis [oˈeɪsɪs] *n, pl* **oases** [-ˌsiːz] : oasis *f*

oath [ˈoːθ] *n, pl* **oaths** [ˈoːðz, ˈoːθs] **1** : serment *m* **2** SWEARWORD : juron *m*

oats [ˈoːts] *npl* : avoine *f* — **oatmeal** [ˈoːtˌmiːl] *n* : farine *f* d'avoine

obedient [oˈbiːdiənt] *adj* : obéissant — **obedience** [oˈbiːdiənts] *n* : obéissance *f* — **obediently** [oˈbiːdiəntli] *adv* : docilement

obese [oˈbiːs] *adj* : obèse — **obesity** [oˈbiːsəti] *n* : obésité *f*

obey [oˈbeɪ] *v* **obeyed; obeying** *vt* : obéir à — *vi* : obéir

obituary [əˈbɪtʃuˌɛri] *n, pl* **-aries** : nécrologie *f*

object [ˈɑbʤɪkt] *n* **1** : objet *m* **2** AIM : objectif *m*, but *m* **3** : complément *m* d'objet (en grammaire) — ∼ [əbˈʤɛkt] *vi* : protester, s'opposer — *vt* : objecter — **objection** [əbˈʤɛkʃən] *n* : objection *f* — **objectionable** [əbˈʤɛkʃənəbəl] *adj* : désagréable — **objective** [əbˈʤɛktɪv] *adj* : objectif — ∼ *n* : objectif *m*

oblige [əˈblaɪʤ] *vt* **obliged; obliging 1** : obliger **2** **be much** ∼**d** : être très reconnaissant **3** ∼ **s.o.** : rendre service à qqn — **obligation** [ˌɑbləˈɡeɪʃən] *n* : obligation *f* — **obligatory** [əˈblɪɡəˌtori] *adj* : obligatoire — **obliging** [əˈblaɪʤɪŋ] *adj* : obligeant, aimable

oblique [oˈbliːk] *adj* : oblique

obliterate [əˈblɪtəˌreɪt] *vt* **-ated; -ating** : effacer, détruire

oblivion [əˈblɪviən] *n* : oubli *m* — **oblivious** [əˈblɪviəs] *adj* : inconscient

oblong [ˈɑˌblɑŋ] *adj* : oblong

obnoxious [ɑbˈnɑkʃəs, əb-] *adj* : odieux

oboe [ˈoːˌboː] *n* : hautbois *m*

obscene [ab'siːn, əb-] *adj* : obscène — **obscenity** [ab'sɛnəṭi, əb-] *n, pl* **-ties** : obscénité *f*

obscure [ab'skjur, əb-] *vt* **-scured; -scuring 1** DARKEN : obscurcir **2** HIDE : cacher — *~ adj* : obscur — **obscurity** [ab'skjurəṭi, əb-] *n, pl* **-ties** : obscurité *f*

observe [əb'zərv] *vt* **-served; -serving** : observer — **observant** [əb'zərvənt] *adj* : observateur — **observation** [ˌabsər'veɪʃən, -zər-] *n* : observation *f* — **observatory** [əb'zərvəˌtori] *n, pl* **-ries** : observatoire *m* — **observer** [əb'zərvər] *n* : observateur *m*, -trice *f*

obsess [əb'sɛs] *vt* : obséder — **obsession** [ab'sɛʃən, əb-] *n* : obsession *f* — **obsessive** [ab'sɛsɪv, əb-] *adj* : obsessionnel, obsédant

obsolete [ˌabsə'liːt, 'absəˌ-] *adj* : obsolète, démodé

obstacle ['abstɪkəl] *n* : obstacle *m*

obstetrics [əb'stɛtrɪks] *ns & pl* : obstétrique *f*

obstinate ['abstənət] *adj* : obstiné

obstruct [əb'strʌkt] *vt* **1** BLOCK : obstruer **2** HINDER : entraver — **obstruction** [əb'strʌkʃən] *n* : obstruction *f*

obtain [əb'teɪn] *vt* : obtenir

obtrusive [əb'truːsɪv] *adj* : trop voyant (se dit des choses), importun (se dit des personnes)

obtuse [ab'tuːs, əb-, -'tjuːs] *adj* : obtus

obvious ['abviəs] *adj* : évident — **obviously** ['abviəsli] *adv* **1** CLEARLY : manifestement **2** OF COURSE : évidemment, bien sûr

occasion [ə'keɪʒən] *n* **1** : occasion *f* **2** EVENT : événement *m* — *~ vt* : occasionner, provoquer — **occasional** [ə'keɪʒənəl] *adj* : occasionnel — **occasionally** [ə'keɪʒənəli] *adv* : de temps en temps

occult [ə'kʌlt, 'aˌkʌlt] *adj* : occulte

occupy ['akjəˌpai] *vt* **-pied; -pying 1** : occuper **2** **~ oneself with** : s'occuper de — **occupancy** ['akjəpəntsi] *n, pl* **-cies** : occupation *f* — **occupant** ['akjəpənt] *n* : occupant *m*, -pante *f* — **occupation** [ˌakjə'peiʃən] *n* **1** : occupation *f* **2** JOB : profession *f*, métier *m* — **occupational** [ˌakjə'peiʃənəl] *adj* **1** : professionnel **2** **~ hazard** : risque *m* du métier

occur [ə'kər] *vi* **occurred; occurring 1** HAPPEN : avoir lieu, se produire, arriver **2** APPEAR : se trouver **3** **~ to s.o.** : venir à l'esprit de qqn — **occurrence** [ə'kərənts] *n* **1** EVENT : événement *m* **2** INSTANCE : cas *m*, apparition *f*

ocean ['oːʃən] *n* : océan *m* — **oceanic** [ˌoːʃi-'ænɪk] *adj* : océanique

ocher *or* **ochre** ['oːkər] *n* : ocre *mf*

o'clock [ə'klak] *adv* **1 at six ~** : à six heures **2 it's ten ~** : il est dix heures

octagon ['aktəˌgan] *n* : octogone *m*

octave ['aktɪv] *n* : octave *f*

October [ak'toːbər] *n* : octobre *m*

octopus ['aktəˌpus, -pəs] *n, pl* **-puses** *or* **-pi** [-ˌpai] : pieuvre *f*

ocular ['akjələr] *adj* : oculaire — **oculist** ['akjəlist] *n* : oculiste *mf*

odd ['ad] *adj* **1** STRANGE : étrange, bizarre **2** : dépareillé (se dit d'une chaussette, etc.) **3** **~ jobs** : travaux *mpl* divers **4 ~ number** : nombre *m* impair **5 a hundred ~ dollars** : cent dollars et quelques — **oddity** ['adəṭi] *n, pl* **-ties** : étrangeté *f* — **oddly** ['adli] *adv* : étrangement — **odds** ['adz] *npl* **1** RATIO : cote *f* **2** CHANCES : chances *fpl* **3 at ~s** : en conflit — **odds and ends** *npl* : objets *mpl* divers

ode ['oːd] *n* : ode *f*

odious ['oːdiəs] *adj* : odieux

odor *or Brit* **odour** ['oːdər] *n* : odeur *f* — **odorless** *or Brit* **odourless** ['oːdərləs] *adj* : inodore

of [ʌv, əv] *prep* **1** : de **2 five minutes ~ ten** : dix heures moins cinq **3 made ~ wood** : en bois **4 the eighth ~ April** : le huit avril

off ['ɔf] *adv* **1 be ~** LEAVE : s'en aller **2 come ~** : se détacher **3 cut ~** : couper **4 day ~** : jour *m* de congé **5 far ~** : éloigné **6 ~ and on** : par périodes **7 take ~** REMOVE : enlever **8 ten miles ~** : à dix milles d'ici **9 three weeks ~** : en trois semaines — *~ prep* **1** : de **2 be ~ duty** : être libre **3 be ~ the point** : ne pas être la question **4 ~ center** : mal centré — *~ adj* **1** OUT : éteint, fermé **2** CANCELED : annulé **3 on the ~ chance** : au cas où

offend [ə'fɛnd] *vt* : offenser — **offender** [ə-'fɛndər] *n* : délinquant *m*, -quante *f*; coupable *mf* — **offense** *or* **offence** [ə'fɛnts, 'ɔˌfɛnts] *n* **1** INSULT : offense *f* **2** CRIME : délit *m* **3** : attaque *f* (aux sports) **4 take ~** : s'offenser — **offensive** [ə'fɛntsɪv, 'ɔˌfɛnt-] *adj* : offensif — *~ n* : offensive *f*

offer ['ɔfər] *vt* : offrir, présenter — *~ n* : proposition *f*, offre *f* — **offering** ['ɔfərɪŋ] *n* : offre *f*, offrande *f* (en religion)

offhand ['ɔf'hænd] *adv* : spontanément, au pied levé — *~ adj* : désinvolte

office ['ɔfəs] *n* **1** : bureau *m* **2** POSITION : fonction *f*, poste *m* — **officer** ['ɔfəsər] *n* **1** *or* **police ~** : policier *m*, agent *m* (de police) **2** OFFICIAL : fonctionnaire *mf* **3** : officier *m* (dans l'armée) — **official** [ə'fɪʃəl] *adj* : officiel — *~ n* : officiel *m*, -cielle *f*

offing ['ɔfɪŋ] *n* **in the ~** : en perspective, imminent

offset ['ɔfˌsɛt] *vt* **-set; -setting** : compenser

offshore ['ɔf'ʃor] *adv* : en mer — ~ *adj* : côtier, marin

offspring ['ɔf,sprɪŋ] *ns & pl* : progéniture *f*

often ['ɔfən, 'ɔftən] *adv* **1** : souvent, fréquemment **2 every so** ~ : de temps en temps

ogle ['o:gəl] *vt* **ogled; ogling** : lorgner

ogre ['o:gər] *n* : ogre *m*, ogresse *f*

oh ['o:] *interj* **1** : oh **2** ~ **really?** : vraiment?

oil ['ɔɪl] *n* **1** : huile *f* (d'olive, etc.) **2** PETRO-LEUM : pétrole *m* **3** *or* **heating** ~ : mazout *m* — ~ *vt* : huiler, lubrifier — **oilskin** ['ɔɪl-,skɪn] *n* : ciré *m* — **oily** ['ɔɪli] *adj* **oilier; -est** : huileux

ointment ['ɔɪntmənt] *n* : pommade *f*

OK *or* **okay** [,o:'keɪ] *adv* **1** WELL : bien **2** YES : oui — ~ *adj* **1** ALL RIGHT : bien **2 are you** ~? : ça va? — ~ *vt* **OK'd** *or* **okayed; OK'ing** *or* **okaying** : approuver — ~ *n* **1** APPROVAL : accord *m* **2 give the** ~ : donner le feu vert

okra ['o:krə, *south also* -kri] *n* : gombo *m*

old ['o:ld] *adj* **1** : vieux **2** FORMER : ancien **3 any** ~ : n'importe quel **4 be ten years** ~ : avoir dix ans **5** ~ **age** : vieillesse *f* **6** ~ **man** : vieux *m* **7** ~ **woman** : vieille *f* — ~ *n* **the** ~ : les vieux, les personnes âgées — **old–fashioned** ['o:ld'fæʃənd] *adj* : démodé

olive ['ɑlɪv, -ləv] *n* **1** : olive *f* (fruit) **2** *or* ~ **green** : vert *m* olive

Olympic [o'lɪmpɪk] *adj* : olympique — **Olympic Games** [o'lɪmpɪk] *or* **Olympics** [-pɪks] *npl* : jeux *mpl* Olympiques

omelet *or* **omelette** ['ɑmlət, 'ɑmə-] *n* : omelette *f*

omen ['o:mən] *n* : augure *m*, présage *m*

omit [o'mɪt] *vt* **omitted; omitting** : omettre — **omission** [o'mɪʃən] *n* : omission *f*

omnipotent [ɑm'nɪpətənt] *adj* : omnipotent

on ['ɑn, 'ɔn] *prep* **1** : sur **2** ~ **fire** : en feu **3** ~ **foot** : à pied **4** ~ **Friday** : vendredi **5** ~ **the plane** : dans l'avion **6** ~ **the right** : à droite — ~ *adv* **1 from that moment** ~ : à partir de ce moment-là **2 later** ~ : plus tard **3 put** ~ : mettre — ~ *adj* **1** : allumé (se dit d'une lumière), en marche (se dit d'un moteur), ouvert (se dit d'un robinet) **2 be** ~ : avoir lieu (se dit d'un événement)

once ['wʌnts] *adv* **1** : une fois **2** FORMERLY : autrefois — ~ *n* **1** : une seule fois **2 at** ~ SIMULTANEOUSLY : en même temps **3 at** ~ IMMEDIATELY : tout de suite — ~ *conj* : dès que, une fois que

oncoming ['ɑn,kʌmɪŋ, 'ɔn-] *adj* : qui approche

one ['wʌn] *n* **1** : un *m* (numéro) **2** ~ **o'clock** : une heure — ~ *adj* **1** : un, une **2**

ONLY : seul, unique **3** SAME : même — ~ *pron* **1** : un, une **2** ~ **another** : l'un l'autre **3** ~ **never knows** : on ne sait jamais **4 this** ~ : celui-ci, celle-ci **5 that** ~ : celui-là, celle-là **6 which** ~? : lequel?, laquelle? — **oneself** [,wən'self] *pron* **1** (*used reflexively*) : se **2** (*used for emphasis*) : soi-même **3** (*used after prepositions*) : soi **4 by** ~ : seul — **one–sided** ['wʌn'saɪdəd] *adj* **1** UNEQUAL : inégal **2** BIASED : partial — **one–way** ['wʌn'weɪ] *adj* **1** : à sens unique (se dit d'une route) **2** ~ **ticket** : aller *m* simple

ongoing ['ɑn,go:ɪŋ] *adj* : continu, en cours

onion ['ʌnjən] *n* : oignon *m*

online ['ɑn,laɪn, 'ɔn-] *adj or adv* : en ligne

only ['o:nli] *adj* : seul, unique — ~ *adv* **1** : seulement, ne...que **2 if** ~ : si, si seulement **3** ~ **too well** : trop bien — ~ *conj* BUT : mais

onset ['ɑn,set] *n* : début *m*

onslaught ['ɑn,slɔt, 'ɔn-] *n* : attaque *f*

onto ['ɑn,tu:, 'ɔn-] *prep* : sur

onus ['o:nəs] *n* : responsabilité *f*, charge *f*

onward ['ɑnwərd, 'ɔn-] *adv & adj* **1** : en avant **2 from today** ~ : à partir d'aujourd'hui

onyx ['ɑnɪks] *n* : onyx *m*

ooze ['u:z] *vi* **oozed; oozing** : suinter

opal ['o:pəl] *n* : opale *f*

opaque [o'peɪk] *adj* : opaque

open ['o:pən] *adj* **1** : ouvert **2** FRANK : franc, sincère **3** CLEAR : dégagé **4** PUBLIC : public **5** UNCOVERED : découvert — ~ *vt* **1** : ouvrir **2** START : commencer — *vi* **1** : s'ouvrir **2** BEGIN : commencer **3** ~ **onto** : donner sur — ~ *n* **1 in the** ~ OUTDOORS : au grand air, dehors **2 in the** ~ KNOWN : connu — **open–air** ['o:pən-'ær] *adj* : en plein air — **opener** ['o:pənər] *n or* **can** ~ : ouvre-boîtes — **opening** ['o:pənɪŋ] *n* **1** : ouverture *f* **2** START : début *m* **3** OPPORTUNITY : occasion *f* — ~ *adj* : premier, préliminaire — **openly** ['o:pənli] *adv* : ouvertement, franchement

opera ['ɑprə, 'ɑpərə] *n* : opéra *m*

operate ['ɑpə,reɪt] *v* **-ated; -ating** *vi* **1** FUNCTION : fonctionner, marcher **2** ~ **on s.o.** : opérer qqn — *vt* **1** : faire fonctionner (une machine) **2** MANAGE : diriger, gérer — **operation** [,ɑpə'reɪʃən] *n* **1** : opération *f* **2 in** ~ : en marche, en service — **operational** [,ɑpə'reɪʃənəl] *adj* : opérationnel — **operative** ['ɑpərətɪv, -,reɪ-] *adj* : en vigueur — **operator** ['ɑpə,reɪtər] *n* **1** : opérateur *m*, -trice *f* **2 or telephone** ~ : standardiste *mf*

opinion [ə'pɪnjən] *n* : opinion *f*, avis *m* — **opinionated** [ə'pɪnjə,neɪtəd] *adj* : opiniâtre

opium ['o:piəm] *n* : opium *m*

opossum [ə'pɑsəm] *n* : opossum *m*

opponent [ə'po:nənt] *n* : adversaire *mf*
opportunity [ˌapər'tu:nəṭi, -'tju:-] *n, pl* **-ties**
: occasion *f* — **opportune** [ˌapər'tu:n,
-'tju:n] *adj* : opportun — **opportunism**
[ˌapər'tu:ˌnizəm, -'tju:-] *n* : opportunisme
m — **opportunist** [ˌapər'tu:nist, -'tju:-] *n*
: opportuniste *mf* — **opportunistic**
[ˌapərtu:'nistik, -tju:-] *adj* : opportuniste
oppose [ə'po:z] *vt* **-posed; -posing** : s'opposer à — **opposed** [ə'po:zd] *adj* ~ **to**
: opposé à
opposite ['apəzət] *adj* **1** FACING : d'en face
2 CONTRARY : opposé, inverse — ~ *n*
: contraire *m* — ~ *adv* : en face — ~ *prep*
: en face de — **opposition** [ˌapə'zɪʃ ən] *n*
: opposition *f*
oppress [ə'prɛs] *vt* **1** PERSECUTE : opprimer
2 BURDEN : oppresser — **oppression** [ə-
'prɛʃ ən] *n* : oppression *f* — **oppressive**
[ə'prɛsɪv] *adj* : oppressif — **oppressor** [ə-
'prɛsər] *n* : oppresseur *m*
opt ['apt] *vi* : opter
optic ['aptɪk] *or* **optical** ['aptɪkəl] *adj* : optique — **optician** [ap'tɪʃ ən] *n* : opticien *m*,
-cienne *f*
optimism ['aptəˌmɪzəm] *n* : optimisme *m* —
optimist ['aptəmɪst] *n* : optimiste *mf* — **optimistic** [ˌaptə'mɪstɪk] *adj* : optimiste
optimum ['aptəməm] *adj* : optimum — ~
n, pl **-ma** ['aptəmə] : optimum *m*
option ['apʃ ən] *n* : option *f* — **optional**
['apʃ ənəl] *adj* : facultatif, optionnel
opulence ['apjələnts] *n* : opulence *f* — **opulent** [-lənt] *adj* : opulent
or ['ɔr] *conj* **1** (*indicating an alternative*)
: ou **2** (*following a negative*) : ni **3** ~ **else**
OTHERWISE : sinon
oracle ['ɔrəkəl] *n* : oracle *m*
oral ['ɔrəl] *adj* : oral
orange ['ɔrɪndʒ] *n* **1** : orange *f* (fruit) **2** : orange *m* (couleur)
orator ['ɔrəṭər] *n* : orateur *m*, -trice *f*
orbit ['ɔrbət] *n* : orbite *f* — ~ *vt* : graviter
autour de
orchard ['ɔrtʃ ərd] *n* : verger *m*
orchestra ['ɔrkəstrə] *n* : orchestre *m*
orchid ['ɔrkɪd] *n* : orchidée *f*
ordain [ɔr'deɪn] *vt* **1** DECREE : décréter **2**
: ordonner (en religion)
ordeal [ɔr'di:l, 'ɔrˌdi:l] *n* : épreuve *f*
order ['ɔrdər] *vt* **1** COMMAND : ordonner **2**
REQUEST : commander (un repas, etc.) **3**
ORGANIZE : organiser — ~ *n* **1** : ordre *m* **2**
COMMAND, REQUEST : commande *f* **3** in
good ~ : en bon état **4** in ~ to : afin de
5 out of ~ : en panne — **orderly** ['ɔrdərli]
adj **1** TIDY : en ordre, ordonné **2** DISCI-
PLINED : discipliné
ordinary ['ɔrdənˌɛri] *adj* **1** USUAL : normal,
habituel **2** AVERAGE : ordinaire, moyen —

ordinarily [ˌɔrdən'ɛrəli] *adv* : d'ordinaire,
d'habitude
ore ['ɔr] *n* : minerai *m*
oregano [ə'rɛgəˌno:] *n* : origan *m*
organ ['ɔrgən] *n* **1** : orgue *m* (instrument de
musique) **2** : organe *m* (du corps) — **organic** [ɔr'gænɪk] *adj* **1** : organique **2** NA-
TUREL : biologique — **organism** ['ɔrgə-
ˌnizəm] *n* : organisme *m* — **organist**
['ɔrgənɪst] *n* : organiste *mf* — **organize**
['ɔrgəˌnaɪz] *vt* **-nized; -nizing 1** : organiser
2 get organized : s'organiser — **organization** [ˌɔrgənə'zeɪʃ ən] *n* : organisation *f* —
organizer ['ɔrgəˌnaɪzər] *n* : organisateur *m*,
-trice *f*
orgasm ['ɔrˌgæzəm] *n* : orgasme *m*
orgy ['ɔrdʒi] *n, pl* **-gies** : orgie *f*
Orient ['oriˌɛnt] *n* the ~ : l'Orient *m* — **orient** *vt* : orienter — **oriental** [ˌori'ɛntəl] *adj*
: oriental, d'Orient — **orientation** [ˌoriən-
'teɪʃ ən] *n* : orientation *f*
orifice ['ɔrəfəs] *n* : orifice *m*
origin ['ɔrədʒən] *n* : origine *f* — **original** [ə-
'rɪdʒ ənəl] *adj* **1** : original **2** FIRST : premier
— ~ *n* : original *m* — **originality** [əˌrɪdʒ ə-
'næləṭi] *n* : originalité *f* — **originally**
[ə'rɪdʒ ənəli] *adv* : à l'origine — **originate** [ə-
'rɪdʒ əˌneɪt] *v* **-nated; -nating** *vt* : donner
naissance à — *vi* : provenir, prendre naissance
ornament ['ɔrnəmənt] *n* : ornement *m* — **ornamental** [ˌɔrnə'mɛntəl] *adj* : ornemental
— **ornate** [ɔr'neɪt] *adj* : orné
ornithology [ˌɔrnə'θalədʒi] *n, pl* **-gies** : ornithologie *f*
orphan ['ɔrfən] *n* : orphelin *m*, -line *f*
orthodox ['ɔrθəˌdaks] *adj* : orthodoxe — **orthodoxy** ['ɔrθəˌdaksi] *n, pl* **-doxies** : orthodoxie *f*
orthopedic [ˌɔrθə'pi:dɪk] *adj* : orthopédique
— **orthopedics** [ˌɔrθə'pi:dɪks] *ns & pl* : orthopédie *f*
oscillate ['asəˌleɪt] *vi* **-lated; -lating** : osciller — **oscillation** [ˌasə'leɪʃ ən] *n* : oscillation *f*
ostensible [a'stɛntsəbəl] *adj* : apparent —
ostentation [ˌastən'teɪʃ ən] *n* : ostentation *f*
osteopath ['astiəˌpæθ] *n* : ostéopathe *mf*
ostracism ['astrəˌsɪzəm] *n* : ostracisme *m* —
ostracize ['astrəˌsaɪz] *vt* **-cized; -cizing**
: mettre au ban de la société
ostrich ['astrɪtʃ, 'ɔs-] *n* : autruche *f*
other ['ʌðər] *adj* **1** : autre **2** every ~ **day**
: tous les deux jours **3** on the ~ **hand**
: d'autre part — ~ *pron* **1** : autre **2** the
~**s** : les autres **3** someone or ~
: quelqu'un — **other than** *prep* : autrement
que, à part — **otherwise** ['ʌðərˌwaɪz] *adv* **1**
: autrement **2** OR ELSE : sinon — ~ *adj*
: autre

otter ['ɑtər] *n* : loutre *f*

ought ['ɔt] *v aux* **1** : devoir **2 you ~ to have done it** : tu aurais dû le faire

ounce ['aunts] *n* : once *f*

our ['ɑr, 'aur] *adj* : notre, nos — **ours** ['aurz, 'ɑrz] *pron* **1** : le nôtre, la nôtre **2 a friend of ~** : un de nos amis **3 that's ~** : c'est à nous — **ourselves** [ɑr'sɛlvz, aur-] *pron* **1** (*used reflexively*) : nous **2** (*used for emphasis*) : nous-mêmes

oust ['aust] *vt* : évincer

out ['aut] *adv* **1** OUTSIDE : dehors **2 cry ~** : crier **3 eat ~** : aller au restaurant **4 go ~** : sortir **5 turn ~** : éteindre — **~ prep → out of — ~** *adj* **1** ABSENT : absent, sorti **2** RELEASED : sorti **3** UNFASHIONABLE : démodé **4** EXTINGUISHED : éteint **5 the sun is ~** : il fait soleil

outboard motor ['aut,bord] *n* : hors-bord *m*

outbreak ['aut,breɪk] *n* : éruption *f* (d'une maladie, etc.), déclenchement *m* (des hostilités, etc.)

outburst ['aut,bərst] *n* : explosion *f*, accès *m*

outcast ['aut,kæst] *n* : paria *m*

outcome ['aut,kʌm] *n* : résultat *m*

outcry ['aut,kraɪ] *n*, *pl* **-cries** : tollé *m*

outdated [,aut'deɪtəd] *adj* : démodé

outdo [,aut'du:] *vt* **-did** [-'dɪd]; **-done** [-'dʌn]; **-doing** [-'du:ɪŋ]; **-does** [-'dʌz] : surpasser

outdoor ['aut'dor] *adj* : en plein air, de plein air — **outdoors** ['aut'dorz] *adv* : dehors

outer ['autər] *adj* : extérieur — **outer space** *n* : espace *m* cosmique

outfit ['aut,fɪt] *n* **1** EQUIPMENT : équipement *m* **2** COSTUME : tenue *f* **3** GROUP : équipe *f* — **~** *vt* **-fitted**; **-fitting** : équiper

outgoing ['aut,goːɪŋ] *adj* **1** LEAVING : en partance (se dit d'un train, etc.), sortant (se dit d'une personne) **2** EXTROVERTED : ouvert **3 ~ mail** : courrier *m* à expédier

outgrow [,aut'groː] *vt* **-grew** [-'gruː]; **-grown** [-'groːn]; **-growing** : devenir trop grand pour

outing ['autɪŋ] *n* : excursion *f*, sortie *f*

outlandish [aut'lændɪʃ] *adj* : bizarre

outlast [,aut'læst] *vt* : durer plus longtemps que

outlaw ['aut,lɔ] *n* : hors-la-loi *m* — **~** *vt* : proscrire

outlay ['aut,leɪ] *n* : dépenses *fpl*

outlet ['aut,lɛt, -lət] *n* **1** EXIT : sortie *f*, issue *f* **2** MARKET : débouché *m* **3** RELEASE : exutoire *m* **4** *or* **electrical ~** : prise *f* de courant **5** *or* **retail ~** : point *m* de vente

outline ['aut,laɪn] *n* **1** CONTOUR : contour *m* **2** SKETCH : esquisse *f* — **~** *vt* **-lined**; **-lining 1** : souligner le contour de **2** SUMMARIZE : exposer dans ses grandes lignes

outlive [,aut'lɪv] *vt* **-lived**; **-living** : survivre à

outlook ['aut,luk] *n* : perspective *f*

outlying ['aut,laɪɪŋ] *adj* : écarté, périphérique

outmoded [,aut'moːdəd] *adj* : démodé

outnumber [,aut'nʌmbər] *vt* : surpasser en nombre

out of *prep* **1** OUTSIDE : en dehors de **2** FROM : de **3 four ~ five** : quatre sur cinq **4 made ~ plastic** : fait en plastique **5 ~ control** : hors de contrôle **6 ~ money** : sans argent **7 ~ spite** : par dépit — **out—of—date** [,autəv'deɪt] *adj* **1** OLD-FASHIONED : démodé **2** EXPIRED : périmé — **out—of—doors** [autəv'dorz] → **outdoors**

outpost ['aut,poːst] *n* : avant-poste *m*

output ['aut,put] *n* : rendement *m*, production *f*

outrage ['aut,reɪdʒ] *n* **1** AFFRONT : outrage *m*, affront *m* **2** ANGER : indignation *f* — **~** *vt* **-raged**; **-raging** : outrager — **outrageous** [,aut'reɪdʒəs] *adj* **1** DISGRACEFUL : scandaleux **2** EXCESSIVE : outrancier

outright ['aut,raɪt] *adv* **1** COMPLETELY : complètement **2** INSTANTLY : sur le coup **3** FRANKLY : carrément — **~** *adj* : total, absolu

outset ['aut,sɛt] *n* : début *m*, commencement *m*

outside [,aut'saɪd, 'aut,-] *n* : extérieur *m* — **~** *adj* : extérieur — **~** *adv* : à l'extérieur, dehors — **~** *prep or* **~ of** : en dehors de, à part — **outsider** [,aut'saɪdər] *n* : étranger *m*, -gère *f*

outskirts ['aut,skərts] *npl* : banlieue *f*, périphérie *f*

outspoken [,aut'spoːkən] *adj* : franc, direct

outstanding [,aut'stændɪŋ] *adj* **1** UNPAID : impayé **2** UNRESOLVED : en suspens **3** NOTABLE : exceptionnel

outstretched [,aut'strɛtʃt] *adj* : tendu

outstrip [,aut'strɪp] *vt* **-stripped**; **-stripping** : devancer

outward ['autwərd] *or* **outwards** [-wərdz] *adv* **1** : vers l'extérieur **2 ~ bound** : en partance — **~** *adj* : extérieur — **outwardly** ['autwərdli] *adv* : en apparence

outweigh [,aut'weɪ] *vt* : l'emporter sur

outwit [,aut'wɪt] *vt* **-witted**; **-witting** : se montrer plus malin que

oval ['oːvəl] *adj* : ovale — **~** *n* : ovale *m*

ovary ['oːvəri] *n*, *pl* **-ries** : ovaire *m*

ovation [oː'veɪʃən] *n* : ovation *f*

oven ['ʌvən] *n* : four *m*

over ['oːvər] *adv* **1** ABOVE : au-dessus **2** MORE : de trop **3** AGAIN : encore **4 all ~** : partout **5 ask ~** : inviter **6 four times ~** : quatre fois de suite **7 ~ here** : ici **8 ~ there** : là-bas **9 start ~** : recommencer

— ~ *prep* **1** ABOVE : au-dessus de, par-dessus **2** MORE THAN : plus de **3** ACROSS : de l'autre côté de **4** DURING : pendant, au cours de **5** CONCERNING : au sujet de — ~ *adj* : fini, terminé

overall [‚o:vər'ɔl] *adv* GENERALLY : en général — ~ *adj* : d'ensemble, total — **overalls** ['o:vər‚ɔlz] *npl* : salopette *f*

overbearing [‚o:vər'bærɪŋ] *adj* : impérieux, autoritaire

overboard ['o:vər‚bord] *adv* : par-dessus bord

overburden [‚o:vər'bərdən] *vt* : surcharger

overcast ['o:vər‚kæst] *adj* : couvert

overcharge [‚o:vər'ʧardʒ] *vt* **-charged; -charging** : faire payer trop cher à

overcoat ['o:vər‚ko:t] *n* : pardessus *m*

overcome [‚o:vər'kʌm] *vt* **-came** [-'keɪm]; **-come; -coming 1** CONQUER : vaincre, surmonter **2** OVERWHELM : accabler

overcook [‚o:vər'kʊk] *vt* : faire trop cuire

overcrowded [‚o:vər'kraʊdəd] *adj* : bondé

overdo [‚o:vər'du:] *vt* **-did** [-'dɪd]; **-done** [-'dʌn]; **-doing; -does** [-'dʌz] **1** : exagérer **2** → **overcook**

overdose ['o:vər‚do:s] *n* : overdose *f*

overdraw [‚o:vər'drɔ:] *v* **-drew** [-'dru:]; **-drawn** [-'drɔn]; **-drawing** : mettre à découvert — **overdraft** ['o:vər‚dræft] *n* : découvert *m*

overdue [‚o:vər'du:] *adj* **1** UNPAID : arriéré **2** LATE : en retard

overestimate [‚o:vər'estə‚meɪt] *vt* **-mated; -mating** : surestimer

overflow [‚o:vər'flo:] *v* : déborder — ~ ['o:vər‚flo:] *n* : trop-plein *m*, débordement *m*

overgrown [‚o:vər'gro:n] *adj* : envahi par la végétation

overhand ['o:vər‚hænd] *adv* : par-dessus la tête

overhang [‚o:vər'hæŋ] *vt* **-hung** [-'hʌŋ]; **-hanging** : surplomber

overhaul [‚o:vər'hɔl] *vt* : réviser (un moteur, etc.), remanier (un système, etc.)

overhead [‚o:vər'hɛd] *adv* : au-dessus — ~ *adj* : aérien — ~ *n* : frais *mpl* généraux

overhear [‚o:vər'hɪr] *vt* **-heard** [-'hərd]; **-hearing** : entendre par hasard

overheat [‚o:vər'hi:t] *vt* : surchauffer

overjoyed [‚o:vər'ʤɔɪd] *adj* : ravi

overland ['o:vər‚lænd, -lənd] *adv & adj* : par voie de terre

overlap [‚o:vər'læp] *v* **-lapped; -lapping** *vt* : chevaucher — *vi* : se chevaucher

overload [‚o:vər'lo:d] *vt* : surcharger

overlook [‚o:vər'lʊk] *vt* **1** : donner sur (un jardin, la mer, etc.) **2** IGNORE : négliger, laisser passer

overly ['o:vərli] *adv* : trop

overnight [‚o:vər'naɪt] *adv* **1** : (pendant) la nuit **2** SUDDENLY : du jour au lendemain — ~ ['o:vər‚naɪt] *adj* **1** : de nuit, d'une nuit **2** SUDDEN : soudain

overpass ['o:vər‚pæs] *n* : voie *f* surélevée *Can*, pont *m* autoroutier

overpopulated [‚o:vər'pɑpjə‚leɪtəd] *adj* : surpeuplé

overpower [‚o:vər'paʊər] *vt* **1** CONQUER : vaincre **2** OVERWHELM : accabler

overrate [‚o:vər'reɪt] *vt* **-rated; -rating** : surestimer

override [‚o:vər'raɪd] *vt* **-rode** [-'ro:d]; **-ridden** [-'rɪdən]; **-riding 1** : passer outre à **2** ANNUL : annuler — **overriding** [o:vər'raɪdɪŋ] *adj* : primordial

overrule [‚o:vər'ru:l] *vt* **-ruled; -ruling** : rejeter

overrun [‚o:vər'rʌn] *vt* **-ran** [-'ræn]; **-running 1** INVADE : envahir **2** EXCEED : dépasser

overseas [‚o:vər'si:z] *adv* : à l'étranger, outre-mer — ~ ['o:vər‚si:z] *adj* : à l'étranger, extérieur

oversee [‚o:vər'si:] *vt* **-saw** [-'sɔ]; **-seen** [-'si:n]; **-seeing** : surveiller

overshadow [‚o:vər'ʃæ‚do:] *vt* : éclipser

oversight ['o:vər‚saɪt] *n* : oubli *m*, omission *f*

oversleep [‚o:vər'sli:p] *vi* **-slept** [-'slɛpt]; **-sleeping** : se réveiller trop tard

overstep [‚o:vər'stɛp] *vt* **-stepped; -stepping** : outrepasser

overt [o'vərt, 'o:‚vərt] *adj* : manifeste

overtake [‚o:vər'teɪk] *vt* **-took** [-'tʊk]; **-taken** [-'teɪkən]; **-taking** : dépasser

overthrow [‚o:vər'θro:] *vt* **-threw** [-'θru:]; **-thrown** [-'θro:n]; **-throwing** : renverser

overtime ['o:vər‚taɪm] *n* **1** : heures *fpl* supplémentaires **2** : prolongations *fpl* (aux sports)

overtone ['o:vər‚to:n] *n* : nuance *f*, sous-entendu *m*

overture ['o:vər‚ʧʊr, -ʧər] *n* : ouverture *f* (en musique)

overturn [‚o:vər'tərn] *vt* : renverser — *vi* : se renverser

overweight [‚o:vər'weɪt] *adj* : trop gros, obèse

overwhelm [‚o:vər'ʰwɛlm] *vt* **1** : submerger, accabler **2** DEFEAT : écraser — **overwhelming** [‚oɪvər'ʰwɛlmɪŋ] *adj* : accablant, écrasant

overwork [‚o:vər'wərk] *vt* : surmener — ~ *n* : surmenage *m*

overwrought [‚o:vər'rɔt] *adj* : à bout de nerfs

owe ['o:] *vt* **owed; owing** : devoir — **owing to** *prep* : à cause de

owl ['aʊl] *n* : hibou *m*

own ['o:n] *adj* : propre — ~ *vt* : posséder

avoir — *vi* ~ **up** : avouer — ~ *pron* **1 my** (**your, his/her, our, their**) ~ : le mien, la mienne; le tien, la tienne; le vôtre, la vôtre; le sien, la sienne; le nôtre, la nôtre; le leur, la leur **2 on one's** ~ : tout seul **3 to each his** ~ : chacun son goût — **owner** [ˈoːnər]

n : propriétaire *mf* — **ownership** [ˈoːnər-ˌʃɪp] *n* : possession *f*
ox [ˈɑks] *n, pl* **oxen** [ˈɑksən] : bœuf *m*
oxygen [ˈɑksɪʤən] *n* : oxygène *m*
oyster [ˈɔɪstər] *n* : huître *f*
ozone [ˈoːˌzoːn] *n* : ozone *m*

P

p [ˈpiː] *n, pl* **p's** *or* **ps** [ˈpiːz] : p *m*, seizième lettre de l'alphabet
pace [ˈpeɪs] *n* **1** STEP : pas *m* **2** SPEED : allure *f* **3 keep** ~ **with** : suivre — ~ *v* **paced; pacing** *vt* : arpenter — *vi* ~ **to and fro** : faire les cent pas
pacify [ˈpæsəˌfaɪ] *vt* **-fied; -fying** : pacifier, apaiser — **pacifier** [ˈpæsəˌfaɪər] *n* : tétine *f*, sucette *f* — **pacifist** [ˈpæsəfɪst] *n* : pacifiste *mf*
pack [ˈpæk] *n* **1** PACKAGE : paquet *m* **2** BAG : sac *m* **3** GROUP : bande *f*, meute *f* (de chiens) **4** : jeu *m* (de cartes) — ~ *vt* **1** PACKAGE : emballer **2** FILL : remplir **3** : faire (ses bagages) — **package** [ˈpækɪʤ] *vt* **-aged; -aging** : empaqueter — ~ *n* : paquet *m*, colis *m* — **packet** [ˈpækət] *n* : paquet *m*
pact [ˈpækt] *n* : pacte *m*
pad [ˈpæd] *n* **1** CUSHION : coussin *m* **2** TABLET : bloc *m* (de papier) **3 ink** ~ : tampon *m* encreur **4 launching** ~ : rampe *m* de lancement **5** : protection *f* (aux sports) — ~ *vt* **padded; padding** : rembourrer — **padding** [ˈpædɪŋ] *n* STUFFING : rembourrage *m*
paddle [ˈpædəl] *n* **1** : pagaie *f*, aviron *m* Can **2** : raquette *f* (aux sports) — ~ *vt* **-dled; -dling** : pagayer
padlock [ˈpædˌlɑk] *n* : cadenas *m* — ~ *vt* : cadenasser
pagan [ˈpeɪgən] *n* : païen *m*, païenne *f* — ~ *adj* : païen
page[1] [ˈpeɪʤ] **paged; paging** *vt* : appeler
page[2] *n* : page *f* (d'un livre)
pageant [ˈpæʤənt] *n* : spectacle *m* — **pageantry** [ˈpæʤəntri] *n* : apparat *m*
paid → **pay**
pail [ˈpeɪl] *n* : seau *m*
pain [ˈpeɪn] *n* **1** : douleur *f* **2 take** ~**s** *npl* : se donner de la peine — ~ *vt* : peiner, faire souffrir — **painful** [ˈpeɪnfəl] *adj* : douloureux — **painkiller** [ˈpeɪnˌkɪlər] *n* : analgésique *m* — **painless** [ˈpeɪnləs] *adj*

: indolore, sans douleur — **painstaking** [ˈpeɪnˌsteɪkɪŋ] *adj* : soigneux, méticuleux
paint [ˈpeɪnt] *v* : peindre, peinturer Can — ~ *n* : peinture *f* — **paintbrush** [ˈpeɪnt-ˌbrʌʃ] *n* : pinceau *m* (d'un artiste), brosse *f* — **painter** [ˈpeɪntər] *n* : peintre *m* — **painting** [ˈpeɪntɪŋ] *n* : peinture *f*
pair [ˈpær] *n* **1** : paire *f* **2** COUPLE : couple *m* — ~ *vi* : accoupler
pajamas *or Brit* **pyjamas** [pəˈʤɑməz, -ˈʤæ-] *npl* : pyjama *m*
pal [ˈpæl] *n* : copain *m*, -pine *f*
palace [ˈpæləs] *n* : palais *m*
palate [ˈpælət] *n* : palais *m* — **palatable** [ˈpælətəbəl] *adj* : savoureux
pale [ˈpeɪl] *adj* **paler; palest** : pâle — ~ *vi* **paled; paling** : pâlir — **paleness** [ˈpeɪlnəs] *n* : pâleur *f*
palette [ˈpælət] *n* : palette *f*
pallid [ˈpæləd] *adj* : pâle
palm[1] [ˈpɑm, ˈpɑlm] *n* : paume *f* (de la main)
palm[2] *or* ~ **tree** : palmier *m* — **Palm Sunday** *n* : dimanche *m* des Rameaux
palpitate [ˈpælpəˌteɪt] *vi* **-tated; -tating** : palpiter — **palpitation** [ˌpælpəˈteɪʃən] *n* : palpitation *f*
paltry [ˈpoltri] *adj* **-trier; -est** : dérisoire
pamper [ˈpæmpər] *vt* : dorloter
pamphlet [ˈpæmpflət] *n* : dépliant *m*, brochure *f*
pan [ˈpæn] *n* **1** SAUCEPAN : casserole *f* **2** FRYING PAN : poêle *f*
pancake [ˈpænˌkeɪk] *n* : crêpe *f*
pancreas [ˈpæŋkriəs, ˈpæn-] *n* : pancréas *m*
panda [ˈpændə] *n* : panda *m*
pandemonium [ˌpændəˈmoːniəm] *n* : tumulte *m*
pander [ˈpændər] *vi* : flatter (bassement)
pane [ˈpeɪn] *n* : vitre *f*, carreau *m*
panel [ˈpænəl] *n* **1** : panneau *m* **2** COMMITTEE : comité *m* **3** *or* **control** ~ : tableau *m* (de bord) — **paneling** [ˈpænəlɪŋ] *n* : lambris *m*
pang [ˈpæŋ] *n* : tiraillement *m*

panic ['pænɪk] *n* : panique *f* — ～ *v* **-icked;**
-icking : paniquer

panorama [ˌpænə'ræmə, -'rɑ-] *n* : panorama
m — **panoramic** [ˌpænə'ræmɪk, -'rɑ-] *adj*
: panoramique

pansy ['pænzi] *n, pl* **-sies** : pensée *f*

pant ['pænt] *vi* : haleter

panther ['pænθər] *n* : panthère *f*

panties ['pæntiz] *npl* : (petite) culotte *f*, slip
m France

pantomime ['pæntəˌmaɪm] *n* : pantomime *f*

pantry ['pæntri] *n, pl* **-tries** : garde-manger
m

pants ['pænts] *npl* : pantalon *m*

panty hose ['pæntiˌhoːz] *npl* : collant *m*

papaya [pə'paɪə] *n* : papaye *f*

paper ['peɪpər] *n* **1** : papier *m* **2** DOCUMENT
: document *m* **3** NEWSPAPER : journal *m* **4**
: devoir *m* (scolaire) — ～ *vt* WALLPAPER
: tapisser — ～ *adj* : de papier, en papier —
paperback ['peɪpərˌbæk] *n* : livre *m* de
poche — **paper clip** *n* : trombone *m* — **pa-**
perwork ['peɪpərˌwərk] *n* : paperasserie *f*

par ['pɑr] *n* **1** EQUALITY : égalité *f* **2 on a**
～ **with** : de pair avec

parable ['pærəbəl] *n* : parabole *f*

parachute ['pærəˌʃuːt] *n* : parachute *m*

parade [pə'reɪd] *n* **1** : défilé *m*, parade *f*
(militaire) **2** DISPLAY : étalage *m* — ～ *v*
-raded; -rading *vi* MARCH : défiler — *vt*
DISPLAY : faire étalage de

paradise ['pærəˌdaɪs, -ˌdaɪz] *n* : paradis *m*

paradox ['pærəˌdɑks] *n* : paradoxe *m* —
paradoxical [ˌpærə'dɑksɪkəl] *adj* : paradoxal

paragraph ['pærəˌgræf] *n* : paragraphe *m*

parakeet ['pærəˌkiːt] *n* : perruche *f*

parallel ['pærəˌlɛl, -ləl] *adj* : parallèle — ～
n **1** : parallèle *f* (en géometrie) **2** SIMILAR-
ITY : parallèle *m* — ～ *vt* MATCH : égaler

paralysis [pə'ræləsɪs] *n, pl* **-yses** [-ˌsiːz]
: paralysie *f* — **paralyze** *or Brit* **paralyse**
['pærəˌlaɪz] *vt* **-lyzed** *or Brit* **-lysed; -lyzing**
or Brit **-lysing** : paralyser

parameter [pə'ræmətər] *n* : paramètre *m*

paramount ['pærəˌmaʊnt] *adj* : suprême

paranoia [ˌpærə'nɔɪə] *n* : paranoïa *f* — **para-**
noid ['pærəˌnɔɪd] *adj* : paranoïaque

parapet ['pærəpət, -ˌpɛt] *n* : parapet *m*

paraphernalia [ˌpærəfə'neɪljə, -fər-] *ns & pl*
: attirail *m*

paraphrase ['pærəˌfreɪz] *n* : paraphrase *f* —
～ *vt* **-phrased; -phrasing** : paraphraser

paraplegic ['pærə'pliːdʒɪk] *n* : paraplégique
mf

parasite ['pærəˌsaɪt] *n* : parasite *m*

parasol ['pærəˌsɔl] *n* : parasol *m*

paratrooper ['pærəˌtruːpər] *n* : parachutiste
m (militaire)

parcel ['pɑrsəl] *n* : paquet *m*

parch ['pɑrtʃ] *vt* : dessécher

parchment ['pɑrtʃmənt] *n* : parchemin *m*

pardon ['pɑrdən] *n* **1** FORGIVENESS : pardon
m **2** : grâce *f* (en droit) — ～ *vt* **1** FORGIVE
: pardonner **2** ABSOLVE : gracier

parent ['pærənt] *n* **1** : mère *f*, père *m* **2** ～**s**
npl : parents *mpl* — **parental** [pə'rɛntəl] *adj*
: parental

parenthesis [pə'rɛnθəsəs] *n, pl* **-ses** [-ˌsiːz]
: parenthèse *f*

parish ['pærɪʃ] *n* : paroisse *f* — **parishioner**
[pə'rɪʃənər] *n* : paroissien *m*, -sienne *f*

Parisian [pə'rɪʒən, -'ri-] *adj* : parisien

parity ['pærəti] *n, pl* **-ties** : parité *f*

park ['pɑrk] *n* : parc *m* — ～ *vt* : garer — *vi*
: se garer, stationner

parka ['pɑrkə] *n* : parka *m*

parliament ['pɑrləmənt] *n* : parlement *m* —
parliamentary [ˌpɑrlə'mɛntəri] *adj* : parlementaire

parlor *or Brit* **parlour** ['pɑrlər] *n* : salon *m*

parochial [pə'roːkiəl] *adj* **1** : paroissial **2**
PROVINCIAL : de clocher, provincial

parody ['pærədi] *n, pl* **-dies** : parodie *f* — ～
vt **-died; -dying** : parodier

parole [pə'roːl] *n* : liberté *f* conditionnelle

parquet ['pɑrˌkeɪ, pɑr'keɪ] *n* : parquet *m*

parrot ['pærət] *n* : perroquet *m*

parry ['pæri] *vt* **-ried; -rying 1** : parer (un
coup) **2** EVADE : éluder (une question)

parsley ['pɑrsli] *n* : persil *m*

parsnip ['pɑrsnɪp] *n* : panais *m*

part ['pɑrt] *n* **1** : partie *f* **2** PIECE : pièce *f* **3**
ROLE : rôle *m* **4** SHARE : part *f* **5** SIDE : parti
m **6** : raie *f* (entre les cheveux) — ～ *vi* **1**
or ～ **company** : se séparer **2** ～ **with** : se
défaire de — *vt* SEPARATE : séparer

partake [pɑr'teɪk, pər-] *vi* **-took** [-'tʊk];
-taken [-'teɪkən]; **-taking** ～ **in** : participer
à

partial ['pɑrʃəl] *adj* **1** INCOMPLETE : partiel
2 BIASED : partial

participate [pər'tɪsəˌpeɪt, pɑr-] *vi* **-pated;**
-pating : participer — **participant** [pər-
'tɪsəpənt, pɑr-] *n* : participant *m*, -pante *f*

participle ['pɑrtəˌsɪpəl] *n* : participe *m*

particle ['pɑrtɪkəl] *n* : particule *f*

particular [pər'tɪkjələr] *adj* **1** : particulier **2**
FUSSY : exigeant — ～ *n* **1 in** ～ : en particulier **2** ～**s** *npl* DETAILS : détails *mpl* —
particularly [pər'tɪkjələrli] *adv* : particulièrement

partisan ['pɑrtəzən, -sən] *n* : partisan *m*,
-sane *f*

partition [pər'tɪʃən, pɑr-] *n* **1** DISTRIBUTION
: division *f* **2** DIVIDER : cloison *f* — ～ *vt* **1**
: diviser **2** : cloisonner (une pièce)

partly ['pɑrtli] *adv* : en partie

partner ['pɑrtnər] *n* **1** ASSOCIATE : associé
m, -ciée *f* **2** : partenaire *mf* (aux sports, en

danse) — **partnership** ['pɑrtnər‚ʃɪp] n : association f

party ['pɑrti] n, pl **-ties** **1** : parti m (politique) **2** PARTICIPANT : partie f **3** GATHERING : fête f **4** GROUP : groupe m

pass ['pæs] vi **1** MOVE : passer **2** **come to ~** : se passer, advenir **3** or **~ away** DIE : mourir **4 ~ out** FAINT : s'évanouir — vt **1** : passer **2** OVERTAKE : dépasser **3** : réussir (un examen) **4 ~ up** : laisser passer — **~** n **1** PERMIT : permis m, laissez-passer m **2** : passe f (aux sports) **3** or **mountain ~** : col m de montagne — **passable** ['pæsəbəl] adj ACCEPTABLE : passable — **passage** ['pæsɪʤ] n **1** : passage m **2** CORRIDOR : couloir m — **passageway** ['pæsɪʤ‚weɪ] n : passage m, couloir m

passenger ['pæsənʤər] n : passager m, -gère f

passerby [‚pæsər'baɪ, 'pæsər‚-] n, pl **passersby** : passant m, -sante f

passing ['pæsɪŋ] adj : passager

passion ['pæʃən] n : passion f — **passionate** ['pæʃənət] adj : passionné

passive ['pæsɪv] adj : passif

Passover ['pæs‚o:vər] n : Pâque f (juive)

passport ['pæs‚pɔrt] n : passeport m

password ['pæs‚wərd] n : mot de passe

past ['pæst] adj **1** : dernier, passé **2** FORMER : ancien — **~** prep **1** BEYOND : au-delà de **2** IN FRONT OF : devant **3** **half ~ one** : une heure et demie — **~** n : passé m — **~** adv : devant

pasta ['pɑstə, 'pæs-] n : pâtes fpl

paste ['peɪst] n **1** GLUE : colle f **2** DOUGH : pâte f — **~** vt **pasted; pasting** : coller

pastel [pæ'stɛl] n : pastel m — **~** adj : pastel

pasteurize ['pæstʃə‚raɪz, 'pæstjə-] vt **-ized; -izing** : pasteuriser

pastime ['pæs‚taɪm] n : passe-temps m

pastor ['pæstər] n : pasteur m

pastry ['peɪstri] n, pl **-tries** : pâtisserie f

pasture ['pæstʃər] n : pâturage m

pasty ['peɪsti] adj **-tier; -est** **1** DOUGHY : pâteux **2** PALLID : terreux

pat ['pæt] n **1** TAP : (petite) tape f **2** : noix f (de beurre, etc.) — **~** vt **patted; patting** : tapoter — **~** adv **have down ~** : connaître par cœur

patch ['pætʃ] n **1** : pièce f (d'étoffe) **2** : plaque f (de glace) — **~** vt **1** REPAIR : rapiécer **2 ~ up** : réparer — **patchy** ['pætʃi] adj **patchier; patchiest** : inégal, irrégulier

patent ['pætənt] adj **1** or **patented** [-təd] : breveté **2** ['pætənt, 'peɪt-] OBVIOUS : patent, évident — **~** ['pætənt] n : brevet m — **~** ['pætənt] vt : breveter

paternal [pə'tərnəl] adj : paternel — **paternity** [pə'tərnəti] n : paternité f

path ['pæθ, 'pɑθ] n **1** : allée f (dans un parc) **2** TRAIL : chemin m, sentier m **3** COURSE : trajectoire f

pathetic [pə'θɛtɪk] adj : pitoyable

pathology [pə'θɑləʤi] n, pl **-gies** : pathologie f

pathway ['pæθ‚weɪ] n : chemin m, sentier m

patience ['peɪʃənts] n : patience f — **patient** ['peɪʃənt] adj : patient — **~** n : patient m, -tiente f; malade mf — **patiently** ['peɪʃəntli] adv : patiemment

patio ['pæti‚o:, 'pɑt-] n, pl **-tios** : patio m

patriot ['peɪtriət, -‚ɑt] n : patriote mf — **patriotic** [‚peɪtri'ɑtɪk] adj : patriote

patrol [pə'tro:l] n : patrouille f — **~** vi **-trolled; -trolling** : patrouiller

patron ['peɪtrən] n **1** SPONSOR : mécène m **2** CUSTOMER : client m, cliente f — **patronage** ['peɪtrənɪʤ, 'pæ-] n **1** SPONSORSHIP : patronage m **2** CLIENTELE : clientèle f — **patronize** ['peɪtrə‚naɪz, 'pæ-] vt **-ized; -izing** **1** SUPPORT : patronner, parrainer **2** : traiter avec condescendance

patter ['pætər] n : crépitement m

pattern ['pætərn] n **1** MODEL : modèle m **2** DESIGN : dessin m, motif m **3** NORM : mode m, norme f — **~** vt : modeler

paunch ['pɒntʃ] n : bedaine f

pause ['pɒz] n : pause f — **~** vi **paused; pausing** : faire une pause

pave ['peɪv] vt **paved; paving** : paver — **pavement** ['peɪvmənt] n : chaussée f

pavilion [pə'vɪljən] n : pavillon m

paw ['pɒ] n : patte f — **~** vt : tripoter

pawn¹ ['pɒn] n : gage m

pawn² vt : mettre en gage — **pawnbroker** ['pɒn‚bro:kər] n : prêteur m, -teuse f sur gages — **pawnshop** ['pɒn‚ʃɑp] n : mont-de-piété m France

pay ['peɪ] v **paid** ['peɪd]; **paying** vt **1** : payer **2 ~ attention to** : prêter attention à **3 ~ back** : rembourser **4 ~ one's respects** : présenter ses respects **5 ~ s.o. a visit** : rendre visite à qqn — vi : payer — **~** n : paie f, salaire m — **payable** ['peɪebəl] adj : payable — **paycheck** ['peɪ‚tʃɛk] n : chèque m de paie — **payment** ['peɪmənt] n : paiement m

PC [‚pi:'si:] n, pl **PCs** or **PC's** COMPUTER : PC m, micro-ordinateur m

pea ['pi:] n : pois m

peace ['pi:s] n : paix f — **peaceful** ['pi:sfəl] adj : paisible

peach ['pi:tʃ] n : pêche f

peacock ['pi:‚kɑk] n : paon m

peak ['pi:k] n **1** SUMMIT : sommet m, pic m **2** APEX : apogée f — **~** adj : maximal — **~** vi : atteindre un sommet

perform

peanut ['piː,nʌt] *n* : cacahouète *f*
pear ['pær] *n* : poire *f*
pearl ['pərl] *n* : perle *f*
peasant ['pɛzənt] *n* : paysan *m*, -sanne *f*
peat ['piːt] *n* : tourbe *f*
pebble ['pɛbəl] *n* : caillou *m*
pecan [pɪ'kɑn, -'kæn, 'piː,kæn] *n* : noix *f* de pécan *France*, noix *f* de pacane *Can*
peck ['pɛk] *vt* : picorer — ~ *n* **1** : coup *m* de bec **2** KISS : bécot *m*
peculiar [pɪ'kjuːljər] *adj* **1** DISTINCTIVE : particulier **2** STRANGE : bizarre — **peculiarity** [pɪ,kjuːl'jærəti, -,kjuːli'ær-] *n*, *pl* **-ties 1** DISTINCTIVENESS : particularité *f* **2** STRANGENESS : bizarrerie *f*
pedal ['pɛdəl] *n* : pédale *f* — ~ *vt* **-aled** *or* **-alled; -aling** *or* **-alling** : pédaler
pedantic [pɪ'dæntɪk] *adj* : pédant
peddle ['pɛdəl] *vt* **-dled; -dling** : colporter — **peddler** ['pɛdlər] *n* : colporteur *m*, -teuse *f*
pedestal ['pɛdəstəl] *n* : piédestal *m*
pedestrian [pə'dɛstriən] *n* — ~ *adj* ~ **crossing** : passage *m* pour piétons
pediatrics [,piː,di'ætrɪks] *ns & pl* : pédiatrie *f* — **pediatrician** [,piː,diə'trɪʃən] *n* : pédiatre *mf*
pedigree ['pɛdə,griː] *n* : pedigree *m* (d'un animal)
peek ['piːk] *vi* GLANCE : jeter un coup d'œil — ~ *n* : coup *m* d'œil furtif
peel ['piːl] *vt* : peler (un fruit), éplucher (un oignon, etc.) — *vi* **1** : peler (se dit de la peau) **2** : s'écailler (se dit de la peinture) — ~ *n* : pelure *f* (de pomme), écorce *f* (d'orange), épluchure *f* (de pomme de terre)
peep[1] ['piːp] *vi* : pépier (se dit d'un oiseau) — ~ *n* : pépiement *m* (d'un oiseau)
peep[2] *vi* PEEK : jeter un coup d'œil — ~ *n* GLANCE : coup *m* d'œil
peer[1] ['pɪr] *n* : pair *m*
peer[2] *vi* : regarder attentivement
peeve ['piːv] *vt* **peeved; peeving** : irriter — **peevish** ['piːvɪʃ] *adj* : grincheux
peg ['pɛg] *n* **1** HOOK : patère *f* **2** STAKE : piquet *m*
pelican ['pɛlɪkən] *n* : pélican *m*
pellet ['pɛlət] *n* **1** BALL : boulette *f* **2** SHOT : plomb *m*
pelt[1] ['pɛlt] *n* : peau *f* (d'un animal)
pelt[2] *vt* THROW : bombarder
pelvis ['pɛlvɪs] *n*, *pl* **-vises** [-vɪsəz] *or* **-ves** [-,viːz] : bassin *m*
pen[1] ['pɛn] *vt* **penned; penning** ENCLOSE : enfermer — ~ *n* : parc *m*, enclos *m*
pen[2] *n* : stylo *m*
penal ['piːnəl] *adj* : pénal — **penalize** ['piːnə,laɪz, 'pɛn-] *vt* **-ized; -izing** : pénaliser — **penalty** ['pɛnəlti] *n*, *pl* **-ties 1** : peine *f* (en droit) **2** : pénalité *f* (aux sports)
penance ['pɛnənts] *n* : pénitence *f*

pencil ['pɛntsəl] *n* : crayon *m*
pending ['pɛndɪŋ] *adj* **1** UNDECIDED : en instance **2** IMMINENT : imminent — ~ *prep* **1** DURING : pendant **2** AWAITING : en attendant
penetrate ['pɛnə,treɪt] *v* **-trated; -trating** : pénétrer — **penetration** [,pɛnə'treɪʃən] *n* : pénétration *f*
penguin ['pɛŋgwɪn, 'pɛn-] *n* : manchot *m*
penicillin [,pɛnə'sɪlən] *n* : pénicilline *f*
peninsula [pə'nɪntsələ, -'nɪntʃʊlə] *n* : péninsule *f*
penis ['piːnəs] *n*, *pl* **-nes** [-,niːz] *or* **-nises** : pénis *m*
penitentiary [,pɛnə'tɛntʃəri] *n*, *pl* **-ries** : pénitencier *m*, prison *f*
pen name *n* : nom *m* de plume
penny ['pɛni] *n*, *pl* **-nies** : centime *m*, cent *m*, sou *m* — **penniless** ['pɛnɪləs] *adj* : sans le sou
pension ['pɛntʃən] *n* : pension *f*, retraite *f*
pensive ['pɛntsɪv] *adj* : pensif
pentagon ['pɛntə,gɑn] *n* : pentagone *m*
people ['piːpəl] *ns & pl* **1** people *npl* : personnes *fpl*, gens *mfpl* **2** *pl* ~**s** : peuple *m* — ~ *vt* **-pled; -pling** : peupler
pep ['pɛp] *n* : entrain *m*
pepper ['pɛpər] *n* **1** : poivre *m* (condiment) **2** : poivron *m* (légume) — **peppermint** ['pɛpər,mɪnt] *n* : menthe *f* poivrée
per ['pər] *prep* **1** : par **2** ACCORDING TO : selon **3 ten miles** ~ **hour** : dix miles à l'heure
perceive [pər'siːv] *vt* **-ceived; -ceiving** : percevoir
percent [pər'sɛnt] *adv* : pour cent — **percentage** [pər'sɛntɪʤ] *n* : pourcentage *m*
perceptible [pər'sɛptəbəl] *adj* : perceptible
perception [pər'sɛpʃən] *n* : perception *f* — **perceptive** [pər'sɛptɪv] *adj* : perspicace
perch[1] ['pərtʃ] *n* : perchoir *m* — ~ *vi* : se percher
perch[2] *n* : perche *f* (poisson)
percolate ['pərkə,leɪt] *v* **-lated; -lating** *vi* SEEP : filtrer — *vt* : passer (du café) — **percolator** ['pərkə,leɪtər] *n* : cafetière *f* à pression
percussion [pər'kʌʃən] *n* : percussion *f*
perennial [pə'rɛniəl] *adj* **1** RECURRING : perpétuel **2** ~ **flowers** : fleurs *fpl* vivaces
perfect ['pərfɪkt] *adj* : parfait — ~ [pər'fɛkt] *vt* : perfectionner — **perfection** [pər'fɛkʃən] *n* : perfection *f* — **perfectionist** [pər'fɛkʃənɪst] *n* : perfectionniste *mf*
perforate ['pərfə,reɪt] *vt* **-rated; -rating** : perforer
perform [pər'fɔrm] *vt* **1** CARRY OUT : exécuter, faire **2** PRESENT : jouer — *vi* **1** ACT : jouer **2** FUNCTION : fonctionner — **performance** [pər'fɔr,mənts] *n* **1** EXECUTION

: exécution *f* **2** : interprétation *f* (d'un acteur), performance *f* (d'un athlète) **3** PRESENTATION : représentation *f* — **performer** [pər'fɔrmər] *n* : interprète *mf*
perfume ['pər,fju:m, pər'-] *n* : parfum *m*
perhaps [pər'hæps] *adv* : peut-être
peril ['pɛrəl] *n* : péril *m* — **perilous** ['pɛrələs] *adj* : périlleux
perimeter [pə'rɪmətər] *n* : périmètre *m*
period ['pɪriəd] *n* **1** : point *m* (signe de ponctuation) **2** TIME : période *f* **3** ERA : époque *f* **4** *or* **menstrual** ~ : règles *fpl* — **periodic** [,pɪri'adɪk] *adj* : périodique — **periodical** [,pɪri'adɪkəl] *n* : périodique *m*
peripheral [pə'rɪfərəl] *adj* : périphérique
perish ['pɛrɪʃ] *vi* : périr — **perishable** ['pɛrɪʃəbəl] *adj* : périssable — **perishables** ['pɛrɪʃəbəlz] *npl* : denrées *fpl* périssables
perjury ['pərdʒəri] *n* : faux témoignage *m*
perk ['pərk] *vi* ~ **up** : se ragaillardir — ~ *n* : avantage *m* — **perky** ['pərki] *adj* **perkier; perkiest** : guilleret
permanence ['pərmənənts] *n* : permanence *f* — **permanent** ['pərmənənt] *adj* : permanent — ~ *n* : permanente *f*
permeate ['pərmi,eɪt] *vt* **-ated; -ating** : pénétrer
permission [pər'mɪʃən] *n* : permission *f* — **permissible** [pər'mɪsəbəl] *adj* : permis, admissible — **permissive** [pər'mɪsɪv] *adj* : permissif — **permit** [pər'mɪt] *v* **-mitted; -mitting** : permettre — ~ ['pər,mɪt, pər'-] *n* : permis *m*
peroxide [pə'rak,saɪd] *n* : peroxyde *m*
perpendicular [,pərpən'dɪkjələr] *adj* : perpendiculaire
perpetrate ['pərpə,treɪt] *vt* **-trated; -trating** : perpétrer — **perpetrator** ['pərpə,treɪtər] *n* : auteur *m* (d'un délit)
perpetual [pər'pɛtʃuəl] *adj* : perpétuel
perplex [pər'plɛks] *vt* : laisser perplexe — **perplexity** [pər'plɛksəti] *n, pl* **-ties** : perplexité *f*
persecute ['pərsɪ,kju:t] *vt* **-cuted; -cuting** : persécuter — **persecution** [,pərsɪ'kju:ʃən] *n* : persécution *f*
persevere [,pərsə'vɪr] *vi* **-vered; -vering** : persévérer — **perseverance** [,pərsə'vɪrənts] *n* : persévérance *f*
persist [pər'sɪst] *vi* : persister — **persistence** [pər'sɪstənts] *n* : persistance *f* — **persistent** [pər'sɪstənt] *adj* : persistant
person ['pərsən] *n* : personne *f* — **personal** ['pərsənəl] *adj* : personnel — **personality** [,pərsən'æləti] *n, pl* **-ties** : personnalité *f* — **personally** ['pərsənəli] *adv* : personnellement — **personnel** [,pərsə'nɛl] *n* : personnel *m*
perspective [pər'spɛktɪv] *n* : perspective *f*
perspiration [,pərspə'reɪʃən] *n* : trans-

piration *f* — **perspire** [pər'spaɪr] *vi* **-spired; -spiring** : transpirer
persuade [pər'sweɪd] *vt* **-suaded; -suading** : persuader — **persuasion** [pər'sweɪʒən] *n* **1** : persuasion *f* **2** BELIEF : conviction *f*
pertain [pər'teɪn] *vi* ~ **to** : avoir rapport à — **pertinent** ['pərtənənt] *adj* : pertinent
perturb [pər'tərb] *vt* : troubler
pervade [pər'veɪd] *vt* **-vaded; -vading** : se répandre dans — **pervasive** [pər'veɪsɪv, -zɪv] *adj* : envahissant
perverse [pər'vərs] *adj* **1** CORRUPT : pervers **2** STUBBORN : obstiné — **pervert** ['pər,vərt] *n* : pervers *m*, -verse *f*
pessimism ['pɛsə,mɪzəm] *n* : pessimisme *m* — **pessimist** ['pɛsəmɪst] *n* : pessimiste *mf* — **pessimistic** [,pɛsə'mɪstɪk] *adj* : pessimiste
pest ['pɛst] *n* **1** : plante *f* ou animal *m* nuisible **2** NUISANCE : peste *f*
pester ['pɛstər] *vt* **-tered; -tering** : importuner, harceler
pesticide ['pɛstə,saɪd] *n* : pesticide *m*
pet ['pɛt] *n* **1** : animal *m* domestique **2** FAVORITE : chouchou *m fam* — ~ *vt* **petted; petting** : caresser
petal ['pɛtəl] *n* : pétale *m*
petition [pə'tɪʃən] *n* : pétition *f* — ~ *vt* : adresser une pétition à
petrify ['pɛtrə,faɪ] *vt* **-fied; -fying** : pétrifier
petroleum [pə'tro:liəm] *n* : pétrole *m*
petty ['pɛti] *adj* **-tier; -est 1** INSIGNIFICANT : insignifiant **2** MEAN : mesquin
petulant ['pɛtʃələnt] *adj* : irritable
pew ['pju:] *n* : banc *m* d'église
pewter ['pju:tər] *n* : étain *m*
pharmacy ['farməsi] *n, pl* **-cies** : pharmacie *f* — **pharmacist** [,farməsɪst] *n* : pharmacien *m*, -cienne *f*
phase ['feɪz] *n* : phase *f* — ~ *vt* **phased; phasing 1** ~ **in** : introduire graduellement **2** ~ **out** : discontinuer progressivement
phenomenon [fɪ'namə,nan, -nən] *n, pl* **-na** [-nə] *or* **-nons** : phénomène *m* — **phenomenal** [fɪ'namənəl] *adj* : phénoménal
philanthropy [fə'lænθrəpi] *n, pl* **-pies** : philanthropie *f* — **philanthropist** [fə'lænθrəpɪst] *n* : philanthrope *mf*
philosophy [fə'lasəfi] *n, pl* **-phies** : philosophie *f* — **philosopher** [fə'lasəfər] *n* : philosophe *mf*
phlegm ['flɛm] *n* : mucosité *f*
phobia ['fo:biə] *n* : phobie *f*
phone ['fo:n] → **telephone**
phonetic [fə'nɛtɪk] *adj* : phonétique
phony *or* **phoney** ['fo:ni] *adj* **-nier; -est** : faux — ~ *n, pl* **-nies** : charlatan *m*
phosphorus ['fasfərəs] *n* : phosphore *m*
photo ['fo:to:] *n, pl* **-tos** : photo *f* — **photocopier** ['fo:to,kapiər] *n* : photocopieur *m*,

photocopieuse *f* — **photocopy** [ˈfoːtoˌkɑpi] *n, pl* **-pies** : photocopie *f* — ~ *vt* **-copied;** **-copying** : photocopier — **photograph** [ˈfoːtəˌgræf] *n* : photographie *f,* photo *f* — ~ *vt* : photographier — **photographer** [fəˈtɑgrəfər] *n* : photographe *mf* — **photographic** [ˌfoːtəˈgræfɪk] *adj* : photographique — **photography** [fəˈtɑgrəfi] *n* : photographie *f*

phrase [ˈfreɪz] *n* : expression *f* — ~ *vt* **phrased; phrasing** : formuler, exprimer

physical [ˈfɪzɪkəl] *adj* : physique — ~ *n* : examen *m* médical

physician [fəˈzɪʃən] *n* : médecin *mf*

physics [ˈfɪzɪks] *ns & pl* : physique *f* — **physicist** [ˈfɪzəsɪst] *n* : physicien *m,* -cienne *f*

physiology [ˌfɪziˈɑlədʒi] *n* : physiologie *f*

physique [fəˈziːk] *n* : physique *m*

piano [piˈænoː] *n, pl* **-anos** : piano *m* — **pianist** [piˈænɪst, ˈpiːənɪst] *n* : pianiste *mf*

pick [ˈpɪk] *vt* **1** CHOOSE : choisir **2** GATHER : cueillir **3** REMOVE : enlever **4** ~ **a fight** : chercher la bagarre — *vi* **1** CHOOSE : choisir **2** ~ **on** : harceler — ~ *n* **1** CHOICE : choix *m* **2** BEST : meilleur *m* **3** *or* **pickax** [ˈpɪkˌæks] : pic *m*

picket [ˈpɪkət] *n* **1** STAKE : piquet *m* **2** *or* ~ **line** : piquet *m* de grève — ~ *vi* : faire un piquet de grève

pickle [ˈpɪkəl] *n* **1** : cornichon *m* **2** JAM : pétrin *m fam* — ~ *vt* **-led; -ling** : conserver dans la saumure

pickpocket [ˈpɪkˌpɑkət] *n* : voleur *m,* -leuse *f* à la tire

pickup [ˈpɪkˌəp] *n or* ~ **truck** : camionnette *f* — **pick up** *vt* **1** LIFT : ramasser **2** LEARN : apprendre **3** RESUME : reprendre **4** TIDY : mettre en ordre **5** COLLECT : prendre — *vi* IMPROVE : s'améliorer

picnic [ˈpɪkˌnɪk] *n* : pique-nique *m* — ~ *vi* **-nicked; -nicking** : pique-niquer

picture [ˈpɪktʃər] *n* **1** PAINTING : tableau *m* **2** DRAWING : dessin *m* **3** PHOTO : photo *f,* photographie *f* **4** IMAGE : image *f* **5** MOVIE : film *m* — ~ *vt* **-tured; -turing 1** DEPICT : dépeindre **2** IMAGINE : s'imaginer — **picturesque** [ˌpɪktʃəˈrɛsk] *adj* : pittoresque

pie [ˈpaɪ] *n* **1** : tarte *f* (dessert) **2** : pâté *m,* tourte *f*

piece [ˈpiːs] *n* **1** : pièce *f* **2** FRAGMENT : morceau *m* — ~ *vt* **pieced; piecing** *or* ~ **together** : rassembler — **piecemeal** [ˈpiːsˌmiːl] *adv* : graduellement — ~ *adj* : fragmentaire

pier [ˈpɪr] *n* : jetée *f*

pierce [ˈpɪrs] *vt* **pierced; piercing** : percer — **piercing** [ˈpɪrsɪŋ] *adj* : perçant

piety [ˈpaɪəti] *n, pl* **-eties** : piété *f*

pig [ˈpɪg] *n* : porc *m,* cochon *m*

pigeon [ˈpɪdʒən] *n* : pigeon *m* — **pigeonhole** [ˈpɪdʒənˌhoːl] *n* : casier *m*

piggyback [ˈpɪgiˌbæk] *adv & adj* : sur le dos

pigment [ˈpɪgmənt] *n* : pigment *m*

pigpen [ˈpɪgˌpɛn] *n* : porcherie *f*

pigtail [ˈpɪgˌteɪl] *n* : natte *f*

pile[1] [ˈpaɪəl] *n* HEAP : pile *f,* tas *m* — ~ *v* **piled; piling** *vt* **1** STACK : empiler **2** LOAD : remplir — *vi or* ~ **up** : s'accumuler **2** CROWD : s'empiler

pile[2] *n* NAP : poil *m* (d'un tapis, etc.)

pilfer [ˈpɪlfər] *vt* : chaparder *fam*

pilgrim [ˈpɪlgrəm] *n* : pèlerin *m,* -rine *f* — **pilgrimage** [ˈpɪlgrəmɪdʒ] *n* : pèlerinage *m*

pill [ˈpɪl] *n* : pilule *f,* cachet *m*

pillage [ˈpɪlɪdʒ] *n* : pillage *m* — ~ *vt* **-laged; -laging** : piller

pillar [ˈpɪlər] *n* : pilier *m*

pillow [ˈpɪˌloː] *n* : oreiller *m* — **pillowcase** [ˈpɪloːˌkeɪs] *n* : taie *f* d'oreiller

pilot [ˈpaɪlət] *n* — ~ *vt* : piloter — **pilot light** *n* : veilleuse *f*

pimple [ˈpɪmpəl] *n* : bouton *m*

pin [ˈpɪn] *n* **1** : épingle *f* **2** BROOCH : broche *f* **3** *or* **bowling** ~ : quille *f* — ~ *vt* **pinned; pinning 1** FASTEN : épingler **2** *or* ~ **down** : fixer

pincers [ˈpɪntsərz] *npl* : tenailles *fpl*

pinch [ˈpɪntʃ] *vt* **1** : pincer **2** STEAL : piquer — *vi* : serrer — ~ *n* **1** SQUEEZE : pincement *m* **2** LITTLE : pincée *f* **3 in a** ~ : à la rigueur

pine[1] [ˈpaɪn] *n* : pin *m*

pine[2] *vi* **pined; pining 1** LANGUISH : languir **2** ~ **for** : désirer ardemment

pineapple [ˈpaɪnˌæpəl] *n* : ananas *m*

pink [ˈpɪŋk] *adj* : rose — ~ *n* : rose *m*

pinnacle [ˈpɪnɪkəl] *n* : pinacle *m*

pinpoint [ˈpɪnˌpɔɪnt] *vt* : préciser

pint [ˈpaɪnt] *n* : pinte *f*

pioneer [ˌpaɪəˈnɪr] *n* : pionnier *m,* -nière *f*

pious [ˈpaɪəs] *adj* : pieux

pipe [ˈpaɪp] *n* **1** : tuyau *m* **2** : pipe *f* (pour fumer du tabac) — **pipeline** [ˈpaɪpˌlaɪn] *n* : pipeline *m*

piquant [ˈpiːkənt, ˈpɪkwənt] *adj* : piquant

pirate [ˈpaɪrət] *n* : pirate *m*

pistachio [pəˈstæʃiˌoː, -ˈstɑ-] *n, pl* **-chios** : pistache *f*

pistol [ˈpɪstəl] *n* : pistolet *m*

piston [ˈpɪstən] *n* : piston *m*

pit [ˈpɪt] *n* **1** HOLE : trou *m,* fosse *f* **2** MINE : mine *f* **3** : creux *m* (de l'estomac) **4** : noyau *m* (d'un fruit) — ~ *vt* **pitted; pitting 1** MARK : marquer **2** : dénoyauter (un fruit) **3** ~ **against** : opposer à

pitch [ˈpɪtʃ] *vt* **1** : dresser (une tente, etc.) **2** THROW : lancer — *vi* LURCH : tanguer (se dit d'un navire, etc.) — ~ *n* **1** DEGREE, LEVEL : degré *m,* niveau *m* **2** TONE : ton *m* **3**

THROW : lancement *m* **4** *or* **sales** ~ : boniment *m* de vente — **pitcher** [ˈpɪtʃər] *n* **1** JUG : cruche *f* **2** : artilleur *m Can* (au baseball) — **pitchfork** [ˈpɪtʃˌfɔrk] *n* : fourche *f*

pitfall [ˈpɪtˌfɔl] *n* : piège *m*

pith [ˈpɪθ] *n* : moelle *f* — **pithy** [ˈpɪθi] *adj* **pithier; pithiest** : concis

pity [ˈpɪti] *n, pl* **pities 1** : pitié *f* **2 what a** ~**!** : quel dommage! — ~ *vt* **pitied; pitying** : avoir pitié de — **pitiful** [ˈpɪtɪfəl] *adj* : pitoyable — **pitiless** [ˈpɪtɪləs] *adj* : impitoyable

pivot [ˈpɪvət] *n* : pivot *m* — ~ *vi* : pivoter

pizza [ˈpiːtsə] *n* : pizza *f*

placard [ˈplækərd, -ˌkɑrd] *n* POSTER : affiche *f*

placate [ˈpleɪˌkeɪt, ˈplæ-] *vt* **-cated; -cating** : calmer

place [ˈpleɪs] *n* **1** : place *f* **2** LOCATION : endroit *m*, lieu *m* **3 in the first** ~ : tout d'abord **4 take** ~ : avoir lieu — ~ *vt* **placed; placing 1** PUT, SET : placer, mettre **2** RECOGNIZE : remettre **3** ~ **an order** : passer une commande — **placement** [ˈpleɪsmənt] *n* : placement *m*

placid [ˈplæsəd] *adj* : placide

plagiarism [ˈpleɪdʒəˌrɪzəm] *n* : plagiat *m* — **plagiarize** [ˈpleɪdʒəˌraɪz] *vt* **-rized; -rizing** : plagier

plague [ˈpleɪg] *n* **1** : peste *f* **2** CALAMITY : fléau *m*

plaid [ˈplæd] *n* : tissu *m* écossais — ~ *adj* : écossais

plain [ˈpleɪn] *adj* **1** SIMPLE : simple **2** CLEAR : clair, évident **3** FRANK : franc **4** HOMELY : ordinaire — ~ *n* : plaine *f* — **plainly** [ˈpleɪnli] *adv* **1** SIMPLY : simplement **2** CLEARLY : clairement **3** FRANKLY : franchement

plaintiff [ˈpleɪntɪf] *n* : demandeur *m*, -deresse *f*; plaignant *m*, -gnante *f*

plan [ˈplæn] *n* **1** DIAGRAM : plan *m* **2** IDEA : projet *m* — ~ *v* **planned; planning 1** INTEND : projeter **2** PREPARE : organiser — *vi* : faire des projets

plane¹ [ˈpleɪn] *n* **1** SURFACE : plan *m* **2** AIRPLANE : avion *m*

plane² *n or* **carpenter's** ~ : rabot *m*

planet [ˈplænət] *n* : planète *f*

plank [ˈplæŋk] *n* : planche *f*

planning [ˈplænɪŋ] *n* : organisation *f*, planification *f*

plant [ˈplænt] *vt* : planter — ~ *n* **1** : plante *f* **2** FACTORY : usine *f*

plaque [ˈplæk] *n* : plaque *f*

plaster [ˈplæstər] *n* : plâtre *m* — ~ *vt* **1** : plâtrer **2** COVER : couvrir

plastic [ˈplæstɪk] *adj* **1** : de plastique, en plastique **2** ~ **surgery** : chirurgie *f* esthétique — ~ *n* : plastique *m*

plate [ˈpleɪt] *n* **1** SHEET : plaque *f* **2** DISH : assiette *f* **3** ILLUSTRATION : planche *f* — ~ *vt* **plated; plating** : plaquer (avec un métal)

plateau [plæˈtoː] *n, pl* **-teaus** *or* **-teaux** [-ˈtoːz] : plateau *m*

platform [ˈplætˌfɔrm] *n* **1** STAGE : tribune *f*, estrade *f* **2** : quai *m* (d'une gare) **3** *or* **political** ~ : plate-forme *f* (électorale)

platinum [ˈplætənəm] *n* : platine *m*

platoon [pləˈtuːn] *n* : section *f* (dans l'armée)

platter [ˈplætər] *n* : plat *m*

plausible [ˈplɔzəbəl] *adj* : plausible

play [ˈpleɪ] *n* **1** : jeu *m* **2** DRAMA : pièce *f* de théâtre — ~ *vi* : jouer — *vt* **1** : jouer à (un jeu, un sport) **2** : jouer de (un instrument de musique) **3** PERFORM : jouer **4** ~ **down** : minimiser **5** ~ **up** EMPHASIZE : souligner — **player** [ˈpleɪər] *n* : joueur *m*, joueuse *f* — **playful** [ˈpleɪfəl] *adj* : enjoué — **playground** [ˈpleɪˌgraʊnd] *n* : cour *f* de récréation — **playing card** *n* : carte *f* à jouer — **playmate** [ˈpleɪˌmeɪt] *n* : camarade *mf* de jeu — **play-off** [ˈpleɪˌɔf] *n* : match *m* crucial — **playpen** [ˈpleɪˌpɛn] *n* : parc *m* (pour bébés) — **plaything** [ˈpleɪˌθɪŋ] *n* : jouet *m* — **playwright** [ˈpleɪˌraɪt] *n* : dramaturge *mf*, auteur *m* dramatique

plea [ˈpliː] *n* **1** : défense *f* (en droit) **2** REQUEST : appel *m*, requête *f* — **plead** [ˈpliːd] *v* **pleaded** *or* **pled** [ˈplɛd]; **pleading** : plaider

pleasant [ˈplɛzənt] *adj* : agréable — **please** [ˈpliːz] *v* **pleased; pleasing** *vt* **1** GRATIFY : plaire à, faire plaisir à **2** SATISFY : contenter — *vi* : plaire, faire plaisir — ~ *adv* : s'il vous plaît — **pleasing** [ˈpliːzɪŋ] *adj* : agréable — **pleasure** [ˈplɛʒər] *n* : plaisir *m*

pleat [ˈpliːt] *n* : pli *m*

pledge [ˈplɛdʒ] *n* **1** SECURITY : gage *m* **2** PROMISE : promesse *f* — ~ *vt* **pledged; pledging 1** PAWN : mettre en gage **2** PROMISE : promettre

plenty [ˈplɛnti] *n* **1** ABUNDANCE : abondance *f* **2** ~ **of** : beaucoup de — **plentiful** [ˈplɛntɪfəl] *adj* : abondant

pliable [ˈplaɪəbəl] *adj* : flexible, malléable

pliers [ˈplaɪərz] *npl* : pinces *fpl*

plight [ˈplaɪt] *n* : situation *f* difficile

plod [ˈplɑd] *vi* **plodded; plodding 1** : marcher lourdement **2** LABOR : peiner

plot [ˈplɑt] *n* **1** LOT : lopin *m*, parcelle *f* (de terre) **2** STORY : intrigue *f* **3** CONSPIRACY : complot *m* — ~ *v* **plotted; plotting** *vt* **1** : faire un plan de — *vi* CONSPIRE : comploter

plow *or* **plough** [ˈplaʊ] *n* **1** : charrue *f* **2** → **snowplow** — ~ *vt* **1** : labourer (la terre) **2** : déneiger

ploy [ˈplɔɪ] *n* : stratagème *m*

pluck [ˈplʌk] *vt* **1** : cueillir (une fleur) **2** : plumer (un oiseau) **3** : pincer (une corde) **4 ~ one's eyebrows** : s'épiler les sourcils

plug [ˈplʌg] *n* **1** STOPPER : bouchon *m*, tampon *m* **2** : prise *f* (électrique) — **~** *vt* **plugged; plugging 1** BLOCK : boucher **2** ADVERTISE : faire de la publicité pour **3 ~ in** : brancher

plum [ˈplʌm] *n* : prune *f*, pruneau *m* Can

plumb [ˈplʌm] *adj* : vertical, droit — **plumber** [ˈplʌmər] *n* : plombier *m* — **plumbing** [ˈplʌmɪŋ] *n* **1** : plomberie *f* **2** PIPES : tuyauterie *f*

plummet [ˈplʌmət] *vi* : tomber

plump [ˈplʌmp] *adj* : grassouillet, dodu

plunder [ˈplʌndər] *vt* : piller — **~** *n* : pillage *m*

plunge [ˈplʌndʒ] *v* **plunged; plunging** *vt* : plonger — *vi* **1** DIVE : plonger **2** DROP : chuter — **~** *n* **1** DIVE : plongeon *m* **2** DROP : chute *f* — **plunger** [ˈplʌndʒər] *n* : ventouse *f*

plural [ˈplʊrəl] *adj* : pluriel — **~** *n* : pluriel *m*

plus [ˈplʌs] *adj* : positif — **~** *n* **1** *or* **~ sign** : plus *m* **2** ADVANTAGE : plus *m*, avantage *m* — **~** *prep* : plus — **~** *conj* AND : et

plush [ˈplʌʃ] *n* : peluche *f* — **~** *adj* : somptueux

Pluto [ˈpluːˌtoː] *n* : Pluton *f*

plutonium [pluːˈtoːniəm] *n* : plutonium *m*

ply [ˈplaɪ] *vt* **plied; plying 1** USE : manier (un outil) **2** PRACTICE : exercer

plywood [ˈplaɪˌwʊd] *n* : contre-plaqué *m*

pneumatic [nʊˈmætɪk, njʊ-] *adj* : pneumatique

pneumonia [nʊˈmoːnjə, njʊ-] *n* : pneumonie *f*

poach[1] [ˈpoːtʃ] *vt* : pocher (des œufs)

poach[2] *vt or* **~ game** : braconner le gibier — **poacher** [ˈpoːtʃər] *n* : braconnier *m*, -nière *f*

pocket [ˈpakət] *n* : poche *f* — **~** *vt* : empocher — **pocketbook** [ˈpakətˌbʊk] *n* PURSE : sac *m* à main, sacoche *f* Can — **pocketknife** [ˈpakətˌnaɪf] *n, pl* **-knives** : canif *m*

pod [ˈpad] *n* : cosse *f*

poem [ˈpoːəm] *n* : poème *m* — **poet** [ˈpoːət] *n* : poète *mf* — **poetic** [poˈɛtɪk] *or* **poetical** [-tɪkəl] *adj* : poétique — **poetry** [ˈpoːətri] *n* : poésie *f*

poignant [ˈpɔɪnjənt] *adj* : poignant

point [ˈpɔɪnt] *n* **1** : point *m* **2** PURPOSE : utilité *f*, but *m* **3** TIP : pointe *f* **4** FEATURE : qualité *f* **5 at one** : à un moment donné — **~** *vt* **1** AIM : braquer **2** *or* **~ out** INDICATE : indiquer — **point–blank** [ˈpɔɪntˈblæŋk] *adv* : à bout portant — **pointer**

[ˈpɔɪntər**]** *n* **1** ROD : baguette *f* **2** TIP : conseil *m* — **pointless** [ˈpɔɪntləs] *adj* : inutile — **point of view** *n* : point *m* de vue

poise [ˈpɔɪz] *n* **1** EQUILIBRIUM : équilibre *m* **2** COMPOSURE : assurance *f*

poison [ˈpɔɪzən] *n* : poison *m* — **~** *vt* : empoisonner — **poisonous** [ˈpɔɪzənəs] *adj* : vénéneux (se dit d'une plante), vénimeux (se dit d'un animal), toxique (se dit d'une substance)

poke [ˈpoːk] *v* **poked; poking** *vt* **1** JAB : pousser **2** THRUST : fourrer *fam* — **~** *n* JAB : coup *m*

poker[1] [ˈpoːkər] *n* : tisonnier *m* (pour le feu)

poker[2] *n* : poker *m* (jeu de cartes)

polar [ˈpoːlər] *adj* : polaire — **polar bear** *n* : ours *m* polaire, ours *m* blanc — **polarize** [ˈpoːləˌraɪz] *vt* **-ized; -izing** : polariser

pole[1] [ˈpoːl] *n* ROD : perche *f*

pole[2] *n* : pôle *m* (en géographie)

police [pəˈliːs] *vt* **-liced; -licing** : surveiller — **~** *ns & pl* **the ~** : la police — **policeman** [pəˈliːsmən] *n, pl* **-men** [-mən, -ˌmɛn] : policier *m* — **police officer** *n* : agent *m* de police — **policewoman** [pəˈliːsˌwʊmən] *n, pl* **-women** [-ˌwɪmən] : femme *f* policier

policy [ˈpaləsi] *n, pl* **-cies 1** : politique *f* **2** *or* **insurance ~** : police *f* d'assurance

polio [ˈpoːliˌoː] *or* **poliomyelitis** [ˌpoːliˌoːˌmaɪəˈlaɪtəs] *n* : polio *f*, poliomyélite *f*

polish [ˈpalɪʃ] *vt* **1** : polir **2** : cirer (se dit des chaussures, etc) — **~** *n* **1** LUSTER : poli *m*, éclat *m* **2** WAX : cire *f* (pour les meubles, etc.), cirage *m* (pour les chaussures) **3** nail **~** : vernis *m* à ongles

polite [pəˈlaɪt] *adj* **-liter; -est** : poli — **politeness** [pəˈlaɪtnəs] *n* : politesse *f*

political [pəˈlɪtɪkəl] *adj* : politique — **politician** [ˌpaləˈtɪʃən] *n* : politicien *m*, -cienne *f* — **politics** [ˈpaləˌtɪks] *ns & pl* : politique *f*

polka [ˈpoːlkə, ˈpoːkə] *n* : polka *f* — **polka dot** *n* : pois *m*, picot *m* Can

poll [ˈpoːl] *n* **1** SURVEY : sondage *m* **2 ~s** *npl* : urnes *fpl* — **~** *vt* **1** : obtenir (des voix) **2** CANVASS : sonder

pollen [ˈpalən] *n* : pollen *m*

pollute [pəˈluːt] *vt* **-luted; -luting** : polluer — **pollution** [pəˈluːʃən] *n* : pollution *f*

polyester [ˈpaliˌɛstər, ˌpaliˈ-] *n* : polyester *m*

polymer [ˈpaləmər] *n* : polymère *m*

pomegranate [ˈpaməˌgrænət, ˈpamˌgræ-] *n* : grenade *f* (fruit)

pomp [ˈpamp] *n* : pompe *f* — **pompous** [ˈpampəs] *adj* : pompeux

pond [ˈpand] *n* : étang *m*, mare *f*

ponder [ˈpandər] *vt* : considérer — *vi* **~ over** : réfléchir à, méditer sur

pontoon [panˈtuːn] *n* : ponton *m*

pony [ˈpoːni] *n, pl* **-nies** : poney *m* — **ponytail** [ˈpoːniˌteɪl] *n* : queue *f* de cheval

poodle ['pu:dəl] *n* : caniche *m*

pool ['pu:l] *n* **1** PUDDLE : flaque *f* (d'eau), mare *f* (de sang) **2** RESERVE : fonds *m* commun **3** BILLIARDS : billard *m* américain **4** *or* **swimming ~** : piscine *f* — **~** *vt* : mettre en commun

poor ['pur, 'por] *adj* **1** : pauvre **2** INFERIOR : mauvais — **poorly** ['purli, 'por-] *adv* BADLY : mal

pop[1] ['pap] *v* **popped; popping** *vt* **1** BURST : faire éclater **2** PUT : mettre — *vi* **1** BURST : éclater, exploser **2** *or* **~ in** : faire une petite visite **3** *or* **~ out** : sortir **4 ~ up** APPEAR : surgir — **~** *n* **1** : bruit *m* sec **2** SODA : boisson *f* gazeuse — **~** *adj* : pop

pop[2] *n or* **~ music** : musique *f* pop

popcorn ['pap,korn] *n* : pop-corn *m*

pope ['po:p] *n* : pape *m*

poplar ['paplər] *n* : peuplier *m*

poppy ['papi] *n, pl* **-pies** : coquelicot *m*

popular ['papjələr] *adj* : populaire — **popularity** [,papjə'lærəṭi] *n* : popularité *f* — **popularize** ['papjələ,raɪz] *vt* **-ized; -izing** : populariser

populate ['papjə,leɪt] *vt* **-lated; -lating** : peupler — **population** [,papjə'leɪʃən] *n* : population *f*

porcelain ['porsələn] *n* : porcelaine *f*

porch ['portʃ] *n* : porche *m*

porcupine ['porkjə,paɪn] *n* : porc-épic *m*

pore[1] ['por] *vi* **pored; poring ~ over** : étudier de près

pore[2] *n* : pore *m*

pork ['pork] *n* : porc *m*

pornography [por'nagrəfi] *n* : pornographie *f* — **pornographic** [,pornə'græfɪk] *adj* : pornographique

porous ['porəs] *adj* : poreux

porpoise ['porpəs] *n* : marsouin *m*

porridge ['porɪdʒ] *n* : porridge *m France*, gruau *m Can*

port[1] ['port] *n* HARBOR : port *m*

port[2] *n or* **~ side** : bâbord *m*

port[3] *n or* **~ wine** : porto *m*

portable ['portəbəl] *adj* : portatif

porter ['portər] *n* : porteur *m*, -teuse *f*

portfolio [port'fo:li,o] *n, pl* **-lios** : portefeuille *m*

porthole ['port,ho:l] *n* : hublot *m*

portion ['porʃən] *n* : portion *f*

portrait ['portrət, -,treɪt] *n* : portrait *m*

portray ['por'treɪ] *vt* DEPICT : représenter

Portuguese [,portʃə'gi:z, -'gi:s] *adj* : portugais — **~** *n* : portugais *m* (langue)

pose ['po:z] *v* **posed; posing** *vt* : poser — *vi* **1** : poser **2 ~ as** : se faire passer pour — **~** *n* : pose *f*

posh ['paʃ] *adj* : chic

position [pə'zɪʃən] *n* **1** : position *f* **2** JOB : poste *m* — **~** *vt* **1** PLACE : placer **2** ORIENT : positionner

positive ['pazəṭɪv] *adj* **1** : positif **2** SURE : sûr, certain

possess [pə'zɛs] *vt* : posséder — **possession** [pə'zɛʃən] *n* **1** : possession *f* **2 ~s** *npl* BELONGINGS : biens *mpl* — **possessive** [pə'zɛsɪv] *adj* : possessif

possible ['pasəbəl] *adj* : possible — **possibility** [,pasə'bɪləṭi] *n, pl* **-ties** : possibilité *f* — **possibly** ['pasəbli] *adv* : peut-être, possiblement *Can*

post[1] ['po:st] *n* POLE : poteau *m*

post[2] *n* POSITION : poste *m*

post[3] *n* MAIL : poste *f*, courrier *m* — **~** *vt* **1** MAIL : poster **2 keep ~ed** : tenir au courant — **postage** ['po:stɪdʒ] *n* : affranchissement *m* — **postal** ['po:stəl] *adj* : postal — **postcard** ['po:st,kard] *n* : carte *f* postale

poster ['po:stər] *n* : poster *m*, affiche *f*

posterity [pa'stɛrəṭi] *n* : postérité *f*

posthumous ['pastʃəməs] *adj* : posthume

postman ['po:stmən, -,mæn] *n, pl* **-men** [-mən, -,mɛn] → **mailman** — **post office** *n* : bureau *m* de poste

postpone [,po:st'po:n] *vt* **-poned; -poning** : remettre, reporter — **postponement** [,po:st'po:nmənt] *n* : renvoi *m*, remise *f*

postscript ['po:st,skrɪpt] *n* : post-scriptum *m*

posture ['pastʃər] *n* : posture *f*

postwar [,po:st'wor] *adj* : d'après-guerre

pot ['pat] *n* **1** SAUCEPAN : marmite *f*, casserole *f* **2** CONTAINER : pot *m*

potassium [pə'tæsiəm] *n* : potassium *m*

potato [pə'teɪto] *n, pl* **-toes** : pomme *f* de terre, patate *f fam*

potent ['po:tənt] *adj* **1** POWERFUL : puissant **2** EFFECTIVE : efficace

potential [pə'tɛntʃəl] *adj* : potentiel — **~** *n* : potentiel *m*

pothole ['pat,ho:l] *n* : nid-de-poule *m*

potion ['po:ʃən] *n* : potion *f*

pottery ['paṭəri] *n, pl* **-teries** : poterie *f*

pouch ['pautʃ] *n* **1** BAG : petit sac *m* **2** : poche *f* (des marsupiaux)

poultry ['po:ltri] *n* : volaille *f*

pounce ['paunts] *vi* **pounced; pouncing** : bondir

pound[1] ['paund] *n* **1** : livre *f* (unité de mesure) **2** : livre *f* sterling

pound[2] *n* SHELTER : fourrière *f*

pound[3] *vt* **1** CRUSH : piler **2** HAMMER : marteler **3** BEAT : battre — *vi* BEAT : battre

pour ['por] *vt* : verser — *vi* **1** FLOW : couler **2** RAIN : pleuvoir à verse

pout ['paut] *vi* : faire la moue — **~** *n* : moue *f*

poverty ['pavərṭi] *n* : pauvreté *f*

powder ['paʊdər] vt **1** : poudrer **2** CRUSH : pulvériser — ~ n : poudre f — **powdery** ['paʊdəri] adj : poudreux

power ['paʊər] n **1** AUTHORITY : pouvoir m **2** ABILITY : capacité f **3** STRENGTH : puissance f **4** CURRENT : courant m — ~ vt : faire fonctionner, faire marcher — **powerful** ['paʊərfəl] adj : puissant — **powerless** ['paʊərləs] adj : impuissant

practical ['præktɪkəl] adj : pratique — **practically** ['præktɪkli] adv : pratiquement

practice or **practise** ['præktəs] v **-ticed** or **-tised; -ticing** or **-tising** vt **1** : pratiquer **2** : exercer (une profession) — vi **1** : s'exercer **2** TRAIN : s'entraîner — ~ n **1** : pratique f **2** : exercice m (d'une profession) **3** TRAINING : entraînement m — **practitioner** [præk'tɪʃənər] n : praticien m, -cienne f

pragmatic [præg'mætɪk] adj : pragmatique

prairie ['preri] n : prairie f

praise ['preɪz] vt **praised; praising** : louer — ~ n : louange f — **praiseworthy** ['preɪz,wərði] adj : louable, digne d'éloges

prance ['prænts] vt **pranced; prancing** : caracoler (se dit d'un cheval), cabrioler (se dit d'une personne)

prank ['præŋk] n : farce f

prawn ['prɔn] n : crevette f (rose)

pray ['preɪ] vi : prier — **prayer** ['prɛr] n : prière f

preach ['priːtʃ] v : prêcher — **preacher** ['priːtʃər] n : pasteur m

precarious [prɪ'kæriəs] adj : précaire

precaution [prɪ'kɔʃən] n : précaution f

precede [prɪ'siːd] vt **-ceded; -ceding** : précéder — **precedence** ['presədənts, prɪ'siːdənts] n **1** : préséance f **2** PRIORITY : priorité f — **precedent** ['presədənt] n : précédent m

precinct ['priː,sɪŋkt] n **1** DISTRICT : arrondissement m (en France), circonscription f (au Canada) **2** ~s npl : environs mpl

precious ['prɛʃəs] adj : précieux

precipice ['presəpəs] n : précipice m

precipitate [prɪ'sɪpə,teɪt] v **-tated; -tating** : précipiter — **precipitation** [prɪ,sɪpə'teɪʃən] n **1** HASTE : précipitation f, hâte f **2** : précipitations fpl (en météorologie)

precise [prɪ'saɪs] adj : précis — **precisely** [prɪ'saɪsli] adv : précisément — **precision** [prɪ'sɪʒən] n : précision f

preclude [prɪ'kluːd] vt **-cluded; -cluding** : empêcher

precocious [prɪ'koʃəs] adj : précoce

preconceived [,priːkən'siːvd] adj : préconçu

predator ['predətər] n : prédateur m

predecessor ['predə,sɛsər, 'priː-] n : prédécesseur m

predicament [prɪ'dɪkəmənt] n : situation f difficile

predict [prɪ'dɪkt] vt : prédire — **predictable** [prɪ'dɪktəbəl] adj : prévisible — **prediction** [prɪ'dɪkʃən] n : prédiction f

predispose [,priːdɪ'spoːz] vt : prédisposer

predominant [prɪ'damənənt] adj : prédominant

preen ['priːn] vt : lisser (ses plumes)

prefabricated [,priː'fæbrə,keɪtəd] adj : préfabriqué

preface ['prefəs] n : préface f

prefer [prɪ'fər] vt **-ferred; -ferring** : préférer — **preferable** ['prefərəbəl] adj : préférable — **preference** ['prefərəns, 'prefər-] n : préférence f — **preferential** [,prefə'rɛntʃəl] adj : pré-férentiel

prefix ['priː,fɪks] n : préfixe m

pregnancy ['pregnəntsi] n, pl **-cies** : grossesse f — **pregnant** ['pregnənt] adj : enceinte

prehistoric [,priːhɪs'tɔrɪk] or **prehistorical** [-ɪkəl] adj : préhistorique

prejudice ['predʒədəs] n **1** HARM : préjudice m **2** BIAS : préjugés mpl — ~ vt **-diced; -dicing** **1** : porter préjudice à (en droit) **2** be ~d : avoir des préjugés

preliminary [prɪ'lɪmə,neri] adj : préliminaire

prelude ['pre,luːd, 'prɛl,juːd; 'preɪ,luːd, 'priː-] n : prélude m

premature [,priːmə'tʊr, -'tjʊr, -'tʃʊr] adj : prématuré

premeditated [prɪ'medə,teɪtəd] adj : prémédité

premier [prɪ'mɪr, -'mjɪr; 'priː,mɪər] adj : premier — ~ n → **prime minister**

premiere [prɪ'mjɛr, -'mɪr] n : première f (d'un spectacle)

premise ['premɪs] n **1** : prémisse f (d'un raisonnement) **2** ~s npl : lieux mpl

premium ['priːmiəm] n : prime f

preoccupied [prɪ'akjə,paɪd] adj : préoccupé

prepare [prɪ'pær] v **-pared; -paring** vt : préparer — vi : se préparer — **preparation** [,prepə'reɪʃən] n **1** PREPARING : préparation f **2** ~s npl ARRANGEMENTS : préparatifs mpl — **preparatory** [prɪ'pærə,tori] adj : préparatoire

prepay [,priː'peɪ] vt **-paid; -paying** : payer d'avance

preposition [,prepə'zɪʃən] n : préposition f

preposterous [prɪ'pastərəs] adj : absurde, insensé

prerequisite [priː'rɛkwəzət] n : préalable m

prerogative [prɪ'ragətɪv] n : prérogative f

prescribe [prɪ'skraɪb] vt **-scribed; -scribing** : prescrire — **prescription** [prɪ'skrɪpʃən] n : prescription f

presence ['prezənts] n : présence f

present¹ ['prezənt] adj **1** CURRENT : actuel

2 ATTENDING : présent — ~ *n or* ~ **time**
: présent *m*
present² ['prɛzənt] *n* GIFT : cadeau *m* — ~
[prɪ'zɛnt] *vt* : présenter — **presentation**
[ˌpriːˌzɛn'teɪʃən, ˌprɛzən-] *n* : présentation *f*
presently ['prɛzəntli] *adv* **1** SOON : bientôt
2 NOW : actuellement, en ce moment
preserve [prɪ'zərv] *vt* **-served; -serving 1**
PROTECT : préserver **2** MAINTAIN : conserver — ~ *n* **1** *or* **game** ~ : réserve *f* **2**
~**s** *npl* : confitures *fpl* — **preservation**
[ˌprɛzər'veɪʃən] *n* : préservation *f*, maintien
m — **preservative [prɪ'zərvətɪv]** *n* : agent
m de conservation
president ['prɛzədənt] *n* : président *m* —
presidency ['prɛzədəntsi] *n, pl* **-cies**
: présidence *f* — **presidential [ˌprɛzə-**
'dɛntʃəl] *adj* : présidentiel
press ['prɛs] *n* : presse *f* — ~ *vt* **1** PUSH
: presser, appuyer sur **2** IRON : repasser —
vi **1** PUSH : appuyer **2** CROWD : se presser
— **pressing ['prɛsɪŋ]** *adj* : urgent — **pres-**
sure ['prɛʃər] *n* : pression *f* — ~ *vt*
-sured; -suring : pousser, faire pression sur
prestige [prɛ'stiːʒ, -'stiːdʒ] *n* : prestige *m* —
prestigious [prɛ'stɪdʒəs, -'sti-, prə-] *adj*
: prestigieux
presume [prɪ'zuːm] *vt* **-sumed; -suming**
: présumer — **presumably [prɪ'zuːməbli]**
adv : vraisemblablement — **presumption**
[prɪ'zʌmpʃən] *n* : présomption *f* — **pre-**
sumptuous [prɪ'zʌmptʃuəs] *adj* : présomptueux
pretend [prɪ'tɛnd] *vt* **1** PROFESS : prétendre
2 FEIGN : faire semblant de — *vi* : faire semblant — **pretense** *or* **pretence ['priːˌtɛnts,**
prɪ'tɛnts] *n* **1** CLAIM : prétention *f* **2** PRE-
TEXT : prétexte *m* — **pretentious [prɪ-**
'tɛnʃəs] *adj* : prétentieux
pretext ['priːˌtɛkst] *n* : prétexte *m*
pretty ['prɪti] *adj* **-tier; -est** : joli, beau — ~
adv FAIRLY : assez
pretzel ['prɛtsəl] *n* : bretzel *m*
prevail [prɪ'veɪl] *vi* : prévaloir — **prevalent**
['prɛvələnt] *adj* : répandu
prevent [prɪ'vɛnt] *vt* : empêcher — **preven-**
tion [prɪ'vɛntʃən] *n* : prévention *f* — **pre-**
ventive [prɪ'vɛntɪv] *adj* : préventif
preview ['priːˌvjuː] *n* : avant-première *f*
previous ['priːviəs] *adj* : antérieur, précédent
— **previously ['priːviəsli]** *adv* : antérieurement, auparavant
prey ['preɪ] *ns & pl* : proie *f* — **prey on** *vt*
: faire sa proie de
price ['praɪs] *n* : prix *m* — ~ *vt* **priced;**
pricing : fixer un prix sur — **priceless**
['praɪsləs] *adj* : inestimable
prick ['prɪk] *n* : piqûre *f* — ~ *vt* **1** : piquer
2 ~ **up one's ears** : dresser l'oreille —
prickly ['prɪkəli] *adj* **-lier; -est** : épineux

pride ['praɪd] *n* : fierté *f*, orgueil *m* — ~ *vt*
prided; priding ~ **oneself on** : être fier
de
priest ['priːst] *n* : prêtre *m* — **priesthood**
['priːstˌhʊd] *n* : prêtrise *f*
prim ['prɪm] *adj* **primmer; primmest**
: guindé
primary ['praɪˌmɛri, 'praɪməri] *adj* **1** FIRST
: primaire **2** PRINCIPAL : principal — **pri-**
marily [praɪ'mɛrəli] *adv* : principalement
prime¹ ['praɪm] *vt* **primed; priming 1** LOAD
: charger **2** PREPARE : apprêter **3** COACH
: préparer
prime² ['praɪm] *n* **the** ~ **of life** : la force de l'âge —
~ *adj* **1** MAIN : principal **2** EXCELLENT
: excellent — **prime minister** *n* : Premier
ministre *m*
primer¹ ['praɪmər] *n* : apprêt *m*
primer² ['prɪmər] *n* : premier livre *m* de lecture
primitive ['prɪmətɪv] *adj* : primitif
primrose ['prɪmˌroːz] *n* : primevère *f*
prince ['prɪnts] *n* : prince *m* — **princess**
['prɪntsəs, 'prɪnˌsɛs] *n* : princesse *f*
principal ['prɪntsəpəl] *adj* : principal — ~ *n*
1 DIRECTOR : directeur *m*, -trice *f* **2** : principal *m* (d'une dette), capital *m* (d'une
somme)
principle ['prɪntsəpəl] *n* : principe *m*
print ['prɪnt] *n* **1** MARK : empreinte *f* **2** LET-
TER : caractère *m* **3** ENGRAVING : gravure *f*
4 : imprimé *m* (d'un tissu) **5** : épreuve *f* (en
photographie) **6 in** ~ : disponible — ~ *vt*
: imprimer (un texte, etc.) — *vi* : écrire en
lettres moulées — **printer ['prɪntər]** *n* **1**
: imprimeur *m* (personne) **2** : imprimante *f*
(machine) — **printing ['prɪntɪŋ]** *n* **1** : imprimerie *f* (technique) **2** IMPRESSION : impression *f* **3** LETTERING : écriture *f* en lettres
moulées
prior ['praɪər] *adj* **1** : antérieur, précédent **2**
~ **to** : avant — **priority [praɪ'ɔrəti]** *n, pl*
-ties : priorité *f*
prison ['prɪzən] *n* : prison *f* — **prisoner**
['prɪzənər] *n* : prisonnier *m*, -nière *f*
privacy ['praɪvəsi] *n, pl* **-cies** : intimité *f* —
private ['praɪvət] *adj* **1** : privé **2** PER-
SONAL : personnel — ~ *n* : (simple) soldat
m — **privately ['praɪvətli]** *adv* : en privé
privilege ['prɪvlɪdʒ, 'prɪvə-] *n* : privilège *m*
— **privileged ['prɪvlɪdʒd, 'prɪvə-]** *adj* : privilégié
prize ['praɪz] *n* : prix *m* — ~ *adj* : primé —
~ *vt* **prized; prizing** : priser — **prizewin-**
ning ['praɪzˌwɪnɪŋ] *adj* : primé, gagnant
pro ['proː] *n* **1** → **professional 2 the** ~**s**
and cons : le pour et le contre
probability [ˌprɑbə'bɪləti] *n, pl* **-ties** : probabilité *f* — **probable ['prɑbəbəl]** *adj* : probable — **probably [-bli]** *adv* : probablement

probation [pro'beɪʃən] *n* : période *f* d'essai (d'un employé)

probe ['pro:b] *n* **1** : sonde *f* (en médecine) **2** INVESTIGATION : enquête *f* — ~ *vt* **probed; probing** : sonder

problem ['prɑbləm] *n* : problème *m*

procedure [prə'si:dʒər] *n* : procédure *f*

proceed [pro'si:d] *vi* **1** ACT : procéder **2** CONTINUE : continuer **3** ADVANCE : avancer, aller — **proceedings** [pro'si:dɪŋz] *npl* **1** EVENTS : événements *mpl* **2** or **legal** ~ : poursuites *fpl* — **proceeds** ['pro:,si:dz] *npl* : recette *f*

process ['prɑ,sɛs, 'pro:-] *n, pl* **-cesses** ['prɑ,sɛsəz, 'pro:-, -,sɛsəz, -sə,si:z] **1** : processus *m* **2** METHOD : procédé *m* **3 in the** ~ **of** : en train de — ~ *vt* : traiter — **procession** [prə'sɛʃən] *n* : procession *f*

proclaim [pro'kleɪm] *vt* : proclamer — **proclamation** [,prɑklə'meɪʃən] *n* : proclamation *f*

procrastinate [prə'kræstə,neɪt] *vi* **-nated; -nating** : remettre à plus tard

procure [prə'kjʊr] *vt* **-cured; -curing** : obtenir

prod ['prɑd] *vt* **prodded; prodding** : pousser

prodigal ['prɑdɪɡəl] *adj* : prodigue

prodigious [prə'dɪdʒəs] *adj* : prodigieux

prodigy ['prɑdədʒi] *n, pl* **-gies** : prodige *m*

produce [prə'du:s, -'dju:s] *vt* **-duced; -ducing 1** : produire **2** SHOW : présenter **3** CAUSE : causer — ~ ['prɑ,du:s, 'pro:-, -,dju:s] *n* : produits *mpl* agricoles — **producer** [prə'du:sər, -'dju:-] *n* : producteur *m*, -trice *f* — **product** ['prɑ,dʌkt] *n* : produit *m* — **productive** [prə'dʌktɪv] *adj* : productif

profane [pro'feɪn] *adj* **1** SECULAR : profane **2** IRREVERENT : sacrilège — **profanity** [pro'fænəti] *n, pl* **-ties** : juron *m*

profess [prə'fɛs] *vt* : professer — **profession** [prə'fɛʃən] *n* : profession *f* — **professional** [prə'fɛʃənəl] *adj* : professionnel — ~ *n* : professionnel *m*, -nelle *f* — **professor** [prə'fɛsər] *n* : professeur *m*

proficiency [prə'fɪʃəntsi] *n, pl* **-cies** : compétence *f* — **proficient** [prə'fɪʃənt] *adj* : compétent

profile ['pro:,faɪl] *n* : profil *m*

profit ['prɑfət] *n* : profit *m*, bénéfice *m* — ~ *vi* ~ **from** : tirer profit de — *vt* BENEFIT : profiter à — **profitable** ['prɑfətəbəl] *adj* : profitable

profound [prə'faʊnd] *adj* : profond

profuse [prə'fju:s] *adj* **1** ABUNDANT : abondant **2** LAVISH : prodigue — **profusion** [prə'fju:ʒən] *n* : profusion *f*

prognosis [prɑg'no:sɪs] *n, pl* **-ses** [-,si:z] : pronostic *m*

program *or Brit* **programme** ['pro:,ɡræm, -ɡrəm] *n* **1** : programme *m* **2 television** ~ : émission *f* de télévision — ~ *vt* **-grammed** *or* **-gramed; -gramming** *or* **-graming** : programmer

progress ['prɑgrəs, -,ɡrɛs] *n* **1** : progrès *m* **2 in** ~ : en cours — ~ [prə'ɡrɛs] *vi* : progresser — **progressive** [prə'ɡrɛsɪv] *adj* **1** : progressiste (en politique, etc.) **2** : progressif

prohibit [pro'hɪbət] *vt* : interdire — **prohibition** [,pro:ə'bɪʃən, ,pro:hə-] *n* : prohibition *f*

project ['prɑ,dʒɛkt, -dʒɪkt] *n* : projet *m* — ~ [prə'dʒɛkt] *vt* : projeter — *vi* PROTRUDE : faire saillie — **projectile** [prə'dʒɛktəl, -,taɪl] *n* : projectile *m* — **projection** [prə'dʒɛkʃən] *n* **1** : projection *f* **2** BULGE : saillie *f* — **projector** [prə'dʒɛktər] *n* : projecteur *m*

proliferate [prə'lɪfə,reɪt] *vi* **-ated; -ating** : proliférer — **proliferation** [prə,lɪfə'reɪʃən] *n* : prolifération *f* — **prolific** [prə'lɪfɪk] *adj* : prolifique

prologue ['pro:,lɔg, -,lɑg] *n* : prologue *m*

prolong [prə'lɔŋ] *vt* : prolonger

prom ['prɑm] *n* : bal *m* d'étudiants

prominent ['prɑmənənt] *adj* **1** : proéminent **2** IMPORTANT : important — **prominence** ['prɑmənənts] *n* **1** : proéminence *f* **2** IMPORTANCE : importance *f*

promiscuous [prə'mɪskjuəs] *adj* : de mœurs légères

promise ['prɑməs] *n* : promesse *f* — ~ *v* **-mised; -mising** : promettre — **promising** ['prɑməsɪŋ] *adj* : prometteur

promote [prə'mo:t] *vt* **-moted; -moting** : promouvoir — **promoter** [prə'mo:tər] *n* : promoteur *m*, -trice *f* — **promotion** [prə'mo:ʃən] *n* : promotion *f*

prompt ['prɑmpt] *vt* **1** INCITE : inciter **2** CAUSE : provoquer — ~ *adj* **1** QUICK : prompt **2** PUNCTUAL : ponctuel

prone ['pro:n] *adj* **1** APT : sujet, enclin **2** FLAT : à plat ventre

prong ['prɔŋ] *n* : dent *f*

pronoun ['pro:,naʊn] *n* : pronom *m*

pronounce [prə'naʊnts] *vt* **-nounced; -nouncing** : prononcer — **pronouncement** [prə'naʊntsmənt] *n* : déclaration *f* — **pronunciation** [prə,nʌntsi'eɪʃən] *n* : prononciation *f*

proof ['pru:f] *n* **1** EVIDENCE : preuve *f* **2** PRINT : épreuve *f* — **proofread** ['pru:f,ri:d] *vt* **-read** [-,rɛd]; **-reading** : corriger les épreuves de

prop ['prɑp] *n* **1** SUPPORT : étai *m* **2** ~**s** *npl* : accessoires *mpl* — ~ *vt* **propped; propping 1** LEAN : appuyer **2** ~ **up** SUPPORT : étayer

propaganda [,prɑpə'ɡændə, ,pro:-] *n* : propagande *f*

propagate ['prɑpə,geɪt] v **-gated; -gating** vt : propager — vi : se propager

propel [prə'pɛl] vt **-pelled; -pelling** : propulser — **propeller** [prə'pɛlər] n : hélice f

propensity [prə'pɛnʦəti] n, pl **-ties** : propension f

proper ['prɑpər] adj 1 SUITABLE : convenable 2 REAL : vrai 3 CORRECT : correct 4 ~ **name** : nom propre — **properly** ['prɑpərli] adv : correctement

property ['prɑpərti] n, pl **-ties** 1 POSSESSIONS : biens mpl, propriété f 2 REAL ESTATE : biens mpl immobiliers 3 QUALITY : propriété f

prophet ['prɑfət] n : prophète m — **prophecy** ['prɑfəsi] n, pl **-cies** : prophétie f — **prophesy** ['prɑfə,saɪ] vt **-sied; -sying** : prophétiser — **prophetic** [prə'fɛtɪk] adj : prophétique

proponent [prə'po:nənt] n : partisan m, -sane f

proportion [prə'porʃən] n 1 : proportion f 2 SHARE : part f — **proportional** [prə'porʃənəl] adj : proportionnel — **proportionate** [prə'porʃənət] adj : proportionnel

proposal [prə'po:zəl] n : proposition f

propose [prə'po:z] v **-posed; -posing** vt : proposer — vi : faire une demande en mariage — **proposition** [,prɑpə'zɪʃən] n : proposition f

proprietor [prə'praɪətər] n : propriétaire mf

propriety [prə'praɪəti] n, pl **-ties** : convenance f

propulsion [prə'pʌlʃən] n : propulsion f

prose ['pro:z] n : prose f

prosecute ['prɑsɪ,kju:t] vt **-cuted; -cuting** : poursuivre — **prosecution** [,prɑsɪ'kju:ʃən] n : poursuites fpl judiciaires — **prosecutor** ['prɑsɪ,kju:tər] n : procureur m

prospect ['prɑ,spɛkt] n 1 VIEW : vue f 2 POSSIBILITY : perspective f 3 ~s : espérances fpl — **prospective** [prə'spɛktɪv, 'prɑ,spɛk-] adj : éventuel

prosper ['prɑspər] vt : prospérer — **prosperity** [prɑ'spɛrəti] n : prospérité f — **prosperous** ['prɑspərəs] adj : prospère

prostitute ['prɑstə,tu:t, -,tju:t] n : prostituée f — **prostitution** [,prɑstə'tu:ʃən, -'tju:-] n : prostitution f

prostrate ['prɑ,streɪt] adj 1 : allongé à plat ventre 2 STRICKEN : prostré

protagonist [pro'tægənɪst] n : protagoniste mf

protect [prə'tɛkt] vt : protéger — **protection** [prə'tɛkʃən] n : protection f — **protective** [prə'tɛktɪv] adj : protecteur — **protector** [prə'tɛktər] n : protecteur m, -trice f

protein ['pro:,ti:n] n : protéine f

protest ['pro:,tɛst] n 1 DEMONSTRATION : manifestation f 2 OBJECTION : protestation f — ~ [pro'tɛst] v : protester — **Protestant** ['prɑtəstənt] n : protestant m, -tante f — **protester** or **protestor** ['pro:,tɛstər, prə'-] n : manifestant m, -tante f

protocol ['pro:tə,kɔl] n : protocole m

protrude [pro'tru:d] vi **-truded; -truding** : dépasser

proud ['praʊd] adj 1 : fier 2 ARROGANT : orgueilleux

prove ['pru:v] v **proved; proved** or **proven** ['pru:vən], **proving** vt : prouver — vi : s'avérer, se montrer

proverb ['prɑ,vərb] n : proverbe m

provide [prə'vaɪd] v **-vided; -viding** vt : fournir — vi ~ **for** SUPPORT : subvenir aux besoins de — **provided** [prə'vaɪdəd] or ~ **that** conj : à condition que — **providence** ['prɑvədənʦ] n : providence f

province ['prɑvɪnʦ] n 1 : province f 2 SPHERE : domaine m — **provincial** [prə'vɪnʧəl] adj : provincial

provision [prə'vɪʒən] n 1 SUPPLYING : approvisionnement m 2 STIPULATION : stipulation f 3 ~s npl : provisions fpl — **provisional** [prə'vɪʒənəl] adj : provisoire

provoke [prə'vo:k] vt **-voked; -voking** : provoquer — **provocative** [prə'vɑkətɪv] adj : provocant, provocateur

prow ['praʊ] n : proue f

prowess ['praʊəs] n : prouesse f

prowl ['praʊl] vi : rôder — ~ n **be on the** ~ : rôder — **prowler** ['praʊlər] n : rôdeur m, -deuse f

proximity [prɑk'sɪməti] n : proximité f — **proxy** ['prɑksi] n, pl **proxies** : procuration f

prude ['pru:d] n : prude f

prudence ['pru:dənʦ] n : prudence f — **prudent** ['pru:dənt] adj : prudent

prune¹ ['pru:n] n : pruneau m

prune² vt **pruned; pruning** : élaguer, tailler

pry ['praɪ] v **pried; prying** vi ~ **into** : mettre son nez dans — vt or ~ **open** : forcer avec un levier

psalm ['sɑm, 'sɑlm] n : psaume m

pseudonym ['su:də,nɪm] n : pseudonyme m

psychiatry [sə'kaɪətri, saɪ-] n : psychiatrie f — **psychiatric** [,saɪki'ætrɪk] adj : psychiatrique — **psychiatrist** [sə'kaɪətrɪst, saɪ-] n : psychiatre mf

psychic ['saɪkɪk] adj : psychique

psychoanalysis [,saɪkoə'næləsɪs] n : psychanalyse f — **psychoanalyst** [,saɪko-'ænəlɪst] n : psychanalyste mf — **psychoanalyze** [,saɪko'ænəl,aɪz] vt **-lyzed; -lyzing** : psychanalyser

psychology [saɪ'kɑləʤi] n, pl **-gies** : psychologie f — **psychological** [,saɪkə-'lɑʤɪkəl] adj : psychologique — **psychologist** [saɪ'kɑləʤɪst] n : psychologue mf

psychotherapy [ˌsaɪkoˈθɛrəpi] *n* : psychothérapie *f*
puberty [ˈpjuːbərti] *n* : puberté *f*
public [ˈpʌblɪk] *adj* : public — ~ *n* : public *m* — **publication** [ˌpʌbləˈkeɪʃən] *n* : publication *f* — **publicity** [pəˈblɪsəti] *n* : publicité *f* — **publicize** [ˈpʌbləˌsaɪz] *vt* **-cized; -cizing** : rendre public, faire connaître
publish [ˈpʌblɪʃ] *vt* : publier — **publisher** [ˈpʌblɪʃər] *n* **1** : éditeur *m*, -trice *f* **2** : maison *f* d'édition (entreprise)
puck [ˈpʌk] *n* : palet *m*, rondelle *f* Can (au hockey)
pucker [ˈpʌkər] *vt* : plisser — *vi* : se plisser
pudding [ˈpʊdɪŋ] *n* : pudding *m*, pouding *m*
puddle [ˈpʌdəl] *n* : flaque *f* (d'eau)
puff [ˈpʌf] *vi* **1** BLOW : souffler **2** PANT : haleter **3** ~ **up** SWELL : enfler — *vt or* ~ **out** : gonfler — ~ *n* **1** : bouffée *f* **2 cream** ~ : chou *m* à la crème **3** *or* **powder** ~ : houppette *f* — **puffy** [ˈpʌfi] *adj* **puffier; puffiest** : enflé, bouffi
pull [ˈpʊl, ˈpʌl] *vt* **1** : tirer **2** STRAIN : se froisser **3** EXTRACT : arracher **4** DRAW : sortir **5** ~ **off** : enlever **6** ~ **oneself together** : se ressaisir **7** ~ **up** RAISE : remonter — *vi* **1** ~ **away** : se retirer **2** ~ **out of** : quitter **3** ~ **through** RECOVER : s'en tirer **4** ~ **together** COOPERATE : agir en concert **5** ~ **up** STOP : s'arrêter — ~ *n* **1** TUG : coup *m* **2** INFLUENCE : influence *f* — **pulley** [ˈpʊli] *n, pl* **-leys** : poulie *f* — **pullover** [ˈpʊlˌoːvər] *n* : chandail *m*, pullover *m France*
pulmonary [ˈpʊlməˌnɛri, ˈpʌl-] *adj* : pulmonaire
pulp [ˈpʌlp] *n* : pulpe *f*
pulpit [ˈpʊlˌpɪt] *n* : chaire *f*
pulsate [ˈpʌlˌseɪt] *vi* **-sated; -sating 1** BEAT : palpiter **2** VIBRATE : vibrer — **pulse** [ˈpʌls] *n* : pouls *m*
pummel [ˈpʌməl] *vt* **-meled; -meling** : bourer de coups
pump[1] [ˈpʌmp] *n* : pompe *f* — ~ *vt* **1** : pomper (de l'eau) **2** ~ **up** : gonfler
pump[2] *n* SHOE : escarpin *m*
pumpernickel [ˈpʌmpərˌnɪkəl] *n* : pain *m* noir
pumpkin [ˈpʌmpkɪn, ˈpʌŋkən] *n* : citrouille *f*, potiron *m France*
pun [ˈpʌn] *n* : jeu *m* de mots
punch[1] [ˈpʌntʃ] *vt* **1** : donner un coup de poing à **2** PERFORATE : poinçonner — ~ *n* BLOW : coup *m* de poing
punch[2] *n* : punch *m* (boisson)
punctual [ˈpʌŋktʃuəl] *adj* : ponctuel — **punctuality** [ˌpʌŋktʃuˈæləti] *n* : ponctualité *f*
punctuate [ˈpʌŋktʃuˌeɪt] *vt* **-ated; -ating**

: ponctuer — **punctuation** [ˌpʌŋktʃuˈeɪʃən] *n* : ponctuation *f*
puncture [ˈpʌŋktʃər] *n* **1** HOLE : perforation *f* **2** PRICK : piqûre *f* — ~ *vt* **-tured; -turing 1** PIERCE : perforer **2** : crever (un ballon, un pneu, etc.)
pungent [ˈpʌndʒənt] *adj* : âcre
punish [ˈpʌnɪʃ] *vt* : punir — **punishment** [ˈpʌnɪʃmənt] *n* : punition *f* — **punitive** [ˈpjuːnətɪv] *adj* : punitif
puny [ˈpjuːni] *adj* **-nier; -est** : chétif
pup [ˈpʌp] *n* : chiot *m*, jeune animal *m*
pupil[1] [ˈpjuːpəl] *n* STUDENT : élève *mf*
pupil[2] *n* : pupille *f* (de l'œil)
puppet [ˈpʌpət] *n* : marionnette *f*
puppy [ˈpʌpi] *n, pl* **-pies** : chiot *m*
purchase [ˈpərtʃəs] *vt* **-chased; -chasing** : acheter — ~ *n* : achat *m*
pure [ˈpjʊr] *adj* **purer; purest** : pur
puree [pjuˈreɪ, -ˈriː] *n* : purée *f*
purely [ˈpjʊrli] *adv* : purement
purgatory [ˈpərgəˌtori] *n, pl* **-ries** : purgatoire *m* — **purge** [ˈpərdʒ] *vt* **purged; purging** : purger — ~ *n* : purge *f*
purify [ˈpjʊrəˌfaɪ] *vt* **-fied; -fying** : purifier — **purifier** [ˈpjʊrəˌfaɪər] *n* : purificateur *m*
puritan [ˈpjʊrətən] *n* : puritain *m*, -taine *f* — **puritanical** [ˌpjʊrəˈtænɪkəl] *adj* : puritain
purity [ˈpjʊrəti] *n* : pureté *f*
purple [ˈpərpəl] *adj* : violet, pourpre — ~ *n* : violet *m*, pourpre *m*
purpose [ˈpərpəs] *n* **1** AIM : intention *f*, but *m* **2** DETERMINATION : résolution *f* **3 on** ~ : exprès — **purposeful** [ˈpərpəsfəl] *adj* **1** MEANINGFUL : significatif **2** INTENTIONAL : réfléchi **3** DETERMINED : résolu — **purposely** [ˈpərpəsli] *adv* : exprès
purr [ˈpər] *n* : ronronnement *m* — ~ *vi* : ronronner
purse [ˈpərs] *n* **1** *or* **change** ~ : porte-monnaie *m* **2** HANDBAG : sac *m* à main, sacoche *f Can*
pursue [pərˈsuː] *vt* **-sued; -suing** : poursuivre — **pursuer** [pərˈsuːər] *n* : poursuivant *m*, -vante *f* — **pursuit** [pərˈsuːt] *n* **1** : poursuite *f* **2** OCCUPATION : activité *f*
pus [ˈpʌs] *n* : pus *m*
push [ˈpʊʃ] *vt* **1** : pousser **2** PRESS : appuyer sur **3** THRUST : enfoncer **4** ~ **away** : repousser — *vi* **1** : pousser **2** ~ **on** : continuer **3** ~ **(oneself)** : s'exercer — ~ *n* **1** SHOVE : poussée *f* **2** EFFORT : effort *m* — **pushy** [ˈpʊʃi] *adj* **pushier; pushiest** : arriviste
pussycat [ˈpʊsiˌkæt] *n* : minet *m*, minou *m fam*
put [ˈpʊt] *v* **put; putting** *vt* **1** : mettre **2** PLACE : placer, poser **3** EXPRESS : dire **4** ~ **forward** PROPOSE : avancer, proposer —

vi **~ up with** TOLERATE : supporter — **put away** *vt* **1** STORE : ranger **2** *or* **~ aside** : mettre de côté — **put down** *vt* **1** : poser, déposer **2** WRITE : mettre (par écrit) — **put off** *vt* POSTPONE : remettre à plus tard, retarder — **put on** *vt* **1** ASSUME : prendre **2** PRESENT : monter (un spectacle, etc.) **3** WEAR : mettre — **put out** *vt* **1** EXTINGUISH, TURN OFF : éteindre **2** INCONVENIENCE : déranger — **put up** *vt* **1** BUILD : ériger **2** LODGE : loger **3** HANG : accrocher

putrefy ['pju:trə,faɪ] *v* **-fied; -fying** *vt* : putréfier — *vi* : se putréfier

putty ['pʌti] *n, pl* **-ties** : mastic *m*

puzzle ['pʌzəl] *vt* **-zled; -zling** CONFUSE : intriguer, laisser perplexe — **~** *n* **1** : casse-tête *m* **2** *or* **jigsaw ~** : puzzle *m* **3** MYSTERY : énigme *f*, mystère *m*

pyjamas *Brit* → **pajamas**

pylon ['paɪ,lɑn, -lən] *n* : pylône *m*

pyramid ['pɪrə,mɪd] *n* : pyramide *f*

python ['paɪ,θɑn, -θən] *n* : python *m*

Q

q ['kju:] *n, pl* **q's** *or* **qs** ['kju:z] : q *m*, dix-septième lettre de l'alphabet

quack[1] ['kwæk] *vi* : faire des coin-coin

quack[2] *n* CHARLATAN : charlatan *m*

quadruped ['kwɑdrə,pɛd] *n* : quadrupède *m*

quadruple [kwɑ'dru:pəl, -'drʌ-; 'kwɑ-drə-] *v* **-pled; -pling** : quadrupler — **~** *adj* : quadruple

quagmire ['kwæg,maɪr, 'kwɑg-] *n* : bourbier *m*

quail ['kweɪl] *n, pl* **quail** *or* **quails** : caille *f*

quaint ['kweɪnt] *adj* **1** ODD : bizarre **2** PICTURESQUE : pittoresque

quake ['kweɪk] *vi* **quaked; quaking** : trembler

qualify ['kwɑlə,faɪ] *v* **-fied; -fying** *vt* **1** LIMIT : poser des conditions sur **2** AUTHORIZE : qualifier, autoriser **3** MODERATE : mitiger — *vi* : se qualifier — **qualification** [,kwɑləfə'keɪʃən] *n* **1** : qualification *f* **2** LIMITATION : réserve *f* **3** ABILITY : compétence *f* — **qualified** ['kwɑlə,faɪd] *adj* : qualifié, compétent

quality ['kwɑləti] *n, pl* **-ties** : qualité *f*

qualm ['kwɑm, 'kwɑlm, 'kwɔm] *n* : scrupule *m*

quandary ['kwɑndri] *n, pl* **-ries** : dilemme *m*

quantity ['kwɑntəti] *n, pl* **-ties** : quantité *f*

quarantine ['kwɔrən,ti:n] *n* : quarantaine *f* — **~** *vt* **-tined; -tining** : mettre en quarantaine

quarrel ['kwɔrəl] *n* : dispute *f*, querelle *f* — **~** *vi* **-reled** *or* **-relled; -reling** *or* **-relling** : se quereller, se disputer — **quarrelsome** ['kwɔrəlsəm] *adj* : querelleur

quarry ['kwɔri] *n, pl* **-ries** EXCAVATION : carrière *f*

quart ['kwɔrt] *n* : quart *m* de gallon

quarter ['kwɔrtər] *n* **1** : quart *m* **2** : (pièce de) vingt-cinq cents *m* **3** DISTRICT : quartier

m **4** : trimestre *m* (de l'année fiscale) **5** **~ after three** : trois heures et quart **6** **~s** *npl* LODGINGS : logement *m* — *vt* : diviser en quatre — **quarterly** ['kwɔrtərli] *adv* : tous les trois mois, trimestriellement — **~** *adj* : trimestriel — **~** *n, pl* **-lies** : publication *f* trimestrielle

quartet [kwɔr'tɛt] *n* : quatuor *m*

quartz ['kwɔrts] *n* : quartz *m*

quash ['kwɑʃ, 'kwɔʃ] *vt* : étouffer, réprimer

quaver ['kweɪvər] *vi* : trembloter

quay ['ki:, 'keɪ, 'kweɪ] *n* WHARF : quai *m*

queasy ['kwi:zi] *adj* **-sier; -est** : nauséeux

Quebecer [kwɪ'bɛkər] *adj* : québécois

Quebecois *or* **Québécois** [kebe'kwɑ:] *adj* : québécois

queen ['kwi:n] *n* : reine *f*

queer ['kwɪr] *adj* : étrange, bizarre

quell ['kwɛl] *vt* SUPPRESS : réprimer

quench ['kwɛntʃ] *vt* **1** EXTINGUISH : éteindre **2** **~ one's thirst** : étancher la soif

query ['kwɪri, 'kwɛr-] *n, pl* **-ries** : question *f* — **~** *vt* **-ried; -rying** ASK : poser une question à

quest ['kwɛst] *n* : quête *f*

question ['kwɛstʃən] *n* : question *f* — **~** *vt* **1** ASK : poser une question à **2** INTERROGATE : questionner **3** DOUBT : mettre en doute — **questionable** ['kwɛstʃənəbəl] *adj* : discutable — **question mark** *n* : point m d'interrogation — **questionnaire** [,kwɛstʃə'nær] *n* : questionnaire *m*

queue ['kju:] *n* LINE : queue *f*, file *f* — **~** *vi* **queued; queuing** *or* **queueing** : faire la queue

quibble ['kwɪbəl] *vi* **-bled; -bling** : chicaner — **~** *n* : chicane *f*

quick ['kwɪk] *adj* : rapide — **~** *adv* : rapidement, vite — **quicken** ['kwɪkən] *vt* : accélérer — **~** *vi* : s'accélérer — **quickly**

['kwɪkli] *adv* : rapidement, vite — **quick-ness** ['kwɪknəs] *n* : rapidité *f*, vitesse *f* — **quicksand** ['kwɪk,sænd] *n* : sables *mpl* mouvants

quiet ['kwaɪət] *n* **1** : silence *m* **2** CALM : calme *m* — ~ *adj* **1** SILENT : silencieux **2** CALM : tranquille — ~ *vt* **1** SILENCE : faire taire **2** CALM : calmer — *vi or* ~ **down** : se calmer — **quietly** ['kwaɪətli] *adv* **1** SILENTLY : sans bruit, doucement **2** CALMLY : tranquillement

quilt ['kwɪlt] *n* : édredon *m*

quintet [kwɪn'tɛt] *n* : quintette *m* — **quintuple** [kwɪn'tu:pəl, -'tju:-, -'tʌ-; 'kwɪntə-] *adj* : quintuple

quip ['kwɪp] *n* : raillerie *f*

quirk ['kwərk] *n* : bizarrerie *f* — **quirky** ['kwərki] *adj* **quirkier; quirkiest** : excentrique

quit ['kwɪt] *v* **quit; quitting** *vt* **1** LEAVE

: quitter **2** STOP : arrêter — *vi* **1** GIVE UP : abandonner **2** RESIGN : démissionner

quite ['kwaɪt] *adv* **1** COMPLETELY : tout à fait **2** RATHER : assez **3** POSITIVELY : vraiment

quits ['kwɪts] *adj* **1** : quitte **2 we called it** ~ : nous y avons renoncé

quiver ['kwɪvər] *vi* : trembler

quiz ['kwɪz] *n, pl* **quizzes** TEST : interrogation *f* — ~ *vt* **quizzed; quizzing** : questionner, interroger

quota ['kwo:tə] *n* : quota *m*

quotation [kwo'teɪʃən] *n* **1** CITATION : citation *f* **2** ESTIMATE : devis *m* — **quotation marks** *npl* : guillemets *mpl* — **quote** ['kwo:t] *vt* **quoted; quoting 1** CITE : citer **2** STATE : indiquer (un prix) **3** : coter (un prix à la Bourse) — ~ *n* **1** → **quotation 2** ~s *npl* → **quotation marks**

quotient ['kwo:ʃənt] *n* : quotient *m*

R

r ['ɑr] *n, pl* **r's** *or* **rs** ['ɑrz] : r *m*, dix-huitième lettre de l'alphabet

rabbi ['ræ,baɪ] *n* : rabbin *m*

rabbit ['ræbət] *n, pl* **-bit** *or* **-bits** : lapin *m*, -pine *f*

rabies ['reɪbi:z] *ns & pl* : rage *f* — **rabid** ['ræbɪd] *adj* **1** : enragé (se dit d'un chien) **2** FURIOUS : furieux

raccoon [ræ'ku:n] *n, pl* **-coon** *or* **-coons** : raton *m* laveur

race¹ ['reɪs] *n* **1** : race *f* **2 human** ~ : genre *m* humain

race² *n* **1** : course *f* (à pied, etc.) — ~ *vi* **raced; racing** : courir — **racehorse** ['reɪs-ˌhors] *n* : cheval *m* de course — **racetrack** ['reɪsˌtræk] *n* : hippodrome *m*

racial ['reɪʃəl] *adj* : racial — **racism** ['reɪ-ˌsɪzəm] *n* : racisme *m* — **racist** ['reɪsɪst] *n* : raciste *mf*

rack ['ræk] *n* **1** SHELF : étagère *f* **2 luggage** ~ : porte-bagages *m* — ~ *vt* **1** ~**ed with** : tourmenté par **2** ~ **one's brains** : se creuser les méninges

racket¹ ['rækət] *n* : raquette *f* (de tennis, etc.)

racket² **1** DIN : vacarme *m* **2** SWINDLE : escroquerie *f*

racy ['reɪsi] *adj* **racier; -est** : osé, risqué

radar ['reɪˌdɑr] *n* : radar *m*

radiant ['reɪdiənt] *adj* : radieux — **radiance** ['reɪdiənts] *n* : éclat *m* — **radiate** ['reɪdiˌeɪt]

v **-ated; -ating** *vt* : irradier — *vi* : rayonner — **radiation** [ˌreɪdi'eɪʃən] *n* : rayonnement *m* — **radiator** ['reɪdiˌeɪtər] *n* : radiateur *m*

radical ['rædɪkəl] *adj* : radical — ~ *n* : radical *m*, -cale *f*

radii → **radius**

radio ['reɪdiˌo:] *n, pl* **-dios** : radio *f* — ~ *vt* : transmettre par radio — **radioactive** ['reɪdio'æktɪv] *adj* : radioactif

radish ['rædɪʃ] *n* : radis *m*

radius ['reɪdiəs] *n, pl* **radii** [-diˌaɪ] : rayon *m*

raffle ['ræfəl] *vt* **-fled; -fling** : mettre en tombola — ~ *n* : tombola *f*

raft ['ræft] *n* : radeau *m*

rafter ['ræftər] *n* : chevron *m*

rag ['ræg] *n* **1** : chiffon *m*, guenille *f Can* **2 in** ~**s** : en haillons

rage ['reɪdʒ] *n* **1** : colère *f*, rage *f* **2 be all the** ~ : faire fureur — ~ *vi* **raged; raging 1** : être furieux **2** : hurler (se dit du vent, etc.)

ragged ['rægəd] *adj* **1** UNEVEN : inégal **2** TATTERED : en loques

raid ['reɪd] *n* **1** : invasion *f*, raid *m* **2** *or* **police** ~ : descente *f*, rafle *f* — ~ *vt* INVADE : envahir

rail¹ ['reɪl] *vi* ~ **at** : invectiver contre

rail² *n* **1** BAR : barre *f* **2** HANDRAIL : balustrade *f* **3** TRACK : rail *m* **4 by** ~ : par train — **railing** ['reɪlɪŋ] *n* **1** : rampe *f* (d'un escalier), balustrade *f* (d'un balcon) **2** RAILS : grille *f* — **railroad** ['reɪlˌro:d] *n*

: chemin *m* de fer — **railway** ['reɪl,weɪ] →
railroad

rain ['reɪn] *n* : pluie *f* — ~ *vi* : pleuvoir —
rainbow ['reɪn,bo:] *n* : arc-en-ciel *m* —
raincoat ['reɪn,ko:t] *n* : imperméable *m*
— **rainfall** ['reɪn,fɔl] *n* : précipitations *fpl*
— **rainy** ['reɪni] *adj* **rainier; -est** : pluvieux

raise ['reɪz] *vt* **raised; raising** 1 : lever 2
REAR : élever 3 GROW : cultiver 4 IN-
CREASE : augmenter 5 : soulever (des ob-
jections) 6 ~ **money** : collecter des fonds
— ~ *n* : augmentation *f*

raisin ['reɪzən] *n* : raisin *m* sec

rake ['reɪk] *n* : râteau *m* — ~ *vt* **raked; rak-
ing** : ratisser

rally ['ræli] *v* **-lied; -lying** *vi* : se rallier, se
rassembler — *vt* : rallier, rassembler — ~
n, pl **-lies** : ralliement *m*, rassemblement *m*

ram ['ræm] *n* : bélier *m* (mouton) — ~ *vt*
rammed; ramming 1 CRAM : fourrer 2 *or*
~ **into** : percuter

RAM ['ræm] *n* (random-*access* *memory*)
: RAM *f*

ramble ['ræmbəl] *vi* **-bled; -ling** 1 WANDER
: se balader 2 *or* ~ **on** : divaguer — ~ *n*
: randonnée *f*, excursion *f*

ramp ['ræmp] *n* 1 : rampe *f* 2 : passerelle *f*
(pour accéder à un avion)

rampage ['ræm,peɪdʒ] *vi* **-paged; -paging**
: se déchaîner

rampant ['ræmpənt] *adj* : déchaîné

ramshackle ['ræm,ʃækəl] *adj* : délabré

ran → **run**

ranch ['ræntʃ] *n* : ranch *m*

rancid ['ræntsɪd] *adj* : rance

rancor *or Brit* **rancour** ['ræŋkər] *n* : rancœur *f*, rancune *f*

random ['rændəm] *adj* 1 : aléatoire 2 **at** ~
: au hasard

rang → **ring**

range ['reɪndʒ] *n* 1 : chaîne *f* (de montagnes)
2 STOVE : cuisinière *f* 3 VARIETY : gamme *f*
4 SCOPE : portée *f* — ~ *vi* **ranged; ranging**
1 EXTEND : s'étendre 2 ~ **from ... to ...**
: varier entre ... et ... — **ranger** ['reɪndʒər] *n*
or **forest** ~ : garde *m* forestier

rank[1] ['ræŋk] *adj* : fétide

rank[2] *n* 1 ROW : rang *m* 2 : grade *m* (militaire) 3 ~**s** : simples soldats *mpl* 4 **the** ~
and file : la base — ~ *vt* RATE : classer,
ranger — *vi* : se classer, compter

rankle ['ræŋkəl] *vi* **-kled; -kling** : rester sur
le cœur

ransack ['ræn,sæk] *vt* 1 SEARCH : fouiller
2 LOOT : saccager

ransom ['ræntsəm] *n* : rançon *f* — ~ *vt*
: payer une rançon pour

rant ['rænt] *vi or* ~ **and rave** : fulminer

rap[1] ['ræp] *n* KNOCK : coup *m* sec — ~ *v*
rapped; rapping : cogner

rap[2] *n or* ~ **music** : rap *m*

rapacious [rə'peɪʃəs] *adj* : rapace

rape ['reɪp] *vt* **raped; raping** : violer — ~ *n*
: viol *m*

rapid ['ræpɪd] *adj* : rapide — **rapids**
['ræpɪdz] *npl* : rapides *mpl*

rapture ['ræptʃər] *n* : extase *f*

rare ['rær] *adj* **rarer; rarest** 1 FINE : exceptionnel 2 UNCOMMON : rare 3 : saignant (se
dit de la viande) — **rarely** ['rærli] *adv*
: rarement — **rarity** ['rærəti] *n, pl* **-ties**
: rareté *f*

rascal ['ræskəl] *n* : polisson *m*, -sonne *f*

rash[1] ['ræʃ] *adj* : irréfléchi

rash[2] *n* : rougeurs *fpl*

raspberry ['ræz,bɛri] *n, pl* **-ries** : framboise
f

rat ['ræt] *n* : rat *m*

rate ['reɪt] *n* 1 PACE : vitesse *f*, rythme *m* 2
: taux *m* (d'intérêt, etc.) 3 PRICE : tarif *m* 4
at any ~ : de toute manière — ~ *vt* **rated;
rating** 1 REGARD : considérer 2 RANK
: classer

rather ['ræðər, 'rʌ-, 'rɑ-] *adv* 1 FAIRLY
: assez, plutôt 2 **I'd** ~ **decide** : je préférerais décider

ratify ['ræṭə,faɪ] *vt* **-fied; -fying** : ratifier
— **ratification** [,ræṭəfə'keɪʃən] *n* : ratification *f*

rating ['reɪṭɪŋ] *n* 1 : classement *m*, cote *f* 2
~**s** *npl* : indice *m* d'écoute

ratio ['reɪʃio] *n, pl* **-tios** : rapport *m*, proportion *f*

ration ['ræʃən, 'reɪʃən] *n* 1 : ration *f* 2 ~**s**
npl : vivres *mpl* — ~ *vt* **rationed; ra-
tioning** : rationner

rational ['ræʃənəl] *adj* : rationnel — **rationale** [,ræʃə'næl] *n* : logique *f*, raisons *fpl* —
rationalize ['ræʃənə,laɪz] *vt* **-ized; -izing**
: rationaliser

rattle ['ræṭəl] *v* **-tled; -tling** *vi* : faire du bruit
— *vt* 1 SHAKE : agiter 2 UPSET : décon-
certer 3 ~ **off** : débiter à toute vitesse —
~ *n* 1 : succession *f* de bruits secs 2 *or*
baby's ~ : hochet *m* — **rattlesnake**
['ræṭəl,sneɪk] *n* : serpent *m* à sonnettes

ravage ['rævɪdʒ] *vt* **-aged; -aging** : ravager
— **ravages** ['rævɪdʒəz] *npl* : ravages *mpl*

rave ['reɪv] *vi* **raved; raving** 1 : délirer 2 ~
about : parler avec enthousiasme de

raven ['reɪvən] *n* : grand corbeau *m*

ravenous ['rævənəs] *adj* 1 HUNGRY : affamé 2 VORACIOUS : vorace

ravine [rə'vi:n] *n* : ravin *m*

ravishing ['rævɪʃɪŋ] *adj* : ravissant

raw ['rɔ] *adj* **rawer; rawest** 1 UNCOOKED
: cru 2 INEXPERIENCED : novice 3 CHAFED
: à vif (se dit d'une plaie) 4 : cru et humide
(se dit de la température) 5 ~ **materials**
: matières *fpl* premières

ray ['reɪ] *n* : rayon *m* (de lumière), lueur *f* (d'espoir, etc.)

rayon ['reɪˌɑn] *n* : rayonne *f*

raze ['reɪz] *vt* **razed; razing** : raser, détruire

razor ['reɪzər] *n* : rasoir *m* — **razor blade** *n* : lame *f* de rasoir

reach ['ri:tʃ] *vt* **1** : atteindre **2** *or* ~ **out** : tendre **3** : parvenir à (une entente, etc.) **4** CONTACT : rejoindre — *vi* EXTEND : s'étendre — ~ *n* **1** : portée *f*, proximité *f* **2** **within** ~ : à portée de la main

react [ri'ækt] *vi* : réagir — **reaction** [ri-'ækʃən] *n* : réaction *f* — **reactionary** [ri-'ækʃəˌnɛri] *adj* : réactionnaire — ~ *n, pl* **-ries** : réactionnaire *mf* — **reactor** [ri-'æktər] *n* : réacteur *m*

read ['ri:d] *v* **read** ['rɛd]; **reading** *vt* **1** : lire **2** INTERPRET : interpréter **3** SAY : dire **4** INDICATE : indiquer — *vi* : se lire — **readable** ['ri:dəbəl] *adj* : lisible — **reader** ['ri:dər] *n* : lecteur *m*, -trice *f*

readily ['rɛdəli] *adv* **1** WILLINGLY : volontiers **2** EASILY : facilement

reading ['ri:dɪŋ] *n* : lecture *f*

readjust [ˌri:ə'dʒʌst] *vt* : réajuster — *vi* : se réadapter

ready ['rɛdi] *adj* **readier; -est 1** : prêt, disposé **2** AVAILABLE : disponible **3** **get** ~ : se préparer — ~ *vt* **readied; readying** : préparer

real ['ri:l] *adj* **1** : véritable, réel **2** GENUINE : authentique — ~ *adv* VERY : très — **real estate** *n* : biens *mpl* immobiliers — **realistic** [ˌri:ə'lɪstɪk] *adj* : réaliste — **reality** [ri-'æləti] *n, pl* **-ties** : réalité *f*

realize ['ri:əˌlaɪz] *vt* **-ized; -izing 1** : se rendre compte de **2** ACHIEVE : réaliser

really ['rɪli, 'rɪ-] *adv* : vraiment

realm ['rɛlm] *n* **1** KINGDOM : royaume *m* **2** SPHERE : domaine *m*

reap ['ri:p] *vt* : moissonner, récolter

reappear [ˌri:ə'pɪr] *vi* : réapparaître

rear¹ ['rɪr] *vt* : élever (des enfants, etc.)

rear² *n* : arrière *m*, derrière *m* — ~ *adj* : postérieur

rearrange [ˌri:ə'reɪndʒ] *vt* **-ranged; -ranging** : réarranger

reason ['ri:zən] *n* : raison *f* — ~ *vi* : raisonner — **reasonable** ['ri:zənəbəl] *adj* : raisonnable — **reasoning** ['ri:zənɪŋ] *n* : raisonnement *m*

reassure [ˌri:ə'ʃʊr] *vt* **-sured; -suring** : rassurer — **reassurance** [ˌri:ə'ʃʊrənts] *n* : réconfort *m*

rebate ['ri:ˌbeɪt] *n* : ristourne *f*

rebel ['rɛbəl] *n* : rebelle *mf* — ~ [rɪ'bɛl] *vi* **-belled; -belling** : se rebeller — **rebellion** [rɪ'bɛljən] *n* : rébellion *f* — **rebellious** [rɪ-'bɛljəs] *adj* : rebelle

rebirth [ˌri:'bərθ] *n* : renaissance *f*

reboot [ˌri:'bu:t] *vt* : réamorcer, redémarrer (en informatique)

rebound ['ri:ˌbaʊnd, rɪ'baʊnd] *vi* : rebondir — ~ ['ri:ˌbaʊnd] *n* : rebond *m*

rebuff [rɪ'bʌf] *vt* : rabrouer — ~ *n* : rebuffade *f*

rebuild [ˌri:'bɪld] *vt* **-built** [-'bɪlt]; **-building** : reconstruire

rebuke [rɪ'bju:k] *vt* **-buked; -buking** : reprocher — ~ *n* : réprimande *f*

rebut [rɪ'bʌt] *vt* **-butted; -butting** : réfuter — **rebuttal** [rɪ'bʌtəl] *n* : réfutation *f*

recall [rɪ'kɔl] *vt* **1** : rappeler (au devoir, etc.) **2** REMEMBER : se rappeler **3** REVOKE : annuler — ~ [rɪ'kɔl, 'ri:ˌkɔl] *n* : rappel *m*

recapitulate [ˌri:kə'pɪtʃəˌleɪt] *v* **-lated; -lating** : récapituler

recapture [ˌri:'kæptʃər] *vt* **-tured; -turing 1** : reprendre **2** RELIVE : revivre

recede [rɪ'si:d] *vi* **-ceded; -ceding** : se retirer

receipt [rɪ'si:t] *n* **1** : reçu *m* **2** ~**s** *npl* : recettes *fpl*

receive [rɪ'si:v] *vt* **-ceived; -ceiving** : recevoir — **receiver** [rɪ'si:vər] *n* : récepteur *m*, combiné *m*

recent ['ri:sənt] *adj* : récent — **recently** [-li] *adv* : récemment

receptacle [rɪ'sɛptɪkəl] *n* : récipient *m*

reception [rɪ'sɛpʃən] *n* : réception *f* — **receptionist** [rɪ'sɛpʃənɪst] *n* : réceptionniste *mf* — **receptive** [rɪ'sɛptɪv] *adj* : réceptif

recess ['ri:ˌsɛs, rɪ'sɛs] *n* **1** ALCOVE : recoin *m* **2** BREAK : récréation *f* (scolaire) — **recession** [rɪ'sɛʃən] *n* : récession *f*

recharge [ˌri:'tʃɑrdʒ] *vt* **-charged; -charging** : recharger — **rechargeable** [ˌri:-'tʃɑrdʒəbəl] *adj* : rechargeable

recipe ['rɛsəˌpi:] *n* : recette *f*

recipient [rɪ'sɪpiənt] *n* : récipiendaire *mf*

reciprocal [rɪ'sɪprəkəl] *adj* : réciproque

recite [rɪ'saɪt] *vt* **-cited; -citing 1** : réciter (un poème, etc.) **2** LIST : énumérer — **recital** [rɪ'saɪtəl] *n* : récital *m*

reckless ['rɛkləs] *adj* : imprudent — **recklessness** ['rɛkləsnəs] *n* : imprudence *f*

reckon ['rɛkən] *vt* : estimer, penser — **reckoning** ['rɛkənɪŋ] *n* : calculs *mpl*

reclaim [rɪ'kleɪm] *vt* : récupérer

recline [rɪ'klaɪn] *vi* **-clined; -clining** : s'allonger — **reclining** [rɪ'klaɪnɪŋ] *adj* : réglable (se dit d'un siège)

recluse ['rɛˌklu:s, rɪ'klu:s] *n* : reclus *m*, -cluse *f*

recognition [ˌrɛkɪg'nɪʃən] *n* : reconnaissance *f* — **recognizable** ['rɛkəgˌnaɪzəbəl] *adj* : reconnaissable — **recognize** ['rɛkɪgˌnaɪz] *vt* **-nized; -nizing** : reconnaître

recoil [rɪ'kɔɪl] *vi* : reculer — ~ ['ri:ˌkɔɪl, rɪ'-] *n* : recul *m* (d'une arme à feu)

recollect [ˌrɛkə'lɛkt] v : se souvenir — **recollection** [ˌrɛkə'lɛkʃən] n : souvenir m

recommend [ˌrɛkə'mɛnd] vt : recommander — **recommendation** [ˌrɛkəmən'deɪʃən] n : recommandation f

reconcile ['rɛkən,saɪl] v -ciled; -ciling vt 1 : réconcilier (des personnes), concilier (des dates, etc.) 2 ~ oneself to : se résigner à — vi MAKE UP : se réconcilier — **reconciliation** [ˌrɛkən,sɪli'eɪʃən] n : réconciliation f

reconsider [ˌri:kən'sɪdər] vt : reconsidérer

reconstruct [ˌri:kən'strʌkt] vt : reconstruire

record [rɪ'kɔrd] vt 1 : enregistrer 2 WRITE DOWN : noter — ~ ['rɛkərd] n 1 DOCUMENT : dossier m 2 REGISTER : registre m 3 HISTORY : passé m 4 : disque m (de musique) 5 or police ~ : casier m judiciaire 6 world ~ : record m mondial — **recorder** [rɪ'kɔrdər] n 1 : flûte f à bec 2 or tape ~ : magnétophone m — **recording** [rɪ'kɔrdɪŋ] n : enregistrement m

recount[1] [rɪ'kaʊnt] vt NARRATE : raconter

recount[2] ['ri:,kaʊnt, ,rɪ'-] vt : recompter (des votes, etc.) — ~ n : décompte m

recourse ['ri:,kɔrs, rɪ'-] n 1 : recours m 2 have ~ to : recourir à

recover [rɪ'kʌvər] vt : récupérer — vi RECUPERATE : se remettre, se rétablir — **recovery** [rɪ'kʌvəri] n, pl -ries : rétablissement m

recreation [ˌrɛkri'eɪʃən] n : loisirs mpl, récréation f — **recreational** [ˌrɛkri'eɪʃənəl] adj : récréatif

recruit [rɪ'kru:t] vt : recruter — ~ n : recrue f — **recruitment** [rɪ'kru:tmənt] n : recrutement m

rectangle ['rɛk,tæŋɡəl] n : rectangle m — **rectangular** [rɛk'tæŋɡjələr] adj : rectangulaire

rectify ['rɛktə,faɪ] vt -fied; -fying : rectifier

rector ['rɛktər] n : pasteur m — **rectory** ['rɛktəri] n, pl -ries : presbytère m

rectum ['rɛktəm] n, pl -tums or -ta [-tə] : rectum m

recuperate [rɪ'ku:pə,reɪt, -'kju:-] v -ated; -ating vt : récupérer — vi : se rétablir

recur [rɪ'kər] vi -curred; -curring : réapparaître — **recurrence** [rɪ'kərənts] n : répétition f — **recurrent** [rɪ'kərənt] adj : qui se répète

recycle [rɪ'saɪkəl] vt -cled; -cling : recycler

red ['rɛd] adj : rouge — ~ n : rouge m — **redden** ['rɛdən] v : rougir — **reddish** ['rɛdɪʃ] adj : rougeâtre

redecorate [ˌri:'dɛkə,reɪt] vt -rated; -rating : repeindre

redeem [rɪ'di:m] vt : racheter, sauver — **redemption** [rɪ'dɛmpʃən] n : rédemption f

red–handed ['rɛd'hændəd] adv & adj : la main dans le sac

redhead ['rɛd,hɛd] n : roux m, rousse f

red–hot ['rɛd'hɑt] adj : brûlant

redness ['rɛdnəs] n : rougeur f

redo [ˌri:'du:] vt -did [-dɪd]; -done [-'dʌn]; -doing : refaire

red tape n : paperasserie f

reduce [rɪ'du:s, -'dju:s] vt -duced; -ducing : réduire — **reduction** [rɪ'dʌkʃən] n : réduction f

redundant [rɪ'dʌndənt] adj : superflu

reed ['ri:d] n : roseau m

reef ['ri:f] n : récif m

reek ['ri:k] vi : empester

reel ['ri:l] n : bobine f (de fil, etc.) — ~ vt ~ in : enrouler (une ligne de pêche), ramener (un poisson) — vi 1 STAGGER : tituber 2 SPIN : tournoyer

reestablish [ˌri:ɪ'stæblɪʃ] vt : rétablir

refer [rɪ'fər] v -ferred; -ferring vt DIRECT : renvoyer — vi ~ to 1 : faire allusion à 2 CONSULT : consulter

referee [ˌrɛfə'ri:] n : arbitre m — ~ v -eed; -eeing : arbitrer

reference ['rɛfrənts, 'rɛfə-] n 1 : référence f 2 in ~ to : en ce qui concerne

refill [ˌri:'fɪl] vt : remplir à nouveau — ~ ['ri:,fɪl] n : recharge f (d'encre)

refine [rɪ'faɪn] vt -fined; -fining : raffiner — **refined** [rɪ'faɪnd] adj : raffiné — **refinement** [rɪ'faɪnmənt] n : raffinement m — **refinery** [rɪ'faɪnəri] n, pl -eries : raffinerie f

reflect [rɪ'flɛkt] vt : réfléchir (la lumière), refléter (une image, etc.) — vi 1 PONDER : réfléchir 2 ~ badly on : faire du tort à — **reflection** [rɪ'flɛkʃən] n 1 : réflexion f 2 IMAGE : reflet m

reflex ['ri:,flɛks] n : réflexe m

reflexive [rɪ'flɛksɪv] adj : réfléchi

reform [rɪ'fɔrm] vt : réformer — ~ n : réforme f — **reformer** [rɪ'fɔrmər] n : réformateur m, -trice f

refrain[1] [rɪ'freɪn] vi ~ from : se retenir de

refrain[2] n : refrain m (en musique)

refresh [rɪ'frɛʃ] vt : rafraîchir — **refreshments** [rɪ'frɛʃmənts] npl : rafraîchissements mpl

refrigerate [rɪ'frɪdʒə,reɪt] vt -ated; -ating : réfrigérer — **refrigeration** [rɪ,frɪdʒə'reɪʃən] n : réfrigération f — **refrigerator** [rɪ'frɪdʒə,reɪtər] n : réfrigérateur m

refuel [rɪ:'fju:əl] v -eled or -elled; -eling or -elling vt : ravitailler en carburant — vi : se ravitailler

refuge ['rɛ,fju:dʒ] n : refuge m, abri m — **refugee** [ˌrɛfju'dʒi:] n : réfugié m, -giée f

refund [rɪ'fʌnd, 'ri:,fʌnd] vt : rembourser — ~ ['ri:,fʌnd] n : remboursement m

refurbish [rɪ'fərbɪʃ] vt : remettre à neuf

refuse[1] [rɪ'fju:z] vt -fused; -fusing 1 : refuser 2 ~ to do sth : se refuser à faire qqch — **refusal** [rɪ'fju:zəl] n : refus m

refuse² ['rɛ,fju:s, -,fju:z] *n* : ordures *fpl*, déchets *mpl*

refute [rɪ'fju:t] *vt* **-futed; -futing** : réfuter

regain [ri:'geɪn] *vt* : retrouver

regal ['ri:gəl] *adj* : royal, majestueux — **regalia** [rɪ'geɪljə] *npl* : insignes *mpl*, vêtements *mpl* de cérémonie

regard [rɪ'gɑrd] *n* **1** : égard *m*, considération *f* **2** ESTEEM : estime *f* **3 ~s** *npl* : amitiés *fpl* **4 with ~ to** : en ce qui concerne — **~** *vt* **1** HEED : tenir compte de **2** ESTEEM : estimer **3 as ~s** : en ce qui concerne **4 ~ as** : considérer — **regarding** [rɪ'gɑrdɪŋ] *prep* : concernant — **regardless** [rɪ'gɑrdləs] *adv* : malgré tout — **regardless of** *prep* **1** : sans tenir compte de **2** IN SPITE OF : malgré

regime [reɪ'ʒi:m, rɪ-] *n* : régime *m* — **regimen** ['rɛdʒəmən] *n* : régimen *m*

regiment ['rɛdʒəmənt] *n* : régiment *m*

region ['ri:dʒən] *n* : région *f* — **regional** ['ri:dʒənəl] *adj* : régional

register ['rɛdʒəstər] *n* : registre *m* — **~** *vt* **1** : inscrire, enregistrer **2** SHOW : exprimer **3** RECORD : indiquer (la température, etc.) **4** : immatriculer (un véhicule) — *vi* ENROLL : s'inscrire — **registration** [,rɛdʒə'streɪʃən] *n* **1** : inscription *f*, enregistrement *m* **2 ~ number** : numéro *m* d'immatriculation — **registry** ['rɛdʒəstri] *n, pl* **-tries** : registre *m*

regret [rɪ'grɛt] *vt* **-gretted; -gretting** : regretter — **~** *n* **1** REMORSE : remords *m* **2** SORROW : regret *m* — **regrettable** [rɪ'grɛtəbəl] *adj* : lamentable

regular ['rɛgjələr] *adj* **1** : régulier **2** CUSTOMARY : habituel — **~** *n* : habitué *m*, -tuée *f* — **regularity** [,rɛgjə'lærəti] *n, pl* **-ties** : régularité *f* — **regularly** ['rɛgjələrli] *adv* : régulièrement — **regulate** ['rɛgjə,leɪt] *vt* **-lated; -lating** : régler — **regulation** [,rɛgjə'leɪʃən] *n* **1** RULE : règlement *m*, règle *f* **2** CONTROL : réglementation *f*

rehabilitate [,ri:hə'bɪlə,teɪt, ,ri:ə-] *vt* **-tated; -tating** : réhabiliter — **rehabilitation** [,ri:hə,bɪlə'teɪʃən, ,ri:ə-] *n* : réhabilitation *f*

rehearse [rɪ'hərs] *vt* **-hearsed; -hearsing** : répéter — **rehearsal** [rɪ'hərsəl] *n* : répétition *f*

reign ['reɪn] *n* : règne *m* — **~** *vi* : régner

reimburse [,ri:əm'bərs] *vt* **-bursed; -bursing** : rembourser — **reimbursement** [,ri:əm'bərsmənt] *n* : remboursement *m*

rein ['reɪn] *n* : rêne *f*

reindeer ['reɪn,dɪr] *n* : renne *m*

reinforce [,ri:ən'fors] *vt* **-forced; -forcing** : renforcer — **reinforcement** [,ri:ən'forsmənt] *n* : renfort *m*

reinstate [,ri:ən'steɪt] *vt* **-stated; -stating** : rétablir (dans ses fonctions)

reiterate [ri'ɪtə,reɪt] *vt* **-ated; -ating** : réitérer

reject [rɪ'dʒɛkt] *vt* : rejeter — **rejection** [rɪ-'dʒɛkʃən] *n* : rejet *m*

rejoice [rɪ'dʒɔɪs] *vi* **-joiced; -joicing** : se réjouir

rejuvenate [rɪ'dʒu:və,neɪt] *vt* **-nated; -nating** : rajeunir

rekindle [ri:'kɪndəl] *vt* **-dled; -dling** : raviver, ranimer

relapse ['ri:,læps, rɪ'læps] *n* : rechute *f* — **~** [rɪ'læps] *vi* **-lapsed; -lapsing** : rechuter

relate [rɪ'leɪt] *v* **-lated; -lating** *vt* **1** TELL : raconter **2** ASSOCIATE : relier — *vi* **1 ~ to** : se rapporter à **2 ~ to** : s'entendre (avec) **3 ~ to** : apprécier, comprendre — **related** [rɪ'leɪtəd] *adj* **~ to** : apparenté à — **relation** [rɪ'leɪʃən] *n* **1** : rapport *m*, lien *m* **2** RELATIVE : parent *m*, -rente *f* **3 in ~ to** : par rapport à **4 ~s** *npl* : rapports *mpl*, relations *fpl* — **relationship** [rɪ'leɪʃən,ʃɪp] *n* **1** : rapport *m*, relations *fpl* **2** KINSHIP : liens *mpl* de parenté — **relative** ['rɛlətɪv] *n* : parent *m*, -rente *f* — **~** *adj* : relatif — **relatively** ['rɛlətɪvli] *adv* : relativement

relax [rɪ'læks] *vt* : détendre — *vi* : se détendre — **relaxation** [,ri:,læk'seɪʃən] *n* : détente *f*, relaxation *f*

relay ['ri:,leɪ] *n* **1** : relève *m* **2 or ~ race** : course *f* de relais — **~** ['ri:,leɪ, rɪ'leɪ] *vt* **-layed; -laying** : relayer, transmettre

release [rɪ'li:s] *vt* **-leased; -leasing 1** FREE : libérer, mettre en liberté **2** : relâcher (une bride, etc.) **3** EMIT : émettre **4** : publier (un livre), sortir (un nouveau film) — **~** *n* **1** : libération *f* **2** : sortie *f* (d'un film), parution *f* (d'un livre)

relegate ['rɛlə,geɪt] *vt* **-gated; -gating** : reléguer

relent [rɪ'lɛnt] *vi* **1** GIVE IN : céder **2** ABATE : se calmer — **relentless** [rɪ'lɛntləs] *adj* : implacable

relevant ['rɛləvənt] *adj* : pertinent — **relevance** ['rɛləvənts] *n* : pertinence *f*

reliable [rɪ'laɪəbəl] *adj* : fiable, sûr — **reliability** [rɪ,laɪə'bɪləti] *n, pl* **-ties** : fiabilité *f* — **reliance** [rɪ'laɪənts] *n* **1** : dépendance *f* **2** TRUST : confiance *f*

relic ['rɛlɪk] *n* : relique *f*

relief [rɪ'li:f] *n* **1** : soulagement *m* **2** AID : aide *f*, secours *m* **3** : relief *m* (d'une carte géographique) **4** REPLACEMENT : relève *f* — **relieve** [rɪ'li:v] *vt* **-lieved; -lieving 1** : soulager **2** REPLACE : relayer (qqn) **3 ~ s.o. of** : libérer qqn de

religion [rɪ'lɪdʒən] *n* : religion *f* — **religious** [rɪ'lɪdʒəs] *adj* : religieux

relinquish [rɪ'lɪŋkwɪʃ, -'lɪn-] *vt* : renoncer à

relish ['rɛlɪʃ] *n* **1** : condiment *m* à base de cornichons **2 with ~** : avec un plaisir évident — **~** *vt* : savourer

relocate [,ri:'lo:,keɪt, ,ri:lo'keɪt] *v* **-cated;**

-cating *vt* : transférer — *vi* : déménager, s'établir ailleurs — **relocation** [‚ri:loˈkeɪʃən] *n* : déménagement *m*

reluctance [rɪˈlʌktənts] *n* : réticence *f* — **reluctant** [rɪˈlʌktənt] *adj* : réticent — **reluctantly** [rɪˈlʌktəntli] *adv* : à contrecœur

rely [rɪˈlaɪ] *vi* **-lied; -lying** ~ **on 1** : dépendre de **2** TRUST : se fier à

remain [rɪˈmeɪn] *vi* : rester — **remainder** [rɪˈmeɪndər] *n* : reste *m*, restant *m* — **remains** [rɪˈmeɪnz] *npl* : restes *mpl*

remark [rɪˈmɑrk] *n* : remarque *f*, observation *f* — ~ *vt* **1** : remarquer **2** SAY : mentionner — *vi* ~ **on** : observer que — **remarkable** [rɪˈmɑrkəbəl] *adj* : remarquable

remedy [ˈrɛmədi] *n, pl* **-dies** : remède *m* — ~ *vt* **-died; -dying** : remédier à — **remedial** [rɪˈmiːdiəl] *adj* : de rattrapage

remember [rɪˈmɛmbər] *vt* **1** : se rappeler, se souvenir de **2** ~ **to** : ne pas oublier de — *vi* : se rappeler, se souvenir — **remembrance** [rɪˈmɛmbrənts] *n* : souvenir *m*

remind [rɪˈmaɪnd] *vt* ~ **s.o. of sth** : rappeler qqch à qqn — **reminder** [rɪˈmaɪndər] *n* : rappel *m*

reminisce [‚rɛməˈnɪs] *vi* **-nisced; -niscing** : se rappeler le bon vieux temps — **reminiscent** [‚rɛməˈnɪsənt] *adj* ~ **of** : qui rappelle, qui fait penser à

remission [rɪˈmɪʃən] *n* : rémission *f*

remit [rɪˈmɪt] *vt* **-mitted; -mitting** : envoyer (de l'argent)

remnant [ˈrɛmnənt] *n* **1** : reste *m*, restant *m* **2** TRACE : vestige *m*

remorse [rɪˈmɔrs] *n* : remords *m* — **remorseful** [rɪˈmɔrsfəl] *adj* : plein de remords

remote [rɪˈmoːt] *adj* **-moter; -est 1** : lointain, éloigné **2** ALOOF : distant — **remote control** *n* : télécommande *f*

remove [rɪˈmuːv] *vt* **-moved; -moving 1** : enlever, ôter **2** DISMISS : renvoyer **3** ELIMINATE : supprimer, dissiper — **removable** [rɪˈmuːvəbəl] *adj* : amovible — **removal** [rɪˈmuːvəl] *n* : élimination *f*

remunerate [rɪˈmjuːnə‚reɪt] *vt* **-ated; -ating** : rémunérer

render [ˈrɛndər] *vt* : rendre

rendition [rɛnˈdɪʃən] *n* : interprétation *f*

renegade [ˈrɛnɪ‚geɪd] *n* : renégat *m*, -gate *f*

renew [rɪˈnuː, -ˈnjuː] *vt* **1** : renouveler **2** RESUME : reprendre — **renewal** [rɪˈnuːəl, -ˈnjuː-] *n* : renouvellement *m*

renounce [rɪˈnaʊnts] *vt* **-nounced; -nouncing** : renoncer à

renovate [ˈrɛnə‚veɪt] *vt* **-vated; -vating** : rénover — **renovation** [‚rɛnəˈveɪʃən] *n* : rénovation *f*

renown [rɪˈnaʊn] *n* : renommée *f*, renom *m* — **renowned** [rɪˈnaʊnd] *adj* : renommé, célèbre

rent [ˈrɛnt] *n* **1** : loyer *m* (somme d'argent) **2 for** ~ : à louer — ~ *vt* : louer — **rental** [ˈrɛntəl] *n* : location *f* — ~ *adj* : de location — **renter** [ˈrɛntər] *n* : locataire *mf*

renunciation [rɪ‚nʌntsiˈeɪʃən] *n* : renonciation *f*

reorganize [‚riːˈɔrgə‚naɪz] *vt* **-nized; -nizing** : réorganiser — **reorganization** [‚riː‚ɔrgənəˈzeɪʃən] *n* : réorganisation *f*

repair [rɪˈpær] *vt* : réparer — ~ *n* **1** : réparation *f* **2 in bad** ~ : en mauvais état

repay [rɪˈpeɪ] *vt* **-paid; -paying** : rembourser (un emprunt), rendre (une faveur, etc.)

repeal [rɪˈpiːl] *vt* : abroger, révoquer — ~ *n* : abrogation *f*, révocation *f*

repeat [rɪˈpiːt] *vt* : répéter — ~ *n* **1** : répétition *f* **2** : rediffusion *f* (se dit d'une émission) — **repeatedly** [rɪˈpiːtədli] *adv* : à plusieurs reprises

repel [rɪˈpɛl] *vt* **-pelled; -pelling** : repousser — **repellent** [rɪˈpɛlənt] *adj* : repoussant

repent [rɪˈpɛnt] *vi* : se repentir — **repentance** [rɪˈpɛntənts] *n* : repentir *m*

repercussion [‚riːpərˈkʌʃən, ‚rɛpər-] *n* : répercussion *f*

repertoire [ˈrɛpər‚twɑr] *n* : répertoire *m*

repetition [‚rɛpəˈtɪʃən] *n* : répétition *f* — **repetitious** [‚rɛpəˈtɪʃəs] *adj* : répétitif — **repetitive** [rɪˈpɛtətɪv] *adj* : répétitif

replace [rɪˈpleɪs] *vt* **-placed; -placing 1** : remettre (à sa place) **2** SUBSTITUTE : remplacer **3** EXCHANGE : échanger — **replacement** [rɪˈpleɪsmənt] *n* **1** : remplacement *m* **2** SUBSTITUTE : remplaçant *m*, -çante *f* **3** ~ **part** : pièce *f* de rechange

replenish [rɪˈplɛnɪʃ] *vt* **1** : réapprovisionner **2** : remplir (de nouveau)

replica [ˈrɛplɪkə] *n* : réplique *f*

reply [rɪˈplaɪ] *vi* **-plied; -plying** : répondre, répliquer — ~ *n, pl* **-plies** : réponse *f*, réplique *f*

report [rɪˈpɔrt] *n* **1** : rapport *m*, compte rendu *m* **2** *or* **news** ~ : reportage *m* **3 weather** ~ : bulletin *m* (météorologique) — ~ *vt* **1** RELATE : raconter **2** ~ **an accident** : signaler un accident — *vi* ~ **to s.o.** : se présenter à qqn — **report card** *n* : bulletin *m* scolaire — **reporter** [rɪˈpɔrtər] *n* : journaliste *mf*, reporter *m*

reprehensible [‚rɛprɪˈhɛntsəbəl] *adj* : répréhensible

represent [‚rɛprɪˈzɛnt] *vt* : représenter — **representation** [‚rɛprɪ‚zɛnˈteɪʃən, -zən-] *n* : représentation *f* — **representative** [‚rɛprɪˈzɛntətɪv] *adj* : représentatif — ~ *n* : représentant *m*, -tante *f*

repress [rɪˈprɛs] *vt* : réprimer — **repression** [rɪˈprɛʃən] *n* : répression *f*

reprieve [rɪˈpriːv] *n* : sursis *m*

reprimand ['rɛprə,mænd] *n* : réprimande *f*
— **~** *vt* : réprimander
reprint [ri'prɪnt] *vt* : réimprimer — **~** ['ri:-
,prɪnt, ri'prɪnt] *n* : réimpression *f*
reprisal [rɪ'praɪzəl] *n* : représailles *fpl*
reproach [rɪ'proːʃ] *n* **1** : reproche *m* **2 be-**
yond ~ : irréprochable — **~** *vt* : reprocher à — **reproachful** [rɪ'proːtʃfəl] *adj*
: de reproche
reproduce [,ri:prə'duːs, -'djuːs] *v* **-duced;**
-ducing *vt* : reproduire — *vi* : se reproduire
— **reproduction** [,ri:prə'dʌkʃən] *n* : reproduction *f*
reptile ['rɛp,taɪl] *n* : reptile *m*
republic [rɪ'pʌblɪk] *n* : république *f* — **re-**
publican [rɪ'pʌblɪkən] *n* : républicain *m*,
-caine *f* — **~** *adj* : républicain
repudiate [rɪ'pjuːdi,eɪt] *vt* **-ated; -ating**
: répudier
repugnant [rɪ'pʌgnənt] *adj* : répugnant —
repugnance [rɪ'pʌgnənts] *n* : répugnance *f*
repulse [rɪ'pʌls] *vt* **-pulsed; -pulsing** : repousser — **repulsive** [rɪ'pʌlsɪv] *adj* : repoussant
reputation [,rɛpjə'teɪʃən] *n* : réputation *f* —
reputable ['rɛpjətəbəl] *adj* : de bonne
réputation — **reputed** [rɪ'pjuːtəd] *adj*
: réputé
request [rɪ'kwɛst] *n* : demande *f* — **~** *vt*
: demander
require [rɪ'kwaɪr] *vt* **-quired; -quiring 1**
CALL FOR : requérir **2** NEED : avoir besoin
de — **requirement** [rɪ'kwaɪrmənt] *n* **1**
NEED : besoin *m* **2** DEMAND : exigence *f* —
requisite ['rɛkwəzɪt] *adj* : nécessaire
resale ['riː,seɪl, ,riː'seɪl] *n* : revente *f*
rescind [rɪ'sɪnd] *vt* : annuler, abroger
rescue ['rɛs,kjuː] *vt* **-cued; -cuing** : sauver,
secourir — **~** *n* : sauvetage *m* — **rescuer**
['rɛs,kjuːər] *n* : sauveteur *m*, secouriste *mf*
research [rɪ'sərtʃ, 'riː,-] *vt* : faire des recherches
fpl — **~** *vt* : faire des recherches sur — **re-**
searcher [rɪ'sərtʃər, 'riː,-] *n* : chercheur *m*,
-cheuse *f*
resemble [rɪ'zɛmbəl] *vt* **-bled; -bling**
: ressembler à — **resemblance** [rɪ'zɛm-
blənts] *n* : ressemblance *f*
resent [rɪ'zɛnt] *vt* : en vouloir à, s'offenser
de — **resentful** [rɪ'zɛntfəl] *adj* : éprouver
du ressentiment — **resentment** [rɪ-
'zɛntmənt] *n* : ressentiment *m*
reserve [rɪ'zərv] *vt* **-served; -serving**
: réserver — **~** *n* : réserve *f* — **reservation**
[,rɛzər'veɪʃən] *n* **1** : réserve *f* (indienne) **2**
RESERVING : réservation *f* — **reserved** [rɪ-
'zərvd] *adj* : réservé, discret — **reservoir**
['rɛzər,vwɑr, -,vwɔr, -,vɔr] *n* : réservoir *m*
reset [,riː'sɛt] *vt* **-set; -setting** : remettre à
l'heure (une montre), remettre à zéro (un
compteur)

residence ['rɛzədənts] *n* : résidence *f* — **re-**
side [rɪ'zaɪd] *vi* **-sided; -siding** : résider —
resident ['rɛzədənt] *adj* : résidant — **~** *n*
: résident *m*, -dente *f* — **residential** [,rɛzə-
'dɛntʃəl] *adj* : résidentiel
residue ['rɛzə,duː, -,djuː] *n* : résidu *m*
resign [rɪ'zaɪn] *vt* **1** QUIT : démissionner **2**
~ oneself to : se résigner à — **resigna-**
tion [,rɛzɪg'neɪʃən] *n* **1** : démission *f* **2** AC-
CEPTANCE : résignation *f*
resilient [rɪ'zɪljənt] *adj* **1** : résistant **2** ELAS-
TIC : élastique — **resilience** [rɪ'zɪljənts] *n* **1**
: résistance *f* **2** ELASTICITY : élasticité *f*
resin ['rɛzən] *n* : résine *f*
resist [rɪ'zɪst] *vt* : résister à — **resistance**
[rɪ'zɪstənts] *n* : résistance *f* — **resistant** [rɪ-
'zɪstənt] *adj* : résistant
resolve [rɪ'zɑlv] *vt* **-solved; -solving 1** : résoudre **2 ~ to do** : décider de faire — **~**
n : résolution *f*, détermination *f* — **resolu-**
tion [,rɛzə'luːʃən] *n* : résolution *f* — **res-**
olute ['rɛzə,luːt] *adj* : résolu
resonance ['rɛzənənts] *n* : résonance *f* —
resonant ['rɛzənənt] *adj* : résonant
resort [rɪ'zɔrt] *n* **1** : recours *m* **2** : centre *m*
touristique, station *f* (de ski, etc.) — **~** *vi*
~ to : recourir à, avoir recours à
resound [rɪ'zaʊnd] *vi* : résonner, retentir —
resounding [rɪ'zaʊndɪŋ] *adj* : retentissant
resource ['riː,sors, rɪ'sors] *n* : ressource *f* —
resourceful [rɪ'sorsfəl, -'zors-] *adj* : ingénieux, débrouillard
respect [rɪ'spɛkt] *n* **1** : respect *m* **2 ~s** *npl*
: respects *mpl*, hommages *mpl* **3 in ~ to**
: en ce qui concerne **4 in some ~s** : à
certains égards — **~** *vt* : respecter — **re-**
spectable [rɪ'spɛktəbəl] *adj* : respectable
— **respectful** [rɪ'spɛktfəl] *adj* : respectueux — **respective** [rɪ'spɛktɪv] *adj*
: respectif — **respectively** [rɪ'spɛktɪvli]
adv : respectivement
respiratory ['rɛspərə,tori, rɪ'spaɪrə-] *adj*
: respiratoire
respite ['rɛspɪt, rɪ'spaɪt] *n* : répit *m*, sursis *m*
response [rɪ'spɑnts] *n* : réponse *f* — **re-**
spond [rɪ'spɑnd] *vi* : répondre — **responsi-**
bility [rɪ,spɑntsə'bɪləti] *n, pl* **-ties** : responsabilité *f* — **responsible** [rɪ'spɑntsəbəl] *adj*
: responsable — **responsive** [rɪ'spɑntsɪv]
adj : réceptif
rest[1] ['rɛst] *n* **1** : repos *m* **2** SUPPORT : appui
m **3** : silence *m* (en musique) **4 ~ area**
: aire *f* de repos, halte *f* routière *Can* — **~**
vi **1** : se reposer **2** LEAN : s'appuyer **3 ~**
on DEPEND : dépendre de — *vt* **1** : reposer
2 LEAN : appuyer
rest[2] *n* REMAINDER : reste *m*
restaurant ['rɛstə,rɑnt, -rənt] *n* : restaurant
m
restful ['rɛstfəl] *adj* : reposant, paisible

restless ['rɛstləs] *adj* : inquiet, agité
restore [rɪ'stor] *vt* **-stored; -storing 1** RE-
TURN : retourner **2** REESTABLISH : rétablir
3 REPAIR : restaurer — **restoration** [,rɛstə-
'reɪʃən] *n* **1** : rétablissement *m* **2** REPAIR
: restauration *f*
restrain [rɪ'streɪn] *vt* **1** : retenir **2 ~ oneself** : se retenir — **restrained** [rɪ'streɪnd]
adj : contenu, maîtrisé — **restraint** [rɪ-
'streɪnt] *n* **1** : restriction *f*, contrainte *f* **2**
SELF-CONTROL : retenue *f*, maîtrise *f* de soi
restrict [rɪ'strɪkt] *vt* : restreindre — **restriction** [rɪ'strɪkʃən] *n* : restriction *f* — **restrictive** [rɪ'strɪktɪv] *adj* : restrictif
result [rɪ'zʌlt] *vi* **1 ~ from** : résulter de **2
~ in** : avoir pour résultat — **~** *n* **1** : résultat *m* **2 as a ~ of** : à la suite de
resume [rɪ'zu:m] *v* **-sumed; -suming**
: reprendre
résumé *or* **resume** *or* **resumé** ['rɛzə,meɪ,
,rɛzə'-] *n* : curriculum *m* vitæ
resumption [rɪ'zʌmpʃən] *n* : reprise *f*
resurgence [rɪ'sərdʒənts] *n* : réapparition *f*
resurrection [,rɛzə'rɛkʃən] *n* : résurrection *f*
— **resurrect** [,rɛzə'rɛkt] *vt* : ressusciter
resuscitate [rɪ'sʌsə,teɪt] *vt* **-tated; -tating**
: réanimer
retail ['ri:,teɪl] *vt* : vendre au détail — **~** *n*
: vente *f* au détail — **~** *adj* : de détail — **~**
adv : au détail — **retailer** ['ri:,teɪlər] *n* : dé-
taillant *m*, -lante *f*
retain [rɪ'teɪn] *vt* : retenir
retaliate [rɪ'tæli,eɪt] *vi* **-ated; -ating** : riposter — **retaliation** [rɪ,tæli'eɪʃən] *n* : riposte *f*, représailles *fpl*
retarded [rɪ'tardəd] *adj* : arriéré
retention [rɪ'tɛnʃən] *n* : rétention *f*
reticence ['rɛtəsənts] *n* : réticence *f* — **reticent** ['rɛtəsənt] *adj* : réticent, hésitant
retina ['rɛtənə] *n, pl* **-nas** *or* **-nae** [-ən,i:,
-ən,aɪ] : rétine *f*
retire [rɪ'taɪr] *vi* **-tired; -tiring 1** WITHDRAW
: se retirer **2** : prendre sa retraite **3** : aller se
coucher — **retirement** [rɪ'taɪrmənt] *n* : retraite *f*
retort [rɪ'tort] *vt* : rétorquer, riposter — **~** *n*
: riposte *f*
retrace [,ri:'treɪs] *vt* **-traced; -tracing ~
one's steps** : revenir sur ses pas
retract [rɪ'trækt] *vt* **1** WITHDRAW : retirer **2**
: rentrer (ses griffes, etc.) — **retractable** [rɪ-
'træktəbəl] *adj* : escamotable
retrain [,ri:'treɪn] *vt* : recycler
retreat [rɪ'tri:t] *n* **1** : retraite *f* **2** REFUGE
: refuge *m* — **~** *vi* : se retirer, reculer
retribution [,rɛtrə'bju:ʃən] *n* : châtiment *m*
retrieve [rɪ'tri:v] *vt* **-trieved; -trieving**
: retrouver, récupérer — **retrieval** [rɪ'tri:vəl]
n : récupération *f*
retroactive [,rɛtro'æktɪv] *adj* : rétroactif

retrospect ['rɛtrə,spɛkt] *n* **in ~** : avec le
recul — **retrospective** [,rɛtrə'spɛktɪv] *adj*
: rétrospectif
return [rɪ'tərn] *vi* **1** : retourner, revenir **2**
REAPPEAR : réapparaître — *vt* **1** : rapporter,
rendre **2** YIELD : produire — **~** *n* **1** : retour *m* **2** YIELD : rapport *m*, rendement *m* **3
in ~ for** : en échange de **4** *or* **tax ~** : déclaration *f* d'impôts — **~** *adj* : de retour
reunite [,ri:ju'naɪt] *vt* **-nited; -niting** : réunir
— **reunion** [ri'ju:njən] *n* : réunion *f*
revamp [,ri:'væmp] *vt* : retaper (une maison), réviser (un texte)
reveal [rɪ'vi:l] *vt* **1** : révéler **2** SHOW : laisser
voir
revel ['rɛvəl] *vi* **-eled** *or* **-elled; -eling** *or*
-elling ~ in : se délecter de
revelation [,rɛvə'leɪʃən] *n* : révélation *f*
revelry ['rɛvəlri] *n, pl* **-ries** : festivités *fpl*,
réjouissances *fpl*
revenge [rɪ'vɛndʒ] *vt* **-venged; -venging**
: venger — **~** *n* **1** : vengeance *f* **2 take ~
on** : se venger sur
revenue ['rɛvə,nu:, -,nju:] *n* : revenu *m*
reverberate [rɪ'vərbə,reɪt] *vi* **-ated; -ating**
: retentir, résonner
reverence ['rɛvərənts] *n* : révérence *f*,
vénération *f* — **revere** [rɪ'vir] *vt* **-vered;
-vering** : révérer, vénérer — **reverend**
['rɛvərənd] *adj* : révérend — **reverent**
['rɛvərənt] *adj* : respectueux
reverse [rɪ'vərs] *adj* : inverse, contraire —
~ *v* **-versed; -versing** *vt* **1** : inverser **2**
CHANGE : renverser, annuler — *vi* **1** : faire
marche arrière (se dit d'une voiture) — **~** *n*
1 BACK : dos *m*, envers *m* **2** *or* **~ gear**
: marche *f* arrière **3 the ~** : le contraire —
reversal [rɪ'vərsəl] *n* **1** : renversement *m* **2**
CHANGE : revirement *m* **3** SETBACK : revers
m — **reversible** [rɪ'vərsəbəl] *adj* : réversible
— **revert** [rɪ'vərt] *vi* **~ to** : revenir à
review [rɪ'vju:] *n* **1** : révision *f* **2** OVERVIEW
: résumé *m* **3** : critique *f* **4** : revue *f* (militaire) — **~** *vt* **1** EXAMINE : examiner **2**
: repasser (une leçon) **3** : faire la critique de
(un roman, etc.) — **reviewer** [rɪ'vju:ər] *n*
: critique *mf*
revile [rɪ'vaɪl] *vt* **-viled; -viling** : injurier
revise [rɪ'vaɪz] *vt* **-vised; -vising 1** : réviser,
corriger **2** : modifier (une politique) — **revision** [rɪ'vɪʒən] *n* : révision *f*
revive [rɪ'vaɪv] *v* **-vived; -viving** *vt* **1**
: ranimer, raviver **2** : réanimer (une personne) **3** RESTORE : rétablir — *vi* COME TO
: reprendre connaissance — **revival** [rɪ-
'vaɪvəl] *n* : renouveau *m*, renaissance *f*
revoke [rɪ'vo:k] *vt* **-voked; -voking** : révoquer
revolt [rɪ'vo:lt] *vt* : révolter, dégoûter — *vi*
~ against : se révolter contre — **~** *n* : ré-

volte *f*, insurrection *f* — **revolting** [rɪ-
ˈvoːltɪŋ] *adj* : révoltant, dégoûtant
revolution [ˌrɛvəˈluːʃən] *n* : révolution *f* —
revolutionary [ˌrɛvəˈluːʃənˌɛri] *adj* : révolutionnaire — ~ *n, pl* **-aries** : révolutionnaire *mf* — **revolutionize** [ˌrɛvəˈluːʃənˌaɪz]
vt **-ized; -izing** : révolutionner
revolve [rɪˈvalv] *v* **-volved; -volving** *vt*
: faire tourner — *vi* : tourner
revolver [rɪˈvalvər] *n* : revolver *m*
revulsion [rɪˈvʌlʃən] *n* : répugnance *f*
reward [rɪˈwɔrd] *vt* : récompenser — ~ *n*
: récompense *f*
rewrite [ˌriːˈraɪt] *vt* **-wrote** [-ˈroːt]; **-written**
[-ˈrɪtən] **-writing** : récrire
rhetoric [ˈrɛtərɪk] *n* : rhétorique *f* — **rhetorical** [rɪˈtɔrɪkəl] *adj* : rhétorique
rheumatism [ˈruːməˌtɪzəm, ˈruː-] *n* : rhumatisme *m*
rhino [ˈraɪˌnoː] *n, pl* **-no** *or* **-nos** → **rhinoceros** — **rhinoceros** [raɪˈnasərəs] *n, pl* **-no-
ceros** *or* **-noceros** *or* **-noceri** [-ˌraɪ]
: rhinocéros *m*
rhubarb [ˈruːˌbarb] *n* : rhubarbe *f*
rhyme [ˈraɪm] *n* **1** : rime *f* **2** VERSE : vers *m*
— ~ *vi* **rhymed; rhyming** : rimer
rhythm [ˈrɪðəm] *n* : rythme *m* — **rhythmic**
[ˈrɪðmɪk] *or* **rhythmical** [-mɪkəl] *adj* : rythmique
rib [ˈrɪb] *n* : côte *f* (en anatomie) — ~ *vt*
ribbed; ribbing : taquiner
ribbon [ˈrɪbən] *n* : ruban *m*
rice [ˈraɪs] *n* : riz *m*
rich [ˈrɪtʃ] *adj* **1** : riche **2** ~ **meal** : repas *m*
lourd — **riches** [ˈrɪtʃəz] *npl* : richesses *fpl* —
richness [ˈrɪtʃnəs] *n* : richesse *f*
rickety [ˈrɪkəti] *adj* : branlant
ricochet [ˈrɪkəˌʃeɪ] *n* : ricochet *m* — ~ *vi*
-cheted [-ˌʃeɪd] *or* **-chetted** [-ˌʃɛtəd];
-cheting [-ˌʃeɪɪŋ] *or* **-chetting** [-ˌʃɛtɪŋ] : ricocher
rid [ˈrɪd] *vt* **rid; ridding 1** : débarrasser **2** ~
oneself of : se débarrasser de — **riddance**
[ˈrɪdənts] *n* **good** ~**!** : bon débarras!
riddle[1] [ˈrɪdəl] *n* : énigme *f*, devinette *f*
riddle[2] *vt* **-dled; -dling 1** : cribler **2** ~ **with**
: plein de
ride [ˈraɪd] *v* **rode** [ˈroːd]; **ridden** [ˈrɪdən];
riding *vt* **1** : monter (à cheval, à bicyclette),
prendre (le bus, etc.) **2** TRAVEL : parcourir
— *vi* **1** *or* ~ **horseback** : monter à cheval
2 : aller (en auto, etc.) — ~ *n* **1** : tour *m*,
promenade *f* **2** : manège *m* (à la foire) **3**
give s.o. a ~ : conduire qqn en voiture —
rider [ˈraɪdər] *n* **1** : cavalier *m*, -lière *f* **2**
CYCLIST : cycliste *mf*, motocycliste *mf*
ridge [ˈrɪdʒ] *n* : chaîne *f* (de montagnes)
ridiculous [rəˈdɪkjələs] *adj* : ridicule —
ridicule [ˈrɪdəˌkjuːl] *n* : ridicule *m*, dérision
f — ~ *vt* **-culed; -culing** : ridiculiser

rife [ˈraɪf] *adj* **be** ~ **with** : être abondant en
rifle[1] [ˈraɪfəl] *vi* **-fled; -fling** ~ **through**
: fouiller dans
rifle[2] *n* : carabine *f*, fusil *m*
rift [ˈrɪft] *n* **1** : fente *f*, fissure *f* **2** BREACH
: désaccord *m*
rig[1] [ˈrɪg] *vt* : truquer (une élection)
rig[2] *vt* **rigged; rigging 1** : gréer (un navire) **2**
EQUIP : équiper **3** *or* ~ **out** DRESS : habiller
4 *or* ~ **up** : bricoler — ~ *n* **1** : gréement
m **2** *or* **oil** ~ : plateforme *f* pétrolière —
rigging [ˈrɪgɪŋ, -gən] *n* : gréement *m*
right [ˈraɪt] *adj* **1** JUST : bien, juste **2** COR-
RECT : exact **3** APPROPRIATE : convenable **4**
STRAIGHT : droit **5 be** ~ : avoir raison **6** →
right–hand — ~ *n* **1** GOOD : bien *m* **2** EN-
TITLEMENT : droit *m* **3 on the** ~ : à droite
4 *or* ~ **side** : droite *f* — ~ *adv* **1** WELL
: bien, comme il faut **2** EXACTLY : précisément **3** DIRECTLY : droit **4** IMMEDIATELY
: tout de suite **5** COMPLETELY : tout à fait **6**
or **to the** ~ : à la droite — ~ *vt* **1** RESTORE
: redresser **2** ~ **a wrong** : réparer un tort —
right angle *n* : angle *m* droit — **righteous**
[ˈraɪtʃəs] *adj* : juste, droit — **rightful**
[ˈraɪtfəl] *adj* : légitime — **right–hand** [ˈraɪt-
ˈhænd] *adj* **1** : du côté droit **2** ~ **man** : bras
m droit — **right–handed** [ˈraɪtˈhændəd] *adj*
: droitier — **rightly** [ˈraɪtli] **1** : à juste titre **2**
CORRECTLY : correctement — **right–of–
way** [ˌraɪtəˈweɪ, -əv-] *n, pl* **rights–of–way**
: priorité *f* (sur la route) — **right–wing**
[ˈraɪtˈwɪŋ] *adj* : de droite (en politique)
rigid [ˈrɪdʒɪd] *adj* : rigide
rigor *or Brit* **rigour** [ˈrɪgər] *n* : rigueur *f* —
rigorous [ˈrɪgərəs] *adj* : rigoureux
rim [ˈrɪm] *n* **1** EDGE : bord *m* **2** : jante *f*
(d'une roue)
rind [ˈraɪnd] *n* : écorce *f* (de citron, etc.)
ring[1] [ˈrɪŋ] *v* **rang** [ˈræŋ]; **rung** [ˈrʌŋ]; **ringing** *vi* **1** : sonner **2** RESOUND : résonner —
vt : sonner (une cloche, etc.) — ~ *n* **1** : son
m, tintement *m* **2** CALL : coup *m* de téléphone
ring[2] *n* **1** : bague *f*, anneau *m* **2** CIRCLE : cercle *m* **3** *or* **boxing** ~ : ring *m* (de boxe) **4**
NETWORK : réseau *m* (clandestin) — ~ *vt*
ringed; ringing : encercler — **ringleader**
[ˈrɪŋˌliːdər] *n* : meneur *m*, -neuse *f*
rink [ˈrɪŋk] *n* : piste *f*, patinoire *f*
rinse [ˈrɪnts] *vt* **rinsed; rinsing** : rincer —
~ *n* : rinçage *m*
riot [ˈraɪət] *n* : émeute *f* — ~ *vi* : faire une
émeute — **rioter** [ˈraɪətər] *n* : émeutier *m*,
-tière *f*
rip [ˈrɪp] *v* **ripped; ripping** *vt* **1** : déchirer **2**
~ **off** : arracher — *vi* : se déchirer — ~ *n*
: déchirure *f*
ripe [ˈraɪp] *adj* **riper; ripest** : mûr, prêt —
ripen [ˈraɪpən] *v* : mûrir

ripple 318

ripple ['rɪpəl] *v* **-pled; -pling** *vi* : onduler (se
dit de l'eau) — *vt* : rider — ~ *n* : ondulation *f*, ride *f*
rise ['raɪz] *vi* **rose** ['ro:z]; **risen** ['rɪzən]; **rising 1** : se lever (se dit d'une personne, du
soleil, etc.) **2** INCREASE : augmenter, monter **3** ~ **up** REBEL : se soulever (contre) —
~ *n* **1** ASCENT : montée *f* **2** INCREASE
: augmentation *f* **3** INCLINE : pente *f* —
riser ['raɪzər] *n* **1** early ~ : lève-tôt *mf* **2**
late ~ : lève-tard *mf*
risk ['rɪsk] *n* : risque *m* — ~ *vt* : risquer —
risky ['rɪski] *adj* **riskier; -est** : risqué,
hasardeux
rite ['raɪt] *n* : rite *m* — **ritual** ['rɪtʃuəl] *adj*
: rituel — ~ *n* : rituel *m*
rival ['raɪvəl] *n* : rival *m*, -vale *f* — ~ *adj*
: rival — ~ *vt* **-valed** *or* **-valled; -valing** *or*
-valling : rivaliser avec — **rivalry** ['raɪvəlri]
n, pl **-ries** : rivalité *f*
river ['rɪvər] *n* : rivière *f*, fleuve *m* — ~ *adj*
: fluvial
rivet ['rɪvət] *n* : rivet *m* — ~ *vt* **1** : river,
fixer **2** be ~ed by : être fasciné par
road ['ro:d] *n* **1** : route *f* **2** STREET : rue *f* **3**
PATH : chemin *m* — **roadblock** ['ro:d,blak]
n : barrage *m* routier — **roadside** ['ro:d-
,saɪd] *n* : bord *m* de la route — **roadway**
['ro:d,weɪ] *n* : chaussée *f*
roam ['ro:m] *vi* : errer
roar ['ror] *vi* **1** : rugir **2** ~ **with laughter**
: éclater de rire — *vt* : hurler — ~ *n* **1**
: rugissement *m* **2** : grondement *m* (d'un
avion, etc.)
roast ['ro:st] *vt* : rôtir (de la viande, etc.),
griller (des noix, etc.) — ~ *n* : rôti *m* —
roast beef *n* : rosbif *m*
rob ['rab] *vt* **robbed; robbing 1** : dévaliser
(une banque), cambrioler (une maison) **2**
STEAL : voler — **robber** ['rabər] *n* : voleur
m, -leuse *f* — **robbery** ['rabəri] *n, pl* **-beries**
: vol *m*
robe ['ro:b] *n* **1** : toge *f* (d'un juge) **2** →
bathrobe
robin ['rabən] *n* : rouge-gorge *m*
robot ['ro:,bat, -bət] *n* : robot *m*
robust [ro'bʌst, 'ro:,bʌst] *adj* : robuste
rock[1] ['rak] *vt* **1** : bercer (un enfant), balancer (un berceau) **2** SHAKE : secouer — *vi*
: se balancer — ~ *n or* ~ **music**
: musique *f* rock
rock[2] *n* **1** : roche *f*, roc *m* **2** BOULDER
: rocher *m* **3** STONE : pierre *f*
rocket ['rakət] *n* : fusée *f*
rocking chair *n* : fauteuil *m* à bascule
rocky ['raki] *adj* **rockier; -est 1** : rocheux **2**
SHAKY : précaire
rod ['rad] *n* **1** : baguette *f* (de bois), tige *f* (de
métal) **2** *or* **fishing** ~ : canne *f* à pêche
rode → **ride**

rodent ['ro:dənt] *n* : rongeur *m*
rodeo ['ro:di,o:, ro'deɪ,o:] *n, pl* **-deos**
: rodéo *m*
roe ['ro:] *n* : œufs *mpl* de poisson
roe deer *n* : chevreuil *m*
role ['ro:l] *n* : rôle *m*
roll ['ro:l] *n* **1** : rouleau *m* **2** LIST : liste *f* **3**
BUN : petit pain *m* **4** : roulement *m* (de tam-
bour) — ~ *vt* **1** : rouler **2** ~ **down**
: baisser **3** ~ **out** : dérouler **4** ~ **up**
: retrousser (ses manches) — *vi* **1** : (se)
rouler **2** ~ **over** : se retourner — **roller**
['ro:lər] *n* : rouleau *m* — **roller coaster**
['ro:lər,ko:stər] *n* : montagnes *fpl* russes —
roller-skate ['ro:lər,skeɪt] *vi* **-skated;
-skating** : faire du patin à roulettes — **roller
skates** *npl* : patins *mpl* à roulettes
Roman ['ro:mən] *adj* : romain — **Roman
Catholic** *adj* : catholique
romance [ro'mænts, 'ro:,mænts] *n* **1**
: roman *m* d'amour **2** AFFAIR : liaison *f*
amoureuse
romantic [ro'mæntɪk] *adj* : romantique
roof ['ru:f, 'rʊf] *n, pl* **roofs** ['ru:fs, 'rʊfs,
'ru:vz, 'rʊvz] **1** : toit *m* **2** ~ **of the mouth**
: palais *m* — **roofing** ['ru:fɪŋ, 'rʊfɪŋ] *n* : toiture *f* — **rooftop** ['ru:f,tap, 'rʊf-] *n* → **roof**
rook ['rʊk] *n* : tour *f* (aux échecs)
rookie ['rʊki] *n* : novice *mf*
room ['ru:m, 'rʊm] *n* **1** : chambre *f* (à
coucher), salle *f* (de conférence) **2** SPACE
: espace *m* **3** OPPORTUNITY : possibilité *f* —
roommate ['ru:m,meɪt, 'rʊm-] *n* : camarade *mf* de chambre — **roomy** ['ru:mi,
'rʊmi] *adj* **roomier; -est** : spacieux
roost ['ru:st] *n* : perchoir *m* — ~ *vi* : se
percher — **rooster** ['ru:stər, 'rʊs-] *n* : coq *m*
root[1] ['ru:t, 'rʊt] *n* **1** : racine *f* **2** SOURCE
: origine *f* **3** CORE : fond *m*, cœur *m* — *vt* ~
out : extirper
root[2] *vi* ~ **for** SUPPORT : encourager
rope ['ro:p] *n* : corde *f* — ~ *vt* **roped; rop-
ing 1** : attacher (avec une corde) **2** ~ **off**
: interdire l'accès à
rosary ['ro:zəri] *n, pl* **-ries** : chapelet *m*
rose[1] → **rise**
rose[2] ['ro:z] *n* : rose *f* (fleur), rose *m* (couleur)
— **rosebush** ['ro:z,bʊʃ] *n* : rosier *m*
rosemary ['ro:z,mɛri] *n, pl* **-maries** : ro-
marin *m*
Rosh Hashanah [,rɑʃə'ʃanə, ,ro:ʃ-] *n* : le
Nouvel An juif
rostrum ['rastrəm] *n, pl* **-tra** [-trə] *or* **-trums**
: tribune *f*
rosy ['ro:zi] *adj* **rosier; -est 1** : rose, rosé **2**
PROMISING : prometteur
rot ['rat] *v* **rotted; rotting** : pourrir — ~ *n*
: pourriture *f*
rotary ['ro:təri] *adj* : rotatif — ~ *n* : rond-
point *m*

rotate ['roː,teɪt] *v* **-tated; -tating** *vi* : tourner — *vt* **1** : tourner **2** ALTERNATE : faire à tour de rôle — **rotation** [roʲteɪʃən] *n* : rotation *f*

rote ['roːt] *n* **by ~** : par cœur

rotten ['rɑtən] *adj* **1** : pourri **2** BAD : mauvais

rouge ['ruːʒ] *n* : rouge *m* à joues

rough ['rʌf] *adj* **1** COARSE : rugueux **2** RUGGED : accidenté **3** CHOPPY : agité **4** DIFFICULT : difficile **5** FORCEFUL : brusque **6** APPROXIMATE : approximatif **7 ~ draft** : brouillon *m* — *vt* **1 → roughen 2 ~ up** BEAT : tabasser *fam* — **roughage** ['rʌfɪʤ] *n* : fibres *mpl* alimentaires — **roughen** ['rʌfən] *vt* : rendre rugueux — **roughly** ['rʌfli] *adv* **1** : rudement **2** ABOUT : environ — **roughness** ['rʌfnəs] *n* : rugosité *f*

roulette [ˌruːˈlɛt] *n* : roulette *f*

round ['raʊnd] *adj* : rond — **~** *adv* → **around** — **~** *n* **1** : série *f* (de négociations, etc.) **2** : manche *f* (d'un match) **3 ~ of applause** : salve *f* d'applaudissements **4 ~s** *npl* : visites *fpl* (d'un médecin, etc.), rondes *fpl* (d'un policier, etc.) — **~** *vt* **1** TURN : tourner **2 ~ off** : arrondir **3 ~ off** *or* **~ out** COMPLETE : compléter **4 ~ up** GATHER : rassembler — **~** *prep* → **around** — **roundabout** ['raʊndəˌbaʊt] *adj* : indirect — **round–trip** ['raʊndˌtrɪp] *adj* : voyage *m* aller et retour — **roundup** ['raʊndˌʌp] *n* : rassemblement *m*

rouse ['raʊz] *vt* **roused; rousing 1** AWAKEN : réveiller **2** EXCITE : susciter

rout ['raʊt] *n* : déroute *f* — **~** *vt* : mettre en déroute

route ['ruːt, 'raʊt] *n* **1** : route *f* **2** *or* **delivery ~** : tournée *f* de livraison

routine [ruːˈtiːn] *n* : routine *f* — **~** *adj* : routinier

row[1] ['roː] *vi* : ramer

row[2] ['roː] *n* **1** : file *f* (de gens), rangée *f* (de maisons, etc.) **2 in a ~** SUCCESSIVELY : de suite

row[3] ['raʊ] *n* **1** RACKET : vacarme *m* **2** QUARREL : dispute *f*

rowboat ['roːˌboːt] *n* : bateau *m* à rames

rowdy ['raʊdi] *adj* **-dier; -est** : tapageur

royal ['rɔɪəl] *adj* : royal — **royalty** ['rɔɪəlti] *n*, *pl* **-ties 1** : royauté *f* **2 royalties** *npl* : droits *mpl* d'auteur

rub ['rʌb] *v* **rubbed; rubbing** *vt* **1** : frotter **2 ~ in** : faire pénétrer — *vi* **1 ~ against** : frotter contre **2 ~ off** : enlever (en frottant) — **~** *n* : friction *f*, massage *m*

rubber ['rʌbər] *n* : caoutchouc *m* — **rubber band** *n* : élastique *m* — **rubber stamp** *n* : tampon *m* (de caoutchouc) — **rubbery** ['rʌbəri] *adj* : caoutchouteux

rubbish ['rʌbɪʃ] *n* **1** : ordures *fpl*, déchets *mpl* **2** NONSENSE : bêtises *fpl*

rubble ['rʌbəl] *n* : décombres *mpl*

ruby ['ruːbi] *n*, *pl* **-bies** : rubis *m*

rudder ['rʌdər] *n* : gouvernail *m*

ruddy ['rʌdi] *adj* **-dier; -est** : rougeaud

rude ['ruːd] *adj* **ruder; rudest 1** IMPOLITE : grossier **2** ABRUPT : brusque — **rudely** ['ruːdli] *adv* : grossièrement — **rudeness** ['ruːdnəs] *n* : manque *m* d'éducation

rudiment ['ruːdəmənt] *n* : rudiment *m* — **rudimentary** [ˌruːdəˈmɛntəri] *adj* : rudimentaire

ruffle ['rʌfəl] *vt* **-fled; -fling 1** : ébouriffer (ses cheveux), hérisser (ses plumes) **2** VEX : contrarier — **~** *n* : volant *m* (d'une jupe, etc.)

rug ['rʌg] *n* : tapis *m*, carpette *f*

rugged ['rʌgəd] *adj* **1** : accidenté (se dit d'un terrain), escarpé (se dit d'une montagne) **2** STURDY : robuste

ruin ['ruːən] *n* : ruine *f* — **~** *vt* : ruiner

rule ['ruːl] *n* **1** : règle *f*, règlement *m* **2** CONTROL : autorité *f* **3 as a ~** : en général — **~** *v* **ruled; ruling** *vt* **1** GOVERN : gouverner **2** : juger, décider (d'un juge) **3 ~ out** : écarter — *vi* : gouverner, régner — **ruler** ['ruːlər] *n* **1** : dirigeant *m*, -geante *f*; souverain *m*, -raine *f* **2** : règle *f* (pour mesurer) — **ruling** ['ruːlɪŋ] *n* VERDICT : décision *f*

rum ['rʌm] *n* : rhum *m*

rumble ['rʌmbəl] *vi* **-bled; -bling 1** : gronder **2** : gargouiller (se dit de l'estomac) — **~** *n* : grondement *m*

rummage ['rʌmɪʤ] *vi* **-maged; -maging ~ in** : fouiller dans

rumor *or Brit* **rumour** ['ruːmər] *n* : rumeur *f* — **~** *vt* **be ~ed that** : il paraît que

rump ['rʌmp] *n* **1** : croupe *f* (d'un animal) **2** *or* **~ steak** : romsteck *m*

run ['rʌn] *v* **ran** ['ræn]; **run; running** *vi* **1** : courir **2** FUNCTION : marcher **3** LAST : durer **4** : déteindre (se dit des couleurs) **5** EXTEND : passer (se dit d'un câble) **6** : se présenter (comme candidat) **7 ~ away** : s'enfuir **8 ~ into** ENCOUNTER : rencontrer **9 ~ into** HIT : heurter **10 ~ late** : être en retard **11 ~ out of** : manquer de **12 ~ over** : écraser — *vt* **1** : courir **2** OPERATE : faire marcher **3** : faire couler (de l'eau) **4** MANAGE : diriger **5 ~ a fever** : faire de la température — **~** *n* **1** : course *f* **2** TRIP : tour *m*, excursion *f* **3** SERIES : série *f* **4 in the long ~** : à la longue — **runaway** ['rʌnəˌweɪ] *n* : fugitif *m*, -tive *f* — **~** *adj* : fugueur — **rundown** ['rʌnˌdaʊn] *n* : résumé *m* — **run–down** ['rʌnˈdaʊn] *adj* **1** : délabré **2** EXHAUSTED : fatigué

rung[1] **→ ring**[1]

rung[2] ['rʌŋ] *n* : barreau *m* (d'une échelle, etc.)

runner ['rʌnər] *n* : coureur *m*, -reuse *f* — **runner–up** [,rʌnər'ʌp] *n, pl* **runners–up** : second *m*, -conde *f* — **running** ['rʌnɪŋ] *adj* **1** FLOWING : courant **2** CONTINUOUS : continuel **3** CONSECUTIVE : de suite

runway ['rʌn,weɪ] *n* : piste *f* (d'envol ou d'atterrissage)

rupture ['rʌptʃər] *n* : rupture *f* — ~ *v* **-tured; -turing** *vt* : rompre — *vi* : se rompre

rural ['rʊrəl] *adj* : rural

ruse ['ru:s, 'ru:z] *n* : ruse *f*, stratagème *m*

rush[1] ['rʌʃ] *n* **1** : jonc *m* (plante) **2 in a** ~ : pressé

rush[2] *vi* : se précipiter — *vt* **1** : presser, bousculer **2** ATTACK : prendre d'assaut **3**

: transporter d'urgence (à l'hôpital, etc.) — ~ *n* **1** : hâte *f*, empressement *m* **2** : bouffée *f* (d'air), torrent *m* (d'eau) — **rush hour** *n* : heure *f* de pointe

russet ['rʌsət] *adj* : roux

Russian ['rʌʃən] *adj* : russe — ~ *n* : russe (langue)

rust ['rʌst] *n* : rouille *f* — ~ *vi* : se rouiller — *vt* : rouiller

rustic ['rʌstɪk] *adj* : rustique, champêtre

rustle ['rʌsəl] *vi* **-tled; -tling** bruire — ~ *n* : bruissement *m*

rusty ['rʌsti] *adj* **rustier; -est** : rouillé

rut ['rʌt] *n* **1** : ornière *f* **2 be in a** ~ : s'enliser dans une routine

ruthless ['ru:θləs] *adj* : impitoyable, cruel

rye ['raɪ] *n* : seigle *m*

S

s ['ɛs] *n, pl* **s's** *or* **ss** ['ɛsəz] : s *m*, dix-neuvième lettre de l'alphabet

Sabbath ['sæbəθ] *n* **1** : sabbat *m* (judaïsme) **2** : dimanche *m* (christianisme)

sabotage ['sæbə,tɑʒ] *n* : sabotage *m* — ~ *vt* **-taged; -taging** : saboter

sack ['sæk] *n* : sac *m* — ~ *vt* **1** FIRE : virer *fam* **2** PLUNDER : saccager

sacred ['seɪkrəd] *adj* : sacré

sacrifice ['sækrə,faɪs] *n* : sacrifice *m* — ~ *vt* **-ficed; -ficing** : sacrifier

sad ['sæd] *adj* **sadder; saddest** : triste — **sadden** ['sædən] *vt* : attrister

saddle ['sædəl] *n* : selle *f* — ~ *vt* **-dled; -dling** : seller

sadistic [sə'dɪstɪk] *adj* : sadique

sadness ['sædnəs] *n* : tristesse *f*

safari [sə'fɑri, -'fær-] *n* : safari *m*

safe ['seɪf] *adj* **safer; safest 1** : sûr **2** UNHARMED : en sécurité **3** CAREFUL : prudent **4** ~ **and sound** : sain et sauf — ~ *n* : coffre-fort *m* — **safeguard** ['seɪf,gɑrd] *n* : sauvegarde *f* — ~ *vt* : sauvegarder — **safely** ['seɪfli] *adv* **1** : sûrement **2 arrive** ~ : bien arriver — **safety** ['seɪfti] *n, pl* **-ties** : sécurité *f* — **safety belt** *n* : ceinture *f* de sécurité — **safety pin** *n* : épingle *f* de sûreté

sag ['sæg] *vi* **sagged; sagging** : s'affaisser

sage[1] ['seɪdʒ] *n* : sauge *f* (plante)

sage[2] *n* : sage *m*

said → **say**

sail ['seɪl] *n* **1** : voile *f* (d'un bateau) **2 go for a** ~ : faire un tour en bateau **3 set** ~ : prendre la mer — ~ *vi* : naviguer — *vt* **1**

: manœuvrer (un bateau) **2** ~ **the seas** : parcourir les mers — **sailboat** ['seɪl,bo:t] *n* : voilier *m* — **sailor** ['seɪlər] *n* : marin *m*, matelot *m*

saint ['seɪnt, *before a name* ,seɪnt *or* sənt] *n* : saint *m*, sainte *f*

sake ['seɪk] *n* **1 for goodness'** ~! : pour l'amour de Dieu! **2 for the** ~ **of** : pour le bien de

salad ['sæləd] *n* : salade *f*

salary ['sæləri] *n, pl* **-ries** : salaire *m*

sale ['seɪl] *n* **1** : vente *f* **2 for** ~ : à vendre **3 on** ~ : en solde — **salesman** ['seɪlzmən] *n, pl* **-men** [-mən, -,mɛn] : vendeur *m*, représentant *m* — **saleswoman** ['seɪlz,wʊmən] *n, pl* **-women** [-,wɪmən] : vendeuse *f*, représentante *f*

salient ['seɪljənt] *adj* : saillant

saliva [sə'laɪvə] *n* : salive *f*

salmon ['sæmən] *ns & pl* : saumon *m*

salon [sə'lɑn, 'sæ,lɑn] *n* : salon *m*

saloon [sə'lu:n] *n* : bar *m*

salt ['sɔlt] *n* : sel *m* — ~ *vt* : saler — **saltwater** ['sɔlt,wɔtər, -,wɑ-] *adj* : de mer — **salty** ['sɔlti] *adj* **saltier; -est** : salé

salute [sə'lu:t] *vt* **-luted; -luting** : saluer — ~ *n* : salut *m*

salvage ['sælvɪdʒ] *vt* **-vaged; -vaging** : sauver, récupérer

salvation [sæl'veɪʃən] *n* : salut *m*

salve ['sæv, 'sɑv] *n* : onguent *m*, pommade *f*

same ['seɪm] *adj* **1** : même **2 be the** ~ **(as)** : être comme **3 the** ~ **thing (as)** : la même chose (que) — ~ *pron* **1 all the** ~ : pareil

2 the ~ : le même — ~ *adv* **the** ~ : pareil

sample ['sæmpəl] *n* : échantillon *m* — ~ *vt* **-pled; -pling** : essayer

sanctify ['sæŋktə,faɪ] *vt* **-fied; -fying** : sanctifier

sanction ['sæŋkʃən] *n* : sanction *f* — ~ *vt* : sanctionner

sanctuary ['sæŋktʃu,ɛri] *n, pl* **-aries** : sanctuaire *m*

sand ['sænd] *n* : sable *m* — ~ *vt* **1** : sabler (une route) **2** : poncer (du bois)

sandal ['sændəl] *n* : sandale *f*

sandpaper ['sænd,peɪpər] *n* : papier *m* de verre — ~ *vt* : poncer

sandwich ['sænd,wɪtʃ] *n* : sandwich *m* — ~ *vt* **between** : mettre entre

sandy ['sændi] *adj* **sandier; -est** : sablonneux

sane ['seɪn] *adj* **saner; -est 1** : sain d'esprit **2** SENSIBLE : raisonnable

sang → **sing**

sanitary ['sænətɛri] *adj* **1** : sanitaire **2** HYGIENIC : hygiénique — **sanitary napkin** *n* : serviette *f* hygiénique — **sanitation** [,sænə'teɪʃən] *n* : système *m* sanitaire

sanity ['sænəti] *n* : équilibre *m* mental

sank → **sink**

Santa Claus ['sæntə,klɔz] *n* : père *m* Noël

sap¹ ['sæp] *n* : sève *f* (d'un arbre)

sap² *vt* **sapped; sapping** : saper, miner

sapphire ['sæ,faɪr] *n* : saphir *m*

sarcasm ['sɑr,kæzəm] *n* : sarcasme *m* — **sarcastic** [sɑr'kæstɪk] *adj* : sarcastique

sardine [sɑr'di:n] *n* : sardine *f*

sash ['sæʃ] *n* : large ceinture *f* (d'une robe), écharpe *f* (d'un uniforme)

sat → **sit**

satellite ['sætə,laɪt] *n* : satellite *m*

satin ['sætən] *n* : satin *m*

satire ['sæ,taɪr] *n* : satire *f* — **satiric** [sə'tɪrɪk] *or* **satirical** [-ɪkəl] *adj* : satirique

satisfaction [,sætəs'fækʃən] *n* : satisfaction *f* — **satisfactory** [,sætəs'fæktəri] *adj* : satisfaisant — **satisfy** ['sætəs,faɪ] *vt* **-fied; -fying** : satisfaire — **satisfying** ['sætəs,faɪɪ] *adj* : satisfaisant

saturate ['sætʃə,reɪt] *vt* **-rated; -rating 1** : saturer **2** DRENCH : tremper

Saturday ['sætər,deɪ, -di] *n* : samedi *m*

Saturn ['sætərn] *n* : Saturne *f*

sauce ['sɔs] *n* : sauce *f* — **saucepan** ['sɔs,pæn] *n* : casserole *f* — **saucer** ['sɔsər] *n* : soucoupe *f*

Saudi ['saudi] *or* **Saudi Arabian** ['saudɪə'reɪbiən] *adj* : saoudien

sauna ['sɔnə, 'saunə] *n* : sauna *m*

saunter ['sɔntər, 'sɑn-] *vi* : se promener

sausage ['sɔsɪdʒ] *n* : saucisse *f* (crue), saucisson *m* (cuit)

sauté [sɔ'teɪ, so:-] *vt* **-téed** *or* **-téd; -téing** : faire revenir

savage ['sævɪdʒ] *adj* : sauvage, féroce — ~ *n* : sauvage *mf* — **savagery** ['sævɪdʒri, -dʒəri] *n, pl* **-ries** : férocité *f*

save ['seɪv] *vt* **saved; saving 1** RESCUE : sauver **2** RESERVE : garder **3** : gagner (temps), économiser (de l'argent) **4** : sauvegarder (en informatique) — ~ *prep* EXCEPT : sauf

savior ['seɪvjər] *n* : sauveur *m*

savor ['seɪvər] *vt* : savourer — **savory** ['seɪvəri] *adj* : savoureux

saw¹ → **see**

saw² ['sɔ] *n* : scie *f* — ~ *vt* **sawed; sawed** *or* **sawn** ['sɔn]; **sawing** : scier — **sawdust** ['sɔ,dʌst] *n* : sciure *f* — **sawmill** ['sɔ,mɪl] *n* : scierie *f*

saxophone ['sæksə,fo:n] *n* : saxophone *m*

say ['seɪ] *v* **said** ['sɛd]; **saying; says** ['sɛz] *vt* **1** : dire **2** INDICATE : indiquer (se dit d'une montre, etc.) — *vi* **1** : dire **2 that is to** ~ : c'est-à-dire — ~ *n, pl* **says** ['seɪz] **1 have no** ~ : ne pas avoir son mot à dire **2 have one's** ~ : dire son mot — **saying** ['seɪɪ] *n* : dicton *m*

scab ['skæb] *n* **1** : croûte *f*, gale *f* *Can* **2** STRIKEBREAKER : jaune *mf*

scaffold ['skæfəld, -,fo:ld] *n* : échafaudage *m* (en construction)

scald ['skɔld] *vt* : ébouillanter

scale¹ ['skeɪl] *n* : pèse-personne *m*, balance *f*

scale² *n* : écaille *f* (d'un poisson, etc.) — ~ *vt* **scaled; scaling** : écailler

scale³ *n* : gamme *f* (en musique), échelle *f* (salariale)

scallion ['skæljən] *n* : ciboule *f*, échalote *f*

scallop ['skɑləp, 'skæ-] *n* : coquille *f* Saint-Jacques

scalp ['skælp] *n* : cuir *m* chevelu

scam ['skæm] *n* : escroquerie *f*

scan ['skæn] *vt* **scanned; scanning 1** EXAMINE : scruter **2** SKIM : lire attentivement **3** : balayer (en informatique)

scandal ['skændəl] *n* : scandale *m* — **scandalous** ['skændələs] *adj* : scandaleux

Scandinavian [,skændə'neɪviən] *adj* : scandinave

scant ['skænt] *adj* : insuffisant

scapegoat ['skeɪp,go:t] *n* : bouc *m* émissaire

scar ['skɑr] *n* : cicatrice *f* — ~ *v* **scarred; scarring** *vt* : laisser une cicatrice sur — *vi* : se cicatriser

scarce ['skɛrs] *adj* **scarcer; scarcest** : rare — **scarcely** ['skɛrsli] *adv* : à peine — **scarcity** ['skɛrsəti] *n, pl* **-ties** : pénurie *f*

scare ['skɛr] *vt* **scared; scaring 1** : faire peur à **2 be** ~**d of** : avoir peur de — ~ *n* **1** FRIGHT : peur *f* **2** PANIC : panique *f* — **scarecrow** ['skɛr,kro:] *n* : épouvantail *m*

scarf ['skɑrf] *n, pl* **scarves** ['skɑrvz] *or*
scarfs : écharpe *f*, foulard *m*
scarlet ['skɑrlət] *adj* : écarlate — **scarlet
fever** *n* : scarlatine *f*
scary ['skɛri] *adj* **scarier, -est** : qui fait peur
scathing ['skeɪðɪŋ] *adj* : cinglant
scatter ['skæt̬ər] *vt* **1** STREW : éparpiller **2**
DISPERSE : disperser — *vi* : se disperser
scavenger ['skævəndʒər] *n* : charognard *m*,
-gnarde *f*
scenario [sə'næri,o:, -'nɑr-] *n, pl* **-ios** : scénario *m*
scene ['si:n] *n* **1** : scène *f* **2 behind the ~s**
: dans les coulisses — **scenery** ['si:nəri] *n,
pl* **-eries 1** : décor *m* **2** LANDSCAPE
: paysages *mpl* — **scenic** ['si:nɪk] *adj* : pittoresque
scent ['sɛnt] *n* **1** : arôme *m* **2** PERFUME
: parfum *m* **3** TRAIL : piste *f* — **scented**
['sɛntəd] *adj* : parfumé
sceptic ['skɛptɪk] → **skeptic**
schedule ['skɛ,dʒu:l, -dʒəl, *esp Brit* 'ʃɛd-
ju:l] *n* **1** : programme *m* **2** TIMETABLE : horaire *m* **3 behind ~** : en retard **4 on ~** : à
l'heure — ~ *vt* **-uled; -uling** : prévoir
scheme ['ski:m] *n* **1** PLAN : plan *m* **2** PLOT
: intrigue *f* — ~ *vi* **schemed; scheming**
: conspirer
schizophrenia [,skɪtsə'fri:niə, ,skɪzə-,
-'frɛ-] *n* : schizophrénie *f*
scholar ['skɑlər] *n* : savant *m*, -vante *f*; érudit *m*, -dite *f* — **scholarship** ['skɑlər,ʃɪp] *n*
: bourse *f*
school[1] ['sku:l] *n* : banc *m* (de poissons)
school[2] *n* **1** : école *f*, lycée *m* **2** COLLEGE
: université *f* **3** DEPARTMENT : faculté *f* —
~ *vt* : instruire — **schoolboy** ['sku:l,bɔɪ] *n*
: écolier *m* — **schoolgirl** ['sku:l,gərl] *n*
: écolière *f*
science ['saɪən̩ts] *n* : science *f* — **scientific**
[,saɪən'tɪfɪk] *adj* : scientifique — **scientist**
['saɪəntɪst] *n* : scientifique *mf*
scissors ['sɪzərz] *npl* : ciseaux *mpl*
scoff ['skɑf] *vi* ~ **at** : se moquer de
scold ['sko:ld] *vt* : gronder, réprimander
scoop ['sku:p] *n* **1** : pelle *f* **2** : exclusivité *f*
(en journalisme) — ~ *vt* **1** : enlever (avec
une pelle) **2 ~ out** : évider **3 ~ up** : ramasser
scooter ['sku:t̬ər] *n* **1** : trottinette *f* **2** *or*
motor ~ : scooter *m*
scope ['sko:p] *n* **1** RANGE : étendue *f*, portée
f **2** OPPORTUNITY : possibilités *fpl*
scorch ['skɔrtʃ] *vt* : roussir
score ['skor] *n, pl* **scores 1** : score *m*,
pointage *m Can* (aux sports) **2** RATING
: note *f*, résultat *m* **3** : partition *f* (en
musique) **4 keep ~** : marquer les points
— ~ *vt* **scored; scoring 1** : marquer (un
point) **2** : obtenir (une note)

scorn ['skɔrn] *n* : mépris *m*, dédain *m* — ~
vt : mépriser, dédaigner — **scornful**
['skɔrnfəl] *adj* : méprisant
scorpion ['skɔrpiən] *n* : scorpion *m*
scotch ['skɑtʃ] *n or* ~ **whiskey** : scotch *m*
— **Scottish** ['skɑtɪʃ] *adj* : écossais
scoundrel ['skaʊndrəl] *n* : chenapan *m*
scour ['skaʊər] *vt* **1** SCRUB : récurer **2**
SEARCH : parcourir
scourge ['skərdʒ] *n* : fléau *m*
scout ['skaʊt] *n* : éclaireur *m*, -reuse *f*; scout
m, scoute *f*
scowl ['skaʊl] *vi* : faire la grimace — ~ *n*
: air *m* renfrogné
scram ['skræm] *vi* **scrammed; scramming**
: filer *fam*
scramble ['skræmbəl] *vt* **-bled; -bling**
: brouiller, mêler — ~ *n* : bousculade *f*,
ruée *f* — **scrambled eggs** *npl* : œufs *mpl*
brouillés
scrap ['skræp] *n* **1** PIECE : bout *m* **2** *or* ~
metal : ferraille *f* **3 ~s** *npl* LEFTOVERS
: restes *mpl* — ~ *vt* **scrapped; scrapping**
: mettre au rebut
scrapbook ['skræp,bʊk] *n* : album *m* de
coupures de journaux
scrape ['skreɪp] *v* **scraped; scraping** *vt* **1**
: racler **2** : s'écorcher (le genou, etc.) **3** *or*
~ **off** : enlever en grattant — *vi* **1** ~
against : érafler **2 ~ by** : se débrouiller —
~ *n* **1** : éraflure *f* **2** PREDICAMENT : pétrin
m fam — **scraper** ['skreɪpər] *n* : grattoir *m*
scratch ['skrætʃ] *vt* **1** : égratigner **2** MARK
: rayer **3** : se gratter (la tête, etc.) **4 ~ out**
: biffer — ~ *n* **1** : éraflure *f*, égratignure *f*
2 from ~ : à partir de zéro
scrawny ['skrɔni] *adj* **-nier; -niest** : maigre
scream ['skri:m] *vi* : hurler, crier — ~ *n*
: hurlement *m*, cri *m*
screech ['skri:tʃ] *n* **1** : cri *m* perçant **2**
: crissement *m* (de pneus, etc.) — ~ *vi* **1**
: pousser un cri **2** : crisser (se dit des pneus,
etc.)
screen ['skri:n] *n* **1** : écran *m* (de télévision,
etc.) **2** PARTITION : paravent *m* **3** *or* **window ~** : moustiquaire *f* — ~ *vt* **1** SHIELD
: protéger **2** HIDE : cacher **3** EXAMINE
: passer au crible
screw ['skru:] *n* : vis *f* — ~ *vt* **1** : visser **2**
~ **up** RUIN : bousiller — **screwdriver**
['skru:,draɪvər] *n* : tournevis *m*
scribble ['skrɪbəl] *v* **-bled; -bling** : gribouiller, griffonner — ~ *n* : gribouillage *m*
script ['skrɪpt] *n* : scénario *m* (d'un film, etc.)
scroll ['skro:l] *n* : rouleau *m* (de parchemin)
— ~ *vi* : défiler (en informatique)
scrub ['skrʌb] *vt* **scrubbed; scrubbing**
SCOUR : récurer — ~ *n* : nettoyage *m*
scruple ['skru:pəl] *n* : scrupule *m* —
scrupulous ['skru:pjələs] *adj* : scrupuleux

scrutiny ['skru:təni] *n, pl* **-nies** : analyse *f* attentive

scuffle ['skʌfəl] *n* : bagarre *f*

sculpture ['skʌlptʃər] *n* : sculpture *f* — **sculptor** ['skʌlptər] *n* : sculpteur *m*

scum ['skʌm] *n* : écume *f*

scurry ['skəri] *vi* **-ried; -rying** : se précipiter

scuttle ['skʌtəl] *vt* **-tled; -tling** : saborder (un navire)

scythe ['saɪð] *n* : faux *f*

sea ['si:] *n* **1** : mer *f* **2 at ~** : en mer — **~** *adj* : de mer — **seafood** ['si:ˌfu:d] *n* : fruits *mpl* de mer — **seagull** ['si:ˌgʌl] *n* : mouette *f*

seal[1] ['si:l] *n* : phoque *m*

seal[2] *n* **1** STAMP : sceau *m* **2** CLOSURE : fermeture *f* (hermétique) — **~** *vt* : sceller, cacheter

seam ['si:m] *n* : couture *f*

search ['sərtʃ] *vt* : fouiller — *vi* **~ for** : chercher — **~** *n* **1** : recherche *f* **2** EXAMINATION : fouille *f*

seashell ['si:ˌʃɛl] *n* : coquillage *m* — **seashore** ['si:ˌʃor] *n* : bord *m* de la mer — **seasick** ['si:ˌsɪk] *adj* **be ~** : avoir le mal de mer — **seasickness** ['si:ˌsɪknəs] *n* : mal *m* de mer

season ['si:zən] *n* : saison *f* — **~** *vt* : assaisonner, épicer — **seasonal** ['si:zənəl] *adj* : saisonnier — **seasoned** ['si:zənd] *adj* : expérimenté — **seasoning** ['si:zənɪŋ] *n* : assaisonnement *m*

seat ['si:t] *n* **1** : siège *m* **2** : fond *m* (de pantalon) **3 take a ~** : asseyez-vous — **~** *vt* **1 be ~ed** : s'asseoir **2 the bus ~s 30** : l'autobus peut accueillir 30 personnes — **seat belt** *n* : ceinture *f* de sécurité

seaweed ['si:ˌwi:d] *n* : algue *f* marine

secede [sɪ'si:d] *vi* **-ceded; -ceding** : faire sécession

secluded [sɪ'klu:dəd] *adj* : isolé — **seclusion** [sɪ'klu:ʒən] *n* : isolement *m*

second ['sɛkənd] *adj* : second, deuxième — **~** *or* **secondly** ['sɛkəndli] *adv* : deuxièmement — **~** *n* **1** : deuxième *mf*; second *m*, -conde *f* **2** MOMENT : seconde *f* **3 have ~s** : prendre une deuxième portion (de nourriture) — **~** *vt* : affirmer, appuyer — **secondary** ['sɛkənˌdɛri] *adj* : secondaire — **secondhand** ['sɛkənd'hænd] *adj* : d'occasion — **second–rate** ['sɛkənd'reɪt] *adj* : médiocre

secret ['si:krət] *adj* : secret — **~** *n* : secret *m* — **secrecy** ['si:krəsi] *n, pl* **-cies** : secret *m*

secretary ['sɛkrəˌtɛri] *n, pl* **-taries 1** : secrétaire *mf* **2** : ministre *m* (du gouvernement)

secrete [sɪ'kri:t] *vt* **-creted; -creting** : sécréter

secretive ['si:krətɪv, sɪ'kri:tɪv] *adj* : cachottier — **secretly** ['si:krətli] *adv* : en secret

sect ['sɛkt] *n* : secte *f*

section ['sɛkʃən] *n* : section *f*, partie *f*

sector ['sɛktər] *n* : secteur *m*

secular ['sɛkjələr] *adj* : séculier, laïque

secure [sɪ'kjʊr] *adj* **-curer; -est** : sûr, en sécurité — **~** *vt* **-cured; -curing 1** FASTEN : attacher **2** GET : obtenir — **security** [sɪ'kjʊrəti] *n, pl* **-ties 1** : sécurité *f* **2** GUARANTEE : garantie *f* **3 securities** *npl* : valeurs *fpl*

sedan [sɪ'dæn] *n* : berline *f*

sedative ['sɛdətɪv] *n* : calmant *m*, sédatif *m*

sedentary ['sɛdənˌtɛri] *adj* : sédentaire

seduce [sɪ'du:s, -'dju:s] *vt* **-duced; -ducing** : séduire — **seduction** [sɪ'dʌkʃən] *n* : séduction *f* — **seductive** [sɪ'dʌktɪv] *adj* : séduisant

see ['si:] *v* **saw** ['sɔ]; **seen** ['si:n]; **seeing** *vt* **1** : voir **2** UNDERSTAND : comprendre **3** ESCORT : accompagner **4 ~ through** : mener à terme **5 ~ you later** : au revoir — *vi* **1** : voir **2** UNDERSTAND : comprendre **3 let's ~** : voyons **4 ~ to** : s'occuper de

seed ['si:d] *n, pl* **seed** *or* **seeds 1** : graine *f* **2** SOURCE : germe *m* — **seedling** ['si:dlɪŋ] *n* : semis *m*, jeune plant *m* — **seedy** ['si:di] *adj* **seedier; seediest** SQUALID : miteux

seek ['si:k] *v* **sought** ['sɔt]; **seeking** *vt* **1** *or* **~ out** : chercher **2** REQUEST : demander — *vi* : rechercher

seem ['si:m] *vi* : paraître, sembler, avoir l'air

seep ['si:p] *vi* : suinter

seesaw ['si:ˌsɔ] *n* : balançoire *f*, bascule *f*

seethe ['si:ð] *vi* **seethed; seething** : bouillonner (de rage)

segment ['sɛgmənt] *n* : segment *m*

segregate ['sɛgrɪˌgeɪt] *vt* **-gated; -gating** : séparer — **segregation** [ˌsɛgrɪ'geɪʃən] *n* : ségrégation *f*

seize ['si:z] *vt* **seized; seizing 1** GRASP : saisir **2** CAPTURE : prendre — **seizure** ['si:ʒər] *n* : attaque *f*, crise *f* (en médecine)

seldom ['sɛldəm] *adv* : rarement

select [sə'lɛkt] *adj* : privilégié — **~** *vt* : choisir, sélectionner — **selection** [sə'lɛkʃən] *n* : sélection *f*

self ['sɛlf] *n, pl* **selves** ['sɛlvz] **1** : moi *m* **2 her better ~** : son meilleur côté — **self–addressed** [ˌsɛlfə'drɛst] *adj* **~ envelope** : enveloppe *f* affranchie — **self–assured** [ˌsɛlfə'ʃʊrd] *adj* : sûr de soi — **self–centered** [ˌsɛlf'sɛntərd] *adj* : égocentrique — **self–confidence** [ˌsɛlf'kɑnfədənts] *n* : confiance *f* en soi — **self–confident** [ˌsɛlf'kɑnfədənt] *adj* : sûr de soi — **self–conscious** [ˌsɛlf'kɑntʃəs] *adj* : gêné, timide — **self–control** [ˌsɛlfkən'tro:l] *n* : maîtrise *f* de soi — **self–defense** [ˌsɛlfdɪ'fɛnts] *n* : autodéfense *f* — **self–employed** [ˌsɛlfɪm'plɔɪd] *adj* : qui travaille à son compte —

self—esteem [ˌsɛlfɪˈstiːm] n : amour-propre m — **self—evident** [ˌsɛlfˈɛvədənt] adj : qui va de soi — **self—explanatory** [ˌsɛlfɪkˈsplænəˌtori] adj : explicite — **self—help** [ˌsɛlfˈhɛlp] n : initiative f personnelle — **self—important** [ˌsɛlfɪmˈpɔrtənt] adj : vaniteux — **self—interest** [ˌsɛlfˈɪntrəst, -təˌrɛst] n : intérêt m personnel — **selfish** [ˈsɛlfɪʃ] adj : égoïste — **selfishness** [ˈsɛlfɪʃnəs] n : égoïsme m — **self—pity** [ˌsɛlfˈpɪti] n, pl -ties : apitoiement m sur soi-même — **self—portrait** [ˌsɛlfˈpɔrtrət] n : autoportrait m — **self—respect** [ˌsɛlfrɪˈspɛkt] n : amour m propre — **self—righteous** [ˌsɛlfˈraɪtʃəs] adj : suffisant — **self—service** [ˌsɛlfˈsərvɪs] n : libre-service m — **self—sufficient** [ˌsɛlfsəˈfɪʃənt] adj : autosuffisant — **self—taught** [ˌsɛlfˈtɔt] adj : autodidacte

sell [ˈsɛl] v **sold** [ˈsoːld]; **selling** vt : vendre — vi : se vendre — **seller** [ˈsɛlər] n : vendeur m, -deuse f

selves → **self**

semantics [sɪˈmæntɪks] ns & pl : sémantique f

semblance [ˈsɛmbləns] n : semblant m, apparence f

semester [səˈmɛstər] n : semestre m

semicolon [ˈsɛmiˌkoːlən, ˈsɛˌmaɪ-] n : point-virgule m

semifinal [ˈsɛmiˌfaɪnəl, ˈsɛˌmaɪ-] n : demi-finale f

seminary [ˈsɛməˌnɛri] n, pl -naries : séminaire m — **seminar** [ˈsɛməˌnɑr] n : séminaire m

senate [ˈsɛnət] n : sénat m — **senator** [ˈsɛnətər] n : sénateur m

send [ˈsɛnd] vt **sent** [ˈsɛnt]; **sending** 1 : envoyer, expédier 2 ~ **away for** : commander 3 ~ **back** : renvoyer (de la marchandise, etc.) 4 ~ **for** : appeler, faire venir — **sender** [ˈsɛndər] n : expéditeur m, -trice f

Senegalese [ˌsɛnəgəˈliːz, -ˈliːs] adj : sénégalais

senile [ˈsiːˌnaɪl] adj : sénile — **senility** [sɪˈnɪləti] n : sénilité f

senior [ˈsiːnjər] n 1 SUPERIOR : supérieur m 2 : étudiant m, -diante f de dernière année (en éducation) 3 or ~ **citizen** : personne f du troisième âge 4 **be s.o.'s** ~ : être plus âgé que qqn — ~ adj 1 : haut placé 2 ELDER : aîné, plus âgé — **seniority** [ˌsiːˈnjɔrəti] n : ancienneté f

sensation [sɛnˈseɪʃən] n : sensation f — **sensational** [sɛnˈseɪʃənəl] adj : sensationnel

sense [ˈsɛnts] n 1 : sens m 2 FEELING : sensation f 3 COMMON SENSE : bon sens m 4 **make** ~ : être logique — ~ vt **sensed**; **sensing** : sentir — **senseless** [ˈsɛntsləs]

adj : insensé — **sensible** [ˈsɛntsəbəl] adj : raisonnable, pratique — **sensibility** [ˌsɛntsəˈbɪləti] n, pl -ties : sensibilité f — **sensitive** [ˈsɛntsətɪv] adj 1 : sensible 2 TOUCHY : susceptible — **sensitivity** [ˌsɛntsəˈtɪvəti] n, pl -ties : sensibilité f — **sensor** [ˈsɛnˌsɔr, ˈsɛntsər] n : détecteur n — **sensual** [ˈsɛntʃuəl] adj : sensuel — **sensuous** [ˈsɛntʃuəs] adj : sensuel

sent → **send**

sentence [ˈsɛntənts, -ənz] n 1 : phrase f 2 JUDGMENT : sentence f, condamnation f — ~ vt -tenced; -tencing : condamner

sentiment [ˈsɛntəmənt] n 1 : sentiment m 2 BELIEF : opinion f, avis m — **sentimental** [ˌsɛntəˈmɛntəl] adj : sentimental — **sentimentality** [ˌsɛntəˌmɛnˈtæləti] n, pl -ties : sentimentalité f

sentry [ˈsɛntri] n, pl -tries : sentinelle f

separation [ˌsɛpəˈreɪʃən] n : séparation f — **separate** [ˈsɛpəˌreɪt] v -rated; -rating vt 1 : séparer 2 DISTINGUISH : distinguer — vi : se séparer — ~ [ˈsɛprət, ˈsɛpə-] adj 1 : séparé 2 DETACHED : à part 3 DISTINCT : distinct — **separately** [ˈsɛprətli, ˈsɛpə-] adv : séparément

September [sɛpˈtɛmbər] n : septembre m

sequel [ˈsiːkwəl] n : continuation f, suite f

sequence [ˈsiːkwənts] n 1 ORDER : ordre m, suite f 2 : série f, succession f (de nombres)

serene [səˈriːn] adj : serein, calme — **serenity** [səˈrɛnəti] n : sérénité f

sergeant [ˈsɑrdʒənt] n : sergent m

serial [ˈsɪriəl] adj : en série — ~ n : feuilleton m — **series** [ˈsɪrˌiːz] n, pl : série f

serious [ˈsɪriəs] adj : sérieux — **seriously** [ˈsɪriəsli] adv 1 : sérieusement 2 GRAVELY : gravement 3 **take** ~ : prendre au sérieux

sermon [ˈsərmən] n : sermon m

serpent [ˈsərpənt] n : serpent m

servant [ˈsərvənt] n : domestique mf

serve [ˈsərv] v **served**; **serving** vi 1 : servir 2 ~ **as** : servir de — vt 1 : servir (une personne, etc.), desservir (une région, etc.) 2 ~ **time** : purger une peine — **server** [ˈsərvər] n 1 WAITER : serveur m, -veuse f 2 : serveur m (en informatique)

service [ˈsərvəs] n 1 : service m 2 CEREMONY : office m (en religion) 3 MAINTENANCE : entretien m 4 **armed** ~s : forces fpl armées — ~ vt -viced; -vicing : réviser (un véhicule, etc.) — **serviceman** [ˈsərvəsˌmæn, -mən] n, pl -men [-mən, -ˌmɛn] : militaire m — **service station** n : station-service f, poste m d'essence — **serving** [ˈsərvɪŋ] n : portion f, ration f

session [ˈsɛʃən] n : séance f, session f

set [ˈsɛt] n 1 : ensemble m, série f, jeu m 2 : set m (au tennis) 3 or **stage** ~ : scène f, plateau *m* **4** *or* **television** ～ : poste *m* de télévision — ～ *v* **set; setting** *vt* **1** *or* ～ **down** : mettre, placer 2 : régler (une montre) **3** FIX : fixer (un rendez-vous, etc.) **4** ～ **fire to** : mettre le feu à **5** ～ **free** : mettre en liberté **6** ～ **off** : déclencher (une alarme), faire détoner (une bombe) **7** ～ **out to do sth** : se proposer de faire qqch **8** ～ **up** ASSEMBLE : installer **9** ～ **up** ESTABLISH : établir — *vi* **1** : prendre (se dit de la gélatine, etc.) **2** : se coucher (se dit du soleil) **3** ～ **in** BEGIN : commencer **4** ～ **off** *or* ～ **out** : partir (en voyage) — ～ *adj* **1** FIXED : fixe **2** READY : prêt — **setback** ['sɛt,bæk] *n* : revers *m* — **setting** ['sɛtɪŋ] *n* **1** : réglage *m* (d'une machine) **2** MOUNTING : monture *f* (d'un bijou) **3** SCENE : décor *m*

settle ['sɛt̬əl] *v* **settled; settling** *vi* **1** : se poser (se dit d'un oiseau), se déposer (se dit de la poussière) **2** ～ **down** RELAX : se calmer **3** ～ **for** : se contenter de **4** ～ **in** : s'installer — *vt* **1** DECIDE : fixer, décider **2** RESOLVE : résoudre **3** PAY : régler (un compte) **4** CALM : calmer **5** COLONIZE : coloniser — **settlement** ['sɛt̬əlmənt] *n* **1** PAYMENT : règlement *m* **2** COLONY : colonie *f*, village *m* **3** AGREEMENT : accord *m* — **settler** ['sɛt̬ələr] *n* : colonisateur *m*, -trice *f*; colon *m*

seven ['sɛvən] *n* : sept *m* — ～ *adj* : sept — **seven hundred** *adj* : sept cents — **seventeen** [,sɛvən'ti:n] *n* : dix-sept *m* — ～ *adj* : dix-sept — **seventeenth** [,sɛvən'ti:nθ] *n* **1** : dix-septième *mf* **2 April** ～ : le dix-sept avril — ～ *adj* : dix-septième — **seventh** [,sɛvənθ] *n* **1** : septième *mf* **2 July** ～ : le sept juillet — ～ *adj* : septième — **seventieth** ['sɛvəntiəθ] *n* : soixante-dixième *mf* — ～ *adj* : soixante-dixième — **seventy** ['sɛvənti] *n, pl* **-ties** : soixante-dix *m* — ～ *adj* : soixante-dix

sever ['sɛvər] *vt* **-ered; -ering 1** : couper **2** BREAK : rompre

several ['sɛvrəl, 'sɛvə-] *adj & pron* : plusieurs

severance ['sɛvrənts, 'sɛvə-] *n* **1** : rupture *f* **2** ～ **pay** : indemnité *f* de départ

severe [sə'vɪr] *adj* **-verer; -verest 1** : sévère **2** SERIOUS : grave — **severely** [sə'vɪrli] *adv* **1** : sévèrement **2** SERIOUSLY : gravement

sew ['so:] *v* **sewed; sewn** ['so:n] *or* **sewed; sewing** : coudre

sewer ['su:ər] *n* : égout *m* — **sewage** ['su:ɪdʒ] *n* : eaux *fpl* d'égout

sewing ['so:ɪŋ] *n* : couture *f*

sex ['sɛks] *n* **1** : sexe *m* **2** INTERCOURSE : relations *fpl* sexuelles — **sexism** ['sɛk,sɪzəm] *n* : sexisme *m* — **sexist** ['sɛksɪst] *adj* : sexiste — **sexual** ['sɛkʃʊəl] *adj* : sexuel —

sexuality [,sɛkʃʊ'ælət̬i] *n* : sexualité *f* — **sexy** ['sɛksi] *adj* **sexier; sexiest** : sexy

shabby ['ʃæbi] *adj* **-bier; -biest 1** WORN : miteux **2** UNFAIR : mal, injuste

shack ['ʃæk] *n* : cabane *f*

shackles ['ʃækəlz] *npl* : fers *mpl*, chaînes *fpl*

shade ['ʃeɪd] *n* **1** : ombre *f* **2** : ton *m* (d'une couleur) **3** NUANCE : nuance *f* **4** *or* **lampshade** : abat-jour *m* **5** **window** ～ : store *m* — ～ *vt* **shaded; shading** : protéger de la lumière — **shadow** ['ʃædo:] *n* : ombre *f* — **shadowy** ['ʃædowi] *adj* INDISTINCT : vague — **shady** ['ʃeɪdi] *adj* **shadier; shadiest 1** : ombragé **2** DISREPUTABLE : suspect

shaft ['ʃæft] *n* **1** : tige *f* (d'une flèche, etc.) **2** HANDLE : manche *m* **3** AXLE : arbre *m* **4** *or* **mine** ～ : puits *m*

shaggy ['ʃægi] *adj* **-gier; -est** : poilu

shake ['ʃeɪk] *v* **shook** ['ʃʊk]; **shaken** ['ʃeɪkən]; **shaking** *vt* **1** : secouer **2** MIX : agiter **3** ～ **hands with s.o.** : serrer la main à qqn **4** ～ **one's head** : secouer la tête **5** ～ **up** UPSET : ébranler — *vi* : trembler — ～ *n* **1** : secousse *f* **2** → **handshake** — **shaker** ['ʃeɪkər] *n* **1 salt** ～ : salière *f* **2 pepper** ～ : poivrière *f* — **shaky** ['ʃeɪki] *adj* **shakier; shakiest 1** : tremblant **2** UNSTABLE : peu ferme

shall ['ʃæl] *v aux, past* **should** ['ʃʊd]; *pres sing & pl* **shall 1** (*expressing volition or futurity*) → **will 2** (*expressing possibility or obligation*) → **should 3** ～ **we go?** : nous y allons?

shallow ['ʃælo:] *adj* **1** : peu profond **2** SUPERFICIAL : superficiel

sham ['ʃæm] *n* : faux-semblant *m*

shambles ['ʃæmbəlz] *ns & pl* : désordre *m*

shame ['ʃeɪm] *n* **1** : honte *f* **2 what a** ～! : quel dommage! — ～ *vt* **shamed; shaming** : faire honte à — **shameful** ['ʃeɪmfəl] *adj* : honteux

shampoo [ʃæm'pu:] *vt* : se laver (les cheveux) — ～ *n, pl* **-poos** : shampooing *m*

shan't ['ʃænt] (*contraction of* **shall not**) → **shall**

shape ['ʃeɪp] *v* **shaped; shaping** *vt* **1** : façonner **2** DETERMINE : déterminer **3 be** ～**d like** : avoir la forme de — *vi or* ～ **up** : prendre forme — ～ *n* **1** : forme *f* **2 get in** ～ : se mettre en forme — **shapeless** ['ʃeɪpləs] *adj* : informe

share ['ʃɛr] *n* **1** : portion *f*, part *f* **2** : action *f* (d'une compagnie) — ～ *v* **shared; sharing** *vt* **1** : partager **2** DIVIDE : diviser — *vi* : partager — **shareholder** ['ʃɛr,ho:ldər] *n* : actionnaire *mf*

shark ['ʃɑrk] *n* : requin *m*

sharp ['ʃɑrp] *adj* **1** : affilé **2** POINTY : pointu **3** ACUTE : aigu **4** HARSH : dur, sévère **5** CLEAR : net **6** : dièse (en musique)

— ~ *adv* **at two o'clock** ~ : à deux heures pile — ~ *n* : dièse *m* (en musique) — **sharpen** [ˈʃɑrpən] *vt* : aiguiser (un couteau, etc.), tailler (un crayon) — **sharpener** [ˈʃɑrpənər] *n* **1** *or* **knife** ~ : aiguisoir *m* **2** *or* **pencil** ~ : taille-crayon *m* — **sharply** [ˈʃɑrpli] *adv* : brusquement

shatter [ˈʃæt̬ər] *vt* **1** : briser, fracasser **2** DEVASTATE : détruire — *vi* : se briser, se fracasser

shave [ˈʃeɪv] *v* **shaved; shaved** *or* **shaven** [ˈʃeɪvən]; **shaving** *vt* **1** : raser **2** SLICE : couper — *vi* : se raser — ~ *n* : rasage — **shaver** [ˈʃeɪvər] *n* : rasoir *m*

shawl [ˈʃɔl] *n* : châle *m*

she [ˈʃi] *pron* : elle

sheaf [ˈʃif] *n, pl* **sheaves** [ˈʃivz] : gerbe *f* (de céréales), liasse *f* (de papiers)

shear [ˈʃɪr] *vt* **sheared; sheared** *or* **shorn** [ˈʃɔrn]; **shearing** : tondre — **shears** [ˈʃɪrz] *npl* : cisailles *fpl*

sheath [ˈʃiθ] *n, pl* **sheaths** [ˈʃiðz, ˈʃiːθs] : fourreau *m* (d'épée), gaine *f* (de poignard)

shed[1] [ˈʃɛd] *v* **shed; shedding** *vt* **1** : verser (des larmes) **2** : perdre (ses poils, etc.) ~ **light on** : éclairer — *vi* : perdre ses poils, muer

shed[2] *n* : abri *m*, remise *f*

she'd [ˈʃiːd] (*contraction of* **she had** *or* **she would**) → **have, would**

sheen [ˈʃin] *n* : lustre *m*, éclat *m*

sheep [ˈʃiːp] *n, pl* **sheep** : mouton *m* — **sheepish** [ˈʃiːpɪʃ] *adj* : penaud

sheer [ˈʃɪr] *adj* **1** PURE : pur **2** STEEP : escarpé

sheet [ˈʃiːt] *n* **1** : drap *m* (de lit) **2** : feuille *f* (de papier) **3** : plaque *f* (de glace, etc.)

shelf [ˈʃɛlf] *n, pl* **shelves** [ˈʃɛlvz] : étagère *f*, rayon *m*

shell [ˈʃɛl] *n* **1** : coquillage *m* **2** : carapace *f* (d'un crustacé, etc.) **3** : coquille *f* (d'œuf, etc.) **4** POD : cosse *f* **5** MISSILE : obus *m* — ~ *vt* **1** : décortiquer (des noix), écosser (des pois) **2** BOMBARD : bombarder

she'll [ˈʃiːl, ˈʃɪl] (*contraction of* **she shall** *or* **she will**) → **shall, will**

shellfish [ˈʃɛlˌfɪʃ] *n* : crustacé *m*

shelter [ˈʃɛltər] *n* **1** : abri *m*, refuge *m* **2** **take** ~ : se réfugier — ~ *vt* **1** PROTECT : protéger **2** HARBOR : abriter

shepherd [ˈʃɛpərd] *n* : berger *m*

sherbet [ˈʃərbət] *n* : sorbet *m*

sheriff [ˈʃɛrɪf] *n* : shérif *m*

sherry [ˈʃɛri] *n, pl* **-ries** : xérès *m*

she's [ˈʃiːz] (*contraction of* **she is** *or* **she has**) → **be, have**

shield [ˈʃiːld] *n* : bouclier *m* — ~ *vt* : protéger

shier, shiest → **shy**

shift [ˈʃɪft] *vt* : bouger, changer — *vi* **1** : se

déplacer, bouger **2** CHANGE : changer **3** *o* ~ **gears** : changer de vitesse — ~ *n* : changement *m* **2** : équipe *f* (au travail)

shimmer [ˈʃɪmər] *vi* : briller, reluire

shin [ˈʃɪn] *n* : tibia *m*

shine [ˈʃaɪn] *v* **shone** [ˈʃoːn] *or* **shined shining** *vi* : briller — *vt* POLISH : cirer (de chaussures) — ~ *n* : éclat *m*

shingle [ˈʃɪŋɡəl] *n* : bardeau *m* — **shingle** [ˈʃɪŋɡəlz] *npl* : zona *m*

shiny [ˈʃaɪni] *adj* **shinier; shiniest** : brillan

ship [ˈʃɪp] *n* : bateau *m*, navire *m* — ~ *v* **shipped; shipping** : expédier (par bateau) transporter (par avion) — **shipbuilding** [ˈʃɪpˌbɪldɪŋ] *n* : construction *f* navale — **shipment** [ˈʃɪpmənt] *n* : cargaison *f* chargement *m* — **shipping** [ˈʃɪpɪŋ] *n* : transport *m* (maritime) — **shipwreck** [ˈʃɪpˌrɛk] : naufrage *m* — ~ *vt* **be** ~**ed** : fair naufrage — **shipyard** [ˈʃɪpˌjɑrd] *n* : chantie *m* naval

shirt [ˈʃərt] *n* : chemise *f*

shiver [ˈʃɪvər] *vi* : frissonner — ~ *n* : fris son *m*

shoal [ˈʃoːl] *n* : banc *m* (de poissons, etc.)

shock [ˈʃɑk] *n* **1** : choc *m* **2** *or* **electric** ~ : décharge *f* (électrique) — ~ *vt* : choquer scandaliser — **shock absorber** *n* : amortis seur *m* — **shocking** [ˈʃɑkɪŋ] *adj* : choquan

shoddy [ˈʃɑdi] *adj* **-dier; -est** : de mauvais qualité

shoe [ˈʃuː] *n* : chaussure *f*, soulier *m* — **shoelace** [ˈʃuːˌleɪs] *n* : lacet *m* — **shoe maker** [ˈʃuːˌmeɪkər] *n* : cordonnier *m* -nière *f*

shone → **shine**

shook → **shake**

shoot [ˈʃuːt] *v* **shot** [ˈʃɑt]; **shooting** *vt* **1** : tirer (une balle, etc.) **2** : lancer (un re gard) **3** PHOTOGRAPH : photographier FILM : tourner — *vi* **1** : tirer **2** ~ **by** : passer en trombe — ~ *n* : rejeton *m* pousse *f* (d'une plante) — **shooting star** *n* : étoile *f* filante

shop [ˈʃɑp] *n* **1** : magasin *m*, boutique *f* **2** WORKSHOP : atelier *m* — ~ *vi* **shopped shopping 1** : faire des courses **2 go shop ping** : faire les magasins — **shopkeeper** [ˈʃɑpˌkiːpər] *n* : commerçant *m*, -çante *f* marchand *m*, -chande *f* — **shoplift** [ˈʃɑp ˌlɪft] *vt* : voler à l'étalage — **shoplifte** [ˈʃɑpˌlɪftər] *n* : voleur *m*, -leuse *f* à l'étalag — **shopper** [ˈʃɑpər] *n* : personne *f* qui fai ses courses

shore [ˈʃor] *n* : rivage *m*, bord *m*

shorn → **shear**

short [ˈʃort] *adj* **1** : court **2** : petit, de petit taille **3** CURT : brusque **4 a** ~ **time ago** : i y a peu de temps **5 be** ~ **of** : être à court d — ~ *adv* **1 fall** ~ : ne pas atteindre **2**

stop ~ : s'arrêter net — **shortage** ['ʃɔrtɪʤ] *n* : manque *m*, carence *f* — **short-cake** ['ʃɔrt,keɪk] *n* : tarte *f* sablée — **short-coming** ['ʃɔrt,kʌmɪŋ] *n* : défaut *m* — **short-cut** ['ʃɔrt,kʌt] *n* : raccourci *m* — **shorten** ['ʃɔrtən] *vt* : raccourcir — **shorthand** ['ʃɔrt,hænd] *n* : sténographie *f* — **short–lived** ['ʃɔrt'lɪvd, -'laɪvd] *adj* : éphémère — **shortly** ['ʃɔrtli] *adv* : bientôt — **shortness** ['ʃɔrtnəs] *n* 1 : petite taille *f* 2 ~ **of breath** : manque *m* de souffle — **shorts** *npl* : short *m*, pantalons *mpl* courts — **shortsighted** ['ʃɔrt,saɪtəd] → **nearsighted**

shot ['ʃɑt] *n* 1 : coup *m* (de feu) 2 : coup *m*, tir *m* (aux sports) 3 ATTEMPT : essai *m*, tentative *f* 4 PHOTOGRAPH : photo *f* 5 INJECTION : piqûre *f* 6 : verre *m* (de liqueur) — **shotgun** ['ʃɑt,gʌn] *n* : fusil *m*

should ['ʃʊd] *past of* **shall** 1 **if she ~ call** : si elle appelle 2 **I ~ have gone** : j'aurais dû y aller 3 **they ~ arrive soon** : ils devraient arriver bientôt 4 **what ~ we do?** : qu'allons nous faire?

shoulder ['ʃoːldər] *n* 1 : épaule *f* 2 : accotement *m* (d'une chaussée) — **shoulder blade** *n* : omoplate *f*

shouldn't ['ʃʊdənt] (*contraction of* **should not**) → **should**

shout ['ʃaʊt] *v* : crier — ~ *n* : cri *m*

shove ['ʃʌv] *vt* **shoved; shoving** : pousser, bousculer — ~ *n* **give s.o. a ~** : pousser qqn

shovel ['ʃʌvəl] *n* : pelle *f* — ~ *vt* **-veled** *or* **-velled; -veling** *or* **-velling** : pelleter

show ['ʃoː] *v* **showed; shown** ['ʃoːn] *or* **showed; showing** *vt* 1 : montrer 2 TEACH : enseigner 3 PROVE : démontrer 4 ESCORT : accompagner 5 : passer (une émission, un film, etc.) 6 ~ **off** : faire étalage de — *vi* 1 : se voir 2 ~ **off** : faire le fier 3 ~ **up** ARRIVE : arriver — ~ *n* 1 : démonstration *f* 2 EXHIBITION : exposition *f* 3 : spectacle *m* (de théâtre), émission *f* (de télévision, etc.) — **showdown** ['ʃoː,daʊn] *n* : confrontation *f*

shower ['ʃaʊər] *n* 1 : douche *f* 2 : averse *f* (de pluie, etc.) 3 PARTY : fête *f* — ~ *vt* 1 SPRAY : arroser 2 ~ **s.o. with** : couvrir qqn de — *vi* : prendre une douche

showy ['ʃoːi] *adj* **showier; showiest** : tape-à-l'œil

shrank → **shrink**

shrapnel ['ʃræpnəl] *ns & pl* : éclats *mpl* d'obus

shred ['ʃrɛd] *n* 1 : brin *m*, parcelle *f* 2 **in ~s** : en lambeaux — ~ *vt* **shredded; shredding** 1 : déchirer 2 GRATE : râper

shrewd ['ʃruːd] *adj* : astucieux

shriek ['ʃriːk] *vi* : pousser un cri perçant — ~ *n* : cri *m* perçant

shrill ['ʃrɪl] *adj* : perçant, strident

shrimp ['ʃrɪmp] *n* : crevette *f*

shrine ['ʃraɪn] *n* : lieu *m* saint

shrink ['ʃrɪŋk] *v* **shrank** ['ʃræŋk]; **shrunk** ['ʃrʌŋk] *or* **shrunken** ['ʃrʌŋkən]; **shrinking** : rétrécir

shrivel ['ʃrɪvəl] *vi* **-eled** *or* **-elled; -eling** *or* **-elling** *or* ~ **up** : se dessécher, se rider

shroud ['ʃraʊd] *n* 1 : linceul *m* 2 VEIL : voile *m* — ~ *vt* : envelopper

shrub ['ʃrʌb] *n* : arbuste *m*, arbrisseau *m*

shrug ['ʃrʌg] *vi* **shrugged; shrugging** : hausser les épaules

shrunk → **shrink**

shudder ['ʃʌdər] *vi* : frissonner, frémir — ~ *n* : frisson *m*

shuffle ['ʃʌfəl] *v* **-fled; -fling** *vt* : mélanger (des papiers), battre (des cartes) — *vi* : marcher en traînant les pieds

shun ['ʃʌn] *vt* **shunned; shunning** : éviter, esquiver

shut ['ʃʌt] *v* **shut; shutting** *vt* 1 CLOSE : fermer 2 ~ **turn off** 3 ~ **up** CONFINE : enfermer — *vi* 1 *or* ~ **down** : fermer 2 ~ **up** : se taire — **shutter** ['ʃʌtər] *n or* **window ~** : volet *m* (d'une fenêtre)

shuttle ['ʃʌtəl] *n* 1 : navette *f* (à l'aéroport, etc.) 2 ~ **space shuttle** — ~ *vt* **-tled; -tling** : transporter — **shuttlecock** ['ʃʌtəl,kɑk] *n* : volant *m*

shy ['ʃaɪ] *adj* **shier** *or* **shyer** ['ʃaɪər]; **shiest** *or* **shyest** ['ʃaɪəst] : timide, gêné — ~ *vi* **shied; shying** *or* ~ **away** : éviter — **shyness** ['ʃaɪnəs] *n* : timidité *f*

sibling ['sɪblɪŋ] *n* : frère *m*, sœur *f*

sick ['sɪk] *adj* 1 : malade 2 **be ~** VOMIT : vomir 3 **be ~ of** : en avoir assez de 4 **feel ~** : avoir des nausées — **sicken** ['sɪkən] *vt* DISGUST : écœurer — **sickening** ['sɪkənɪŋ] *adj* : écœurant — **sick leave** *n* : congé *m* de maladie

sickle ['sɪkəl] *n* : faucille *f*

sickly ['sɪkli] *adj* **-lier; -est** : maladif — **sickness** ['sɪknəs] *n* : maladie *f*

side ['saɪd] *n* 1 : bord *m* 2 : côté *m* (d'une personne), flanc *m* (d'un animal) 3 : côté *m*, camp *m* (de l'opposition, etc.) 4 ~ **by ~** : côte à côte 5 **take ~s** : prendre parti — ~ *adj* : latéral — *vi* ~ **with** : prendre le parti de — **sideboard** ['saɪd,bɔrd] *n* : buffet *m* — **sideburns** ['saɪd,bərnz] *npl* : favoris *mpl* — **side effect** *n* : effet *m* secondaire — **sideline** ['saɪd,laɪn] *n* : travail *m* d'appoint — **sidewalk** ['saɪd,wɔk] *n* : trottoir *m* — **sideways** ['saɪd,weɪz] *adv & adj* : de côté — **siding** ['saɪdɪŋ] *n* : revêtement *m* extérieur

siege ['siːʤ, 'siːʒ] *n* : siège *m*

sieve ['sɪv] *n* : tamis *m*, crible *m*

sift ['sɪft] *vt* 1 : tamiser 2 *or* ~ **through** : examiner

sigh ['saɪ] *vi* : soupirer — ~ *n* : soupir *m*

sight ['saɪt] *n* **1** : vue *f* **2** SPECTACLE : spectacle *m* **3** : centre *m* d'intérêt (touristique) **4 catch ~ of** : apercevoir — **sightseer** ['saɪt,si:ər] *n* : touriste *mf*

sign ['saɪn] *n* **1** : signe *m* **2** NOTICE : panneau *m*, enseigne *f* — ~ *vt* : signer (un chèque, etc.) — *vi* **1** : signer **2 ~ up** ENROLL : s'inscrire

signal ['sɪgnəl] *n* : signal *m* — ~ *v* **-naled** *or* **-nalled; -naling** *or* **-nalling** *vt* **1** : faire signe à **2** INDICATE : signaler — *vi* **1** : faire des signes **2** : mettre son clignotant (dans un véhicule)

signature ['sɪgnə,tʃʊr] *n* : signature *f*

significance [sɪg'nɪfɪkənts] *n* **1** : signification *f*, sens *m* **2** IMPORTANCE : importance *f* — **significant** [sɪg'nɪfɪkənt] *adj* **1** : significatif **2** IMPORTANT : considérable — **significantly** [sɪg'nɪfɪkəntli] *adv* : sensiblement — **signify** ['sɪgnə,faɪ] *vt* **-fied; -fying** : signifier — **sign language** *n* : langage *m* des signes — **signpost** ['saɪn,po:st] *n* : poteau *m* indicateur

silence ['saɪlənts] *n* : silence *m* — ~ *vt* **-lenced; -lencing** : faire taire — **silent** ['saɪlənt] *adj* **1** : silencieux **2** : muet (se dit d'un film, etc.)

silhouette [,sɪlə'wɛt] *n* : silhouette *f*

silicon ['sɪlɪkən, -,kɑn] *n* : silicium *m*

silk ['sɪlk] *n* : soie *f* — **silky** ['sɪlki] *adj* **silkier; -est** : soyeux

sill ['sɪl] *n* : rebord *m* (d'une fenêtre), seuil *m* (d'une porte)

silly ['sɪli] *adj* **-lier; -est** : stupide, bête

silt ['sɪlt] *n* : limon *m*

silver ['sɪlvər] *n* **1** : argent *m* **2** → **silverware** — ~ *adj* : d'argent, en argent — **silverware** ['sɪlvər,wær] *n* : argenterie *f*, coutellerie *f* *Can* — **silvery** ['sɪlvəri] *adj* : argenté

similar ['sɪmələr] *adj* : semblable, pareil — **similarity** [,sɪmə'lærəṭi] *n*, *pl* **-ties** : ressemblance *f*, similarité *f*

simmer ['sɪmər] *vi* : mijoter

simple ['sɪmpəl] *adj* **-pler; -plest** **1** : simple **2** EASY : facile — **simplicity** [sɪm'plɪsəṭi] *n* : simplicité *f* — **simplify** ['sɪmplə,faɪ] *vt* **-fied; -fying** : simplifier — **simply** ['sɪmpli] *adv* **1** : simplement **2** ABSOLUTELY : absolument

simulate ['sɪmjə,leɪt] *vt* **-lated; -lating** : simuler

simultaneous [,saɪməl'teɪniəs] *adj* : simultané

sin ['sɪn] *n* : péché *m* — ~ *vi* **sinned; sinning** : pécher

since ['sɪnts] *adv* **1** *or* **~ then** : depuis **2 long ~** : il y a longtemps — ~ *conj* **1** : depuis que **2** BECAUSE : puisque, comme

3 it's been years ~ ... : il y a des années que ... — ~ *prep* : depuis

sincere [sɪn'sɪr] *adj* **-cerer; -cerest** : sincère — **sincerely** [sɪn'sɪrli] *adv* : sincèrement — **sincerity** [sɪn'sɛrəṭi] *n* : sincérité *f*

sinful ['sɪnfəl] *adj* : immoral

sing ['sɪŋ] *v* **sang** ['sæŋ] *or* **sung** ['sʌŋ]; **sung; singing** : chanter

singer ['sɪŋər] *n* : chanteur *m*, -teuse *f*

single ['sɪŋgəl] *adj* **1** : seul, unique **2** UNMARRIED : célibataire **3 every ~ day** : tous les jours **4 every ~ time** : chaque fois — ~ *vt* **-gled; -gling ~ out 1** SELECT : choisir **2** DISTINGUISH : distinguer

singular ['sɪŋgjələr] *adj* : singulier — ~ *n* : singulier *m*

sinister ['sɪnəstər] *adj* : sinistre

sink ['sɪŋk] *v* **sank** ['sæŋk] *or* **sunk** ['sʌŋk]; **sunk; sinking** *vi* **1** : couler **2** DROP : baisser, tomber — *vt* **1** : couler **2 ~ sth into** : enfoncer qqch dans — ~ *n* **1** *or* **bathroom ~** : lavabo *m* **2** *or* **kitchen ~** : évier *m*

sinner ['sɪnər] *n* : pécheur *m*, -cheresse *f*

sip ['sɪp] *vt* **sipped; sipping** : boire à petites gorgées, siroter *fam* — ~ *n* : petite gorgée *f*

siphon ['saɪfən] *n* : siphon *m* — ~ *vt* : siphonner

sir ['sər] *n* **1** (*as a form of address*) : monsieur *m* **2** (*in titles*) : sir *m*

siren ['saɪrən] *n* : sirène *f*

sirloin ['sər,lɔɪn] *n* : aloyau *m*

sissy ['sɪsi] *n*, *pl* **-sies** : poule *f* mouillée *fam*

sister ['sɪstər] *n* : sœur *f* — **sister-in-law** ['sɪstərɪn,lɔ] *n*, *pl* **sisters-in-law** : belle-sœur *f*

sit ['sɪt] *v* **sat** ['sæt]; **sitting** *vi* **1** *or* **~ down** : s'asseoir **2** LIE : être, se trouver **3** MEET : siéger **4** *or* **~ up** : se redresser — *vt* : asseoir

site ['saɪt] *n* **1** : site *m*, emplacement *m* **2** LOT : terrain *m*

sitting room → **living room**

situated ['sɪtʃʊ,eɪṭəd] *adj* : situé — **situation** [,sɪtʃʊ'eɪʃən] *n* : situation *f*

six ['sɪks] *n* : six *m* — ~ *adj* : six — **six hundred** *adj* : six cents — **sixteen** [sɪks'ti:n] *n* : seize *m* — ~ *adj* : seize — **sixteenth** [sɪks'ti:nθ] *n* **1** : seizième *mf* **2** October ~ : le seize octobre — ~ *adj* : seizième — **sixth** ['sɪksθ, 'sɪkst] *n* **1** : sixième *mf* **2** March ~ : le six mars — ~ *adj* : sixième — **sixtieth** ['sɪkstiəθ] *n* : soixantième *mf* — ~ *adj* : soixantième — **sixty** ['sɪksti] *n*, *pl* **-ties** : soixante *m* — ~ *adj* : soixante

size ['saɪz] *n* **1** : taille *f* (d'un vêtement), pointure *f* (de chaussures, etc.) **2** EXTENT : ampleur *f* — ~ *vt* **sized; sizing** *or* **~ up** : jauger, évaluer

sizzle ['sɪzəl] *vi* **-zled; -zling** : grésiller

skate ['skeɪt] *n* : patin *m* — ~ *vi* **skated; skating** : patiner, faire du patin — **skateboard** ['skeɪt,bɔrd] *n* : planche *f* à roulettes — **skater** ['skeɪtər] *n* : patineur *m*, -neuse *f*

skeleton ['skɛlətən] *n* : squelette *m*

skeptical ['skɛptɪkəl] *adj* : sceptique

sketch ['skɛtʃ] *n* : esquisse *f*, croquis *m* — ~ *vt* : esquisser

skewer ['skju:ər] *n* : brochette *f*, broche *f*

ski ['ski:] *n, pl* **skis** : ski *m* — ~ *vi* **skied; skiing** : faire du ski

skid ['skɪd] *n* : dérapage *m* — ~ *vi* **skidded; skidding** : déraper, patiner

skier ['ski:ər] *n* : skieur *m*, skieuse *f*

skill ['skɪl] *n* **1** : habileté *f*, dextérité *f* **2** TECHNIQUE : technique *f* **3** ~**s** *npl* : compétences *fpl* — **skilled** ['skɪld] *adj* : habile

skillet ['skɪlət] *n* : poêle *f* (à frire)

skillful *or Brit* **skilful** ['skɪlfəl] *adj* : habile, adroit

skim ['skɪm] *vt* **skimmed; skimming 1** : écumer (de la soupe), écrémer (du lait) **2** : effleurer (une surface) **3** *or* ~ **through** : parcourir (un livre, etc.) — ~ *adj* : écrémé

skimpy ['skɪmpi] *adj* **skimpier; skimpiest 1** : maigre (se dit d'une portion) **2** : étriqué (se dit d'un vêtement)

skin ['skɪn] *n* **1** : peau *f* **2** : pelure *f* (de pomme, etc.) — ~ *vt* **skinned; skinning 1** : dépouiller (un animal) **2** : s'écorcher (le genou, etc.) — **skin diving** *n* : plongée *f* sous-marine — **skinny** ['skɪni] *adj* **-nier; -est** : maigre

skip ['skɪp] *v* **skipped; skipping** *vi* : sautiller — *vt* OMIT : sauter — ~ *n* : petit saut *m*, petit bond *m*

skirmish ['skərmɪʃ] *n* : escarmouche *f*

skirt ['skərt] *n* : jupe *f*

skull ['skʌl] *n* : crâne *m*

skunk ['skʌŋk] *n* : mouffette *f*

sky ['skaɪ] *n, pl* **skies** : ciel *m* — **skylight** ['skaɪ,laɪt] *n* : lucarne *f* — **skyline** ['skaɪ,laɪn] *n* : horizon *m* — **skyscraper** ['skaɪ,skreɪpər] *n* : gratte-ciel *m*

slab ['slæb] *n* : dalle *f*, bloc *m*

slack ['slæk] *adj* **1** LOOSE : mou, lâche **2** CARELESS : négligent — **slacks** ['slæks] *npl* : pantalon *m* — **slacken** ['slækən] *vt* : relâcher

slain → **slay**

slam ['slæm] *n* : claquement *m* (de porte) — ~ *v* **slammed; slamming** *vt* **1** : claquer (une porte, etc.) **2** *or* ~ **down** : flanquer **3** *or* ~ **shut** : fermer brusquement — *vi* ~ **into** : heurter

slander ['slændər] *vt* : calomnier, diffamer — ~ *n* : calomnie *f*, diffamation *f*

slang ['slæŋ] *n* : argot *m*

slant ['slænt] *n* : pente *f*, inclinaison *f* — ~ *vi* : pencher, s'incliner

slap ['slæp] *vt* **slapped; slapping** : gifler, donner une claque à — ~ *n* : gifle *f*, claque *f*

slash ['slæʃ] *vt* : entailler

slat ['slæt] *n* : lame *f*, lamelle *f*

slate ['sleɪt] *n* : ardoise *f*

slaughter ['slɔtər] *n* : massacre *m* — ~ *vt* **1** : abattre (des animaux) **2** MASSACRE : massacrer — **slaughterhouse** ['slɔtər,haʊs] *n* : abattoir *m*

slave ['sleɪv] *n* : esclave *mf* — **slavery** ['sleɪvəri] *n* : esclavage *m*

sled ['slɛd] *n* : traîneau *m*, luge *f*

sledgehammer ['slɛdʒ,hæmər] *n* : masse *f*

sleek ['sli:k] *adj* : lisse, luisant

sleep ['sli:p] *n* **1** : sommeil *m* **2 go to** ~ : s'endormir — ~ *vi* **slept** ['slɛpt]; **sleeping** : dormir — **sleeper** ['sli:pər] *n* **be a light** ~ : avoir le sommeil léger — **sleepless** ['sli:pləs] *adj* **have a** ~ **night** : passer une nuit blanche — **sleepwalker** ['sli:p,wɔkər] *n* : somnambule *mf* — **sleepy** ['sli:pi] *adj* **sleepier; -est 1** : somnolent **2 be** ~ : avoir sommeil

sleet ['sli:t] *n* : grésil *m* — ~ *vi* : grésiller

sleeve ['sli:v] *n* : manche *f* — **sleeveless** ['sli:vləs] *adj* : sans manches

sleigh ['sleɪ] *n* : traîneau *m*, carriole *f Can*

slender ['slɛndər] *adj* : svelte, mince

slept → **sleep**

slice ['slaɪs] *vt* **sliced; slicing** : trancher — ~ *n* : tranche *f*, rondelle *f*

slick ['slɪk] *adj* SLIPPERY : glissant

slide ['slaɪd] *v* **slid** ['slɪd]; **sliding** ['slaɪdɪŋ] *vi* : glisser — *vt* : faire glisser — ~ *n* **1** : glissoire *f* **2** : toboggan *m* (dans un terrain de jeu) **3** : diapositive *f* (en photographie) **4** DECLINE : baisse *f*

slier, sliest → **sly**

slight ['slaɪt] *adj* **1** SLENDER : mince **2** MINOR : léger — ~ *vt* : offenser — **slightly** ['slaɪtli] *adv* : légèrement, un peu

slim ['slɪm] *adj* **slimmer; slimmest 1** : svelte **2 a** ~ **chance** : une faible chance — ~ *v* **slimmed; slimming** : maigrir

slime ['slaɪm] *n* MUD : vase *f*, boue *f*

sling ['slɪŋ] *vt* **slung** ['slʌŋ]; **slinging** THROW : lancer — ~ *n* **1** : fronde *f* **2** : écharpe *f* (en médecine) — **slingshot** ['slɪŋ,ʃɑt] *n* : lance-pierres *m*

slip[1] ['slɪp] *v* **slipped; slipping** *vi* **1** SLIDE : glisser **2** ~ **away** : partir furtivement **3** ~ **up** : faire une gaffe — *vt* **1** : glisser **2** ~ **into** : enfiler (un vêtement, etc.) — ~ *n* **1** MISTAKE : erreur *f* **2** : jupon *m* **3 a** ~ **of the tongue** : un lapsus

slip[2] *n* ~ **of paper** : bout *m* (de papier)

slipper ['slɪpər] *n* : pantoufle *f*

slippery ['slɪpəri] *adj* **-perier; -est** : glissant

slit ['slɪt] *n* **1** OPENING : fente *f* **2** CUT : incision *f* — ∼ *vt* **slit; slitting** : couper

slither ['slɪðər] *vi* : ramper

sliver ['slɪvər] *n* : éclat *m* (de bois)

slogan ['slo:gən] *n* : slogan *m*

slope ['slo:p] *vi* **sloped; sloping** : pencher — ∼ *n* : pente *f*

sloppy ['slɑpi] *adj* **-pier; -piest 1** CARELESS : peu soigné **2** UNKEMPT : débraillé

slot ['slɑt] *n* **1** : fente *f* **2** GROOVE : rainure *f*

sloth ['slɔθ, 'slo:θ] *n* : paresse *f*

slouch ['slaʊʧ] *vi* : marcher avec les épaules rentrées

slow ['slo:] *adj* **1** : lent **2** be ∼ : retarder (se dit d'une horloge) — ∼ *adv* → **slowly** — ∼ *vt* : retarder — *vi or* ∼ **down** : ralentir — **slowly** ['slo:li] *adv* : lentement — **slowness** ['slo:nəs] *n* : lenteur *f*

slug ['slʌg] *n* : limace *f* (mollusque)

sluggish ['slʌgɪʃ] *adj* : lent

slum ['slʌm] *n* : taudis *m*

slumber ['slʌmbər] *vi* : sommeiller — ∼ *n* : sommeil *m*

slump ['slʌmp] *vi* **1** DROP : baisser, chuter **2** COLLAPSE : s'effondrer — ∼ *n* : crise *f* (économique)

slung → **sling**

slur[1] ['slər] *n* : calomnie *f*, diffamation *f*

slur[2] *vt* **slurred; slurring** : mal articuler (ses mots)

slurp ['slərp] *v* : boire bruyamment

slush ['slʌʃ] *n* : neige *f* fondue, gadoue *f Can*

sly ['slaɪ] *adj* **slier** ['slaɪər]; **sliest** ['slaɪəst] **1** : rusé, sournois **2** on the ∼ : en cachette

smack[1] ['smæk] *vi* ∼ **of** : sentir

smack[2] *vt* **1** : donner une claque à **2** KISS : donner un baiser à — ∼ *n* **1** SLAP : claque *f*, gifle *f* **2** KISS : gros baiser *m* — ∼ *adv* : juste, exactement

small ['smɔl] *adj* : petit — **smallpox** ['smɔl-ˌpɑks] *n* : variole *f*

smart ['smɑrt] *adj* **1** : intelligent **2** STYLISH : élégant

smash ['smæʃ] *n* **1** COLLISION : choc *m* **2** BANG, CRASH : fracas *m* — ∼ *vt* BREAK : fracasser — *vi* **1** SHATTER : se briser **2** ∼ **into** : s'écraser contre

smattering ['smætərɪŋ] *n* : notions *fpl* vagues

smear ['smɪr] *n* : tache *f* — ∼ *vt* **1** : barbouiller, faire des taches sur **2** ∼ **sth on** : enduire qqch de

smell ['smɛl] *v* **smelled** ['smɛld] *or* **smelt** ['smɛlt]; **smelling** : sentir — ∼ *n* **1** : odorat *m* **2** ODOR : odeur *f* — **smelly** ['smɛli] *adj* **smellier; -est** : qui sent mauvais

smile ['smaɪl] *vi* **smiled; smiling** : sourire — ∼ *n* : sourire *m*

smirk ['smərk] *n* : petit sourire *m* satisfait

smitten ['smɪtən] *adj* be ∼ **with** : être épris de

smock ['smɑk] *n* : blouse *f*, sarrau *m*

smog ['smɑg, 'smɔg] *n* : smog *m*

smoke ['smo:k] *n* : fumée *f* — ∼ *v* **smoked; smoking** : fumer — **smoke detector** *n* : détecteur *m* de fumée — **smoker** ['smo:kər] *n* : fumeur *m*, -meuse *f* — **smokestack** ['smo:kˌstæk] *n* : cheminée *f* — **smoky** ['smo:ki] *adj* **smokier; -est** : enfumé

smolder ['smo:ldər] *vi* : couver

smooth ['smu:ð] *adj* : lisse (se dit d'une surface, etc.), calme (se dit de la mer), doux (se dit de la peau, etc.) — ∼ *or* ∼ **out** *vt* : défroisser — **smoothly** ['smu:ðli] *adv* : sans heurts

smother ['smʌðər] *vt* **1** : recouvrir (un feu) **2** : étouffer (qqn)

smudge ['smʌʤ] *vt* **smudged; smudging** : salir, faire des taches sur — ∼ *n* : tache *f*, bavure *f*

smug ['smʌg] *adj* **smugger; smuggest** : suffisant

smuggle ['smʌgəl] *vt* **-gled; -gling** : faire passer en contrebande — **smuggler** ['smʌgələr] *n* : contrebandier *m*, -dière *f*

snack ['snæk] *n* : casse-croûte *m*, collation *f*

snag ['snæg] *n* : accroc *m* — ∼ *vt* **snagged; snagging** : faire un accroc à (un bas)

snail ['sneɪl] *n* : escargot *m*

snake ['sneɪk] *n* : serpent *m*

snap ['snæp] *v* **snapped; snapping** *vi* **1** BREAK : se casser, se briser **2** ∼ **at** : répondre brusquement à — *vt* **1** BREAK : casser, briser **2** ∼ **one's fingers** : claquer des doigts **3** ∼ **open/shut** : s'ouvrir, se fermer d'un coup sec — ∼ *n* **1** : claquement *m* **2** FASTENER : bouton-pression *m* **3** be a ∼ : être facile — **snappy** ['snæpi] *adj* **-pier; -piest 1** FAST : vite **2** STYLISH : élégant — **snapshot** ['snæpˌʃɑt] *n* : instantané *m*

snare ['snær] *n* : piège *m*

snarl[1] ['snɑrl] *vi* TANGLE : enchevêtrer

snarl[2] *vi* GROWL : grogner — ∼ *n* : grognement *m*

snatch ['snæʧ] *vt* : saisir

sneak ['sni:k] *vi* : se glisser, se faufiler — *vt* : faire furtivement — **sneakers** ['sni:kərz] *npl* : tennis *mpl France*, espadrilles *fpl Can* — **sneaky** ['sni:ki] *adj* **sneakier; -est** : sournois

sneer ['snɪr] *vi* : ricaner — ∼ *n* : ricanement *m*

sneeze ['sni:z] *vi* **sneezed; sneezing** : éternuer — ∼ *n* : éternuement *m*

snide ['snaɪd] *adj* : sarcastique

sniff ['snɪf] *vi* : renifler — ∼ *n* : inhalation *f*

— **sniffle** ['snɪfəl] *vi* **-fled; -fling** : renifler
— **sniffles** ['snɪfəlz] *npl* **have the ~** : être enrhumé
snip ['snɪp] *n* : coup *m* de ciseaux — **~** *vt* **snipped; snipping** : couper
snivel ['snɪvəl] *vi* **-eled** *or* **-elled; -eling** *or* **-elling** : pleurnicher *fam*
snob ['snɑb] *n* : snob *mf* — **snobbish** ['snɑbɪʃ] *adj* : snob
snoop ['snu:p] *vi* *or* **~ around** : fouiner
snooze ['snu:z] *vi* **snoozed; snoozing** : sommeiller — **~** *n* : petit somme *m*, sieste *f*
snore ['snor] *vi* **snored; snoring** : ronfler — **~** *n* : ronflement *m*
snort ['snort] *vi* : grogner (se dit d'un cochon, d'une personne) — **~** *n* : grognement *m*
snout ['snaʊt] *n* : museau *m*, groin *m*
snow ['sno:] *n* : neige *f* — **~** *vi* : neiger — **snowbank** ['sno:ˌbæŋk] *n* : banc *m* de neige *Can* — **snowfall** ['sno:ˌfɔl] *n* : chute *f* de neige — **snowflake** ['sno:ˌfleɪk] *n* : flocon *m* de neige — **snowman** ['sno:ˌmæn] *n* : bonhomme *m* de neige — **snowplow** ['sno:ˌplaʊ] *n* : chasse-neige *m* — **snowshoe** ['sno:ˌʃu:] *n* : raquette *f* — **snowstorm** ['sno:ˌstorm] *n* : tempête *f* de neige — **snowy** ['sno:i] *adj* **snowier; -est 1** : neigeux **2** : enneigé (se dit d'une montagne, etc.)
snub ['snʌb] *vt* **snubbed; snubbing** : rabrouer — **~** *n* : rebuffade *f*
snuff ['snʌf] *vt* *or* **~ out** : moucher (une chandelle)
snug ['snʌg] *adj* **snugger; snuggest 1** : confortable, douillet **2** TIGHT : ajusté — **snuggle** ['snʌgəl] *vi* **-gled; -gling** : se blottir
so ['so:] *adv* **1** LIKEWISE : aussi **2** THUS : ainsi **3** THEREFORE : alors **4** *or* **~ much** : tant **5** *or* **~ very** : si **6 and ~ on** : et cetera **7 I think ~** : je pense que oui **8 I told you ~** : je te l'avais bien dit — **~** *conj* **1** THEREFORE : donc **2** *or* **~ that** : pour que **3 ~ what?** : et alors? — **~** *adj* TRUE : vrai — **~** *pron* **or ~** : plus ou moins
soak ['so:k] *vt* **1** : tremper **2 ~ up** : absorber — **~** *n* : trempage *m*
soap ['so:p] *n* : savon *m* — **~** *vt* **~ up** : savonner — **soapy** ['so:pi] *adj* **soapier; -est** : savonneux
soar ['sor] *vi* **1** : planer **2** INCREASE : monter (en flèche)
sob ['sɑb] *vi* **sobbed; sobbing** : sangloter — **~** *n* : sanglot *m*
sober ['so:bər] *adj* **1** : sobre **2** SERIOUS : sérieux — **sobriety** [sə'braɪəti, so-] *n* **1** : sobriété *f* **2** SERIOUSNESS : sérieux *m*

so–called ['so:'kɔld] *adj* : présumé
soccer ['sɑkər] *n* : football *m France*, soccer *m Can*
social ['so:ʃəl] *adj* : social — **~** *n* : réunion *f* — **sociable** ['so:ʃəbəl] *adj* : sociable — **socialism** ['so:ʃəˌlɪzəm] *n* : socialisme *m* — **socialist** ['so:ʃəlɪst] *n* : socialiste *mf* — **~** *adj* : socialiste — **socialize** ['so:ʃəˌlaɪz] *v* **-ized; -izing** *vt* : socialiser — *vi* **~ with** : fréquenter des gens — **society** [sə'saɪəti] *n*, *pl* **-eties** : société *f* — **sociology** [ˌso:si-'ɑlədʒi] *n* : sociologie *f*
sock[1] ['sɑk] *n*, *pl* **socks** *or* **sox** : chaussette *f*
sock[2] *vt* : donner un coup de poing à
socket ['sɑkət] *n* **1** *or* **electric ~** : prise *f* de courant **2** *or* **eye ~** : orbite *f*
soda ['so:də] *n* **1** *or* **~ pop** : boisson *f* gazeuse, soda *m France*, liqueur *f Can* **2** *or* **~ water** : soda *m*
sodium ['so:diəm] *n* : sodium *m*
sofa ['so:fə] *n* : canapé *m*
soft ['sɔft] *adj* **1** : mou **2** SMOOTH : doux — **softball** ['sɔftˌbɔl] *n* : balle-molle *f Can* — **soft drink** *n* : boisson *f* non alcoolisée, boisson *f* gazeuse — **soften** ['sɔfən] *vt* **1** : amollir, ramollir **2** EASE : adoucir, atténuer — *vi* **1** : se ramollir **2** EASE : s'adoucir — **softly** ['sɔftli] *adv* : doucement — **softness** ['sɔftnəs] *n* : douceur *f* — **software** ['sɔftˌwær] *n* : logiciel *m*
soggy ['sɑgi] *adj* **-gier; -est** : détrempé
soil ['sɔɪl] *vt* : salir, souiller — **~** *n* DIRT : terre *f*
solace ['sɑləs] *n* : consolation *f*
solar ['so:lər] *adj* : solaire
sold → sell
solder ['sɑdər, 'sɔ-] *n* : soudure *f* — **~** *vt* : souder
soldier ['so:ldʒər] *n* : soldat *m*
sole[1] ['so:l] *n* : sole *f* (poisson)
sole[2] *n* : plante *f* (du pied), semelle *f* (d'un soulier)
sole[3] *adj* : seul — **solely** ['so:li] *adv* : uniquement
solemn ['sɑləm] *adj* : solennel — **solemnity** [sə'lɛmnəti] *n*, *pl* **-ties** : solennité *f*
solicit [sə'lɪsət] *vt* : solliciter
solid ['sɑləd] *adj* **1** : solide **2** UNBROKEN : continu **3** *or* **~ gold** : massif **4 two ~ hours** : deux heures de suite — **~** *n* : solide *m* — **solidarity** [ˌsɑlə'dærəti] *n* : solidarité *f* — **solidify** [sə'lɪdəˌfaɪ] *v* **-fied; -fying** *vt* : solidifier — *vi* : se solidifier — **solidity** [sə'lɪdəti] *n*, *pl* **-ties** : solidité *f*
solitary ['sɑləˌtɛri] *adj* : solitaire — **solitude** ['sɑləˌtu:d, -ˌtju:d] *n* : solitude *f*
solo ['so:ˌlo:] *n*, *pl* **-los** : solo *m* — **soloist** ['so:loɪst] *n* : soliste *mf*
solution [sə'lu:ʃən] *n* : solution *f* — **soluble** ['sɑljəbəl] *adj* : soluble — **solve** ['sɑlv] *vt*

solved; solving : résoudre — **solvent** ['salvənt] *n* : solvent *m*

somber ['sambər] *adj* : sombre

some ['sʌm] *adj* **1** (*of unspecified identity*) : un **2** (*of an unspecified amount*) : de, un peu de **3** (*of an unspecified number*) : certains **4** SEVERAL : quelques **5 that was** ~ **game!** : ça c'était un match! — ~ *pron* **1** SEVERAL : certains, quelques-uns **2 do you want** ~? : en voulez vous? — ~ *adv* ~ **twenty people** : une vingtaine de personnes — **somebody** ['sʌmbədi, -,badi] *pron* : quelqu'un — **someday** ['sʌm,deɪ] *adv* : un jour — **somehow** ['sʌm,haʊ] *adv* **1** : pour quelque raison **2** ~ **or other** : d'une manière ou d'une autre — **someone** ['sʌm-,wʌn] *pron* : quelqu'un

somersault ['sʌmər,sɔlt] *n* : culbute *f*

something ['sʌmθɪŋ] *pron* **1** : quelque chose **2** ~ **else** : autre chose — **sometime** ['sʌm,taɪm] *adv* **1** : un jour, un de ces jours **2** ~ **next month** : dans le courant du mois à venir — **sometimes** ['sʌm,taɪmz] *adv* : quelquefois, parfois — **somewhat** ['sʌm-,hwɑt, -,hwɑt] *adv* : un peu — **somewhere** ['sʌm,hwɛr] *adv* **1** : quelque part **2** ~ **around** : autour de **3** ~ **else** → **elsewhere**

son ['sʌn] *n* : fils *m*

song ['sɔŋ] *n* : chanson *f*

son–in–law ['sʌnɪn,lɔ] *n, pl* **sons–in–law** : gendre *m*, beau-fils *m*

soon ['su:n] *adv* **1** : bientôt **2** SHORTLY : sous peu **3 as** ~ **as** : aussitôt que **4** ~ **after** : peu après **5** ~**er or later** : tôt ou tard **6 the** ~**er the better** : le plus tôt sera le mieux

soot ['sʊt, 'su:t, 'sʌt] *n* : suie *f*

soothe ['su:ð] *vt* **soothed; soothing 1** : calmer, apaiser **2** RELIEVE : soulager

sophisticated [sə'fɪstə,keɪtəd] *adj* **1** : perfectionné **2** WORLDLY : sophistiqué

sophomore ['saf,mor, 'safə,mor] *n* : étudiant *m*, -diante *f* de deuxième année

soprano [sə'præ,no:] *n, pl* **-nos** : soprano *mf*

sorcerer ['sɔrsərər] *n* : sorcier *m* — **sorcery** ['sɔrsəri] *n* : sorcellerie *f*

sordid ['sɔrdɪd] *adj* : sordide

sore ['sor] *adj* **sorer; sorest 1** : douloureux **2** ~ **loser** : mauvais perdant **3** ~ **throat** : mal *m* de gorge — ~ *n* : plaie *f* — **sorely** ['sorli] *adv* : grandement — **soreness** ['sornəs] *n* : douleur *f*

sorrow ['sar,o:] *n* : chagrin *m*, peine *f*

sorry ['sari] *adj* **-rier; -est 1** PITIFUL : lamentable **2 feel** ~ **for** : plaindre **3 I'm** ~ : je suis désolé, je regrette

sort ['sɔrt] *n* **1** : genre *m*, sorte *f* **2 a** ~ **of** : une espèce de — ~ *vt* : trier, classer — **sort of** *adv* **1** SOMEWHAT : plutôt **2** MORE OR LESS : plus ou moins

SOS [,ɛs,o:'ɛs] *n* : S.O.S. *m*

so–so ['so:'so:] *adv* : comme ci comme ça — ~ *adj* : moyen

soufflé [su:'fleɪ] *n* : soufflé *m*

sought → **seek**

soul ['so:l] *n* **1** : âme *f* **2 not a** ~ : pas un chat

sound[1] ['saʊnd] *adj* **1** HEALTHY : sain **2** FIRM : solide **3** SENSIBLE : logique **4 a** ~ **sleep** : un sommeil profond **5 safe and** ~ : sain et sauf

sound[2] *n* **1** : son *m* **2** NOISE : bruit *m* — ~ *vt* : sonner, retentir — *vi* **1** : sonner **2** SEEM : sembler, paraître

sound[3] *n* CHANNEL : détroit *m* — ~ *v*. : sonder

soundproof ['saʊnd,pru:f] *adj* : insonorisé

soup ['su:p] *n* : soupe *f*

sour ['saʊər] *adj* : aigre — ~ *vt* : aigrir

source ['sors] *n* : source *f*, origine *f*

south ['saʊθ] *adv* : au sud, vers le sud — ~ *adj* : (du) sud — ~ *n* : sud *m* — **southeast** [saʊ'θi:st] *adv* : au sud-est, vers le sud-est — ~ *adj* : (du) sud-est — ~ *n* : sud-est *m* — **southeastern** [saʊ'θi:stərn] *adj* → **southeast** — **southerly** ['sʌðərli] *adv & adj* : (du) sud — **southern** ['sʌðərn] *adj* : du sud, méridional — **southwest** [saʊθ'west] *adv* : au sud-ouest, vers le sud-ouest — ~ *adj* : (du) sud-ouest — ~ *n* : sud-ouest *m* — **southwestern** [saʊθ'westərn] *adj* → **southwest**

souvenir [,su:və'nɪr, 'su:və,-] *n* : souvenir *m*

sovereign ['savərən] *n* : souverain *m*, -raine *f* — ~ *adj* : souverain — **sovereignty** ['savərənti] *n, pl* **-ties** : souveraineté *f*

sow[1] ['saʊ] *n* : truie *f*

sow[2] ['so:] *vt* **sowed; sown** ['so:n] *or* **sowed; sowing** : semer

sox → **sock**

soybean ['sɔɪ,bi:n] *n* : graine *f* de soja

spa ['spɑ] *n* : station *f* thermale

space ['speɪs] *n* **1** : espace *m* **2** ROOM, SPOT : place *f* — ~ *vt* **spaced; spacing** *or* ~ **out** : espacer — **spaceship** ['speɪs,ʃɪp] *n* : vaisseau *m* spatial — **space shuttle** *n* : navette *f* spatiale — **spacious** ['speɪʃəs] *adj* : spacieux, ample

spade[1] ['speɪd] *n* SHOVEL : bêche *f*, pelle *f*

spade[2] *n* : pique *f* (aux cartes)

spaghetti [spə'gɛti] *n* : spaghetti *mpl*

span ['spæn] *n* **1** PERIOD : espace *m* **2** : travée *f* (d'un pont) — ~ *vt* **spanned; spanning 1** : couvrir (une période) **2** CROSS : s'étendre sur

spaniel ['spænjəl] *n* : épagneul *m*

Spanish ['spænɪʃ] *adj* : espagnol — ~ *n* : espagnol *m* (langue)

spank ['spæŋk] *vt* : donner une fessée à

spare ['spær] *vt* **spared; sparing 1** PARDON

: pardonner **2** SAVE : épargner **3 can you
~ a dollar?** : avez-vous un dollar à me
prêter? **4 I can't ~ the time** : je n'ai pas le
temps **5 ~ no expense** : ne pas ménager
ses efforts — **~** *adj* **1** : de rechange **2** EX-
CESS : de trop — **~** *n or* **~ part** : pièce *f*
de rechange — **spare time** *n* : temps *m* libre
— **sparing** ['spærɪŋ] *adj* : économe

spark ['spark] *n* : étincelle *f* — **~** *vt*
: éveiller, susciter — **sparkle** ['sparkəl] *vi*
-kled; -kling : étinceler, scintiller — **~** *n*
: scintillement *m* — **spark plug** *n* : bougie *f*

sparrow ['spæro:] *n* : moineau *m*

sparse ['spars] *adj* **sparser; sparsest**
: clairsemé, épars — **sparsely** ['sparsli] *adv*
: peu

spasm ['spæzəm] *n* : spasme *m*

spat[1] ['spæt] → **spit**

spat[2] *n* QUARREL : prise *f* de bec

spatter ['spætər] *vt* : éclabousser

spawn ['spɔn] *vi* : frayer — *vt* : engendrer,
produire — **~** *n* : frai *m*

speak ['spi:k] *v* **spoke** ['spo:k]; **spoken**
['spo:kən]; **speaking** *vi* **1** : parler **2 ~ out
against** : dénoncer **3 ~ up** : parler plus
fort **4 ~ up for** : défendre — *vt* **1** : dire **2**
: parler (une langue) — **speaker** ['spi:kər] *n*
1 : personne *f* qui parle (une langue) **2** OR-
ATOR : orateur *m*, -trice *f* **3** LOUDSPEAKER
: haut-parleur *m*

spear ['spɪr] *n* : lance *f* — **spearhead** ['spɪr-
ˌhɛd] *n* : fer *m* de lance — **~** *vt* : mener,
être à la tête de — **spearmint** ['spɪrˌmɪnt] *n*
: menthe *f* verte

special ['spɛʃəl] *adj* : spécial, particulier —
specialist ['spɛʃəlɪst] *n* : spécialiste *mf* —
specialize ['spɛʃəˌlaɪz] *vi* **-ized; -izing** : se
spécialiser — **specially** ['spɛʃəli] *adv* : spécialement — **specialty** ['spɛʃəlti] *n, pl* **-ties**
: spécialité *f*

species ['spi:ˌʃi:z, -ˌsi:z] *ns & pl* : espèce *f*

specify ['spɛsəˌfaɪ] *vt* **-fied; -fying** : spécifier
— **specific** [spɪˈsɪfɪk] *adj* : précis, explicite
— **specifically** [spɪˈsɪfɪkli] *adv* **1** : spécialement **2** EXPLICITLY : expressément

specimen ['spɛsəmən] *n* : spécimen *m*,
échantillon *m*

speck ['spɛk] *n* **1** SPOT : tache *f* **2** BIT : brin
m — **speckled** ['spɛkəld] *adj* : tacheté,
moucheté

spectacle ['spɛktɪkəl] *n* **1** : spectacle *m* **2**
~s *npl* GLASSES : lunettes *fpl* — **spectacular** [spɛkˈtækjələr] *adj* : spectaculaire —
spectator ['spɛkˌteɪtər] *n* : spectateur *m*,
-trice *f*

specter *or* **spectre** ['spɛktər] *n* : spectre *m*

spectrum ['spɛktrəm] *n, pl* **-tra** [-trə] *or*
-trums 1 : spectre *m* **2** RANGE : gamme *f*

speculation [ˌspɛkjəˈleɪʃən] *n* : conjectures
fpl, spéculations *fpl*

speech ['spi:tʃ] *n* **1** : parole *f* **2** ADDRESS
: discours *m* — **speechless** ['spi:tʃləs] *adj*
: muet

speed ['spi:d] *n* **1** : vitesse *f* **2** VELOCITY
: rapidité *f* — **~** *v* **sped** ['spɛd] *or*
speeded; speeding *vi* **1** : faire un excès de
vitesse **2 ~ off** : aller à toute vitesse — *vt*
or **~ up** : accélérer — **speed limit** *n* : limitation *f* de vitesse — **speedometer** [spɪ-
ˈdamətər] *n* : compteur *m* (de vitesse) —
speedy ['spi:di] *adj* **speedier; -est** : rapide

spell[1] ['spɛl] *vt* **1** : écrire, orthographier **2**
or **~ out** : épeler **3** MEAN : signifier

spell[2] *n* ENCHANTMENT : sortilège *m*

spell[3] *n* : période *f* (de temps)

spellbound ['spɛlˌbaʊnd] *adj* : captivé

spelling ['spɛlɪŋ] *n* : orthographe *f*

spend ['spɛnd] *vt* **spent** ['spɛnt]; **spending
1** : dépenser (de l'argent) **2** : passer (ses vacances, etc.)

sperm ['spərm] *n, pl* **sperm** *or* **sperms**
: sperme *m*

sphere ['sfɪr] *n* : sphère *f* — **spherical**
['sfɪrɪkəl, 'sfɛr-] *adj* : sphérique

spice ['spaɪs] *n* : épice *f* — **~** *vt* **spiced;
spicing** : assaisonner — **spicy** ['spaɪsi] *adj*
spicier; -est : épicé, piquant

spider ['spaɪdər] *n* : araignée *f*

spigot ['spɪgət, -kət] *n* : robinet *m*

spike ['spaɪk] *n* **1** : gros clou *m* **2** POINT
: pointe *f* — **spiky** ['spaɪki] *adj* **-kier; -est**
: pointu

spill ['spɪl] *vt* : renverser, répandre — *vi* : se
répandre

spin ['spɪn] *v* **spun** ['spʌn]; **spinning** *vi*
: tourner, tournoyer — *vt* **1** : faire tourner **2**
: filer (de la laine) — **~** *n* **1** : tour *m* **2 go
for a ~** : faire une balade (en auto)

spinach ['spɪnɪtʃ] *n* : épinards *mpl*

spinal cord ['spaɪnəl] *n* : moelle *f* épinière

spindle ['spɪndəl] *n* : fuseau *m* (en textile)

spine ['spaɪn] *n* **1** : colonne *f* vertébrale **2**
: piquant *m* (d'un animal) **3** : dos *m* (d'un
livre)

spinster ['spɪnstər] *n* : vieille fille *f*

spiral ['spaɪrəl] *adj* : en spirale — **~** *n* : spirale *f* — **~** *vi* **-raled** *or* **-ralled; -raling** *or*
-ralling : aller en spirale

spire ['spaɪr] *n* : flèche *f*

spirit ['spɪrət] *n* **1** : esprit *m* **2 in good ~s**
: de bonne humeur **3 ~s** *npl* : spiritueux
mpl — **spirited** ['spɪrətəd] *adj* : animé —
spiritual ['spɪrɪtʃʊəl, -tʃəl] *adj* : spirituel —
spirituality [ˌspɪrɪtʃʊˈæləti] *n* : spiritualité *f*

spit[1] ['spɪt] *n* : broche *f*

spit[2] *v* **spit** *or* **spat** ['spæt]; **spitting**
: cracher — **~** *n* SALIVA : salive *f*

spite ['spaɪt] *n* **1** : rancune *f* **2 in ~ of**
: malgré — **~** *vt* **spited; spiting** : contrarier — **spiteful** ['spaɪtfəl] *adj* : rancunier

splash ['splæʃ] vt : éclabousser — vi or ~ **about** : patauger — ~ n 1 : éclaboussement m 2 : plouf m (bruit)

splatter ['splæt̬ər] → **spatter**

spleen ['spli:n] n : rate f (organe)

splendid ['splɛndəd] adj : splendide — ~ **splendor** or Brit **splendour** ['splɛndər] n : splendeur f

splint ['splɪnt] n : attelle f

splinter ['splɪntər] n : éclat m — ~ vi : se briser en éclats

split ['splɪt] v split; splitting vt 1 : fendre (du bois), déchirer (un pantalon) 2 or ~ up : diviser — vi ~ up : se séparer — ~ n 1 CRACK : fente f 2 or ~ seam : déchirure f

splurge ['splərdʒ] vi splurged; splurging : faire des folles dépenses

spoil ['spɔɪl] vt spoiled or spoilt ['spɔɪlt]; spoiling 1 RUIN : gâcher 2 PAMPER : gâter — **spoils** ['spɔɪlz] npl : butin m

spoke[1] ['spo:k] → **speak**

spoke[2] n : rayon m (d'une roue)

spoken → **speak**

spokesman ['spo:ksmən] n, pl -men [-mən, -ˌmɛn] : porte-parole m — **spokeswoman** ['spo:ksˌwʊmən] n, pl -women [-ˌwɪmən] : porte-parole f

sponge ['spʌndʒ] n : éponge f — ~ vt sponged; sponging : éponger — **spongy** ['spʌndʒi] adj spongier; -est : spongieux

sponsor ['spɑntsər] n : parrain m (d'une cause, etc.) — ~ vt : patronner — **sponsorship** ['spɑntsərˌʃɪp] n : parrainage m, patronage m

spontaneity ['spɑntə'ni:əţi, -'neɪ-] n : spontanéité f — **spontaneous** [spɑn'teɪniəs] adj : spontané

spooky ['spu:ki] adj spookier; -est : qui donne la chair de poule

spool ['spu:l] n : bobine f

spoon ['spu:n] n : cuillère f — **spoonful** ['spu:nˌfʊl] n : cuillerée f

sporadic [spə'rædɪk] adj : sporadique

sport ['sport] n 1 : sport m 2 be a good ~ : avoir l'esprit d'équipe — **sportsman** ['sportsmən] n, pl -men [-mən, -ˌmɛn] : sportif m — **sportswoman** ['sportsˌwʊmən] n, pl -women [-ˌwɪmən] : sportive f — **sporty** ['sporţi] adj sportier; -est : sportif

spot ['spɑt] n 1 : tache f 2 DOT : pois m 3 PLACE : endroit m, lieu m 4 in a tight ~ : dans l'embarras 5 on the ~ INSTANTLY : immédiatement — ~ vt spotted; spotting 1 STAIN : tacher 2 DETECT, NOTICE : apercevoir, repérer — **spotless** ['spɑtləs] adj : impeccable — **spotlight** ['spɑtˌlaɪt] n 1 : projecteur m, spot m 2 be in the ~ : être le centre de l'attention — **spotty** ['spɑţi] adj -tier; -est : irrégulier

spouse ['spaʊs] n : époux m, épouse f

spout ['spaʊt] vi : jaillir — ~ n : bec m (d'une cruche)

sprain ['spreɪn] n : entorse f, foulure f — ~ vt : se faire une entorse à, se fouler (la cheville, etc.)

sprawl ['sprɔl] vi 1 : être affalé (dans un fauteuil, etc.) 2 EXTEND : s'étendre — ~ n : étendue f

spray[1] ['spreɪ] n BOUQUET : gerbe f, bouquet m

spray[2] n 1 MIST : gouttelettes fpl fines 2 or **aerosol** ~ : vaporisateur m, bombe f 3 ~ **bottle** : atomiseur m — ~ vt : vaporiser, pulvériser

spread ['sprɛd] v spread; spreading vt 1 : propager (une nouvelle), répandre (de l'information) 2 or ~ out : écarter 3 : étaler, tartiner (avec de la confiture, etc.) — vi 1 : se propager (se dit d'une maladie) 2 or ~ out : s'étendre (se dit d'un feu) — ~ n 1 : propagation f, diffusion f 2 PASTE : pâte f à tartiner — **spreadsheet** ['sprɛdˌʃi:t] n : tableur m

spree ['spri] n go on a spending ~ : faire de folles dépenses

sprightly ['spraɪtli] adj -lier; -est : vif, alerte

spring ['sprɪŋ] v sprang ['spræŋ] or sprung ['sprʌŋ]; sprung; springing vi 1 : sauter, bondir 2 ~ from : surgir de — vt 1 ACTIVATE : actionner 2 ~ sth on s.o. : surprendre qqn avec qqch — ~ n 1 : puits m 2 : printemps m (saison) 3 LEAP : bond m, saut m 4 RESILIENCE : élasticité f 5 : ressort m (mécanisme) 6 or bedspring : sommier m — **springboard** ['sprɪŋˌbord] n : tremplin m — **springtime** ['sprɪŋˌtaɪm] n : printemps m — **springy** ['sprɪŋi] adj springier; -est : élastique

sprinkle ['sprɪŋkəl] v -kled; -kling vt 1 : arroser 2 DUST : saupoudrer — ~ n : petite averse f — **sprinkler** ['sprɪŋk'lər] n : arroseur m

sprint ['sprɪnt] vi : courir — ~ n : sprint m (aux sports)

sprout ['spraʊt] vi : germer, pousser — ~ n : pousse f

spruce[1] ['spru:s] vt spruced; sprucing ~ up : embellir

spruce[2] n : épicéa m

spun → **spin**

spur ['spər] n 1 : éperon m 2 STIMULUS : incitation f 3 on the ~ of the moment : sur le coup — ~ vt spurred; spurring 1 or ~ on : éperonner (un cheval) 2 ~ on MOTIVATE : motiver

spurn ['spərn] vt : repousser, rejeter

spurt[1] ['spərt] vi : jaillir — ~ n : jaillissement m, jet m

spurt[2] *n* **1** : sursaut *m* (d'énergie, etc.) **2 work in —s** : travailler par à-coups

spy ['spaɪ] *vi* **spied; spying — on** : espionner — *~ n* : espion *m*

squabble ['skwɑbəl] *n* : dispute *f*, querelle *f* — *~ vi* **-bled; -bling** : se disputer, se chamailler

squad ['skwɑd] *n* : peloton *m* (militaire), brigade *f* (de police)

squadron ['skwɑdrən] *n* : escadron *m* (de soldats), escadre *f* (de navires ou d'avions)

squalid ['skwɑlɪd] *adj* : sordide

squalor ['skwɑlər] *n* : conditions *fpl* sordides

squander ['skwɑndər] *vt* : gaspiller

square ['skwær] *n* **1** : carré *m* **2** : place *f* (d'une ville) — *~ adj* **squarer; squarest 1** : carré **2** EVEN : quitte — *~ vt* **squared; squaring** : carrer (un nombre) — **square root** *n* : racine *f* carrée

squash[1] ['skwɑʃ, 'skwɔʃ] *vt* : écraser, aplatir

squash[2] *n*, *pl* **squashes** *or* **squash** : courge *f*

squat ['skwɑt] *vi* **squatted; squatting** : s'accroupir — *~ adj* **squatter; squattest** : trapu

squawk ['skwɔk] *n* : cri *m* rauque — *~ vi* : pousser des cris rauques

squeak ['skwi:k] *vi* : grincer — *~ n* : grincement *m*

squeal ['skwi:l] *vi* **1** : pousser des cris aigus **2** : crisser (se dit des pneus), grincer (se dit des freins) **3 ~ on** : dénoncer — *~ n* : petit cri *m* aigu

squeamish ['skwi:mɪʃ] *adj* : impressionnable, délicat

squeeze ['skwi:z] *vt* **squeezed; squeezing 1** : presser, serrer **2** : extraire (du jus) — *~ n* : pression *f*, resserrement *m*

squid ['skwɪd] *n*, *pl* **squid** *or* **squids** : calmar *m*

squint ['skwɪnt] *vi* : loucher

squirm ['skwərm] *vi* : se tortiller

squirrel ['skwərəl] *n* : écureuil *m*

squirt ['skwərt] *vt* : lancer un jet de — *vi* : jaillir — *~ n* : jet *m*

stab ['stæb] *n* **1** : coup *m* de couteau **2 ~ of pain** : élancement *m* **3 take a ~ at sth** : tenter de faire qqch — *~ vt* **stabbed; stabbing 1** KNIFE : poignarder **2** THRUST : planter

stable ['steɪbəl] *n* **1** : étable *f* (pour le bétail) **2** *or* **horse ~** : écurie *f* — *~ adj* **-bler; -est** : stable — **stability** [stə'bɪləti] *n*, *pl* **-ties** : stabilité *f* — **stabilize** ['steɪbə,laɪz] *vt* **-lized; -lizing** : stabiliser

stack ['stæk] *n* : tas *m*, pile *f* — *~ vt* : entasser, empiler

stadium ['steɪdiəm] *n*, *pl* **-dia** [-diə] *or* **-diums** : stade *m*

staff ['stæf] *n*, *pl* **staffs** ['stæfs, 'stævz] *or* **staves** ['stævz, 'steɪvz] **1** : bâton *m* **2** *pl* **staffs** PERSONNEL : personnel *m*

stag ['stæg] *n*, *pl* **stags** *or* **stag** : cerf *m*

stage ['steɪdʒ] *n* **1** : scène *f* (au théâtre) **2** PHASE : étape *f* **3 the ~** : le théâtre — *~ vt* **staged; staging 1** : mettre en scène **2** ORGANIZE : organiser

stagger ['stægər] *vi* : tituber, chanceler — *vt* **1** : échelonner **2 be ~ed by** : être stupéfié par — **staggering** ['stægərɪŋ] *adj* : stupéfiant

stagnant ['stægnənt] *adj* : stagnant — **stagnate** ['stæg,neɪt] *vi* **-nated; -nating** : stagner

stain ['steɪn] *vt* **1** : tacher **2** : teindre (du bois) — *~ n* **1** : tache *f* **2** DYE : teinture *f* — **stainless steel** ['steɪnləs] *n* : acier *m* inoxydable

stair ['stær] *n* **1** STEP : marche *f* **2 ~s** *npl* : escalier *m* — **staircase** ['stær,keɪs] *n* : escalier *m* — **stairway** ['stær,weɪ] *n* : escalier *m*

stake ['steɪk] *n* **1** POST : poteau *m*, pieu *m*, piquet *m* **2** INTEREST : intérêts *mpl* **3 be at ~** : être en jeu — *~ vt* **staked; staking 1** BET : miser, parier **2 ~ a claim to** : revendiquer

stale ['steɪl] *adj* **staler; stalest 1** : rassis **2** OLD : vieux **3** STUFFY : vicié

stalk[1] ['stɔk] *n* : tige *f* (d'une plante)

stalk[2] *vt* : traquer, suivre

stall[1] ['stɔl] *n* **1** : stalle *f* (d'un cheval, etc.) **2** STAND : stand *m*, kiosque *m* — *~ vi* : caler (se dit d'un moteur)

stall[2] *vt* : retarder

stallion ['stæljən] *n* : étalon *m*

stalwart ['stɔlwərt] *adj* **1** STRONG : robuste **2 ~ supporter** : partisan *m* inconditionnel

stamina ['stæmənə] *n* : résistance *f*

stammer ['stæmər] *vi* : bégayer — *~ n* : bégaiement *m*

stamp ['stæmp] *n* **1** SEAL : cachet *m* **2** MARK : tampon *m* **3** *or* **postage ~** : timbre *m* — *~ vt* **1** : affranchir (une lettre, etc.) **2** IMPRINT : estamper **3** MINT : frapper (la monnaie) **4 ~ one's feet** : taper des pieds

stampede [stæm'pi:d] *n* : débandade *f*, ruée *f*

stance ['stænts] *n* : position *f*

stand ['stænd] *v* **stood** ['stʊd]; **standing** *vi* **1** : être debout **2** BE : être, se trouver **3** CONTINUE : rester valable **4** LIE, REST : reposer **5 ~ back** : reculer **6 ~ out** : ressortir **7** *or* **~ up** : se mettre debout — *vt* **1** PLACE : mettre **2** ENDURE : supporter **3 ~ a chance** : avoir de bonnes chances — **stand by** *vt* **1** : s'en tenir à (une promesse, etc.) **2** SUPPORT : appuyer — **stand for** *vt* **1** MEAN : signifier **2** PERMIT : tolérer —

stand up vi 1 ~ **for** : défendre 2 ~ **up to** : tenir tête à — **stand** n 1 RESISTANCE : résistance f 2 STALL : stand m 3 BASE : pied m 4 POSITION : position f 5 ~**s** npl : tribune f

standard ['stændərd] n 1 : norme f 2 BANNER : étendard m 3 CRITERION : critère m 4 ~ **of living** : niveau m de vie — ~ adj : standard

standing ['stændıŋ] n 1 RANK : position f, standing m 2 DURATION : durée f

standpoint ['stænd,pɔɪnt] n : point m de vue

standstill ['stænd,stıl] n 1 **be at a** ~ : être paralysé 2 **come to a** ~ : s'arrêter

stank → **stink**

stanza ['stænzə] n : strophe f

staple[1] ['steɪpəl] n : produit m de base — ~ adj : principal, de base

staple[2] n : agrafe f — ~ vt -pled; -pling : agrafer — **stapler** ['steɪplər] n : agrafeuse f

star ['star] n : étoile f — ~ v **starred**; **starring** vt FEATURE : avoir pour vedette — vi ~ **in** : être la vedette de

starboard ['starbərd] n : tribord m

starch ['startʃ] vt : amidonner — ~ n 1 : amidon m 2 : fécule f (aliment)

stardom ['stardəm] n : célébrité f

stare ['stær] vi **stared**; **staring** : regarder fixement — ~ n : regard m fixe

starfish ['star,fıʃ] n : étoile f de mer

stark ['stark] adj 1 PLAIN : austère 2 HARSH : sévère, dur

starling ['starlıŋ] n : étourneau m

starry ['stari] adj -rier; -est : étoilé

start ['start] vi 1 : débuter, commencer 2 SET OUT : partir 3 JUMP : sursauter 4 or ~ **up** : démarrer — vt 1 : commencer 2 CAUSE : provoquer 3 or ~ **up** ESTABLISH : établir 4 or ~ **up** : mettre en marche (un moteur, etc.) — ~ n 1 : commencement m, début m 2 **get an early** ~ : commencer tôt 3 **give s.o. a** ~ : faire sursauter qqn — **starter** ['startər] n : démarreur m (d'un véhicule)

startle ['startəl] vt -tled; -tling : surprendre

starve ['starv] v **starved**; **starving** vi : mourir de faim — vt : affamer — **starvation** [star'veɪʃən] n : faim f

state ['steɪt] n 1 : état m 2 **the States** : les États-Unis — ~ vt **stated**; **stating** 1 SAY : déclarer 2 REPORT : exposer — **statement** ['steɪtmənt] n 1 : déclaration f 2 or **bank** ~ : relevé m de compte — **statesman** ['steɪtsmən] n, pl -**men** [-mən, -,mɛn] : homme m d'État

static ['stætık] adj : statique — ~ n : parasites mpl (en radio, etc.)

station ['steɪʃən] n 1 : gare f (de train) 2 : chaîne f (de télévision), poste m (de radio)

3 → **fire station**, **police station** — ~ vt : poster, placer — **stationary** ['steɪʃə,nɛri] adj : stationnaire

stationery ['steɪʃə,nɛri] n : papeterie f, papier m à lettres

station wagon n : familiale f

statistic [stə'tɪstɪk] n : statistique f

statue ['stæ,tʃu:] n : statue f

stature ['stætʃər] n : stature f, taille f

status ['steɪtəs, 'stæ-] n 1 : statut m 2 or **marital** ~ : situation f (de famille) 3 or **social** ~ : rang m (social)

statute ['stæ,tʃu:t] n : loi f, règle f

staunch ['stɔntʃ] adj : dévoué

stay[1] ['steɪ] vi 1 REMAIN : rester, demeurer 2 LODGE : séjourner 3 ~ **awake** : rester éveillé 4 ~ **in** : rester à la maison — ~ n : séjour m

stay[2] n SUPPORT : soutien m

stead ['stɛd] n **in s.o.'s** ~ : à la place de qqn — **steadfast** ['stɛd,fæst] adj 1 FIRM : ferme 2 LOYAL : fidèle — **steady** ['stɛdi] adj **steadier**; -**est** 1 FIRM, SURE : ferme, stable 2 FIXED : fixe 3 CONSTANT : constant — ~ vt **steadied**; **steadying** : stabiliser

steak ['steɪk] n : bifteck m, steak m

steal ['sti:l] v **stole** ['sto:l]; **stolen** ['sto:lən]; **stealing** : voler

stealthy ['stɛlθi] adj **stealthier**; -**est** : furtif

steam ['sti:m] n 1 : vapeur f 2 **let off** ~ : se défouler — vt 1 : cuire à la vapeur 2 or ~ **up** : s'embuer

steel ['sti:l] n 1 : acier m 2 ~ **industry** : sidérurgie — ~ adj : en acier, d'acier

steep[1] ['sti:p] adj : raide, à pic

steep[2] vt : infuser (du thé, etc.)

steeple ['sti:pəl] n : clocher m, flèche f

steer[1] ['stɪr] n : bœuf m

steer[2] vt 1 : conduire (une voiture, etc.), gouverner (un navire) 2 GUIDE : diriger — **steering wheel** n : volant m

stem ['stɛm] n : tige f (d'une plante), pied m (d'un verre) — ~ vi ~ **from** : provenir de

stench ['stɛntʃ] n : puanteur f

step ['stɛp] n 1 : pas m 2 RUNG, STAIR : marche f 3 ~ **by** ~ : petit à petit 4 **take** ~**s** : prendre des mesures 5 **watch your** ~ : faites attention (à la marche) — ~ vi **stepped**; **stepping** 1 : faire un pas 2 ~ **back** : reculer 3 ~ **down** RESIGN : se retirer 4 ~ **in** : intervenir 5 ~ **out** : sortir (pour un moment) 6 ~ **this way** : par ici — **step up** vt INCREASE : augmenter

stepbrother ['stɛp,brʌðər] n : beau-frère m — **stepdaughter** ['stɛp,dɔtər] n : belle-fille f — **stepfather** ['stɛp,faðər, -,fa-] n : beau-père m

stepladder ['stɛp,lædər] n : escabeau m

stepmother ['stɛp,mʌðər] n : belle-mère f

— **stepsister** ['stɛp,sɪstər] *n* : belle-sœur *f*
—**stepson** ['stɛp,sʌn] *n* : beau-fils *m*
stereo ['steri,o:, 'stɪr-] *n, pl* **stereos** : stéréo
f — *~ adj* : stéréo
stereotype ['sterio,taɪp, 'stɪr-] *vt* **-typed;**
-typing : stéréotyper — *~ n* : stéréotype *m*
sterile ['sterəl] *adj* : stérile — **sterility**
[stə'rɪləti] *n* : stérilité *f* — **sterilization**
[,sterələ'zeɪʃən] *n* : stérilisation *f* — **steril-**
ize ['sterə,laɪz] *vt* **-ized; -izing** : stériliser
sterling silver ['stərlɪŋ] *n* : argent *m* fin
stern[1] ['stərn] *adj* : sévère
stern[2] *n* : poupe *f*
stethoscope ['stɛθə,sko:p] *n* : stéthoscope
m
stew ['stu:, 'stju:] *n* : ragoût *m* — *~ vi* **1**
: cuire **2** FRET : être préoccupé
steward ['stu:ərd, 'stju:-] *n* **1** : administrateur *m*, -trice *f* **2** : steward *m* (d'un
avion, etc.) — **stewardess** ['stu:ərdəs,
'stju:-] *n* : hôtesse *f*
stick[1] ['stɪk] *n* **1** : bâton *m* **2** WALKING
STICK : canne *f*
stick[2] *v* **stuck** ['stʌk]; **sticking** *vt* **1** : coller
2 STAB : enfoncer **3** PUT : mettre **4** *~* **out**
: sortir, tirer (la langue) — *vi* **1** : se coller **2**
JAM : se bloquer **3** *~* **around** : rester **4** *~*
out PROTRUDE : dépasser **5** *~* **up for**
: défendre — **sticker** ['stɪkər] *n* : autocollant *m* — **sticky** ['stɪki] *adj* **stickier; -est**
: collant
stiff ['stɪf] *adj* **1** RIGID : rigide, raide **2**
STILTED : guindé **3** : courbaturé (se dit des
muscles) — **stiffen** ['stɪfən] *vt* : renforcer,
raidir — *vi* : se durcir, se raidir — **stiffness**
['stɪfnəs] *n* : raideur *f*, rigidité *f*
stifle ['staɪfəl] *vt* **-fled; -fling** : étouffer
stigmatize ['stɪgmə,taɪz] *vt* **-tized; -tizing**
: stigmatiser
still ['stɪl] *adj* **1** : immobile **2** SILENT : tranquille — *~ adv* **1** : encore, toujours **2** NEV-
ERTHELESS : quand même, tout de même **3**
sit *~*! : reste tranquille! — *~ n* : quiétude
f, calme *m* — **stillness** ['stɪlnəs] *n* : calme *m*,
silence *m*
stilt ['stɪlt] *n* : échasse *f* — **stilted** ['stɪltəd]
adj : forcé
stimulate ['stɪmjə,leɪt] *vt* **-lated; -lating**
: stimuler — **stimulant** ['stɪmjələnt] *n*
: stimulant *m* — **stimulation** [,stɪmjə-
'leɪʃən] *n* : stimulation *f* — **stimulus**
['stɪmjələs] *n, pl* **-li** [-,laɪ] : stimulant *m*
sting ['stɪŋ] *v* **stung** ['stʌŋ]; **stinging** : piquer — *~ n* : piqûre *f* — **stinger** ['stɪŋər] *n*
: dard *m*, aiguillon *m*
stingy ['stɪndʒi] *adj* **stingier; -est** : avare,
pingre — **stinginess** ['stɪndʒinəs] *n*
: avarice *f*
stink ['stɪŋk] *vi* **stank** ['stæŋk] *or* **stunk**

['stʌŋk]; **stunk; stinking** : puer — *~ n*
: puanteur *f*
stint ['stɪnt] *vi* *~* **on** : lésiner sur — *~ n*
: période *f* (de travail)
stipulate ['stɪpjə,leɪt] *vt* **-lated; -lating**
: stipuler — **stipulation** [,stɪpjə'leɪʃən] *n*
: stipulation *f*
stir ['stər] *v* **stirred; stirring** *vt* **1** : agiter, remuer **2** MOVE : émouvoir **3** INCITE : inciter
4 *or* *~* **up** PROVOKE : susciter — *vi* : remuer, bouger — *~ n* COMMOTION : émoi *m*
stirrup ['stərəp, 'stɪr-] *n* : étrier *m*
stitch ['stɪtʃ] *n* : point *m* (en couture, en
médecine) — *~ v* : coudre
stock ['stak] *n* **1** INVENTORY : réserve *f*,
stock *m* **2** SECURITIES : actions *fpl*, valeurs
fpl **3** ANCESTRY : lignée *f*, souche *f* **4**
BROTH : bouillon *m* **5 out of** *~* : épuisé **6**
take *~* **of** : évaluer — *~ vt* : approvisionner — *vi* *~* **up on** : s'approvisionner en —
stockbroker ['stak,bro:kər] *n* : agent *m* de
change
stocking ['stakɪŋ] *n* : bas *m*
stock market *n* : Bourse *f*
stocky ['staki] *adj* **stockier; -est** : trapu
stodgy ['stadʒi] *adj* **stodgier; -est 1** DULL
: lourd **2** OLD-FASHIONED : vieux-jeu
stoic ['sto:ɪk] *n* : stoïque *mf* — *~ or* **stoical**
[-ɪkəl] *adj* : stoïque
stoke ['sto:k] *vt* **stoked; stoking** : alimenter
(un feu, etc.)
stole[1] ['sto:l] → **steal**
stole[2] *n* : étole *f*
stolen → **steal**
stomach ['stʌmɪk] *n* : estomac *m* — *~ vt*
: supporter, tolérer — **stomachache**
['stʌmɪk,eɪk] *n* : mal *m* de ventre
stone ['sto:n] *n* **1** : pierre *f* **2** : noyau *m*
(d'un fruit) — *~ vt* **stoned; stoning** : lapider — **stony** ['sto:ni] *adj* **stonier; -est**
: pierreux
stood → **stand**
stool ['stu:l] *n* : tabouret *m*
stoop ['stu:p] *vi* **1** : se baisser, se pencher **2**
~ **to** : s'abaisser à
stop ['stap] *v* **stopped; stopping** *vt* **1** PLUG
: boucher **2** PREVENT : empêcher **3** HALT
: arrêter, mettre fin à **4** CEASE : cesser de —
vi **1** : s'arrêter, stopper **2** CEASE : cesser **3**
~ **by** : passer — *~ n* **1** : arrêt *m*, halte *f*
2 come to a *~* : s'arrêter **3 put a** *~* **to**
: mettre fin à — **stoplight** ['stap,laɪt] *n*
: feu *m* rouge — **stopper** ['stapər] *n* : bouchon *m*
store ['stor] *vt* **stored; storing** : emmagasiner, entreposer — *~ n* **1** SUPPLY
: réserve *f*, provision *f* **2** SHOP : magasin *m*
— **storage** ['storɪdʒ] *n* : entreposage *m* —
storehouse ['stor,haus] *n* : entrepôt *m* —
storekeeper ['stor,ki:pər] *n* : commerçant

m, -çante *f* — **storeroom** ['stor,ru:m, -,rʊm] *n* : magasin *m*, réserve *f*

stork ['stork] *n* : cigogne *f*

storm ['storm] *n* : orage *m*, tempête *f* — ~ *vi* **1** RAGE : tempêter **2** ~ **out** : partir furieux — *vt* ATTACK : prendre d'assaut — **stormy** ['stormi] *adj* stormier; -est : orageux

story[1] ['stori] *n*, *pl* **stories** **1** TALE : conte *m* **2** ACCOUNT : histoire *f*, récit *m* **3** RUMOR : rumeur *f*

story[2] *n* FLOOR : étage *m*

stout ['staʊt] *adj* **1** RESOLUTE : tenace **2** STURDY : fort **3** FAT : corpulent

stove ['sto:v] *n* **1** : poêle *m* (pour chauffer) **2** RANGE : cuisinière *f*

stow ['sto:] *vt* **1** : ranger **2** LOAD : charger — *vi* ~ **away** : voyager clandestinement

straddle ['strædəl] *vt* **-dled; -dling** : s'asseoir à califourchon sur

straggle ['strægəl] *vi* -gled; -gling : traîner — **straggler** ['strægələr] *n* : traînard *m*, -narde *f*

straight ['streɪt] *adj* **1** : droit **2** : raide (se dit des cheveux) **3** HONEST : franc — ~ *adv* **1** DIRECTLY : (tout) droit, directement **2** FRANKLY : carrément — **straightaway** [,streɪtə'weɪ] *adv* : immédiatement — **straighten** ['streɪtən] *vt* **1** : redresser, rendre droit **2** *or* ~ **up** : ranger — **straightforward** [streɪt'fɔrwərd] *adj* **1** FRANK : franc, honnête **2** CLEAR : clair, simple

strain ['streɪn] *vt* **1** : se forcer (la voix), se fatiguer (les yeux), se froisser (un muscle) **2** FILTER : égoutter **3** ~ **oneself** : faire un grand effort — *vi* : s'efforcer — ~ *n* **1** STRESS : stress *m*, tension *f* **2** SPRAIN : foulure *f* — **strainer** ['streɪnər] *n* : passoire *f*

strait ['streɪt] *n* **1** : détroit *m* **2 in dire** ~**s** : aux abois

strand[1] ['strænd] *vt* **be left** ~**ed** : être abandonné

strand[2] *n* : fil *m*, brin *m*

strange ['streɪndʒ] *adj* **stranger; strangest** **1** : étrange, bizarre **2** UNFAMILIAR : inconnu — **strangely** ['streɪndʒli] *adv* : étrangement — **strangeness** ['streɪndʒnəs] *n* : étrangeté *f* — **stranger** ['streɪndʒər] *n* : étranger *m*, -gère *f*

strangle ['stræŋgəl] *vt* -gled; -gling : étrangler

strap ['stræp] *n* **1** : courroie *f*, sangle *f* **2** *or* **shoulder** ~ : bretelle *f* — *vt* **strapped; strapping** : attacher — **strapless** ['stræpləs] *n* : sans bretelles — **strapping** ['stræpɪŋ] *adj* : robuste, costaud *fam*

strategy ['strætədʒi] *n*, *pl* **-gies** : stratégie *f* — **strategic** [strə'ti:dʒɪk] *adj* : stratégique

straw ['strɔ] *n* **1** : paille *f* **2 the last** ~ : le comble

strawberry ['strɔ,bɛri] *n*, *pl* **-ries** : fraise *f*

stray ['streɪ] *n* : animal *m* errant — ~ *vi* **1** : errer, vagabonder **2** DEVIATE : s'écarter — ~ *adj* : errant, perdu

streak ['stri:k] *n* **1** : raie *f*, bande *f* **2** VEIN : veine *f*

stream ['stri:m] *n* **1** : ruisseau *m* **2** FLOW : flot *m*, courant *m* — ~ *vi* : couler — **streamer** ['stri:mər] *n* **1** : banderole *f* **2** : serpentin *m* (de papier) — **streamlined** ['stri:m,laɪnd] *adj* **1** : aérodynamique **2** EFFICIENT : efficace

street ['stri:t] *n* : rue *f* — **streetcar** ['stri:t-,kɑr] *n* : tramway *m* — **streetlight** ['stri:t-,laɪt] *n* : réverbère *m*

strength ['streŋkθ] *n* **1** : force *f* **2** TOUGHNESS : résistance *f* **3** INTENSITY : intensité *f* **4** ~**s and weaknesses** : qualités et faiblesses — **strengthen** ['streŋkθən] *vt* **1** : fortifier **2** REINFORCE : renforcer **3** INTENSIFY : intensifier

strenuous ['strenjʊəs] *adj* **1** : énergique **2** ARDUOUS : ardu — **strenuously** ['strenjʊəsli] *adv* : vigoureusement

stress ['stres] *n* **1** : stress *m*, tension *f* **2** EMPHASIS : accent *m* — ~ *vt* **1** EMPHASIZE : mettre l'accent sur **2** *or* ~ **out** : stresser — **stressful** ['stresfəl] *adj* : stressant

stretch ['stretʃ] *vt* **1** : étirer (des muscles, un élastique, etc.) **2** EXTEND : tendre **3** ~ **the truth** : exagérer — *vi* **1** : s'étirer **2** ~ **out** EXTEND : s'étendre — ~ *n* **1** : étirement *m* **2** EXPANSE : étendue *f* **3** : période *f* (de temps) — **stretcher** ['stretʃər] *n* : civière *f*, brancard *m*

strew ['stru:] *vt* **strewed; strewed** *or* **strewn** ['stru:n]; **strewing** : éparpiller

stricken ['strɪkən] *adj* ~ **with** : affligé de (une émotion), atteint de (une maladie)

strict ['strɪkt] *adj* : strict — **strictly** *adv* ~ **speaking** : à proprement parler

stride ['straɪd] *vi* **strode** ['stro:d]; **stridden** ['strɪdən]; **striding** : marcher à grandes enjambées — ~ *n* **1** : grand pas *m*, enjambée *f* **2 make great** ~**s** : faire de grands progrès

strident ['straɪdənt] *adj* : strident

strife ['straɪf] *n* : conflit *m*

strike ['straɪk] *v* **struck** ['strʌk]; **struck; striking** *vt* **1** HIT : frapper **2** *or* ~ **against** : heurter **3** *or* ~ **out** DELETE : rayer **4** : sonner (l'heure) **5** IMPRESS : impressionner **6** : découvrir (de l'or, du pétrole) **7 it** ~**s me that** ... : il m'apparaît que ... **8** ~ **up** START : commencer — *vi* **1** : frapper **2** ATTACK : attaquer **3** : faire grève — ~ *n* **1** BLOW : coup *m* **2** : grève *f* (des transports, etc.) **3** ATTACK : attaque *f* **4** : prise *f* *Can* (au baseball) — **striker** ['straɪkər] *n*

: gréviste *mf* — **striking** ['straikiŋ] *adj*
: frappant, saisissant

string ['striŋ] *n* **1** : ficelle *f* **2** SERIES : suite
f **3** ~**s** *npl* : cordes *fpl* (d'un orchestre) —
~ *vt* **strung** ['strʌŋ]; **stringing** : enfiler —
string bean *n* : haricot *m* vert

stringent ['strindʒənt] *adj* : rigoureux, strict

strip¹ ['strip] *v* **stripped; stripping** *vt* RE-
MOVE : enlever — *vi* UNDRESS : se déshabiller

strip² *n* : bande *f*

stripe ['straip] *n* : rayure *f*, bande *f* —
striped ['straipt, 'straipəd] *adj* : rayé, à
rayures

strive ['straiv] *vi* **strove** ['stro:v]; **striven**
['strivən] *or* **strived; striving 1** ~ **for** : lutter pour **2** ~ **to** : s'efforcer de

strode → **stride**

stroke ['stro:k] *vt* **stroked; stroking** : caresser — ~ *n* : attaque *f* (cérébrale)

stroll ['stro:l] *vi* : se promener — ~ *n*
: promenade *f* — **stroller** ['stro:lər] *n*
: poussette *f* (pour enfants)

strong ['strɔŋ] *adj* : fort, robuste — **stronghold** ['strɔŋ,ho:ld] *n* : bastion *m* —
strongly ['strɔŋli] *adv* **1** DEEPLY : profondément **2** TOTALLY : totalement **3** VIGOROUSLY : énergiquement

strove → **strive**

struck → **strike**

structure ['strʌktʃər] *n* : structure *f* — **structural** ['strʌktʃərəl] *adj* : structural

struggle ['strʌgəl] *vi* **-gled; -gling 1** : lutter,
se débattre **2** STRIVE : s'efforcer — ~ *n*
: lutte *f*

strung → **string**

strut ['strʌt] *vi* **strutted; strutting** : se pavaner

stub ['stʌb] *n* : mégot *m* (de cigarette), bout
m (de crayon, etc.), talon *m* (de chèque) —
~ *vt* **stubbed; stubbing** ~ **one's toe** : se
cogner le doigt de pied

stubble ['stʌbəl] *n* : barbe *f* de plusieurs
jours

stubborn ['stʌbərn] *adj* **1** : têtu, obstiné **2**
PERSISTENT : tenace

stuck → **stick** — **stuck–up** ['stʌk'ʌp] *adj*
: prétentieux

stud¹ ['stʌd] *n* : étalon *m*

stud² *n* **1** NAIL : clou *m* **2** : montant *m* (en
construction)

student ['stu:dənt, 'stju:-] *n* : élève *m*, élève
f (au primaire); étudiant *m*, -diante *f* (universitaire) — **studio** ['stu:di,o:, 'stju:-] *n, pl*
-dios : studio *m*, atelier *m* — **study** ['stʌdi]
n, pl **studies 1** : étude *f* **2** OFFICE : bureau
m — ~ *v* **studied; studying** : étudier —
studious ['stu:diəs, 'stju:-] *adj* : studieux

stuff ['stʌf] *n* **1** : affaires *fpl*, choses *fpl* **2**
MATTER, SUBSTANCE : chose *f* — ~ *vt* **1**

FILL : rembourrer **2** CRAM : fourrer —
stuffing ['stʌfiŋ] *n* : rembourrage *m* —
stuffy ['stʌfi] *adj* **stuffier; -est 1** STODGY
: ennuyeux **2** : bouché (se dit du nez) **3** ~
rooms : pièces *fpl* mal aérées

stumble ['stʌmbəl] *vi* **-bled; -bling 1**
: trébucher **2** ~ **across** *or* ~ **upon**
: tomber sur

stump ['stʌmp] *n* **1** : moignon *m* (d'un
membre) **2** *or* **tree** ~ : souche *f* — ~ *vt*
: laisser perplexe

stun ['stʌn] *vt* **stunned; stunning 1** : assommer (avec un coup) **2** ASTONISH : étonner

stung → **sting**

stunk → **stink**

stunning ['stʌniŋ] *adj* **1** : incroyable, sensationnel **2** STRIKING : frappant

stunt¹ ['stʌnt] *vt* : rabougrir

stunt² *n* : prouesse *f* (acrobatique)

stupid ['stu:pəd, 'stju:-] *adj* **1** : stupide **2**
SILLY : bête — **stupidity** [stʊ'pidəti, stju:-]
n, pl **-ties** : stupidité *f*

sturdy ['stərdi] *adj* **-dier; -est 1** : fort, résistant **2** ROBUST : robuste — **sturdiness**
['stərdinəs] *n* : solidité *f*

stutter ['stʌtər] *vi* : bégayer — ~ *n* : bégaiement *m*

sty ['stai] *n* **1** *pl* **sties** PIGPEN : porcherie *f* **2**
pl **sties** *or* **styes** : orgelet *m*

style ['stail] *n* **1** : style *m* **2** FASHION : mode
f — ~ *vt* **styled; styling** : coiffer (les
cheveux) — **stylish** ['stailiʃ] *adj* : chic, élégant

suave ['swɑv] *adj* : raffiné et affable

subconscious [,sʌb'kɑntʃəs] *adj* : subconscient — ~ *n* : subconscient *m*

subdivision ['sʌbdə,viʒən] *n* : subdivision *f*

subdue [səb'du:, -'dju:] *vt* **-dued; -duing 1**
CONQUER : subjuguer **2** CONTROL
: dominer **3** SOFTEN : atténuer — **subdued**
[səb'du:d, -'dju:d] *adj* : atténué

subject ['sʌbdʒikt] *n* **1** : sujet *m* **2** TOPIC
: matière *f* — ~ *adj* **1** : asservi **2** ~ **to**
: sujet à — ~ [səb'dʒekt] *vt* ~ **to** : soumettre à — **subjective** [səb'dʒektiv] *adj*
: subjectif

subjunctive [səb'dʒʌnktiv] *n* : subjonctif *m*

sublet ['sʌb,let] *vt* **-let; -letting** : sous-louer

sublime [sə'blaim] *adj* : sublime

submarine ['sʌbmə,ri:n, ,sʌbmə'-] *n* : sous-marin *m*

submerge [səb'mərdʒ] *vt* **-merged; -merging** : submerger

submit [səb'mit] *v* **-mitted; -mitting** *vi* **1**
YIELD : se rendre **2** ~ **to** : se soumettre à
— *vt* : soumettre — **submission** [səb-
'miʃən] *n* : soumission *f* — **submissive**
[səb'misiv] *adj* : soumis

subordinate [sə'bɔrdənət] *adj* : subordonné

— ~ *n* : subordonné *m*, -née *f* — ~ [sə-'bɔrdən,eɪt] *vt* **-nated; -nating** : subordonner

subpoena [sə'pi:nə] *n* : assignation *f*

subscribe [səb'skraɪb] *vi* **-scribed; -scribing** ~ **to** : s'abonner à (un magazine, etc.) — **subscriber** [səb'skraɪbər] *n* : abonné *m*, -née *f* — **subscription** [səb'skrɪpʃən] *n* : abonnement *m*

subsequent ['sʌbsɪkwənt, -sə,kwɛnt] *adj* **1** : subséquent, suivant **2** ~ **to** : postérieur à — **subsequently** ['sʌbsɪ,kwɛntli, -,kwənt-] *adv* : par la suite

subservient [səb'sərviənt] *adj* : servile

subside [səb'saɪd] *vi* **-sided; -siding** : s'atténuer

subsidiary [səb'sɪdi,ɛri] *adj* : secondaire — ~ *n, pl* **-aries** : filiale *f*

subsidy ['sʌbsədi] *n, pl* **-dies** : subvention *f* — **subsidize** ['sʌbsə,daɪz] *vt* **-dized; -dizing** : subventionner

subsistence [səb'sɪstənʦ] *n* : subsistance *f* — **subsist** [səb'sɪst] *vi* : subsister

substance ['sʌbstənʦ] *n* : substance *f*

substandard [,sʌb'stændərd] *adj* : inférieur

substantial [səb'stænʧəl] *adj* : substantiel — **substantially** [səb'stænʧəli] *adv* : considérablement

substitute ['sʌbstə,tu:t, -,tju:t] *n* **1** : remplaçant *m*, -çante *f*; suppléant *m*, -pléante *f* **2** : succédané *m* (d'une chose) — ~ *vt* **-tuted; -tuting** : substituer, remplacer

subtitle ['sʌb,taɪtəl] *n* : sous-titre *m*

subtle ['sʌtəl] *adj* **-tler; -tlest** : subtil — **subtlety** ['sʌtəlti] *n, pl* **-ties** : subtilité *f*

subtraction [səb'trækʃən] *n* : soustraction *f* — **subtract** [səb'trækt] *vt* : soustraire

suburb ['sʌ,bərb] *n* **1** : quartier *m* résidentiel **2 the** ~**s** : la banlieue — **suburban** [sə'bərbən] *adj* : de banlieue

subversive [səb'vərsɪv] *adj* : subversif

subway ['sʌb,weɪ] *n* : métro *m*

succeed [sək'si:d] *vt* : succéder à — *vi* : réussir — **success** [sək'sɛs] *n* : réussite *f*, succès *m* — **successful** [sək'sɛsfəl] *adj* : réussi — **successfully** [sək'sɛsfəli] *adv* : avec succès

succession [sək'sɛʃən] *n* **1** : succession *f* **2 in** ~ : successivement, de suite — **successive** [sək'sɛsɪv] *adj* : successif — **successor** [sək'sɛsər] *n* : successeur *m*

succinct [sək'sɪŋkt, sə'sɪŋkt] *adj* : succinct

succumb [sə'kʌm] *vi* : succomber

such ['sʌʧ] *adj* **1** : tel, pareil **2** ~ **as** : comme **3** ~ **a pity!** : quel dommage! — ~ *pron* **1** : tel **2 as** ~ : comme tel — ~ *adv* **1** VERY : très **2** ~ **a nice man!** : un homme si gentil! **3** ~ **that** : de façon à ce que

suck ['sʌk] *vt* **1** *or* ~ **on** : sucer **2** *or* ~ **up**

: absorber (un liquide), aspirer (avec une machine) — **suckle** ['sʌkəl] *v* **-led; -ling** *vt* : allaiter — *vi* : téter — **suction** ['sʌkʃən] *n* : succion *f*

sudden ['sʌdən] *adj* **1** : soudain, subit **2 all of a** ~ : tout à coup — **suddenly** ['sʌdənli] *adv* : soudainement, subitement

suds ['sʌdz] *npl* : mousse *f* (de savon)

sue ['su:] *vt* **sued; suing** : poursuivre en justice

suede ['sweɪd] *n* : daim *m*, suède *m*

suet ['su:ət] *n* : graisse *f* de rognon

suffer ['sʌfər] *vi* : souffrir — **suffering** ['sʌfərɪŋ] *n* : souffrance *f*

suffice [sə'faɪs] *vi* **-ficed; -ficing** : être suffisant, suffir — **sufficient** [sə'fɪʃənt] *adj* : suffisant — **sufficiently** [sə'fɪʃəntli] *adv* : suffisamment

suffix ['sʌ,fɪks] *n* : suffixe *m*

suffocate ['sʌfə,keɪt] *v* **-cated; -cating** *vt* : asphyxier, suffoquer — *vi* : s'asphyxier, suffoquer

suffrage ['sʌfrɪʤ] *n* : suffrage *m*

sugar ['ʃʊgər] *n* : sucre *m* — **sugarcane** ['ʃʊgər,keɪn] *n* : canne *f* à sucre — **sugarhouse** ['ʃʊgər,haʊs] *n* : cabane *f* (à sucre) *Can*

suggestion [səg'ʤɛsʧən, sə-] *n* : suggestion *f*, proposition *f* — **suggest** [səg'ʤɛst, sə-] *vt* **1** : proposer, suggérer **2** INDICATE : laisser supposer

suicide ['su:ə,saɪd] *n* **1** : suicide *m* **2 commit** ~ : se suicider — **suicidal** [,su:ə-'saɪdəl] *adj* : suicidaire

suit ['su:t] *n* **1** : complet *m* (d'homme), tailleur *m* (de femme) **2** : couleur *f* (aux cartes) — ~ *vt* : convenir à, aller à — **suitable** ['su:təbəl] *adj* : convenable, approprié — **suitcase** ['su:t,keɪs] *n* : valise *f*

suite ['swi:t] *n* : suite *f*

suitor ['su:tər] *n* : prétendant *m*

sulfur *or Brit* **sulphur** ['sʌlfər] *n* : soufre *m*

sulk ['sʌlk] *vi* : bouder — **sulky** ['sʌlki] *adj* **sulkier; -est** : boudeur

sullen ['sʌlən] *adj* : maussade, morose

sulphur *Brit* → **sulfur**

sultry ['sʌltri] *adj* **-trier; -est 1** : étouffant, lourd **2** SENSUAL : sensuel

sum ['sʌm] *n* : somme *f* — ~ *vt* **summed; summing** ~ **up** : résumer — **summarize** ['sʌmə,raɪz] *v* **-rized; -rizing** *vt* : résumer — *vi* : se résumer — **summary** ['sʌməri] *n, pl* **-ries** : sommaire *m*, résumé *m*

summer ['sʌmər] *n* : été *m*

summit ['sʌmət] *n* : sommet *m*, cime *f*

summon ['sʌmən] *vt* **1** : appeler (qqn), convoquer (une réunion) **2** : citer (en droit) — **summons** ['sʌmənz] *n, pl* **summonses** SUBPOENA : assignation *f*

sumptuous ['sʌmpʧʊəs] *adj* : somptueux

sun ['sʌn] n : soleil m — **sunbathe** ['sʌn‚beɪð] vi **-bathed; -bathing** : prendre un bain de soleil — **sunburn** ['sʌn‚bərn] n : coup m de soleil

Sunday ['sʌn‚deɪ, -di] n : dimanche m

sunflower ['sʌn‚flaʊər] n : tournesol m

sung → **sing**

sunglasses ['sʌn‚glæsəz] npl : lunettes fpl de soleil

sunk → **sink**

sunlight ['sʌn‚laɪt] n : (lumière f du) soleil m — **sunny** ['sʌni] adj **-nier; -est** : ensoleillé — **sunrise** ['sʌn‚raɪz] n : lever m du soleil — **sunset** ['sʌn‚sɛt] n : coucher m du soleil — **sunshine** ['sʌn‚ʃaɪn] n : (lumière f du) soleil m — **suntan** ['sʌn‚tæn] n : hâle m, bronzage m

super ['su:pər] adj : super fam, génial

superb [su'pərb] adj : superbe

superficial [‚su:pər'fɪʃəl] adj : superficiel

superfluous [su'pərfluəs] adj : superflu

superintendent [‚su:pərɪn'tɛndənt] n **1** : commissaire m (de police) **2** or **building ~** : concierge mf **3** or **school ~** : inspecteur m, -trice f

superior [su'pɪriər] adj : supérieur — **~** n : supérieur m, -rieure f — **superiority** [su‚pɪri'ɔrəti] n, pl **-ties** : supériorité f

superlative [su'pərlətɪv] n : superlatif m

supermarket ['su:pər‚mɑrkət] n : supermarché m

supernatural [‚su:pər'nætʃərəl] adj : surnaturel

superpower ['su:pər‚paʊər] n : superpuissance f

supersede [‚su:pər'si:d] vt **-seded; -seding** : remplacer, supplanter

superstition [‚su:pər'stɪʃən] n : superstition f — **superstitious** [‚su:pər'stɪʃəs] adj : superstitieux

supervise ['su:pər‚vaɪz] vt **-vised; -vising** : surveiller, superviser — **supervision** [‚su:pər'vɪʒən] n : surveillance f, supervision f — **supervisor** ['su:pər‚vaɪzər] n : surveillant m, -lante f

supper ['sʌpər] n : dîner m, souper m Can

supplant [sə'plænt] vt : supplanter

supple ['sʌpəl] adj **-pler; -plest** : souple

supplement ['sʌpləmənt] n : supplément m — **~** ['sʌplə‚mɛnt] vt : compléter, augmenter

supply [sə'plaɪ] vt **-plied; -plying 1** : fournir **2 ~ with** : approvisionner en — **~** n, pl **-plies 1** : provision f, réserve f **2 ~ and demand** : l'offre et la demande **3 supplies** npl : provisions fpl, vivres mpl **4 supplies** npl : fournitures fpl (de bureau, etc.) — **supplier** [sə'plaɪər] n : fournisseur m, -seuse f

support [sə'port] vt **1** BACK : soutenir, appuyer **2** : subvenir aux besoins de (une famille, etc.) **3** PROP UP : supporter — **~** n **1** : appui m, soutien m **2** PROP : support m — **supporter** [sə'portər] n **1** : partisan m, -sane f **2** FAN : supporter m

suppose [sə'po:z] vt **-posed; -posing 1** : supposer **2 be ~d to do sth** : être censé faire qqch — **supposedly** [sə'po:zədli] adv : soi-disant

suppress [sə'prɛs] vt **1** : réprimer **2** WITHHOLD : supprimer

supreme [su'pri:m] adj : suprême — **supremacy** [su'prɛməsi] n, pl **-cies** : suprématie f

sure ['ʃʊr] adj **surer; surest 1** : sûr **2 make ~ that** : s'assurer que — **~** adv **1** OF COURSE : bien sûr **2 it ~ is hot!** : quelle chaleur! — **surely** ['ʃʊrli] adv : sûrement

surfing ['sərfɪŋ] n : surf m

surface ['sərfəs] n **1** : surface f **2** AREA : superficie f — **~** vi **-faced; -facing** : faire surface, remonter à la surface — vt : revêtir (une chaussée)

surfboard ['sərf‚bord] n : planche f de surf

surfeit ['sərfət] n : excès m

surfing ['sərfɪŋ] n : surf m

surge ['sərdʒ] vi **surged; surging** : déferler — **~** n **1** : déferlement m (de la mer), ruée f (de personnes, etc.) **2** INCREASE : augmentation f (subite)

surgeon ['sərdʒən] n : chirurgien m, -gienne f — **surgery** ['sərdʒəri] n, pl **-geries** : chirurgie f — **surgical** ['sərdʒɪkəl] adj : chirurgical

surly ['sərli] adj **-lier; -est** : revêche, bourru

surname ['sər‚neɪm] n : nom m de famille

surpass [sər'pæs] vt : surpasser

surplus ['sər‚plʌs] n : excédent m, surplus m

surprise [sər'praɪz, sə-] n **1** : surprise f **2 take by ~** : prendre au dépourvu — **~** vt **-prised; -prising** : surprendre — **surprising** [sə'praɪzɪŋ, sər-] adj : surprenant

surrender [sə'rɛndər] vt : rendre, céder — vi : se rendre — **~** n : capitulation f, reddition f

surround [sə'raʊnd] vt : entourer — **surroundings** [sə'raʊndɪŋz] npl : environs mpl, alentours mpl

surveillance [sər'veɪlənts, -'veɪljənts, -'veɪənts] n : surveillance f

survey [sər'veɪ] vt **-veyed; -veying 1** : arpenter (un terrain) **2** INSPECT : inspecter **3** POLL : sonder — **~** ['sər‚veɪ] n, pl **-veys 1** INSPECTION : inspection f **2** POLL : sondage m — **surveyor** [sər'veɪər] n : arpenteur m, -teuse f

survive [sər'vaɪv] v **-vived; -viving** vi : survivre — vt : survivre à — **survival** [sər'vaɪvəl] n : survie f — **survivor** [sər'vaɪvər] n : survivant m, -vante f

susceptible [sə'sɛptəbəl] *adj* ~ **to** : prédisposé à

suspect ['sʌs,pɛkt, sə'spɛkt] *adj* : suspect — ~ ['sʌs,pɛkt] *n* : suspect *m*, -pecte *f* — ~ [sə'spɛkt] *vt* **1** : douter de, se méfier de **2** ~ **s.o. of** : soupçonner qqn de

suspend [sə'spɛnd] *vt* : suspendre — **suspenders** [sə'spɛndərz] *npl* : bretelles *fpl* — **suspense** [sə'spɛnʦ] *n* **1** : incertitude *f* **2** : suspense *m* (au cinéma, etc.)

suspicion [sə'spɪʃən] *n* : soupçon *m* — **suspicious** [sə'spɪʃəs] *adj* **1** QUESTIONABLE : suspect **2** DISTRUSTFUL : soupçonneux

sustain [sə'steɪn] *vt* **1** SUPPORT : soutenir **2** NOURISH : nourrir **3** SUFFER : subir

swagger ['swægər] *vi* : se pavaner

swallow[1] ['swɑloː] *vt* **1** : avaler **2** *or* ~ **up** : engloutir — ~ *n* : gorgée *f*

swallow[2] *n* : hirondelle *f*

swam → **swim**

swamp ['swɑmp] *n* : marais *m*, marécage *m* — ~ *vt* : inonder — **swampy** ['swɑmpi] *adj* **swampier; -est** : marécageux

swan ['swɑn] *n* : cygne *m*

swap ['swɑp] *vt* **swapped; swapping** : échanger — ~ *n* : échange *m*

swarm ['swɔrm] *n* : essaim *m* (d'abeilles, etc.) — ~ *vi* ~ **with** : grouiller de

swat ['swɑt] *vt* **swatted; swatting** : écraser (un insecte)

sway ['sweɪ] *n* **1** : balancement *m* **2** INFLUENCE : influence *f* — ~ *vi* : se balancer — *vt* : influencer

swear ['swær] *v* **swore** ['swor]; **sworn** ['sworn]; **swearing** *vi* CURSE : jurer — *vt* VOW : jurer — **swearword** ['swær,wərd] *n* : juron *m*

sweat ['swɛt] *vi* **sweat** *or* **sweated; sweating** : transpirer — ~ *n* : sueur *f*, transpiration *f*

sweater ['swɛtər] *n* : pull-over *m France*, chandail *m*

sweaty ['swɛti] *adj* **sweatier; -est** : en sueur

sweep ['swiːp] *v* **swept** ['swɛpt] **sweeping** *vt* **1** : balayer **2** *or* ~ **aside** : écarter — *vi* : balayer — ~ *n* **1** : coup *m* de balai **2** SCOPE : étendue *f* — **sweeping** ['swiːpɪŋ] *adj* **1** WIDE : large **2** EXTENSIVE : de grande portée

sweet ['swiːt] *adj* **1** : doux, sucré **2** PLEASANT : agréable, gentil — ~ *n* : bonbon *m*, dessert *m* — **sweeten** ['swiːtən] *vt* : sucrer — **sweetener** ['swiːtənər] *n* : édulcorant *m* — **sweetheart** ['swiːt,hɑrt] *n* **1** : petit ami *m*, petite amie *f* **2** (*used as a term of address*) : chéri *m*, -rie *f* — **sweetness** ['swiːtnəs] *n* : douceur *f* — **sweet potato** *n* : patate *f* douce

swell ['swɛl] *vi* **swelled; swelled** *or* **swollen** ['swoːlən, 'swʌl-]; **swelling 1** *or* ~ **up**

: enfler, gonfler **2** INCREASE : augmenter — ~ *n* : houle *f* (de la mer) — **swelling** ['swɛlɪŋ] *n* : enflure *f*, gonflement *m*

sweltering ['swɛltərɪŋ] *adj* : étouffant

swept → **sweep**

swerve ['swərv] *vi* **swerved; swerving** : faire une embardée — ~ *n* : embardée *f*

swift ['swɪft] *adj* : rapide — **swiftly** ['swɪftli] *adv* : rapidement

swim ['swɪm] *vi* **swam** ['swæm]; **swum** ['swʌm]; **swimming 1** : nager **2** REEL : tourner — ~ *n* **1** : baignade *f* **2 go for a** ~ : aller se baigner — **swimmer** ['swɪmər] *n* : nageur *m*, -geuse *f*

swindle ['swɪndəl] *vt* **-dled; -dling** : escroquer — ~ *n* : escroquerie *f* — **swindler** ['swɪndələr] *n* : escroc *m*

swine ['swaɪn] *ns & pl* : porc *m*

swing ['swɪŋ] *v* **swung** ['swʌŋ]; **swinging** *vt* : balancer, faire osciller — *vi* **1** : se balancer, osciller **2** SWIVEL : tourner — ~ *n* **1** : va-et-vient *m*, balancement *m* **2** : balançoire *f* (dans un terrain de jeu) **3 be in full** ~ : battre son plein

swipe ['swaɪp] *vt* **swiped; swiping 1** : passer dans un lecteur de cartes **2** STEAL : piquer *fam*

swirl ['swərl] *vi* : tourbillonner — ~ *n* : tourbillon *m*

swish ['swɪʃ] *vi* RUSTLE : faire un bruit léger

Swiss ['swɪs] *adj* : suisse

switch ['swɪʧ] *n* **1** CHANGE : changement *m* **2** : interrupteur *m* (d'électricité), bouton *m* (d'une radio ou d'une télévision) — ~ *vt* **1** CHANGE : changer de **2** ~ **on** : ouvrir, allumer **3** ~ **off** : couper, fermer, éteindre — *vi* SWAP : échanger — **switchboard** ['swɪʧ,bord] *n or* **telephone** ~ : standard *m*

swivel ['swɪvəl] *vi* **-eled** *or* **-elled; -eling** *or* **-elling** : pivoter

swollen → **swell**

swoop ['swuːp] *vi* ~ **down on** : s'abattre sur — ~ *n* : descente *f* en piqué

sword ['sord] *n* : épée *f*

swordfish ['sord,fɪʃ] *n* : espadon *m*

swore, sworn → **swear**

swum → **swim**

swung → **swing**

syllable ['sɪləbəl] *n* : syllabe *f*

syllabus ['sɪləbəs] *n, pl* **-bi** [-,baɪ] *or* **-buses** : programme *m* (d'études)

symbol ['sɪmbəl] *n* : symbole *m* — **symbolic** ['sɪm'bɑlɪk] *adj* : symbolique — **symbolism** ['sɪmbə,lɪzəm] *n* : symbolisme *m* — **symbolize** ['sɪmbə,laɪz] *vt* **-ized; -izing** : symboliser

symmetry ['sɪmətri] *n, pl* **-tries** : symétrie *f* — **symmetrical** [sə'mɛtrɪkəl] *adj* : symétrique

sympathy ['sɪmpəθi] *n, pl* **-thies 1** COMPASSION : sympathie *f* **2** UNDERSTANDING : compréhension *f* **3** CONDOLENCES : condoléances *fpl* — **sympathetic** [ˌsɪmpə'θɛtɪk] *adj* **1** COMPASSIONATE : compatissant **2** UNDERSTANDING : compréhensif — **sympathize** ['sɪmpəˌθaɪz] *vi* **-thized; -thizing** ~ **with 1** PITY : plaindre **2** UNDERSTAND : comprendre

symphony ['sɪmpfəni] *n, pl* **-nies** : symphonie *f*

symposium [sɪm'poːziəm] *n, pl* **-sia** [-ziə] *or* **-siums** : symposium *m*

symptom ['sɪmptəm] *n* : symptôme *m*

synagogue ['sɪnəˌɡɑɡ, -ˌɡɔɡ] *n* : synagogue *f*

synchronize ['sɪŋkrəˌnaɪz, 'sɪn-] *vt* **-nized; -nizing** : synchroniser

syndrome ['sɪnˌdroːm] *n* : syndrome *m*

synonym ['sɪnəˌnɪm] *n* : synonyme *m* — **synonymous** [sə'nɑnəməs] *adj* : synonyme

syntax ['sɪnˌtæks] *n* : syntaxe *f*

synthesis ['sɪnθəsɪs] *n, pl* **-ses** [-ˌsiːz] : synthèse *f* — **synthetic** [sɪn'θɛtɪk] *adj* : synthétique

syringe [sə'rɪndʒ, 'sɪrɪndʒ] *n* : seringue *f*

syrup ['sərəp, 'sɪrəp] *n* : sirop *m*

system ['sɪstəm] *n* **1** : système *m* **2** BODY : organisme *m* **3** digestive ~ : appareil *m* digestif — **systematic** [ˌsɪstə'mætɪk] *adj* : systématique

T

t ['tiː] *n, pl* **t's** *or* **ts** ['tiːz] : t *m*, vingtième lettre de l'alphabet

tab ['tæb] *n* **1** FLAP : languette *f* **2** keep ~s on : surveiller

table ['teɪbəl] *n* : table *f* — **tablecloth** ['teɪbəlˌklɔθ] *n* : nappe *f* — **tablespoon** ['teɪbəlˌspuːn] *n* : cuillère *f* à soupe

tablet ['tæblət] *n* **1** : bloc-notes *m* **2** PILL : comprimé *m*

tabloid ['tæˌblɔɪd] *n* : quotidien *m* populaire, tabloïde *m*

taboo [tə'buː, tæ-] *adj* : tabou — ~ *n, pl* **-boos** : tabou *m*

tacit ['tæsɪt] *adj* : tacite

taciturn ['tæsɪˌtərn] *adj* : taciturne

tack ['tæk] *vt* **1** ATTACH : clouer **2** ~ on ADD : ajouter

tackle ['takəl] *n* **1** GEAR : équipement *m*, matériel *m* **2** : plaquage *m* (au football) — ~ *vt* **-led; -ling 1** : plaquer (au football) **2** CONFRONT : s'attaquer à

tacky ['tæki] *adj* **tackier; tackiest 1** STICKY : collant **2** GAUDY : de mauvais goût

tact ['tækt] *n* : tact *m* — **tactful** ['tæktfəl] *adj* : plein de tact

tactical ['tæktɪkəl] *adj* : tactique — **tactic** ['tæktɪk] *n* : tactique *f* — **tactics** ['tæktɪks] *ns & pl* : tactique *f*

tactless ['tæktləs] *adj* : qui manque de tact

tadpole ['tædˌpoːl] *n* : têtard *m*

tag[1] ['tæg] *n* LABEL : étiquette *f* — ~ *v* **tagged; tagging** *vt* LABEL : étiqueter — *vi* ~ along : suivre

tag[2] *vt* : toucher (au jeu de chat)

tail ['teɪl] *n* **1** : queue *f* **2** ~s *npl* : pile *f*

(d'une pièce de monnaie) — ~ *vt* FOLLOW : suivre

tailor ['teɪlər] *n* : tailleur *m* — ~ *vt* **1** : faire sur mesure (un vêtement) **2** ADAPT : adapter

taint ['teɪnt] *vt* : entacher, souiller

Taiwanese [ˌtaɪwə'niːz, -'niːs] *adj* : taiwanais

take ['teɪk] *v* **took** ['tʊk]; **taken** ['teɪkən]; **taking** *vt* **1** : prendre **2** BRING : emmener **3** CARRY : porter **4** REQUIRE : demander **5** ACCEPT : accepter **6** BEAR : supporter **7** : passer (un examen) **8 I** ~ it that : je suppose que **9** ~ a walk : se promener **10** ~ apart DISMANTLE : démonter **11** ~ back : retirer **12** ~ in ALTER : reprendre **13** ~ in UNDERSTAND : saisir **14** ~ in DECEIVE : tromper **15** ~ off REMOVE : enlever **16** ~ on : assumer (une responsabilité) **17** ~ over : prendre le pouvoir **18** ~ place : avoir lieu **19** ~ up SHORTEN : raccourcir **20** ~ up OCCUPY : prendre — *vi* **1** WORK : faire effet **2** ~ off DEPART : s'en aller **3** ~ off : décoller (se dit d'un avion) — ~ *n* **1** PROCEEDS : recette *f* **2** : prise *f* (au cinéma) — **takeoff** ['teɪkˌɔf] *n* : décollage *m* (d'un avion) — **takeover** ['teɪkˌoːvər] *n* : prise *f* de contrôle (d'une compagnie)

talcum powder ['tælkəm] *n* : talc *m*

tale ['teɪl] *n* : conte *m*, histoire *f*

talent ['tælənt] *n* : talent *m* — **talented** ['tæləntəd] *adj* : talentueux, doué

talk ['tɔk] *vt* **1** : parler **2** ~ about : parler de **3** ~ to/with : parler avec — *vi* **1** SPEAK : parler **2** ~ over : parler de, discuter —

~ *n* **1** CONVERSATION : entretien *m*, conversation *f* **2** SPEECH : discours *m*, exposé *m* — **talkative** ['tɔkətɪv] *adj* : bavard

tall ['tɔl] *adj* **1** : grand **2 how ~ are you?** : combien mesures-tu?

tally ['tæli] *n, pl* **-lies** : compte *m* — ~ *v* **-lied; -lying** *vt* RECKON : calculer — *vi* MATCH : correspondre

tambourine [ˌtæmbə'riːn] *n* : tambourin *m*

tame ['teɪm] *adj* **tamer; tamest 1** : apprivoisé **2** : docile — ~ *vt* **tamed; taming** : apprivoiser, dompter

tamper ['tæmpər] *vi* ~ **with** : forcer (une serrure), falsifier (un document)

tampon ['tæmˌpɑn] *n* : tampon *m* (hygiénique)

tan ['tæn] *v* **tanned; tanning** *vt* : tanner (du cuir) — *vi* : bronzer — ~ *n* **1** SUNTAN : bronzage *m* **2** : brun *m* clair (couleur)

tang ['tæŋ] *n* : goût *m* piquant

tangent ['tændʒənt] *n* : tangente *f*

tangerine ['tændʒəˌriːn, ˌtændʒə'-] *n* : mandarine *f*

tangible ['tændʒəbəl] *adj* : tangible

tangle ['tæŋgəl] *v* **-gled; -gling** *vt* : enchevêtrer — *vi* : s'emmêler — ~ *n* : enchevêtrement *m*

tango ['tæŋˌgoː] *n, pl* **-gos** : tango *m*

tank ['tæŋk] *n* **1** : réservoir *m*, cuve *f* **2** : char *m* (militaire) — **tanker** ['tæŋkər] *n* **1** *or* **oil ~** : pétrolier *m* **2** *or* ~ **truck** : camion-citern *m*

tantalizing ['tæntəˌlaɪzɪŋ] *adj* : alléchant

tantrum ['tæntrəm] *n* **throw a ~** : piquer une crise

tap¹ ['tæp] *n* FAUCET : robinet *m* — ~ *vt* **tapped; tapping** : mettre sur écoute

tap² *v* **tapped; tapping** *vt* TOUCH : tapoter, taper — *vi* : taper légèrement — ~ *n* : petit coup *m*

tape ['teɪp] *n or* **adhesive ~** : ruban *m* adhésif — ~ *vt* **taped; taping 1** : coller avec un ruban adhésif **2** RECORD : enregistrer — **tape measure** *n* : mètre *m* ruban

taper ['teɪpər] *vi* **1** : s'effiler **2** *or* ~ **off** : diminuer

tapestry ['tæpəstri] *n, pl* **-tries** : tapisserie *f*

tar ['tɑr] *n* : goudron *m* — ~ *vt* **tarred; tarring** : goudronner

tarantula [tə'ræntʃələ, -'ræntələ] *n* : tarentule *f*

target ['tɑrgət] *n* **1** : cible *f* **2** GOAL : objectif *m*, but *m*

tariff ['tærɪf] *n* : tarif *m* douanier

tarnish ['tɑrnɪʃ] *vt* : ternir — *vi* : se ternir

tarpaulin [tɑr'pɔlən, 'tɑrpə-] *n* : bâche *f*

tart¹ ['tɑrt] *adj* SOUR : aigre

tart² *n* : tartelette *f*

tartan ['tɑrtən] *n* : tartan *m*, tissu *m* écossais

task ['tæsk] *n* : tâche *f*

tassel ['tæsəl] *n* : gland *m*

taste ['teɪst] *v* **tasted; tasting** *vt* : goûter (à) — *vi* ~ **like** : avoir le goût de — ~ *n* : goût *m* — **tasteful** ['teɪstfəl] *adj* : de bon goût — **tasteless** ['teɪstləs] *adj* **1** FLAVORLESS : sans goût **2** COARSE : de mauvais goût — **tasty** ['teɪsti] *adj* **tastier; tastiest** : savoureux

tattered ['tætərd] *adj* : en lambeaux

tattle ['tætəl] *vi* **-tled; -tling** ~ **on s.o.** : dénoncer qqn

tattoo [tæ'tuː] *vt* : tatouer — ~ *n* : tatouage *m*

taught → **teach**

taunt ['tɔnt] *n* : raillerie *f* — ~ *vt* : railler

taut ['tɔt] *adj* : tendu

tavern ['tævərn] *n* : taverne *f*

tax ['tæks] *vt* **1** : imposer (une personne), taxer (de l'argent, des marchandises) **2** STRAIN : mettre à l'épreuve — ~ *n* : taxe *f*, impôt *m* — **taxable** ['tæksəbəl] *adj* : imposable — **taxation** [tæk'seɪʃən] *n* : taxation *f*, imposition *f* — **tax–exempt** ['tæksɪg'zɛmpt, -ɛg-] *adj* : exempt d'impôts

taxi ['tæksi] *n, pl* **taxis** : taxi *m*

taxpayer ['tæksˌpeɪər] *n* : contribuable *mf*

tea ['tiː] *n* : thé *m*

teach ['tiːtʃ] *v* **taught** ['tɔt]; **teaching** *vt* **1** : enseigner (un sujet) **2** ~ **s.o. to** : apprendre qqn à — *vi* : enseigner — **teacher** ['tiːtʃər] *n* : instituteur *m*, -trice *f* (à l'école primaire); professeur *m* — **teaching** ['tiːtʃɪŋ] *n* : enseignement *m*

teacup ['tiːˌkʌp] *n* : tasse *f* à thé

team ['tiːm] *n* : équipe *f* — ~ *vi* ~ **up with** : faire équipe avec — ~ *adj* : d'équipe — **teammate** ['tiːmˌmeɪt] *n* : coéquipier *m*, -pière *f* — **teamwork** ['tiːmˌwərk] *n* : travail *m* d'équipe

teapot ['tiːˌpɑt] *n* : théière *f*

tear¹ ['tær] *v* **tore** ['tor]; **torn** ['tɔrn]; **tearing** *vt* **1** RIP : déchirer **2** ~ **down** : démolir **3** ~ **off** *or* ~ **out** : arracher **4** ~ **up** : déchirer — *vi* **1** : se déchirer **2** RUSH : se précipiter — ~ *n* : déchirure *f*

tear² ['tɪr] *n* : larme *f* — **tearful** ['tɪrfəl] *adj* : larmoyant

tease ['tiːz] *vt* **teased; teasing** : taquiner — ~ *n* : taquin *m*, -quine *f*

teaspoon ['tiːˌspuːn] *n* : petite cuillère *f*, cuillère *f* à café

technical ['tɛknɪkəl] *adj* : technique — **technicality** [ˌtɛknə'kæləti] *n, pl* **-ties** : détail *m* technique — **technician** [tɛk'nɪʃən] *n* : technicien *m*, -cienne *f*

technique [tɛk'niːk] *n* : technique *f*

technological [ˌtɛknə'lɑdʒɪkəl] *adj* : technologique — **technology** [tɛk'nɑlədʒi] *n, pl* **-gies** : technologie *f*

tedious ['ti:diəs] *adj* : fastidieux — **tedium** ['ti:diəm] : ennui *m*

teem ['ti:m] *vi* ~ **with** : foisonner de, abonder en

teenage ['ti:n͵eɪʤ] *or* **teenaged** [-͵eɪʤd] *adj* : adolescent, d'adolescence — **teenager** ['ti:n͵eɪʤər] *n* : adolescent *m*, -cente *f* — **teens** ['ti:nz] *npl* : adolescence *f*

teepee → **tepee**

teeter ['ti:tər] *vi* : chanceler

teeth → **tooth** — **teethe** ['ti:ð] *vi* **teethed**; **teething** : faire ses dents

telecommunication [͵tɛləkə͵mju:nə'keɪʃən] *n* : télécommunication *f*

telegram ['tɛlə͵græm] *n* : télégramme *m*

telegraph ['tɛlə͵græf] *n* : télégraphe *m*

telephone ['tɛlə͵fo:n] *n* : téléphone *m* — ~ *v* **-phoned**; **-phoning** *vt* : téléphoner à — *vi* : appeler, téléphoner

telescope ['tɛlə͵sko:p] *n* : télescope *m*

televise ['tɛlə͵vaɪz] *vt* **-vised**; **-vising** : téléviser — **television** ['tɛlə͵vɪʒən] *n* **1** : télévision *f* **2** *or* ~ **set** : téléviseur *m*

tell ['tɛl] *v* **told** ['to:ld]; **telling** *vt* **1** : dire **2** RELATE : raconter **3** DISTINGUISH : distinguer **4** ~ **s.o. off** : réprimander qqn — *vi* **1** : dire **2** KNOW : savoir **3** SHOW : se faire sentir **4** ~ **on s.o.** : dénoncer qqn — **teller** ['tɛlər] *n or* **bank** ~ : caissier *m*, -sière *f*

temp ['tɛmp] *n* : intérimaire *mf*; occasionnel *m*, -nelle *f Can*

temper ['tɛmpər] *vt* MODERATE : tempérer — ~ *n* **1** MOOD : humeur *f* **2 lose one's** ~ : se mettre en colère — **temperament** ['tɛmpərmənt, -prə-, -pərə-] *n* : tempérament *m* — **temperamental** [͵tɛmpər'mɛntəl, -prə-, -pərə-] *adj* : capricieux — **temperate** ['tɛmpərət] *adj* **1** MILD : tempéré **2** MODERATE : modéré

temperature ['tɛmpər͵ʧur, -prə-, -ʧər] *n* **1** : température *f* **2 have a** ~ : avoir de la température

temple ['tɛmpəl] *n* **1** : temple *m* **2** : tempe *f* (en anatomie)

tempo ['tɛm͵po:] *n, pl* **-pi** [-͵pi:] *or* **-pos 1** : tempo *m* **2** PACE : rythme *m*

temporarily [͵tɛmpə'rɛrəli] *adv* : temporairement — **temporary** ['tɛmpə͵rɛri] *adj* : temporaire

tempt ['tɛmpt] *vt* : tenter — **temptation** [tɛmp'teɪʃən] *n* : tentation *f*

ten ['tɛn] *n* : dix *m* — ~ *adj* : dix

tenacious [tə'neɪʃəs] *adj* : tenace — **tenacity** [tə'næsəti] *n* : ténacité *f*

tenant ['tɛnənt] *n* : locataire *mf*

tend[1] ['tɛnd] *vt* : s'occuper de

tend[2] *vi* ~ **to** : avoir tendance à — **tendency** ['tɛndənsi] *n, pl* **-cies** : tendance *f*

tender[1] ['tɛndər] *adj* **1** : tendre **2** PAINFUL : douloureux

tender[2] *vt* : présenter — ~ *n* **1** : soumission *f* **2 legal** ~ : cours *m* légal

tenderloin ['tɛndər͵lɔɪn] *n* : filet *m* (de porc, etc.)

tenderness ['tɛndərnəs] *n* : tendresse *f*

tendon ['tɛndən] *n* : tendon *m*

tenet ['tɛnət] *n* : principe *m*

tennis ['tɛnəs] *n* : tennis *m*

tenor ['tɛnər] *n* : ténor *m*

tense[1] ['tɛns] *n* : temps *m* (en grammaire)

tense[2] *v* **tensed**; **tensing** *vt* : tendre — *vi or* ~ **up** : se raidir — ~ *adj* **tenser**; **tensest** : tendu — **tension** ['tɛnʧən] *n* : tension *f*

tent ['tɛnt] *n* : tente *f*

tentacle ['tɛntɪkəl] *n* : tentacule *m*

tentative ['tɛntətɪv] *adj* **1** HESITANT : hésitant **2** PROVISIONAL : provisoire

tenth ['tɛnθ] *n* **1** : dixième *mf* **2 September** ~ : le dix septembre — ~ *adj* : dixième

tenuous ['tɛnjuəs] *adj* : ténu

tepee ['ti:͵pi:] *n* : tipi *m*

tepid ['tɛpɪd] *adj* : tiède

term ['tərm] *n* **1** WORD : terme *m* **2** : trimestre *m* (scolaire) **3 be on good** ~**s** : être en bons termes — ~ *vt* : appeler, nommer

terminal ['tərmənəl] *adj* : terminal — ~ *n* **1** : borne *f* (en électricité) **2** *or* **computer** ~ : terminal *m* **3** : terminus *m* (de train, de bus)

terminate ['tərmə͵neɪt] *v* **-nated**; **-nating** *vi* : se terminer — *vt* : terminer — **termination** [͵tərmə'neɪʃən] *n* : fin *f*

terminology [͵tərmə'naləʤi] *n, pl* **-gies** : terminologie *f*

termite ['tər͵maɪt] *n* : termite *m*

terrace ['tɛrəs] *n* : terrasse *f*

terrain [tə'reɪn] *n* : terrain *m*

terrestrial [tə'rɛstriəl] *adj* : terrestre

terrible ['tɛrəbəl] *adj* : terrible, épouvantable — **terribly** ['tɛrəbli] *adv* : terriblement

terrier ['tɛriər] *n* : terrier *m*

terrific [tə'rɪfɪk] *adj* **1** FRIGHTFUL : terrible **2** EXCELLENT : formidable

terrify ['tɛrə͵faɪ] *vt* **-fied**; **-fying** : terrifier — **terrifying** ['tɛrə͵faɪɪŋ] *adj* : terrifiant

territory ['tɛrə͵tori] *n, pl* **-ries** : territoire *m* — **territorial** [͵tɛrə'toriəl] *adj* : territorial

terror ['tɛrər] *n* : terreur *f* — **terrorism** ['tɛrər͵ɪzəm] *n* : terrorisme *m* — **terrorist** ['tɛrərɪst] *n* : terroriste *mf* — **terrorize** ['tɛrər͵aɪz] *vt* **-ized**; **-izing** : terroriser

terse ['tərs] *adj* **terser**; **tersest** : concis, succinct

test ['tɛst] *n* **1** TRIAL : épreuve *f* **2** EXAM : examen *m*, test *m* **3 blood** ~ : analyse *f* de sang — ~ *vt* **1** TRY : essayer **2** QUIZ : examiner, tester **3** : analyser (le sang, etc.), examiner (les yeux, etc.)

testament ['tɛstəmənt] *n* **1** WILL : testament
m **2 the Old/New Testament** : l'Ancien, le
Nouveau Testament
testicle ['tɛstɪkəl] *n* : testicule *m*
testify ['tɛstə,faɪ] *v* **-fied; -fying** : témoigner
testimony ['tɛstə,mo:ni] *n, pl* **-nies** : témoignage *m*
test tube *n* : éprouvette *f*
tetanus ['tɛtənəs] *n* : tétanos *m*
tether ['tɛðər] *vt* : attacher
text ['tɛkst] *n* : texte *m* — **textbook** ['tɛkst-
,bʊk] *n* : manuel *m* scolaire
textile ['tɛk,staɪl, 'tɛkstəl] *n* : textile *m*
texture ['tɛkstʃər] *n* : texture *f*
than ['ðæn] *conj* : que — ~ *prep* : que, de
thank ['θæŋk] *vt* **1** : remercier **2** ~ **you**
: merci — **thankful** ['θæŋkfəl] *adj* : reconnaissant — **thankfully** ['θæŋkfəli] *adv* **1**
: avec reconnaissance **2** FORTUNATELY
: heureusement — **thankless** ['θæŋkləs]
adj : ingrat — **thanks** ['θæŋks] *npl* **1** : re-
merciements *mpl* **2** ~ **to** : grâce à
Thanksgiving [θæŋks'gɪvɪŋ, 'θæŋks,-] *n*
: jour *m* d'Action de Grâces
that ['ðæt] *pron, pl* **those** ['ðo:z] **1** : cela, ce,
ça **2** (*more distant*) : celui-là, celle-là, ceux-
là, celles-là **3** WHO : qui **4** (*used to introduce relative clauses*) : que **5 is** ~ **you?**
: c'est toi? **6** ~ **is** : c'est-à-dire — ~ *conj*
1 : que **2 in order** ~ : afin que — ~ *adj,
pl* **those 1** : ce, cet, cette, ces **2** ~ **one**
: celui-là, celle-là — ~ *adv* VERY : tellement, très
thaw ['θɔ] *vt* : dégeler (des aliments) — *vi* **1**
: se dégeler **2** MELT : fondre — ~ *n* : dégel
m
the [ðə, *before vowel sounds usu* ði:] *art* **1**
: le, la, l', les **2** PER : le, la **3** ~ **English**
: les Anglais — ~ *adv* **1** : le **2** ~ **sooner**
~ **better** : le plus tôt sera le mieux
theater *or* **theatre** ['θi:ətər] *n* : théâtre *m* —
theatrical [θi'ætrɪkəl] *adj* : théâtral
theft ['θɛft] *n* : vol *m*
their ['ðɛr] *adj* : leur — **theirs** ['ðɛrz] *pron*
: le leur, la leur, les leurs **2 some friends of**
~ : des amis à eux
them ['ðɛm] *pron* **1** (*used as direct object*)
: les **2** (*used as indirect object*) : leur **3**
(*used as object of a preposition*) : eux, elles
theme ['θi:m] *n* : thème *m*
themselves [ðəm'sɛlvz, ðɛm-] *pron* **1** (*used
reflexively*) : se **2** (*used emphatically*)
: eux-mêmes, elles-mêmes **3** (*used after a
preposition*) : eux, elles, eux-mêmes, elles-
mêmes **4 by** ~ : tous seuls, toutes seules
then ['ðɛn] *adv* **1** : alors **2** NEXT : ensuite,
puis **3** BESIDES : et puis — ~ *adj* : d'alors,
de l'époque
theology [θi'ɑlədʒi] *n, pl* **-gies** : théologie *f*
theorem ['θi:ərəm, 'θɪrəm] *n* : théorème *m*

— **theoretical** [,θi:ə'rɛtɪkəl] *adj* : théorique
— **theory** ['θi:əri, 'θɪri] *n, pl* **-ries** : théorie *f*
therapeutic [,θɛrə'pju:tɪk] *adj* : thérapeutique — **therapist** ['θɛrəpɪst] *n* : thérapeute
mf — **therapy** ['θɛrəpi] *n, pl* **-pies** : thérapie *f*
there ['ðɛr] *adv* **1** *or* **over** ~ : là-bas **2**
down/up ~ : là-dessous, là-haut **3 in** ~
: là-dedans **4** ~, **it's done!** : voilà, c'est
fini! **5 who's** ~? : qui est là? — ~ *pron*
1 ~ **is/are** : il y a **2** ~ **are three of us**
: nous sommes trois — **thereabouts** *or*
thereabout [ðærə'baʊts, -'baʊt, 'ðærə,-]
adv : dans les environs, par là — **thereafter**
[ðær'æftər] *adv* : par la suite — **thereby**
[ðær'baɪ, 'ðær,baɪ] *adv* : ainsi — **therefore**
['ðær,for] *adv* : donc, par conséquent
thermal ['θərməl] *adj* : thermal, thermique
thermometer [θər'mɑmətər] *n* : thermomètre *m*
thermos ['θərməs] *n* : thermos *mf*
thermostat ['θərmə,stæt] *n* : thermostat *m*
thesaurus [θɪ'sɔrəs] *n, pl* **-sauri** [-'sɔr,aɪ] *or*
-sauruses [-'sɔrəsəz] : dictionnaire *m*
analogique, dictionnaire *m* des synonymes
these → **this**
thesis ['θi:sɪs] *n, pl* **theses** ['θi:,si:z] : thèse *f*
they ['ðeɪ] *pron* **1** : ils, elles **2 as** ~ **say**
: comme on dit **3 there** ~ **are** : les voici
— **they'd** ['ðeɪd] (*contraction of* **they had** *or*
they would) → **have, would** — **they'll**
['ðeɪl, 'ðɛl] (*contraction of* **they shall** *or*
they will) → **shall, will** — **they're** ['ðɛr]
(*contraction of* **they are**) → **be** — **they've**
['ðeɪv] (*contraction of* **they have**) → **have**
thick ['θɪk] *adj* **1** : épais **2** DENSE : bête **3 a**
~ **accent** : un accent prononcé **4 two**
inches ~ : deux pouces d'épaisseur — ~
n in the ~ **of** : au plus fort de — **thicken**
['θɪkən] *vt* : épaissir (une sauce, etc.) — ~
vi : s'épaissir — **thicket** ['θɪkət] *n* : fourré *m*
— **thickness** ['θɪknəs] *n* : épaisseur *f*,
grosseur *f*
thief ['θi:f] *n, pl* **thieves** ['θi:vz] : voleur *m*,
-leuse *f*
thigh ['θaɪ] *n* : cuisse *f*
thimble ['θɪmbəl] *n* : dé *m* à coudre
thin ['θɪn] *adj* **thinner; thinnest 1** : mince **2**
SPARSE : clairsemé **3** WATERY : clair (se dit
d'une soupe, etc.) — ~ *v* **thinned; thinning** *vt* DILUTE : diluer — *vi* : s'éclaircir
thing ['θɪŋ] *n* **1** : chose *f* **2** ~**s** *npl* BELONG-
INGS : affaires *fpl* **3 for one** ~ : en premier
lieu **4 how are** ~**s?** : comment ça va? **5
the important** ~ **is...** : l'important c'est...
think ['θɪŋk] *v* **thought** ['θɔt]; **thinking** *vt* **1**
: penser **2** BELIEVE : croire **3** ~ **up** : inventer — *vi* **1** : penser **2** ~ **about** *or*
CONSIDER : penser à **3** ~ **of** REMEMBER
: se rappeler

thinness ['θɪnnəs] *n* : minceur *f*

third ['θərd] *adj* : troisième — ~ *or* **thirdly** [-li] *adv* : troisième, troisièmement — ~ *n* **1** : troisième *mf* (dans une série) **2** : tiers *m* (en mathématiques) **3 December** ~ : le trois décembre — **Third World** *n* : le tiers-monde

thirst ['θərst] *n* : soif *f* — **thirsty** ['θərsti] *adj* **thirstier; thirstiest 1** : assoiffé **2 be** ~ : avoir soif

thirteen [,θər'ti:n] *n* : treize *m* — ~ *adj* : treize — **thirteenth** [,θər'ti:nθ] *n* **1** : treizième *mf* **2 January** ~ : le treize janvier — ~ *adj* : treizième

thirty ['θərṭi] *n, pl* **-ties** : trente *m* — ~ *adj* : trente — **thirtieth** ['θərṭiəθ] *n* **1** : trentième *mf* **2 May** ~ : le trente mai — ~ *adj* : trentième

this ['ðɪs] *pron, pl* **these 1** : ce, ceci **2** (*in comparisons*) : celui-ci, celle-ci, ceux-ci, celles-ci **3** ~ **is your room** : voici ta chambre — ~ *adj, pl* **these** ['ði:z] **1** : ce, cet, cette, ces **2** ~ **one** : celui-ci, celle-ci **3** ~ **way** : par ici — ~ *adv* : si, aussi

thistle ['θɪsəl] *n* : chardon *m*

thorn ['θɔrn] *n* : épine *f* — **thorny** ['θɔrni] *adj* **thornier; thorniest** : épineux

thorough ['θə,ro:] *adj* **1** : consciencieux **2** COMPLETE : complet — **thoroughly** ['θəroli] *adv* **1** : à fond **2** COMPLETELY : absolument — **Thoroughbred** ['θəro,brɛd] *n* : pur-sang *m* — **thoroughfare** ['θəro,fær] *n* : voie *f* publique

those → **that**

though ['ðo:] *conj* : bien que, quoique — ~ *adv* **1** : cependant, pourtant **2 as** ~ : comme si

thought ['θɔt] → **think** — ~ *n* **1** : pensée *f* **2** IDEA : idée *f* — **thoughtful** ['θɔtfəl] *adj* **1** : pensif **2** KIND : aimable — **thoughtless** ['θɔtləs] *adj* **1** : irréfléchi **2** RUDE : manquer d'égard (envers qqn)

thousand ['θauzənd] *n, pl* **-sands** *or* **-sand** : mille *m* — ~ *adj* : mille — **thousandth** ['θauzənṭθ] *n* : millième *mf* — ~ *adj* : millième

thrash ['θræʃ] *vi or* ~ **about** : se débattre

thread ['θrɛd] *n* : fil *m* — ~ *vt* : enfiler (une aiguille, des perles, etc.) — **threadbare** ['θrɛd'bær] *adj* : usé

threat ['θrɛt] *n* : menace *f* — **threaten** ['θrɛtən] *v* : menacer — **threatening** ['θrɛtənɪŋ] *adj* : menaçant

three ['θri:] *n* : trois *m* — ~ *adj* : trois — **three hundred** *adj* : trois cent

threshold ['θrɛʃ,ho:ld, -,o:ld] *n* : seuil *m*

threw → **throw**

thrift ['θrɪft] *n* : économie *f* — **thrifty** ['θrɪfti] *adj* **thriftier; thriftiest** : économe

thrill ['θrɪl] *vt* : transporter (de joie) — ~ *n*

: frisson *m* — **thriller** ['θrɪlər] *n* : thriller *m* — **thrilling** ['θrɪlɪŋ] *adj* : excitant

thrive ['θraɪv] *vi* **throve** ['θro:v] *or* **thrived; thriven** ['θrɪvən] **1** FLOURISH : réussir **2** PROSPER : prospérer

throat ['θro:t] *n* : gorge *f*

throb ['θrɑb] *vi* **throbbed; throbbing 1** : battre, palpiter **2** VIBRATE : vibrer **3** ~ **with pain** : lanciner

throes ['θro:] *npl* **1** : agonie *f* **2 in the** ~ **of** : en proie à

throne ['θro:n] *n* : trône *m*

throng ['θrɔŋ] *n* : foule *f*

through ['θru:] *prep* **1** : à travers **2** BECAUSE OF : à cause de **3** BY : par **4** DURING : pendant **5 Monday** ~ **Friday** : du lundi au vendredi **6** → **throughout** — ~ *adv* **1** : à travers **2** COMPLETELY : complètement **3 let** ~ : laisser passer — ~ *adj* **1 be** ~ : avoir terminé **2** ~ **traffic** : trafic en transit — **throughout** [θru:'aut] *prep* **1** : partout dans **2** DURING : pendant

throw ['θro:] *vt* **threw** ['θru:]; **thrown** ['θro:n]; **throwing 1** : lancer (une balle, etc.) **2** CONFUSE : déconcerter **3** ~ **a party** : organiser une fête **4** ~ **away** *or* ~ **out** : jeter — ~ *n* TOSS : lancer *m*, jet *m* — **throw up** *vt* : vomir, renvoyer *Can fam*, restituer *Can fam*

thrush ['θrʌʃ] *n* : grive *f* (oiseau)

thrust ['θrʌst] *vt* **thrust; thrusting 1** : enfoncer, planter **2** ~ **upon** : imposer à — ~ *n* : poussée *f*

thud ['θʌd] *n* : bruit *m* sourd

thug ['θʌg] *n* : voyou *m*

thumb ['θʌm] *n* : pouce *m* — ~ *vt or* ~ **through** : feuilleter — **thumbnail** ['θʌm,neɪl] *n* : ongle *m* du pouce — **thumbtack** ['θʌm,tæk] *n* : punaise *f*

thump ['θʌmp] *vt* : cogner — *vi* : battre fort (se dit du cœur) — ~ *n* : bruit *m* sourd

thunder ['θʌndər] *n* : tonnerre *m* — ~ *vi* : tonner — ~ *vt* SHOUT : vociférer — **thunderbolt** ['θʌndər,bo:lt] *n* : foudre *f* — **thunderous** ['θʌndərəs] *adj* : étourdissant — **thunderstorm** ['θʌndər,storm] *n* : orage *m*

Thursday ['θərz,deɪ, -di] *n* : jeudi *m*

thus ['ðʌs] *adv* **1** : ainsi, donc **2** ~ **far** : jusqu'à présent

thwart ['θwɔrt] *vt* : contrecarrer

thyme ['taɪm, 'θaɪm] *n* : thym *m*

thyroid ['θaɪ,rɔɪd] *n* : thyroïde *f*

tic ['tɪk] *n* : tic *m* (nerveux)

tick¹ ['tɪk] *n* : tique *f* (insecte)

tick² *n* **1** : tic-tac *m* (bruit) **2** CHECK : coche *f* — ~ *vi* : faire tic-tac — *vt* **1** *or* ~ **off** CHECK : cocher **2** ~ **off** ANNOY : agacer

ticket ['tɪkət] *n* **1** : billet *m* (d'avion, de train, etc.), ticket *m* (d'autobus, de métro) **2** *or* **parking** ~ : contravention *f*

tickle ['tɪkəl] *v* **-led; -ling** *vt* **1** : chatouiller **2** AMUSE : amuser — *vi* : chatouiller — **~** *n* : chatouillement *m* — **ticklish** ['tɪkəlɪʃ] *adj* : chatouilleux

tidal wave ['taɪdəl] *n* : raz-de-marée *m*

tidbit ['tɪd,bɪt] *n* : détail *m* intéressant

tide ['taɪd] *n* : marée *f* — **~** *vt* **tided; tiding** **~ over** : dépanner

tidy ['taɪdi] *adj* **-dier; -est** NEAT : propre — **~** *vt* **-died; -dying** *or* **~ up** : ranger

tie ['taɪ] *n* **1** : attache *f*, cordon *m* **2** BOND : lien **3** : match *m* nul (aux sports) **4** NECKTIE : cravate *f* — **~** *v* **tied; tying** *or* **tieing** *vt* **1** : attacher **2 ~ a knot** : faire un nœud — *vi* : faire match nul, être ex æquo

tier ['tɪr] *n* : étage *m*, gradin *m* (d'un stade)

tiger ['taɪgər] *n* : tigre *m*

tight ['taɪt] *adj* **1** : serré, étroit **2** TAUT : tendu **3** STINGY : avare **4 a ~ seal** : une fermeture étanche — **~** *adv* **closed ~** : bien fermé — **tighten** ['taɪtən] *vt* : serrer, resserrer — **tightly** ['taɪtli] *adv* : fermement, bien — **tightrope** ['taɪt,ro:p] *n* : corde *f* raide — **tights** ['taɪts] *npl* : collants *mpl*

tile ['taɪl] *n* : carreau *m*, tuile *f* — **~** *vt* **tiled; tiling** : carreler, poser des tuiles sur

till¹ ['tɪl] *prep & conj* → **until**

till² *vt* : labourer

till³ *n* : tiroir-caisse *m*

tilt ['tɪlt] *n* **1** : inclinaison *f* **2 at full ~** : à toute vitesse — **~** *vt* : pencher, incliner — *vi* : se pencher, s'incliner

timber ['tɪmbər] *n* **1** : bois *m* de construction **2** BEAM : poutre *f*

time ['taɪm] *n* **1** : temps *m* **2** AGE : époque *f* **3** : rythme *m* (en musique) **4 at ~s** : parfois **5 at this ~** : en ce moment **6 for the ~ being** : pour le moment **7 from ~ to ~** : de temps à autre **8 have a good ~** : amusez-vous bien **9 on ~** : à l'heure **10 several ~s** : plusieurs fois **11 ~ after ~** : à maintes reprises **12 what ~ is it?** : quelle heure est-il? — **~** *vt* **timed; timing 1** SCHEDULE : prévoir, fixer **2** : chronométrer (une course, etc.) — **timeless** ['taɪmləs] *adj* : éternel — **timely** ['taɪmli] *adj* **-lier; -est** : opportun — **timer** ['taɪmər] *n* : minuteur *m* (en cuisine) — **times** ['taɪmz] *prep* **3 ~ 4 is 12** : 3 fois 4 égale 12 — **timetable** ['taɪm,teɪbəl] *n* : horaire *m*

timid ['tɪmɪd] *adj* : timide

tin ['tɪn] *n* **1** : étain *m* (métal) **2** *or* **~ can** : boîte *f* — **tinfoil** ['tɪn,fɔɪl] *n* : papier *m* d'aluminium

tinge ['tɪndʒ] *vt* **tinged; tingeing** *or* **tinging** ['tɪndʒɪŋ] : teinter — **~** *n* : teinte *f*

tingle ['tɪngəl] *vi* **-gled; -gling** : picoter — **~** *n* : picotement *m*

tinker ['tɪŋkər] *vi* **~ with** : bricoler

tinkle ['tɪŋkəl] *vi* **-kled; -kling** : tinter — **~** *n* : tintement *m*

tint ['tɪnt] *n* : teinte *f* — **~** *vt* : teinter

tiny ['taɪni] *adj* **-nier; -niest** : minuscule

tip¹ ['tɪp] *v* **tipped; tipping** *vt* **1** TILT : incliner **2** *or* **~ over** : renverser — *vi* : pencher

tip² *n* END : pointe *f*, bout *m* (d'un crayon)

tip³ *n* ADVICE : conseil *m*, tuyau *m fam* — **~** *vt* **~ off** : prévenir

tip⁴ *vt* : donner un pourboire à — **~** *n* GRATUITY : pourboire *m*

tipsy ['tɪpsi] *adj* **-sier; -est** : gris *fam*, éméché *fam*

tiptoe ['tɪp,to:] *n* **on ~** : sur la pointe des pieds — **~** *vi* **-toed; -toeing** : marcher sur la pointe des pieds

tire¹ ['taɪr] *n* : pneu *m*

tire² *v* **tired; tiring** *vt* : fatiguer — *vi* : se fatiguer — **tired** ['taɪrd] *adj* **1** : fatigué **2 be ~ of** : en avoir assez de — **tiresome** ['taɪrsəm] *adj* : ennuyeux

tissue ['tɪ,ʃu:] *n* **1** : tissu *m* (en biologie) **2** : mouchoir *m* en papier, papier *m* mouchoir *Can*

title ['taɪtəl] *n* : titre *m* — **~** *vt* **-tled; -tling** : intituler

to ['tu:] *prep* **1** : à **2** TOWARD : vers **3** IN ORDER TO : afin de, pour **4** UP TO : jusqu'à **5 a quarter ~ three** : trois heures moins le quart **6 be nice ~ him** : sois gentil envers lui **7 ten ~ the box** : dix par boîte **8 two ~ four years old** : entre deux et quatre ans **9 want ~ do** : vouloir faire — **~** *adv* **1 come ~** : reprendre connaissance **2 go ~ and fro** : aller et venir

toad ['to:d] *n* : crapaud *m*

toast ['to:st] *vt* **1** : griller (du pain), toaster *Can* **2** : boire à la santé de (une personne) — **~** *n* **1** : toast *m*, pain *m* grillé, rôtie *f* **2 drink a ~ to** : porter un toast à — **toaster** ['to:stər] *n* : grille-pain *m*

tobacco [tə'bæko:] *n, pl* **-cos** : tabac *m*

toboggan [tə'bagən] *n* : toboggan *m*, traîne *f Can*

today [tə'deɪ] *adv* : aujourd'hui — **~** *n* : aujourd'hui *m*

toddler ['tadələr] *n* : bambin *m*, -bine *f*

toe ['to:] *n* : orteil *m*, doigt *m* de pied — **toenail** ['to:,neɪl] *n* : ongle *m* d'orteil

together [tə'gɛðər] *adv* **1** : ensemble **2 ~ with** : ainsi que

toil ['tɔɪl] *n* : labeur *m* — **~** *vi* : peiner

toilet ['tɔɪlət] *n* BATHROOM : toilettes *fpl*, toilette *f Can* — **toilet paper** *n* : papier *m* hygiénique — **toiletries** ['tɔɪlətriz] *npl* : articles *mpl* de toilette

token ['to:kən] *n* **1** SIGN : signe *m*, marque *f* **2** : jeton *m* (pour le métro, etc.)

told → **tell**

tolerable ['tɑlərəbəl] *adj* : tolérable — **tolerance** ['tɑlərənts] *n* : tolérance *f* — **tolerant** ['tɑlərənt] *adj* : tolérant — **tolerate** ['tɑlə,reɪt] *vt* -**ated; -ating** : tolérer

toll[1] ['to:l] *n* **1** : péage *m* **2 death ~** : nombre *m* de morts **3 take a ~ on** : affecter

toll[2] *v* RING : sonner

tomato [tə'meɪto, -'mɑ-] *n, pl* -**toes** : tomate *f*

tomb ['tu:m] *n* : tombeau *m* — **tombstone** ['tu:m,sto:n] *n* : pierre *f* tombale

tomorrow [tə'mɑro] *adv* : demain — **~** *n* : demain *m*

ton ['tən] *n* : tonne *f*

tone ['to:n] *n* **1** : ton *m* **2** BEEP : tonalité *f* — **~** *vt* **toned; toning** *or* **~ down** : atténuer

tongs ['tɑŋz, 'tɔŋz] *npl* : pinces *fpl*

tongue ['tʌŋ] *n* : langue *f*

tonic ['tɑnɪk] *n* : tonique *m*

tonight [tə'naɪt] *adv* : ce soir — **~** *n* : ce soir, cette nuit

tonsil ['tɑntsəl] *n* : amygdale *f*

too ['tu:] *adv* **1** ALSO : aussi **2** VERY : très

took → take

tool ['tu:l] *n* : outil *m* — **toolbox** ['tu:l,bɑks] *n* : boîte *f* à outils

toot ['tu:t] *vi* : klaxonner — **~** *n* : coup *m* de klaxon

tooth ['tu:θ] *n, pl* **teeth** ['ti:θ] : dent *f* — **toothache** ['tu:θ,eɪk] *n* : mal *m* de dents — **toothbrush** ['tu:θ,brʌʃ] *n* : brosse *f* à dents — **toothpaste** ['tu:θ,peɪst] *n* : dentifrice *m*

top[1] ['tɑp] *n* **1** : haut *m* **2** SUMMIT : cime *f* **3** COVER : couvercle *m* **4 on ~ of** : sur — **~** *vt* **topped; topping 1** COVER : couvrir **2** SURPASS : dépasser — **~** *adj* **1** : de haut, du haut **2** LEADING : premier, principal **3 the ~ floor** : le dernier étage

top[2] *n* : toupie *f* (jouet)

topic ['tɑpɪk] *n* : sujet *m* — **topical** ['tɑpɪkəl] *adj* : d'actualité

topple ['tɑpəl] *v* -**pled; -pling** *vi* : basculer — *vt* : renverser

torch ['tɔrʧ] *n* : torche *f*

tore → tear[1]

torment ['tɔr,mɛnt] *n* : tourment *m* — **~** ['tɔr,mɛnt, tɔr'-] *vt* : tourmenter

torn → tear[1]

tornado [tɔr'neɪdo] *n, pl* -**does** *or* -**dos** : tornade *f*

torpedo [tɔr'pi:do] *n, pl* -**does** : torpille *f* — **~** *vt* : torpiller

torrent ['tɔrənt] *n* : torrent *m*

torrid ['tɔrɪd] *adj* : torride

torso ['tɔr,so:] *n, pl* -**sos** *or* -**si** [-,si:] : torse *m*

tortoise ['tɔrtəs] *n* : tortue *f* — **tortoiseshell** ['tɔrtəs,ʃɛl] *n* : écaille *f*

tortuous ['tɔrtluəs] *adj* : tortueux

torture ['tɔrʧər] *n* : torture *f* — **~** *vt* -**tured; -turing** : torturer

toss ['tɔs, 'tɑs] *vt* : tirer, lancer — *vi* **~ and turn** : se tourner et se retourner — **~** *n* : lancer *m*

tot ['tɑt] *n* : petit enfant *m*

total ['to:təl] *adj* : total — **~** *n* : total *m* — **~** *vt* -**taled** *or* -**talled; -taling** *or* -**talling** : totaliser, additionner

totalitarian [,to:,tælə'tɛriən] *adj* : totalitaire

touch ['tʌʧ] *vt* **1** : toucher **2** AFFECT : émouvoir **3 ~ up** : retoucher — *vi* : se toucher — **~** *n* **1** : toucher *m* (sens) **2** HINT : touche *f* **3 a ~ of** : un peu de **4 keep in ~** : demeurer en contact — **touchdown** ['tʌʧ,daʊn] *n* **1** : atterrissage *m* (d'un avion) **2** : but *m* (au football américain) — **touchy** ['tʌʧi] *adj* **touchier; touchiest 1** : susceptible **2 a ~ subject** : un sujet épineux

tough ['tʌf] *adj* **1** : dur **2** STRONG : solide **3** STRICT : sévère **4** DIFFICULT : difficile — **toughen** ['tʌfən] *vt or* **~ up** : endurcir — *vi* : s'endurcir — **toughness** ['tʌfnəs] *n* : dureté *f*

tour ['tʊr] *n* **1** : tour *m* (d'une ville, etc.), visite *f* (d'un musée, etc.) **2 go on ~** : faire une tournée — **~** *vi* **1** TRAVEL : voyager **2** : être en tournée (se dit d'une équipe, etc.) — *vt* : visiter — **tourist** ['tʊrɪst, 'tər-] *n* : touriste *mf*

tournament ['tʊrnəmənt, 'tur-] *n* : tournoi *m*

tousle ['taʊzəl] *vt* -**sled; -sling** : ébouriffer (les cheveux)

tout ['taʊt] *vt* : vanter les mérites de

tow ['to:] *vt* : remorquer — **~** *n* : remorquage *m*

toward ['tɔrd, tə'wɔrd] *or* **towards** ['tɔrdz, tə'wɔrdz] *prep* : vers

towel ['taʊəl] *n* : serviette *f*

tower ['taʊər] *n* : tour *f* — **~** *vi* **~ over** : dominer — **towering** ['taʊərɪŋ] *adj* : imposant

town ['taʊn] *n* **1** VILLAGE : village *m* **2** CITY : ville *f* — **township** ['taʊn,ʃɪp] *n* **1** : municipalité *f* **2** : canton *m* Can (division territoriale)

tow truck ['to:,trʌk] *n* : dépanneuse *f*, remorqueuse *f* Can

toxic ['tɑksɪk] *adj* : toxique

toy ['tɔɪ] *n* : jouet *m* — **~** *vi* **~ with** : jouer avec

trace ['treɪs] *n* : trace *f* — **~** *vt* **traced; tracing 1** : tracer, calquer (un dessin) **2** FOLLOW : suivre **3** LOCATE : retrouver

track ['træk] *n* **1** : piste *f* **2** FOOTPRINT : trace *f* **3** *or* **railroad ~** : voie *f* ferrée **4 keep ~ of** : suivre — **~** *vt* : suivre la trace de, suivre la piste de

tract[1] ['trækt] *n* **1** EXPANSE : étendue *f* **2** : appareil *m* (en physiologie)

tract[2] *n* LEAFLET : brochure *f*

traction ['trækʃən] *n* : traction *f*

tractor ['træktər] n 1 : tracteur m 2 or **trac-tor–trailer** : semi-remorque m
trade ['treɪd] n 1 PROFESSION : métier m 2 COMMERCE : commerce m 3 INDUSTRY : industrie f 4 EXCHANGE : échange m — ~ v **traded; trading** vi : faire du commerce — vt ~ **sth for** : échanger qqch pour — **trademark** ['treɪd,mɑrk] n : marque f de fabrique
tradition [trə'dɪʃən] n : tradition f — **traditional** [trə'dɪʃənəl] adj : traditionnel
traffic ['træfɪk] n 1 : circulation f (routière) 2 **drug** ~ : trafic m de drogue — ~ vi **-ficked; -ficking** : trafiquer — **traffic light** n : feu m (de signalisation)
tragedy ['trædʒədi] n, pl **-dies** : tragédie f — **tragic** ['trædʒɪk] adj : tragique
trail ['treɪl] vi 1 DRAG : traîner 2 LAG : être à la traîne 3 ~ **off** : s'estomper — vt 1 : traîner 2 PURSUE : suivre la piste de — ~ n 1 : trace f, piste f 2 PATH : sentier m, chemin m — **trailer** ['treɪlər] n 1 : remorque f 2 CAMPER : caravane f, roulotte f Can
train ['treɪn] n 1 : train m 2 : traîne f (d'une robe) 3 SERIES : suite f, série f 4 ~ **of thought** : fil m des pensées — ~ vt 1 : former, entraîner (un athlète, etc.) 2 AIM : braquer — vi : s'entraîner (aux sports) — **trainer** ['treɪnər] n 1 : entraîneur m, -neuse f (aux sports) 2 : dresseur m, -seuse f (d'animaux)
trait ['treɪt] n : trait m
traitor ['treɪtər] n : traître m, -tresse f
tramp ['træmp] vi : marcher (d'un pas lourd) — ~ n VAGRANT : clochard m, -charde f
trample ['træmpəl] vt **-pled; -pling** : piétiner
trampoline [,træmpə'li:n, 'træmpə,-] n : trampoline m
trance ['trænts] n : transe f
tranquility or **tranquility** [træŋ'kwɪləti] : tranquillité f — **tranquilizer** ['træŋkwə,laɪzər] n : tranquillisant m
transaction [træn'zækʃən] n : transaction f
transcribe [træn'skraɪb] vt **-scribed; -scribing** : transcrire — **transcript** ['træn,skrɪpt] n : transcription f
transfer [trænts'fər, 'trænts,fər] v **-ferred; -ferring** vt 1 : transférer 2 : muter (un employé) — vi 1 : être transféré 2 : changer (d'université) — ~ ['trænts,fər] n 1 : transfert m, mutation f 2 : virement m (de fonds)
transform [trænts'fɔrm] vt : transformer — **transformation** [,træntsfər'meɪʃən] n : transformation f
transfusion [trænts'fju:ʒən] n : transfusion f
transgression [trænts'grɛʃən, trænz-] n : transgression f — **transgress** [trænts'grɛs, trænz-] vt : transgresser
transient ['træntʃənt, 'trænsiənt] adj : transitoire, passager

transit ['træntsɪt, 'trænzɪt] n 1 : transit m 2 TRANSPORTATION : transport m — **transition** [træn'sɪʃən, -'zɪʃ-] n : transition f — **transitive** ['træntsətɪv, 'trænzə-] adj : transitif — **transitory** ['træntsə,tori, 'trænzə-] adj : transitoire, passager
translate [trænts'leɪt, trænz-; 'trænts,-'trænz,-] vt **-lated; -lating** : traduire — **translation** [trænts'leɪʃən, trænz-] n : traduction f — **translator** [trænts'leɪtər, trænz-; 'trænts,-, 'trænz,-] n : traducteur m, -trice f
translucent [trænts'lu:sənt, trænz-] adj : translucide
transmit [trænts'mɪt, trænz-] vt **-mitted; -mitting** : transmettre — **transmission** [trænts'mɪʃən, trænz-] n : transmission f — **transmitter** [trænts'mɪtər, trænz-; 'trænts,-, 'trænz,-] n : émetteur m
transparent [trænts'pærənt] adj : transparent — **transparency** [trænts'pærəntsi] n, pl **-cies** : transparence f
transplant [trænts'plænt] vt : transplanter — ~ ['trænts,plænt] n : transplantation f
transport [trænts'port, 'trænts,-] vt : transporter — ~ ['trænts,port] n : transport m — **transportation** [,træntspər'teɪʃən] n : transport m
transpose [trænts'po:z] vt **-posed; -posing** : transposer
trap ['træp] n : piège m — ~ vt **trapped; trapping** : prendre au piège, attraper — **trapdoor** ['træp'dor] n : trappe f
trapeze [træ'pi:z] n : trapèze m
trappings ['træpɪŋz] npl SIGNS : attributs mpl
trash ['træʃ] n : déchets mpl, ordures fpl
trauma ['trɔmə, 'traʊ-] n : traumatisme m — **traumatic** [trə'mætɪk, trɔ-, traʊ-] adj : traumatisant
travel ['trævəl] vi **-eled** or **-elled; -eling** or **-elling** 1 : voyager 2 SPREAD : circuler, se répandre 3 MOVE : aller, rouler — ~ n : voyages mpl — **traveler** or **traveller** ['trævələr] n : voyageur m, -geuse f
trawl ['trɔl] vi : pêcher au chalut — **trawler** ['trɔlər] n : chalutier m
tray ['treɪ] n : plateau m
treachery ['trɛtʃəri] n, pl **-eries** : traîtrise f — **treacherous** ['trɛtʃərəs] adj 1 : traître 2 DANGEROUS : dangereux
tread ['trɛd] v **trod** ['trɑd]; **trodden** ['trɑdən] or **trod; treading** vt ~ **water** : nager sur place — vi or ~ **on** : marcher sur — ~ n 1 STEP : pas m 2 : bande f de roulement (d'un pneu) — **treadmill** ['trɛd,mɪl] n : exerciseur m
treason ['tri:zən] n : trahison f
treasure ['trɛʒər, 'treɪ-] n : trésor m — ~ vt **-sured; -suring** : tenir beaucoup à — **treas-**

urer ['trɛʒərər, 'treɪ-] *n* : trésorier *m*, -rière *f* — **treasury** ['trɛʒəri, 'treɪ-] *n, pl* **-suries** **1** : trésorerie *f* **2 Treasury** : ministère *m* des Finances

treat ['tri:t] *vt* **1** : traiter **2 ∼ s.o. to sth** : offrir qqch à qqn — **∼** *n* : régal *m*, plaisir *m*

treatise ['tri:ṭəs] *n* : traité *m*

treatment ['tri:tmənt] *n* : traitement *m*

treaty ['tri:ṭi] *n, pl* **-ties** : traité *m*

treble ['trɛbəl] *adj* **1** TRIPLE : triple **2** : de soprano (en musique) — **treble clef** *n* : clé *f* de sol

tree ['tri:] *n* : arbre *m*

trek ['trɛk] *n* : randonnée *f*

trellis ['trɛlɪs] *n* : treillis *m*, treillage *m*

tremble ['trɛmbəl] *vi* **-bled; -bling** : trembler

tremendous [trɪ'mɛndəs] *adj* **1** HUGE : énorme **2** EXCELLENT : formidable

tremor ['trɛmər] *n* : tremblement *m*

trench ['trɛntʃ] *n* : tranchée *f*

trend ['trɛnd] *n* **1** : tendance *f* **2** FASHION : mode *f* — **trendy** ['trɛndi] *adj* **trendier; trendiest** : à la mode

trepidation [ˌtrɛpə'deɪʃən] *n* : inquiétude *f*

trespass ['trɛspəs, -ˌpæs] *vi* : s'introduire illégalement

trial ['traɪəl] *n* **1** HEARING : procès *m* **2** TEST : essai *m* **3** ORDEAL : épreuve *f* — **∼** *adj* : d'essai

triangle ['traɪˌæŋgəl] *n* : triangle *m* — **triangular** [traɪ'æŋgjələr] *adj* : triangulaire

tribe ['traɪb] *n* : tribu *f* — **tribal** ['traɪbəl] *adj* : tribal

tribulation [ˌtrɪbjə'leɪʃən] *n* : tourment *m*

tribunal [traɪ'bju:nəl, trɪ-] *n* : tribunal *m*

tribute ['trɪˌbju:t] *n* : hommage *m* — **tributary** ['trɪbjəˌteri] *n, pl* **-taries** : affluent *m*

trick ['trɪk] *n* **1** PRANK : farce *f*, tour *m* **2** KNACK : truc *m*, astuce *f* — **∼** *vt* : duper — **trickery** ['trɪkəri] *n* : tromperie *f*

trickle ['trɪkəl] *vi* **-led; -ling** DRIP : dégouliner — **∼** *n* : filet *m* (d'eau)

tricky ['trɪki] *adj* **trickier; trickiest** **1** SLY : rusé **2** DIFFICULT : difficile

tricycle ['traɪsəkəl, -ˌsɪkəl] *n* : tricycle *m*

trifle ['traɪfəl] *n* : bagatelle *f*, rien *m* — **trifling** ['traɪflɪŋ] *adj* : insignifiant

trigger ['trɪgər] *n* : détente *f*, gâchette *f* — **∼** *vt* : déclencher

trillion ['trɪljən] *n* : billion *m*

trilogy ['trɪlədʒi] *n, pl* **-gies** : trilogie *f*

trim ['trɪm] *vt* **trimmed; trimming 1** CUT : tailler **2** ADORN : décorer — **∼** *adj* **trimmer; trimmest 1** SLIM : mince **2** NEAT : soigné — **∼** *n* **1** HAIRCUT : coupe *f* **2** DECORATION : garniture *f* — **trimmings** ['trɪmɪŋs] *npl* : garniture *f*

Trinity ['trɪnəṭi] *n* : Trinité *f*

trinket ['trɪŋkət] *n* : babiole *f*

trio ['tri:ˌo:] *n, pl* **trios** : trio *m*

trip ['trɪp] *v* **tripped; tripping** *vi* : trébucher, s'enfarger *Can* — *vt* **1** : faire trébucher (une personne) **2** ACTIVATE : déclencher — **∼** *n* **1** : voyage *m* **2** STUMBLE : trébuchement *m*

tripe ['traɪp] *n* : tripes *fpl* (d'un animal)

triple ['trɪpəl] *v* **-pled; -pling** : tripler — **∼** *n* : triple *m* — **∼** *adj* : triple — **triplets** ['trɪpləts] *npl* : triplés *mpl* — **triplicate** ['trɪplɪkət] *n* **in ∼** : en trois exemplaires

tripod ['traɪˌpɑd] *n* : trépied *m*

trite ['traɪt] *adj* **triter; tritest** : banal

triumph ['traɪəmpf] *n* : triomphe *m* — **∼** *vi* : triompher — **triumphal** [traɪ'ʌmpfəl] *adj* : triomphal — **triumphant** [traɪ'ʌmpfənt] *adj* : triomphant

trivial ['trɪviəl] *adj* : insignifiant — **trivia** ['trɪviə] *ns & pl* : futilités *fpl* — **triviality** [ˌtrɪvi'æləṭi] *n, pl* **-ties** : insignifiance *f*

trod, trodden → **tread**

trolley ['trɑli] *n, pl* **-leys** : tramway *m*

trombone [trɑm'bo:n] *n* : trombone *m*

troop ['tru:p] *n* **1** GROUP : bande *f*, groupe *m* **2 ∼s** *npl* : troupes *fpl* — **trooper** ['tru:pər] *n* **1** : soldat *m* **2** *or* **state ∼** : gendarme *m France*, policier *m*

trophy ['tro:fi] *n, pl* **-phies** : trophée *m*

tropic ['trɑpɪk] *n* **1** : tropique *m* **2 the ∼s** : les tropiques *mpl* — **∼** *or* **tropical** ['trɑpɪkəl] *adj* : tropical

trot ['trɑt] *n* : trot *m* — **∼** *vi* **trotted; trotting** : trotter

trouble ['trʌbəl] *vt* **-bled; -bling 1** WORRY : inquiéter **2** BOTHER : déranger — **∼** *n* **1** PROBLEMS : ennuis *mpl* **2** EFFORT : mal *m*, peine *f* **3 be in ∼** : avoir des ennuis **4 I had ∼ doing it** : j'ai eu du mal à le faire — **troublemaker** ['trʌbəlˌmeɪkər] *n* : fauteur *m*, -trice *f* de troubles — **troublesome** ['trʌbəlsəm] *adj* : gênant, pénible

trough ['trɔf] *n, pl* **troughs** ['trɔfs, 'trɔvz] **1** : abreuvoir *m* (pour les animaux) **2** *or* **feeding ∼** : auge *f*

trousers ['trauzərz] *npl* : pantalon *m*

trout ['traut] *ns & pl* : truite *f*

trowel ['trauəl] *n* : truelle *f* (pour le mortier), déplantoir *m* (pour le jardinage)

truant ['tru:ənt] *n* : élève *mf* absentéiste

truce ['tru:s] *n* : trêve *f*

truck ['trʌk] *n* : camion *m* — **trucker** ['trʌkər] *n* : camionneur *m*, -neuse *f*; routier *m*

trudge ['trʌdʒ] *vi* **trudged; trudging** : marcher péniblement

true ['tru:] *adj* **truer; truest 1** FACTUAL : vrai **2** LOYAL : fidèle **3** GENUINE : authentique

truffle ['trʌfəl] *n* : truffe *f*

truly ['tru:li] *adv* : vraiment

trump ['trʌmp] *n* : atout *m*

trumpet ['trʌmpət] *n* : trompette *f*

trunk ['trʌŋk] *n* **1** STEM, TORSO : tronc *m* **2** : trompe *f* (d'un éléphant) **3** : coffre *m* (d'une voiture) **4** SUITCASE : malle *f* **5 ~s** *npl* : maillot *m* de bain

trust ['trʌst] *n* **1** CONFIDENCE : confiance *f* **2** HOPE : espoir *m* **3** : trust *m* (en finances) **4** **in ~** : par fidéicommis — **~** *vi* **1** HOPE : espérer **2 ~ in** : faire confiance à — *vt* **1** ENTRUST : confier **2 l ~ him** : j'ai confiance en lui — **trustee** [ˌtrʌs'ti:] *n* : fidéicommissaire *mf* — **trustworthy** ['trʌstˌwərði] *adj* : digne de confiance

truth ['tru:θ] *n, pl* **truths** ['tru:ðz, 'tru:θs] : vérité *f* — **truthful** ['tru:θfəl] *adj* : sincère, vrai

try ['traɪ] *v* **tried; trying** *vt* **1** ATTEMPT : essayer **2** : juger (un accusé) **3** TEST : éprouver, mettre à l'épreuve **4** TASTE : goûter — *vi* : essayer — **~** *n, pl* **tries** : essai *m* — **trying** ['traɪɪŋ] *adj* : pénible — **tryout** ['traɪˌaʊt] *n* : essai *m*

tsar ['zɑr, 'tsɑr, 'sɑr] → **czar**

T–shirt ['ti:ˌʃərt] *n* : tee-shirt *m*, t-shirt *m*

tub ['tʌb] *n* **1** VAT : cuve *f* **2** CONTAINER : pot *m* **3** BATHTUB : baignoire *f*

tuba ['tu:bə, 'tju:-] *n* : tuba *m*

tube ['tu:b, 'tju:b] *n* **1** : tube *m* **2** *or* **inner ~** : chambre *f* à air **3 the ~** : la télé

tuberculosis [tʊˌbərkjə'lo:səs, tjʊ-] *n, pl* **-loses** [-ˌsi:z] : tuberculose *f*

tubing ['tu:bɪŋ, 'tju:-] *n* : tubes *mpl* — **tubular** ['tu:bjələr, 'tju:-] *adj* : tubulaire

tuck ['tʌk] *vt* **1** *or* **~ away** : ranger **2 ~ in** : rentrer (une chemise, etc.) — **~** *n* : pli *m*

Tuesday ['tu:zˌdeɪ, 'tju:z-, -di] *n* : mardi *m*

tuft ['tʌft] *n* : touffe *f* (de cheveux, d'herbe, etc.)

tug ['tʌɡ] *vt* **tugged; tugging** *or* **~ at** : tirer sur — **~** *n* : petit coup *m* — **tugboat** ['tʌɡˌbo:t] *n* : remorqueur *m* — **tug-of-war** [ˌtʌɡə'wɔr] *n, pl* **tugs-of-war** : lutte *f* à la corde

tuition [tʊ'ɪʃən, 'tju:-] *n* : frais *mpl* de scolarité

tulip ['tu:lɪp, 'tju:-] *n* : tulipe *f*

tumble ['tʌmbəl] *vi* **-bled; -bling** : tomber — **~** *n* : chute *f* — **tumbler** ['tʌmblər] *n* : verre *m* droit

tummy ['tʌmi] *n, pl* **-mies** : ventre *m*

tumor *or Brit* **tumour** ['tu:mər, 'tju:-] *n* : tumeur *f*

tumult ['tu:ˌmʌlt 'tju:-] *n* : tumulte *m* — **tumultuous** [tʊ'mʌltʃʊəs, tju:-] *adj* : tumultueux

tuna ['tu:nə 'tju:-] *n, pl* **-na** *or* **-nas** : thon *m*

tune ['tu:n, 'tju:n] *n* **1** MELODY : air *m* **2 in ~** : accordé, juste **3 out of ~** : désac-

cordé, faux — **~** *v* **tuned; tuning** *vt* **1** : accorder (un piano, etc.) **2** *or* **~ up** : régler (un moteur) — *vi* **~ in** : se mettre à l'écoute — **tuner** ['tu:nər, 'tju:-] *n* : accordeur *m* (de pianos, etc.)

tunic ['tu:nɪk, 'tju:-] *n* : tunique *f*

Tunisian [tu:'ni:ʒən, tju:'nɪziən] *adj* : tunisien

tunnel ['tʌnəl] *n* : tunnel *m* — **~** *vi* **-neled** *or* **-nelled; -neling** *or* **-nelling** : creuser un tunnel

turban ['tərbən] *n* : turban *m*

turbine ['tərbən, -ˌbaɪn] *n* : turbine *f*

turbulent ['tərbjələnt] *adj* : turbulent — **turbulence** ['tərbjələnts] *n* : turbulence *f*

turf ['tərf] *n* : gazon *m*

turkey ['tərki] *n, pl* **-keys** : dinde *f*

Turkish ['tərkɪʃ] *adj* : turc — **~** *n* : turc *m* (langue)

turmoil ['tərˌmɔɪl] *n* : désarroi *m*, confusion *f*

turn ['tərn] *vt* **1** : tourner **2** SPRAIN : tordre **3 ~ down** REFUSE : refuser **4 ~ down** LOWER : baisser **5 ~ in** : rendre **6 ~ into** : convertir en **7 ~ off** : éteindre (la lumière, etc.), couper (le contact, etc.) **8 ~ out** EXPEL : expulser **9 ~ out** PRODUCE : produire **10 ~ out** → **turn off 11** *or* **~ over** FLIP : retourner **12 ~ over** TRANSFER : remettre **13 ~ s.o.'s stomach** : soulever le cœur à qqn **14 ~ up** RAISE : augmenter — *vi* **1** ROTATE : tourner **2** BECOME : devenir **3** SOUR : tourner **4** CHANGE : se transformer **5 ~ head** : se diriger **6** *or* **~ around** : se retourner **7 ~ in** RETIRE : se coucher **8 ~ in** DELIVER : livrer **9 ~ into** : se changer en **10 ~ out** COME : venir **11 ~ out** RESULT : se terminer **12 ~ out to be** : s'avérer, se révéler **13 ~ up** APPEAR : se présenter — **~** *n* **1** ROTATION : tour *m* **2** CHANGE : changement *m* **3** CURVE : virage *m* **4** DEED : service *m* **5 wait your ~** : attendez votre tour

turnip ['tərnəp] *n* : navet *m*

turnout ['tərnˌaʊt] *n* : participation *f* — **turnover** ['tərnˌo:vər] *n* **1** REVERSAL : renversement *m* **2** : roulement *m* (du personnel) **3 apple ~** : chausson *m* aux pommes — **turnpike** ['tərnˌpaɪk] *n* : autoroute *f* à péage — **turntable** ['tərnˌteɪbəl] *n* : platine *f*

turpentine ['tərpənˌtaɪn] *n* : térébenthine *f*

turret ['tərət] *n* : tourelle *f*

turtle ['tərtəl] *n* : tortue *f* — **turtleneck** ['tərtəlˌnɛk] *n* : col *m* roulé, col *m* montant

tusk ['tʌsk] *n* : défense *f* (d'un animal)

tutor ['tu:tər, 'tju:-] *n* : précepteur *m*, -trice *f*; professeur *m* particulier — **~** *vt* : donner des cours particuliers à

tuxedo [ˌtək'si:ˌdo:] *n, pl* **-dos** *or* **-does** : smoking *m*

TV [ˌti:'vi:, 'ti:ˌvi:] → **television**

twang ['twæŋ] *n* : ton *m* nasillard (de la voix)

tweed ['twiːd] *n* : tweed *m*

tweet ['twiːt] *n* : pépiement *m* — ~ *vi* : pépier

tweezers ['twiːzərz] *ns & pl* : pince *f* à épiler

twelve ['twɛlv] *n* : douze *m* — ~ *adj* : douze — **twelfth** ['twɛlfθ] *n* 1 : douzième *mf* 2 **February** ~ : le douze février — ~ *adj* : douzième

twenty ['twʌnti, 'twɛn-] *n, pl* **-ties** : vingt *m* — ~ *adj* : vingt — **twentieth** ['twʌntiəθ, 'twɛn-] *n* 1 : vingtième *mf* 2 **March** ~ : le vingt mars — ~ *adj* : vingtième

twice ['twaɪs] *adv* 1 : deux fois 2 ~ **as much** : deux fois plus

twig ['twɪg] *n* : brindille *f*

twilight ['twaɪˌlaɪt] *n* : crépuscule *m*

twin ['twɪn] *n* : jumeau *m*, -melle *f* — ~ *adj* : jumeau

twine ['twaɪn] *n* : ficelle *f*

twinge ['twɪndʒ] *n* : élancement *m* (de douleur)

twinkle ['twɪŋkəl] *vi* **-kled; -kling** 1 : scintiller (se dit des étoiles, etc.) 2 : pétiller (se dit des yeux) — ~ *n* : scintillement *m* (des étoiles), pétillement *m* (des yeux)

twirl ['twərl] *vt* : faire tournoyer — *vi* : tournoyer — ~ *n* : tournoiement *m*

twist ['twɪst] *vt* 1 TURN : tourner 2 SPRAIN : tordre 3 DISTORT : déformer — *vi* 1 : serpenter (se dit d'une route) 2 COIL : s'enrouler 3 ~ **and turn** : se tortiller 4 ~ **off** : dévisser — ~ *n* 1 TURN : tour *m* 2 BEND : tournant *m* 3 **a** ~ **of fate** : un coup du sort — **twister** ['twɪstər] → **tornado**

twitch ['twɪtʃ] *vi* : se contracter — ~ *n or* **nervous** ~ : tic *m* (nerveux)

two ['tuː] *n, pl* **twos** : deux *m* — ~ *adj* : deux — **twofold** ['tuːˈfoːld] *adj* : double — ~ *adv* : doublement — **two hundred** *adj* : deux cents

tycoon [taɪˈkuːn] *n* : magnat *m*

tying → **tie**

type ['taɪp] *n* 1 KIND : type *m* 2 : caractère *m* (d'imprimerie) — ~ *v* **typed; typing** : taper (à la machine) — **typewriter** ['taɪpˌraɪtər] *n* : machine *f* à écrire, dactylo *f Can*

typhoon [taɪˈfuːn] *n* : typhon *m*

typical ['tɪpɪkəl] *adj* : typique — **typify** ['tɪpəˌfaɪ] *vt* **-fied; -fying** : être typique de

typist ['taɪpɪst] *n* : dactylo *mf*

typography [taɪˈpɑgrəfi] *n* : typographie *f*

tyranny ['tɪrəni] *n, pl* **-nies** : tyrannie *f* — **tyrant** ['taɪrənt] *n* : tyran *m*

tzar ['zɑr, 'tsɑr, 'sɑr] → **czar**

U

u ['juː] *n, pl* **u's** *or* **us** ['juːz] : u *m*, vingt et unième lettre de l'alphabet

udder ['ʌdər] *n* : pis *m*

UFO [ˌjuːˌɛfˈoː, 'juːˌfoː] *n* (*unidentified flying object*), *pl* **UFO's** *or* **UFOs** : ovni *m*

ugly ['ʌgli] *adj* **-lier; -est** : laid — **ugliness** ['ʌglinəs] *n* : laideur *f*

ulcer ['ʌlsər] *n* : ulcère *f*

ulterior [ˌʌlˈtɪriər] *adj* ~ **motive** : arrière-pensée *f*

ultimate ['ʌltəmət] *adj* 1 : ultime, final 2 SUPREME : suprême — **ultimately** ['ʌltəmətli] *adv* 1 : finalement, en fin de compte 2 EVENTUALLY : par la suite

ultimatum [ˌʌltəˈmeɪtəm, -ˈmɑ-] *n, pl* **-tums** *or* **-ta** [-tə] : ultimatum *m*

ultraviolet [ˌʌltrəˈvaɪələt] *adj* : ultraviolet

umbilical cord [ˌʌmˈbɪlɪkəl] *n* : cordon *m* ombilical

umbrella [ˌʌmˈbrɛlə] *n* : parapluie *m*

umpire ['ʌmˌpaɪr] *n* : arbitre *m* — ~ *vt* **-pired; -piring** : arbitrer

umpteenth ['ʌmpˌtinθ, ˌʌmpˈ-] *adj* : énième

unable [ˌʌnˈeɪbəl] *adj* 1 : incapable 2 **be** ~ **to** : ne pas pouvoir

unabridged [ˌʌnəˈbrɪdʒd] *adj* : intégral

unacceptable [ˌʌnɪkˈsɛptəbəl] *adj* : inacceptable

unaccountable [ˌʌnəˈkaʊntəbəl] *adj* : inexplicable

unaccustomed [ˌʌnəˈkʌstəmd] *adj* **be** ~ **to** : ne pas avoir l'habitude de

unadulterated [ˌʌnəˈdʌltəˌreɪtəd] *adj* : pur, naturel

unaffected [ˌʌnəˈfɛktəd] *adj* 1 : indifférent 2 NATURAL : sans affectation

unafraid [ˌʌnəˈfreɪd] *adj* : sans peur

unaided [ˌʌnˈeɪdəd] *adj* : sans aide

unanimous [juˈnænəməs] *adj* : unanime

unannounced [ˌʌnəˈnaʊnst] *adj* : inattendu, sans se faire annoncer

unarmed [ˌʌnˈɑrmd] *adj* : non armé, sans armes

unassuming [ˌʌnəˈsuːmɪŋ] *adj* : modeste

unattached [ˌʌnəˈtætʃt] *adj* 1 : détaché 2 UNMARRIED : libre

unattractive [ˌʌnəˈtræktɪv] *adj* : peu attrayant

unauthorized [ˌʌnˈɔθəˌraɪzd] *adj* : non autorisé

unavailable [ˌʌnəˈveɪləbəl] *adj* : indisponible

unavoidable [ˌʌnəˈvɔɪdəbəl] *adj* : inévitable

unaware [ˌʌnəˈwær] *adj* **1** : ignorant **2 be ~ of** : ignorer, ne pas être conscient de

unbalanced [ˌʌnˈbælən̯st] *adj* : déséquilibré

unbearable [ˌʌnˈbærəbəl] *adj* : insupportable

unbelievable [ˌʌnbəˈliːvəbəl] *adj* : incroyable

unbending [ˌʌnˈbɛndɪŋ] *adj* : inflexible

unbiased [ˌʌnˈbaɪəst] *adj* : impartial

unborn [ˌʌnˈbɔrn] *adj* : qui n'est pas encore né

unbreakable [ˌʌnˈbreɪkəbəl] *adj* : incassable

unbroken [ˌʌnˈbroːkən] *adj* **1** INTACT : intact **2** CONTINUOUS : continu

unbutton [ˌʌnˈbʌtən] *vt* : déboutonner

uncalled–for [ˌʌnˈkɔldˌfɔr] *adj* : déplacé, injustifié

uncanny [ənˈkæni] *adj* **1** STRANGE : mystérieux, troublant **2** REMARKABLE : remarquable

unceasing [ˌʌnˈsiːsɪŋ] *adj* : incessant

uncertain [ˌʌnˈsərtən] *adj* : incertain — **uncertainty** [ˌʌnˈsərtənti] *n, pl* **-ties** : incertitude *f*

unchanged [ˌʌnˈtʃeɪndʒd] *adj* : inchangé — **unchanging** [ˌʌnˈtʃeɪndʒɪŋ] *adj* : immuable

uncivilized [ˌʌnˈsɪvəˌlaɪzd] *adj* : barbare

uncle [ˈʌŋkəl] *n* : oncle *m*

unclear [ˌʌnˈklɪr] *adj* : peu clair

uncomfortable [ˌʌnˈkʌmpfərtəbəl] *adj* **1** : inconfortable **2** AWKWARD : mal à l'aise

uncommon [ˌʌnˈkɑmən] *adj* : rare, peu commun

uncompromising [ˌʌnˈkɑmprəˌmaɪzɪŋ] *adj* : intransigeant

unconcerned [ˌʌnkənˈsərnd] *adj* : indifférent

unconditional [ˌʌnkənˈdɪʃənəl] *adj* : inconditionnel

unconscious [ˌʌnˈkɑnʃəs] *adj* : inconscient

uncontrollable [ˌʌnkənˈtroːləbəl] *adj* : incontrôlable

unconventional [ˌʌnkənˈvɛntʃənəl] *adj* : peu conventionnel

uncouth [ˌʌnˈkuːθ] *adj* : grossier

uncover [ˌʌnˈkʌvər] *vt* : découvrir

undecided [ˌʌndɪˈsaɪdəd] *adj* : indécis

undeniable [ˌʌndɪˈnaɪəbəl] *adj* : indéniable

under [ˈʌndər] *adv* **1** : en dessous **2** LESS : moins **3** *or* **~ anesthetic** : sous anesthésie — **~** *prep* **1** BELOW, BENEATH : sous, en dessous de **2** ACCORDING TO : d'après, selon

underage [ˌʌndərˈeɪdʒ] *adj* : mineur

underclothes [ˈʌndərˌkloːz, -ˌkloːðz] *npl* → **underwear**

undercover [ˌʌndərˈkʌvər] *adj* : secret

underdeveloped [ˌʌndərdɪˈvɛləpt] *adj* : sous-développé

underestimate [ˌʌndərˈɛstəˌmeɪt] *vt* **-mated; -mating** : sous-estimer

undergo [ˌʌndərˈgoː] *vt* **-went** [-ˈwɛnt]; **-gone** [-ˈgɔn]; **-going** : subir, éprouver

undergraduate [ˌʌndərˈgrædʒuət] *n* : étudiant *m*, -diante *f* de premier cycle; étudiant *m*, -diante *f* qui prépare une licence *France*

underground [ˌʌndərˈgraund] *adv* : sous terre — **~** [ˈʌndərˌgraund] *adj* **1** : souterrain **2** SECRET : clandestin — **~** [ˈʌndərˌgraund] *n* SUBWAY : métro *m*

undergrowth [ˈʌndərˌgroːθ] *n* : sous-bois *m*, broussailles *fpl*

underhanded [ˌʌndərˈhændəd] *adj* SLY : sournois

underline [ˈʌndərˌlaɪn] *vt* **-lined; -lining** : souligner

underlying [ˌʌndərˈlaɪɪŋ] *adj* : sous-jacent

undermine [ˌʌndərˈmaɪn] *vt* **-mined; -mining** : saper, miner

underneath [ˌʌndərˈniːθ] *prep* : sous, au-dessous de — **~** *adv* : en dessous, dessous

underpants [ˈʌndərˌpænts] *npl* : caleçon *m*, slip *m France*

underpass [ˈʌndərˌpæs] *n* : voie *f* inférieure (de l'autoroute), passage *m* souterrain (pour piétons)

underprivileged [ˌʌndərˈprɪvlɪdʒd] *adj* : défavorisé

undershirt [ˈʌndərˌʃərt] *n* : maillot *m* de corps

understand [ˌʌndərˈstænd] *vt* **-stood** [-ˈstud]; **-standing 1** : comprendre **2** BELIEVE : croire — **understandable** [ˌʌndərˈstændəbəl] *adj* : compréhensible — **understanding** [ˌʌndərˈstændɪŋ] *n* **1** : compréhension *f* **2** AGREEMENT : entente *f*, accord *m* — **~** *adj* : compréhensif

understudy [ˈʌndərˌstʌdi] *n, pl* **-dies** : doublure *f* (au théâtre)

undertake [ˌʌndərˈteɪk] *vt* **-took** [-ˈtuk]; **-taken** [-ˈteɪkən]; **-taking** : entreprendre (une tâche), assumer (une responsabilité) — **undertaker** [ˈʌndərˌteɪkər] *n* : entrepreneur *m* de pompes funèbres — **undertaking** [ˈʌndərˌteɪkɪŋ, ˌʌndər-] *n* : entreprise *f*

undertone [ˈʌndərˌtoːn] *n* : voix *f* basse

undertow [ˈʌndərˌtoː] *n* : courant *m* sous-marin

underwater [ˌʌndərˈwɔtər, -ˈwɑ-] *adj* : sous-marin — **~** *adv* : sous l'eau

under way [ˌʌndərˈweɪ] *adv* : en cours, en route

underwear [ˈʌndərˌwær] *n* : sous-vêtements *mpl*

underwent → **undergo**

underworld [ˈʌndərˌwərld] *n or* **criminal ~** : milieu *m*, pègre *f*

undesirable [ˌʌndɪˈzaɪrəbəl] *adj* : indésirable

undisputed [ˌʌndɪˈspjuːtəd] *adj* : incontesté

undo [ˌʌnˈduː] *vt* **-did; -done; -doing 1** UNFASTEN : défaire, détacher **2 ~ a wrong** : réparer un tort

undoubtedly [ˌʌnˈdaʊtədli] *adv* : sans aucun doute

undress [ˌʌnˈdrɛs] *vt* : déshabiller — *vi* : se déshabiller

undue [ˌʌnˈduː, -ˈdjuː] *adj* : excessif, démesuré

undulate [ˈʌndʒəˌleɪt] *vi* **-lated; -lating** : onduler

unduly [ˌʌnˈduːli] *adv* : excessivement

unearth [ˌʌnˈərθ] *vt* : déterrer

uneasy [ˌʌnˈiːzi] *adj* **1** : mal à l'aise, gêné **2** WORRIED : inquiet **3** UNSTABLE : précaire — **uneasily** [ˌʌnˈiːzəli] *adv* : avec inquiétude — **uneasiness** [ˌʌnˈiːzinəs] *n* : inquiétude *f*

uneducated [ˌʌnˈɛdʒəˌkeɪtəd] *adj* : sans éducation

unemployed [ˌʌnɪmˈplɔɪd] *adj* : en chômage, sans travail — **unemployment** [ˌʌnɪmˈplɔɪmənt] *n* : chômage *m*

unequal [ˌʌnˈiːkwəl] *adj* : inégal

uneven [ˌʌnˈiːvən] *adj* **1** : inégal **2** ODD : impair

unexpected [ˌʌnɪkˈspɛktəd] *adj* : inattendu, imprévu

unfailing [ˌʌnˈfeɪlɪŋ] *adj* **1** CONSTANT : infaillible **2** INEXHAUSTIBLE : inépuisable

unfair [ˌʌnˈfær] *adj* : injuste — **unfairly** [ˌʌnˈfærli] *adj* : injustement — **unfairness** [ˌʌnˈfærnəs] *n* : injustice *f*

unfaithful [ˌʌnˈfeɪθfəl] *adj* : infidèle — **unfaithfulness** [ˌʌnˈfeɪθfəlnəs] *n* : infidélité *f*

unfamiliar [ˌʌnfəˈmiljər] *adj* **1** : inconnu, peu familier **2 be ~ with** : mal connaître

unfasten [ˌʌnˈfæsən] *vt* : déboucler (une ceinture)

unfavorable [ˌʌnˈfeɪvərəbəl] *adj* : défavorable

unfeeling [ˌʌnˈfiːlɪŋ] *adj* : insensible

unfinished [ˌʌnˈfɪnɪʃd] *adj* : inachevé

unfit [ˌʌnˈfɪt] *adj* : inapte, impropre

unfold [ˌʌnˈfoːld] *vt* **1** : déplier **2** REVEAL : dévoiler — *vi* : se dérouler

unforeseen [ˌʌnfɔrˈsiːn] *adj* : imprévu

unforgettable [ˌʌnfərˈgɛtəbəl] *adj* : inoubliable

unforgivable [ˌʌnfərˈgɪvəbəl] *adj* : impardonnable

unfortunate [ˌʌnˈfɔrtʃənət] *adj* **1** UNLUCKY : malheureux **2** REGRETTABLE : regrettable, fâcheux — **unfortunately** [ˌʌnˈfɔrtʃənətli] *adv* : malheureusement

unfounded [ˌʌnˈfaʊndəd] *adj* : sans fondement

unfurl [ˌʌnˈfərl] *vt* : déployer

unfurnished [ˌʌnˈfərnɪʃt] *adj* : non meublé

ungainly [ˌʌnˈgeɪnli] *adj* : gauche

ungodly [ˌʌnˈgɑdli, -ˈgɑd-] *adj* UNSEEMLY : indu, impossible

ungrateful [ˌʌnˈgreɪtfəl] *adj* : ingrat

unhappy [ˌʌnˈhæpi] *adj* **-pier; -est 1** SAD : malheureux, triste **2** DISSATISFIED : mécontent — **unhappiness** [ˌʌnˈhæpinəs] *n* : tristesse *f*

unharmed [ˌʌnˈhɑrmd] *adj* : indemne

unhealthy [ˌʌnˈhɛlθi] *adj* **-healthier; -healthiest 1** : insalubre, malsain **2** SICKLY : malade, maladif

unheard-of [ˌʌnˈhərdəv] *adj* : sans précédent, inconnu

unhook [ˌʌnˈhʊk] *vt* **1** REMOVE : décrocher **2** UNFASTEN : dégrafer

unhurt [ˌʌnˈhərt] *adj* : indemne

unicorn [ˈjuːnəˌkɔrn] *n* : licorne *f*

unification [ˌjuːnəfəˈkeɪʃən] *n* : unification *f*

uniform [ˈjuːnəˌfɔrm] *adj* : uniforme — **~** *n* : uniforme *m* — **uniformity** [ˌjuːnəˈfɔrməti] *n, pl* **-ties** : uniformité *f*

unify [ˈjuːnəˌfaɪ] *vt* **-fied; -fying** : unifier

unilateral [ˌjuːnəˈlætərəl] *adj* : unilatéral

uninhabited [ˌʌnɪnˈhæbətəd] *adj* : inhabité

union [ˈjuːnjən] *n* **1** : union *f* **2** *or* **labor ~** : syndicat *m*

unique [jʊˈniːk] *adj* : unique — **uniquely** [jʊˈniːkli] *adv* : exceptionnellement

unison [ˈjuːnəsən, -zən] *n* **in ~** : à l'unisson

unit [ˈjuːnɪt] *n* **1** : unité *f* **2** GROUP : groupe *m*

unite [jʊˈnaɪt] *v* **united; uniting** *vt* : unir — *vi* : s'unir — **unity** [ˈjuːnəti] *n, pl* **-ties** : unité *f*

universe [ˈjuːnəˌvərs] *n* : univers *m* — **universal** [ˌjuːnəˈvərsəl] *adj* : universel

university [ˌjuːnəˈvərsəti] *n, pl* **-ties** : université *f*

unjust [ˌʌnˈdʒʌst] *adj* : injuste — **unjustified** [ˌʌnˈdʒʌstəˌfaɪd] *adj* : injustifié

unkempt [ˌʌnˈkɛmpt] *adj* : en désordre, négligé

unkind [ˌʌnˈkaɪnd] *adj* : peu aimable, pas gentil — **unkindness** [ˌʌnˈkaɪndnəs] *n* : méchanceté *f*

unknown [ˌʌnˈnoːn] *adj* : inconnu

unlawful [ˌʌnˈlɔfəl] *adj* : illégal

unless [ənˈlɛs] *conj* : à moins que, à moins de

unlike [ˌʌnˈlaɪk] *adj* : différent — **~** *prep* **1** : différent de **2** : contrairement à — **unlikelihood** [ˌʌnˈlaɪkliˌhʊd] *n* : improbabilité *f* —

unlimited 356

unlikely [,ʌn'laɪkli] *adj* **-lier; -liest** : improbable

unlimited [,ʌn'lɪmət̬əd] *adj* : illimité

unload [,ʌn'loːd] *vt* : décharger

unlock [,ʌn'lɑk] *vt* : ouvrir, débarrer *Can* (une porte, etc.)

unlucky [,ʌn'lʌki] *adj* **-luckier; -luckiest 1** : malchanceux **2** : qui porte malheur (se dit d'un numéro)

unmarried [,ʌn'mærid] *adj* : célibataire

unnecessary [,ʌn'nɛsə,sɛri] *adj* : inutile

unnerving [,ʌn'nərvɪŋ] *adj* : déconcertant

unnoticed [,ʌn'noːt̬əst] *adj* : inaperçu

unoccupied [,ʌn'ɑkjə,paɪd] *adj* **1** IDLE : inoccupé **2** EMPTY : libre

unofficial [,ʌnə'fɪʃəl] *adj* : officieux, non officiel

unpack [,ʌn'pæk] *vi* : défaire ses bagages

unparalleled [,ʌn'pærə,lɛld] *adj* : sans égal, sans pareil

unpleasant [,ʌn'plɛzənt] *adj* : désagréable

unplug [,ʌn'plʌg] *vt* **-plugged; -plugging 1** UNCLOG : déboucher **2** DISCONNECT : débrancher

unpopular [,ʌn'pɑpjələr] *adj* : impopulaire

unprecedented [,ʌn'prɛsə,dɛnt̬əd] *adj* : sans précédent

unpredictable [,ʌnprɪ'dɪktəbəl] *adj* : imprévisible

unprepared [,ʌnpri'pærd] *adj* : mal préparé

unqualified [,ʌn'kwɑlə,faɪd] *adj* : non qualifié

unquestionable [,ʌn'kwɛstʃənəbəl] *adj* : incontestable

unravel [,ʌn'rævəl] *vt* **-eled** *or* **-elled; -eling** *or* **elling** : démêler, dénouer

unreal [,ʌn'riːl] *adj* : irréel — **unrealistic** [,ʌn,riːə'lɪstɪk] *adj* : irréaliste

unreasonable [,ʌn'riːzənəbel] *adj* : déraisonnable

unrecognizable [,ʌn'rɛkəg,naɪzəb'l] *adj* : méconnaissable

unrelated [,ʌnri'leɪt̬əd] *adj* : sans rapport

unrelenting [,ʌnri'lɛntɪŋ] *adj* : implacable

unreliable [,ʌnri'laɪəbəl] *adj* : peu fiable, peu sûr

unrepentant [,ʌnri'pɛntənt] *adj* : impénitent

unrest [,ʌn'rɛst] *n* : agitation *f,* troubles *mpl*

unripe [,ʌn'raɪp] *adj* : pas mûr, vert

unrivaled *or* **unrivalled** [,ʌn'raɪvəld] *adj* : sans égal, incomparable

unroll [,ʌn'roːl] *vt* : dérouler

unruly [,ʌn'ruːli] *adj* : indiscipliné

unsafe [,ʌn'seɪf] *adj* : dangereux

unsatisfactory [,ʌn,sæt̬əs'fæktəri] *adj* : peu satisfaisant

unscrew [,ʌn'skruː] *vt* : dévisser

unseemly [,ʌn'siːmli] *adj* **-lier; -est** : inconvenant

unseen [,ʌn'siːn] *adj* : invisible

unsettle [,ʌn'sɛt̬əl] *vt* **-tled; -tling** DISTURB : perturber — **unsettled** [,ʌn'sɛt̬əld] *adj* **1** UNSTABLE : instable **2** DISTURBED : troublé

unsightly [,ʌn'saɪtli] *adj* : laid

unskilled [,ʌn'skɪld] *adj* : non spécialisé — **unskillful** [,ʌn'skɪlfəl] *adj* : malhabile

unsound [,ʌn'saʊnd] *adj* : peu judicieux

unspeakable [,ʌn'spiːkəbəl] *adj* **1** : indicible **2** TERRIBLE : atroce

unstable [,ʌn'steɪbəl] *adj* : instable

unsteady [,ʌn'stɛdi] *adj* **1** : instable **2** SHAKY : tremblant

unsuccessful [,ʌnsək'sɛsfəl] *adj* **1** : infructueux **2 be ~** : échouer

unsuitable [,ʌn'suːt̬əbəl] *adj* : qui ne convient pas, inapproprié — **unsuited** [,ʌn'suːt̬əd] *adj* : inapte

unsure [,ʌn'ʃʊr] *adj* **1** : incertain **2 be ~ of oneself** : manquer de confiance en soi

unsuspecting [,ʌnsə'spɛktɪŋ] *adj* : qui ne se doute de rien

unthinkable [,ʌn'θɪŋkəbəl] *adj* : impensable, inconcevable

untidy [,ʌn'taɪdi] *adj* **-dier; -est** : en désordre

untie [,ʌn'taɪ] *vt* **-tied; -tying** *or* **-tieing** : dénouer, défaire

until [,ʌn'tɪl] *prep* **1** UP TO : jusqu'à **2** BEFORE : avant — **~** *conj* : jusqu'à ce que, avant que, avant de

untimely [,ʌn'taɪmli] *adj* **1** : prématuré **2** INOPPORTUNE : déplacé

untoward [,ʌn'tord, -'toːərd, -tə'word] *adj* : fâcheux

untroubled [,ʌn'trʌbəld] *adj* **1** : tranquille **2 be ~ by** : ne pas être affecté par

untrue [,ʌn'truː] *adj* : faux

unused *adj* [,ʌn'juːzd, *in sense 1 usually* -'juːst] **1** UNACCUSTOMED : pas habitué **2** NEW : neuf, nouveau

unusual [,ʌn'juːʒʊəl] *adj* : peu commun, rare — **unusually** [,ʌn'juːʒʊəli] *adv* : exceptionnellement

unveil [,ʌn'veɪl] *vt* : dévoiler

unwanted [,ʌn'wɑnt̬əd] *adj* : non désiré

unwarranted [,ʌn'wɔrəntəd] *adj* : injustifié

unwelcome [,ʌn'wɛlkəm] *adj* : inopportun

unwell [,ʌn'wɛl] *adj* : indisposé

unwieldy [,ʌn'wiːldi] *adj* : encombrant

unwilling [,ʌn'wɪlɪŋ] *adj* : peu disposé — **unwillingly** [,ʌn'wɪlɪŋli] *adv* : à contrecœur

unwind [,ʌn'waɪnd] *v* **-wound; -winding** *vt* : dérouler — *vi* **1** : se dérouler **2** RELAX : se détendre

unwise [,ʌn'waɪz] *adj* : imprudent

unworthy [,ʌn'wərði] *adj* **~ of** : indigne de

unwrap [,ʌn'ræp] *vt* **-wrapped; -wrapped** : déballer

up ['ʌp] *adv* **1** ABOVE : en haut **2** UPWARDS : vers le haut **3 farther ~** : plus loin **4 go ~** : augmenter, monter **5 speak ~** : par-

ler plus fort **6 stand** ~ : se lever **7** ~
until : jusqu'à — ~ *adj* **1** AWAKE : levé **2**
INCREASING : qui augmente **3** UP-TO-DATE
: au courant, à jour **4** FINISHED : fini **5 be**
~ **for** : être prêt pour **6 what's** ~?
: qu'est-ce qui se passe? — ~ *prep* **1** : en
haut de **2 go** ~ : monter **3 sail** ~ **the**
river : remonter la rivière en bateau **4** ~ **to**
: jusqu'à — ~ *v* upped; upping *vt* : augmenter — *vi* ~ **and leave** : partir sans mot
dire

upbringing [ˈʌpˌbrɪŋɪŋ] *n* : éducation *f*
upcoming [ˌʌpˈkʌmɪŋ] *adj* : prochain, à
venir
update [ˌʌpˈdeɪt] *vt* -dated; -dating : mettre
à jour — ~ [ˈʌpˌdeɪt] *n* : mise *f* à jour
upgrade [ˈʌpˌgreɪd, ˌʌpˈ-] *vt* -graded;
-grading **1** IMPROVE : améliorer **2** PRO-
MOTE : promouvoir
upheaval [ˌʌpˈhiːvəl] *n* : bouleversement *m*
uphill [ˌʌpˈhɪl] *adv* **go** ~ : monter — ~
[ˈʌpˌhɪl] *adj* **1** ASCENDING : qui monte **2**
DIFFICULT : pénible
uphold [ˌʌpˈhoːld] *vt* -held; -holding
: soutenir, maintenir
upholstery [ˌʌpˈhoːlstəri] *n, pl* -steries
: rembourrage *m*
upkeep [ˈʌpˌkiːp] *n* : entretien *m*
upon [əˈpɔn, əˈpɑn] *prep* **1** : sur **2** ~ leaving : en partant
upper [ˈʌpər] *adj* : supérieur
upper class *n* : aristocratie *f*
upper hand *n* **have the** ~ : avoir le dessus
uppermost [ˈʌpərˌmoːst] *adj* : le plus haut,
le plus élevé
upright [ˈʌpˌraɪt] *adj* : droit — ~ *n* : montant *m* (en construction)
uprising [ˈʌpˌraɪzɪŋ] *n* : soulèvement *m*
uproar [ˈʌpˌroːr] *n* : tumulte *m*
uproot [ˌʌpˈruːt, -ˈrʊt] *vt* : déraciner
upset [ˌʌpˈsɛt] *vt* -set; -setting **1** OVER-
TURN : renverser **2** DISRUPT : déranger **3**
ANNOY : ennuyer — ~ *adj* **1** DISTRESSED
: bouleversé **2** ANNOYED : ennuyé, vexé **3**
have an ~ **stomach** : avoir l'estomac
dérangé — ~ [ˈʌpˌsɛt] *n* : bouleversement
m
upshot [ˈʌpˌʃɑt] *n* : résultat *m*
upside down *adv* **1** : à l'envers **2 turn** ~
: mettre sens dessus dessous — **upside-**
down [ˌʌpˌsaɪdˈdaʊn] *adj* : à l'envers
upstairs [ˌʌpˈstærz] *adv* : en haut — ~ [ˈʌp-
ˌstærz, ˌʌpˈ-] *adj* : d'en haut, à l'étage — ~
[ˈʌpˌstærz, ˌʌpˈ-] *ns & pl* : étage *m*
upstart [ˈʌpˌstɑrt] *n* : arriviste *mf*
upstream [ˈʌpˈstriːm] *adv* : en amont
up–to–date [ˌʌptəˈdeɪt] *adj* **1** : à jour **2**
MODERN : moderne
uptown [ˈʌpˈtaʊn] *adv* : dans les quartiers
résidentiels

upturn [ˈʌpˌtərn] *n* : amélioration *f*, reprise *f*
(économique)
upward [ˈʌpwərd] *or* **upwards** [-wərdz] *adv*
1 : vers le haut **2** ~ **of** : plus de — **upward**
adj : ascendant
uranium [jʊˈreɪniəm] *n* : uranium *m*
Uranus [jʊˈreɪnəs, ˈjʊrənəs] *n* : Uranus *f*
urban [ˈərbən] *adj* : urbain
urbane [ˌərˈbeɪn] *adj* : raffiné, courtois
urge [ˈərdʒ] *vt* **urged; urging** : pousser, inciter — ~ *n* **1** DESIRE : envie *f* **2** IMPULSE
: pulsion *f* — **urgency** [ˈərdʒəntsi] *n, pl*
-cies : urgence *f* — **urgent** [ˈərdʒənt] *adj* **1**
: urgent **2 be** ~ : presser
urinal [ˈjʊrənəl, *esp Brit* jʊˈraɪnəl] *n* : urinoir
m
urine [ˈjʊrən] *n* : urine *f* — **urinate** [ˈjʊrə-
ˌneɪt] *vi* -nated; -nating : uriner
urn [ˈərn] *n* : urne *f*
us [ˈʌs] *pron* : nous
usable [ˈjuːzəbəl] *adj* : utilisable
usage [ˈjuːsɪdʒ, -zɪdʒ] *n* : usage *m*
use [ˈjuːz] *v* used [ˈjuːzd; *in phrase "used*
to" usually ˈjuːstuː]; using *vt* **1** : employer,
utiliser, se servir de **2** CONSUME : consommer **3** ~ **up** : épuiser — *vi* **she** ~**d to**
dance : elle dansait avant — ~ [ˈjuːs] *n* **1**
: emploi *m*, usage *m* **2** USEFULNESS : utilité
f **3 in** ~ : occupé **4 what's the** ~? : à
quoi bon? — **used** [ˈjuːzd] *adj* **1** SECOND-
HAND : d'occasion **2 be** ~ **to** : avoir
l'habitude de, être habitué à — **useful** [ˈjuː-
sfəl] *adj* : utile, pratique — **usefulness**
[ˈjuːsfəlnəs] *n* : utilité *f* — **useless** [ˈjuːsləs]
adj : inutile — **user** [ˈjuːzər] *n* : usager *m*;
utilisateur *m*, -trice *f*
usher [ˈʌʃər] *vt* **1** : conduire, accompagner
2 ~ **in** : inaugurer — ~ *n* : huissier *m* (à
un tribunal); placeur *m*, -ceuse *f* (au théâtre)
usual [ˈjuːʒʊəl] *adj* **1** : habituel **2 as** ~
: comme d'habitude — **usually** [ˈjuːʒʊəli]
adv : habituellement, d'habitude
usurp [jʊˈsərp, -ˈzərp] *vt* : usurper
utensil [jʊˈtɛntsəl] *n* : ustensile *m*
uterus [ˈjuːtərəs] *n, pl* uteri [-ˌraɪ] : utérus *m*
utility [juːˈtɪləti] *n, pl* -ties **1** : utilité *f* **2** *or*
public ~ : service *m* public
utilize [ˈjuːtəˌlaɪz] *vt* -lized; -lizing : utiliser
utmost [ˈʌtˌmoːst] *adj* **1** FARTHEST : extrême **2 of** ~ **importance** : de la plus
haute importance — ~ *n* **do one's** ~
: faire tout son possible
utopia [jʊˈtoːpiə] *n* : utopie *f* — **utopian** [jʊ-
ˈtoːpiən] *adj* : utopique
utter[1] [ˈʌtər] *adj* : absolu, total
utter[2] *vt* : émettre (un son), pousser (un cri)
— **utterance** [ˈʌtərənts] *n* : déclaration *f*,
paroles *fpl*
utterly [ˈʌtərli] *adv* : complètement

V

v [ˈviː] *n, pl* **v's** *or* **vs** [ˈviːz] : v *m*, vingt-deuxième lettre de l'alphabet

vacant [ˈveɪkənt] *adj* **1** AVAILABLE : libre **2** UNOCCUPIED : vacant — **vacancy** [ˈveɪkəntsi] *n, pl* **-cies 1** : chambre *f* disponible **2** : poste *m* vacant **3** no ~ : complet

vacate [ˈveɪˌkeɪt] *vt* **-cated; -cating** : quitter

vacation [veɪˈkeɪʃən, və-] *n* : vacances *fpl*

vaccination [ˌvæksəˈneɪʃən] *n* : vaccination *f* — **vaccinate** [ˈvæksəˌneɪt] *vt* **-nated; -nating** : vacciner — **vaccine** [vækˈsiːn, ˈvækˌ-] *n* : vaccin *m*

vacuum [ˈvæˌkjuːm, -kjəm] *n, pl* **vacuums** *or* **vacua** [ˈvækjuə] : vide *m* — ~ *vt* : passer l'aspirateur sur — **vacuum cleaner** *n* : aspirateur *m*, balayeuse *f Can*

vagina [vəˈdʒaɪnə] *n, pl* **-nae** [-ˌniː, -ˌnaɪ] *or* **-nas** : vagin *m*

vagrant [ˈveɪgrənt] *n* : vagabond *m*, -bonde *f*

vague [ˈveɪg] *adj* **vaguer; vaguest** : vague

vain [ˈveɪn] *adj* **1** FUTILE : vain **2** CONCEITED : vaniteux

valentine [ˈvælənˌtaɪn] *n* : carte *f* de Saint-Valentin

valiant [ˈvæljənt] *adj* : vaillant

valid [ˈvæləd] *adj* : valable, valide — **validate** [ˈvæləˌdeɪt] *vt* **-dated; -dating** : valider

valley [ˈvæli] *n, pl* **-leys** : vallée *f*

valor *or Brit* **valour** [ˈvælər] *n* : bravoure *f*

value [ˈvælˌjuː] *n* : valeur *f* — ~ *vt* **valued; valuing 1** : estimer, évaluer **2** APPRECIATE : apprécier — **valuable** [ˈvæljuəbəl, -jəbəl] *adj* **1** : de valeur **2** WORTHWHILE : précieux — **valuables** [ˈvæljuəbəlz, -jəbəlz] *npl* : objets *mpl* de valeur

valve [ˈvælv] *n* : valve *f* (d'un pneu), soupape *f*

vampire [ˈvæmˌpaɪr] *n* : vampire *m*

van [ˈvæn] *n* : camionnette *f*, fourgonnette *f*

vandal [ˈvændəl] *n* : vandale *mf* — **vandalism** [ˈvændəˌlɪzəm] *n* : vandalisme *m* — **vandalize** [ˈvændəˌlaɪz] *vt* **-ized; -izing** : saccager

vane [ˈveɪn] *n or* **weather ~** : girouette *f*

vanguard [ˈvænˌgɑrd] *n* : avant-garde *f*

vanilla [vəˈnɪlə, -ˈnɛ-] *n* : vanille *f*

vanish [ˈvænɪʃ] *vi* : disparaître

vanity [ˈvænəti] *n, pl* **-ties** : vanité *f*

vantage point [ˈvæntɪdʒ] *n* : point *m* de vue

vapor [ˈveɪpər] *n* : vapeur *f*

variable [ˈvɛriəbəl] *adj* : variable — ~ *n* : variable *f* — **variant** [ˈvɛriənt] *n* : variante *f* — **variation** [ˌvɛriˈeɪʃən] *n* : variation *f* —

varied [ˈvɛrid] *adj* : varié, divers — **variety** [vəˈraɪəti] *n, pl* **-eties 1** DIVERSITY : variété *f* **2** SORT : espèce *f*, sorte *f* — **various** [ˈvɛriəs] *adj* : divers, varié

varnish [ˈvɑrnɪʃ] *n* : vernis *m* — ~ *vt* : vernir

vary [ˈvɛri] *v* **varied; varying** : varier

vase [ˈveɪs, ˈveɪz, ˈvɑz] *n* : vase *m*

vast [ˈvæst] *adj* : vaste — **vastness** [ˈvæstnəs] *n* : immensité *f*

vat [ˈvæt] *n* : cuve *f*, bac *m*

vault [ˈvɔlt] *n* **1** ARCH : voûte *f* **2** *or* **bank ~** : chambre *f* forte

VCR [ˌviːˌsiːˈɑr] *n* (videocassette recorder) : magnétoscope *m*

veal [ˈviːl] *n* : veau *m*

veer [ˈvɪr] *vi* : virer

vegetable [ˈvɛdʒtəbəl, ˈvɛdʒətə-] *adj* **1** : végétal **2** ~ **soup** : soupe *f* aux légumes — ~ *n* : légume *m* — **vegetarian** [ˌvɛdʒəˈtɛriən] *n* : végétarien *m*, -rienne *f* — **vegetation** [ˌvɛdʒəˈteɪʃən] *n* : végétation *f*

vehement [ˈviːəmənt] *adj* : véhément

vehicle [ˈviːəkəl, ˈviːˌhɪkəl] *n* : véhicule *m*

veil [ˈveɪl] *n* : voile *m* — ~ *vt* : voiler

vein [ˈveɪn] *n* **1** : veine *f* **2** : filon *m* (d'un minéral, etc.) **3** : nervure *f* (d'une feuille)

velocity [vəˈlɑsəti] *n, pl* **-ties** : vélocité *f*

velvet [ˈvɛlvət] *n* : velours *m* — **velvety** [ˈvɛlvəti] *adj* : velouté

vending machine [ˈvɛndɪŋ-] *n* : distributeur *m* automatique

vendor [ˈvɛndər] *n* : vendeur *m*, -deuse *f*

veneer [vəˈnɪr] *n* **1** : placage *m* (de bois) **2** FACADE : vernis *m*

venerable [ˈvɛnərəbəl] *adj* : vénérable — **venerate** [ˈvɛnəˌreɪt] *vt* **-ated; -ating** : vénérer

venereal [vəˈnɪriəl] *adj* : vénérien

venetian blind [vəˈniːʃən] *n* : store *m* vénitien

vengeance [ˈvɛndʒənts] *n* **1** : vengeance *f* **2** **take ~ on** : se venger sur — **vengeful** [ˈvɛndʒfəl] *adj* : vengeur, vindicatif

venison [ˈvɛnəsən, -zən] *n* : venaison *f*

venom [ˈvɛnəm] *n* : venin *m* — **venomous** [ˈvɛnəməs] *adj* : venimeux

vent [ˈvɛnt] *vt* : décharger — ~ *n* **1** : orifice *m*, conduit *m* **2** *or* **air ~** : bouche *f* d'aération — **ventilate** [ˈvɛntəˌleɪt] *vt* **-lated; -lating** : ventiler — **ventilation** [ˌvɛntəˈleɪʃən] *n* : ventilation *f*

venture [ˈvɛntʃər] *v* **-tured; -turing** *vt* RISK : risquer — *vi or* ~ **out** : s'aventurer — ~ *n* : entreprise *f*

Venus ['vi:nəs] *n* : Vénus *f*

veranda *or* **verandah** [və'rændə] *n* : véranda *f*

verb ['vərb] *n* : verbe *m* — **verbal** ['vərbəl] *adj* : verbal — **verbatim** [vər'beitəm] *adv & adj* : mot pour mot

verdict ['vərdikt] *n* : verdict *m*

verge ['vərdʒ] *n* **1** EDGE : bordure *f* **2 on the ~ of** : sur le point de

verify ['verə,fai] *vt* -**fied**; -**fying** : vérifier

vermin ['vərmən] *ns & pl* : vermine *f*

versatile ['vərsətəl] *adj* : polyvalent

verse ['vərs] *n* **1** STANZA : strophe *f* **2** PO-ETRY : vers *mpl* **3** : verset *m* (de la Bible) — **versed** ['vərst] *adj* **be well ~ in** : être versé dans

version ['vərʒən] *n* : version *f*

versus ['vərsəs] *prep* : contre

vertebra ['vərtəbrə] *n, pl* -**brae** [-,brei, -,bri:] *or* -**bras** : vertèbre *f*

vertical ['vərtikəl] *adj* : vertical — **~** *n* : verticale *f*

vertigo ['vərti,go:] *n, pl* -**goes** *or* -**gos** : vertige *m*

very ['veri] *adv* **1** : très **2 ~ much** : beaucoup — **~** *adj* **1** EXACT : même **2 at the ~ least** : tout au moins **3 the ~ thought!** : quelle idée!

vessel ['vesəl] *n* **1** : vaisseau *m* **2** CON-TAINER : récipient *m*

vest ['vest] *n* : gilet *m*

vestige ['vestidʒ] *n* : vestige *m*

veteran ['vetərən, 'vetrən] *n* : vétéran *m*, ancien combattant *m*

veterinarian [,vetərə'neriən, ,vetrə-] *n* : vétérinaire *mf*

veto ['vi:to] *n, pl* -**toes** : veto *m* — **~** *vt* : mettre son veto à

vex ['veks] *vt* **vexed; vexing** : vexer, contrarier

via ['vaiə, 'vi:ə] *prep* : via, par

viable ['vaiəbəl] *adj* : viable

vial ['vaiəl] *n* : ampoule *f*

vibrant ['vaibrənt] *adj* : vibrant — **vibrate** ['vai,breit] *vi* -**brated; -brating** : vibrer — **vibration** [vai'breiʃən] *n* : vibration *f*

vicar ['vikər] *n* : vicaire *m*

vice ['vais] *n* : vice *m*

vice president *n* : vice-président *m*, -dente *f*

vice versa [,vaisi'vərsə, ,vais'vər-] *adv* : vice versa

vicinity [və'sinəti] *n, pl* -**ties** : environs *mpl*

vicious ['viʃəs] *adj* **1** SAVAGE : brutal **2** MA-LICIOUS : méchant

victim ['viktəm] *n* : victime *f*

victor ['viktər] *n* : vainqueur *m* — **victorious** [vik'to:riəs] *adj* : victorieux — **victory** ['viktəri] *n, pl* -**ries** : victoire *f*

video ['vidi,o:] *n* : vidéo *f* — **~** *adj* : vidéo — **videocassette** [,vidioka'set] *n* : vidéo-

cassette *f* — **videotape** ['vidio,teip] *n* : bande *f* vidéo — **~** *vt* -**taped; -taping** : enregistrer (sur magnétoscope)

vie ['vai] *vi* **vied; vying** ['vaiiŋ] **~ for** : lutter pour

Vietnamese [vi,etnə'mi:z, -'mi:s] *adj* : vietnamien

view ['vju:] *n* **1** : vue *f* **2** OPINION : opinion *f*, avis *m* **3 come into ~** : apparaître **4 in ~ of** : vu, étant donné — **~** *vt* **1** : voir **2** CONSIDER : considérer — **viewer** ['vju:ər] *n* *or* **television ~** : téléspectateur *m*, -trice *f* — **viewpoint** ['vju:,pɔint] *n* : point *m* de vue

vigil ['vidʒəl] *n* : veille *f* — **vigilance** ['vidʒələnts] *n* : vigilance *f* — **vigilant** ['vidʒələnt] *adj* : vigilant, attentif

vigor *or* *Brit* **vigour** ['vigər] *n* : vigueur *f* — **vigorous** ['vigərəs] *adj* : vigoureux

vile ['vail] *adj* **viler; vilest 1** BASE : vil **2** AWFUL : abominable, exécrable

villa ['vilə] *n* : villa *f*

village ['vilidʒ] *n* : village *m* — **villager** ['vilidʒər] *n* : villageois *m*, -geoise *f*

villain ['vilən] *n* : scélérat *m*, -rate *f*; méchant *m*, -chante *f*

vindicate ['vində,keit] *vt* -**cated; -cating** : justifier

vindictive [vin'diktiv] *adj* : vindicatif

vine ['vain] *n* : vigne *f*

vinegar ['vinigər] *n* : vinaigre *m*

vineyard ['vinjərd] *n* : vignoble *m*

vintage ['vintidʒ] *n* **1** *or* **~ wine** : vin *m* de grand cru **2** *or* **~ year** : millésime *m*

vinyl ['vainəl] *n* : vinyle *m*

violate ['vaiə,leit] *vt* -**lated; -lating** : violer — **violation** [,vaiə'leiʃən] *n* : violation *f*

violence ['vaiələnts] *n* : violence *f* — **violent** ['vaiələnt] *adj* : violent

violet ['vaiələt] *adj* : violet — **~** *n* **1** : violette *f* (plante) **2** : violet *m* (couleur)

violin [,vaiə'lin] *n* : violon *m* — **violinist** [,vaiə'linist] *n* : violoniste *mf*

VIP [,vi:,ai'pi:] *n, pl* **VIPs** [-'pi:z] (*very important person*) : personnage *m* de marque

viper ['vaipər] *n* : vipère *f*

virgin ['vərdʒən] *adj* : vierge — **~** *n* : vierge *f* — **virginity** [vər'dʒinəti] *n, pl* -**ties** : virginité *f*

virile ['virəl, -,ail] *adj* : viril

virtual ['vərtʃuəl] *adj* : virtuel (en informatique) — **virtually** ['vərtʃuəli] *adv* : pratiquement

virtue ['vər,tʃu:] *n* **1** : vertu *f* **2 by ~ of** : en raison de

virtuoso [,vərtʃu'o:,so:, -,zo:] *n, pl* -**sos** *or* -**si** [-,si:, -,zi:] : virtuose *mf*

virtuous ['vərtʃuəs] *adj* : vertueux

virulent ['virələnt, -jələnt] *adj* : virulent

virus ['vairəs] *n* : virus *m*

visa ['vi:zə, -sə] n : visa m

viscous ['vɪskəs] adj : visqueux

vise or Brit **vice** ['vaɪs] n : étau m

visible ['vɪzəbəl] adj : visible — **visibility** [ˌvɪzə'bɪləti] n, pl **-ties** : visibilité f

vision ['vɪʒən] n : vision f — **visionary** ['vɪʒəˌnɛri] adj : visionnaire

visit ['vɪzət] vt : rendre visite à (qqn), visiter (un lieu) — ~ n : visite f — **visitor** ['vɪzətər] n : visiteur m, -teuse f

visor ['vaɪzər] n : visière f

vista ['vɪstə] n : vue f

visual ['vɪʒʊəl] adj : visuel — **visualize** ['vɪʒʊəˌlaɪz] vt **-ized; -izing** : visualiser

vital ['vaɪtəl] adj 1 : vital 2 ESSENTIAL : essentiel — **vitality** [vaɪ'tæləti] n, pl **-ties** : vitalité f

vitamin ['vaɪtəmən] n : vitamine f

vivacious [və'veɪʃəs, vaɪ-] adj : vif, animé

vivid ['vɪvəd] adj : vivant, vif

vocabulary [voː'kæbjəˌlɛri] n, pl **-laries** : vocabulaire m

vocal ['voːkəl] adj 1 : vocal 2 OUTSPOKEN : franc — **vocal cords** npl : cordes fpl vocales — **vocalist** ['voːkəlɪst] n : chanteur m, -teuse f

vocation [voʹkeɪʃən] n 1 : vocation f (religieuse) 2 OCCUPATION : profession f, métier m — **vocational** [voʹkeɪʃənəl] adj : professionnel

vodka ['vadkə] n : vodka m

vogue ['voːg] n 1 : vogue f, mode f 2 **be in** ~ : être à la mode

voice ['vɔɪs] n : voix f — ~ ['vɔɪs] vt **voiced; voicing** : exprimer, formuler

void ['vɔɪd] adj 1 NULL : nul 2 ~ **of** : dépourvu de — ~ n : vide m — ~ vt ANNUL : annuler

volatile ['valətəl] adj : volatil, instable

volcano [val'keɪˌnoː, val-] n, pl **-noes** or **-nos** : volcan m — **volcanic** [val'kænɪk, val-] adj : volcanique

volley ['vali] n, pl **-leys** : volée f — **volleyball** ['valiˌbɔl] n : volley-ball m

volt ['voːlt] n : volt m — **voltage** ['voːltɪʤ] n 1 : voltage m 2 **high** ~ : de haute tension

volume ['valjəm, -juːm] n : volume m

voluntary ['valənˌtɛri] adj 1 : volontaire 2 UNPAID : bénévole — **volunteer** [ˌvalən'tɪr] n : volontaire mf — ~ vt : offrir — vi : se porter volontaire

voluptuous [və'lʌptʃʊəs] adj : volup-tueux

vomit ['vamət] n : vomi m — ~ v : vomir

voracious [vɔ'reɪʃəs, və-] adj : vorace

vote ['voːt] n 1 : vote m 2 SUFFRAGE : droit m de vote — ~ v **voted; voting** : voter — **voter** ['voːtər] n : électeur m, -trice f — **voting** ['voːtɪŋ] n : scrutin m, vote m

vouch ['vaʊtʃ] vi ~ **for** : répondre de — **voucher** ['vaʊtʃər] n : bon m

vow ['vaʊ] n : vœu m, serment m — ~ vt : jurer

vowel ['vaʊəl] n : voyelle f

voyage ['vɔɪɪʤ] n : voyage m

vulgar ['vʌlgər] adj 1 COMMON : vulgaire 2 CRUDE : grossier — **vulgarity** [ˌvʌl'gærəti] n, pl **-ties** : vulgarité f

vulnerable ['vʌlnərəbəl] adj : vulnérable — **vulnerability** [ˌvʌlnərə'bɪləti] n : vulnérabilité f

vulture ['vʌltʃər] n : vautour m

vying → vie

W

w ['dʌbəlˌjuː] n, pl **w's** or **ws** [-juːz] : w m, vingt-troisième lettre de l'alphabet

wad ['wad] n : tampon m (d'ouate, etc.), liasse f (de billets)

waddle ['wadəl] vi **-dled; -dling** : se dandiner

wade ['weɪd] v **waded; wading** vi : patauger — vt or ~ **across** : traverser

wafer ['weɪfər] n : gaufrette f

waffle ['wafəl] n : gaufre f

waft ['waft, 'wæft] vi : flotter

wag ['wæg] vt **wagged; wagging** : agiter, remuer

wage ['weɪʤ] n or **wages** npl : salaire m, paie f — ~ vt **waged; waging** ~ **war** : faire la guerre

wager ['weɪʤər] n : pari m — ~ v : parier

wagon ['wægən] n : chariot m

wail ['weɪl] vi : se lamenter — ~ n : lamentation f

waist ['weɪst] n : taille f — **waistline** ['weɪstˌlaɪn] n : taille f

wait ['weɪt] vi : attendre — vt 1 AWAIT : attendre 2 ~ **tables** : servir à table — ~ n 1 : attente f 2 **lie in** ~ **for** : guetter — **waiter** ['weɪtər] n : serveur m, garçon m — **waiting room** n : salle f d'attente — **waitress** ['weɪtrəs] n : serveuse f

waive ['weɪv] vt **waived; waiving** : renoncer à

wake[1] ['weɪk] v **woke** ['woːk]; **woken**

['wo:kən] *or* **waked; waking** *vi or* ~ **up**
: se réveiller — *vt* : réveiller — ~ *n* : veillée
f funèbre
wake[2] *n* **1** : sillage *m* (laissé par un bateau)
2 in the ~ **of** : à la suite de
waken ['weɪkən] *vt* : réveiller — *vi* : se
réveiller
walk ['wɔk] *vi* **1** : marcher, aller à pied **2**
STROLL : se promener — *vt* **1** : faire à pied **2**
: raccompagner (qqn), promener (un chien)
— ~ *n* **1** : marche *f*, promenade *f* **2** PATH
: chemin *m* **3** GAIT : démarche *f* (d'une personne) — **walker** ['wɔkər] *n* : marcheur *m*,
-cheuse *f*; promeneur *m*, -neuse *f* — **walking
stick** : canne *f* — **walkout** ['wɔk,aʊt] *n*
STRIKE : grève *f* — **walk out** *vi* **1** STRIKE
: faire la grève **2** LEAVE : partir, sortir **3** ~
on : quitter, abandonner
wall ['wɔl] *n* **1** : mur *m* (extérieur), paroi *f*
(intérieur) **2** : remparts *mpl* (d'une ville)
wallet ['wɑlət] *n* : portefeuille *m*
Walloon [wɑ'lu:n] *adj* : wallon
wallop ['wɑləp] *vt* : donner une raclée à —
~ *n* : raclée *f*
wallow ['wɑ,lo:] *vi* **1** : se vautrer **2** ~ **in**
: s'apitoyer sur
wallpaper ['wɔl,peɪpər] *n* : tapisserie *f* — ~
vt : tapisser
walnut ['wɔl,nʌt] *n* **1** : noyer *m* (arbre) **2**
: noix *f* (fruit)
walrus ['wɔlrəs, 'wɑl-] *n, pl* **-rus** *or* **-ruses**
: morse *m*
waltz ['wɔlts] *n* : valse *f* — ~ *vi* : valser
wan ['wɑn] *adj* **wanner; wannest** : blême,
pâle
wand ['wɑnd] *n* : baguette *f* (magique)
wander ['wɑndər] *vi* **1** : se promener, se
balader **2** STRAY : errer — *vt* : parcourir —
wanderer ['wɑndərər] *n* : vagabond *m*,
-bonde *f*
wane ['weɪn] *vi* **waned; waning** : diminuer
— ~ *n* **be on the** ~ : être sur le déclin
want ['wɑnt, 'wɔnt] *vt* **1** DESIRE : vouloir **2**
NEED : avoir besoin de **3** LACK : manquer
de **4** ~**ed** : recherché par la police — ~ *n*
1 NEED : besoin *m* **2** LACK : manque *m* **3**
DESIRE : désir *m* **4 for** ~ **of** : faute de —
wanting ['wɑntɪŋ, 'wɔn-] *adj* **be** ~ : manquer
wanton ['wɑntən, 'wɔn-] *adj* **1** LEWD : lascif **2** ~ **cruelty** : cruauté *f* gratuite
war ['wɔr] *n* : guerre *f*
ward ['wɔrd] *n* **1** : salle *f* (d'un hôpital, etc.)
2 : circonscription *f* électorale **3** ~ **of the
court** : pupille *f* — ~ *vt or* ~ **off** : parer,
éviter — **warden** ['wɔrdən] *n* **1** : gardien *m*,
-dienne *f* **2** *or* **prison** ~ : directeur *m*,
-trice *f* de prison
wardrobe ['wɔrd,ro:b] *n* **1** CLOSET : armoire
f, penderie *f* **2** CLOTHES : garde-robe *f*

warehouse ['wær,haʊs] *n* : entrepôt *m*, magasin *m* — **wares** ['wærz] *npl* : marchandises *fpl*
warfare ['wɔr,fær] *n* : guerre *f*
warhead ['wɔr,hed] *n* : ogive *f*
warily ['wærəli] *adv* : avec précaution
warlike ['wɔr,laɪk] *adj* : guerrier, belliqueux
warm ['wɔrm] *adj* **1** : chaud **2** LUKEWARM
: tiède **3** CARING : chaleureux **4 I feel** ~
: j'ai chaud — ~ *vt or* ~ **up** : chauffer,
réchauffer — *vi* **1** *or* ~ **up** : se réchauffer
2 ~ **to** : se prendre de sympathie pour
(qqn), s'enthousiasmer pour (qqch) —
warm–blooded ['wɔrm'blʌdəd] *adj* : à
sang chaud — **warmhearted** ['wɔrm-
'hɑrtəd] *adj* : chaleureux — **warmly**
['wɔrmli] *adv* **1** : chaleureusement **2 dress**
~ : s'habiller chaudement — **warmth**
['wɔrmpθ] *n* **1** : chaleur *f* **2** AFFECTION : affection *f*
warn ['wɔrn] *vt* **1** : avertir **2** INFORM : aviser
— **warning** ['wɔrnɪŋ] *n* **1** : avertissement *m*
2 NOTICE : avis *m*
warp ['wɔrp] *vt* **1** : voiler (bois, etc.) **2** DIS-
TORT : déformer
warrant ['wɔrənt] *n* **1** : autorisation *f* **2 arrest** ~ : mandat *m* d'arrêt — ~ *vt* : justifier — **warranty** ['wɔrənti, ,wɔrən'ti:] *n, pl*
-ties : garantie *f*
warrior ['wɔriər] *n* : guerrier *m*, -rière *f*
warship ['wɔr,ʃɪp] *n* : navire *m* de guerre
wart ['wɔrt] *n* : verrue *f*
wartime ['wɔr,taɪm] *n* : temps *m* de guerre
wary ['wæri] *adj* **warier; -est 1** : prudent,
circonspect **2 be** ~ **of** : se méfier de
was → **be**
wash ['wɔʃ, 'wɑʃ] *vt* **1** : laver, se laver **2** ~
away : emporter — *vi* : se laver — ~ *n* **1**
: lavage *m* **2** LAUNDRY : linge *m* sale —
washable ['wɔʃəbəl, 'wɑ-] *adj* : lavable —
washcloth ['wɔʃ,klɔθ, 'wɑʃ-] *n* : gant *m*
de toilette, débarbouillette *f Can* —
washed–out ['wɔʃt'aʊt, 'wɑʃt-] *adj* **1** : décoloré **2** EXHAUSTED : épuisé — **washer**
['wɔʃər, 'wɑ-] *n* **1** → **washing machine 2**
: rondelle *f*, joint *m* — **washing machine** *n*
: machine *f* à laver — **washroom** ['wɔʃ-
,ru:m, 'wɑʃ-, -,rʊm] *n* : toilettes *fpl*
wasn't ['wʌzənt] (*contraction of* **was not**) →
be
wasp ['wɑsp] *n* : guêpe *f*
waste ['weɪst] *v* **wasted; wasting** *vt*
: gaspiller, perdre — *vi or* ~ **away** : dépérir
— ~ *adj* : de rebut — ~ *n* **1** : gaspillage
m (d'argent), perte *f* (de temps) **2** RUBBISH
: déchets *mpl*, ordures *fpl* — **wastebasket**
['weɪst,bæskət] *n* : corbeille *f* à papier —
wasteful ['weɪstfəl] *adj* : gaspilleur —
wasteland ['weɪst,lænd, -lənd] *n* : terre *f*
inculte

watch ['wɑtʃ] *vi* **1** : regarder **2** *or* **keep ~**
: faire le guet **3 ~ out** : faire attention
— *vt* **1** : regarder **2** *or* **~ over** : veiller —
~ *n* **1** : montre *f* **2** SURVEILLANCE
: surveillance *f* — **watchdog** ['wɑtʃ,dɔg] *n*
: chien *m* de garde, chienne *f* de garde —
watchful ['wɑtʃfəl] *adj* : vigilant — **watchman** ['wɑtʃmən] *n, pl* **-men** [-mən, -,mɛn]
: gardien *m*
water ['wɔtər, 'wɑ-] *n* : eau *f* — **~** *vt* **1** : arroser (un jardin, etc.) **2** *or* **~ down** DILUTE
: diluer, couper (du vin, etc.) — *vi* **1** : lar-
moyer (se dit des yeux) **2 my mouth is**
~ing : j'ai l'eau à la bouche — **watercolor**
['wɔtər,kʌlər, 'wɑ-] *n* : aquarelle *f* — **watercress** ['wɔtər,krɛs, 'wɑ-] *n* : cresson *m*
— **waterfall** ['wɔtər,fɔl, 'wɑ-] *n* : chute *f*
(d'eau), cascade *f* — **water lily** *n* : nénuphar
m — **watermark** ['wɔtər,mɑrk, 'wɑ-] *n*
: filigrane *m* — **watermelon** ['wɔtər,mɛlən,
'wɑ-] *n* : pastèque *f*, melon *m* d'eau — **waterproof** ['wɔtər,pru:f, 'wɑ-] *adj* : imperméable — **watershed** ['wɔtər,ʃɛd, 'wɑ-] *n*
1 : ligne *m* de partage des eaux **2** : moment
m critique — **waterskiing** ['wɔtər,ski:ɪŋ,
'wɑ-] *n* : ski *m* nautique — **watertight**
['wɔtər,taɪt, wɑ-] *adj* : étanche — **waterway**
['wɔtər,weɪ, 'wɑ-] *n* : cours *m* d'eau navigable — **waterworks** ['wɔtər,wərks, wɑ-] *npl*
: système *m* hydraulique — **watery**
['wɔtəri, 'wɑ-] *adj* **1** : larmoyant (se dit des
yeux) **2** DILUTED : trop liquide, dilué
watt ['wɑt] *n* : watt *m* — **wattage** ['wɑtɪdʒ] *n*
: puissance *f* en watts
wave ['weɪv] *v* **waved; waving** *vi* **1** : faire
un signe de la main **2** : flotter au vent (se dit
d'un drapeau) — *vt* **1** SHAKE : agiter,
brandir **2** CURL : onduler **3** SIGNAL : faire
signe à — **~** *n* **1** : vague *f* (d'eau) **2** CURL
: ondulation *f* **3** : onde *f* (en physique) **4**
: geste *m* de la main **4** SURGE : vague *f* —
wavelength ['weɪv,lɛŋkθ] *n* : longueur *f*
d'onde
waver ['weɪvər] *vi* : vaciller, chanceler
wavy ['weɪvi] *adj* **wavier; -est** : ondulé
wax[1] ['wæks] *vi* : croître (se dit de la lune)
wax[2] *n* : cire *f* — **~** *vt* : cirer (le plancher,
etc.), farter (des skis) — **waxy** ['wæksi] *adj*
waxier; -est : cireux
way ['weɪ] *n* **1** : chemin *m* **2** MEANS : façon
f, manière *f* **3 by the ~** : à propos **4 by ~**
of : par, via **5 come a long ~** : faire de
grands progrès **6 get in the ~** : gêner le
passage **7 get one's own ~** : arriver à ses
fins **8 out of the ~** REMOTE : éloigné,
isolé **9 which ~ did he go?** : où est-il
passé?
we ['wi:] *pron* : nous
weak ['wi:k] *adj* : faible — **weaken** ['wi:-
kən] *vt* : affaiblir — *vi* : s'affaiblir, faiblir —

weakling ['wi:klɪŋ] *n* : mauviette *f* —
weakly ['wi:kli] *adv* : faiblement — **weakness** ['wi:knəs] *n* **1** : faiblesse *f* **2** FLAW
: défaut *m*
wealth ['wɛlθ] *n* **1** : richesse *f* **2 a ~ of**
: une profusion de — **wealthy** ['wɛlθi] *adj*
wealthier; -est : riche
wean ['wi:n] *vt* : sevrer (un bébé)
weapon ['wɛpən] *n* : arme *f*
wear ['wær] *v* **wore** ['wor]; **worn** ['worn];
wearing *vt* **1** : mettre, porter **2 ~ oneself**
out : s'épuiser **3** *or* **~ out** : user — *vi* **1**
LAST : durer **2 ~ off** : diminuer **3 ~ out**
: s'user, se détériorer — **~** *n* **1** USE : usage
m **2** CLOTHES : vêtements *mpl* — **wear and
tear** : usure *f*
weary ['wɪri] *adj* **-rier; -est** : fatigué, las —
~ *vt* **-ried; -rying** : lasser, fatiguer —
weariness ['wɪrinəs] *n* : lassitude *f* —
wearisome ['wɪrisəm] *adj* : fastidieux
weasel ['wi:zəl] *n* : belette *f*
weather ['wɛðər] *n* **1** : temps *m* **2 be under**
the ~ : ne pas être dans son assiette — **~**
vt OVERCOME : surmonter — **weather-
beaten** ['wɛðər,bi:tən] *adj* **1** : battu, usé
(par les intempéries) **2** : hâlé (se dit d'un
visage) — **weatherman** ['wɛðər,mæn] *n, pl*
-men [-mən, -,mɛn] : météorologiste *mf* —
weather vane *n* : girouette *f*
weave ['wi:v] *v* **wove** ['wo:v] *or* **weaved;**
woven ['wo:vən] *or* **weaved; weaving** *vt* **1**
: tisser **2 ~ one's way through** : se faufiler à travers — *vi* : tisser — **~** *n* : tissage *m*
web ['wɛb] *n* **1** : toile *f* (d'araignée) **2** : pal-
mure *f* (d'un oiseau) **3** NETWORK : réseau *m*
4 Web → World Wide Web
webbed ['wɛbd] *adj* : palmé
webmaster ['wɛb,mæstər] *n* : webmestre *m*
wed ['wɛd] *v* **wedded; wedding** *vt* : se
marier à, épouser — *vi* : marier
we'd ['wi:d] (*contraction of* **we had, we**
should, *or* **we would**) → **have, should,
would**
wedding ['wɛdɪŋ] *n* : mariage *m*, noces *fpl*
wedge ['wɛdʒ] *n* **1** : cale *f* **2** PIECE : morceau
m (de fromage), part *m* (de gâteau, etc.) —
~ *vt* **wedged; wedging 1** : caler, fixer **2**
CRAM : enfoncer
Wednesday ['wɛnz,deɪ, -di] *n* : mercredi *m*
wee ['wi:] *adj* **1** : très petit **2 in the ~**
hours : aux petites heures (du matin)
weed ['wi:d] *n* : mauvaise herbe *f* — **~** *vt* **1**
: désherber **2 ~ out** : se débarrasser de
week ['wi:k] *n* : semaine *f* — **weekday**
['wi:k,deɪ] *n* : jour *m* de semaine — **weekend** ['wi:k,ɛnd] *n* : fin *f* de semaine, weekend *m* — **weekly** ['wi:kli] *adv* : à la semaine,
chaque semaine — **~** *adj* : hebdomadaire
— **~** *n, pl* **-lies** : hebdomadaire *m*
weep ['wi:p] *vi* **wept** ['wɛpt]; **weeping**

: pleurer — **weeping willow** *n* : saule *m* pleureur — **weepy** ['wi:pi] *adj* **weepier; -est** : au bord des larmes

weigh ['wei] *vt* **1** : peser **2** CONSIDER : considérer **3 ~ down** : accabler — *vi* **1** : peser **2 ~ on s.o.'s mind** : préoccuper qqn

weight ['weit] *n* **1** : poids *m* **2** IMPORTANCE : influence *f* **3 gain ~** : engraisser **4 lose ~** : maigrir — **weighty** ['weiti] *adj* **weightier; -est 1** HEAVY : pesant, lourd **2** IMPORTANT : de poids

weird ['wird] *adj* **1** : mystérieux **2** STRANGE : étrange, bizarre

welcome ['wɛlkəm] *vt* **-comed; -coming** : accueillir, souhaiter la bienvenue à — ~ *adj* **1** : bienvenu **2 you're ~** : de rien, je vous en prie — ~ *n* : accueil *m*

weld ['wɛld] *vt* : souder — ~ *n* : soudure *f*

welfare ['wɛl,fær] *n* **1** WELL-BEING : bien-être *m* **2** AID : aide *f* sociale, assistance *f* publique

well[1] ['wɛl] *n* : puits *m* (d'eau, de pétrole, etc.) — ~ *vi or* ~ **up** : monter, jaillir

well[2] *adv* **better** ['bɛtər]; **best** ['bɛst] **1** : bien **2 as ~** : aussi — ~ *adj* : bien — ~ *interj* **1** (*used to introduce a remark*) : bon, bien, enfin **2** (*used to express surprise*) : ça alors!, eh bien!

we'll ['wi:l, wil] (*contraction of* **we shall** *or* **we will**) → **shall, will**

well–being ['wɛl'bi:iŋ] *n* : bien-être *m* — **well–bred** ['wɛl'brɛd] *adj* : bien élevé, poli — **well–done** ['wɛl'dʌn] *adj* **1** : bien fait **2** : bien cuit (se dit de la viande, etc.) — **well–known** ['wɛl'no:n] *adj* : bien connu — **well–meaning** ['wɛl'mi:niŋ] *adj* : bien intentionné — **well–off** ['wɛl'ɔf] *adj* : prospère — **well–rounded** ['ɕwɛlˈraʊndəd] *adj* : complet — **well–to–do** [,wɛltə'du:] *adj* : riche, aisé

Welsh ['wɛlʃ] *adj* : gallois — ~ *n* : gallois *m* (langue)

welt ['wɛlt] *n* : zébrure *f*, marque *f* (sur la peau)

went → **go**
wept → **weep**
were → **be**

we're ['wir, 'wər, 'wi:ər] (*contraction of* **we are**) → **be**

weren't ['wərənt, 'wərnt] (*contraction of* **were not**) → **be**

west ['wɛst] *adv* : à l'ouest, vers l'ouest — ~ *adj* : ouest, d'ouest — ~ *n* **1** : ouest *m* **2 the West** : l'Ouest *m*, l'Occident *m* — **westerly** ['wɛstərli] *adv* : vers l'ouest — ~ *adj* : à l'ouest, d'ouest — **western** ['wɛstərn] *adj* **1** : ouest, de l'ouest, occidental **2 Western** : de l'Ouest, occidental — **Westerner** ['wɛstərnər] *n* : habitant *m*,

-tante *f* de l'Ouest — **westward** ['wɛstwərd] *adv & adj* : vers l'ouest

wet ['wɛt] *adj* **wetter; wettest 1** : mouillé **2** RAINY : pluvieux **3 ~ paint** : peinture *f* fraîche — ~ *vt* **wet** *or* **wetted; wetting** : mouiller, humecter

we've ['wi:v] (*contraction of* **we have**) → **have**

whack ['hwæk] *vt* : donner une claque à — ~ *n* : coup *m*, claque *f*

whale ['hweil] *n, pl* **whales** *or* **whale** : baleine *f*

wharf ['hwɔrf] *n, pl* **wharves** ['hwɔrvz] : quai *m*

what ['hwɑt, 'hwʌt] *adj* **1** (*used in questions and exclamations*) : quel **2** WHATEVER : tout — ~ *pron* **1** (*used in questions*) : qu'est-ce que, qu'est-ce qui **2** (*used in indirect statements*) : ce que, ce qui **3 ~ does it cost?** : combien est-ce que ça coûte? **4 ~ for?** : pourquoi? **5 ~ if** : et si — **whatever** [hwɑt'ɛvər, ,hwʌt-] *adj* **1** : n'importe quel **2 there's no chance ~** : il n'y a pas la moindre possibilité **3 nothing ~** : rien du tout — ~ *pron* **1** ANYTHING : (tout) ce que **2** (*used in questions*) : qu'est-ce que, qu'est-ce qui **3 ~ it may be** : quoi que ce soit — **whatsoever** [,hwɑtso'ɛvər, ,hwʌt-] *adj & pron* → **whatever**

wheat ['hwi:t] *n* : blé *m*

wheedle ['hwi:dəl] *vt* **-dled; -dling** : enjôler

wheel ['hwi:l] *n* **1** : roue *f* **2 or steering ~** : volant *m* — ~ *vt* : pousser (quelque chose sur des roulettes) — **wheelbarrow** ['hwi:l-,bær,o:] *n* : brouette *f* — **wheelchair** ['hwi:l,tʃær] *n* : fauteuil *m* roulant

wheeze ['hwi:z] *vi* **wheezed; wheezing** : respirer bruyamment

when ['hwɛn] *adv* : quand — ~ *conj* **1** : quand, lorsque **2 the days ~ I go to the bank** : les jours où je vais à la banque — ~ *pron* : quand — **whenever** [hwɛn'ɛvər] *adv* : quand (donc) — ~ *conj* **1** : chaque fois que **2 ~ you like** : quand vous voulez

where ['hwær] *adv* **1** : où **2 ~ are you going?** : où vas-tu? — ~ *conj & pron* : où — **whereabouts** ['hwærə,baʊts] *adv* : où (donc) — ~ *ns & pl* **know s.o.'s ~** : savoir où se trouve qqn

whereas [hwær'æz] *conj* : alors que, tandis que

wherever [hwær'ɛvər] *conj* **1** : n'importe où **2** WHERE : où, où donc

whet ['hwɛt] *vt* **whetted; whetting 1** : affûter, aiguiser (un couteau) **2 ~ one's appetite** : ouvrir l'appétit

whether ['hwɛðər] *conj* **1** : si **2 we doubt ~ he'll show up** : nous doutons qu'il vienne **3 ~ you like it or not** : que cela te plaise ou non

which [*ʰwɪtʃ*] *adj* **1** : quel **2 in ~ case** : auquel cas — ~ *pron* **1** (*used in questions*) : lequel, quel **2** (*used in relative clauses*) : qui, que — **whichever** [*ʰwɪtʃ-ˈɛvər*] *adj* : peu importe quel — ~ *pron* : quel que

whiff [*ʰwɪf*] *n* **1** PUFF : bouffée *f* **2** SMELL : odeur *f*

while [*ʰwaɪl*] *n* **1** : temps *m*, moment *m* **be worth one's ~** : valoir la peine **3 in a ~** : sous peu — ~ *conj* **1** : pendant que **2** WHEREAS : tandis que, alors que **3** ALTHOUGH : bien que — ~ *vt* **whiled**; **whiling ~ away** : (faire) passer

whim [*ʰwɪm*] *n* : caprice *m*, lubie *f*

whimper [*ʰwɪmpər*] *vi* : gémir, pleurnicher *fam* — ~ *n* : gémissement *m*

whimsical [*ʰwɪmzɪkəl*] *adj* : capricieux, fantasque

whine [*ʰwaɪn*] *vi* **whined**; **whining 1** WHIMPER : gémir **2** COMPLAIN : se plaindre — ~ *n* : gémissement *m*

whip [*ʰwɪp*] *v* **whipped**; **whipping** *vt* **1** : fouetter **2** BEAT : battre (des œufs, etc.) — *vi* FLAP : battre, claquer — ~ *n* : fouet *m*

whir [*ʰwər*] *vi* **whirred**; **whirring** : ronronner, vrombir

whirl [*ʰwərl*] *vi* : tourner, tourbillonner — ~ *n* : tourbillon *m* — **whirlpool** [*ʰwərl-ˌpu:l*] *n* : tourbillon *m* (d'eau) — **whirlwind** [*ʰwərl,wɪnd*] *n* : tourbillon *m* (de vent)

whisk [*ʰwɪsk*] *vt* **1** : fouetter (des œufs) **2** *or* ~ **away** : enlever — ~ *n* : fouet *m* (en cuisine)

whisker [*ʰwɪskər*] *n* **1** : poil *m* de barbe **2** ~**s** *npl* : barbe *f* (d'un homme), moustaches *fpl* (d'un chat, etc.)

whiskey *or* **whisky** [*ʰwɪski*] *n, pl* **-keys** *or* **-kies** : whisky *m*

whisper [*ʰwɪspər*] *v* : chuchoter — ~ *n* : chuchotement *m*

whistle [*ʰwɪsəl*] *v* **-tled**; **-tling** : siffler — ~ *n* **1** : sifflement *m* (son) **2** : sifflet *m* (objet)

white [*ʰwaɪt*] *adj* **whiter**; **-est** : blanc — ~ *n* **1** : blanc *m* (couleur) **2** *or* ~ **person** : Blanc *m*, Blanche *f* — **white—collar** [*ʰwaɪtˈkɑlər*] *adj* : de bureau — **whiten** [*ʰwaɪtən*] *v* : blanchir — **whiteness** [*ʰwaɪtnəs*] *n* : blancheur *f* — **whitewash** [*ʰwaɪt,wɔʃ*] *n* : lait *m* de chaux

whittle [*ʰwɪtəl*] *vt* **-tled**; **-tling ~ down** : réduire

whiz *or* **whizz** [*ʰwɪz*] *vi* **whizzed**; **whizzing 1** BUZZ : bourdonner **2** ~ **by** : passer à toute vitesse — ~ *or* **whizz** *n, pl* **whizzes** : expert *m*, as *m* — **whiz kid** *n* : jeune prodige *m*

who [*ʰhu:*] *pron* **1** (*used in direct and indirect questions*) : qui, qui est-ce qui **2** (*used in relative clauses*) : qui — **whoever** [hu:-ˈevər] *pron* **1** : qui que ce soit, quiconque **2** (*used in questions*) : qui

whole [*ho:l*] *adj* **1** : entier **2** INTACT : intact **3 a ~ lot** : beaucoup — ~ *n* **1** : tout *m*, ensemble *m* **2 as a ~** : dans son ensemble **3 on the ~** : en général — **wholehearted** [*ho:lˈhɑrtəd*] *adj* : sincère — **wholesale** [*ho:l,seɪl*] *n* : vente *f* en gros — ~ *adj* : de gros — ~ *adv* : en gros — **wholesaler** [*ho:l,seɪlər*] *n* : grossiste *mf* — **wholesome** [*ho:lsəm*] *adj* : sain — **whole wheat** *adj* : de blé entier — **wholly** [*ho:li*] *adv* : entièrement

whom [*hu:m*] *pron* **1** (*used in direct and indirect questions*) : qui, à qui **2** (*used in relative clauses*) : que

whooping cough [*hu:pɪŋ*] *n* : coqueluche *f*

whore [*hor*] *n* : prostituée *f*

whose [*hu:z*] *adj* **1** (*used in questions*) : de qui, à qui **2** (*used in relative clauses*) : dont — ~ *pron* : à qui

why [*ʰwaɪ*] *adv* : pourquoi — ~ *n, pl* **whys** : pourquoi *m* — ~ *conj* : pourquoi — ~ *interj* (*used to express surprise*) : mais!, tiens!

wick [*wɪk*] *n* : mèche *f*

wicked [*wɪkəd*] *adj* **1** : méchant **2** MISCHIEVOUS : espiègle **3** TERRIBLE : terrible — **wickedness** [*wɪkədnəs*] *n* : méchanceté *f*

wicker [*wɪkər*] *n* : osier *m*

wide [*waɪd*] *adj* **wider**; **widest 1** : de large, de largeur **2** VAST : étendu, vaste — ~ *adv* **1** ~ **apart** : très écarté **2 far and ~** : partout **3 open ~** : ouvrir grand (la bouche) — **wide—awake** [*waɪdəˈweɪk*] *adj* : éveillé, alerte — **widely** [*waɪdli*] *adv* : largement — **widen** [*waɪdən*] *vt* : élargir — **widespread** [*waɪdˈspred*] *adj* : généralisé

widow [*wɪ,do:*] *n* : veuve *f* — ~ *vt* : devenir veuf — **widower** [*wɪdowər*] *n* : veuf *m*

width [*wɪdθ*] *n* : largeur *f*

wield [*wi:ld*] *vt* **1** : manier **2** EXERT : exercer

wife [*waɪf*] *n, pl* **wives** [*waɪvz*] : femme *f*, épouse *f*

wig [*wɪg*] *n* : perruque *f*

wiggle [*wɪgəl*] *v* **-gled**; **-gling** *vi* : remuer — *vt* : faire bouger (ses orteils, etc.)

wigwam [*wɪg,wɑm*] *n* : wigwam *m*

wild [*waɪld*] *adj* **1** : sauvage **2** UNRULY : indiscipliné **3** RANDOM : au hasard **4** FRANTIC : frénétique **5** OUTRAGEOUS : extravagant — ~ *adv* **1** → **wildly 2 run ~** : se déchaîner — **wild boar** *n* : sanglier *m* — **wilderness** [*wɪldərnəs*] *n* : région *f* sauvage — **wildfire** [*waɪld,faɪr*] *n* **1** : feu *m* de forêt **2 spread like ~** : se répandre comme une traînée de poudre — **wildflower** [*waɪld,flauər*] *n* : fleur *f* des champs —

wildlife ['waɪld,laɪf] *n* : faune *f* — **wildly** ['waɪldli] *adv* **1** FRANTICALLY : frénétiquement **2** EXTREMELY : extrêmement

will[1] ['wɪl] *v, past* **would** ['wʊd]; *pres sing & pl* **will** *vt* WISH : vouloir — *v aux* **1 tomorrow we ～ go shopping** : demain nous irons faire les magasins **2 he ～ get angry over nothing** : il se fâche pour des riens **3 I ～ go despite them** : j'irai malgré eux **4 I won't do it** : je ne le ferai pas **5 that ～ be the mailman** : ça doit être le facteur **6 the back seat ～ hold three people** : le siège arrière peut accommoder trois personnes **7 accidents ～ happen** : les accidents arrivent **8 you ～ do as I say** : je t'ordonne de faire ce que je te dis

will[2] *n* **1** : volonté *f* **2** TESTAMENT : testament *m* **3 free ～** : de son propre gré — **willful** *or* **wilful** ['wɪlfəl] *adj* **1** OBSTINATE : volontaire **2** INTENTIONAL : délibéré — **willing** ['wɪlɪŋ] *adj* **1** : complaisant **2 be ～ to** : être prêt à, être disposé à — **willingly** ['wɪlɪŋli] *adv* : volontiers, de bon cœur — **willingness** ['wɪlɪŋnəs] *n* : bonne volonté *f*

willow ['wɪ,lo:] *n* : saule *m*

willpower ['wɪl,paʊər] *n* : volonté *f*

wilt ['wɪlt] *vi* : se faner

wily ['waɪli] *adj* **wilier; -est** : rusé, malin

win ['wɪn] *v* **won** ['wʌn]; **winning** *vi* : gagner — *vt* **1** : gagner, remporter **2 ～ over** : convaincre — *～ n* : victoire *f*

wince ['wɪnts] *vi* **winced; wincing** : tressaillir — *～ n* : tressaillement *m*

winch ['wɪntʃ] *n* : treuil *m*

wind[1] ['wɪnd] *n* **1** : vent *m* **2** BREATH : souffle *m* **3** : gaz *mpl* intestinaux **4 get ～ of** : apprendre

wind[2] ['waɪnd] *v* **wound** ['waʊnd]; **winding** *vi* : serpenter — *vt* **1** COIL : enrouler **2 ～ a clock** : remonter une horloge

wind down *vi* RELAX : se détendre

windfall ['wɪnd,fɔl] *n* : bénéfice *m* inattendu

winding ['waɪndɪŋ] *adj* : sinueux

wind instrument *n* : instrument *m* à vent

windmill ['wɪnd,mɪl] *n* : moulin *m* à vent

window ['wɪn,do:] *n* : fenêtre *f* (d'une maison), vitre *f* (d'une voiture), guichet *m* (dans une banque, etc.), vitrine *f* (d'un magasin) — **windowpane** ['wɪn,do:,peɪn] *n* : vitre *f*, carreau *m* — **windowsill** ['wɪndo,sɪl] *n* : rebord *m* de fenêtre

windpipe ['wɪnd,paɪp] *n* : trachée *f*

windshield ['wɪnd,ʃi:ld] *n* **1** : pare-brise *m* **2 ～ wiper** : essuie-glace *m*

wind up ['waɪnd,ʌp] *vt* : terminer, conclure — *vi* : finir

windy ['wɪndi] *adj* **windier; -est 1** : venteux **2 it's ～** : il vente

wine ['waɪn] *n* : vin *m* — **wine cellar** *n* : cave *f* à vin

wing ['wɪŋ] *n* : aile *f*

wink ['wɪŋk] *vi* : faire un clin d'œil — *～ n* **1** : clin *m* d'œil **2 not sleep a ～** : ne pas fermer l'œil

winner ['wɪnər] *n* : gagnant *m*, -gnante *f* — **winning** ['wɪnɪŋ] *adj* : gagnant — **winnings** ['wɪnɪŋz] *npl* : gains *mpl*

winter ['wɪntər] *n* : hiver *m* — *～ adj* : d'hiver — **wintergreen** ['wɪntər,gri:n] *n* : gaulthérie *f* — **wintertime** ['wɪntər,taɪm] *n* : hiver *m* — **wintry** ['wɪntri] *adj* **-trier; -est** : hivernal

wipe ['waɪp] *vt* **wiped; wiping 1** : essuyer **2 ～ away** : effacer (un souvenir) **3 ～ out** : détruire — *～ n* : coup *m* d'éponge

wire ['waɪr] *n* **1** : fil *m* métallique **2** : câble *m* (électrique ou téléphonique) — *～ vt* **wired; wiring 1** : faire l'installation électrique de **2** BIND : relier, attacher — **wireless** ['waɪrləs] *adj* : sans fil — **wiring** ['waɪrɪŋ] *n* : installation *f* électrique — **wiry** ['waɪri] *adj* **wirier** ['waɪriər]; **-est** : mince et musclé

wisdom ['wɪzdəm] *n* : sagesse *f* — **wisdom tooth** *n* : dent *f* de sagesse

wise ['waɪz] *adj* **wiser; wisest 1** : sage **2** SENSIBLE : prudent — **wisecrack** ['waɪz,kræk] *n* : vanne *f* — **wisely** ['waɪzli] *adv* : sagement

wish ['wɪʃ] *vt* **1** : souhaiter, désirer **2 ～ s.o. well** : souhaiter le meilleur à qqn — *vi* **1** : souhaiter, vouloir **2 as you ～** : comme vous voulez — *～ n* **1** : souhait *m*, désir *m*, vœu *m* **2 best ～es** *npl* : meilleurs vœux *mpl* — **wishful** ['wɪʃfəl] *adj* **1** : désireux **2 ～ thinking** : illusions *fpl*

wishy-washy ['wɪʃi,wɔʃi, -,wɑʃi] *adj* : faible, insipide

wisp ['wɪsp] *n* **1** : mèche *f* (de cheveux) **2** HINT : trace *f*, soupçon *m*

wistful ['wɪstfəl] *adj* : mélancolique

wit ['wɪt] *n* **1** CLEVERNESS : ingénuosité *f* **2** HUMOR : esprit *m* **3 at one's ～'s end** : désespéré **4 scared out of one's ～s** : mort de peur

witch ['wɪtʃ] *n* : sorcière *f* — **witchcraft** ['wɪtʃ,kræft] *n* : sorcellerie *f*

with ['wɪð, 'wɪθ] *prep* **1** : avec **2 I'm going ～ you** : je vais avec toi **3 it varies ～ the season** : ça varie selon la saison **4 the girl ～ red hair** : la fille aux cheveux roux **5 ～ all his faults, he's still my friend** : malgré tous ses défauts, il est quand même mon ami

withdraw [wɪð'drɔ, wɪθ-] *v* **-drew** [-'dru:]; **-drawn** [-'drɔn]; **-drawing** *vt* : retirer, rétracter (une parole, etc.) — *vi* LEAVE : se retirer — **withdrawal** [wɪð'drɔəl, wɪθ-] *n* : retrait *m* — **withdrawn** [wɪð'drɔn, wɪθ-] *adj* : renfermé, replié sur soi-même

wither [ˈwɪðər] *vi* : se faner, se flétrir

withhold [wɪθˈhoːld, wɪθ-] *vt* **-held** [-ˈhɛld]; **-holding** : retenir (des fonds), refuser (la permission, etc.)

within [wɪðˈɪn, wɪθ-] *adv* : à l'intérieur — **~** *prep* **1** : dans, à l'intérieur de **2** (*in expressions of distance*) : à moins de **3** (*in expressions of time*) : en moins de **4 ~ reach** : à (la) portée de la main

without [wɪðˈaʊt, wɪθ-] *adv* **do ~** : se passer de — **~** *prep* : sans

withstand [wɪθˈstænd, wɪð-] *vt* **-stood** [-ˈstʊd]; **-standing 1** BEAR : supporter **2** RESIST : résister à

witness [ˈwɪtnəs] *n* **1** : témoin *m* **2** EVIDENCE : témoignage *m* **3 bear ~** : témoigner — **~** *vt* **1** SEE : être témoin de **2** : servir de témoin lors de (une signature)

witty [ˈwɪti] *adj* **-tier; -est** : ingénieux

wives → **wife**

wizard [ˈwɪzərd] *n* **1** : magicien *m*, sorcier *m* **2 a math ~** : un génie en mathématiques

wobble [ˈwɑbəl] *vi* **-bled; -bling 1** : branler, osciller **2** : trembler (se dit de la voix, etc.) — **wobbly** [ˈwɑbəli] *adj* : bancal

woe [ˈwoː] *n* **1** : affliction *f* **2 ~s** *npl* TROUBLES : peines *fpl* — **woeful** [ˈwoːfəl] *adj* : triste

woke, woken → **wake**

wolf [ˈwʊlf] *n, pl* **wolves** [ˈwʊlvz] : loup *m*, louve *f* — **~** *vt or* **~ down** : engloutir, engouffrer

woman [ˈwʊmən] *n, pl* **women** [ˈwɪmən] : femme *f* — **womanly** [ˈwʊmənli] *adj* : féminin

womb [ˈwuːm] *n* : utérus *m*

won → **win**

wonder [ˈwʌndər] *n* **1** MARVEL : merveille *f* **2** AMAZEMENT : émerveillement *m* — **~** *vi* : penser, songer — *vt* : se demander — **wonderful** [ˈwʌndərfəl] *adj* : merveilleux, formidable

won't [ˈwoːnt] (*contraction of* **will not**) → **will**

woo [ˈwuː] *vt* **1** COURT : courtiser, faire la cour à **2** : rechercher les faveurs de (un client, etc.)

wood [ˈwʊd] *n* **1** : bois *m* (matière) **2** *or* **~s** *npl* FOREST : bois *m* — **~** *adj* : de bois, en bois — **woodchuck** [ˈwʊdˌtʃʌk] *n* : marmotte *f* d'Amérique — **wooded** [ˈwʊdəd] *adj* : boisé — **wooden** [ˈwʊdən] *adj* : en bois, de bois — **woodpecker** [ˈwʊdˌpɛkər] *n* : pic *m* — **woodwind** [ˈwʊdˌwɪnd] *n* : bois *m* (en musique) — **woodwork** [ˈwʊdˌwərk] *n* : boiseries *fpl* (en menuiserie)

wool [ˈwʊl] *n* : laine *f* — **woolen** *or* **woollen** [ˈwʊlən] *adj* **1** : de laine, en laine **2 ~s** *npl* : lainages *mpl* — **woolly** [ˈwʊli] *adj* **-lier; -est** : laineux

woozy [ˈwuːzi] *adj* **-zier; -est** : qui a la tête qui tourne

word [ˈwərd] *n* **1** : mot *m* **2** NEWS : nouvelles *fpl* **3 ~s** *npl* : texte *m*, paroles *fpl* (d'une chanson, etc.) **4 have a ~ with s.o.** : parler avec qqn **5 keep one's ~** : tenir sa parole — **~** *vt* : formuler, rédiger — **wording** [ˈwərdɪŋ] *n* : termes *mpl* (d'un document) — **word processing** *n* : traitement *m* de texte — **word processor** *n* : machine *f* à traitement de textes — **wordy** [ˈwərdi] *adj* **wordier; -est** : prolixe

wore → **wear**

work [ˈwərk] *n* **1** LABOR : travail *m* **2** EMPLOYMENT : travail *m*, emploi *m* **3** : œuvre *f* (d'art, etc.) **4 ~s** *npl* FACTORY : usine *f* **5 ~s** *npl* MECHANISM : rouages *mpl* (d'une horloge, etc.) — **~** *v* **worked** [ˈwərkt] *or* **wrought** [ˈrɔt]; **working** *vt* **1** : faire travailler (qqn) **2** OPERATE : faire marcher — *vi* **1** : travailler **2** FUNCTION : fonctionner **3** SUCCEED : réussir — **workbench** [ˈwərkˌbɛntʃ] *n* : établi *m* — **worked up** *adj* : nerveux — **worker** [ˈwərkər] *n* : travailleur *m*, -leuse *f*; employé *m*, -ployée *f* — **working** [ˈwərkɪŋ] *adj* **1** : qui travaille (se dit d'une personne), de travail (de sit d'un vêtement, etc.) **2 be in ~ order** : en état de marche — **working class** *n* : classe *f* ouvrière — **workman** [ˈwərkmən] *n, pl* **-men** [-mən, -ˌmɛn] : ouvrier *m* — **workmanship** [ˈwərkmənˌʃɪp] *n* : habileté *f*, dextérité *f* — **workout** [ˈwərkˌaʊt] *n* : exercices *mpl* physiques — **work out** *vt* **1** DEVELOP : élaborer **2** SOLVE : résoudre — *vi* **1** TURN OUT : marcher **2** SUCCEED : fonctionner, bien tourner **3** EXERCISE : s'entraîner, faire de l'exercice — **workshop** [ˈwərkˌʃɑp] *n* : atelier *m* — **work up** *vt* **1** EXCITE : stimuler **2** GENERATE : produire

world [ˈwərld] *n* **1** : monde *m* **2 think the ~ of s.o.** : tenir qqn en haute estime — **~** *adj* : du monde, mondial — **worldly** [ˈwərldli] *adj* : matériel, de ce monde — **worldwide** [ˈwərldˌwaɪd] *adv* : partout dans le monde — **~** *adj* : mondial, universel

World Wide Web *n* : Web *m*

worm [ˈwərm] *n* **1** : ver *m* **2 ~s** *npl* : vers *mpl* (intestinaux)

worn → **wear** — **worn–out** [ˈwornˈaʊt] *adj* **1** USED : usé, fini **2** EXHAUSTED : épuisé, éreinté

worry [ˈwəri] *v* **-ried; -rying** *vt* : inquiéter, préoccuper — *vi* : s'inquiéter — **~** *n, pl* **-ries** : inquiétude *f*, souci *m* — **worried** [ˈwəriːd] *adj* : inquiet — **worrisome** [ˈwərisəm] *adj* : inquiétant

worse [ˈwərs] *adv* (*comparative of* **bad** *or of* **ill**) : moins bien, plus mal — **~** *adj* (*comparative of* **bad** *or of* **ill**) **1** : pire, plus mauvais **2 get ~** : s'empirer — **~** *n* **1 the ~** : le pire **2 take a turn for the ~** : s'aggraver, empirer — **worsen** ['wərsən] *vi* : empirer, rempirer *Can fam* — *vt* : aggraver

worship ['wərʃəp] *v* **-shiped** *or* **-shipped; -shiping** *or* **-shipping** *vt* : adorer, vénérer — *vi* : pratiquer une religion — **~** *n* : adoration *f*, culte *m* — **worshiper** *or* **worshipper** ['wərləpər] *n* : fidèle *mf* (en religion)

worst ['wərst] *adv* (*superlative of* **ill** *or of* **bad** *or* **badly**) : plus mal — **~** *adj* (*superlative of* **bad** *or of* **ill**) : pire, plus mauvais — **~** *n* **the ~** : le pire

worth ['wərθ] *n* **1** : valeur *f* (monétaire) **2** MERIT : mérite *m* **3 ten dollars' ~ of gas** : dix dollars d'essence — **~** *prep* **1 be ~ doing** : valoir l'effort **2 it's ~ $ 10** : cela vaut 10 $ — **worthless** ['wərθləs] *adj* **1** : sans valeur **2** USELESS : inutile — **worthwhile** [wərθ'hwaɪl] *adj* : qui en vaut la peine — **worthy** ['wərði] *adj* **-thier; -est** : digne

would ['wʊd] *past of* **will 1 he ~ often take his children to the park** : il amenait souvent ses enfants au parc **2 I ~ go if I had the money** : j'irais si j'avais les moyens **3 I ~ rather go alone** : je préférerais y aller seul **4 she ~ have won if she hadn't tripped** : elle aurait gagné si elle n'avait pas trébuché **5 ~ you kindly help them?** : auriez-vous la gentillesse de les aider? — **wouldn't** ['wʊdʰnt] (*contraction of* **would not**) → **would**

wound[1] ['wuːnd] *n* : blessure *f* — **~** *vt* : blesser

wound[2] ['waʊnd] → **wind**

wove, woven → **weave**

wrangle ['ræŋgəl] *vi* **-gled; -gling** : se disputer

wrap ['ræp] *vt* **wrapped; wrapping 1** : envelopper, emballer **2** *or* **~ up** FINISH : conclure — **~** *n* — **wrapper** — **wrapper** ['ræpər] *n* : papier *m*, emballage *m* — **wrapping** ['ræpɪŋ] *n* : emballage *m*

wrath ['ræθ] *n* : furie *f*, colère *f*

wreath ['riːθ] *n, pl* **wreaths** ['riːðz, 'riːθs] : couronne *f* (de fleurs, etc.)

wreck ['rɛk] *n* **1** WRECKAGE : épave *f* (d'un

navire) **2** ACCIDENT : accident *m* (de voiture), écrasement *m* (d'avion) **3 be a nervous ~** : être à bout — *vt* : détruire (une automobile), faire échouer (un navire) — **wreckage** ['rɛkɪʤ] *n* **1** : épave *f* (d'un navire) **2** : décombres *mpl* (d'un édifice)

wren ['rɛn] *n* : roitelet *m*

wrench ['rɛntʃ] *vt* PULL : tirer brusquement — **~** *n* **1** TUG : secousse *f* **2** *or* **monkey ~** : clef *f*

wrestle ['rɛsəl] *vi* **-tled; -tling** : lutter, pratiquer la lutte (aux sports) — **wrestler** ['rɛsələr] *n* : lutteur *m*, -teuse *f* — **wrestling** ['rɛsəlɪŋ] *n* : lutte *f* (sport)

wretch ['rɛtʃ] *n* : pauvre diable *m* — **wretched** ['rɛtʃəd] *adj* **1** : misérable **2 ~ weather** : temps *m* affreux

wriggle ['rɪgəl] *vi* **-gled; -gling** : gigoter

wring ['rɪŋ] *vt* **wrung** ['rʌŋ]; **wringing 1** *or* **~ out** : essorer (du linge) **2** TWIST : tordre

wrinkle ['rɪŋkəl] *n* : ride *f* — **~** *v* **-kled; -kling** *vt* : rider — *vi* : se rider

wrist ['rɪst] *n* : poignet *m* — **wristwatch** ['rɪst,wɑtʃ] *n* : montre-bracelet *f*

writ ['rɪt] *n* : ordonnance *f* (en droit)

write ['raɪt] *v* **wrote** ['roːt]; **written** ['rɪtən]; **writing** : écrire — **write down** *vt* : mettre par écrit, noter — **write off** *vt* CANCEL : annuler — **writer** ['raɪtər] *n* : écrivain *m*, écrivaine *f Can*

writhe ['raɪð] *vi* **writhed; writhing** : se tordre, se tortiller

writing ['raɪtɪŋ] *n* : écriture *f*

wrong ['rɔŋ] *n* **1** : mal *m* **2** INJUSTICE : tort *m* — **~** *adj* **wronger; wrongest 1** : mal **2** UNSUITABLE : inapproprié **3** INCORRECT : mauvais, faux **4 be ~** : se tromper, avoir tort **5 what's ~?** : qu'est-ce qui ne va pas? — **~** *adv* **1** : à tort **2** INCORRECTLY : mal — **~** *vt* **wronged; wronging** : faire du tort à — **wrongful** ['rɔŋfəl] *adj* **1** UNJUST : injustifié **2** UNLAWFUL : illégal — **wrongly** ['rɔŋli] *adv* : à tort

wrote → **write**

wrought iron ['rɔt] *n* : fer *m* forgé

wrung → **wring**

wry ['raɪ] *adj* **wrier** ['raɪər]; **wriest** ['raɪəst] : narquois

XYZ

x [ˈɛks] *n*, *pl* **x's** *or* **xs** [ˈɛksəz] : x *m*, vingt–quatrième lettre de l'alphabet

xenophobia [ˌzɛnəˈfoːbiə, ˌziː-] *n* : xénophobie *f*

Xmas [ˈkrɪsməs] → **Christmas**

X ray [ˈɛksˌreɪ] *n* **1** : rayon *m* X **2** *or* **~ photograph** : radiographie *f* — **x–ray** *vt* : radiographier

xylophone [ˈzaɪləˌfoːn] *n* : xylophone *m*

y [ˈwaɪ] *n*, *pl* **y's** *or* **ys** [ˈwaɪz] : y *m*, vingt–cinquième lettre de l'alphabet

yacht [ˈjɑt] *n* : yacht *m*

yam [ˈjæm] *n* SWEET POTATO : patate *f* douce

yank [ˈjæŋk] *vt* : tirer d'un coup sec — **~** *n* : coup *m* sec

yap [ˈjæp] *vi* **yapped; yapping 1** : japper **2** CHATTER : jacasser — **~** *n* : jappement *m*

yard [ˈjɑrd] *n* **1** : yard *m*, verge *f* *Can* (unité de mesure) **2** COURTYARD : cour *f* **3** : jardin *m* (d'une maison) — **yardstick** [ˈjɑrdˌstɪk] *n* **1** : mètre *m* **2** CRITERION : critère *m*

yarn [ˈjɑrn] *n* **1** : fil *m* (à tisser) **2** TALE : histoire *f*

yawn [ˈjɔn] *vi* : bâiller — **~** *n* : bâillement *m*

year [ˈjɪr] *n* **1** : an *m*, année *f* **2 he's ten ~s old** : il a dix ans **3 I haven't seen them in ~s** : je ne les ai pas vus depuis des années — **yearbook** [ˈjɪrˌbʊk] *n* : recueil *m* annuel, annuaire *m* — **yearly** [ˈjɪrli] *adv* **1** : annuellement **2 three times ~** : trois fois par an — **~** *adj* : annuel

yearn [ˈjərn] *vi* **~ for** : désirer ardemment — **yearning** [ˈjərnɪŋ] *n* : désir *m* ardent

yeast [ˈjiːst] *n* : levure *f*

yell [ˈjɛl] *vi* : crier — *vt* : crier, hurler — **~** *n* : cri *m*, hurlement *m*

yellow [ˈjɛlo] *adj* : jaune — **~** *n* : jaune *m* — **~** *v* : jaunir — **yellowish** [ˈjɛloɪʃ] *adj* : jaunâtre

yelp [ˈjɛlp] *n* : glapissement *m* — **~** *vi* : glapir

yes [ˈjes] *adv* **1** : oui **2 you're not ready, are you? ~, I am** : vous n'êtes pas prêt? mais si, je le suis — **~** *n* : oui *m*

yesterday [ˈjestərˌdeɪ, -di] *adv* : hier — **~** *n* **1** : hier *m* **2 the day before ~** : avant–hier *m*

yet [ˈjɛt] *adv* **1** : encore **2 has he come ~?** : est-il déjà arrivé? **3 not ~** : pas encore **4 ~ more problems** : encore des problèmes **5** NEVERTHELESS : néanmoins — **~** *conj* : mais

yield [ˈjiːld] *vt* **1** PRODUCE : produire, rapporter **2 ~ the right of way** : céder le passage — *vi* **1** GIVE : céder **2** SURRENDER : se rendre — **~** *n* : rendement *m*, rapport *m*

yoga [ˈjoːgə] *n* : yoga *m*

yogurt [ˈjoːgərt] *n* : yaourt *m*, yogourt *m*

yoke [ˈjoːk] *n* : joug *m*

yolk [ˈjoːk] *n* : jaune *m* (d'œuf)

you [ˈjuː] *pron* **1** (*used as subject — singular*) : tu (familier), vous (forme polie) **2** (*used as subject — plural*) : vous **3** (*used as the direct or indirect object of a verb*) : te (familier), vous (forme polie), vous (pluriel) **4** (*used as the object of a preposition*) : toi (familier), vous (forme polie), vous (pluriel) **5 ~ never know** : on ne sait jamais — **you'd** [ˈjuɪd, ˈjʊd] (*contraction of* **you had** *or* **you would**) → **have, would** — **you'll** [ˈjuːl, ˈjʊl] (*contraction of* **you shall** *or* **you will**) → **shall, will**

young [ˈjʌŋ] *adj* **younger** [ˈjʌŋgər]; **youngest** [-gəst] **1** : jeune **2 my ~er brother** : mon frère cadet **3 she is the ~est** : elle est la plus jeune — **~** *npl* : jeunes *mfpl* (personnes), petits *mpl* (animaux) — **youngster** [ˈjʌŋkstər] *n* **1** : jeune *mf* **2** CHILD : enfant *mf*

your [ˈjʊr, ˈjoːr, jər] *adj* **1** (*familiar singular*) : ta, ton **2** (*formal singular*) : votre **3** (*familiar plural*) : tes **4** (*formal plural*) : vos **5 on ~ left** : à votre gauche

you're [ˈjʊr, ˈjoɪr, ˈjər, ˈjuɪər] (*contraction of* **you are**) → **be**

yours [ˈjʊrz, ˈjoːrz] *pron* **1** (*familiar singular*) : le tien, la tienne **2** (*formal singular*) : le vôtre, la vôtre **3** (*familiar plural*) : les tiens, les tiennes **4** (*formal plural*) : les vôtres

yourself [jərˈsɛlf] *pron*, *pl* **yourselves** [jərˈsɛlvz] **1** (*used reflexively*) : tu (familier), vous (forme polie), vous (pluriel) **2** (*used for emphasis*) : toi–même (familier), vous–même (forme polie), vous–mêmes (pluriel)

youth [ˈjuːθ] *n*, *pl* **youths** [ˈjuːðz, ˈjuːθs] **1** : jeunesse *f* **2** BOY : jeune *m* **3 today's ~** : les jeunes d'aujourd'hui — **youthful** [ˈjuːθfəl] *adj* **1** : juvénile, de jeunesse **2** YOUNG : jeune

you've [ˈjuːv] (*contraction of* **you have**) → **have**

yowl [ˈjæʊl] *vi* : hurler (se dit d'un chien ou d'une personne) — **~** *n* : hurlement *m*

yule [ˈjuːl] *n* : Noël *m* — **yuletide** [ˈjuːlˌtaɪd] *n* : temps *m* de Noël

z [ˈziː] *n*, *pl* **z's** *or* **zs** : z *m*, vingt-sixième lettre de l'alphabet

zany ['zeɪni] *adj* **-nier; -est** : farfelu *fam*

zeal ['ziːl] *n* : zèle *m*, ferveur *f* — **zealous** ['zɛləs] *adj* : zélé

zebra ['ziːbrə] *n* : zèbre *m*

zed ['zɛd] *Brit* → **z**

zenith ['ziːnəθ] *n* : zénith *m*

zero ['ziːro, 'zɪro] *n, pl* **-ros** : zéro *m* — ~ *adj* : zéro, nul

zest ['zɛst] *n* **1** : enthousiasme *m*, entrain *m* **2** FLAVOR : piquant *m*

zigzag ['zɪg,zæg] *n* : zigzag *m* — ~ *vi* **-zagged; -zagging** : zigzaguer

zinc ['zɪŋk] *n* : zinc *m*

zip ['zɪp] *v* **zipped; zipping** *vt or* ~ **up** : fermer avec une fermeture à glissière — *vi* SPEED : filer à toute allure — **zip code** *n* : code *m* postal — **zipper** ['zɪpər] *n* : fermeture *f* à glissière

zodiac ['zoːdi,æk] *n* : zodiaque *m*

zone ['zoːn] *n* : zone *f*

zoo ['zuː] *n, pl* **zoos** : zoo *m* — **zoology** [zo-'ɑlədʒi, zuː-] *n* : zoologie *f*

zoom ['zuːm] *vi* : passer comme une trombe — ~ *n or* ~ **lens** : zoom *m*

zucchini [zʊ'kiːni] *n, pl* **-ni** *or* **-nis** : courgette *f*

Common French Abbreviations

FRENCH ABBREVIATION AND EXPANSION		ENGLISH EQUIVALENT	
EPS	éducation physique et sportive	**PE**	physical education
etc.	et caetera, et cetera	**etc.**	et cetera
É.-U.	États-Unis	**US**	United States
F	Fahrenheit	**F**	Fahrenheit
F	franc	**fr.**	franc
FAB	franco à bord	**FOB**	free on board
févr.	février	**Feb.**	February
FMI	Fonds monétaire international	**IMF**	International Monetary Fund
g	gauche	**l., L**	left
g	gramme	**g**	gram
h	heure(s)	**hr.**	hour
HS	hors service	—	out of order
i.e.	c'est-à-dire	**i.e.**	that is
IPC	indice des prix à la consommation	**CPI**	consumer price index
Î.P.-É	île-du-Prince-Édouard	**PE, P.E.I.**	Prince Edward Island
janv.	janvier	**Jan.**	January
jeu.	jeudi	**Thurs.**	Thursday
juill.	juillet	**Jul.**	July
kg	kilogramme	**kg**	kilogram
km	kilomètre	**km**	kilometer
l	litre	**l**	liter
lun.	lundi	**Mon.**	Monday
m	mètre	**m.**	meter
M.	monsieur	**Mr.**	mister
mar.	mardi	**Tues.**	Tuesday
MB, Man.	Manitoba	**MB, Man.**	Manitoba
mer.	mercredi	**Wed.**	Wednesday
MLF	mouvement de libération des femmes	—	—
Mlle	Mademoiselle	**Ms., Miss**	—
Mme	Madame	**Ms., Mrs.**	—
MST	maladie sexuellement transmissible	**STD**	sexually transmitted disease
N	Nord, nord	**N**	North, north
N°, n°	numéro	**no.**	number
NB, N.-B.	Nouveau-Brunswick	**NB, N.B.**	New Brunswick
n.d.	non disponible	**NA**	not available
NL, T.-N.-L.	Terre-Neuve et Labrador	**NL**	Newfoundland and Labrador
nov.	novembre	**Nov.**	November
NS, N.-É.	Nouvelle-Écosse	**NS, N.S.**	Nova Scotia
NT	Territoires du Nord-Ouest	**NT, N.T.**	Northwest Territories
NU	Nunavut	**Nu**	Nunavut
O	Ouest, ouest	**W**	West, west

FRENCH ABBREVIATION AND EXPANSION		ENGLISH EQUIVALENT	
oc	ondes courtes	**s-w**	short wave
oct.	octobre	**Oct.**	October
OIT	Organisation internationale du travail	**ILO**	International Labor Organization
OMS	Organisation mondiale de la santé	**WHO**	World Health Organization
ON, Ont.	Ontario	**ON, Ont.**	Ontario
ONG	organisation non gouvernementale	**NGO**	nongovernmental organization
ONU	Organisation des Nations Unies	**UN**	United Nations
OTAN	Organisation du traité de l'Atlantique Nord	**NATO**	North Atlantic Treaty Organization
OVNI, ovni	objet volant non identifié	**UFO**	unidentified flying object
p.	page	**p.**	page
PCV	paiement contre vérification	—	collect call
PDG	président-directeur général	**CEO**	chief executive officer
PE	Île-du-Prince-Édouard	**PE, P.E.I.**	Prince Edward Island
p. ex.	par exemple	**e.g.**	for example
PIB	produit intérieur brut	**GDP**	gross domestic product
PNB	produit national brut	**GNP**	gross national product
P.-S.	post-scriptum	**P.S.**	postscript
QC	Québec	**QC, Que.**	Quebec
QG	quartier général	**HQ**	headquarters
QI	quotient intellectuel	**IQ**	intelligence quotient
R-D	recherche-développement	**R and D**	research and development
réf.	référence	**ref.**	reference
RF	République Française	—	France
RN	route nationale	—	interstate highway
RV	rendez-vous	**rdv., R.V.**	rendezvous
s.	siècle	**c., cent.**	century
S	Sud, sud	**S, so.**	South, south
SA	société anonyme	**Inc.**	incorporated (company)
sam.	samedi	**Sat.**	Saturday
SARL	société à responsabilité limitée	**Ltd.**	limited (corporation)
Sask.	Saskatchewan	**SK, Sask.**	Saskatchewan
SDF	sans domicile fixe	—	homeless (person)
sept.	septembre	**Sept.**	September
SK	Saskatchewan	**SK, Sask.**	Saskatchewan
SM	Sa Majesté	**HM**	His Majesty, Her Majesty
SME	Système monétaire européen	—	European Monetary System
St	saint	**St.**	Saint
Ste	sainte	**St.**	Saint
SVP	s'il vous plaît	**pls.**	please

FRENCH ABBREVIATION AND EXPANSION		ENGLISH EQUIVALENT	
t	tonne	t., tn.	ton
tél.	téléphone	tel.	telephone
T.-N.	Terre-Neuve	NF, Nfld.	Newfoundland
T.N.-O.	Territoires du Nord-Ouest	NT, N.T.	Northwest Territories
TVA	taxe à valeur ajoutée	VAT	value-added tax
UE	Union européenne	EU	European Union
univ.	université	U., univ.	university
V., v.	voir	vid.	see
ven.	vendredi	Fri.	Friday
vol.	volume	vol.	volume
VPC	vente par correspondance	—	mail-order selling
W-C	water closet	w.c.	water closet
YT, Yuk.	Yukon	YT, Y.T.	Yukon Territory

Italo Calvino

MARCOVALDO

or

The seasons in the city

Translated from the Italian by
William Weaver

A Harvest/HBJ Book
A Helen and Kurt Wolff Book
Harcourt Brace Jovanovich, Publishers
San Diego New York London

Requests for permission to make copies of any part of the work should be mailed to: Permissions, Harcourt Brace Jovanovich, Publishers, Orlando, Florida 32887

Library of Congress Cataloging in Publication Data
Calvino, Italo.

Marcovaldo, or, The seasons in the city.
Translation of: Marcovaldo, ovvero, Le stagioni in città.
"A Helen and Kurt Wolff book."
I. Title
PQ4809.A45M313   1983   853′.914   83-4372
ISBN 0-15-157081-7
ISBN 0-15-657204-4 (pbk.)

Printed in the United States of America

First American edition

B C D E F G H I J

Author's note:

These stories take place in an industrial city of northern Italy. The first in the series were written in the early 1950s and thus are set in a very poor Italy, the Italy of neo-realistic movies. The last stories date from the mid-60s, when the illusions of an economic boom flourished.

I.C.

SPRING

1. *Mushrooms in the city*

The wind, coming to the city from far away, brings it unusual gifts, noticed by only a few sensitive souls, such as hay-fever victims, who sneeze at the pollen from flowers of other lands.

One day, to the narrow strip of ground flanking a city avenue came a gust of spores from God knows where; and some mushrooms germinated. Nobody noticed them except Marcovaldo, the worker who caught his tram just there every morning.

This Marcovaldo possessed an eye ill-suited to city life: billboards, traffic-lights, shop-windows, neon signs, posters, no matter how carefully devised to catch the attention, never arrested his gaze, which might have been running over the desert sands. Instead, he would never miss a leaf yellowing on a branch, a feather trapped by a roof-tile; there was no horsefly on a horse's back, no worm-hole in a plank, or fig-peel squashed on the sidewalk that Marcovaldo didn't remark and ponder over, discovering the changes of season, the yearnings of his heart, and the woes of his existence.

Thus, one morning, as he was waiting for the tram that would take him to Sbav and Co., where he was employed as an unskilled laborer, he noticed something unusual near the stop, in the sterile, encrusted strip of earth beneath the

1

avenue's line of trees; at certain points, near the tree trunks, some bumps seemed to rise and, here and there, they had opened, allowing roundish subterranean bodies to peep out.

Bending to tie his shoes, he took a better look: they were mushrooms, real mushrooms, sprouting right in the heart of the city! To Marcovaldo the gray and wretched world surrounding him seemed suddenly generous with hidden riches; something could still be expected of life, beyond the hourly wage of his stipulated salary, with inflation index, family grant, and cost-of-living allowance.

On the job he was more absent-minded than usual; he kept thinking that while he was there unloading cases and boxes, in the darkness of the earth the slow, silent mushrooms, known only to him, were ripening their porous flesh, were assimilating underground humors, breaking the crust of clods. "One night's rain would be enough," he said to himself, "then they would be ready to pick." And he couldn't wait to share his discovery with his wife and his six children.

"I'm telling you!" he announced during their scant supper. "In a week's time we'll be eating mushrooms! A great fry! That's a promise!"

And to the smaller children, who did not know what mushrooms were, he explained ecstatically the beauty of the numerous species, the delicacy of their flavor, the way they should be cooked; and so he also drew into the discussion his wife, Domitilla, who until then had appeared rather incredulous and abstracted.

"Where are these mushrooms?" the children asked. "Tell us where they grow!"

At this question Marcovaldo's enthusiasm was curbed by a suspicious thought: Now if I tell them the place, they'll go and hunt for them with the usual gang of kids, word will spread through the neighborhood, and the mushrooms will end up in somebody else's pan! And so that discovery, which had promptly filled his heart with universal love, now made him wildly possessive, surrounded him with jealous and distrusting fear.

"I know where the mushrooms are, and I'm the only one who knows," he said to his children, "and God help you if you breathe a word to anybody."

The next morning, as he approached the tram stop, Marcovaldo was filled with apprehension. He bent to look at the ground and, to his relief, saw that the mushrooms had grown a little, but not much, and were still almost completely hidden by the earth.

He was bent in this position when he realized there was someone behind him. He straightened up at once and tried to act indifferent. It was the street-cleaner, leaning on his broom and looking at him.

This street-cleaner, whose jurisdiction included the place where the mushrooms grew, was a lanky youth with eye-glasses. His name was Amadigi, and Marcovaldo had long harbored a dislike of him, perhaps because of those eye-glasses that examined the pavement of the streets, seeking any trace of nature, to be eradicated by his broom.

It was Saturday; and Marcovaldo spent his free half-day circling the bed of dirt with an absent air, keeping an eye on the street-cleaner in the distance and on the mushrooms, and calculating how much time they needed to ripen.

That night it rained: like peasants who, after months of drought, wake up and leap with joy at the sound of the first drops, so Marcovaldo, alone in all the city, sat up in bed and called to his family: "It's raining! It's raining!" and breathed in the smell of moistened dust and fresh mold that came from outside.

At dawn – it was Sunday – with the children and a borrowed basket, he ran immediately to the patch. There were the mushrooms, erect on their stems, their caps high over the still-soaked earth. "Hurrah!" – and they fell to gathering them.

"Papà! Look how many that man over there has found," Michelino said, and his father, raising his eyes, saw Amadigi standing beside them, also with a basket full of mushrooms under his arm.

"Ah, you're gathering them, too?" the street-cleaner said. "Then they're edible? I picked a few, but I wasn't sure . . . Farther down the avenue some others have sprouted, even bigger ones . . . Well, now that I know, I'll tell my relatives; they're down there arguing whether it's a good idea to pick them or not . . ." And he walked off in a hurry.

Marcovaldo was speechless: even bigger mushrooms, which he hadn't noticed, an unhoped-for harvest, being taken from him like this, before his very eyes. For a moment he was almost frozen with anger, fury, then – as sometimes happens – the collapse of individual passion led to a generous impulse. At that hour, many people were waiting for the tram, umbrellas over their arms, because the weather was still damp and uncertain. "Hey, you! Do you want to eat fried mushrooms tonight?" Marcovaldo shouted to the crowd of people at the stop. "Mushrooms are growing here by the street! Come along! There's plenty for all!" And he walked off after Amadigi, with a string of people behind him.

They all found plenty of mushrooms, and lacking baskets, they used their open umbrellas. Somebody said: "It would be nice to have a big feast, all of us together!" But, instead, each took his own share and went home.

They saw one another again soon, however; that very evening, in fact, in the same ward of the hospital, after the stomach-pump had saved them all from poisoning. It was not serious, because the number of mushrooms eaten by each person was quite small.

Marcovaldo and Amadigi had adjacent beds; they glared at each other.

SUMMER

2. Park-bench vacation

On his way to work each morning, Marcovaldo walked beneath the green foliage of a square with trees, a bit of public garden, isolated in the junction of four streets. He raised his eyes among the boughs of the horse-chestnuts, where they were at their thickest and allowed yellow rays only to glint in the shade transparent with sap; and he listened to the racket of the sparrows, tone-deaf, invisible on the branches. To him they seemed nightingales, and he said to himself: "Oh, if I could wake just once at the twitter of birds and not at the sound of the alarm and the crying of little Paolino and the yelling of my wife, Domitilla!" or else: "Oh, if I could sleep here, alone, in the midst of this cool green shade and not in my cramped, hot room; here amid the silence, not amid the snoring and sleep-talking of my whole family and the racing of trams down below in the street; here in the natural darkness of the night, not in the artificial darkness of closed blinds, streaked by the glare of headlights; oh, if I could see leaves and sky on opening my eyes!" With these thoughts every day Marcovaldo began his eight daily hours – plus overtime – as an unskilled laborer.

In one corner of the square, under a dome of horse-chestnuts, there was a remote, half-hidden bench. And Marcovaldo had picked it as his own. On those summer nights, in the room where five of them slept, when he

5

couldn't get to sleep, he would dream of the bench as a vagabond dreams of a bed in a palace. One night, quietly, while his wife snored and the children kicked in their sleep, he got out of bed, dressed, tucked his pillow under his arm, left the house and went to the square.

There it was cool, peaceful. He was already savoring the contact of those planks, whose wood – he knew – was soft and cozy, preferable in every respect to the flattened mattress of his bed; he would look for a moment at the stars, then close his eyes in a sleep that would compensate him for all the insults of the day.

Cool and peace he found, but not the empty bench. A couple of lovers were sitting there, looking into each other's eyes. Discreetly, Marcovaldo withdrew. "It's late," he thought, "they surely won't spend the whole night outdoors! They'll come to an end of their billing and cooing."

But the two were not billing or cooing: they were quarreling. And when lovers start to quarrel there's no telling how long it will go on.

He was saying: "Why don't you admit that when you said what you said you knew you were going to hurt me and not make me happy the way you were pretending you thought?"

Marcovaldo realized it was going to last quite a while.

"No, I will not admit it," she answered, as Marcovaldo had already expected.

"Why won't you admit it?"

"I'll never admit it."

Damn, Marcovaldo thought. His pillow clutched under his arm, he went for a stroll. He went and looked at the moon, which was full, big above trees and roofs. He came back towards the bench, giving it a fairly wide berth out of fear of disturbing them, but actually hoping to irritate them a little and persuade them to go away. But they were too caught up in the argument to notice him.

"You admit it then?"

"No, no, I don't admit it in the least!"

"But what if you did admit it?"

"Even if I did admit something, I wouldn't admit what you want me to admit!"

Marcovaldo went back to look at the moon, then he went to look at a traffic-light, a bit farther on. The light flashed yellow, yellow, yellow, constantly blinking on and off. Marcovaldo compared the moon with the traffic-light. The moon with her mysterious pallor, also yellow, but also green, in its depths, and even blue; the traffic-light with its common little yellow. And the moon, all calm, casting her light without haste, streaked now and then by fine wisps of clouds, which she majestically allowed to fall around her shoulders; and the traffic-light meanwhile, always there, on and off, on and off, throbbing with a false vitality, but actually weary and enslaved.

He went back to see if the girl had admitted anything. Not on your life: no admission from her. In fact, she wasn't now the one who refused to admit; he was. The situation had changed completely, and it was she who kept saying to him: "Then you admit it?", and he kept saying no. A half hour went by like this. In the end, he admitted, or she did; anyway, Marcovaldo saw them get up and walk off, hand in hand.

He ran to the bench, flung himself on it; but meanwhile, in his waiting, he had lost some of his propensity to feel the sweetness he had been expecting to find there, and his bed at home, as he now remembered it, wasn't as hard as it had been. But these were minor points; his determination to enjoy the night in the open air remained firm. He stuck his face in the pillow and prepared for sleep, the kind of sleep to which he had long become unaccustomed.

Now he had found the most comfortable position. He wouldn't have shifted a fraction of an inch for anything in the world. Too bad, though, that when he lay like this, his gaze didn't fall on a prospect of trees and sky alone, so that in sleep his eyes would close on a view of absolute natural serenity. Before him, foreshortened, a tree was followed by the sword of a general from the height of his monument, then another tree, a notice-board, a third tree, and then, a bit farther, that false, flashing moon, the traffic-light, still ticking off its yellow, yellow, yellow.

It must be said that Marcovaldo's nervous system had been in such poor shape lately that even when he was dead tired a trifle sufficed to keep him awake; he had only to think something was annoying him, and sleep was out of the question. And now he was annoyed by that traffic-light blinking on and off. It was there in the distance, a yellow eye, winking, alone: it was nothing to bother about. But Marcovaldo must have been suffering from nervous exhaustion: he stared at that blinking and repeated to himself: "How I would sleep if that thing wasn't there! How I would sleep!" He closed his eyes and seemed to feel, under his eyelids, that silly yellow blinking; he screwed his eyes shut and he could see dozens of traffic-lights; he reopened his eyes, it was the same thing all over again.

He got up. He had to put some screen between himself and the traffic-light. He went as far as the general's monument and looked around. At the foot of the monument there was a laurel wreath, nice and thick, but now dry and coming apart, standing on props, with a broad, faded ribbon: "*The 15th Lancers on the Anniversary of The Glorious Victory.*" Marcovaldo climbed up on the pedestal, raised the wreath, and hung it on the general's sabre.

Tornaquinci, the night watchman, making his rounds, crossed the square on his bicycle; Marcovaldo hid behind the statue. Tornaquinci saw the shadow of the monument move on the ground: he stopped, filled with suspicion. He studied that wreath on the sabre: he realized something was out of place, but didn't know quite what. He aimed the beam of his flashlight up there; he read: "*The 15th Lancers on the Anniversary of The Glorious Victory.*" He nodded approvingly and went away.

To give him time to go off, Marcovaldo made another turn around the square. In a nearby street, a team of workmen was repairing a switch of the tram-track. At night, in the deserted streets, those little groups of men huddling in the glow of the welding torches, their voices ringing, then dying immediately, have a secret look, as of people preparing things the inhabitants of the daytime must never know. Marcovaldo approached, stood looking at the flame, the workmen's movements, with a somewhat embarrassed attention, his eyes growing smaller and smaller with sleepiness. He hunted for a cigarette in his pocket, to keep himself awake; but he had no matches. "Who'll give me a light?" he asked the workmen. "With this?" the man with the torch said, spraying a flurry of sparks.

Another workman stood up, handed him a lighted cigarette. "Do you work nights, too?"

"No, I work days," Marcovaldo said.

"Then what are you doing up at this time of night? We're about to quit."

He went back to the bench. He stretched out. Now the traffic-light was hidden from his eyes; he could fall asleep, at last.

He hadn't noticed the noise, before. Now, that buzz, like a grim, inhaling breath and an endless scraping and also a scratching, filled his ears completely. There is no sound more heart-rending than that of a welding torch, a kind of muffled scream. Without moving, huddled as he was on the bench, his face against the crumpled pillow, Marcovaldo could find no escape, and the noise continued to conjure up the scene illuminated by the gray flame scattering golden sparks all around, the men hunkered on the ground, smoked-glass vizors over their faces, the torch grasped in the hand shaken by a rapid tremor, the halo of shadow around the tool cart, at the tall trellis-like apparatus that reached the wires. He opened his eyes, turned on the bench, looked at the stars among the boughs. The insensitive sparrows continued sleeping up there among the leaves.

To fall asleep like a bird, to have a wing you could stick

your head under, a world of branches suspended above the earthly world, barely glimpsed down below, muffled and remote. Once you begin rejecting your present state, there is no knowing where you can arrive. Now Marcovaldo, in order to sleep, needed something; but he himself didn't know quite what; at this point not even a genuine silence would have been enough. He had to have a basis of sound, softer than silence, a faint wind passing through the thick undergrowth of a forest, a murmur of water bubbling up and disappearing in a meadow.

He had an idea and he rose to his feet. It wasn't exactly an idea, because half-dazed by the sleepiness that filled him, he couldn't form any thought properly; but it was like a re-collection that somewhere around there was something connected with the idea of water, with its loquacious and subdued flow.

In fact, there was a fountain, nearby, a distinguished work of sculpture and hydraulics, with nymphs, fauns, river gods, who enlaced jets, cascades, a play of water. Only it was dry: at night, in summer, since the aqueduct was functioning less, they turned it off. Marcovaldo wandered around for a little while like a sleep-walker; more by instinct than by reason he knew that a tub must have a tap. A man who has a good eye can find what he is looking for even with his eyes closed. He turned on the tap: from the conch-shells, from the beards, from the nostrils of the horses, great jets rose, the feigned caverns were cloaked in glistening mantles, and all this water resounded like the organ of a choir loft in the great empty square, with all the rustling and turbulence that water can create. The night watchman, Tornaquinci, was coming along again on his coal-black bicycle, thrusting his tickets under doorways, when he suddenly saw the whole fountain explode before his eyes like a liquid firework. He nearly fell off his seat.

Trying to open his eyes as little as possible, to retain that shred of sleep he felt he had grasped, Marcovaldo ran and flung himself again on the bench. There, now it was as if he lay on the bank of a stream, with the woods above him; he slept.

He dreamed of a dinner, the dish was covered as if to keep the pasta warm. He uncovered it and there was a dead mouse, which stank. He looked into his wife's plate: another dead mouse. Before his children, more mice, smaller, but also rotting. He uncovered the tureen and found a cat, belly in the air; and the stink woke him.

Not far away there was the garbage truck that passes at night to empty the garbage cans. He could make out in the dim glow from the headlights, the crane, cackling and jerking, the shadows of men standing on the top of the mountain of refuse, their hands guiding the receptacle attached to the pulley, emptying it into the truck, pounding it with blows of their shovels, their voices grim and jerky like the movement of the crane: "Higher . . . let it go . . . to hell with you . . .," with metallic clashes like opaque gongs, and then the engine picking up, slowly, only to stop a bit farther on, as the maneuver began all over again.

But by now Marcovaldo's sleep had reached a zone where sounds no longer arrived, and these, even so graceless and rasping, came as if muffled in a soft halo, perhaps because of the very consistency of the garbage packed into the trucks. It was the stink that kept him awake, the stink sharpened by an unbearable idea of stink, whereby even the sounds, those dampened and remote sounds, and the image, outlined against the light, of the truck with the crane didn't reach his mind as sound and sight but only as stink. And Marcovaldo was delirious, vainly pursuing with his nostrils' imagination the fragrance of a rose arbor.

The night watchman, Tornaquinci, felt sweat bathe his forehead as he glimpsed a human form running on all fours along a flower-bed, then saw it angrily rip up some buttercups, then disappear. But he thought it must have been either a dog, the responsibility of dog-catchers, or a hallucination, the responsibility of the alienist, or a

were-wolf, the responsibility of God knows who but prefer-
ably not him; and he turned the corner.

Meanwhile, having gone back to his sleeping place,
Marcovaldo pressed the bedraggled clump of buttercups to
his nose, trying to fill his sense of smell to the brim with
their perfume: but he could press very little from those
almost odorless flowers. Still the fragrance of dew, of earth,
and of trampled grass was already a great balm. He dispelled
the obsession of garbage and slept. It was dawn.

His waking was a sudden explosion of sun-filled sky
above his head, a sun that virtually obliterated the leaves,
then restored them gradually to his half-blinded sight. But
Marcovaldo could not stay because a shiver had made him
jump up: the spatter of a hydrant, which the city gardeners
use for watering the flowerbeds, made cold streams trickle
down his clothes. And all around there were trams clamor-
ing, trucks going to market, hand-carts, pickups, workers
on motorbikes rushing to factories, and the blinds being
rolled up at house windows whose panes were glittering.
His mouth and eyes sticky, his back stiff and one hip
bruised, bewildered, Marcovaldo rushed to work.

AUTUMN

3. The municipal pigeon

The routes birds follow, as they migrate southwards or northwards, in autumn or in spring, rarely cross the city. Their flights cleave the heavens high above the striped humps of fields and along the edge of woods; at one point they seem to follow the curving line of a river or the furrow of a valley; at another, the invisible paths of the wind. But they sheer off as soon as the range of a city's rooftops looms up before them.

And yet, once, a flight of autumn woodcock appeared in a street's slice of sky. And the only person to notice was Marcovaldo, who always walked with his nose in the air. He was on a little tricycle-truck, and seeing the birds he pedaled harder, as if he were chasing them, in the grip of a hunter's fantasy, though the only gun he had ever held was an army rifle.

And as he proceeded, his eyes on the flying birds, he found himself at an intersection, the light red, in the midst of the automobiles; and he came within a hair's breadth of being run over. As a traffic cop, his face purple, wrote name and address in a notebook, Marcovaldo sought again with his eyes those wings in the sky; but they had vanished.

At work, his fine brought him harsh reproaches.

"Can't you even get traffic-lights straight?" his foreman,

13

Signor Viligelmo, shouted at him. "What were you looking at anyway, knuckle-head?"

"I was looking at a flight of woodcock . . ." he said.

"What?" Signor Viligelmo was an old man; his eyes glistened. And Marcovaldo told him the story.

"Saturday I'm going out with dog and gun!" the foreman said, full of vigor, now forgetting his outburst. "The migration's begun, up in the hills. Those birds were certainly scared off by the hunters up there, and they flew over the city . . ."

All that day Marcovaldo's brain ground and ground, like a mill. "Saturday, if the hills are full of hunters, as is quite likely, God knows how many woodcock will fly over the city. If I handle it right, Sunday I'll eat roast woodcock."

The building where Marcovaldo lived had a flat roof, with wires strung for drying laundry. Marcovaldo climbed up there with three of his children, carrying a can of bird-lime, a brush, and a sack of corn. While the children scattered kernels of corn everywhere, he spread birdlime on the parapets, the wires, the frames of the chimneypots. He put so much on that Filippetto, while he was playing, almost got stuck fast.

That night Marcovaldo dreamed of the roof dotted with fluttering, trapped woodcock. His wife, Domitilla, more greedy and lazy, dreamed of ducks already roasted, lying on the chimneys. His daughter Isolina, romantic, dreamed of humming-birds to decorate her hat. Michelino dreamed of finding a stork up there.

The next day, every hour one of the children went up to inspect the roof: he would just peek out from the trap-door so, if they were about to alight, they wouldn't be scared; then he would come down and report. The reports were not good. But then, towards noon, Pietruccio came back, shouting: "They're here! Papà! Come and see!"

Marcovaldo went up with a sack. Trapped in the birdlime there was a poor pigeon, one of those gray urban doves, used to the crowds and racket of the squares. Fluttering around, other pigeons contemplated him sadly, as he tried to unstick his wings from the mess on which he had unwisely lighted.

Marcovaldo and his family were sucking the little bones of that thin and stringy pigeon, which had been roasted, when they heard a knocking at the door.

It was the landlady's maid. "The Signora wants you! Come at once!"

Very concerned, because he was six months behind with the rent and feared eviction, Marcovaldo went to the Signora's apartment, on the main floor. As he entered the living room, he saw that there was already a visitor: the purple-faced cop.

"Come in, Marcovaldo," the Signora said. "I am informed that on our roof someone is trapping the city's pigeons. Do you know anything about it?"

Marcovaldo felt himself freeze.

"Signora! Signora!" a woman's voice cried at that moment.

"What is it, Guendalina?"

The laundress came in. "I went up to hang out the laundry, and all the wash is stuck to the lines. I pulled on it, to get it loose, but it tore. Everything's ruined. What can it be?"

Marcovaldo rubbed his hand over his stomach, as if his digestion were giving him trouble.

WINTER

4. *The city lost in the snow*

That morning the silence woke him. Marcovaldo pulled himself out of bed with the sensation there was something strange in the air. He couldn't figure out what time it was, the light between the slats of the blinds was different from all other hours of day and night. He opened the window: the city was gone; it had been replaced by a white sheet of paper. Narrowing his eyes, he could make out, in the whiteness, some almost-erased lines, which corresponded to those of the familiar view: the windows and the roofs and the lamp-posts all around, but they were lost under all the snow that had settled over them during the night.

"Snow!" Marcovaldo cried to his wife; that is, he meant to cry, but his voice came out muffled. As it had fallen on lines and colors and views, the snow had fallen on noises, or rather on the very possibility of making noise; sounds, in a padded space, did not vibrate.

He went to work on foot; the trams were blocked by the snow. Along the street, making his own path, he felt free as he had never felt before. In the city all differences between sidewalk and street had vanished; vehicles could not pass, and Marcovaldo, even if he sank up to his thighs at every step and felt the snow get inside his socks, had become master, free to walk in the middle of the street, to trample on flower-beds, to cross outside the prescribed lines, to proceed in a zig-zag.

Streets and avenues stretched out, endless and deserted, like blanched chasms between mountainous cliffs. There was no telling whether the city hidden under that mantle was still the same or whether, in the night, another had taken its place. Who could say if under those white mounds there were still gasoline pumps, news-stands, tram stops, or if there were only sack upon sack of snow? As he walked along, Marcovaldo dreamed of getting lost in a different city: instead, his footsteps were taking him straight to his everyday place of work, the usual shipping department, and, once he had crossed the threshold, the worker was amazed at finding himself among those walls, the same as ever, as if the change that had cancelled the outside world had spared only his firm.

There, waiting for him, was a shovel, taller than he was. The department foreman, Signor Viligelmo, handing it to him, said: "Shoveling the snow off the sidewalk in front of the building is up to us. To you, that is." Marcovaldo took the shovel and went outside again.

Shoveling snow is no game, especially on an empty stomach; but Marcovaldo felt the snow was a friend, an element that erased the cage of walls which imprisoned his life. And he set to work with a will, sending great shovel-fuls of snow flying from the sidewalk to the center of the street.

The jobless Sigismondo was also filled with gratitude for the snow, because having enrolled in the ranks of the municipal snow-shovelers that morning, he now had before him a few days of guaranteed employment. But this feeling, instead of inspiring in him vague fantasies like Marcovaldo's, led him to quite specific calculations, to determine how many cubic feet of snow had to be shoveled to clear so many square feet. In other words, he aimed at impressing the captain of his team; and thus – his secret ambition – at getting ahead in the world.

Now Sigismondo turned, and what did he see? The stretch of road he had just cleared was being covered again with snow, by the helter-skelter shoveling of a character panting there on the sidewalk. Sigismondo almost had a fit. He ran and confronted the other man, thrusting at the stranger's chest his shovel piled high with snow. "Hey, you! Are you the one who's been throwing that snow there?"

"Eh? What?" Marcovaldo started, but admitted, "Ah, maybe I am."

"Well, either you take it right back with your shovel, or I'll make you eat it, down to the last flake."

"But I have to clear the sidewalk."

"And I have to clear the street. So?"

"Where'll I put it?"

"Do you work for the City?"

"No. For Sbav and Co."

Sigismondo taught him how to pile up the snow along the edge of the sidewalk, and Marcovaldo cleared his whole stretch. Content, sticking their shovels into the snow, the two men stood and contemplated their achievement.

"Got a butt?" Sigismondo asked.

They were lighting half a cigarette apiece, when a snow-plow came along the street, raising two big white waves that fell at either side. Every sound that morning was a mere rustle: by the time the men raised their heads, the whole section they had shoveled was again covered with snow. "What happened? Has it started snowing again?" And they looked up at the sky. The machine, spinning its huge brushes, was already turning at the corner.

Marcovaldo learned to pile the snow into a compact little wall. If he went on making little walls like that, he could build some streets for himself alone; only he would know where those streets led, and everybody else would be lost there. He could remake the city, pile up mountains high as houses, which no one would be able to tell from real houses. But perhaps by now all the houses had turned to snow, inside and out; a whole city of snow with monuments and spires and trees, a city that could be unmade by shovel and remade in a different way.

On the edge of the sidewalk at a certain point there was a considerable heap of snow. Marcovaldo was about to level it to the height of his little walls when he realized it was an automobile: the de-luxe car of Commendatore Alboino, chairman of the board, all covered with snow. Since the difference between an automobile and a pile of snow was so slight, Marcovaldo began creating the form of an automobile with his shovel. It came out well: you really couldn't tell which of the two was real. To put the final touches on his work Marcovaldo used some rubbish that had turned up in his shovel: a rusted tin served to model the shape of a headlight; an old tap gave the door its handle.

A great bowing and scraping of doormen, attendants and flunkies, and the chairman, Commendatore Alboino, came out of the main entrance. Short-sighted and efficient, he strode straight to his car, grasped the protruding tap, pulled it down, bowed his head, and stepped into the pile of snow up to his neck.

Marcovaldo had already turned the corner and was shoveling in the courtyard.

The boys in the yard had made a snow man. "He needs a nose!" one of them said. "What'll we use? A carrot!" And they ran to their various kitchens to hunt among the vegetables.

Marcovaldo contemplated the snow man. "There, under the snow you can't tell what is snow and what is only covered. Except in one case: man; because it's obvious I am I and not this man here."

Absorbed in his meditations, he didn't hear two men shouting from the rooftop: "Hey, mister, get out of the way!" They were the men responsible for pushing the snow off the roof-tiles. And all of a sudden, about three hundred-weight of snow fell right on top of him.

The children returned with their looted carrots. "Oh, they've made another snow man!" In the courtyard there were two identical dummies, side by side.

"We'll give them each a nose!" And they thrust carrots into the heads of the two snow men.

More dead than alive, Marcovaldo, through the sheath in which he was buried and frozen, felt some nourishment reach him. And he chewed on it.

"Hey, look! The carrot's gone!" The children were very frightened.

The bravest of the boys didn't lose heart. He had a spare nose: a pepper, and he stuck it into the snow man. The snow man ate that, too.

Then they tried giving him a nose made out of coal, a big lump. Marcovaldo spat it out with all his might. "Help! He's alive! He's alive!" The children ran away.

In a corner of the courtyard there was a grille from which a cloud of warmth emerged. With the heavy tread of a snow man, Marcovaldo went and stood there. The snow melted over him, trickled in rivulets down his clothes: a Marcovaldo reappeared, all swollen and stuffed up with a cold.

He took the shovel, mostly to warm himself, and began to work in the courtyard. There was a sneeze blocked at the top of his nose, all ready and waiting, but refusing to make up its mind and burst forth. Marcovaldo shoveled, his eyes half-closed, and the sneeze remained nested in the top of his nose. All of a sudden: the "Aaaaaah . . ." was almost a roar, and the "choo!" was louder than the explosion of a mine. The blast flung Marcovaldo against the wall.

Blast, indeed: that sneeze had caused a genuine tornado. All the snow in the courtyard rose and whirled in a blizzard, drawn upwards, pulverized in the sky.

When Marcovaldo reopened his eyes, after being stunned, the courtyard was completely cleared, with not even one flake of snow. And to his gaze there appeared the familiar courtyard, the gray walls, the boxes from the warehouse, the things of every day, sharp and hostile.

SPRING

5. *The wasp treatment*

Winter departed and left rheumatic aches behind. A faint noonday sun came to cheer the days, and Marcovaldo would spend a few hours watching the leaves sprout, as he sat on a bench, waiting to go back to work. Near him a little old man would come and sit, hunched in his overcoat, all patches: he was a certain Signor Rizieri, retired, all alone in the world, and also a regular visitor of sunny park benches. From time to time this Signor Rizieri would jerk and cry – "Ow!" – and hunch even deeper into his coat. He was a mass of rheumatism, arthritis, lumbago, collected during the damp, cold winter, which continued to pursue him for the rest of the year. To console him, Marcovaldo would explain the various stages of his own rheumatic pains, as well as those of his wife and of his oldest daughter, Isolina, who, poor thing, was turning out to be rather delicate.

Every day Marcovaldo carried his lunch wrapped in newspaper; seated on the bench he would unwrap it and give the crumpled piece of newspaper to Signor Rizieri, who would hold out his hand impatiently, saying: "Let's see what the news is." He always read it with the same interest, even if it was two years old.

And so one day he came upon an article about a method of curing rheumatism with bee venom.

"They must mean honey," Marcovaldo said, always inclined to be optimistic.

21

"No," Rizieri said, "venom, it says here: the poison in the sting." And he read a few passages aloud. The two of them discussed bees at length, their virtues, attributes, and also the possible cost of this treatment.

After that, as he walked along the avenues, Marcovaldo pricked up his ears at every buzz, his gaze followed every insect that flew around him. And so, observing the circling of a wasp with a big black-and-yellow-striped belly, he saw it burrow into the hollow of a tree, where other wasps then came out: a thrumming, a bustle that announced the presence of a whole wasp-nest inside the trunk. Marcovaldo promptly began his hunt. He had a glass jar, in the bottom of which there was still a thick layer of jam. He placed it, open, near the tree. Soon a wasp buzzed around it, then went inside, attracted by the sugary smell. Marcovaldo was quick to cover the jar with a paper lid.

And the moment he saw Signor Rizieri, he could say to him: "Come, I'll give you the injection!", showing him the jar with the infuriated wasp trapped inside.

The old man hesitated, but Marcovaldo refused to postpone the experiment for any reason, and insisted on performing it right there, on their bench: the patient didn't even have to undress. With a mixture of fear and hope, Signor Rizieri raised the hem of his overcoat, his jacket, his shirt; and opening a space through his tattered undershirts, he uncovered a part of his loins where he ached. Marcovaldo stuck the top of the jar there and slipped away the paper that was acting as a lid. At first nothing happened; the wasp didn't move. Had he gone to sleep? To waken him, Marcovaldo gave the bottom of the jar a whack. That whack was just what was needed: the insect darted forward and jabbed his sting into Signor Rizieri's loins. The old man let out a yell, jumped to his feet, and began walking like a soldier on parade, rubbing the stung part and emitting a string of confused curses.

Marcovaldo was all content; the old man had never been so erect, so martial. But a policeman had stopped nearby, and was staring wide-eyed; Marcovaldo took Rizieri by the arm and went off, whistling.

He came home with another wasp in the jar. To convince his wife to allow the sting was no easy matter, but in the end he succeeded. For a while, at least Domitilla complained only of the wasp sting.

Marcovaldo started catching wasps full tilt. He gave Isolina an injection, and Domitilla a second one, because only systematic treatment could bring about an improvement. Then he decided to have a shot himself. The children, you know how they are, were saying: "Me, too; me, too," but Marcovaldo preferred to equip them with jars and set them to catching more wasps, to supply the daily requirements.

Signor Rizieri came to Marcovaldo's house looking for him; he had another old man with him, Cavalier Ulrico, who dragged one leg and wanted to start the treatment at once.

Word spread; Marcovaldo now had an assembly-line set up: he always kept half a dozen wasps in stock, each in its glass jar, lined up on a shelf. He applied the jar to the patient's behind as if it were a syringe, he pulled away the paper lid, and when the wasp had stung, he rubbed the place with alcohol-soaked cotton, with the nonchalant hand of an experienced physician. His house consisted of a single room, in which the whole family slept; they divided it with a makeshift screen, waiting-room on one side, doctor's office on the other. In the waiting-room Marcovaldo's wife received the clients and collected the fees. The children took the empty jars and ran off towards the wasps' nest for refills. Sometimes a wasp would sting them, but they hardly cried any more, because they knew it was good for their health.

That year rheumatic aches and pains twisted among the population like the tentacles of an octopus; Marcovaldo's cure acquired great renown; and on Saturday afternoon he saw his poor garret invaded by a little throng of suffering men and women, pressing a hand to their back or hip, some with the tattered aspect of beggars, others looking like well-off people, drawn by the novelty of this treatment.

"Hurry," Marcovaldo said to his three boys, "take the jars, go and catch as many wasps as you can." The boys went off.

It was a sunny day, many wasps were buzzing along the avenue. The boys usually hunted them at a certain distance from the tree where their nest was, trying to catch isolated insects. But that day, Michelino, to save time and catch more, began hunting right at the entrance to the nest. "This is the way to do it," he said to his brothers, and he tried to catch a wasp by putting the jar over it the moment it landed. But, every time, that wasp flew away and came back to light closer and and closer to the nest. Now it was at the very edge of the hollow in the trunk, and Michelino was about to lower the jar on it, when he felt two other big wasps fling themselves on him as if they wanted to sting him on the head. He shielded himself, but he felt the prick of the stings and, crying out in pain, he dropped the jar. Immediately, dismay at what he had done erased his pain: the jar had fallen into the mouth of the nest. No further buzzing was heard, no more wasps came out; Michelino, without even the strength to yell, took a step backwards. Then from the nest a thick, black cloud burst out, with a deafening hum: all the wasps were advancing at once in an enraged swarm!

His brothers heard Michelino let out a scream as he began running as he had never run in his life. He seemed steam-driven, as that cloud he trailed after him seemed the smoke from a chimney.

Where does a child run when he is being chased? He runs home! And that's what Michelino did.

The passers-by didn't have time to realize what that sight was, something between a cloud and a human being, darting along the streets with a roar mixed with a loud buzz.

Marcovaldo was saying to his patients: "Just one moment,

the wasps will soon be here," when the door opened and the swarm invaded the room. They didn't even see Michelino, who went to stick his head in a basin of water: the whole room was full of wasps and the patients flapped their arms in the futile effort to drive them away, and the rheumatics performed wonders of agility and the benumbed limbs were released in furious movements.

The fire department came, and then the Red Cross. Lying on his cot in the hospital, swollen beyond recognition by the stings, Marcovaldo didn't dare react to the curses that were hurled at him from the other cots of the ward by his patients.

SUMMER

6. A Saturday of sun, sand, and sleep

"For your rheumatism," the Public Health doctor had said, "this summer you should take some sand treatments." And so, one Saturday afternoon, Marcovaldo was exploring the banks of the river, looking for a place where the sand was dry and in the sun. But wherever there was sand, the river was only a clank of rusty chains; dredgers and derricks were at work: machines as old as dinosaurs digging into the river and emptying giant spoonfuls of sand into the contractors' dump-trucks parked there among the willows. The conveyor line of buckets rose erect and descended overturned, and the cranes lifted on their long neck a pelican-like gullet spilling gobbets of the black muck of the river-bed. Marcovaldo bent to touch the sand, crushed it in his palm; it was wet, a mush, a mire: even where the sun had formed a dry and crumbling crust, an inch below it was still damp.

Marcovaldo's children, whom their father had brought along hoping to put them to work covering him with sand, couldn't contain their desire to go swimming. "Papà, papà, we're going to dive! We're going to swim in the river!"

"Are you crazy? There's a sign: 'All swimming forbidden.' You'd drown, you'd sink like stones!" And he explained that, where the river-bed has been excavated by dredgers, there remain hollow funnels that suck the stream down in eddies or whirlpools.

"Whirlpools! Show us the whirlpools!" For the children, the word had a jolly sound.

"You can't see one; it grabs you by the foot, while you're swimming, and drags you down."

"What about that? Why doesn't it go down? Is it a fish?"

"No, it's a dead cat," Marcovaldo explained. "It floats because its belly is full of water."

"Does the whirlpool catch the cat by its tail?" Michelino asked.

The slope of the grassy bank, at a certain point, opened out in a rather flat clearing where a big sifter had been set up. Two men were sifting a pile of sand, using shovels, and with the same shovels they then loaded it on a black, shallow barge, a kind of raft, which floated there, tied to a willow. The two bearded men worked under the fierce sun wearing hats and jackets, but torn and moldy, and trousers ending in shreds at the knee, leaving legs and feet bare.

In that sand, left to dry for days and days, fine, cleansed of impurities, pale as the sand at the seaside, Marcovaldo recognized what was needed for him. But he had discovered it too late: they were already loading it onto that barge, to take it away . . .

No, not yet: the sandmen, having completed their loading, broke out a flask of wine, and after passing it back and forth a couple of times drinking in gulps, they lay down in the shade of the willows while the hour of greatest heat passed.

"As long as they are sleeping, I can lie down in their sand and have a sand pack!" Marcovaldo thought, and he ordered the children, in a low voice: "Quick, help me!"

He jumped on the barge, took off shirt, trousers and shoes, and burrowed into the sand. "Cover me! With the shovel!" he said to the children. "No, not my head; I need that to breathe with. It has to stay outside. All the rest!"

For the children it was like building a sand-castle. "Shall we make sand-pies? No, a castle with ramparts! No, no, it makes a nice track for marbles!"

"Go away now!" Marcovaldo huffed, from beneath his sarcophagus of sand. "No, first put a paper hat over my forehead and eyes. And then jump ashore and go play a bit farther off, otherwise the men will wake up and drive me away."

"We can tow you down the river, pulling the barge–rope from the shore," Filippetto suggested, when he had already half–untied the mooring.

Marcovaldo, immobilized, twisted his mouth and eyes to scold them. "If you don't go away right now, if you make me get up from here, I'll beat you with the shovel!" The kids ran off.

The sun blazed, the sand burned, and Marcovaldo, dripping sweat under his paper hat, felt, as he lay there motionless, enduring the baking, the sense of satisfaction produced by painful treatments or nasty medicines, when you think: "The worse it is, the more good it's doing me."

He dozed off, rocked by the slight current that first tautened the mooring a little, then loosened it. In this pulling to and fro, the knot, which Filippetto had already half undone, became undone altogether. And the barge laden with sand moved down the river, free.

It was the hottest hour of the afternoon. Everything slept: the man buried in the sand, the arbors over the little jetties, the deserted bridges, the houses rising, windows shuttered, above the embankments. The river was low, but the barge, driven by the current, skirted the muddy shoals which rose now and then; otherwise, a light bump on the bottom was enough to send it back into the flow of water, gradually becoming deeper.

One of these bumps made Marcovaldo open his eyes. He saw the sky charged with sunlight, the low summer clouds passing. "How they run," he thought, of the clouds, "and there isn't a breath of wind!" Then he saw some electric wires: they too were running, like the clouds. He looked to one side, as much as he could, with the hundredweight of sand on top of him. The right bank was far away, green, and it was running; the left was gray, far off, also in flight. He realized he was in the midst of the river, voyaging. Nobody answered: he was alone, buried on a sand barge, adrift, without oars or rudder. He knew he should get up, try to land, call for help; but at the same time the thought that sand-packs require absolute immobility held him, made him feel committed to stay there as long as he could, so as not to lose precious instants of his cure.

At that moment he saw the bridge; and from the statues and lamps that adorned the railings, from the breadth of the arches that touched the sky, he recognized it: he hadn't realized how far he had come. And as he entered the opaque region of shade that the arches cast, he remembered the rapids. About a hundred yards beyond the bridge, the river-bed made a drop; the barge would drop down the falls and overturn, and he would be smothered by the sand, the water, the barge, with no hope of emerging alive. Still, even at that moment, his greatest concern was the sand cure, whose beneficent effects would be promptly lost.

He waited for the plunge. And it came: but it was a thud coming upwards from below. On the brink of the falls, in that dry season, shoals of mud had collected, some greening with slender clumps of cane and rushes. The barge ran aground, on all its flat keel, flinging up the whole load of sand and the man buried in it. Marcovaldo found himself hurled into the air as if by a catapult, and at that moment he saw the river below him. Or rather: he didn't see it at all, he saw only the teeming crowd of people who filled the river.

On this Saturday afternoon, a great throng of swimmers crowded that stretch of river, where the shallow water came only up to the navel; children wallowed in it, whole classes of them, and fat women, and gentlemen who did the dead-man's float, and girls in bikinis, and young toughs who wrestled with each other, and mattresses, balls, life-savers, inner-tubes, row boats, kayaks, rubber boats, motor boats, life-saving boats, yawls from yacht clubs, fishermen with nets, fishermen with rods, old women with parasols, young ladies in straw hats, and dogs, dogs, dogs, from toy poodles to Saint Bernards: you couldn't see even an inch of the river's surface. And Marcovaldo, as he flew, was uncertain whether he would fall onto a rubber mattress or into the arms of a Junoesque matron, but of one thing he was certain: not even a drop of water would touch him.

AUTUMN

7. *The lunch-box*

The joys of that round and flat vessel, or lunch-box, known as the "pietanziera", consist first of all in its having a screw-on top. The action of unscrewing the cover already makes your mouth water, especially if you don't yet know what is inside, because, for example, it's your wife who prepares the vessel for you every morning. Once the box is uncovered, you see your food packed there: salami and lentils, or hard-boiled eggs and beets, or else polenta and codfish, all neatly arranged within that circumference as the continents and oceans are set on the maps of the globe; and even if the food is scant it gives the effect of being substantial and compact. The cover, once it has been removed, serves as a plate, and so there are two receptacles and you can begin to divide the contents.

Marcovaldo, the handyman, having unscrewed the lid of his box and swiftly inhaled its aroma, grabs the cutlery that he has always carried in his pocket, wrapped in a bundle, ever since he began eating his noon meal from the lunch-box instead of returning home. The fork's first jabs serve to rouse those benumbed victuals a bit, to give the prominence and attraction of a dish just set on the table to those foods that have been cramped inside there for so many hours. Then you begin to see that there isn't much, and you think:

31

"Best to eat it slowly." But, rapid and ravenous, the first forkfuls have already been raised to the mouth.

The immediate sensation is the sadness of eating cold food, but the joys promptly begin again as you find the flavors of the family board transported to an unusual setting. Marcovaldo has now begun chewing slowly: he is seated on a bench by an avenue, near the place where he works; since his house is far away and to go there at noon costs time and tram tickets, he brings his lunch in the box, bought for the purpose, and he eats in the open air, watching the people go by, and then he refreshes himself at a drinking fountain. If it's autumn and the sun is out, he chooses places where an occasional ray strikes; the shiny red leaves that fall from the trees serve him as napkins; the salami skins go to stray dogs, who are quick to become his friends; and the sparrows collect the bread crumbs, at a moment when no one is going past in the avenue.

As he eats, he thinks: "Why am I so happy to taste the flavor of my wife's cooking here, when at home, among the quarrels and tears, the debts that crop up in every conversation, I can't enjoy it?" And then he thinks: "Now I remember. These are the leftovers from last night's supper." And he is immediately seized again by discontent, perhaps because he has to eat leftovers, cold and a bit soured, perhaps because the aluminum of the lunch-box gives the food a metallic taste, but the notion lodged in his head is: The thought of Domitilla manages to spoil my meals even when I'm far away from her.

At that point, he realizes he has come almost to the end, and again this dish seems to him something very special and rare, and he eats with enthusiasm and devotion the final remains on the bottom of the plate, the ones that taste most of metal. Then, gazing at the empty, greasy receptacle, he is again overcome by sadness.

Then he wraps everything up, puts it in his pocket, and stands; it's still early to go back to work; in the big pocket of his heavy jacket the cutlery drums against the empty lunch-box. Marcovaldo goes to a wine-shop and has them pour him a glass, filled to the brim; or else to a café where he sips a little cup of coffee; then he looks at the pastries in the glass case, the boxes of candies and nougat, persuades himself that he doesn't want any, that he doesn't want anything at all; for a moment he watches the table-football to convince himself that he wants to kill time, not appetite. He goes back into the street. The trams are crowded again; it is almost the hour to return to work, and he heads in that direction.

It so happened that his wife, Domitilla, for personal reasons, bought a great quantity of sausage and turnips. And for three evenings in a row, Marcovaldo found sausage and turnips for supper. Now that sausage must have been made of dog meat; the smell alone was enough to kill your appetite. As for the turnips, this pale and shifty vegetable was the only one Marcovaldo had never been able to bear.

At noon, there they were again: his sausage and turnips, cold and greasy, in the lunch-box. Forgetful as he was, he always unscrewed the lid with curiosity and gluttony, never remembering what he had eaten for supper the previous night; and every day brought the same disappointment. The fourth day, he stuck his fork into it, sniffed once again, rose from the bench, and holding the open lunch-box in his hand, walked absently along the street. The passers-by saw this man carrying a fork in one hand and a plate of sausage in the other, apparently unable to bring himself to raise the first forkful to his mouth.

From a window a voice said: "Hey, mister!"

Marcovaldo raised his eyes. On the mezzanine floor of a grand villa, a boy was standing at a window, his elbows on the sill, where a dish had been set.

"Hey, mister! What are you eating?"

"Sausage and turnips!"

"Lucky you," the boy said.

"Mmm . . ." Marcovaldo replied, vaguely.

"Imagine! I'm supposed to eat fried brains . . ."

Marcovaldo looked at the dish on the sill. There were fried brains, soft and curly as a pile of clouds. His nostrils twitched.

"What? Don't you like brains?" he asked the little boy.

"No. They locked me up in here to punish me, because I wouldn't eat it. But I'll throw it out of the window."

"And you like sausage?"

"Oh, yes, it looks like a snake . . . We never eat it at our house . . ."

"Then you give me your plate and I'll give you mine."

"Hurrah!" The child was overjoyed. He held out to the man his porcelain plate with heavy silver fork, and the man gave him the lunch-box with the tin fork.

And so both fell to eating: the boy at the window-sill and Marcovaldo seated on a bench opposite, both licking their lips and declaring they had never tasted such good food.

But then, behind the boy, a governess appears, with her hands on her hips.

"Well, young man! My goodness! What are you eating?"

"Sausage!" the boy says.

"And who gave it to you?"

"That gentleman there," and he pointed to Marcovaldo, who interrupted his slow and earnest chewing of a morsel of brains.

"Throw it away! The smell! Throw it away!"

"But it's good . . ."

"And your plate? The fork?"

"The gentleman has them . . ." and he pointed again to Marcovaldo, who was holding the fork in the air with a bit of half-eaten brains stuck on it.

The woman began yelling. "Thief! Thief! The silver!"

Marcovaldo stood up, looked for another moment at the half-finished dish of fried brains, went to the window, set plate and fork on the sill, stared at the governess with contempt, and withdrew. He heard the clatter of the lunch-box on the pavement, the boy's crying, the rude slam of the window. He bent to pick up the lunch-box and its cover. They were a bit dented; the cover no longer fit properly. He jammed everything into his pocket and went off to work.

WINTER

8. The forest on the superhighway

Cold has a thousand shapes and a thousand ways of moving in the world: on the sea it gallops like a troop of horses, on the countryside it falls like a swarm of locusts, in the cities like a knife-blade it slashes the streets and penetrates the chinks of unheated houses. In Marcovaldo's house that evening they had burned the last kindling, and the family, all bundled in overcoats, was watching the embers fade in the stove, and the little clouds rise from their own mouths at every breath. They had stopped talking; the little clouds spoke for them: the wife emitted great long ones like sighs, the children puffed them out like assorted soap-bubbles, and Marcovaldo blew them upwards in jerks, like flashes of genius that promptly vanish.

In the end Marcovaldo made up his mind: "I'm going to look for wood. Who knows? I might find some." He stuffed four or five newspapers between his shirt and his jacket as breastplates against gusts of air, he hid a long, snaggle-tooth saw under his overcoat, and thus he went out into the night, followed by the long, hopeful looks of his family. He made a papery rustle at every step; the saw peeped out now and then above his collar.

Looking for wood in the city: easier said than done! Marcovaldo headed at once towards a little patch of public park that stood between two streets. All was deserted.

Marcovaldo studied the naked trees, one by one, thinking of his family, waiting for him with their teeth chattering.

Little Michelino, his teeth chattering, was reading a book of fairy-tales, borrowed from the small library at school. The book told of a child, son of a woodsman, who went out with a hatchet to chop wood in the forest. "That's the place to go!" Michelino said. "The forest! There's wood there, all right!" Born and raised in the city, he had never seen a forest, not even at a distance.

Then and there, he worked it out with his brothers: one took a hatchet, one a hook, one a rope; they said good-bye to their Mamma and went out in search of a forest.

They walked around the city, illuminated by street-lamps, and they saw only houses: not a sign of a forest. They encountered an occasional passer-by, but they didn't dare ask him where a forest was. And so they reached the area where the houses of the city ended and the street turned into a highway.

At the sides of the highway, the children saw the forest: a thick growth of strange trees blocked the view of the plain. Their trunks were very very slender, erect or slanting; and their crowns were flat and outspread, revealing the strangest shapes and the strangest colors when a passing car illuminated them with its headlights. Boughs in the form of a toothpaste tube, a face, cheese, hand, razor, bottle, cow, tire, all dotted with a foliage of letters of the alphabet.

"Hurrah!" Michelino said. "This is the forest!"

And, spellbound, the brothers watched the moon rise among those strange shadows: "How beautiful it is . . ."

Michelino immediately reminded them of their purpose in coming there: wood. So they chopped down a little tree in the form of a yellow primrose blossom, cut it into bits, and took it home.

Marcovaldo came home with his scant armful of damp branches, and found the stove burning.

"Where did you find it?" he cried, pointing to what

remained of a billboard, which, being of plywood, had burned very quickly.

"In the forest!" the children said.

"What forest?"

"The one by the highway. It's full of wood!"

Since it was so simple, and there was need of more wood, he thought he might as well follow the children's example, and Marcovaldo again went out with his saw. He went to the highway.

Officer Astolfo, of the highway police, was a bit short-sighted, and on night duty, racing on his motorcycle, he should have worn eyeglasses; but he didn't say so, for fear it would block his advancement.

That evening, there was a report that on the super-highway a bunch of kids was knocking down billboards. Officer Astolfo set out to inspect.

On either side of the road, the forest of strange figures, admonishing and gesticulating, accompanied Astolfo, who peered at them one by one, widening his near-sighted eyes. There, in the beam of his motorcycle's headlight, he caught a little urchin who had climbed up on a billboard. Astolfo put on the brakes. "Hey, what are you doing there? Jump down this minute!" The kid didn't move and stuck out its tongue. Astolfo approached and saw it was an ad for processed cheese, with a big child licking his lips. "Yes, of course," Astolfo said, and zoomed off.

A little later, in the shadow of a huge billboard, he illuminated a sad, frightened face. "Don't make a move! Don't try running away!" But nobody ran away. It was a suffering human face painted in the midst of a foot covered with corns: an ad for a corn-remover. "Oh, sorry," Astolfo said, and dashed away.

The billboard for a headache tablet was a gigantic head of a man, his hands over his eyes, in pain. Astolfo sped past, and the headlight illuminated Marcovaldo, who had scrambled to the top with his saw, trying to cut off a slice. Dazzled by the light, Marcovaldo huddled down and remained motionless, clinging to an ear of the big head, where the saw had already reached the middle of the brow.

Astolfo examined it carefully and said: "Oh, yes. Stappa tablets! Very effective ad! Smart idea! That little man up there with the saw represents the migraine that is cutting the head in two. I got it right away!" And he went off, content.

All was silence and cold. Marcovaldo heaved a sigh of relief, settled on his uncomfortable perch, and resumed work. The muffled scrape of the saw against the wood spread through the moonlit sky.

SPRING

9. The good air

"These children," the Public Health doctor said, "need to breathe some good air, at a certain altitude; they should run through meadows . . ."

He was between the beds of the half-basement where the family lived, and was pressing his stethoscope against little Teresa's back, between her shoulder-blades, frail as the wings of a tiny featherless bird. The beds were two, and the four children, all ill, peeked out at the head and foot of each bed, with flushed cheeks and glistening eyes.

"On meadows like the flower-bed in the square?" Michelino asked.

"The altitude of a skyscraper?" asked Filippetto.

"Air that's good to eat?" asked Pietruccio.

Marcovaldo, tall and skinny, and his wife, Domitilla, short and squat, were leaning on one elbow on either side of a rickety chest of drawers. Without moving the elbow, each raised the other arm and then dropped it, grumbling together: "Where are we supposed to find those things, six mouths to feed, loaded with debts? How are we supposed to manage?"

"The most beautiful place we can send them," Marcovaldo declared, "is into the streets."

"We'll find good air," Domitilla concluded, "when we're evicted and have to sleep under the stars."

40

One Saturday afternoon, as soon as they were well again, Marcovaldo took the children and led them off on a walk in the hills. The part of the city where they lived is the farthest from the hills. To reach the slopes they made a long journey on a crowded tram and the children saw only the legs of passengers around them. Little by little the tram emptied; at the windows, finally freed, an avenue appeared, climbing up. And so they reached the end of the line and set forth.

It was early spring; the trees were just budding in a tepid sun. The children looked around, slightly disoriented. Marcovaldo led them up a little path of steps, rising among the green.

"Why is there a stairway without a house over it?" Michelino asked.

"It's not a house stairway; it's like a street."

"A street . . . And how can the cars manage the steps?"

Around them there were garden walls, with trees inside.

"Walls without a roof . . . Did they bomb them?"

"They're gardens . . . like courtyards . . ." the father explained. "The house is farther back, beyond those trees."

Michelino shook his head, unconvinced. "But courtyards are inside houses, not outside."

Teresina asked: "Do the trees live in these houses?"

As they climbed up, it seemed to Marcovaldo that he was gradually shedding the moldy smell of the warehouse in which he shifted packages for eight hours a day and the damp stains on the walls of his house and the dust that settled, gilded, in the cone of light from the little window, and the fits of coughing in the darkness. His children now seemed to him less sallow and frail, already somehow part of that light and that green.

"You like it here, don't you?"

"Yes."

"Why?"

"There aren't any police. You can pull up the flowers, throw stones."

"What about breathing? Are you breathing?"

"No."

"The air's good here."

They chewed it. "What are you talking about? It doesn't have any taste at all."

They climbed almost to the top of the hill. At one turn, the city appeared, way down below, spread flat on the gray cobweb of the streets. The children rolled around on a meadow as if they had never done anything else in their life. A little breeze sprang up; it was already evening. In the city a few lights came on, in a confused sparkle. Marcovaldo felt again a rush of the feeling he had had as a young man, arriving in the city, when those streets, those lights attracted him as if he expected something unknown from them. The swallows plunged headlong through the air onto the city.

Then he was seized by the sadness of having to go back down there, and in the clotted landscape he figured out the shadow of his neighborhood: it seemed to him a leaden wasteland, stagnant, covered by the thick scales of the roofs and the shreds of smoke flapping on the stick-like chimney-pots.

It had turned cool: perhaps he should call the children. But seeing them swinging peacefully on the lower limbs of a tree, he dismissed that thought. Michelino came over to him and asked: "Papà, why don't we come and live here?"

"Stupid, there aren't any houses; nobody lives up here!" Marcovaldo said, with irritation, because he had actually been daydreaming of being able to live up there.

And Michelino said: "Nobody? What about those gentlemen? Look!"

The air was turning gray and down from the meadows came a troop of men, of various ages, all dressed in heavy gray suits, buttoned up like pyjamas, all with cap and cane. They came in bunches, some talking in loud voices or laughing, sticking those canes into the grass or carrying them, hung by the curved handle, over their arm.

"Who are they? Where are they going?" Michelino asked his father, but Marcovaldo was looking at them, silent.

One passed nearby; he was a heavy man of about forty. "Good evening!" he said. "Well, what news do you bring us, from down in the city?"

"Good evening," Marcovaldo said. "What do you mean by news?"

"Nothing. I was just talking," the man said, and stopped; he had a broad, white face, with only a splotch of pink, or red, like a shadow, over his cheekbones. "I always say that, to anybody from the city. I've been up here for three months, you understand."

"And you never go down?"

"Hmph, when the doctors decide to let me!" And he laughed briefly. "And this!" And he tapped his fingers on his chest, with some more brief laughter, a bit breathless. "They've already discharged me twice, as cured, but as soon as I went back to the factory, wham, all over again. And they ship me back up here. Some fun!"

"Them too?" Marcovaldo asked, nodding at the other men, who had scattered over the grass; and at the same time, his eyes sought Filippetto and Teresa and Pietruccio, whom he had lost sight of.

"All comrades on the same holiday," the man said, and winked. "We're let out on a pass, before taps . . . We go to bed early . . . Obviously, we can't go beyond the grounds . . ."

"What grounds?"

"This is part of the sanatorium. Didn't you know?"

Marcovaldo took the hand of Michelino, who had stood there listening, a bit scared. Evening was climbing up the slopes; there below, their neighborhood was no longer discernible, and it seemed not so much to have been swallowed by the shadows, but to have spread its own shadow everywhere. It was time to go back. "Teresa! Filippetto!" Marcovaldo called and started to look for them. "Sorry," he said to the man, "I don't see the other children anywhere."

The man stepped to a parapet. "They're down there," he said, "they're picking cherries."

In a ditch, Marcovaldo saw a cherry tree and around it were the men dressed in gray, pulling down the branches with their curved sticks, and picking the fruit. And Teresa and the two boys, all delighted, were also picking cherries and taking them from the men's hands and laughing with them.

"It's late," Marcovaldo said. "It's cold. Let's go home . . ."

The heavy man pointed the tip of his cane towards the rows of lights that were coming on, down below.

"In the evening," he said, "with this stick I take my walk in the city. I choose a street, a row of lamps, and I follow it, like this . . . I stop at the windows, I meet people, I say hello to them . . . When you walk in the city, think of it sometimes: my cane is following you . . ."

The children came back crowned with leaves, made by the inmates.

"This is a wonderful place, Papà!" Teresa said. "We'll come and play here again, won't we?"

"Papà!" Michelino blurted. "Why don't we come and live here, too, with these gentlemen?"

"It's late. Say good-bye to the gentlemen! Say thanks for the cherries. Come on! We're going!"

They headed home. They were tired. Marcovaldo didn't answer any questions. Filippetto wanted to be carried, Pietruccio wanted to ride piggy-back, Teresa made him drag her by the hand, and Michelino, the oldest, went ahead by himself, kicking stones.

SUMMER

10. A journey with the cows

The city noises that on summer nights come through the open windows into the rooms of those who are made sleepless by the heat, the true noises of the night-time city, are audible at a certain hour, when the anonymous din of motors dies away and is silent, and from the silence, discreet, distinct, graduated according to the distance, emerge the step of a noctambulant, the rustle of a night watchman's bike, a remote muddled brawl, and a snoring from the upper floors, the groan of a sick man, the continued striking of an old clock every hour. Until, at dawn, the orchestra of alarm clocks in the working-class houses tunes up, and a tram goes by on its tracks.

And so, one night, between his wife and the children all sweating in their sleep, Marcovaldo lay with his eyes closed, to listen to as much of this powdering of frail sounds as filtered from the pavement down through the low windows into his half-basement. He heard the swift, cheerful heel of a woman who was late, the patched sole of the man who stopped irregularly to collect cigarette butts, the whistle of someone who felt alone, and every now and then a broken clash of words in a dialogue between friends, enough to suggest they were talking about sports or money. But in the hot night those sounds lost all relief, they dissolved as if dampened by the sultry heat that crammed

45

the void of the streets, and yet they seemed to want to impose themselves, to assert their dominion over that uninhabited realm. In every human presence Marcovaldo recognized sadly a brother, stuck like him, even in vacation time, to that oven of cooked and dusty cement, by debts, by the burden of the family, by the meagerness of his wages.

And as if the impossible thought of vacation had suddenly opened the gates of a dream to him, he seemed to hear a distant clank of bells, and a dog's bark, and also a brief lowing. But his eyes were open, he wasn't dreaming: and, pricking up his ears, he sought to regain a grip on those vague impressions, or a denial of them; and he actually did hear a sound as of hundreds and hundreds of steps, slow, scattered, hollow, which came closer and drowned out all other sounds, except, indeed, that rusty clanking.

Marcovaldo got up, slipped on his shirt and trousers. "Where are you going?" asked his wife, who slept with one eye open.

"There's a herd of cattle passing in the street. I'm going to see it."

"Me, too! Me, too!" cried the children, who knew how to wake up at the right moment.

It was the sort of herd that used to cross the city at night, in early summer, going towards the mountains for the alpine pasture. Climbing into the street with their eyes still half-closed in sleep, the children saw the stream of dun or piebald withers which invaded the sidewalk, brushed against the walls covered with bills, the lowered shutters, the stakes of no-parking signs, the gasoline pumps. Cautiously extending their hoofs from the step at the intersections, their muzzles never betraying a jolt of curiosity, pressed against the loins of those ahead of them, the cows brought with them the odor of dung, wild flowers, milk and the languid sound of their bells, and the city seemed not to touch them, already absorbed as they were into their world of damp meadows, mountain mists and the fords of streams.

Impatient, on the contrary, as if made nervous by the looming city, the cowherds wore themselves out in brief, futile dashes along the side of the line, raising their sticks and bursting out in broken, guttural cries. The dogs, to whom nothing human is alien, made a display of nonchalance, proceeding with noses erect, little bells tinkling, intent on their job; but clearly they too were uneasy and restless, otherwise they would have allowed themselves to be distracted and would have begun sniffing corners, lamp-posts, stains on the pavement, as is every city dog's first thought.

"Papà," the children said. "Are cows like trams? Do they have stops? Where's the beginning of the cows' line?"

"There's no connection between them and trams," Marcovaldo explained. "They're going to the mountains."

"Can they wear skis?" Pietruccio asked.

"They're going to pasture, to eat grass."

"Don't they get fined if they trample the lawns?"

The only one not asking questions was Michelino, who, older than the others, already had his own ideas about cows, and was now intent simply on checking them, observing the mild horns, the withers, and variegated coats. And so he followed the herd, trotting along at its side like the sheep dogs.

When the last group had passed, Marcovaldo took the children's hands to go back to sleep, but he couldn't see Michelino. He went down into the room and asked his wife: "Has Michelino already come home?"

"Michelino? Wasn't he with you?"

"He started following the herd, and God only knows where he's got to," Marcovaldo thought, and ran back to the street. The herd had already crossed the square, and Marcovaldo had to look for the street it had turned into. But that night, it seemed, various herds were crossing the city, each along a different street, each heading for its own valley. Marcovaldo tracked down and overtook one herd, then realized it wasn't his; at an intersection he saw, four streets farther on, another herd proceeding along a parallel, and he ran that way; there, the cowherds told him they had met another heading in the opposite direction. And so, until the last sound of a cow-bell had died away in the dawn light, Marcovaldo went on combing the city in vain.

The captain to whom he went to report his son's disappearance said: "Followed a herd of cows? He's probably gone off to the mountains, for a summer holiday, lucky kid. Don't worry: he'll come back all tanned and fattened up."

The captain's opinion was confirmed a few days later by a clerk in the place where Marcovaldo worked who had returned from his first-shift holiday. At a mountain pass he had encountered the boy: he was with the herd, he sent greetings to his father, and he was fine.

In the dusty city heat Marcovaldo kept thinking of his lucky son, who now was surely spending his hours in a fir tree's shade, whistling with a wisp of grass in his mouth, looking down at the cows moving slowly over the meadow, and listening to a murmur of waters in the shadows of the valley.

His Mamma, on the contrary, couldn't wait for him to return: "Will he come back by train? By bus? It's been a week . . . It's been a month . . . The weather must be bad . . ." And she could find no peace, even though having one fewer at table every day was in itself a relief.

"Lucky kid, up in the cool, stuffing himself with butter and cheese," Marcovaldo said, and every time, at the end of the street, there appeared, in a light haze, the jagged white and gray of the mountains, he felt as if he had sunk into a well, in whose light, up at the top, he seemed to see maple and chestnut fronds glinting, and to hear wild bees buzzing, and Michelino up there, lazy and happy, amid milk and honey and blackberry thickets.

But he too was expecting his son's return evening after evening, though, unlike the boy's mother, he wasn't thinking of the schedules of trains and buses: he was listening at night to the footsteps on the street as if the little window of the room were the mouth of a seashell, re-echoing, when you put your ear to it, the sounds of the mountain.

One night he sat abruptly up in bed: it wasn't an illusion; he heard approaching on the cobbles that unmistakable trample of cloven hoofs, mixed with the tinkling of bells.

They ran to the street, he and the whole family. The herd was returning, slow and grave. And in the midst of the herd, astride a cow's back, his hands clutching its collar, his head bobbing at every step, was Michelino, half asleep.

They lifted him down, a dead weight; they hugged and kissed him. He was dazed.

"How are you? Was it beautiful?"

"Oh . . . yes . . ."

"Were you homesick?"

"Yes . . ."

"Is it beautiful in the mountains?"

He was standing, facing them, his brows knit, his gaze hard.

"I worked like a mule," he said, and spat on the ground. He now had a man's face. "Carrying the buckets to the milkers every evening, from one cow to the next, and then emptying them into the cans, in a hurry, always in a worse hurry, until late. And then early in the morning, rolling the cans down to the trucks that take them to the city. And counting . . . always counting: the cows, the cans, and if you made a mistake there was trouble . . ."

"But weren't you in the meadows? When the cows were grazing?"

"There was never enough time. Always something to be done. The milk, the bedding, the dung. And all for what? With the excuse that I didn't have a work–contract, what did they pay me? Practically nothing. But if you think I'm going to hand it over to you now, you're wrong. Come on, let's go to sleep; I'm dead tired."

He shrugged, blew his nose, and went into the house.

The herd was still moving away along the street, carrying with it the lying, languid odor of hay and the sound of bells.

AUTUMN

11. The poisonous rabbit

When the day comes to leave the hospital, you already know it in the morning and if you're in good shape you move around the wards, practising the way you're going to walk when you're outside; you whistle, act like a well man with those still sick, not to arouse envy but for the pleasure of adopting a tone of encouragement. You see the sun beyond the big panes, or the fog if there's fog; you hear the sounds of the city; and everything is different from before, when every morning you felt them enter – the light and sound of an unattainable world – as you woke behind the bars of that bed. Now, outside, there is your world again. The healed man recognizes it as natural and usual; and suddenly he notices once more the smell of the hospital.

Marcovaldo, one morning, was sniffing around like that, cured, waiting for them to write certain things in his health insurance book so that he could leave. The doctor took his papers, said to him, "Wait here", and left him alone in the office. Marcovaldo looked at the white-enameled furniture he had so hated, the test-tubes full of grim substances, and tried to cheer himself with the thought that he was about to leave it all. But he couldn't manage to feel the joy he would have expected. Perhaps it was the idea of going back to the warehouse to shift packing cases, or of the mischief his children had surely been up to in his absence, and especially

of the fog outside that made him think of having to step out
into the void, to dissolve in a damp nothingness. And so he
looked around, with a vague need to feel affection towards
something in here; but everything he saw reminded him of
torture or discomfort.

Then he saw a rabbit in a cage. It was a white rabbit, with
a long, fluffy coat, a pink triangle of a nose, amazed red
eyes, ears almost furless flattened against its back. It wasn't
all that big, but in the narrow cage its crouching oval body
made the wire screen bulge and clumps of fur stuck out,
ruffled by a slight trembling. Outside the cage, on the table,
there was some grass and the remains of a carrot. Marcovaldo
thought of how unhappy the animal must be, shut up in
there, seeing that carrot but not being able to eat it. And he
opened the door of the cage. The rabbit didn't come out:
it stayed there, still, with only a slight twitch of its face, as
if it were pretending to chew in order to seem nonchalant.
Marcovaldo took the carrot and held it closer, then slowly
drew it back, to urge the rabbit to come out. The rabbit
followed him, cautiously bit the carrot and began gnawing
it diligently, in Marcovaldo's hand. The man stroked it on
the back and, meanwhile, squeezed it, to see if it was fat. He
felt it was somewhat bony, under its coat. From this fact,
and from the way it pulled on the carrot, it was obvious that
they kept it on short rations. If it belonged to me,
Marcovaldo thought, I would stuff it until it became a ball.
And he looked at it with the loving eye of the breeder who
manages to allow kindness towards the animal to coexist
with anticipation of the roast, all in one emotion. There,
after days and days of sordid stay in the hospital, at the
moment of leaving, he discovered a friendly presence, which
would have sufficed to fill his hours and his thoughts. And
he had to leave it, go back into the foggy city, where you
don't encounter rabbits.

The carrot was almost finished. Marcovaldo took the
animal into his arms while he looked around for something
else to feed him. He held its nose to a potted geranium on

the doctor's desk, but the animal indicated it didn't like the plant. At that same moment Marcovaldo heard the doctor's step, coming back: how could he explain why he was holding the rabbit in his arms? He was wearing his heavy work coat, tight at the waist. In a hurry, he stuck the rabbit inside, buttoned his coat all the way up, and to keep the doctor from seeing that wriggling bulge at his stomach, he shifted it around to his back. The rabbit, frightened, behaved itself. Marcovaldo collected his papers and moved the rabbit to his chest, because he had to turn and leave. And so, with the rabbit hidden under his coat, he left the hospital and went to work.

"Ah, you're cured at last?" the foreman, Signor Viligelmo, said, seeing him arrive. "And what's that growth there?" and he pointed to the bulging chest.

"I'm wearing a hot poultice to prevent cramps," Marcovaldo said.

At that, the rabbit twitched, and Marcovaldo jumped up like an epileptic.

"Now what's come over you?" Viligelmo said.

"Nothing. Hiccups," he answered, and with one hand he shoved the rabbit behind his back.

"You're still a bit seedy, I notice," the boss said.

The rabbit was trying to crawl up his back, and Marcovaldo shrugged hard to send it down again.

"You're shivering. Go home for another day. And make sure you're well tomorrow."

Marcovaldo came home, carrying the rabbit by its ears, like a lucky hunter.

"Papà! Papà!" the children hailed him, running to meet him. "Where did you catch it? Can we have it? Is it a present for us?" And they tried to grab it at once.

"You're back?" his wife said, and from the look she gave him, Marcovaldo realized that his period of hospitalization had served only to enable her to accumulate new grievances against him. "A live animal? What are you going to do with it? It'll make messes all over the place."

Marcovaldo cleared the table and set the rabbit down in the middle, where it huddled flat, as if trying to vanish. "Don't anybody dare touch it!" he said. "This is our rabbit, and it's going to fatten up peacefully till Christmas."

"Is it a male or a female?" Michelino asked.

Marcovaldo had given no thought to the possibility of its being a female. A new plan immediately occurred to him: if it was a female, he could mate her and start raising rabbits. And already in his imagination the damp walls disappeared and the room was a green farm among the fields.

But it was a male, all right. Still Marcovaldo had now got this idea of raising rabbits into his head. It was a male, but a very handsome male, for whom a bride should be found and the means to raise a family.

"What are we going to feed it, when we don't have enough for ourselves?" his wife asked, sharply.

"Let me give it some thought," Marcovaldo said.

The next day, at work, from some green potted plants in the Management Office, which he was supposed to take out every morning, water, then put back, he removed one leaf each—broad leaves, shiny on one side and opaque on the other—and stuck them into his overalls. Then, when one of the girls came in with a bunch of flowers, he asked her, "Did your boy-friend give them to you? Aren't you going to give me one?" and he pocketed that, too. To a boy peeling a pear, he said, "Leave me the peel." And so, a leaf here, a peeling there, a petal somewhere else, he hoped to feed the animal.

At a certain point, Signor Viligelmo sent for him. Can they have noticed the plants are missing leaves? Marcovaldo wondered, accustomed always to feeling guilty.

In the foreman's office there was the doctor from the hospital, two Red Cross men, and a city policeman. "Listen," the doctor said, "a rabbit has disappeared from my laboratory. If you know anything about it, you'd better not try to act smart. Because we've injected it with the germs of a terrible disease and it can spread it through the whole city. I needn't ask if you've eaten it; if you had, you'd be dead and gone by now."

An ambulance was waiting outside; they rushed and got in it, and with the siren screaming constantly, they went through streets and avenues to Marcovaldo's house, and along the way there remained a wake of leaves and peelings and flowers that Marcovaldo sadly threw out of the window.

Marcovaldo's wife that morning simply didn't know what to put in the pot. She looked at the rabbit her husband had brought home the day before, now in a makeshift cage, filled with shavings. "It arrived just at the right moment," she said to herself. "There's no money; his wages have already gone for the extra medicines the Public Health doesn't cover; the shops won't give us any more credit. Raise rabbits, indeed! Or wait till Christmas to roast it! We're skipping meals, and we're supposed to fatten a rabbit!"

"Isolina," she said to her daughter, "you're a big girl now, you have to learn how to cook a rabbit. You begin by killing it and skinning it, and then I'll tell you what to do next."

Isolina was reading a magazine of sentimental romances. "No," she whined, "*you* begin by killing it and skinning it, and then I'll watch how you cook it."

"What a help!" her mother said. "I don't have the heart to kill it. But I know it's a very easy matter; you just have to hold it by the ears and hit it hard on the back of the head. As for skinning, we'll see."

"We won't see anything," the daughter said, without raising her nose from the magazine. "I'm not hitting a live rabbit on the head. And I haven't the slightest notion of skinning it, either."

The three little ones had listened to this dialogue with wide eyes.

Their mother pondered for a moment, looked at them, then said, "Children . . ."

The children, as if by agreement, turned their backs on their mother and left the room.

"Wait, children!" their mother said. "I wanted to ask you if you'd like to take the rabbit outside. We'll tie a pretty ribbon around his neck and you can go for a walk with him."

The children stopped and exchanged looks. "A walk where?" Michelino asked.

"Oh, a little stroll. Then go call on Signora Diomira, show her the rabbit, and ask her if she'll please kill it and skin it for us. She's so good at that."

The mother had found the right method: children, as everyone knows, are caught up by the thing they like most, and they prefer not to think of the rest. And so they found a long, lilac-colored ribbon, tied it around the animal's neck, and used it as a leash, fighting over it, and pulling after them the reluctant, half-strangled rabbit.

"Tell Signora Diomira," the mother insisted, "that she can keep a leg for herself! No, better the head. Oh, she can take her pick."

The children had barely gone out when Marcovaldo's room was surrounded and invaded by orderlies, doctors, guards, and policemen. Marcovaldo was in their midst, more dead than alive. "Where is the rabbit that was taken from the hospital? Hurry: show us where it is, but don't touch it; it's infected with the germs of a terrible disease!" Marcovaldo led them to the cage, but it was empty. "Already eaten?" "No, no!" "Where is it then?" "At Signora Diomira's!" And the pursuers resumed their hunt.

They knocked at Signora Diomira's door. "Rabbit? What rabbit? Are you crazy?" Seeing her house invaded by strangers, in white jackets or uniforms, looking for a rabbit, the old woman nearly had a stroke. She knew nothing about Marcovaldo's rabbit.

In fact, the three children, trying to save the rabbit from death, had decided to take it to a safe place, play with it for a while, and then let it go; and instead of stopping at Signora

Diomira's landing, they decided to climb up to a terrace over the rooftops. They would tell their mother it had broken the leash and had run off. But no animal seemed so ill-suited to an escape as that rabbit. Making it climb all those steps was a problem: it huddled, frightened, on each step. In the end they picked it up and carried it.

On the terrace they wanted to make it run: it wouldn't run. They tried setting it on the edge of the roof, to see if it would walk the way cats do; but it seemed to suffer vertigo. They tried hoisting it onto a TV antenna, to see if it could keep its balance: no, it fell down. Bored, the children ripped away the leash, turned the animal loose at a place where all the paths of the roofs opened out, an oblique and angular sea, and they left.

When it was alone, the rabbit began moving. It ventured a few steps, looked around, changed direction, turned, then, in little hops and skips, it started over the roofs. It was an animal born prisoner: its yearning for liberty did not have broad horizons. The greatest gift it had known in life was the ability to have a few moments free of fear. Now, now it could move, with nothing around to frighten it, perhaps for the first time in its life. The place was unfamiliar, but a clear concept of familiar and unfamiliar was something it had never been able to formulate. And ever since it had begun to feel an undefined, mysterious ailment gnawing inside itself, the whole world was of less and less interest to it. And so it went onto the roofs; and the cats that saw it hopping didn't understand what it was and they drew back, in awe.

Meanwhile, from skylights, from dormer windows, from flat decks, the rabbit's itinerary had not gone unremarked. Some people began to display basins of salad on their sills, peeking then from behind the curtains, others threw a pear core on the roof-tiles and spread a string lasso around it, someone else arranged a row of bits of carrot along the parapet, leading to his own window. And a rallying-cry ran through all the families living in the garrets: "Stewed rabbit today" – or "fricasseed rabbit" – or "roast rabbit".

The animal had noticed these lures, these silent offers of food. And though it was hungry, it didn't trust them. It knew that every time humans tried to attract it with offers of food, something obscure and painful happened: either they stuck a syringe into its flesh, or a scalpel, or they forced it into a buttoned-up jacket, or they dragged it along with a ribbon around its neck . . . And the memory of these misfortunes merged with the pain it felt inside, with the slow change of organs that it sensed, with the prescience of death. And hunger. But as if it knew that, of all these discomforts, only hunger could be allayed, and recognized that these treacherous human beings could provide, in addition to cruel sufferings, a sense – which it also needed – of protection, of domestic warmth, it decided to surrender to play the humans' game: then whatever had to happen, would happen. So, it began to eat the bits of carrot, following the trail that, as the rabbit well knew, would make it prisoner and martyr again, but savoring once more, and perhaps for the last time, the good earthy flavor of vegetables. Now it was approaching the garret window, now a hand would stretch out to catch it: instead, all of a sudden, the window slammed and closed it out. This was an event alien to its experience: a trap that refused to snap shut. The rabbit turned, looked for other signs of treachery around, to choose the best one to give in to. But meanwhile the leaves of salad had been drawn indoors, the lassos thrown away, the lurking people had vanished, windows and skylights were now barred, terraces were deserted.

It so happened that a police truck had passed through the city, with a loudspeaker shouting: "Attention, attention! A long-haired white rabbit has been lost; it is affected by a serious, contagious disease! Anyone finding it should be informed that it is poisonous to eat; even its touch can transmit harmful germs! Anyone seeing it should alert the nearest police station, hospital, or fire house!"

Terror spread over the rooftops. Everyone was on guard, and the moment they sighted the rabbit, which, with a limp flop, moved from one roof to the next, they gave the alarm, and all disappeared as if at the approach of a swarm of locusts. The rabbit proceeded, teetering on the cornices; this sense of solitude, just at the moment when it had discovered the necessity of human nearness, seemed even more menacing to it, unbearable.

Meanwhile Cavalier Ulrico, an old hunter, had loaded his rifle with cartridges for hare, and had gone to take his stand on a terrace, hiding behind a chimney. When he saw the white shadow of the rabbit emerge from the fog, he fired; but his emotion at the thought of the animal's evil bane was so great that the spatter of shot fell a bit off the mark onto the tiles, like hail. The rabbit heard the shot rattle all around, and one pellet pierced its ear. It understood: this was a declaration of war; at this point all relations with mankind were broken off. And in its contempt of humans, at what seemed, to the rabbit, somehow a base ingratitude, it decided to end it all.

A roof covered with corrugated iron sloped down, oblique, and ended at the void, in the opaque nothingness of the fog. The rabbit planted itself there on all four paws, first cautiously, then letting itself go. And so, slipping, surrounded and consumed by its pain, it went towards death. At the edge, the drainpipe delayed it for a second, then it tumbled down . . .

And it landed in the gloved hands of a fireman, perched at the top of a portable ladder. Foiled even in that extreme act of animal dignity, the rabbit was bundled into the ambulance, which set off full-tilt towards the hospital. Also aboard were Marcovaldo, his wife, and his children, to be interned for observation and for a series of vaccine tests.

WINTER

12. The wrong stop

For anyone who dislikes his home and finds it inhospitable, the favorite refuge on cold evenings is the movies. Marcovaldo had a passion for Technicolor films on the wide screen, which can embrace the most vast horizons: prairies, rocky mountains, equatorial forests, islands where you live with a garland around your head. He would see the picture twice, and he never came out until they were closing the theater; and in his thoughts he continued living in those landscapes and breathing those colors. But the return home in the drizzling night, the wait at the stop for tram number 30, the realization that his life would know no other setting beyond trams, traffic-lights, rooms in the half-basement, gas stoves, drying laundry, warehouses and shipping rooms, made the film's splendor fade for him to a worn and gray sadness.

That evening, the film he had seen took place in the forests of India: steam rose in clouds from the swampy undergrowth, and serpents slithered along the lianas and climbed up the statues of ancient temples swallowed up by the jungle.

Coming out of the theater, he opened his eyes at the street, closed them again, reopened them: he saw nothing. Absolutely nothing. Not even in front of his nose. In the hours he had spent inside, fog had invaded the city, a thick, opaque fog, which engulfed things and sounds, flattened distances into a space without dimensions, mixed lights into the darkness and transformed them into glows without shape or place.

Marcovaldo headed mechanically for the stop of the 30 tram and banged his nose against the signpost. At that moment he realized he was happy: the fog, erasing the world around him, allowed him to hold in his eyes the visions of the wide screen. Even the cold was muffled, as if the city had pulled a cloud over it, like a blanket. Bundled up in his overcoat, Marcovaldo felt protected from every external sensation, suspended in the void; and he could color this void with the images of India, the Ganges, the jungle, Calcutta.

The tram arrived, evanescent as a phantom, slowly jangling; things existed just to the slight extent that sufficed; for Marcovaldo staying at the rear of the tram that evening, his back to the other passengers, as he stared beyond the panes at the empty night traversed only by undefined luminous presences and by an occasional shadow blacker than the darkness, offered the perfect situation for day-dreaming, for projecting in front of himself, wherever he went, a never-ending film on a boundless screen.

With these fantasies he lost count of the stops; all at once he asked himself where he was; he saw the tram was now almost empty; he peered out of the windows, interpreted the glimmers that surfaced, decided his stop was the next, ran to the door just in time, and got out. He looked around, seeking some reference-point. But the few shadows and lights his eyes could discern refused to form any known image. He had got off at the wrong stop and didn't know where he was.

If he met a passer-by it would be easy to ask him the way; but whether because of the loneliness of this place or because of the hour or the bad weather, there wasn't a shadow of a human being to be seen. Finally he saw one, a shadow, and waited for it to come closer. No, it was moving away; perhaps it was crossing the street, or walking down the middle of it; it might not be a pedestrian, but a cyclist, on a bicycle without a headlight.

Marcovaldo cried out: "Hey! Hey, mister! Please, can you tell me where Via Pancrazio Pancrazietti is?"

The shape moved farther away, was now almost invisible. "That way . . ." But there was no telling which way he had pointed.

"Right or left?" shouted Marcovaldo, but he could have been addressing the void.

An answer came, the wake of an answer: ". . . eft!" but it could also have been ". . . ight!" In any case, since there was no seeing which way the other man faced, right and left meant nothing.

Now Marcovaldo was walking towards a glow that seemed to come from the opposite sidewalk, a bit farther on. But the distance proved to be much greater: he had to cross a kind of square, with a little island of grass in the middle, and arrows (the only intelligible sign) indicating that traffic had to keep right. It was late, but surely some café was still open, some tavern; the sign he was just beginning to decipher said: Bar . . . Then it went out; on what must have been an illuminated window a shaft of darkness fell, like a blind. The bar was closing, and it was still—he seemed to understand at that moment—very far away.

So he might as well head for another light. As he walked, Marcovaldo didn't know if he was following a straight line, if the luminous dot he was now heading for was always the same or had doubled or trebled or changed position. The soot, a somewhat milky black, within which he moved was so fine that already he felt it infiltrating his overcoat, as if through a sieve, between the threads of the cloth, which soaked it up like a sponge.

The light he reached was the smoky entrance to a tavern. Inside, there were people seated or standing at the counter, but, because of the poor illumination or because the fog had penetrated everywhere, even here forms seemed blurred, like certain taverns you see in the movies, situated in ancient times or in distant lands.

"I was looking . . . maybe you gentlemen know where it is . . . for Via Pancrazietti . . ." he began saying, but there was noise in the tavern, drunks who laughed, believing him drunk, and the questions he managed to ask, the explanations he managed to obtain, were also foggy and blurred. Especially since, to warm himself, he ordered—or rather, he allowed the men standing at the counter to force on him – a quarter-liter of wine, at first, and then another half-liter, plus a few glasses which, with great slaps on the back, were offered him by the others. In short, when he came out of the tavern, his notions of the way home were no clearer than before, though, in compensation, the fog was more than ever capable of containing all continents and colors.

With the warmth of the wine inside him, Marcovaldo walked for a good quarter of an hour, with steps that constantly felt the need of stretching to the left and to the right, to gauge the width of the sidewalk (if he was still following a sidewalk), and hands that felt the need to touch continuously the walls (if he was still following a wall). The fog in his thoughts, as he walked, was gradually dispelled; but the fog outside remained dense. He remembered that at the tavern they had told him to take a certain avenue, follow it for a hundred yards, then ask again. But now he didn't know how far he had come from the tavern, or if he had only walked around the block.

The spaces seemed uninhabited, within brick walls like the confines of factories. At one corner there was surely the marble plaque with the name of the street, but the light of the lamp-post, suspended between the two lanes, didn't reach that far. To approach the words, Marcovaldo climbed up a no-parking sign. He climbed until he could put his nose on the plaque, but the letters had faded and he had no matches to illuminate them better. Above the plaque, the wall ended in a flat, broad top, and leaning out from the no-parking sign, Marcovaldo managed to hoist himself up there. He had glimpsed, set above the top of the wall, a big whitish sign. He took a few steps along the top of the wall, reaching the sign; here the street-light illuminated the black letters on the white ground, but the words: "Access to unauthorized persons strictly prohibited" gave him no enlightenment.

The top of the wall was so wide that he could balance himself on it and walk; indeed, when he thought about it, it was better than the sidewalk, because the street-lights were high enough to illuminate his steps, making a bright stripe in the midst of the darkness. At a certain point the wall ended and Marcovaldo found himself against the capital of a gate-post. No: the wall made a right angle and went on . . .

And so, what with angles, niches, junctures, posts, Marcovaldo's route followed an irregular pattern; several times he thought the wall was ending, then discovered it continued in another direction; after so many turns he no longer knew what direction he was headed in, or rather, on which side he should jump, if he wanted to move down to the street. Jump . . . And what if the height had increased? He crouched on the top of a column, tried to peer down, on one side and the other, but no ray of light reached the ground: it might be a little drop of a couple of yards, or an abyss. The only thing he could do was continue advancing up where he was.

The avenue of escape was not long in appearing. It was a flat surface, a pale glimmer, next to the wall: perhaps the roof of a building, of cement – as Marcovaldo realized, when he began to walk on it – which extended into the darkness. He immediately regretted having ventured onto it; now he had lost all reference-points, he had moved away from the line of street-lights, and every step he took might bring him to the edge of the roof or, beyond it, into the void.

The void really was a chasm. From below little lights glowed, as if at a great distance, and if those were the street-lights down there, the ground must be much lower still. Marcovaldo found himself suspended in a space impossible to imagine: at times, up above, red and green lights appeared, arranged in irregular figures, like constellations. Peering at those lights, with his nose in the air, he soon took a step into the void and fell headlong.

"I'm dead!" he thought; but at the same moment he found himself seated on some soft earth; his hands touched some grass; he had fallen, unharmed, into the midst of a meadow. The low lights, which had seemed so distant to him, were a line of little bulbs at ground-level.

A peculiar place to put lights, but convenient all the same, because they marked out a path for him. His foot now was not treading on grass but on asphalt: in the midst of the meadow a broad paved street passed, illuminated by those luminous beams at ground-level. Around him, nothing: only the very high, colored lights, which appeared and disappeared.

"A paved road is sure to lead somewhere," Marcovaldo thought, and started following it. He arrived at a fork, or rather, at an intersection, where every branch of the road was flanked by those little low bulbs and huge white numbers were marked on the ground.

He lost heart. What did it matter which direction he chose to follow if, all around, there was only this flat grassy meadow and this empty fog? It was at this point that he saw, at a man's height, a movement of beams of light. A man, really a man, with his arms open, dressed – it seemed – in a yellow overall, was waving two luminous little disks like the kind station-masters wave.

Marcovaldo ran towards this man and, even before reaching him, he started saying breathlessly: "Hey, hey, listen, here in the midst of the fog, how do I – "

"Don't worry," the voice of the man in yellow replied. "Above a thousand meters there's no fog, you can proceed safely. The steps are just ahead; the others have already boarded."

The words were obscure, but heartening: Marcovaldo

was particularly pleased to hear there were other people not far away; he advanced to join them, without asking further questions.

The mysteriously announced steps were a little stairway with comfortable steps and two railings, white in the darkness. Marcovaldo climbed up. On the threshold of a low doorway, a girl greeted him so cordially it seemed impossible she was actually addressing him.

Marcovaldo bowed and scraped. "My humble respects, Signorina." Steeped in cold and dampness as he was, he was dazed at finding refuge under a roof . . .

He entered, blinked, his eyes blinded by the light. He wasn't in a house. He was – where? In a bus, he thought, a long bus with many empty places. He sat down. As a rule, going home from work, he never took the bus, but chose the tram because the ticket cost a bit less. This time, however, he was lost in a neighborhood so remote that surely there was only a bus service. How lucky he was to have arrived in time to catch this one, no doubt the last! And what soft, comfortable seats! Marcovaldo, now that he had found out about it, would always take the bus, even if the passengers were obliged to obey some rules (". . . Please," a loudspeaker was saying, "refrain from smoking and fasten your seatbelts . . ."), even if the roar of the motor, as it started, was excessive.

A man in uniform passed among the seats. "Excuse me, conductor," Marcovaldo said. "Do you know if there's a stop anywhere near Via Pancrazio Pancrazietti?"

"What are you talking about, sir? Our first stop is Bombay, then we go on to Calcutta and Singapore."

Marcovaldo looked around. In the other places were seated impassive Indians, with beards and turbans. There were also a few women, wrapped in embroidered saris, a painted spot on their brow. The night beyond the windows was full of stars, now that the plane had passed through the thick blanket of fog, and was flying in the limpid sky of the great altitudes.

SPRING

13. Where the river is more blue?

It was a time when the simplest foods contained threats, traps, and frauds. Not a day went by without some newspaper telling of ghastly discoveries in the housewife's shopping: cheese was made of plastic, butter from tallow candles; in fruit and vegetables the arsenic of insecticides was concentrated in percentages higher than the vitamin content; to fatten chickens they stuffed them with synthetic pills that could transform the man who ate a drumstick into a chicken himself. Fresh fish had been caught the previous year in Iceland and they put make-up on the eyes to make it seem yesterday's catch. Mice had been found in several milk-bottles, whether dead or alive was not made clear. From the tins of oil it was no longer the golden juice of the olive that flowed, but the fat of old mules, cleverly distilled.

At work or in the café Marcovaldo heard them discussing these things, and every time he felt something like a mule's kick in his stomach, or a mouse running down his esophagus. At home, when his wife, Domitilla, came back from the market, the sight of her shopping-bag, which once had given him such joy with its celery and eggplant, the rough, absorbent paper of the packages from the grocer or the delicatessen, now filled him with fear, as if hostile presences had infiltrated the walls of his house.

"I must bend all my efforts," he vowed to himself,

"towards providing my family with food that hasn't passed through the treacherous hands of speculators." In the morning, going to work, he sometimes encountered men with fishing-poles and rubber boots, heading for the river. "That's the way," Marcovaldo said to himself. But the river, there in the city, which collected garbage and waste and the emptying of sewers, filled him with deep repugnance. "I have to look for a place," he said to himself, "where the water is really water, and fish are really fish. There I'll drop my line."

The days were growing longer: with his motorbike, after work, Marcovaldo set to exploring the river along its course before the city, and the little streams, its tributaries. He was specially interested in the stretches where the water flowed farthest from the paved road. He proceeded along paths, among the clumps of willows, riding his motorbike as far as he could go, then – after leaving it in a bush – on foot, until he reached the stream. Once he got lost: he roamed among steep, overgrown slopes, and could find no trail, nor did he know in which direction the river lay. Then, all of a sudden, pushing some branches aside, he saw the silent water a few feet below him – it was a widening of the river, practically a calm little pool – of such a blue that it seemed a mountain lake.

His emotion didn't prevent him from peering down among the little ripples of the stream. And there, his stubbornness was rewarded! A flicker, the unmistakable flash of a fin at the surface, and then another, another still: such happiness, he could hardly believe his eyes. This was the place where the fish of the whole river assembled, the fisherman's paradise, perhaps still unknown to everyone but him. On his way home (it was already growing dark) he stopped and cut signs on the bark of the elms, and made piles of stones at certain spots, to be able to find the way again.

Now he had only to equip himself. Actually, he had already thought about it: among the neighbors and the personnel of his firm he had already identified about ten dedicated fishermen. With hints and allusions, promising each to inform him, the moment he was really sure, of a place full of tench that only he knew about, he managed to borrow, a bit from one, a bit from another, the most complete fisherman's outfit ever seen.

Now he lacked nothing: pole, line, hooks, bait, net, boots, creel. One fine morning, in a couple of hours – from six to eight, before going to work, at the river with the tench – could he fail to catch some? And in fact, he had only to drop his line and he caught them; the tench bit, without any suspicion. Since it was so easy with hook and line, he tried with the net; the tench were so good-natured that they rushed headlong into the net, too.

When it was time to leave, his creel was already full. He looked for a path, moving up the river.

"Hey, you!" At a curve in the shore, among the poplars, there was a character wearing a guard's cap, and giving him an ugly stare.

"Me? What is it?" Marcovaldo asked, sensing an unknown threat to his tench.

"Where did you catch those fish there?" the guard asked.

"Eh? Why?" And Marcovaldo's heart was already in his mouth.

"If you caught them down below, throw them back right now: didn't you see the factory up there?" And the man pointed out a long, low building that now, having come around the bend of the river, Marcovaldo could discern, beyond the willows, throwing smoke into the air and, into the water, a dense cloud of an incredible color somewhere between turquoise and violet. "You must at least have seen the color of the water! A paint factory: the river's poisoned because of that blue, and the fish are poisoned, as well. Throw them back right now, or I'll confiscate them!"

Marcovaldo would have liked to fling them far away as fast as possible, get rid of them, as if the mere smell were enough to poison him. But in front of the guard, he didn't want to humble himself. "What if I caught them farther up?"

"Then that's another story. I'll confiscate them and fine you, too. Above the factory there's a fishing preserve. Can't you see the sign?"

"Actually," Marcovaldo hastened to say, "I carry a fishing-pole just for looks, to fool my friends. I really bought the fish at the village shop nearby."

"Then everything's all right. You only have to pay the tax, to take them into the city: we're beyond the city limits here."

Marcovaldo had already opened the creel and was empty-ing it into the river. Some of the tench must have been still alive, because they darted off with great joy.

SUMMER

14. Moon and GNAC

The night lasted twenty seconds, then came twenty seconds of GNAC. For twenty seconds you could see the blue sky streaked with black clouds, the gilded sickle of the waxing moon, outlined by an impalpable halo, and stars that, the more you looked at them, the denser their poignant smallness became, to the sprinkle of the Milky Way: all this seen in great haste; every detail you dwelt on was something of the whole that you lost, because the twenty seconds quickly ended and the GNAC took over.

The GNAC was a part of the neon sign SPAAK-COGNAC on the roof opposite, which shone for twenty seconds then went off for twenty, and when it was lighted you couldn't see anything else. The moon suddenly faded, the sky became a flat, uniform black, the stars lost their radiance, and the cats, male and female, that for ten seconds had been letting out howls of love, moving languidly towards each other along the drainpipes and the roof-trees, squatted on the tiles, their fur bristling in the phosphorescent neon light.

Leaning out of the attic where they lived, Marcovaldo's family was traversed by conflicting trains of thought. It was night, and Isolina, a big girl by now, felt carried away by the moonlight; her heart yearned, and even the faintest croaking of a radio from the lower floors of the building came to her

like the notes of a serenade; there was the GNAC, and that
radio seemed to take on a different rhythm, a jazz beat, and
Isolina thought of the dance-hall full of blazing lights and
herself, poor thing, up here all alone. Pietruccio and
Michelino stared wide-eyed into the night and let themselves
be invaded by a warm, soft fear of being surrounded by
forests full of brigands; then, GNAC!, and they sprang
up with thumbs erect and forefingers extended, one against
the other: "Hands up! I'm the Lone Ranger!" Domitilla,
their mother, every time the light was turned off, thought:
"Now the children must be sent to bed; this air could be
bad for them; and Isolina shouldn't be looking out of the
window at this hour: it's not proper!" But then everything
was again luminous, electric, outside and inside, and
Domitilla felt as if she were paying a visit to the home of
someone important.

Fiordaligi, on the contrary, a melancholy youth, every
time the GNAC went off, saw the dimly lighted window of
a garret appear behind the curl of the G, and beyond the
pane the face of a moon-colored girl, neon-colored, the
color of light in the night, a mouth still almost a child's that,
the moment he smiled at her, parted imperceptibly and
seemed almost to open in a smile; then all of a sudden from
the darkness that implacable G of GNAC burst out again,
and the face lost its outline, was transformed into a weak,
pale shadow, and he could no longer tell if the girlish mouth
had responded to his smile.

In the midst of this storm of passions, Marcovaldo was
trying to teach his children the positions of the celestial
bodies.

"That's the Great Bear: one, two, three, four, and there,
the tail. And that's the Little Bear. And the Pole-Star that
means North."

"What does that one over there mean?"

"It means *C*. But that doesn't have anything to do with the
stars. It's the last letter of the word COGNAC. The stars
mark the four cardinal points. North South East West. The

moon's hump is to the west. Hump to the west, waxing
moon. Hump to the east, waning moon."

"Is cognac waning, Papà? The *C*'s hump is to the east!"

"Waxing and waning have nothing to do with that: it's a
sign the Spaak company has put there."

"What company put up the moon then?"

"The moon wasn't put up by a company. It's a satellite,
and it's always there."

"If it's always there, why does it keep changing its
hump?"

"It's the quarters. You only see a part of it."

"You only see a part of COGNAC too."

"Because the roof of the Pierbernardi building is higher."

"Higher than the moon?"

And so, every time the GNAC came on, Marcovaldo's
stars became mixed up with terrestrial commerce, and
Isolina transformed a sigh into a low humming of a mambo,
and the girl of the garret disappeared in that cold and dazzling
arc, hiding her response to the kiss that Fiordaligi had finally
summoned the courage to blow her on his fingertips, and
Filippetto and Michelino, their fists to their faces, played at
strafing: Tat–tat–tat–tat . . . against the glowing sign, which,
after its twenty seconds, went off.

"Tat–tat–tat . . . Did you see that, Papà? I shot it out with
just one burst." Filippetto said, but already, outside the
neon light, his warlike mania had vanished and his eyes
were filling with sleep.

"If you only had!" his father blurted. "If it had only been
blown to bits! I'd show you Leo the lion, the Twins . . ."

"Leo the lion!" Michelino was overcome with enthusiasm. "Wait!" He had an idea. He took his slingshot,
loaded it with gravel, of which he always carried a reserve
pocketful, and fired a volley of pebbles, with all his strength,
at the GNAC.

They heard the shower fall, scattered, on the tiles of the
roof opposite, on the tin of the drainpipes, the tinkle at the
panes of a window that had been struck, the gong of a

pebble plunging down on the metal shield of a street-light, a voice from below: "It's raining stones! Hey, you up there! Hoodlum." But at the very moment of the shooting the neon sign had turned off at the end of its twenty seconds. And everyone in the attic room began counting mentally: one two three, ten eleven, up to twenty. They counted nineteen, held their breath, they counted twenty, they counted twenty-one twenty-two, for fear of having counted too fast. But no, not at all: the GNAC didn't come on again; it remained a black curlicue, hard to decipher, twined around its scaffolding like a vine around a pergola. "Aaaah!" they all shouted and the hood of the sky rose, infinitely starry, above them.

Marcovaldo, his hand frozen halfway towards the slap he meant to give Michelino, felt as if he had been flung into space. The darkness that now reigned at roof-level made a kind of obscure barrier that shut out the world below, where yellow and green and red hieroglyphics continued to whirl, and the winking eyes of traffic-lights, and the luminous navigation of empty trams, and the invisible cars that cast in front of them the bright cone of their headlights. From this world only a diffuse phosphorescence rose up this high, vague as smoke. And raising your eyes, no longer blinded, you saw the perspective of space unfold, the constellations expanded in depth, the firmament turning in every direction, a sphere that contains everything and is contained by no boundary, and only a thinning of its weft, like a breach, opened towards Venus, to make it stand out alone over the frame of the earth, with its steady slash of light exploded and concentrated at one point.

Suspended in this sky, the new moon – rather than display the abstract appearance of a half-moon – revealed its true nature as an opaque sphere, its whole outline illuminated by the oblique rays of a sun the earth had lost, though it retained (as you can see only on certain early-summer nights) its warm color. And Marcovaldo, looking at that narrow shore of moon cut there between shadow and light, felt a nostalgia, as if yearning to arrive at a beach which had stayed miraculously sunny in the night.

And so they remained at the window of the garret, the children frightened by the measureless consequences of their act, Isolina carried away as if in ecstasy, Fiordaligi, who, alone among all, discerned the dimly lighted garret and finally the girl's lunar smile. Their Mamma recovered herself: "Come on now, it's night. What are you doing at the window? You'll catch something, in this moonlight!"

Michelino aimed his slingshot up high. "Now I'll turn off the moon!" He was seized and put to bed.

And so for the rest of that night and all through the night following, the neon sign on the other roof said only SPAAK-CO, and from Marcovaldo's garret you could see the firmament. Fiordaligi and the lunar girl blew each other kisses, and perhaps, speaking to each other in sign language, they would manage to make a date to meet.

But on the morning of the second day, on the roof, in the scaffolding that supported the neon sign, the tiny forms of two electricians in overalls were visible, as they checked the tubes and wires. With the air of old men who predict changes in the weather, Marcovaldo stuck his head out and said: "Tonight there'll be GNAC again."

Somebody knocked at the garret. They opened the door. It was a gentleman wearing eyeglasses. "I beg your pardon, could I take a look at your window? Thanks." And he introduced himself: "Godifredo, neon advertising agent."

"We're ruined! They want us to pay the damages!" Marcovaldo thought, and he was already devouring his children with his eyes, forgetting his astronomical transports. "Now he'll look at the window and realize the stones could only have come from here." He tried to ward this off. "You know how it is, the kids shoot at the sparrows. Pebbles. I don't know how that Spaak sign went out. But I punished them, all right. Oh yes indeed, I punished them! And you can be sure it won't happen again."

Signor Godifredo's face became alert. "Actually, I'm

employed by 'Tomahawk Cognac', not by Spaak. I had come to examine the possibility of a sign on this roof. But do go on: I'm interested in what you're saying."

And so it was that Marcovaldo, half an hour later, concluded a deal with Tomahawk Cognac, Spaak's chief rival. The children should empty their slingshots at the GNAC every time the sign was turned on again.

"That should be the straw that will break the camel's back," Signor Godifredo said. He was not mistaken: already on the verge of bankruptcy because of its large advertising outlay, Spaak and Co. took the constant damaging of its most beautiful neon signs as a bad omen. The sign that now sometimes said COGAC and sometimes CONAC or CONC spread among the firm's creditors the impression of financial difficulties; at a certain point, the advertising agency refused to make further repairs if arrears were not paid; the turned-off sign increased the alarm among the creditors; and Spaak went out of business.

In the sky of Marcovaldo the full moon shone, round, in all its splendor.

It was in the last quarter when the electricians came back to clamber over the roof opposite. And that night, in letters of fire, letters twice as high and broad as before, they could read TOMAHAWK COGNAC, and there was no longer moon or firmament or sky or night, only TOMAHAWK COGNAC, TOMAHAWK COGNAC, TOMAHAWK COGNAC, which blinked on and off every two seconds.

The worst hit was Fiordaligi; the garret of the lunar girl had vanished behind an enormous, impenetrable *W*.

AUTUMN

15. *The rain and the leaves*

At his job, among his various other responsibilities, Marcovaldo had to water every morning the potted plant in the entrance hall. It was one of those green house-plants with an erect, thin stalk from which, on both sides, broad, long-stemmed, shiny leaves stick out: in other words, one of those plants that are so plant-shaped, with leaves so leaf-shaped, that they don't seem real. But still it was a plant, and as such it suffered, because staying there, between the curtain and the umbrella-stand, it lacked light, air, and dew. Every morning Marcovaldo discovered some nasty sign: the stem of one leaf drooped as if it could no longer support the weight, another leaf was becoming spotted like the cheek of a child with measles, the tip of a third leaf was turning yellow; until, one or the other, plop!, was found on the floor. Meanwhile (what most wrung his heart) the plant's stalk grew taller, taller, no longer making orderly fronds, but naked as a pole, with a clump at the top that made it resemble a palm-tree.

Marcovaldo cleared away the fallen leaves, dusted the healthy ones, poured at the foot of the plant (slowly, so the pot wouldn't spill over and dirty the tiles) half a watering-can of water, immediately absorbed by the earth in the pot. And to these simple actions he devoted an attention he gave no other task of his, almost like the compassion felt for the

77

troubles of a relative. And he sighed, whether for the plant or himself: because in that lanky, yellowing bush within the company walls he recognized a companion in misfortune.

The plant (this was how it was called, simply, as if any more specific name were useless in a setting where it alone had to represent the vegetable kingdom) had become such a part of Marcovaldo's life that it dominated his thoughts at every hour of the day and night. When he examined the gathering clouds in the sky, his gaze now was no longer that of a city-dweller, wondering whether or not he should wear his raincoat, but that of a farmer expecting from day to day the end of a drought. And the moment when he raised his head from his work and saw, against the light, beyond the little window of the warehouse, the curtain of rain that had begun to fall, thick and silent, he would drop everything, run to the plant, take the pot in his arms, and set it outside in the courtyard.

The plant, feeling the water run over its leaves, seemed to expand, to offer the greatest possible surface to the drops, and in its joy it seemed to don its most brilliant green: or at least so Marcovaldo thought, as he lingered to observe it, forgetting to take shelter.

They stayed there in the courtyard, man and plant, facing each other, the man almost feeling plant-sensations under the rain, the plant – no longer accustomed to the open air and to the phenomena of nature – amazed, much like a man who finds himself suddenly drenched from head to foot, his clothes soaked. Marcovaldo, his nose in the air, sniffed the smell of the rain, a smell – for him – already of woods and fields, and he pursued with his mind some vague memories. But among these memories there surfaced, clearer and closer, that of the rheumatic aches that afflicted him every year; and then, hastily, he went back inside.

When working hours were over, the place had to be locked up. Marcovaldo asked the warehouse foreman: "Can I leave the plant outside there, in the courtyard?"

The foreman, Signor Viligelmo, was the kind of man

who avoided burdensome responsibilities: "Are you crazy? What if somebody steals it? Who'll answer for that?"

But Marcovaldo, seeing how much good the rain did the plant, couldn't bring himself to put it back inside: it would mean wasting that gift of heaven. "I could keep it until tomorrow morning . . ." he suggested. "I'll load it on the rack of my bike and take it home . . . That way it'll get as much rain as possible."

Signor Viligelmo thought it over a moment, then concluded: "Then you're taking the responsibility." And he gave his consent.

Under the pouring rain, Marcovaldo crossed the city, bent over the handle-bars of his motorbike, bundled up in a rain-proof wind-breaker. Behind him, on the rack, he had tied the pot; and bike, man, and plant seemed a sole thing; indeed the hunched and bundled man disappeared, and you saw only a plant on a bicycle. Every now and then, from beneath his hood, Marcovaldo looked around until he could see a dripping leaf flapping behind him: and every time it seemed to him that the plant had become taller and more leafy.

At home, a garret with its window-sill on the roof, the moment Marcovaldo arrived with the pot in his arms, the children started dancing around it.

"The Christmas tree! The Christmas tree!"

"No, no, what are you talking about? Christmas is a long way off yet!" Marcovaldo protested. "Watch out for those leaves, they're delicate!"

"We're already like sardines in a can, in this house," Domitilla grumbled. "If you bring a tree in, too, we'll have to move out . . ."

"It's only a plant! I'll put it on the window-sill . . ."

The shadowy form of the plant on the sill could be seen from the room. Marcovaldo, at supper, didn't look at his plate, but beyond the window-panes.

Ever since they had left the half-basement for the garret, the life of Marcovaldo and family had greatly improved.

However, living up under the roof also had its drawbacks: the ceiling, for example, leaked a little. The drops fell in four or five distinct places, at regular intervals; and Marcovaldo put basins under them, or pots. On rainy nights when all of them were in bed, they could hear the tic-toc-tuc of the various drips, which made him shudder as if at a premonition of rheumatism. That night, on the contrary, every time Marcovaldo woke from his restless sleep and pricked up his ears, the tic-toc-tuc seemed cheery music to him: it told him the rain was continuing, mild and steady, and was nourishing the plant, driving the sap up along its delicate stalks, unfolding the leaves like sails. Tomorrow, when I look out, I'll find it has grown! he thought.

But even though he had thought about this, when he opened the window in the morning, he couldn't believe his eyes: the plant now filled half the window, the leaves had at least doubled in number, and no longer drooped under their own weight, but were erect and sharp as swords. He climbed down the steps, with the pot clutched to him, tied it to the rack, and rushed to work.

The rain had stopped, but the weather was still uncertain. Marcovaldo hadn't even climbed out of his seat when a few drops started falling again. "Since the rain does it so much good, I'll leave it in the courtyard again," he thought.

In the warehouse, every now and then he went to peek out of the window onto the courtyard. His distraction from work did not please the foreman. "Well, what's wrong with you this morning? Always looking out of the window."

"It's growing! Come and see for yourself, Signor Viligelmo!" And Marcovaldo motioned to him, speaking almost in a whisper, as if the plant were not to overhear. "Look how it's growing! It really has grown, hasn't it?"

"Yes, it's grown quite a bit," the boss conceded, and for Marcovaldo this was one of those satisfactions that life on the job rarely grants the personnel.

It was Saturday. Work ended at one and they were all off until Monday. Marcovaldo would have liked to take the plant home with him again, but now, since it was no longer raining, he couldn't think of any pretext. The sky, however, was not clear: black cumulus clouds were scattered here and there. He went to the foreman, who, a meteorology enthusiast, kept a barometer hanging over his desk. "What's the forecast, Signor Viligelmo?"

"Bad, still bad," he said. "For that matter, though it's not raining here, it is in the neighborhood where I live. I just telephoned my wife."

"In that case," Marcovaldo quickly proposed, "I'll take the plant on a little trip where it's raining," and, no sooner said than done, he fixed the pot again on the rack of his bike.

Saturday afternoon and Sunday Marcovaldo spent in this fashion: bouncing on the seat of his motorbike, the plant behind him, he studied the sky, seeking a cloud that seemed in the right mood, then he would race through the streets until he encountered rain. From time to time, turning around, he saw the plant a bit taller: high as the taxis, as the delivery trucks, as the trams! And with broader and broader leaves, from which the rain slid onto his rain-proof hood like a shower.

By now it was a tree on two wheels, speeding through the city, bewildering traffic cops, drivers, pedestrians. And the clouds, at the same time, sped along the paths of the wind, spattering a neighborhood with rain, then abandoning it; and the passers-by, one after another, stuck out their hands and closed their umbrellas; and along streets and avenues and squares, Marcovaldo chased his cloud, bent over his handle-bars, bundled in his hood from which only his nose protruded, his little motor putt-putting along at full tilt, as he kept the plant in the trajectory of the drops, as if the trail of rain that the cloud drew after itself had got caught in the leaves and thus all rushed ahead, drawn by the same power: wind, cloud, rain, plant, wheels.

On Monday Marcovaldo presented himself, empty-handed, to Signor Viligelmo.

"Where's the plant?" the foreman asked at once.

"Outside. Come."

"Where?" Viligelmo said. "I don't see it."

"It's that one over there. It's grown a bit . . ." and he pointed to a tree that reached the third floor. It was no longer planted in its old pot but in a kind of barrel, and instead of using his bike Marcovaldo had had to borrow a little motor-truck.

"Now what?" The boss was infuriated. "How can we get it into the entrance hall? It won't go through the doors any more!"

Marcovaldo shrugged.

"The only thing," Viligelmo said, "is to give it back to the nursery, in exchange for a plant of the right size!"

Marcovaldo climbed onto his bike again. "I'll go."

He resumed his dash through the city. The tree filled the center of the streets with green. The cops, concerned about traffic, stopped him at every intersection; then – when Marcovaldo explained that he was taking the plant back to the nursery, to get rid of it – they let him go on. But, taking first this street then that, Marcovaldo couldn't bring himself to turn into the one to the nursery. He hadn't the heart to give up his creature, now that he had raised it with such success: nothing in his whole life, it seemed to him, had given him the satisfaction he had received from that plant.

And so he went on, to and fro among streets and squares and embankments and bridges. And foliage worthy of a tropical forest spread out until it covered his head, back, arms, until he had disappeared into the green. And all these leaves and stems of leaves and the stalk, too (which had remained very slim), swayed and swayed as if in a constant trembling, whether a downpour of rain was still striking them, or whether the drops became rarer or stopped altogether.

The rain ceased. It was the hour towards sunset. At the end of the streets, in the space between the houses, a light mixed with rainbow settled. The plant, after that impetuous effort of growth that had involved it as long as the rain lasted, was virtually exhausted. Continuing his aimless race, Marcovaldo didn't notice that, behind him, the intense green of the leaves, one by one, was turning to yellow, a golden yellow.

For quite a while already, a procession of motorbikes and cars and bicycles and children had been following the tree that was moving about the city, without Marcovaldo's becoming aware of them, and they were shouting: "The baobab! The babobab!" and with great "Ooooh's!" of wonder they watched the yellowing of the leaves. When one leaf dropped and flew off, many hands were raised to catch it in flight.

A wind sprang up; the golden leaves, in gusts, darted off in midair, spinning. Marcovaldo still thought that, behind him, he had the green, thick tree, when all of a sudden – perhaps feeling himself unsheltered in the wind – he looked back. The tree was gone: there was only a thin stick, from which extended a monstrance of bare stems, and one last yellow leaf at the top still. In the light of the rainbow everything else seemed black: the people on the sidewalks, the façades of the houses that served as backdrop; and over this black, in midair, the golden leaves twirled, shining, hundreds of them; and hundreds of hands, red and pink, rose from the darkness to grab them; and the wind lifted the golden leaves towards the rainbow there at the end of the street, and the hands, and the shouts; and it detached even the last leaf, which turned from yellow to orange, then red, violet, blue, green, then yellow again, and then vanished.

WINTER

16. Marcovaldo at the supermarket

At six in the evening the city fell into the hands of the consumers. All during the day the big occupation of the productive public was to produce: they produced consumer goods. At a certain hour, as if a switch had been thrown, they stopped production and, away!, they were all off, to consume. Every day an impetuous flowering barely had time to blossom inside the lighted shop-windows, the red salamis to hang, the towers of porcelain dishes to rise to the ceiling, the rolls of fabric to unfurl folds like peacock's tails, when lo! the consuming throng burst in, to dismantle, to gnaw, to grope, to plunder. An uninterrupted line wound along all the sidewalks and under the arcades, extended through the glass doors of the shops to all the counters, nudged onwards by each individual's elbows in the ribs of the next, like the steady throb of pistons. Consume! And they touched the goods and put them back and picked them up again and tore them from one another's hands; consume! and they forced the pale salesladies to display on the counter linen and more linen; consume! and the spools of colored string spun like tops, the sheets of flowered paper fluttered their wings, enfolding purchases in little packages, and the little packages in big packages, bound, each, with its butterfly knot. And off went packages and bundles and wallets and bags; they whirled around the cashier's desk in a clutter, hands digging into pocketbooks seeking change-purses, and fingers rummaging in change-purses for coins, and down below, in a forest of alien legs and hems of overcoats, children no longer held by the hand became lost and started crying.

One of these evenings Marcovaldo was taking his family out for a walk. Since they had no money, their entertainment was to watch others go shopping; for the more money circulates, the more those without any can hope — sooner or later a bit of it will come into my pockets. But, on the contrary, Marcovaldo's wages, because they were scant and the family was large, and there were instalments and debts to be paid, flowed away the moment he collected them. Anyhow, watching was always lovely, especially if you took a turn around the supermarket.

This was a self-service supermarket. It provided those carts, like iron baskets on wheels; and each customer pushed his cart along, filling it with every sort of delicacy. Marcovaldo, on entering, also took a cart; his wife, another; and his four children took one each. And so they marched in procession, their carts before them, among counters piled high with mountains of good things to eat, pointing out to one another the salamis and the cheeses, naming them, as if in a crowd they had recognized the faces of friends, or acquaintances, anyway.

"Papà, can we take this, at least?" the children asked every minute.

"No, hands off! Mustn't touch," Marcovaldo said, remembering that, at the end of this stroll, the check-out girl was waiting, to total up the sum.

"Then why is that lady taking one?" they insisted, seeing all these good housewives who, having come in to buy only a few carrots and a bunch of celery, couldn't resist the sight of a pyramid of jars and plonk plonk plonk! with a partly absent and partly resigned movement, they sent cans of tomatoes, peaches, anchovies, thudding into their carts.

In other words, if your cart is empty and the others are

full, you can hold out only so long: then you're over-whelmed by envy, heartbreak, and you can't stand it. So Marcovaldo, having told his wife and children not to touch anything, made a rapid turn at one of the intersections, eluded his family's gaze, and, having taken a box of dates from a shelf, put it in his cart. He wanted only to experience the pleasure of pushing it around for ten minutes, displaying his purchases like everyone else, and then replace it where he had taken it. This box, plus a red bottle of ketchup and a package of coffee and a blue pack of spaghetti. Marcovaldo was sure that, restraining himself for at least a quarter of an hour, and without spending a cent, he could savor the joy of those who know how to choose the product. But if the children were to see him, that would spell trouble! They would immediately start imitating him and God only knows the confusion that would lead to!

Marcovaldo tried to cover his tracks, moving along a zig-zag course through the departments, now following busy maidservants, now be-furred ladies. And as one or the other extended her hand to select a fragrant yellow squash or a box of triangular processed cheeses, he would imitate her. The loudspeakers were broadcasting gay little tunes: the consumers moved or paused, following the rhythm, and at the right moment they stretched out their arms, picked up an object and set it in their baskets, all to the sound of music.

Marcovaldo's cart was now filled with merchandise; his footsteps led him into the less frequented departments, where products with more and more undecipherable names were sealed in boxes with pictures from which it was not clear whether these were fertilizer for lettuce or lettuce seeds or actual lettuce or poison for lettuce-caterpillars or feed to attract the birds that eat those caterpillars or else seasoning for lettuce or for the roasted birds. In any case, Marcovaldo took two or three boxes.

And so he was proceeding between two high hedges of shelves. All at once the aisle ended and there was a long space, empty and deserted, with neon lights that made the tiles gleam. Marcovaldo was there, alone with his cart full of things, and at the end of that empty space there was the exit with the cash-desk.

His first instinct was to break into a run, head down, pushing the cart before him like a tank, to escape from the supermarket with his booty before the check-out girl could give the alarm. But at that moment, from a nearby aisle, another cart appeared, even more loaded than his, and the person pushing it was his wife, Domitilla. And from somewhere else, yet another emerged, and Filippetto was pushing it with all his strength. At this area the aisles of many departments converged, and from each opening one of Marcovaldo's children appeared, all pushing carts laden like freighters. Each had had the same idea, and now, meeting, they realized they had assembled a complete sampling of all the supermarket's possibilities. "Papà, are we rich then?" Michelino asked. "Will we have food to eat for a year?"

"Go back! Hurry! Get away from the desk!" Marcovaldo cried, doing an about-face and hiding, himself and his victuals, behind the counters; and he began to dash, bent double as if under enemy fire, to become lost once more among the various departments. A rumble resounded behind him; he turned and saw the whole family, galloping at his heels, pushing their carts in line, like a train.

"They'll charge us a million for this!"

The supermarket was large and complex as a labyrinth: you could roam around it for hours and hours. With all these provisions at their disposal, Marcovaldo and family could have spent the winter there, never coming out. But the loudspeakers had already stopped their tunes, and were saying: "Attention, please! In fifteen minutes the supermarket will close! Please proceed to the check-out counters!"

It was time to get rid of their cargo: now or never. At the summons of the loudspeaker, the crowd of customers was gripped by a frantic haste, as if these were the last minutes in the last supermarket of the whole world, an urgency either to grab everything there was or to leave it there – the motive wasn't clear – and there was a pushing and shoving around all the shelves. Marcovaldo, Domitilla and the children took advantage of it to replace goods on the counters or to slip things into other people's carts. The replacements were somewhat random: the flypaper ended on the ham shelf, a cabbage landed among the cakes. They didn't realise that, instead of a cart, one lady was pushing a baby carriage with an infant inside: they stuck a bottle of Barbera in with it.

Depriving themselves of things like this, without even having tasted them, was a torment that brought tears to the eyes. And so, at the very moment they abandoned a jar of mayonnaise, they came upon a bunch of bananas, and took it; or a roast chicken to substitute for a nylon broom; with this system the more they emptied their carts, the more they filled them.

The family with their provisions went up and down the escalators, and at every level, on all sides they found themselves facing obligatory routes that led to a check-out cashier, who aimed an adding machine, chattering like a machine gun, at all those who showed signs of leaving. The wandering of Marcovaldo and family resembled more and more that of caged animals or of prisoners in a luminous prison with walls of colored panels.

In one place, the panels of one wall had been dismantled; there was a ladder set there, hammers, carpenter's and mason's tools. A contractor was building an annex to the supermarket. Their working day over, the men had gone off, leaving everything where it was. Marcovaldo, his provisions before him, passed through the hole in the wall. Ahead there was darkness: he advanced. And his family, with their carts, came after him.

The rubber wheels of the carts jolted over the ground, sandy at times, as if cobbles had been removed, then on a floor of loose planks. Marcovaldo proceeded, poised, along a plank; the others followed him. All of a sudden they saw, before and behind, above and below, many lights strewn in the darkness, and all around, the void.

They were on the wooden structure of a scaffolding, at the level of seven-storey houses. The city opened below them in a luminous sparkle of windows and signs and the electric spray from tram antennae; higher up, the sky was dotted with stars and red lights of radio stations' antennae. The scaffolding shook under the weight of all those goods teetering up there. Michelino said: "I'm scared!"

From the darkness a shadow advanced. It was an enormous mouth, toothless, that opened, stretching forward on a long metal neck: a crane. It descended on them, stopped at their level, the lower jaw against the edge of the scaffolding. Marcovaldo tilted the cart, emptied the goods into the iron maw, and moved forward. Domitilla did the same. The children imitated their parents. The crane closed its jaws, with all the supermarket loot inside, and, pulley creaking, drew back its neck and moved away. Below, the multicolored neon signs glowed and turned, inviting everyone to buy the products on sale in the great supermarket.

SPRING

17. *Smoke, wind, and soap-bubbles*

Every day the postman left some envelopes in the tenants' boxes; only in Marcovaldo's there was never anything, because nobody ever wrote him, and if it hadn't been for an occasional dun from the light or the gas company, his box would have been absolutely useless.

"Papà! There's mail!" Michelino shouted.

"Come off it!" he answered. "The same old ads!"

From all the letter-boxes a blue-and-yellow folded sheet was protruding. It said that to achieve really good suds, Blancasol was the best of products; anyone who presented this blue-and-yellow paper would be given a free sample.

Since these sheets were narrow and long, some of them jutted from the slot of the boxes; others lay on the ground, crumpled, or only a bit mussed, because many tenants, opening the box, would promptly throw away all the advertising matter that crammed it. Filippetto, Pietruccio, and Michelino, collecting some from the floor, slipping some from the slots, and actually fishing others out with a bit of wire, began to make a collection of Blancasol coupons.

"I have the most!"

"No! Count them! I have the most! You want to bet?"

Blancasol had conducted the advertising campaign through the whole neighborhood, house to house. And house to house, the young brothers started covering the

90

area, trying to corner the coupons. Some concierges drove them away, shouting: "You little crooks! What are you trying to steal? I'm going to call the police." Others were pleased to see the kids clean up some of the waste paper deposited there every day.

In the evening, Marcovaldo's two poor rooms were all blue and yellow with Blancasol ads; the children counted and recounted them and piled them into packs like bank tellers with banknotes.

"Papà, we have so many; couldn't we start a laundry?" Filippetto asked.

In those days, the detergent world was in great upheaval. Blancasol's advertising campaign had alarmed all the rival companies. To launch their products, they distributed through all the mailboxes of the city similar coupons, which entitled the recipient to larger and larger free samples.

Marcovaldo's children, in the days that followed, were kept very busy. Every morning the letter-boxes blossomed like peach-trees in spring: slips of paper with green drawings or pink, blue, orange, promised snow-white wash for those who used Washrite or Lavolux or Beautisuds or Handikleen. For the boys, the collecting of coupons and free-sample cards ramified into more and more new classifications. At the same time, their collection territory expanded, extending to the buildings on other streets.

Naturally, these maneuvers could not go unnoticed. The neighborhood kids soon realized what Michelino and his brothers went out hunting for all day, and immediately those papers, to which none of them had paid any attention before, became a sought-after booty. There was a period of rivalry among the various bands of kids, when the collection in one zone rather than another gave rise to disputes and brawling. Then, after a series of exchanges and negotiations, they reached an agreement: an organized system of hunting was more profitable than helter-skelter grabbing. And the collection of coupons became so methodical that the moment the man from Washrite or Rinsequik went by on his round of doorways, his route was observed and shadowed, step by step, and as fast as the material was distributed, it was confiscated by the kids.

Commanding operations, naturally, were still Filippetto, Pietruccio, and Michelino, because the idea had been theirs in the first place. They even succeeded in convincing the other boys that the coupons were common property and should be preserved all together. "Like in a bank!" Pietruccio explained.

"Do we own a laundry or a bank?" Michelino asked.

"Whatever it is, we're millionaires!"

The boys were so excited they couldn't sleep any more, and they made plans for the future.

"We only have to redeem all these samples and we'll have a huge amount of detergent."

"Where are we going to keep it?"

"We'll rent a warehouse!"

"Why not a freighter?"

Advertising, like fruits and flowers, has its seasons. After a few weeks, the detergent season ended; in the letter-boxes you found only ads for corn-removers.

"Shall we start collecting these, too?" someone suggested. But the prevailing view was that they should devote themselves at once to the redemption of their accumulated wealth of detergents. It was merely a matter of going to the prescribed shops and making them give a sample for every coupon. But this new phase of their plan, apparently quite simple, proved to be much longer and more complicated than the first.

Operations had to be conducted in skirmishing order: one kid at a time in one shop at a time. They could present three or even four coupons at once, provided they were of different brands; and if the clerks wanted to give only one sample of one brand, they had to say: "My Mamma wants to try them all to see which one's best."

Things became difficult when, in many shops, they would give the free sample only to those who bought something;

never had Mammas seen their children so eager to run errands to the grocery.

In other words, the transformation of coupons into goods was dragging out and required supplementary expenses because errands with Mamma's money were few and the shops to be covered were many. To procure funds the only course was to initiate phase three of the plan, namely the sale of the detergent already redeemed.

They decided to sell it door to door, ringing bells: "Signora! Are you interested? Perfect wash!" and they would hold out the box of Rinsequik or the packet of Blancasol.

"Yes, yes, thanks. Give it here," some of them said, and the moment they had the sample, they would slam the door in the boy's face.

"Hey? Where's the money?" And they would hammer their fists on the door.

"Money? Isn't it free? Go home, you naughty kids!"

In that same period, in fact, men hired by the various brands were going from home to home, leaving free samples: this was a new advertising offensive undertaken by the whole detergent industry, since the coupon campaign had not proved fruitful.

Marcovaldo's house looked like the basement of a grocery store, full as it was of products by Beautisuds, Handikleen, Lavolux; but from all this quantity of merchandise not a cent could be squeezed; it was stuff that's given away, like the water of drinking-fountains.

Naturally, among the company representatives the rumor soon spread that some kids were making the same rounds, door to door, selling the very product their representatives were begging housewives to accept free. In the world of trade waves of pessimism are frequent: they began to report that they, who were giving the stuff away, were told by housewives that they didn't have any use for detergents, while the same women actually bought the products from those who demanded money. The planning offices of the various firms got together, market research specialists were consulted: the conclusion they reached was that such unfair competition could be carried out only by receivers of stolen goods. The police, after bringing formal charges against criminals unknown, began to patrol the neighborhood, hunting for thieves and the hiding-place of their loot.

In a moment the detergents became as dangerous as dynamite. Marcovaldo was afraid. "I won't have even an ounce of this powder in my house!" But they didn't know where to put it; nobody wanted it at home. It was decided that the children would go and throw all of it into the river.

It was before dawn; on the bridge a little cart arrived, drawn by Pietruccio and pushed by his brothers, laden with boxes of Washrite and Lavolux, then another similar cart drawn by Uguccione, the son of the concierge across the street, and then others, many others. In the center of the bridge they stopped, they allowed a cyclist to pass. After he had cast a curious glance behind him, they cried: "Go!" Michelino began hurling boxes into the river.

"Stupid! Can't you see they float?" Filippetto cried. "You have to empty the powder into the river, not dump the box!"

And from the boxes, opened one by one, a soft white cloud drifted down, rested on the current that seemed to absorb it, reappeared in a swarm of tiny bubbles, then seemed to sink. "That's the way!" And the kids began emptying pounds and pounds.

"Look! Over there!" Michelino shouted, and pointed farther downstream.

After the bridge there were the falls. Where the stream began its descent, the bubbles were no longer visible; they reappeared farther down, but now they had become huge bubbles that swelled and pushed one another upwards from below, a wave of suds that rose and became gigantic, already it was as high as the falls, a whitish foam like a barber's mug lathered by his shaving-brush. It was as if all those powders of rival brands had made a point of demonstrating their frothiness: and the river was brimming with suds at the piers, and the fishermen, who at the first light were already in the water wearing their hip-boots, pulled in their lines and ran off.

A little breeze stirred the morning air. A clump of bubbles broke from the water's surface, and flew off, lightly. It was dawn and the bubbles took on a pink hue. The children saw them go off, high over their heads, and cried: "Ooooo . . ."

The bubbles flew on, following the invisible tracks of the city's currents of air; they turned into the streets at roof-level, always avoiding bumps with cornices and drainpipes. Now the compactness of the bunch had dissolved: the bubbles, first one then another, had flown off on their own, and each following a route different because of altitude and speed and path; they wandered in mid-air. They had multiplied, it seemed; indeed, they really had, because the river continued spilling over with foam like a pan of milk on the stove. And the wind, the wind raised up froths and frills and clumps that stretched out into rainbow garlands (the rays of the oblique sun, having climbed over the roofs, had now taken possession of the city and the river), and invaded the sky above the wires and antennae.

Dark shadows of workers rushed to the factories on their chattering motorbikes and the blue-green swarm hovering over them followed as if each man were pulling behind him a bunch of balloons tied by a long string to his handle-bars.

It was some people on a tram who first took notice. "Look! Look! What's that up there?" The tram-driver stopped and got out: all the passengers got out and started looking into the sky, the bikes and motorbikes stopped and the cars and the news-vendors and the bakers and all the morning passers-by and among them Marcovaldo on his way to work, and all stuck their noses in the air, following the flight of the soap-bubbles.

"Surely it's not some atomic thing?" an old woman asked, and fear ran through the crowd, and one man, seeing a bubble about to light on him, ran off, yelling: "It's radio-active!"

But the bubbles continued to glisten, multi-hued and fragile and so light that one puff, whoosh, and they were gone; and soon, in the crowd, the alarm died as it had flared up. "Radioactive my foot! It's soap! Soap-bubbles like kids blow!" And a frantic gaiety seized them. "Look at that one! And that! And that!" because they saw some enormous ones, of incredible dimensions, flying over, and as these bubbles grazed each other, they merged, they became double and triple, and the sky, the roofs, the tall buildings, through these transparent cupolas, appeared in shapes and colors never seen before.

From their smoke-stacks the factories had begun belching forth black smoke, as they did every morning. And the swarms of bubbles encountered the smoke-clouds and the sky was divided between currents of black smoke and currents of rainbow foam, and in the eddying wind they seemed to fight, and for a moment, only one moment, it looked as if the tops of the smoke-stacks were conquered by the bubbles, but soon there was such a mixture – between the smoke that imprisoned the rainbow foam and the globes of soap that imprisoned a veil of grains of soot – that you couldn't understand anything. Until, at a certain point, after seeking and seeking in the sky, Marcovaldo couldn't see the bubbles any longer, but only smoke, smoke, smoke.

SUMMER

18. The city all to himself

For eleven months of the year the inhabitants loved their city and woe to anyone who cast aspersions: the skyscrapers, the cigarette machines, the wide-screen movie theaters, all undeniable sources of constant attraction. The only citizen to whom this feeling could not be attributed with certitude was Marcovaldo; but what he thought – first – was hard to know since he didn't have great powers of communication, and – second – it mattered so little that it made no difference.

At a certain point in the year, the month of August began. And then you witnessed a general change of feeling. Nobody loved the city any more: even the skyscrapers and the pedestrian subways and the car-parks, till yesterday so cherished, had become disagreeable and tiresome. The inhabitants wanted only to get away as quickly as possible: and so, filling trains and clogging superhighways, by the 15th of the month all of them were actually gone. Except one. Marcovaldo was the only inhabitant not to leave the city.

He would go out to take a walk downtown, in the morning. The streets opened before him, broad and endless, drained of cars and deserted; the façades of the buildings, a gray fence of lowered iron shutters and the countless slats of the blinds, were sealed, like ramparts. For the whole year Marcovaldo had dreamed of being able to use the streets as streets, that is, walking in the middle of them: now he could do it, and he could also cross on the red light, and jay-walk, and stop in the center of squares. But he realized that the pleasure didn't come so much from doing these unaccustomed things as from seeing a whole different world: streets like the floors of valleys, or dry river-beds, houses like blocks of steep mountains, or the walls of a cliff.

To be sure, you immediately noticed the absence of something: but not the line of parked cars, or the jam at the intersection, or the flow of the crowd at the entrance to the department store, or the clump of people waiting for the tram; what was missing to fill the empty spaces and bend the squared surfaces was, say, a flood due to the bursting of water mains or an invasion of roots of the trees along the avenue which would crack the asphalt. Marcovaldo's eyes peered around seeking the emergence of a different city, a city of bark and scales and clots and nerve-systems under the city of paint and tar and glass and stucco. And there, the building which he passed every day was revealed to him, in its reality, as a quarry of porous gray sandstone; the fence of a building-site was of pine-planks still fresh, with knots that looked like buds; on the sign of the big fabric shop rested a host of little moths, asleep.

You would have said that, the moment human beings had deserted the city, it had fallen prey to inhabitants hidden till yesterday, who now gained the upper hand. For a bit Marcovaldo's stroll followed the itinerary of a file of ants, then let itself be turned aside by the flight of a bewildered scarab beetle, then lingered to accompany the twisting progress of a caterpillar. It wasn't only animals that invaded the area: Marcovaldo discovered that at the newspaper kiosks, on the northern side, a fine layer of mold had formed, that the potted trees outside restaurants made an effort to thrust their leaves beyond the frame of shadow of the sidewalk. But did the city still exist? That agglomerate of synthetic matter that confined Marcovaldo's days now proved to be a mosaic of disparate stones, each quite distinct from the others to sight and touch, in its hardness and heat and consistency.

And so, forgetting the function of sidewalks and zebra-stripes, Marcovaldo was moving through the streets with a butterfly's zig-zag, when all of a sudden the radiator of a sports car going at eighty miles per hour missed his hip by a fraction of an inch. Half in fear and half because of the blast, Marcovaldo leaped up and fell back, stunned.

The car, with a great snarl, braked, almost spinning full circle. A group of young men, in shirt sleeves, jumped out. "Now they'll beat me up," Marcovaldo thought, "because I was walking in the middle of the street!"

The young men were armed with strange implements. "At last we've found him! At last!" they said, surrounding Marcovaldo. "Here he is then," said one of them, holding a silvery little stick to his mouth, "the only inhabitant left in the city on the mid-August holiday. Excuse me, sir, would you mind telling our viewers your impressions?" and he stuck the silvery stick under Marcovaldo's nose.

A dazzling glow exploded, it was hot as a furnace, and Marcovaldo was about to faint. They had trained spot-lights on him, cameras, microphones. He stammered something: at every three syllables he uttered, the young man moved in, twisting the microphone towards himself. "Ah, so you mean to say that . . ." and he would go on talking for ten minutes.

To put it simply: they were interviewing him.

"Can I go now?"

"Of course. Thank you very much . . . Actually, if you have nothing else to do . . . and feel like earning a little something . . . would you mind staying here and lending us a hand?"

The whole square was topsy-turvy: trucks, sound-trucks, cameras with dollies, batteries, lamps, teams of men in overalls, trundling from one place to another, all sweating.

"Here she is! She's here! She's here!" From an open limousine a movie star got out.

"Come on, guys, we can start the fountain sequence!"

The director of the TV report *August Follies* began to issue orders for shooting the famous star diving into the main fountain of the city.

To Marcovaldo, the grip, they had given the job of shifting around the square the bank of floodlights on a heavy stand. The great square now buzzed with machinery and sizzling arc-lights, resounded to hammering on make-shift metal scaffoldings, shouted commands . . . To Marcovaldo's eyes, blinded and dazed, the everyday city had resumed the place of that other city, glimpsed for a moment, or perhaps only dreamed.

AUTUMN

19. The garden of stubborn cats

The city of cats and the city of men exist one inside the other, but they are not the same city. Few cats recall the time when there was no distinction: the streets and squares of men were also streets and squares of cats, and the lawns, courtyards, balconies, and fountains: you lived in a broad and various space. But for several generations now domestic felines have been prisoners of an uninhabitable city: the streets are uninterruptedly overrun by the mortal traffic of cat-crushing automobiles; in every square foot of terrain where once a garden extended or a vacant lot or the ruins of an old demolition, now condominiums loom up, welfare housing, brand-new skyscrapers; every entrance is crammed with parked cars; the courtyards, one by one, have been roofed by reinforced concrete and transformed into garages or movie houses or storerooms or workshops. And where a rolling plateau of low roofs once extended, copings, terraces, water tanks, balconies, skylights, corrugated-iron sheds, now one general superstructure rises wherever structures can rise; the intermediate differences in height, between the low ground of the street and the supernal heaven of the penthouses, disappear; the cat of a recent litter seeks in vain the itinerary of its fathers, the point from which to make the soft leap from balustrade to cornice to drainpipe, or for the quick climb on the roof-tiles.

But in this vertical city, in this compressed city where all voids tend to fill up and every block of cement tends to mingle with other blocks of cement, a kind of counter-city opens, a negative city, that consists of empty slices between wall and wall, of the minimal distances ordained by the building regulations between two constructions, between the rear of one construction and the rear of the next; it is a city of cavities, wells, air conduits, driveways, inner yards, accesses to basements, like a network of dry canals on a planet of stucco and tar, and it is through this network, grazing the walls, that the ancient cat population still scurries.

On occasion, to pass the time, Marcovaldo would follow a cat. It was during the work-break, between noon and three, when all the personnel except Marcovaldo went home to eat, and he – who brought his lunch in his bag – laid his place among the packing-cases in the warehouse, chewed his snack, smoked a half-cigar, and wandered around, alone and idle, waiting for work to resume. In those hours, a cat that peeped in at a window was always welcome company, and a guide for new explorations. He had made friends with a tabby, well-fed, a blue ribbon around its neck, surely living with some well-to-do family. This tabby shared with Marcovaldo the habit of an afternoon stroll right after lunch; and naturally a friendship sprang up.

Following his tabby friend, Marcovaldo had started looking at places as if through the round eyes of a cat and even if these places were the usual environs of his firm he saw them in a different light, as settings for cattish stories, with connections practicable only by light, velvety paws. Though from the outside the neighborhood seemed poor in cats, every day on his rounds Marcovaldo made the acquaintance of some new face, and a miau, a hiss, a stiffening of fur on an arched back was enough for him to sense ties and intrigues and rivalries among them. At those moments he thought he had already penetrated the secrecy of the felines' society: and then he felt himself scrutinized by pupils that became slits, under the surveillance of the antennae of taut whiskers, and all the cats around him sat impassive as sphinxes, the pink triangle of their noses convergent on the black triangles of their lips, and the only things that moved were the tips of the ears, with a vibrant jerk like radar. They reached the end of a narrow passage, between squalid blank walls; and, looking around, Marcovaldo saw that the cats that had led him this far had vanished, all of them together, no telling in which direction, even his tabby friend, and they had left him alone. Their realm had territories, cere-monies, customs that it was not yet granted to him to discover.

On the other hand, from the cat city there opened un-suspected peep-holes onto the city of men: and one day the same tabby led him to discover the great Biarritz Restaurant.

Anyone wishing to see the Biarritz Restaurant had only to assume the posture of a cat, that is, proceed on all fours. Cat and man, in this fashion, walked around a kind of dome, at whose foot some low, rectangular little windows opened. Following the tabby's example, Marcovaldo looked down. They were transoms through which the luxurious hall received air and light. To the sound of gypsy violins, partridges and quails swirled by on silver dishes balanced by the white-gloved fingers of waiters in tailcoats. Or, more precisely, above the partridges and quails the dishes whirled, and above the dishes the white gloves, and poised on the waiters' patent-leather shoes, the gleaming parquet floor, from which hung dwarf potted palms and table-cloths and crystal and buckets like bells with the champagne bottle for their clapper: everything was turned upside-down because Marcovaldo, for fear of being seen, wouldn't stick his head inside the window and confined himself to looking at the reversed reflection of the room in the tilted pane.

But it was not so much the windows of the dining-room as those of the kitchens that interested the cat: looking through the former you saw, distant and somehow trans-figured, what in the kitchens presented itself – quite concrete and within paw's reach – as a plucked bird or a fresh fish. And it was towards the kitchens, in fact, that the tabby wanted to lead Marcovaldo, either through a gesture of altruistic friendship or else because it counted on the man's help for one of its raids. Marcovaldo, however, was reluctant to leave his belvedere over the main room: first as he was fascinated by the luxury of the place, and then because something down there had riveted his attention. To such an extent that, overcoming his fear of being seen, he kept peeking in, with his head in the transom.

In the midst of the room, directly under that pane, there was a little glass fish–tank, a kind of aquarium, where some fat trout were swimming. A special customer approached, a man with a shiny bald pate, black suit, black beard. An old waiter in tailcoat followed him, carrying a little net as if he were going to catch butterflies. The gentleman in black looked at the trout with a grave, intent air; then he raised one hand and with a slow, solemn gesture singled out a fish. The waiter dipped the net into the tank, pursued the appointed trout, captured it, headed for the kitchens, holding out in front of him, like a lance, the net in which the fish wriggled. The gentleman in black, solemn as a magistrate who has handed down a capital sentence, went to take his seat and wait for the return of the trout, sautéed "à la meunière".

If I found a way to drop a line from up here and make one of those trout bite, Marcovaldo thought, I couldn't be accused of theft; at worst, of fishing in an unauthorized place. And ignoring the miaus that called him towards the kitchens, he went to collect his fishing tackle.

Nobody in the crowded dining-room of the Biarritz saw the long, fine line, armed with hook and bait, as it slowly dropped into the tank. The fish saw the bait, and flung themselves on it. In the fray one trout managed to bite the worm: and immediately it began to rise, rise, emerge from the water, a silvery flash, it darted up high, over the laid tables and the trolleys of hors d'oeuvres, over the blue flames of the crêpes Suzette, until it vanished into the heavens of the transom.

Marcovaldo had yanked the rod with the brisk snap of the expert fisherman, so the fish landed behind his back. The trout had barely touched the ground when the cat sprang. What little life the trout still had was lost between the tabby's teeth. Marcovaldo, who had abandoned his line at that moment to run and grab the fish, saw it snatched from under his nose, hook and all. He was quick to put one foot on the rod, but the snatch had been so strong that the rod was all the man had left, while the tabby ran off with the fish, pulling the line after it. Treacherous kitty! It had vanished.

But this time it wouldn't escape him: there was that long line trailing after him and showing the way he had taken. Though he had lost sight of the cat, Marcovaldo followed the end of the line: there it was, running along a wall; it climbed a parapet, wound through a doorway, was swallowed up by a basement . . . Marcovaldo, venturing into more and more cattish places, climbed roofs, straddled railings, always managed to catch a glimpse – perhaps only a second before it disappeared – of that moving trace that indicated the thief's path.

Now the line played out down a sidewalk, in the midst of the traffic, and Marcovaldo, running after it, almost managed to grab it. He flung himself down on his belly: there, he grabbed it! He managed to seize one end of the line before it slipped between the bars of a gate.

Beyond a half-rusted gate and two bits of wall buried under climbing plants, there was a little rank garden, with a small, abandoned-looking building at the far end of it. A carpet of dry leaves covered the path, and dry leaves lay everywhere under the boughs of the two plane-trees, forming actually some little mounds in the yard. A layer of leaves was yellowing in the green water of a pool. Enormous buildings rose all around, skyscrapers with thousands of windows, like so many eyes trained disapprovingly on that

little square patch with two trees, a few tiles, and all those
yellow leaves, surviving right in the middle of an area of
great traffic.

And in this garden, perched on the capitals and balus-
trades, lying on the dry leaves of the flower-beds, climbing
on the trunks of the trees or on the drainpipes, motionless
on their four paws, their tails making a question-mark,
seated to wash their faces, there were tiger cats, black cats,
white cats, calico cats, tabbies, angoras, Persians, house cats
and stray cats, perfumed cats and mangy cats. Marcovaldo
realized he had finally reached the heart of the cats' realm,
their secret island. And, in his emotion, he almost forgot his
fish.

It had remained, that fish, hanging by the line from the
branch of a tree, out of reach of the cats' leaps; it must have
dropped from its kidnapper's mouth at some clumsy
movement, perhaps as it was defended from the others, or
perhaps displayed as an extraordinary prize. The line had
got tangled, and Marcovaldo, tug as he would, couldn't
manage to yank it loose. A furious battle had meanwhile
been joined among the cats, to reach that unreachable fish,
or rather, to win the right to try and reach it. Each wanted to
prevent the others from leaping: they hurled themselves on
one another, they tangled in mid-air, they rolled around
clutching each other, and finally a general war broke out in a
whirl of dry, crackling leaves.

After many futile yanks, Marcovaldo now felt the line
was free, but he took care not to pull it: the trout would have
fallen right in the midst of that infuriated scrimmage of
felines.

It was at this moment that, from the top of the walls of
the gardens, a strange rain began to fall: fish-bones, heads,
tails, even bits of lung and lights. Immediately the cats'
attention was distracted from the suspended trout and they
flung themselves on the new delicacies. To Marcovaldo, this
seemed the right moment to pull the line and regain his fish.
But, before he had time to act, from a blind of the little villa,

two yellow, skinny hands darted out: one was brandishing scissors; the other, a frying-pan. The hand with the scissors was raised above the trout, the hand with the frying-pan was thrust under it. The scissors cut the line, the trout fell into the pan; hands, scissors and pan withdrew, the blind closed: all in the space of a second. Marcovaldo was totally bewildered.

"Are you also a cat-lover?" A voice at his back made him turn round. He was surrounded by little old women, some of them ancient, wearing old-fashioned hats on their heads; others, younger, but with the look of spinsters; and all were carrying in their hands or their bags packages of leftover meat or fish, and some even had little pans of milk. "Will you help me throw this package over the fence, for those poor creatures?"

All the ladies, cat-lovers, gathered at this hour around the garden of dry leaves to take food to their protégés.

"Can you tell me why they are all here, these cats?" Marcovaldo inquired.

"Where else could they go? This garden is all they have left! Cats come here from other neighborhoods, too, from miles and miles around . . ."

"And birds, as well," another lady added. "They're forced to live by the hundreds and hundreds on these few trees . . ."

"And the frogs, they're all in that pool, and at night they never stop croaking . . . You can hear them even on the eighth floor of the buildings around here."

"Who does this villa belong to anyway?" Marcovaldo asked. Now, outside the gate, there weren't just the cat-loving ladies but also other people: the man from the gas pump opposite, the apprentices from a mechanic's shop, the postman, the grocer, some passers-by. And none of them, men and women, had to be asked twice: all wanted to have their say, as always when a mysterious and controversial subject comes up.

"It belongs to a Marchesa. She lives there, but you never see her . . ."

"She's been offered millions and millions, by developers, for this little patch of land, but she won't sell . . ."

"What would she do with millions, an old woman all alone in the world? She wants to hold on to her house, even if it's falling to pieces, rather than be forced to move . . ."

"It's the only undeveloped bit of land in the downtown area . . . Its value goes up every year . . . They've made her offers —"

"Offers! That's not all. Threats, intimidation, persecution . . . You don't know the half of it! Those contractors!"

"But she holds out. She's held out for years . . ."

"She's a saint. Without her, where would those poor animals go?"

"A lot she cares about the animals, the old miser! Have you ever seen her give them anything to eat?"

"How can she feed the cats when she doesn't have food for herself? She's the last descendant of a ruined family!"

"She hates cats. I've seen her chasing them and hitting them with an umbrella!"

"Because they were tearing up her flowerbeds!"

"What flower-beds? I've never seen anything in this garden but a great crop of weeds!"

Marcovaldo realized that with regard to the old Marchesa opinions were sharply divided: some saw her as an angelic being, others as an egoist and a miser.

"It's the same with the birds; she never gives them a crumb!"

"She gives them hospitality. Isn't that plenty?"

"Like she gives the mosquitoes, you mean. They all come from here, from that pool. In the summertime the mosquitoes eat us alive, and it's all the fault of that Marchesa!"

"And the mice? This villa is a mine of mice. Under the dead leaves they have their burrows, and at night they come out . . ."

"As far as the mice go, the cats take care of them . . ."

"Oh, you and your cats! If we had to rely on them . . ."

"Why? Have you got something to say against cats?"

Here the discussion degenerated into a general quarrel.

"The authorities should do something: confiscate the villa!" one man cried.

"What gives them the right?" another protested.

"In a modern neighborhood like ours, a mouse-nest like this . . . it should be forbidden . . ."

"Why, I picked my apartment precisely because it overlooked this little bit of green . . ."

"Green, hell! Think of the fine skyscraper they could build here!"

Marcovaldo would have liked to add something of his own, but he couldn't get a word in. Finally, all in one breath, he exclaimed: "The Marchesa stole a trout from me!"

The unexpected news supplied fresh ammunition to the old woman's enemies, but her defenders exploited it as proof of the indigence to which the unfortunate noblewoman was reduced. Both sides agreed that Marcovaldo should go and knock at her door to demand an explanation.

It wasn't clear whether the gate was locked or unlocked; in any case, it opened, after a push, with a mournful creak. Marcovaldo picked his way among the leaves and cats, climbed the steps to the porch, knocked hard at the entrance.

At a window (the very one where the frying-pan had appeared), the blind was raised slightly and in one corner a round, pale blue eye was seen, and a clump of hair dyed an undefinable color, and a dry skinny hand. A voice was heard, asking: "Who is it? Who's at the door?", the words accompanied by a cloud smelling of fried oil.

"It's me, Marchesa. The trout man," Marcovaldo explained. "I don't mean to trouble you. I only wanted to tell you, in case you didn't know, that the trout was stolen from me, by that cat, and I'm the one who caught it. In fact the line . . ."

"Those cats! It's always those cats . . ." the Marchesa said, from behind the shutter, with a shrill, somewhat nasal voice. "All my troubles come from the cats! Nobody knows

what I go through! Prisoner night and day of those horrid
beasts! And with all the refuse people throw over the walls,
to spite me!"

"But my trout . . ."

"Your trout! What am I supposed to know about your
trout!" The Marchesa's voice became almost a scream, as if
she wanted to drown out the sizzle of the oil in the pan,
which came through the window along with the aroma of
fried fish. "How can I make sense of anything, with all the
stuff that rains into my house?"

"I understand, but did you take the trout or didn't you?"

"When I think of all the damage I suffer because of the
cats! Ah, fine state of affairs! I'm not responsible for anything! I can't tell you what I've lost! Thanks to those cats,
who've occupied house and garden for years! My life at the
mercy of those animals! Go and find the owners! Make
them pay damages! Damages? A whole life destroyed! A
prisoner here, unable to move a step!"

"Excuse me for asking: but who's forcing you to stay?"

From the crack in the blind there appeared sometimes a
round, pale blue eye, sometimes a mouth with two protruding teeth; for a moment the whole face was visible, and
to Marcovaldo it seemed, bewilderingly, the face of a cat.

"They keep me prisoner, they do, those cats! Oh, I'd be
glad to leave! What wouldn't I give for a little apartment all
my own, in a nice clean modern building! But I can't go out
. . . They follow me, they block my path, they trip me up!"
The voice became a whisper, as if to confide a secret.
"They're afraid I'll sell the lot . . . They won't leave me . . .
won't allow me . . . When the builders come to offer me a
contract, you should see them, those cats! They get in the
way, pull out their claws; they even chased a lawyer off!
Once I had the contract right here, I was about to sign it, and
they dived in through the window, knocked over the
inkwell, tore up all the pages . . ."

All of a sudden Marcovaldo remembered the time, the
shipping department, the boss. He tiptoed off over the dried

leaves, as the voice continued to come through the slats of the blind, enfolded in that cloud apparently from the oil of a frying-pan. "They even scratched me . . . I still have the scar . . . All alone here at the mercy of these demons . . ."

Winter came. A blossoming of white flakes decked the branches and capitals and the cats' tails. Under the snow, the dry leaves dissolved into mush. The cats were rarely seen, the cat-lovers even less; the packages of fish-bones were consigned only to cats who came to the door. Nobody, for quite a while, had seen anything of the Marchesa. No smoke came now from the chimneypot of the villa.

One snowy day, the garden was again full of cats, who had returned as if it were spring, and they were miauing as if on a moonlight night. The neighbors realized that something had happened: they went and knocked at the Marchesa's door. She didn't answer: she was dead.

In the spring, instead of the garden, there was a huge building site that a contractor had set up. The steam shovels dug down to great depths to make room for the foundations, cement poured into the iron armatures, a very high crane passed beams to the workmen who were making the scaffoldings. But how could they get on with their work? Cats walked along all the planks, they made bricks fall and upset buckets of mortar, they fought in the midst of the piles of sand. When you started to raise an armature, you found a cat perched on the top of it, hissing fiercely. More treacherous pusses climbed onto the masons' backs as if to purr, and there was no getting rid of them. And the birds continued making their nests in all the trestles, the cab of the crane looked like an aviary . . . And you couldn't dip up a bucket of water that wasn't full of frogs, croaking and hopping . . .

WINTER

20. Santa's Children

No period of the year is more gentle and good, for the
world of industry and commerce, than Christmas and the
weeks preceding it. From the streets rises the tremulous
sound of the mountaineers' bagpipes; and the big companies, till yesterday coldly concerned with calculating gross
product and dividends, open their hearts to human affections
and to smiles. The sole thought of Boards of Directors now
is to give joy to their fellow-man, sending gifts accompanied
by messages of goodwill both to other companies and to
private individuals; every firm feels obliged to buy a great
stock of products from a second firm to serve as presents to
third firms; and those firms, for their part, buy from yet
another firm further stocks of presents for the others; the
office windows remain aglow till late, specially those of the
shipping department, where the personnel work overtime
wrapping packages and boxes; beyond the misted panes, on
the sidewalks covered by a crust of ice, the pipers advance.
Having descended from the dark mysterious mountains,
they stand at the downtown intersections, a bit dazzled by
the excessive lights, by the excessively rich shop-windows;
and heads bowed, they blow into their instruments; at that
sound among the businessmen the heavy conflicts of interest
are placated and give way to a new rivalry: to see who can

present the most conspicuous and original gift in the most attractive way.

At Sbav and Co. that year the Public Relations Office suggested that the Christmas presents for the most important persons should be delivered at home by a man dressed as Santa Claus.

The idea won the unanimous approval of the top executives. A complete Santa Claus outfit was bought: white beard, red cap and tunic edged in white fur, big boots. They had the various delivery men try it on, to see whom it fitted best, but one man was too short and the beard touched the ground; another was too stout and couldn't get into the tunic; another was too young; yet another was too old and it wasn't worth wasting make-up on him.

While the head of the Personnel Office was sending for other possible Santas from the various departments, the assembled executives sought to develop the idea: the Human Relations Office wanted the employees' Christmas packages also to be distributed by Santa Claus, at a collective ceremony; the Sales Office wanted Santa to make a round of the shops as well; the Advertising Office was worried about the prominence of the firm's name, suggesting that perhaps they should tie four balloons to a string with the letters S.B.A.V.

All were caught up in the lively and cordial atmosphere spreading through the festive, productive city; nothing is more beautiful than the sensation of material goods flowing on all sides and, with it, the good will each feels towards the others; for this, this above all, as the skirling sound of the pipes reminds us, is what really counts.

In the shipping department, goods – material and spiritual – passed through Marcovaldo's hands, since it represented merchandise to load and unload. And it was not only through loading and unloading that he shared in the general festivity, but also by thinking that at the end of that labyrinth of hundreds of thousands of packages there waited a package belonging to him alone, prepared by the Human Relations

Office; and even more, by figuring how much was due him at the end of the month, counting the Christmas bonus and his overtime hours. With that money, he too would be able to rush to the shops and buy, buy, buy, to give presents, presents, presents, as his most sincere feelings and the general interests of industry and commerce decreed.

The head of the Personnel Office came into the shipping department with a fake beard in his hand. "Hey, you!" he said to Marcovaldo. "See how this beard looks on you. Perfect! You're Santa then. Come upstairs. Get moving. You'll be given a special bonus if you make fifty home deliveries per day."

Got up as Santa Claus, Marcovaldo rode through the city, on the saddle of the motorbike-truck laden with packages wrapped in vari-colored paper, tied with pretty ribbons, and decorated with twigs of mistletoe and holly. The white cotton beard tickled him a little but it protected his throat from the cold air.

His first trip was to his own home, because he couldn't resist the temptation of giving his children a surprise. At first, he thought, they won't recognize me. Then I bet they'll laugh!

The children were playing on the stairs. They barely looked up. "Hi, Papà."

Marcovaldo was let down. "Hmph . . . Don't you see how I'm dressed?"

"How are you supposed to be dressed?" Pietruccio said. "Like Santa Claus, right?"

"And you recognized me first thing?"

"Easy! We recognized Signor Sigismondo, too; and he was disguised better than you!"

"And the janitor's brother-in-law!"

"And the father of the twins across the street!"

"And the uncle of Ernestina – the girl with the braids!"

"All dressed like Santa Claus?" Marcovaldo asked, and

the disappointment in his voice wasn't due only to the failure of the family surprise, but also because he felt that the company's prestige had somehow been impaired.

"Of course. Just like you," the children answered. "Like Santa Claus. With a fake beard, as usual." And turning their backs on him, the children became absorbed again in their games.

It so happened that the Public Relations Offices of many firms had had the same idea at the same time; and they had recruited a great number of people, jobless for the most part, pensioners, street-vendors, and had dressed them in the red tunic, with the cotton-wool beard. The children, the first few times, had been amused, recognizing acquaintances under that disguise, neighborhood figures, but after a while they were jaded and paid no further attention.

The game they were involved in seemed to absorb them entirely. They had gathered on a landing and were seated in a circle. "May I ask what you're plotting?" Marcovaldo inquired.

"Leave us alone, Papà; we have to fix our presents."

"Presents for who?"

"For a poor child. We have to find a poor child and give him presents."

"Who said so?"

"It's in our school reader."

Marcovaldo was about to say: "You're poor children yourselves!" But during this past week he had become so convinced that he was an inhabitant of the Land of Plenty, where all purchased and enjoyed themselves and exchanged presents, that it seemed bad manners to mention poverty; and he preferred to declare: "Poor children don't exist any more!"

Michelino stood up and asked: "Is that why you don't bring us presents, Papà?"

Marcovaldo felt a pang at his heart. "I have to earn some overtime now," he said hastily, "and then I'll bring you some."

"How do you earn it?"

"Delivering presents," Marcovaldo said.

"To us?"

"No, to other people."

"Why not to us? It'd be quicker."

Marcovaldo tried to explain. "Because I'm not the Human Relations Santa Claus, after all; I'm the Public Relations Santa Claus. You understand?"

"No."

"Never mind." But since he wanted somehow to apologize for coming home empty-handed, he thought he might take Michelino with him, on his round of deliveries. "If you're good, you can come and watch your Papà taking presents to people," he said, straddling the seat of the little delivery wagon.

"Let's go. Maybe I'll find a poor child," Michelino said and jumped on, clinging to his father's shoulders.

In the streets of the city Marcovaldo encountered only other red-and-white Santas, absolutely identical with him, who were driving panel-trucks or delivery carts or opening the doors of shops for customers laden with packages or helping carry their purchases to the car. And all these Santas seemed concentrated, busy, as if they were responsible for the operation of the enormous machine of the Holiday Season.

And exactly like them, Marcovaldo ran from one address to another, following his list, dismounted from his seat, sorted the packages in the wagon, selected one, presented it to the person opening the door, pronouncing the words: "Sbav and Company wish a Merry Christmas and a Happy New Year", and pocketed the tip.

This tip could be substantial and Marcovaldo might have been considered content, but something was missing. Every time, before ringing at a door, followed by Michelino, he anticipated the wonder of the person who, on opening the door, would see Santa Claus himself standing there before him; he expected some fuss, curiosity, gratitude. And every time he was received like the postman, who brings the newspaper day after day.

He rang at the door of a luxurious house. A governess answered the door. "Oh, another package. Who's this one from?"

"Sbav and Company wish a . . ."

"Well, bring it in," and she led Santa Claus down a corridor filled with tapestries, carpets, and majolica vases. Michelino, all eyes, followed his father.

The governess opened a glass door. They entered a room with a high ceiling, so high that a great fir tree could fit beneath it. It was a Christmas tree lighted by glass bubbles of every color, and from its branches hung presents and sweets of every description. From the ceiling hung heavy crystal chandeliers, and the highest branches of the fir caught some of the glistening drops. Over a large table were arrayed glass, silver, boxes of candied fruit and cases of bottles. The toys, scattered over a great rug, were as numerous as in a toyshop, mostly complicated electronic devices and model space-ships. On that rug, in an empty corner, there was a little boy about nine years old, lying prone, with a bored, sullen look. He was leafing through an illustrated volume, as if everything around him were no concern of his.

"Gianfranco, look. Gianfranco," the governess said. "You see? Santa Claus has come back with another present?"

"Three hundred twelve," the child sighed, without looking up from his book. "Put it over there."

"It's the three hundred and twelfth present that's arrived," the governess said. "Gianfranco is so clever. He keeps count; he doesn't miss one. Counting is his great passion."

On tiptoe Marcovaldo and Michelino left the house.

"Papà is that little boy a poor child?" Michelino asked.

Marcovaldo was busy rearranging the contents of the truck and didn't answer immediately. But after a moment, he hastened to protest: "Poor? What are you talking about?

You know who his father is? He's the president of the Society for the Implementation of Christmas Consumption. Commendatore–"

He broke off, because he didn't see Michelino anywhere. "Michelino! Michelino! Where are you?" He had vanished.

I bet he saw another Santa Claus go by, took him for me, and has gone off after him . . . Marcovaldo continued his rounds, but he was a bit concerned, and couldn't wait to get home again.

At home, he found Michelino with his brothers, good as gold.

"Say, where did you go?"

"I came home, to collect our presents . . . the presents for that poor child . . ."

"What? Who?"

"The one that was so sad . . . the one in the villa, with the Christmas tree . . ."

"Him? What kind of a present could you give him?"

"Oh, we fixed them up very nice . . . three presents, all wrapped in silver paper."

The younger boys spoke up: "We all went together to take them to him! You should have seen how happy he was!"

"I'll bet!" Marcovaldo said. "That was just what he needed to make him happy: your presents!"

"Yes, ours! . . . He ran over right away to tear off the paper and see what they were . . ."

"And what were they?"

"The first was a hammer: that big round hammer, the wooden kind . . ."

"What did he do then?"

"He was jumping with joy! He grabbed it and began to use it!"

"How?"

"He broke all the toys! And all the glassware! Then he took the second present . . ."

"What was that?"

"A slingshot. You should of seen him. He was so happy! He hit all the glass balls on the Christmas tree. Then he started on the chandeliers . . ."

"That's enough. I don't want to hear any more! And the . . . third present?"

"We didn't have anything left to give, so we took some silver paper and wrapped up a box of kitchen matches. That was the present that made him happiest of all. He said: They never let me touch matches! He began to strike them, and . . ."

"And?"

". . . and he set fire to everything!"

Marcovaldo was tearing his hair. "I'm ruined!"

The next day, turning up at work, he felt the storm brewing. He dressed again as Santa Claus, in great haste, loaded the presents to be delivered onto the truck, already amazed that no one had said anything to him, and then he saw, coming towards him, the three section chiefs: the one from Public Relations, the one from Advertising, and the one from Sales.

"Stop!" they said to him. "Unload everything. At once!"

This is it, Marcovaldo said to himself, and could already picture himself fired.

"Hurry up! We have to change all the packages!" the three section chiefs said. "The Society for the Implementation of Christmas Consumption has launched a campaign to push the Destructive Gift!"

"On the spur of the moment like this," one of the men remarked. "They might have thought of it sooner . . ."

"It was a sudden inspiration the President had," another chief explained. "It seems his little boy was given some ultra-modern gift-articles, Japanese, I believe, and for the first time the child was obviously enjoying himself . . ."

"The important thing," the third added, "is that the Destructive Gift serves to destroy articles of every sort: just

what's needed to speed up the pace of consumption and give
the market a boost . . . All in minimum time and within a
child's capacities . . . The President of the Society sees a
whole new horizon opening out. He's in seventh heaven,
he's so enthusiastic . . ."

"But this child . . ." Marcovaldo asked, in a faint voice:
"did he really destroy much stuff?"

"It's hard to make an estimate, even a hazy one, because
the house was burned down . . ."

Marcovaldo went back to the street, illuminated as if it
were night, crowded with Mammas and children and uncles
and grannies and packages and balloons and rocking horses
and Christmas trees and Santa Clauses and chickens and
turkeys and fruit cakes and bottles and bagpipers and
chimney-sweeps and chestnut vendors shaking pans of
chestnuts over round, glowing, black stoves.

And the city seemed smaller, collected in a luminous
vessel, buried in the dark heart of a forest, among the
age-old trunks of the chestnut trees and an endless cloak of
snow. Somewhere in the darkness the howl of the wolf was
heard; the hares had a hole buried in the snow, in the warm
red earth under a layer of chestnut burrs.

A jack-hare came out, white, onto the snow, he twitched
his ears, ran beneath the moon, but he was white and
couldn't be seen, as if he weren't there. Only his little paws
left a light print on the snow, like little clover leaves. Nor
could the wolf be seen, for he was black and stayed in the
black darkness of the forest. Only if he opened his mouth,
his teeth were visible, white and sharp.

There was a line where the forest, all black, ended and the
snow began, all white. The hare ran on this side, and the
wolf on that.

The wolf saw the hare's prints on the snow and followed
them, always keeping in the black, so as not to be seen. At
the point where the prints ended there should be the hare,
and the wolf came out of the black, opened wide his red
maw and his sharp teeth, and bit the wind.

The hare was a bit farther on, invisible; he scratched one ear with his paw, and escaped, hopping away.

Is he here? There? Is he a bit farther on?

Only the expanse of snow could be seen, white as this page.